TENTH EDITION

BUSINESS INTELLIGENCE AND ANALYTICS:

SYSTEMS FOR DECISION SUPPORT

Ramesh Sharda

Oklahoma State University

Dursun Delen

Oklahoma State University

Efraim Turban

University of Hawaii

With contributions by

J. E. Aronson

The University of Georgia

Ting-Peng Liang

National Sun Yat-sen University

David King

JDA Software Group, Inc.

PEARSON

Boston   Columbus   Indianapolis   New York   San Francisco   Upper Saddle River
Amsterdam   Cape Town   Dubai   London   Madrid   Milan   Munich   Paris   Montréal   Toronto
Delhi   Mexico City   São Paulo   Sydney   Hong Kong   Seoul   Singapore   Taipei   Tokyo

Editor in Chief: Stephanie Wall
Executive Editor: Bob Horan
Program Manager Team Lead: Ashley Santora
Program Manager: Denise Vaughn
Executive Marketing Manager: Anne Fahlgren
Project Manager Team Lead: Judy Leale
Project Manager: Tom Benfatti
Operations Specialist: Michelle Klein
Creative Director: Jayne Conte

Cover Designer: Suzanne Behnke
Digital Production Project Manager: Lisa Rinaldi
Full-Service Project Management: George Jacob, Integra Software Solutions.
Printer/Binder: Edwards Brothers Malloy-Jackson Road
Cover Printer: Lehigh/Phoenix-Hagerstown
Text Font: Garamond

Credits and acknowledgments borrowed from other sources and reproduced, with permission, in this textbook appear on the appropriate page within text.

Microsoft and/or its respective suppliers make no representations about the suitability of the information contained in the documents and related graphics published as part of the services for any purpose. All such documents and related graphics are provided "as is" without warranty of any kind. Microsoft and/or its respective suppliers hereby disclaim all warranties and conditions with regard to this information, including all warranties and conditions of merchantability, whether express, implied or statutory, fitness for a particular purpose, title and non-infringement. In no event shall Microsoft and/or its respective suppliers be liable for any special, indirect or consequential damages or any damages whatsoever resulting from loss of use, data or profits, whether in an action of contract, negligence or other tortious action, arising out of or in connection with the use or performance of information available from the services.

The documents and related graphics contained herein could include technical inaccuracies or typographical errors. Changes are periodically added to the information herein. Microsoft and/or its respective suppliers may make improvements and/or changes in the product(s) and/or the program(s) described herein at any time. Partial screen shots may be viewed in full within the software version specified.

Microsoft® Windows®, and Microsoft Office® are registered trademarks of the Microsoft Corporation in the U.S.A. and other countries. This book is not sponsored or endorsed by or affiliated with the Microsoft Corporation.

Many of the designations by manufacturers and sellers to distinguish their products are claimed as trademarks. Where those designations appear in this book, and the publisher was aware of a trademark claim, the designations have been printed in initial caps or all caps.

Library of Congress Cataloging-in-Publication Data

Turban, Efraim.
[Decision support and expert systems]
Business intelligence and analytics: systems for decision support/Ramesh Sharda, Oklahoma State University, Dursun Delen, Oklahoma State University, Efraim Turban, University of Hawaii; With contributions by J. E. Aronson, The University of Georgia, Ting-Peng Liang, National Sun Yat-sen University, David King, JDA Software Group, Inc.—Tenth edition.
     pages cm
     ISBN-13: 978-0-13-305090-5
     ISBN-10: 0-13-305090-4
     1. Management—Data processing. 2. Decision support systems. 3. Expert systems (Computer science)
4. Business intelligence. I. Title.
     HD30.2.T87 2014
     658.4'038011—dc23
                                                                                      2013028826

10 9 8 7 6 5 4 3 2 1

ISBN 10: 0-13-305090-4
ISBN 13: 978-0-13-305090-5

BRIEF CONTENTS

CONTENTS

Part II Descriptive Analytics 77

PREFACE

Analytics has become the technology driver of this decade. Companies such as IBM, Oracle, Microsoft, and others are creating new organizational units focused on analytics that help businesses become more effective and efficient in their operations. Decision makers are using more computerized tools to support their work. Even consumers are using analytics tools directly or indirectly to make decisions on routine activities such as shopping, healthcare, and entertainment. The field of decision support systems (DSS)/ business intelligence (BI) is evolving rapidly to become more focused on innovative applications of data streams that were not even captured some time back, much less analyzed in any significant way. New applications turn up daily in healthcare, sports, entertainment, supply chain management, utilities, and virtually every industry imaginable.

The theme of this revised edition is BI and analytics for enterprise decision support. In addition to traditional decision support applications, this edition expands the reader's understanding of the various types of analytics by providing examples, products, services, and exercises by discussing Web-related issues throughout the text. We highlight Web intelligence/Web analytics, which parallel BI/business analytics (BA) for e-commerce and other Web applications. The book is supported by a Web site (**pearsonhighered.com/ sharda**) and also by an independent site at **dssbibook.com**. We will also provide links to software tutorials through a special section of the Web site.

The purpose of this book is to introduce the reader to these technologies that are generally called *analytics* but have been known by other names. The core technology consists of DSS, BI, and various decision-making techniques. We use these terms interchangeably. This book presents the fundamentals of the techniques and the manner in which these systems are constructed and used. We follow an EEE approach to introducing these topics: **Exposure, Experience,** and **Explore**. The book primarily provides **exposure** to various analytics techniques and their applications. The idea is that a student will be inspired to learn from how other organizations have employed analytics to make decisions or to gain a competitive edge. We believe that such **exposure** to what is being done with analytics and how it can be achieved is the key component of learning about analytics. In describing the techniques, we also introduce specific software tools that can be used for developing such applications. The book is not limited to any one software tool, so the students can **experience** these techniques using any number of available software tools. Specific suggestions are given in each chapter, but the student and the professor are able to use this book with many different software tools. Our book's companion Web site will include specific software guides, but students can gain **experience** with these techniques in many different ways. Finally, we hope that this **exposure** and **experience** enable and motivate readers to **explore** the potential of these techniques in their own domain. To facilitate such **exploration,** we include exercises that direct them to Teradata University Network and other sites as well that include team-oriented exercises where appropriate. We will also highlight new and innovative applications that we learn about on the book's companion Web sites.

Most of the specific improvements made in this tenth edition concentrate on three areas: reorganization, content update, and a sharper focus. Despite the many changes, we have preserved the comprehensiveness and user friendliness that have made the text a market leader. We have also reduced the book's size by eliminating older and redundant material and by combining material that was not used by a majority of professors. At the same time, we have kept several of the classical references intact. Finally, we present accurate and updated material that is not available in any other text. We next describe the changes in the tenth edition.

WHAT'S NEW IN THE TENTH EDITION?

With the goal of improving the text, this edition marks a major reorganization of the text to reflect the focus on analytics. The last two editions transformed the book from the traditional DSS to BI and fostered a tight linkage with the Teradata University Network (TUN). This edition is now organized around three major types of analytics. The new edition has many timely additions, and the dated content has been deleted. The following major specific changes have been made:

- ***New organization.*** The book is now organized around three types of analytics: descriptive, predictive, and prescriptive, a classification promoted by INFORMS. After introducing the topics of DSS/BI and analytics in Chapter 1 and covering the foundations of decision making and decision support in Chapter 2, the book begins with an overview of data warehousing and data foundations in Chapter 3. This part then covers descriptive or reporting analytics, specifically, visualization and business performance measurement. Chapters 5–8 cover predictive analytics. Chapters 9–12 cover prescriptive and decision analytics as well as other decision support systems topics. Some of the coverage from Chapter 3–4 in previous editions will now be found in the new Chapters 9 and 10. Chapter 11 covers expert systems as well as the new rule-based systems that are commonly built for implementing analytics. Chapter 12 combines two topics that were key chapters in earlier editions—knowledge management and collaborative systems. Chapter 13 is a new chapter that introduces big data and analytics. Chapter 14 concludes the book with discussion of emerging trends and topics in business analytics, including location intelligence, mobile computing, cloud-based analytics, and privacy/ethical considerations in analytics. This chapter also includes an overview of the analytics ecosystem to help the user explore all of the different ways one can participate and grow in the analytics environment. Thus, the book marks a significant departure from the earlier editions in organization. Of course, it is still possible to teach a course with a traditional DSS focus with this book by covering Chapters 1–4, Chapters 9–12, and possibly Chapter 14.

- ***New chapters.*** The following chapters have been added:

  Chapter 8, *"Web Analytics, Web Mining, and Social Analytics."* This chapter covers the popular topics of Web analytics and social media analytics. It is an almost entirely new chapter (95% new material).

  Chapter 13, *"Big Data and Analytics."* This chapter introduces the hot topics of Big Data and analytics. It covers the basics of major components of Big Data techniques and charcteristics. It is also a new chapter (99% new material).

  Chapter 14, *"Business Analytics: Emerging Trends and Future Impacts."* This chapter examines several new phenomena that are already changing or are likely to change analytics. It includes coverage of geospatial in analytics, location-based analytics applications, consumer-oriented analytical applications, mobile platforms, and cloud-based analytics. It also updates some coverage from the previous edition on ethical and privacy considerations. It concludes with a major discussion of the analytics ecosystem (90% new material).

- ***Streamlined coverage.*** We have made the book shorter by keeping the most commonly used content. We also mostly eliminated the preformatted online content. Instead, we will use a Web site to provide updated content and links on a regular basis. We also reduced the number of references in each chapter.

- ***Revamped author team.*** Building upon the excellent content that has been prepared by the authors of the previous editions (Turban, Aronson, Liang, King, Sharda, and Delen), this edition was revised by Ramesh Sharda and Dursun Delen.

Both Ramesh and Dursun have worked extensively in DSS and analytics and have industry as well as research experience.

- *A live-update Web site.* Adopters of the textbook will have access to a Web site that will include links to news stories, software, tutorials, and even YouTube videos related to topics covered in the book. This site will be accessible at **http://dssbibook.com**.

- *Revised and updated content.* Almost all of the chapters have new opening vignettes and closing cases that are based on recent stories and events. In addition, application cases throughout the book have been updated to include recent examples of applications of a specific technique/model. These application case stories now include suggested questions for discussion to encourage class discussion as well as further exploration of the specific case and related materials. New Web site links have been added throughout the book. We also deleted many older product links and references. Finally, most chapters have new exercises, Internet assignments, and discussion questions throughout.

Specific changes made in chapters that have been retained from the previous editions are summarized next:

Chapter 1, "An Overview of Business Intelligence, Analytics, and Decision Support," introduces the three types of analytics as proposed by INFORMS: descriptive, predictive, and prescriptive analytics. A noted earlier, this classification is used in guiding the complete reorganization of the book itself. It includes about 50 percent new material. All of the case stories are new.

Chapter 2, "Foundations and Technologies for Decision Making," combines material from earlier Chapters 1, 2, and 3 to provide a basic foundation for decision making in general and computer-supported decision making in particular. It eliminates some duplication that was present in Chapters 1–3 of the previous editions. It includes 35 percent new material. Most of the cases are new.

Chapter 3, "Data Warehousing"
- 30 percent new material, including the cases
- New opening case
- Mostly new cases throughout
- NEW: A historic perspective to data warehousing—how did we get here?
- Better coverage of multidimensional modeling (star schema and snowflake schema)
- An updated coverage on the future of data warehousing

Chapter 4, "Business Reporting, Visual Analytics, and Business Performance Management"
- 60 percent of the material is new—especially in visual analytics and reporting
- Most of the cases are new

Chapter 5, "Data Mining"
- 25 percent of the material is new
- Most of the cases are new

Chapter 6, "Techniques for Predictive Modeling"
- 55 percent of the material is new
- Most of the cases are new
- New sections on SVM and kNN

Chapter 7, "Text Analytics, Text Mining, and Sentiment Analysis"
- 50 percent of the material is new
- Most of the cases are new
- New section (1/3 of the chapter) on sentiment analysis

Chapter 8, "Web Analytics, Web Mining, and Social Analytics" (New Chapter)
- 95 percent of the material is new

Chapter 9, "Model-Based Decision Making: Optimization and Multi-Criteria Systems"
- All new cases
- Expanded coverage of analytic hierarchy process
- New examples of mixed-integer programming applications and exercises
- About 50 percent new material

In addition, all the Microsoft Excel–related coverage has been updated to work with Microsoft Excel 2010.

Chapter 10, "Modeling and Analysis: Heuristic Search Methods and Simulation"
- This chapter now introduces genetic algorithms and various types of simulation models
- It includes new coverage of other types of simulation modeling such as agent-based modeling and system dynamics modeling
- New cases throughout
- About 60 percent new material

Chapter 11, "Automated Decision Systems and Expert Systems"
- Expanded coverage of automated decision systems including examples from the airline industry
- New examples of expert systems
- New cases
- About 50 percent new material

Chapter 12, "Knowledge Management and Collaborative Systems"
- Significantly condensed coverage of these two topics combined into one chapter
- New examples of KM applications
- About 25 percent new material

Chapters 13 and 14 are mostly new chapters, as described earlier.

We have retained many of the enhancements made in the last editions and updated the content. These are summarized next:

- **Links to Teradata University Network (TUN).** Most chapters include new links to TUN (**teradatauniversitynetwork.com**). We encourage the instructors to register and join teradatauniversitynetwork.com and explore various content available through the site. The cases, white papers, and software exercises available through TUN will keep your class fresh and timely.
- **Book title.** As is already evident, the book's title and focus have changed substantially.
- **Software support.** The TUN Web site provides software support at no charge. It also provides links to free data mining and other software. In addition, the site provides exercises in the use of such software.

THE SUPPLEMENT PACKAGE: PEARSONHIGHERED.COM/SHARDA

A comprehensive and flexible technology-support package is available to enhance the teaching and learning experience. The following instructor and student supplements are available on the book's Web site, **pearsonhighered.com/sharda**:

- **Instructor's Manual.** The Instructor's Manual includes learning objectives for the entire course and for each chapter, answers to the questions and exercises at the end of each chapter, and teaching suggestions (including instructions for projects). The Instructor's Manual is available on the secure faculty section of **pearsonhighered.com/sharda**.

- ***Test Item File and TestGen Software.*** The Test Item File is a comprehensive collection of true/false, multiple-choice, fill-in-the-blank, and essay questions. The questions are rated by difficulty level, and the answers are referenced by book page number. The Test Item File is available in Microsoft Word and in TestGen. Pearson Education's test-generating software is available from **www.pearsonhighered. com/irc**. The software is PC/MAC compatible and preloaded with all of the Test Item File questions. You can manually or randomly view test questions and drag-and-drop to create a test. You can add or modify test-bank questions as needed. Our TestGens are converted for use in BlackBoard, WebCT, Moodle, D2L, and Angel. These conversions can be found on **pearsonhighered.com/sharda**. The TestGen is also available in Respondus and can be found on **www.respondus.com**.
- ***PowerPoint slides.*** PowerPoint slides are available that illuminate and build on key concepts in the text. Faculty can download the PowerPoint slides from **pearsonhighered.com/sharda**.

ACKNOWLEDGMENTS

Many individuals have provided suggestions and criticisms since the publication of the first edition of this book. Dozens of students participated in class testing of various chapters, software, and problems and assisted in collecting material. It is not possible to name everyone who participated in this project, but our thanks go to all of them. Certain individuals made significant contributions, and they deserve special recognition.

First, we appreciate the efforts of those individuals who provided formal reviews of the first through tenth editions (school affiliations as of the date of review):

Robert Blanning, Vanderbilt University
Ranjit Bose, University of New Mexico
Warren Briggs, Suffolk University
Lee Roy Bronner, Morgan State University
Charles Butler, Colorado State University
Sohail S. Chaudry, University of Wisconsin–La Crosse
Kathy Chudoba, Florida State University
Wingyan Chung, University of Texas
Woo Young Chung, University of Memphis
Paul "Buddy" Clark, South Carolina State University
Pi'Sheng Deng, California State University–Stanislaus
Joyce Elam, Florida International University
Kurt Engemann, Iona College
Gary Farrar, Jacksonville University
George Federman, Santa Clara City College
Jerry Fjermestad, New Jersey Institute of Technology
Joey George, Florida State University
Paul Gray, Claremont Graduate School
Orv Greynholds, Capital College (Laurel, Maryland)
Martin Grossman, Bridgewater State College
Ray Jacobs, Ashland University
Leonard Jessup, Indiana University
Jeffrey Johnson, Utah State University
Jahangir Karimi, University of Colorado Denver
Saul Kassicieh, University of New Mexico
Anand S. Kunnathur, University of Toledo

Shao-ju Lee, California State University at Northridge
Yair Levy, Nova Southeastern University
Hank Lucas, New York University
Jane Mackay, Texas Christian University
George M. Marakas, University of Maryland
Dick Mason, Southern Methodist University
Nick McGaughey, San Jose State University
Ido Millet, Pennsylvania State University–Erie
Benjamin Mittman, Northwestern University
Larry Moore, Virginia Polytechnic Institute and State University
Simitra Mukherjee, Nova Southeastern University
Marianne Murphy, Northeastern University
Peter Mykytyn, Southern Illinois University
Natalie Nazarenko, SUNY College at Fredonia
Souren Paul, Southern Illinois University
Joshua Pauli, Dakota State University
Roger Alan Pick, University of Missouri–St. Louis
W. "RP" Raghupaphi, California State University–Chico
Loren Rees, Virginia Polytechnic Institute and State University
David Russell, Western New England College
Steve Ruth, George Mason University
Vartan Safarian, Winona State University
Glenn Shephard, San Jose State University
Jung P. Shim, Mississippi State University
Meenu Singh, Murray State University
Randy Smith, University of Virginia
James T.C. Teng, University of South Carolina
John VanGigch, California State University at Sacramento
David Van Over, University of Idaho
Paul J.A. van Vliet, University of Nebraska at Omaha
B. S. Vijayaraman, University of Akron
Howard Charles Walton, Gettysburg College
Diane B. Walz, University of Texas at San Antonio
Paul R. Watkins, University of Southern California
Randy S. Weinberg, Saint Cloud State University
Jennifer Williams, University of Southern Indiana
Steve Zanakis, Florida International University
Fan Zhao, Florida Gulf Coast University

Several individuals contributed material to the text or the supporting material. Susan Baxley and Dr. David Schrader of Teradata provided special help in identifying new TUN content for the book and arranging permissions for the same. Peter Horner, editor of *OR/MS Today,* allowed us to summarize new application stories from *OR/MS Today* and *Analytics Magazine.* We also thank INFORMS for their permission to highlight content from *Interfaces.* Prof. Rick Wilson contributed some examples and exercise questions for Chapter 9. Assistance from Natraj Ponna, Daniel Asamoah, Amir Hassan-Zadeh, Kartik Dasika, Clara Gregory, and Amy Wallace (all of Oklahoma State University) is gratefully acknowledged for this edition. We also acknowledge Narges Kasiri (Ithaca College) for the write-up on system dynamics modeling and Jongswas Chongwatpol (NIDA, Thailand) for the material on SIMIO software. For the previous edition, we acknowledge the contributions of Dave King (JDA Software Group, Inc.) and

Jerry Wagner (University of Nebraska–Omaha). Major contributors for earlier editions include Mike Goul (Arizona State University) and Leila A. Halawi (Bethune-Cookman College), who provided material for the chapter on data warehousing; Christy Cheung (Hong Kong Baptist University), who contributed to the chapter on knowledge management; Linda Lai (Macau Polytechnic University of China); Dave King (JDA Software Group, Inc.); Lou Frenzel, an independent consultant whose books *Crash Course in Artificial Intelligence and Expert Systems* and *Understanding of Expert Systems* (both published by Howard W. Sams, New York, 1987) provided material for the early editions; Larry Medsker (American University), who contributed substantial material on neural networks; and Richard V. McCarthy (Quinnipiac University), who performed major revisions in the seventh edition.

Previous editions of the book have also benefited greatly from the efforts of many individuals who contributed advice and interesting material (such as problems), gave feedback on material, or helped with class testing. These individuals are Warren Briggs (Suffolk University), Frank DeBalough (University of Southern California), Mei-Ting Cheung (University of Hong Kong), Alan Dennis (Indiana University), George Easton (San Diego State University), Janet Fisher (California State University, Los Angeles), David Friend (Pilot Software, Inc.), the late Paul Gray (Claremont Graduate School), Mike Henry (OSU), Dustin Huntington (Exsys, Inc.), Subramanian Rama Iyer (Oklahoma State University), Angie Jungermann (Oklahoma State University), Elena Karahanna (The University of Georgia), Mike McAulliffe (The University of Georgia), Chad Peterson (The University of Georgia), Neil Rabjohn (York University), Jim Ragusa (University of Central Florida), Alan Rowe (University of Southern California), Steve Ruth (George Mason University), Linus Schrage (University of Chicago), Antonie Stam (University of Missouri), Ron Swift (NCR Corp.), Merril Warkentin (then at Northeastern University), Paul Watkins (The University of Southern California), Ben Mortagy (Claremont Graduate School of Management), Dan Walsh (Bellcore), Richard Watson (The University of Georgia), and the many other instructors and students who have provided feedback.

Several vendors cooperated by providing development and/or demonstration software: Expert Choice, Inc. (Pittsburgh, Pennsylvania), Nancy Clark of Exsys, Inc. (Albuquerque, New Mexico), Jim Godsey of GroupSystems, Inc. (Broomfield, Colorado), Raimo Hämäläinen of Helsinki University of Technology, Gregory Piatetsky-Shapiro of KDNuggets.com, Logic Programming Associates (UK), Gary Lynn of NeuroDimension Inc. (Gainesville, Florida), Palisade Software (Newfield, New York), Jerry Wagner of Planners Lab (Omaha, Nebraska), Promised Land Technologies (New Haven, Connecticut), Salford Systems (La Jolla, California), Sense Networks (New York, New York), Gary Miner of StatSoft, Inc. (Tulsa, Oklahoma), Ward Systems Group, Inc. (Frederick, Maryland), Idea Fisher Systems, Inc. (Irving, California), and Wordtech Systems (Orinda, California).

Special thanks to the Teradata University Network and especially to Hugh Watson, Michael Goul, and Susan Baxley, Program Director, for their encouragement to tie this book with TUN and for providing useful material for the book.

Many individuals helped us with administrative matters and editing, proofreading, and preparation. The project began with Jack Repcheck (a former Macmillan editor), who initiated this project with the support of Hank Lucas (New York University). Judy Lang collaborated with all of us, provided editing, and guided us during the entire project through the eighth edition.

Finally, the Pearson team is to be commended: Executive Editor Bob Horan, who orchestrated this project; Kitty Jarrett, who copyedited the manuscript; and the production team, Tom Benfatti at Pearson, George and staff at Integra Software Services, who transformed the manuscript into a book.

We would like to thank all these individuals and corporations. Without their help, the creation of this book would not have been possible. Ramesh and Dursun want to specifically acknowledge the contributions of previous coauthors Janine Aronson, David King, and T. P. Liang, whose original contributions constitute significant components of the book.

R.S.

D.D.

E.T.

Note that Web site URLs are dynamic. As this book went to press, we verified that all the cited Web sites were active and valid. Web sites to which we refer in the text sometimes change or are discontinued because companies change names, are bought or sold, merge, or fail. Sometimes Web sites are down for maintenance, repair, or redesign. Most organizations have dropped the initial "www" designation for their sites, but some still use it. If you have a problem connecting to a Web site that we mention, please be patient and simply run a Web search to try to identify the new site. Most times, the new site can be found quickly. Some sites also require a free registration before allowing you to see the content. We apologize in advance for this inconvenience.

ABOUT THE AUTHORS

Ramesh Sharda (M.B.A., Ph.D., University of Wisconsin–Madison) is director of the Ph.D. in Business for Executives Program and Institute for Research in Information Systems (IRIS), ConocoPhillips Chair of Management of Technology, and a Regents Professor of Management Science and Information Systems in the Spears School of Business at Oklahoma State University (OSU). About 200 papers describing his research have been published in major journals, including *Operations Research, Management Science, Information Systems Research, Decision Support Systems,* and *Journal of MIS.* He cofounded the AIS SIG on Decision Support Systems and Knowledge Management (SIGDSS). Dr. Sharda serves on several editorial boards, including those of *INFORMS Journal on Computing, Decision Support Systems,* and *ACM Transactions on Management Information Systems.* He has authored and edited several textbooks and research books and serves as the co-editor of several book series (Integrated Series in Information Systems, Operations Research/Computer Science Interfaces, and Annals of Information Systems) with Springer. He is also currently serving as the executive director of the Teradata University Network. His current research interests are in decision support systems, business analytics, and technologies for managing information overload.

Dursun Delen (Ph.D., Oklahoma State University) is the Spears and Patterson Chairs in Business Analytics, Director of Research for the Center for Health Systems Innovation, and Professor of Management Science and Information Systems in the Spears School of Business at Oklahoma State University (OSU). Prior to his academic career, he worked for a privately owned research and consultancy company, Knowledge Based Systems Inc., in College Station, Texas, as a research scientist for five years, during which he led a number of decision support and other information systems–related research projects funded by federal agencies such as DoD, NASA, NIST, and DOE. Dr. Delen's research has appeared in major journals including *Decision Support Systems, Communications of the ACM, Computers and Operations Research, Computers in Industry, Journal of Production Operations Management, Artificial Intelligence in Medicine,* and *Expert Systems with Applications,* among others. He recently published four textbooks: *Advanced Data Mining Techniques* with Springer, 2008; *Decision Support and Business Intelligence Systems* with Prentice Hall, 2010; *Business Intelligence: A Managerial Approach,* with Prentice Hall, 2010; and *Practical Text Mining,* with Elsevier, 2012. He is often invited to national and international conferences for keynote addresses on topics related to data/text mining, business intelligence, decision support systems, and knowledge management. He served as the general co-chair for the 4th International Conference on Network Computing and Advanced Information Management (September 2–4, 2008, in Seoul, South Korea) and regularly chairs tracks and mini-tracks at various information systems conferences. He is the associate editor-in-chief for *International Journal of Experimental Algorithms,* associate editor for *International Journal of RF Technologies* and *Journal of Decision Analytics,* and is on the editorial boards of five other technical journals. His research and teaching interests are in data and text mining, decision support systems, knowledge management, business intelligence, and enterprise modeling.

Efraim Turban (M.B.A., Ph.D., University of California, Berkeley) is a visiting scholar at the Pacific Institute for Information System Management, University of Hawaii. Prior to this, he was on the staff of several universities, including City University of Hong Kong; Lehigh University; Florida International University; California State University, Long

Beach; Eastern Illinois University; and the University of Southern California. Dr. Turban is the author of more than 100 refereed papers published in leading journals, such as *Management Science, MIS Quarterly,* and *Decision Support Systems.* He is also the author of 20 books, including *Electronic Commerce: A Managerial Perspective* and *Information Technology for Management.* He is also a consultant to major corporations worldwide. Dr. Turban's current areas of interest are Web-based decision support systems, social commerce, and collaborative decision making.

Decision Making and Analytics
An Overview

LEARNING OBJECTIVES FOR PART I

- Understand the need for business analytics
- Understand the foundations and key issues of managerial decision making
- Understand the major categories and applications of business analytics
- Learn the major frameworks of computerized decision support: analytics, decision support systems (DSS), and business intelligence (BI)

This book deals with a collection of computer technologies that support managerial work—essentially, decision making. These technologies have had a profound impact on corporate strategy, performance, and competitiveness. These techniques broadly encompass analytics, business intelligence, and decision support systems, as shown throughout the book. In Part I, we first provide an overview of the whole book in one chapter. We cover several topics in this chapter. The first topic is managerial decision making and its computerized support; the second is frameworks for decision support. We then introduce business analytics and business intelligence. We also provide examples of applications of these analytical techniques, as well as a preview of the entire book. The second chapter within Part I introduces the foundational methods for decision making and relates these to computerized decision support. It also covers the components and technologies of decision support systems.

An Overview of Business Intelligence, Analytics, and Decision Support

LEARNING OBJECTIVES

- Understand today's turbulent business environment and describe how organizations survive and even excel in such an environment (solving problems and exploiting opportunities)
- Understand the need for computerized support of managerial decision making
- Understand an early framework for managerial decision making

- Learn the conceptual foundations of the decision support systems (DSS[1]) methodology
- Describe the business intelligence (BI) methodology and concepts and relate them to DSS
- Understand the various types of analytics
- List the major tools of computerized decision support

The business environment (climate) is constantly changing, and it is becoming more and more complex. Organizations, private and public, are under pressures that force them to respond quickly to changing conditions and to be innovative in the way they operate. Such activities require organizations to be agile and to make frequent and quick strategic, tactical, and operational decisions, some of which are very complex. Making such decisions may require considerable amounts of relevant data, information, and knowledge. Processing these, in the framework of the needed decisions, must be done quickly, frequently in real time, and usually requires some computerized support. This book is about using business analytics as computerized support for managerial decision making. It concentrates on both the theoretical and conceptual foundations of decision support, as well as on the commercial tools and techniques that are available. This introductory chapter provides more details of these topics as well as an overview of the book. This chapter has the following sections:

---

[1]The acronym *DSS* is treated as both singular and plural throughout this book. Similarly, other acronyms, such as *MIS* and *GSS*, designate both plural and singular forms. This is also true of the word *analytics*.

1.1   OPENING VIGNETTE: Magpie Sensing Employs Analytics to Manage a Vaccine Supply Chain Effectively and Safely

Cold chain in healthcare is defined as the temperature-controlled supply chain involving a system of transporting and storing vaccines and pharmaceutical drugs. It consists of three major components—transport and storage equipment, trained personnel, and efficient management procedures. The majority of the vaccines in the cold chain are typically maintained at a temperature of 35–46 degrees Fahrenheit [2–8 degrees Centigrade]. Maintaining cold chain integrity is extremely important for healthcare product manufacturers.

Especially for the vaccines, improper storage and handling practices that compromise vaccine viability prove a costly, time-consuming affair. Vaccines must be stored properly from manufacture until they are available for use. Any extreme temperatures of heat or cold will reduce vaccine potency; such vaccines, if administered, might not yield effective results or could cause adverse effects.

Effectively maintaining the temperatures of storage units throughout the healthcare supply chain in real time—i.e., beginning from the gathering of the resources, manufacturing, distribution, and dispensing of the products—is the most effective solution desired in the cold chain. Also, the location-tagged real-time environmental data about the storage units helps in monitoring the cold chain for spoiled products. The chain of custody can be easily identified to assign product liability.

A study conducted by the Centers for Disease Control and Prevention (CDC) looked at the handling of cold chain vaccines by 45 healthcare providers around United States and reported that three-quarters of the providers experienced serious cold chain violations.

A WAY TOWARD A POSSIBLE SOLUTION

Magpie Sensing, a start-up project under Ebers Smith and Douglas Associated LLC, provides a suite of cold chain monitoring and analysis technologies for the healthcare industry. It is a shippable, wireless temperature and humidity monitor that provides real-time, location-aware tracking of cold chain products during shipment. Magpie Sensing's solutions rely on rich analytics algorithms that leverage the data gathered from the monitoring devices to improve the efficiency of cold chain processes and predict cold storage problems before they occur.

Magpie sensing applies all three types of analytical techniques—descriptive, predictive, and prescriptive analytics—to turn the raw data returned from the monitoring devices into actionable recommendations and warnings.

The properties of the cold storage system, which include the set point of the storage system's thermostat, the typical range of temperature values in the storage system, and the duty cycle of the system's compressor, are monitored and reported in real time. This information helps trained personnel to ensure that the storage unit is properly configured to store a particular product. All the temperature information is displayed on a Web dashboard that shows a graph of the temperature inside the specific storage unit.

Based on information derived from the monitoring devices, Magpie's predictive analytic algorithms can determine the set point of the storage unit's thermostat and alert the system's users if the system is incorrectly configured, depending upon the various types of products stored. This offers a solution to the users of consumer refrigerators where the thermostat is not temperature graded. Magpie's system also sends alerts about possible temperature violations based on the storage unit's average temperature and subsequent compressor cycle runs, which may drop the temperature below the freezing point. Magpie's predictive analytics further report possible human errors, such as failure to shut the storage unit doors or the presence of an incomplete seal, by analyzing the temperature trend and alerting users via Web interface, text message, or audible alert before the temperature bounds are actually violated. In a similar way, a compressor or a power failure can be detected; the estimated time before the storage unit reaches an unsafe temperature also is reported, which prepares the users to look for backup solutions such as using dry ice to restore power.

In addition to predictive analytics, Magpie Sensing's analytics systems can provide prescriptive recommendations for improving the cold storage processes and business decision making. Prescriptive analytics help users dial in the optimal temperature setting, which helps to achieve the right balance between freezing and spoilage risk; this, in turn, provides a cushion-time to react to the situation before the products spoil. Its prescriptive analytics also gather useful meta-information on cold storage units, including the times of day that are busiest and periods where the system's doors are opened, which can be used to provide additional design plans and institutional policies that ensure that the system is being properly maintained and not overused.

Furthermore, prescriptive analytics can be used to guide equipment purchase decisions by constantly analyzing the performance of current storage units. Based on the storage system's efficiency, decisions on distributing the products across available storage units can be made based on the product's sensitivity.

Using Magpie Sensing's cold chain analytics, additional manufacturing time and expenditure can be eliminated by ensuring that product safety can be secured throughout the supply chain and effective products can be administered to the patients. Compliance with state and federal safety regulations can be better achieved through automatic data gathering and reporting about the products involved in the cold chain.

QUESTIONS FOR THE OPENING VIGNETTE

1. What information is provided by the descriptive analytics employed at Magpie Sensing?
2. What type of support is provided by the predictive analytics employed at Magpie Sensing?
3. How does prescriptive analytics help in business decision making?
4. In what ways can actionable information be reported in real time to concerned users of the system?
5. In what other situations might real-time monitoring applications be needed?

WHAT WE CAN LEARN FROM THIS VIGNETTE

This vignette illustrates how data from a business process can be used to generate insights at various levels. First, the graphical analysis of the data (termed *reporting analytics*) allows users to get a good feel for the situation. Then, additional analysis using **data mining** techniques can be used to estimate what future behavior would be like. This is the domain of predictive analytics. Such analysis can then be taken to create specific recommendations for operators. This is an example of what we call prescriptive analytics. Finally, this opening vignette also suggests that innovative applications of analytics can create new business ventures. Identifying opportunities for applications of analytics and assisting with decision making in specific domains is an emerging entrepreneurial opportunity.

Sources: Magpiesensing.com, "Magpie Sensing Cold Chain Analytics and Monitoring," **magpiesensing.com/wp-content/uploads/2013/01/ColdChainAnalyticsMagpieSensing-Whitepaper.pdf** (accessed July 2013); Centers for Disease Control and Prevention, Vaccine Storage and Handling, **http://www.cdc.gov/vaccines/pubs/pinkbook/vac-storage.html#storage** (accessed July 2013); A. Zaleski, "Magpie Analytics System Tracks Cold-Chain Products to Keep Vaccines, Reagents Fresh" (2012), **technicallybaltimore.com/profiles/startups/magpie-analytics-system-tracks-cold-chain-products-to-keep-vaccines-reagents-fresh** (accessed February 2013).

1.2 CHANGING BUSINESS ENVIRONMENTS AND COMPUTERIZED DECISION SUPPORT

The opening vignette illustrates how a company can employ technologies to make sense of data and make better decisions. Companies are moving aggressively to computerized support of their operations. To understand why companies are embracing computerized support, including business intelligence, we developed a model called the *Business Pressures–Responses–Support Model*, which is shown in Figure 1.1.

The Business Pressures–Responses–Support Model

The Business Pressures–Responses–Support Model, as its name indicates, has three components: business pressures that result from today's business climate, responses (actions taken) by companies to counter the pressures (or to take advantage of the opportunities available in the environment), and computerized support that facilitates the monitoring of the environment and enhances the response actions taken by organizations.

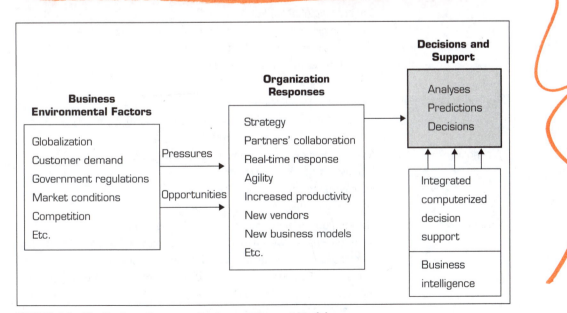

FIGURE 1.1 The Business Pressures–Responses–Support Model.

THE BUSINESS ENVIRONMENT The environment in which organizations operate today is becoming more and more complex. This complexity creates opportunities on the one hand and problems on the other. Take globalization as an example. Today, you can easily find suppliers and customers in many countries, which means you can buy cheaper materials and sell more of your products and services; great opportunities exist. However, globalization also means more and stronger competitors. Business environment factors can be divided into four major categories: *markets, consumer demands, technology,* and *societal.* These categories are summarized in Table 1.1.

Note that the *intensity* of most of these factors increases with time, leading to more pressures, more competition, and so on. In addition, organizations and departments within organizations face decreased budgets and amplified pressures from top managers to increase performance and profit. In this kind of environment, managers must respond quickly, innovate, and be agile. Let's see how they do it.

ORGANIZATIONAL RESPONSES: BE REACTIVE, ANTICIPATIVE, ADAPTIVE, AND PROACTIVE
Both private and public organizations are aware of today's business environment and pressures. They use different actions to counter the pressures. Vodafone New Zealand Ltd (Krivda, 2008), for example, turned to BI to improve communication and to support executives in its effort to retain existing customers and increase revenue from these customers. Managers may take other actions, including the following:

- Employ strategic planning.
- Use new and innovative business models.
- Restructure business processes.
- Participate in business alliances.
- Improve corporate information systems.
- Improve partnership relationships.

TABLE 1.1 Business Environment Factors That Create Pressures on Organizations

Factor	Description
Markets	Strong competition
	Expanding global markets
	Booming electronic markets on the Internet
	Innovative marketing methods
	Opportunities for outsourcing with IT support
	Need for real-time, on-demand transactions
Consumer demands	Desire for customization
	Desire for quality, diversity of products, and speed of delivery
	Customers getting powerful and less loyal
Technology	More innovations, new products, and new services
	Increasing obsolescence rate
	Increasing information overload
	Social networking, Web 2.0 and beyond
Societal	Growing government regulations and deregulation
	Workforce more diversified, older, and composed of more women
	Prime concerns of homeland security and terrorist attacks
	Necessity of Sarbanes-Oxley Act and other reporting-related legislation
	Increasing social responsibility of companies
	Greater emphasis on sustainability

- Encourage innovation and creativity.
- Improve customer service and relationships.
- Employ social media and mobile platforms for e-commerce and beyond.
- Move to make-to-order production and on-demand manufacturing and services.
- Use new IT to improve communication, data access (discovery of information), and collaboration.
- Respond quickly to competitors' actions (e.g., in pricing, promotions, new products and services).
- Automate many tasks of white-collar employees.
- Automate certain decision processes, especially those dealing with customers.
- Improve decision making by employing analytics.

Many, if not all, of these actions require some computerized support. These and other response actions are frequently facilitated by computerized decision support (DSS).

CLOSING THE STRATEGY GAP One of the major objectives of computerized decision support is to facilitate closing the gap between the current performance of an organization and its desired performance, as expressed in its mission, objectives, and goals, and the strategy to achieve them. In order to understand why computerized support is needed and how it is provided, especially for decision-making support, let's look at managerial decision making.

SECTION 1.2 REVIEW QUESTIONS

1. List the components of and explain the Business Pressures–Responses–Support Model.
2. What are some of the major factors in today's business environment?
3. What are some of the major response activities that organizations take?

1.3 MANAGERIAL DECISION MAKING

Management is a process by which organizational goals are achieved by using resources. The resources are considered inputs, and attainment of goals is viewed as the output of the process. The degree of success of the organization and the manager is often measured by the ratio of outputs to inputs. This ratio is an indication of the organization's *productivity*, which is a reflection of the *organizational and managerial performance*.

The level of productivity or the success of management depends on the performance of managerial functions, such as planning, organizing, directing, and controlling. To perform their functions, managers engage in a continuous process of making decisions. Making a decision means selecting the best alternative from two or more solutions.

The Nature of Managers' Work

Mintzberg's (2008) classic study of top managers and several replicated studies suggest that managers perform 10 major roles that can be classified into three major categories: *interpersonal, informational*, and *decisional* (see Table 1.2).

To perform these roles, managers need information that is delivered efficiently and in a timely manner to personal computers (PCs) on their desktops and to mobile devices. This information is delivered by networks, generally via Web technologies.

In addition to obtaining information necessary to better perform their roles, managers use computers directly to support and improve decision making, which is a key task

TABLE 1.2	Mintzberg's 10 Managerial Roles
Role	**Description**
Interpersonal	
Figurehead	Is symbolic head; obliged to perform a number of routine duties of a legal or social nature
Leader	Is responsible for the motivation and activation of subordinates; responsible for staffing, training, and associated duties
Liaison	Maintains self-developed network of outside contacts and informers who provide favors and information
Informational	
Monitor	Seeks and receives a wide variety of special information (much of it current) to develop a thorough understanding of the organization and environment; emerges as the nerve center of the organization's internal and external information
Disseminator	Transmits information received from outsiders or from subordinates to members of the organization; some of this information is factual, and some involves interpretation and integration
Spokesperson	Transmits information to outsiders about the organization's plans, policies, actions, results, and so forth; serves as an expert on the organization's industry
Decisional	
Entrepreneur	Searches the organization and its environment for opportunities and initiates improvement projects to bring about change; supervises design of certain projects
Disturbance handler	Is responsible for corrective action when the organization faces important, unexpected disturbances
Resource allocator	Is responsible for the allocation of organizational resources of all kinds; in effect, is responsible for the making or approval of all significant organizational decisions
Negotiator	Is responsible for representing the organization at major negotiations

Sources: Compiled from H. A. Mintzberg, *The Nature of Managerial Work.* Prentice Hall, Englewood Cliffs, NJ, 1980; and H. A. Mintzberg, *The Rise and Fall of Strategic Planning.* The Free Press, New York, 1993.

that is part of most of these roles. Many managerial activities in all roles revolve around decision making. *Managers, especially those at high managerial levels, are primarily decision makers.* We review the decision-making process next but will study it in more detail in the next chapter.

The Decision-Making Process

For years, managers considered decision making purely an art—a talent acquired over a long period through experience (i.e., learning by trial-and-error) and by using intuition. Management was considered an art because a variety of individual styles could be used in approaching and successfully solving the same types of managerial problems. These styles were often based on creativity, judgment, intuition, and experience rather than on systematic quantitative methods grounded in a scientific approach. However, recent research suggests that companies with top managers who are more focused on persistent work (almost dullness) tend to outperform those with leaders whose main strengths are interpersonal communication skills (Kaplan et al., 2008; Brooks, 2009). It is more important to emphasize methodical, thoughtful, analytical decision making rather than flashiness and interpersonal communication skills.

Managers usually make decisions by following a four-step process (we learn more about these in Chapter 2):

1. Define the problem (i.e., a decision situation that may deal with some difficulty or with an opportunity).
2. Construct a model that describes the real-world problem.
3. Identify possible solutions to the modeled problem and evaluate the solutions.
4. Compare, choose, and recommend a potential solution to the problem.

To follow this process, one must make sure that sufficient alternative solutions are being considered, that the consequences of using these alternatives can be reasonably predicted, and that comparisons are done properly. However, the environmental factors listed in Table 1.1 make such an evaluation process difficult for the following reasons:

- Technology, information systems, advanced search engines, and globalization result in more and more alternatives from which to choose.
- Government regulations and the need for compliance, political instability and terrorism, competition, and changing consumer demands produce more uncertainty, making it more difficult to predict consequences and the future.
- Other factors are the need to make rapid decisions, the frequent and unpredictable changes that make trial-and-error learning difficult, and the potential costs of making mistakes.
- These environments are growing more complex every day. Therefore, making decisions today is indeed a complex task.

Because of these trends and changes, it is nearly impossible to rely on a trial-and-error approach to management, especially for decisions for which the factors shown in Table 1.1 are strong influences. Managers must be more sophisticated; they must use the new tools and techniques of their fields. Most of those tools and techniques are discussed in this book. Using them to support decision making can be extremely rewarding in making effective decisions. In the following section, we look at why we need computer support and how it is provided.

SECTION 1.3 REVIEW QUESTIONS

1. Describe the three major managerial roles, and list some of the specific activities in each.
2. Why have some argued that management is the same as decision making?
3. Describe the four steps managers take in making a decision.

1.4 INFORMATION SYSTEMS SUPPORT FOR DECISION MAKING

From traditional uses in payroll and bookkeeping functions, computerized systems have penetrated complex managerial areas ranging from the design and management of automated factories to the application of analytical methods for the evaluation of proposed mergers and acquisitions. Nearly all executives know that information technology is vital to their business and extensively use information technologies.

Computer applications have moved from transaction processing and monitoring activities to problem analysis and solution applications, and much of the activity is done with Web-based technologies, in many cases accessed through mobile devices. Analytics and BI tools such as data warehousing, data mining, online analytical processing (OLAP), dashboards, and the use of the Web for decision support are the cornerstones of today's modern management. Managers must have high-speed, networked information systems (wireline or wireless) to assist them with their most important task: making decisions. Besides the obvious growth in hardware, software, and network capacities, some developments have clearly contributed to facilitating growth of decision support and analytics in a number of ways, including the following:

- ***Group communication and collaboration.*** Many decisions are made today by groups whose members may be in different locations. Groups can collaborate and communicate readily by using Web-based tools as well as the ubiquitous smartphones. Collaboration is especially important along the supply chain, where partners—all the way from vendors to customers—must share information. Assembling a group of decision makers, especially experts, in one place can be costly. Information systems can improve the collaboration process of a group and enable its members to be at different locations (saving travel costs). We will study some applications in Chapter 12.

- ***Improved data management.*** Many decisions involve complex computations. Data for these can be stored in different databases anywhere in the organization and even possibly at Web sites outside the organization. The data may include text, sound, graphics, and video, and they can be in different languages. It may be necessary to transmit data quickly from distant locations. Systems today can search, store, and transmit needed data quickly, economically, securely, and transparently.

- ***Managing giant data warehouses and Big Data.*** Large data warehouses, like the ones operated by Walmart, contain terabytes and even petabytes of data. Special methods, including parallel computing, are available to organize, search, and mine the data. The costs related to data warehousing are declining. Technologies that fall under the broad category of Big Data have enabled massive data coming from a variety of sources and in many different forms, which allows a very different view into organizational performance that was not possible in the past.

- ***Analytical support.*** With more data and analysis technologies, more alternatives can be evaluated, forecasts can be improved, risk analysis can be performed quickly, and the views of experts (some of whom may be in remote locations) can be collected quickly and at a reduced cost. Expertise can even be derived directly from analytical systems. With such tools, decision makers can perform complex simulations, check many possible scenarios, and assess diverse impacts quickly and economically. This, of course, is the focus of several chapters in the book.

- ***Overcoming cognitive limits in processing and storing information.*** According to Simon (1977), the human mind has only a limited ability to process and store information. People sometimes find it difficult to recall and use information in an error-free fashion due to their cognitive limits. The term *cognitive limits* indicates that an individual's problem-solving capability is limited when a wide range of diverse information and knowledge is required. Computerized systems enable people to overcome their cognitive limits by quickly accessing and processing vast amounts of stored information (see Chapter 2).

- ***Knowledge management.*** Organizations have gathered vast stores of information about their own operations, customers, internal procedures, employee interactions, and so forth through the unstructured and structured communications taking place among the various stakeholders. Knowledge management systems (KMS, Chapter 12) have become sources of formal and informal support for decision making to managers, although sometimes they may not even be called *KMS*.

- ***Anywhere, any time support.*** Using wireless technology, managers can access information anytime and from any place, analyze and interpret it, and communicate with those involved. This perhaps is the biggest change that has occurred in the last few years. The speed at which information needs to be processed and converted into decisions has truly changed expectations for both consumers and businesses.

These and other capabilities have been driving the use of computerized decision support since the late 1960s, but especially since the mid-1990s. The growth of mobile technologies, social media platforms, and analytical tools has enabled a much higher level of information systems support for managers. In the next sections we study a historical classification of decision support tasks. This leads us to be introduced to decision support systems. We will then study an overview of technologies that have been broadly referred to as business intelligence. From there we will broaden our horizons to introduce various types of analytics.

SECTION 1.4 REVIEW QUESTIONS

1. What are some of the key system-oriented trends that have fostered IS-supported decision making to a new level?
2. List some capabilities of information systems that can facilitate managerial decision making.
3. How can a computer help overcome the cognitive limits of humans?

1.5 AN EARLY FRAMEWORK FOR COMPUTERIZED DECISION SUPPORT

An early framework for computerized decision support includes several major concepts that are used in forthcoming sections and chapters of this book. Gorry and Scott-Morton created and used this framework in the early 1970s, and the framework then evolved into a new technology called *DSS*.

The Gorry and Scott-Morton Classical Framework

Gorry and Scott-Morton (1971) proposed a framework that is a 3-by-3 matrix, as shown in Figure 1.2. The two dimensions are the degree of structuredness and the types of control.

Type of Decision	Type of Control		
	Operational Control	**Managerial Control**	**Strategic Planning**
Structured	**1** Accounts receivable Accounts payable Order entry	**2** Budget analysis Short-term forecasting Personnel reports Make-or-buy	**3** Financial management Investment portfolio Warehouse location Distribution systems
Semistructured	**4** Production scheduling Inventory control	**5** Credit evaluation Budget preparation Plant layout Project scheduling Reward system design Inventory categorization	**6** Building a new plant Mergers & acquisitions New product planning Compensation planning Quality assurance HR policies Inventory planning

Unstructured	**7**
	Buying software
	Approving loans
	Operating a help desk
	Selecting a cover for
	  a magazine
		8
		Negotiating
		Recruiting an executive
		Buying hardware
		Lobbying
			9
			R & D planning
			New tech development
			Social responsibility
			  planning

FIGURE 1.2 Decision Support Frameworks.

DEGREE OF STRUCTUREDNESS The left side of Figure 1.2 is based on Simon's (1977) idea that decision-making processes fall along a continuum that ranges from highly structured (sometimes called *programmed*) to highly unstructured (i.e., *nonprogrammed*) decisions. Structured processes are routine and typically repetitive problems for which standard solution methods exist. *Unstructured processes* are fuzzy, complex problems for which there are no cut-and-dried solution methods.

An **unstructured problem** is one where the articulation of the problem or the solution approach may be unstructured in itself. In a **structured problem**, the procedures for obtaining the best (or at least a good enough) solution are known. Whether the problem involves finding an appropriate inventory level or choosing an optimal investment strategy, the objectives are clearly defined. Common objectives are cost minimization and profit maximization.

Semistructured problems fall between structured and unstructured problems, having some structured elements and some unstructured elements. Keen and Scott-Morton (1978) mentioned trading bonds, setting marketing budgets for consumer products, and performing capital acquisition analysis as semistructured problems.

TYPES OF CONTROL The second half of the Gorry and Scott-Morton framework (refer to Figure 1.2) is based on Anthony's (1965) taxonomy, which defines three broad categories that encompass all managerial activities: *strategic planning*, which involves defining long-range goals and policies for resource allocation; *management control*, the acquisition and efficient use of resources in the accomplishment of organizational goals; and *operational control*, the efficient and effective execution of specific tasks.

THE DECISION SUPPORT MATRIX Anthony's and Simon's taxonomies are combined in the nine-cell decision support matrix shown in Figure 1.2. The initial purpose of this matrix was to suggest different types of computerized support to different cells in the matrix. Gorry and Scott-Morton suggested, for example, that for *semistructured decisions* and *unstructured decisions*, conventional management information systems (MIS) and management science (MS) tools are insufficient. Human intellect and a different approach to computer technologies are necessary. They proposed the use of a supportive information system, which they called a *DSS*.

Note that the more structured and operational control-oriented tasks (such as those in cells 1, 2, and 4) are usually performed by lower-level managers, whereas the tasks in cells 6, 8, and 9 are the responsibility of top executives or highly trained specialists.

Computer Support for Structured Decisions

Computers have historically supported structured and some semistructured decisions, especially those that involve operational and managerial control, since the 1960s. Operational and managerial control decisions are made in all functional areas, especially in finance and production (i.e., operations) management.

Structured problems, which are encountered repeatedly, have a high level of structure. It is therefore possible to abstract, analyze, and classify them into specific categories. For example, a make-or-buy decision is one category. Other examples of categories are capital budgeting, allocation of resources, distribution, procurement, planning, and inventory control decisions. For each category of decision, an easy-to-apply prescribed model and solution approach have been developed, generally as quantitative formulas. Therefore, it is possible to use a *scientific approach* for automating portions of managerial decision making.

Computer Support for Unstructured Decisions

Unstructured problems can be only partially supported by standard computerized quantitative methods. It is usually necessary to develop customized solutions. However, such solutions may benefit from data and information generated from corporate or external data sources. Intuition and judgment may play a large role in these types of decisions, as may computerized communication and collaboration technologies, as well as knowledge management (see Chapter 12).

Computer Support for Semistructured Problems

Solving semistructured problems may involve a combination of standard solution procedures and human judgment. Management science can provide models for the portion of a decision-making problem that is structured. For the unstructured portion, a DSS can improve the quality of the information on which the decision is based by providing, for example, not only a single solution but also a range of alternative solutions, along with their potential impacts. These capabilities help managers to better understand the nature of problems and, thus, to make better decisions.

SECTION 1.5 REVIEW QUESTIONS

1. What are structured, unstructured, and semistructured decisions? Provide two examples of each.
2. Define *operational control, managerial control*, and *strategic planning*. Provide two examples of each.
3. What are the nine cells of the decision framework? Explain what each is for.
4. How can computers provide support for making structured decisions?
5. How can computers provide support to semistructured and unstructured decisions?

1.6 THE CONCEPT OF DECISION SUPPORT SYSTEMS (DSS)

In the early 1970s, Scott-Morton first articulated the major concepts of DSS. He defined **decision support systems (DSS)** as "interactive computer-based systems, which help decision makers utilize *data* and *models* to solve unstructured problems" (Gorry and Scott-Morton, 1971). The following is another classic DSS definition, provided by Keen and Scott-Morton (1978):

> Decision support systems couple the intellectual resources of individuals with the capabilities of the computer to improve the quality of decisions. It is a computer-based support system for management decision makers who deal with semistructured problems.

Note that the term *decision support system*, like *management information system* (MIS) and other terms in the field of IT, is a content-free expression (i.e., it means different things to different people). Therefore, there is no universally accepted definition of DSS. (We present additional definitions in Chapter 2.) Actually, DSS can be viewed as a *conceptual methodology*—that is, a broad, umbrella term. However, some view DSS as a narrower, specific decision support application.

DSS as an Umbrella Term

The term *DSS* can be used as an umbrella term to describe any computerized system that supports decision making in an organization. An organization may have a knowledge management system to guide all its personnel in their problem solving. Another organization may have separate support systems for marketing, finance, and accounting; a supply chain management (SCM) system for production; and several rule-based systems for product repair diagnostics and help desks. DSS encompasses them all.

Evolution of DSS into Business Intelligence

In the early days of DSS, managers let their staff do some supportive analysis by using DSS tools. As PC technology advanced, a new generation of managers evolved—one that was comfortable with computing and knew that technology can directly help make intelligent business decisions faster. New tools such as OLAP, data warehousing, data mining, and intelligent systems, delivered via Web technology, added promised capabilities and easy access to tools, models, and data for computer-aided decision making. These tools started to appear under the names *BI* and *business analytics* in the mid-1990s. We introduce these concepts next, and relate the DSS and BI concepts in the following sections.

SECTION 1.6 REVIEW QUESTIONS

1. Provide two definitions of *DSS*.
2. Describe *DSS* as an umbrella term.

1.7 A FRAMEWORK FOR BUSINESS INTELLIGENCE (BI)

The decision support concepts presented in Sections 1.5 and 1.6 have been implemented incrementally, under different names, by many vendors that have created tools and methodologies for decision support. As the enterprise-wide systems grew, managers were able to access user-friendly reports that enabled them to make decisions quickly. These systems, which were generally called *executive information systems* (EIS), then began to offer additional visualization, alerts, and performance measurement capabilities. By 2006, the major *commercial* products and services appeared under the umbrella term *business intelligence* (BI).

Definitions of BI

Business intelligence (BI) is an umbrella term that combines architectures, tools, databases, analytical tools, applications, and methodologies. It is, like DSS, a content-free expression, so it means different things to different people. Part of the confusion about BI lies in the flurry of acronyms and buzzwords that are associated with it (e.g., business performance management [BPM]). BI's major objective is to enable interactive access (sometimes in real time) to data, to enable manipulation of data, and to give business managers and analysts the ability to conduct appropriate analyses. By analyzing historical and current data, situations, and performances, decision makers get valuable insights that enable them to make more informed and better decisions. The process of BI is based on the *transformation* of data to information, then to decisions, and finally to actions.

A Brief History of BI

The term *BI* was coined by the Gartner Group in the mid-1990s. However, the concept is much older; it has its roots in the MIS reporting systems of the 1970s. During that period, reporting systems were static, two dimensional, and had no analytical capabilities. In the early 1980s, the concept of *executive information systems* (EIS) emerged. This concept expanded the computerized support to top-level managers and executives. Some of the

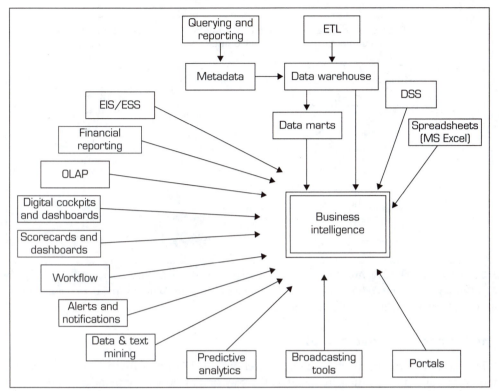

FIGURE 1.3   **Evolution of Business Intelligence (BI).**

capabilities introduced were dynamic multidimensional (ad hoc or on-demand) reporting, forecasting and prediction, trend analysis, drill-down to details, status access, and critical success factors. These features appeared in dozens of commercial products until the mid-1990s. Then the same capabilities and some new ones appeared under the name BI. Today, a good BI-based enterprise information system contains all the information executives need. So, the original concept of EIS was transformed into BI. By 2005, BI systems started to include *artificial intelligence* capabilities as well as powerful analytical capabilities. Figure 1.3 illustrates the various tools and techniques that may be included in a BI system. It illustrates the evolution of BI as well. The tools shown in Figure 1.3 provide the capabilities of BI. The most sophisticated BI products include most of these capabilities; others specialize in only some of them. We will study several of these capabilities in more detail in Chapters 5 through 9.

The Architecture of BI

A BI system has four major components: a *data warehouse*, with its source data; *business analytics*, a collection of tools for manipulating, mining, and analyzing the data in the data warehouse; *business performance management (BPM)* for monitoring and analyzing performance; and a *user interface* (e.g., a dashboard). The relationship among these components is illustrated in Figure 1.4. We will discuss these components in detail in Chapters 3 through 9.

Styles of BI

The architecture of BI depends on its applications. MicroStrategy Corp. distinguishes five styles of BI and offers special tools for each. The five styles are report delivery and alerting; enterprise reporting (using dashboards and scorecards); cube analysis (also known as slice-and-dice analysis); ad hoc queries; and statistics and data mining.

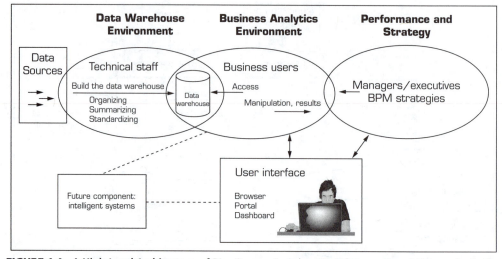

FIGURE 1.4 **A High-Level Architecture of BI.** *Source:* Based on W. Eckerson, *Smart Companies in the 21st Century: The Secrets of Creating Successful Business Intelligent Solutions.* The Data Warehousing Institute, Seattle, WA, 2003, p. 32, Illustration 5.

The Origins and Drivers of BI

Where did modern approaches to data warehousing (DW) and BI come from? What are their roots, and how do those roots affect the way organizations are managing these initiatives today? Today's investments in information technology are under increased scrutiny in terms of their bottom-line impact and potential. The same is true of DW and the BI applications that make these initiatives possible.

Organizations are being compelled to capture, understand, and harness their data to support decision making in order to improve business operations. Legislation and regulation (e.g., the Sarbanes-Oxley Act of 2002) now require business leaders to document their business processes and to sign off on the legitimacy of the information they rely on and report to stakeholders. Moreover, business cycle times are now extremely compressed; faster, more informed, and better decision making is therefore a competitive imperative. Managers need the *right information* at the *right time* and in the *right place*. This is the mantra for modern approaches to BI.

Organizations have to work smart. Paying careful attention to the management of BI initiatives is a necessary aspect of doing business. It is no surprise, then, that organizations are increasingly championing BI. You will hear about more BI successes and the fundamentals of those successes in Chapters 3 through 9. Examples of many applications of BI are provided in Table 1.3. Application Case 1.1 illustrates one such application of BI that has helped many airlines, as well as the companies offering such services to the airlines.

A Multimedia Exercise in Business Intelligence

Teradata University Network (TUN) includes some videos along the lines of the television show *CSI* to illustrate concepts of analytics in different industries. These are called "BSI Videos (Business Scenario Investigations)." Not only these are entertaining, but they also provide the class with some questions for discussion. For starters, please go to **teradatauniversitynetwork.com/teach-and-learn/library-item/?LibraryItemId=889**. Watch the video that appears on YouTube. Essentially, you have to assume the role of a customer service center professional. An incoming flight is running late, and several passengers are likely to miss their connecting flights. There are seats on one outgoing flight that can accommodate two of the four passengers. Which two passengers should be given

TABLE 1.3 Business Value of BI Analytical Applications

Analytic Application	Business Question	Business Value
Customer segmentation	What market segments do my customers fall into, and what are their characteristics?	Personalize customer relationships for higher satisfaction and retention.
Propensity to buy	Which customers are most likely to respond to my promotion?	Target customers based on their need to increase their loyalty to your product line. Also, increase campaign profitability by focusing on the most likely to buy.
Customer profitability	What is the lifetime profitability of my customer?	Make individual business interaction decisions based on the overall profitability of customers.
Fraud detection	How can I tell which transactions are likely to be fraudulent?	Quickly determine fraud and take immediate action to minimize cost.
Customer attrition	Which customer is at risk of leaving?	Prevent loss of high-value customers and let go of lower-value customers.
Channel optimization	What is the best channel to reach my customer in each segment?	Interact with customers based on their preference and your need to manage cost.

Source: A. Ziama and J. Kasher, *Data Mining Primer for the Data Warehousing Professional.* Teradata, Dayton, OH, 2004.

Application Case 1.1

Sabre Helps Its Clients Through Dashboards and Analytics

Sabre is one of the world leaders in the travel industry, providing both business-to-consumer services as well as business-to-business services. It serves travelers, travel agents, corporations, and travel suppliers through its four main companies: Travelocity, Sabre Travel Network, Sabre Airline Solutions, and Sabre Hospitality Solutions. The current volatile global economic environment poses significant competitive challenges to the airline industry. To stay ahead of the competition, Sabre Airline Solutions recognized that airline executives needed enhanced tools for managing their business decisions by eliminating the traditional, manual, time-consuming process of collecting and aggregating financial and other information needed for actionable initiatives. This enables real-time decision support at airlines throughout the world that maximize their (and, in turn, Sabre's) return on information by driving insights, actionable intelligence, and value for customers from the growing data.

Sabre developed an Enterprise Travel Data Warehouse (ETDW) using Teradata to hold its massive reservations data. ETDW is updated in near-real time with batches that run every 15 minutes, gathering data from all of Sabre's businesses. Sabre uses its ETDW to create Sabre Executive Dashboards that provide near–real-time executive insights using a Cognos 8 BI platform with Oracle Data Integrator and Oracle Goldengate technology infrastructure. The Executive Dashboards offer their client airlines' top-level managers and decision makers a timely, automated, user-friendly solution, aggregating critical performance metrics in a succinct way and providing at a glance a 360-degree view of the overall health of the airline. At one airline, Sabre's Executive Dashboards provide senior management with a daily and intra-day snapshot of key performance indicators in a single application, replacing the once-a-week, 8-hour process of generating the same report from various data sources. The use of dashboards is not limited to the external customers; Sabre also uses them for their assessment of internal operational performance.

The dashboards help Sabre's customers to have a clear understanding of the data through the visual displays that incorporate interactive drill-down capabilities. It replaces flat presentations and allows for more focused review of the data with less effort and

(Continued)

Application Case 1.1 (Continued)

time. This facilitates team dialog by making the data/metrics pertaining to sales performance, including ticketing, seats sold and flown, operational performance such as data on flight movement and tracking, customer reservations, inventory, and revenue across an airline's multiple distribution channels, available to many stakeholders. The dashboard systems provide scalable infrastructure, graphical user interface (GUI) support, data integration, and data aggregation that empower airline executives to be more proactive in taking actions that lead to positive impacts on the overall health of their airline.

With its ETDW, Sabre could also develop other Web-based analytical and reporting solutions that leverage data to gain customer insights through analysis of customer profiles and their sales interactions to calculate customer value. This enables better customer segmentation and insights for value-added services.

QUESTIONS FOR DISCUSSION

1. What is traditional reporting? How is it used in organizations?
2. How can analytics be used to transform traditional reporting?
3. How can interactive reporting assist organizations in decision making?

What We Can Learn from This Application Case

This Application Case shows that organizations that earlier used reporting only for tracking their internal business activities and meeting compliance requirements set out by the government are now moving toward generating actionable intelligence from their transactional business data. Reporting has become broader as organizations are now trying to analyze archived transactional data to understand underlying hidden trends and patterns that would enable them to make better decisions by gaining insights into problematic areas and resolving them to pursue current and future market opportunities. Reporting has advanced to interactive online reports that enable users to pull and quickly build custom reports as required and even present the reports aided by visualization tools that have the ability to connect to the database, providing the capabilities of digging deep into summarized data.

Source: Teradata.com, "Sabre Airline Solutions," **teradata.com/t/case-studies/Sabre-Airline-Solutions-EB6281** (accessed February 2013).

---

priority? You are given information about customers' profiles and relationship with the airline. Your decisions might change as you learn more about those customers' profiles.

Watch the video, pause it as appropriate, and answer the questions on which passengers should be given priority. Then resume the video to get more information. After the video is complete, you can see the slides related to this video and how the analysis was prepared on a slide set at **teradatauniversitynetwork.com/templates/Download.aspx?ContentItemId=891.** Please note that access to this content requires initial registration.

This multimedia excursion provides an example of how additional information made available through an enterprise data warehouse can assist in decision making.

The DSS–BI Connection

By now, you should be able to see some of the similarities and differences between DSS and BI. First, their architectures are very similar because BI evolved from DSS. However, BI implies the use of a data warehouse, whereas DSS may or may not have such a feature. BI is, therefore, more appropriate for large organizations (because data warehouses are expensive to build and maintain), but DSS can be appropriate to any type of organization.

Second, most DSS are constructed to *directly* support specific decision making. BI systems, in general, are geared to provide accurate and timely information, and they support decision support *indirectly*. This situation is changing, however, as more and more decision support tools are being added to BI software packages.

Third, BI has an executive and strategy orientation, especially in its BPM and dash-board components. DSS, in contrast, is oriented toward analysts.

Fourth, most BI systems are constructed with commercially available tools and components that are fitted to the needs of organizations. In building DSS, the interest may be in constructing solutions to very unstructured problems. In such situations, more programming (e.g., using tools such as Excel) may be needed to customize the solutions.

Fifth, DSS methodologies and even some tools were developed mostly in the academic world. BI methodologies and tools were developed mostly by software companies. (See Zaman, 2005, for information on how BI has evolved.)

Sixth, many of the tools that BI uses are also considered DSS tools. For example, data mining and predictive analysis are core tools in both areas.

Although some people equate DSS with BI, these systems are not, at present, the same. It is interesting to note that some people believe that DSS is a part of BI—one of its analytical tools. Others think that BI is a special case of DSS that deals mostly with reporting, communication, and collaboration (a form of data-oriented DSS). Another explanation (Watson, 2005) is that BI is a result of a continuous revolution and, as such, DSS is one of BI's original elements. In this book, we separate DSS from BI. However, we point to the DSS–BI connection frequently. Further, as noted in the next section onward, in many circles BI has been subsumed by the new term *analytics* or *data science*.

SECTION 1.7 REVIEW QUESTIONS

1. Define *BI*.

2. List and describe the major components of BI.

3. What are the major similarities and differences of DSS and BI?

1.8 BUSINESS ANALYTICS OVERVIEW

The word "analytics" has replaced the previous individual components of computerized decision support technologies that have been available under various labels in the past. Indeed, many practitioners and academics now use the word *analytics* in place of BI. Although many authors and consultants have defined it slightly differently, one can view analytics as the process of developing actionable decisions or recommendation for actions based upon insights generated from historical data. The Institute for Operations Research and Management Science (INFORMS) has created a major initiative to organize and promote analytics. According to INFORMS, analytics represents the combination of computer technology, management science techniques, and statistics to solve real problems. Of course, many other organizations have proposed their own interpretations and motivation for analytics. For example, SAS Institute Inc. proposed eight levels of analytics that begin with standardized reports from a computer system. These reports essentially provide a sense of what is happening with an organization. Additional technologies have enabled us to create more customized reports that can be generated on an ad hoc basis. The next extension of reporting takes us to online analytical processing (OLAP)–type queries that allow a user to dig deeper and determine the specific source of concern or opportunities. Technologies available today can also automatically issue alerts for a decision maker when performance issues warrant such alerts. At a consumer level we see such alerts for weather or other issues. But similar alerts can also be generated in specific settings when sales fall above or below a certain level within a certain time period or when the inventory for a specific product is running low. All of these applications are made possible through analysis and queries on data being collected by an organization. The next level of analysis might entail statistical analysis to better understand patterns. These can then be taken a step further to develop forecasts or models for predicting how customers might respond to

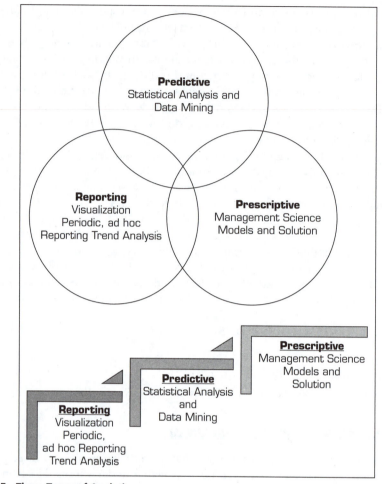

FIGURE 1.5 Three Types of Analytics.

a specific marketing campaign or ongoing service/product offerings. When an organization has a good view of what is happening and what is likely to happen, it can also employ other techniques to make the best decisions under the circumstances. These eight levels of analytics are described in more detail in a white paper by SAS (**sas.com/news/sascom/analytics_levels.pdf**).

This idea of looking at all the data to understand what is happening, what will happen, and how to make the best of it has also been encapsulated by INFORMS in proposing three levels of analytics. These three levels are identified (**informs.org/Community/Analytics**) as descriptive, predictive, and prescriptive. Figure 1.5 presents two graphical views of these three levels of analytics. One view suggests that these three are somewhat independent steps (of a ladder) and one type of analytics application leads to another. The interconnected circles view suggests that there is actually some overlap across these three types of analytics. In either case, the interconnected nature of different types of analytics applications is evident. We next introduce these three levels of analytics.

Descriptive Analytics

Descriptive or reporting analytics refers to knowing what is happening in the organization and understanding some underlying trends and causes of such occurrences. This involves, first of all, consolidation of data sources and availability of all relevant data in a form that enables appropriate reporting and analysis. Usually development of this data infrastructure is part of data warehouses, which we study in Chapter 3. From this data infrastructure we can develop appropriate reports, queries, alerts, and trends using various reporting tools and techniques. We study these in Chapter 4.

A significant technology that has become a key player in this area is visualization. Using the latest visualization tools in the marketplace, we can now develop powerful insights into the operations of our organization. Application Cases 1.2 and 1.3 highlight some such applications in the healthcare domain. Color renderings of such applications are available on the companion Web site and also on Tableau's Web site. Chapter 4 covers visualization in more detail.

Application Case 1.2

Eliminating Inefficiencies at Seattle Children's Hospital

Seattle Children's was the seventh highest ranked children's hospital in 2011, according to *U.S. News & World Report*. For any organization that is committed to saving lives, identifying and removing the inefficiencies from systems and processes so that more resources become available to cater to patient care become very important. At Seattle Children's, management is continuously looking for new ways to improve the quality, safety, and processes from the time a patient is admitted to the time they are discharged. To this end, they spend a lot of time in analyzing the data associated with the patient visits.

To quickly turn patient and hospital data into insights, Seattle Children's implemented Tableau Software's business intelligence application. It provides a browser based on easy-to-use analytics to the stakeholders; this makes it intuitive for individuals to create visualizations and to understand what the data has to offer. The data analysts, business managers, and financial analysts as well as clinicians, doctors, and researchers are all using descriptive analytics to solve different problems in a much faster way. They are developing visual systems on their own, resulting in dashboards and scorecards that help in defining the standards, the current performance achieved measured against the standards, and how these systems will grow into the future. Through the use of monthly and daily dashboards, day-to-day decision making at Seattle Children's has improved significantly.

Seattle Children's measures patient wait-times and analyzes them with the help of visualizations to discover the root causes and contributing factors for patient waiting. They found that early delays cascaded during the day. They focused on on-time appointments of patient services as one of the solutions to improving patient overall waiting time and increasing the availability of beds. Seattle Children's saved about $3 million from the supply chain, and with the help of tools like Tableau, they are finding new ways to increase savings while treating as many patients as possible by making the existing processes more efficient.

QUESTIONS FOR DISCUSSION

1. Who are the users of the tool?
2. What is a dashboard?
3. How does visualization help in decision making?
4. What are the significant results achieved by the use of Tableau?

What We Can Learn from This Application Case

This Application Case shows that reporting analytics involving visualizations such as dashboards can offer major insights into existing data and show how a variety of users in different domains and departments can contribute toward process and quality improvements in an organization. Furthermore, exploring the data visually can help in identifying the root causes of problems and provide a basis for working toward possible solutions.

Source: Tableausoftware.com, "Eliminating Waste at Seattle Children's," **tableausoftware.com/eliminating-waste-at-seattle-childrens** (accessed February 2013).

Application Case 1.3

Analysis at the Speed of Thought

Kaleida Health, the largest healthcare provider in western New York, has more than 10,000 employees, five hospitals, a number of clinics and nursing homes, and a visiting-nurse association that deals with millions of patient records. Kaleida's traditional reporting tools were inadequate to handle the growing data, and they were faced with the challenge of finding a business intelligence tool that could handle large data sets effortlessly, quickly, and with a much deeper analytic capability.

At Kaleida, many of the calculations are now done in Tableau, primarily pulling the data from Oracle databases into Excel and importing the data into Tableau. For many of the monthly analytic reports, data is directly extracted into Tableau from the data warehouse; many of the data queries are saved and rerun, resulting in time savings when dealing with millions of records—each having more than 40 fields per record. Besides speed, Kaleida also uses Tableau to merge different tables for generating extracts.

Using Tableau, Kaleida can analyze emergency room data to determine the number of patients who visit more than 10 times a year. The data often reveal that people frequently use emergency room and ambulance services inappropriately for stomachaches, headaches, and fevers. Kaleida can manage resource utilizations—the use and cost of supplies—which will ultimately lead to efficiency and standardization of supplies management across the system.

Kaleida now has its own business intelligence department and uses Tableau to compare itself to other hospitals across the country. Comparisons are made on various aspects, such as length of patient stay, hospital practices, market share, and partnerships with doctors.

QUESTIONS FOR DISCUSSION

1. What are the desired functionalities of a reporting tool?
2. What advantages were derived by using a reporting tool in the case?

What We Can Learn from This Application Case

Correct selection of a reporting tool is extremely important, especially if an organization wants to derive value from reporting. The generated reports and visualizations should be easily discernible; they should help people in different sectors make sense out of the reports, identify the problematic areas, and contribute toward improving them. Many future organizations will require reporting analytic tools that are fast and capable of handling huge amounts of data efficiently to generate desired reports without the need for third-party consultants and service providers. A truly useful reporting tool can exempt organizations from unnecessary expenditure.

Source: Tableausoftware.com, "Kaleida Health Finds Efficiencies, Stays Competitive," **tableausoftware.com/learn/stories/user-experience-speed-thought-kaleida-health** (accessed February 2013).

Predictive Analytics

Predictive analytics aims to determine what is likely to happen in the future. This analysis is based on statistical techniques as well as other more recently developed techniques that fall under the general category of data mining. The goal of these techniques is to be able to predict if the customer is likely to switch to a competitor ("churn"), what the customer is likely to buy next and how much, what promotion a customer would respond to, or whether this customer is a creditworthy risk. A number of techniques are used in developing predictive analytical applications, including various classification algorithms. For example, as described in Chapters 5 and 6, we can use classification techniques such as decision tree models and neural networks to predict how well a motion picture will do at the box office. We can also use clustering algorithms for segmenting customers into different clusters to be able to target specific promotions to them. Finally, we can use association mining techniques to estimate relationships between different purchasing behaviors. That is, if a customer buys one product, what else is the customer likely to purchase? Such analysis can assist a retailer in recommending or promoting related products. For example, any product search on Amazon.com results in the retailer also suggesting other similar products that may interest a customer. We will study these techniques and their applications in Chapters 6 through 9. Application Cases 1.4 and 1.5 highlight some similar applications. Application Case 1.4 introduces a movie you may have heard of: *Moneyball*. It is perhaps one of the best examples of applications of predictive analysis in sports.

Application Case 1.4

Moneyball: Analytics in Sports and Movies

Moneyball, a biographical, sports, drama film, was released in 2011 and directed by Bennett Miller. The film was based on Michael Lewis's book, *Moneyball*. The movie gave a detailed account of the Oakland Athletics baseball team during the 2002 season and the Oakland general manager's efforts to assemble a competitive team.

The Oakland Athletics suffered a big loss to the New York Yankees in 2001 postseason. As a result, Oakland lost many of its star players to free agency and ended up with a weak team with unfavorable financial prospects. The general manager's efforts to reassemble a competitive team were denied because Oakland had limited payroll. The scouts for the Oakland Athletics followed the old baseball custom of making subjective decisions when selecting the team members. The general manager then met a young, computer whiz with an economics degree from Yale. The general manager decided to appoint him as the new assistant general manager.

The assistant general manager had a deep passion for baseball and had the expertise to crunch the numbers for the game. His love for the game made him develop a radical way of understanding baseball statistics. He was a disciple of Bill James, a marginal figure who offered rationalized techniques to analyze baseball. James looked at baseball statistics in a different way, crunching the numbers purely on facts and eliminating subjectivity. James pioneered the nontraditional analysis method called the Sabermetric approach, which derived from SABR—Society for American Baseball Research.

The assistant general manager followed the Sabermetric approach by building a prediction model to help the Oakland Athletics select players based on their "on-base percentage" (OBP), a statistic that measured how often a batter reached base for any reason other than fielding error, fielder's choice, dropped/uncaught third strike, fielder's obstruction, or catcher's interference. Rather than relying on the scout's experience and intuition, the assistant general manager selected players based almost exclusively on OBP.

Spoiler Alert: The new team beat all odds, won 20 consecutive games, and set an American League record.

Questions for Discussion

1. How is predictive analytics applied in *Moneyball*?
2. What is the difference between objective and subjective approaches in decision making?

What We Can Learn from This Application Case

Analytics finds its use in a variety of industries. It helps organizations rethink their traditional problem-solving abilities, which are most often subjective, relying on the same old processes to find a solution. Analytics takes the radical approach of using historical data to find fact-based solutions that will remain appropriate for making even future decisions.

Source: Wikipedia, "On-Base Percentage," **en.wikipedia.org/ wiki/On_base_percentage** (accessed January 2013); Wikipedia, "Sabermetricsm," **wikipedia.org/wiki/Sabermetrics** (accessed January 2013).

Application Case 1.5

Analyzing Athletic Injuries

Any athletic activity is prone to injuries. If the injuries are not handled properly, then the team suffers. Using analytics to understand injuries can help in deriving valuable insights that would enable the coaches and team doctors to manage the team composition, understand player profiles, and ultimately aid in better decision making concerning which players might be available to play at any given time.

In an exploratory study, Oklahoma State University analyzed American football-related sport injuries by using reporting and predictive analytics. The project followed the CRISP-DM methodology to understand the problem of making recommendations on managing injuries, understanding the various data elements collected about injuries, cleaning the data, developing visualizations to draw various inferences, building predictive models to analyze the injury healing time period, and drawing sequence rules to predict the relationship among the injuries and the various body part parts afflicted with injuries.

The injury data set consisted of more than 560 football injury records, which were categorized into injury-specific variables—body part/site/laterality, action taken, severity, injury type, injury start and healing dates—and player/sport-specific variables—player ID, position played, activity, onset, and game location. Healing time was calculated for each record, which was classified into different sets of time periods: 0–1 month, 1–2 months, 2–4 months, 4–6 months, and 6–24 months.

Various visualizations were built to draw inferences from injury data set information depicting the healing time period associated with players' positions, severity of injuries and the healing time period, treatment offered and the associated healing time period, major injuries afflicting body parts, and so forth.

Neural network models were built to predict each of the healing categories using IBM SPSS Modeler. Some of the predictor variables were current status of injury, severity, body part, body site, type of injury, activity, event location, action taken, and position played. The success of classifying the healing category was quite good: Accuracy was 79.6 percent. Based on the analysis, many business recommendations were suggested, including employing more specialists' input from injury onset instead of letting the training room staff screen the injured players; training players at defensive positions to avoid being injured; and holding practice to thoroughly safety-check mechanisms.

QUESTIONS FOR DISCUSSION

1. What types of analytics are applied in the injury analysis?
2. How do visualizations aid in understanding the data and delivering insights into the data?
3. What is a classification problem?
4. What can be derived by performing sequence analysis?

What We Can Learn from This Application Case

For any analytics project, it is always important to understand the business domain and the current state of the business problem through extensive analysis of the only resource—historical data. Visualizations often provide a great tool for gaining the initial insights into data, which can be further refined based on expert opinions to identify the relative importance of the data elements related to the problem. Visualizations also aid in generating ideas for obscure business problems, which can be pursued in building predictive models that could help organizations in decision making.

Prescriptive Analytics

The third category of analytics is termed **prescriptive analytics**. The goal of prescriptive analytics is to recognize what is going on as well as the likely forecast and make decisions to achieve the best performance possible. This group of techniques has historically been studied under the umbrella of operations research or management sciences and has generally been aimed at optimizing the performance of a system. The goal here is to provide a decision or a recommendation for a specific action. These recommendations can be in the forms of a specific yes/no decision for a problem, a specific amount (say, price for a specific item or airfare to charge), or a complete set of production plans. The decisions may be presented to a decision maker in a report or may directly be used in an automated decision rules system (e.g., in airline pricing systems). Thus, these types of analytics can also be termed **decision or normative analytics**. Application Case 1.6 gives an example of such prescriptive analytic applications. We will learn about some of these techniques and several additional applications in Chapters 10 through 12.

Application Case 1.6

Industrial and Commercial Bank of China (ICBC) Employs Models to Reconfigure Its Branch Network

The Industrial and Commercial Bank of China (ICBC) has more than 16,000 branches and serves over 230 million individual customers and 3.6 million corporate clients. Its daily financial transactions total about $180 million. It is also the largest publicly traded bank in the world in terms of market capitalization, deposit volume, and profitability. To stay competitive and increase profitability, ICBC was faced with the challenge to quickly adapt to the fast-paced economic growth, urbanization, and increase in personal wealth of the Chinese. Changes had to be implemented in over 300 cities with high variability in customer behavior and financial status. Obviously, the nature of the challenges in such a huge economy meant that a large-scale optimization solution had to be developed to locate branches in the right places, with right services, to serve the right customers.

With their existing method, ICBC used to decide where to open new branches through a scoring model in which different variables with varying weight were used as inputs. Some of the variables were customer flow, number of residential households, and number of competitors in the intended geographic region. This method was deficient in determining the customer distribution of a geographic area. The existing method was also unable to optimize the distribution of bank branches in the branch network. With support from IBM, a branch reconfiguration (BR) tool was developed. Inputs for the BR system are in three parts:

a. Geographic data with 83 different categories
b. Demographic and economic data with 22 different categories
c. Branch transactions and performance data that consisted of more than 60 million transaction records each day

These three inputs helped generate accurate customer distribution for each area and, hence, helped the bank optimize its branch network. The BR system consisted of a market potential calculation model, a branch network optimization model, and a branch site evaluation model. In the market potential model, the customer volume and value is measured based on input data and expert knowledge. For instance, expert knowledge would help determine if personal income should be weighted more than gross domestic product (GDP). The geographic areas are also demarcated into cells, and the preference of one cell over the other is determined. In the branch network optimization model, mixed integer programming is used to locate branches in candidate cells so that they cover the largest market potential areas. In the branch site evaluation model, the value for establishing bank branches at specific locations is determined.

Since 2006, the development of the BR has been improved through an iterative process. ICBC's branch reconfiguration tool has increased deposits by $21.2 billion since its inception. This increase in deposit is because the bank can now reach more customers with the right services by use of its optimization tool. In a specific example, when BR was implemented in Suzhou in 2010, deposits increased to $13.67 billion from an initial level of $7.56 billion in 2007. Hence, the BR tool assisted in an increase of deposits to the tune of $6.11 billion between 2007 and 2010. This project was selected as a finalist in the Edelman Competition 2011, which is run by INFORMS to promote actual applications of management science/operations research models.

(Continued)

Application Case 1.6   (Continued)

QUESTIONS FOR DISCUSSION

1. How can analytical techniques help organizations to retain competitive advantage?
2. How can descriptive and predictive analytics help in pursuing prescriptive analytics?
3. What kinds of prescriptive analytic techniques are employed in the case study?
4. Are the prescriptive models once built good forever?

What We Can Learn from This Application Case

Many organizations in the world are now embracing analytical techniques to stay competitive and achieve growth. Many organizations provide consulting solutions to the businesses in employing prescriptive analytical solutions. It is equally important to have proactive decision makers in the organizations who are aware of the changing economic environment as well as the advancements in the field of analytics to ensure that appropriate models are employed. This case shows an example of geographic market segmentation and customer behavioral segmentation techniques to isolate the profitability of customers and employ optimization techniques to locate the branches that deliver high profitability in each geographic segment.

Source: X. Wang et al., "Branch Reconfiguration Practice Through Operations Research in Industrial and Commercial Bank of China," *Interfaces*, January/February 2012, Vol. 42, No. 1, pp. 33–44; DOI: 10.1287/inte.1110.0614.

Analytics Applied to Different Domains

Applications of analytics in various industry sectors have spawned many related areas or at least buzzwords. It is almost fashionable to attach the word *analytics* to any specific industry or type of data. Besides the general category of text analytics—aimed at getting value out of text (to be studied in Chapter 6)—or Web analytics—analyzing Web data streams (Chapter 7)—many industry- or problem-specific analytics professions/streams have come up. Examples of such areas are marketing analytics, retail analytics, fraud analytics, transportation analytics, health analytics, sports analytics, talent analytics, behavioral analytics, and so forth. For example, Application Case 1.1 could also be termed as a case study in airline analytics. Application Cases 1.2 and 1.3 would belong to health analytics; Application Cases 1.4 and 1.5 to sports analytics; Application Case 1.6 to bank analytics; and Application Case 1.7 to retail analytics. The End-of-Chapter Application Case could be termed insurance analytics. Literally, any systematic analysis of data in a specific sector is being labeled as "(fill-in-blanks)" Analytics. Although this may result in overselling the concepts of analytics, the benefit is that more people in specific industries are aware of the power and potential of analytics. It also provides a focus to professionals developing and applying the concepts of analytics in a vertical sector. Although many of the techniques to develop analytics applications may be common, there are unique issues within each vertical segment that influence how the data may be collected, processed, analyzed, and the applications implemented. Thus, the differentiation of analytics based on a vertical focus is good for the overall growth of the discipline.

Analytics or Data Science?

Even as the concept of analytics is getting popular among industry and academic circles, another term has already been introduced and is becoming popular. The new term is *data science*. Thus the practitioners of data science are data scientists. Mr. D. J. Patil of LinkedIn is sometimes credited with creating the term *data science*. There have been some attempts to describe the differences between data analysts and data scientists (e.g., see this study at **emc.com/collateral/about/news/emc-data-science-study-wp.pdf**). One view is that *data analyst* is just another term for professionals who were doing business intelligence in the form of data compilation, cleaning, reporting, and perhaps some visualization. Their skill sets included Excel, some SQL knowledge, and reporting. A reader of Section 1.8 would recognize that as descriptive or reporting analytics. In contrast, a data scientist is responsible for predictive analysis, statistical analysis, and more advanced analytical tools and algorithms. They may have a deeper knowledge of algorithms and may recognize them under various labels—data mining, knowledge discovery, machine learning, and so forth. Some of these professionals may also need deeper programming knowledge to be able to write code for data cleaning and analysis in current Web-oriented languages such as Java and Python. Again, our readers should recognize these as falling under the predictive and prescriptive analytics umbrella. Our view is that the distinction between analytics and data science is more of a degree of technical knowledge and skill sets than the functions. It may also be more of a distinction across disciplines. Computer science, statistics, and applied mathematics programs appear to prefer the data science label, reserving the analytics label for more business-oriented professionals. As another example of this, applied physics professionals have proposed using *network science* as the term for describing analytics that relate to a group of people—social networks, supply chain networks, and so forth. See **barabasilab.neu.edu/networksciencebook/downlPDF. html** for an evolving textbook on this topic.

Aside from a clear difference in the skill sets of professionals who only have to do descriptive/reporting analytics versus those who engage in all three types of analytics, the distinction is fuzzy between the two labels, at best. We observe that graduates of our analytics programs tend to be responsible for tasks more in line with data science professionals (as defined by some circles) than just reporting analytics. This book is clearly aimed at introducing the capabilities and functionality of all analytics (which includes data science), not just reporting analytics. From now on, we will use these terms interchangeably.

SECTION 1.8 REVIEW QUESTIONS

1. Define *analytics*.

2. What is descriptive analytics? What various tools are employed in descriptive analytics?

3. How is descriptive analytics different from traditional reporting?

4. What is a data warehouse? How can data warehousing technology help in enabling analytics?

5. What is predictive analytics? How can organizations employ predictive analytics?

6. What is prescriptive analytics? What kinds of problems can be solved by prescriptive analytics?

7. Define modeling from the analytics perspective.

8. Is it a good idea to follow a hierarchy of descriptive and predictive analytics before applying prescriptive analytics?

9. How can analytics aid in objective decision making?

1.9 BRIEF INTRODUCTION TO BIG DATA ANALYTICS

What Is Big Data?

Our brains work extremely quickly and are efficient and versatile in processing large amounts of all kinds of data: images, text, sounds, smells, and video. We process all different forms of data relatively easily. Computers, on the other hand, are still finding it hard to keep up with the pace at which data is generated—let alone analyze it quickly. We have the problem of Big Data. So what is Big Data? Simply put, it is data that cannot be stored in a single storage unit. Big Data typically refers to data that is arriving in many different forms, be they structured, unstructured, or in a stream. Major sources of such data are clickstreams from Web sites, postings on social media sites such as Facebook, or data from traffic, sensors, or weather. A Web search engine like Google needs to search and index billions of Web pages in order to give you relevant search results in a fraction of a second. Although this is not done in real time, generating an index of all the Web pages on the Internet is not an easy task. Luckily for Google, it was able to solve this problem. Among other tools, it has employed Big Data analytical techniques.

There are two aspects to managing data on this scale: storing and processing. If we could purchase an extremely expensive storage solution to store all the data at one place on one unit, making this unit fault tolerant would involve major expense. An ingenious solution was proposed that involved storing this data in chunks on different machines connected by a network, putting a copy or two of this chunk in different locations on the network, both logically and physically. It was originally used at Google (then called *Google File System*) and later developed and released as an Apache project as the Hadoop Distributed File System (HDFS).

However, storing this data is only half the problem. Data is worthless if it does not provide business value, and for it to provide business value, it has to be analyzed. How are such vast amounts of data analyzed? Passing all computation to one powerful computer does not work; this scale would create a huge overhead on such a powerful computer. Another ingenious solution was proposed: Push computation to the data, instead of pushing data to a computing node. This was a new paradigm, and it gave rise to a whole new way of processing data. This is what we know today as the MapReduce programming paradigm, which made processing Big Data a reality. MapReduce was originally developed at Google, and a subsequent version was released by the Apache project called Hadoop MapReduce.

Today, when we talk about storing, processing, or analyzing Big Data, HDFS and MapReduce are involved at some level. Other relevant standards and software solutions have been proposed. Although the major toolkit is available as open source, several companies have been launched to provide training or specialized analytical hardware or software services in this space. Some examples are HortonWorks, Cloudera, and Teradata Aster.

Over the past few years, what was called Big Data changed more and more as Big Data applications appeared. The need to process data coming in at a rapid rate added velocity to the equation. One example of fast data processing is algorithmic trading. It is the use of electronic platforms based on algorithms for trading shares on the financial market, which operates in the order of microseconds. The need to process different kinds of data added variety to the equation. Another example of the wide variety of data is sentiment analysis, which uses various forms of data from social media platforms and customer responses to gauge sentiments. Today Big Data is associated with almost any kind of large data that has the characteristics of volume, velocity, and variety. Application Case 1.7 illustrates one example of Big Data analytics. We will study Big Data characteristics in more detail in Chapters 3 and 13.

SECTION 1.9 REVIEW QUESTIONS

1. What is Big Data analytics?

2. What are the sources of Big Data?

3. What are the characteristics of Big Data?

4. What processing technique is applied to process Bi ta?

Application Case 1.7

Gilt Groupe's Flash Sales Streamlined by Big Data Analytics

Gilt Groupe is an online destination offering flash sales for major brands by selling their clothing and accessories. It offers its members exclusive discounts on high-end clothing and other apparel. After registering with Gilt, customers are sent e-mails containing a variety of offers. Customers are given a 36-48 hour window to make purchases using these offers. There are about 30 different sales each day. While a typical department store turns over its inventory two or three times a year, Gilt does it eight to 10 times a year. Thus, they have to manage their inventory extremely well or they could incur extremely high inventory costs. In order to do this, analytics software developed at Gilt keeps track of every customer click—ranging from what brands the customers click on, what colors they choose, what styles they pick, and what they end up buying. Then Gilt tries to predict what these customers are more likely to buy and stocks inventory according to these predictions. Customers are sent customized alerts to sale offers depending on the suggestions by the analytics software.

That, however, is not the whole process. The software also monitors what offers the customers choose from the recommended offers to make more accurate predictions and to increase the effectiveness of its personalized recommendations. Some customers do not check e-mail that often. Gilt's analytics

software keeps track of responses to offers and sends the same offer 3 days later to those customers who haven't responded. Gilt also keeps track of what customers are saying in general about Gilt's products by analyzing Twitter feeds to analyze sentiment. Gilt's recommendation software is based on Teradata Aster's technology solution that includes Big Data analytics technologies.

QUESTIONS FOR DISCUSSION

1. What makes this case study an example of Big Data analytics?
2. What types of decisions does Gilt Groupe have to make?

What We Can Learn From this Application Case

There is continuous growth in the amount of structured and unstructured data, and many organizations are now tapping these data to make actionable decisions. Big Data analytics is now enabled by the advancements in technologies that aid in storage and processing of vast amounts of rapidly growing data.

Source: Asterdata.com, "Gilt Groupe Speaks on Digital Marketing Optimization," **asterdata.com/gilt_groupe_video.php** (accessed February 2013).

1.10 PLAN OF THE BOOK

The previous sections have given you an understanding of the need for using information technology in decision making; an IT-oriented view of various types of decisions; and the evolution of decision support systems into business intelligence, and now into analytics. In the last two sections we have seen an overview of various types of analytics and their applications. Now we are ready for a more detailed managerial excursion into these topics, along with some potentially deep hands-on experience in some of the technical topics. The 14 chapters of this book are organized into five parts, as shown in Figure 1.6.

Part I: Business Analytics: An Overview

In Chapter 1, we provided an introduction, definitions, and an overview of decision support systems, business intelligence, and analytics, including Big Data analytics. Chapter 2 covers the basic phases of the decision-making process and introduces decision support systems in more detail.

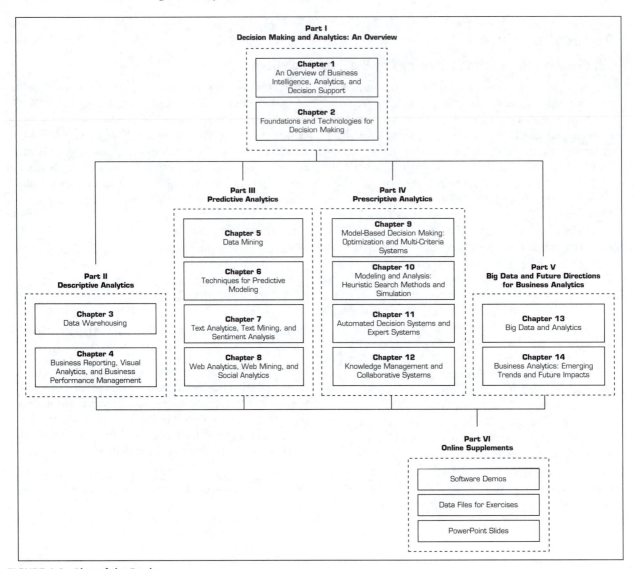

FIGURE 1.6 Plan of the Book.

Part II: Descriptive Analytics

Part II begins with an introduction to data warehousing issues, applications, and technologies in Chapter 3. Data represent the fundamental backbone of any decision support and analytics application. Chapter 4 describes business reporting, visualization technologies, and applications. It also includes a brief overview of business performance management techniques and applications, a topic that has been a key part of traditional BI.

Part III: Predictive Analytics

Part III comprises a large part of the book. It begins with an introduction to predictive analytics applications in Chapter 5. It includes many of the common application techniques: classification, clustering, association mining, and so forth. Chapter 6 includes a technical description of selected data mining techniques, especially neural network models. Chapter 7 focuses on text mining applications. Similarly, Chapter 8 focuses on Web analytics, including social media analytics, sentiment analysis, and other related topics.

Part IV: Prescriptive Analytics

Part IV introduces decision analytic techniques, which are also called prescriptive analytics. Specifically, Chapter 9 covers selected models that may be implemented in spreadsheet environments. It also covers a popular multi-objective decision technique—analytic hierarchy processes.

Chapter 10 then introduces other model-based decision-making techniques, especially heuristic models and simulation. Chapter 11 introduces automated decision systems including expert systems. This part concludes with a brief discussion of knowledge management and group support systems in Chapter 12.

Part V: Big Data and Future Directions for Business Analytics

Part V begins with a more detailed coverage of Big Data and analytics in Chapter 13.

Chapter 14 attempts to integrate all the material covered in this book and concludes with a discussion of emerging trends, such as how the ubiquity of wireless and GPS devices and other sensors is resulting in the creation of massive new databases and unique applications. A new breed of data mining and BI companies is emerging to analyze these new databases and create a much better and deeper understanding of customers' behaviors and movements. The chapter also covers cloud-based analytics, recommendation systems, and a brief discussion of security/privacy dimensions of analytics. It concludes the book by also presenting a discussion of the analytics ecosystem. An understanding of the ecosystem and the various players in the analytics industry highlights the various career opportunities for students and practitioners of analytics.

1.11 RESOURCES, LINKS, AND THE TERADATA UNIVERSITY NETWORK CONNECTION

The use of this chapter and most other chapters in this book can be enhanced by the tools described in the following sections.

Resources and Links

We recommend the following major resources and links:

- The Data Warehousing Institute (**tdwi.org**)
- Information Management (**information-management.com**)
- DSS Resources (**dssresources.com**)
- Microsoft Enterprise Consortium (**enterprise.waltoncollege.uark.edu/mec.asp**)

Vendors, Products, and Demos

Most vendors provide software demos of their products and applications. Information about products, architecture, and software is available at **dssresources.com**.

Periodicals

We recommend the following periodicals:

- *Decision Support Systems*
- *CIO Insight* (**cioinsight.com**)
- *Technology Evaluation* (**technologyevaluation.com**)
- *Baseline Magazine* (**baselinemag.com**)

The Teradata University Network Connection

This book is tightly connected with the free resources provided by Teradata University Network (TUN; see **teradatauniversitynetwork.com**). The TUN portal is divided into two major parts: one for students and one for faculty. This book is connected to the TUN portal via a special section at the end of each chapter. That section includes appropriate links for the specific chapter, pointing to relevant resources. In addition, we provide hands-on exercises, using software and other material (e.g., cases) available at TUN.

The Book's Web Site

This book's Web site, **pearsonhighered.com/turban**, contains supplemental textual material organized as Web chapters that correspond to the printed book's chapters. The topics of these chapters are listed in the online chapter table of contents. Other content is also available on an independent Web site (**dssbibook.com**).[2]

Chapter Highlights

- The business environment is becoming complex and is rapidly changing, making decision making more difficult.
- Businesses must respond and adapt to the changing environment rapidly by making faster and better decisions.
- The time frame for making decisions is shrinking, whereas the global nature of decision making is expanding, necessitating the development and use of computerized DSS.
- Computerized support for managers is often essential for the survival of an organization.
- An early decision support framework divides decision situations into nine categories, depending on the degree of structuredness and managerial activities. Each category is supported differently.
- Structured repetitive decisions are supported by standard quantitative analysis methods, such as MS, MIS, and rule-based automated decision support.
- DSS use data, models, and sometimes knowledge management to find solutions for semistructured and some unstructured problems.
- BI methods utilize a central repository called a data warehouse that enables efficient data mining, OLAP, BPM, and data visualization.

- BI architecture includes a data warehouse, business analytics tools used by end users, and a user interface (such as a dashboard).
- Many organizations employ descriptive analytics to replace their traditional flat reporting with interactive reporting that provides insights, trends, and patterns in the transactional data.
- Predictive analytics enable organizations to establish predictive rules that drive the business outcomes through historical data analysis of the existing behavior of the customers.
- Prescriptive analytics help in building models that involve forecasting and optimization techniques based on the principles of operations research and management science to help organizations to make better decisions.
- Big Data analytics focuses on unstructured, large data sets that may also include vastly different types of data for analysis.
- Analytics as a field is also known by industry-specific application names such as sports analytics. It is also known by other related names such as data science or network science.

---

[2]As this book went to press, we verified that all the cited Web sites were active and valid. However, URLs are dynamic. Web sites to which we refer in the text sometimes change or are discontinued because companies change names, are bought or sold, merge, or fail. Sometimes Web sites are down for maintenance, repair, or redesign. Many organizations have dropped the initial "www" designation for their sites, but some still use it. If you have a problem connecting to a Web site that we mention, please be patient and simply run a Web search to try to identify the possible new site. Most times, you can quickly find the new site through one of the popular search engines. We apologize in advance for this inconvenience.

Key Terms

business intelligence (BI)	decision (or normative) analytics	descriptive (or reporting) analytics	semistructured problem
dashboard	decision support system (DSS)	predictive analytics	structured problem
data mining		prescriptive analytics	unstructured problem

Questions for Discussion

1. Give examples for the content of each cell in Figure 1.2.
2. Survey the literature from the past 6 months to find one application each for DSS, BI, and analytics. Summarize the applications on one page and submit it with the exact sources.
3. Observe an organization with which you are familiar. List three decisions it makes in each of the following categories: strategic planning, management control (tactical planning), and operational planning and control.
4. Distinguish BI from DSS.
5. Compare and contrast predictive analytics with prescriptive and descriptive analytics. Use examples.

Exercises

Teradata University Network (TUN) and Other Hands-On Exercises

1. Go to **teradatauniversitynetwork.com**. Using the registration your instructor provides, log on and learn the content of the site. You will receive assignments related to this site. Prepare a list of 20 items in the site that you think could be beneficial to you.
2. Enter the TUN site and select "cases, projects and assignments." Then select the case study: "Harrah's High Payoff from Customer Information." Answer the following questions about this case:
   a. What information does the data mining generate?
   b. How is this information helpful to management in decision making? (Be specific.)
   c. List the types of data that are mined.
   d. Is this a DSS or BI application? Why?
3. Go to **teradatauniversitynetwork.com** and find the paper titled "Data Warehousing Supports Corporate Strategy at First American Corporation" (by Watson, Wixom, and Goodhue). Read the paper and answer the following questions:
   a. What were the drivers for the DW/BI project in the company?
   b. What strategic advantages were realized?
   c. What operational and tactical advantages were achieved?
   d. What were the critical success factors (CSF) for the implementation?
4. Go to **analytics-magazine.org/issues/digital-editions** and find the January/February 2012 edition titled "Special Issue: The Future of Healthcare." Read the article "Predictive Analytics—Saving Lives and Lowering Medical Bills." Answer the following questions:
   a. What is the problem that is being addressed by applying predictive analytics?
   b. What is the FICO Medication Adherence Score?
   c. How is a prediction model trained to predict the FICO Medication Adherence Score? Did the prediction model classify FICO Medication Adherence Score?
   d. Zoom in on Figure 4 and explain what kind of technique is applied on the generated results.
   e. List some of the actionable decisions that were based on the results of the predictions.
5. Go to **analytics-magazine.org/issues/digital-editions** and find the January/February 2013 edition titled "Work Social." Read the article "Big Data, Analytics and Elections" and answer the following questions:
   a. What kinds of Big Data were analyzed in the article? Comment on some of the sources of Big Data.
   b. Explain the term *integrated system*. What other technical term suits integrated system?
   c. What kinds of data analysis techniques are employed in the project? Comment on some initiatives that resulted from data analysis.
   d. What are the different prediction problems answered by the models?
   e. List some of the actionable decisions taken that were based on the predication results.
   f. Identify two applications of Big Data analytics that are not listed in the article.

6. Search the Internet for material regarding the work of managers and the role analytics play. What kind of references to consulting firms, academic departments, and programs do you find? What major areas are represented? Select five sites that cover one area and report your findings.

7. Explore the public areas of **dssresources.com**. Prepare a list of its major available resources. You might want to refer to this site as you work through the book.

8. Go to **microstrategy.com**. Find information on the five styles of BI. Prepare a summary table for each style.

9. Go to **oracle.com** and click the Hyperion link under Applications. Determine what the company's major products are. Relate these to the support technologies cited in this chapter.

End-of-Chapter Application Case

Nationwide Insurance Used BI to Enhance Customer Service

Nationwide Mutual Insurance Company, headquartered in Columbus, Ohio, is one of the largest insurance and financial services companies, with $23 billion in revenues and more than $160 billion in statutory assets. It offers a comprehensive range of products through its family of 100-plus companies with insurance products for auto, motorcycle, boat, life, homeowners, and farms. It also offers financial products and services including annuities, mortgages, mutual funds, pensions, and investment management.

Nationwide strives to achieve greater efficiency in all operations by managing its expenses along with its ability to grow its revenue. It recognizes the use of its strategic asset of information combined with analytics to outpace competitors in strategic and operational decision making even in complex and unpredictable environments.

Historically, Nationwide's business units worked independently and with a lot of autonomy. This led to duplication of efforts, widely dissimilar data processing environments, and extreme data redundancy, resulting in higher expenses. The situation got complicated when Nationwide pursued any mergers or acquisitions.

Nationwide, using enterprise data warehouse technology from Teradata, set out to create, from the ground up, a single, authoritative environment for clean, consistent, and complete data that can be effectively used for best-practice analytics to make strategic and tactical business decisions in the areas of customer growth, retention, product profitability, cost containment, and productivity improvements. Nationwide transformed its siloed business units, which were supported by stove-piped data environments, into integrated units by using cutting-edge analytics that work with clear, consolidated data from all of its business units. The Teradata data warehouse at Nationwide has grown from 400 gigabytes to more than 100 terabytes and supports 85 percent of Nationwide's business with more than 2,500 users.

Integrated Customer Knowledge

Nationwide's Customer Knowledge Store (CKS) initiative developed a customer-centric database that integrated customer, product, and externally acquired data from more than 48 sources into a single customer data mart to deliver a holistic view of customers. This data mart was coupled with Teradata's customer relationship management application to create and manage effective customer marketing campaigns that use behavioral analysis of customer interactions to drive customer management actions (CMAs) for target segments. Nationwide added more sophisticated customer analytics that looked at customer portfolios and the effectiveness of various marketing campaigns. This data analysis helped Nationwide to initiate proactive customer communications around customer lifetime events like marriage, birth of child, or home purchase and had significant impact on improving customer satisfaction. Also, by integrating customer contact history, product ownership, and payment information, Nationwide's behavioral analytics teams further created prioritized models that could identify which specific customer interaction was important for a customer at any given time. This resulted in one percentage point improvement in customer retention rates and significant improvement in customer enthusiasm scores. Nationwide also achieved 3 percent annual growth in incremental sales by using CKS. There are other uses of the customer database. In one of the initiatives, by integrating customer telephone data from multiple systems into CKS, the relationship managers at Nationwide try to be proactives in contacting customers in advance of a possible weather catastrophe, such as a hurricane or flood, to provide the primary policyholder information and explain the claims processes. These and other analytic insights now drive Nationwide to provide extremely personal customer service.

Financial Operations

A similar performance payoff from integrated information was also noted in financial operations. Nationwide's decentralized management style resulted in a fragmented financial reporting environment that included more than 14 general ledgers, 20 charts of accounts, 17 separate data repositories, 12 different reporting tools, and hundreds of thousands of spreadsheets. There was no common central view of the business, which resulted in labor-intensive slow and inaccurate reporting.

About 75 percent of the effort was spent on acquiring, cleaning, and consolidating and validating the data, and very little time was spent on meaningful analysis of the data.

The Financial Performance Management initiative implemented a new operating approach that worked on a single data and technology architecture with a common set of systems standardizing the process of reporting. It enabled Nationwide to operate analytical centers of excellence with world-class planning, capital management, risk assessment, and other decision support capabilities that delivered timely, accurate, and efficient accounting, reporting, and analytical services.

The data from more than 200 operational systems was sent to the enterprise-wide data warehouse and then distributed to various applications and analytics. This resulted in a 50 percent improvement in the monthly closing process with closing intervals reduced from 14 days to 7 days.

Postmerger Data Integration

Nationwide's Goal State Rate Management initiative enabled the company to merge Allied Insurance's automobile policy system into its existing system. Both Nationwide and Allied source systems were custom-built applications that did not share any common values or process data in the same manner. Nationwide's IT department decided to bring all the data from source systems into a centralized data warehouse, organized in an integrated fashion that resulted in standard dimensional reporting and helped Nationwide in performing what-if analyses. The data analysis team could identify previously unknown potential differences in the data environment where premiums rates were calculated differently between Nationwide and Allied sides. Correcting all of these benefited Nationwide's policyholders because they were safeguarded from experiencing wide premium rate swings.

Enhanced Reporting

Nationwide's legacy reporting system, which catered to the needs of property and casualty business units, took weeks to compile and deliver the needed reports to the agents. Nationwide determined that it needed better access to sales and policy information to reach its sales targets. It chose a single data warehouse approach and, after careful assessment of the needs of sales management and individual agents, selected a business intelligence platform that would integrate dynamic enterprise dashboards into its reporting systems, making it easy for the agents and associates to view policy information at a glance. The new reporting system, dubbed Revenue Connection, also enabled users to analyze the information with a lot of interactive and drill-down-to-details capabilities at various levels that eliminated the need to generate custom ad hoc reports. Revenue Connection virtually eliminated requests for manual policy audits, resulting in huge savings in time and money for the business and technology teams. The reports were produced in 4 to 45 seconds, rather than days or weeks, and productivity in some units improved by 20 to 30 percent.

QUESTIONS FOR DISCUSSION

1. Why did Nationwide need an enterprise-wide data warehouse?
2. How did integrated data drive the business value?
3. What forms of analytics are employed at Nationwide?
4. With integrated data available in an enterprise data warehouse, what other applications could Nationwide potentially develop?

What We Can Learn from This Application Case

The proper use of integrated information in organizations can help achieve better business outcomes. Many organizations now rely on data warehousing technologies to perform the online analytical processes on the data to derive valuable insights. The insights are used to develop predictive models that further enable the growth of the organizations by more precisely assessing customer needs. Increasingly, organizations are moving toward deriving value from analytical applications in real time with the help of integrated data from real-time data warehousing technologies.

Source: Teradata.com, "Nationwide, Delivering an On Your Side Experience," **teradata.com/WorkArea/linkit.aspx?LinkIdentifier=id&ItemID=14714** (accessed February 2013).

References

Anthony, R. N. (1965). *Planning and Control Systems: A Framework for Analysis.* Cambridge, MA: Harvard University Graduate School of Business.

Asterdata.com. "Gilt Groupe Speaks on Digital Marketing Optimization." **www.asterdata.com/gilt_groupe_video. php** (accessed February 2013).

Barabasilab.neu.edu. "Network Science." **barabasilab.neu. edu/networksciencebook/downlPDF.html** (accessed February 2013).

Brooks, D. (2009, May 18). "In Praise of Dullness." *New York Times,* **nytimes.com/2009/05/19/opinion/19brooks. html** (accessed February 2013).

Centers for Disease Control and Prevention, Vaccines for Children Program, "Module 6 of the VFC Operations Guide." **cdc.gov/vaccines/pubs/pinkbook/vac-storage.html#storage** (accessed January 2013).

Eckerson, W. (2003). *Smart Companies in the 21st Century: The Secrets of Creating Successful Business Intelligent Solutions.* Seattle, WA: The Data Warehousing Institute.

Emc.com. "Data Science Revealed: A Data-Driven Glimpse into the Burgeoning New Field." **emc.com/collateral/about/news/emc-data-science-study-wp.pdf** (accessed February 2013).

Gorry, G. A., and M. S. Scott-Morton. (1971). "A Framework for Management Information Systems." *Sloan Management Review*, Vol. 13, No. 1, pp. 55–70.

INFORMS. "Analytics Section Overview." **informs.org/Community/Analytics** (accessed February 2013).

Keen, P. G. W., and M. S. Scott-Morton. (1978). *Decision Support Systems: An Organizational Perspective.* Reading, MA: Addison-Wesley.

Krivda, C. D. (2008, March). "Dialing Up Growth in a Mature Market." *Teradata Magazine*, pp. 1–3.

Magpiesensing.com. "MagpieSensing Cold Chain Analytics and Monitoring." **magpiesensing.com/wp-content/uploads/2013/01/ColdChainAnalyticsMagpieSensing-Whitepaper.pdf** (accessed January 2013).

Mintzberg, H. A. (1980). *The Nature of Managerial Work.* Englewood Cliffs, NJ: Prentice Hall.

Mintzberg, H. A. (1993). *The Rise and Fall of Strategic Planning.* New York: The Free Press.

Simon, H. (1977). *The New Science of Management Decision.* Englewood Cliffs, NJ: Prentice Hall.

Tableausoftware.com. "Eliminating Waste at Seattle Children's." **tableausoftware.com/eliminating-waste-at-seattle-childrens** (accessed February 2013).

Tableausoftware.com. "Kaleida Health Finds Efficiencies, Stays Competitive." **tableausoftware.com/learn/stories/user-experience-speed-thought-kaleida-health** (accessed February 2013).

Teradata.com. "Nationwide, Delivering an On Your Side Experience." **teradata.com/case-studies/delivering-on-your-side-experience** (accessed February 2013).

Teradata.com. "Sabre Airline Solutions." **teradata.com/t/case-studies/Sabre-Airline-Solutions-EB6281** (accessed February 2013).

Wang, X., et al. (2012, January/February). "Branch Reconfiguration Practice Through Operations Research in Industrial and Commercial Bank of China." *Interfaces*, Vol. 42, No. 1, pp. 33–44.

Watson, H. (2005, Winter). "Sorting Out What's New in Decision Support." *Business Intelligence Journal.*

Wikipedia. "On Base Percentage." **en.wikipedia.org/wiki/On_base_percentage** (accessed January 2013).

Wikipedia. "Sabermetrics." **en.wikipedia.org/wiki/Sabermetrics** (accessed January 2013).

Zaleski, A. (2012). "Magpie Analytics System Tracks Cold-Chain Products to Keep Vaccines, Reagents Fresh." **TechnicallyBaltimore.com** (accessed February 2013).

Zaman, M. (2009, April). "Business Intelligence: Its Ins and Outs." **technologyevaluation.com** (accessed February 2013).

Ziama, A., and J. Kasher. (2004). "Data Mining Primer for the Data Warehousing Professional." Dayton, OH: *Teradata*.

Foundations and Technologies for Decision Making

LEARNING OBJECTIVES

- Understand the conceptual foundations of decision making
- Understand Simon's four phases of decision making: intelligence, design, choice, and implementation
- Understand the essential definition of DSS

- Understand important DSS classifications
- Learn how DSS support for decision making can be provided in practice
- Understand DSS components and how they integrate

Our major focus in this book is the support of decision making through computer-based information systems. The purpose of this chapter is to describe the conceptual foundations of decision making and how decision support is provided. This chapter includes the following sections:

2.1   OPENING VIGNETTE: Decision Modeling at HP Using Spreadsheets

HP is a major manufacturer of computers, printers, and many industrial products. Its vast product line leads to many decision problems. Olavson and Fry (2008) have worked on many spreadsheet models for assisting decision makers at HP and have identified several lessons from both their successes and their failures when it comes to constructing and applying spreadsheet-based tools. They define a *tool* as "a reusable, analytical solution designed to be handed off to nontechnical end users to assist them in solving a repeated business problem."

When trying to solve a problem, HP developers consider the three phases in developing a model. The first phase is problem framing, where they consider the following questions in order to develop the best solution for the problem:

- Will analytics solve the problem?
- Can an existing solution be leveraged?
- Is a tool needed?

The first question is important because the problem may not be of an analytic nature, and therefore, a spreadsheet tool may not be of much help in the long run without fixing the nonanalytical part of the problem first. For example, many inventory-related issues arise because of the inherent differences between the goals of marketing and supply chain groups. Marketing likes to have the maximum variety in the product line, whereas supply chain management focuses on reducing the inventory costs. This difference is partially outside the scope of any model. Coming up with nonmodeling solutions is important as well. If the problem arises due to "misalignment" of incentives or unclear lines of authority or plans, no model can help. Thus, it is important to identify the root issue.

The second question is important because sometimes an existing tool may solve a problem that then saves time and money. Sometimes modifying an existing tool may solve the problem, again saving some time and money, but sometimes a custom tool is necessary to solve the problem. This is clearly worthwhile to explore.

The third question is important because sometimes a new computer-based system is not required to solve the problem. The developers have found that they often use analytically derived decision guidelines instead of a tool. This solution requires less time for development and training, has lower maintenance requirements, and also provides simpler and more intuitive results. That is, after they have explored the problem deeper, the developers may determine that it is better to present decision rules that can be easily implemented as guidelines for decision making rather than asking the managers to run some type of a computer model. This results in easier training, better understanding of the rules being proposed, and increased acceptance. It also typically leads to lower development costs and reduced time for deployment.

If a model has to be built, the developers move on to the second phase—the actual design and development of the tools. Adhering to five guidelines tends to increase the probability that the new tool will be successful. The first guideline is to develop a prototype as quickly as possible. This allows the developers to test the designs, demonstrate various features and ideas for the new tools, get early feedback from the end users to see what works for them and what needs to be changed, and test adoption. Developing a prototype also prevents the developers from overbuilding the tool and yet allows them to construct more scalable and standardized software applications later. Additionally, by developing a prototype, developers can stop the process once the tool is "good enough," rather than building a standardized solution that would take longer to build and be more expensive.

The second guideline is to "build insight, not black boxes." The HP spreadsheet model developers believe that this is important, because often just entering some data and receiving a calculated output is not enough. The users need to be able to think of alternative scenarios, and the tool does not support this if it is a "black box" that provides only one recommendation. They argue that a tool is best only if it provides information to help make and support decisions rather than just give the answers. They also believe that an interactive tool helps the users to understand the problem better, therefore leading to more informed decisions.

The third guideline is to "remove unneeded complexity before handoff." This is important, because as a tool becomes more complex it requires more training and expertise, more data, and more recalibrations. The risk of bugs and misuse also increases. Sometimes it is best to study the problem, begin modeling and analysis, and then start shaping the program into a simple-to-use tool for the end user.

The fourth guideline is to "partner with end users in discovery and design." By working with the end users the developers get a better feel of the problem and a better idea of what the end users want. It also increases the end users' ability to use analytic tools. The end users also gain a better understanding of the problem and how it is solved using the new tool. Additionally, including the end users in the development process enhances the decision makers' analytical knowledge and capabilities. By working together, their knowledge and skills complement each other in the final solution.

The fifth guideline is to "develop an Operations Research (OR) champion." By involving end users in the development process, the developers create champions for the new tools who then go back to their departments or companies and encourage their coworkers to accept and use them. The champions are then the experts on the tools in their areas and can then help those being introduced to the new tools. Having champions increases the possibility that the tools will be adopted into the businesses successfully.

The final stage is the handoff, when the final tools that provide complete solutions are given to the businesses. When planning the handoff, it is important to answer the following questions:

- Who will use the tool?
- Who owns the decisions that the tool will support?
- Who else must be involved?
- Who is responsible for maintenance and enhancement of the tool?
- When will the tool be used?
- How will the use of the tool fit in with other processes?
- Does it change the processes?
- Does it generate input into those processes?
- How will the tool impact business performance?
- Are the existing metrics sufficient to reward this aspect of performance?
- How should the metrics and incentives be changed to maximize impact to the business from the tool and process?

By keeping these lessons in mind, developers and proponents of computerized decision support in general and spreadsheet-based models in particular are likely to enjoy greater success.

QUESTIONS FOR THE OPENING VIGNETTE

1. What are some of the key questions to be asked in supporting decision making through DSS?
2. What guidelines can be learned from this vignette about developing DSS?
3. What lessons should be kept in mind for successful model implementation?

WHAT WE CAN LEARN FROM THIS VIGNETTE

This vignette relates to providing decision support in a large organization:

- Before building a model, decision makers should develop a good understanding of the problem that needs to be addressed.
- A model may not be necessary to address the problem.
- Before developing a new tool, decision makers should explore reuse of existing tools.
- The goal of model building is to gain better insight into the problem, not just to generate more numbers.
- Implementation plans should be developed along with the model.

Source: Based on T. Olavson and C. Fry, "Spreadsheet Decision-Support Tools: Lessons Learned at Hewlett-Packard," *Interfaces*, Vol. 38, No. 4, July/August 2008, pp. 300–310.

2.2 DECISION MAKING: INTRODUCTION AND DEFINITIONS

We are about to examine how decision making is practiced and some of the underlying theories and models of decision making. You will also learn about the various traits of decision makers, including what characterizes a good decision maker. Knowing this can help you to understand the types of decision support tools that managers can use to make more effective decisions. In the following sections, we discuss various aspects of decision making.

Characteristics of Decision Making

In addition to the characteristics presented in the opening vignette, **decision making** may involve the following:

- Groupthink (i.e., group members accept the solution without thinking for themselves) can lead to bad decisions.
- Decision makers are interested in evaluating what-if scenarios.
- Experimentation with a real system (e.g., develop a schedule, try it, and see how well it works) may result in failure.
- Experimentation with a real system is possible only for one set of conditions at a time and can be disastrous.
- Changes in the decision-making environment may occur continuously, leading to invalidating assumptions about a situation (e.g., deliveries around holiday times may increase, requiring a different view of the problem).
- Changes in the decision-making environment may affect decision quality by imposing time pressure on the decision maker.
- Collecting information and analyzing a problem takes time and can be expensive. It is difficult to determine when to stop and make a decision.
- There may not be sufficient information to make an intelligent decision.
- Too much information may be available (i.e., information overload).

To determine how real decision makers make decisions, we must first understand the process and the important issues involved in decision making. Then we can understand appropriate methodologies for assisting decision makers and the contributions information systems can make. Only then can we develop DSS to help decision makers.

This chapter is organized based on the three key words that form the term *DSS*: *decision, support,* and *systems*. A decision maker should not simply apply IT tools blindly. Rather, the decision maker gets support through a rational approach that simplifies reality and provides a relatively quick and inexpensive means of considering various alternative courses of action to arrive at the best (or at least a very good) solution to the problem.

A Working Definition of Decision Making

Decision making is a process of choosing among two or more alternative courses of action for the purpose of attaining one or more goals. According to Simon (1977), managerial decision making is synonymous with the entire management process. Consider the important managerial function of planning. Planning involves a series of decisions: What should be done? When? Where? Why? How? By whom? Managers set goals, or plan; hence, planning implies decision making. Other managerial functions, such as organizing and controlling, also involve decision making.

Decision-Making Disciplines

Decision making is directly influenced by several major disciplines, some of which are behavioral and some of which are scientific in nature. We must be aware of how their philosophies can affect our ability to make decisions and provide support. Behavioral disciplines include anthropology, law, philosophy, political science, psychology, social psychology, and sociology. Scientific disciplines include computer science, decision analysis, economics, engineering, the hard sciences (e.g., biology, chemistry, physics), management science/operations research, mathematics, and statistics.

An important characteristic of management support systems (MSS) is their emphasis on the **effectiveness**, or "goodness," of the decision produced rather than on the computational efficiency of obtaining it; this is usually a major concern of a transaction processing system. Most Web-based DSS are focused on improving decision effectiveness. **Efficiency** may be a by-product.

Decision Style and Decision Makers

In the following sections, we examine the notion of decision style and specific aspects about decision makers.

DECISION STYLE   **Decision style** is the manner by which decision makers think and react to problems. This includes the way they perceive a problem, their cognitive responses, and how values and beliefs vary from individual to individual and from situation to situation. As a result, people make decisions in different ways. Although there is a general process of decision making, it is far from linear. People do not follow the same steps of the process in the same sequence, nor do they use all the steps. Furthermore, the emphasis, time allotment, and priorities given to each step vary significantly, not only from one person to another, but also from one situation to the next. The manner in which managers make decisions (and the way they interact with other people) describes their decision style. Because decision styles depend on the factors described earlier, there are many decision styles. Personality temperament tests are often used to determine decision styles. Because there are many such tests, it is important to try to equate them in determining decision style. However, the various tests measure somewhat different aspects of personality, so they cannot be equated.

Researchers have identified a number of decision-making styles. These include heuristic and analytic styles. One can also distinguish between autocratic versus democratic styles. Another style is consultative (with individuals or groups). Of course, there are many combinations and variations of styles. For example, a person can be analytic and autocratic, or consultative (with individuals) and heuristic.

For a computerized system to successfully support a manager, it should fit the decision situation as well as the decision style. Therefore, the system should be flexible and adaptable to different users. The ability to ask what-if and goal-seeking questions provides flexibility in this direction. A Web-based interface using graphics is a desirable feature in supporting certain decision styles. If a DSS is to support varying styles, skills, and knowledge, it should not attempt to enforce a specific process. Rather, it should help decision makers use and develop their own styles, skills, and knowledge.

Different decision styles require different types of support. A major factor that determines the type of support required is whether the decision maker is an individual or a group. Individual decision makers need access to data and to experts who can provide advice, whereas groups additionally need collaboration tools. Web-based DSS can provide support to both.

A lot of information is available on the Web about cognitive styles and decision styles (e.g., see Birkman International, Inc., **birkman.com**; Keirsey Temperament Sorter and Keirsey Temperament Theory-II, **keirsey.com**). Many personality/temperament tests are available to help managers identify their own styles and those of their employees. Identifying an individual's style can help establish the most effective communication patterns and ideal tasks for which the person is suited.

DECISION MAKERS Decisions are often made by individuals, especially at lower managerial levels and in small organizations. There may be conflicting objectives even for a sole decision maker. For example, when making an investment decision, an individual investor may consider the rate of return on the investment, liquidity, and safety as objectives. Finally, decisions may be fully automated (but only after a human decision maker decides to do so!).

This discussion of decision making focuses in large part on an individual decision maker. Most major decisions in medium-sized and large organizations are made by groups. Obviously, there are often conflicting objectives in a group decision-making setting. Groups can be of variable size and may include people from different departments or from different organizations. Collaborating individuals may have different cognitive styles, personality types, and decision styles. Some clash, whereas others are mutually enhancing. Consensus can be a difficult political problem. Therefore, the process of decision making by a group can be very complicated. Computerized support can greatly enhance group decision making. Computer support can be provided at a broad level, enabling members of whole departments, divisions, or even entire organizations to collaborate online. Such support has evolved over the past few years into enterprise information systems (EIS) and includes group support systems (GSS), enterprise resource management (ERM)/enterprise resource planning (ERP), supply chain management (SCM), knowledge management systems (KMS), and customer relationship management (CRM) systems.

SECTION 2.2 REVIEW QUESTIONS

1. What are the various aspects of decision making?
2. Identify similarities and differences between individual and group decision making.
3. Define *decision style* and describe why it is important to consider in the decision-making process.
4. What are the benefits of mathematical models?

2.3 PHASES OF THE DECISION-MAKING PROCESS

It is advisable to follow a systematic decision-making process. Simon (1977) said that this involves three major phases: intelligence, design, and choice. He later added a fourth phase, implementation. Monitoring can be considered a fifth phase—a form of feedback. However,

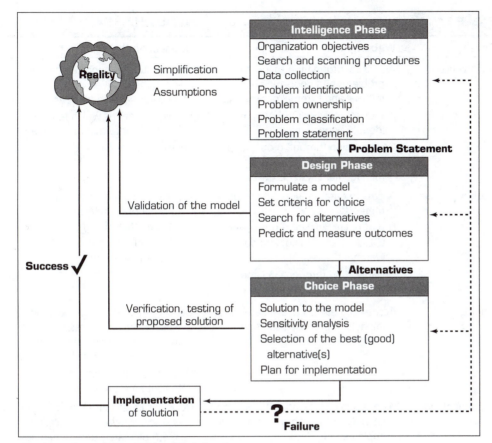

FIGURE 2.1 The Decision-Making/Modeling Process.

we view monitoring as the *intelligence phase* applied to the *implementation phase*. Simon's model is the most concise and yet complete characterization of rational decision making. A conceptual picture of the decision-making process is shown in Figure 2.1.

There is a continuous flow of activity from intelligence to design to choice (see the bold lines in Figure 2.1), but at any phase, there may be a return to a previous phase (feedback). Modeling is an essential part of this process. The seemingly chaotic nature of following a haphazard path from problem discovery to solution via decision making can be explained by these feedback loops.

The decision-making process starts with the **intelligence phase**; in this phase, the decision maker examines reality and identifies and defines the problem. *Problem ownership* is established as well. In the **design phase**, a model that represents the system is constructed. This is done by making assumptions that simplify reality and writing down the relationships among all the variables. The model is then validated, and criteria are determined in a principle of choice for evaluation of the alternative courses of action that are identified. Often, the process of model development identifies alternative solutions and vice versa.

The **choice phase** includes selection of a proposed solution to the model (not necessarily to the problem it represents). This solution is tested to determine its viability. When the proposed solution seems reasonable, we are ready for the last phase: implementation of the decision (not necessarily of a system). Successful implementation results in solving the real problem. Failure leads to a return to an earlier phase of the process. In fact, we can return to an earlier phase during any of the latter three phases. The decision-making situations described in the opening vignette follow Simon's four-phase model, as do almost all other decision-making situations. Web impacts on the four phases, and vice versa, are shown in Table 2.1.

TABLE 2.1 Simon's Four Phases of Decision Making and the Web

Phase	Web Impacts	Impacts on the Web
Intelligence	Access to information to identify problems and opportunities from internal and external data sources Access to analytics methods to identify opportunities Collaboration through group support systems (GSS) and knowledge management systems (KMS)	Identification of opportunities for e-commerce, Web infrastructure, hardware and software tools, etc. Intelligent agents, which reduce the burden of information overload Smart search engines
Design	Access to data, models, and solution methods Use of online analytical processing (OLAP), data mining, and data warehouses Collaboration through GSS and KMS Similar solutions available from KMS	Brainstorming methods (e.g., GSS) to collaborate in Web infrastructure design Models and solutions of Web infrastructure issues
Choice	Access to methods to evaluate the impacts of proposed solutions	Decision support system (DSS) tools, which examine and establish criteria from models to determine Web, intranet, and extranet infrastructure DSS tools, which determine how to route messages
Implementation	Web-based collaboration tools (e.g., GSS) and KMS, which can assist in implementing decisions Tools, which monitor the performance of e-commerce and other sites, including intranets, extranets, and the Internet	Decisions implemented on browser and server design and access, which ultimately determined how to set up the various components that have evolved into the Internet

Note that there are many other decision-making processes. Notable among them is the Kepner-Tregoe method (Kepner and Tregoe, 1998), which has been adopted by many firms because its tools are readily available from Kepner-Tregoe, Inc. (**kepner-tregoe. com**). We have found that these alternative models, including the Kepner-Tregoe method, readily map into Simon's four-phase model.

We next turn to a detailed discussion of the four phases identified by Simon.

SECTION 2.3 REVIEW QUESTIONS

1. List and briefly describe Simon's four phases of decision making.

2. What are the impacts of the Web on the phases of decision making?

2.4 DECISION MAKING: THE INTELLIGENCE PHASE

Intelligence in decision making involves scanning the environment, either intermittently or continuously. It includes several activities aimed at identifying problem situations or opportunities. It may also include monitoring the results of the implementation phase of a decision-making process.

Problem (or Opportunity) Identification

The intelligence phase begins with the identification of organizational goals and objectives related to an issue of concern (e.g., inventory management, job selection, lack of or incorrect Web presence) and determination of whether they are being met. Problems occur because of dissatisfaction with the status quo. Dissatisfaction is the result of a difference between what people desire (or expect) and what is occurring. In this first phase, a decision maker attempts to determine whether a problem exists, identify its symptoms, determine its magnitude, and explicitly define it. Often, what is described as a problem (e.g., excessive costs) may be only a symptom (i.e., measure) of a problem (e.g., improper inventory levels). Because real-world problems are usually complicated by many interrelated factors, it is sometimes difficult to distinguish between the symptoms and the real problem. New opportunities and problems certainly may be uncovered while investigating the causes of symptoms. For example, Application Case 2.1 describes a classic story of recognizing the correct problem.

The existence of a problem can be determined by monitoring and analyzing the organization's productivity level. The measurement of productivity and the construction of a model are based on real data. The collection of data and the estimation of future data are among the most difficult steps in the analysis. The following are some issues that may arise during data collection and estimation and thus plague decision makers:

- Data are not available. As a result, the model is made with, and relies on, potentially inaccurate estimates.
- Obtaining data may be expensive.
- Data may not be accurate or precise enough.
- Data estimation is often subjective.
- Data may be insecure.
- Important data that influence the results may be qualitative (soft).
- There may be too many data (i.e., information overload).

Application Case 2.1

Making Elevators Go Faster!

This story has been reported in numerous places and has almost become a classic example to explain the need for problem identification. Ackoff (as cited in Larson, 1987) described the problem of managing complaints about slow elevators in a tall hotel tower. After trying many solutions for reducing the complaint: staggering elevators to go to different floors, adding operators, and so on, the management determined that the real problem was not about the *actual* waiting time but rather the *perceived* waiting time. So the solution was to install full-length mirrors on elevator doors on each floor. As Hesse and Woolsey (1975) put it, "the women would look at themselves in the mirrors and make adjustments, while the men would look at the women, and before they knew it, the elevator was there." By reducing the perceived waiting time, the problem went away. Baker and

Cameron (1996) give several other examples of distractions, including lighting, displays, and so on, that organizations use to reduce perceived waiting time. If the real problem is identified as *perceived* waiting time, it can make a big difference in the proposed solutions and their costs. For example, full-length mirrors probably cost a whole lot less than adding an elevator!

Sources: Based on J. Baker and M. Cameron, "The Effects of the Service Environment on Affect and Consumer Perception of Waiting Time: An Integrative Review and Research Propositions," *Journal of the Academy of Marketing Science,* Vol. 24, September 1996, pp. 338–349; R. Hesse and G. Woolsey, *Applied Management Science: A Quick and Dirty Approach,* SRA Inc., Chicago, 1975; R. C. Larson, "Perspectives on Queues: Social Justice and the Psychology of Queuing," *Operations Research,* Vol. 35, No. 6, November/December 1987, pp. 895–905.

- Outcomes (or results) may occur over an extended period. As a result, revenues, expenses, and profits will be recorded at different points in time. To overcome this difficulty, a present-value approach can be used if the results are quantifiable.
- It is assumed that future data will be similar to historical data. If this is not the case, the nature of the change has to be predicted and included in the analysis.

When the preliminary investigation is completed, it is possible to determine whether a problem really exists, where it is located, and how significant it is. A key issue is whether an information system is reporting a problem or only the symptoms of a problem. For example, if reports indicate that sales are down, there is a problem, but the situation, no doubt, is symptomatic of the problem. It is critical to know the real problem. Sometimes it may be a problem of perception, incentive mismatch, or organizational processes rather than a poor decision model.

Problem Classification

Problem classification is the conceptualization of a problem in an attempt to place it in a definable category, possibly leading to a standard solution approach. An important approach classifies problems according to the degree of structuredness evident in them. This ranges from totally structured (i.e., programmed) to totally unstructured (i.e., unprogrammed), as described in Chapter 1.

Problem Decomposition

Many complex problems can be divided into subproblems. Solving the simpler subproblems may help in solving a complex problem. Also, seemingly poorly structured problems sometimes have highly structured subproblems. Just as a semistructured problem results when some phases of decision making are structured whereas other phases are unstructured, so when some subproblems of a decision-making problem are structured with others unstructured, the problem itself is semistructured. As a DSS is developed and the decision maker and development staff learn more about the problem, it gains structure. Decomposition also facilitates communication among decision makers. Decomposition is one of the most important aspects of the analytical hierarchy process. (AHP is discussed in Chapter 11, which helps decision makers incorporate both qualitative and quantitative factors into their decision-making models.)

Problem Ownership

In the intelligence phase, it is important to establish problem ownership. A problem exists in an organization only if someone or some group takes on the responsibility of attacking it and if the organization has the ability to solve it. The assignment of authority to solve the problem is called **problem ownership**. For example, a manager may feel that he or she has a problem because interest rates are too high. Because interest rate levels are determined at the national and international levels, and most managers can do nothing about them, high interest rates are the problem of the government, not a problem for a specific company to solve. The problem companies actually face is how to operate in a high–interest-rate environment. For an individual company, the interest rate level should be handled as an uncontrollable (environmental) factor to be predicted.

When problem ownership is not established, either someone is not doing his or her job or the problem at hand has yet to be identified as belonging to anyone. It is then important for someone to either volunteer to own it or assign it to someone.

The intelligence phase ends with a formal problem statement.

SECTION 2.4 REVIEW QUESTIONS

1. What is the difference between a problem and its symptoms?

2. Why is it important to classify a problem?

3. What is meant by *problem decomposition*?

4. Why is establishing problem ownership so important in the decision-making process?

2.5 DECISION MAKING: THE DESIGN PHASE

The design phase involves finding or developing and analyzing possible courses of action. These include understanding the problem and testing solutions for feasibility. A model of the decision-making problem is constructed, tested, and validated. Let us first define a model.

Models[1]

A major characteristic of a DSS and many BI tools (notably those of business analytics) is the inclusion of at least one model. The basic idea is to perform the DSS analysis on a model of reality rather than on the real system. A *model* is a simplified representation or abstraction of reality. It is usually simplified because reality is too complex to describe exactly and because much of the complexity is actually irrelevant in solving a specific problem.

Mathematical (Quantitative) Models

The complexity of relationships in many organizational systems is described mathematically. Most DSS analyses are performed numerically with mathematical or other quantitative models.

The Benefits of Models

We use models for the following reasons:

- Manipulating a model (changing decision variables or the environment) is much easier than manipulating a real system. Experimentation is easier and does not interfere with the organization's daily operations.
- Models enable the compression of time. Years of operations can be simulated in minutes or seconds of computer time.
- The cost of modeling analysis is much lower than the cost of a similar experiment conducted on a real system.
- The cost of making mistakes during a trial-and-error experiment is much lower when models are used than with real systems.
- The business environment involves considerable uncertainty. With modeling, a manager can estimate the risks resulting from specific actions.
- Mathematical models enable the analysis of a very large, sometimes infinite, number of possible solutions. Even in simple problems, managers often have a large number of alternatives from which to choose.
- Models enhance and reinforce learning and training.
- Models and solution methods are readily available.

Modeling involves conceptualizing a problem and abstracting it to quantitative and/or qualitative form (see Chapter 9). For a mathematical model, the variables are

---

[1]Caution: Many students and professionals view models strictly as those of "data modeling" in the context of systems analysis and design. Here, we consider analytical models such as those of linear programming, simulation, and forecasting.

identified, and their mutual relationships are established. Simplifications are made, whenever necessary, through assumptions. For example, a relationship between two variables may be assumed to be linear even though in reality there may be some non-linear effects. A proper balance between the level of model simplification and the representation of reality must be obtained because of the cost–benefit trade-off. A simpler model leads to lower development costs, easier manipulation, and a faster solution but is less representative of the real problem and can produce inaccurate results. However, a simpler model generally requires fewer data, or the data are aggregated and easier to obtain.

The process of modeling is a combination of art and science. As a science, there are many standard model classes available, and, with practice, an analyst can determine which one is applicable to a given situation. As an art, creativity and finesse are required when determining what simplifying assumptions can work, how to combine appropriate features of the model classes, and how to integrate models to obtain valid solutions. Models have **decision variables** that describe the alternatives from among which a manager must choose (e.g., how many cars to deliver to a specific rental agency, how to advertise at specific times, which Web server to buy or lease), a result variable or a set of result variables (e.g., profit, revenue, sales) that describes the objective or goal of the decision-making problem, and uncontrollable variables or parameters (e.g., economic conditions) that describe the environment. The process of modeling involves determining the (usually mathematical, sometimes symbolic) relationships among the variables. These topics are discussed in Chapter 9.

Selection of a Principle of Choice

A **principle of choice** is a criterion that describes the acceptability of a solution approach. In a model, it is a result variable. Selecting a principle of choice is not part of the choice phase but involves how a person establishes decision-making objective(s) and incorporates the objective(s) into the model(s). Are we willing to assume high risk, or do we prefer a low-risk approach? Are we attempting to optimize or satisfice? It is also important to recognize the difference between a criterion and a constraint (see Technology Insights 2.1). Among the many principles of choice, normative and descriptive are of prime importance.

TECHNOLOGY INSIGHTS 2.1   The Difference Between a Criterion and a Constraint

Many people new to the formal study of decision making inadvertently confuse the concepts of criterion and constraint. Often, this is because a criterion may imply a constraint, either implicit or explicit, thereby adding to the confusion. For example, there may be a distance criterion that the decision maker does not want to travel too far from home. However, there is an implicit constraint that the alternatives from which he selects must be within a certain distance from his home. This constraint effectively says that if the distance from home is greater than a certain amount, then the alternative is not feasible—or, rather, the distance to an alternative must be less than or equal to a certain number (this would be a formal relationship in some models; in the model in this case, it reduces the search, considering fewer alternatives). This is similar to what happens in some cases when selecting a university, where schools beyond a single day's driving distance would not be considered by most people, and, in fact, the utility function (criterion value) of distance can start out low close to home, peak at about 70 miles (about 100 km)—say, the distance between Atlanta (home) and Athens, Georgia—and sharply drop off thereafter.

Normative Models

Normative models are models in which the chosen alternative is demonstrably the best of all possible alternatives. To find it, the decision maker should examine all the alternatives and prove that the one selected is indeed the best, which is what the person would normally want. This process is basically **optimization**. This is typically the goal of what we call prescriptive analytics (Part IV). In operational terms, optimization can be achieved in one of three ways:

1. Get the highest level of goal attainment from a given set of resources. For example, which alternative will yield the maximum profit from an investment of $10 million?
2. Find the alternative with the highest ratio of goal attainment to cost (e.g., profit per dollar invested) or maximize productivity.
3. Find the alternative with the lowest cost (or smallest amount of other resources) that will meet an acceptable level of goals. For example, if your task is to select hardware for an intranet with a minimum bandwidth, which alternative will accomplish this goal at the least cost?

Normative decision theory is based on the following assumptions of rational decision makers:

- Humans are economic beings whose objective is to maximize the attainment of goals; that is, the decision maker is rational. (More of a good thing [revenue, fun] is better than less; less of a bad thing [cost, pain] is better than more.)
- For a decision-making situation, all viable alternative courses of action and their consequences, or at least the probability and the values of the consequences, are known.
- Decision makers have an order or preference that enables them to rank the desirability of all consequences of the analysis (best to worst).

Are decision makers really rational? Though there may be major anomalies in the presumed rationality of financial and economic behavior, we take the view that they could be caused by incompetence, lack of knowledge, multiple goals being framed inadequately, misunderstanding of a decision maker's true expected utility, and time-pressure impacts. There are other anomalies, often caused by time pressure. For example, Stewart (2002) described a number of researchers working with intuitive decision making. The idea of "thinking with your gut" is obviously a heuristic approach to decision making. It works well for firefighters and military personnel on the battlefield. One critical aspect of decision making in this mode is that many scenarios have been thought through in advance. Even when a situation is new, it can quickly be matched to an existing one on-the-fly, and a reasonable solution can be obtained (through *pattern recognition*). Luce et al. (2004) described how emotions affect decision making, and Pauly (2004) discussed inconsistencies in decision making.

We believe that irrationality is caused by the factors listed previously. For example, Tversky et al. (1990) investigated the phenomenon of preference reversal, which is a known problem in applying the AHP to problems. Also, some criterion or preference may be omitted from the analysis. Ratner et al. (1999) investigated how variety can cause individuals to choose less-preferred options, even though they will enjoy them less. But we maintain that variety clearly has value, is part of a decision maker's utility, and is a criterion and/or constraint that should be considered in decision making.

Suboptimization

By definition, optimization requires a decision maker to consider the impact of each alternative course of action on the entire organization because a decision made in one area may have significant effects (positive or negative) on other areas. Consider, for example, a marketing department that implements an electronic commerce (e-commerce) site. Within hours, orders far exceed production capacity. The production department, which plans its own schedule, cannot meet demand. It may gear up for as high demand as possible. Ideally and independently, the department should produce only a few products in extremely large quantities to minimize manufacturing costs. However, such a plan might result in large, costly inventories and marketing difficulties caused by the lack of a variety of products, especially if customers start to cancel orders that are not met in a timely way. This situation illustrates the sequential nature of decision making.

A systems point of view assesses the impact of every decision on the entire system. Thus, the marketing department should make its plans in conjunction with other departments. However, such an approach may require a complicated, expensive, time-consuming analysis. In practice, the MSS builder may close the system within narrow boundaries, considering only the part of the organization under study (the marketing and/or production department, in this case). By simplifying, the model then does not incorporate certain complicated relationships that describe interactions with and among the other departments. The other departments can be aggregated into simple model components. Such an approach is called **suboptimization**.

If a suboptimal decision is made in one part of the organization without considering the details of the rest of the organization, then an optimal solution from the point of view of that part may be inferior for the whole. However, suboptimization may still be a very practical approach to decision making, and many problems are first approached from this perspective. It is possible to reach tentative conclusions (and generally usable results) by analyzing only a portion of a system, without getting bogged down in too many details. After a solution is proposed, its potential effects on the remaining departments of the organization can be tested. If no significant negative effects are found, the solution can be implemented.

Suboptimization may also apply when simplifying assumptions are used in modeling a specific problem. There may be too many details or too many data to incorporate into a specific decision-making situation, and so not all of them are used in the model. If the solution to the model seems reasonable, it may be valid for the problem and thus be adopted. For example, in a production department, parts are often partitioned into A/B/C inventory categories. Generally, A items (e.g., large gears, whole assemblies) are expensive (say, $3,000 or more each), built to order in small batches, and inventoried in low quantities; C items (e.g., nuts, bolts, screws) are very inexpensive (say, less than $2) and ordered and used in very large quantities; and B items fall in between. All A items can be handled by a detailed scheduling model and physically monitored closely by management; B items are generally somewhat aggregated, their groupings are scheduled, and management reviews these parts less frequently; and C items are not scheduled but are simply acquired or built based on a policy defined by management with a simple economic order quantity (EOQ) ordering system that assumes constant annual demand. The policy might be reviewed once a year. This situation applies when determining all criteria or modeling the entire problem becomes prohibitively time-consuming or expensive.

Suboptimization may also involve simply bounding the search for an optimum (e.g., by a heuristic) by considering fewer criteria or alternatives or by eliminating large portions of the problem from evaluation. If it takes too long to solve a problem, a good-enough solution found already may be used and the optimization effort terminated.

Descriptive Models

Descriptive models describe things as they are or as they are believed to be. These models are typically mathematically based. Descriptive models are extremely useful in DSS for investigating the consequences of various alternative courses of action under different configurations of inputs and processes. However, because a descriptive analysis checks the performance of the system for a given set of alternatives (rather than for all alternatives), there is no guarantee that an alternative selected with the aid of descriptive analysis is optimal. In many cases, it is only satisfactory.

Simulation is probably the most common descriptive modeling method. **Simulation** is the imitation of reality and has been applied to many areas of decision making. Computer and video games are a form of simulation: An artificial reality is created, and the game player lives within it. Virtual reality is also a form of simulation because the environment is simulated, not real. A common use of simulation is in manufacturing. Again, consider the production department of a firm with complications caused by the marketing department. The characteristics of each machine in a job shop along the supply chain can be described mathematically. Relationships can be established based on how each machine physically runs and relates to others. Given a trial schedule of batches of parts, it is possible to measure how batches flow through the system and to use the statistics from each machine. Alternative schedules may then be tried and the statistics recorded until a reasonable schedule is found. Marketing can examine access and purchase patterns on its Web site. Simulation can be used to determine how to structure a Web site for improved performance and to estimate future purchases. Both departments can therefore use primarily experimental modeling methods.

Classes of descriptive models include the following:

- Complex inventory decisions
- Environmental impact analysis
- Financial planning
- Information flow
- Markov analysis (predictions)
- Scenario analysis
- Simulation (alternative types)
- Technological forecasting
- Waiting-line (queuing) management

A number of nonmathematical descriptive models are available for decision making. One is the cognitive map (see Eden and Ackermann, 2002; and Jenkins, 2002). A cognitive map can help a decision maker sketch out the important qualitative factors and their causal relationships in a messy decision-making situation. This helps the decision maker (or decision-making group) focus on what is relevant and what is not, and the map evolves as more is learned about the problem. The map can help the decision maker understand issues better, focus better, and reach closure. One interesting software tool for cognitive mapping is Decision Explorer from Banxia Software Ltd. (**banxia.com**; try the demo).

Another descriptive decision-making model is the use of narratives to describe a decision-making situation. A *narrative* is a story that helps a decision maker uncover the important aspects of the situation and leads to better understanding and framing. This is extremely effective when a group is making a decision, and it can lead to a more common viewpoint, also called a *frame*. Juries in court trials typically use narrative-based approaches in reaching verdicts (see Allan, Frame, and Turney, 2003; Beach, 2005; and Denning, 2000).

Good Enough, or Satisficing

According to Simon (1977), most human decision making, whether organizational or individual, involves a willingness to settle for a satisfactory solution, "something less than the best." When **satisficing**, the decision maker sets up an aspiration, a goal, or a desired level of performance and then searches the alternatives until one is found that achieves this level. The usual reasons for satisficing are time pressures (e.g., decisions may lose value over time), the ability to achieve optimization (e.g., solving some models could take a really long time, and recognition that the marginal benefit of a better solution is not worth the marginal cost to obtain it (e.g., in searching the Internet, you can look at only so many Web sites before you run out of time and energy). In such a situation, the decision maker is behaving rationally, though in reality he or she is satisficing. Essentially, satisficing is a form of suboptimization. There may be a best solution, an optimum, but it would be difficult, if not impossible, to attain it. With a normative model, too much computation may be involved; with a descriptive model, it may not be possible to evaluate all the sets of alternatives.

Related to satisficing is Simon's idea of *bounded rationality*. Humans have a limited capacity for rational thinking; they generally construct and analyze a simplified model of a real situation by considering fewer alternatives, criteria, and/or constraints than actually exist. Their behavior with respect to the simplified model may be rational. However, the rational solution for the simplified model may not be rational for the real-world problem. Rationality is bounded not only by limitations on human processing capacities, but also by individual differences, such as age, education, knowledge, and attitudes. Bounded rationality is also why many models are descriptive rather than normative. This may also explain why so many good managers rely on intuition, an important aspect of good decision making (see Stewart, 2002; and Pauly, 2004).

Because rationality and the use of normative models lead to good decisions, it is natural to ask why so many bad decisions are made in practice. Intuition is a critical factor that decision makers use in solving unstructured and semistructured problems. The best decision makers recognize the trade-off between the marginal cost of obtaining further information and analysis versus the benefit of making a better decision. But sometimes decisions must be made quickly, and, ideally, the intuition of a seasoned, excellent decision maker is called for. When adequate planning, funding, or information is not available, or when a decision maker is inexperienced or ill trained, disaster can strike.

Developing (Generating) Alternatives

A significant part of the model-building process is generating alternatives. In optimization models (such as linear programming), the alternatives may be generated automatically by the model. In most decision situations, however, it is necessary to generate alternatives manually. This can be a lengthy process that involves searching and creativity, perhaps utilizing electronic brainstorming in a GSS. It takes time and costs money. Issues such as when to stop generating alternatives can be very important. Too many alternatives can be detrimental to the process of decision making. A decision maker may suffer from information overload.

Generating alternatives is heavily dependent on the availability and cost of information and requires expertise in the problem area. This is the least formal aspect of **problem solving**. Alternatives can be generated and evaluated using heuristics. The generation of alternatives from either individuals or groups can be supported by electronic brainstorming software in a Web-based GSS.

Note that the search for alternatives usually occurs after the criteria for evaluating the alternatives are determined. This sequence can ease the search for alternatives and reduce the effort involved in evaluating them, but identifying potential alternatives can sometimes aid in identifying criteria.

The outcome of every proposed alternative must be established. Depending on whether the decision-making problem is classified as one of certainty, risk, or uncertainty, different modeling approaches may be used (see Drummond, 2001; and Koller, 2000). These are discussed in Chapter 9.

Measuring Outcomes

The value of an alternative is evaluated in terms of goal attainment. Sometimes an outcome is expressed directly in terms of a goal. For example, profit is an outcome, profit maximization is a goal, and both are expressed in dollar terms. An outcome such as customer satisfaction may be measured by the number of complaints, by the level of loyalty to a product, or by ratings found through surveys. Ideally, a decision maker would want to deal with a single goal, but in practice, it is not unusual to have multiple goals (see Barba-Romero, 2001; and Koksalan and Zionts, 2001). When groups make decisions, each group participant may have a different agenda. For example, executives might want to maximize profit, marketing might want to maximize market penetration, operations might want to minimize costs, and stockholders might want to maximize the bottom line. Typically, these goals conflict, so special multiple-criteria methodologies have been developed to handle this. One such method is the AHP. We will study AHP in Chapter 9.

Risk

All decisions are made in an inherently unstable environment. This is due to the many unpredictable events in both the economic and physical environments. Some risk (measured as probability) may be due to internal organizational events, such as a valued employee quitting or becoming ill, whereas others may be due to natural disasters, such as a hurricane. Aside from the human toll, one economic aspect of Hurricane Katrina was that the price of a gallon of gasoline doubled overnight due to uncertainty in the port capabilities, refining, and pipelines of the southern United States. What can a decision maker do in the face of such instability?

In general, people have a tendency to measure uncertainty and risk badly. Purdy (2005) said that people tend to be overconfident and have an illusion of control in decision making. The results of experiments by Adam Goodie at the University of Georgia indicate that most people are overconfident most of the time (Goodie, 2004). This may explain why people often feel that one more pull of a slot machine will definitely pay off.

However, methodologies for handling extreme uncertainty do exist. For example, Yakov (2001) described a way to make good decisions based on very little information, using an information gap theory and methodology approach. Aside from estimating the potential utility or value of a particular decision's outcome, the best decision makers are capable of accurately estimating the risk associated with the outcomes that result from making each decision. Thus, one important task of a decision maker is to attribute a level of risk to the outcome associated with each potential alternative being considered. Some decisions may lead to unacceptable risks in terms of success and can therefore be discarded or discounted immediately.

In some cases, some decisions are assumed to be made under conditions of certainty simply because the environment is assumed to be stable. Other decisions are made under conditions of uncertainty, where risk is unknown. Still, a good decision maker can make working estimates of risk. Also, the process of developing BI/DSS involves learning more about the situation, which leads to a more accurate assessment of the risks.

Scenarios

A **scenario** is a statement of assumptions about the operating environment of a particular system at a given time; that is, it is a narrative description of the decision-situation setting. A scenario describes the decision and uncontrollable variables and parameters for a specific modeling situation. It may also provide the procedures and constraints for the modeling.

Scenarios originated in the theater, and the term was borrowed for war gaming and large-scale simulations. Scenario planning and analysis is a DSS tool that can capture a whole range of possibilities. A manager can construct a series of scenarios (i.e., what-if cases), perform computerized analyses, and learn more about the system and decision-making problem while analyzing it. Ideally, the manager can identify an excellent, possibly optimal, solution to the model of the problem.

Scenarios are especially helpful in simulations and what-if analyses. In both cases, we change scenarios and examine the results. For example, we can change the anticipated demand for hospitalization (an input variable for planning), thus creating a new scenario. Then we can measure the anticipated cash flow of the hospital for each scenario.

Scenarios play an important role in decision making because they:

- Help identify opportunities and problem areas
- Provide flexibility in planning
- Identify the leading edges of changes that management should monitor
- Help validate major modeling assumptions
- Allow the decision maker to explore the behavior of a system through a model
- Help to check the sensitivity of proposed solutions to changes in the environment, as described by the scenario

Possible Scenarios

There may be thousands of possible scenarios for every decision situation. However, the following are especially useful in practice:

- The worst possible scenario
- The best possible scenario
- The most likely scenario
- The average scenario

The scenario determines the context of the analysis to be performed.

Errors in Decision Making

The model is a critical component in the decision-making process, but a decision maker may make a number of errors in its development and use. Validating the model before it is used is critical. Gathering the right amount of information, with the right level of precision and accuracy, to incorporate into the decision-making process is also critical. Sawyer (1999) described "the seven deadly sins of decision making," most of which are behavior or information related.

SECTION 2.5 REVIEW QUESTIONS

1. Define *optimization* and contrast it with *suboptimization*.
2. Compare the normative and descriptive approaches to decision making.
3. Define *rational decision making*. What does it really mean to be a rational decision maker?
4. Why do people exhibit bounded rationality when solving problems?

5. Define *scenario*. How is a scenario used in decision making?

6. Some "errors" in decision making can be attributed to the notion of decision making from the gut. Explain what is meant by this and how such errors can happen.

2.6 DECISION MAKING: THE CHOICE PHASE

Choice is the critical act of decision making. The choice phase is the one in which the actual decision and the commitment to follow a certain course of action are made. The boundary between the design and choice phases is often unclear because certain activities can be performed during both of them and because the decision maker can return frequently from choice activities to design activities (e.g., generate new alternatives while performing an evaluation of existing ones). The choice phase includes the search for, evaluation of, and recommendation of an appropriate solution to a model. A solution to a model is a specific set of values for the decision variables in a selected alternative. Choices can be evaluated as to their viability and profitability.

Note that solving a model is not the same as solving the problem the model represents. The solution to the model yields a recommended solution to the problem. The problem is considered solved only if the recommended solution is successfully implemented.

Solving a decision-making model involves searching for an appropriate course of action. Search approaches include **analytical techniques** (i.e., solving a formula), **algorithms** (i.e., step-by-step procedures), heuristics (i.e., rules of thumb), and blind searches (i.e., shooting in the dark, ideally in a logical way). These approaches are examined in Chapter 9.

Each alternative must be evaluated. If an alternative has multiple goals, they must all be examined and balanced against each other. **Sensitivity analysis** is used to determine the robustness of any given alternative; slight changes in the parameters should ideally lead to slight or no changes in the alternative chosen. **What-if analysis** is used to explore major changes in the parameters. Goal seeking helps a manager determine values of the decision variables to meet a specific objective. All this is discussed in Chapter 9.

SECTION 2.6 REVIEW QUESTIONS

1. Explain the difference between a principle of choice and the actual choice phase of decision making.

2. Why do some people claim that the choice phase is the point in time when a decision is really made?

3. How can sensitivity analysis help in the choice phase?

2.7 DECISION MAKING: THE IMPLEMENTATION PHASE

In *The Prince*, Machiavelli astutely noted some 500 years ago that there was "nothing more difficult to carry out, nor more doubtful of success, nor more dangerous to handle, than to initiate a new order of things." The implementation of a proposed solution to a problem is, in effect, the initiation of a new order of things or the introduction of change. And change must be managed. User expectations must be managed as part of change management.

The definition of *implementation* is somewhat complicated because implementation is a long, involved process with vague boundaries. Simplistically, the **implementation phase** involves putting a recommended solution to work, not necessarily implementing a computer system. Many generic implementation issues, such as resistance to change, degree of support of top management, and user training, are important in dealing with information system supported decision making. Indeed, many previous technology-related waves (e.g., business process reengineering (BPR), knowledge management, etc.) have faced mixed results mainly because of change management challenges and issues. Management of change is almost an entire discipline in itself, so we recognize its importance and encourage the readers to focus on it independently. Implementation also includes a thorough understanding of project management. Importance of project management goes far beyond analytics, so the last few years have witnessed a major growth in certification programs for project managers. A very popular certification now is Project Management Professional (PMP). See **pmi.org** for more details.

Implementation must also involve collecting and analyzing data to learn from the previous decisions and improve the next decision. Although analysis of data is usually conducted to identify the problem and/or the solution, analytics should also be employed in the feedback process. This is especially true for any public policy decisions. We need to be sure that the data being used for problem identification is valid. Sometimes people find this out only after the implementation phase.

The decision-making process, though conducted by people, can be improved with computer support, which is the subject of the next section.

SECTION 2.7 REVIEW QUESTIONS

1. Define *implementation*.

2. How can DSS support the implementation of a decision?

2.8 HOW DECISIONS ARE SUPPORTED

In Chapter 1, we discussed the need for computerized decision support and briefly described some decision aids. Here we relate specific technologies to the decision-making process (see Figure 2.2). Databases, data marts, and especially data warehouses are important technologies in supporting all phases of decision making. They provide the data that drive decision making.

Support for the Intelligence Phase

The primary requirement of decision support for the intelligence phase is the ability to scan external and internal information sources for opportunities and problems and to interpret what the scanning discovers. Web tools and sources are extremely useful for environmental

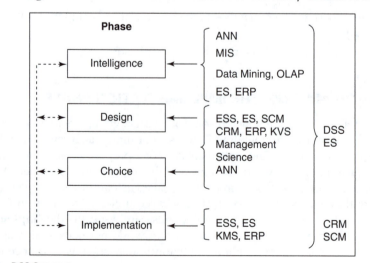

FIGURE 2.2 DSS Support.

scanning. Web browsers provide useful front ends for a variety of tools, from OLAP to data mining and data warehouses. Data sources can be internal or external. Internal sources may be accessible via a corporate intranet. External sources are many and varied.

Decision support/BI technologies can be very helpful. For example, a data warehouse can support the intelligence phase by continuously monitoring both internal and external information, looking for early signs of problems and opportunities through a Web-based enterprise information portal (also called a dashboard). Similarly, (automatic) data (and Web) mining (which may include expert systems [ES], CRM, genetic algorithms, neural networks, and other analytics systems) and (manual) OLAP also support the intelligence phase by identifying relationships among activities and other factors. Geographic information systems (GIS) can be utilized either as stand-alone systems or integrated with these systems so that a decision maker can determine opportunities and problems in a spatial sense. These relationships can be exploited for competitive advantage (e.g., CRM identifies classes of customers to approach with specific products and services). A KMS can be used to identify similar past situations and how they were handled. GSS can be used to share information and for brainstorming. As seen in Chapter 14, even cell phone and GPS data can be captured to create a micro-view of customers and their habits.

Another aspect of identifying internal problems and capabilities involves monitoring the current status of operations. When something goes wrong, it can be identified quickly and the problem can be solved. Tools such as business activity monitoring (BAM), business process management (BPM), and product life-cycle management (PLM) provide such capability to decision makers. Both routine and ad hoc reports can aid in the intelligence phase. For example, regular reports can be designed to assist in the problem-finding activity by comparing expectations with current and projected performance. Web-based OLAP tools are excellent at this task. So are visualization tools and electronic document management systems.

Expert systems (ES), in contrast, can render advice regarding the nature of a problem, its classification, its seriousness, and the like. ES can advise on the suitability of a solution approach and the likelihood of successfully solving the problem. One of the primary areas of ES success is interpreting information and diagnosing problems. This capability can be exploited in the intelligence phase. Even intelligent agents can be used to identify opportunities.

Much of the information used in seeking new opportunities is qualitative, or soft. This indicates a high level of unstructuredness in the problems, thus making DSS quite useful in the intelligence phase.

The Internet and advanced database technologies have created a glut of data and information available to decision makers—so much that it can detract from the quality and speed of decision making. It is important to recognize some issues in using data and analytics tools for decision making. First, to paraphrase baseball great Vin Scully, "data should be used the way a drunk uses a lamppost. For support, not for illumination." It is especially true when the focus is on understanding the problem. We should recognize that not all the data that may help understand the problem is available. To quote Einstein, "Not everything that counts can be counted, and not everything that can be counted counts." There might be other issues that have to be recognized as well.

Support for the Design Phase

The design phase involves generating alternative courses of action, discussing the criteria for choices and their relative importance, and forecasting the future consequences of using various alternatives. Several of these activities can use standard models provided by a DSS (e.g., financial and forecasting models, available as applets). Alternatives for structured problems can be generated through the use of either standard or special models.

However, the generation of alternatives for complex problems requires expertise that can be provided only by a human, brainstorming software, or an ES. OLAP and data mining software are quite useful in identifying relationships that can be used in models. Most DSS have quantitative analysis capabilities, and an internal ES can assist with qualitative methods as well as with the expertise required in selecting quantitative analysis and forecasting models. A KMS should certainly be consulted to determine whether such a problem has been encountered before or whether there are experts on hand who can provide quick understanding and answers. CRM systems, revenue management systems, ERP, and SCM systems software are useful in that they provide models of business processes that can test assumptions and scenarios. If a problem requires brainstorming to help identify important issues and options, a GSS may prove helpful. Tools that provide cognitive mapping can also help. Cohen et al. (2001) described several Web-based tools that provide decision support, mainly in the design phase, by providing models and reporting of alternative results. Each of their cases has saved millions of dollars annually by utilizing these tools. Such DSS are helping engineers in product design as well as decision makers solving business problems.

Support for the Choice Phase

In addition to providing models that rapidly identify a best or good-enough alternative, a DSS can support the choice phase through what-if and goal-seeking analyses. Different scenarios can be tested for the selected option to reinforce the final decision. Again, a KMS helps identify similar past experiences; CRM, ERP, and SCM systems are used to test the impacts of decisions in establishing their value, leading to an intelligent choice. An ES can be used to assess the desirability of certain solutions as well as to recommend an appropriate solution. If a group makes a decision, a GSS can provide support to lead to consensus.

Support for the Implementation Phase

This is where "making the decision happen" occurs. The DSS benefits provided during implementation may be as important as or even more important than those in the earlier phases. DSS can be used in implementation activities such as decision communication, explanation, and justification.

Implementation-phase DSS benefits are partly due to the vividness and detail of analyses and reports. For example, one chief executive officer (CEO) gives employees and external parties not only the aggregate financial goals and cash needs for the near term, but also the calculations, intermediate results, and statistics used in determining the aggregate figures. In addition to communicating the financial goals unambiguously, the CEO signals other messages. Employees know that the CEO has thought through the assumptions behind the financial goals and is serious about their importance and attainability. Bankers and directors are shown that the CEO was personally involved in analyzing cash needs and is aware of and responsible for the implications of the financing requests prepared by the finance department. Each of these messages improves decision implementation in some way.

As mentioned earlier, reporting systems and other tools variously labeled as BAM, BPM, KMS, EIS, ERP, CRM, and SCM are all useful in tracking how well an implementation is working. GSS is useful for a team to collaborate in establishing implementation effectiveness. For example, a decision might be made to get rid of unprofitable customers. An effective CRM can identify classes of customers to get rid of, identify the impact of doing so, and then verify that it really worked that way.

All phases of the decision-making process can be supported by improved communication through collaborative computing via GSS and KMS. Computerized systems can facilitate communication by helping people explain and justify their suggestions and opinions.

Decision implementation can also be supported by ES. An ES can be used as an advisory system regarding implementation problems (such as handling resistance to change). Finally, an ES can provide training that may smooth the course of implementation.

Impacts along the value chain, though reported by an EIS through a Web-based enterprise information portal, are typically identified by BAM, BPM, SCM, and ERP systems. CRM systems report and update internal records, based on the impacts of the implementation. These inputs are then used to identify new problems and opportunities—a return to the intelligence phase.

SECTION 2.8 REVIEW QUESTIONS

1. Describe how DSS/BI technologies and tools can aid in each phase of decision making.

2. Describe how new technologies can provide decision-making support.

Now that we have studied how technology can assist in decision making, we study some details of decision support systems (DSS) in the next two sections.

2.9 DECISION SUPPORT SYSTEMS: CAPABILITIES

The early definitions of a DSS identified it as a system intended to support managerial decision makers in semistructured and unstructured decision situations. DSS were meant to be adjuncts to decision makers, extending their capabilities but not replacing their judgment. They were aimed at decisions that required judgment or at decisions that could not be completely supported by algorithms. Not specifically stated but implied in the early definitions was the notion that the system would be computer based, would operate interactively online, and preferably would have graphical output capabilities, now simplified via browsers and mobile devices.

A DSS Application

A DSS is typically built to support the solution of a certain problem or to evaluate an opportunity. This is a key difference between DSS and BI applications. In a very strict sense, **business intelligence (BI)** systems monitor situations and identify problems and/or opportunities, using analytic methods. Reporting plays a major role in BI; the user generally must identify whether a particular situation warrants attention, and then analytical methods can be applied. Again, although models and data access (generally through a data warehouse) are included in BI, DSS typically have their own databases and are developed to solve a specific problem or set of problems. They are therefore called **DSS applications**.

Formally, a DSS is an approach (or methodology) for supporting decision making. It uses an interactive, flexible, adaptable computer-based information system (CBIS) especially developed for supporting the solution to a specific unstructured management problem. It uses data, provides an easy user interface, and can incorporate the decision maker's own insights. In addition, a DSS includes models and is developed (possibly by end users) through an interactive and iterative process. It can support all phases of decision making and may include a knowledge component. Finally, a DSS can be used by a single user or can be Web based for use by many people at several locations.

Because there is no consensus on exactly what a DSS is, there is obviously no agreement on the standard characteristics and capabilities of DSS. The capabilities in Figure 2.3 constitute an ideal set, some members of which are described in the definitions of DSS and illustrated in the application cases.

The key characteristics and capabilities of DSS (as shown in Figure 2.3) are:

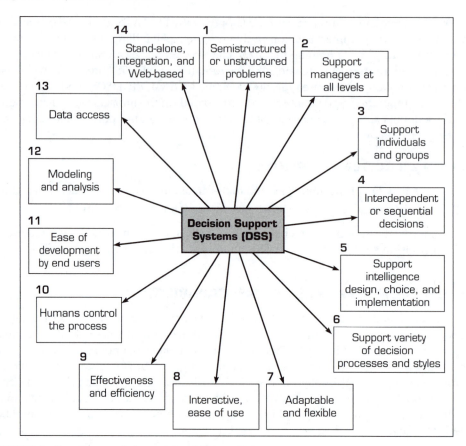

FIGURE 2.3 Key Characteristics and Capabilities of DSS.

1. Support for decision makers, mainly in semistructured and unstructured situations, by bringing together human judgment and computerized information. Such problems cannot be solved (or cannot be solved conveniently) by other computerized systems or through use of standard quantitative methods or tools. Generally, these problems gain structure as the DSS is developed. Even some structured problems have been solved by DSS.

2. Support for all managerial levels, ranging from top executives to line managers.

3. Support for individuals as well as groups. Less-structured problems often require the involvement of individuals from different departments and organizational levels or even from different organizations. DSS support virtual teams through collaborative Web tools. DSS have been developed to support individual and group work, as well as to support individual decision making and groups of decision makers working somewhat independently.

4. Support for interdependent and/or sequential decisions. The decisions may be made once, several times, or repeatedly.

5. Support in all phases of the decision-making process: intelligence, design, choice, and implementation.

6. Support for a variety of decision-making processes and styles.

7. The decision maker should be reactive, able to confront changing conditions quickly, and able to adapt the DSS to meet these changes. DSS are flexible, so users can add, delete, combine, change, or rearrange basic elements. They are also flexible in that they can be readily modified to solve other, similar problems.

8. User-friendliness, strong graphical capabilities, and a natural language interactive human–machine interface can greatly increase the effectiveness of DSS. Most new DSS applications use Web-based interfaces or mobile platform interfaces.

9. Improvement of the effectiveness of decision making (e.g., accuracy, timeliness, quality) rather than its efficiency (e.g., the cost of making decisions). When DSS are deployed, decision making often takes longer, but the decisions are better.

10. The decision maker has complete control over all steps of the decision-making process in solving a problem. A DSS specifically aims to support, not to replace, the decision maker.

11. End users are able to develop and modify simple systems by themselves. Larger systems can be built with assistance from information system (IS) specialists. Spreadsheet packages have been utilized in developing simpler systems. OLAP and data mining software, in conjunction with data warehouses, enable users to build fairly large, complex DSS.

12. Models are generally utilized to analyze decision-making situations. The modeling capability enables experimentation with different strategies under different configurations.

13. Access is provided to a variety of data sources, formats, and types, including GIS, multimedia, and object-oriented data.

14. The DSS can be employed as a stand-alone tool used by an individual decision maker in one location or distributed throughout an organization and in several organizations along the supply chain. It can be integrated with other DSS and/or applications, and it can be distributed internally and externally, using networking and Web technologies.

These key DSS characteristics and capabilities allow decision makers to make better, more consistent decisions in a timely manner, and they are provided by the major DSS components, which we will describe after discussing various ways of classifying DSS (next).

SECTION 2.9 REVIEW QUESTIONS

1. List the key characteristics and capabilities of DSS.
2. Describe how providing support to a workgroup is different from providing support to group work. Explain why it is important to differentiate these concepts.
3. What kinds of DSS can end users develop in spreadsheets?
4. Why is it so important to include a model in a DSS?

2.10 DSS CLASSIFICATIONS

DSS applications have been classified in several different ways (see Power, 2002; Power and Sharda, 2009). The design process, as well as the operation and implementation of DSS, depends in many cases on the type of DSS involved. However, remember that not every DSS fits neatly into one category. Most fit into the classification provided by the Association for Information Systems Special Interest Group on Decision Support Systems (AIS SIGDSS). We discuss this classification but also point out a few other attempts at classifying DSS.

The AIS SIGDSS Classification for DSS

The AIS SIGDSS (**ais.site-ym.com/group/SIGDSS**) has adopted a concise classification scheme for DSS that was proposed by Power (2002). It includes the following categories:

- Communications-driven and group DSS (GSS)
- Data-driven DSS

- Document-driven DSS
- Knowledge-driven DSS, data mining, and management ES applications
- Model-driven DSS

There may also be hybrids that combine two or more categories. These are called *compound DSS*. We discuss the major categories next.

COMMUNICATIONS-DRIVEN AND GROUP DSS   Communications-driven and group DSS (GSS) include DSS that use computer, collaboration, and communication technologies to support groups in tasks that may or may not include decision making. Essentially, all DSS that support any kind of group work fall into this category. They include those that support meetings, design collaboration, and even supply chain management. Knowledge management systems (KMS) that are developed around communities that practice collaborative work also fall into this category. We discuss these in more detail in later chapters.

DATA-DRIVEN DSS   Data-driven DSS are primarily involved with data and processing them into information and presenting the information to a decision maker. Many DSS developed in OLAP and reporting analytics software systems fall into this category. There is minimal emphasis on the use of mathematical models.

In this type of DSS, the database organization, often in a data warehouse, plays a major role in the DSS structure. Early generations of database-oriented DSS mainly used the *relational* database configuration. The information handled by relational databases tends to be voluminous, descriptive, and rigidly structured. A database-oriented DSS features strong report generation and query capabilities. Indeed, this is primarily the current application of the tools marked under the BI umbrella or under the label of reporting/business analytics. The chapters on data warehousing and business performance management (BPM) describe several examples of this category of DSS.

DOCUMENT-DRIVEN DSS   Document-driven DSS rely on knowledge coding, analysis, search, and retrieval for decision support. They essentially include all DSS that are text based. Most KMS fall into this category. These DSS also have minimal emphasis on utilizing mathematical models. For example, a system that we built for the U.S. Army's Defense Ammunitions Center falls in this category. The main objective of document-driven DSS is to provide support for decision making using documents in various forms: oral, written, and multimedia.

KNOWLEDGE-DRIVEN DSS, DATA MINING, AND MANAGEMENT EXPERT SYSTEMS APPLICATIONS   These DSS involve the application of knowledge technologies to address specific decision support needs. Essentially, all artificial intelligence–based DSS fall into this category. When symbolic storage is utilized in a DSS, it is generally in this category. ANN and ES are included here. Because the benefits of these *intelligent DSS* or *knowledge-based DSS* can be large, organizations have invested in them. These DSS are utilized in the creation of *automated decision-making systems*, as described in Chapter 12. The basic idea is that rules are used to automate the decision-making process. These rules are basically either an ES or structured like one. This is important when decisions must be made quickly, as in many e-commerce situations.

MODEL-DRIVEN DSS   The major emphases of DSS that are primarily developed around one or more (large-scale/complex) optimization or simulation models typically include significant activities in model formulation, model maintenance, model management in distributed computing environments, and what-if analyses. Many large-scale applications fall into this category. Notable examples include those used by Procter & Gamble (Farasyn et al., 2008), HP (Olavson and Fry, 2008), and many others.

The focus of such systems is on using the model(s) to optimize one or more objectives (e.g., profit). The most common end-user tool for DSS development is Microsoft Excel. Excel includes dozens of statistical packages, a linear programming package (Solver), and many financial and management science models. We will study these in more detail in Chapter 9. These DSS typically can be grouped under the new label of *prescriptive analytics*.

COMPOUND DSS   A compound, or hybrid, DSS includes two or more of the major categories described earlier. Often, an ES can benefit by utilizing some optimization, and clearly a data-driven DSS can feed a large-scale optimization model. Sometimes documents are critical in understanding how to interpret the results of visualizing data from a data-driven DSS.

An emerging example of a compound DSS is a product offered by WolframAlpha (**wolframalpha.com**). It compiles knowledge from outside databases, models, algorithms, documents, and so on to provide answers to specific questions. For example, it can find and analyze current data for a stock and compare it with other stocks. It can also tell you how many calories you will burn when performing a specific exercise or the side effects of a particular medicine. Although it is in early stages as a collection of knowledge components from many different areas, it is a good example of a compound DSS in getting its knowledge from many diverse sources and attempting to synthesize it.

Other DSS Categories

Many other proposals have been made to classify DSS. Perhaps the first formal attempt was by Alter (1980). Several other important categories of DSS include (1) institutional and ad hoc DSS; (2) personal, group, and organizational support; (3) individual support system versus GSS; and (4) custom-made systems versus ready-made systems. We discuss some of these next.

INSTITUTIONAL AND AD HOC DSS   **Institutional DSS** (see Donovan and Madnick, 1977) deal with decisions of a recurring nature. A typical example is a portfolio management system (PMS), which has been used by several large banks for supporting investment decisions. An institutionalized DSS can be developed and refined as it evolves over a number of years, because the DSS is used repeatedly to solve identical or similar problems. It is important to remember that an institutional DSS may not be used by everyone in an organization; it is the *recurring nature of the decision-making problem* that determines whether a DSS is institutional versus ad hoc.

Ad hoc DSS deal with specific problems that are usually neither anticipated nor recurring. Ad hoc decisions often involve strategic planning issues and sometimes management control problems. Justifying a DSS that will be used only once or twice is a major issue in DSS development. Countless ad hoc DSS applications have evolved into institutional DSS. Either the problem recurs and the system is reused or others in the organization have similar needs that can be handled by the formerly ad hoc DSS.

Custom-Made Systems Versus Ready-Made Systems

Many DSS are custom made for individual users and organizations. However, a comparable problem may exist in similar organizations. For example, hospitals, banks, and universities share many similar problems. Similarly, certain nonroutine problems in a functional area (e.g., finance, accounting) can repeat themselves in the same functional area of different areas or organizations. Therefore, it makes sense to build generic DSS that can be used (sometimes with modifications) in several organizations. Such DSS are called *ready-made* and are sold by various vendors (e.g., Cognos, MicroStrategy, Teradata). Essentially, the database, models, interface, and other support features are built in: Just add an organization's data and logo. The major OLAP and analytics vendors provide DSS templates for a variety of functional areas, including finance, real estate, marketing, and accounting. The number of ready-made DSS continues to increase because of their flexibility and low cost. They are typically developed using Internet technologies for database access and communications, and Web browsers for interfaces. They also readily incorporate OLAP and other easy-to-use DSS generators.

One complication in terminology results when an organization develops an institutional system but, because of its structure, uses it in an ad hoc manner. An organization can build a large data warehouse but then use OLAP tools to query it and perform ad hoc analysis to solve nonrecurring problems. The DSS exhibits the traits of ad hoc and institutional systems and also of custom and ready-made systems. Several ERP, CRM, knowledge management (KM), and SCM companies offer DSS applications online. These kinds of systems can be viewed as ready-made, although typically they require modifications (sometimes major) before they can be used effectively.

SECTION 2.10 REVIEW QUESTIONS

1. List the DSS classifications of the AIS SIGDSS.
2. Define *document-driven DSS*.
3. List the capabilities of institutional DSS and ad hoc DSS.
4. Define the term *ready-made DSS*.

2.11 COMPONENTS OF DECISION SUPPORT SYSTEMS

A DSS application can be composed of a data management subsystem, a model management subsystem, a user interface subsystem, and a knowledge-based management subsystem. We show these in Figure 2.4.

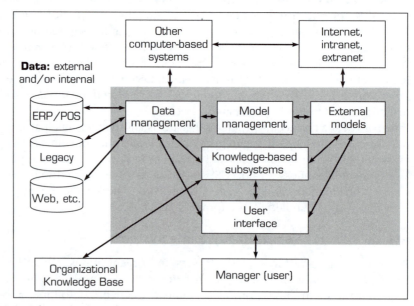

FIGURE 2.4   Schematic View of DSS.

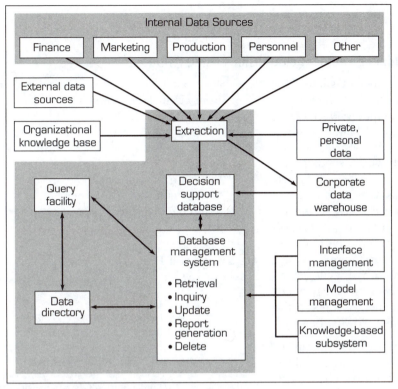

FIGURE 2.5   Structure of the Data Management Subsystem.

The Data Management Subsystem

The data management subsystem includes a database that contains relevant data for the situation and is managed by software called the **database management system (DBMS)**.[2] The data management subsystem can be interconnected with the corporate **data warehouse**, a repository for corporate relevant decision-making data. Usually, the data are stored or accessed via a database Web server. The data management subsystem is composed of the following elements:

- DSS database
- Database management system
- Data directory
- Query facility

These elements are shown schematically in Figure 2.5 (in the shaded area). The figure also shows the interaction of the data management subsystem with the other parts of the DSS, as well as its interaction with several data sources. Many of the BI or descriptive analytics applications derive their strength from the data management side of the subsystems. Application Case 2.2 provides an example of a DSS that focuses on data.

The Model Management Subsystem

The model management subsystem is the component that includes financial, statistical, management science, or other quantitative models that provide the system's analytical capabilities and appropriate software management. Modeling languages for building custom models are also included. This software is often called a **model base management**

---

[2]*DBMS* is used as both singular and plural (*system* and *systems*), as are many other acronyms in this text.

Application Case 2.2

Station Casinos Wins by Building Customer Relationships Using Its Data

Station Casinos is a major provider of gaming for Las Vegas–area residents. It owns about 20 properties in Nevada and other states, employs over 12,000 people, and has revenue of over $1 billion.

Station Casinos wanted to develop an in-depth view of each customer/guest who visited Casino Station properties. This would permit them to better understand customer trends as well as enhance their one-to-one marketing for each guest. The company employed the Teradata warehouse to develop the "Total Guest Worth" solution. The project used used Aprimo Relationship Manager, Informatica, and Cognos to capture, analyze, and segment customers. Almost 500 different data sources were integrated to develop the full view of a customer. As a result, the company was able to realize the following benefits:

- Customer segments were expanded from 14 (originally) to 160 segments so as to be able to target more specific promotions to each segment.
- A 4 percent to 6 percent increase in monthly slot profit.

- Slot promotion costs were reduced by $1 million (from $13 million per month) by better targeting the customer segments.
- A 14 percent improvement in guest retention.
- Increased new-member acquisition by 160 percent.
- Reduction in data error rates from as high as 80 percent to less than 1 percent.
- Reduced the time to analyze a campaign's effectiveness from almost 2 weeks to just a few hours.

QUESTIONS FOR DISCUSSION

1. Why is this decision support system classified as a data-focused DSS?
2. What were some of the benefits from implementing this solution?

Source: Teradata.com, "No Limits: Station Casinos Breaks the Mold on Customer Relationships," **teradata.com/case-studies/Station-Casinos-No-Limits-Station-Casinos-Breaks-the-Mold-on-Customer-Relationships-Executive-Summary-eb6410** (accessed February 2013).

system (MBMS). This component can be connected to corporate or external storage of models. Model solution methods and management systems are implemented in Web development systems (such as Java) to run on application servers. The model management subsystem of a DSS is composed of the following elements:

- Model base
- MBMS
- Modeling language
- Model directory
- Model execution, integration, and command processor

These elements and their interfaces with other DSS components are shown in Figure 2.6.

At a higher level than building blocks, it is important to consider the different types of models and solution methods needed in the DSS. Often at the start of development, there is some sense of the model types to be incorporated, but this may change as more is learned about the decision problem. Some DSS development systems include a wide variety of components (e.g., Analytica from Lumina Decision Systems), whereas others have a single one (e.g., Lindo). Often, the results of one type of model component (e.g., forecasting) are used as input to another (e.g., production scheduling). In some cases, a modeling language is a component that generates input to a solver, whereas in other cases, the two are combined.

Because DSS deal with semistructured or unstructured problems, it is often necessary to customize models, using programming tools and languages. Some examples of these are .NET Framework languages, C++, and Java. OLAP software may also be used to work with models in data analysis. Even languages for simulation such as Arena and statistical packages such as those of SPSS offer modeling tools developed through the use of a proprietary

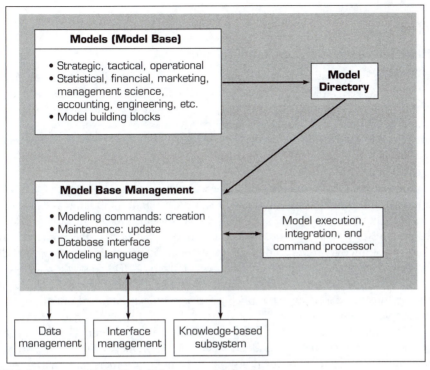

FIGURE 2.6   **Structure of the Model Management Subsystem.**

programming language. For small and medium-sized DSS or for less complex ones, a spreadsheet (e.g., Excel) is usually used. We will use Excel for many key examples in this book. Application Case 2.3 describes a spreadsheet-based DSS. However, using a spreadsheet for modeling a problem of any significant size presents problems with documentation and error diagnosis. It is very difficult to determine or understand nested, complex relationships in spreadsheets created by someone else. This makes it difficult to modify a model built by someone else. A related issue is the increased likelihood of errors creeping into the formulas. With all the equations appearing in the form of cell references, it is challenging to figure out where an error might be. These issues were addressed in an early generation of DSS development software that was available on mainframe computers in the 1980s. One such product was called Interactive Financial Planning System (IFPS). Its developer, Dr. Gerald Wagner, then released a desktop software called Planners Lab. Planners Lab includes the following components: (1) an easy-to-use algebraically oriented model-building language and (2) an easy-to-use state-of-the-art option for visualizing model output, such as answers to what-if and goal seek questions to analyze results of changes in assumptions. The combination of these components enables business managers and analysts to build, review, and challenge the assumptions that underlie decision-making scenarios.

Planners Lab makes it possible for the decision makers to "play" with assumptions to reflect alternative views of the future. Every Planners Lab model is an assemblage of assumptions about the future. Assumptions may come from databases of historical performance, market research, and the decision makers' minds, to name a few sources. Most assumptions about the future come from the decision makers' accumulated experiences in the form of opinions.

The resulting collection of equations is a Planners Lab model that *tells a readable story for a particular scenario.* Planners Lab lets decision makers describe their plans in their own words and with their own assumptions. The product's *raison d'être* is that a simulator should facilitate a conversation with the decision maker in the process of

Application Case 2.3

SNAP DSS Helps OneNet Make Telecommunications Rate Decisions

Telecommunications network services to educational institutions and government entities are typically provided by a mix of private and public organizations. Many states in the United States have one or more state agencies that are responsible for providing network services to schools, colleges, and other state agencies. One example of such an agency is OneNet in Oklahoma. OneNet is a division of the Oklahoma State Regents for Higher Education and operated in cooperation with the Office of State Finance.

Usually agencies such as OneNet operate as an enterprise-type fund. They must recover their costs through billing their clients and/or by justifying appropriations directly from the state legislatures. This cost recovery should occur through a pricing mechanism that is efficient, simple to implement, and equitable. This pricing model typically needs to recognize many factors: convergence of voice, data, and video traffic on the same infrastructure; diversity of user base in terms of educational institutions, state agencies, and so on; diversity of applications in use by state clients, from e-mail to videoconferences, IP telephoning, and distance learning; recovery of current costs, as well as planning for upgrades

and future developments; and leverage of the shared infrastructure to enable further economic development and collaborative work across the state that leads to innovative uses of OneNet.

These considerations led to the development of a spreadsheet-based model. The system, SNAP-DSS, or Service Network Application and Pricing (SNAP)-based DSS, was developed in Microsoft Excel 2007 and used the VBA programming language.

The SNAP-DSS offers OneNet the ability to select the rate card options that best fit the preferred pricing strategies by providing a real-time, user-friendly, graphical user interface (GUI). In addition, the SNAP-DSS not only illustrates the influence of the changes in the pricing factors on each rate card option, but also allows the user to analyze various rate card options in different scenarios using different parameters. This model has been used by OneNet financial planners to gain insights into their customers and analyze many what-if scenarios of different rate plan options.

Source: Based on J. Chongwatpol and R. Sharda, "SNAP: A DSS to Analyze Network Service Pricing for State Networks," *Decision Support Systems*, Vol. 50, No. 1, December 2010, pp. 347–359.

describing business assumptions. All assumptions are described in English equations (or the user's native language).

The best way to learn how to use Planners Lab is to launch the software and follow the tutorials. The software can be downloaded at **plannerslab.com**.

The User Interface Subsystem

The user communicates with and commands the DSS through the **user interface** subsystem. The user is considered part of the system. Researchers assert that some of the unique contributions of DSS are derived from the intensive interaction between the computer and the decision maker. The Web browser provides a familiar, consistent graphical user interface (GUI) structure for most DSS. For locally used DSS, a spreadsheet also provides a familiar user interface. A difficult user interface is one of the major reasons managers do not use computers and quantitative analyses as much as they could, given the availability of these technologies. The Web browser has been recognized as an effective DSS GUI because it is flexible, user friendly, and a gateway to almost all sources of necessary information and data. Essentially, Web browsers have led to the development of portals and dashboards, which front end many DSS.

Explosive growth in portable devices including smartphones and tablets has changed the DSS user interfaces as well. These devices allow either handwritten input or typed input from internal or external keyboards. Some DSS user interfaces utilize natural-language input (i.e., text in a human language) so that the users can easily express themselves in a meaningful way. Because of the fuzzy nature of human language, it is fairly difficult to develop software to interpret it. However, these packages increase in accuracy every year, and they will ultimately lead to accurate input, output, and language translators.

Cell phone inputs through SMS are becoming more common for at least some consumer DSS-type applications. For example, one can send an SMS request for search on any topic to GOOGL (46645). It is most useful in locating nearby businesses, addresses, or phone numbers, but it can also be used for many other decision support tasks. For example, users can find definitions of words by entering the word "define" followed by a word, such as "define extenuate." Some of the other capabilities include:

- Translations: "Translate thanks in Spanish."
- Price lookups: "Price 32GB iPhone."
- Calculator: Although you would probably just want to use your phone's built-in calculator function, you can send a math expression as an SMS for an answer.
- Currency conversions: "10 usd in euros."
- Sports scores and game times: Just enter the name of a team ("NYC Giants"), and Google SMS will send the most recent game's score and the date and time of the next match.

This type of SMS-based search capability is also available for other search engines, including Yahoo! and Microsoft's new search engine Bing.

With the emergence of smartphones such as Apple's iPhone and Android smartphones from many vendors, many companies are developing applications (commonly called *apps*) to provide purchasing-decision support. For example, Amazon.com's app allows a user to take a picture of any item in a store (or wherever) and send it to Amazon.com. Amazon.com's graphics-understanding algorithm tries to match the image to a real product in its databases and sends the user a page similar to Amazon.com's product info pages, allowing users to perform price comparisons in real time. Thousands of other apps have been developed that provide consumers support for decision making on finding and selecting stores/restaurants/service providers on the basis of location, recommendations from others, and especially from your own social circles.

Voice input for these devices and PCs is common and fairly accurate (but not perfect). When voice input with accompanying speech-recognition software (and readily available text-to-speech software) is used, verbal instructions with accompanied actions and outputs can be invoked. These are readily available for DSS and are incorporated into the portable devices described earlier. An example of voice inputs that can be used for a general-purpose DSS is Apple's Siri application and Google's Google Now service. For example, a user can give her zip code and say "pizza delivery." These devices provide the search results and can even place a call to a business.

Recent efforts in business process management (BPM) have led to inputs directly from physical devices for analysis via DSS. For example, radio-frequency identification (RFID) chips can record data from sensors in railcars or in-process products in a factory. Data from these sensors (e.g., recording an item's status) can be downloaded at key locations and immediately transmitted to a database or data warehouse, where they can be analyzed and decisions can be made concerning the status of the items being monitored. Walmart and Best Buy are developing this technology in their SCM, and such *sensor networks* are also being used effectively by other firms.

The Knowledge-Based Management Subsystem

The knowledge-based management subsystem can support any of the other subsystems or act as an independent component. It provides intelligence to augment the decision maker's own. It can be interconnected with the organization's knowledge repository (part of a knowledge management system [KMS]), which is sometimes called the **organizational knowledge base**. Knowledge may be provided via Web servers. Many artificial intelligence methods have been implemented in Web development systems such as Java and are easy to integrate into the other DSS components. One of the most widely publicized knowledge-based DSS is IBM's Watson computer system. It is described in Application Case 2.4.

We conclude the sections on the three major DSS components with information on some recent technology and methodology developments that affect DSS and decision making. Technology Insights 2.2 summarizes some emerging developments in user

Application Case 2.4
From a Game Winner to a Doctor!

The television show *Jeopardy!* inspired an IBM research team to build a supercomputer named Watson that successfully took on the challenge of playing *Jeopardy!* and beat the other human competitors. Since then, Watson has evolved into a question-answering computing platform that is now being used commercially in the medical field and is expected to find its use in many other areas.

Watson is a cognitive system built on clusters of powerful processors supported by IBM's DeepQA® software. Watson employs a combination of techniques like natural-language processing, hypothesis generation and evaluation, and evidence-based learning to overcome the constraints imposed by programmatic computing. This enables Watson to work on massive amounts of real-world, unstructured Big Data efficiently.

In the medical field, it is estimated that the amount of medical information doubles every 5 years. This massive growth limits a physician's decision-making ability in diagnosis and treatment of illness using an evidence-based approach. With the advancements being made in the medical field every day, physicians do not have enough time to read every journal that can help them in keeping up-to-date with the latest advancements. Patient histories and electronic medical records contain lots of data. If this information can be analyzed in combination with vast amounts of existing medical knowledge, many useful clues can be provided to the physicians to help them identify diagnostic and treatment options. Watson, dubbed Dr. Watson, with its advanced machine learning capabilities, now finds a new role as a computer companion that assists physicians by providing relevant real-time information for critical decision making in choosing the right diagnostic and treatment procedures. (Also see the opening vignette for Chapter 7.)

Memorial Sloan-Kettering Cancer Center (MSKCC), New York, and WellPoint, a major insurance provider, have begun using Watson as a treatment advisor in oncology diagnosis. Watson learned the process of diagnosis and treatment through its natural-language processing capabilities, which enabled it to leverage the unstructured data with an enormous amount of clinical expertise data, molecular and genomic data from existing cancer case histories, journal articles, physicians' notes, and guidelines and best practices from the National Comprehensive Cancer Network. It was then trained by oncologists to apply the knowledge gained in comparing an individual patient's medical information against a wide variety of treatment guidelines, published research, and other insights to provide individualized, confidence-scored recommendations to the physicians.

At MSKCC, Watson facilitates evidence-based support for every suggestion it makes while analyzing an individual case by bringing out the facts from medical literature that point to a particular suggestion. It also provides a platform for the physicians to look at the case from multiple directions by doing further analysis relevant to the individual case. Its voice recognition capabilities allow physicians to speak to Watson, enabling it to be a perfect assistant that helps physicians in critical evidence-based decision making.

WellPoint also trained Watson with a vast history of medical cases and now relies on Watson's hypothesis generation and evidence-based learning to generate recommendations in providing approval for medical treatments based on the clinical and patient data. Watson also assists the insurance providers in detecting fraudulent claims and protecting physicians from malpractice claims.

Watson provides an excellent example of a knowledge-based DSS that employs multiple advanced technologies.

QUESTIONS FOR DISCUSSION

1. What is a cognitive system? How can it assist in real-time decision making?
2. What is evidence-based decision making?
3. What is the role played by Watson in the discussion?
4. Does Watson eliminate the need for human decision making?

What We Can Learn from This Application Case

Advancements in technology now enable the building of powerful, cognitive computing platforms combined with complex analytics. These systems are impacting the decision-making process radically by shifting them from an opinion-based process to a more real-time, evidence-based process, thereby turning available information intelligence into actionable wisdom that can be readily employed across many industrial sectors.

Sources: Ibm.com, "IBM Watson: Ushering In a New Era of Computing," **www-03.ibm.com/innovation/us/watson** (accessed February 2013); Ibm.com, "IBM Watson Helps Fight Cancer with Evidence-Based Diagnosis and Treatment Suggestions," **www-03.ibm.com/innovation/us/watson/pdf/MSK_Case_Study_IMC14794.pdf** (accessed February 2013); Ibm.com, "IBM Watson Enables More Effective Healthcare Preapproval Decisions Using Evidence-Based Learning," **www-03.ibm.com/innovation/us/watson/pdf/WellPoint_Case_Study_IMC14792.pdf** (accessed February 2013).

TECHNOLOGY INSIGHTS 2.2

Next Generation of Input Devices

The last few years have seen exciting developments in user interfaces. Perhaps the most common example of the new user interfaces is the iPhone's multi-touch interface that allows a user to zoom, pan, and scroll through a screen just with the use of a finger. The success of iPhone has spawned developments of similar user interfaces from many other providers including Blackberry, HTC, LG, Motorola (a part of Google), Microsoft, Nokia, Samsung, and others. Mobile platform has become the major access mechanism for all decision support applications.

In the last few years, gaming devices have evolved significantly to be able to receive and process gesture-based inputs. In 2007, Nintendo introduced the Wii game platform, which is able to process motions and gestures. Microsoft's Kinect is able to recognize image movements and use that to discern inputs. The next generation of these technologies is in the form of mind-reading platforms. A company called Emotiv (**en.wikipedia.org/wiki/Emotiv**) made big news in early 2008 with a promise to deliver a game controller that a user would be able to control by thinking about it. These technologies are to be based on *electroencephalography (EEG),* the technique of reading and processing the electrical activity at the scalp level as a result of specific thoughts in the brain. The technical details are available on Wikipedia (**en.wikipedia.org/wiki/Electroencephalography**) and the Web. Although EEG has not yet been known to be used as a DSS user interface (at least to the authors), its potential is significant for many other DSS-type applications. Many other companies are developing similar technologies.

It is also possible to speculate on other developments on the horizon. One major growth area is likely to be in wearable devices. Google's wearable glasses that are labeled "augmented reality" glasses will likely emerge as a new user interface for decision support in both consumer and corporate decision settings. Similarly, Apple is supposed to be working on iOS-based wristwatch-type computers. These devices will significantly impact how we interact with a system and use the system for decision support. So it is a safe bet that user interfaces are going to change significantly in the next few years. Their first use will probably be in gaming and consumer applications, but the business and DSS applications won't be far behind.

Sources: Various Wikipedia sites and the company Web sites provided in the feature.

interfaces. Many developments in DSS components are the result of new developments in hardware and software computer technology, data warehousing, data mining, OLAP, Web technologies, integration of technologies, and DSS application to various and new functional areas. There is also a clear link between hardware and software capabilities and improvements in DSS. Hardware continues to shrink in size while increasing in speed and other capabilities. The sizes of databases and data warehouses have increased dramatically. Data warehouses now provide hundreds of petabytes of sales data for retail organizations and content for major news networks.

We expect to see more seamless integration of DSS components as they adopt Web technologies, especially XML. These Web-based technologies have become the center of activity in developing DSS. Web-based DSS have reduced technological barriers and have made it easier and less costly to make decision-relevant information and model-driven DSS available to managers and staff users in geographically distributed locations, especially through mobile devices.

DSS are becoming more embedded in other systems. Similarly, a major area to expect improvements in DSS is in GSS in supporting collaboration at the enterprise level. This is true even in the educational arena. Almost every new area of information systems involves some level of decision-making support. Thus, DSS, either directly or indirectly, has impacts on CRM, SCM, ERP, KM, PLM, BAM, BPM, and other EIS. As these systems evolve, the active decision-making component that utilizes mathematical, statistical, or even descriptive models increases in size and capability, although it may be buried deep within the system.

Finally, different types of DSS components are being integrated more frequently. For example, GIS are readily integrated with other, more traditional, DSS components and tools for improved decision making.

By definition, a DSS must include the three major components—DBMS, MBMS, and user interface. The knowledge-based management subsystem is optional, but it can provide many benefits by providing intelligence in and to the three major components. As in any other MIS, the user may be considered a component of DSS.

Chapter Highlights

- Managerial decision making is synonymous with the whole process of management.
- Human decision styles need to be recognized in designing systems.
- Individual and group decision making can both be supported by systems.
- Problem solving is also opportunity evaluation.
- A model is a simplified representation or abstraction of reality.
- Decision making involves four major phases: intelligence, design, choice, and implementation.
- In the intelligence phase, the problem (opportunity) is identified, classified, and decomposed (if needed), and problem ownership is established.
- In the design phase, a model of the system is built, criteria for selection are agreed on, alternatives are generated, results are predicted, and a decision methodology is created.

- In the choice phase, alternatives are compared, and a search for the best (or a good-enough) solution is launched. Many search techniques are available.
- In implementing alternatives, a decision maker should consider multiple goals and sensitivity-analysis issues.
- Satisficing is a willingness to settle for a satisfactory solution. In effect, satisficing is suboptimizing. Bounded rationality results in decision makers satisficing.
- Computer systems can support all phases of decision making by automating many of the required tasks or by applying artificial intelligence.
- A DSS is designed to support complex managerial problems that other computerized techniques cannot. DSS is user oriented, and it uses data and models.
- DSS are generally developed to solve specific managerial problems, whereas BI systems typically

report status, and, when a problem is discovered, their analysis tools are utilized by decision makers.
- DSS can provide support in all phases of the decision-making process and to all managerial levels for individuals, groups, and organizations.
- DSS is a user-oriented tool. Many applications can be developed by end users, often in spreadsheets.
- DSS can improve the effectiveness of decision making, decrease the need for training, improve management control, facilitate communication, save effort by the users, reduce costs, and allow for more objective decision making.
- The AIS SIGDSS classification of DSS includes communications-driven and group DSS (GSS), data-driven DSS, document-driven DSS, knowledge-driven DSS, data mining and management ES applications, and model-driven DSS. Several other classifications map into this one.
- Several useful classifications of DSS are based on why they are developed (institutional versus ad hoc), what level within the organization they support (personal, group, or organizational), whether they support individual work or group work (individual DSS versus GSS), and how they are developed (custom versus ready-made).
- The major components of a DSS are a database and its management, a model base and its management, and a user-friendly interface. An intelligent (knowledge-based) component can also be included. The user is also considered to be a component of a DSS.
- Data warehouses, data mining, and OLAP have made it possible to develop DSS quickly and easily.
- The data management subsystem usually includes a DSS database, a DBMS, a data directory, and a query facility.
- The model base includes standard models and models specifically written for the DSS.
- Custom-made models can be written in programming languages, in special modeling languages, and in Web-based development systems (e.g., Java, the .NET Framework).
- The user interface (or dialog) is of utmost importance. It is managed by software that provides the needed capabilities. Web browsers and smartphones/tablets commonly provide a friendly, consistent DSS GUI.
- The user interface capabilities of DSS have moved into small, portable devices, including smartphones, tablets, and so forth.

Key Terms

ad hoc DSS	decision making	institutional DSS	problem ownership
algorithm	decision style	intelligence phase	problem solving
analytical techniques	decision variable	model base management	satisficing
business intelligence	descriptive model	system (MBMS)	scenario
(BI)	design phase	normative model	sensitivity analysis
choice phase	DSS application	optimization	simulation
data warehouse	effectiveness	organizational	suboptimization
database management	efficiency	knowledge base	user interface
system (DBMS)	implementation phase	principle of choice	what-if analysis

Questions for Discussion

1. Why is intuition still an important aspect of decision making?
2. Define *efficiency* and *effectiveness*, and compare and contrast the two.
3. Why is it important to focus on the effectiveness of a decision, not necessarily the efficiency of making a decision?
4. What are some of the measures of effectiveness in a toy manufacturing plant, a restaurant, an educational institution, and the U.S. Congress?
5. Even though implementation of a decision involves change, and change management is very difficult, explain how change management has *not* changed very much in thousands of years. Use specific examples throughout history.
6. Your company is considering opening a branch in China. List typical activities in each phase of the decision (intelligence, design, choice, implementation) of whether to open a branch.

7. You are about to buy a car. Using Simon's four-phase model, describe your activities at each step.
8. Explain, through an example, the support given to decision makers by computers in each phase of the decision process.
9. Some experts believe that the major contribution of DSS is to the implementation of a decision. Why is this so?
10. Review the major characteristics and capabilities of DSS. How do each of them relate to the major components of DSS?

11. List some internal data and external data that could be found in a DSS for a university's admissions office.
12. Why does a DSS need a DBMS, a model management system, and a user interface, but not necessarily a knowledge-based management system?
13. What are the benefits and the limitations of the AIS SIGDSS classification for DSS?
14. Search for a ready-made DSS. What type of industry is its market? Explain why it is a ready-made DSS.

Exercises

Teradata University Network TUN) and Other Hands-On Exercises

1. Choose a case at TUN or use the case that your instructor chooses. Describe in detail what decisions were to be made in the case and what process was actually followed. Be sure to describe how technology assisted or hindered the decision-making process and what the decision's impacts were.
2. Most companies and organizations have downloadable demos or trial versions of their software products on the Web so that you can copy and try them out on your own computer. Others have online demos. Find one that provides decision support, try it out, and write a short report about it. Include details about the intended purpose of the software, how it works, and how it supports decision making.
3. Comment on Simon's (1977) philosophy that managerial decision making is synonymous with the whole process

of management. Does this make sense? Explain. Use a real-world example in your explanation.
4. Consider a situation in which you have a preference about where you go to college: You want to be not too far away from home and not too close. Why might this situation arise? Explain how this situation fits with rational decision-making behavior.
5. Explore **teradatauniversitynetwork.com**. In a report, describe at least three interesting DSS applications and three interesting DSS areas (e.g., CRM, SCM) that you have discovered there.
6. Examine Daniel Power's DSS Resources site at **dssresources.com**. Take the Decision Support Systems Web Tour (**dssresources.com/tour/index.html**). Explore other areas of the Web site.

End-of-Chapter Application Case

Logistics Optimization in a Major Shipping Company (CSAV)

Introduction

Compañía Sud Americana de Vapores (CSAV) is a shipping company headquartered in Chile, South America, and is the sixth largest shipping company in the world. Its operations in over 100 countries worldwide are managed from seven regional offices. CSAV operates 700,000 containers valued at $2 billion. Less than 10 percent of these containers are owned by CSAV. The rest are acquired from other third-party companies on lease. At the heart of CSAV's business operations is their container fleet, which is only second to vessel fuel in terms of cost. As part of their strategic planning, the company recognized that addressing the problem of empty container logistics would help reduce operational cost. In a typical cycle of a cargo container, a shipper first acquires an empty container from a container depot. The container is then loaded onto a truck and sent to the merchant, who then fills it with his products. Finally, the container is sent by truck to the ship for

onward transport to the destination. Typically, there are transshipments along the way where a container may be moved from one vessel to another until it gets to its destination. At the destination, the container is transported to the consignee. After emptying the container, it is sent to the nearest CSAV depot, where maintenance is done on the container.

There were four main challenges recognized by CSAV to its empty container logistics problem:

- **Imbalance.** Some geographic regions are net exporters while others are net ivmporters. Places like China are net exporters; hence, there are always shortages of containers. North America is a net importer; it always has a surplus of containers. This creates an imbalance of containers as a result of uneven flow of containers.
- **Uncertainty.** Factors like demand, date of return of empty containers, travel times, and the ship's capacity

for empty containers create uncertainty in the location and availability of containers.

- **_Information handling and sharing._** Huge loads of data need to be processed every day. CSAV processes 400,000 container transactions every day. Timely decisions based on accurate information had to be generated in order to help reduce safety stocks of empty containers.
- **_Coordination of interrelated decisions worldwide._** Previously, decisions were made at the local level. Consequently, in order to alleviate the empty container problem, decisions regarding movement of empty containers at various locations had to be coordinated.

Methodology/Solution

CSAV developed an integrated system called Empty Container Logistics Optimization (ECO) using moving average, trended and seasonal time series, and sales force forecast (CFM) methods. The ECO system comprises a forecasting model, inventory model, multi-commodity (MC) network flow model, and a Web interface. The forecasting model draws data from the regional offices, processes it, and feeds the resultant information to the inventory model. Some of the information the forecasting model generates are the space in the vessel for empty containers and container demand. The forecasting module also helps reduce forecast error and, hence, allows CSAV's depot to maintain lower safety stocks. The inventory model calculates the safety stocks and feeds it to the MC Network Flow model. The MC Network Flow model is the core of the ECO system. It provides information for optimal decisions to be made regarding inventory levels, container repositioning flows, and the leasing and return of empty containers. The objective function is to minimize empty container logistics cost, which is mostly a result of leasing, repositioning, storage, loading, and discharge operations.

Results/Benefits

The ECO system activities in all regional centers are well coordinated while still maintaining flexibility and creativity in their operations. The system resulted in a 50 percent reduction in inventory stock. The generation of intelligent information from historical transactional data helped increase efficiency of operation. For instance, the empty time per container cycle decreased from a high of 47.2 days in 2009 to only 27.3 days the following year, resulting in an increase of 60 percent of the average empty container turnover. Also, container cycles

increased from a record low of 3.8 cycles in 2009 to 4.8 cycles in 2010. Moreover, when the ECO system was implemented in 2010, the excess cost per full voyage became $35 cheaper than the average cost for the period between 2006 and 2009. This resulted in cost savings of $101 million on all voyages in 2010. It was estimated that ECO's direct contribution to this cost reduction was about 80 percent ($81 million). CSAV projected that ECO will help generate $200 million profits over the next 2 years since its implementation in 2010.

CASE QUESTIONS

1. Explain why solving the empty container logistics problem contributes to cost savings for CSAV.
2. What are some of the qualitative benefits of the optimization model for the empty container movements?
3. What are some of the key benefits of the forecasting model in the ECO system implemented by CSAV?
4. Perform an online search to determine how other shipping companies handle the empty container problem. Do you think the ECO system would directly benefit those companies?
5. Besides shipping logistics, can you think of any other domain where such a system would be useful in reducing cost?

What We Can Learn from This End-of-Chapter Application Case

The empty container problem is faced by most shipping companies. The problem is partly caused by an imbalance in the demand of empty containers between different geographic areas. CSAV used an optimization system to solve the empty container problem. The case demonstrates a situation where a business problem is solved not just by one method or model, but by a combination of different operations research and analytics methods. For instance, we realize that the optimization model used by CSAV consisted of different submodels such as the forecasting and inventory models. The shipping industry is only one sector among a myriad of sectors where optimization models are used to decrease the cost of business operations. The lessons learned in this case could be explored in other domains such as manufacturing and supply chain.

Source: R. Epstein et al., "A Strategic Empty Container Logistics Optimization in a Major Shipping Company," _Interfaces_, Vol. 42, No. 1, January–February 2012, pp. 5–16.

References

Allan, N., R. Frame, and I. Turney. (2003). "Trust and Narrative: Experiences of Sustainability." _The Corporate Citizen_, Vol. 3, No. 2.

Alter, S. L. (1980). _Decision Support Systems: Current Practices and Continuing Challenges._ Reading, MA: Addison-Wesley.

Baker, J., and M. Cameron. (1996, September). "The Effects of the Service Environment on Affect and Consumer Perception of Waiting Time: An Integrative Review and Research Propositions." _Journal of the Academy of Marketing Science,_ Vol. 24, pp. 338–349.

Barba-Romero, S. (2001, July/August). "The Spanish Government Uses a Discrete Multicriteria DSS to Determine Data Processing Acquisitions." *Interfaces*, Vol. 31, No. 4, pp. 123–131.

Beach, L. R. (2005). *The Psychology of Decision Making: People in Organizations*, 2nd ed. Thousand Oaks, CA: Sage.

Birkman International, Inc., **birkman.com**; Keirsey Temperament Sorter and Keirsey Temperament Theory-II, **keirsey.com**.

Chongwatpol, J., and R. Sharda. (2010, December). "SNAP: A DSS to Analyze Network Service Pricing for State Networks." *Decision Support Systems,* Vol. 50, No. 1, pp. 347–359.

Cohen, M.-D., C. B. Charles, and A. L. Medaglia. (2001, March/April). "Decision Support with Web-Enabled Software." *Interfaces*, Vol. 31, No. 2, pp. 109–129.

Denning, S. (2000). *The Springboard: How Storytelling Ignites Action in Knowledge-Era Organizations*. Burlington, MA: Butterworth-Heinemann.

Donovan, J. J., and S. E. Madnick. (1977). "Institutional and Ad Hoc DSS and Their Effective Use." *Data Base*, Vol. 8, No. 3, pp. 79–88.

Drummond, H. (2001). *The Art of Decision Making: Mirrors of Imagination, Masks of Fate*. New York: Wiley.

Eden, C., and F. Ackermann. (2002). "Emergent Strategizing." In A. Huff and M. Jenkins (eds.). *Mapping Strategic Thinking*. Thousand Oaks, CA: Sage Publications.

Epstein, R., et al. (2012, January/February). "A Strategic Empty Container Logistics Optimization in a Major Shipping Company." *Interfaces*, Vol. 42, No. 1, pp. 5–16.

Farasyn, I., K. Perkoz, and W. Van de Velde. (2008, July/August). "Spreadsheet Models for Inventory Target Setting at Procter and Gamble." *Interfaces*, Vol. 38, No. 4, pp. 241–250.

Goodie, A. (2004, Fall). "Goodie Studies Pathological Gamblers' Risk-Taking Behavior." *The Independent Variable*. Athens, GA: The University of Georgia, Institute of Behavioral Research. **ibr.uga.edu/publications/fall2004.pdf** (accessed February 2013).

Hesse, R., and G. Woolsey. (1975). *Applied Management Science: A Quick and Dirty Approach*. Chicago: SRA Inc.

Ibm.com. "IBM Watson: Ushering In a New Era of Computing." **www-03.ibm.com/innovation/us/watson** (accessed February 2013).

Ibm.com. "IBM Watson Helps Fight Cancer with Evidence-Based Diagnosis and Treatment Suggestions." **www-03.ibm.com/innovation/us/watson/pdf/MSK_Case_Study_IMC14794.pdf** (accessed February 2013).

Ibm.com. "IBM Watson Enables More Effective Healthcare Preapproval Decisions Using Evidence-Based Learning." **www-03.ibm.com/innovation/us/watson/pdf/WellPoint_Case_Study_IMC14792.pdf** (accessed February 2013).

Jenkins, M. (2002). "Cognitive Mapping." In D. Partington (ed.). *Essential Skills for Management Research*. Thousand Oaks, CA: Sage Publications.

Kepner, C., and B. Tregoe. (1998). *The New Rational Manager*. Princeton, NJ: Kepner-Tregoe.

Koksalan, M., and S. Zionts (eds.). (2001). *Multiple Criteria Decision Making in the New Millennium*. Heidelberg: Springer-Verlag.

Koller, G. R. (2000). *Risk Modeling for Determining Value and Decision Making*. Boca Raton, FL: CRC Press.

Larson, R. C. (1987, November/December). "Perspectives on Queues: Social Justice and the Psychology of Queueing." *Operations Research*, Vol. 35, No. 6, pp. 895–905.

Luce, M. F., J. W. Payne, and J. R. Bettman. (2004). "The Emotional Nature of Decision Trade-offs." In S. J. Hoch, H. C. Kunreuther, and R. E. Gunther (eds.). *Wharton on Making Decisions*. New York: Wiley.

Olavson, T., and C. Fry. (2008, July/August). "Spreadsheet Decision-Support Tools: Lessons Learned at Hewlett-Packard." *Interfaces*, Vol. 38, No. 4, pp. 300–310.

Pauly, M. V. (2004). "Split Personality: Inconsistencies in Private and Public Decisions." In S. J. Hoch, H. C. Kunreuther, and R. E. Gunther (eds.). *Wharton on Making Decisions*. New York: Wiley.

Power, D. J. (2002). *Decision Making Support Systems: Achievements, Trends and Challenges*. Hershey, PA: Idea Group Publishing.

Power, D. J., and R. Sharda. (2009). "Decisions Support Systems." In S.Y. Nof (ed.), *Springer Handbook of Automation*. New York: Springer.

Purdy, J. (2005, Summer). "Decisions, Delusions, & Debacles." *UGA Research Magazine*.

Ratner, R. K., B. E. Kahn, and D. Kahneman. (1999, June). "Choosing Less-Preferred Experiences for the Sake of Variety." *Journal of Consumer Research*, Vol. 26, No. 1.

Sawyer, D. C. (1999). *Getting It Right: Avoiding the High Cost of Wrong Decisions*. Boca Raton, FL: St. Lucie Press.

Simon, H. (1977). *The New Science of Management Decision*. Englewood Cliffs, NJ: Prentice Hall.

Stewart, T. A. (2002, November). "How to Think with Your Gut." *Business 2.0*.

Teradata.com. "No Limits: Station Casinos Breaks the Mold on Customer Relationships." **teradata.com/case-studies/Station-Casinos-No-Limits-Station-Casinos-Breaks-the-Mold-on-Customer-Relationships-Executive-Summary-eb6410** (accessed February 2013).

Tversky, A., P. Slovic, and D. Kahneman. (1990, March). "The Causes of Preference Reversal." *American Economic Review*, Vol. 80, No. 1.

Yakov, B.-H. (2001). *Information Gap Decision Theory: Decisions Under Severe Uncertainty*. New York: Academic Press.

Descriptive Analytics

LEARNING OBJECTIVES FOR PART II

- Learn the role of descriptive analytics (DA) in solving business problems
- Learn the basic definitions, concepts, and architectures of data warehousing (DW)
- Learn the role of data warehouses in managerial decision support
- Learn the capabilities of business reporting and visualization as enablers of DA
- Learn the importance of information visualization in managerial decision support
- Learn the foundations of the emerging field of visual analytics
- Learn the capabilities and limitations of dashboards and scorecards
- Learn the fundamentals of business performance management (BPM)

Descriptive analytics, often referred to as business intelligence, uses data and models to answer the "what happened?" and "why did it happen?" questions in business settings. It is perhaps the most fundamental echelon in the three-step analytics continuum upon which predictive and prescriptive analytics capabilities are built. As you will see in the following chapters, the key enablers of descriptive analytics include data warehousing, business reporting, decision dashboard/ scorecards, and visual analytics.

Data Warehousing

LEARNING OBJECTIVES

- Understand the basic definitions and concepts of data warehouses
- Understand data warehousing architectures
- Describe the processes used in developing and managing data warehouses
- Explain data warehousing operations
- Explain the role of data warehouses in decision support
- Explain data integration and the extraction, transformation, and load (ETL) processes
- Describe real-time (active) data warehousing
- Understand data warehouse administration and security issues

The concept of data warehousing has been around since the late 1980s. This chapter provides the foundation for an important type of database, called a *data warehouse,* which is primarily used for decision support and provides improved analytical capabilities. We discuss data warehousing in the following sections:

3.1 OPENING VIGNETTE: Isle of Capri Casinos Is Winning with Enterprise Data Warehouse

Isle of Capri is a unique and innovative player in the gaming industry. After entering the market in Biloxi, Mississippi, in 1992, Isle has grown into one of the country's largest publicly traded gaming companies, mostly by establishing properties in the southeastern United States and in the country's heartland. Isle of Capri Casinos, Inc., is currently operating 18 casinos in seven states, serving nearly 2 million visitors each year.

CHALLENGE

Even though they seem to have a differentiating edge, compared to others in the highly competitive gaming industry, Isle is not entirely unique. Like any gaming company, Isle's success depends largely on its relationship with its customers—its ability to create a gaming, entertainment, and hospitality atmosphere that anticipates customers' needs and exceeds their expectations. Meeting such a goal is impossible without two important components: a company culture that is laser-focused on making the customer experience an enjoyable one, and a data and technology architecture that enables Isle to constantly deepen its understanding of its customers, as well as the various ways customer needs can be efficiently met.

SOLUTION

After an initial data warehouse implementation was derailed in 2005, in part by Hurricane Katrina, Isle decided to reboot the project with entirely new components and Teradata as the core solution and key partner, along with IBM Cognos for Business Intelligence. Shortly after that choice was made, Isle brought on a management team that clearly understood how the Teradata and Cognos solution could enable key decision makers throughout the operation to easily frame their own initial queries, as well as timely follow-up questions, thus opening up a wealth of possibilities to enhance the business.

RESULTS

Thanks to its successful implementation of a comprehensive data warehousing and business intelligence solution, Isle has achieved some deeply satisfying results. The company has dramatically accelerated and expanded the process of information gathering and dispersal, producing about 150 reports on a daily basis, 100 weekly, and 50 monthly, in addition to ad hoc queries, completed within minutes, all day every day. Prior to an enterprise data warehouse (EDW) from Teradata, Isle produced about 5 monthly reports per property, but because they took a week or more to produce, properties could not begin to analyze monthly activity until the second week of the following month. Moreover, none of the reports analyzed anything less than an entire month at a time; today, reports using up-to-the minute data on specific customer segments at particular properties are available, often the same day, enabling the company to react much more quickly to a wide range of customer needs.

Isle has cut the time in half needed to construct its core monthly direct-mail campaigns and can generate less involved campaigns practically on the spot. In addition to moving faster, Isle has honed the process of segmentation and now can cross-reference a wide range of attributes, such as overall customer value, gaming behaviors, and hotel preferences. This enables them to produce more targeted campaigns aimed at particular customer segments and particular behaviors.

Isle also has enabled its management and employees to further deepen their understanding of customer behaviors by connecting data from its hotel systems and data from its customer-tracking systems—and to act on that understanding through improved marketing campaigns and heightened levels of customer service. For example, the addition of hotel data offered new insights about the increased gaming local patrons do when they stay at a hotel. This, in turn, enabled new incentive programs (such as a free hotel night) that have pleased locals and increased Isle's customer loyalty.

The hotel data also has enhanced Isle's customer hosting program. By automatically notifying hosts when a high-value guest arrives at a hotel, hosts have forged deeper relationships with their most important clients. "This is by far the best tool we've had since I've been at the company," wrote one of the hosts.

Isle of Capri can now do more accurate property-to-property comparisons and analyses, largely because Teradata consolidated disparate data housed at individual properties and centralized it in one location. One result: A centralized intranet site posts daily figures for each individual property, so they can compare such things as performance of revenue from slot machines and table games, as well as complimentary redemption values. In addition, the IBM Cognos Business Intelligence tool enables additional comparisons, such as direct-mail redemption values, specific direct-mail program response rates, direct-mail–incented gaming revenue, hotel-incented gaming revenue, noncomplimentary (cash) revenue from hotel room reservations, and hotel room occupancy. One clear benefit is that it holds individual properties accountable for constantly raising the bar.

Beginning with an important change in marketing strategy that shifted the focus to customer days, time and again the Teradata/IBM Cognos BI implementation has demonstrated the value of extending the power of data throughout Isle's enterprise. This includes immediate analysis of response rates to marketing campaigns and the addition of profit and loss data that has successfully connected customer value and total property value. One example of the power of this integration: By joining customer value and total property value, Isle gains a better understanding of its retail customers—a population invisible to them before—enabling them to more effectively target marketing efforts, such as radio ads.

Perhaps most significantly, Isle has begun to add slot machine data to the mix. The most important and immediate impact will be the way in which customer value will inform purchasing of new machines and product placement on the customer floor. Down the road, the addition of this data also might position Isle to take advantage of server-based gaming, where slot machines on the casino floor will essentially be computer terminals that enable the casino to switch a game to a new one in a matter of seconds.

In short, as Isle constructs its solutions for regularly funneling slot machine data into the warehouse, its ability to use data to re-imagine the floor and forge ever deeper and more lasting relationships will exceed anything it might have expected when it embarked on this project.

QUESTIONS FOR THE OPENING VIGNETTE

1. Why is it important for Isle to have an EDW?
2. What were the business challenges or opportunities that Isle was facing?
3. What was the process Isle followed to realize EDW? Comment on the potential challenges Isle might have had going through the process of EDW development.
4. What were the benefits of implementing an EDW at Isle? Can you think of other potential benefits that were not listed in the case?
5. Why do you think large enterprises like Isle in the gaming industry can succeed without having a capable data warehouse/business intelligence infrastructure?

WHAT WE CAN LEARN FROM THIS VIGNETTE

The opening vignette illustrates the strategic value of implementing an enterprise data warehouse, along with its supporting BI methods. Isle of Capri Casinos was able to leverage its data assets spread throughout the enterprise to be used by knowledge workers (wherever and whenever they are needed) to make accurate and timely decisions. The data warehouse integrated various databases throughout the organization into a single, in-house enterprise unit to generate a single version of the truth for the company, putting all decision makers, from planning to marketing, on the same page. Furthermore, by regularly funneling slot machine data into the warehouse, combined with customer-specific rich data that comes from variety of sources, Isle significantly improved its ability to discover patterns to re-imagine/reinvent the gaming floor operations and forge ever deeper and more lasting relationships with its customers. The key lesson here is that an enterprise-level data warehouse combined with a strategy for its use in decision support can result in significant benefits (financial and otherwise) for an organization.

Sources: Teradata, Customer Success Stories, **teradata.com/t/case-studies/Isle-of-Capri-Casinos-Executive-Summary-EB6277** (accessed February 2013); **www-01.ibm.com/software/analytics/cognos**.

3.2 DATA WAREHOUSING DEFINITIONS AND CONCEPTS

Using real-time data warehousing in conjunction with DSS and BI tools is an important way to conduct business processes. The opening vignette demonstrates a scenario in which a real-time active data warehouse supported decision making by analyzing large amounts of data from various sources to provide rapid results to support critical processes. The single version of the truth stored in the data warehouse and provided in an easily digestible form expands the boundaries of Isle of Capri's innovative business processes. With real-time data flows, Isle can view the current state of its business and quickly identify problems, which is the first and foremost step toward solving them analytically.

Decision makers require concise, dependable information about current operations, trends, and changes. Data are often fragmented in distinct operational systems, so managers often make decisions with partial information, at best. Data warehousing cuts through this obstacle by accessing, integrating, and organizing key operational data in a form that is consistent, reliable, timely, and readily available, wherever and whenever needed.

What Is a Data Warehouse?

In simple terms, a **data warehouse (DW)** is a pool of data produced to support decision making; it is also a repository of current and historical data of potential interest to managers throughout the organization. Data are usually structured to be available in a form ready for analytical processing activities (i.e., online analytical processing [OLAP], data mining, querying, reporting, and other decision support applications). A data warehouse is a subject-oriented, integrated, time-variant, nonvolatile collection of data in support of management's decision-making process.

A Historical Perspective to Data Warehousing

Even though data warehousing is a relatively new term in information technology, its roots can be traced way back in time, even before computers were widely used. In the early 1900s, people were using data (though mostly via manual methods) to formulate trends to help business users make informed decisions, which is the most prevailing purpose of data warehousing.

The motivations that led to developing data warehousing technologies go back to the 1970s, when the computing world was dominated by the mainframes. Real business data-processing applications, the ones run on the corporate mainframes, had complicated file structures using early-generation databases (not the table-oriented relational databases most applications use today) in which they stored data. Although these applications did a decent job of performing routine transactional data-processing functions, the data created as a result of these functions (such as information about customers, the products they ordered, and how much money they spent) was locked away in the depths of the files and databases. When aggregated information such as sales trends by region and by product type was needed, one had to formally request it from the data-processing department, where it was put on a waiting list with a couple hundred other report requests (Hammergren and Simon, 2009). Even though the need for information and the data that could be used to generate it existed, the database technology was not there to satisfy it. Figure 3.1 shows a timeline where some of the significant events that led to the development of data warehousing are shown.

Later in this decade, commercial hardware and software companies began to emerge with solutions to this problem. Between 1976 and 1979, the concept for a new company, Teradata, grew out of research at the California Institute of Technology (Caltech), driven from discussions with Citibank's advanced technology group. Founders worked to design a database management system for parallel processing with multiple microprocessors, targeted specifically for decision support. Teradata was incorporated on July 13, 1979, and started in a garage in Brentwood, California. The name Teradata was chosen to symbolize the ability to manage terabytes (trillions of bytes) of data.

The 1980s were the decade of personal computers and minicomputers. Before anyone knew it, real computer applications were no longer only on mainframes; they were all over the place—everywhere you looked in an organization. That led to a portentous problem called *islands of data*. The solution to this problem led to a new type of software, called a *distributed database management system,* which would magically pull the requested data from databases across the organization, bring all the data back to the same place, and then consolidate it, sort it, and do whatever else was necessary to answer the user's question. Although the concept was a good one and early results from research were promising, the results were plain and simple: They just didn't work efficiently in the real world, and the islands-of-data problem still existed.

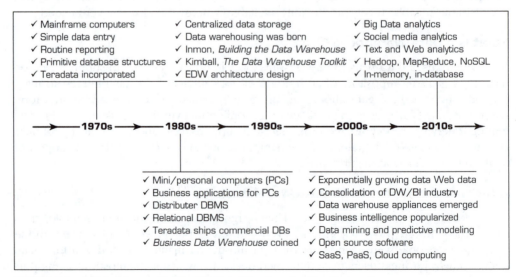

FIGURE 3.1   A List of Events That Led to Data Warehousing Development.

Meanwhile, Teradata began shipping commercial products to solve this problem. Wells Fargo Bank received the first Teradata test system in 1983, a parallel RDBMS (relational database management system) for decision support—the world's first. By 1984, Teradata released a production version of their product, and in 1986, *Fortune* magazine named Teradata Product of the Year. Teradata, still in existence today, built the first data warehousing appliance—a combination of hardware and software to solve the data warehousing needs of many. Other companies began to formulate their strategies, as well.

During this decade several other events happened, collectively making it the decade of data warehousing innovation. For instance, Ralph Kimball founded Red Brick Systems in 1986. Red Brick began to emerge as a visionary software company by discussing how to improve data access; in 1988, Barry Devlin and Paul Murphy of IBM Ireland introduced the term *business data warehouse* as a key component of business information systems.

In the 1990s a new approach to solving the islands-of-data problem surfaced. If the 1980s approach of reaching out and accessing data directly from the files and databases didn't work, the 1990s philosophy involved going back to the 1970s method, in which data from those places was copied to another location—only doing it right this time; hence, data warehousing was born. In 1993, Bill Inmon wrote the seminal book *Building the Data Warehouse*. Many people recognize Bill as the father of data warehousing. Additional publications emerged, including the 1996 book by Ralph Kimball, *The Data Warehouse Toolkit*, which discussed general-purpose dimensional design techniques to improve the data architecture for query-centered decision support systems.

In the 2000s, in the world of data warehousing, both popularity and the amount of data continued to grow. The vendor community and options have begun to consolidate. In 2006, Microsoft acquired ProClarity, jumping into the data warehousing market. In 2007, Oracle purchased Hyperion, SAP acquired Business Objects, and IBM merged with Cognos. The data warehousing leaders of the 1990s have been swallowed by some of the largest providers of information system solutions in the world. During this time, other innovations have emerged, including data warehouse appliances from vendors such as Netezza (acquired by IBM), Greenplum (acquired by EMC), DATAllegro (acquired by Microsoft), and performance management appliances that enable real-time performance monitoring. These innovative solutions provided cost savings because they were plug-compatible to legacy data warehouse solutions.

In the 2010s the big buzz has been *Big Data*. Many believe that Big Data is going to make an impact on data warehousing as we know it. Either they will find a way to coexist (which seems to be the most likely case, at least for several years) or Big Data (and the technologies that come with it) will make traditional data warehousing obsolete. The technologies that came with Big Data include Hadoop, MapReduce, NoSQL, Hive, and so forth. Maybe we will see a new term coined in the world of data that combines the needs and capabilities of traditional data warehousing and the Big Data phenomenon.

Characteristics of Data Warehousing

A common way of introducing data warehousing is to refer to its fundamental characteristics (see Inmon, 2005):

- ***Subject oriented.*** Data are organized by detailed subject, such as sales, products, or customers, containing only information relevant for decision support. Subject orientation enables users to determine not only how their business is performing, but why. A data warehouse differs from an operational database in that most operational databases have a product orientation and are tuned to handle transactions that update the database. Subject orientation provides a more comprehensive view of the organization.
- ***Integrated.*** Integration is closely related to subject orientation. Data warehouses must place data from different sources into a consistent format. To do so, they must

deal with naming conflicts and discrepancies among units of measure. A data warehouse is presumed to be totally integrated.

- **Time variant (time series).** A warehouse maintains historical data. The data do not necessarily provide current status (except in real-time systems). They detect trends, deviations, and long-term relationships for forecasting and comparisons, leading to decision making. Every data warehouse has a temporal quality. Time is the one important dimension that all data warehouses must support. Data for analysis from multiple sources contains multiple time points (e.g., daily, weekly, monthly views).
- **Nonvolatile.** After data are entered into a data warehouse, users cannot change or update the data. Obsolete data are discarded, and changes are recorded as new data.

These characteristics enable data warehouses to be tuned almost exclusively for data access. Some additional characteristics may include the following:

- **Web based.** Data warehouses are typically designed to provide an efficient computing environment for Web-based applications.
- **Relational/multidimensional.** A data warehouse uses either a relational structure or a multidimensional structure. A recent survey on multidimensional structures can be found in Romero and Abelló (2009).
- **Client/server.** A data warehouse uses the client/server architecture to provide easy access for end users.
- **Real time.** Newer data warehouses provide real-time, or active, data-access and analysis capabilities (see Basu, 2003; and Bonde and Kuckuk, 2004).
- **Include metadata.** A data warehouse contains metadata (data about data) about how the data are organized and how to effectively use them.

Whereas a data warehouse is a repository of data, data warehousing is literally the entire process (see Watson, 2002). Data warehousing is a discipline that results in applications that provide decision support capability, allows ready access to business information, and creates business insight. The three main types of data warehouses are data marts, operational data stores (ODS), and enterprise data warehouses (EDW). In addition to discussing these three types of warehouses next, we also discuss metadata.

Data Marts

Whereas a data warehouse combines databases across an entire enterprise, a **data mart** is usually smaller and focuses on a particular subject or department. A data mart is a subset of a data warehouse, typically consisting of a single subject area (e.g., marketing, operations). A data mart can be either dependent or independent. A **dependent data mart** is a subset that is created directly from the data warehouse. It has the advantages of using a consistent data model and providing quality data. Dependent data marts support the concept of a single enterprise-wide data model, but the data warehouse must be constructed first. A dependent data mart ensures that the end user is viewing the same version of the data that is accessed by all other data warehouse users. The high cost of data warehouses limits their use to large companies. As an alternative, many firms use a lower-cost, scaled-down version of a data warehouse referred to as an *independent data mart*. An **independent data mart** is a small warehouse designed for a strategic business unit (SBU) or a department, but its source is not an EDW.

Operational Data Stores

An **operational data store (ODS)** provides a fairly recent form of customer information file (CIF). This type of database is often used as an interim staging area for a data warehouse. Unlike the static contents of a data warehouse, the contents of an ODS are updated throughout the course of business operations. An ODS is used for short-term decisions involving mission-critical applications rather than for the medium- and long-term decisions associated with an EDW. An ODS is similar to short-term memory in that it stores only very recent information. In comparison, a data warehouse is like long-term memory because it stores permanent information. An ODS consolidates data from multiple source systems and provides a near–real-time, integrated view of volatile, current data. The exchange, transfer, and load (ETL) processes (discussed later in this chapter) for an ODS are identical to those for a data warehouse. Finally, **oper marts** (see Imhoff, 2001) are created when operational data needs to be analyzed multidimensionally. The data for an oper mart come from an ODS.

Enterprise Data Warehouses (EDW)

An **enterprise data warehouse (EDW)** is a large-scale data warehouse that is used across the enterprise for decision support. It is the type of data warehouse that Isle of Capri developed, as described in the opening vignette. The large-scale nature provides integration of data from many sources into a standard format for effective BI and decision support applications. EDW are used to provide data for many types of DSS, including CRM, supply chain management (SCM), business performance management (BPM), business activity monitoring (BAM), product life-cycle management (PLM), revenue management, and sometimes even knowledge management systems (KMS). Application Case 3.1 shows the variety of benefits that telecommunication companies leverage from implementing data warehouse driven analytics solutions.

Metadata

Metadata are data about data (e.g., see Sen, 2004; and Zhao, 2005). Metadata describe the structure of and some meaning about data, thereby contributing to their effective or

---

Application Case 3.1

A Better Data Plan: Well-Established TELCOs Leverage Data Warehousing and Analytics to Stay on Top in a Competitive Industry

Mobile service providers (i.e., Telecommunication Companies, or TELCOs in short) that helped trigger the explosive growth of the industry in the mid- to late-1990s have long reaped the benefits of being first to market. But to stay competitive, these companies must continuously refine everything from customer service to plan pricing. In fact, veteran carriers face many of the same challenges that up-and-coming carriers do: retaining customers, decreasing costs, fine-tuning pricing models, improving customer satisfaction, acquiring new customers and understanding the role of social media in customer loyalty

Highly targeted data analytics play an ever-more-critical role in helping carriers secure or improve their standing in an increasingly competitive marketplace. Here's how some of the world's leading providers are creating a strong future based on solid business and customer intelligence.

Customer Retention

It's no secret that the speed and success with which a provider handles service requests directly affects customer satisfaction and, in turn, the propensity to churn. But getting down to which factors have the greatest impact is a challenge.

"If we could trace the steps involved with each process, we could understand points of failure and acceleration," notes Roxanne Garcia, manager of the Commercial Operations Center for Telefónica de Argentina. "We could measure workflows both within and across functions, anticipate rather than react to performance indicators, and improve the overall satisfaction with onboarding new customers."

The company's solution was its traceability project, which began with 10 dashboards in 2009. It has since realized US$2.4 million in annualized revenues

(Continued)

Application Case 3.1 (Continued)

and cost savings, shortened customer provisioning times and reduced customer defections by 30%.

Cost Reduction

Staying ahead of the game in any industry depends, in large part, on keeping costs in line. For France's Bouygues Telecom, cost reduction came in the form of automation. Aladin, the company's Teradata-based marketing operations management system, automates marketing/communications collateral production. It delivered more than US$1 million in savings in a single year while tripling email campaign and content production.

"The goal is to be more productive and responsive, to simplify teamwork, [and] to standardize and protect our expertise," notes Catherine Corrado, the company's project lead and retail communications manager. "[Aladin lets] team members focus on value-added work by reducing low-value tasks. The end result is more quality and more creative [output]."

An unintended but very welcome benefit of Aladin is that other departments have been inspired to begin deploying similar projects for everything from call center support to product/offer launch processes.

Customer Acquisition

With market penetration near or above 100% in many countries, thanks to consumers who own multiple devices, the issue of new customer acquisition is no small challenge. Pakistan's largest carrier, Mobilink, also faces the difficulty of operating in a market where 98% of users have a pre-paid plan that requires regular purchases of additional minutes.

"Topping up, in particular, keeps the revenues strong and is critical to our company's growth," says Umer Afzal, senior manager, BI. "Previously we lacked the ability to enhance this aspect of incremental growth. Our sales information model gave us that ability because it helped the distribution team plan sales tactics based on smarter data-driven strategies that keep our suppliers [of SIM cards, scratch cards and electronic top-up capability] fully stocked."

As a result, Mobilink has not only grown subscriber recharges by 2% but also expanded new customer acquisition by 4% and improved the profitability of those sales by 4%.

Social Networking

The expanding use of social networks is changing how many organizations approach everything from customer service to sales and marketing. More carriers are turning their attention to social networks to better understand and influence customer behavior.

Mobilink has initiated a social network analysis project that will enable the company to explore the concept of viral marketing and identify key influencers who can act as brand ambassadors to cross-sell products. Velcom is looking for similar key influencers as well as low-value customers whose social value can be leveraged to improve existing relationships. Meanwhile, Swisscom is looking to combine the social network aspect of customer behavior with the rest of its analysis over the next several months.

Rise to the Challenge

While each market presents its own unique challenges, most mobile carriers spend a great deal of time and resources creating, deploying and refining plans to address each of the challenges outlined here. The good news is that just as the industry and mobile technology have expanded and improved over the years, so also have the data analytics solutions that have been created to meet these challenges head on.

Sound data analysis uses existing customer, business and market intelligence to predict and influence future behaviors and outcomes. The end result is a smarter, more agile and more successful approach to gaining market share and improving profitability.

QUESTIONS FOR DISCUSSION

1. What are the main challenges for TELCOs?
2. How can data warehousing and data analytics help TELCOs in overcoming their challenges?
3. Why do you think TELCOs are well suited to take full advantage of data analytics?

Source: Teradata Magazine, Case Study by Colleen Marble, "A Better Data Plan: Well-Established Telcos Leverage Analytics to Stay on Top in a Competitive Industry" **http://www.teradatamagazine.com/v13n01/Features/A-Better-Data-Plan/** (accessed September 2013).

ineffective use. Mehra (2005) indicated that few organizations really understand metadata, and fewer understand how to design and implement a metadata strategy. Metadata are generally defined in terms of usage as technical or business metadata. Pattern is another way to view metadata. According to the pattern view, we can differentiate between syntactic metadata (i.e., data describing the syntax of data), structural metadata (i.e., data describing the structure of the data), and semantic metadata (i.e., data describing the meaning of the data in a specific domain).

We next explain traditional metadata patterns and insights into how to implement an effective metadata strategy via a holistic approach to enterprise metadata integration. The approach includes ontology and metadata registries; enterprise information integration (EII); extraction, transformation, and load (ETL); and service-oriented architectures (SOA). Effectiveness, extensibility, reusability, interoperability, efficiency and performance, evolution, entitlement, flexibility, segregation, user interface, versioning, versatility, and low maintenance cost are some of the key requirements for building a successful metadata-driven enterprise.

According to Kassam (2002), business metadata comprise information that increases our understanding of traditional (i.e., structured) data. The primary purpose of metadata should be to provide context to the reported data; that is, it provides enriching information that leads to the creation of knowledge. Business metadata, though difficult to provide efficiently, release more of the potential of structured data. The context need not be the same for all users. In many ways, metadata assist in the conversion of data and information into knowledge. Metadata form a foundation for a metabusiness architecture (see Bell, 2001). Tannenbaum (2002) described how to identify metadata requirements. Vaduva and Vetterli (2001) provided an overview of metadata management for data warehousing. Zhao (2005) described five levels of metadata management maturity: (1) ad hoc, (2) discovered, (3) managed, (4) optimized, and (5) automated. These levels help in understanding where an organization is in terms of how and how well it uses its metadata.

The design, creation, and use of metadata—descriptive or summary data about data—and its accompanying standards may involve ethical issues. There are ethical considerations involved in the collection and ownership of the information contained in metadata, including privacy and intellectual property issues that arise in the design, collection, and dissemination stages (for more, see Brody, 2003).

SECTION 3.2 REVIEW QUESTIONS

1. What is a data warehouse?
2. How does a data warehouse differ from a database?
3. What is an ODS?
4. Differentiate among a data mart, an ODS, and an EDW.
5. Explain the importance of metadata.

3.3 DATA WAREHOUSING PROCESS OVERVIEW

Organizations, private and public, continuously collect data, information, and knowledge at an increasingly accelerated rate and store them in computerized systems. Maintaining and using these data and information becomes extremely complex, especially as scalability issues arise. In addition, the number of users needing to access the information continues to increase as a result of improved reliability and availability of network access, especially the Internet. Working with multiple databases, either integrated in a data warehouse or not, has become an extremely difficult task requiring considerable expertise, but it can provide immense benefits far exceeding its cost. As an illustrative example, Figure 3.2 shows business benefits of the enterprise data warehouse built by Teradata for a major automobile manufacturer.

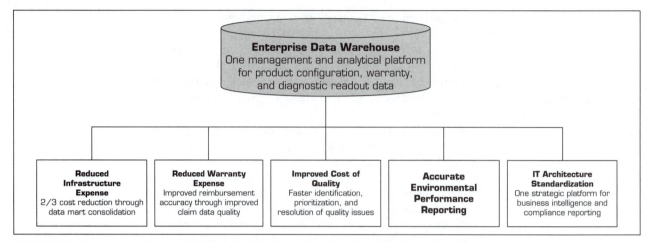

FIGURE 3.2   Data-Driven Decision Making—Business Benefits of an Enterprise Data Warehouse.

Application Case 3.2

Data Warehousing Helps MultiCare Save More Lives

In the spring of 2012, leadership at MultiCare Health System (MultiCare)—a Tacoma, Washington–based health system—realized the results of a 12-month journey to reduce septicemia.

The effort was supported by the system's top leadership, who participated in a data-driven approach to prioritize care improvement based on an analysis of resources consumed and variation in care outcomes. Reducing septicemia (mortality rates) was a top priority for MultiCare as a result of three hospitals performing below, and one that was performing well below, national mortality averages.

In September 2010, MultiCare implemented Health Catalyst's Adaptive Data Warehouse, a healthcare-specific data model, and subsequent clinical and process improvement services to measure and effect care through organizational and process improvements. Two major factors contributed to the rapid reduction in septicemia mortality.

Clinical Data to Drive Improvement

The Adaptive Data Warehouse™ organized and simplified data from multiple data sources across the continuum of care. It became the single source of truth requisite to see care improvement opportunities and to measure change. It also proved to be an important means to unify clinical, IT, and financial

leaders and to drive accountability for performance improvement.

Because it proved difficult to define sepsis due to the complex comorbidity factors leading to septicemia, MultiCare partnered with Health Catalyst to refine the clinical definition of sepsis. Health Catalyst's data work allowed MultiCare to explore around the boundaries of the definition and to ultimately settle on an algorithm that defined a septic patient. The iterative work resulted in increased confidence in the severe sepsis cohort.

System-Wide Critical Care Collaborative

The establishment and collaborative efforts of permanent, integrated teams consisting of clinicians, technologists, analysts, and quality personnel were essential for accelerating MultiCare's efforts to reduce septicemia mortality. Together the collaborative addressed three key bodies of work—standard of care definition, early identification, and efficient delivery of defined-care standard.

Standard of Care: Severe Sepsis Order Set

The Critical Care Collaborative streamlined several sepsis order sets from across the organization into one system-wide standard for the care of severely septic patients. Adult patients presenting with sepsis receive the same care, no matter at which MultiCare hospital they present.

Early Identification: Modified Early Warning System (MEWS)

MultiCare developed a modified early warning system (MEWS) dashboard that leveraged the cohort definition and the clinical EMR to quickly identify patients who were trending toward a sudden downturn. Hospital staff constantly monitor MEWS, which serves as an early detection tool for caregivers to provide preemptive interventions.

Efficient Delivery: Code Sepsis ("Time Is Tissue")

The final key piece of clinical work undertaken by the Collaborative was to ensure timely implementation of the defined standard of care to patients who are more efficiently identified. That model already exists in healthcare and is known as the "code" process. Similar to other "code" processes (code trauma,

code neuro, code STEMI), code sepsis at MultiCare is designed to bring together essential caregivers in order to efficiently deliver time-sensitive, life-saving treatments to the patient presenting with severe sepsis.

In just 12 months, MultiCare was able to reduce septicemia mortality rates by an average of 22 percent, leading to more than $1.3 million in validated cost savings during that same period. The sepsis cost reductions and quality of care improvements have raised the expectation that similar results can be realized in other areas of MultiCare, including heart failure, emergency department performance, and inpatient throughput.

Questions for Discussion

1. What do you think is the role of data warehousing in healthcare systems?
2. How did MultiCare use data warehousing to improve health outcomes?

Source: **healthcatalyst.com/success_stories/multicare-2** (accessed February 2013).

Many organizations need to create data warehouses—massive data stores of time-series data for decision support. Data are imported from various external and internal resources and are cleansed and organized in a manner consistent with the organization's needs. After the data are populated in the data warehouse, data marts can be loaded for a specific area or department. Alternatively, data marts can be created first, as needed, and then integrated into an EDW. Often, though, data marts are not developed, but data are simply loaded onto PCs or left in their original state for direct manipulation using BI tools.

In Figure 3.3, we show the data warehouse concept. The following are the major components of the data warehousing process:

- ***Data sources.*** Data are sourced from multiple independent operational "legacy" systems and possibly from external data providers (such as the U.S. Census). Data may also come from an OLTP or ERP system. Web data in the form of Web logs may also feed a data warehouse.
- ***Data extraction and transformation.*** Data are extracted and properly transformed using custom-written or commercial software called ETL.
- ***Data loading.*** Data are loaded into a staging area, where they are transformed and cleansed. The data are then ready to load into the data warehouse and/or data marts.
- ***Comprehensive database.*** Essentially, this is the EDW to support all decision analysis by providing relevant summarized and detailed information originating from many different sources.
- ***Metadata.*** Metadata are maintained so that they can be assessed by IT personnel and users. Metadata include software programs about data and rules for organizing data summaries that are easy to index and search, especially with Web tools.

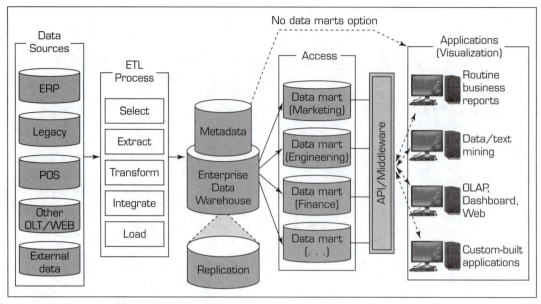

FIGURE 3.3 A Data Warehouse Framework and Views.

- ***Middleware tools.*** Middleware tools enable access to the data warehouse. Power users such as analysts may write their own SQL queries. Others may employ a managed query environment, such as Business Objects, to access data. There are many front-end applications that business users can use to interact with data stored in the data repositories, including data mining, OLAP, reporting tools, and data visualization tools.

SECTION 3.3 REVIEW QUESTIONS

1. Describe the data warehousing process.
2. Describe the major components of a data warehouse.
3. Identify and discuss the role of middleware tools.

3.4 DATA WAREHOUSING ARCHITECTURES

There are several basic information system architectures that can be used for data warehousing. Generally speaking, these architectures are commonly called client/server or n-tier architectures, of which two-tier and three-tier architectures are the most common (see Figures 3.4 and 3.5), but sometimes there is simply one tier. These types of multi-tiered

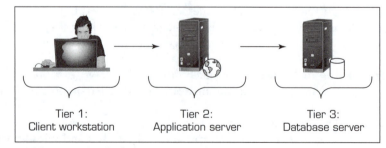

FIGURE 3.4 Architecture of a Three-Tier Data Warehouse.

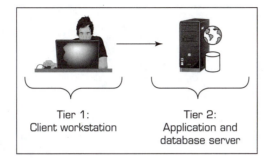

FIGURE 3.5   Architecture of a Two-Tier Data Warehouse.

architectures are known to be capable of serving the needs of large-scale, performance-demanding information systems such as data warehouses. Referring to the use of n-tiered architectures for data warehousing, Hoffer et al. (2007) distinguished among these architectures by dividing the data warehouse into three parts:

1. The data warehouse itself, which contains the data and associated software
2. Data acquisition (back-end) software, which extracts data from legacy systems and external sources, consolidates and summarizes them, and loads them into the data warehouse
3. Client (front-end) software, which allows users to access and analyze data from the warehouse (a DSS/BI/business analytics [BA] engine)

In a three-tier architecture, operational systems contain the data and the software for data acquisition in one tier (i.e., the server), the data warehouse is another tier, and the third tier includes the DSS/BI/BA engine (i.e., the application server) and the client (see Figure 3.4). Data from the warehouse are processed twice and deposited in an additional multidimensional database, organized for easy multidimensional analysis and presentation, or replicated in data marts. The advantage of the three-tier architecture is its separation of the functions of the data warehouse, which eliminates resource constraints and makes it possible to easily create data marts.

In a two-tier architecture, the DSS engine physically runs on the same hardware platform as the data warehouse (see Figure 3.5). Therefore, it is more economical than the three-tier structure. The two-tier architecture can have performance problems for large data warehouses that work with data-intensive applications for decision support.

Much of the common wisdom assumes an absolutist approach, maintaining that one solution is better than the other, despite the organization's circumstances and unique needs. To further complicate these architectural decisions, many consultants and software vendors focus on one portion of the architecture, therefore limiting their capacity and motivation to assist an organization through the options based on its needs. But these aspects are being questioned and analyzed. For example, Ball (2005) provided decision criteria for organizations that plan to implement a BI application and have already determined their need for multidimensional data marts but need help determining the appropriate tiered architecture. His criteria revolve around forecasting needs for space and speed of access (see Ball, 2005, for details).

Data warehousing and the Internet are two key technologies that offer important solutions for managing corporate data. The integration of these two technologies produces Web-based data warehousing. In Figure 3.6, we show the architecture of Web-based data warehousing. The architecture is three tiered and includes the PC client, Web server, and application server. On the client side, the user needs an Internet connection and a Web browser (preferably Java enabled) through the familiar graphical user interface (GUI). The Internet/intranet/extranet is the communication medium between client

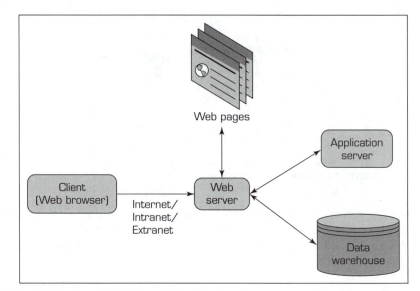

FIGURE 3.6 **Architecture of Web-Based Data Warehousing.**

and servers. On the server side, a Web server is used to manage the inflow and outflow of information between client and server. It is backed by both a data warehouse and an application server. Web-based data warehousing offers several compelling advantages, including ease of access, platform independence, and lower cost.

The Vanguard Group moved to a Web-based, three-tier architecture for its enterprise architecture to integrate all its data and provide customers with the same views of data as internal users (Dragoon, 2003). Likewise, Hilton migrated all its independent client/ server systems to a three-tier data warehouse, using a Web design enterprise system. This change involved an investment of $3.8 million (excluding labor) and affected 1,500 users. It increased processing efficiency (speed) by a factor of six. When it was deployed, Hilton expected to save $4.5 to $5 million annually. Finally, Hilton experimented with Dell's clustering (i.e., parallel computing) technology to enhance scalability and speed (see Anthes, 2003).

Web architectures for data warehousing are similar in structure to other data warehousing architectures, requiring a design choice for housing the Web data warehouse with the transaction server or as a separate server(s). Page-loading speed is an important consideration in designing Web-based applications; therefore, server capacity must be planned carefully.

Several issues must be considered when deciding which architecture to use. Among them are the following:

- ***Which database management system (DBMS) should be used?*** Most data warehouses are built using relational database management systems (RDBMS). Oracle (Oracle Corporation, **oracle.com**), SQL Server (Microsoft Corporation, **microsoft. com/sql**), and DB2 (IBM Corporation, **http://www-01.ibm.com/software/data/ db2/**) are the ones most commonly used. Each of these products supports both client/server and Web-based architectures.
- ***Will parallel processing and/or partitioning be used?*** Parallel processing enables multiple CPUs to process data warehouse query requests simultaneously and provides scalability. Data warehouse designers need to decide whether the database tables will be partitioned (i.e., split into smaller tables) for access efficiency and what the criteria will be. This is an important consideration that is necessitated by

the large amounts of data contained in a typical data warehouse. A recent survey on parallel and distributed data warehouses can be found in Furtado (2009). Teradata (**teradata.com**) has successfully adopted and often commended on its novel implementation of this approach.

- ***Will data migration tools be used to load the data warehouse?*** Moving data from an existing system into a data warehouse is a tedious and laborious task. Depending on the diversity and the location of the data assets, migration may be a relatively simple procedure or (in contrast) a months-long project. The results of a thorough assessment of the existing data assets should be used to determine whether to use migration tools and, if so, what capabilities to seek in those commercial tools.

- ***What tools will be used to support data retrieval and analysis?*** Often it is necessary to use specialized tools to periodically locate, access, analyze, extract, transform, and load necessary data into a data warehouse. A decision has to be made on (1) developing the migration tools in-house, (2) purchasing them from a third-party provider, or (3) using the ones provided with the data warehouse system. Overly complex, real-time migrations warrant specialized third-part ETL tools.

Alternative Data Warehousing Architectures

At the highest level, data warehouse architecture design viewpoints can be categorized into enterprise-wide data warehouse (EDW) design and data mart (DM) design (Golfarelli and Rizzi, 2009). In Figure 3.7 (parts a–e), we show some alternatives to the basic architectural design types that are neither pure EDW nor pure DM, but in between or beyond the traditional architectural structures. Notable new ones include hub-and-spoke and federated architectures. The five architectures shown in Figure 3.7 (parts a–e) are proposed by Ariyachandra and Watson (2005, 2006a, and 2006b). Previously, in an extensive study, Sen and Sinha (2005) identified 15 different data warehousing methodologies. The sources of these methodologies are classified into three broad categories: core-technology vendors, infrastructure vendors, and information-modeling companies.

a. ***Independent data marts.*** This is arguably the simplest and the least costly architecture alternative. The data marts are developed to operate independently of each another to serve the needs of individual organizational units. Because of their independence, they may have inconsistent data definitions and different dimensions and measures, making it difficult to analyze data across the data marts (i.e., it is difficult, if not impossible, to get to the "one version of the truth").

b. ***Data mart bus architecture.*** This architecture is a viable alternative to the independent data marts where the individual marts are linked to each other via some kind of middleware. Because the data are linked among the individual marts, there is a better chance of maintaining data consistency across the enterprise (at least at the metadata level). Even though it allows for complex data queries across data marts, the performance of these types of analysis may not be at a satisfactory level.

c. ***Hub-and-spoke architecture.*** This is perhaps the most famous data warehousing architecture today. Here the attention is focused on building a scalable and maintainable infrastructure (often developed in an iterative way, subject area by subject area) that includes a centralized data warehouse and several dependent data marts (each for an organizational unit). This architecture allows for easy customization of user interfaces and reports. On the negative side, this architecture lacks the holistic enterprise view, and may lead to data redundancy and data latency.

d. ***Centralized data warehouse.*** The centralized data warehouse architecture is similar to the hub-and-spoke architecture except that there are no dependent data marts; instead, there is a gigantic enterprise data warehouse that serves the needs

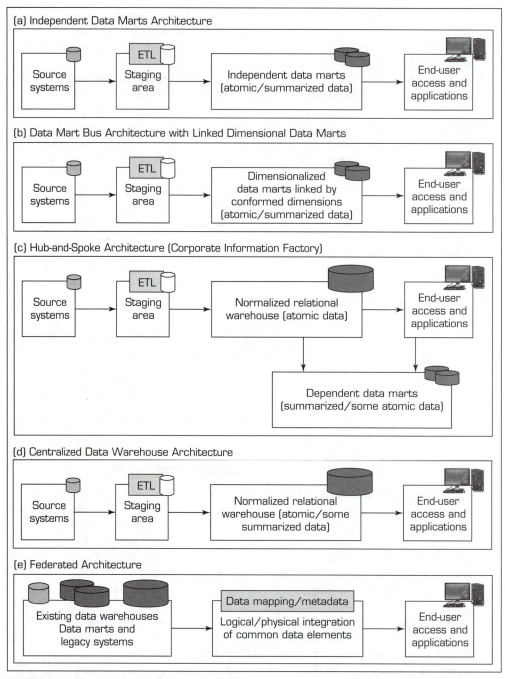

FIGURE 3.7 Alternative Data Warehouse Architectures. *Source:* Adapted from T. Ariyachandra and H. Watson, "Which Data Warehouse Architecture Is Most Successful?" *Business Intelligence Journal,* Vol. 11, No. 1, First Quarter, 2006, pp. 4–6.

of all organizational units. This centralized approach provides users with access to all data in the data warehouse instead of limiting them to data marts. In addition, it reduces the amount of data the technical team has to transfer or change, therefore simplifying data management and administration. If designed and implemented properly, this architecture provides a timely and holistic view of the enterprise to

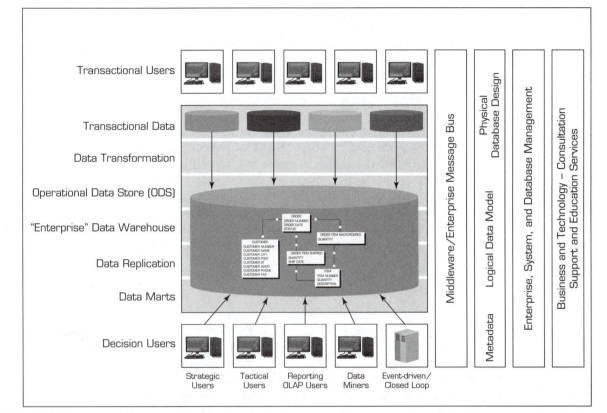

FIGURE 3.8   Teradata Corporation's Enterprise Data Warehouse.   *Source:* Teradata Corporation (**teradata.com**). Used with permission.

whomever, whenever, and wherever they may be within the organization. The central data warehouses architecture, which is advocated mainly by Teradata Corp., advises using data warehouses without any data marts (see Figure 3.8).

e. ***Federated data warehouse.***   The federated approach is a concession to the natural forces that undermine the best plans for developing a perfect system. It uses all possible means to integrate analytical resources from multiple sources to meet changing needs or business conditions. Essentially, the federated approach involves integrating disparate systems. In a federated architecture, existing decision support structures are left in place, and data are accessed from those sources as needed. The federated approach is supported by middleware vendors that propose distributed query and join capabilities. These eXtensible Markup Language (XML)–based tools offer users a global view of distributed data sources, including data warehouses, data marts, Web sites, documents, and operational systems. When users choose query objects from this view and press the submit button, the tool automatically queries the distributed sources, joins the results, and presents them to the user. Because of performance and data quality issues, most experts agree that federated approaches work well to supplement data warehouses, not replace them (see Eckerson, 2005).

Ariyachandra and Watson (2005) identified 10 factors that potentially affect the architecture selection decision:

1. Information interdependence between organizational units
2. Upper management's information needs
3. Urgency of need for a data warehouse

4. Nature of end-user tasks
5. Constraints on resources
6. Strategic view of the data warehouse prior to implementation
7. Compatibility with existing systems
8. Perceived ability of the in-house IT staff
9. Technical issues
10. Social/political factors

These factors are similar to many success factors described in the literature for information systems projects and DSS and BI projects. Technical issues, beyond providing technology that is feasibly ready for use, are important, but often not as important as behavioral issues, such as meeting upper management's information needs and user involvement in the development process (a social/political factor). Each data warehousing architecture has specific applications for which it is most (and least) effective and thus provides maximal benefits to the organization. However, overall, the data mart structure seems to be the least effective in practice. See Ariyachandra and Watson (2006a) for some additional details.

Which Architecture Is the Best?

Ever since data warehousing became a critical part of modern enterprises, the question of which data warehouse architecture is the best has been a topic of regular discussion. The two gurus of the data warehousing field, Bill Inmon and Ralph Kimball, are at the heart of this discussion. Inmon advocates the hub-and-spoke architecture (e.g., the Corporate Information Factory), whereas Kimball promotes the data mart bus architecture with conformed dimensions. Other architectures are possible, but these two options are fundamentally different approaches, and each has strong advocates. To shed light on this controversial question, Ariyachandra and Watson (2006b) conducted an empirical study. To collect the data, they used a Web-based survey targeted at individuals involved in data warehouse implementations. Their survey included questions about the respondent, the respondent's company, the company's data warehouse, and the success of the data warehouse architecture.

In total, 454 respondents provided usable information. Surveyed companies ranged from small (less than $10 million in revenue) to large (in excess of $10 billion). Most of the companies were located in the United States (60%) and represented a variety of industries, with the financial services industry (15%) providing the most responses. The predominant architecture was the hub-and-spoke architecture (39%), followed by the bus architecture (26%), the centralized architecture (17%), independent data marts (12%), and the federated architecture (4%). The most common platform for hosting the data warehouses was Oracle (41%), followed by Microsoft (19%), and IBM (18%). The average (mean) gross revenue varied from $3.7 billion for independent data marts to $6 billion for the federated architecture.

They used four measures to assess the success of the architectures: (1) information quality, (2) system quality, (3) individual impacts, and (4) organizational impacts. The questions used a seven-point scale, with the higher score indicating a more successful architecture. Table 3.1 shows the average scores for the measures across the architectures.

As the results of the study indicate, independent data marts scored the lowest on all measures. This finding confirms the conventional wisdom that independent data marts are a poor architectural solution. Next lowest on all measures was the federated architecture. Firms sometimes have disparate decision support platforms resulting from mergers and acquisitions, and they may choose a federated approach, at least in the short run. The findings suggest that the federated architecture is not an optimal long-term solution. What is interesting, however, is the similarity of the averages for the bus, hub-and-spoke, and centralized architectures. The differences are sufficiently small that no claims can be

TABLE 3.1	Average Assessment Scores for the Success of the Architectures				
	Independent Data Marts	Bus Architecture	Hub-and Spoke Architecture	Centralized Architecture (No Dependent Data Marts)	Federated Architecture
Information Quality	4.42	5.16	5.35	5.23	4.73
System Quality	4.59	5.60	5.56	5.41	4.69
Individual Impacts	5.08	5.80	5.62	5.64	5.15
Organizational Impacts	4.66	5.34	5.24	5.30	4.77

made for a particular architecture's superiority over the others, at least based on a simple comparison of these success measures.

They also collected data on the domain (e.g., varying from a subunit to company-wide) and the size (i.e., amount of data stored) of the warehouses. They found that the hub-and-spoke architecture is typically used with more enterprise-wide implementations and larger warehouses. They also investigated the cost and time required to implement the different architectures. Overall, the hub-and-spoke architecture was the most expensive and time-consuming to implement.

SECTION 3.4 REVIEW QUESTIONS

1. What are the key similarities and differences between a two-tiered architecture and a three-tiered architecture?
2. How has the Web influenced data warehouse design?
3. List the alternative data warehousing architectures discussed in this section.
4. What issues should be considered when deciding which architecture to use in developing a data warehouse? List the 10 most important factors.
5. Which data warehousing architecture is the best? Why?

3.5 DATA INTEGRATION AND THE EXTRACTION, TRANSFORMATION, AND LOAD (ETL) PROCESSES

Global competitive pressures, demand for return on investment (ROI), management and investor inquiry, and government regulations are forcing business managers to rethink how they integrate and manage their businesses. A decision maker typically needs access to multiple sources of data that must be integrated. Before data warehouses, data marts, and BI software, providing access to data sources was a major, laborious process. Even with modern Web-based data management tools, recognizing what data to access and providing them to the decision maker is a nontrivial task that requires database specialists. As data warehouses grow in size, the issues of integrating data grow as well.

The business analysis needs continue to evolve. Mergers and acquisitions, regulatory requirements, and the introduction of new channels can drive changes in BI requirements. In addition to historical, cleansed, consolidated, and point-in-time data, business users increasingly demand access to real-time, unstructured, and/or remote data. And everything must be integrated with the contents of an existing data warehouse. Moreover, access via PDAs and through speech recognition and synthesis is becoming more commonplace, further complicating integration issues (Edwards, 2003). Many integration projects involve enterprise-wide systems. Orovic (2003) provided a checklist of what works and what does not work when attempting such a project. Properly integrating data from various databases and other disparate sources is difficult. But when it is not done properly, it can lead to disaster in enterprise-wide systems such as CRM, ERP, and supply chain projects (Nash, 2002).

Data Integration

Data integration comprises three major processes that, when correctly implemented, permit data to be accessed and made accessible to an array of ETL and analysis tools and the data warehousing environment: data access (i.e., the ability to access and extract data from any data source), data federation (i.e., the integration of business views across multiple data stores), and change capture (based on the identification, capture, and delivery of the changes made to enterprise data sources). See Application Case 3.3 for an example of how BP Lubricant benefits from implementing a data warehouse that integrates data

Application Case 3.3

BP Lubricants Achieves BIGS Success

BP Lubricants established the BIGS program following recent merger activity to deliver globally consistent and transparent management information. As well as timely business intelligence, BIGS provides detailed, consistent views of performance across functions such as finance, marketing, sales, and supply and logistics.

BP is one of the world's largest oil and petrochemicals groups. Part of the BP plc group, BP Lubricants is an established leader in the global automotive lubricants market. Perhaps best known for its Castrol brand of oils, the business operates in over 100 countries and employs 10,000 people. Strategically, BP Lubricants is concentrating on further improving its customer focus and increasing its effectiveness in automotive markets. Following recent merger activity, the company is undergoing transformation to become more effective and agile and to seize opportunities for rapid growth.

Challenge

Following recent merger activity, BP Lubricants wanted to improve the consistency, transparency, and accessibility of management information and business intelligence. In order to do so, it needed to integrate data held in disparate source systems, without the delay of introducing a standardized ERP system.

Solution

BP Lubricants implemented the pilot for its Business Intelligence and Global Standards (BIGS) program, a

strategic initiative for management information and business intelligence. At the heart of BIGS is Kalido, an adaptive enterprise data warehousing solution for preparing, implementing, operating, and managing data warehouses.

Kalido's federated enterprise data warehousing solution supported the pilot program's complex data integration and diverse reporting requirements. To adapt to the program's evolving reporting requirements, the software also enabled the underlying information architecture to be easily modified at high speed while preserving all information. The system integrates and stores information from multiple source systems to provide consolidated views for:

- *Marketing.* Customer proceeds and margins for market segments with drill down to invoice-level detail
- *Sales.* Sales invoice reporting augmented with both detailed tariff costs and actual payments
- *Finance.* Globally standard profit and loss, balance sheet, and cash flow statements—with audit ability; customer debt management supply and logistics; consolidated view of order and movement processing across multiple ERP platforms

Benefits

By improving the visibility of consistent, timely data, BIGS provides the information needed to assist the business in identifying a multitude of business opportunities to maximize margins and/or manage associated costs. Typical responses to the benefits of consistent data resulting from the BIGS pilot include:

- Improved consistency and transparency of business data
- Easier, faster, and more flexible reporting
- Accommodation of both global and local standards
- Fast, cost-effective, and flexible implementation cycle
- Minimal disruption of existing business processes and the day-to-day business

- Identifies data quality issues and encourages their resolution
- Improved ability to respond intelligently to new business opportunities

QUESTIONS FOR DISCUSSION

1. What is BIGS at BP Lubricants?
2. What were the challenges, the proposed solution, and the obtained results with BIGS?

Sources: Kalido, "BP Lubricants Achieves BIGS, Key IT Solutions," **http://www.kalido.com/customer-stories/bp-plc.htm** (accessed on August 2013). Kalido, "BP Lubricants Achieves BIGS Success," **kalido.com/collateral/Documents/English-US/ CS-BP%20BIGS.pdf** (accessed August 2013); and BP Lubricant homepage, **bp.com/lubricanthome.do** (accessed August 2013).

from many sources. Some vendors, such as SAS Institute, Inc., have developed strong data integration tools. The SAS enterprise data integration server includes customer data integration tools that improve data quality in the integration process. The Oracle Business Intelligence Suite assists in integrating data as well.

A major purpose of a data warehouse is to integrate data from multiple systems. Various integration technologies enable data and metadata integration:

- Enterprise application integration (EAI)
- Service-oriented architecture (SOA)
- Enterprise information integration (EII)
- Extraction, transformation, and load (ETL)

Enterprise application integration (EAI) provides a vehicle for pushing data from source systems into the data warehouse. It involves integrating application functionality and is focused on sharing functionality (rather than data) across systems, thereby enabling flexibility and reuse. Traditionally, EAI solutions have focused on enabling application reuse at the application programming interface (API) level. Recently, EAI is accomplished by using SOA coarse-grained services (a collection of business processes or functions) that are well defined and documented. Using Web services is a specialized way of implementing an SOA. EAI can be used to facilitate data acquisition directly into a near–real-time data warehouse or to deliver decisions to the OLTP systems. There are many different approaches to and tools for EAI implementation.

Enterprise information integration (EII) is an evolving tool space that promises real-time data integration from a variety of sources, such as relational databases, Web services, and multidimensional databases. It is a mechanism for pulling data from source systems to satisfy a request for information. EII tools use predefined metadata to populate views that make integrated data appear relational to end users. XML may be the most important aspect of EII because XML allows data to be tagged either at creation time or later. These tags can be extended and modified to accommodate almost any area of knowledge (see Kay, 2005).

Physical data integration has conventionally been the main mechanism for creating an integrated view with data warehouses and data marts. With the advent of EII tools (see Kay, 2005), new virtual data integration patterns are feasible. Manglik and Mehra (2005) discussed the benefits and constraints of new data integration patterns that can expand traditional physical methodologies to present a comprehensive view for the enterprise.

We next turn to the approach for loading data into the warehouse: ETL.

Extraction, Transformation, and Load

At the heart of the technical side of the data warehousing process is **extraction, transformation, and load (ETL)**. ETL technologies, which have existed for some time, are instrumental in the process and use of data warehouses. The ETL process is an integral component in any data-centric project. IT managers are often faced with challenges because the ETL process typically consumes 70 percent of the time in a data-centric project.

The ETL process consists of extraction (i.e., reading data from one or more databases), transformation (i.e., converting the extracted data from its previous form into the form in which it needs to be so that it can be placed into a data warehouse or simply another database), and load (i.e., putting the data into the data warehouse). Transformation occurs by using rules or lookup tables or by combining the data with other data. The three database functions are integrated into one tool to pull data out of one or more databases and place them into another, consolidated database or a data warehouse.

ETL tools also transport data between sources and targets, document how data elements (e.g., metadata) change as they move between source and target, exchange metadata with other applications as needed, and administer all runtime processes and operations (e.g., scheduling, error management, audit logs, statistics). ETL is extremely important for data integration as well as for data warehousing. The purpose of the ETL process is to load the warehouse with integrated and cleansed data. The data used in ETL processes can come from any source: a mainframe application, an ERP application, a CRM tool, a flat file, an Excel spreadsheet, or even a message queue. In Figure 3.9, we outline the ETL process.

The process of migrating data to a data warehouse involves the extraction of data from all relevant sources. Data sources may consist of files extracted from OLTP databases, spreadsheets, personal databases (e.g., Microsoft Access), or external files. Typically, all the input files are written to a set of staging tables, which are designed to facilitate the load process. A data warehouse contains numerous business rules that define such things as how the data will be used, summarization rules, standardization of encoded attributes, and calculation rules. Any data quality issues pertaining to the source files need to be corrected before the data are loaded into the data warehouse. One of the benefits of a

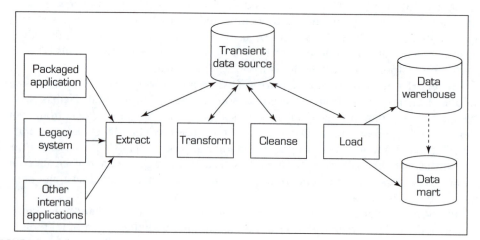

FIGURE 3.9 The ETL Process.

well-designed data warehouse is that these rules can be stored in a metadata repository and applied to the data warehouse centrally. This differs from an OLTP approach, which typically has data and business rules scattered throughout the system. The process of loading data into a data warehouse can be performed either through data transformation tools that provide a GUI to aid in the development and maintenance of business rules or through more traditional methods, such as developing programs or utilities to load the data warehouse, using programming languages such as PL/SQL, C++, Java, or .NET Framework languages. This decision is not easy for organizations. Several issues affect whether an organization will purchase data transformation tools or build the transformation process itself:

- Data transformation tools are expensive.
- Data transformation tools may have a long learning curve.
- It is difficult to measure how the IT organization is doing until it has learned to use the data transformation tools.

In the long run, a transformation-tool approach should simplify the maintenance of an organization's data warehouse. Transformation tools can also be effective in detecting and scrubbing (i.e., removing any anomalies in the data). OLAP and data mining tools rely on how well the data are transformed.

As an example of effective ETL, Motorola, Inc., uses ETL to feed its data warehouses. Motorola collects information from 30 different procurement systems and sends it to its global SCM data warehouse for analysis of aggregate company spending (see Songini, 2004).

Solomon (2005) classified ETL technologies into four categories: sophisticated, enabler, simple, and rudimentary. It is generally acknowledged that tools in the sophisticated category will result in the ETL process being better documented and more accurately managed as the data warehouse project evolves.

Even though it is possible for programmers to develop software for ETL, it is simpler to use an existing ETL tool. The following are some of the important criteria in selecting an ETL tool (see Brown, 2004):

- Ability to read from and write to an unlimited number of data source architectures
- Automatic capturing and delivery of metadata
- A history of conforming to open standards
- An easy-to-use interface for the developer and the functional user

Performing extensive ETL may be a sign of poorly managed data and a fundamental lack of a coherent data management strategy. Karacsony (2006) indicated that there is a direct correlation between the extent of redundant data and the number of ETL processes. When data are managed correctly as an enterprise asset, ETL efforts are significantly reduced, and redundant data are completely eliminated. This leads to huge savings in maintenance and greater efficiency in new development while also improving data quality. Poorly designed ETL processes are costly to maintain, change, and update. Consequently, it is crucial to make the proper choices in terms of the technology and tools to use for developing and maintaining the ETL process.

A number of packaged ETL tools are available. Database vendors currently offer ETL capabilities that both enhance and compete with independent ETL tools. SAS acknowledges the importance of data quality and offers the industry's first fully integrated solution that merges ETL and data quality to transform data into strategic valuable assets. Other ETL software providers include Microsoft, Oracle, IBM, Informatica, Embarcadero, and Tibco. For additional information on ETL, see Golfarelli and Rizzi (2009), Karaksony (2006), and Songini (2004).

SECTION 3.5 REVIEW QUESTIONS

1. Describe data integration.

2. Describe the three steps of the ETL process.

3. Why is the ETL process so important for data warehousing efforts?

3.6 DATA WAREHOUSE DEVELOPMENT

A data warehousing project is a major undertaking for any organization and is more complicated than a simple, mainframe selection and implementation project because it comprises and influences many departments and many input and output interfaces and it can be part of a CRM business strategy. A data warehouse provides several benefits that can be classified as direct and indirect. Direct benefits include the following:

- End users can perform extensive analysis in numerous ways.
- A consolidated view of corporate data (i.e., a single version of the truth) is possible.
- Better and more timely information is possible. A data warehouse permits information processing to be relieved from costly operational systems onto low-cost servers; therefore, many more end-user information requests can be processed more quickly.
- Enhanced system performance can result. A data warehouse frees production processing because some operational system reporting requirements are moved to DSS.
- Data access is simplified.

Indirect benefits result from end users using these direct benefits. On the whole, these benefits enhance business knowledge, present competitive advantage, improve customer service and satisfaction, facilitate decision making, and help in reforming business processes; therefore, they are the strongest contributions to competitive advantage. (For a discussion of how to create a competitive advantage through data warehousing, see Parzinger and Frolick, 2001.) For a detailed discussion of how organizations can obtain exceptional levels of payoffs, see Watson et al. (2002). Given the potential benefits that a data warehouse can provide and the substantial investments in time and money that such a project requires, it is critical that an organization structure its data warehouse project to maximize the chances of success. In addition, the organization must, obviously, take costs into consideration. Kelly (2001) described a ROI approach that considers benefits in the categories of keepers (i.e., money saved by improving traditional decision support functions); gatherers (i.e., money saved due to automated collection and dissemination of information); and users (i.e., money saved or gained from decisions made using the data warehouse). Costs include those related to hardware, software, network bandwidth, internal development, internal support, training, and external consulting. The net present value (NPV) is calculated over the expected life of the data warehouse. Because the benefits are broken down approximately as 20 percent for keepers, 30 percent for gatherers, and 50 percent for users, Kelly indicated that users should be involved in the development process, a success factor typically mentioned as critical for systems that imply change in an organization.

Application Case 3.4 provides an example of a data warehouse that was developed and delivered intense competitive advantage for the Hokuriku (Japan) Coca-Cola Bottling Company. The system was so successful that plans are underway to expand it to encompass the more than 1 million Coca-Cola vending machines in Japan.

Clearly defining the business objective, gathering project support from management end users, setting reasonable time frames and budgets, and managing expectations are critical to a successful data warehousing project. A data warehousing strategy is a

Application Case 3.4

Things Go Better with Coke's Data Warehouse

In the face of competitive pressures and consumer demand, how does a successful bottling company ensure that its vending machines are profitable? The answer for Hokuriku Coca-Cola Bottling Company (HCCBC) is a data warehouse and analytical software implemented by Teradata Corp. HCCBC built the system in response to a data warehousing system developed by its rival, Mikuni. The data warehouse collects not only historical data but also near–real-time data from each vending machine (viewed as a store) that could be transmitted via wireless connection to headquarters. The initial phase of the project was deployed in 2001. The data warehouse approach provides detailed product information, such as time and date of each sale, when a product sells out, whether someone was short-changed, and whether the machine is malfunctioning. In each case, an alert is triggered, and the vending machine immediately reports it to the data center over a wireless transmission system. (Note that Coca-Cola in the United States has used modems to link vending machines to distributors for over a decade.)

In 2002, HCCBC conducted a pilot test and put all its Nagano vending machines on a wireless network to gather near–real-time point of sale (POS) data from each one. The results were astounding because they accurately forecasted demand and identified problems quickly. Total sales immediately increased 10 percent. In addition, due to the more accurate machine servicing, overtime and other costs decreased 46 percent. In addition, each salesperson was able to service up to 42 percent more vending machines.

The test was so successful that planning began to expand it to encompass the entire enterprise (60,000 machines), using an active data warehouse. Eventually, the data warehousing solution will ideally expand across corporate boundaries into the entire Coca-Cola Bottlers network so that the more than 1 million vending machines in Japan will be networked, leading to immense cost savings and higher revenue.

QUESTIONS FOR DISCUSSION

1. How did Coca-Cola in Japan use data warehousing to improve its business processes?
2. What were the results of their enterprise active data warehouse implementation?

Sources: Adapted from K. D. Schwartz, "Decisions at the Touch of a Button," *Teradata Magazine,* **teradata.com/t/page/117774/index.html** (accessed June 2009); K. D. Schwartz, "Decisions at the Touch of a Button," *DSS Resources,* March 2004, pp. 28–31, **dssresources.com/cases/coca-colajapan/index.html** (accessed April 2006); and Teradata Corp., "Coca-Cola Japan Puts the Fizz Back in Vending Machine Sales," **teradata.com/t/page/118866/index.html** (accessed June 2009).

blueprint for the successful introduction of the data warehouse. The strategy should describe where the company wants to go, why it wants to go there, and what it will do when it gets there. It needs to take into consideration the organization's vision, structure, and culture. See Matney (2003) for the steps that can help in developing a flexible and efficient support strategy. When the plan and support for a data warehouse are established, the organization needs to examine data warehouse vendors. (See Table 3.2 for a sample list of vendors; also see The Data Warehousing Institute [**twdi.org**] and *DM Review* [**information-management.com**].) Many vendors provide software demos of their data warehousing and BI products.

Data Warehouse Development Approaches

Many organizations need to create the data warehouses used for decision support. Two competing approaches are employed. The first approach is that of Bill Inmon, who is often called "the father of data warehousing." Inmon supports a top-down development approach that adapts traditional relational database tools to the development needs of an

TABLE 3.2 Sample List of Data Warehousing Vendors

Vendor	Product Offerings
Business Objects (**businessobjects.com**)	A comprehensive set of business intelligence and data visualization software (now owned by SAP)
Computer Associates (**cai.com**)	Comprehensive set of data warehouse (DW) tools and products
DataMirror (**datamirror.com**)	DW administration, management, and performance products
Data Advantage Group (**dataadvantagegroup.com**)	Metadata software
Dell (**dell.com**)	DW servers
Embarcadero Technologies (**embarcadero.com**)	DW administration, management, and performance products
Greenplum (**greenplum.com**)	Data warehousing and data appliance solution provider (now owned by EMC)
Harte-Hanks (**harte-hanks.com**)	Customer relationship management (CRM) products and services
HP (**hp.com**)	DW servers
Hummingbird Ltd. (**hummingbird.com**, now is a subsidiary of Open Text.)	DW engines and exploration warehouses
Hyperion Solutions (**hyperion.com**, now an Oracle company)	Comprehensive set of DW tools, products, and applications
IBM InfoSphere (**www-01.ibm.com/software/data/infosphere/**)	Data integration, DW, master data management, big data products
Informatica (**informatica.com**)	DW administration, management, and performance products
Microsoft (**microsoft.com**)	DW tools and products
Netezza	DW software and hardware (DW appliance) provider (now owned by IBM)
Oracle (including PeopleSoft and Siebel) (**oracle.com**)	DW, ERP, and CRM tools, products, and applications
SAS Institute (**sas.com**)	DW tools, products, and applications
Siemens (**siemens.com**)	DW servers
Sybase (**sybase.com**)	Comprehensive set of DW tools and applications
Teradata (**teradata.com**)	DW tools, DW appliances, DW consultancy, and applications

enterprise-wide data warehouse, also known as the EDW approach. The second approach is that of Ralph Kimball, who proposes a bottom-up approach that employs dimensional modeling, also known as the data mart approach.

Knowing how these two models are alike and how they differ helps us understand the basic data warehouse concepts (e.g., see Breslin, 2004). Table 3.3 compares the two approaches. We describe these approaches in detail next.

THE INMON MODEL: THE EDW APPROACH Inmon's approach emphasizes top-down development, employing established database development methodologies and tools, such as entity-relationship diagrams (ERD), and an adjustment of the spiral development approach. The EDW approach does not preclude the creation of data marts. The EDW is the ideal in this approach because it provides a consistent and comprehensive view of the enterprise. Murtaza (1998) presented a framework for developing EDW.

THE KIMBALL MODEL: THE DATA MART APPROACH Kimball's data mart strategy is a "plan big, build small" approach. A data mart is a subject-oriented or department-oriented data warehouse. It is a scaled-down version of a data warehouse that focuses on the requests

TABLE 3.3 Contrasts Between the Data Mart and EDW Development Approaches

Effort	Data Mart Approach	EDW Approach
Scope	One subject area	Several subject areas
Development time	Months	Years
Development cost	$10,000 to $100,000+	$1,000,000+
Development difficulty	Low to medium	High
Data prerequisite for sharing	Common (within business area)	Common (across enterprise)
Sources	Only some operational and external systems	Many operational and external systems
Size	Megabytes to several gigabytes	Gigabytes to petabytes
Time horizon	Near-current and historical data	Historical data
Data transformations	Low to medium	High
Update frequency	Hourly, daily, weekly	Weekly, monthly
Technology		
Hardware	Workstations and departmental servers	Enterprise servers and mainframe computers
Operating system	Windows and Linux	Unix, Z/OS, OS/390
Databases	Workgroup or standard database servers	Enterprise database servers
Usage		
Number of simultaneous users	10s	100s to 1,000s
User types	Business area analysts and managers	Enterprise analysts and senior executives
Business spotlight	Optimizing activities within the business area	Cross-functional optimization and decision making

Sources: Adapted from J. Van den Hoven, "Data Marts: Plan Big, Build Small," in *IS Management Handbook,* 8th ed., CRC Press, Boca Raton, FL, 2003; and T. Ariyachandra and H. Watson, "Which Data Warehouse Architecture Is Most Successful?" *Business Intelligence Journal,* Vol. 11, No. 1, First Quarter 2006, pp. 4–6.

of a specific department, such as marketing or sales. This model applies dimensional data modeling, which starts with tables. Kimball advocated a development methodology that entails a bottom-up approach, which in the case of data warehouses means building one data mart at a time.

WHICH MODEL IS BEST?   There is no one-size-fits-all strategy to data warehousing. An enterprise's data warehousing strategy can evolve from a simple data mart to a complex data warehouse in response to user demands, the enterprise's business requirements, and the enterprise's maturity in managing its data resources. For many enterprises, a data mart is frequently a convenient first step to acquiring experience in constructing and managing a data warehouse while presenting business users with the benefits of better access to their data; in addition, a data mart commonly indicates the business value of data warehousing. Ultimately, engineering an EDW that consolidates old data marts and data warehouses is the ideal solution (see Application Case 3.5). However, the development of individual data marts can often provide many benefits along the way toward developing an EDW, especially if the organization is unable or unwilling to invest in a large-scale project. Data marts can also demonstrate feasibility and success in providing benefits. This could potentially lead to an investment in an EDW. Table 3.4 summarizes the most essential characteristic differences between the two models.

Application Case 3.5

Starwood Hotels & Resorts Manages Hotel Profitability with Data Warehousing

Starwood Hotels & Resorts Worldwide, Inc., is one of the leading hotel and leisure companies in the world with 1,112 properties in nearly 100 countries and 154,000 employees at its owned and managed properties. Starwood is a fully integrated owner, operator and franchisor of hotels, resorts, and residences with the following internationally renowned brands: St. Regis®, The Luxury Collection®, W®, Westin®, Le Méridien®, Sheraton®, Four Points® by Sheraton, Aloft®, and ElementSM. The Company boasts one of the industry's leading loyalty programs, Starwood Preferred Guest (SPG), allowing members to earn and redeem points for room stays, room upgrades, and flights, with no blackout dates. Starwood also owns Starwood Vacation Ownership Inc., a premier provider of world-class vacation experiences through villa-style resorts and privileged access to Starwood brands.

Challenge

Starwood Hotels has significantly increased the number of hotels it operates over the past few years through global corporate expansion, particularly in the Asia/Pacific region. This has resulted in a dramatic rise in the need for business critical information about Starwood's hotels and customers. All Starwood hotels globally use a single enterprise data warehouse to retrieve information critical to efficient hotel management, such an that regarding revenue, central reservations, and rate plan reports. In addition, Starwood Hotels' management runs important daily operating reports from the data warehouse for a wide range of business functions. Starwood's enterprise data warehouse spans almost all areas within the company, so it is essential not only for central-reservation and consumption information, but also to Starwood's loyalty program, which relies on all guest information, sales information, corporate sales information, customer service, and other data that managers, analysts, and executives depend on to make operational decisions.

The company is committed to knowing and servicing its guests, yet, "as data growth and demands grew too great for the company's legacy system, it was falling short in delivering the information hotel managers and administrators required on a daily

basis, since central reservation system (CRS) reports could take as long as 18 hours," said Richard Chung, Starwood Hotels' director of data integration. Chung added that hotel managers would receive the transient pace report—which presents market-segmented information on reservations—5 hours later than it was needed. Such delays prevented managers from adjusting rates appropriately, which could result in lost revenue.

Solution and Results

After reviewing several vendor offerings, Starwood Hotels selected Oracle Exadata Database Machine X2-2 HC Full Rack and Oracle Exadata Database Machine X2-2 HP Full Rack, running on Oracle Linux. "With the implementation of Exadata, Starwood Hotels can complete extract, transform, and load (ETL) operations for operational reports in 4 to 6 hours, as opposed to 18 to 24 hours previously, a six-fold improvement," Chung said. Real-time feeds, which were not possible before, now allow transactions to be posted immediately to the data warehouse, and users can access the changes in 5 to 10 minutes instead of 24 hours, making the process up to 288 times faster.

Accelerated data access allows all Starwood properties to get the same, up-to-date data needed for their reports, globally. Previously, hotel managers in some areas could not do same-day or next-day analyses. There were some locations that got fresh data and others that got older data. Hotel managers, worldwide, now have up-to-date data for their hotels, increasing efficiency and profitability, improving customer service by making sure rooms are available for premier customers, and improving the company's ability to manage room occupancy rates. Additional reporting tools, such as those used for CRM and sales and catering, also benefited from the improved processing. Other critical reporting has benefited as well. Marketing campaign management is also more efficient now that managers can analyze results in days or weeks instead of months.

"Oracle Exadata Database Machine enables us to move forward with an environment that provides our hotel managers and corporate executives with near–real-time information to make optimal business decisions and provide ideal amenities for our guests." —Gordon Light, Business Relationship Manager, Starwood Hotels & Resorts Worldwide, Inc.

QUESTIONS FOR DISCUSSION

1. How big and complex are the business operations of Starwood Hotels & Resorts?

2. How did Starwood Hotels & Resorts use data warehousing for better profitability?

3. What were the challenges, the proposed solution, and the obtained results?

Source: Oracle customer success story, **www.oracle.com/us/corporate/customers/customersearch/starwood-hotels-1-exadata-sl-1855106.html; Starwood Hotels and Resorts, starwoodhotels.com (accessed July 2013).**

Additional Data Warehouse Development Considerations

Some organizations want to completely outsource their data warehousing efforts. They simply do not want to deal with software and hardware acquisitions, and they do not want to manage their information systems. One alternative is to use hosted data warehouses. In this scenario, another firm—ideally, one that has a lot of experience

TABLE 3.4   Essential Differences Between Inmon's and Kimball's Approaches

Characteristic	Inmon	Kimball
Methodology and Architecture		
Overall approach	Top-down	Bottom-up
Architecture structure	Enterprise-wide (atomic) data warehouse "feeds" departmental databases	Data marts model a single business process, and enterprise consistency is achieved through a data bus and conformed dimensions
Complexity of the method	Quite complex	Fairly simple
Comparison with established development methodologies	Derived from the spiral methodology	Four-step process; a departure from relational database management system (RDBMS) methods
Discussion of physical design	Fairly thorough	Fairly light
Data Modeling		
Data orientation	Subject or data driven	Process oriented
Tools	Traditional (entity-relationship diagrams [ERD], data flow diagrams [DFD])	Dimensional modeling; a departure from relational modeling
End-user accessibility	Low	High
Philosophy		
Primary audience	IT professionals	End users
Place in the organization	Integral part of the corporate information factory	Transformer and retainer of operational data
Objective	Deliver a sound technical solution based on proven database methods and technologies	Deliver a solution that makes it easy for end users to directly query the data and still get reasonable response times

Sources: Adapted from M. Breslin, "Data Warehousing Battle of the Giants: Comparing the Basics of Kimball and Inmon Models," *Business Intelligence Journal,* Vol. 9, No. 1, Winter 2004, pp. 6–20; and T. Ariyachandra and H. Watson, "Which Data Warehouse Architecture Is Most Successful?" *Business Intelligence Journal,* Vol. 11, No. 1, First Quarter 2006.

TECHNOLOGY INSIGHTS 3.1   Hosted Data Warehouses

A hosted data warehouse has nearly the same, if not more, functionality as an on-site data ware-house, but it does not consume computer resources on client premises. A hosted data warehouse offers the benefits of BI minus the cost of computer upgrades, network upgrades, software licenses, in-house development, and in-house support and maintenance.

A hosted data warehouse offers the following benefits:

- Requires minimal investment in infrastructure
- Frees up capacity on in-house systems
- Frees up cash flow
- Makes powerful solutions affordable
- Enables powerful solutions that provide for growth
- Offers better quality equipment and software
- Provides faster connections
- Enables users to access data from remote locations
- Allows a company to focus on core business
- Meets storage needs for large volumes of data

Despite its benefits, a hosted data warehouse is not necessarily a good fit for every organi-zation. Large companies with revenue upwards of $500 million could lose money if they already have underused internal infrastructure and IT staff. Furthermore, companies that see the para-digm shift of outsourcing applications as loss of control of their data are not likely to use a business intelligence service provider (BISP). Finally, the most significant and common argument against implementing a hosted data warehouse is that it may be unwise to outsource sensitive applications for reasons of security and privacy.

Sources: Compiled from M. Thornton and M. Lampa, "Hosted Data Warehouse," *Journal of Data Warehousing,* Vol. 7, No. 2, 2002, pp. 27–34; and M. Thornton, "What About Security? The Most Common, but Unwarranted, Objection to Hosted Data Warehouses," *DM Review,* Vol. 12, No. 3, March 18, 2002, pp. 30–43.

and expertise—develops and maintains the data warehouse. However, there are security and privacy concerns with this approach. See Technology Insights 3.1 for some details.

Representation of Data in Data Warehouse

A typical data warehouse structure is shown in Figure 3.3. Many variations of data ware-house architecture are possible (see Figure 3.7). No matter what the architecture was, the design of data representation in the data warehouse has always been based on the concept of dimensional modeling. **Dimensional modeling** is a retrieval-based system that supports high-volume query access. Representation and storage of data in a data warehouse should be designed in such a way that not only accommodates but also boosts the processing of complex multidimensional queries. Often, the star schema and the snowflakes schema are the means by which dimensional modeling is implemented in data warehouses.

The **star schema** (sometimes referenced as star join schema) is the most commonly used and the simplest style of dimensional modeling. A star schema contains a central fact table surrounded by and connected to several **dimension tables** (Adamson, 2009). The fact table contains a large number of rows that correspond to observed facts and external links (i.e., foreign keys). A fact table contains the descriptive attributes needed to perform decision analysis and query reporting, and foreign keys are used to link to dimension tables. The decision analysis attributes consist of performance measures, operational metrics, aggregated measures (e.g., sales volumes, customer retention rates, profit margins, production costs, crap rates, and so forth), and all the other metrics needed to analyze the organization's performance. In other words, the fact table primarily addresses what the data warehouse supports for decision analysis.

Surrounding the central fact tables (and linked via foreign keys) are dimension tables. The dimension tables contain classification and aggregation information about the central fact rows. Dimension tables contain attributes that describe the data contained within the fact table; they address how data will be analyzed and summarized. Dimension tables have a one-to-many relationship with rows in the central fact table. In querying, the dimensions are used to slice and dice the numerical values in the fact table to address the requirements of an ad hoc information need. The star schema is designed to provide fast query-response time, simplicity, and ease of maintenance for read-only database structures. A simple star schema is shown in Figure 3.10a. The star schema is considered a special case of the snowflake schema.

The **snowflake schema** is a logical arrangement of tables in a multidimensional database in such a way that the entity-relationship diagram resembles a snowflake in shape. Closely related to the star schema, the snowflake schema is represented by centralized fact tables (usually only one) that are connected to multiple dimensions. In the snowflake schema, however, dimensions are normalized into multiple related tables whereas the star schema's dimensions are denormalized with each dimension being represented by a single table. A simple snowflake schema is shown in Figure 3.10b.

Analysis of Data in the Data Warehouse

Once the data is properly stored in a data warehouse, it can be used in various ways to support organizational decision making. OLAP (online analytical processing) is arguably the most commonly used data analysis technique in data warehouses, and it has been growing in popularity due to the exponential increase in data volumes and the recognition of the business value of data-driven analytics. Simply, OLAP is an approach to quickly answer ad hoc questions by executing multidimensional analytical queries against organizational data repositories (i.e., data warehouses, data marts).

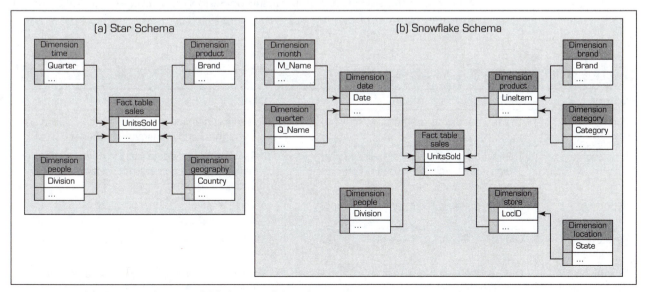

FIGURE 3.10 (a) The Star Schema, and (b) the Snowflake Schema.

OLAP Versus OLTP

OLTP (online transaction processing system) is a term used for a transaction system, which is primarily responsible for capturing and storing data related to day-to-day business functions such as ERP, CRM, SCM, point of sale, and so forth. The OLTP system addresses a critical business need, automating daily business transactions and running real-time reports and routine analyses. But these systems are not designed for ad hoc analysis and complex queries that deal with a number of data items. OLAP, on the other hand, is designed to address this need by providing ad hoc analysis of organizational data much more effectively and efficiently. OLAP and OLTP rely heavily on each other: OLAP uses the data captures by OLTP, and OLTP automates the business processes that are managed by decisions supported by OLAP. Table 3.5 provides a multi-criteria comparison between OLTP and OLAP.

OLAP Operations

The main operational structure in OLAP is based on a concept called *cube*. A **cube** in OLAP is a multidimensional data structure (actual or virtual) that allows fast analysis of data. It can also be defined as the capability of efficiently manipulating and analyzing data from multiple perspectives. The arrangement of data into cubes aims to overcome a limitation of relational databases: Relational databases are not well suited for near instantaneous analysis of large amounts of data. Instead, they are better suited for manipulating records (adding, deleting, and updating data) that represent a series of transactions. Although many report-writing tools exist for relational databases, these tools are slow when a multidimensional query that encompasses many database tables needs to be executed.

Using OLAP, an analyst can navigate through the database and screen for a particular subset of the data (and its progression over time) by changing the data's orientations and defining analytical calculations. These types of user-initiated navigation of data through the specification of slices (via rotations) and **drill down**/up (via aggregation and disaggregation) is sometimes called "slice and dice." Commonly used OLAP operations include slice and dice, drill down, roll up, and pivot.

- *Slice.* A slice is a subset of a multidimensional array (usually a two-dimensional representation) corresponding to a single value set for one (or more) of the dimensions not in the subset. A simple slicing operation on a three-dimensional cube is shown in Figure 3.11.

TABLE 3.5 A Comparison Between OLTP and OLAP

Criteria	OLTP	OLAP
Purpose	To carry out day-to-day business functions	To support decision making and provide answers to business and management queries
Data source	Transaction database (a normalized data repository primarily focused on efficiency and consistency)	Data warehouse or data mart (a nonnormalized data repository primarily focused on accuracy and completeness)
Reporting	Routine, periodic, narrowly focused reports	Ad hoc, multidimensional, broadly focused reports and queries
Resource requirements	Ordinary relational databases	Multiprocessor, large-capacity, specialized databases
Execution speed	Fast (recording of business transactions and routine reports)	Slow (resource intensive, complex, large-scale queries)

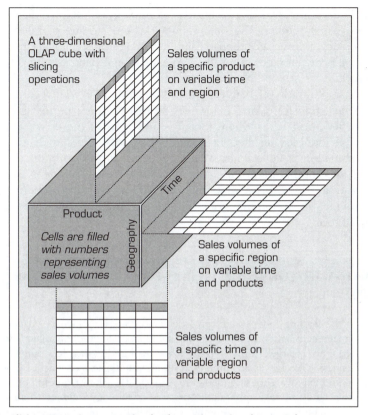

FIGURE 3.11 **Slicing Operations on a Simple Three-Dimensional Data Cube.**

- *Dice.* The dice operation is a slice on more than two dimensions of a data cube.
- *Drill Down/Up* Drilling down or up is a specific OLAP technique whereby the user navigates among levels of data ranging from the most summarized (up) to the most detailed (down).
- *Roll-up.* A roll-up involves computing all of the data relationships for one or more dimensions. To do this, a computational relationship or formula might be defined.
- *Pivot:* A pivot is a means of changing the dimensional orientation of a report or ad hoc query-page display.

VARIATIONS OF OLAP OLAP has a few variations; among them ROLAP, MOLAP, and HOLAP are the most common ones.

ROLAP stands for Relational Online Analytical Processing. ROLAP is an alternative to the MOLAP (Multidimensional OLAP) technology. Although both ROLAP and MOLAP analytic tools are designed to allow analysis of data through the use of a multidimensional data model, ROLAP differs significantly in that it does not require the precomputation and storage of information. Instead, ROLAP tools access the data in a relational database and generate SQL queries to calculate information at the appropriate level when an end user requests it. With ROLAP, it is possible to create additional database tables (summary tables or aggregations) that summarize the data at any desired combination of dimensions. While ROLAP uses a relational database source, generally the database must be carefully designed for ROLAP use. A database that was designed for OLTP will not function well as a ROLAP database. Therefore, ROLAP still involves creating an additional copy of the data.

MOLAP is an alternative to the ROLAP technology. MOLAP differs from ROLAP significantly in that it requires the precomputation and storage of information in the cube—the operation known as preprocessing. MOLAP stores this data in an optimized multidimensional array storage, rather than in a relational database (which is often the case for ROLAP).

The undesirable trade-off between ROLAP and MOLAP with regards to the additional ETL (extract, transform, and load) cost and slow query performance has led to inquiries for better approaches where the pros and cons of these two approaches are optimized. These inquiries resulted in HOLAP (Hybrid Online Analytical Processing), which is a combination of ROLAP and MOLAP. HOLAP allows storing part of the data in a MOLAP store and another part of the data in a ROLAP store. The degree of control that the cube designer has over this partitioning varies from product to product. Technology Insights 3.2 provides an opportunity for conducting a simple hands-on analysis with the MicroStrategy BI tool.

TECHNOLOGY INSIGHTS 3.2   Hands-On Data Warehousing with MicroStrategy

MicroStrategy is the leading independent provider of business intelligence, data warehousing performance management, and business reporting solutions. The other big players in this market were recently acquired by large IT firms: Hyperion was acquired by Oracle; Cognos was acquired by IBM; and Business Objects was acquired by SAP. Despite these recent acquisitions, the business intelligence and data warehousing market remains active, vibrant, and full of opportunities.

Following is a step-by-step approach to using MicroStrategy software to analyze a hypothetical business situation. A more comprehensive version of this hands-on exercise can be found at the TUN Web site. According to this hypothetical scenario, you (the vice president of sales at a global telecommunications company) are planning a business visit to the European region. Before meeting with the regional salespeople on Monday, you want to know the sale representatives' activities for the last quarter (Quarter 4 of 2004). You are to create such an ad hoc report using MicroStrategy's Web access. In order to create this and many other OLAP reports, you will need the access code for the **TeradataUniversityNetwork.com** Web site. It is free of charge for educational use and only your professor will be able to get the necessary access code for you to utilize not only MicroStrategy software but also a large collection of other business intelligence resources at this site.

Once you are in TeradataUniversityNetwork, you need to go to "APPLY & DO" and select "MicroStrategy BI" from the "Software" section. On the "MicroStrategy/BI" Web page, follow these steps:

1. Click on the link for "MicroStrategy Application Modules." This will lead you to a page that shows a list of previously built MicroStrategy applications.
2. Select the "Sales Force Analysis Module." This module is designed to provide you with in-depth insight into the entire sales process. This insight in turn allows you to increase lead conversions, optimize product lines, take advantage of your organization's most successful sales practices, and improve your sales organization's effectiveness.
3. In the "Sales Force Analysis Module" site you will see three sections: View, Create, and Tolls. In the View section, click on the link for "Shared Reports." This link will take you to a place where a number of previously created sales reports are listed for everybody's use.
4. In the "Shared Reports" page, click on the folder named "Pipeline Analysis." Pipeline Analysis reports provide insight into all open opportunities and deals in the sales pipeline. These reports measure the current status of the sales pipeline, detect changing trends and key events, and identify key open opportunities. You want to review what is in the pipeline for each sales rep, as well as whether or not they hit their sales quota last quarter.
5. In the "Pipeline Analysis" page, click on the report named "Current Pipeline vs. Quota by Sales Region and District." This report presents the current pipeline status for each sales

district within a sales region. It also projects whether target quotas can be achieved for the current quarter.

6. In the "Current Pipeline vs. Quota by Sales Region and District" page, select (with single click) "2004 Q4" as the report parameter, indicating that you want to see how the representatives performed against their quotas for the last quarter.

7. Run the report by clicking on the "Run Report" button at the bottom of the page. This will lead you to a sales report page where the values for each Metric are calculated for all three European sales regions. In this interactive report, you can easily change the region from Europe to United States or Canada using the pull-down combo box, or you can drill-in one of the three European regions by simply clicking on the appropriate region's heading to see more detailed analysis of the selected region.

SECTION 3.6 REVIEW QUESTIONS

1. List the benefits of data warehouses.
2. List several criteria for selecting a data warehouse vendor, and describe why they are important.
3. What is OLAP and how does it differ from OLTP?
4. What is a cube? What do drill down, roll up, and slice and dice mean?
5. What are ROLAP, MOLAP, and HOLAP? How do they differ from OLAP?

3.7 DATA WAREHOUSING IMPLEMENTATION ISSUES

Implementing a data warehouse is generally a massive effort that must be planned and executed according to established methods. However, the project life cycle has many facets, and no single person can be an expert in each area. Here we discuss specific ideas and issues as they relate to data warehousing.

People want to know how successful their BI and data warehousing initiatives are in comparison to those of other companies. Ariyachandra and Watson (2006a) proposed some benchmarks for BI and data warehousing success. Watson et al. (1999) researched data warehouse failures. Their results showed that people define a "failure" in different ways, and this was confirmed by Ariyachandra and Watson (2006a). The Data Warehousing Institute (**tdwi.org**) has developed a data warehousing maturity model that an enterprise can apply in order to benchmark its evolution. The model offers a fast means to gauge where the organization's data warehousing initiative is now and where it needs to go next. The maturity model consists of six stages: prenatal, infant, child, teenager, adult, and sage. Business value rises as the data warehouse progresses through each succeeding stage. The stages are identified by a number of characteristics, including scope, analytic structure, executive perceptions, types of analytics, stewardship, funding, technology platform, change management, and administration. See Eckerson et al. (2009) and Eckerson (2003) for more details.

Data warehouse projects have many risks. Most of them are also found in other IT projects, but data warehousing risks are more serious because data warehouses are expensive, time-and-resource demanding, large-scale projects. Each risk should be assessed at the inception of the project. When developing a successful data warehouse, it is important to carefully consider various risks and avoid the following issues:

- ***Starting with the wrong sponsorship chain.*** You need an executive sponsor who has influence over the necessary resources to support and invest in the data warehouse. You also need an executive project driver, someone who has earned the respect of other executives, has a healthy skepticism about technology, and is decisive but flexible. You also need an IS/IT manager to head up the project.

- ***Setting expectations that you cannot meet.*** You do not want to frustrate executives at the moment of truth. Every data warehousing project has two phases: Phase 1 is the selling phase, in which you internally market the project by selling the benefits to those who have access to needed resources. Phase 2 is the struggle to meet the expectations described in Phase 1. For a mere $1 to $7 million, hopefully, you can deliver.

- ***Engaging in politically naive behavior.*** Do not simply state that a data warehouse will help managers make better decisions. This may imply that you feel they have been making bad decisions until now. Sell the idea that they will be able to get the information they need to help in decision making.

- ***Loading the warehouse with information just because it is available.*** Do not let the data warehouse become a data landfill. This would unnecessarily slow the use of the system. There is a trend toward real-time computing and analysis. Data warehouses must be shut down to load data in a timely way.

- ***Believing that data warehousing database design is the same as transactional database design.*** In general, it is not. The goal of data warehousing is to access aggregates rather than a single or a few records, as in transaction-processing systems. Content is also different, as is evident in how data are organized. DBMS tend to be nonredundant, normalized, and relational, whereas data warehouses are redundant, not normalized, and multidimensional.

- ***Choosing a data warehouse manager who is technology oriented rather than user oriented.*** One key to data warehouse success is to understand that the users must get what they need, not advanced technology for technology's sake.

- ***Focusing on traditional internal record-oriented data and ignoring the value of external data and of text, images, and, perhaps, sound and video.*** Data come in many formats and must be made accessible to the right people at the right time and in the right format. They must be cataloged properly.

- ***Delivering data with overlapping and confusing definitions.*** Data cleansing is a critical aspect of data warehousing. It includes reconciling conflicting data definitions and formats organization-wide. Politically, this may be difficult because it involves change, typically at the executive level.

- ***Believing promises of performance, capacity, and scalability.*** Data warehouses generally require more capacity and speed than is originally budgeted for. Plan ahead to scale up.

- ***Believing that your problems are over when the data warehouse is up and running.*** DSS/BI projects tend to evolve continually. Each deployment is an iteration of the prototyping process. There will always be a need to add more and different data sets to the data warehouse, as well as additional analytic tools for existing and additional groups of decision makers. High energy and annual budgets must be planned for because success breeds success. Data warehousing is a continuous process.

- ***Focusing on ad hoc data mining and periodic reporting instead of alerts.*** The natural progression of information in a data warehouse is (1) extract the data from legacy systems, cleanse them, and feed them to the warehouse; (2) support ad hoc reporting until you learn what people want; and (3) convert the ad hoc reports into regularly scheduled reports. This process of learning what people want in order to provide it seems natural, but it is not optimal or even practical. Managers are busy and need time to read reports. Alert systems are better than periodic reporting systems and can make a data warehouse mission critical. Alert systems monitor the data flowing into the warehouse and inform all key people who have a need to know as soon as a critical event occurs.

In many organizations, a data warehouse will be successful only if there is strong senior management support for its development and if there is a project champion who is high up in the organizational chart. Although this would likely be true for any large-scale IT project, it is especially important for a data warehouse realization. The successful implementation of a data warehouse results in the establishment of an architectural framework that may allow for decision analysis throughout an organization and in some cases also provides comprehensive SCM by granting access to information on an organization's customers and suppliers. The implementation of Web-based data warehouses (sometimes called *Webhousing*) has facilitated ease of access to vast amounts of data, but it is difficult to determine the hard benefits associated with a data warehouse. Hard benefits are defined as benefits to an organization that can be expressed in monetary terms. Many organizations have limited IT resources and must prioritize projects. Management support and a strong project champion can help ensure that a data warehouse project will receive the resources necessary for successful implementation. Data warehouse resources can be a significant cost, in some cases requiring high-end processors and large increases in direct-access storage devices (DASD). Web-based data warehouses may also have special security requirements to ensure that only authorized users have access to the data.

User participation in the development of data and access modeling is a critical success factor in data warehouse development. During data modeling, expertise is required to determine what data are needed, define business rules associated with the data, and decide what aggregations and other calculations may be necessary. Access modeling is needed to determine how data are to be retrieved from a data warehouse, and it assists in the physical definition of the warehouse by helping to define which data require indexing. It may also indicate whether dependent data marts are needed to facilitate information retrieval. The team skills needed to develop and implement a data warehouse include in-depth knowledge of the database technology and development tools used. Source systems and development technology, as mentioned previously, reference the many inputs and the processes used to load and maintain a data warehouse.

Application Case 3.6 presents an excellent example for a large-scale implementation of an integrated data warehouse by a state government.

Application Case 3.6

EDW Helps Connect State Agencies in Michigan

Through customer service, resource optimization, and the innovative use of information and technology, the Michigan Department of Technology, Management & Budget (DTMB) impacts every area of government. Nearly 10,000 users in five major departments, 20 agencies, and more than 100 bureaus rely on the EDW to do their jobs more effectively and better serve Michigan residents. The EDW achieves $1 million per business day in financial benefits.

The EDW helped Michigan achieve $200 million in annual financial benefits within the Department of Community Health alone, plus another $75 million

per year within the Department of Human Services (DHS). These savings include program integrity benefits, cost avoidance due to improved outcomes, sanction avoidance, operational efficiencies, and the recovery of inappropriate payments within its Medicaid program.

The Michigan DHS data warehouse (DW) provides unique and innovative information critical to the efficient operation of the agency from both a strategic and tactical level. Over the last 10 years, the DW has yielded a 15:1 cost-effectiveness ratio. Consolidated information from the DW now contributes to nearly every function of DHS, including

(Continued)

Application Case 3.6 (Continued)

accurate delivery of and accounting for benefits delivered to almost 2.5 million DHS public assistance clients.

Michigan has been ambitious in its attempts to solve real-life problems through the innovative sharing and comprehensive analyses of data. Its approach to BI/DW has always been "enterprise" (statewide) in nature, rather than having separate BI/DW platforms for each business area or state agency. By removing barriers to sharing enterprise data across business units, Michigan has leveraged massive amounts of data to create innovative approaches to the use of BI/DW, delivering efficient, reliable enterprise solutions using multiple channels.

QUESTIONS FOR DISCUSSION

1. Why would a state invest in a large and expensive IT infrastructure (such as an EDW)?

2. What are the size and complexity of EDW used by state agencies in Michigan?

3. What were the challenges, the proposed solution, and the obtained results of the EDW?

Source: Compiled from TDWI Best Practices Awards 2012 Winner, Enterprise Data Warehousing, Government and Non-Profit Category, "Michigan Departments of Technology, Management & Budget (DTMB), Community Health (DCH), and Human Services (DHS)," featured in *TDWI What Works*, Vol. 34, p. 22; and **michigan.michigan.gov.**

Massive Data Warehouses and Scalability

In addition to flexibility, a data warehouse needs to support scalability. The main issues pertaining to scalability are the amount of data in the warehouse, how quickly the warehouse is expected to grow, the number of concurrent users, and the complexity of user queries. A data warehouse must scale both horizontally and vertically. The warehouse will grow as a function of data growth and the need to expand the warehouse to support new business functionality. Data growth may be a result of the addition of current cycle data (e.g., this month's results) and/or historical data.

Hicks (2001) described huge databases and data warehouses. Walmart is continually increasing the size of its massive data warehouse. Walmart is believed to use a warehouse with hundreds of terabytes of data to study sales trends, track inventory, and perform other tasks. IBM recently publicized its 50-terabyte warehouse benchmark (IBM, 2009). The U.S. Department of Defense is using a 5-petabyte data warehouse and repository to hold medical records for 9 million military personnel. Because of the storage required to archive its news footage, CNN also has a petabyte-sized data warehouse.

Given that the size of data warehouses is expanding at an exponential rate, scalability is an important issue. Good scalability means that queries and other data-access functions will grow (ideally) linearly with the size of the warehouse. See Rosenberg (2006) for approaches to improve query performance. In practice, specialized methods have been developed to create scalable data warehouses. Scalability is difficult when managing hundreds of terabytes or more. Terabytes of data have considerable inertia, occupy a lot of physical space, and require powerful computers. Some firms use parallel processing, and others use clever indexing and search schemes to manage their data. Some spread their data across different physical data stores. As more data warehouses approach the petabyte size, better and better solutions to scalability continue to be developed.

Hall (2002) also addressed scalability issues. AT&T is an industry leader in deploying and using massive data warehouses. With its 26-terabyte data warehouse, AT&T can detect fraudulent use of calling cards and investigate calls related to kidnappings and other crimes. It can also compute millions of call-in votes from television viewers selecting the next American Idol.

For a sample of successful data warehousing implementations, see Edwards (2003). Jukic and Lang (2004) examined the trends and specific issues related to the use of off-shore resources in the development and support of data warehousing and BI applications. Davison (2003) indicated that IT-related offshore outsourcing had been growing at 20 to 25 percent per year. When considering offshoring data warehousing projects, careful consideration must be given to culture and security (for details, see Jukic and Lang, 2004).

SECTION 3.7 REVIEW QUESTIONS

1. What are the major DW implementation tasks that can be performed in parallel?
2. List and discuss the most pronounced DW implementation guidelines.
3. When developing a successful data warehouse, what are the most important risks and issues to consider and potentially avoid?
4. What is scalability? How does it apply to DW?

3.8 REAL-TIME DATA WAREHOUSING

Data warehousing and BI tools traditionally focus on assisting managers in making strategic and tactical decisions. Increased data volumes and accelerating update speeds are fundamentally changing the role of the data warehouse in modern business. For many businesses, making fast and consistent decisions across the enterprise requires more than a traditional data warehouse or data mart. Traditional data warehouses are not business critical. Data are commonly updated on a weekly basis, and this does not allow for responding to transactions in near–real-time.

More data, coming in faster and requiring immediate conversion into decisions, means that organizations are confronting the need for real-time data warehousing. This is because decision support has become operational, integrated BI requires closed-loop analytics, and yesterday's ODS will not support existing requirements.

In 2003, with the advent of real-time data warehousing, there was a shift toward using these technologies for operational decisions. **Real-time data warehousing (RDW)**, also known as **active data warehousing (ADW)**, is the process of loading and providing data via the data warehouse as they become available. It evolved from the EDW concept. The active traits of an RDW/ADW supplement and expand traditional data warehouse functions into the realm of tactical decision making. People throughout the organization who interact directly with customers and suppliers will be empowered with information-based decision making at their fingertips. Even further leverage results when an ADW provides information directly to customers and suppliers. The reach and impact of information access for decision making can positively affect almost all aspects of customer service, SCM, logistics, and beyond. E-business has become a major catalyst in the demand for active data warehousing (see Armstrong, 2000). For example, online retailer Overstock.com, Inc. (**overstock.com**) connected data users to a real-time data warehouse. At Egg plc, the world's largest purely online bank, a customer data warehouse is refreshed in near–real-time. See Application Case 3.7.

As business needs evolve, so do the requirements of the data warehouse. At this basic level, a data warehouse simply reports what happened. At the next level, some analysis occurs. As the system evolves, it provides prediction capabilities, which lead to the next level of operationalization. At its highest evolution, the ADW is capable of making events happen (e.g., activities such as creating sales and marketing campaigns or identifying and exploiting opportunities). See Figure 3.12 for a graphic description of this evolutionary process. A recent survey on managing evolution of data warehouses can be found in Wrembel (2009).

Application Case 3.7

Egg Plc Fries the Competition in Near Real Time

Egg plc, now a part of Yorkshire Building Society (**egg.com**) is the world's largest online bank. It provides banking, insurance, investments, and mortgages to more than 3.6 million customers through its Internet site. In 1998, Egg selected Sun Microsystems to create a reliable, scalable, secure infrastructure to support its more than 2.5 million daily transactions. In 2001, the system was upgraded to eliminate latency problems. This new customer data warehouse (CDW) used Sun, Oracle, and SAS software products. The initial data warehouse had about 10 terabytes of data and used a 16-CPU server. The system provides near–real-time data access. It provides data warehouse and data mining services to internal users, and it provides a requisite set of customer data to the customers themselves. Hundreds of sales and marketing campaigns are constructed using near–real-time data (within several minutes). And better, the system enables faster decision making about specific customers and customer classes.

QUESTIONS FOR DISCUSSION

1. Why kind of business is Egg plc in? What is the competitive landscape?
2. How did Egg plc use near–real-time data warehousing for competitive advantage?

Sources: Compiled from "Egg's Customer Data Warehouse Hits the Mark," *DM Review*, Vol. 15, No. 10, October 2005, pp. 24–28; Sun Microsystems, "Egg Banks on Sun to Hit the Mark with Customers," September 19, 2005, **sun.com/smi/Press/sunflash/2005-09/sunflash.20050919.1.xml** (accessed April 2006); and ZD Net UK, "Sun Case Study: Egg's Customer Data Warehouse," **whitepapers.zdnet.co.uk/0,39025945,60159401p-39000449q,00.htm** (accessed June 2009).

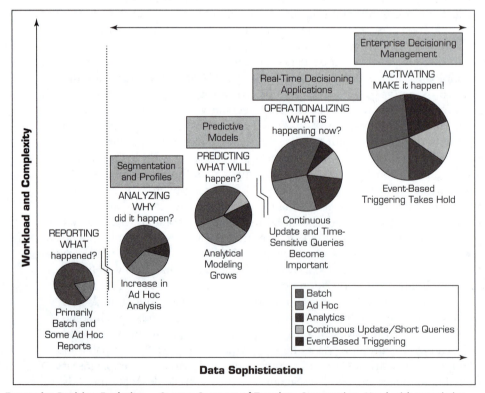

FIGURE 3.12 **Enterprise Decision Evolution.** *Source:* Courtesy of Teradata Corporation. Used with permission.

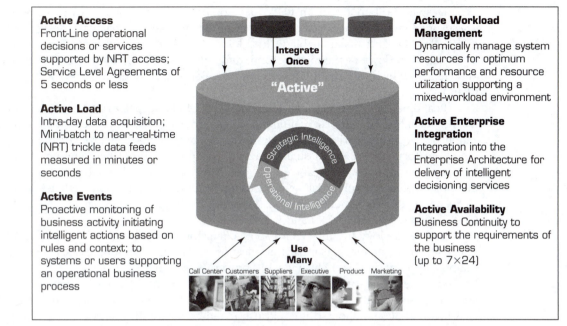

Active Access
Front-Line operational decisions or services supported by NRT access; Service Level Agreements of 5 seconds or less

Active Load
Intra-day data acquisition; Mini-batch to near-real-time (NRT) trickle data feeds measured in minutes or seconds

Active Events
Proactive monitoring of business activity initiating intelligent actions based on rules and context; to systems or users supporting an operational business process

Active Workload Management
Dynamically manage system resources for optimum performance and resource utilization supporting a mixed-workload environment

Active Enterprise Integration
Integration into the Enterprise Architecture for delivery of intelligent decisioning services

Active Availability
Business Continuity to support the requirements of the business (up to 7×24)

FIGURE 3.13 The Teradata Active EDW. *Source:* Courtesy of Teradata Corporation. Used with permission.

Teradata Corporation provides the baseline requirements to support an EDW. It also provides the new traits of active data warehousing required to deliver data freshness, performance, and availability and to enable enterprise decision management (see Figure 3.13 for an example).

An ADW offers an integrated information repository to drive strategic and tactical decision support within an organization. With real-time data warehousing, instead of extracting operational data from an OLTP system in nightly batches into an ODS, data are assembled from OLTP systems as and when events happen and are moved at once into the data warehouse. This permits the instant updating of the data warehouse and the elimination of an ODS. At this point, tactical and strategic queries can be made against the RDW to use immediate as well as historical data.

According to Basu (2003), the most distinctive difference between a traditional data warehouse and an RDW is the shift in the data acquisition paradigm. Some of the business cases and enterprise requirements that led to the need for data in real time include the following:

- A business often cannot afford to wait a whole day for its operational data to load into the data warehouse for analysis.
- Until now, data warehouses have captured snapshots of an organization's fixed states instead of incremental real-time data showing every state change and almost analogous patterns over time.
- With a traditional hub-and-spoke architecture, keeping the metadata in sync is difficult. It is also costly to develop, maintain, and secure many systems as opposed to one huge data warehouse so that data are centralized for BI/BA tools.
- In cases of huge nightly batch loads, the necessary ETL setup and processing power for large nightly data warehouse loading might be very high, and the processes might take too long. An EAI with real-time data collection can reduce or eliminate the nightly batch processes.

Despite the benefits of an RDW, developing one can create its own set of issues. These problems relate to architecture, data modeling, physical database design, storage and scalability, and maintainability. In addition, depending on exactly when data are accessed, even down to the microsecond, different versions of the truth may be extracted and created, which can confuse team members. For details, refer to Basu (2003) and Terr (2004).

Real-time solutions present a remarkable set of challenges to BI activities. Although it is not ideal for all solutions, real-time data warehousing may be successful if the organization develops a sound methodology to handle project risks, incorporate proper planning, and focus on quality assurance activities. Understanding the common challenges and applying best practices can reduce the extent of the problems that are often a part of implementing complex data warehousing systems that incorporate BI/BA methods. Details and real implementations are discussed by Burdett and Singh (2004) and Wilk (2003). Also see Akbay (2006) and Ericson (2006).

See Technology Insights 3.3 for some details on how the real-time concept evolved. The flight management dashboard application at Continental Airlines (see the End-of-Chapter Application Case) illustrates the power of real-time BI in accessing a data warehouse for use in face-to-face customer interaction situations. The operations staff uses the real-time system to identify issues in the Continental flight network. As another example, UPS invested $600 million so it could use real-time data and processes. The investment was expected to cut 100 million delivery miles and save 14 million gallons of fuel annually by managing its real-time package-flow technologies (see Malykhina, 2003). Table 3.6 compares traditional and active data warehousing environments.

Real-time data warehousing, near–real-time data warehousing, zero-latency warehousing, and *active data warehousing* are different names used in practice to describe the same concept. Gonzales (2005) presented different definitions for ADW. According to Gonzales, ADW is only one option that provides blended tactical and strategic data on demand. The architecture to build an ADW is very similar to the corporate information factory architecture developed by Bill Inmon. The only difference between a corporate information factory and an ADW is the implementation of both data stores in a single

---

TECHNOLOGY INSIGHTS 3.3   The Real-Time Realities of Active Data Warehousing

By 2003, the role of data warehousing in practice was growing rapidly. Real-time systems, though a novelty, were the latest buzz, along with the major complications of providing data and information instantaneously to those who need them. Many experts, including Peter Coffee, *eWeek*'s technology editor, believe that real-time systems must feed a real-time decision-making process. Stephen Brobst, CTO of the Teradata division of NCR, indicated that active data warehousing is a process of evolution in how an enterprise uses data. *Active* means that the data warehouse is also used as an operational and tactical tool. Brobst provided a five-stage model that fits Coffee's experience (2003) of how organizations "grow" in their data utilization (see Brobst et al., 2005). These stages (and the questions they purport to answer) are reporting (What happened?), analysis (Why did it happen?), prediction (What will happen?), operationalizing (What is happening?), and active warehousing (What do I want to happen?). The last stage, active warehousing, is where the greatest benefits may be obtained. Many organizations are enhancing centralized data warehouses to serve both operational and strategic decision making.

Sources: Adapted from P. Coffee, "'Active' Warehousing," *eWeek,* Vol. 20, No. 25, June 23, 2003, p. 36; and Teradata Corp., "Active Data Warehousing," **teradata.com/active-data-warehousing/** (accessed August 2013).

TABLE 3.6 Comparison Between Traditional and Active Data Warehousing Environments

Traditional Data Warehouse Environment	Active Data Warehouse Environment
Strategic decisions only	Strategic and tactical decisions
Results sometimes hard to measure	Results measured with operations
Daily, weekly, monthly data currency acceptable; summaries often appropriate	Only comprehensive detailed data available within minutes is acceptable
Moderate user concurrency	High number (1,000 or more) of users accessing and querying the system simultaneously
Highly restrictive reporting used to confirm or check existing processes and patterns; often uses predeveloped summary tables or data marts	Flexible ad hoc reporting, as well as machine-assisted modeling (e.g., data mining) to discover new hypotheses and relationships
Power users, knowledge workers, internal users	Operational staffs, call centers, external users

Sources: Adapted from P. Coffee, "'Active' Warehousing," *eWeek*, Vol. 20, No. 25, June 23, 2003, p. 36; and Teradata Corp., "Active Data Warehousing," **teradata.com/active-data-warehousing/** (accessed August 2013).

environment. However, an SOA based on XML and Web services provides another option for blending tactical and strategic data on demand.

One critical issue in real-time data warehousing is that not all data should be updated continuously. This may certainly cause problems when reports are generated in real time, because one person's results may not match another person's. For example, a company using Business Objects Web Intelligence noticed a significant problem with real-time intelligence. Real-time reports produced at slightly different times differ (see Peterson, 2003). Also, it may not be necessary to update certain data continuously (e.g., course grades that are 3 or more years old).

Real-time requirements change the way we view the design of databases, data warehouses, OLAP, and data mining tools because they are literally updated concurrently while queries are active. But the substantial business value in doing so has been demonstrated, so it is crucial that organizations adopt these methods in their business processes. Careful planning is critical in such implementations.

SECTION 3.8 REVIEW QUESTIONS

1. What is an RDW?
2. List the benefits of an RDW.
3. What are the major differences between a traditional data warehouse and an RDW?
4. List some of the drivers for RDW.

3.9 DATA WAREHOUSE ADMINISTRATION, SECURITY ISSUES, AND FUTURE TRENDS

Data warehouses provide a distinct competitive edge to enterprises that effectively create and use them. Due to its huge size and its intrinsic nature, a data warehouse requires especially strong monitoring in order to sustain satisfactory efficiency and productivity. The successful administration and management of a data warehouse entails skills and proficiency that go past what is required of a traditional database administrator (DBA).

A **data warehouse administrator (DWA)** should be familiar with high-performance software, hardware, and networking technologies. He or she should also possess solid business insight. Because data warehouses feed BI systems and DSS that help managers with their decision-making activities, the DWA should be familiar with the decision-making processes so as to suitably design and maintain the data warehouse structure. It is particularly significant for a DWA to keep the existing requirements and capabilities of the data warehouse stable while simultaneously providing flexibility for rapid improvements. Finally, a DWA must possess excellent communications skills. See Benander et al. (2000) for a description of the key differences between a DBA and a DWA.

Security and privacy of information are main and significant concerns for a data warehouse professional. The U.S. government has passed regulations (e.g., the Gramm-Leach-Bliley privacy and safeguards rules, the Health Insurance Portability and Accountability Act of 1996 [HIPAA]), instituting obligatory requirements in the management of customer information. Hence, companies must create security procedures that are effective yet flexible to conform to numerous privacy regulations. According to Elson and LeClerc (2005), effective security in a data warehouse should focus on four main areas:

1. Establishing effective corporate and security policies and procedures. An effective security policy should start at the top, with executive management, and should be communicated to all individuals within the organization.
2. Implementing logical security procedures and techniques to restrict access. This includes user authentication, access controls, and encryption technology.
3. Limiting physical access to the data center environment.
4. Establishing an effective internal control review process with an emphasis on security and privacy.

See Technology Insights 3.4 for a description of Ambeo's important software tool that monitors security and privacy of data warehouses. Finally, keep in mind that accessing a data warehouse via a mobile device should always be performed cautiously. In this instance, data should only be accessed as read-only.

In the near term, data warehousing developments will be determined by noticeable factors (e.g., data volumes, increased intolerance for latency, the diversity and complexity of data types) and less noticeable factors (e.g., unmet end-user requirements for

---

TECHNOLOGY INSIGHTS 3.4   Ambeo Delivers Proven Data-Access Auditing Solution

Since 1997, Ambeo (**ambeo.com**; now Embarcadero Technologies, Inc.) has deployed technology that provides performance management, data usage tracking, data privacy auditing, and monitoring to *Fortune* 1000 companies. These firms have some of the largest database environments in existence. Ambeo data-access auditing solutions play a major role in an enterprise information security infrastructure.

The Ambeo technology is a relatively easy solution that records everything that happens in the databases, with low or zero overhead. In addition, it provides data-access auditing that identifies exactly who is looking at data, when they are looking, and what they are doing with the data. This real-time monitoring helps quickly and effectively identify security breaches.

Sources: Adapted from "Ambeo Delivers Proven Data Access Auditing Solution," *Database Trends and Applications*, Vol. 19, No. 7, July 2005; and Ambeo, "Keeping Data Private (and Knowing It): Moving Beyond Conventional Safeguards to Ensure Data Privacy," **am-beo.com/why_ambeo_white_papers.html** (accessed May 2009).

dashboards, balanced scorecards, master data management, information quality). Given these drivers, Moseley (2009) and Agosta (2006) suggested that data warehousing trends will lean toward simplicity, value, and performance.

The Future of Data Warehousing

The field of data warehousing has been a vibrant area in information technology in the last couple of decades, and the evidence in the BI/BA and Big Data world shows that the importance of the field will only get even more interesting. Following are some of the recently popularized concepts and technologies that will play a significant role in defining the future of data warehousing.

Sourcing (mechanisms for acquisition of data from diverse and dispersed sources):

- ***Web, social media, and Big Data.***   The recent upsurge in the use of the Web for personal as well as business purposes coupled with the tremendous interest in social media creates opportunities for analysts to tap into very rich data sources. Because of the sheer volume, velocity, and variety of the data, a new term, *Big Data*, has been coined to name the phenomenon. Taking advantage of Big Data requires development of new and dramatically improved BI/BA technologies, which will result in a revolutionized data warehousing world.

- ***Open source software.***   Use of open source software tools is increasing at an unprecedented level in warehousing, business intelligence, and data integration. There are good reasons for the upswing of open source software used in data warehousing (Russom, 2009): (1) The recession has driven up interest in low-cost open source software; (2) open source tools are coming into a new level of maturity, and (3) open source software augments traditional enterprise software without replacing it.

- ***SaaS (software as a service),***   "The Extended ASP Model." SaaS is a creative way of deploying information system applications where the provider licenses its applications to customers for use as a service on demand (usually over the Internet). SaaS software vendors may host the application on their own servers or upload the application to the consumer site. In essence, SaaS is the new and improved version of the ASP model. For data warehouse customers, finding SaaS-based software applications and resources that meet specific needs and requirements can be challenging. As these software offerings become more agile, the appeal and the actual use of SaaS as the choice of data warehousing platform will also increase.

- ***Cloud computing.***   Cloud computing is perhaps the newest and the most innovative platform choice to come along in years. Numerous hardware and software resources are pooled and virtualized, so that they can be freely allocated to applications and software platforms as resources are needed. This enables information system applications to dynamically scale up as workloads increase. Although cloud computing and similar virtualization techniques are fairly well established for operational applications today, they are just now starting to be used as data warehouse platforms of choice. The dynamic allocation of a cloud is particularly useful when the data volume of the warehouse varies unpredictably, making capacity planning difficult.

Infrastructure (architectural—hardware and software—enhancements):

- ***Columnar (a new way to store and access data in the database).***   A column-oriented database management system (also commonly called a *columnar database*) is a system that stores data tables as sections of columns of data rather than as rows of data (which is the way most relational database management systems do it). That is, these columnar databases store data by columns instead of rows (all values of a single column are stored consecutively on disk memory). Such a structure gives a much finer grain of control to the relational database management system. It can access only the columns required for the query as opposed to being forced to access all columns of the row. It performs significantly better for queries that need a small percentage of the columns in the tables they are in but performs significantly worse when you need most of the columns due to the overhead in attaching all of the columns together to form the result sets. Comparisons between row-oriented and column-oriented data layouts are typically concerned with the efficiency of hard-disk access for a given workload (which happens to be one of the most time-consuming operations in a computer). Based on the task at hand, one may be significantly advantageous over the other. Column-oriented organizations are more efficient when (1) an aggregate needs to be computed over many rows but only for a notably smaller subset of all columns of data, because reading that smaller subset of data can be faster than reading all data, and (2) new values of a column are supplied for all rows at once, because that column data can be written efficiently and replace old column data without touching any other columns for the rows. Row-oriented organizations are more efficient when (1) many columns of a single row are required at the same time, and when row size is relatively small, as the entire row can be retrieved with a single disk seek, and (2) writing a new row if all of the column data is supplied at the same time, as the entire row can be written with a single disk seek. Additionally, since the data stored in a column is of uniform type, it lends itself better for compression. That is, significant storage size optimization is available in column-oriented data that is not available in row-oriented data. Such optimal compression of data reduces storage size, making it more economically justifiable to pursue in-memory or solid state storage alternatives.

- ***Real-time data warehousing.*** Real-time data warehousing implies that the refresh cycle of an existing data warehouse updates the data more frequently (almost at the same time as the data becomes available at operational databases). These real-time data warehouse systems can achieve near–real-time update of data, where the data latency typically is in the range from minutes to hours. As the latency gets smaller, the cost of data update seems to increase exponentially. Future advancements in many technological fronts (ranging from automatic data acquisition to intelligent software agents) are needed to make real-time data warehousing a reality with an affordable price tag.

- ***Data warehouse appliances (all-in-one solutions to DW).*** A data warehouse appliance consists of an integrated set of servers, storage, operating system(s), database management systems, and software specifically preinstalled and preoptimized for data warehousing. In practice, data warehouse appliances provide solutions for the mid-to-big data warehouse market, offering low-cost performance on data volumes in the terabyte to petabyte range. In order to improve performance, most data warehouse appliance vendors use massively parallel processing architectures. Even though most database and data warehouse vendors provide appliances nowadays, many believe that Teradata was the first to provide a commercial data warehouse appliance product. What is often observed now is the emergence of data warehouse bundles, where vendors combine their hardware and database software as a data warehouse platform. From a benefits standpoint, data warehouse appliances have significantly low total cost of ownership, which includes initial purchase costs, ongoing maintenance costs, and the cost of changing capacity as the data grows. The resource cost for monitoring and tuning the data warehouse makes up a large part of the total cost of ownership, often as much as 80 percent. DW appliances reduce administration for day-to-day operations, setup, and integration. Since data warehouse appliances provide a single-vendor solution, they tend to better optimize the hardware and software within the appliance. Such a unified integration maximizes the chances of successful integration and testing of the DBMS storage and operating system by avoiding some of the compatibility issues that arise from multi-vendor solutions. A data warehouse appliance also provides a single point of contact for problem resolution and a much simpler upgrade path for both software and hardware.

- ***Data management technologies and practices.***   Some of the most pressing needs for a next-generation data warehouse platform involve technologies and practices that we generally don't think of as part of the platform. In particular, many users need to update the data management tools that process data for use through data warehousing. The future holds strong growth for master data management (MDM). This relatively new, but extremely important, concept is gaining popularity for many reasons, including the following: (1) Tighter integration with operational systems demands MDM; (2) most data warehouses still lack MDM and data quality functions; and (3) regulatory and financial reports must be perfectly clean and accurate.

- ***In-database processing technology (putting the algorithms where the data is).***   In-database processing (also called *in-database analytics*) refers to the integration of the algorithmic extent of data analytics into data warehouse. By doing so, the data and the analytics that work off the data live within the same environment. Having the two in close proximity increases the efficiency of the computationally intensive analytics procedures. Today, many large database-driven decision support systems, such as those used for credit card fraud detection and investment risk management, use this technology because it provides significant performance improvements over traditional methods in a decision environment where time is of the essence. In-database processing is a complex endeavor compared to the traditional way of conducting analytics, where the data is moved out of the database (often in a flat file format that consists of rows and columns) into a separate analytics environment (such as SAS Enterprise Modeler, Statistica Data Miner, or IBM SPSS Modeler) for processing. In-database processing makes more sense for high-throughput, real-time application environments, including fraud detection, credit scoring, risk management, transaction processing, pricing and margin analysis, usage-based micro-segmenting, behavioral ad targeting, and recommendation engines, such as those used by customer service organizations to determine next-best actions. In-database processing is performed and promoted as a feature by many of the major data warehousing vendors, including Teradata (integrating SAS analytics capabilities into the data warehouse appliances), IBM Netezza, EMC Greenplum, and Sybase, among others.

- ***In-memory storage technology (moving the data in the memory for faster processing).***   Conventional database systems, such as relational database management systems, typically use physical hard drives to store data for an extended period of time. When a data-related process is requested by an application, the database management system loads the data (or parts of the data) into the main memory, processes it, and responds back to the application. Although data (or parts of the data) is temporarily cached in the main memory in a database management system, the primary storage location remains a magnetic hard disk. In contrast, an in-memory database system keeps the data permanently in the main memory. When a data-related process is requested by an application, the database management system directly accesses the data, which is already in the main memory, processes it, and responds back to the requesting application. This direct access to data in main memory makes the processing of data orders much faster than the traditional method. The main benefit of in-memory technology (maybe the only benefit of it) is the incredible speed at which it accesses the data. The disadvantages include cost of paying for a very large main memory (even though it is getting cheaper, it still costs a great deal to have a large enough main memory that can hold all of company's data) and the need for sophisticated data recovery strategies (since main memory is volatile and can be wiped out accidentally).

- **New database management systems.** A data warehouse platform consists of several basic components, of which the most critical is the database management system (DBMS). This is only natural, given the fact that DBMS is the component of the platform where the most work must be done to implement a data model and optimize it for query performance. Therefore, the DBMS is where many next-generation innovations are expected to happen.

- **Advanced analytics.** Users can choose different analytic methods as they move beyond basic OLAP-based methods and into advanced analytics. Some users choose advanced analytic methods based on data mining, predictive analytics, statistics, artificial intelligence, and so on. Still, the majority of users seem to be choosing SQL-based methods. Either SQL-based or not, advanced analytics seem to be among the most important promises of next-generation data warehousing.

The future of data warehousing seems to be full of promises and significant challenges. As the world of business becomes more global and complex, the need for business intelligence and data warehousing tools will also become more prominent. The fast-improving information technology tools and techniques seem to be moving in the right direction to address the needs of future business intelligence systems.

SECTION 3.9 REVIEW QUESTIONS

1. What steps can an organization take to ensure the security and confidentiality of customer data in its data warehouse?
2. What skills should a DWA possess? Why?
3. What recent technologies may shape the future of data warehousing? Why?

3.10 RESOURCES, LINKS, AND THE TERADATA UNIVERSITY NETWORK CONNECTION

The use of this chapter and most other chapters in this book can be enhanced by the tools described in the following sections.

Resources and Links

We recommend looking at the following resources and links for further reading and explanations:

- The Data Warehouse Institute (**tdwi.org**)
- *DM Review* (**information-management.com**)
- DSS Resources (**dssresources.com**)

Cases

All major MSS vendors (e.g., MicroStrategy, Microsoft, Oracle, IBM, Hyperion, Cognos, Exsys, Fair Isaac, SAP, Information Builders) provide interesting customer success stories. Academic-oriented cases are available at the Harvard Business School Case Collection (**harvardbusinessonline.hbsp.harvard.edu**), Business Performance Improvement Resource (**bpir.com**), IGI Global Disseminator of Knowledge (**igi-global.com**), Ivy League Publishing (**ivylp.com**), ICFAI Center for Management Research (**icmr.icfai.org/casestudies/**

icmr_case_studies.htm), KnowledgeStorm (**knowledgestorm.com**), and other sites. For additional case resources, see Teradata University Network (**teradatauniversitynetwork. com**). For data warehousing cases, we specifically recommend the following from the Teradata University Network (**teradatauniversitynetwork.com**): "Continental Airlines Flies High with Real-Time Business Intelligence," "Data Warehouse Governance at Blue Cross and Blue Shield of North Carolina," "3M Moves to a Customer Focus Using a Global Data Warehouse," "Data Warehousing Supports Corporate Strategy at First American Corporation," "Harrah's High Payoff from Customer Information," and "Whirlpool." We also recommend the Data Warehousing Failures Assignment, which consists of eight short cases on data warehousing failures.

Vendors, Products, and Demos

A comprehensive list of vendors, products, and demos is available at *DM Review* (**dmreview.com**). Vendors are listed in Table 3.2. Also see **technologyevaluation.com**.

Periodicals

We recommend the following periodicals:

- *Baseline* (**baselinemag.com**)
- *Business Intelligence Journal* (**tdwi.org**)
- *CIO* (**cio.com**)
- *CIO Insight* (**cioinsight.com**)
- *Computerworld* (**computerworld.com**)
- *Decision Support Systems* (**elsevier.com**)
- *DM Review* (**dmreview.com**)
- *eWeek* (**eweek.com**)
- *InfoWeek* (**infoweek.com**)
- *InfoWorld* (**infoworld.com**)
- *InternetWeek* (**internetweek.com**)
- *Management Information Systems Quarterly* (*MIS Quarterly*; **misq.org**)
- *Technology Evaluation* (**technologyevaluation.com**)
- *Teradata Magazine* (**teradata.com**)

Additional References

For additional information on data warehousing, see the following:

- C. Imhoff, N. Galemmo, and J. G. Geiger. (2003). *Mastering Data Warehouse Design: Relational and Dimensional Techniques.* New York: Wiley.
- D. Marco and M. Jennings. (2004). *Universal Meta Data Models.* New York: Wiley.
- J. Wang. (2005). *Encyclopedia of Data Warehousing and Mining.* Hershey, PA: Idea Group Publishing.

For more on databases, the structure on which data warehouses are developed, see the following:

- R. T. Watson. (2006). *Data Management,* 5th ed., New York: Wiley.

The Teradata University Network (TUN) Connection

TUN (**teradatauniversitynetwork.com**) provides a wealth of information and cases on data warehousing. One of the best is the Continental Airlines case, which we require you to solve in a later exercise. Other recommended cases are mentioned earlier in this chapter. At TUN, if you click the Courses tab and select Data Warehousing, you will see links to many relevant articles, assignments, book chapters, course Web sites, PowerPoint presentations, projects, research reports, syllabi, and Web seminars. You will also find links to active data warehousing software demonstrations. Finally, you will see links to Teradata (**teradata.com**), where you can find additional information, including excellent data warehousing success stories, white papers, Web-based courses, and the online version of *Teradata Magazine*.

Chapter Highlights

- A data warehouse is a specially constructed data repository where data are organized so that they can be easily accessed by end users for several applications.
- Data marts contain data on one topic (e.g., marketing). A data mart can be a replication of a subset of data in the data warehouse. Data marts are a less expensive solution that can be replaced by or can supplement a data warehouse. Data marts can be independent of or dependent on a data warehouse.
- An ODS is a type of customer-information-file database that is often used as a staging area for a data warehouse.
- Data integration comprises three major processes: data access, data federation, and change

capture. When these three processes are correctly implemented, data can be accessed and made accessible to an array of ETL and analysis tools and data warehousing environments.
- ETL technologies pull data from many sources, cleanse them, and load them into a data warehouse. ETL is an integral process in any data-centric project.
- Real-time or active data warehousing supplements and expands traditional data warehousing, moving into the realm of operational and tactical decision making by loading data in real time and providing data to users for active decision making.
- The security and privacy of data and information are critical issues for a data warehouse professional.

Key Terms

active data warehousing (ADW)	dependent data mart	enterprise information integration (EII)	oper mart
cube	dimensional modeling	extraction,	operational data store (ODS)
data integration	dimension table	transformation,	real-time data
data mart	drill down	and load (ETL)	warehousing (RDW)
data warehouse (DW)	enterprise application integration (EAI)	independent data mart	snowflake schema
data warehouse administrator (DWA)	enterprise data warehouse (EDW)	metadata OLTP	star schema

Questions for Discussion

1. Compare data integration and ETL. How are they related?
2. What is a data warehouse, and what are its benefits? Why is Web accessibility important with a data warehouse?
3. A data mart can replace a data warehouse or complement it. Compare and discuss these options.
4. Discuss the major drivers and benefits of data warehousing to end users.
5. List the differences and/or similarities between the roles of a database administrator and a data warehouse administrator.

6. Describe how data integration can lead to higher levels of data quality.
7. Compare the Kimball and Inmon approaches toward data warehouse development. Identify when each one is most effective.
8. Discuss security concerns involved in building a data warehouse.

9. Investigate current data warehouse development implementation through offshoring. Write a report about it. In class, debate the issue in terms of the benefits and costs, as well as social factors.

Exercises

Teradata University and Other Hands-On Exercises

1. Consider the case describing the development and application of a data warehouse for Coca-Cola Japan (a summary appears in Application Case 3.4), available at the DSS Resources Web site, **http://dssresources.com/cases/coca-colajapan/**. Read the case and answer the nine questions for further analysis and discussion.
2. Read the Ball (2005) article and rank-order the criteria (ideally for a real organization). In a report, explain how important each criterion is and why.
3. Explain when you should implement a two- or three-tiered architecture when considering developing a data warehouse.
4. Read the full Continental Airlines case (summarized in the End-of-Chapter Application Case) at **teradatauniversitynetwork.com** and answer the questions.
5. At **teradatauniversitynetwork.com**, read and answer the questions to the case "Harrah's High Payoff from Customer Information." Relate Harrah's results to how airlines and other casinos use their customer data.
6. At **teradatauniversitynetwork.com**, read and answer the questions of the assignment "Data Warehousing Failures." Because eight cases are described in that assignment, the class may be divided into eight groups, with one case assigned per group. In addition, read Ariyachandra and Watson (2006a), and for each case identify how the failure occurred as related to not focusing on one or more of the reference's success factor(s).
7. At **teradatauniversitynetwork.com**, read and answer the questions with the assignment "Ad-Vent Technology: Using the MicroStrategy Sales Analytic Model." The MicroStrategy software is accessible from the TUN site. Also, you might want to use Barbara Wixom's PowerPoint presentation about the MicroStrategy software ("Demo Slides for MicroStrategy Tutorial Script"), which is also available at the TUN site.
8. At **teradatauniversitynetwork.com**, watch the Web seminars titled "Real-Time Data Warehousing: The Next Generation of Decision Support Data Management" and "Building the Real-Time Enterprise." Read the article "Teradata's Real-Time Enterprise Reference Architecture: A Blueprint for the Future of IT," also available at this site. Describe how real-time concepts and technologies work and how they can be used to extend existing data warehousing and BI architectures to support day-to-day decision making. Write a report indicating how real-time data warehousing is specifically providing competitive advantage for organizations. Describe in detail the difficulties in such implementations and operations and describe how they are being addressed in practice.

9. At **teradatauniversitynetwork.com**, watch the Web seminars "Data Integration Renaissance: New Drivers and Emerging Approaches," "In Search of a Single Version of the Truth: Strategies for Consolidating Analytic Silos," and "Data Integration: Using ETL, EAI, and EII Tools to Create an Integrated Enterprise." Also read the "Data Integration" research report. Compare and contrast the presentations. What is the most important issue described in these seminars? What is the best way to handle the strategies and challenges of consolidating data marts and spreadsheets into a unified data warehousing architecture? Perform a Web search to identify the latest developments in the field. Compare the presentation to the material in the text and the new material that you found.
10. Consider the future of data warehousing. Perform a Web search on this topic. Also, read these two articles: L. Agosta, "Data Warehousing in a Flat World: Trends for 2006," *DM Direct Newsletter,* March 31, 2006; and J. G. Geiger, "CIFe: Evolving with the Times," *DM Review,* November 2005, pp. 38–41. Compare and contrast your findings.
11. Access **teradatauniversitynetwork.com**. Identify the latest articles, research reports, and cases on data warehousing. Describe recent developments in the field. Include in your report how data warehousing is used in BI and DSS.

Team Assignments and Role-Playing Projects

1. Kathryn Avery has been a DBA with a nationwide retail chain (Big Chain) for the past 6 years. She has recently been asked to lead the development of Big Chain's first data warehouse. The project has the sponsorship of senior management and the CIO. The rationale for developing the data warehouse is to advance the reporting systems, particularly in sales and marketing, and, in the longer term, to improve Big Chain's CRM. Kathryn has been to a Data Warehousing Institute conference and has been doing some reading, but she is still mystified

about development methodologies. She knows there are two groups—EDW (Inmon) and architected data marts (Kimball)—that have robust features.

Initially, she believed that the two methodologies were extremely dissimilar, but as she has examined them more carefully, she isn't so certain. Kathryn has a number of questions that she would like answered:

a. What are the real differences between the methodologies?

b. What factors are important in selecting a particular methodology?

c. What should be her next steps in thinking about a methodology?

Help Kathryn answer these questions. (This exercise was adapted from K. Duncan, L. Reeves, and J. Griffin, "BI Experts' Perspective," *Business Intelligence Journal,* Vol. 8, No. 4, Fall 2003, pp. 14–19.)

2. Jeet Kumar is the administrator of data warehousing at a big regional bank. He was appointed 5 years ago to implement a data warehouse to support the bank's CRM business strategy. Using the data warehouse, the bank has been successful in integrating customer information, understanding customer profitability, attracting customers, enhancing customer relationships, and retaining customers.

Over the years, the bank's data warehouse has moved closer to real time by moving to more frequent refreshes of the data warehouse. Now, the bank wants to implement customer self-service and call center applications that require even fresher data than is currently available in the warehouse.

Jeet wants some support in considering the possibilities for presenting fresher data. One alternative is to entirely commit to implementing real-time data warehousing. His ETL vendor is prepared to assist him make this change. Nevertheless, Jeet has been informed about EAI and EII technologies and wonders how they might fit into his plans.

In particular, he has the following questions:

a. What exactly are EAI and EII technologies?

b. How are EAI and EII related to ETL?

c. How are EAI and EII related to real-time data warehousing?

d. Are EAI and EII required, complementary, or alternatives to real-time data warehousing?

Help Jeet answer these questions. (This exercise was adapted from S. Brobst, E. Levy, and C. Muzilla, "Enterprise Application Integration and Enterprise Information Integration," *Business Intelligence Journal,* Vol. 10, No. 2, Spring 2005, pp. 27–33.)

3. Interview administrators in your college or executives in your organization to determine how data warehousing could assist them in their work. Write a proposal describing your findings. Include cost estimates and benefits in your report.

4. Go through the list of data warehousing risks described in this chapter and find two examples of each in practice.

5. Access **teradata.com** and read the white papers "Measuring Data Warehouse ROI" and "Realizing ROI: Projecting and Harvesting the Business Value of an Enterprise Data Warehouse." Also, watch the Web-based course "The ROI Factor: How Leading Practitioners Deal with the Tough Issue of Measuring DW ROI." Describe the most important issues described in them. Compare these issues to the success factors described in Ariyachandra and Watson (2006a).

6. Read the article by K. Liddell Avery and Hugh J. Watson, "Training Data Warehouse End Users," *Business Intelligence Journal,* Vol. 9, No. 4, Fall 2004, pp. 40–51 (which is available at **teradatauniversitynetwork.com**). Consider the different classes of end users, describe their difficulties, and discuss the benefits of appropriate training for each group. Have each member of the group take on one of the roles and have a discussion about how an appropriate type of data warehousing training would be good for each of you.

Internet Exercises

1. Search the Internet to find information about data warehousing. Identify some newsgroups that have an interest in this concept. Explore ABI/INFORM in your library, e-library, and Google for recent articles on the topic. Begin with **tdwi.org, technologyevaluation.com**, and the major vendors: **teradata.com, sas.com, oracle.com**, and **ncr.com**. Also check **cio.com, information-management.com, dssresources.com**, and **db2mag.com**.

2. Survey some ETL tools and vendors. Start with **fairisaac.com** and **egain.com**. Also consult **information-management.com**.

3. Contact some data warehouse vendors and obtain information about their products. Give special attention to vendors that provide tools for multiple purposes, such as Cognos, Software A&G, SAS Institute, and Oracle. Free online demos are available from some of these vendors. Download a demo or two and try them. Write a report describing your experience.

4. Explore **teradata.com** for developments and success stories about data warehousing. Write a report about what you have discovered.

5. Explore **teradata.com** for white papers and Web-based courses on data warehousing. Read the former and watch the latter. (Divide the class so that all the sources are covered.) Write what you have discovered in a report.

6. Find recent cases of successful data warehousing applications. Go to data warehouse vendors' sites and look for cases or success stories. Select one and write a brief summary to present to your class.

End-of-Chapter Application Case

Continental Airlines Flies High with Its Real-Time Data Warehouse

As business intelligence (BI) becomes a critical component of daily operations, real-time data warehouses that provide end users with rapid updates and alerts generated from transactional systems are increasingly being deployed. Real-time data warehousing and BI, supporting its aggressive Go Forward business plan, have helped Continental Airlines alter its industry status from "worst to first" and then from "first to favorite." Continental airlines (now a part of United Airlines) is a leader in real-time DW and BI. In 2004, Continental won the Data Warehousing Institute's Best Practices and Leadership Award. Even though it has been a while since Continental Airlines deployed its hugely successful real-time DW and BI infrastructure, it is still regarded as one of the best examples and a seminal success story for real-time active data warehousing.

Problem(s)

Continental Airlines was founded in 1934, with a single-engine Lockheed aircraft in the Southwestern United States. As of 2006, Continental was the fifth largest airline in the United States and the seventh largest in the world. Continental had the broadest global route network of any U.S. airline, with more than 2,300 daily departures to more than 227 destinations.

Back in 1994, Continental was in deep financial trouble. It had filed for Chapter 11 bankruptcy protection twice and was heading for its third, and probably final, bankruptcy. Ticket sales were hurting because performance on factors that are important to customers was dismal, including a low percentage of on-time departures, frequent baggage arrival problems, and too many customers turned away due to overbooking.

Solution

The revival of Continental began in 1994, when Gordon Bethune became CEO and initiated the Go Forward plan, which consisted of four interrelated parts to be implemented simultaneously. Bethune targeted the need to improve customer-valued performance measures by better understanding customer needs as well as customer perceptions of the value of services that were and could be offered. Financial management practices were also targeted for a significant overhaul. As early as 1998, the airline had separate databases for marketing and operations, all hosted and managed by outside vendors. Processing queries and instigating marketing programs to its high-value customers were time-consuming and ineffective. In additional, information that the workforce needed to make quick decisions was simply not available. In 1999, Continental chose to integrate its marketing, IT, revenue, and operational data sources into a single, in-house, EDW. The data warehouse provided a variety of early, major benefits.

As soon as Continental returned to profitability and ranked first in the airline industry in many performance metrics, Bethune and his management team raised the bar by escalating the vision. Instead of just performing best, they wanted Continental to be their customers' favorite airline. The Go Forward plan established more actionable ways to move from first to favorite among customers. Technology became increasingly critical for supporting these new initiatives. In the early days, having access to historical, integrated information was sufficient. This produced substantial strategic value. But it became increasingly imperative for the data warehouse to provide real-time, actionable information to support enterprise-wide tactical decision making and business processes.

Luckily, the warehouse team had expected and arranged for the real-time shift. From the very beginning, the team had created an architecture to handle real-time data feeds into the warehouse, extracts of data from legacy systems into the warehouse, and tactical queries to the warehouse that required almost immediate response times. In 2001, real-time data became available from the warehouse, and the amount stored grew rapidly. Continental moves real-time data (ranging from to-the-minute to hourly) about customers, reservations, check-ins, operations, and flights from its main operational systems to the warehouse. Continental's real-time applications include the following:

- Revenue management and accounting
- Customer relationship management (CRM)
- Crew operations and payroll
- Security and fraud
- Flight operations

Results

In the first year alone, after the data warehouse project was deployed, Continental identified and eliminated over $7 million in fraud and reduced costs by $41 million. With a $30 million investment in hardware and software over 6 years, Continental has reached over $500 million in increased revenues and cost savings in marketing, fraud detection, demand forecasting and tracking, and improved data center management. The single, integrated, trusted view of the business (i.e., the single version of the truth) has led to better, faster decision making.

Because of its tremendous success, Continental's DW implementation has been recognized as an excellent example for real-time BI, based on its scalable and extensible architecture, practical decisions on what data are captured in real time, strong relationships with end users, a small and highly competent data warehouse staff, sensible weighing of strategic and tactical decision support requirements, understanding of the synergies between decision support and operations, and changed business processes that use real-time data.

QUESTIONS FOR THE END-OF-CHAPTER APPLICATION CASE

1. Describe the benefits of implementing the Continental Go Forward strategy.
2. Explain why it is important for an airline to use a real-time data warehouse.

3. Identify the major differences between the traditional data warehouse and a real-time data warehouse, as was implemented at Continental.

4. What strategic advantage can Continental derive from the real-time system as opposed to a traditional information system?

Sources: Adapted from H. Wixom, J. Hoffer, R. Anderson-Lehman, and A. Reynolds, "Real-Time Business Intelligence: Best Practices at Continental Airlines," *Information Systems Management Journal,* Winter 2006, pp. 7–18; R. Anderson-Lehman, H. Watson, B. Wixom, and J. Hoffer, "Continental Airlines Flies High with Real-Time Business Intelligence," *MIS Quarterly Executive,* Vol. 3, No. 4, December 2004, pp. 163–176 (available at **teradatauniversitynetwork.com**); H. Watson, "Real Time: The Next Generation of Decision-Support Data Management," *Business Intelligence Journal,* Vol. 10, No. 3, 2005, pp. 4–6; M. Edwards, "2003 Best Practices Awards Winners: Innovators in Business Intelligence and Data Warehousing," *Business Intelligence Journal,* Fall 2003, pp. 57–64; R. Westervelt, "Continental Airlines Builds Real-Time Data Warehouse," August 20, 2003, **searchoracle.techtarget.com**; R. Clayton, "Enterprise Business Performance Management: Business Intelligence + Data Warehouse = Optimal Business Performance," *Teradata Magazine,* September 2005, and The Data Warehousing Institute, "2003 Best Practices Summaries: Enterprise Data Warehouse," 2003.

References

Adamson, C. (2009). *The Star Schema Handbook: The Complete Reference to Dimensional Data Warehouse Design.* Hoboken, NJ: Wiley.

Adelman, S., and L. Moss. (2001, Winter). "Data Warehouse Risks." *Journal of Data Warehousing,* Vol. 6, No. 1.

Agosta, L. (2006, January). "The Data Strategy Adviser: The Year Ahead—Data Warehousing Trends 2006." *DM Review,* Vol. 16, No. 1.

Akbay, S. (2006, Quarter 1). "Data Warehousing in Real Time." *Business Intelligence Journal,* Vol. 11, No. 1.

Ambeo. (2005, July). "Ambeo Delivers Proven Data Access Auditing Solution." *Database Trends and Applications,* Vol. 19, No. 7.

Anthes, G. H. (2003, June 30). "Hilton Checks into New Suite." *Computerworld,* Vol. 37, No. 26.

Ariyachandra, T., and H. Watson. (2005). "Key Factors in Selecting a Data Warehouse Architecture." *Business Intelligence Journal,* Vol. 10, No. 3.

Ariyachandra, T., and H. Watson. (2006a, January). "Benchmarks for BI and Data Warehousing Success." *DM Review,* Vol. 16, No. 1.

Ariyachandra, T., and H. Watson. (2006b). "Which Data Warehouse Architecture Is Most Successful?" *Business Intelligence Journal,* Vol. 11, No. 1.

Armstrong, R. (2000, Quarter 3). "E-nalysis for the E-business." *Teradata Magazine Online,* **teradata.com**.

Ball, S. K. (2005, November 14). "Do You Need a Data Warehouse Layer in Your Business Intelligence Architecture?" **datawarehouse.ittoolbox.com/documents/industry-articles/do-you-need-a-data-warehouse-layer-in-your-business-intelligencearchitecture-2729** (accessed June 2009).

Barquin, R., A. Paller, and H. Edelstein. (1997). "Ten Mistakes to Avoid for Data Warehousing Managers." In R. Barquin and H. Edelstein (eds.). *Building, Using, and Managing the Data Warehouse.* Upper Saddle River, NJ: Prentice Hall.

Basu, R. (2003, November). "Challenges of Real-Time Data Warehousing." *DM Review.*

Bell, L. D. (2001, Spring). "MetaBusiness Meta Data for the Masses: Administering Knowledge Sharing for Your Data Warehouse." *Journal of Data Warehousing,* Vol. 6, No. 3.

Benander, A., B. Benander, A. Fadlalla, and G. James. (2000, Winter). "Data Warehouse Administration and Management." *Information Systems Management,* Vol. 17, No. 1.

Bonde, A., and M. Kuckuk. (2004, April). "Real World Business Intelligence: The Implementation Perspective." *DM Review,* Vol. 14, No. 4.

Breslin, M. (2004, Winter). "Data Warehousing Battle of the Giants: Comparing the Basics of Kimball and Inmon Models." *Business Intelligence Journal,* Vol. 9, No. 1.

Brobst, S., E. Levy, and C. Muzilla. (2005, Spring). "Enterprise Application Integration and Enterprise Information Integration." *Business Intelligence Journal,* Vol. 10, No. 3.

Brody, R. (2003, Summer). "Information Ethics in the Design and Use of Metadata." *IEEE Technology and Society Magazine,* Vol. 22, No. 3.

Brown, M. (2004, May 9–12). "8 Characteristics of a Successful Data Warehouse." *Proceedings of the Twenty-Ninth Annual SAS Users Group International Conference* (SUGI 29). Montreal, Canada.

Burdett, J., and S. Singh. (2004). "Challenges and Lessons Learned from Real-Time Data Warehousing." *Business Intelligence Journal,* Vol. 9, No. 4.

Coffee, P. (2003, June 23). "'Active' Warehousing." *eWeek,* Vol. 20, No. 25.

Cooper, B. L., H. J. Watson, B. H. Wixom, and D. L. Goodhue. (1999, August 15–19). "Data Warehousing Supports Corporate Strategy at First American Corporation." SIM International Conference, Atlanta.

Cooper, B. L., H. J. Watson, B. H. Wixom, and D. L. Goodhue. (2000). "Data Warehousing Supports Corporate Strategy at First American Corporation." *MIS Quarterly,* Vol. 24, No. 4, pp. 547–567.

Dasu, T., and T. Johnson. (2003). *Exploratory Data Mining and Data Cleaning.* New York: Wiley.

Davison, D. (2003, November 14). "Top 10 Risks of Offshore Outsourcing." META Group Research Report, now Gartner, Inc., Stamford, CT.

Devlin, B. (2003, Quarter 2). "Solving the Data Warehouse Puzzle." *DB2 Magazine.*

Dragoon, A. (2003, July 1). "All for One View." *CIO.*

Eckerson, W. (2003, Fall). "The Evolution of ETL." *Business Intelligence Journal,* Vol. 8, No. 4.

Eckerson, W. (2005, April 1). "Data Warehouse Builders Advocate for Different Architectures." *Application Development Trends.*

Eckerson, W., R. Hackathorn, M. McGivern, C. Twogood, and G. Watson. (2009). "Data Warehousing Appliances." *Business Intelligence Journal,* Vol. 14, No. 1, pp. 40–48.

Edwards, M. (2003, Fall). "2003 Best Practices Awards Winners: Innovators in Business Intelligence and Data Warehousing." *Business Intelligence Journal,* Vol. 8, No. 4.

"Egg's Customer Data Warehouse Hits the Mark." (2005, October). *DM Review,* Vol. 15, No. 10, pp. 24–28.

Elson, R., and R. LeClerc. (2005). "Security and Privacy Concerns in the Data Warehouse Environment." *Business Intelligence Journal,* Vol. 10, No. 3.

Ericson, J. (2006, March). "Real-Time Realities." *BI Review.*

Furtado, P. (2009). "A Survey of Parallel and Distributed Data Warehouses." *International Journal of Data Warehousing and Mining,* Vol. 5, No. 2, pp. 57–78.

Golfarelli, M., and Rizzi, S. (2009). *Data Warehouse Design: Modern Principles and Methodologies.* San Francisco: McGraw-Hill Osborne Media.

Gonzales, M. (2005, Quarter 1). "Active Data Warehouses Are Just One Approach for Combining Strategic and Technical Data." *DB2 Magazine.*

Hall, M. (2002, April 15). "Seeding for Data Growth." *Computerworld,* Vol. 36, No. 16.

Hammergren, T. C., and A. R. Simon. (2009). *Data Warehousing for Dummies,* 2nd ed. Hoboken, NJ: Wiley.

Hicks, M. (2001, November 26). "Getting Pricing Just Right." *eWeek,* Vol. 18, No. 46.

Hoffer, J. A., M. B. Prescott, and F. R. McFadden. (2007). *Modern Database Management,* 8th ed. Upper Saddle River, NJ: Prentice Hall.

Hwang, M., and H. Xu. (2005, Fall). "A Survey of Data Warehousing Success Issues." *Business Intelligence Journal,* Vol. 10, No. 4.

IBM. (2009). *50 Tb Data Warehouse Benchmark on IBM System Z.* Armonk, NY: IBM Redbooks.

Imhoff, C. (2001, May). "Power Up Your Enterprise Portal." *E-Business Advice.*

Inmon, W. H. (2005). *Building the Data Warehouse,* 4th ed. New York: Wiley.

Inmon, W. H. (2006, January). "Information Management: How Do You Tune a Data Warehouse?" *DM Review,* Vol. 16, No. 1.

Jukic, N., and C. Lang. (2004, Summer). "Using Offshore Resources to Develop and Support Data Warehousing Applications." *Business Intelligence Journal,* Vol. 9, No. 3.

Kalido. "BP Lubricants Achieves BIGS Success." **kalido.com/ collateral/Documents/English-US/CS-BP%20BIGS. pdf** (accessed August 2009).

Karacsony, K. (2006, January). "ETL Is a Symptom of the Problem, not the Solution." *DM Review,* Vol. 16, No. 1.

Kassam, S. (2002, April 16). "Freedom of Information." *Intelligent Enterprise,* Vol. 5, No. 7.

Kay, R. (2005, September 19). "EII." *Computerworld,* Vol. 39, No. 38.

Kelly, C. (2001, June 14). "Calculating Data Warehousing ROI." **SearchSQLServer.com** *Tips.*

Malykhina, E. (2003, January 3). "The Real-Time Imperative." *InformationWeek,* Issue 1020.

Manglik, A., and V. Mehra. (2005, Winter). "Extending Enterprise BI Capabilities: New Patterns for Data Integration." *Business Intelligence Journal,* Vol. 10, No. 1.

Martins, C. (2005, December 13). "HP to Consolidate Data Marts into Single Warehouse." *Computerworld.*

Matney, D. (2003, Spring). "End-User Support Strategy." *Business Intelligence Journal,* Vol. 8, No. 3.

McCloskey, D. W. (2002). *Choosing Vendors and Products to Maximize Data Warehousing Success.* New York: Auerbach Publications.

Mehra, V. (2005, Summer). "Building a Metadata-Driven Enterprise: A Holistic Approach." *Business Intelligence Journal,* Vol. 10, No. 3.

Moseley, M. (2009). "Eliminating Data Warehouse Pressures with Master Data Services and SOA." *Business Intelligence Journal,* Vol. 14, No. 2, pp. 33–43.

Murtaza, A. (1998, Fall). "A Framework for Developing Enterprise Data Warehouses." *Information Systems Management,* Vol. 15, No. 4.

Nash, K. S. (2002, July). "Chemical Reaction." *Baseline.*

Orovic, V. (2003, June). "To Do & Not to Do." *eAI Journal.*

Parzinger, M. J., and M. N. Frolick. (2001, July). "Creating Competitive Advantage Through Data Warehousing." *Information Strategy,* Vol. 17, No. 4.

Peterson, T. (2003, April 21). "Getting Real About Real Time." *Computerworld,* Vol. 37, No. 16.

Raden, N. (2003, June 30). "Real Time: Get Real, Part II." *Intelligent Enterprise.*

Reeves, L. (2009). *Manager's Guide to Data Warehousing.* Hoboken, NJ: Wiley.

Romero, O., and A. Abelló. (2009). "A Survey of Multidimensional Modeling Methodologies." *International Journal of Data Warehousing and Mining,* Vol. 5, No. 2, pp. 1–24.

Rosenberg, A. (2006, Quarter 1). "Improving Query Performance in Data Warehouses." *Business Intelligence Journal,* Vol. 11, No. 1.

Russom, P. (2009). Next Generation Data Warehouse Platforms. TDWI Best Practices Report, available at **www. tdwi.org** (accessed January 2010).

Sammon, D., and P. Finnegan. (2000, Fall). "The Ten Commandments of Data Warehousing." *Database for Advances in Information Systems,* Vol. 31, No. 4.

Sapir, D. (2005, May). "Data Integration: A Tutorial." *DM Review,* Vol. 15, No. 5.

Saunders, T. (2009). "Cooking up a Data Warehouse." *Business Intelligence Journal,* Vol. 14, No. 2, pp. 16–23.

Schwartz, K. D. "Decisions at the Touch of a Button." *Teradata Magazine,* (accessed June 2009).

Schwartz, K. D. (2004, March). "Decisions at the Touch of a Button." *DSS Resources,* pp. 28–31. **dssresources.com/ cases/coca-colajapan/index.html** (accessed April 2006).

Sen, A. (2004, April). "Metadata Management: Past, Present and Future." *Decision Support Systems,* Vol. 37, No. 1.

Sen, A., and P. Sinha. (2005). "A Comparison of Data Warehousing Methodologies." *Communications of the ACM,* Vol. 48, No. 3.

Solomon, M. (2005, Winter). "Ensuring a Successful Data Warehouse Initiative." *Information Systems Management Journal.*

Songini, M. L. (2004, February 2). "ETL Quickstudy." *Computerworld,* Vol. 38, No. 5.

Sun Microsystems. (2005, September 19). "Egg Banks on Sun to Hit the Mark with Customers." **sun.com/smi/ Press/sunflash/2005-09/sunflash.20050919.1.xml** (accessed April 2006; no longer available online).

Tannenbaum, A. (2002, Spring). "Identifying Meta Data Requirements." *Journal of Data Warehousing,* Vol. 7, No. 3.

Tennant, R. (2002, May 15). "The Importance of Being Granular." *Library Journal,* Vol. 127, No. 9.

Teradata Corp. "A Large US-Based Insurance Company Masters Its Finance Data." (accessed July 2009).

Teradata Corp. "Active Data Warehousing." **teradata.com/ active-data-warehousing/** (accessed April 2006).

Teradata Corp. "Coca-Cola Japan Puts the Fizz Back in Vending Machine Sales." (accessed June 2009).

Teradata. "Enterprise Data Warehouse Delivers Cost Savings and Process Efficiencies." **teradata.com/t/resources/case-studies/NCR-Corporation-eb4455** (accessed June 2009).

Terr, S. (2004, February). "Real-Time Data Warehousing: Hardware and Software." *DM Review,* Vol. 14, No. 3.

Thornton, M. (2002, March 18). "What About Security? The Most Common, but Unwarranted, Objection to Hosted Data Warehouses." *DM Review,* Vol. 12, No. 3, pp. 30–43.

Thornton, M., and M. Lampa. (2002). "Hosted Data Warehouse." *Journal of Data Warehousing,* Vol. 7, No. 2, pp. 27–34.

Turban, E., D. Leidner, E. McLean, and J. Wetherbe. (2006). *Information Technology for Management,* 5th ed. New York: Wiley.

Vaduva, A., and T. Vetterli. (2001, September). "Metadata Management for Data Warehousing: An Overview." *International Journal of Cooperative Information Systems,* Vol. 10, No. 3.

Van den Hoven, J. (1998). "Data Marts: Plan Big, Build Small." *Information Systems Management,* Vol. 15, No. 1.

Watson, H. J. (2002). "Recent Developments in Data Warehousing." *Communications of the ACM,* Vol. 8, No. 1.

Watson, H. J., D. L. Goodhue, and B. H. Wixom. (2002). "The Benefits of Data Warehousing: Why Some Organizations Realize Exceptional Payoffs." *Information & Management,* Vol. 39.

Watson, H., J. Gerard, L. Gonzalez, M. Haywood, and D. Fenton. (1999). "Data Warehouse Failures: Case Studies and Findings." *Journal of Data Warehousing,* Vol. 4, No. 1.

Weir, R. (2002, Winter). "Best Practices for Implementing a Data Warehouse." *Journal of Data Warehousing,* Vol. 7, No. 1.

Wilk, L. (2003, Spring). "Data Warehousing and Real-Time Computing." *Business Intelligence Journal,* Vol. 8, No. 3.

Wixom, B., and H. Watson. (2001, March). "An Empirical Investigation of the Factors Affecting Data Warehousing Success." *MIS Quarterly,* Vol. 25, No. 1.

Wrembel, R. (2009). "A Survey of Managing the Evolution of Data Warehouses." *International Journal of Data Warehousing and Mining,* Vol. 5, No. 2, pp. 24–56.

ZD Net UK. "Sun Case Study: Egg's Customer Data Warehouse." **whitepapers.zdnet.co.uk/0,39025945,60159401p-39000449q,00.htm** (accessed June 2009).

Zhao, X. (2005, October 7). "Meta Data Management Maturity Model." *DM Direct Newsletter.*

Business Reporting, Visual Analytics, and Business Performance Management

LEARNING OBJECTIVES

- Define business reporting and understand its historical evolution
- Recognize the need for and the power of business reporting
- Understand the importance of data/ information visualization
- Learn different types of visualization techniques
- Appreciate the value that visual analytics brings to BI/BA
- Know the capabilities and limitations of dashboards
- Understand the nature of business performance management (BPM)
- Learn the closed-loop BPM methodology
- Describe the basic elements of the balanced scorecard

A report is a communication artifact prepared with the specific intention of relaying information in a presentable form. If it concerns business matters, then it is called a **business report**. Business reporting is an essential part of the business intelligence movement toward improving managerial decision making. Nowadays, these reports are more visually oriented, often using colors and graphical icons that collectively look like a dashboard to enhance the information content. Business reporting and business performance management (BPM) are both enablers of business intelligence and analytics. As a decision support tool, BPM is more than just a reporting technology. It is an integrated set of processes, methodologies, metrics, and applications designed to drive the overall financial and operational performance of an enterprise. It helps enterprises translate their strategies and objectives into plans, monitor performance against those plans, analyze variations between actual results and planned results, and adjust their objectives and actions in response to this analysis.

This chapter starts with examining the need for and the power of business reporting. With the emergence of analytics, business reporting evolved into dashboards and visual analytics, which, compared to traditional descriptive reporting, is much more predictive and prescriptive. Coverage of dashboards and visual analytics is followed by a comprehensive introduction to BPM. As you will see and appreciate, BPM and visual analytics have a symbiotic relationship (over scorecards and dashboards) where they benefit from each other's strengths.

4.1   OPENING VIGNETTE: Self-Service Reporting Environment Saves Millions for Corporate Customers

Headquartered in Omaha, Nebraska, Travel and Transport, Inc., is the sixth largest travel management company in the United States, with more than 700 employee-owners located nationwide. The company has extensive experience in multiple verticals, including travel management, loyalty solutions programs, meeting and incentive planning, and leisure travel services.

CHALLENGE

In the field of employee travel services, the ability to effectively communicate a value proposition to existing and potential customers is critical to winning and retaining business. With travel arrangements often made on an ad hoc basis, customers find it difficult to analyze costs or instate optimal purchase agreements. Travel and Transport wanted to overcome these challenges by implementing an integrated reporting and analysis system to enhance relationships with existing clients, while providing the kind of value-added services that would attract new prospects.

SOLUTION

Travel and Transport implemented Information Builders' WebFOCUS business intelligence (BI) platform (called eTTek Review) as the foundation of a dynamic customer self-service BI environment. This dashboard-driven expense-management application helps more than 800 external clients like Robert W. Baird & Co., MetLife, and American Family Insurance to plan, track, analyze, and budget their travel expenses more efficiently and to benchmark them against similar companies, saving them millions of dollars. More than 200 internal employees, including customer service specialists, also have access to the system, using it to generate more precise forecasts for clients and to streamline and accelerate other key support processes such as quarterly reviews.

Thanks to WebFOCUS, Travel and Transport doesn't just tell its clients how much they are saving by using its services—it shows them. This has helped the company to differentiate itself in a market defined by aggressive competition. Additionally, WebFOCUS eliminates manual report compilation for client service specialists, saving the company close to $200,000 in lost time each year.

AN INTUITIVE, GRAPHICAL WAY TO MANAGE TRAVEL DATA

Using stunning graphics created with WebFOCUS and Adobe Flex, the business intelligence system provides access to thousands of reports that show individual client metrics, benchmarked information against aggregated market data, and even ad hoc reports that users can specify as needed. "For most of our corporate customers, we thoroughly manage their travel from planning and reservations to billing, fulfillment, and ongoing analysis," says Mike Kubasik, senior vice president and CIO at Travel and Transport. "WebFOCUS is important to our business. It helps our customers monitor employee spending, book travel with preferred vendors, and negotiate corporate purchasing agreements that can save them millions of dollars per year."

Clients love it, and it's giving Travel and Transport a competitive edge in a crowded marketplace. "I use Travel and Transport's eTTek Review to automatically e-mail reports throughout the company for a variety of reasons, such as monitoring travel trends and company expenditures and assisting with airline expense reconciliation and allocations," says Cathy Moulton, vice president and travel manager at Robert W. Baird & Co., a prominent financial services company. What she loves about the WebFOCUS-enabled Web portal is that it makes all of the company's travel information available in just a few clicks. "I have the data at my fingertips," she adds. "I don't have to wait for someone to go in and do it for me. I can set up the reports on my own. Then we can go to the hotels and preferred vendors armed with detailed information that gives us leverage to negotiate our rates."

Robert W. Baird & Co. isn't the only firm benefiting from this advanced access to reporting. Many of Travel and Transport's other clients are also happy with the technology. "With Travel and Transport's state-of-the-art reporting technology, MetLife is able to measure its travel program through data analysis, standard reporting, and the ability to create ad hoc reports dynamically," says Tom Molesky, director of travel services at MetLife. "Metrics derived from actionable data provide direction and drive us toward our goals. This is key to helping us negotiate with our suppliers, enforce our travel policy, and save our company money. Travel and Transport's leading-edge product has helped us to meet and, in some cases, exceed our travel goals."

READY FOR TAKEOFF

Travel and Transport used WebFOCUS to create an online system that allows clients to access information directly, so they won't have to rely on the IT department to run reports for them. Its objective was to give customers online tools to monitor corporate travel expenditures throughout their companies. By giving clients access to the right data, Travel and Transport can help make sure its customers are getting the best pricing from airlines, hotels, car rental companies, and other vendors. "We needed more than just pretty reports," Kubasik recalls, looking back on the early phases of the BI project. "We wanted to build a reporting environment that was powerful enough to handle transaction-intensive operations, yet simple enough to deploy over the Web." It was a winning formula. Clients and customer service specialists continue to use eTTek Review to create forecasts for the coming year and to target specific areas of business travel expenditures. These users can choose from dozens of management reports. Popular reports include travel summary, airline compliance, hotel analysis, and car analysis.

Travel managers at about 700 corporations use these reports to analyze corporate travel spending on a daily, weekly, monthly, quarterly, and annual basis. About 160 standard reports and more than 3,000 custom reports are currently set up in eTTek Review, including everything from noncompliance reports that reveal why an employee did not obtain the lowest airfare for a particular flight to executive overviews that summarize spending patterns. Most reports are parameter driven with Information Builders' unique guided ad hoc reporting technology.

PEER REVIEW SYSTEM KEEPS EXPENSES ON TRACK

Users can also run reports that compare their own travel metrics with aggregated travel data from other Travel and Transport clients. This benchmarking service lets them gauge whether their expenditures, preferred rates, and other metrics are in line with those of other companies of a similar size or within the same industry. By pooling the data, Travel and Transport helps protect individual clients' information while also enabling its entire customer base to achieve lower rates by giving them leverage for their negotiations.

Reports can be run interactively or in batch mode, with results displayed on the screen, stored in a library, saved to a PDF file, loaded into an Excel spreadsheet, or sent as an Active Report that permits additional analysis. "Our clients love the visual metaphors provided by Information Builders' graphical displays, including Adobe Flex and WebFOCUS Active PDF files," explains Steve Cords, IT manager at Travel and Transport and team leader for the eTTek Review project. "Most summary reports have drill-down capability to a detailed report. All reports can be run for a particular hierarchy structure, and more than one hierarchy can be selected."

Of course, users never see the code that makes all of this possible. They operate in an intuitive dashboard environment with drop-down menus and drillable graphs, all accessible through a browser-based interface that requires no client-side software. This architecture makes it easy and cost-effective for users to tap into eTTek Review from any location. Collectively, customers run an estimated 50,000 reports per month. About 20,000 of those reports are automatically generated and distributed via WebFOCUS ReportCaster.

AN EFFICIENT ARCHITECTURE THAT YIELDS SOARING RESULTS

Travel and Transport captures travel information from reservation systems known as Global Distribution Systems (GDS) via a proprietary back-office system that resides in a DB2 database on an IBM iSeries computer. They use SQL tables to store user IDs and passwords, and use other databases to store the information. "The database can be sorted according to a specific hierarchy to match the breakdown of reports required by each company," continues Cords. "If they want to see just marketing and accounting information, we can deliver it. If they want to see the particular level of detail reflecting a given cost center, we can deliver that, too."

Because all data is securely stored for three years, clients can generate trend reports to compare current travel to previous years. They can also use the BI system to monitor where employees are traveling at any point in time. The reports are so easy to use that Cords and his team have started replacing outdated processes with new automated ones using the same WebFOCUS technology. The company also uses WebFOCUS to streamline their quarterly review process. In the past, client service managers had to manually create these quarterly reports by aggregating data from a variety of clients. The 80-page report took one week to create at the end of every quarter.

Travel and Transport has completely automated the quarterly review system using WebFOCUS so the managers can select the pages, percentages, and specific data they want to include. This gives them more time to do further analysis and make better use of the information. Cords estimates that the time savings add up to about $200,000 every year for this project alone. "Metrics derived from actionable data are key to helping us negotiate with our suppliers, enforce our travel policy, and save our company money," continues Cords. "During the recession, the travel industry was hit particularly hard, but Travel and

Transport managed to add new multimillion dollar accounts even in the worst of times. We attribute a lot of this growth to the cutting-edge reporting technology we offer to clients."

QUESTIONS FOR THE OPENING VIGNETTE

1. What does Travel and Transport, Inc., do?
2. Describe the complexity and the competitive nature of the business environment in which Travel and Transport, Inc., functions.
3. What were the main business challenges?
4. What was the solution? How was it implemented?
5. Why do you think a multi-vendor, multi-tool solution was implemented?
6. List and comment on at least three main benefits of the implemented system. Can you think of other potential benefits that are not mentioned in the case?

WHAT WE CAN LEARN FROM THIS VIGNETTE

Trying to survive (and thrive) in a highly competitive industry, Travel and Transport, Inc., was aware of the need to create and effectively communicate a value proposition to its existing and potential customers. As is the case in many industries, in the travel business, success or mere survival depends on continuously winning new customers while retaining the existing ones. The key was to provide value-added services to the client so that they can efficiently analyze costs and other options to quickly instate optimal purchase agreements. Using WebFOCUS (an integrated reporting and information visualization environment by Information Builders), Travel and Transport empowered their clients to access information whenever and wherever they need it. Information is the power that decision makers need the most to make better and faster decisions. When economic conditions are tight, every managerial decision—every business transaction—counts. Travel and Transport used a variety of reputable vendors/products (hardware and software) to create a cutting-edge reporting technology so that their clients can make better, faster decisions to improve their financial well-being.

Source: Information Builders, Customer Success Story, **informationbuilders.com/applications/travel-and-transport** (accessed February 2013).

4.2 BUSINESS REPORTING DEFINITIONS AND CONCEPTS

Decision makers are in need of information to make accurate and timely decisions. Information is essentially the contextualization of data. Information is often provided in the form of a written **report** (digital or on paper), although it can also be provided orally. Simply put, a report is any communication artifact prepared with the specific intention of conveying information in a presentable form to whoever needs it, whenever and wherever they may need it. It is usually a document that contains information (usually driven from data and personal experiences) organized in a narrative, graphic, and/or tabular form, prepared periodically (recurring) or on an as-required (ad hoc) basis, referring to specific time periods, events, occurrences, or subjects.

In business settings, types of reports include memos, minutes, lab reports, sales reports, progress reports, justification reports, compliance reports, annual reports, and policies and procedures. Reports can fulfill many different (but often related) functions. Here are a few of the most prevailing ones:

- To ensure that all departments are functioning properly
- To provide information

- To provide the results of an analysis
- To persuade others to act
- To create an organizational memory (as part of a knowledge management system)

Reports can be lengthy at times. For those reports, there usually is an executive summary for those who do not have the time and interest to go through it all. The summary (or abstract, or more commonly called executive brief) should be crafted carefully, expressing only the important points in a very concise and precise manner, and lasting no more than a page or two.

In addition to business reports, examples of other types of reports include crime scene reports, police reports, credit reports, scientific reports, recommendation reports, white papers, annual reports, auditor's reports, workplace reports, census reports, trip reports, progress reports, investigative reports, budget reports, policy reports, demographic reports, credit reports, appraisal reports, inspection reports, and military reports, among others. In this chapter we are particularly interested in business reports.

What Is a Business Report?

A business report is a written document that contains information regarding business matters. Business reporting (also called enterprise reporting) is an essential part of the larger drive toward improved managerial decision making and organizational knowledge management. The foundation of these reports is various sources of data coming from both inside and outside the organization. Creation of these reports involves ETL (extract, transform, and load) procedures in coordination with a data warehouse and then using one or more reporting tools. While reports can be distributed in print form or via e-mail, they are typically accessed via a corporate intranet.

Due to the expansion of information technology coupled with the need for improved competitiveness in businesses, there has been an increase in the use of computing power to produce unified reports that join different views of the enterprise in one place. Usually, this reporting process involves querying structured data sources, most of which are created by using different logical data models and data dictionaries to produce a human-readable, easily digestible report. These types of business reports allow managers and coworkers to stay informed and involved, review options and alternatives, and make informed decisions. Figure 4.1 shows the continuous cycle of data acquisition → information generation → decision making → business process management. Perhaps the most critical task in this cyclic process is the reporting (i.e., information generation)—converting data from different sources into actionable information.

The key to any successful report is clarity, brevity, completeness, and correctness. In terms of content and format, there are only a few categories of business report: informal, formal, and short. Informal reports are usually up to 10 pages long; are routine and internal; follow a letter or memo format; and use personal pronouns and contractions. Formal reports are 10 to 100 pages long; do not use personal pronouns or contractions; include a title page, table of contents, and an executive summary; are based on deep research or an analytic study; and are distributed to external or internal people with a need-to-know designation. Short reports are to inform people about events or system status changes and are often periodic, investigative, compliance, and situational focused.

The nature of the report also changes significantly based on whom the report is created for. Most of the research in effective reporting is dedicated to internal reports that inform stakeholders and decision makers within the organization. There are also external reports between businesses and the government (e.g., for tax purposes or for regular filings to the Securities and Exchange Commission). These formal reports are mostly standardized and periodically filed either nationally or internationally. Standard Business Reporting, which is a collection of international programs instigated by a

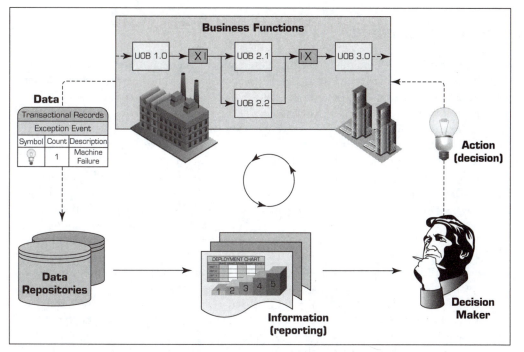

FIGURE 4.1   **The Role of Information Reporting in Managerial Decision Making.**

number of governments, aims to reduce the regulatory burden for business by simplifying and standardizing reporting requirements. The idea is to make business the epicenter when it comes to managing business-to-government reporting obligations. Businesses conduct their own financial administration; the facts they record and decisions they make should drive their reporting. The government should be able to receive and process this information without imposing undue constraints on how businesses administer their finances. Application Case 4.1 illustrates an excellent example for overcoming the challenges of financial reporting.

Application Case 4.1

Delta Lloyd Group Ensures Accuracy and Efficiency in Financial Reporting

Delta Lloyd Group is a financial services provider based in the Netherlands. It offers insurance, pensions, investing, and banking services to its private and corporate clients through its three strong brands: Delta Lloyd, OHRA, and ABN AMRO Insurance. Since its founding in 1807, the company has grown in the Netherlands, Germany, and Belgium, and now employs around 5,400 permanent staff. Its 2011 full-year financial reports show €5.5 billion in gross written premiums, with shareholders' funds amounting to €3.9 billion and investments under management worth nearly €74 billion.

Challenges

Since Delta Lloyd Group is publicly listed on the NYSE Euronext Amsterdam, it is obliged to produce annual and half-year reports. Various subsidiaries in Delta Lloyd Group must also produce reports to fulfill local legal requirements: for example, banking and

(Continued)

Application Case 4.1 (Continued)

insurance reports are obligatory in the Netherlands. In addition, Delta Lloyd Group must provide reports to meet international requirements, such as the IFRS (International Financial Reporting Standards) for accounting and the EU Solvency I Directive for insurance companies. The data for these reports is gathered by the group's finance department, which is divided into small teams in several locations, and then converted into XML so that it can be published on the corporate Web site.

Importance of Accuracy

The most challenging part of the reporting process is the "last mile"—the stage at which the consolidated figures are cited, formatted, and described to form the final text of the report. Delta Lloyd Group was using Microsoft Excel for the last-mile stage of the reporting process. To minimize the risk of errors, the finance team needed to manually check all the data in its reports for accuracy. These manual checks were very time-consuming. Arnold Honig, team leader for reporting at Delta Lloyd Group, comments: "Accuracy is essential in financial reporting, since errors could lead to penalties, reputational damage, and even a negative impact on the company's stock price. We needed a new solution that would automate some of the last mile processes and reduce the risk of manual error."

Solution

The group decided to implement IBM Cognos Financial Statement Reporting (FSR). The implementation of the software was completed in just 6 weeks during the late summer. This rapid implementation gave the finance department enough time to prepare a trial draft of the annual report in FSR, based on figures from the third financial quarter. The successful creation of this draft gave Delta Lloyd Group enough confidence to use Cognos FSR for the final version of the annual report, which was published shortly after the end of the year.

Results

Employees are delighted with the IBM Cognos FSR solution. Delta Lloyd Group has divided the annual report into chapters, and each member of the reporting team is responsible for one chapter. Arnold Honig says, "Since employees can work on documents simultaneously, they can share the huge workload involved in report generation. Before, the reporting process was inefficient, because only one person could work on the report at a time."

Since the workload can be divided up, staff can complete the report with less overtime. Arnold Honig comments, "Previously, employees were putting in 2 weeks of overtime during the 8 weeks required to generate a report. This year, the 10 members of staff involved in the report generation process worked 25 percent less overtime, even though they were still getting used to the new software. This is a big win for Delta Lloyd Group and its staff." The group is expecting further reductions in employee overtime in the future as staff becomes more familiar with the software.

Accurate Reports

The IBM Cognos FSR solution automates key stages in the report-writing process by populating the final report with accurate, up-to-date financial data. Wherever the text of the report needs to mention a specific financial figure, the finance team simply inserts a "variable"—a tag that is linked to an underlying data source. Wherever the variable appears in the document, FSR will pull the figure through from the source into the report. If the value of the figure needs to be changed, the team can simply update it in the source, and the new value will automatically flow through into the text, maintaining accuracy and consistency of data throughout the report.

Arnold Honig comments, "The ability to update figures automatically across the whole report reduces the scope for manual error inherent in spreadsheet-based processes and activities. Since we have full control of our reporting processes, we can produce better quality reports more efficiently and reduce our business risk." IBM Cognos FSR also provides a comparison feature, which highlights any changes made to reports. This feature makes it quicker and easier for users to review new versions of documents and ensure the accuracy of their reports.

Adhering to Industry Regulations

In the future, Delta Lloyd Group is planning to extend its use of IBM Cognos FSR to generate internal management reports. It will also help Delta Lloyd Group to meet industry regulatory standards, which are becoming stricter. Arnold Honig comments, "The EU Solvency II Directive will come into effect soon, and our Solvency II reports will need to be tagged with eXtensible Business Reporting Language [XBRL]. By implementing IBM Cognos FSR, which fully supports XBRL tagging, we have equipped ourselves to meet both current and future regulatory requirements."

QUESTIONS FOR DISCUSSION

1. How did Delta Lloyd Group improve accuracy and efficiency in financial reporting?
2. What were the challenges, the proposed solution, and the obtained results?
3. Why is it important for Delta Lloyd Group to comply with industry regulations?

Source: IBM, Customer Success Story, "Delta Lloyd Group Ensures Accuracy in Financial Reporting," **public.dhe.ibm.com/common/ssi/ecm/en/ytc03561nlen/YTC03561NLEN.PDF** (accessed February 2013); and **www.deltalloydgroep.com**.

Even though there are a wide variety of business reports, the ones that are often used for managerial purposes can be grouped into three major categories (Hill, 2013).

METRIC MANAGEMENT REPORTS   In many organizations, business performance is managed through outcome-oriented metrics. For external groups, these are service-level agreements (SLAs). For internal management, they are key performance indicators (KPIs). Typically, there are enterprise-wide agreed targets to be tracked over a period of time. They may be used as part of other management strategies such as Six Sigma or Total Quality Management (TQM).

DASHBOARD-TYPE REPORTS   A popular idea in business reporting in recent years has been to present a range of different performance indicators on one page, like a dashboard in a car. Typically, dashboard vendors would provide a set of predefined reports with static elements and fixed structure, but also allow for customization of the dashboard widgets, views, and set targets for various metrics. It's common to have color-coded traffic lights defined for performance (red, orange, green) to draw management attention to particular areas. More details on dashboards are given later in this chapter.

BALANCED SCORECARD–TYPE REPORTS   This is a method developed by Kaplan and Norton that attempts to present an integrated view of success in an organization. In addition to financial performance, balanced scorecard–type reports also include customer, business process, and learning and growth perspectives. More details on balanced scorecards are provided later in this chapter.

Components of the Business Reporting System

Although each business reporting system has its unique characteristics, there seems to be a generic pattern that is common across organizations and technology architectures. Think of this generic pattern as having the business user on one end of the reporting continuum and the data sources on the other end. Based on the needs and requirements of the business user, the data is captured, stored, consolidated, and converted to desired reports using a set of predefined business rules. To be successful, such a system needs an overarching assurance process that covers the entire value chain and moves back and forth, ensuring that reporting requirements and information delivery are properly aligned (Hill, 2008). Following are the most common components of a business reporting system.

- **OLTP (online transaction processing).** A system that measures some aspect of the real world as events (e.g., transactions) and records them into enterprise databases. Examples include ERP systems, POS systems, Web servers, RFID readers, handheld inventory readers, card readers, and so forth.
- **Data supply.** A system that takes recorded events/transactions and delivers them reliably to the reporting system. The data access can be push or pull, depending on whether or not it is responsible for initiating the delivery process. It can also be polled (or batched) if the data are transferred periodically, or triggered (or online) if data are transferred in case of a specific event.
- **ETL (extract, transform, and load).** This is the intermediate step where these recorded transactions/events are checked for quality, put into the appropriate format, and inserted into the desired data format.
- **Data storage.** This is the storage area for the data and metadata. It could be a flat file or a spreadsheet, but it is usually a relational database management system (RDBMS) set up as a data mart, data warehouse, or operational data store (ODS); it often employs online analytical processing (OLAP) functions like cubes.
- **Business logic.** The explicit steps for how the recorded transactions/events are to be converted into metrics, scorecards, and dashboards.
- **Publication.** The system that builds the various reports and hosts them (for users) or disseminates them (to users). These systems may also provide notification, annotation, collaboration, and other services.
- **Assurance.** A good business reporting system is expected to offer a quality service to its users. This includes determining if and when the right information is to be delivered to the right people in the right way/format.

Application Case 4.2 is an excellent example to illustrate the power and the utility of automated report generation for a large (and, at a time of natural crisis, somewhat chaotic) organization like FEMA.

Application Case 4.2
Flood of Paper Ends at FEMA

Staff at the Federal Emergency Management Agency (FEMA), a U.S. federal agency that coordinates disaster response when the President declares a national disaster, always got two floods at once. First, water covered the land. Next, a flood of paper, required to administer the National Flood Insurance Program (NFIP), covered their desks—pallets and pallets of green-striped reports poured off a mainframe printer and into their offices. Individual reports were sometimes 18 inches thick, with a nugget of information about insurance claims, premiums, or payments buried in them somewhere.

Bill Barton and Mike Miles don't claim to be able to do anything about the weather, but the project manager and computer scientist, respectively, from Computer Sciences Corporation (CSC) have used WebFOCUS software from Information Builders to turn back the flood of paper generated by the NFIP. The program allows the government to work together with national insurance companies to collect flood insurance premiums and pay claims for flooding in communities that adopt flood control measures. As a result of CSC's work, FEMA staff no longer leaf through paper reports to find the data they need. Instead, they browse insurance data posted on NFIP's BureauNet intranet site, select just the information they want to see, and get an on-screen report or download the data as a spreadsheet.

And that is only the start of the savings that WebFOCUS has provided. The number of times that NFIP staff asks CSC for special reports has dropped in half, because NFIP staff can generate many of the special reports they need without calling on a programmer to develop them. Then there is the cost of creating BureauNet in the first place. Barton estimates that using conventional Web and database software to export data from FEMA's mainframe, store it in a new database, and link that to a Web server would have cost about 100 times as much—more than $500,000—and taken about two years to complete, compared with the few months Miles spent on the WebFOCUS solution.

When Tropical Storm Allison, a huge slug of sodden, swirling clouds, moved out of the Gulf of Mexico onto the Texas and Louisiana coastline in June 2001, it killed 34 people, most from drowning; damaged or destroyed 16,000 homes and businesses; and displaced more than 10,000 families. President George W. Bush declared 28 Texas counties disaster areas, and FEMA moved in to help. This was the first serious test for BureauNet, and it delivered. This first comprehensive use of BureauNet resulted in FEMA field staff readily accessing what they needed and when they needed it, and asking for many new types of reports. Fortunately, Miles and WebFOCUS were up to the task. In some cases, Barton says, "FEMA would ask for a new type of report one day, and Miles would have it on BureauNet the next day, thanks to the speed with which he could create new reports in WebFOCUS."

The sudden demand on the system had little impact on its performance, notes Barton. "It handled the demand just fine," he says. "We had no problems with it at all." "And it made a huge difference to FEMA and the job they had to do. They had never had that level of access before, never had been able to just click on their desktop and generate such detailed and specific reports."

QUESTIONS FOR DISCUSSION

1. What is FEMA and what does it do?
2. What are the main challenges that FEMA faces?
3. How did FEMA improve its inefficient reporting practices?

Sources: Information Builders, Customer Success Story, "Useful Information Flows at Disaster Response Agency," **informationbuilders.com/applications/fema** (accessed January 2013); and **fema.gov**.

SECTION 4.2 REVIEW QUESTIONS

1. What is a report? What are they used for?
2. What is a business report? What are the main characteristics of a good business report?
3. Describe the cyclic process of management and comment on the role of business reports.
4. List and describe the three major categories of business reports.
5. What are the main components of a business reporting system?

4.3 DATA AND INFORMATION VISUALIZATION

Data visualization (or more appropriately, information visualization) has been defined as, "the use of visual representations to explore, make sense of, and communicate data" (Few, 2008). Although the name that is commonly used is *data visualization*, usually what is meant by this is information visualization. Since information is the aggregation, summarizations, and contextualization of data (raw facts), what is portrayed in visualizations is the information and not the data. However, since the two terms *data visualization* and *information visualization* are used interchangeably and synonymously, in this chapter we will follow suit.

Data visualization is closely related to the fields of information graphics, information visualization, scientific visualization, and statistical graphics. Until recently, the major forms of data visualization available in both business intelligence applications have included charts and graphs, as well as the other types of visual elements used to create scorecards and dashboards. Application Case 4.3 shows how visual reporting tools can help facilitate cost-effective business information creations and sharing.

Application Case 4.3
Tableau Saves Blastrac Thousands of Dollars with Simplified Information Sharing

Blastrac, a self-proclaimed global leader in portable surface preparation technologies and equipment (e.g., shot blasting, grinding, polishing, scarifying, scraping, milling, and cutting equipment), depended on the creation and distribution of reports across the organization to make business decisions. However, the company did not have a consistent reporting method in place and, consequently, preparation of reports for the company's various needs (sales data, working capital, inventory, purchase analysis, etc.) was tedious. Blastrac's analysts each spent nearly one whole day per week (a total of 20 to 30 hours) extracting data from the multiple enterprise resource planning (ERP) systems, loading it into several Excel spreadsheets, creating filtering capabilities and establishing predefined pivot tables.

Not only were these massive spreadsheets often inaccurate and consistently hard to understand, but also they were virtually useless for the sales team, which couldn't work with the complex format. In addition, each consumer of the reports had different needs.

Blastrac Vice President and CIO Dan Murray began looking for a solution to the company's reporting troubles. He quickly ruled out the rollout of a single ERP system, a multimillion-dollar proposition. He also eliminated the possibility of an enterprise-wide business intelligence (BI) platform deployment because of cost—quotes from five different vendors ranged from $130,000 to over $500,000. What Murray needed was a solution that was affordable, could deploy quickly without disrupting current systems, and was able to represent data consistently regardless of the multiple currencies Blastrac operates in.

The Solution and the Results

Working with IT services consultant firm, Interworks, Inc., out of Oklahoma, Murray and team finessed the data sources. Murray then deployed two data visualization tools from Tableau Software: Tableau Desktop, a visual data analysis solution that allowed Blastrac analysts to quickly and easily create intuitive and visually compelling reports, and Tableau Reader, a free application that enabled everyone across the company to directly interact with the reports, filtering, sorting, extracting, and printing data as it fit their needs—and at a total cost of less than one-third the lowest competing BI quote.

With only one hour per week now required to create reports—a 95 percent increase in productivity—and updates to these reports happening automatically through Tableau, Murray and his team are able to proactively identify major business events reflected in company data—such as an exceptionally large sale—instead of reacting to incoming questions from employees as they had been forced to do previously.

"Prior to deploying Tableau, I spent countless hours customizing and creating new reports based on individual requests, which was not efficient or productive for me," said Murray. "With Tableau, we create one report for each business area, and, with very little training, they can explore the data themselves. By deploying Tableau, I not only saved thousands of dollars and endless months of deployment, but I'm also now able to create a product that is infinitely more valuable for people across the organization.

QUESTIONS FOR DISCUSSION

1. How did Blastrac achieve significant cost savingin reporting and information sharing?
2. What were the challenge, the proposed solution, and the obtained results?

Sources: **tableausoftware.com/learn/stories/spotlight-blastric**; **blastrac.com/about-us**; and **interworks.com.**

To better understand the current and future trends in the field of data visualization, it helps to begin with some historical context.

A Brief History of Data Visualization

Despite the fact that predecessors to data visualization date back to the second century AD, most developments have occurred in the last two and a half centuries, predominantly during the last 30 years (Few, 2007). Although visualization has not been widely recognized as a discipline until fairly recently, today's most popular visual forms date back a few centuries. Geographical exploration, mathematics, and popularized history spurred the creation of early maps, graphs, and timelines as far back as the 1600s, but William Playfair is widely credited as the inventor of the modern chart, having created the first widely distributed line and bar charts in his Commercial and Political Atlas of 1786 and what is generally considered to be the first pie chart in his Statistical Breviary, published in 1801 (see Figure 4.2).

Perhaps the most notable innovator of information graphics during this period was Charles Joseph Minard, who graphically portrayed the losses suffered by Napoleon's army in the Russian campaign of 1812 (see Figure 4.3). Beginning at the Polish–Russian border, the thick band shows the size of the army at each position. The path of Napoleon's retreat from Moscow in the bitterly cold winter is depicted by the dark lower band, which is tied to temperature and time scales. Popular visualization expert, author, and critic

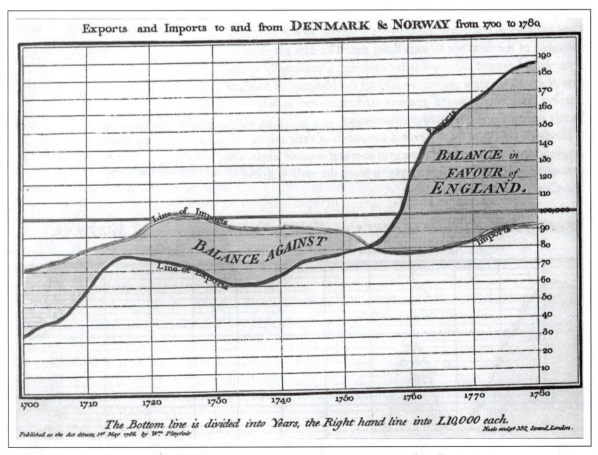

FIGURE 4.2   The First Pie Chart Created by William Playfair in 1801.   *Source:* en.wikipedia.org.

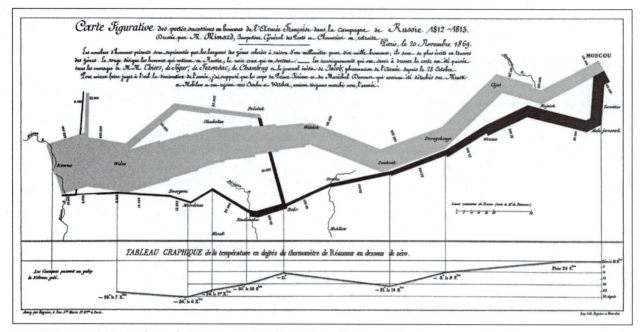

FIGURE 4.3   Decimation of Napoleon's Army During the 1812 Russian Campaign.   *Source:* **en.wikipedia.org**.

Edward Tufte says that this "may well be the best statistical graphic ever drawn." In this graphic Minard managed to simultaneously represent several data dimensions (the size of the army, direction of movement, geographic locations, outside temperature, etc.) in an artistic and informative manner. Many more great visualizations were created in the 1800s, and most of them are chronicled in Tufte's Web site (**edwardtufte.com**) and his visualization books.

The 1900s saw the rise of a more formal, empirical attitude toward visualization, which tended to focus on aspects such as color, value scales, and labeling. In the mid-1900s, cartographer and theorist Jacques Bertin published his Semiologie Graphique, which some say serves as the theoretical foundation of modern information visualization. While most of his patterns are either outdated by more recent research or completely inapplicable to digital media, many are still very relevant.

In the 2000s the Internet has emerged as a new medium for visualization and brought with it a whole lot of new tricks and capabilities. Not only has the worldwide, digital distribution of both data and visualization made them more accessible to a broader audience (raising visual literacy along the way), but it has also spurred the design of new forms that incorporate interaction, animation, graphics-rendering technology unique to screen media, and real-time data feeds to create immersive environments for communicating and consuming data.

Companies and individuals are, seemingly all of a sudden, interested in data; that interest has, in turn, sparked a need for visual tools that help them understand it. Cheap hardware sensors and do-it-yourself frameworks for building your own system are driving down the costs of collecting and processing data. Countless other applications, software tools, and low-level code libraries are springing up to help people collect, organize, manipulate, visualize, and understand data from practically any source. The Internet has also served as a fantastic distribution channel for visualizations; a diverse community of designers, programmers, cartographers, tinkerers, and data wonks has assembled to disseminate all sorts of new ideas and tools for working with data in both visual and nonvisual forms.

Google Maps has also single-handedly democratized both the interface conventions (click to pan, double-click to zoom) and the technology (256-pixel square map tiles with predictable file names) for displaying interactive geography online, to the extent that most people just know what to do when they're presented with a map online. Flash has served well as a cross-browser platform on which to design and develop rich, beautiful Internet applications incorporating interactive data visualization and maps; now, new browser-native technologies such as canvas and SVG (sometimes collectively included under the umbrella of HTML5) are emerging to challenge Flash's supremacy and extend the reach of dynamic visualization interfaces to mobile devices.

The future of data/information visualization is very hard to predict. We can only extrapolate from what has already been invented: more three-dimensional visualization, more immersive experience with multidimensional data in a virtual reality environment, and holographic visualization of information. There is a pretty good chance that we will see something that we have never seen in the information visualization realm invented before the end of this decade. Application Case 4.4 shows how Dana-Farber Cancer Institute used information visualization to better understand the cancer vaccine clinical trials.

Application Case 4.4

TIBCO Spotfire Provides Dana-Farber Cancer Institute with Unprecedented Insight into Cancer Vaccine Clinical Trials

When Karen Maloney, business development manager of the Cancer Vaccine Center (CVC) at Dana-Farber Cancer Institute in Boston, decided to investigate the competitive landscape of the cancer vaccine field, she looked to a strategic planning and marketing MBA class at Babson College in Wellesley, Massachusetts, for help with the research project. There she met Xiaohong Cao, whose bioinformatics background led to the decision to focus on clinical vaccine trials as representative of potential competition. This became Dana-Farber CVC's first organized attempt to assess in-depth the cancer vaccine market.

Cao focused on the analysis of 645 clinical trials related to cancer vaccines. The data was extracted in XML from the **ClinicalTrials.gov** Web site, and included categories such as "Summary of Purpose," "Trial Sponsor," "Phase of the Trial," "Recruiting Status," and "Location." Additional statistics on cancer types, including incidence and survival rates, were retrieved from the National Cancer Institute Surveillance data.

Challenge and Solution

Although information from clinical vaccine trials is organized fairly well into categories and can be downloaded, there is great inconsistency and redundancy inherent in the data registry. To gain a good understanding of the landscape, both an overview and an in-depth analytic capability were required simultaneously. It would have been very difficult, not to mention incredibly time-consuming, to analyze information from the multiple data sources separately, in order to understand the relationships underlying the data or identify trends and patterns using spreadsheets. And to attempt to use a traditional business intelligence tool would have required significant IT resources. Cao proposed using the TIBCO Spotfire DXP (Spotfire) computational and visual analysis tool for data exploration and discovery.

Results

With the help of Cao and Spotfire software, Dana-Farber's CVC developed a first-of-its-kind analysis approach to rapidly extract complex data specifically for cancer vaccines from the major clinical trial repository. Summarization and visualization of these data represents a cost-effective means of making informed decisions about future cancer vaccine clinical trials. The findings are helping the CVC at Dana-Farber understand its competition and the diseases they are working on to help shape its strategy in the marketplace.

(Continued)

Application Case 4.4 (Continued)

Spotfire software's visual and computational analysis approach provides the CVC at Dana-Farber and the research community at large with a better understanding of the cancer vaccine clinical trials landscape and enables rapid insight into the hotspots of cancer vaccine activity, as well as into the identification of neglected cancers.

"The whole field of medical research is going through an enormous transformation, in part driven by information technology," adds Brusic. "Using a tool like Spotfire for analysis is a promising area in this field because it helps integrate information from multiple sources, ask specific questions, and rapidly extract new knowledge from the data that was previously not easily attainable."

QUESTIONS FOR DISCUSSION

1. How did Dana-Farber Cancer Institute use TIBCO Spotfire to enhance information reporting and visualization?

2. What were the challenge, the proposed solution, and the obtained results?

Sources: TIBCO Spotfire, Customer Success Story, "TIBCO Spotfire Provides Dana-Farber Cancer Institute with Unprecedented Insight into Cancer Vaccine Clinical Trials," **spotfire.tibco.com/~/media/content-center/case-studies/dana-farber.ashx** (accessed March 2013); and Dana-Farber Cancer Institute, **dana-farber.org.**

SECTION 4.3 REVIEW QUESTIONS

1. What is data visualization? Why is it needed?
2. What are the historical roots of data visualization?
3. Carefully analyze Charles Joseph Minard's graphical portrayal of Napoleon's march. Identify and comment on all of the information dimensions captured in this ancient diagram.
4. Who is Edward Tufte? Why do you think we should know about his work?
5. What do you think the "next big thing" is in data visualization?

4.4 DIFFERENT TYPES OF CHARTS AND GRAPHS

Often end users of business analytics systems are not sure what type of chart or graph to use for a specific purpose. Some charts and/or graphs are better at answering certain types of questions. What follows is a short description of the types of charts and/or graphs commonly found in most business analytics tools and what types of question that they are better at answering/analyzing.

Basic Charts and Graphs

What follows are the basic charts and graphs that are commonly used for information visualization.

LINE CHART Line charts are perhaps the most frequently used graphical visuals for time-series data. Line charts (or line graphs) show the relationship between two variables; they most often are used to track changes or trends over time (having one of the variables set to time on the *x*-axis). Line charts sequentially connect individual data points to help infer changing trends over a period of time. Line charts are often used to show time-dependent changes in the values of some measure such as changes on a specific stock price over a 5-year period or changes in the number of daily customer service calls over a month.

BAR CHART   Bar charts are among the most basic visuals used for data representation. Bar charts are effective when you have nominal data or numerical data that splits nicely into different categories so you can quickly see comparative results and trends within your data. Bar charts are often used to compare data across multiple categories such as percent advertising spending by departments or by product categories. Bar charts can be vertically or horizontally oriented. They can also be stacked on top of each other to show multiple dimensions in a single chart.

PIE CHART   Pie charts are visually appealing, as the name implies, pie-looking charts. Because they are so visually attractive, they are often incorrectly used. Pie charts should only be used to illustrate relative proportions of a specific measure. For instance, they can be used to show relative percentage of advertising budget spent on different product lines or they can show relative proportions of majors declared by college students in their sophomore year. If the number of categories to show are more than just a few (say, more than 4), one should seriously consider using a bar chart instead of a pie chart.

SCATTER PLOT   Scatter plots are often used to explore relationships between two or three variables (in 2D or 2D visuals). Since they are visual exploration tools, having more than three variables, translating into more than three dimensions, is not easily achievable. Scatter plots are an effective way to explore the existence of trends, concentrations, and outliers. For instance, in a two-variable (two-axis) graph, a scatter plot can be used to illustrate the co-relationship between age and weight of heart disease patients or it can illustrate the relationship between number of customer care representatives and number of open customer service claims. Often, a trend line is superimposed on a two-dimensional scatter plot to illustrate the nature of the relationship.

BUBBLE CHART   Bubble charts are often enhanced versions of scatter plots. The bubble chart is not a new visualization type; instead, it should be viewed as a technique to enrich data illustrated in scatter plots (or even geographic maps). By varying the size and/ or color of the circles, one can add additional data dimensions, offering more enriched meaning about the data. For instance, it can be used to show a competitive view of college-level class attendance by major and by time of the day or it can be used to show profit margin by product type and by geographic region.

Specialized Charts and Graphs

The graphs and charts that we review in this section are either derived from the basic charts as special cases or they are relatively new and specific to a problem type and/or an application area.

HISTOGRAM   Graphically speaking, a histogram looks just like a bar chart. The difference between histograms and generic bar charts is the information that is portrayed in them. Histograms are used to show the frequency distribution of a variable, or several variables. In a histogram, the x-axis is often used to show the categories or ranges, and the y-axis is used to show the measures/values/frequencies. Histograms show the distributional shape of the data. That way, one can visually examine if the data is distributed normally, exponentially, and so on. For instance, one can use a histogram to illustrate the exam performance of a class, where distribution of the grades as well as comparative analysis of individual results can be shown; or one can use a histogram to show age distribution of their customer base.

GANTT CHART Gantt charts are a special case of horizontal bar charts that are used to portray project timelines, project tasks/activity durations, and overlap amongst the tasks/activities. By showing start and end dates/times of tasks/activities and the overlapping relationships, Gantt charts make an invaluable aid for management and control of projects. For instance, Gantt charts are often used to show project timeline, talk overlaps, relative task completions (a partial bar illustrating the completion percentage inside a bar that shows the actual task duration), resources assigned to each task, milestones, and deliverables.

PERT CHART PERT charts (also called network diagrams) are developed primarily to simplify the planning and scheduling of large and complex projects. A PERT chart shows precedence relationships among the project activities/tasks. It is composed of nodes (represented as circles or rectangles) and edges (represented with directed arrows). Based on the selected PERT chart convention, either nodes or the edges may be used to represent the project activities/tasks (activity-on-node versus activity-on-arrow representation schema).

GEOGRAPHIC MAP When the data set includes any kind of location data (e.g., physical addresses, postal codes, state names or abbreviations, country names, latitude/longitude, or some type of custom geographic encoding), it is better and more informative to see the data on a map. Maps usually are used in conjunction with other charts and graphs, as opposed to by themselves. For instance, one can use maps to show distribution of customer service requests by product type (depicted in pie charts) by geographic locations. Often a large variety of information (e.g., age distribution, income distribution, education, economic growth, population changes, etc.) can be portrayed in a geographic map to help decide where to open a new restaurant or a new service station. These types of systems are often called geographic information systems (GIS).

BULLET Bullet graphs are often used to show progress toward a goal. A bullet graph is essentially a variation of a bar chart. Often they are used in place of gauges, meters, and thermometers in dashboards to more intuitively convey the meaning within a much smaller space. Bullet graphs compare a primary measure (e.g., year-to-date revenue) to one or more other measures (e.g., annual revenue target) and present this in the context of defined performance metrics (e.g., sales quota). A bullet graph can intuitively illustrate how the primary measure is performing against overall goals (e.g., how close a sales representative is to achieving his/her annual quota).

HEAT MAP Heat maps are great visuals to illustrate the comparison of continuous values across two categories using color. The goal is to help the user quickly see where the intersection of the categories is strongest and weakest in terms of numerical values of the measure being analyzed. For instance, heat maps can be used to show segmentation analysis of the target market where the measure (color gradient would be the purchase amount) and the dimensions would be age and income distribution.

HIGHLIGHT TABLE Highlight tables are intended to take heat maps one step further. In addition to showing how data intersects by using color, highlight tables add a number on top to provide additional detail. That is, it is a two-dimensional table with cells populated with numerical values and gradients of colors. For instance, one can show sales representative performance by product type and by sales volume.

TREE MAP Tree maps display hierarchical (tree-structured) data as a set of nested rectangles. Each branch of the tree is given a rectangle, which is then tiled with smaller rectangles representing sub-branches. A leaf node's rectangle has an area proportional to a specified dimension on the data. Often the leaf nodes are colored to show a separate dimension of the data. When the color and size dimensions are correlated in some way with the tree structure, one can often easily see patterns that would be difficult to spot in other ways, such as if a certain color is particularly relevant. A second advantage of tree maps is that, by construction, they make efficient use of space. As a result, they can legibly display thousands of items on the screen simultaneously.

Even though these charts and graphs cover a major part of what is commonly used in information visualization, they by no means cover it all. Nowadays, one can find many other specialized graphs and charts that serve a specific purpose. Furthermore, current trends are to combine/hybridize and animate these charts for better looking and more intuitive visualization of today's complex and volatile data sources. For instance, the interactive, animated, bubble charts available at the Gapminder Web site (**gapminder. org**) provide an intriguing way of exploring world health, wealth, and population data from a multidimensional perspective. Figure 4.4 depicts the sorts of displays available at the site. In this graph, population size, life expectancy, and per capita income at the continent level are shown; also given is a time-varying animation that shows how these variables changed over time.

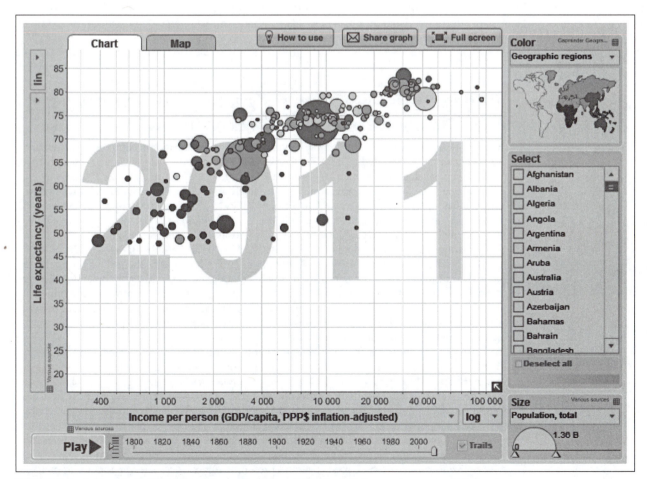

FIGURE 4.4   A Gapminder Chart That Shows Wealth and Health of Nations.   *Source:* **gapminder.org**.

SECTION 4.4 REVIEW QUESTIONS

1. Why do you think there are large numbers of different types of charts and graphs?
2. What are the main differences among line, bar, and pie charts? When should you choose to use one over the other?
3. Why would you use a geographic map? What other types of charts can be combined with a geographic map?
4. Find two more charts that are not covered in this section, and comment on their usability.

4.5 THE EMERGENCE OF DATA VISUALIZATION AND VISUAL ANALYTICS

As Seth Grimes (2009) has noted, there is a "growing palette" of data visualization techniques and tools that enable the users of business analytics and business intelligence systems to better "communicate relationships, add historical context, uncover hidden correlations and tell persuasive stories that clarify and call to action." The latest Magic Quadrant on Business Intelligence and Analytics Platforms released by Gartner in February 2013 further emphasizes the importance of visualization in business intelligence. As the chart shows, most of the solution providers in the *Leaders* quadrant are either relatively recently founded information visualization companies (e.g., Tableau Software, QlikTech, Tibco Spotfire) or are well-established, large analytics companies (e.g., SAS, IBM, Microsoft, SAP, MicroStrategy) that are increasingly focusing their efforts in information visualization and visual analytics. Details on the Gartner's latest Magic Quadrant are given in Technology Insights 4.1.

TECHNOLOGY INSIGHTS 4.1   Gartner Magic Quadrant for Business Intelligence and Analytics Platforms

Gartner, Inc., the creator of Magic Quadrants, is a leading information technology research and advisory company. Founded in 1979, Gartner has 5,300 associates, including 1,280 research analysts and consultants, and numerous clients in 85 countries.

Magic Quadrant is a research method designed and implemented by Gartner to monitor and evaluate the progress and positions of companies in a specific, technology-based market. By applying a graphical treatment and a uniform set of evaluation criteria, Magic Quadrant helps users to understand how technology providers are positioned within a market.

Gartner changed the name of this Magic Quadrant from "Business Intelligence Platforms" to "Business Intelligence and Analytics Platforms" in 2012 to emphasize the growing importance of analytics capabilities to the information systems that organizations are now building. Gartner defines the business intelligence and analytics platform market as a software platform that delivers 15 capabilities across three categories: integration, information delivery, and analysis. These capabilities enable organizations to build precise systems of classification and measurement to support decision making and improve performance.

Figure 4.5 illustrates the latest Magic Quadrant for Business Intelligence and Analytics platforms. Magic Quadrant places providers in four groups (niche players, challengers, visionaries, and leaders) along two dimensions: completeness of vision (*x*-axis) and ability to execute (*y*-axis). As the quadrant clearly shows, most of the well-known BI/BA providers are positioned in the "leaders" category while many of the lesser known, relatively new, emerging providers are positioned in the "niche players" category.

Right now, most of the activity in the business intelligence and analytics platform market is from organizations that are trying to mature their visualization capabilities and to move from descriptive to diagnostic (i.e., predictive and prescriptive) analytics. The vendors in the market have overwhelmingly concentrated on meeting this user demand. If there were a single market

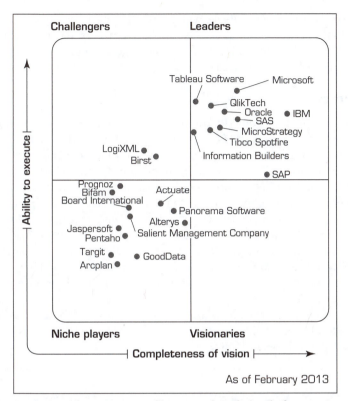

FIGURE 4.5   **Magic Quadrant for Business Intelligence and Analytics Platforms.**   *Source:* **gartner.com**.

theme in 2012, it would be that data discovery/visualization became a mainstream architecture. For years, data discovery/visualization vendors—such as QlikTech, Salient Management Company, Tableau Software, and Tibco Spotfire—received more positive feedback than vendors offering OLAP cube and semantic-layer-based architectures. In 2012, the market responded:

- MicroStrategy significantly improved Visual Insight.
- SAP launched Visual Intelligence.
- SAS launched Visual Analytics.
- Microsoft bolstered PowerPivot with Power View.
- IBM launched Cognos Insight.
- Oracle acquired Endeca.
- Actuate acquired Quiterian.

This emphasis on data discovery/visualization from most of the leaders in the market—which are now promoting tools with business-user-friendly data integration, coupled with embedded storage and computing layers (typically in-memory/columnar) and unfettered drilling—accelerates the trend toward decentralization and user empowerment of BI and analytics, and greatly enables organizations' ability to perform diagnostic analytics.

Source: Gartner Magic Quadrant, released on February 5, 2013, **gartner.com** (accessed February 2013).

In business intelligence and analytics, the key challenges for visualization have revolved around the intuitive representation of large, complex data sets with multiple dimensions and measures. For the most part, the typical charts, graphs, and other visual elements used in these applications usually involve two dimensions, sometimes three, and fairly small subsets of data sets. In contrast, the data in these systems reside in a data warehouse. At a minimum, these warehouses involve a range of dimensions (e.g., product, location, organizational structure, time), a range of measures, and millions of cells of data. In an effort to address these challenges, a number of researchers have developed a variety of new visualization techniques.

Visual Analytics

Visual analytics is a recently coined term that is often used loosely to mean nothing more than information visualization. What is meant by **visual analytics** is the combination of visualization and predictive analytics. While information visualization is aimed at answering "what happened" and "what is happening" and is closely associated with business intelligence (routine reports, scorecards, and dashboards), visual analytics is aimed at answering "why is it happening," "what is more likely to happen," and is usually associated with business analytics (forecasting, segmentation, correlation analysis). Many of the information visualization vendors are adding the capabilities to call themselves visual analytics solution providers. One of the top, long-time analytics solution providers, SAS Institute, is approaching it from another direction. They are embedding their analytics capabilities into a high-performance data visualization environment that they call visual analytics.

Visual or not visual, automated or manual, online or paper based, business reporting is not much different than telling a story. Technology Insights 4.2 provides a different, unorthodox viewpoint to better business reporting.

TECHNOLOGY INSIGHTS 4.2   Telling Great Stories with Data and Visualization

Everyone who has data to analyze has stories to tell, whether it's diagnosing the reasons for manufacturing defects, selling a new idea in a way that captures the imagination of your target audience, or informing colleagues about a particular customer service improvement program. And when it's telling the story behind a big strategic choice so that you and your senior management team can make a solid decision, providing a fact-based story can be especially challenging. In all cases, it's a big job. You want to be interesting and memorable; you know you need to keep it simple for your busy executives and colleagues. Yet you also know you have to be factual, detail oriented, and data driven, especially in today's metric-centric world.

It's tempting to present just the data and facts, but when colleagues and senior management are overwhelmed by data and facts without context, you lose. We have all experienced presentations with large slide decks, only to find that the audience is so overwhelmed with data that they don't know what to think, or they are so completely tuned out, they take away only a fraction of the key points.

Start engaging your executive team and explaining your strategies and results more powerfully by approaching your assignment as a story. You will need the "what" of your story (the facts and data) but you also need the "who?," the "how?," the "why?," and the often missed "so what?" It's these story elements that will make your data relevant and tangible for your audience. Creating a good story can aid you and senior management in focusing on what is important.

Why Story?

Stories bring life to data and facts. They can help you make sense and order out of a disparate collection of facts. They make it easier to remember key points and can paint a vivid picture of what the future can look like. Stories also create interactivity—people put themselves into stories and can relate to the situation.

Cultures have long used storytelling to pass on knowledge and content. In some cultures, storytelling is critical to their identity. For example, in New Zealand, some of the Maori people tattoo their faces with *mokus*. A *moku* is a facial tattoo containing a story about ancestors—the family tribe. A man may have a tattoo design on his face that shows features of a hammerhead to highlight unique qualities about his lineage. The design he chooses signifies what is part of his "true self" and his ancestral home.

Likewise, when we are trying to understand a story, the storyteller navigates to finding the "true north." If senior management is looking to discuss how they will respond to a competitive change, a good story can make sense and order out of a lot of noise. For example, you may have facts and data from two studies, one including results from an advertising study and one from a product satisfaction study. Developing a story for what you measured across both studies can help people see the whole where there were disparate parts. For rallying your distributors around a new product, you can employ a story to give vision to what the future can look like. Most importantly, storytelling is interactive—typically the presenter uses words and pictures that audience members can put themselves into. As a result, they become more engaged and better understand the information.

So What Is a Good Story?

Most people can easily rattle off their favorite film or book. Or they remember a funny story that a colleague recently shared. Why do people remember these stories? Because they contain certain characteristics. First, a good story has great characters. In some cases, the reader or viewer has a vicarious experience where they become involved with the character. The character then has to be faced with a challenge that is difficult but believable. There must be hurdles that the character overcomes. And finally, the outcome or prognosis is clear by the end of the story. The situation may not be resolved—but the story has a clear endpoint.

Think of Your Analysis as a Story—Use a Story Structure

When crafting a data-rich story, the first objective is to find the story. Who are the characters? What is the drama or challenge? What hurdles have to be overcome? And at the end of your story, what do you want your audience to do as a result?

Once you know the core story, craft your other story elements: define your characters, understand the challenge, identify the hurdles, and crystallize the outcome or decision question. Make sure you are clear with what you want people to do as a result. This will shape how your audience will recall your story. With the story elements in place, write out the storyboard, which represents the structure and form of your story. Although it's tempting to skip this step, it is better first to understand the story you are telling and then to focus on the presentation structure and form. Once the storyboard is in place, the other elements will fall into place. The storyboard will help you to think about the best analogies or metaphors, to clearly set up challenge or opportunity, and to finally see the flow and transitions needed. The storyboard also helps you focus on key visuals (graphs, charts, and graphics) that you need your executives to recall.

In summary, don't be afraid to use data to tell great stories. Being factual, detail oriented, and data driven is critical in today's metric-centric world but it does not have to mean being boring and lengthy. In fact, by finding the real stories in your data and following the best practices, you can get people to focus on your message—and thus on what's important. Here are those best practices:

1. Think of your analysis as a story—use a story structure.
2. Be authentic—your story will flow.
3. Be visual—think of yourself as a film editor.
4. Make it easy for your audience and you.
5. Invite and direct discussion.

Source: Elissa Fink and Susan J. Moore, "Five Best Practices for Telling Great Stories with Data," 2012, white paper by Tableau Software, Inc., **tableausoftware.com/whitepapers/telling-stories-with-data** (accessed February 2013).

High-Powered Visual Analytics Environments

Due to the increasing demand for visual analytics coupled with fast-growing data volumes, there is an exponential movement toward investing in highly efficient visualization systems. With their latest move into visual analytics, the statistical software giant SAS Institute is now among the ones who are leading this wave. Their new product, SAS Visual Analytics, is a very **high-performance**, in-memory solution for exploring massive amounts of data in a very short time (almost instantaneously). It empowers users to spot patterns, identify opportunities for further analysis, and convey visual results via Web reports or a mobile platform such as tablets and smartphones. Figure 4.6 shows the high-level architecture of the SAS Visual Analytics platform. On one end of the architecture, there are universal Data Builder and Administrator capabilities, leading into Explorer, Report Designer, and Mobile BI modules, collectively providing an end-to-end visual analytics solution.

Some of the key benefits proposed by SAS analytics are:

- Empower all users with data exploration techniques and approachable analytics to drive improved decision making. SAS Visual Analytics enables different types of users to conduct fast, thorough explorations on all available data. Subsetting or sampling of data is not required. Easy-to-use, interactive Web interfaces broaden the audience for analytics, enabling everyone to glean new insights. Users can look at more options, make more precise decisions, and drive success even faster than before.
- Answer complex questions faster, enhancing the contributions from your analytic talent. SAS Visual Analytics augments the data discovery and exploration process by providing extremely fast results to enable better, more focused analysis. Analytically savvy users can identify areas of opportunity or concern from vast amounts of data so further investigation can take place quickly.
- Improve information sharing and collaboration. Large numbers of users, including those with limited analytical skills, can quickly view and interact with reports and charts via the Web, Adobe PDF files, and iPad mobile devices, while IT maintains control of the underlying data and security. SAS Visual Analytics provides the right information to the right person at the right time to improve productivity and organizational knowledge.

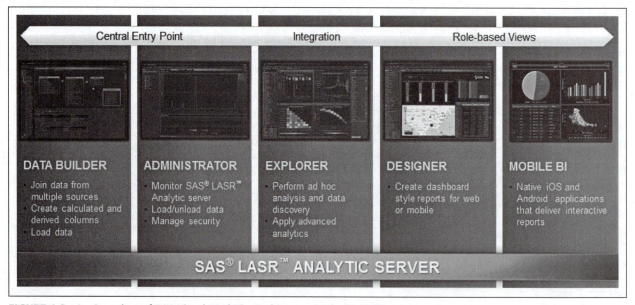

FIGURE 4.6 An Overview of SAS Visual Analytics Architecture. *Source:* SAS.com.

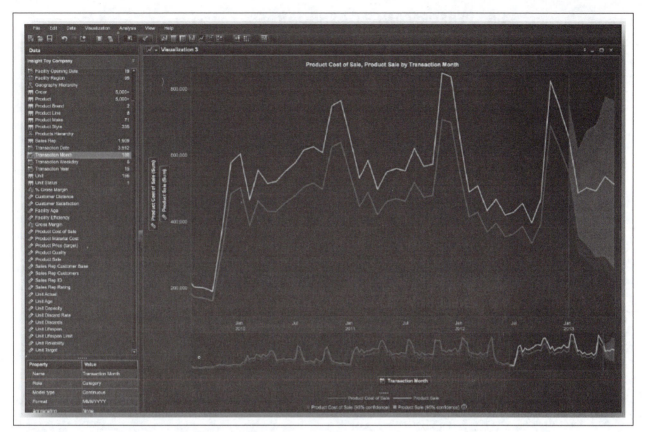

FIGURE 4.7 **A Screenshot from SAS Visual Analytics.** *Source:* **SAS.com.**

- Liberate IT by giving users a new way to access the information they need. Free IT from the constant barrage of demands from users who need access to different amounts of data, different data views, ad hoc reports, and one-off requests for information. SAS Visual Analytics enables IT to easily load and prepare data for multiple users. Once data is loaded and available, users can dynamically explore data, create reports, and share information on their own.
- Provide room to grow at a self-determined pace. SAS Visual Analytics provides the option of using commodity hardware or database appliances from EMC Greenplum and Teradata. It is designed from the ground up for performance optimization and scalability to meet the needs of any size organization.

Figure 4.7 shows a screenshot of an SAS Analytics platform where time-series forecasting and confidence intervals around the forecast are depicted. A wealth of information on SAS Visual Analytics, along with access to the tool itself for teaching and learning purposes, can be found at teradatauniversitynetwork.com.

SECTION 4.5 REVIEW QUESTIONS

1. What are the reasons for the recent emergence of visual analytics?
2. Look at Gartner's Magic Quadrant for Business Intelligence and Analytics Platforms. What do you see? Discuss and justify your observations.
3. What is the difference between information visualization and visual analytics?
4. Why should storytelling be a part of your reporting and data visualization?
5. What is a high-powered visual analytics environment? Why do we need it?

4.6 PERFORMANCE DASHBOARDS

Performance dashboards are common components of most, if not all, performance management systems, performance measurement systems, BPM software suites, and BI platforms. **Dashboards** provide visual displays of important information that is consolidated and arranged on a single screen so that information can be digested at a single glance and easily drilled in and further explored. A typical dashboard is shown in Figure 4.8. This particular executive dashboard displays a variety of KPIs for a hypothetical software company called Sonatica (selling audio tools). This executive dashboard shows a high-level view of the different functional groups surrounding the products, starting from a general overview to the marketing efforts, sales, finance, and support departments. All of this is intended to give executive decision makers a quick and accurate idea of what is going on within the organization. On the left side of the dashbord, we can see (in a time-series fashion) the quarterly changes in revenues, expenses, and margins, as well as the comparison of those figures to previous years' monthly numbers. On the upper-right side we see two dials with color-coded regions showing the amount of monthly expenses for support services (dial on the left) and the amount of other expenses (dial on the right).

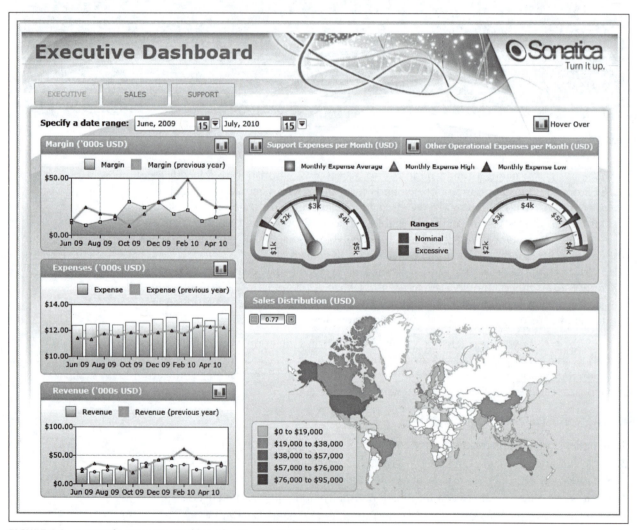

FIGURE 4.8 A Sample Executive Dashboard. *Source:* dundas.com.

As the color coding indicates, while the monthly support expenses are well within the normal ranges, the other expenses are in the red (or darker) region, indicating excessive values. The geographic map on the bottom right shows the distribution of sales at the country level throughput the world. Behind these graphical icons there are variety of mathematical functions aggregating numerous data points to their highest level of meaningul figures. By clicking on these graphical icons, the consumer of this information can drill down to more granular levels of information and data.

Dashboards are used in a wide variety of businesses for a wide variety of reasons. For instance, in Application Case 4.5, you will find the summary of a successful implementation of information dashboards by the Dallas Cowboys football team.

Application Case 4.5

Dallas Cowboys Score Big with Tableau and Teknion

Founded in 1960, the Dallas Cowboys are a professional American football team headquartered in Irving, Texas. The team has a large national following, which is perhaps best represented by the NFL record for number of consecutive games at sold-out stadiums.

Challenge

Bill Priakos, COO of the Dallas Cowboys Merchandising Division, and his team needed more visibility into their data so they could run it more profitably. Microsoft was selected as the baseline platform for this upgrade as well as a number of other sales, logistics, and e-commerce applications. The Cowboys expected that this new information architecture would provide the needed analytics and reporting. Unfortunately, this was not the case, and the search began for a robust dashboarding, analytics, and reporting tool to fill this gap.

Solution and Results

Tableau and Teknion together provided real-time reporting and dashboard capabilities that exceeded the Cowboys' requirements. Systematically and methodically the Teknion team worked side by side with data owners and data users within the Dallas Cowboys to deliver all required functionality, on time and under budget. "Early in the process, we were able to get a clear understanding of what it would take to run a more profitable operation for the Cowboys," said Teknion Vice President Bill Luisi. "This process step is a key step in Teknion's approach with any client, and it always pays huge dividends as the implementation plan progresses."

Added Luisi, "Of course, Tableau worked very closely with us and the Cowboys during the entire project. Together, we made sure that the Cowboys could achieve their reporting and analytical goals in record time."

Now, for the first time, the Dallas Cowboys are able to monitor their complete merchandising activities from manufacture to end customer and see not only what is happening across the life cycle, but drill down even further into why it is happening.

Today, this BI solution is used to report and analyze the business activities of the Merchandising Division, which is responsible for all of the Dallas Cowboys' brand sales. Industry estimates say that the Cowboys generate 20 percent of all NFL merchandise sales, which reflects the fact they are the most recognized sports franchise in the world.

According to Eric Lai, a *ComputerWorld* reporter, Tony Romo and the rest of the Dallas Cowboys may have been only average on the football field in the last few years, but off the field, especially in the merchandising arena, they remain America's team.

QUESTIONS FOR DISCUSSION

1. How did the Dallas Cowboys use information visualization?
2. What were the challenge, the proposed solution, and the obtained results?

Sources: Tableau, Case Study, **tableausoftware.com/learn/stories/tableau-and-teknion-exceed-cowboys-requirements** (accessed February 2013); and E. Lai, "BI Visualization Tool Helps Dallas Cowboys Sell More Tony Romo Jerseys," *ComputerWorld*, October 8, 2009.

Dashboard Design

Dashboards are not a new concept. Their roots can be traced at least to the EIS of the 1980s. Today, dashboards are ubiquitous. For example, a few years back, Forrester Research estimated that over 40 percent of the largest 2,000 companies in the world use the technology (Ante and McGregor, 2006). Since then, one can safely assume that this number has gone up quite significantly. In fact, nowadays it would be rather unusual to see a large company using a BI system that does not employ some sort of performance dashboards. The Dashboard Spy Web site (**dashboardspy.com/about**) provides further evidence of their ubiquity. The site contains descriptions and screenshots of thousands of BI dashboards, scorecards, and BI interfaces used by businesses of all sizes and industries, nonprofits, and government agencies.

According to Eckerson (2006), a well-known expert on BI in general and dashboards in particular, the most distinctive feature of a dashboard is its three layers of information:

1. ***Monitoring.*** Graphical, abstracted data to monitor key performance metrics.
2. ***Analysis.*** Summarized dimensional data to analyze the root cause of problems.
3. ***Management.*** Detailed operational data that identify what actions to take to resolve a problem.

Because of these layers, dashboards pack a lot of information into a single screen. According to Few (2005), "The fundamental challenge of dashboard design is to display all the required information on a single screen, clearly and without distraction, in a manner that can be assimilated quickly." To speed assimilation of the numbers, the numbers need to be placed in context. This can be done by comparing the numbers of interest to other baseline or target numbers, by indicating whether the numbers are good or bad, by denoting whether a trend is better or worse, and by using specialized display widgets or components to set the comparative and evaluative context.

Some of the common comparisons that are typically made in business intelligence systems include comparisons against past values, forecasted values, targeted values, benchmark or average values, multiple instances of the same measure, and the values of other measures (e.g., revenues versus costs). In Figure 4.8, the various KPIs are set in context by comparing them with targeted values, the revenue figure is set in context by comparing it with marketing costs, and the figures for the various stages of the sales pipeline are set in context by comparing one stage with another.

Even with comparative measures, it is important to specifically point out whether a particular number is good or bad and whether it is trending in the right direction. Without these sorts of evaluative designations, it can be time-consuming to determine the status of a particular number or result. Typically, either specialized visual objects (e.g., traffic lights) or visual attributes (e.g., color coding) are used to set the evaluative context. Again, for the dashboard in Figure 4.8, color coding (or varying gray tones) is used with the gauges to designate whether the KPI is good or bad, and green up arrows are used with the various stages of the sales pipeline to indicate whether the results for those stages are trending up or down and whether up or down is good or bad. Although not used in this particular example, additional colors—red and orange, for instance—could be used to represent other states on the various gauges. An interesting and informative dashboard-driven reporting solution built specifically for a very large telecommunication company is featured in Application Case 4.6.

Application Case 4.6

Saudi Telecom Company Excels with Information Visualization

Supplying Internet and mobile services to over 160 million customers across the Middle East, Saudi Telecom Company (STC) is one of the largest providers in the region, extending as far as Africa and South Asia. With millions of customers contacting STC daily for billing, payment, network usage, and support, all of this information has to be monitored somewhere. Located in the headquarters of STC is a data center that features a soccer field–sized wall of monitors all displaying information regarding network statistics, service analytics, and customer calls.

The Problem

When you have acres of information in front of you, prioritizing and contextualizing the data are paramount in understanding it. STC needed to identify the relevant metrics, properly visualize them, and provide them to the right people, often with time-sensitive information. "The executives didn't have the ability to see key performance indicators" said Waleed Al Eshaiwy, manager of the data center at STC. "They would have to contact the technical teams to get status reports. By that time, it would often be too late and we would be reacting to problems rather than preventing them."

The Solution

After carefully evaluating several vendors, STC made the decision to go with Dundas because of its rich data visualization alternatives. Dundas business intelligence consultants worked on-site in STC's headquarters in Riyadh to refine the telecommunication dashboards so they functioned properly. "Even if someone were to show you what was in the database, line by line, without visualizing it, it would be difficult to know what was going on," said Waleed, who worked closely with Dundas consultants. The success that STC experienced led to engagement on an enterprise-wide, mission-critical project to transform their data center and create a more proactive monitoring environment. This project culminated with the monitoring systems in STC's data center finally transforming from reactive to pro-active. Figure 4.9 shows a sample dashboard for call center management.

The Benefits

"Dundas' information visualization tools allowed us to see trends and correct issues before they became problems," said Mr. Eshaiwy. He added, "We decreased the amount of service tickets by 55 percent the year that we started using the information visualization tools and dashboards. The availability of the system increased, which meant customer satisfaction levels increased, which led to an increased customer base, which of course lead to increased revenues." With new, custom KPIs becoming visually available to the STC team, Dundas' dashboards currently occupy nearly a quarter of the soccer field–sized monitor wall. "Everything is on my screen, and I can drill down and find whatever I need to know," explained Waleed. He added, "Because of the design and structure of the dashboards, we can very quickly recognize the root cause of the problems and take appropriate action." According to Mr. Eshaiwy, Dundas is a success: "The adoption rates are excellent, it's easy to use, and it's one of the most successful projects that we have implemented. Even visitors who stop by my office are grabbed right away by the look of the dashboard!"

QUESTIONS FOR DISCUSSION

1. Why do you think telecommunications companies are among the prime users of information visualization tools?
2. How did Saudi Telecom use information visualization?
3. What were their challenges, the proposed solution, and the obtained results?

Source: Dundas, Customer Success Story, "Saudi Telecom Company Used Dundas' Information Visualization Solution," **dundas.com/wp-content/uploads/Saudi-Telecom-Company-Case-Study1.pdf** (accessed February 2013).

(Continued)

Application Case 4.6 (Continued)

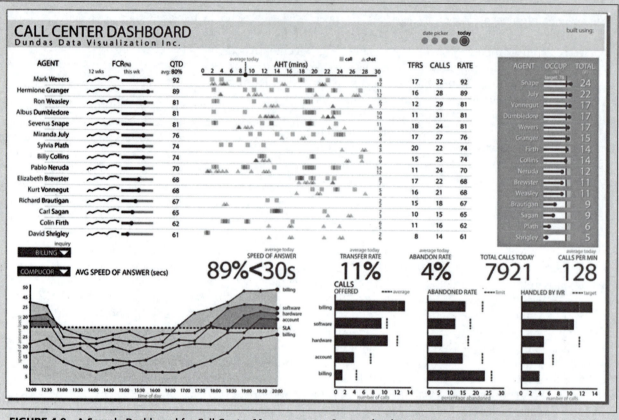

FIGURE 4.9 A Sample Dashboard for Call Center Management. *Source:* dundas.com.

What to Look for in a Dashboard

Although performance dashboards and other information visualization frameworks differ in their purpose, they all share some common design characteristics. First, they all fit within the larger business intelligence and/or performance measurement system. This means that their underlying architecture is the BI or performance management architecture of the larger system. Second, all well-designed dashboard and other information visualizations possess the following characteristics (Novell, 2009):

- They use visual components (e.g., charts, performance bars, sparklines, gauges, meters, stoplights) to highlight, at a glance, the data and exceptions that require action.
- They are transparent to the user, meaning that they require minimal training and are extremely easy to use.
- They combine data from a variety of systems into a single, summarized, unified view of the business.
- They enable drill-down or drill-through to underlying data sources or reports, providing more detail about the underlying comparative and evaluative context.
- They present a dynamic, real-world view with timely data refreshes, enabling the end user to stay up to date with any recent changes in the business.
- They require little, if any, customized coding to implement, deploy, and maintain.

Best Practices in Dashboard Design

The real estate saying "location, location, location" makes it obvious that the most important attribute for a piece of real estate property is where it is located. For dashboards, it is "data, data, data." An often overlooked aspect, data is one of the most important things to consider in designing dashboards (Carotenuto, 2007). Even if a dashboard's appearance looks professional, is aesthetically pleasing, and includes graphs and tables created according to accepted visual design standards, it is also important to ask about the data: Is it reliable? Is it timely? Is any data missing? Is it consistent across all dashboards? Here are some of the experiences-driven best practices in dashboard design (Radha, 2008).

Benchmark Key Performance Indicators with Industry Standards

Many customers, at some point in time, want to know if the metrics they are measuring are the right metrics to monitor. At times, many customers have found that the metrics they are tracking are not the right ones to track. Doing a gap assessment with industry benchmarks aligns you with industry best practices.

Wrap the Dashboard Metrics with Contextual Metadata

Often when a report or a visual dashboard/scorecard is presented to business users, many questions remain unanswered. The following are some examples:

- Where did you source this data?
- While loading the data warehouse, what percentage of the data got rejected/ encountered data quality problems?
- Is the dashboard presenting "fresh" information or "stale" information?
- When was the data warehouse last refreshed?
- When is it going to be refreshed next?
- Were any high-value transactions that would skew the overall trends rejected as a part of the loading process?

Validate the Dashboard Design by a Usability Specialist

In most dashboard environments, the dashboard is designed by a tool specialist without giving consideration to usability principles. Even though it's a well-engineered data warehouse that can perform well, many business users do not use the dashboard because it is perceived as not being user friendly, leading to poor adoption of the infrastructure and change management issues. Upfront validation of the dashboard design by a usability specialist can mitigate this risk.

Prioritize and Rank Alerts/Exceptions Streamed to the Dashboard

Because there are tons of raw data, it is important to have a mechanism by which important exceptions/behaviors are proactively pushed to the information consumers. A business rule can be codified, which detects the alert pattern of interest. It can be coded into a program, using database-stored procedures, which can crawl through the fact tables and detect patterns that need the immediate attention of the business user. This way, information finds the business user as opposed to the business user polling the fact tables for occurrence of critical patterns.

Enrich Dashboard with Business Users' Comments

When the same dashboard information is presented to multiple business users, a small text box can be provided to capture the comments from an end-user perspective. This can often be tagged to the dashboard and put the information in context, adding a lot of perspective to the structured KPIs being rendered.

Present Information in Three Different Levels

Information can be presented in three layers depending upon the granularity of the information: the visual dashboard level, the static report level, and the self-service cube level. When a user navigates the dashboard, a simple set of 8 to 12 KPIs can be presented, which would give a sense of what is going well and what is not.

Pick the Right Visual Construct Using Dashboard Design Principles

In presenting information in a dashboard, some information is presented best with bar charts, some with time-series line graphs, and, when presenting correlations, a scatter plot is useful. Sometimes merely rendering it as simple tables is effective. Once the dashboard design principles are explicitly documented, all the developers working on the front end can adhere to the same principles while rendering the reports and dashboard.

Provide for Guided Analytics

In a typical organization, business users can come at various levels of analytical maturity. The capability of the dashboard can be used to guide the "average" business user in order to access the same navigational path as that of an analytically savvy business user.

SECTION 4.6 REVIEW QUESTIONS

1. What is a performance dashboard? Why are they so popular for BI software tools?
2. What are the graphical widgets commonly used in dashboards? Why?
3. List and describe the three layers of information portrayed on dashboards.
4. What are the common characteristics for dashboards and other information visuals?
5. What are the best practices in dashboard design?

4.7 BUSINESS PERFORMANCE MANAGEMENT

In the business and trade literature, business performance management (BPM) has a number of names, including corporate performance management (CPM), enterprise performance management (EPM), and strategic enterprise management (SEM). CPM was coined by the market analyst firm Gartner (**gartner.com**). EPM is a term associated with Oracle's (**oracle.com**) offering by the same name. SEM is the term that SAP (**sap.com**) uses. In this chapter, BPM is preferred over the other terms because it is the earliest, the most generally used, and the one that does not closely tie to a single-solution provider. The term **business performance management (BPM)** refers to the business processes, methodologies, metrics, and technologies used by enterprises to measure, monitor, and manage business performance. It encompasses three key components (Colbert, 2009):

1. A set of integrated, closed-loop management and analytic processes (supported by technology) that addresses financial as well as operational activities
2. Tools for businesses to define strategic goals and then measure and manage performance against those goals
3. A core set of processes, including financial and operational planning, consolidation and reporting, modeling, analysis, and monitoring of key performance indicators (KPIs), linked to organizational strategy

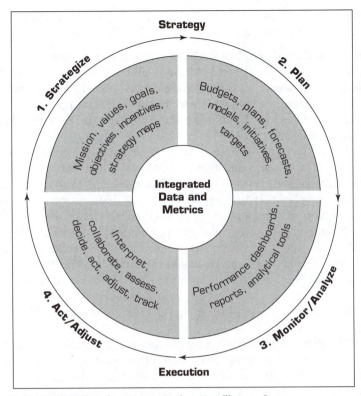

FIGURE 4.10   Closed-Loop BPM Cycle   *Source: Business Intelligence, 2e.*

Closed-Loop BPM Cycle

Maybe the most significant differentiator of BPM from any other BI tools and practices is its strategy focus. BPM encompasses a closed-loop set of processes that link strategy to execution in order to optimize business performance (see Figure 4.10). The loop implies that optimum performance is achieved by setting goals and objectives (i.e., strategize), establishing initiatives and plans to achieve those goals (i.e., plan), monitoring actual performance against the goals and objectives (i.e., monitor), and taking corrective action (i.e., act and adjust). The continuous and repetitive nature of the cycle implies that the completion of an iteration leads to a new and improved one (supporting continues process improvement efforts). In the following section these four processes are described.

1. *Strategize: Where do we want to go?*   Strategy, in general terms, is a high-level plan of action, encompassing a long period of time (often several years) to achieve a defined goal. It is especially necessary in a situation where there are numerous constraints (driven by market conditions, resource availabilities, and legal/political alterations) to deal with on the way to achieving the goal. In a business setting, strategy is the art and the science of crafting decisions that help businesses achieve their goals. More specifically, it is the process of identifying and stating the organization's mission, vision, and objectives, and developing plans (at different levels of granularity—strategic, tactical, and operational) to achieve these objectives.

Business strategies are normally planned and created by a team of corporate executives (often led by the CEO), approved and authorized by the board of directors, and then implemented by the company's management team under the supervision of the senior executives. Business strategy provides an overall direction to the enterprise and is the first and foremost important process in the BPM methodology.

2. Plan: How do we get there? When operational managers know and understand the *what* (i.e., the organizational objectives and goals), they will be able to come up with the *how* (i.e., detailed operational and financial plans). Operational and financial plans answer two questions: What tactics and initiatives will be pursued to meet the performance targets established by the strategic plan? What are the expected financial results of executing the tactics?

An operational plan translates an organization's strategic objectives and goals into a set of well-defined tactics and initiatives, resource requirements, and expected results for some future time period, usually, but not always, a year. In essence, an operational plan is like a project plan that is designed to ensure that an organization's strategy is realized. Most operational plans encompass a portfolio of tactics and initiatives. The key to successful operational planning is integration. Strategy drives tactics, and tactics drive results. Basically, the tactics and initiatives defined in an operational plan need to be directly linked to key objectives and targets in the strategic plan. If there is no linkage between an individual tactic and one or more strategic objectives or targets, management should question whether the tactic and its associated initiatives are really needed at all. The BPM methodologies discussed later in this chapter are designed to ensure that these linkages exist.

The financial planning and budgeting process has a logical structure that typically starts with those tactics that generate some form of revenue or income. In organizations that sell goods or services, the ability to generate revenue is based on either the ability to directly produce goods and services or acquire the right amount of goods and services to sell. After a revenue figure has been established, the associated costs of delivering that level of revenue can be generated. Quite often, this entails input from several departments or tactics. This means the process has to be collaborative and that dependencies between functions need to be clearly communicated and understood. In addition to the collaborative input, the organization also needs to add various overhead costs, as well as the costs of the capital required. This information, once consolidated, shows the cost by tactic as well as the cash and funding requirements to put the plan into operation.

3. Monitor/Analyze: How are we doing? When the operational and financial plans are underway, it is imperative that the performance of the organization be monitored. A comprehensive framework for monitoring performance should address two key issues: what to monitor and how to monitor. Because it is impossible to look at everything, an organization needs to focus on monitoring specific issues. After the organization has identified the indicators or measures to look at, it needs to develop a strategy for monitoring those factors and responding effectively. These measures are most often called key performance indicators (or KPI, in short). An overview of the process of determining KPI is given later in this chapter. A related topic to the selection of the optimal set of KPIs is the balanced scorecard method, which will also be covered in detail later in this chapter.

4. Act and Adjust: What do we need to do differently? Whether a company is interested in growing its business or simply improving its operations, virtually all strategies depend on new projects—creating new products, entering new markets, acquiring new customers or businesses, or streamlining some processes. Most companies approach these new projects with a spirit of optimism rather than objectivity, ignoring the fact that most new projects and ventures fail. What is the chance of failure? Obviously, it depends on the type of project (Slywotzky and Weber, 2007). Hollywood movies have around a 60 percent chance of failure. The same is true for mergers and acquisitions. Large IT projects fail at the rate of 70 percent. For new food products, the failure rate is 80 percent. For new pharmaceutical products, it is even higher, around 90 percent. Overall, the rate of failure for most new projects or ventures runs between 60 and 80 percent. Given these numbers, the answer to the question of "what do we need to do differently?" becomes a vital issue.

Application Case 4.7 shows how a large construction and consultancy company implemented an integrated reporting system to better track their financials and other important KPIs across its international branches.

Application Case 4.7

IBM Cognos Express Helps Mace for Faster and Better Business Reporting

Headquartered in the UK, Mace is an international consultancy and construction company that offers highly integrated services across the full property and infrastructure lifecycle. It employs 3,700 people in more than 60 countries worldwide, and is involved in some of the world's highest-profile projects, such as the construction of London's "Shard", the tallest building in Western Europe.

Many of Mace's international projects are contracted on a fixed-price basis, and their success depends on the company's ability to control costs and maintain profitability. Until recently, the only way for senior managers to gain a full understanding of international operations was a monthly report, based on a complex spreadsheet which drew data from numerous different accounting systems in subsidiaries around the world.

Brendan Kitley, Finance Systems Manager at Mace, comments: "The spreadsheet on which we based our international reports had about 40 tabs and hundreds of cross-links, which meant it was very easy to introduce errors, and the lack of a standardized approach was affecting accuracy and consistency. We wanted to find a more robust process for financial reporting."

Finding the Right Partner

Mace was already using IBM Cognos TM1® software for its domestic business in the UK, and was keen to find a similar solution for the international business.

"We decided to use IBM Cognos Express as the foundation of our international reporting platform," says Brendan Kitley. "We were impressed by its ability to give us many of the same capabilities as our TM1 solution, but at a price-point that was more affordable for an organization the size of our international division. We also liked the web interface, which we knew our international users would be able to access easily."

"We engaged with Barrachd, an IBM Business Partner, to support us during the project, and they did a very professional job. They helped us negotiate a reasonable price for the software licenses, delivered excellent technical support, and provided us with access to the right IBM experts whenever we needed them."

Rapid Implementation

The implementation was completed within six months, despite all the complexities of importing data from multiple accounting systems and handling exchange rate calculations for operations in over 40 countries. Mace is using all four modules of IBM Cognos Express: Xcelerator and Planner for modeling and planning; Reporter for business intelligence; and Advisor for several important dashboards.

"We have been really impressed by the ease of development with Cognos Express," comments Brendan Kitley. "Setting up new applications and cubes is relatively quick and simple, and we feel that we've only scratched the surface of what we can achieve. We have a lot of Cognos skills and experience in-house, so we are keen to build a wider range of functionalities into Cognos Express as we move forward."

Faster, More Sophisticated Reporting

The first major project with Cognos Express was to replicate the default reports that used to be produced by the old spreadsheet-based process. This was achieved relatively quickly, so the team was able to move on to a second phase of developing more sophisticated and detailed reports.

(Continued)

Application Case 4.7 (Continued)

"The reports we have now are much more useful because they allow us to drill down from the group level through all our international subsidiaries to the individual cost-centers, and even to the projects themselves," explains Brendan Kitley. "The ability to get an accurate picture of financial performance in each project empowers our managers to make better decisions."

"Moreover, since the reporting process is now largely automated, we can create reports more quickly and with less effort – which means we can generate them more frequently. Instead of a one-month lead time for reporting, we can do a full profitability analysis in half the time, and give our managers more timely access to the information they need."

Moving Towards a Single Platform

With the success of the international reporting project, Mace is working to unite all its UK and international subsidiaries into this single financial reporting and budgeting system. With a common platform for all reporting processes, the company's central finance team will be able to spend less time and effort on maintaining and customizing the processes, and more on actually analyzing the figures themselves.

Brendan Kitley concludes: "With better visibility and more timely access to more detailed and accurate information, we are in a better position to monitor performance and maintain profitability while ensuring that our projects are delivered on time and within budget. By continuing to work with IBM and Barrachd to develop our Cognos Express solution, we expect to unlock even greater benefits in terms of standardization and financial control."

QUESTIONS FOR DISCUSSION

1. What was the reporting challenge Mace was facing? Do you think this is an unusual challenge specific to Mace?
2. What was the approach for a potential solution?
3. What were the results obtained in the short term, and what were the future plans?

Source: IBM, Customer Success Story, "Mace gains insight into the performance of international projects" **http://www-01. ibm.com/software/success/cssdb.nsf/CS/STRD-99ALBX** (accessed September 2013).

SECTION 4.7 REVIEW QUESTIONS

1. What is business performance management? How does it relate to BI?
2. What are the three key components of a BPM system?
3. List and briefly describe the four phases of the BPM cycle.
4. Why is strategy the most important part of a BPM implementation?

4.8 PERFORMANCE MEASUREMENT

Underlying BPM is a performance measurement system. According to Simons (2002), **performance measurement systems**:

> Assist managers in tracking the implementations of business strategy by comparing actual results against strategic goals and objectives. A performance measurement system typically comprises systematic methods of setting business goals together with periodic feedback reports that indicate progress against goals.

All measurement is about comparisons. Raw numbers are of little value. If you were told that a salesperson completed 50 percent of the deals he or she was working on within a month, that would have little meaning. Now, suppose you were told that the same salesperson had a monthly close rate of 30 percent last year. Obviously, the trend is good. What if you were also told that the average close rate for all salespeople at the company was 80 percent? Obviously, that particular salesperson needs to pick up the pace. As Simons' definition suggests, in performance measurement, the key comparisons revolve around strategies, goals, and objectives. Operational metrics that are used to measure performance are usually called key performance indicators (KPIs).

Key Performance Indicator (KPI)

There is a difference between a "run of the mill" metric and a "strategically aligned" metric. The term **key performance indicator (KPI)** is often used to denote the latter. A KPI represents a strategic objective and measures performance against a goal. According to Eckerson (2009), KPIs are multidimensional. Loosely translated, this means that KPIs have a variety of distinguishing features, including:

- *Strategy.* KPIs embody a strategic objective.
- *Targets.* KPIs measure performance against specific targets. Targets are defined in strategy, planning, or budgeting sessions and can take different forms (e.g., achievement targets, reduction targets, absolute targets).
- *Ranges.* Targets have performance ranges (e.g., above, on, or below target).
- *Encodings.* Ranges are encoded in software, enabling the visual display of performance (e.g., green, yellow, red). Encodings can be based on percentages or more complex rules.
- *Time frames.* Targets are assigned time frames by which they must be accomplished. A time frame is often divided into smaller intervals to provide performance mileposts.
- *Benchmarks.* Targets are measured against a baseline or benchmark. The previous year's results often serve as a benchmark, but arbitrary numbers or external benchmarks may also be used.

A distinction is sometimes made between KPIs that are "outcomes" and those that are "drivers." Outcome KPIs—sometimes known as *lagging indicators*—measure the output of past activity (e.g., revenues). They are often financial in nature, but not always. Driver KPIs—sometimes known as *leading indicators* or *value drivers*—measure activities that have a significant impact on outcome KPIs (e.g., sales leads).

In some circles, driver KPIs are sometimes called *operational KPIs*, which is a bit of an oxymoron (Hatch, 2008). Most organizations collect a wide range of operational metrics. As the name implies, these metrics deal with the operational activities and performance of a company. The following list of examples illustrates the variety of operational areas covered by these metrics:

- *Customer performance.* Metrics for customer satisfaction, speed and accuracy of issue resolution, and customer retention.
- *Service performance.* Metrics for service-call resolution rates, service renewal rates, service-level agreements, delivery performance, and return rates.
- *Sales operations.* New pipeline accounts, sales meetings secured, conversion of inquiries to leads, and average call closure time.
- *Sales plan/forecast.* Metrics for price-to-purchase accuracy, purchase order-to-fulfillment ratio, quantity earned, forecast-to-plan ratio, and total closed contracts.

Whether an operational metric is strategic or not depends on the company and its use of the measure. In many instances, these metrics represent critical drivers of strategic outcomes. For instance, Hatch (2008) recalls the case of a mid-tier wine distributor that was being squeezed upstream by the consolidation of suppliers and downstream by the consolidation of retailers. In response, it decided to focus on four operational measures: on-hand/on-time inventory availability, outstanding "open" order value, net-new accounts, and promotion costs and return on marketing investment. The net result of its efforts was a 12 percent increase in revenues in 1 year. Obviously, these operational metrics were key drivers. However, as described in the following section, in many cases, companies simply measure what is convenient with minimal consideration as to why the data are being collected. The result is a significant waste of time, effort, and money.

Performance Measurement System

There is a difference between a performance measurement system and a performance management system. The latter encompasses the former. That is, any performance management system has a performance measurement system, but not the other way around. If you were to ask, most companies today would claim that they have a performance measurement system but not necessarily a performance management system, even though a performance measurement system has very little, if any, use without the overarching structure of the performance management system.

The most popular performance measurement systems in use are some variant of Kaplan and Norton's balanced scorecard (BSC). Various surveys and benchmarking studies indicate that anywhere from 50 to over 90 percent of all companies have implemented some form of BSC at one time or another. Although there seems to be some confusion about what constitutes "balance," there is no doubt about the originators of the BSC (Kaplan & Norton, 1996): "Central to the BSC methodology is a holistic vision of a measurement system tied to the strategic direction of the organization. It is based on a four-perspective view of the world, with financial measures supported by customer, internal, and learning and growth metrics."

SECTION 4.8 REVIEW QUESTIONS

1. What is a performance management system? Why do we need one?
2. What are the most distinguishing features of KPIs?
3. List and briefly define four of the most commonly cited operational areas for KPIs.
4. What is a performance measurement system? How does it work?

4.9 BALANCED SCORECARDS

Probably the best-known and most widely used performance management system is the balanced scorecard (BSC). Kaplan and Norton first articulated this methodology in their *Harvard Business Review* article, "The Balanced Scorecard: Measures That Drive Performance," which appeared in 1992. A few years later, in 1996, these same authors produced a groundbreaking book—*The Balanced Scorecard: Translating Strategy into Action*—that documented how companies were using the BSC not only to supplement their financial measures with nonfinancial measures, but also to communicate and implement their strategies. Over the past few years, BSC has become a generic term that is used to represent virtually every type of scorecard application and implementation, regardless of whether it is balanced or strategic. In response to this bastardization of the term, Kaplan and Norton released a new book in 2000, *The Strategy-Focused Organization: How Balanced Scorecard Companies Thrive in the New Business Environment*. This book was designed to reemphasize the strategic nature of the BSC methodology. This was followed a few years later, in 2004, by *Strategy Maps: Converting Intangible Assets into Tangible Outcomes*, which describes a detailed process for linking strategic objectives to operational tactics and initiatives. Finally, their latest book, *The Execution Premium*, published in 2008, focuses on the strategy gap—linking strategy formulation and planning with operational execution.

The Four Perspectives

The balanced scorecard suggests that we view the organization from four perspectives—customer, financial, internal business processes, learning and growth—and develop objectives, measures, targets, and initiatives relative to each of these perspectives. Figure 4.11 shows these four objectives and their interrelationship with the organization's vision and strategy.

THE CUSTOMER PERSPECTIVE   Recent management philosophies have shown an increasing realization of the importance of customer focus and customer satisfaction in any business. These are leading indicators: If customers are not satisfied, they will eventually find other suppliers that will meet their needs. Poor performance from this perspective is thus a leading indicator of future decline, even though the current financial picture may look good. In developing metrics for satisfaction, customers should be analyzed in terms of kinds of customers and the kinds of processes for which we are providing a product or service to those customer groups.

THE FINANCIAL PERSPECTIVE   Kaplan and Norton do not disregard the traditional need for financial data. Timely and accurate funding data will always be a priority, and managers will do whatever is necessary to provide it. In fact, often there is more than enough handling and processing of financial data. With the implementation of a corporate database, it is hoped that more of the processing can be centralized and automated. But the point is that the current emphasis on financials leads to the "unbalanced" situation with regard to other perspectives. There is perhaps a need to include additional financial-related data, such as risk assessment and cost–benefit data, in this category.

THE LEARNING AND GROWTH PERSPECTIVE   This perspective aims to answer the question, "To achieve our vision, how will we sustain our ability to change and improve?" It includes employee training, knowledge management, and corporate cultural characteristics related to both individual and corporate-level improvement. In the current climate of rapid technological change, it is becoming necessary for knowledge workers to be in a continuous learning and growing mode. Metrics can be put into place to guide managers

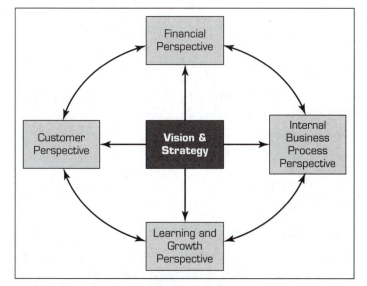

FIGURE 4.11   Four Perspectives in Balanced Scorecard Methodology.

in focusing training funds where they can help the most. In any case, learning and growth constitute the essential foundation for the success of any knowledge-worker organization. Kaplan and Norton emphasize that "learning" is more than "training"; it also includes things like mentors and tutors within the organization, as well as that ease of communication among workers that allows them to readily get help on a problem when it is needed.

THE INTERNAL BUSINESS PROCESS PERSPECTIVE   This perspective focuses on the importance of business processes. Metrics based on this perspective allow the managers to know how well their internal business processes and functions are running, and whether the outcomes of these processes (i.e., products and services) meet and exceed the customer requirements (the mission).

The Meaning of Balance in BSC

From a high-level viewpoint, the **balanced scorecard (BSC)** is both a performance measurement and a management methodology that helps translate an organization's financial, customer, internal process, and **learning** and growth objectives and targets into a set of actionable initiatives. As a measurement methodology, BSC is designed to overcome the limitations of systems that are financially focused. It does this by translating an organization's vision and strategy into a set of interrelated financial and nonfinancial objectives, measures, targets, and initiatives. The nonfinancial objectives fall into one of three perspectives:

- *Customer.* This objective defines how the organization should appear to its customers if it is to accomplish its vision.
- *Internal business process.* This objective specifies the processes the organization must excel at in order to satisfy its shareholders and customers.
- *Learning and growth.* This objective indicates how an organization can improve its ability to change and improve in order to achieve its vision.

Basically, nonfinancial objectives form a simple causal chain with "learning and growth" driving "internal business process" change, which produces "customer" outcomes that are responsible for reaching a company's "financial" objectives. A simple chain of this sort is exemplified in Figure 4.12, where a strategy map and balanced scorecard for a fictitious company are displayed. From the strategy map, we can see that the organization has four objectives across the four BSC perspectives. Like other strategy maps, this one begins at the top with a financial objective (i.e., increase net income). This objective is driven by a customer objective (i.e., increase customer retention). In turn, the customer objective is the result of an internal process objective (i.e., improve call center performance). The map continues down to the bottom of the hierarchy, where the learning objective is found (e.g., reduce employee turnover).

In BSC, the term *balance* arises because the combined set of measures is supposed to encompass indicators that are:

- Financial and nonfinancial
- Leading and lagging
- Internal and external
- Quantitative and qualitative
- Short term and long term

Dashboards Versus Scorecards

In the trade journals, the terms *dashboard* and *scorecard* are used almost interchangeably, even though BPM/BI vendors usually offer separate dashboard and scorecard applications. Although dashboards and scorecards have much in common, there are differences between

	Strategy Map: Linked Objectives	Balanced Scorecard: Measures and Targets		Strategic Initiatives: Action Plans
Financial	Increase Net Income	Net income growth	Increase 25%	
Customer	Increase Customer Retention	Maintenance retention rate	Increase 15%	Change licensing and maintenance contracts
Process	Improve Call Center Performance	Issue turnaround time	Improve 30%	Standardized call center processes
Learning and Growth	Reduce Employee Turnover	Voluntary turnover rate	Reduce 25%	Salary and bonus upgrade

FIGURE 4.12   Strategy Map and Balanced Scorecard.   *Source: Business Intelligence, 2e.*

the two. On the one hand, executives, managers, and staff use scorecards to monitor strategic alignment and success with strategic objectives and targets. As noted, the best-known example is the BSC. On the other hand, dashboards are used at the operational and tactical levels. Managers, supervisors, and operators use operational dashboards to monitor detailed operational performance on a weekly, daily, or even hourly basis. For example, operational dashboards might be used to monitor production quality. In the same vein, managers and staff use tactical dashboards to monitor tactical initiatives. For example, tactical dashboards might be used to monitor a marketing campaign or sales performance.

SECTION 4.9 REVIEW QUESTIONS

1. What is a balanced scorecard (BSC)? Where did it come from?
2. What are the four perspectives that BSC suggests us to use to view organizational performance?
3. Why do we need to define separate objectives, measures, targets, and initiatives for each of these four BSC perspectives?
4. What is the meaning of and motivation for *balance* in BSC?
5. What are the differences and commonalities between dashboards and scorecards?

4.10   SIX SIGMA AS A PERFORMANCE MEASUREMENT SYSTEM

Since its inception in the mid-1980s, Six Sigma has enjoyed widespread adoption by companies throughout the world. For the most part, it has not been used as a performance measurement and management methodology. Instead, most companies use it as a process improvement methodology that enables them to scrutinize their processes, pinpoint problems, and apply remedies. In recent years, some companies, such as Motorola, have recognized the value of using Six Sigma for strategic purposes. In these instances, Six Sigma provides the means to measure and monitor key processes related to a company's profitability and to accelerate improvement in overall business performance. Because of its focus on business processes, Six Sigma also provides a straightforward way to address performance problems after they are identified or detected.

Sigma, σ, is a letter in the Greek alphabet that statisticians use to measure the variability in a process. In the quality arena, *variability* is synonymous with the number of defects. Generally, companies have accepted a great deal of variability in their business processes. In numeric terms, the norm has been 6,200 to 67,000 defects per million opportunities (DPMO). For instance, if an insurance company handles 1 million claims, then under normal operating procedures 6,200 to 67,000 of those claims would be defective (e.g., mishandled, have errors in the forms). This level of variability represents a three- to four-sigma level of performance. To achieve a Six Sigma level of performance, the company would have to reduce the number of defects to no more than 3.4 DPMO. Therefore, **Six Sigma** is a performance management methodology aimed at reducing the number of defects in a business process to as close to zero DPMO as possible.

The DMAIC Performance Model

Six Sigma rests on a simple performance improvement model known as DMAIC. Like BPM, **DMAIC** is a closed-loop business improvement model, and it encompasses the steps of defining, measuring, analyzing, improving, and controlling a process. The steps can be described as follows:

1. ***Define.*** Define the goals, objectives, and boundaries of the improvement activity. At the top level, the goals are the strategic objectives of the company. At lower levels—department or project levels—the goals are focused on specific operational processes.
2. ***Measure.*** Measure the existing system. Establish quantitative measures that will yield statistically valid data. The data can be used to monitor progress toward the goals defined in the previous step.
3. ***Analyze.*** Analyze the system to identify ways to eliminate the gap between the current performance of the system or process and the desired goal.
4. ***Improve.*** Initiate actions to eliminate the gap by finding ways to do things better, cheaper, or faster. Use project management and other planning tools to implement the new approach.
5. ***Control.*** Institutionalize the improved system by modifying compensation and incentive systems, policies, procedures, manufacturing resource planning, budgets, operation instructions, or other management systems.

For new processes, the model that is used is called *DMADV* (define, measure, analyze, design, and verify). Traditionally, DMAIC and DMADV have been used primarily with operational issues. However, nothing precludes the application of these methodologies to strategic issues such as company profitability. In recent years, there has been a focus on combining the Six Sigma methodology with other successful methodologies. For instance, the methodology known as *Lean Manufacturing, Lean Production,* or simply as *Lean* has been combined with Six Sigma in order to improve its impact in performance management.

Balanced Scorecard Versus Six Sigma

While many have combined Six Sigma and Balanced Scorecard for a more holistic solution, some focused on favoring one versus the other. Gupta (2006) in his book titled *Six Sigma Business Scorecard* provides a good summary of the differences between the balanced scorecard and Six Sigma methodologies (see Table 4.1). In a nutshell, the main difference is that BSC is focused on improving overall strategy, whereas Six Sigma is focused on improving processes.

TABLE 4.1 Comparison of Balanced Scorecard and Six Sigma

Balanced Scorecard	Six Sigma
Strategic management system	Performance measurement system
Relates to the longer-term view of the business	Provides snapshot of business's performance and identifies measures that drive performance toward profitability
Designed to develop balanced set of measures	Designed to identify a set of measurements that impact profitability
Identifies measurements around vision and values	Establishes accountability for leadership for wellness and profitability
Critical management processes are to clarify vision/strategy, communicate, plan, set targets, align strategic initiatives, and enhance feedback	Includes all business processes—management and operational
Balances customer and internal operations without a clearly defined leadership role	Balances management and employees' roles; balances costs and revenue of heavy processes
Emphasizes targets for each measurement	Emphasizes aggressive rate of improvement for each measurement, irrespective of target
Emphasizes learning of executives based on the feedback	Emphasizes learning and innovation at all levels based on the process feedback; enlists all employees' participation
Focuses on growth	Focuses on maximizing profitability
Heavy on strategic content	Heavy on execution for profitability
Management system consisting of measures	Measurement system based on process management

Source: P. Gupta, *Six Sigma Business Scorecard,* 2nd ed., McGraw-Hill Professional, New York, 2006.

Effective Performance Measurement

A number of books provide recipes for determining whether a collection of performance measures is good or bad. Among the basic ingredients of a good collection are the following:

- Measures should focus on key factors.
- Measures should be a mix of past, present, and future.
- Measures should balance the needs of shareholders, employees, partners, suppliers, and other stakeholders.
- Measures should start at the top and flow down to the bottom.
- Measures need to have targets that are based on research and reality rather than arbitrary.

As the section on KPIs notes, although all of these characteristics are important, the real key to an effective performance measurement system is to have a good strategy. Measures need to be derived from the corporate and business unit strategies and from an analysis of the key business processes required to achieve those strategies. Of course, this is easier said than done. If it were simple, most organizations would already have effective performance measurement systems in place, but they do not.

Application Case 4.8, which describes the Web-based KPI scorecard system at **Expedia.com**, offers insights into the difficulties of defining both outcome and driver KPIs and the importance of aligning departmental KPIs to overall company objectives.

Application Case 4.8

Expedia.com's Customer Satisfaction Scorecard

Expedia, Inc., is the parent company to some of the world's leading travel companies, providing travel products and services to leisure and corporate travelers in the United States and around the world. It owns and operates a diversified portfolio of well-recognized brands, including **Expedia.com, Hotels.com, Hotwire.com**, TripAdvisor, Egencia, Classic Vacations, and a range of other domestic and international businesses. The company's travel offerings consist of airline flights, hotel stays, car rentals, destination services, cruises, and package travel provided by various airlines, lodging properties, car rental companies, destination service providers, cruise lines, and other travel product and service companies on a stand-alone and package basis. It also facilitates the booking of hotel rooms, airline seats, car rentals, and destination services from its travel suppliers. It acts as an agent in the transaction, passing reservations booked by its travelers to the relevant airline, hotel, car rental company, or cruise line. Together, these popular brands and innovative businesses make Expedia the largest online travel agency in the world, the third largest travel company in the United States, and the fourth largest travel company in the world. Its mission is to become the largest and most profitable seller of travel in the world, by helping everyone everywhere plan and purchase everything in travel.

Problem

Customer satisfaction is key to Expedia's overall mission, strategy, and success. Because **Expedia.com** is an online business, the customer's shopping experience is critical to Expedia's revenues. The online shopping experience can make or break an online business. It is also important that the customer's shopping experience is mirrored by a good trip experience. Because the customer experience is critical, all customer issues need to be tracked, monitored, and resolved as quickly as possible. Unfortunately, a few years back, Expedia lacked visibility into the "voice of the customer." It had no uniform way of measuring satisfaction, of analyzing the drivers of satisfaction, or of determining the impact of satisfaction on the company's profitability or overall business objectives.

Solution

Expedia's problem was not lack of data. The customer satisfaction group at Expedia knew that it had lots of data. In all, there were 20 disparate databases with 20 different owners. Originally, the group charged one of its business analysts with the task of pulling together and aggregating the data from these various sources into a number of key measures for satisfaction. The business analyst spent 2 to 3 weeks every month pulling and aggregating the data, leaving virtually no time for analysis. Eventually, the group realized that it wasn't enough to aggregate the data. The data needed to be viewed in the context of strategic goals, and individuals had to take ownership of the results.

To tackle the problem, the group decided it needed a refined vision. It began with a detailed analysis of the fundamental drivers of the department's performance and the link between this performance and Expedia's overall goals. Next, the group converted these drivers and links into a scorecard. This process involved three steps:

1. ***Deciding how to measure satisfaction.*** This required the group to determine which measures in the 20 databases would be useful for demonstrating a customer's level of satisfaction. This became the basis for the scorecards and KPIs.
2. ***Setting the right performance targets.*** This required the group to determine whether KPI targets had short-term or long-term payoffs. Just because a customer was satisfied with his or her online experience did not mean that the customer was satisfied with the vendor providing the travel service.
3. ***Putting data into context.*** The group had to tie the data to ongoing customer satisfaction projects.

The various real-time data sources are fed into a main database (called the Decision Support

Factory). In the case of the customer satisfaction group, these include customer surveys, CRM systems, interactive voice response systems, and other customer-service systems. The data in the DSS Factory are loaded on a daily basis into several data marts and multidimensional cubes. Users can access the data in a variety of ways that are relevant to their particular business needs.

Benefits

Ultimately, the customer satisfaction group came up with 10 to 12 objectives that linked directly to Expedia's corporate initiatives. These objectives were, in turn, linked to more than 200 KPIs within the customer satisfaction group. KPI owners can build, manage, and consume their own scorecards, and managers and executives have a transparent view of how well actions are aligning with the strategy. The scorecard also provides the customer satisfaction group with the ability to drill down into the data underlying any of the trends or patterns observed. In the past, all of this would have taken weeks or months to do, if it was done at all. With the scorecard, the Customer Service group can immediately see how well it is doing with respect to the KPIs, which, in turn, are reflected in the group's objectives and the company's objectives.

As an added benefit, the data in the system support not only the customer satisfaction group, but also other business units in the company. For example, a frontline manager can analyze airline expenditures on a market-by-market basis to evaluate negotiated contract performance or determine the savings potential for consolidating spending with a single carrier. A travel manager can leverage the business intelligence to discover areas with high volumes of unused tickets or offline bookings and devise strategies to adjust behavior and increase overall savings.

QUESTIONS FOR DISCUSSION

1. Who are the customers for Expedia.com? Why is customer satisfaction a very important part of their business?
2. How did Expedia.com improve customer satisfaction with scorecards?
3. What were the challenges, the proposed solution, and the obtained results?

Sources: Based on Microsoft, "Expedia: Scorecard Solution Helps Online Travel Company Measure the Road to Greatness," **download.microsoft.com/documents/customer evidence/22483_Expedia_Case_Study.doc** (accessed January 2013); and R. Smith, "Expedia-5 Team Blog: Technology," April 5, 2007, **expedia-team5.blogspot.com** (accessed September 2010).

SECTION 4.10 REVIEW QUESTIONS

1. What is Six Sigma? How is it used as a performance measurement system?
2. What is DMAIC? List and briefly describe the steps involved in DMAIC.
3. Compare BSC and Six Sigma as two competing performance measurement systems.
4. What are the ingredients for an effective performance management system?

Chapter Highlights

- A report is any communication artifact prepared with the specific intention of conveying information in a presentable form.
- A business report is a written document that contains information regarding business matters.
- The key to any successful business report is clarity, brevity, completeness, and correctness.
- Data visualization is the use of visual representations to explore, make sense of, and communicate data.

- Perhaps the most notable information graphic of the past was developed by Charles J. Minard, who graphically portrayed the losses suffered by Napoleon's army in the Russian campaign of 1812.
- Basic chart types include line, bar, and pie chart.
- Specialized charts are often derived from the basic charts as exceptional cases.
- Data visualization techniques and tools make the users of business analytics and business intelligence systems better information consumers.

- Visual analytics is the combination of visualization and predictive analytics.
- Increasing demand for visual analytics coupled with fast-growing data volumes led to exponential growth in highly efficient visualization systems investment.
- Dashboards provide visual displays of important information that is consolidated and arranged on a single screen so that information can be digested at a single glance and easily drilled in and further explored.
- BPM refers to the processes, methodologies, metrics, and technologies used by enterprises to measure, monitor, and manage business performance.
- BPM is an outgrowth of BI, and it incorporates many of its technologies, applications, and techniques.
- The primary difference between BI and BPM is that BPM is always strategy driven.
- BPM encompasses a closed-loop set of processes that link strategy to execution in order to optimize business performance.
- The key processes in BPM are strategize, plan, monitor, act, and adjust.
- Strategy answers the question "Where do we want to go in the future?"
- Decades of research highlight the gap between strategy and execution.
- The gap between strategy and execution is found in the broad areas of communication, alignment, focus, and resources.
- Operational and tactical plans address the question "How do we get to the future?"
- An organization's strategic objectives and key metrics should serve as top-down drivers for the allocation of the organization's tangible and intangible assets.
- Monitoring addresses the question of "How are we doing?"
- The overall impact of the planning and reporting practices of the average company is that management has little time to review results from a strategic perspective, decide what should be done differently, and act on the revised plans.

- The drawbacks of using financial data as the core of a performance measurement system are well known.
- Performance measures need to be derived from the corporate and business unit strategies and from an analysis of the key business processes required to achieve those strategies.
- Probably the best-known and most widely used performance management system is the BSC.
- Central to the BSC methodology is a holistic vision of a measurement system tied to the strategic direction of the organization.
- As a measurement methodology, BSC is designed to overcome the limitations of systems that are financially focused.
- As a strategic management methodology, BSC enables an organization to align its actions with its overall strategies.
- In BSC, strategy maps provide a way to formally represent an organization's strategic objectives and the causal connections among them.
- Most companies use Six Sigma as a process improvement methodology that enables them to scrutinize their processes, pinpoint problems, and apply remedies.
- Six Sigma is a performance management methodology aimed at reducing the number of defects in a business process to as close to zero DPMO as possible.
- Six Sigma uses DMAIC, a closed-loop business improvement model that involves the steps of defining, measuring, analyzing, improving, and controlling a process.
- Substantial performance benefits can be gained by integrating BSC and Six Sigma.
- The major BPM applications include strategy management; budgeting, planning, and forecasting; financial consolidation; profitability analysis and optimization; and financial, statutory, and management reporting.
- Over the past 3 to 4 years, the biggest change in the BPM market has been the consolidation of the BPM vendors.

Key Terms

business report
balanced scorecard (BSC)
business performance
   management (BPM)
dashboards

data visualization
DMAIC
high-performance
key performance indicator (KPI)
learning

performance measurement
   systems
report
Six Sigma
visual analytics

Questions for Discussion

1. What are the best practices in business reporting? How can we make our reports stand out?
2. Why has information visualization become a centerpiece in the business intelligence and analytics business? Is there a difference between information visualization and visual analytics?
3. Do you think performance dashboards are here to stay? Or are they about to be outdated? What do you think will be the next big wave in business intelligence and analytics?
4. SAP uses the term *strategic enterprise management* (SEM), Cognos uses the term *corporate performance management* (CPM), and Hyperion uses the term *business performance management* (BPM). Are they referring to the same basic ideas? Provide evidence to support your answer.
5. BPM encompasses five basic processes: strategize, plan, monitor, act, and adjust. Select one of these processes and discuss the types of software tools and applications that are available to support it. Figure 4.10 provides some hints. Also, refer to Bain & Company's list of management tools for assistance (**bain.com/management_tools/home.asp**).
6. Select a public company of interest. Using the company's 2013 annual report, create three strategic financial objectives for 2014. For each objective, specify a strategic goal or target. The goals should be consistent with the company's 2013 financial performance.
7. Netflix's strategy of moving to online video downloads has been widely discussed in a number of articles that can be found online. What are the basic objectives of Netflix's strategy now? What are some of the major assumptions underlying the strategy? Given what you know about discovery-driven planning, do these assumptions seem reasonable?
8. In recent years, the Beyond Budgeting Round Table (BBRT; **bbrt.org**) has called into question traditional budgeting practices. A number of articles on the Web discuss the BBRT's position. In the BBRT's view, what is wrong with today's budgeting practices? What does the BBRT recommend as a substitute?
9. Distinguish between performance management and performance measurement.
10. Create a measure for some strategic objective of interest (you can use one of the objectives formulated in discussion question 6). For the selected measure, complete the measurement template found in Table W4.2.1 in the online file for this chapter.
11. Using the four perspectives of the BSC, create a strategy for a hypothetical company. Express the strategy as a series of strategic objectives. Produce a strategy map depicting the linkages among the objectives.
12. Compare and contrast the DMAIC model with the closed-loop processes of BPM.
13. Select two companies that you are familiar with. What terms do they use to describe their BPM initiatives and software suites? Compare and contrast their offerings in terms of BPM applications and functionality.

Exercises

Teradata University and Other Hands-On Exercises

1. Download Tableau (**tableausoftware.com**). Using the Visualization_MFG_Sample data set (available as an Excel file on this book's Web site), answer the following questions:
   a. What is the relationship between gross box office revenue and other movie-related parameters given in the data set?
   b. How does this relationship vary across different years? Prepare a professional-looking written report that is enhanced with screenshots of your graphical findings.
2. Go to **teradatauniversitynetwork.com**. Select the "Articles" content type. Browse down the list of articles and locate one titled "Business/Corporate Performance Management: Changing Vendor Landscape and New Market Targets." Based on the article, answer the following questions:
   a. What is the basic focus of the article?
   b. What are the major "take aways" from the article?
   c. In the article, which organizational function or role is most intimately involved in CPM?

d. Which applications are covered by CPM?
e. How are these applications similar to or different from the applications covered by Gartner's CPM?
f. What is GRC, and what is its link to corporate performance?
g. What are some of the major acquisitions that occurred in the CPM marketplace over the last couple of years?
h. Select two of the companies discussed by the article (not SAP, Oracle, or IBM). What are the CPM strategies of each of the companies? What do the authors think about these strategies?

3. Go to **teradatauniversitynetwork.com.** Select the "Case Studies" content type. Browse down the list of cases and locate one titled "Real-Time Dashboards at Western Digital." Based on the article, answer the following questions:
   a. What is VIS?
   b. In what ways is the architecture of VIS similar to or different from the architecture of BPM?
   c. What are the similarities and differences between the closed-loop processes of BPM and the processes in the OODA decision cycle?

d. What types of dashboards are in the system? Are they operational or tactical, or are they actually scorecards? Explain.

e. What are the basic benefits provided by Western Digital's VIS and dashboards?

f. What sorts of advice can you provide to a company that is getting ready to create its own VIS and dashboards?

4. Go to Stephen Few's blog "The Perceptual Edge" (**perceptualedge.com**). Go to the section of "Examples." In this section, he provides critiques of various dashboard examples. Read a handful of these examples. Now go to **dundas.com.** Select the "Gallery" section of the site. Once there, click the "Digital Dashboard" selection. You will be shown a variety of different dashboard demos. Run a couple of the demos.

a. What sorts of information and metrics are shown on the demos? What sorts of actions can you take?

b. Using some of the basic concepts from Few's critiques, describe some of the good design points and bad design points of the demos.

5. Download an information visualization tool, such as Tableau, QlikView, or Spotfire. If your school does not have an educational agreement with these companies, then a trial version would be sufficient for this exercise. Use your own data (if you have any) or use one of the data sets that comes with the tool (they usually have one or more data sets for demonstration purposes). Study the data, come up with a couple of business problems, and use data and visualization to analyze, visualize, and potentially solve those problems.

6. Go to **teradatauniversitynetwork.com.** Find the "Tableau Software Project." Read the description, execute the tasks, and answer the questions.

7. Go to **teradatauniversitynetwork.com.** Find the assignment for SAS Visual Analytics. Using the information and step-by-step instructions provided in the assignment, execute the analysis on the SAS Visual Analytics tool (which is a Web-enabled system that does not require any local installation). Answer the questions posed in the assignment.

8. Develop a prototype dashboard to display the financial results of a public company. The prototype can be on paper, on Excel, or on a commercial tool. Use data from the 2012 annual plans of two public companies to illustrate the features of your dashboard.

Team Assignments and Role-Playing Projects

1. Virtually every BPM/CPM vendor provides case studies on their Web sites. As a team, select two of these vendors (you can get their names from the Gartner or AMR lists). Select two case studies from each of these sites. For each, summarize the problem the customer was trying to address, the applications or solutions implemented, and the benefits the customer received from the system.

2. Go to the Dashboard Spy Web site map for executive dashboards (**enterprise-dashboard.com/sitemap**). This site provides a number of examples of executive dashboards. As a team, select a particular industry (e.g., healthcare, banking, airlines). Locate a handful of example dashboards for that industry. Describe the types of metrics found on the dashboards. What types of displays are used to provide the information? Using what you know about dashboard design, provide a paper prototype of a dashboard for this information.

3. Go to **teradatauniversitynetwork.com.** From there, go to University of Arkansas data sources. Choose one of the large data sets, and download a large number of records (this may require you to write an SQL statement that creates the variables that you want to include in the data set). Come up with at least 10 questions that can be addressed with information visualization. Using your favorite data visualization tool, analyze the data and prepare a detail report that includes screenshots and other visuals.

End-of-Chapter Application Case

Smart Business Reporting Helps Healthcare Providers Deliver Better Care

Premier, which serves more than 2,600 U.S. hospitals and 84,000-plus other healthcare sites, exists to help its members improve the cost and quality of the care they provide the communities they serve. Premier also assists its members to prepare for and stay ahead of health reform, including accountable care and other new models of care delivery and reimbursement.

Challenge

As Premier executives looked to execute this vision, they recognized that the company's existing technical infrastructure could not support the new model. Over the years, Premier had developed a series of "siloed" applications, making it difficult for members to connect different data sources and metrics and see the "big picture" of how to drive healthcare transformation.

These platforms and associated software systems also lacked the scalability required to support the massive transaction volumes that were needed. At the same time, as Premier integrates data in new ways, it needs to ensure that the historic high level of data privacy and security is maintained. Moving forward with new technology, Premier had to confirm that it can isolate each healthcare organization's information to continue to meet patient privacy requirements and prevent unauthorized access to sensitive information.

Solution—Bridging the Information Gap

Premier's "re-platforming" effort represents groundbreaking work to enable the sharing and analysis of data from its thousands of member organizations. The new data architecture and infrastructure uses IBM software and hardware to deliver trusted information in the right context at the right time to users based on their roles. Using the new platform, Premier members will be able to use the portal to access the integrated system for various clinical, business, and compliance-related applications. From a clinical aspect, they will have access to best practices from leading hospitals and healthcare experts across the nation and can match patient care protocols with clinical outcomes to improve patient care.

Applications on the new platform will run the gamut from retrospective analysis of patient populations focused on identifying how to reduce readmissions and hospital-acquired conditions to near–real-time identification of patients receiving sub-therapeutic doses of an antibiotic. Business users within the alliance will be able to compare the effectiveness of care locally and with national benchmarks, which will help them improve resource utilization, minimizing waste both in healthcare delivery and in administrative costs. Additionally, this integrated data will help healthcare organizations contract with payers in support of integrated, accountable care.

Premier's commitment to improving healthcare extends beyond its member organizations. As part of its work, it teamed with IBM to create an integrated set of data models and templates that would help other organizations establish a comprehensive data warehouse of clinical, operational, and outcomes information. This data model, called the IBM Healthcare Provider Data Warehouse (HCPDW), can help healthcare organizations provide their staff with accurate and timely information to support the delivery of evidence-based, patient-centric, and accountable care.

Journey to Smarter Decisions

Fundamental to helping Premier turn its vision into reality is an Information Agenda strategy that transforms information into a strategic asset that can be leveraged across applications, processes, and decisions. "In its simplest form, Premier's platform brings together information from all areas of the healthcare system, aggregates it, normalizes it, and benchmarks it, so it impacts performance while the patient is still in the hospital or the physician's office," says Figlioli, senior vice president of healthcare informatics at the Premier healthcare alliance. "We wanted a flexible, nimble partner because this is not a cookie-cutter kind of project," says Figlioli. "Premier and IBM brought to the table an approach that was best of breed and included a cultural and partnering dimension that was fundamentally different from other vendors."

The organization's IT division is building its new infrastructure from the ground up. This includes replacing its existing x86 servers from a variety of hardware vendors with IBM POWER7 processor-based systems to gain greater performance at a lower cost. In fact, an early pilot showed up to a 50 percent increase in processing power with a reduction in costs. Additionally, the company is moving its core data warehouse to IBM DB2 pureScale, which is highly scalable to support the growing amount of data that Premier is collecting from its members. As part of Premier's platform, DB2 pureScale will

help doctors gain the information they need to avoid patient infections that are common in hospitals, and will help pharmacists ensure safe and effective medication use.

Data from facility admission, discharge, and transfer (ADT) systems along with departmental systems, such as pharmacy, microbiology, and lab information systems, will be sent to Premier's core data warehouse as HL7 messages, with near–real-time processing of this data occurring at a rate of 3,000 transactions per second. With the high performance that DB2 data software provides, Premier members can quickly learn of emerging healthcare issues, such as an increased incidence of MRSA (a highly drug-resistant version of *staphylococcus aureus* bacteria) in a particular area.

Data from IBM DB2 database software will be loaded into the IBM Netezza data warehouse appliance to enable members to conduct advanced analytics faster and easier than was previously possible. IBM Cognos Business Intelligence will be used to help members identify and analyze opportunities and trends across their organizations.

IBM InfoSphere software is used to acquire, transform, and create a single, trusted view of each constituent or entity. The data is then integrated and validated, and clinical or business rules management is applied through WebSphere ILOG software. These rules can help automatically notify clinicians of critical issues, such as the appropriate dosing of anti-coagulation medication. IBM Tivoli software provides security and service management. Application development is built upon Rational® software and a common user experience and collaboration are provided through IBM Connections software.

Business Benefits

Potential benefits for saving lives, helping people enjoy healthier lives, and reducing healthcare costs are enormous. In one Premier project, 157 participating hospitals saved an estimated 24,800 lives while reducing healthcare spending by $2.85 billion. The new system helps providers better identify which treatments will enable their patients to live longer, healthier lives. It also supports Premier members' work to address healthcare reform and other legislative requirements.

"When I think about my children, I think about what it will mean for them to live in a society that has solved the complexities of the healthcare system, so that no matter where they live, no matter what they do, no matter what condition they have, they can have the best possible care," says Figlioli.

Over the next 5 years, Premier plans to provide its members with many new applications in support of healthcare reform and other legislative requirements. As capabilities are added, the SaaS model will enable the platform to support its commitment to keep all 2,600 hospital members on the same page, and even expand its user community. With its new approach, Premier IT staff can develop, test, and launch new applications from a central location to provide users with updates concurrently. This is a lower-cost way to give Premier members an analytics solution with a shorter time to value.

1. What is Premier? What does it do?
2. What were the main challenges for Premier to achieve its vision?
3. What was the solution provided by IBM and other partners?

4. What were the results? Can you think of other benefits coming from such an integrated system?

Source: IBM, Customer Success Story, "Premier Healthcare Alliance Making a Quantum Leap Toward More Integrated Care and Improved Provider Performance," **ibm.com/smarterplanet/us/en/leadership/premier/assets/pdf/IBM_Premier.pdf** (accessed February 2013).

References

Allen, S. (2010). "Data Visualization." **interactiondesign.sva.edu** (accessed March 2013).

Ante, S., and J. McGregor. (2006, February 13). "Giving the Boss the Big Picture." *BusinessWeek.* **businessweek.com/magazine/content/06_07/b3971083.htm** (accessed January 2010).

Colbert, J. (2009, June). "Captain Jack and the BPM Market: Performance Management in Turbulent Times." *BPM Magazine.* **bmpmag.net/mag/captain_jack_bpm** (accessed January 2010).

Eckerson, W. (2009, January). "Performance Management Strategies: How to Create and Deploy Effective Metrics." *TDWI Best Practices Report.* **tdwi.org/research/display.aspx?ID=9390** (accessed January 2010).

Eckerson, W. (2006). *Performance Dashboards.* Hoboken, NJ: Wiley.

Few, S. (2005, Winter). "Dashboard Design: Beyond Meters, Gauges, and Traffic Lights." *Business Intelligence Journal,* Vol. 10, No. 1.

Few, S. (2007). "Data Visualization: Past, Present and Future." **perceptualedge.com/articles/Whitepapers/Data_Visualization.pdf** (accessed March 2013).

Few, S. (2008). "Data Visualization and Analysis—BI Blind Spots." *Visual Perceptual Edge.* **perceptualedge.com/blog/?p=367** (accessed January 2010).

Grimes, S. (2009, May 2). "Seeing Connections: Visualizations Makes Sense of Data." *Intelligent Enterprise.* **i.cmpnet.com/intelligententerprise/next-era-business-intelligence/Intelligent_Enterprise_Next_Era_BI_Visualization.pdf** (accessed January 2010).

Gupta, P. (2006). *Six Sigma Business Scorecard,* 2nd ed. New York: McGraw-Hill Professional.

Hammer, M. (2003). *Agenda: What Every Business Must Do to Dominate the Decade.* Pittsburgh, PA: Three Rivers Press.

Hatch, D. (2008, January). "Operational BI: Getting 'Real Time' about Performance." *Intelligent Enterprise.* **intelligententerprise.com/showArticle.jhtml?articleID=205920233** (accessed January 2010).

Hill, G. (2008). "A Guide to Enterprise Reporting." **ghill.customer.netspace.net.au/reporting/components.html** (accessed February 2013).

Kaplan, R., and D. Norton. (2008). *The Execution Premium.* Boston, MA: Harvard Business School Press.

Kaplan, R., and D. Norton. (2004). *Strategy Maps: Converting Intangible Assets into Tangible Outcomes.* Boston, MA: Harvard Business School Press.

Kaplan, R., and D. Norton. (2000). *The Strategy-Focused Organization: How Balanced Scorecard Companies Thrive in the New Business Environment.* Boston, MA: Harvard Business School Press.

Kaplan, R., and D. Norton. (1996). *The Balanced Scorecard: Translating Strategy into Action.* Boston, MA: Harvard University Press.

Kaplan, R., and D. Norton. (1992, January–February). "The Balanced Scorecard—Measures That Drive Performance." *Harvard Business Review,* pp. 71–79.

Knowledge@W. P. Carey. (2009, March 2). "High-Rolling Casinos Hit a Losing Streak." **knowledge.wpcarey.asu.edu/article.cfm?articleid=1752#** (accessed January 2010).

Microsoft. (2006, April 12). "Expedia: Scorecard Solution Helps Online Travel Company Measure the Road to Greatness." **microsoft.com/casestudies/Case_Study_Detail.aspx?CaseStudyID=49076** (accessed January 2010).

Norton, D. (2007). "Strategy Execution—A Competency That Creates Competitive Advantage." The Palladium Group. **thepalladiumgroup.com/KnowledgeObjectRepository/Norton_StrategyExeccreatescompetitiveadvWP.pdf** (accessed December 2012).

Novell. (2009, April). "Executive Dashboards Elements of Success." Novell white paper. **novell.com/rc/docrepository/public/37/basedocument.2009-03-23.4871823014/ExecutiveDashboards_Elements_of_Success_White_Paper_en.pdf** (accessed January 2013).

Simons, R. (2002). *Performance Measurement and Control Systems for Implementing Strategy.* Upper Saddle River, NJ: Prentice Hall.

Six Sigma Institute. (2009). "Lean Enterprise." **sixsigmainstitute.com/lean/index_lean.shtml** (accessed August 2009).

Slywotzky, A., and K. Weber. (2007). *The Upside: The 7 Strategies for Turning Big Threats into Growth Breakthroughs.* New York: Crown Publishing.

Smith, R. (2007, April 5). "Expedia-5 Team Blog: Technology." **expedia-team5.blogspot.com** (accessed January 2012).

Tufte, E. (2013). "Presenting of Data and Information." A resource for Web site designers by Edward Tufte and Dariane Hunt. **edwardtufte.com** (accessed February 2013).

Watson, H., and L. Volonino. (2001, January). "Harrah's High Payoff from Customer Information." *The Data Warehousing Institute Industry Study 2000—Harnessing Customer Information for Strategic Advantage: Technical Challenges and Business Solutions.* **terry.uga.edu/~hwatson/Harrahs.doc** (accessed January 2013).

Predictive Analytics

LEARNING OBJECTIVES FOR PART III

- Learn the role of predictive analytics (PA) and data mining (DM) in solving business problems
- Learn the processes and methods for conducting data mining projects
- Learn the role and capabilities of predictive modeling techniques, including artificial neural networks (ANN) and support vector machines (SVM)
- Learn the contemporary variations to data mining, such as text mining and Web mining

- Gain familiarity with the process, methods, and applications of text analytics and text mining
- Learn the taxonomy of Web mining solutions—Web content mining, Web usage mining, and Web structure mining
- Gain familiarity with the process, methods, and applications of Web analytics and Web mining

Data Mining

LEARNING OBJECTIVES

- Define data mining as an enabling technology for business analytics
- Understand the objectives and benefits of data mining
- Become familiar with the wide range of applications of data mining
- Learn the standardized data mining processes

- Understand the steps involved in data preprocessing for data mining
- Learn different methods and algorithms of data mining
- Build awareness of the existing data mining software tools
- Understand the privacy issues, pitfalls, and myths of data mining

Generally speaking, data mining is a way to develop intelligence (i.e., actionable information or knowledge) from data that an organization collects, organizes, and stores. A wide range of data mining techniques are being used by organizations to gain a better understanding of their customers and their own operations and to solve complex organizational problems. In this chapter, we study data mining as an enabling technology for business analytics, learn about the standard processes of conducting data mining projects, understand and build expertise in the use of major data mining techniques, develop awareness of the existing software tools, and explore privacy issues, common myths, and pitfalls that are often associated with data mining.

5.1 OPENING VIGNETTE: Cabela's Reels in More Customers with Advanced Analytics and Data Mining

Advanced analytics, such as data mining, has become an integral part of many retailers' decision-making processes. Utilizing large and information-rich transactional and customer data (that they collect on a daily basis) to optimize their business processes is not a choice for large-scale retailers anymore, but a necessity to stay competitive. Cabela's is one of those retailers who understands the value proposition and strives to fully utilize their data assets.

BACKGROUND

Started around a kitchen table in Chappell, Nebraska, in 1961, Cabela's has grown to become the largest direct marketer, and a leading specialty retailer, of hunting, fishing, camping, and related outdoor merchandise with $2.3 billion in sales. Credited largely to its information technology and analytics project initiatives, Cabela's has become one of the very few truly omni-channel retailers (an advanced form of multi-channel retailer who concentrate on a seamless approach to the consumer experience through all available shopping channels, including bricks-and-mortar, television, catalog, and e-commerce—through computers and mobile devices).

Essentially, Cabela's wanted to have a single view of the customers across multiple channels to better focus its marketing efforts and drive increased sales. For more than a decade, Cabela's has relied on SAS statistics and data mining tools to help analyze the data it gathers from sales transactions, market research, and demographic data associated with its large database of customers. "Using SAS data mining tools, we create predictive models to optimize customer selection for all customer contacts. Cabela's uses these prediction scores to maximize marketing spend across channels and within each customer's personal contact strategy. These efforts have allowed Cabela's to continue its growth in a profitable manner," says Corey Bergstrom, director of marketing research and analytics for Cabela's. "We're not talking single-digit growth. Over several years, it's double-digit growth."

USING THE BEST OF THE BREED (SAS AND TERADATA) FOR ANALYTICS

By dismantling the information silos existing in different branches, Cabela's was able to create what Tillotson (manager of customer analytics at Cabela's) calls "a holistic view of the customer." "Using SAS and Teradata, our statisticians were able to create the first complete picture of the customers and company activities. The flexibility of SAS in taking data from multiple sources, without help from IT, is critical."

As the volume and complexity of data increases, so does the time spent on preparing and analyzing it. Faster and better analysis results comes from timely and through modeling of large data sources. For that, an integration of data and model building algorithms is needed. To help organizations meet their needs for such integrated solutions, SAS recently joined forces with Teradata (one of the leading providers of data warehousing solutions) to create tools and techniques aimed at improving speed and accuracy for predictive and explanatory models.

Prior to the integration of SAS and Teradata, data for modeling and scoring customers was stored in a data mart. This process required a large amount of time to construct, bringing together disparate data sources and keeping statisticians from working on analytics. On average, the statisticians spent 1 to 2 weeks per month just building the data. Now, with the integration of the two systems, statisticians can leverage the power of SAS using the Teradata warehouse as one source of information rather than the multiple sources that existed before. This change has provided the opportunity to build models faster and with less data latency upon execution.

"With the SAS [and] Teradata integration we have a lot more flexibility. We can use more data and build more models to execute faster," says Dean Wynkoop, manager of data management for Cabela's.

The integration enabled Cabela's to bring its data close to its analytic functions in seconds versus days or weeks. It can also more easily find the highest-value customers in the best locations most likely to buy via the best channels. The integrated solution reduces the need to copy data from one system to another before analyzing the most likely indicators, allowing Cabela's to run related queries and flagging potentially ideal new prospects before the competition does. Analytics helps Cabela's to

- *Improve the return on its direct marketing investment.* Instead of costly mass mailings to every zip code in a 120-mile radius of a store, Cabela's uses predictive modeling to focus its marketing efforts within the geographies of customers most likely to generate the greatest possible incremental sales, resulting in a 60 percent increase in response rates.
- *Select optimal site locations.* "People used to come to us with suggestions on where they'd like our next store to be built," says Sarah Jaeger, marketing statistician. "As we move forward, we proactively leverage data to make retail site selections."
- *Understand the value of customers across all channels.* With detailed customer activity across store, Web site, and catalog purchases, SAS helps Cabela's build prediction, clustering, and association models that rate customers on a five-star system. This system helps enhance the customer experience, offering customer service reps a clear understanding of that customer's value to better personalize their interactions. "We treat all customers well, but we can develop strategies to treat higher-value customers a little better," says Josh Cox, marketing statistician.
- *Design promotional offers that best enhance sales and profitability.* With insights gained from SAS Analytics, Cabela's has learned that while promotions generate only marginal additional customer spending over the long haul, they do bring customers into their stores or to the Internet for catalog purchases.
- *Tailor direct marketing offers to customer preferences.* Cabela's can identify the customer's favorite channel and selectively send related marketing materials. "Does the customer like the 100-page catalogs or the 1,500-page catalogs?" Bergstrom says. "The customer tells us this through his past interactions so we can send the catalog that matches his or her needs. SAS gives Cabela's the power to conceivably personalize a unique marketing message, flyer, or catalog to every customer. The only limitation is the creation of each piece," Bergstrom says.

The integrated analytics solution (SAS Analytics with the Teradata in-database solution) allowed Cabela's to personalize catalog offerings; select new store locations and estimate their first-year sales; choose up-sell offerings that increase profits; and schedule promotions to drive sales. By doing so, the company has experienced double-digit growth. "Our statisticians in the past spent 75 percent of their time just trying to manage data. Now they have more time for analyzing the data with SAS. And we have become more flexible in the marketplace. That is just priceless." Wynkoop says.

Cabela's is currently working on analyzing the clickstream patterns of customers shopping online. Its goal is to put the perfect offer in front of the customer based on historical patterns of similar shoppers. "It is being tested and it works—we just need to productionalize it," Bergstrom says. "This would not be possible without the in-database processing capabilities of SAS, together with Teradata," Wynkoop says.

QUESTIONS FOR THE OPENING VIGNETTE

1. Why should retailers, especially omni-channel retailers, pay extra attention to advanced analytics and data mining?
2. What are the top challenges for multi-channel retails? Can you think of other industry segments that face similar problems?
3. What are the sources of data that retailers such as Cabela's use for their data mining projects?
4. What does it mean to have a "single view of the customer"? How can it be accomplished?
5. What type of analytics help did Cabela's get from their efforts? Can you think of any other potential benefits of analytics for large-scale retailers like Cabela's?
6. What was the reason for Cabela's to bring together SAS and Teradata, the two leading vendors in analytics marketplace?
7. What is in-database analytics, and why would you need it?

WHAT WE CAN LEARN FROM THIS VIGNETTE

The retail industry is amongst the most challenging because of the change that they have to deal with constantly. Understanding customer needs and wants, likes and dislikes, is an ongoing challenge. Ones who are able to create an intimate relationship through a "holistic view of the customer" will be the beneficiaries of this seemingly chaotic environment. In the midst of these challenges, what works in favor of these retailers is the availability of the technologies to collect and analyze data about their customers. Applying advanced analytics tools (i.e., knowledge discovery techniques) to these data sources provide them with the insight that they need for better decision making. Therefore the retail industry has become one of the leading users of the new face of analytics. Data mining is the prime candidate for better management of this data-rich, knowledge-poor business environment. The study described in the opening vignette clearly illustrates the power of analytics and data mining to create a holistic view of the customer for better customer relationship management. In this chapter, you will see a wide variety of data mining applications solving complex problems in a variety of industries where the data is used to leverage competitive business advantage.

Sources: SAS, Customer Case Studies, **sas.com/success/cabelas.html**; and Retail Information Systems News, April 3, 2012, **http://risnews.edgl.com/retail-best-practices/Why-Cabela-s-Has-Emerged-as-the-Top-Omni-Channel-Retailer79470**.

5.2 DATA MINING CONCEPTS AND APPLICATIONS

In an interview with *Computerworld* magazine in January 1999, Dr. Arno Penzias (Nobel laureate and former chief scientist of Bell Labs) identified data mining from organizational databases as a key application for corporations of the near future. In response to *Computerworld*'s age-old question of "What will be the killer applications in the corporation?" Dr. Penzias replied: "Data mining." He then added, "Data mining will become much more important and companies will throw away nothing about their customers because it will be so valuable. If you're not doing this, you're out of business." Similarly, in an article in *Harvard Business Review,* Thomas Davenport (2006) argued that the latest strategic weapon for companies is analytical decision making, providing examples of companies such as **Amazon.com**, Capital One, Marriott International, and others that have used analytics to better understand their customers and optimize their extended supply chains to maximize their returns on investment while providing the best customer service. This level of success is highly dependent on a company under-standing its customers, vendors, business processes, and the extended supply chain very well.

A large portion of "understanding the customer" can come from analyzing the vast amount of data that a company collects. The cost of storing and processing data has decreased dramatically in the recent past, and, as a result, the amount of data stored in electronic form has grown at an explosive rate. With the creation of large databases, the possibility of analyzing the data stored in them has emerged. The term *data mining* was originally used to describe the process through which previously unknown patterns in data were discovered. This definition has since been stretched beyond those limits by some software vendors to include most forms of data analysis in order to increase sales with the popularity of the data mining label. In this chapter, we accept the original defini-tion of data mining.

Although the term *data mining* is relatively new, the ideas behind it are not. Many of the techniques used in data mining have their roots in traditional statistical analysis and artificial intelligence work done since the early part of the 1980s. Why, then, has it suddenly gained the attention of the business world? Following are some of most pro-nounced reasons:

- More intense competition at the global scale driven by customers' ever-changing needs and wants in an increasingly saturated marketplace.
- General recognition of the untapped value hidden in large data sources.
- Consolidation and integration of database records, which enables a single view of customers, vendors, transactions, etc.
- Consolidation of databases and other data repositories into a single location in the form of a data warehouse.
- The exponential increase in data processing and storage technologies.
- Significant reduction in the cost of hardware and software for data storage and processing.
- Movement toward the de-massification (conversion of information resources into nonphysical form) of business practices.

Data generated by the Internet is increasing rapidly in both volume and complexity. Large amounts of genomic data are being generated and accumulated all over the world. Disciplines such as astronomy and nuclear physics create huge quantities of data on a regular basis. Medical and pharmaceutical researchers con-stantly generate and store data that can then be used in data mining applications to identify better ways to accurately diagnose and treat illnesses and to discover new and improved drugs.

On the commercial side, perhaps the most common use of data mining has been in the finance, retail, and healthcare sectors. Data mining is used to detect and reduce fraudulent activities, especially in insurance claims and credit card use (Chan et al., 1999); to identify customer buying patterns (Hoffman, 1999); to reclaim profitable customers (Hoffman, 1998); to identify trading rules from historical data; and to aid in increased profitability using market-basket analysis. Data mining is already widely used to bet-ter target clients, and with the widespread development of e-commerce, this can only become more imperative with time. See Application Case 5.1 for information on how Infinity P&C has used predictive analytics and data mining to improve customer service, combat fraud, and increase profit.

Application Case 5.1

Smarter Insurance: Infinity P&C Improves Customer Service and Combats Fraud with Predictive Analytics

Infinity Property & Casualty Corporation, a provider of nonstandard personal automobile insurance with an emphasis on higher-risk drivers, depends on its ability to identify fraudulent claims for sustained profitability. As a result of implementing analytics tools (from IBM SPSS), Infinity P&C has doubled the accuracy of its fraud identification, contributing to a return on investment of 403 percent per a Nucleus Research study. And the benefits don't stop there: According to Bill Dibble, senior vice president in Claims Operations at Infinity P&C, the use of predictive analytics in serving the company's legitimate claimants is of equal or even greater importance.

Low-Hanging Fruit

Initially, Dibble focused the power of predictive analytics (i.e., data mining) to assist the company's Special Investigative Unit (SIU). "In the early days of SIU, adjusters would use laminated cards with 'red flags' to indicate potential fraud. Taking those 'red flags' and developing rules seemed like an area of low-hanging fruit where we could quickly demonstrate the benefit of our investment in predictive analytics."

Dibble then leveraged a successful approach from another part of the business. "We recognized how important credit was in the underwriting arena, and I thought, 'Let's score our claims in the same way, to give us an indicator of potential fraud.' The larger the number we attach to a case, the more apt we are to have a fraud situation. Lower number, get the claim paid." Dibble notes that fraud represents a $20 billion exposure to the insurance industry and in certain venues could be an element in around 40 percent of claims. "A key benefit of the IBM SPSS system is its ability to continually analyze and score these claims, which helps ensure that we get the claim to the right adjuster at the right time," he says.

Adds Tony Smarrelli, vice president of National Operations: "Industry reports estimate one out of five claims is pure fraud—either opportunity fraud, where someone exaggerates an injury or vehicle damage, or the hard-core criminal rings that work with unethical clinics and attorneys. Rather than putting all five customers through an investigatory process, SPSS helps us 'fast-track' four of them and close their cases within a matter of days. This results in much happier customers, contributes to a more efficient workflow with improved cycle times, and improves retention due to an overall better claims experience."

An Unexpected Benefit

Dibble saw subrogation, the process of collecting damages from the at-fault driver's insurance company, as another piece of low-hanging fruit—and he was right. In the first month of using SPSS, Infinity P&C saw record recovery on paid collision claims, adding about $1 million directly to the company's bottom line and virtually eliminating the third-party collection fees of more than $70,000 per month that the company was used to paying. What's more, each of the following 4 or 5 months was even better than the previous one. "I never thought we would recover the money that we've recovered with SPSS in the subrogation area," he says. "That was a real surprise to us. It brought a lot of attention to SPSS within the company, and to the value of predictive analytics in general."

The rules-based IBM SPSS solution is well suited to Infinity P&C's business. For example, in states that have no-fault benefits, an insurance company can recover commercial vehicles or vehicles over a certain gross vehicle weight. "We can put a rule in IBM SPSS that if medical expenses are paid on a claim involving this type of vehicle, it is immediately referred to the subrogation department," explains Dibble. "This is a real-time ability that keeps us from missing potentially valuable subrogation opportunities, which used to happen a lot when we relied solely on adjuster intuition."

The rules are just as important on the fraud investigation side. Continues Dibble: "If we see an accident that happened around 1:00 A.M. and involved a gas-guzzling GMC Suburban, we need to start looking for fraud. So we dig a little deeper: Is this guy upside-down on his loan, such that he owes more money than the car is worth? Did

(Continued)

Application Case 5.1   (Continued)

the accident happen in a remote spot, suggesting that it may have been staged? Does the individual move frequently or list multiple addresses? As these elements are added to the equation, the score keeps building, and the case is more and more likely to be referred to one of our SIU investigators."

With SPSS, Infinity P&C has reduced SIU referral time from an average of 45–60 days to approximately 1–3 days, which means that investigators can get to work on the case before memories and stories start to change, rental and storage charges mount, and the likelihood of getting an attorney involved increases. The company is also creating a better claim for the SIU to investigate; a higher score correlates to a higher probability of fraud.

Making Us Smarter

SPSS rules start to score the claim immediately on first notice of loss (FNOL) when the claimant reports the accident. "We have completely revised our FNOL screens to collect more data points," says Dibble. "SPSS has made us much smarter in asking questions." Currently SPSS collects data mainly from the company's claims and policy systems; a future initiative to leverage the product's text mining capabilities will make the information in claims notes available as well.

Having proven its value in subrogation and SIU, the SPSS solution is poised for expansion within Infinity P&C. "One of our key objectives moving forward will be what we call 'right scripting,' where

we can script the appropriate questions for call center agents based on the answers they get from the claimant," says Dibble. "We'll also be instituting a process to flag claims with high litigation potential. By reviewing past litigation claims, we can identify predictive traits and handle those cases on a priority basis." Decision management, customer retention, pricing analysis, and dashboards are also potential future applications of SPSS technology.

But at the end of the day, excellent customer service remains the driving force behind Infinity P&C's use of predictive analytics. Concludes Dibble: "My goal is to pay the legitimate customer very quickly and get him on his way. People who are more economically challenged need their car; they typically don't have a spare vehicle. This is the car they use to go back and forth to work, so I want to get them out and on the road without delay. IBM SPSS makes this possible."

QUESTIONS FOR DISCUSSION

1. How did Infinity P&C improve customer service with data mining?
2. What were the challenges, the proposed solution, and the obtained results?
3. What was their implementation strategy? Why is it important to produce results as early as possible in data mining studies?

Source: **public.dhe.ibm.com/common/ssi/ecm/en/ytc03160 usen/YTC03160USEN.PDF** (accessed January 2013).

Definitions, Characteristics, and Benefits

Simply defined, **data mining** is a term used to describe discovering or "mining" knowledge from large amounts of data. When considered by analogy, one can easily realize that the term *data mining* is a misnomer; that is, mining of gold from within rocks or dirt is referred to as "gold" mining rather than "rock" or "dirt" mining. Therefore, data mining perhaps should have been named "knowledge mining" or "knowledge discovery." Despite the mismatch between the term and its meaning, *data mining* has become the choice of the community. Many other names that are associated with data mining include *knowledge extraction, pattern analysis, data archaeology, information harvesting, pattern searching,* and *data dredging*.

Technically speaking, data mining is a process that uses statistical, mathematical, and artificial intelligence techniques to extract and identify useful information and subsequent knowledge (or patterns) from large sets of data. These patterns can be in the form of business rules, affinities, correlations, trends, or prediction models (see Nemati and Barko, 2001). Most literature defines data mining as "the nontrivial process of identifying valid, novel, potentially useful, and ultimately understandable patterns in data stored in structured databases," where the data are organized in records structured by categorical, ordinal, and continuous variables (Fayyad et al., 1996). In this definition, the meanings of the key terms are as follows:

- *Process* implies that data mining comprises many iterative steps.
- *Nontrivial* means that some experimentation-type search or inference is involved; that is, it is not as straightforward as a computation of predefined quantities.
- *Valid* means that the discovered patterns should hold true on new data with sufficient degree of certainty.
- *Novel* means that the patterns are not previously known to the user within the context of the system being analyzed.
- *Potentially useful* means that the discovered patterns should lead to some benefit to the user or task.
- *Ultimately understandable* means that the pattern should make business sense that leads to the user saying "mmm! It makes sense; why didn't I think of that" if not immediately, at least after some post processing.

Data mining is not a new discipline, but rather a new definition for the use of many disciplines. Data mining is tightly positioned at the intersection of many disciplines, including statistics, artificial intelligence, machine learning, management science, information systems, and databases (see Figure 5.1). Using advances in all of these disciplines, data mining strives to make progress in extracting useful information and knowledge from large databases. It is an emerging field that has attracted much attention in a very short time.

The following are the major characteristics and objectives of data mining:

- Data are often buried deep within very large databases, which sometimes contain data from several years. In many cases, the data are cleansed and consolidated into a data warehouse. Data may be presented in a variety of formats (see Technology Insights 5.1 for a brief taxonomy of data).

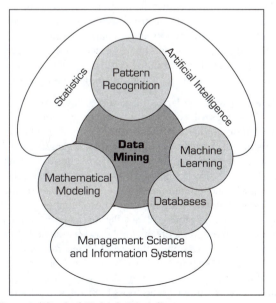

FIGURE 5.1   Data Mining as a Blend of Multiple Disciplines.

- The data mining environment is usually a client/server architecture or a Web-based information systems architecture.
- Sophisticated new tools, including advanced visualization tools, help to remove the information ore buried in corporate files or archival public records. Finding it involves massaging and synchronizing the data to get the right results. Cutting-edge data miners are also exploring the usefulness of soft data (i.e., unstructured text stored in such places as Lotus Notes databases, text files on the Internet, or enterprise-wide intranets).
- The miner is often an end user, empowered by data drills and other power query tools to ask ad hoc questions and obtain answers quickly, with little or no programming skill.
- Striking it rich often involves finding an unexpected result and requires end users to think creatively throughout the process, including the interpretation of the findings.
- Data mining tools are readily combined with spreadsheets and other software development tools. Thus, the mined data can be analyzed and deployed quickly and easily.
- Because of the large amounts of data and massive search efforts, it is sometimes necessary to use parallel processing for data mining.

A company that effectively leverages data mining tools and technologies can acquire and maintain a strategic competitive advantage. Data mining offers organizations an indispensable decision-enhancing environment to exploit new opportunities by transforming data into a strategic weapon. See Nemati and Barko (2001) for a more detailed discussion on the strategic benefits of data mining.

TECHNOLOGY INSIGHTS 5.1   A Simple Taxonomy of Data

Data refers to a collection of facts usually obtained as the result of experiences, observations, or experiments. Data may consist of numbers, letters, words, images, voice recordings, and so on as measurements of a set of variables. Data are often viewed as the lowest level of abstraction from which information and then knowledge is derived.

At the highest level of abstraction, one can classify data as structured and unstructured (or semistructured). Unstructured/semistructured data is composed of any combination of textual, imagery, voice, and Web content. Unstructured/semistructured data will be covered in more detailed in the text mining and Web mining chapters (see Chapters 7 and 8). Structured data is what data mining algorithms use, and can be classified as categorical or numeric. The categorical data can be subdivided into nominal or ordinal data, whereas numeric data can be subdivided into interval or ratio. Figure 5.2 shows a simple taxonomy of data.

- **Categorical data** represent the labels of multiple classes used to divide a variable into specific groups. Examples of categorical variables include race, sex, age group, and educational level. Although the latter two variables may also be considered in a numerical manner by using exact values for age and highest grade completed, it is often more informative to categorize such variables into a relatively small number of ordered classes. The categorical data may also be called *discrete data,* implying that it represents a finite number of values with no continuum between them. Even if the values used for the categorical (or discrete) variables are numeric, these numbers are nothing more than symbols and do not imply the possibility of calculating fractional values.
- **Nominal data** contain measurements of simple codes assigned to objects as labels, which are not measurements. For example, the variable *marital status* can be generally categorized as (1) single, (2) married, and (3) divorced. Nominal data can be represented with binomial values having two possible values (e.g., yes/no, true/false, good/bad), or multinomial values having three or more possible values (e.g., brown/green/blue, white/black/Latino/Asian, single/married/divorced).

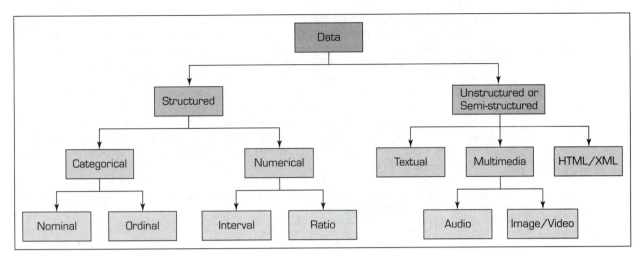

FIGURE 5.2 **A Simple Taxonomy of Data in Data Mining.**

- **Ordinal data** contain codes assigned to objects or events as labels that also represent the rank order among them. For example, the variable *credit score* can be generally categorized as (1) low, (2) medium, or (3) high. Similar ordered relationships can be seen in variables such as age group (i.e., child, young, middle-aged, elderly) and educational level (i.e., high school, college, graduate school). Some data mining algorithms, such as *ordinal multiple logistic regression,* take into account this additional rank-order information to build a better classification model.
- **Numeric data** represent the numeric values of specific variables. Examples of numerically valued variables include age, number of children, total household income (in U.S. dollars), travel distance (in miles), and temperature (in Fahrenheit degrees). Numeric values representing a variable can be integer (taking only whole numbers) or real (taking also the fractional number). The numeric data may also be called *continuous data,* implying that the variable contains continuous measures on a specific scale that allows insertion of interim values. Unlike a discrete variable, which represents finite, countable data, a continuous variable represents scalable measurements, and it is possible for the data to contain an infinite number of fractional values.
- **Interval data** are variables that can be measured on interval scales. A common example of interval scale measurement is temperature on the Celsius scale. In this particular scale, the unit of measurement is 1/100 of the difference between the melting temperature and the boiling temperature of water in atmospheric pressure; that is, there is not an absolute zero value.
- **Ratio data** include measurement variables commonly found in the physical sciences and engineering. Mass, length, time, plane angle, energy, and electric charge are examples of physical measures that are ratio scales. The scale type takes its name from the fact that measurement is the estimation of the ratio between a magnitude of a continuous quantity and a unit magnitude of the same kind. Informally, the distinguishing feature of a ratio scale is the possession of a nonarbitrary zero value. For example, the Kelvin temperature scale has a nonarbitrary zero point of absolute zero, which is equal to –273.15 degrees Celsius. This zero point is nonarbitrary, because the particles that comprise matter at this temperature have zero kinetic energy.

Other data types, including textual, spatial, imagery, and voice, need to be converted into some form of categorical or numeric representation before they can be processed by data mining algorithms. Data can also be classified as static or dynamic (i.e., temporal or time-series).

Some data mining methods and algorithms are very selective about the type of data that they can handle. Providing them with incompatible data types may lead to incorrect models or (more often) halt the model development process. For example, some data mining methods need all of the variables (both input as well as output) represented as numerically valued variables (e.g., neural networks, support vector machines, logistic regression). The nominal or ordinal variables are converted into numeric representations using some type of *1-of-N* pseudo variables (e.g., a categorical variable with three unique values can be transformed into three pseudo variables with binary values—1 or 0). Because this process may increase the number of variables, one should be cautious about the effect of such representations, especially for the categorical variables that have large numbers of unique values.

Similarly, some data mining methods, such as ID3 (a classic decision tree algorithm) and rough sets (a relatively new rule induction algorithm), need all of the variables represented as categorically valued variables. Early versions of these methods required the user to discretize numeric variables into categorical representations before they could be processed by the algorithm. The good news is that most implementations of these algorithms in widely available software tools accept a mix of numeric and nominal variables and internally make the necessary conversions before processing the data.

Application Case 5.2 illustrates an interesting application of data mining where predictive models are used by a police department to identify crime hotspots and better utilize limited crime-fighting resources.

Application Case 5.2

Harnessing Analytics to Combat Crime: Predictive Analytics Helps Memphis Police Department Pinpoint Crime and Focus Police Resources

When Larry Godwin took over as director of the Memphis Police Department (MPD) in 2004, crime across the metro area was surging, and city leaders were growing impatient. "The mayor told me I want this crime problem fixed," recalls Godwin, a 38-year veteran of the MPD. But the new director understood that a business-as-usual approach to crime fighting would no longer be good enough. Early on in his tenure, Godwin convened a meeting of top law enforcement experts to formulate a fresh strategy to turn the tide in the city's crime war. Among the participants in this mini-summit was Dr. Richard Janikowski, a professor of criminology at the University of Memphis, who specialized in using predictive analytics to better understand patterns.

Fighting Crime with Analytics

Janikowski proposed the idea of mining MPD's crime data banks to help zero in on where and when criminals were hitting hardest and then "focus police resources intelligently by putting them in the right place, on the right day, at the right time." By doing so, he said, "you'll either deter criminal activity or you're going to catch people." The idea made sense to Godwin and in short order the MPD and the University of Memphis—along with Project Safe Neighborhoods—teamed up in a pilot program that later became known as Operation Blue CRUSH, or Crime Reduction Utilizing Statistical History.

The data-driven pilot was wildly successful. During one 2-hour operation, officers arrested more criminals than they normally apprehend over an entire weekend. But for Blue CRUSH to be successful on a citywide scale, the MPD would need to align its resources and operations to take full advantage of the power of predictive analytics. If done right, a city-wide rollout of Blue CRUSH had the potential to save money through efficient deployments—a big plus in a city facing serious budget pressures—even as the intelligence-based approach would help drive down overall crime rates. Shortly after, all precincts embraced Blue CRUSH, and predictive analytics has become one of the most potent weapons in MPD's crime-fighting arsenal. At the heart of the system is a versatile statistical analysis tool—IBM SPSS Modeler—that enables officers to unlock the intelligence hidden in the department's huge digital library of crime records and police reports going back nearly a decade.

Safer Streets

All indications are that Blue CRUSH and its intelligence-driven crime fighting techniques are putting a serious dent in Memphis area crime. Since the program was launched, the number of Part One crimes—a category of serious offenses including homicide, rape, aggravated assault, auto theft, and larceny—has plummeted, dropping 27 percent from 2006 to 2010. Intelligent positioning of resources has been a major factor in the decline, helping to deter criminal activity by having more officers patrolling the right area at the right time on the right day.

More intelligent deployments also leads to faster reaction time, since officers are likely to be better positioned to respond to an unfolding crime. In addition, MPD's organized crime units are using data from the predictive analytics solution to run special details that lead to successful multi-agency drug busts and other criminal roundups. Not surprisingly, arrest rates have been steadily improving across the Memphis area, which has a population of 680,000.

Today, the MPD is continuing to explore new ways to exploit statistical analysis in its crime-fighting mission. Of course, predictive analytics and data mining is just one part of MPD's overall strategy for keeping Memphis residents safe. Effective liaisons with community groups and businesses, strong partnerships with regional and federal law enforcement agencies, and intelligent organizational and operational structures all play a part in continuing MPD's success story. "At the end of the day, everybody wants to reduce crime," says Godwin. "Everybody wants a safe community because without it, you don't have anything."

QUESTIONS FOR DISCUSSION

1. How did the Memphis Police Department use data mining to better combat crime?
2. What were the challenges, the proposed solution, and the obtained results?

Source: IBM Customer Story, "Harnessing Analytics to Combat Crime" **public.dhe.ibm.com/common/ssi/ecm/en/imc14541 usen/IMC14541USEN.PDF**.

How Data Mining Works

Using existing and relevant data, data mining builds models to identify patterns among the attributes presented in the data set. Models are the mathematical representations (simple linear relationships and/or complex highly nonlinear relationships) that identify the patterns among the attributes of the objects (e.g., customers) described in the data set. Some of these patterns are explanatory (explaining the interrelationships and affinities among the attributes), whereas others are predictive (foretelling future values of certain attributes). In general, data mining seeks to identify four major types of patterns:

1. *Associations* find the commonly co-occurring groupings of things, such as beer and diapers going together in market-basket analysis.
2. *Predictions* tell the nature of future occurrences of certain events based on what has happened in the past, such as predicting the winner of the Super Bowl or forecasting the absolute temperature of a particular day.
3. *Clusters* identify natural groupings of things based on their known characteristics, such as assigning customers in different segments based on their demographics and past purchase behaviors.
4. *Sequential relationships* discover time-ordered events, such as predicting that an existing banking customer who already has a checking account will open a savings account followed by an investment account within a year.

These types of patterns have been *manually* extracted from data by humans for centuries, but the increasing volume of data in modern times has created a need for more automatic approaches. As data sets have grown in size and complexity, direct manual data analysis has increasingly been augmented with indirect, automatic data processing tools that use sophisticated methodologies, methods, and algorithms. The manifestation of such evolution of automated and semiautomated means of processing large data sets is now commonly referred to as *data mining.*

Generally speaking, data mining tasks can be classified into three main categories: prediction, association, and clustering. Based on the way in which the patterns are extracted from the historical data, the learning algorithms of data mining methods can be classified as either supervised or unsupervised. With supervised learning algorithms, the training data includes both the descriptive attributes (i.e., independent variables or decision variables) as well as the class attribute (i.e., output variable or result variable). In contrast, with unsupervised learning the training data includes only the descriptive attributes. Figure 5.3 shows a simple taxonomy for data mining tasks, along with the learning methods, and popular algorithms for each of the data mining tasks.

PREDICTION   **Prediction** is commonly referred to as the act of telling about the future. It differs from simple guessing by taking into account the experiences, opinions, and other relevant information in conducting the task of foretelling. A term that is commonly associated with prediction is *forecasting.* Even though many believe that these two terms are synonymous, there is a subtle but critical difference between the two. Whereas prediction is largely experience and opinion based, forecasting is data and model based. That is, in order of increasing reliability, one might list the relevant terms as *guessing, predicting,* and *forecasting,* respectively. In data mining terminology, *prediction* and *forecasting* are

Data Mining	Learning Method	Popular Algorithms
Prediction	Supervised	Classification and Regression Trees, ANN, SVM, Genetic Algorithms
Classification	Supervised	Decision Trees, ANN/MLP, SVM, Rough Sets, Genetic Algorithms
Regression	Supervised	Linear/Nonlinear Regression, Regression Trees, ANN/MLP, SVM
Association	Unsupervised	Apriori, OneR, ZeroR, Eclat
Link analysis	Unsupervised	Expectation Maximization Apriori Algorithm, Graph-Based Matching
Sequence analysis	Unsupervised	Apriori Algorithm, FP-Growth technique
Clustering	Unsupervised	K-means, ANN/SOM
Outlier analysis	Unsupervised	K-means, Expectation Maximization (EM)

FIGURE 5.3   **A Simple Taxonomy for Data Mining Tasks.**

used synonymously, and the term *prediction* is used as the common representation of the act. Depending on the nature of what is being predicted, prediction can be named more specifically as classification (where the predicted thing, such as tomorrow's forecast, is a class label such as "rainy" or "sunny") or regression (where the predicted thing, such as tomorrow's temperature, is a real number, such as "65°F").

CLASSIFICATION **Classification**, or supervised induction, is perhaps the most common of all data mining tasks. The objective of classification is to analyze the historical data stored in a database and automatically generate a model that can predict future behavior. This induced model consists of generalizations over the records of a training data set, which help distinguish predefined classes. The hope is that the model can then be used to predict the classes of other unclassified records and, more importantly, to accurately predict actual future events.

Common classification tools include neural networks and decision trees (from machine learning), logistic regression and discriminant analysis (from traditional statistics), and emerging tools such as rough sets, support vector machines, and genetic algorithms. Statistics-based classification techniques (e.g., logistic regression and discriminant analysis) have received their share of criticism—that they make unrealistic assumptions about the data, such as independence and normality—which limit their use in classification-type data mining projects.

Neural networks (see Chapter 6 for a more detailed coverage of this popular machine-learning algorithm) involve the development of mathematical structures (somewhat resembling the biological neural networks in the human brain) that have the capability to learn from past experiences presented in the form of well-structured data sets. They tend to be more effective when the number of variables involved is rather large and the relationships among them are complex and imprecise. Neural networks have disadvantages as well as advantages. For example, it is usually very difficult to provide a good rationale for the predictions made by a neural network. Also, neural networks tend to need considerable training. Unfortunately, the time needed for training tends to increase exponentially as the volume of data increases, and, in general, neural networks cannot be trained on very large databases. These and other factors have limited the applicability of neural networks in data-rich domains.

Decision trees classify data into a finite number of classes based on the values of the input variables. Decision trees are essentially a hierarchy of if-then statements and are thus significantly faster than neural networks. They are most appropriate for categorical and interval data. Therefore, incorporating continuous variables into a decision tree framework requires *discretization,* that is, converting continuous valued numerical variables to ranges and categories.

A related category of classification tools is rule induction. Unlike with a decision tree, with rule induction the if-then statements are induced from the training data directly, and they need not be hierarchical in nature. Other, more recent techniques such as SVM, rough sets, and genetic algorithms are gradually finding their way into the arsenal of classification algorithms.

CLUSTERING **Clustering** partitions a collection of things (e.g., objects, events, etc., presented in a structured data set) into segments (or natural groupings) whose members share similar characteristics. Unlike classification, in clustering the class labels are unknown. As the selected algorithm goes through the data set, identifying the commonalities of things based on their characteristics, the clusters are established. Because the clusters are determined using a heuristic-type algorithm, and because different algorithms may end up with different sets of clusters for the same data set, before the results of clustering techniques are put to actual use it may be necessary for an expert to interpret, and potentially modify, the suggested clusters. After reasonable clusters have been identified, they can be used to classify and interpret new data.

Not surprisingly, clustering techniques include optimization. The goal of clustering is to create groups so that the members within each group have maximum similarity and the members across groups have minimum similarity. The most commonly used clustering techniques include *k*-means (from statistics) and self-organizing maps (from machine learning), which is a unique neural network architecture developed by Kohonen (1982).

Firms often effectively use their data mining systems to perform market segmentation with cluster analysis. Cluster analysis is a means of identifying classes of items so that items in a cluster have more in common with each other than with items in other clusters. It can be used in segmenting customers and directing appropriate marketing products to the segments at the right time in the right format at the right price. Cluster analysis is also used to identify natural groupings of events or objects so that a common set of characteristics of these groups can be identified to describe them.

ASSOCIATIONS **Associations**, or *association rule learning in data mining,* is a popular and well-researched technique for discovering interesting relationships among variables in large databases. Thanks to automated data-gathering technologies such as bar code scanners, the use of association rules for discovering regularities among products in large-scale transactions recorded by point-of-sale systems in supermarkets has become a common knowledge-discovery task in the retail industry. In the context of the retail industry, association rule mining is often called *market-basket analysis.*

Two commonly used derivatives of association rule mining are **link analysis** and **sequence mining**. With link analysis, the linkage among many objects of interest is discovered automatically, such as the link between Web pages and referential relationships among groups of academic publication authors. With sequence mining, relationships are examined in terms of their order of occurrence to identify associations over time. Algorithms used in association rule mining include the popular Apriori (where frequent itemsets are identified) and FP-Growth, OneR, ZeroR, and Eclat.

VISUALIZATION AND TIME-SERIES FORECASTING Two techniques often associated with data mining are *visualization* and *time-series forecasting.* Visualization can be used in conjunction with other data mining techniques to gain a clearer understanding of underlying relationships. As the importance to visualization has increased in recent years, a new term, *visual analytics,* has emerged. The idea is to combine analytics and visualization in a single environment for easier and faster knowledge creation. Visual analytics is covered in detail in Chapter 4. In time-series forecasting, the data consists of values of the same variable that is captured and stored over time in regular intervals. These data are then used to develop forecasting models to extrapolate the future values of the same variable.

Data Mining Versus Statistics

Data mining and statistics have a lot in common. They both look for relationships within data. Most call statistics the foundation of data mining. The main difference between the two is that statistics starts with a well-defined proposition and hypothesis while data mining starts with a loosely defined discovery statement. Statistics collects a sample data (i.e., primary data) to test the hypothesis, while data mining and analytics use all of the existing data (i.e., often observational, secondary data) to discover novel patterns and relationships. Another difference comes from the size of data that they use. Data mining looks for data sets that are as "big" as possible while statistics looks for right size of data (if the data is larger than what is needed/required for the statistical analysis, a sample of the data is used). The meaning of "large data" is rather different between statistics and data mining: Although a few hundred to a thousand data points are large enough to a statistician, several million to a few billion data points are considered large for data mining studies.

SECTION 5.2 REVIEW QUESTIONS

1. Define *data mining*. Why are there many different names and definitions for data mining?
2. What recent factors have increased the popularity of data mining?
3. Is data mining a new discipline? Explain.
4. What are some major data mining methods and algorithms?
5. What are the key differences between the major data mining methods?

5.3 DATA MINING APPLICATIONS

Data mining has become a popular tool in addressing many complex businesses problems and opportunities. It has been proven to be very successful and helpful in many areas, some of which are shown by the following representative examples. The goal of many of these business data mining applications is to solve a pressing problem or to explore an emerging business opportunity in order to create a sustainable competitive advantage.

- *Customer relationship management.* Customer relationship management (CRM) is the extension of traditional marketing. The goal of CRM is to create one-on-one relationships with customers by developing an intimate understanding of their needs and wants. As businesses build relationships with their customers over time through a variety of interactions (e.g., product inquiries, sales, service requests, warranty calls, product reviews, social media connections), they accumulate tremendous amounts of data. When combined with demographic and socioeconomic attributes, this information-rich data can be used to (1) identify most likely responders/buyers of new products/services (i.e., customer profiling); (2) understand the root causes of customer attrition in order to improve customer retention (i.e., churn analysis); (3) discover time-variant associations between products and services to maximize sales and customer value; and (4) identify the most profitable customers and their preferential needs to strengthen relationships and to maximize sales.
- *Banking.* Data mining can help banks with the following: (1) automating the loan application process by accurately predicting the most probable defaulters; (2) detecting fraudulent credit card and online-banking transactions; (3) identifying ways to maximize customer value by selling them products and services that they are most likely to buy; and (4) optimizing the cash return by accurately forecasting the cash flow on banking entities (e.g., ATM machines, banking branches).
- *Retailing and logistics.* In the retailing industry, data mining can be used to (1) predict accurate sales volumes at specific retail locations in order to determine correct inventory levels; (2) identify sales relationships between different products (with market-basket analysis) to improve the store layout and optimize sales promotions; (3) forecast consumption levels of different product types (based on seasonal and environmental conditions) to optimize logistics and hence maximize sales; and (4) discover interesting patterns in the movement of products (especially for the products that have a limited shelf life because they are prone to expiration, perishability, and contamination) in a supply chain by analyzing sensory and RFID data.

- *Manufacturing and production.* Manufacturers can use data mining to (1) predict machinery failures before they occur through the use of sensory data (enabling what is called *condition-based maintenance*); (2) identify anomalies and commonalities in production systems to optimize manufacturing capacity; and (3) discover novel patterns to identify and improve product quality.
- *Brokerage and securities trading.* Brokers and traders use data mining to (1) predict when and how much certain bond prices will change; (2) forecast the range and direction of stock fluctuations; (3) assess the effect of particular issues and events on overall market movements; and (4) identify and prevent fraudulent activities in securities trading.
- *Insurance.* The insurance industry uses data mining techniques to (1) forecast claim amounts for property and medical coverage costs for better business planning; (2) determine optimal rate plans based on the analysis of claims and customer data; (3) predict which customers are more likely to buy new policies with special features; and (4) identify and prevent incorrect claim payments and fraudulent activities.
- *Computer hardware and software.* Data mining can be used to (1) predict disk drive failures well before they actually occur; (2) identify and filter unwanted Web content and e-mail messages; (3) detect and prevent computer network security bridges; and (4) identify potentially unsecure software products.
- *Government and defense.* Data mining also has a number of military applications. It can be used to (1) forecast the cost of moving military personnel and equipment; (2) predict an adversary's moves and hence develop more successful strategies for military engagements; (3) predict resource consumption for better planning and budgeting; and (4) identify classes of unique experiences, strategies, and lessons learned from military operations for better knowledge sharing throughout the organization.
- *Travel industry (airlines, hotels/resorts, rental car companies).* Data mining has a variety of uses in the travel industry. It is successfully used to (1) predict sales of different services (seat types in airplanes, room types in hotels/resorts, car types in rental car companies) in order to optimally price services to maximize revenues as a function of time-varying transactions (commonly referred to as *yield management*); (2) forecast demand at different locations to better allocate limited organizational resources; (3) identify the most profitable customers and provide them with personalized services to maintain their repeat business; and (4) retain valuable employees by identifying and acting on the root causes for attrition.
- *Healthcare.* Data mining has a number of healthcare applications. It can be used to (1) identify people without health insurance and the factors underlying this undesired phenomenon; (2) identify novel cost–benefit relationships between different treatments to develop more effective strategies; (3) forecast the level and the time of demand at different service locations to optimally allocate organizational resources; and (4) understand the underlying reasons for customer and employee attrition.
- *Medicine.* Use of data mining in medicine should be viewed as an invaluable complement to traditional medical research, which is mainly clinical and biological in nature. Data mining analyses can (1) identify novel patterns to improve survivability of patients with cancer; (2) predict success rates of organ transplantation patients to develop better donor-organ matching policies; (3) identify the functions of different genes in the human chromosome (known as genomics); and (4) discover the relationships between symptoms and illnesses (as well as illnesses and successful treatments) to help medical professionals make informed and correct decisions in a timely manner.

- **Entertainment industry.** Data mining is successfully used by the entertainment industry to (1) analyze viewer data to decide what programs to show during prime time and how to maximize returns by knowing where to insert advertisements; (2) predict the financial success of movies before they are produced to make investment decisions and to optimize the returns; (3) forecast the demand at different locations and different times to better schedule entertainment events and to optimally allocate resources; and (4) develop optimal pricing policies to maximize revenues.

- **Homeland security and law enforcement.** Data mining has a number of homeland security and law enforcement applications. Data mining is often used to (1) identify patterns of terrorist behaviors (see Application Case 5.3 for an example of the use of data mining to track funding of terrorists' activities); (2) discover crime patterns (e.g., locations, timings, criminal behaviors, and other related attributes) to help solve criminal cases in a timely manner; (3) predict and eliminate potential biological and chemical attacks to the nation's critical infrastructure by analyzing special-purpose sensory data; and (4) identify and stop malicious attacks on critical information infrastructures (often called *information warfare*).

- **Sports.** Data mining was used to improve the performance of National Basketball Association (NBA) teams in the United States. Major League Baseball teams are into predictive analytics and data mining to optimally utilize their limited resources for a winning season (see Moneyball article in Chapter 1). In fact, most, if not all, of the professional sports employ data crunchers and use data mining to increase their chances of winning. Data mining applications are not limited to professional sports. In recently published article, Delen et al. (2012) developed models to predict NCAA Bowl Game outcomes using a wide range of variables about the two opposing teams' previous game statistics. Wright (2012) used a variety of predictors for examination of the NCAA men's basketball championship bracket (a.k.a. March Madness).

Application Case 5.3

A Mine on Terrorist Funding

The terrorist attack on the World Trade Center on September 11, 2001, underlined the importance of open source intelligence. The USA PATRIOT Act and the creation of the U.S. Department of Homeland Security (DHS) heralded the potential application of information technology and data mining techniques to detect money laundering and other forms of terrorist financing. Law enforcement agencies have been focusing on money laundering activities via normal transactions through banks and other financial service organizations.

Law enforcement agencies are now focusing on international trade pricing as a terrorism funding tool. International trade has been used by money launderers to move money silently out of a country without attracting government attention. This transfer is achieved by overvaluing imports and undervaluing exports. For example, a domestic importer and foreign exporter could form a partnership and overvalue imports, thereby transferring money from the home country, resulting in crimes related to customs fraud, income tax evasion, and money laundering. The foreign exporter could be a member of a terrorist organization.

Data mining techniques focus on analysis of data on import and export transactions from the U.S. Department of Commerce and commerce-related entities. Import prices that exceed the upper quartile import prices and export prices that are lower than the lower quartile export prices are tracked.

(Continued)

Application Case 5.3   (Continued)

The focus is on abnormal transfer prices between corporations that may result in shifting taxable income and taxes out of the United States. An observed price deviation may be related to income tax avoidance/evasion, money laundering, or terrorist financing. The observed price deviation may also be due to an error in the U.S. trade database.

Data mining will result in efficient evaluation of data, which, in turn, will aid in the fight against terrorism. The application of information technology and data mining techniques to financial transactions can contribute to better intelligence information.

Questions for Discussion

1. How can data mining be used to fight terrorism? Comment on what else can be done beyond what is covered in this short application case.

2. Do you think that, although data mining is essential for fighting terrorist cells, it also jeopardizes individuals' rights to privacy?

Sources: J. S. Zdanowic, "Detecting Money Laundering and Terrorist Financing via Data Mining," *Communications of the ACM,* Vol. 47, No. 5, May 2004, p. 53; and R. J. Bolton, "Statistical Fraud Detection: A Review," *Statistical Science,* Vol. 17, No. 3, January 2002, p. 235.

SECTION 5.3 REVIEW QUESTIONS

1. What are the major application areas for data mining?

2. Identify at least five specific applications of data mining and list five common characteristics of these applications.

3. What do you think is the most prominent application area for data mining? Why?

4. Can you think of other application areas for data mining not discussed in this section? Explain.

5.4   DATA MINING PROCESS

In order to systematically carry out data mining projects, a general process is usually followed. Based on best practices, data mining researchers and practitioners have proposed several processes (workflows or simple step-by-step approaches) to maximize the chances of success in conducting data mining projects. These efforts have led to several standardized processes, some of which (a few of the most popular ones) are described in this section.

One such standardized process, arguably the most popular one, Cross-Industry Standard Process for Data Mining—**CRISP-DM**—was proposed in the mid-1990s by a European consortium of companies to serve as a nonproprietary standard methodology for data mining (CRISP-DM, 2013). Figure 5.4 illustrates this proposed process, which is a sequence of six steps that starts with a good understanding of the business and the need for the data mining project (i.e., the application domain) and ends with the deployment of the solution that satisfied the specific business need. Even though these steps are sequential in nature, there is usually a great deal of backtracking. Because the data mining is driven by experience and experimentation, depending on the problem situation and the knowledge/experience of the analyst, the whole process can be very iterative (i.e., one should expect to go back and forth through the steps quite a few times) and time-consuming. Because later steps are built on the outcome of the former ones, one should pay extra attention to the earlier steps in order not to put the whole study on an incorrect path from the onset.

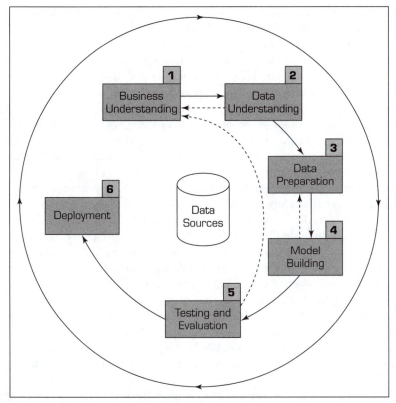

FIGURE 5.4   **The Six-Step CRISP-DM Data Mining Process.**

Step 1: Business Understanding

The key element of any data mining study is to know what the study is for. Answering such a question begins with a thorough understanding of the managerial need for new knowledge and an explicit specification of the business objective regarding the study to be conducted. Specific goals such as "What are the common characteristics of the customers we have lost to our competitors recently?" or "What are typical profiles of our customers, and how much value does each of them provide to us?" are needed. Then a project plan for finding such knowledge is developed that specifies the people responsible for collecting the data, analyzing the data, and reporting the findings. At this early stage, a budget to support the study should also be established, at least at a high level with rough numbers.

Step 2: Data Understanding

A data mining study is specific to addressing a well-defined business task, and different business tasks require different sets of data. Following the business understanding, the main activity of the data mining process is to identify the relevant data from many available databases. Some key points must be considered in the data identification and selection phase. First and foremost, the analyst should be clear and concise about the description of the data mining task so that the most relevant data can be identified. For example, a retail data mining project may seek to identify spending behaviors of female shoppers who purchase seasonal clothes based on their demographics, credit card transactions, and socioeconomic attributes. Furthermore, the analyst should build an intimate understanding of the data sources (e.g., where the relevant data are stored and in what form; what the process of collecting the data is—automated versus manual; who the collectors of the data are and how often the data are updated) and the variables (e.g., What are the most relevant variables? Are there any synonymous and/or homonymous variables? Are the variables independent of each other—do they stand as a complete information source without overlapping or conflicting information?).

In order to better understand the data, the analyst often uses a variety of statistical and graphical techniques, such as simple statistical summaries of each variable (e.g., for numeric variables the average, minimum/maximum, median, and standard deviation are among the calculated measures, whereas for categorical variables the mode and frequency tables are calculated), correlation analysis, scatter plots, histograms, and box plots. A careful identification and selection of data sources and the most relevant variables can make it easier for data mining algorithms to quickly discover useful knowledge patterns.

Data sources for data selection can vary. Normally, data sources for business applications include demographic data (such as income, education, number of households, and age), sociographic data (such as hobby, club membership, and entertainment), transactional data (sales record, credit card spending, issued checks), and so on.

Data can be categorized as quantitative and qualitative. Quantitative data is measured using numeric values. It can be discrete (such as integers) or continuous (such as real numbers). Qualitative data, also known as categorical data, contains both nominal and ordinal data. Nominal data has finite nonordered values (e.g., gender data, which has two values: male and female). Ordinal data has finite ordered values. For example, customer credit ratings are considered ordinal data because the ratings can be excellent, fair, and bad.

Quantitative data can be readily represented by some sort of probability distribution. A probability distribution describes how the data is dispersed and shaped. For instance, normally distributed data is symmetric and is commonly referred to as being a bell-shaped curve. Qualitative data may be coded to numbers and then described by frequency distributions. Once the relevant data are selected according to the data mining business objective, data preprocessing should be pursued.

Step 3: Data Preparation

The purpose of data preparation (or more commonly called *data preprocessing*) is to take the data identified in the previous step and prepare it for analysis by data mining methods. Compared to the other steps in CRISP-DM, data preprocessing consumes the most time and effort; most believe that this step accounts for roughly 80 percent of the total time spent on a data mining project. The reason for such an enormous effort spent on this step is the fact that real-world data is generally incomplete (lacking attribute values, lacking certain attributes of interest, or containing only aggregate data), noisy (containing errors or outliers), and inconsistent (containing discrepancies in codes or names). Figure 5.5 shows the four main steps needed to convert the raw real-world data into minable data sets.

In the first phase of data preprocessing, the relevant data is collected from the identified sources (accomplished in the previous step—Data Understanding—of the CRISP-DM process), the necessary records and variables are selected (based on an intimate understanding of the data, the unnecessary sections are filtered out), and the records coming from multiple data sources are integrated (again, using the intimate understanding of the data, the synonyms and homonyms are to be handled properly).

In the second phase of data preprocessing, the data is cleaned (this step is also known as data scrubbing). In this step, the values in the data set are identified and dealt with. In some cases, missing values are an anomaly in the data set, in which case they

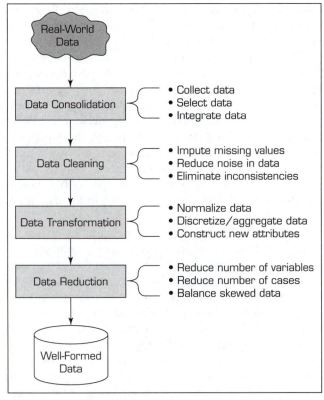

FIGURE 5.5 **Data Preprocessing Steps.**

need to be imputed (filled with a most probable value) or ignored; in other cases, the missing values are a natural part of the data set (e.g., the *household income* field is often left unanswered by people who are in the top income tier). In this step, the analyst should also identify noisy values in the data (i.e., the outliers) and smooth them out. Additionally, inconsistencies (unusual values within a variable) in the data should be handled using domain knowledge and/or expert opinion.

In the third phase of data preprocessing, the data is transformed for better processing. For instance, in many cases the data is normalized between a certain minimum and maximum for all variables in order to mitigate the potential bias of one variable (having large numeric values, such as for household income) dominating other variables (such as *number of dependents* or *years in service,* which may potentially be more important) having smaller values. Another transformation that takes place is discretization and/or aggregation. In some cases, the numeric variables are converted to categorical values (e.g., low, medium, high); in other cases a nominal variable's unique value range is reduced to a smaller set using concept hierarchies (e.g., as opposed to using the individual states with 50 different values, one may choose to use several regions for a variable that shows location) in order to have a data set that is more amenable to computer processing. Still, in other cases one might choose to create new variables based on the existing ones in order to magnify the information found in a collection of variables in the data set. For instance, in an organ transplantation data set one might choose to use a single variable showing the blood-type match (1: match, 0: no-match) as opposed to separate multinominal values for the blood type of both the donor and the recipient. Such simplification may increase the information content while reducing the complexity of the relationships in the data.

The final phase of data preprocessing is data reduction. Even though data miners like to have large data sets, too much data is also a problem. In the simplest sense, one can visualize the data commonly used in data mining projects as a flat file consisting of two dimensions: variables (the number of columns) and cases/records (the number of rows). In some cases (e.g., image processing and genome projects with complex microarray data), the number of variables can be rather large, and the analyst must reduce the number to a manageable size. Because the variables are treated as different dimensions that describe the phenomenon from different perspectives, in data mining this process is commonly called *dimensional reduction*. Even though there is not a single best way to accomplish this task, one can use the findings from previously published literature; consult domain experts; run appropriate statistical tests (e.g., principal component analysis or independent component analysis); and, more preferably, use a combination of these techniques to successfully reduce the dimensions in the data into a more manageable and most relevant subset.

With respect to the other dimension (i.e., the number of cases), some data sets may include millions or billions of records. Even though computing power is increasing exponentially, processing such a large number of records may not be practical or feasible. In such cases, one may need to sample a subset of the data for analysis. The underlying assumption of sampling is that the subset of the data will contain all relevant patterns of the complete data set. In a homogenous data set, such an assumption may hold well, but real-world data is hardly ever homogenous. The analyst should be extremely careful in selecting a subset of the data that reflects the essence of the complete data set and is not specific to a subgroup or subcategory. The data is usually sorted on some variable, and taking a section of the data from the top or bottom may lead to a biased data set on specific values of the indexed variable; therefore, one should always try to randomly select the records on the sample set. For skewed data, straightforward random sampling may not be sufficient, and stratified sampling (a proportional representation of different subgroups in the data is represented in the sample data set) may be required. Speaking of skewed data: It is a good practice to balance the highly skewed data by either oversampling the less represented or undersampling the more represented classes. Research has shown that balanced data sets tend to produce better prediction models than unbalanced ones (Wilson and Sharda, 1994).

The essence of data preprocessing is summarized in Table 5.1, which maps the main phases (along with their problem descriptions) to a representative list of tasks and algorithms.

Step 4: Model Building

In this step, various modeling techniques are selected and applied to an already prepared data set in order to address the specific business need. The model-building step also encompasses the assessment and comparative analysis of the various models built. Because there is no universally known *best* method or algorithm for a data mining task, one should use a variety of viable model types along with a well-defined experimentation and assessment strategy to identify the "best" method for a given purpose. Even for a single method or algorithm, a number of parameters need to be calibrated to obtain optimal results. Some methods may have specific requirements on the way that the data is to be formatted; thus, stepping back to the data preparation step is often necessary. Application Case 5.4 presents a research study where a number of model types are developed and compared to each other.

Depending on the business need, the data mining task can be of a prediction (either classification or regression), an association, or a clustering type. Each of these

TABLE 5.1 **A Summary of Data Preprocessing Tasks and Potential Methods**

Main Task	Subtasks	Popular Methods
Data consolidation	Access and collect the data	SQL queries, software agents, Web services.
	Select and filter the data	Domain expertise, SQL queries, statistical tests.
	Integrate and unify the data	SQL queries, domain expertise, ontology-driven data mapping.
Data cleaning	Handle missing values in the data	Fill-in missing values (imputations) with most appropriate values (mean, median, min/max, mode, etc.); recode the missing values with a constant such as "ML"; remove the record of the missing value; do nothing.
	Identify and reduce noise in the data	Identify the outliers in data with simple statistical techniques (such as averages and standard deviations) or with cluster analysis; once identified either remove the outliers or smooth them by using binning, regression, or simple averages.
	Find and eliminate erroneous data	Identify the erroneous values in data (other than outliers), such as odd values, inconsistent class labels, odd distributions; once identified, use domain expertise to correct the values or remove the records holding the erroneous values.
Data transformation	Normalize the data	Reduce the range of values in each numerically valued variable to a standard range (e.g., 0 to 1 or −1 to +1) by using a variety of normalization or scaling techniques.
	Discretize or aggregate the data	If needed, convert the numeric variables into discrete representations using range or frequency-based binning techniques; for categorical variables reduce the number of values by applying proper concept hierarchies.
	Construct new attributes	Derive new and more informative variables from the existing ones using a wide range of mathematical functions (as simple as addition and multiplication or as complex as a hybrid combination of log transformations).
Data reduction	Reduce number of attributes	Principal component analysis, independent component analysis, Chi-square testing, correlation analysis, and decision tree induction.
	Reduce number of records	Random sampling, stratified sampling, expert–knowledge-driven purposeful sampling.
	Balance skewed data	Oversample the less represented or undersample the more represented classes.

data mining tasks can use a variety of data mining methods and algorithms. Some of these data mining methods were explained earlier in this chapter, and some of the most popular algorithms, including decision trees for classification, *k*-means for clustering, and the Apriori algorithm for association rule mining, are described later in this chapter.

Application Case 5.4

Data Mining in Cancer Research

According to the American Cancer Society, half of all men and one-third of all women in the United States will develop cancer during their lifetimes; approximately 1.5 million new cancer cases will be diagnosed in 2013. Cancer is the second most common cause of death in the United States and in the world, exceeded only by cardiovascular disease. This year, over 500,000 Americans are expected to die of cancer—more than 1,300 people a day—accounting for nearly 1 of every 4 deaths.

Cancer is a group of diseases generally characterized by uncontrolled growth and spread of abnormal cells. If the growth and/or spread is not controlled, it can result in death. Even though the exact reasons are not known, cancer is believed to be caused by both external factors (e.g., tobacco, infectious organisms, chemicals, and radiation) and internal factors (e.g., inherited mutations, hormones, immune conditions, and mutations that occur from metabolism). These causal factors may act together or in sequence to initiate or promote carcinogenesis. Cancer is treated with surgery, radiation, chemotherapy, hormone therapy, biological therapy, and targeted therapy. Survival statistics vary greatly by cancer type and stage at diagnosis.

The 5-year relative survival rate for all cancers is improving, and decline in cancer mortality has reached 20 percent in 2013, translating to the avoidance of about 1.2 million deaths from cancer since 1991. That's more than 400 lives saved per day! The improvement in survival reflects progress in diagnosing certain cancers at an earlier stage and improvements in treatment. Further improvements are needed to prevent and treat cancer.

Even though cancer research has traditionally been clinical and biological in nature, in recent years data-driven analytic studies have become a common complement. In medical domains where data- and analytics-driven research have been applied successfully, novel research directions have been identified to further advance the clinical and biological studies. Using various types of data, including molecular, clinical, literature-based, and clinical-trial data, along with suitable data mining tools and techniques, researchers have been able to identify novel patterns, paving the road toward a cancer-free society.

In one study, Delen (2009) used three popular data mining techniques (decision trees, artificial neural networks, and support vector machines) in conjunction with logistic regression to develop prediction models for prostate cancer survivability. The data set contained around 120,000 records and 77 variables. A k-fold cross-validation methodology was used in model building, evaluation, and comparison. The results showed that support vector models are the most accurate predictor (with a test set accuracy of 92.85%) for this domain, followed by artificial neural networks and decision trees. Furthermore, using a sensitivity–analysis-based evaluation method, the study also revealed novel patterns related to prognostic factors of prostate cancer.

In a related study, Delen et al. (2004) used two data mining algorithms (artificial neural networks and decision trees) and logistic regression to develop prediction models for breast cancer survival using a large data set (more than 200,000 cases). Using a 10-fold cross-validation method to measure the unbiased estimate of the prediction models for performance comparison purposes, the results indicated that the decision tree (C5 algorithm) was the best predictor, with 93.6 percent accuracy on the holdout sample (which was the best prediction accuracy reported in the literature); followed by artificial neural networks, with 91.2 percent accuracy; and logistic regression, with 89.2 percent accuracy. Further analysis of prediction models revealed prioritized importance of the prognostic factors, which can then be used as basis for further clinical and biological research studies.

These examples (among many others in the medical literature) show that advanced data mining techniques can be used to develop models that possess a high degree of predictive as well as explanatory power. Although data mining methods are capable of extracting patterns and relationships hidden deep in large and complex medical databases, without the cooperation and feedback from the medical experts their results are not of much use. The patterns found via data mining methods should be evaluated by medical professionals who have years of experience in the problem domain to decide whether they are logical, actionable, and novel to warrant new research directions. In short, data mining is not meant to replace medical professionals and researchers, but to complement their invaluable efforts to provide data-driven new research directions and to ultimately save more human lives.

QUESTIONS FOR DISCUSSION

1. How can data mining be used for ultimately curing illnesses like cancer?

2. What do you think are the promises and major challenges for data miners in contributing to medical and biological research endeavors?

Sources: D. Delen, "Analysis of Cancer Data: A Data Mining Approach," *Expert Systems,* Vol. 26, No. 1, 2009, pp. 100–112; J. Thongkam, G. Xu, Y. Zhang, and F. Huang, "Toward Breast Cancer Survivability Prediction Models Through Improving Training Space," *Expert Systems with Applications,* Vol. 36, No. 10, 2009, pp. 12200–12209; D. Delen, G. Walker, and A. Kadam, "Predicting Breast Cancer Survivability: A Comparison of Three Data Mining Methods," *Artificial Intelligence in Medicine,* Vol. 34, No. 2, 2005, pp. 113–127.

Step 5: Testing and Evaluation

In step 5, the developed models are assessed and evaluated for their accuracy and generality. This step assesses the degree to which the selected model (or models) meets the business objectives and, if so, to what extent (i.e., do more models need to be developed and assessed). Another option is to test the developed model(s) in a real-world scenario if time and budget constraints permit. Even though the outcome of the developed models is expected to relate to the original business objectives, other findings that are not necessarily related to the original business objectives but that might also unveil additional information or hints for future directions often are discovered.

The testing and evaluation step is a critical and challenging task. No value is added by the data mining task until the business value obtained from discovered knowledge patterns is identified and recognized. Determining the business value from discovered knowledge patterns is somewhat similar to playing with puzzles. The extracted knowledge patterns are pieces of the puzzle that need to be put together in the context of the specific business purpose. The success of this identification operation depends on the interaction among data analysts, business analysts, and decision makers (such as business managers). Because data analysts may not have the full understanding of the data mining objectives and what they mean to the business and the business analysts and decision makers may not have the technical knowledge to interpret the results of sophisticated mathematical solutions, interaction among them is necessary. In order to properly interpret knowledge patterns, it is often necessary to use a variety of tabulation and visualization techniques (e.g., pivot tables, cross-tabulation of findings, pie charts, histograms, box plots, scatter plots).

Step 6: Deployment

Development and assessment of the models is not the end of the data mining project. Even if the purpose of the model is to have a simple exploration of the data, the knowledge gained from such exploration will need to be organized and presented in a way that the end user can understand and benefit from. Depending on the requirements, the deployment phase can be as simple as generating a report or as complex as implementing a repeatable data mining process across the enterprise. In many cases, it is the customer, not the data analyst, who carries out the deployment steps. However, even if the analyst will not carry out the deployment effort, it is important for the customer to understand up front what actions need to be carried out in order to actually make use of the created models.

The deployment step may also include maintenance activities for the deployed models. Because everything about the business is constantly changing, the data that reflect the business activities also are changing. Over time, the models (and the patterns embedded within them) built on the old data may become obsolete, irrelevant, or misleading. Therefore, monitoring and maintenance of the models are important if the data mining results are to become a part of the day-to-day business and its environment. A careful preparation of a maintenance strategy helps to avoid unnecessarily long periods of incorrect usage of data mining results. In order to monitor the deployment of the data mining result(s), the project needs a detailed plan on the monitoring process, which may not be a trivial task for complex data mining models.

Other Data Mining Standardized Processes and Methodologies

In order to be applied successfully, a data mining study must be viewed as a process that follows a standardized methodology rather than as a set of automated software tools and techniques. In addition to CRISP-DM, there is another well-known methodology developed by the SAS Institute, called SEMMA (2009). The acronym **SEMMA** stands for "sample, explore, modify, model, and assess."

Beginning with a statistically representative sample of the data, SEMMA makes it easy to apply exploratory statistical and visualization techniques, select and transform the most significant predictive variables, model the variables to predict outcomes, and confirm a model's accuracy. A pictorial representation of SEMMA is given in Figure 5.6.

By assessing the outcome of each stage in the SEMMA process, the model developer can determine how to model new questions raised by the previous results, and thus proceed back to the exploration phase for additional refinement of the data; that is, as with CRISP-DM, SEMMA is driven by a highly iterative experimentation cycle.

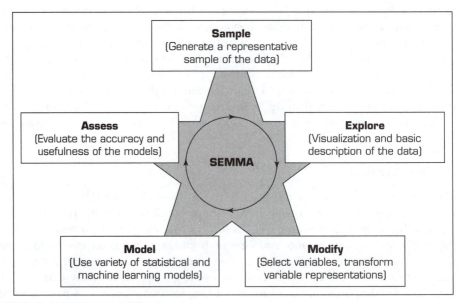

FIGURE 5.6   SEMMA Data Mining Process.

The main difference between CRISP-DM and SEMMA is that CRISP-DM takes a more comprehensive approach—including understanding of the business and the relevant data—to data mining projects, whereas SEMMA implicitly assumes that the data mining project's goals and objectives along with the appropriate data sources have been identified and understood.

Some practitioners commonly use the term **knowledge discovery in databases (KDD)** as a synonym for data mining. Fayyad et al. (1996) defined *knowledge discovery in databases* as a process of using data mining methods to find useful information and patterns in the data, as opposed to data mining, which involves using algorithms to identify patterns in data derived through the KDD process. KDD is a comprehensive process that encompasses data mining. The input to the KDD process consists of organizational data. The enterprise data warehouse enables KDD to be implemented efficiently because it provides a single source for data to be mined. Dunham (2003) summarized the KDD process as consisting of the following steps: data selection, data preprocessing, data transformation, data mining, and interpretation/evaluation. Figure 5.7 shows the polling results for the question "What main methodology are you using for data mining?" (conducted by **kdnuggets.com** in August 2007).

SECTION 5.4 REVIEW QUESTIONS

1. What are the major data mining processes?
2. Why do you think the early phases (understanding of the business and understanding of the data) take the longest in data mining projects?
3. List and briefly define the phases in the CRISP-DM process.
4. What are the main data preprocessing steps? Briefly describe each step and provide relevant examples.
5. How does CRISP-DM differ from SEMMA?

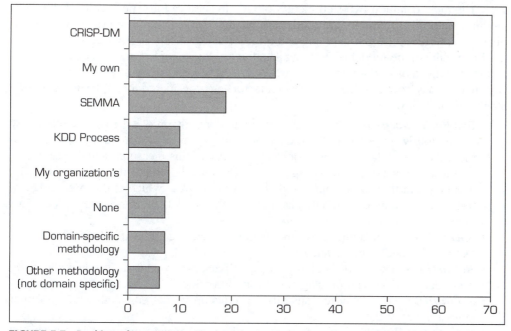

FIGURE 5.7   **Ranking of Data Mining Methodologies/Processes.**   *Source:* Used with permission from **kdnuggets.com**.

5.5 DATA MINING METHODS

A variety of methods are available for performing data mining studies, including classification, regression, clustering, and association. Most data mining software tools employ more than one technique (or algorithm) for each of these methods. This section describes the most popular data mining methods and explains their representative techniques.

Classification

Classification is perhaps the most frequently used data mining method for real-world problems. As a popular member of the machine-learning family of techniques, classification learns patterns from past data (a set of information—traits, variables, features—on characteristics of the previously labeled items, objects, or events) in order to place new instances (with unknown labels) into their respective groups or classes. For example, one could use classification to predict whether the weather on a particular day will be "sunny," "rainy," or "cloudy." Popular classification tasks include credit approval (i.e., good or bad credit risk), store location (e.g., good, moderate, bad), target marketing (e.g., likely customer, no hope), fraud detection (i.e., yes, no), and telecommunication (e.g., likely to turn to another phone company, yes/no). If what is being predicted is a class label (e.g., "sunny," "rainy," or "cloudy"), the prediction problem is called a classification, whereas if it is a numeric value (e.g., temperature such as 68°F), the prediction problem is called a **regression**.

Even though clustering (another popular data mining method) can also be used to determine groups (or class memberships) of things, there is a significant difference between the two. Classification learns the function between the characteristics of things (i.e., independent variables) and their membership (i.e., output variable) through a supervised learning process where both types (input and output) of variables are presented to the algorithm; in clustering, the membership of the objects is learned through an unsupervised learning process where only the input variables are presented to the algorithm. Unlike classification, clustering does not have a supervising (or controlling) mechanism that enforces the learning process; instead, clustering algorithms use one or more heuristics (e.g., multidimensional distance measure) to discover natural groupings of objects.

The most common two-step methodology of classification-type prediction involves model development/training and model testing/deployment. In the model development phase, a collection of input data, including the actual class labels, is used. After a model has been trained, the model is tested against the holdout sample for accuracy assessment and eventually deployed for actual use where it is to predict classes of new data instances (where the class label is unknown). Several factors are considered in assessing the model, including the following:

- **Predictive accuracy.** The model's ability to correctly predict the class label of new or previously unseen data. Prediction accuracy is the most commonly used assessment factor for classification models. To compute this measure, actual class labels of a test data set are matched against the class labels predicted by the model. The accuracy can then be computed as the *accuracy rate,* which is the percentage of test data set samples correctly classified by the model (more on this topic is provided later in the chapter).
- **Speed.** The computational costs involved in generating and using the model, where faster is deemed to be better.
- **Robustness.** The model's ability to make reasonably accurate predictions, given noisy data or data with missing and erroneous values.
- **Scalability.** The ability to construct a prediction model efficiently given a rather large amount of data.
- **Interpretability.** The level of understanding and insight provided by the model (e.g., how and/or what the model concludes on certain predictions).

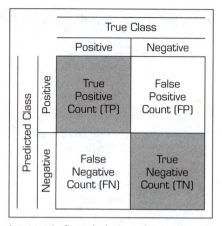

FIGURE 5.8 A Simple Confusion Matrix for Tabulation of Two-Class Classification Results.

Estimating the True Accuracy of Classification Models

In classification problems, the primary source for accuracy estimation is the *confusion matrix* (also called a *classification matrix* or a *contingency table*). Figure 5.8 shows a confusion matrix for a two-class classification problem. The numbers along the diagonal from the upper left to the lower right represent correct decisions, and the numbers outside this diagonal represent the errors.

Table 5.2 provides equations for common accuracy metrics for classification models.

When the classification problem is not binary, the confusion matrix gets bigger (a square matrix with the size of the unique number of class labels), and accuracy metrics become limited to *per class accuracy rates* and the *overall classifier accuracy*.

$$(\textit{True Classification Rate})_i = \frac{(\textit{True Classification})_i}{\sum_{i=1}^{n}(\textit{False Classification})_i}$$

$$(\textit{Overall Classifier Accuracy})_i = \frac{\sum_{i=1}^{n}(\textit{True Classification})_i}{\textit{Total Number of Cases}}$$

Estimating the accuracy of a classification model (or classifier) induced by a supervised learning algorithm is important for the following two reasons: First, it can be used to estimate its future prediction accuracy, which could imply the level of confidence one should have in the classifier's output in the prediction system. Second, it can be used for choosing a classifier from a given set (identifying the "best" classification model among the many trained). The following are among the most popular estimation methodologies used for classification-type data mining models.

SIMPLE SPLIT The **simple split** (or holdout or test sample estimation) partitions the data into two mutually exclusive subsets called a *training set* and a *test set* (or *holdout set*). It is common to designate two-thirds of the data as the training set and the remaining one-third as the test set. The training set is used by the inducer (model builder), and the built classifier is then tested on the test set. An exception to this rule occurs when the classifier is an artificial neural network. In this case, the data is partitioned into three mutually exclusive subsets: training, validation, and testing.

TABLE 5.2 Common Accuracy Metrics for Classification Models

Metric	Description
$\text{True Positive Rate} = \dfrac{TP}{TP + FN}$	The ratio of correctly classified positives divided by the total positive count (i.e., hit rate or recall)
$\text{True Negative Rate} = \dfrac{TN}{TN + FP}$	The ratio of correctly classified negatives divided by the total negative count (i.e., false alarm rate)
$\text{Accuracy} = \dfrac{TP + TN}{TP + TN + FP + FN}$	The ratio of correctly classified instances (positives and negatives) divided by the total number of instances
$\text{Precision} = \dfrac{TP}{TP + FP}$	The ratio of correctly classified positives divided by the sum of correctly classified positives and incorrectly classified positives
$\text{Recall} = \dfrac{TP}{TP + FN}$	Ratio of correctly classified positives divided by the sum of correctly classified positives and incorrectly classified negatives

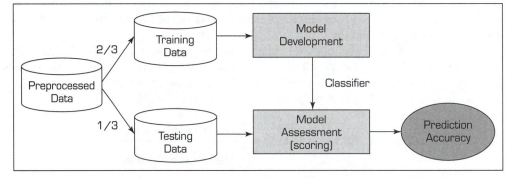

FIGURE 5.9   Simple Random Data Splitting.

The validation set is used during model building to prevent overfitting (more on artificial neural networks can be found in Chapter 6). Figure 5.9 shows the simple split methodology.

The main criticism of this method is that it makes the assumption that the data in the two subsets are of the same kind (i.e., have the exact same properties). Because this is a simple random partitioning, in most realistic data sets where the data are skewed on the classification variable, such an assumption may not hold true. In order to improve this situation, stratified sampling is suggested, where the strata become the output variable. Even though this is an improvement over the simple split, it still has a bias associated from the single random partitioning.

k-FOLD CROSS-VALIDATION   In order to minimize the bias associated with the random sampling of the training and holdout data samples in comparing the predictive accuracy of two or more methods, one can use a methodology called **k-fold cross-validation**. In k-fold cross-validation, also called *rotation estimation,* the complete data set is randomly split into k mutually exclusive subsets of approximately equal size. The classification model is trained and tested k times. Each time it is trained on all but one fold and then tested on the remaining single fold. The cross-validation estimate of the overall accuracy of a model is calculated by simply averaging the k individual accuracy measures, as shown in the following equation:

$$CVA = \frac{1}{k}\sum_{i=1}^{k}A_i$$

where CVA stands for cross-validation accuracy, k is the number of folds used, and A is the accuracy measure (e.g., hit-rate, sensitivity, specificity) of each fold.

ADDITIONAL CLASSIFICATION ASSESSMENT METHODOLOGIES Other popular assessment methodologies include the following:

- ***Leave-one-out.*** The leave-one-out method is similar to the k-fold cross-validation where the k takes the value of 1; that is, every data point is used for testing once on as many models developed as there are number of data points. This is a time-consuming methodology, but sometimes for small data sets it is a viable option.
- ***Bootstrapping.*** With **bootstrapping**, a fixed number of instances from the original data is sampled (with replacement) for training and the rest of the data set is used for testing. This process is repeated as many times as desired.
- ***Jackknifing.*** Similar to the leave-one-out methodology, with jackknifing the accuracy is calculated by leaving one sample out at each iteration of the estimation process.
- ***Area under the ROC curve.*** The **area under the ROC curve** is a graphical assessment technique where the true positive rate is plotted on the y-axis and false positive rate is plotted on the x-axis. The area under the ROC curve determines the accuracy measure of a classifier: A value of 1 indicates a perfect classifier whereas 0.5 indicates no better than random chance; in reality, the values would range between the two extreme cases. For example, in Figure 5.10 A has a better classification performance than B, while C is not any better than the random chance of flipping a coin.

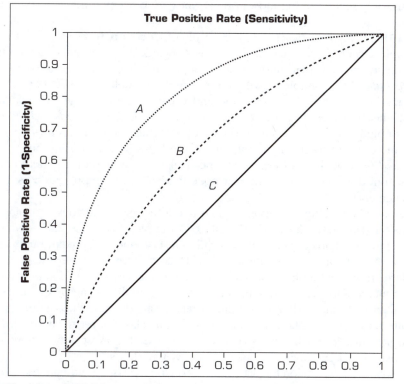

FIGURE 5.10 A Sample ROC Curve.

CLASSIFICATION TECHNIQUES   A number of techniques (or algorithms) are used for classification modeling, including the following:

- *Decision tree analysis.* Decision tree analysis (a machine-learning technique) is arguably the most popular classification technique in the data mining arena. A detailed description of this technique is given in the following section.
- *Statistical analysis.* Statistical techniques were the primary classification algorithm for many years until the emergence of machine-learning techniques. Statistical classification techniques include logistic regression and discriminant analysis, both of which make the assumptions that the relationships between the input and output variables are linear in nature, the data is normally distributed, and the variables are not correlated and are independent of each other. The questionable nature of these assumptions has led to the shift toward machine-learning techniques.
- *Neural networks.* These are among the most popular machine-learning techniques that can be used for classification-type problems. A detailed description of this technique is presented in Chapter 6.
- *Case-based reasoning.* This approach uses historical cases to recognize commonalities in order to assign a new case into the most probable category.
- *Bayesian classifiers.* This approach uses probability theory to build classification models based on the past occurrences that are capable of placing a new instance into a most probable class (or category).
- *Genetic algorithms.* This approach uses the analogy of natural evolution to build directed-search-based mechanisms to classify data samples.
- *Rough sets.* This method takes into account the partial membership of class labels to predefined categories in building models (collection of rules) for classification problems.

A complete description of all of these classification techniques is beyond the scope of this book; thus, only several of the most popular ones are presented here.

DECISION TREES   Before describing the details of **decision trees**, we need to discuss some simple terminology. First, decision trees include many input variables that may have an impact on the classification of different patterns. These input variables are usually called *attributes*. For example, if we were to build a model to classify loan risks on the basis of just two characteristics—income and a credit rating—these two characteristics would be the attributes and the resulting output would be the *class label* (e.g., low, medium, or high risk). Second, a tree consists of branches and nodes. A *branch* represents the outcome of a test to classify a pattern (on the basis of a test) using one of the attributes. A *leaf node* at the end represents the final class choice for a pattern (a chain of branches from the root node to the leaf node, which can be represented as a complex if-then statement).

The basic idea behind a decision tree is that it recursively divides a training set until each division consists entirely or primarily of examples from one class. Each nonleaf node of the tree contains a *split point,* which is a test on one or more attributes and determines how the data are to be divided further. Decision tree algorithms, in general, build an initial tree from the training data such that each leaf node is pure, and they then prune the tree to increase its generalization, and, hence, the prediction accuracy on test data.

In the growth phase, the tree is built by recursively dividing the data until each division is either pure (i.e., contains members of the same class) or relatively small. The basic idea is to ask questions whose answers would provide the most information, similar to what we may do when playing the game "Twenty Questions."

The split used to partition the data depends on the type of the attribute used in the split. For a continuous attribute A, splits are of the form value(A) < x, where x is some "optimal" split value of *A*. For example, the split based on income could be "Income < 50000." For the categorical attribute *A*, splits are of the form value(A) belongs to *x*, where *x* is a subset of *A*. As an example, the split could be on the basis of gender: "Male versus Female."

A general algorithm for building a decision tree is as follows:

1. Create a root node and assign all of the training data to it.
2. Select the *best* splitting attribute.
3. Add a branch to the root node for each value of the split. Split the data into mutually exclusive (nonoverlapping) subsets along the lines of the specific split and mode to the branches.
4. Repeat the steps 2 and 3 for each and every leaf node until the stopping criterion is reached (e.g., the node is dominated by a single class label).

Many different algorithms have been proposed for creating decision trees. These algorithms differ primarily in terms of the way in which they determine the splitting attribute (and its split values), the order of splitting the attributes (splitting the same attribute only once or many times), the number of splits at each node (binary versus ternary), the stopping criteria, and the pruning of the tree (pre- versus postpruning). Some of the most well-known algorithms are ID3 (followed by C4.5 and C5 as the improved versions of ID3) from machine learning, classification and regression trees (CART) from statistics, and the chi-squared automatic interaction detector (CHAID) from pattern recognition.

When building a decision tree, the goal at each node is to determine the attribute and the split point of that attribute that best divides the training records in order to purify the class representation at that node. To evaluate the goodness of the split, some splitting indices have been proposed. Two of the most common ones are the Gini index and information gain. The Gini index is used in CART and SPRINT (Scalable PaRallelizable Induction of Decision Trees) algorithms. Versions of information gain are used in ID3 (and its newer versions, C4.5 and C5).

The **Gini index** has been used in economics to measure the diversity of a population. The same concept can be used to determine the purity of a specific class as a result of a decision to branch along a particular attribute or variable. The best split is the one that increases the purity of the sets resulting from a proposed split. Let us briefly look into a simple calculation of Gini index:

If a data set *S* contains examples from *n* classes, the Gini index is defined as

$$gini(S) = 1 - \sum_{j=1}^{n} p_j^2$$

where p_j is a relative frequency of class *j* in *S*. If a data set *S* is split into two subsets, S_1 and S_2, with sizes N_1 and N_2, respectively, the Gini index of the split data contains examples from *n* classes, and the Gini index is defined as

$$gini_{split}(S) = \frac{N_1}{N} gini(S_1) + \frac{N_2}{N} gini(S_2)$$

The attribute/split combination that provides the smallest $gini_{split}(S)$ is chosen to split the node. In such a determination, one should enumerate all possible splitting points for each attribute.

Information gain is the splitting mechanism used in ID3, which is perhaps the most widely known decision tree algorithm. It was developed by Ross Quinlan in 1986, and since then he has evolved this algorithm into the C4.5 and C5 algorithms. The basic idea behind ID3 (and its variants) is to use a concept called *entropy* in place of the Gini index. **Entropy** measures the extent of uncertainty or randomness in a data set. If all the data in a subset belong to just one class, there is no uncertainty or randomness in that data set, so the entropy is zero. The objective of this approach is to build subtrees so that the entropy of each final subset is zero (or close to zero). Let us also look at the calculation of the information gain.

Assume that there are two classes, P (positive) and N (negative). Let the set of examples S contain p counts of class P and n counts of class N. The amount of information needed to decide if an arbitrary example in S belongs to P or N is defined as

$$I(p, n) = -\frac{p}{p + n} \log_2 \frac{p}{p + n} - \frac{n}{p + n} \log_2 \frac{n}{p + n}$$

Assume that using attribute A a set S will be partitioned into sets $\{S_1, S_2, k, S_v\}$. If S_i contains p_i examples of P and n_i examples of N, the entropy, or the expected information needed to classify objects in all subtrees, S_i, is

$$E(A) = \sum_{i=1}^{n} \frac{p_i + n_i}{p + n} I(p_i, n_i)$$

Then, the information that would be gained by branching on attribute A would be

$$Gain(A) = I(p, n) - E(A)$$

These calculations are repeated for each and every attribute, and the one with the highest information gain is selected as the splitting attribute. The basic ideas behind these splitting indices are rather similar to each other but the specific algorithmic details vary. A detailed definition of the ID3 algorithm and its splitting mechanism can be found in Quinlan (1986).

Application Case 5.5 illustrates how significant the gains may be if the right data mining techniques are used for a well-defined business problem.

Cluster Analysis for Data Mining

Cluster analysis is an essential data mining method for classifying items, events, or concepts into common groupings called *clusters*. The method is commonly used in biology, medicine, genetics, social network analysis, anthropology, archaeology, astronomy, character recognition, and even in MIS development. As data mining has increased in popularity, the underlying techniques have been applied to business, especially to marketing. Cluster analysis has been used extensively for fraud detection (both credit card and e-commerce fraud) and market segmentation of customers in contemporary CRM systems. More applications in business continue to be developed as the strength of cluster analysis is recognized and used.

Cluster analysis is an exploratory data analysis tool for solving classification problems. The objective is to sort cases (e.g., people, things, events) into groups, or clusters, so that the degree of association is strong among members of the same cluster and weak among members of different clusters. Each cluster describes the class to which its members belong. An obvious one-dimensional example of cluster analysis is to establish score ranges into which to assign class grades for a college class. This is similar to the cluster analysis problem that the U.S. Treasury faced when establishing new tax brackets in the 1980s. A fictional example of clustering occurs in J. K. Rowling's *Harry Potter* books. The Sorting Hat determines to which House (e.g., dormitory) to assign first-year students at the Hogwarts School. Another example involves determining how to seat guests at a wedding. As far as data mining goes, the importance of cluster analysis is that it may reveal associations and structures in data that were not previously apparent but are sensible and useful once found.

Application Case 5.5

2degrees Gets a 1275 Percent Boost in Churn Identification

2degrees is New Zealand's fastest growing mobile tele-communications company - In less than 3 years, they have transformed the landscape of New Zealand's mobile telecommunications market. Entering very much as the challenger and battling with incumbents entrenched in the market for over 18 years, 2degrees has won over 580,000 customers and has revenues of more than $100 million in just their third year of operation. Last year's growth was 3761 percent.

Situation

2degrees' information solutions manager, Peter McCallum, explains that predictive analytics had been on the radar at the company for some time. "At 2degrees there are a lot of analytically aware people, from the CEO down. Once we got to the point in our business that we were interested in deploying advanced predictive analytics techniques, we started to look at what was available in the marketplace." It soon became clear that although on paper there were several options, the reality was that the cost of deploying the well-known solutions made it very difficult to build a business case, particularly given that the benefits to the business were as yet unproven.

After careful evaluation, 2degrees decided upon a suite of analytics solutions from 11Ants consisting of Customer Response Analyzer, Customer Churn Analyzer, and Model Builder. "One of the beauties of the 11Ants Analytics solution was that it allowed us to get up and running quickly and very economically. We could test the water and determine what the ROI was likely to be for predictive analytics, making it a lot easier to build a business case for future analytics projects." Peter McCallum said.

When asked why they chose 11Ants Analytics' solutions, Peter said, "One of the beauties of the 11Ants Analytics solution was that it allowed us to get up and running quickly and very economically. We could test the water and determine what the ROI was likely to be for predictive analytics, making it a lot easier to build a business case for future analytics projects. Yet we didn't really have to sacrifice anything in terms of functionality—in fact, the churn models we've built have performed exceptionally well."

11Ants Analytics director of business development, Tom Fuyala, comments: "We are dedicated to getting organizations up and running with predictive analytics faster, without compromising the quality of the results. With other solutions you must [use] trial and error through multiple algorithms manually, but with 11Ants Analytics solutions the entire optimization and management of the algorithms is automated, allowing thousands to be trialed in a few minutes. The benefits of this approach are evidenced in the real-world results."

Peter is also impressed by the ease of use. "The simplicity was a big deal to us. Not having to have the statistical knowledge in-house was definitely a selling point. Company culture was also a big factor in our decision making. 11Ants Analytics felt like a good fit. They've been very responsive and have been great to work with. The turnaround on some of the custom requests we have made has been fantastic."

Peter also likes the fact that models can be built with the desktop modeling tools and then deployed against the enterprise customer database with 11Ants Predictor. "Once the model has been built, it is easy to deploy it in 11Ants Predictor to run against Oracle and score our entire customer base very quickly. The speed with which 11Ants Predictor can re-score hundreds of thousands of customers is fantastic. We presently re-score our customer base monthly, but it is so easy that we could be re-scoring daily if we wanted."

Benefits

2degrees put 11Ants Analytics solutions to work quickly with very satisfying results. The initial project was to focus on an all-too-common problem in the mobile telecommunications industry: customer churn (customers leaving). For this they deployed 11Ants Customer Churn Analyzer.

2degrees was interested in identifying customers most at risk of churning by analyzing data such as time on network, days since last top-up, activation channel, whether the customer ported their number or not, customer plan, and outbound calling behaviors over the preceding 90 days.

(Continued)

Application Case 5.5   (Continued)

A carefully controlled experiment was run over a period of 3 months, and the results were tabulated and analyzed. The results were excellent: Customers identified as churners by 11Ants Customer Churn Analyzer were a game-changing 1275 percent more likely to be churners than customers chosen at random. This can also be expressed as an increase in lift of 12.75 at 5 percent (the 5% of the total population identified as most likely to churn by the model). At 10 percent, lift was 7.28. Other benefits included the various insights that 11Ants Customer Churn Analyzer provided, for instance, validating things that staff had intuitively felt, such as time on network's strong relationship with churn, and highlighting areas where product enhancement would be beneficial.

Armed with the information of which customers were most at risk of defecting, 2degrees could now focus retention efforts on those identified as most at risk, thereby getting substantially higher return on investment on retention marketing expenditure. The bottom line is significantly better results for fewer dollars spent.

2degrees head of customers, Matt Hobbs, provides a perspective on why this is not just important to 2degrees but also to their customers: "Churn prediction is a valuable tool for customer marketing and we are excited about the capabilities 11Ants Analytics provides to identify customers who display indications of churning behavior. This is beneficial to both 2degrees and to our customers."

- To customers go the benefits of identification (if you are not likely to churn, you are not being constantly annoyed by messages asking you to stay) and appropriateness (customers receive offers that actually are appropriate to their usage—minutes for someone who likes to talk, texts for someone who likes to text, etc.).
- To 2degrees go the benefits of targeting (by identifying a smaller group of at-risk customers, retention offers can be richer because of the reduction in the number of people who may receive it but not need it) and appropriateness.

By aligning these benefits for both 2degrees and the customer, the outcomes 2degrees are experiencing are vastly improved.

QUESTIONS FOR DISCUSSION

1. What does 2degrees do? Why is it important for 2degrees to accurately identify churn?
2. What were the challenges, the proposed solution, and the obtained results?
3. How can data mining help in identifying customer churn? How do some companies do it without using data mining tools and techniques?

Source: 11AntsAnalytics Customer Story, "1275% Boost in Churn Identification at 2degrees," **11antsanalytics.com/ casestudies/2degrees_casestudy.aspx** (accessed January 2013).

Cluster analysis results may be used to:

- Identify a classification scheme (e.g., types of customers)
- Suggest statistical models to describe populations
- Indicate rules for assigning new cases to classes for identification, targeting, and diagnostic purposes
- Provide measures of definition, size, and change in what were previously broad concepts
- Find typical cases to label and represent classes
- Decrease the size and complexity of the problem space for other data mining methods
- Identify outliers in a specific domain (e.g., rare-event detection)

DETERMINING THE OPTIMAL NUMBER OF CLUSTERS   Clustering algorithms usually require one to specify the number of clusters to find. If this number is not known from prior knowledge, it should be chosen in some way. Unfortunately, there is no optimal way of calculating what this number is supposed to be. Therefore, several different heuristic methods have been proposed. The following are among the most commonly referenced ones:

- Look at the percentage of variance explained as a function of the number of clusters; that is, choose a number of clusters so that adding another cluster would not give much better modeling of the data. Specifically, if one graphs the percentage of variance explained by the clusters, there is a point at which the marginal gain will drop (giving an angle in the graph), indicating the number of clusters to be chosen.
- Set the number of clusters to $(n/2)^{1/2}$, where n is the number of data points.
- Use the Akaike Information Criterion (AIC), which is a measure of the goodness of fit (based on the concept of entropy) to determine the number of clusters.
- Use Bayesian information criterion (BIC), which is a model-selection criterion (based on maximum likelihood estimation) to determine the number of clusters.

ANALYSIS METHODS   Cluster analysis may be based on one or more of the following general methods:

- Statistical methods (including both hierarchical and nonhierarchical), such as k-means, k-modes, and so on
- Neural networks (with the architecture called self-organizing map, or SOM)
- Fuzzy logic (e.g., fuzzy c-means algorithm)
- Genetic algorithms

Each of these methods generally works with one of two general method classes:

- **Divisive.** With divisive classes, all items start in one cluster and are broken apart.
- **Agglomerative.** With agglomerative classes, all items start in individual clusters, and the clusters are joined together.

Most cluster analysis methods involve the use of a **distance measure** to calculate the closeness between pairs of items. Popular distance measures include Euclidian distance (the ordinary distance between two points that one would measure with a ruler) and Manhattan distance (also called the rectilinear distance, or taxicab distance, between two points). Often, they are based on true distances that are measured, but this need not be so, as is typically the case in IS development. Weighted averages may be used to establish these distances. For example, in an IS development project, individual modules of the system may be related by the similarity between their inputs, outputs, processes, and the specific data used. These factors are then aggregated, pairwise by item, into a single distance measure.

K-MEANS CLUSTERING ALGORITHM   The k-means algorithm (where k stands for the predetermined number of clusters) is arguably the most referenced clustering algorithm. It has its roots in traditional statistical analysis. As the name implies, the algorithm assigns each data point (customer, event, object, etc.) to the cluster whose center (also called *centroid*) is the nearest. The center is calculated as the average of all the points in the cluster; that is, its coordinates are the arithmetic mean for each dimension separately over all the points in the cluster. The algorithm steps are listed below and shown graphically in Figure 5.11:

Initialization step: Choose the number of clusters (i.e., the value of k).

Step 1: Randomly generate k random points as initial cluster centers.

Step 2: Assign each point to the nearest cluster center.

Step 3: Recompute the new cluster centers.

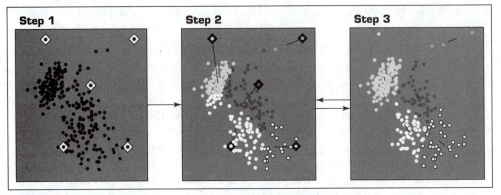

FIGURE 5.11 A Graphical Illustration of the Steps in *k*-Means Algorithm.

Repetition step: Repeat steps 2 and 3 until some convergence criterion is met (usually that the assignment of points to clusters becomes stable).

Association Rule Mining

Association rule mining (also known as *affinity analysis* or *market-basket analysis*) is a popular data mining method that is commonly used as an example to explain what data mining is and what it can do to a technologically less savvy audience. Most of you might have heard the famous (or infamous, depending on how you look at it) relationship discovered between the sales of beer and diapers at grocery stores. As the story goes, a large supermarket chain (maybe Walmart, maybe not; there is no consensus on which supermarket chain it was) did an analysis of customers' buying habits and found a statistically significant correlation between purchases of beer and purchases of diapers. It was theorized that the reason for this was that fathers (presumably young men) were stopping off at the supermarket to buy diapers for their babies (especially on Thursdays), and since they could no longer go to the sports bar as often, would buy beer as well. As a result of this finding, the supermarket chain is alleged to have placed the diapers next to the beer, resulting in increased sales of both.

In essence, association rule mining aims to find interesting relationships (affinities) between variables (items) in large databases. Because of its successful application to retail business problems, it is commonly called *market-basket analysis*. The main idea in market-basket analysis is to identify strong relationships among different products (or services) that are usually purchased together (show up in the same basket together, either a physical basket at a grocery store or a virtual basket at an e-commerce Web site). For example, 65 percent of those who buy comprehensive automobile insurance also buy health insurance; 80 percent of those who buy books online also buy music online; 60 percent of those who have high blood pressure and are overweight have high cholesterol; and 70 percent of the customers who buy laptop computer and virus protection software also buy extended service plan.

The input to market-basket analysis is simple point-of-sale transaction data, where a number of products and/or services purchased together (just like the content of a purchase receipt) are tabulated under a single transaction instance. The outcome of the analysis is invaluable information that can be used to better understand customer-purchase behavior in order to maximize the profit from business transactions. A business can take advantage of such knowledge by (1) putting the items next to each other to make it more convenient for the customers to pick them up together and not forget to buy one when buying the others (increasing sales volume); (2) promoting the items as a package (do not put one on sale if the other(s) are on sale); and (3) placing them apart from each other so that the customer has to walk the aisles to search for it, and by doing so potentially seeing and buying other items.

Applications of market-basket analysis include cross-marketing, cross-selling, store design, catalog design, e-commerce site design, optimization of online advertising, product pricing, and sales/promotion configuration. In essence, market-basket analysis helps businesses infer customer needs and preferences from their purchase patterns. Outside the business realm, association rules are successfully used to discover relationships between symptoms and illnesses, diagnosis and patient characteristics and treatments (which can be used in medical DSS), and genes and their functions (which can be used in genomics projects), among others. Here are a few common areas and uses for association rule mining:

- *Sales transactions:* Combinations of retail products purchased together can be used to improve product placement on the sales floor (placing products that go together in close proximity) and promotional pricing of products (not having promotion on both products that are often purchased together).
- *Credit card transactions:* Items purchased with a credit card provide insight into other products the customer is likely to purchase or fraudulent use of credit card number.
- *Banking services:* The sequential patterns of services used by customers (checking account followed by saving account) can be used to identify other services they may be interested in (investment account).
- *Insurance service products:* Bundles of insurance products bought by customers (car insurance followed by home insurance) can be used to propose additional insurance products (life insurance); or, unusual combinations of insurance claims can be a sign of fraud.
- *Telecommunication services:* Commonly purchased groups of options (e.g., call waiting, caller ID, three-way calling, etc.) help better structure product bundles to maximize revenue; the same is also applicable to multi-channel telecom providers with phone, TV, and Internet service offerings.
- *Medical records:* Certain combinations of conditions can indicate increased risk of various complications; or, certain treatment procedures at certain medical facilities can be tied to certain types of infection.

A good question to ask with respect to the patterns/relationships that association rule mining can discover is "Are all association rules interesting and useful?" In order to answer such a question, association rule mining uses two common metrics: **support**, and **confidence** and **lift**. Before defining these terms, let's get a little technical by showing what an association rule looks like:

$X \Rightarrow Y \, [Supp(\%), \, Conf(\%)]$

{Laptop Computer, Antivirus Software} $\Rightarrow$ {Extended Service Plan} [30%, 70%]

Here, X (products and/or service; called the *left-hand side, LHS,* or the *antecedent*) is associated with Y (products and/or service; called the *right-hand side, RHS,* or *consequent*). S is the support, and C is the confidence for this particular rule. Here are the simple formulas for *Supp, Conf* and Lift.

$$Support = Supp(X \Rightarrow Y) = \frac{number\ of\ baskets\ that\ contains\ both\ X\ and\ Y}{total\ number\ of\ baskets}$$

$$Confidence = Conf(X \Rightarrow Y) = \frac{Supp(X \Rightarrow Y)}{Supp(X)}$$

$$Lift(X \Rightarrow Y) = \frac{Conf(X \Rightarrow Y)}{Expected\ Conf(X \Rightarrow Y)} = \frac{\dfrac{S(X \Rightarrow Y)}{S(X)}}{\dfrac{S(X) * S(Y)}{S(X)}} = \frac{S(X \Rightarrow Y)}{S(X) * S(Y)}$$

The support (S) of a collection of products is the measure of how often these products and/or services (i.e., LHS + RHS = Laptop Computer, Antivirus Software, and Extended Service Plan) appear together in the same transaction, that is, the proportion of transactions in the data set that contain all of the products and/or services mentioned in a specific rule. In this example, 30 percent of all transactions in the hypothetical store database had all three products present in a single sales ticket. The confidence of a rule is the measure of how often the products and/or services on the RHS (consequent) go together with the products and/or services on the LHS (antecedent), that is, the proportion of transactions that include LHS while also including the RHS. In other words, it is the conditional probability of finding the RHS of the rule present in transactions where the LHS of the rule already exists. The lift value of an association rule is the ratio of the confidence of the rule and the expected confidence of the rule. The expected confidence of a rule is defined as the product of the support values of the LHS and the RHS divided by the support of the LHS.

Several algorithms are available for discovering association rules. Some well-known algorithms include Apriori, Eclat, and FP-Growth. These algorithms only do half the job, which is to identify the frequent itemsets in the database. Once the frequent itemsets are identified, they need to be converted into rules with antecedent and consequent parts. Determination of the rules from frequent itemsets is a straightforward matching process, but the process may be time-consuming with large transaction databases. Even though there can be many items on each section of the rule, in practice the consequent part usually contains a single item. In the following section, one of the most popular algorithms for identification of frequent itemsets is explained.

APRIORI ALGORITHM   The **Apriori algorithm** is the most commonly used algorithm to discover association rules. Given a set of itemsets (e.g., sets of retail transactions, each listing individual items purchased), the algorithm attempts to find subsets that are common to at least a minimum number of the itemsets (i.e., complies with a minimum support). Apriori uses a bottom-up approach, where frequent subsets are extended one item at a time (a method known as *candidate generation,* whereby the size of frequent subsets increases from one-item subsets to two-item subsets, then three-item subsets, etc.), and groups of candidates at each level are tested against the data for minimum support. The algorithm terminates when no further successful extensions are found.

As an illustrative example, consider the following. A grocery store tracks sales transactions by SKU (stock-keeping unit) and thus knows which items are typically purchased together. The database of transactions, along with the subsequent steps in identifying the frequent itemsets, is shown in Figure 5.12. Each SKU in the transaction database corresponds to a product, such as "1 = butter," "2 = bread," "3 = water," and so on. The first step in Apriori is to count up the frequencies (i.e., the supports) of each item (one-item itemsets). For this overly simplified example, let us set the minimum support to 3 (or 50%; meaning an itemset is considered to be a frequent

Raw Transaction Data		One-Item Itemsets		Two-Item Itemsets		Three-Item Itemsets	
Transaction No	SKUs (Item No)	Itemset (SKUs)	Support	Itemset (SKUs)	Support	Itemset (SKUs)	Support
1001	1, 2, 3, 4	1	3	1, 2	3	1, 2, 4	3
1002	2, 3, 4	2	6	1, 3	2	2, 3, 4	3
1003	2, 3	3	4	1, 4	3		
1004	1, 2, 4	4	5	2, 3	4		
1005	1, 2, 3, 4			2, 4	5		
1006	2, 4			3, 4	3		

FIGURE 5.12   Identification of Frequent Itemsets in Apriori Algorithm.

itemset if it shows up in at least 3 out of 6 transactions in the database). Because all of the one-item itemsets have at least 3 in the support column, they are all considered frequent itemsets. However, had any of the one-item itemsets not been frequent, they would not have been included as a possible member of possible two-item pairs. In this way, Apriori *prunes* the tree of all possible itemsets. As Figure 5.12 shows, using one-item itemsets, all possible two-item itemsets are generated, and the transaction database is used to calculate their support values. Because the two-item itemset {1, 3} has a support less than 3, it should not be included in the frequent itemsets that will be used to generate the next-level itemsets (three-item itemsets). The algorithm seems deceivingly simple, but only for small data sets. In much larger data sets, especially those with huge amounts of items present in low quantities and small amounts of items present in big quantities, the search and calculation become a computationally intensive process.

SECTION 5.5 REVIEW QUESTIONS

1. Identify at least three of the main data mining methods.
2. Give examples of situations in which classification would be an appropriate data mining technique. Give examples of situations in which regression would be an appropriate data mining technique.
3. List and briefly define at least two classification techniques.
4. What are some of the criteria for comparing and selecting the best classification technique?
5. Briefly describe the general algorithm used in decision trees.
6. Define *Gini index*. What does it measure?
7. Give examples of situations in which cluster analysis would be an appropriate data mining technique.
8. What is the major difference between cluster analysis and classification?
9. What are some of the methods for cluster analysis?
10. Give examples of situations in which association would be an appropriate data mining technique.

5.6 DATA MINING SOFTWARE TOOLS

Many software vendors provide powerful data mining tools. Examples of these vendors include IBM (IBM SPSS Modeler, formerly known as SPSS PASW Modeler and Clementine), SAS (Enterprise Miner), StatSoft (Statistica Data Miner), KXEN (Infinite Insight), Salford (CART, MARS, TreeNet, RandomForest), Angoss (KnowledgeSTUDIO, KnowledgeSeeker), and Megaputer (PolyAnalyst). Noticeably but not surprisingly, the most popular data mining tools are developed by the well-established statistical software companies (SPSS, SAS, and StatSoft)—largely because statistics is the foundation of data mining, and these companies have the means to cost-effectively develop them into full-scale data mining systems. Most of the business intelligence tool vendors (e.g., IBM Cognos, Oracle Hyperion, SAP Business Objects, MicroStrategy, Teradata, and Microsoft) also have some level of data mining capabilities integrated into their software offerings. These BI tools are still primarily focused on multidimensional modeling and data visualization and are not considered to be direct competitors of the data mining tool vendors.

In addition to these commercial tools, several open source and/or free data mining software tools are available online. Probably the most popular free (and open source) data mining tool is **Weka**, which is developed by a number of researchers from the University of Waikato in New Zealand (the tool can be downloaded from **cs.waikato.ac.nz/ml/weka**). Weka includes a large number of algorithms for different data mining tasks and has an intuitive user interface. Another recently released, free (for noncommercial use) data mining tool is **RapidMiner** (developed by Rapid-I; it can be downloaded from **rapid-i.com**). Its graphically enhanced user interface, employment of a rather large number of algorithms, and incorporation of a variety of data visualization features set it apart from the rest of the free tools. Another free and open source data mining tool with an appealing graphical user interface is KNIME (which can be downloaded from **knime.org**). The main difference between commercial tools, such as Enterprise Miner, IBM SPSS Modeler, and Statistica, and free tools, such as Weka, RapidMiner, and KNIME, is computational efficiency. The same data mining task involving a large data set may take a whole lot longer to complete with the free software, and for some algorithms may not even complete (i.e., crashing due to the inefficient use of computer memory). Table 5.3 lists a few of the major products and their Web sites.

A suite of business intelligence capabilities that has become increasingly more popular for data mining projects is **Microsoft SQL Server**, where data and the models are stored in the same relational database environment, making model management a considerably easier task. The **Microsoft Enterprise Consortium** serves as the worldwide source for access to Microsoft's SQL Server 2012 software suite for academic purposes—teaching and research. The consortium has been established to enable universities around the world to access enterprise technology without having to maintain the necessary hardware and software on their own campus. The consortium provides a wide range of business intelligence development tools (e.g., data mining, cube building, business reporting) as well as a number of large, realistic data sets from Sam's Club, Dillard's, and Tyson Foods. The Microsoft Enterprise Consortium is free of charge and can only be used for academic purposes. The Sam M. Walton College of Business at the University of Arkansas hosts the enterprise system and allows consortium members and their students to access these resources by using a simple remote desktop connection. The details about becoming a part of the consortium along with easy-to-follow tutorials and examples can be found at **enterprise. waltoncollege.uark.edu**.

TABLE 5.3 Selected Data Mining Software

Product Name	Web Site (URL)
IBM SPSS Modeler	ibm.com/software/analytics/spss/products/modeler/
SAS Enterprise Miner	sas.com/technologies/bi/analytics/index.html
Statistica	statsoft.com/products/dataminer.htm
Intelligent Miner	ibm.com/software/data/iminer
PolyAnalyst	megaputer.com/polyanalyst.php
CART, MARS, TreeNet, RandomForest	salford-systems.com
Insightful Miner	insightful.com
XLMiner	xlminer.net
KXEN (Knowledge eXtraction ENgines)	kxen.com
GhostMiner	fqs.pl/ghostminer
Microsoft SQL Server Data Mining	microsoft.com/sqlserver/2012/data-mining.aspx
Knowledge Miner	knowledgeminer.net
Teradata Warehouse Miner	ncr.com/products/software/teradata_mining.htm
Oracle Data Mining (ODM)	otn.oracle.com/products/bi/9idmining.html
Fair Isaac Business Science	fairisaac.com/edm
DeltaMaster	bissantz.de
iData Analyzer	infoacumen.com
Orange Data Mining Tool	ailab.si/orange
Zementis Predictive Analytics	zementis.com

In May 2012, **kdnuggets.com** conducted the thirteenth annual Software Poll on the following question: "What Analytics, Data Mining, and Big Data software have you used in the past 12 months for a real project (not just evaluation)?" Here are some of the interesting findings that came out of the poll:

- For the first time (in the last 13 years of polling on the same question), the number of users of free/open source software exceeded the number of users of commercial software.
- Among voters 28 percent used commercial software but not free software, 30 percent used free software but not commercial, and 41 percent used both.
- The usage of Big Data tools grew fivefold: 15 percent used them in 2012, versus about 3 percent in 2011.
- R, RapidMiner, and KNIME are the most popular free/open source tools, while StatSoft's Statistica, SAS's Enterprise Miner, and IBM's SPSS Modeler are the most popular data mining tools.
- Among those who wrote their own analytics code in lower-level languages, R, SQL, Java, and Python were the most popular.

To reduce bias through multiple voting, in this poll **kdnuggets.com** used e-mail verification, which reduced the total number of votes compared to 2011, but made results more representative. The results for data mining software tools are shown in Figure 5.13, while the results for Big Data software tools used, and the platform/language used for your own code, is shown in Figure 5.14.

Application Case 5.6 is about a research study where a number of software tools and data mining techniques are used to build models to predict financial success (box-office receipts) of Hollywood movies while they are nothing more than ideas.

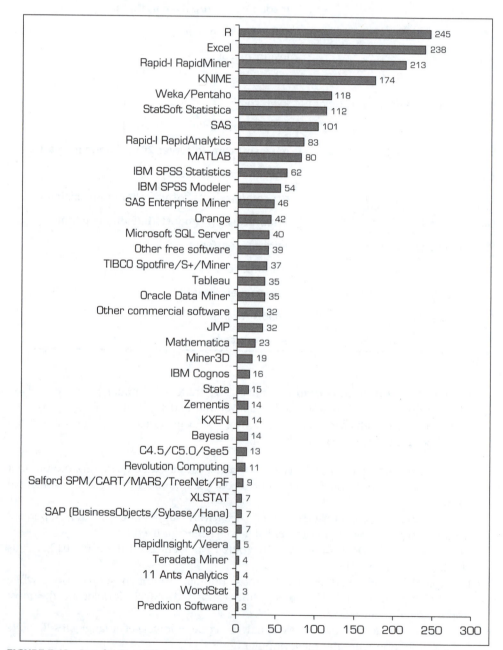

FIGURE 5.13 Popular Data Mining Software Tools (Poll Results). *Source:* Used with permission of kdnuggets.com.

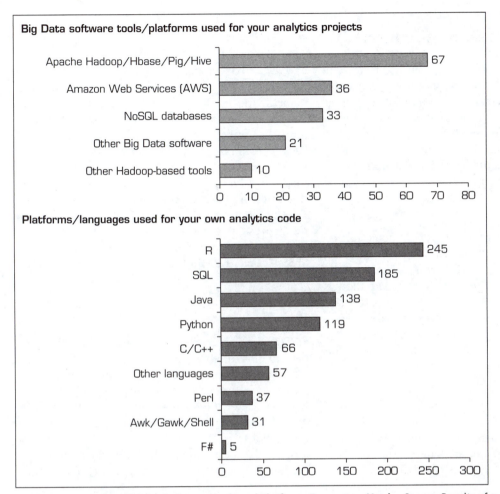

FIGURE 5.14 **Popular Big Data Software Tools and Platforms/Languages Used.** *Source:* Results of a poll conducted by **kdnuggets.com**.

Application Case 5.6

Data Mining Goes to Hollywood: Predicting Financial Success of Movies

Predicting box-office receipts (i.e., financial success) of a particular motion picture is an interesting and challenging problem. According to some domain experts, the movie industry is the "land of hunches and wild guesses" due to the difficulty associated with forecasting product demand, making the movie business in Hollywood a risky endeavor. In support of such observations, Jack Valenti (the longtime president and CEO of the Motion Picture Association of America) once mentioned that "…no one can tell you how a movie is going to do in the marketplace…not until the film opens in darkened theatre and sparks fly up between the screen and the audience." Entertainment industry trade journals and magazines have been full of examples, statements, and experiences that support such a claim.

Like many other researchers who have attempted to shed light on this challenging real-world problem, Ramesh Sharda and Dursun Delen have been exploring the use of data mining to predict the financial performance of a motion picture at the box office before it even enters production (while the movie is nothing more than a conceptual idea). In their highly publicized prediction models, they convert the forecasting

(Continued)

Application Case 5.6   (Continued)

(or regression) problem into a classification problem; that is, rather than forecasting the point estimate of box-office receipts, they classify a movie based on its box-office receipts in one of nine categories, ranging from "flop" to "blockbuster," making the problem a multinomial classification problem. Table 5.4 illustrates the definition of the nine classes in terms of the range of box-office receipts.

Data

Data was collected from variety of movie-related databases (e.g., ShowBiz, IMDb, IMSDb, AllMovie, etc.) and consolidated into a single data set. The data set for the most recently developed models contained 2,632 movies released between 1998 and 2006. A summary of the independent variables along with their specifications is provided in Table 5.5. For more descriptive details and justification for inclusion of these independent variables, the reader is referred to Sharda and Delen (2007).

Methodology

Using a variety of data mining methods, including neural networks, decision trees, support vector machines, and three types of ensembles, Sharda

and Delen developed the prediction models. The data from 1998 to 2005 were used as training data to build the prediction models, and the data from 2006 was used as the test data to assess and compare the models' prediction accuracy. Figure 5.15 shows a screenshot of IBM SPSS Modeler (formerly Clementine data mining tool) depicting the process map employed for the prediction problem. The upper-left side of the process map shows the model development process, and the lower-right corner of the process map shows the model assessment (i.e., testing or scoring) process (more details on IBM SPSS Modeler tool and its usage can be found on the book's Web site).

Results

Table 5.6 provides the prediction results of all three data mining methods as well as the results of the three different ensembles. The first performance measure is the percent correct classification rate, which is called *bingo*. Also reported in the table is the *1-Away* correct classification rate (i.e., within one category). The results indicate that SVM performed the best among the individual prediction models, followed by ANN; the worst of the three

TABLE 5.4 Movie Classification Based on Receipts									
Class No.	1	2	3	4	5	6	7	8	9
Range (in millions of dollars)	<1	>1	>10	>20	>40	>65	>100	>150	>200
	(Flop)	<10	<20	<40	<65	<100	<150	<200	(Blockbuster)

TABLE 5.5 Summary of Independent Variables		
Independent Variable	Number of Values	Possible Values
MPAA Rating	5	G, PG, PG-13, R, NR
Competition	3	High, Medium, Low
Star value	3	High, Medium, Low
Genre	10	Sci-Fi, Historic Epic Drama, Modern Drama, Politically Related, Thriller, Horror, Comedy, Cartoon, Action, Documentary
Special effects	3	High, Medium, Low
Sequel	1	Yes, No
Number of screens	1	Positive integer

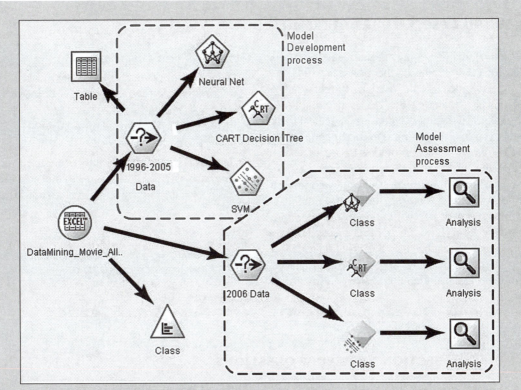

FIGURE 5.15   Process Flow Screenshot for the Box-Office Prediction System.   *Source:* Used with permission from IBM SPSS.

was the CART decision tree algorithm. In general, the ensemble models performed better than the individual predictions models, of which the fusion algorithm performed the best. What is probably more important to decision makers, and standing out in the results table, is the significantly low standard deviation obtained from the ensembles compared to the individual models.

Conclusion

The researchers claim that these prediction results are better than any reported in the published literature for

TABLE 5.6   Tabulated Prediction Results for Individual and Ensemble Models

| | Prediction Models | | | | | |
| | Individual Models | | | Ensemble Models | | |
Performance Measure	SVM	ANN	C&RT	Random Forest	Boosted Tree	Fusion (Average)
Count (Bingo)	192	182	140	189	187	**194**
Count (1-Away)	104	120	126	121	104	**120**
Accuracy (% Bingo)	55.49%	52.60%	40.46%	54.62%	54.05%	**56.07%**
Accuracy (% 1-Away)	85.55%	87.28%	76.88%	89.60%	84.10%	**90.75%**
Standard deviation	0.93	0.87	1.05	0.76	0.84	**0.63**

(Continued)

Application Case 5.6   (Continued)

this problem domain. Beyond the attractive accuracy of their prediction results of the box-office receipts, these models could also be used to further analyze (and potentially optimize) the decision variables in order to maximize the financial return. Specifically, the parameters used for modeling could be altered using the already trained prediction models in order to better understand the impact of different parameters on the end results. During this process, which is commonly referred to as *sensitivity analysis*, the decision maker of a given entertainment firm could find out, with a fairly high accuracy level, how much value a specific actor (or a specific release date, or the addition of more technical effects, etc.) brings to the financial success of a film, making the underlying system an invaluable decision aid.

QUESTIONS FOR DISCUSSION

1. Why is it important for Hollywood professionals to predict the financial success of movies?
2. How can data mining be used to predict the financial success of movies before the start of their production process?
3. How do you think Hollywood performed, and perhaps is still performing, this task without the help of data mining tools and techniques?

Sources: R. Sharda and D. Delen, "Predicting Box-Office Success of Motion Pictures with Neural Networks," *Expert Systems with Applications,* Vol. 30, 2006, pp. 243–254; D. Delen, R. Sharda, and P. Kumar, "Movie Forecast Guru: A Web-based DSS for Hollywood Managers," *Decision Support Systems,* Vol. 43, No. 4, 2007, pp. 1151–1170.

SECTION 5.6 REVIEW QUESTIONS

1. What are the most popular commercial data mining tools?
2. Why do you think the most popular tools are developed by statistics companies?
3. What are the most popular free data mining tools?
4. What are the main differences between commercial and free data mining software tools?
5. What would be your top five selection criteria for a data mining tool? Explain.

5.7   DATA MINING PRIVACY ISSUES, MYTHS, AND BLUNDERS

Data Mining and Privacy Issues

Data that is collected, stored, and analyzed in data mining often contains information about real people. Such information may include identification data (name, address, Social Security number, driver's license number, employee number, etc.), demographic data (e.g., age, sex, ethnicity, marital status, number of children, etc.), financial data (e.g., salary, gross family income, checking or savings account balance, home ownership, mortgage or loan account specifics, credit card limits and balances, investment account specifics, etc.), purchase history (i.e., what is bought from where and when either from the vendor's transaction records or from credit card transaction specifics), and other personal data (e.g., anniversary, pregnancy, illness, loss in the family, bankruptcy filings, etc.). Most of these data can be accessed through some third-party data providers. The main question here is the privacy of the person to whom the data belongs. In order to maintain the privacy and protection of individuals' rights, data mining professionals have ethical (and often legal) obligations. One way to accomplish this is the process of de-identification of the customer records prior to applying data mining applications, so that the records cannot be traced to an individual. Many publicly available data sources (e.g., CDC data, SEER data, UNOS data, etc.) are already de-identified. Prior to accessing these data sources, users are often asked to consent that under no circumstances will they try to identify the individuals behind those figures.

There have been a number of instances in the recent past where companies shared their customer data with others without seeking the explicit consent of their customers. For instance, as most of you might recall, in 2003, JetBlue Airlines provided more than a million passenger records of their customers to Torch Concepts, a U.S. government contractor. Torch then subsequently augmented the passenger data with additional information such as family size and Social Security numbers—information purchased from a data broker called Acxiom. The consolidated personal database was intended to be used for a data mining project in order to develop potential terrorist profiles. All of this was done without notification or consent of passengers. When news of the activities got out, however, dozens of privacy lawsuits were filed against JetBlue, Torch, and Acxiom, and several U.S. senators called for an investigation into the incident (Wald, 2004). Similar, but not as dramatic, privacy-related news has come out in the recent past about the popular social network companies, which allegedly were selling customer-specific data to other companies for personalized target marketing.

There was another peculiar story about privacy concerns that made it into the headlines in 2012. In this instance, the company did not even use any private and/or personal data. Legally speaking, there was no violation of any laws. It was about Target and is summarized in Application Case 5.7.

Application Case 5.7
Predicting Customer Buying Patterns—The Target Story

In early 2012, an infamous story appeared concerning Target's practice of predictive analytics. The story was about a teenager girl who was being sent advertising flyers and coupons by Target for the kinds of things that a new mother-to-be would buy from a store like Target. The story goes like this: An angry man went into a Target outside of Minneapolis, demanding to talk to a manager: "My daughter got this in the mail!" he said. "She's still in high school, and you're sending her coupons for baby clothes and cribs? Are you trying to encourage her to get pregnant?" The manager didn't have any idea what the man was talking about. He looked at the mailer. Sure enough, it was addressed to the man's daughter and contained advertisements for maternity clothing, nursery furniture, and pictures of smiling infants. The manager apologized and then called a few days later to apologize again. On the phone, though, the father was somewhat abashed. "I had a talk with my daughter," he said. "It turns out there's been some activities in my house I haven't been completely aware of. She's due in August. I owe you an apology."

As it turns out, Target figured out a teen girl was pregnant before her father did! Here is how they did it. Target assigns every customer a Guest

ID number (tied to their credit card, name, or e-mail address) that becomes a placeholder that keeps a history of everything they have bought. Target augments this data with any demographic information that they had collected from them or bought from other information sources. Using this information, Target looked at historical buying data for all the females who had signed up for Target baby registries in the past. They analyzed the data from all directions, and soon enough some useful patterns emerged. For example, lotions and special vitamins were among the products with interesting purchase patterns. Lots of people buy lotion, but they have noticed was that women on the baby registry were buying larger quantities of unscented lotion around the beginning of their second trimester. Another analyst noted that sometime in the first 20 weeks, pregnant women loaded up on supplements like calcium, magnesium, and zinc. Many shoppers purchase soap and cotton balls, but when someone suddenly starts buying lots of scent-free soap and extra-big bags of cotton balls, in addition to hand sanitizers and washcloths, it signals that they could be getting close to their delivery date. At the end, they were able to identify about 25 products that, when analyzed together, allowed them to assign each shopper a

(Continued)

Application Case 5.7 (Continued)

"pregnancy prediction" score. More important, they could also estimate a woman's due date to within a small window, so Target could send coupons timed to very specific stages of her pregnancy.

If you look at this practice from a legal perspective, you would conclude that Target did not use any information that violates customer privacy; rather, they used transactional data that most every other retail chain is collecting and storing (and perhaps analyzing) about their customers. What was disturbing in this scenario was perhaps the targeted concept: pregnancy. There are certain events or concepts that should be off limits or treated extremely cautiously, such as terminal disease, divorce, and bankruptcy.

QUESTIONS FOR DISCUSSION

1. What do you think about data mining and its implications concerning privacy? What is the threshold between knowledge discovery and privacy infringement?
2. Did Target go too far? Did they do anything illegal? What do you think they should have done? What do you think they should do now (quit these types of practices)?

Sources: K. Hill, "How Target Figured Out a Teen Girl Was Pregnant Before Her Father Did," *Forbes*, February 13, 2012; and R. Nolan, "Behind the Cover Story: How Much Does Target Know?" **NYTimes.com**, February 21, 2012.

Data Mining Myths and Blunders

Data mining is a powerful analytical tool that enables business executives to advance from describing the nature of the past to predicting the future. It helps marketers find patterns that unlock the mysteries of customer behavior. The results of data mining can be used to increase revenue, reduce expenses, identify fraud, and locate business opportunities, offering a whole new realm of competitive advantage. As an evolving and maturing field, data mining is often associated with a number of myths, including the following (Zaima, 2003):

Myth	Reality
Data mining provides instant, crystal-ball-like predictions.	Data mining is a multistep process that requires deliberate, proactive design and use.
Data mining is not yet viable for business applications.	The current state-of-the-art is ready to go for almost any business.
Data mining requires a separate, dedicated database.	Because of advances in database technology, a dedicated database is not required, even though it may be desirable.
Only those with advanced degrees can do data mining.	Newer Web-based tools enable managers of all educational levels to do data mining.
Data mining is only for large firms that have lots of customer data.	If the data accurately reflect the business or its customers, a company can use data mining.

Data mining visionaries have gained enormous competitive advantage by understanding that these myths are just that: myths.

The following 10 data mining mistakes are often made in practice (Skalak, 2001; Shultz, 2004), and you should try to avoid them:

1. Selecting the wrong problem for data mining.
2. Ignoring what your sponsor thinks data mining is and what it really can and cannot do.

3. Leaving insufficient time for data preparation. It takes more effort than is generally understood.
4. Looking only at aggregated results and not at individual records. IBM's DB2 IMS can highlight individual records of interest.
5. Being sloppy about keeping track of the data mining procedure and results.
6. Ignoring suspicious findings and quickly moving on.
7. Running mining algorithms repeatedly and blindly. It is important to think hard about the next stage of data analysis. Data mining is a very hands-on activity.
8. Believing everything you are told about the data.
9. Believing everything you are told about your own data mining analysis.
10. Measuring your results differently from the way your sponsor measures them.

SECTION 5.7 REVIEW QUESTIONS

1. What are the privacy issues in data mining?
2. How do you think the discussion between privacy and data mining will progress? Why?
3. What are the most common myths about data mining?
4. What do you think are the reasons for these myths about data mining?
5. What are the most common data mining mistakes/blunders? How can they be minimized and/or eliminated?

Chapter Highlights

- Data mining is the process of discovering new knowledge from databases.
- Data mining can use simple flat files as data sources or it can be performed on data in data warehouses.
- There are many alternative names and definitions for data mining.
- Data mining is at the intersection of many disciplines, including statistics, artificial intelligence, and mathematical modeling.
- Companies use data mining to better understand their customers and optimize their operations.
- Data mining applications can be found in virtually every area of business and government, including healthcare, finance, marketing, and homeland security.
- Three broad categories of data mining tasks are prediction (classification or regression), clustering, and association.
- Similar to other information systems initiatives, a data mining project must follow a systematic project management process to be successful.
- Several data mining processes have been proposed: CRISP-DM, SEMMA, KDD, and so forth.
- CRISP-DM provides a systematic and orderly way to conduct data mining projects.

- The earlier steps in data mining projects (i.e., understanding the domain and the relevant data) consume most of the total project time (often more than 80% of the total time).
- Data preprocessing is essential to any successful data mining study. Good data leads to good information; good information leads to good decisions.
- Data preprocessing includes four main steps: data consolidation, data cleaning, data transformation, and data reduction.
- Classification methods learn from previous examples containing inputs and the resulting class labels, and once properly trained they are able to classify future cases.
- Clustering partitions pattern records into natural segments or clusters. Each segment's members share similar characteristics.
- A number of different algorithms are commonly used for classification. Commercial implementations include ID3, C4.5, C5, CART, and SPRINT.
- Decision trees partition data by branching along different attributes so that each leaf node has all the patterns of one class.
- The Gini index and information gain (entropy) are two popular ways to determine branching choices in a decision tree.

- The Gini index measures the purity of a sample. If everything in a sample belongs to one class, the Gini index value is zero.
- Several assessment techniques can measure the prediction accuracy of classification models, including simple split, *k*-fold cross-validation, bootstrapping, and area under the ROC curve.
- Cluster algorithms are used when the data records do not have predefined class identifiers (i.e., it is not known to what class a particular record belongs).
- Cluster algorithms compute measures of similarity in order to group similar cases into clusters.
- The most commonly used similarity measure in cluster analysis is a distance measure.
- The most commonly used clustering algorithms are *k*-means and self-organizing maps.

- Association rule mining is used to discover two or more items (or events or concepts) that go together.
- Association rule mining is commonly referred to as market-basket analysis.
- The most commonly used association algorithm is Apriori, whereby frequent itemsets are identified through a bottom-up approach.
- Association rules are assessed based on their support and confidence measures.
- Many commercial and free data mining tools are available.
- The most popular commercial data mining tools are SPSS PASW and SAS Enterprise Miner.
- The most popular free data mining tools are Weka and RapidMiner.

Key Terms

Apriori algorithm	data mining	lift	ratio data
area under the ROC curve	decision tree	link analysis	regression
	distance measure	Microsoft Enterprise Consortium	SEMMA
association	entropy		sequence mining
bootstrapping	Gini index	Microsoft SQL Server	simple split
categorical data	information gain	nominal data	support
classification	interval data	numeric data	Weka
clustering	*k*-fold cross-validation	ordinal data	
confidence	knowledge discovery in databases (KDD)	prediction	
CRISP-DM		RapidMiner	

Questions for Discussion

1. Define *data mining*. Why are there many names and definitions for data mining?
2. What are the main reasons for the recent popularity of data mining?
3. Discuss what an organization should consider before making a decision to purchase data mining software.
4. Distinguish data mining from other analytical tools and techniques.
5. Discuss the main data mining methods. What are the fundamental differences among them?
6. What are the main data mining application areas? Discuss the commonalities of these areas that make them a prospect for data mining studies.
7. Why do we need a standardized data mining process? What are the most commonly used data mining processes?
8. Discuss the differences between the two most commonly used data mining processes.
9. Are data mining processes a mere sequential set of activities? Explain.
10. Why do we need data preprocessing? What are the main tasks and relevant techniques used in data preprocessing?
11. Discuss the reasoning behind the assessment of classification models.
12. What is the main difference between classification and clustering? Explain using concrete examples.
13. Moving beyond the chapter discussion, where else can association be used?
14. What are the privacy issues with data mining? Do you think they are substantiated?
15. What are the most common myths and mistakes about data mining?

Exercises

Teradata University Network (TUN) and Other Hands-on Exercises

1. Visit **teradatauniversitynetwork.com**. Identify case studies and white papers about data mining. Describe recent developments in the field.

2. Go to **teradatauniversitynetwork.com** or a URL provided by your instructor. Locate Web seminars related to data mining. In particular, locate a seminar given by C. Imhoff and T. Zouqes. Watch the Web seminar. Then answer the following questions:

   a. What are some of the interesting applications of data mining?

   b. What types of payoffs and costs can organizations expect from data mining initiatives?

3. For this exercise, your goal is to build a model to identify inputs or predictors that differentiate risky customers from others (based on patterns pertaining to previous customers) and then use those inputs to predict new risky customers. This sample case is typical for this domain.

   The sample data to be used in this exercise are in Online File W5.1 in the file **CreditRisk.xlsx**. The data set has 425 cases and 15 variables pertaining to past and current customers who have borrowed from a bank for various reasons. The data set contains customer-related information such as financial standing, reason for the loan, employment, demographic information, and the outcome or dependent variable for credit standing, classifying each case as good or bad, based on the institution's past experience.

   Take 400 of the cases as training cases and set aside the other 25 for testing. Build a decision tree model to learn the characteristics of the problem. Test its performance on the other 25 cases. Report on your model's learning and testing performance. Prepare a report that identifies the decision tree model and training parameters, as well as the resulting performance on the test set. Use any decision tree software. (This exercise is courtesy of StatSoft, Inc., based on a German data set from **ftp.ics.uci.edu/pub/machine-learning-databases/statlog/german** renamed CreditRisk and altered.)

4. For this exercise, you will replicate (on a smaller scale) the box-office prediction modeling explained in Application Case 5.6. Download the training data set from Online File W5.2, **MovieTrain.xlsx**, which is in Microsoft Excel format. Use the data description given in Application Case 5.6 to understand the domain and the problem you are trying to solve. Pick and choose your independent variables. Develop at least three classification models (e.g., decision tree, logistic regression, neural networks). Compare the accuracy results using 10-fold cross-validation and percentage split techniques, use confusion matrices, and comment on the outcome. Test the models you have developed on the test set (see Online File W5.3, **MovieTest.xlsx**). Analyze the results with different models and come up with the best classification model, supporting it with your results.

5. This exercise is aimed at introducing you to association rule mining. The Excel data set **baskets1ntrans.xlsx** has around 2800 observations/records of supermarket transaction data. Each record contains the customer's ID and Products that they have purchased. Use this data set to understand the relationships among products (i.e., which products are purchased together). Look for interesting relationships and add screenshots of any subtle association patterns that you might find. More specifically, answer the following questions.

   • Which association rules do you think are most important?

   • Based on some of the association rules you found, make at least three business recommendations that might be beneficial to the company. These recommendations may include ideas about shelf organization, upselling, or cross-selling products. (Bonus points will be given to new/innovative ideas.)

   • What are the Support, Confidence, and Lift values for the following rule?

   • Wine, Canned Veg ⇒ Frozen Meal

Team Assignments and Role-Playing Projects

1. Examine how new data-capture devices such as radio-frequency identification (RFID) tags help organizations accurately identify and segment their customers for activities such as targeted marketing. Many of these applications involve data mining. Scan the literature and the Web and then propose five potential new data mining applications that can use the data created with RFID technology. What issues could arise if a country's laws required such devices to be embedded in everyone's body for a national identification system?

2. Interview administrators in your college or executives in your organization to determine how data warehousing, data mining, OLAP, and visualization tools could assist them in their work. Write a proposal describing your findings. Include cost estimates and benefits in your report.

3. A very good repository of data that has been used to test the performance of many data mining algorithms is available at **ics.uci.edu/~mlearn/MLRepository.html**. Some of the data sets are meant to test the limits of current machine-learning algorithms and to compare their performance with new approaches to learning. However, some of the smaller data sets can be useful for exploring the functionality of any data mining software

or the software that is available as companion software with this book, such as Statistica Data Miner. Download at least one data set from this repository (e.g., Credit Screening Databases, Housing Database) and apply decision tree or clustering methods, as appropriate. Prepare a report based on your results. (Some of these exercises may be used as semester-long term projects, for example.)

4. There are large and feature rich data sets made available by the U.S. government or its subsidiaries on the Internet. For instance Centers for Disease Control and Prevention data sets (**cdc.gov/DataStatistics**); the National Cancer Institute's Surveillance Epidemiology and End Results data sets (**seer.cancer.gov/data**); and the Department of Transportation's Fatality Analysis Reporting System crash data sets (**nhtsa.gov/ FARS**). These data sets are not preprocessed for data mining, which makes them a great resource to experience the complete data mining process. Another rich source for a collection of analytics data sets is listed on **KDNuggets.com** (**kdnuggets.com/datasets/ index.html**).

5. Consider the following data set, which includes three attributes and a classification for admission decisions into an MBA program:

   a. Using the data shown, develop your own manual expert rules for decision making.

   b. Use the Gini index to build a decision tree. You can use manual calculations or a spreadsheet to perform the basic calculations.

   c. Use an automated decision tree software program to build a tree for the same data.

GMAT	GPA	Quantitative GMAT Score (percentile)	Decision
650	2.75	35	No
580	3.50	70	No
600	3.50	75	Yes
450	2.95	80	No
700	3.25	90	Yes
590	3.50	80	Yes
400	3.85	45	No
640	3.50	75	Yes
540	3.00	60	?
690	2.85	80	?
490	4.00	65	?

Internet Exercises

1. Visit the AI Exploratorium at **cs.ualberta.ca/~aixplore**. Click the Decision Tree link. Read the narrative on basketball game statistics. Examine the data and then build a decision tree. Report your impressions of the accuracy of this decision tree. Also, explore the effects of different algorithms.

2. Survey some data mining tools and vendors. Start with **fairisaac.com** and **egain.com**. Consult **dmreview.com** and identify some data mining products and service providers that are not mentioned in this chapter.

3. Find recent cases of successful data mining applications. Visit the Web sites of some data mining vendors and look for cases or success stories. Prepare a report summarizing five new case studies.

4. Go to vendor Web sites (especially those of SAS, SPSS, Cognos, Teradata, StatSoft, and Fair Isaac) and look at success stories for BI (OLAP and data mining) tools. What do the various success stories have in common? How do they differ?

5. Go to **statsoft.com**. Download at least three white papers on applications. Which of these applications may have used the data/text/Web mining techniques discussed in this chapter?

6. Go to **sas.com**. Download at least three white papers on applications. Which of these applications may have used the data/text/Web mining techniques discussed in this chapter?

7. Go to **spss.com**. Download at least three white papers on applications. Which of these applications may have used the data/text/Web mining techniques discussed in this chapter?

8. Go to **teradata.com**. Download at least three white papers on applications. Which of these applications may have used the data/text/Web mining techniques discussed in this chapter?

9. Go to **fairisaac.com**. Download at least three white papers on applications. Which of these applications may have used the data/text/Web mining techniques discussed in this chapter?

10. Go to **salfordsystems.com**. Download at least three white papers on applications. Which of these applications may have used the data/text/Web mining techniques discussed in this chapter?

11. Go to **rulequest.com**. Download at least three white papers on applications. Which of these applications may have used the data/text/Web mining techniques discussed in this chapter?

12. Go to **kdnuggets.com**. Explore the sections on applications as well as software. Find names of at least three additional packages for data mining and text mining.

End-of-Chapter Application Case

Macys.com Enhances Its Customers' Shopping Experience with Analytics

After more than 80 years in business, Macy's Inc. is one of America's most iconic retailers. With annual revenues exceeding $20 billion, Macy's enjoys a loyal base of customers who come to its stores and shop online each day. To continue its legacy of providing stellar customer service and the right selection of products, the retailer's e-commerce division—Macys.com—is using analytics to better understand and enhance its customers' online shopping experience, while helping to increase the retailer's overall profitability.

To more effectively measure and understand the impact of its online marketing initiatives on Macy's store sales, Macys.com increased its analytical capabilities with SAS Enterprise Miner (one of the premier data mining tools in the market), resulting in an e-mail subscription churn reduction of 20 percent. It also uses SAS to automate report generation, saving more than $500,000 a year in comp analyst time.

Ending "One Size Fits All" E-Mail Marketing

"We want to understand customer lifetime value," explains Kerem Tomak, vice president of analytics for Macys.com. "We want to understand how long our customers have been with us, how often an e-mail from us triggers a visit to our site. This helps us better understand who our best customers are and how engaged they are with us. [With that knowledge] we can give our valuable customers the right promotions in order to serve them the best way possible.

"Customers share a lot of information with us—their likes and dislikes—and our task is to support them in return for their loyalty by providing them with what they want, instantly," adds Tomak. Macys.com uses Hadoop as a data platform for SAS Enterprise Miner.

Initially, Tomak was worried that segmenting customers and sending fewer, but more specific, e=mails would reduce traffic to the Web site. "The general belief was that we had to blast everyone," Tomak said. Today, e-mails are sent less frequently, but with more thought, and the retailer has reduced subscription churn rate by approximately 20 percent.

Time Savings, Lower Costs

Tomak's group is responsible for creating a variety of mission critical reports—some daily, some weekly, others monthly—that go to employees in marketing and finance. These data-rich reports were taking analysts 4 to 12 hours to produce—much of it busy work that involved cutting and pasting from Excel spreadsheets. Macys.com is now using SAS to automate the reports. "This cuts the time dramatically. It saves us more than $500,000 a year in terms of comp FTE hours saved—a really big impact," Tomak says, noting that the savings began within about 3 months of installing SAS.

Now his staff can maximize time spent on providing value-added analyses and insights to provide content, products, and offers that guarantee a personalized shopping experience for Macys.com customers.

"Macy's is a very information-hungry organization, and requests for ad hoc reports come from all over the company. These streamlined systems eliminate error, guarantee accuracy, and increase the speed with which we can address requests," Tomak says. "Each time we use the software, we find new ways of doing things, and we are more and more impressed by the speed at which it churns out data and models."

Moving Forward

"With the extra time, the team has moved from being reactionary to proactive, meaning they can examine more data, spend quality time analyzing, and become internal consultants who provide more insight behind the data," he says. "This will be important to supporting the strategy and driving the next generation of Macy's.com."

As competition increases in the online retailing world, Tomak says there is a push toward generating more accurate, real-time decisions about customer preferences. The ability to gain customer insight across channels is a critical part of improving customer satisfaction and revenues, and Macys.com uses SAS Enterprise Miner to validate and guide the site's cross- and up-sell offer algorithms.

Source: **www.sas.com/success/macy.html**.

References

Bhandari, I., E. Colet, J. Parker, Z. Pines, R. Pratap, and K. Ramanujam. (1997). "Advanced Scout: Data Mining and Knowledge Discovery in NBA Data." *Data Mining and Knowledge Discovery,* Vol. 1, No. 1, pp. 121–125.

Buck, N. (December 2000/January 2001). "Eureka! Knowledge Discovery." *Software Magazine.*

Chan, P. K., W. Phan, A. Prodromidis, and S. Stolfo. (1999). "Distributed Data Mining in Credit Card Fraud Detection." *IEEE Intelligent Systems,* Vol. 14, No. 6, pp. 67–74.

CRISP-DM. (2013). "Cross-Industry Standard Process for Data Mining (CRISP-DM)." **www.the-modeling-agency.com/crisp-dm.pdf** (accessed February 2, 2013).

Davenport, T. H. (2006, January). "Competing on Analytics." *Harvard Business Review.*

Delen, D., R. Sharda, and P. Kumar. (2007). "Movie Forecast Guru: A Web-based DSS for Hollywood Managers." *Decision Support Systems,* Vol. 43, No. 4, pp. 1151–1170.

Delen, D., D. Cogdell, and N. Kasap. (2012). "A Comparative Analysis of Data Mining Methods in Predicting NCAA Bowl Outcomes," *International Journal of Forecasting,* Vol. 28, pp. 543–552.

Delen, D. (2009). "Analysis of Cancer Data: A Data Mining Approach." *Expert Systems,* Vol. 26, No. 1, pp. 100–112.

Delen, D., G. Walker, and A. Kadam. (2005). "Predicting Breast Cancer Survivability: A Comparison of Three Data Mining Methods." *Artificial Intelligence in Medicine,* Vol 34, No. 2, pp. 113–127.

Dunham, M. (2003). *Data Mining: Introductory and Advanced Topics.* Upper Saddle River, NJ: Prentice Hall.

EPIC. (2013). Electronic Privacy Information Center. "Case Against JetBlue Airways Corporation and Acxiom Corporation." **http://epic.org/privacy/airtravel/jetblue/ftccomplaint.html** (accessed January 14, 2013).

Fayyad, U., G. Piatetsky-Shapiro, and P. Smyth. (1996). "From Knowledge Discovery in Databases." *AI Magazine,* Vol. 17, No. 3, pp. 37–54.

Hoffman, T. (1998, December 7). "Banks Turn to IT to Reclaim Most Profitable Customers." *Computerworld.*

Hoffman, T. (1999, April 19). "Insurers Mine for Age-Appropriate Offering." *Computerworld.*

Kohonen, T. (1982). "Self-Organized Formation of Topologically Correct Feature Maps." *Biological Cybernetics,* Vol. 43, No. 1, pp. 59–69.

Nemati, H. R., and C. D. Barko. (2001). "Issues in Organizational Data Mining: A Survey of Current Practices." *Journal of Data Warehousing,* Vol. 6, No. 1, pp. 25–36.

North, M. (2012). Data mining for the masses. A Global Text Project Book. **https://sites.google.com/site/dataminingforthemasses** (accessed June 2013).

Quinlan, J. R. (1986). "Induction of Decision Trees." *Machine Learning,* Vol. 1, pp. 81–106.

SEMMA. (2009). "SAS's Data Mining Process: Sample, Explore, Modify, Model, Assess." **sas.com/offices/europe/uk/technologies/analytics/datamining/miner/semma.html** (accessed August 2009).

Sharda, R., and D. Delen. (2006). "Predicting Box-office Success of Motion Pictures with Neural Networks." *Expert Systems with Applications,* Vol. 30, pp. 243–254.

Shultz, R. (2004, December 7). "Live from NCDM: Tales of Database Buffoonery." **directmag.com/news/ncdm-12-07-04/index.html** (accessed April 2009).

Skalak, D. (2001). "Data Mining Blunders Exposed!" *DB2 Magazine,* Vol. 6, No. 2, pp. 10–13.

StatSoft. (2006). "Data Mining Techniques." **statsoft.com/textbook/stdatmin.html** (accessed August 2006).

Wald, M. L. (2004). "U.S. Calls Release of JetBlue Data Improper." *The New York Times,* February 21, 2004.

Wilson, R., and R. Sharda. (1994). "Bankruptcy Prediction Using Neural Networks." *Decision Support Systems,* Vol. 11, pp. 545–557.

Wright, C. (2012). "Statistical Predictors of March Madness: An Examination of the NCAA Men's Basketball Championship." **http://economics-files.pomona.edu/GarySmith/Econ190/Wright%20March%20Madness%20Final%20Paper.pdf** (accessed February 2, 2013).

Zaima, A. (2003). "The Five Myths of Data Mining." *What Works: Best Practices in Business Intelligence and Data Warehousing,* Vol. 15, the Data Warehousing Institute, Chatsworth, CA, pp. 42–43.

CHAPTER

6

Techniques for Predictive Modeling

LEARNING OBJECTIVES

- Understand the concept and definitions of artificial neural networks (ANN)
- Learn the different types of ANN architectures
- Know how learning happens in ANN
- Understand the concept and structure of support vector machines (SVM)
- Learn the advantages and disadvantages of SVM compared to ANN
- Understand the concept and formulation of k-nearest neighbor algorithm (kNN)
- Learn the advantages and disadvantages of kNN compared to ANN and SVM

Predictive modeling is perhaps the most commonly practiced branch in data mining. It allows decision makers to estimate what the future holds by means of learning from the past. In this chapter, we study the internal structures, capabilities/limitations, and applications of the most popular predictive modeling techniques, such as artificial neural networks, support vector machines, and k-nearest neighbor. These techniques are capable of addressing both classification- and regression-type prediction problems. Often, they are applied to complex prediction problems where other techniques are not capable of producing satisfactory results. In addition to these three (that are covered in this chapter), other notable prediction modeling techniques include regression (linear or nonlinear), logistic regression (for classification-type prediction problems), naïve Bayes (probabilistically oriented classification modeling), and different types of decision trees (covered in Chapter 5).

6.1 OPENING VIGNETTE: Predictive Modeling Helps Better Understand and Manage Complex Medical Procedures

Healthcare has become one of the most important issues to have a direct impact on quality of life in the United States and around the world. While the demand for healthcare services is increasing because of the aging population, the supply side is having problems keeping up with the level and quality of service. In order to close the gap, healthcare systems ought to significantly improve their operational effectiveness and efficiency. Effectiveness (doing the right thing, such as diagnosing and treating accurately) and efficiency (doing it the right way, such as using the least amount of resources and time) are the two fundamental pillars upon which the healthcare system can be revived. A promising way to improve healthcare is to take advantage of predictive modeling techniques along with large and feature-rich data sources (true reflections of medical and healthcare experiences) to support accurate and timely decision making.

According to the American Heart Association, cardiovascular disease (CVD) is the underlying cause for over 20 percent of deaths in the United States. Since 1900, CVD has been the number-one killer every year except 1918, which was the year of the great flu pandemic. CVD kills more people than the next four leading causes of deaths combined: cancer, chronic lower respiratory disease, accidents, and diabetes mellitus. Out of all CVD deaths, more than half are attributed to coronary diseases. Not only does CVD take a huge toll on the personal health and well-being of the population, but it is also a great drain on the healthcare resources in the Unites States and elsewhere in the world. The direct and indirect costs associated with CVD for a year are estimated to be in excess of $500 billion. A common surgical procedure to cure a large variant of CVD is called coronary artery bypass grafting (CABG). Even though the cost of a CABG surgery depends on the patient and service provider–related factors, the average rate is between $50,000 and $100,000 in the United States. As an illustrative example, Delen et al. (2012) carried out an analytics study where they used various predictive modeling methods to predict the outcome of a CABG and applied an information fusion-based sensitivity analysis on the trained models to better understand the importance of the prognostic factors. The main goal was to illustrate that predictive and explanatory analysis of large and feature-rich data sets provides invaluable information to make more efficient and effective decisions in healthcare.

RESEARCH METHOD

Figure 6.1 shows the model development and testing process used by Delen et al. They employed four different types of prediction models (artificial neural networks, support vector machines, and two types of decision trees, C5 and CART), and went through a large number of experimental runs to calibrate the modeling parameters for each model type. Once the models were developed, they went on the text data set. Finally, the trained models were exposed to a sensitivity analysis procedure where the contribution of the variables was measured. Table 6.1 shows the test results for the four different types of prediction models.

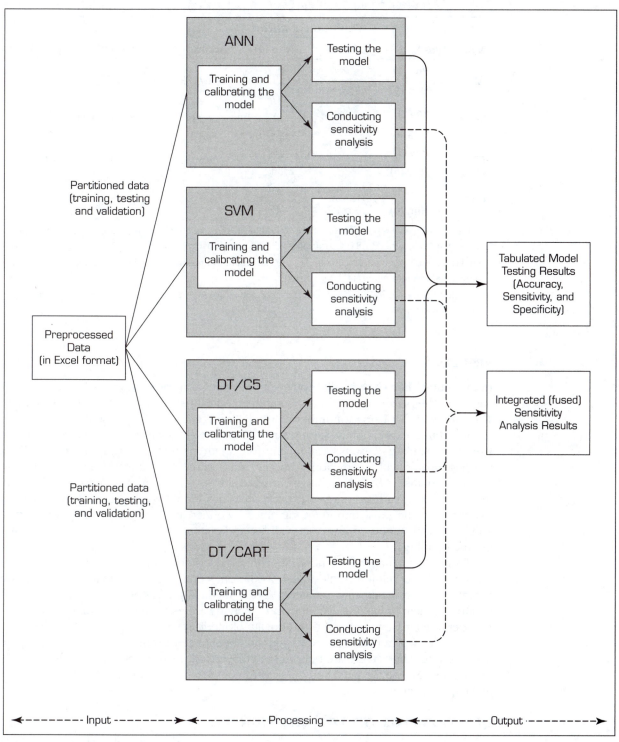

FIGURE 6.1   A Process Map for Training and Testing of the Four Predictive Models.

	Confusion Matrices[2]				
Model Type[1]	**Pos (1)**	**Neg (0)**	**Accuracy**[3]	**Sensitivity**[3]	**Specificity**[3]
ANN Pos (1)	749	230	74.72%	76.51%	72.93%
Neg (0)	265	714			
SVM Pos (1)	876	103	87.74%	89.48%	86.01%
Neg (0)	137	842			
C5 Pos (1)	876	103	79.62%	80.29%	78.96%
Neg (0)	137	842			
CART Pos (1)	660	319	71.15%	67.42%	74.87%
Neg (0)	246	733			

TABLE 6.1 Prediction Accuracy Results for All Four Model Types Based on the Test Data Set

[1]Acronyms for model types: ANN: Artificial Neural Networks; SVM: Support Vector Machines; C5: A popular decision tree algorithm; CART: Classification and Regression Trees.

[2]Prediction results for the test data samples are shown in a confusion matrix, where the rows represent the actuals and columns represent the predicted cases.

[3]Accuracy, Sensitivity, and Specificity are the three performance measures that were used in comparing the four prediction models.

RESULTS

In this study, they showed the power of data mining in predicting the outcome and in analyzing the prognostic factors of complex medical procedures such as CABG surgery. They showed that using a number of prediction methods (as opposed to only one) in a competitive experimental setting has the potential to produce better predictive as well as explanatory results. Among the four methods that they used, SVMs produced the best results with prediction accuracy of 88 percent on the test data sample. The information fusion-based sensitivity analysis revealed the ranked importance of the independent variables. Some of the top variables identified in this analysis having to overlap with the most important variables identified in previously conducted clinical and biological studies confirms the validity and effectiveness of the proposed data mining methodology.

From the managerial standpoint, clinical decision support systems that use the outcome of data mining studies (such as the ones presented in this case study) are not meant to replace healthcare managers and/or medical professionals. Rather, they intend to support them in making accurate and timely decisions to optimally allocate resources in order to increase the quantity and quality of medical services. There still is a long way to go before we can see these decision aids being used extensively in healthcare practices. Among others, there are behavioral, ethical, and political reasons for this resistance to adoption. Maybe the need and the government incentives for better healthcare systems will expedite the adoption.

QUESTIONS FOR THE OPENING VIGNETTE

1. Why is it important to study medical procedures? What is the value in predicting outcomes?
2. What factors do you think are the most important in better understanding and managing healthcare? Consider both managerial and clinical aspects of healthcare.

3. What would be the impact of predictive modeling on healthcare and medicine? Can predictive modeling replace medical or managerial personnel?

4. What were the outcomes of the study? Who can use these results? How can the results be implemented?

5. Search the Internet to locate two additional cases where predictive modeling is used to understand and manage complex medical procedures.

WHAT WE CAN LEARN FROM THIS VIGNETTE

As you will see in this chapter, predictive modeling techniques can be applied to a wide range of problem areas, from standard business problems of assessing customer needs to understanding and enhancing efficiency of production processes to improving healthcare and medicine. This vignette illustrates an innovative application of predictive modeling to better predict, understand, and manage coronary bypass grafting procedures. As the results indicate, these sophisticated predictive modeling techniques are capable of predicting and explaining such complex phenomena. Evidence-based medicine is a relatively new term coined in the healthcare arena, where the main idea is to dig deep into past experiences to discover new and useful knowledge to improve medical and managerial procedures in healthcare. As we all know, healthcare needs all the help that it can get. Compared to traditional research, which is clinical and biological in nature, data-driven studies provide an out-of-the-box view to medicine and management of medical systems.

Sources: D. Delen, A. Oztekin, and L. Tomak, "An Analytic Approach to Better Understanding and Management of Coronary Surgeries," *Decision Support Systems,* Vol. 52, No. 3, 2012, pp. 698–705; and American Heart Association, "Heart Disease and Stroke Statistics—2012 Update," **heart.org** (accessed February 2013).

6.2   BASIC CONCEPTS OF NEURAL NETWORKS

Neural networks represent a brain metaphor for information processing. These models are biologically inspired rather than an exact replica of how the brain actually functions. Neural networks have been shown to be very promising systems in many forecasting and business classification applications due to their ability to "learn" from the data, their nonparametric nature (i.e., no rigid assumptions), and their ability to generalize. **Neural computing** refers to a pattern-recognition methodology for machine learning. The resulting model from neural computing is often called an **artificial neural network (ANN)** or a **neural network**. Neural networks have been used in many business applications for **pattern recognition**, forecasting, prediction, and classification. Neural network computing is a key component of any data mining toolkit. Applications of neural networks abound in finance, marketing, manufacturing, operations, information systems, and so on. Therefore, we devote this chapter to developing a better understanding of neural network models, methods, and applications.

The human brain possesses bewildering capabilities for information processing and problem solving that modern computers cannot compete with in many aspects. It has been postulated that a model or a system that is enlightened and supported by the results from brain research, with a structure similar to that of biological neural networks, could exhibit similar intelligent functionality. Based on this bottom-up approach, ANN (also known as *connectionist models, parallel distributed processing models, neuromorphic systems,* or simply *neural networks*) have been developed as biologically inspired and plausible models for various tasks.

Biological neural networks are composed of many massively interconnected **neurons**. Each neuron possesses **axons** and **dendrites**, fingerlike projections that enable the neuron to communicate with its neighboring neurons by transmitting and receiving electrical and chemical signals. More or less resembling the structure of their biological counterparts, ANN are composed of interconnected, simple processing elements called artificial neurons. When processing information, the processing elements in an ANN operate concurrently and collectively, similar to biological neurons. ANN possess some desirable traits similar to those of biological neural networks, such as the abilities to learn, to self-organize, and to support fault tolerance.

Coming along a winding journey, ANN have been investigated by researchers for more than half a century. The formal study of ANN began with the pioneering work of McCulloch and Pitts in 1943. Inspired by the results of biological experiments and observations, McCulloch and Pitts (1943) introduced a simple model of a binary artificial neuron that captured some of the functions of biological neurons. Using information-processing machines to model the brain, McCulloch and Pitts built their neural network model using a large number of interconnected artificial binary neurons. From these beginnings, neural network research became quite popular in the late 1950s and early 1960s. After a thorough analysis of an early neural network model (called the **perceptron**, which used no hidden layer) as well as a pessimistic evaluation of the research potential by Minsky and Papert in 1969, interest in neural networks diminished.

During the past two decades, there has been an exciting resurgence in ANN studies due to the introduction of new network topologies, new activation functions, and new learning algorithms, as well as progress in neuroscience and cognitive science. Advances in theory and methodology have overcome many of the obstacles that hindered neural network research a few decades ago. Evidenced by the appealing results of numerous studies, neural networks are gaining in acceptance and popularity. In addition, the desirable features in neural information processing make neural networks attractive for solving complex problems. ANN have been applied to numerous complex problems in a variety of application settings. The successful use of neural network applications has inspired renewed interest from industry and business.

Biological and Artificial Neural Networks

The human brain is composed of special cells called *neurons*. These cells do not die and replenish when a person is injured (all other cells reproduce to replace themselves and then die). This phenomenon may explain why humans retain information for an extended period of time and start to lose it when they get old—as the brain cells gradually start to die. Information storage spans sets of neurons. The brain has anywhere from 50 billion to 150 billion neurons, of which there are more than 100 different kinds. Neurons are partitioned into groups called *networks*. Each network contains several thousand highly interconnected neurons. Thus, the brain can be viewed as a collection of neural networks.

The ability to learn and to react to changes in our environment requires intelligence. The brain and the central nervous system control thinking and intelligent behavior. People who suffer brain damage have difficulty learning and reacting to changing environments. Even so, undamaged parts of the brain can often compensate with new learning.

A portion of a network composed of two cells is shown in Figure 6.2. The cell itself includes a **nucleus** (the central processing portion of the neuron). To the left of cell 1, the dendrites provide input signals to the cell. To the right, the axon sends output signals

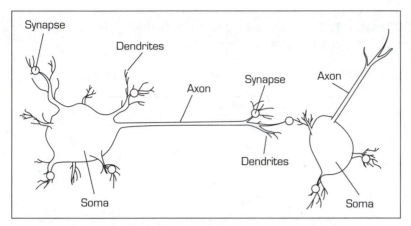

FIGURE 6.2   Portion of a Biological Neural Network: Two Interconnected Cells/Neurons.

to cell 2 via the axon terminals. These axon terminals merge with the dendrites of cell 2. Signals can be transmitted unchanged, or they can be altered by synapses. A **synapse** is able to increase or decrease the strength of the connection between neurons and cause excitation or inhibition of a subsequent neuron. This is how information is stored in the neural networks.

An ANN emulates a biological neural network. Neural computing actually uses a very limited set of concepts from biological neural systems (see Technology Insights 6.1). It is more of an analogy to the human brain than an accurate model of it. Neural concepts usually are implemented as software simulations of the massively parallel processes involved in processing interconnected elements (also called artificial neurons, or *neurodes*) in a network architecture. The artificial neuron receives inputs analogous to the electrochemical impulses that dendrites of biological neurons receive from other neurons. The output of the artificial neuron corresponds to signals sent from a biological neuron over its axon. These artificial signals can be changed by weights in a manner similar to the physical changes that occur in the synapses (see Figure 6.3).

Several ANN paradigms have been proposed for applications in a variety of problem domains. Perhaps the easiest way to differentiate among the various neural models is on the basis of how they structurally emulate the human brain, the way they process information, and how they learn to perform their designated tasks.

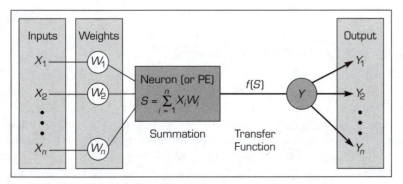

FIGURE 6.3   Processing Information in an Artificial Neuron.

TECHNOLOGY INSIGHTS 6.1 The Relationship Between Biological and Artificial Neural Networks

The following list shows some of the relationships between biological and artificial networks.

Biological	Artificial
Soma	Node
Dendrites	Input
Axon	Output
Synapse	Weight
Slow	Fast
Many neurons (10^9)	Few neurons (a dozen to hundreds of thousands)

Sources: L. Medsker and J. Liebowitz, *Design and Development of Expert Systems and Neural Networks,* Macmillan, New York, 1994, p. 163; and F. Zahedi, *Intelligent Systems for Business: Expert Systems with Neural Networks,* Wadsworth, Belmont, CA, 1993.

Because they are biologically inspired, the main processing elements of a neural network are individual neurons, analogous to the brain's neurons. These artificial neurons receive the information from other neurons or external input stimuli, perform a transformation on the inputs, and then pass on the transformed information to other neurons or external outputs. This is similar to how it is currently thought that the human brain works. Passing information from neuron to neuron can be thought of as a way to activate, or trigger, a response from certain neurons based on the information or stimulus received.

How information is processed by a neural network is inherently a function of its structure. Neural networks can have one or more layers of neurons. These neurons can be highly or fully interconnected, or only certain layers can be connected. Connections between neurons have an associated weight. In essence, the "knowledge" possessed by the network is encapsulated in these interconnection weights. Each neuron calculates a weighted sum of the incoming neuron values, transforms this input, and passes on its neural value as the input to subsequent neurons. Typically, although not always, this input/output transformation process at the individual neuron level is performed in a non-linear fashion.

Application Case 6.1 provides an interesting example of the use of neural networks as a prediction tool in the mining industry.

Application Case 6.1

Neural Networks Are Helping to Save Lives in the Mining Industry

In the mining industry, most of the underground injuries and fatalities are due to rock falls (i.e., fall of hanging wall/roof). The method that has been used for many years in the mines when determining the integrity of the hanging wall is to tap the hanging wall with a sounding bar and listen to the sound emitted. An experienced miner can differentiate an intact/solid hanging wall from a detached/ loose hanging wall by the sound that is emitted. This method is subjective. The Council for Scientific and Industrial Research (CSIR) in South Africa has developed a device that assists any miner in making an objective decision when determining the integrity of the hanging wall. A trained neural network model is embedded into the device. The device then records the sound emitted when a hanging wall is tapped.

The sound is then preprocessed before being input into a trained neural network model, and the trained model classifies the hanging wall as either intact or detached.

Mr. Teboho Nyareli, working as a research engineer at CSIR, who holds a master's degree in electronic engineering from the University of Cape Town in South Africa, used NeuroSolutions, a popular artificial neural network modeling software developed by NeuroDimensions, Inc., to develop the classification type prediction models. The multilayer perceptron-type ANN architecture that he built achieved better than 70 percent prediction accuracy on the hold-out sample. Currently, the prototype system is undergoing a final set of tests before deploying it as a decision aid, followed by the commercialization phase. The following figure shows a snapshot of NeuroSolution's model building platform.

QUESTIONS FOR DISCUSSION

1. How did neural networks help save lives in the mining industry?
2. What were the challenges, the proposed solution, and the obtained results?

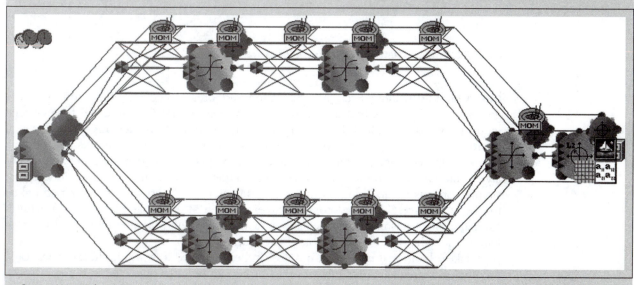

Source: NeuroSolutions customer success story, **neurosolutions.com/resources/nyareli.html** (accessed February 2013).

Elements of ANN

A neural network is composed of processing elements that are organized in different ways to form the network's structure. The basic processing unit is the neuron. A number of neurons are then organized into a network. Neurons can be organized in a number of different ways; these various network patterns are referred to as *topologies*. One popular approach, known as the feedforward-backpropagation paradigm (or simply **backpropagation**), allows all neurons to link the output in one layer to the input of the next layer, but it does not allow any feedback linkage (Haykin, 2009). Backpropagation is the most commonly used network paradigm.

PROCESSING ELEMENTS The **processing elements (PE)** of an ANN are artificial neurons. Each neuron receives inputs, processes them, and delivers a single output, as shown in Figure 6.3. The input can be raw input data or the output of other processing elements. The output can be the final result (e.g., 1 means yes, 0 means no), or it can be input to other neurons.

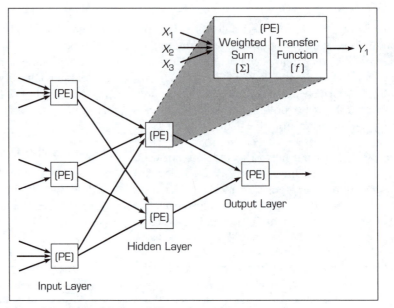

FIGURE 6.4 Neural Network with One Hidden Layer.

NETWORK STRUCTURE Each ANN is composed of a collection of neurons that are grouped into layers. A typical structure is shown in Figure 6.4. Note the three layers: input, intermediate (called the hidden layer), and output. A **hidden layer** is a layer of neurons that takes input from the previous layer and converts those inputs into outputs for further processing. Several hidden layers can be placed between the input and output layers, although it is common to use only one hidden layer. In that case, the hidden layer simply converts inputs into a nonlinear combination and passes the transformed inputs to the output layer. The most common interpretation of the hidden layer is as a feature-extraction mechanism; that is, the hidden layer converts the original inputs in the problem into a higher-level combination of such inputs.

Like a biological network, an ANN can be organized in several different ways (i.e., topologies or architectures); that is, the neurons can be interconnected in different ways. When information is processed, many of the processing elements perform their computations at the same time. This **parallel processing** resembles the way the brain works, and it differs from the serial processing of conventional computing.

Network Information Processing

Once the structure of a neural network is determined, information can be processed. We now present the major concepts related to network information processing.

INPUT Each input corresponds to a single attribute. For example, if the problem is to decide on approval or disapproval of a loan, attributes could include the applicant's income level, age, and home ownership status. The numeric value, or representation, of an attribute is the input to the network. Several types of data, such as text, pictures, and voice, can be used as inputs. Preprocessing may be needed to convert the data into meaningful inputs from symbolic data or to scale the data.

OUTPUTS The output of a network contains the solution to a problem. For example, in the case of a loan application, the output can be *yes* or *no*. The ANN assigns numeric values to the output, such as 1 for "yes" and 0 for "no." The purpose of the network is to compute the output values. Often, postprocessing of the output is required because some networks use two outputs: one for "yes" and another for "no." It is common to round the outputs to the nearest 0 or 1.

CONNECTION WEIGHTS   **Connection weights** are the key elements of an ANN. They express the relative strength (or mathematical value) of the input data or the many connections that transfer data from layer to layer. In other words, weights express the relative importance of each input to a processing element and, ultimately, the output. Weights are crucial in that they store learned patterns of information. It is through repeated adjustments of weights that a network learns.

SUMMATION FUNCTION   The **summation function** computes the weighted sums of all the input elements entering each processing element. A summation function multiplies each input value by its weight and totals the values for a weighted sum Y. The formula for n inputs in one processing element (see Figure 6.5a) is:

$$Y = \sum_{i=1}^{n} X_i W_i$$

For the jth neuron of several processing neurons in a layer (see Figure 6.5b), the formula is:

$$Y_j = \sum_{i=1}^{n} X_i W_{ij}$$

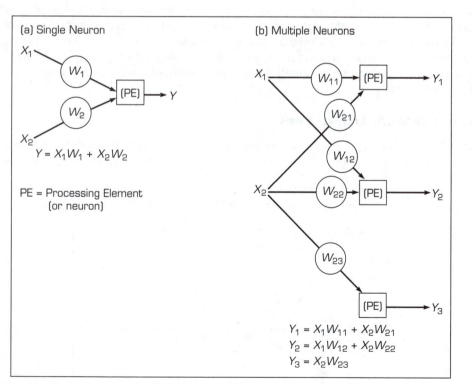

FIGURE 6.5   Summation Function for (a) a Single Neuron and (b) Several Neurons.

TRANSFORMATION (TRANSFER) FUNCTION The summation function computes the internal stimulation, or activation level, of the neuron. Based on this level, the neuron may or may not produce an output. The relationship between the internal activation level and the output can be linear or nonlinear. The relationship is expressed by one of several types of **transformation (transfer) functions**. The transformation function combines (i.e., adds up) the inputs coming into a neuron from other neurons/sources and then produces an output based on the transformation function. Selection of the specific function affects the network's operation. The **sigmoid (logical activation) function** (or *sigmoid transfer function*) is an *S*-shaped transfer function in the range of 0 to 1, and it is a popular as well as useful nonlinear transfer function:

$$Y_T = \frac{1}{(1 + e^{-Y})}$$

where Y_T is the transformed (i.e., normalized) value of Y (see Figure 6.6).

The transformation modifies the output levels to reasonable values (typically between 0 and 1). This transformation is performed before the output reaches the next level. Without such a transformation, the value of the output becomes very large, especially when there are several layers of neurons. Sometimes a threshold value is used instead of a transformation function. A **threshold value** is a hurdle value for the output of a neuron to trigger the next level of neurons. If an output value is smaller than the threshold value, it will not be passed to the next level of neurons. For example, any value of 0.5 or less becomes 0, and any value above 0.5 becomes 1. A transformation can occur at the output of each processing element, or it can be performed only at the final output nodes.

HIDDEN LAYERS Complex practical applications require one or more hidden layers between the input and output neurons and a correspondingly large number of weights. Many commercial ANN include three and sometimes up to five layers, with each containing 10 to 1,000 processing elements. Some experimental ANN use millions of processing elements. Because each layer increases the training effort exponentially and also increases the computation required, the use of more than three hidden layers is rare in most commercial systems.

Neural Network Architectures

There are several neural network architectures (for specifics of models and/or algorithms, see Haykin, 2009). The most common ones include feedforward (multilayer

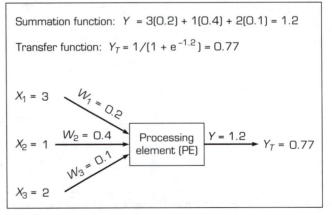

Summation function: $Y = 3(0.2) + 1(0.4) + 2(0.1) = 1.2$

Transfer function: $Y_T = 1/(1 + e^{-1.2}) = 0.77$

$X_1 = 3$ $W_1 = 0.2$

$X_2 = 1$ $W_2 = 0.4$

$W_3 = 0.1$

Processing element (PE) $Y = 1.2$ $Y_T = 0.77$

$X_3 = 2$

FIGURE 6.6   Example of ANN Transfer Function.

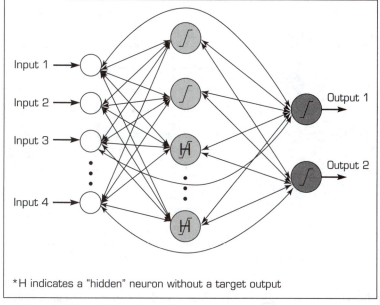

Input 1

Input 2

Input 3

Input 4

Output 1

Output 2

*H indicates a "hidden" neuron without a target output

FIGURE 6.7 **A Recurrent Neural Network Architecture.**

perceptron with backpropagation), associative memory, recurrent networks, Kohonen's self-organizing feature maps, and Hopfield networks. The generic architecture of a feedforward network architecture is shown in Figure 6.4, where the information flows unidirectionally from input layer to hidden layers to output layer. In contrast, Figure 6.7 shows a pictorial representation of a recurrent neural network architecture, where the connections between the layers are not unidirectional; rather, there are many connections in every direction between the layers and neurons, creating a complex connection structure. Many experts believe this better mimics the way biological neurons are structured in the human brain.

KOHONEN'S SELF-ORGANIZING FEATURE MAPS First introduced by the Finnish professor Teuvo Kohonen, **Kohonen's self-organizing feature maps** (Kohonen networks or SOM, in short) provide a way to represent multidimensional data in much lower dimensional spaces, usually one or two dimensions. One of the most interesting aspects of SOM is that they learn to classify data without supervision (i.e., there is no output vector). Remember, in supervised learning techniques, such as backpropagation, the training data consists of vector pairs—an input vector and a target vector. Because of its self-organizing capability, SOM are commonly used for clustering tasks where a group of cases are assigned an arbitrary number of naturals groups. Figure 6.8a illustrates a very small Kohonen network of 4 × 4 nodes connected to the input layer (with three inputs), representing a two-dimensional vector.

HOPFIELD NETWORKS The Hopfield network is another interesting neural network architecture, first introduced by John Hopfield (1982). Hopfield demonstrated in a series of research articles in the early 1980s how highly interconnected networks of nonlinear neurons can be extremely effective in solving complex computational problems. These networks were shown to provide novel and quick solutions to a family of problems stated in terms of a desired objective subject to a number of constraints (i.e., constraint optimization problems). One of the major advantages of Hopfield neural networks is the fact that their structure can be realized on an electronic circuit board, possibly on a VLSI (very large-scale integration) circuit, to be used as an online solver with a parallel-distributed

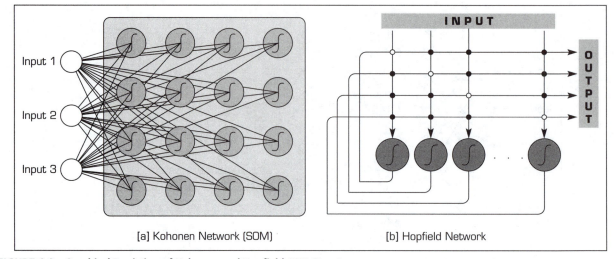

FIGURE 6.8 Graphical Depiction of Kohonen and Hopfield ANN Structures.

process. Architecturally, a general Hopfield network is represented as a single large layer of neurons with total interconnectivity; that is, each neuron is connected to every other neuron within the network (see Figure 6.8b).

Ultimately, the architecture of a neural network model is driven by the task it is intended to carry out. For instance, neural network models have been used as classifiers, as forecasting tools, as customer segmentation mechanisms, and as general optimizers. As shown later in this chapter, neural network classifiers are typically multilayer models in which information is passed from one layer to the next, with the ultimate goal of mapping an input to the network to a specific category, as identified by an output of the network. A neural model used as an optimizer, in contrast, can be a single layer of neurons, highly interconnected, and can compute neuron values iteratively until the model converges to a stable state. This stable state represents an optimal solution to the problem under analysis.

Application Case 6.2 summarizes the use of predictive modeling (e.g., neural networks) in addressing several changing problems in the electric power industry.

Application Case 6.2
Predictive Modeling Is Powering the Power Generators

The electrical power industry produces and delivers electric energy (electricity or power) to both residential and business customers, wherever and whenever they need it. Electricity can be generated from a multitude of sources. Most often, electricity is produced at a power station using electromechanical generators that are driven by heat engines fueled by chemical combustion (by burning coal, petroleum, or natural gas) or nuclear fusion (by a nuclear reactor). Generation of electricity can also be accomplished by other means, such as kinetic energy (through falling/flowing water or wind that activates turbines), solar energy (through the energy emitted by sun, either light or heat), or geothermal energy (through the steam or hot water coming from deep layers of the earth). Once generated, the electric energy is distributed through a power grid infrastructure.

Even though some energy-generation methods are favored over others, all forms of electricity generation have positive and negative aspects. Some are environmentally favored but are economically unjustifiable; others are economically superior but environmentally prohibitive. In a market economy, the options with fewer overall costs are generally chosen above all other sources. It is not clear yet which form can best meet the necessary demand for electricity without permanently damaging the environment. Current trends indicate that increasing the shares of renewable energy and distributed generation from mixed sources has the promise of reducing/balancing environmental and economic risks.

The electrical power industry is a highly regulated, complex business endeavor. There are four distinct roles that companies choose to participate in: power producers, transmitters, distributers, and retailers. Connecting all of the producers to all of the customers is accomplished through a complex structure, called the power grid. Although all aspects of the electricity industry are witnessing stiff competition, power generators are perhaps the ones getting the lion's share of it. To be competitive, producers of power need to maximize the use of their variety of resources by making the right decisions at the right rime.

StatSoft, one of the fastest growing providers of customized analytics solutions, developed integrated decision support tools for power generators. Leveraging the data that comes from the production process, these data mining–driven software tools help technicians and managers rapidly optimize the process parameters maximize the power output while minimizing the risk of adverse effects. Following are a few examples of what these advanced analytics tools, which include ANN and SVM, can accomplish for power generators.

- **Optimize Operation Parameters**
  Problem: A coal-burning 300 MW multicyclone unit required optimization for consistent high flame temperatures to avoid forming slag and burning excess fuel oil.
  Solution: Using StatSoft's predictive modeling tools (along with 12 months of 3-minute historical data), optimized control parameter settings for stoichiometric ratios, coal flows, primary air, tertiary air, and split secondary air damper flows were identified and implemented.
  Results: After optimizing the control parameters, flame temperatures showed strong responses, resulting in cleaner combustion for higher and more stable flame temperatures.

- **Predict Problems Before They Happen**
  Problem: A 400 MW coal-fired DRB-4Z burner required optimization for consistent and robust low NOx operations to avoid excursions

and expensive downtime. Identify root causes of ammonia slip in a selective noncatalytic reduction process for NOx reduction.
  Solution: Apply predictive analytics methodologies (along with historical process data) to predict and control variability; then target processes for better performance, thereby reducing both average NOx and variability.
  Results: Optimized settings for combinations of control parameters resulted in consistently lower NOx emissions with less variability (and no excursions) over continued operations at low load, including predicting failures or unexpected maintenance issues.

- **Reduce Emission (NOx, CO)**
  Problem: While NOx emissions for higher loads were within acceptable ranges, a 400 MW coal-fired DRB-4Z burner was not optimized for low-NOx operations under low load (50–175 MW).
  Solution: Using data-driven predictive modeling technologies with historical data, optimized parameter settings for changes to airflow were identified, resulting in a set of specific, achievable input parameter ranges that were easily implemented into the existing DCS (digital control system).
  Results: After optimization, NOx emissions under low-load operations were comparable to NOx emissions under higher loads.

As these specific examples illustrate, there are numerous opportunities for advanced analytics to make a significant contribution to the power industry. Using data and predictive models could help decision makers get the best efficiency from their production system while minimizing the impact on the environment.

QUESTIONS FOR DISCUSSION

1. What are the key environmental concerns in the electric power industry?
2. What are the main application areas for predictive modeling in the electric power industry?
3. How was predictive modeling used to address a variety of problems in the electric power industry?

Source: StatSoft, Success Stories, **power.statsoft.com/files/ statsoft-powersolutions.pdf** (accessed February 2013).

SECTION 6.2 REVIEW QUESTIONS

1. What is an ANN?

2. Explain the following terms: *neuron, axon,* and *synapse.*

3. How do weights function in an ANN?

4. What is the role of the summation and transformation function?

5. What are the most common ANN architectures? How do they differ from each other?

6.3   DEVELOPING NEURAL NETWORK–BASED SYSTEMS

Although the development process of ANN is similar to the structured design methodologies of traditional computer-based information systems, some phases are unique or have some unique aspects. In the process described here, we assume that the preliminary steps of system development, such as determining information requirements, conducting a feasibility analysis, and gaining a champion in top management for the project, have been completed successfully. Such steps are generic to any information system.

As shown in Figure 6.9, the development process for an ANN application includes nine steps. In step 1, the data to be used for training and testing the network are collected. Important considerations are that the particular problem is amenable to a neural network solution and that adequate data exist and can be obtained. In step 2, training data must be identified, and a plan must be made for testing the performance of the network.

In steps 3 and 4, a network architecture and a learning method are selected. The availability of a particular development tool or the capabilities of the development personnel may determine the type of neural network to be constructed. Also, certain problem types have demonstrated high success rates with certain configurations (e.g., multilayer feedforward neural networks for bankruptcy prediction [Altman (1968), Wilson and Sharda (1994), and Olson et al. (2012)]). Important considerations are the exact number of neurons and the number of layers. Some packages use genetic algorithms to select the network design.

There are several parameters for tuning the network to the desired learning-performance level. Part of the process in step 5 is the initialization of the network weights and parameters, followed by the modification of the parameters as training-performance feedback is received. Often, the initial values are important in determining the efficiency and length of training. Some methods change the parameters during training to enhance performance.

Step 6 transforms the application data into the type and format required by the neural network. This may require writing software to preprocess the data or performing these operations directly in an ANN package. Data storage and manipulation techniques and processes must be designed for conveniently and efficiently retraining the neural network, when needed. The application data representation and ordering often influence the efficiency and possibly the accuracy of the results.

In steps 7 and 8, training and testing are conducted iteratively by presenting input and desired or known output data to the network. The network computes the outputs and adjusts the weights until the computed outputs are within an acceptable tolerance of the known outputs for the input cases. The desired outputs and their relationships to input data are derived from historical data (i.e., a portion of the data collected in step 1).

In step 9, a stable set of weights is obtained. Now the network can reproduce the desired outputs, given inputs such as those in the training set. The network is ready for use as a stand-alone system or as part of another software system where new input data will be presented to it and its output will be a recommended decision.

In the following sections, we examine these steps in more detail.

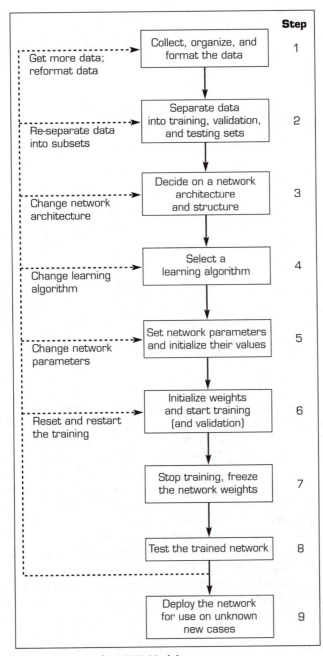

FIGURE 6.9 Development Process of an ANN Model.

The General ANN Learning Process

In **supervised learning,** the learning process is inductive; that is, connection weights are derived from existing cases. The usual process of learning involves three tasks (see Figure 6.10):

1. Compute temporary outputs.
2. Compare outputs with desired targets.
3. Adjust the weights and repeat the process.

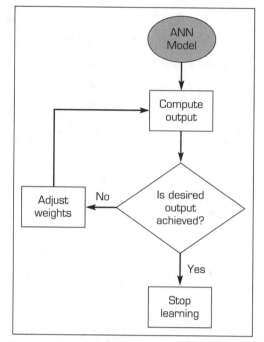

FIGURE 6.10   Supervised Learning Process of an ANN.

When existing outputs are available for comparison, the learning process starts by setting the connection weights. These are set via rules or at random. The difference between the actual output (Y or Y_T) and the desired output (Z) for a given set of inputs is an error called *delta* (in calculus, the Greek symbol delta, Δ, means "difference").

The objective is to minimize delta (i.e., reduce it to 0 if possible), which is done by adjusting the network's weights. The key is to change the weights in the right direction, making changes that reduce delta (i.e., error). We will show how this is done later.

Information processing with an ANN consists of attempting to recognize patterns of activities (i.e., pattern recognition). During the learning stages, the interconnection weights change in response to training data presented to the system.

Different ANN compute delta in different ways, depending on the learning algorithm being used. Hundreds of learning algorithms are available for various situations and configurations of ANN. Perhaps the one that is most commonly used and is easiest to understand is backpropagation.

Backpropagation

Backpropagation (short for *back-error propagation*) is the most widely used supervised learning algorithm in neural computing (Principe et al., 2000). It is very easy to implement. A backpropagation network includes one or more hidden layers. This type of network is considered feedforward because there are no interconnections between the output of a processing element and the input of a node in the same layer or in a preceding layer. Externally provided correct patterns are compared with the neural network's output during (supervised) training, and feedback is used to adjust the weights until the network has categorized all the training patterns as correctly as possible (the error tolerance is set in advance).

Starting with the output layer, errors between the actual and desired outputs are used to correct the weights for the connections to the previous layer (see Figure 6.11).

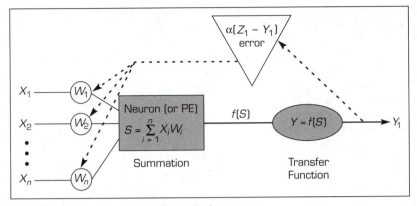

FIGURE 6.11 Backpropagation of Error for a Single Neuron.

For any output neuron j, the error (delta) = $(Z_j - Y_j)$ (df/dx), where Z and Y are the desired and actual outputs, respectively. Using the sigmoid function, $f = [1 + \exp(-x)]^{-1}$, where x is proportional to the sum of the weighted inputs to the neuron, is an effective way to compute the output of a neuron in practice. With this function, the derivative of the sigmoid function $df/dx = f(1 - f)$ and the error is a simple function of the desired and actual outputs. The factor $f(1 - f)$ is the logistic function, which serves to keep the error correction well bounded. The weights of each input to the jth neuron are then changed in proportion to this calculated error. A more complicated expression can be derived to work backward in a similar way from the output neurons through the hidden layers to calculate the corrections to the associated weights of the inner neurons. This complicated method is an iterative approach to solving a nonlinear optimization problem that is very similar in meaning to the one characterizing multiple-linear regression.

The learning algorithm includes the following procedures:

1. Initialize weights with random values and set other parameters.
2. Read in the input vector and the desired output.
3. Compute the actual output via the calculations, working forward through the layers.
4. Compute the error.
5. Change the weights by working backward from the output layer through the hidden layers.

This procedure is repeated for the entire set of input vectors until the desired output and the actual output agree within some predetermined tolerance. Given the calculation requirements for one iteration, a large network can take a very long time to train; therefore, in one variation, a set of cases is run forward and an aggregated error is fed backward to speed up learning. Sometimes, depending on the initial random weights and network parameters, the network does not converge to a satisfactory performance level. When this is the case, new random weights must be generated, and the network parameters, or even its structure, may have to be modified before another attempt is made. Current research is aimed at developing algorithms and using parallel computers to improve this process. For example, genetic algorithms can be used to guide the selection of the network parameters in order to maximize the desired output. In fact, most commercial ANN software tools are now using GA to help users "optimize" the network parameters. Technology Insights 6.2 discusses some of the most popular neural network software and offers some Web links to more comprehensive ANN-related software sites.

TECHNOLOGY INSIGHTS 6.2   ANN Software

Many tools are available for developing neural networks (see this book's Web site and the resource lists at PC AI, **pcai.com**). Some of these tools function like software shells. They provide a set of standard architectures, learning algorithms, and parameters, along with the ability to manipulate the data. Some development tools can support up to several dozen network paradigms and learning algorithms.

Neural network implementations are also available in most of the comprehensive data mining tools, such as the SAS Enterprise Miner, IBM SPSS Modeler (formerly Clementine), and Statistica Data Miner. Weka, RapidMiner, and KNIME are open source free data mining software tools that include neural network capabilities. These free tools can be downloaded from their respective Web sites; simple Internet searches on the names of these tools should lead you to the download pages. Also, most of the commercial software tools are available for download and use for evaluation purposes (usually, they are limited on time of availability and/or functionality).

Many specialized neural network tools enable the building and deployment of a neural network model in practice. Any listing of such tools would be incomplete. Online resources such as Wikipedia (**en.wikipedia.org/wiki/Artificial_neural_network**), Google's or Yahoo!'s software directory, and the vendor listings on **pcai.com** are good places to locate the latest information on neural network software vendors. Some of the vendors that have been around for a while and have reported industrial applications of their neural network software include California Scientific (BrainMaker), NeuralWare, NeuroDimension Inc., Ward Systems Group (Neuroshell), and Megaputer. Again, the list can never be complete.

Some ANN development tools are spreadsheet add-ins. Most can read spreadsheet, database, and text files. Some are freeware or shareware. Some ANN systems have been developed in Java to run directly on the Web and are accessible through a Web browser interface. Other ANN products are designed to interface with expert systems as hybrid development products.

Developers may instead prefer to use more general programming languages, such as C++, or a spreadsheet to program the model and perform the calculations. A variation on this is to use a library of ANN routines. For example, hav.Software (**hav.com**) provides a library of C++ classes for implementing stand-alone or embedded feedforward, simple recurrent, and random-order recurrent neural networks. Computational software such as MATLAB also includes neural network–specific libraries.

SECTION 6.3 REVIEW QUESTIONS

1. List the nine steps in conducting a neural network project.
2. What are some of the design parameters for developing a neural network?
3. How does backpropagation learning work?
4. Describe different types of neural network software available today.
5. How are neural networks implemented in practice when the training/testing is complete?

6.4 ILLUMINATING THE BLACK BOX OF ANN WITH SENSITIVITY ANALYSIS

Neural networks have been used as an effective tool for solving highly complex real-world problems in a wide range of application areas. Even though ANN have been proven in many problem scenarios to be superior predictors and/or cluster identifiers (compared to their traditional counterparts), in some applications there exists an additional need to know "how it does what it does." ANN are typically thought of as black boxes, capable of solving complex problems but lacking the explanation of their capabilities. This phenomenon is commonly referred to as the "black-box" syndrome.

It is important to be able to explain a model's "inner being"; such an explanation offers assurance that the network has been properly trained and will behave as desired once deployed in a business intelligence environment. Such a need to "look under the hood" might be attributable to a relatively small training set (as a result of the high cost of data acquisition) or a very high liability in case of a system error. One example of such an application is the deployment of airbags in automobiles. Here, both the cost of data acquisition (crashing cars) and the liability concerns (danger to human lives) are rather significant. Another representative example for the importance of explanation is loan-application processing. If an applicant is refused for a loan, he or she has the right to know why. Having a prediction system that does a good job on differentiating good and bad applications may not be sufficient if it does not also provide the justification of its predictions.

A variety of techniques has been proposed for analysis and evaluation of trained neural networks. These techniques provide a clear interpretation of how a neural network does what it does; that is, specifically how (and to what extent) the individual inputs factor into the generation of specific network output. Sensitivity analysis has been the front runner of the techniques proposed for shedding light into the "black-box" characterization of trained neural networks.

Sensitivity analysis is a method for extracting the cause-and-effect relationships among the inputs and the outputs of a trained neural network model. In the process of performing sensitivity analysis, the trained neural network's learning capability is disabled so that the network weights are not affected. The basic procedure behind sensitivity analysis is that the inputs to the network are systematically perturbed within the allowable value ranges and the corresponding change in the output is recorded for each and every input variable (Principe et al., 2000). Figure 6.12 shows a graphical illustration of this process. The first input is varied between its mean plus-and-minus a user-defined number of standard deviations (or for categorical variables, all of its possible values are used) while all other input variables are fixed at their respective means (or modes). The network output is computed for a user-defined number of steps above and below the mean. This process is repeated for each input. As a result, a report is generated to summarize the variation of each output with respect to the variation in each input. The generated report often contains a column plot (along with numeric values presented on the x-axis), reporting the relative sensitivity values for each input variable. A representative example of sensitivity analysis on ANN models is provided in Application Case 6.3.

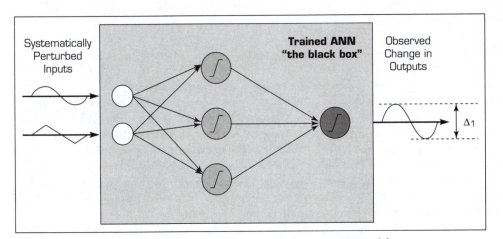

FIGURE 6.12   **A Figurative Illustration of Sensitivity Analysis on an ANN Model.**

Application Case 6.3

Sensitivity Analysis Reveals Injury Severity Factors in Traffic Accidents

According to the National Highway Traffic Safety Administration, over 6 million traffic accidents claim more than 41,000 lives each year in the United States. Causes of accidents and related injury severity are of special interest to traffic-safety researchers. Such research is aimed not only at reducing the number of accidents but also the severity of injury. One way to accomplish the latter is to identify the most profound factors that affect injury severity. Understanding the circumstances under which drivers and passengers are more likely to be severely injured (or killed) in an automobile accident can help improve the overall driving safety situation. Factors that potentially elevate the risk of injury severity of vehicle occupants in the event of an automotive accident include demographic and/or behavioral characteristics of the person (e.g., age, gender, seatbelt usage, use of drugs or alcohol while driving), environmental factors and/or roadway conditions at the time of the accident (e.g., surface conditions, weather or light conditions, the direction of impact, vehicle orientation in the crash, occurrence of a rollover), as well as technical characteristics of the vehicle itself (e.g., vehicle's age, body type).

In an exploratory data mining study, Delen et al. (2006) used a large sample of data—30,358 police-reported accident records obtained from the General Estimates System of the National Highway Traffic Safety Administration—to identify which factors become increasingly more important in escalating the probability of injury severity during a traffic crash. Accidents examined in this study included a geographically representative sample of multiple-vehicle collision accidents, single-vehicle fixed-object collisions, and single-vehicle noncollision (rollover) crashes.

Contrary to many of the previous studies conducted in this domain, which have primarily used regression-type generalized linear models where the functional relationships between injury severity and crash-related factors are assumed to be linear (which is an oversimplification of the reality in most real-world situations), Delen and his colleagues decided to go in a different direction. Because ANN are known to be superior in capturing highly nonlinear complex relationships between the predictor variables (crash factors) and the target variable (severity level of the injuries), they decided to use a series of ANN models to estimate the significance of the crash factors on the level of injury severity sustained by the driver.

From a methodological standpoint, they followed a two-step process. In the first step, they developed a series of prediction models (one for each injury severity level) to capture the in-depth relationships between the crash-related factors and a specific level of injury severity. In the second step, they conducted sensitivity analysis on the trained neural network models to identify the prioritized importance of crash-related factors as they relate to different injury severity levels. In the formulation of the study, the five-class prediction problem was decomposed into a number of binary classification models in order to obtain the granularity of information needed to identify the "true" cause-and-effect relationships between the crash-related factors and different levels of injury severity.

The results revealed considerable differences among the models built for different injury severity levels. This implies that the most influential factors in prediction models highly depend on the level of injury severity. For example, the study revealed that the variable seatbelt use was the most important determinant for predicting higher levels of injury severity (such as incapacitating injury or fatality), but it was one of the least significant predictors for lower levels of injury severity (such as non-incapacitating injury and minor injury). Another interesting finding involved gender: The drivers' gender was among the significant predictors for lower levels of injury severity, but it was not among the significant factors for higher levels of injury severity, indicating that more serious injuries do not depend on the driver being a male or a female. Yet another interesting and somewhat intuitive finding of the study indicated that age becomes an increasingly more significant factor as the level of injury severity increases, implying that older people are more likely to incur severe injuries (and fatalities) in serious automobile crashes than younger people.

QUESTIONS FOR DISCUSSION

1. How does sensitivity analysis shed light on the black box (i.e., neural networks)?

2. Why would someone choose to use a black-box tool like neural networks over theoretically sound, mostly transparent statistical tools like logistic regression?

3. In this case, how did neural networks and sensitivity analysis help identify injury-severity factors in traffic accidents?

Source: D. Delen, R. Sharda, and M. Bessonov, "Identifying Significant Predictors of Injury Severity in Traffic Accidents Using a Series of Artificial Neural Networks," *Accident Analysis and Prevention*, Vol. 38, No. 3, 2006, pp. 434–444.

REVIEW QUESTIONS FOR SECTION 6.4

1. What is the so-called "black-box" syndrome?

2. Why is it important to be able to explain an ANN's model structure?

3. How does sensitivity analysis work?

4. Search the Internet to find other ANN explanation methods.

6.5 SUPPORT VECTOR MACHINES

Support vector machines (SVMs) are one of the popular machine-learning techniques, mostly because of their superior predictive power and their theoretical foundation. SVMs are among the supervised learning methods that produce input-output functions from a set of labeled training data. The function between the input and output vectors can be either a classification function (used to assign cases into predefined classes) or a regression function (used to estimate the continuous numerical value of the desired output). For classification, nonlinear kernel functions are often used to transform the input data (naturally representing highly complex nonlinear relationships) to a high dimensional feature space in which the input data becomes linearly separable. Then, the maximum-margin hyperplanes are constructed to optimally separate the output classes from each other in the training data.

Given a classification-type prediction problem, generally speaking, many linear classifiers (hyperplanes) can separate the data into multiple subsections, each representing one of the classes (see Figure 6.13a, where the two classes are represented with circles ["●"] and squares ["■"]). However, only one hyperplane achieves the maximum separation between the classes (see Figure 6.13b, where the hyperplane and the two maximum margin hyperplanes are separating the two classes).

Data used in SVMs may have more than two dimensions (i.e., two distinct classes). In that case, we would be interested in separating data using the n-1 dimensional hyperplane, where n is the number of dimensions (i.e., class labels). This may be seen as a typical form of linear classifier, where we are interested in finding the n-1 hyperplane so that the distance from the hyperplanes to the nearest data points are maximized. The assumption is that the larger the margin or distance between these parallel hyperplanes, the better the generalization power of the classifier (i.e., prediction power of the SVM model). If such hyperplanes exist, they can be mathematically represented using quadratic optimization modeling. These hyperplanes are known as the maximum-margin hyperplane, and such a linear classifier is known as a maximum margin classifier.

In addition to their solid mathematical foundation in statistical learning theory, SVMs have also demonstrated highly competitive performance in numerous real-world prediction problems, such as medical diagnosis, bioinformatics, face/voice recognition, demand forecasting, image processing, and text mining, which has established SVMs as one of the

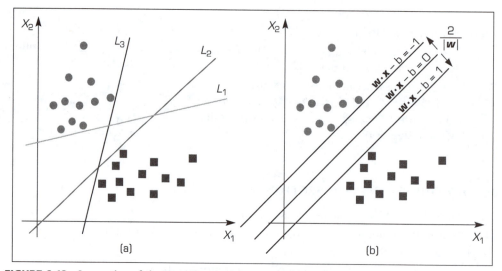

FIGURE 6.13 Separation of the Two Classes Using Hyperplanes.

most popular analytics tools for knowledge discovery and data mining. Similar to artificial neural networks, SVMs possess the well-known ability of being universal approximators of any multivariate function to any desired degree of accuracy. Therefore, they are of particular interest to modeling highly nonlinear, complex problems, systems, and processes. In the research study summarized in Application Case 6.4, SVM are used to successfully predict freshman student attrition.

Application Case 6.4

Managing Student Retention with Predictive Modeling

Generally, student attrition at a university is defined by the number of students who do not complete a degree in that institution. It has become one of the most challenging problems for decision makers in academic institutions. In spite of all of the programs and services to help retain students, according to the U.S. Department of Education, Center for Educational Statistics (**nces.ed.gov**), only about half of those who enter higher education actually graduate with a bachelor's degree. Enrollment management and the retention of students has become a top priority for administrators of colleges and universities in the United States and other developed countries around the world. High rates of student attrition usually result in loss of financial resources, lower graduation rates, and inferior perception of the school in the eyes of all stakeholders. The legislators and policymakers

who oversee higher education and allocate funds, the parents who pay for their children's education in order to prepare them for a better future, and the students who make college choices look for evidence of institutional quality (such as low attrition rate) and reputation to guide their college selection decisions.

The statistics show that the vast majority of students withdraw from the university during their first year (i.e., freshman year) at the college. Since most of the student dropouts occur at the end of the first year, many of the student retention/attrition research studies (including the one summarized here) have focused on first-year dropouts (or the number of students that do not return for the second year). Traditionally, student retention–related research has been survey driven (e.g., surveying a student cohort and following them for a specified period of time to determine whether they continue their education). Using such a research design, researchers worked on developing and validating theoretical models including the famous student integration model developed by Tinto. An alternative (or a complementary) approach to the traditional survey-based retention research is an analytic approach where the data commonly found in institutional databases is used. Educational institutions routinely collect a broad range of information about their students, including demographics, educational background, social involvement, socioeconomic status, and academic progress.

Research Method

In order to improve student retention, one should try to understand the non-trivial reasons behind the attrition. To be successful, one should also be able to accurately identify those students that are at risk of dropping out. This is where analytics come in handy. Using institutional data, prediction models can be developed to accurately identify the students at risk of dropout, so that limited resources (people, money, time, etc., at an institution's student success center) can be optimally used to retain most of them.

In this study, using 5 years of freshman student data (obtained from the university's existing databases) along with several data mining techniques, four types of prediction models are developed and tested to identify the best predictor of freshman attrition. In order to explain the phenomenon (identify the relative importance of variables), a sensitivity analysis of the developed models is also conducted. The main goals of this and other similar analytic studies are to (1) develop models to correctly identify the freshman students who are most likely to drop out after their freshman year, and (2) identify the most important variables by applying sensitivity analyses on developed models. The models that we developed are formulated in such a way that the prediction occurs at the end of the first semester (usually at the end of fall semester) in order for the decision makers to properly craft intervention programs during the next semester (the spring semester) in order to retain them.

Figure 6.14 shows the graphical illustration of the research mythology. First, data from multiple sources about the students are collected and consolidated (see Table 6.2 for the variables used in this study). Next, the data is preprocessed to handle missing values and other anomalies. The preprocessed data is then pushed through a 10-fold cross-validation experiment where for each model type, 10 different models are developed and tested for comparison purposes.

Results

The results (see Table 6.3) showed that, given sufficient data with the proper variables, data mining techniques are capable of predicting freshman student attrition with approximately 80 percent accuracy. Among the four individual prediction models used in this study, support vector machines performed the best, followed by decision trees, neural networks, and logistic regression.

The sensitivity analysis on the trained prediction models indicated that the most important predictors for student attrition are those related to past and present educational success (such as the ratio of completed credit hours into total number of hours enrolled) of the student and whether they are getting financial help.

QUESTIONS FOR DISCUSSION

1. Why is attrition one of the most important issues in higher education?
2. How can predictive analytics (ANN, SVM, and so forth) be used to better manage student retention?
3. What are the main challenges and potential solutions to the use of analytics in retention management?

Sources: Compiled from D. Delen, "A Comparative Analysis of Machine Learning Techniques for Student Retention Management," *Decision Support Systems,* Vol. 49, No. 4, 2010, pp. 498–506; V. Tinto, *Leaving College: Rethinking the Causes and Cures of Student Attrition,* University of Chicago Press, 1987; and D. Delen, "Predicting Student Attrition with Data Mining Methods," *Journal of College Student Retention,* Vol. 13, No. 1, 2011, pp. 17–35.

(Continued)

Application Case 6.4 (Continued)

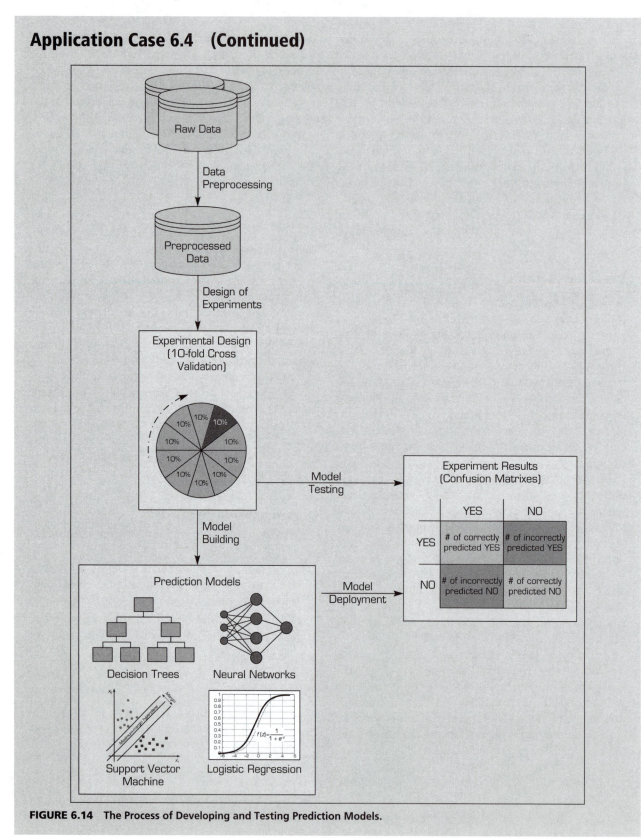

FIGURE 6.14 The Process of Developing and Testing Prediction Models.

TABLE 6.2   List of Variables Used in the Student Retention Project

No.	Variables	Data Type
1	College	Multi Nominal
2	Degree	Multi Nominal
3	Major	Multi Nominal
4	Concentration	Multi Nominal
5	Fall Hours Registered	Number
6	Fall Earned Hours	Number
7	Fall GPA	Number
8	Fall Cumulative GPA	Number
9	Spring Hours Registered	Number
10	Spring Earned Hours	Number
11	Spring GPA	Number
12	Spring Cumulative GPA	Number
13	Second Fall Registered (Y/N)	Nominal
14	Ethnicity	Nominal
15	Sex	Binary Nominal
16	Residential Code	Binary Nominal
17	Marital Status	Binary Nominal
18	SAT High Score Comprehensive	Number
19	SAT High Score English	Number
20	SAT High Score Reading	Number
21	SAT High Score Math	Number
22	SAT High Score Science	Number
23	Age	Number
24	High School GPA	Number
25	High School Graduation Year and Month	Date
26	Starting Term as New Freshmen	Multi Nominal
27	TOEFL Score	Number
28	Transfer Hours	Number
29	CLEP Earned Hours	Number
30	Admission Type	Multi Nominal
31	Permanent Address State	Multi Nominal
32	Received Fall Financial Aid	Binary Nominal
33	Received Spring Financial Aid	Binary Nominal
34	Fall Student Loan	Binary Nominal
35	Fall Grant/Tuition Waiver/Scholarship	Binary Nominal
36	Fall Federal Work Study	Binary Nominal
37	Spring Student Loan	Binary Nominal
38	Spring Grant/Tuition Waiver/Scholarship	Binary Nominal
39	Spring Federal Work Study	Binary Nominal

(Continued)

Application Case 6.4   (Continued)

TABLE 6.3   Prediction Results for the Four Data Mining Methods (A *10*-fold cross-validation with balanced data set is used to obtain these test results.)

		ANN(MLP)		DT(C5)		SVM		LR	
		No	Yes	No	Yes	No	Yes	No	Yes
Confusion Matrix	No	2309	464	2311	417	2313	386	2125	626
	Yes	781	2626	779	2673	777	2704	965	2464
	SUM	3090	3090	3090	3090	3090	3090	3090	3090
Per-class Accuracy		74.72%	84.98%	74.79%	86.50%	74.85%	87.51%	68.77%	79.74%
Overall Accuracy		79.85%		80.65%		81.18%		74.26%	

Mathematical Formulation of SVMs

Consider data points in the training data set of the form:

$$\{(x_1,c_1), (x_2,c_2), \ldots , (x_n,c_n)\}$$

where the c is the class label taking a value of either 1 (i.e., "yes") or 0 (i.e., "no") while $\boldsymbol{x}$ is the input variable vector. That is, each data point is an m-dimensional real vector, usually of scaled [0, 1] or [−1, 1] values. The normalization and/or scaling are important steps to guard against variables/attributes with larger variance that might otherwise dominate the classification formulae. We can view this as training data, which denotes the correct classification (something that we would like the SVM to eventually achieve) by means of a dividing hyperplane, which takes the mathematical form

$$w \cdot x - b = 0.$$

The vector w points perpendicular to the separating hyperplane. Adding the offset parameter b allows us to increase the margin. In its absence, the hyperplane is forced to pass through the origin, restricting the solution. As we are interested in the maximum margin, we are interested in the support vectors and the parallel hyperplanes (to the optimal hyperplane) closest to these support vectors in either class. It can be shown that these parallel hyperplanes can be described by equations

$$w \cdot x - b = 1,$$
$$w \cdot x - b = -1.$$

If the training data are linearly separable, we can select these hyperplanes so that there are no points between them and then try to maximize their distance (see Figure 6.13b). By using geometry, we find the distance between the hyperplanes is $2/|w|$, so we want to minimize $|w|$. To exclude data points, we need to ensure that for all i either

$$w \cdot x_i - b \geq 1 \qquad \text{or}$$
$$w \cdot x_i - b \leq -1.$$

This can be rewritten as:

$$c_i(\mathbf{w} \bullet x_i - b) \geq 1, \qquad 1 \leq i \leq n.$$

Primal Form

The problem now is to minimize $|w|$ subject to the constraint $c_i(\mathbf{w} \bullet x_i - b) \geq 1, \quad 1 \leq i \leq n$. This is a quadratic programming (QP) optimization problem. More clearly,

$$\text{Minimize} \qquad (1/2)\|w\|^2$$
$$\text{Subject to} \qquad c_i(\mathbf{w} \bullet x_i - b) \geq 1, \quad 1 \leq i \leq n.$$

The factor of 1/2 is used for mathematical convenience.

Dual Form

Writing the classification rule in its dual form reveals that classification is only a function of the support vectors, that is, the training data that lie on the margin. The dual of the SVM can be shown to be:

$$\max \sum_{i=1}^{n} \alpha_i - \sum_{i,j} \alpha_i \alpha_j c_i c_j x_i^T x_j$$

where the α terms constitute a dual representation for the weight vector in terms of the training set:

$$w = \sum_{i} \alpha_i c_i x_i$$

Soft Margin

In 1995, Cortes and Vapnik suggested a modified maximum margin idea that allows for mislabeled examples. If there exists no hyperplane that can split the "yes" and "no" examples, the soft margin method will choose a hyperplane that splits the examples as cleanly as possible, while still maximizing the distance to the nearest cleanly split examples. This work popularized the expression support vector machine or SVM. The method introduces slack variables, ξ_i, which measure the degree of misclassification of the datum.

$$c_i(\mathbf{w} \bullet x_i - b) \geq 1 - \xi_i \qquad 1 \leq i \leq n$$

The objective function is then increased by a function that penalizes non-zero ξ_i, and the optimization becomes a trade-off between a large margin and a small error penalty. If the penalty function is linear, the equation now transforms to

$$min \, \|w\|^2 + C\sum_{i} \xi_i \quad \text{such that } c_i(\mathbf{w} \bullet x_i - b) \geq 1 - \xi_i \, 1 \leq i \leq n$$

This constraint along with the objective of minimizing $|w|$ can be solved using Lagrange multipliers. The key advantage of a linear penalty function is that the slack variables vanish from the dual problem, with the constant C appearing only as an vadditional constraint on the Lagrange multipliers. Nonlinear penalty functions have been used, particularly to reduce the effect of outliers on the classifier, but unless care is taken, the problem becomes non-convex, and thus it is considerably more difficult to find a global solution.

Nonlinear Classification

The original optimal hyperplane algorithm proposed by Vladimir Vapnik in 1963, while he was a doctoral student at the Institute of Control Science in Moscow, was a linear classifier. However, in 1992, Boser, Guyon, and Vapnik suggested a way to create nonlinear classifiers by applying the kernel trick (originally proposed by Aizerman et al., 1964) to maximum-margin hyperplanes. The resulting algorithm is formally similar, except that every dot product is replaced by a nonlinear kernel function. This allows the algorithm to fit the maximum-margin hyperplane in the transformed feature space. The transformation may be nonlinear and the transformed space high dimensional; thus, though the classifier is a hyperplane in the high-dimensional feature space it may be nonlinear in the original input space.

If the kernel used is a Gaussian radial basis function, the corresponding feature space is a Hilbert space of infinite dimension. Maximum margin classifiers are well regularized, so the infinite dimension does not spoil the results. Some common kernels include,

Polynomial (homogeneous): $k(x, x') = (x \cdot x')$

Polynomial (inhomogeneous): $k(x, x') = (x \cdot x' + 1)$

Radial basis function: $k(x, x') = \exp(-\gamma \|x - x'\|^2)$, for $\gamma > 0$

Gaussian radial basis function: $k(x, x') = \exp\left(-\dfrac{\|x - x'\|^2}{2\sigma^2}\right)$

Sigmoid: $k(x, x') = \tan h(kx \cdot x' + c)$ for some $k > 0$ and $c < 0$

Kernel Trick

In machine learning, the kernel trick is a method for converting a linear classifier algorithm into a nonlinear one by using a nonlinear function to map the original observations into a higher-dimensional space; this makes a linear classification in the new space equivalent to nonlinear classification in the original space.

This is done using Mercer's theorem, which states that any continuous, symmetric, positive semi-definite kernel function $K(x, y)$ can be expressed as a dot product in a high-dimensional space. More specifically, if the arguments to the kernel are in a measurable space X, and if the kernel is positive semi-definite — i.e.,

$$\sum_{i,j} K(x_i, x_j) c_i c_j \geq 0$$

for any finite subset $\{x_1, \ldots, x_n\}$ of X and subset $\{c_1, \ldots, c_n\}$ of objects (typically real numbers or even molecules)—then there exists a function $\varphi(x)$ whose range is in an inner product space of possibly high dimension, such that

$$K(x, y) = \varphi(x) \cdot \varphi(y)$$

The kernel trick transforms any algorithm that solely depends on the dot product between two vectors. Wherever a dot product is used, it is replaced with the kernel function. Thus, a linear algorithm can easily be transformed into a nonlinear algorithm. This nonlinear algorithm is equivalent to the linear algorithm operating in the range space of φ. However, because kernels are used, the φ function is never explicitly computed. This is desirable, because the high-dimensional space may be infinite-dimensional (as is the case when the kernel is a Gaussian).

Although the origin of the term *kernel trick* is not known, the kernel trick was first published by Aizerman et al. (1964). It has been applied to several kinds of algorithm in machine learning and statistics, including:

- Perceptrons
- Support vector machines
- Principal components analysis
- Fisher's linear discriminant analysis
- Clustering

SECTION 6.5 REVIEW QUESTIONS

1. How do SVM work?
2. What are the advantages and disadvantages of SVM?
3. What is the meaning of "maximum margin hyperplanes"? Why are they important in SVM?
4. What is "kernel trick"? How is it used in SVM?

6.6 A PROCESS-BASED APPROACH TO THE USE OF SVM

Due largely to the better classification results, recently support vector machines (SVMs) have become a popular technique for classification-type problems. Even though people consider them as being easier to use than artificial neural networks, users who are not familiar with the intricacies of SVMs often get unsatisfactory results. In this section we provide a process-based approach to the use of SVM, which is more likely to produce better results. A pictorial representation of the three-step process is given in Figure 6.15.

NUMERICIZING THE DATA SVMs require that each data instance is represented as a vector of real numbers. Hence, if there are categorical attributes, we first have to convert them into numeric data. A common recommendation is to use m pseudo-binary-variables to represent an m-class attribute (where $m \geq 3$). In practice, only one of the m variables assumes the value of "1" and others assume the value of "0" based on the actual class of the case (this is also called 1-of-m representation). For example, a three-category attribute such as {red, green, blue} can be represented as (0,0,1), (0,1,0), and (1,0,0).

NORMALIZING THE DATA As was the case for artificial neural networks, SVMs also require normalization and/or scaling of numerical values. The main advantage of normalization is to avoid attributes in greater numeric ranges dominating those of in smaller numeric ranges. Another advantage is that it helps performing numerical calculations during the iterative process of model building. Because kernel values usually depend on the inner products of feature vectors (e.g., the linear kernel and the polynomial kernel), large attribute values might slow the training process. Use recommendations to normalize each attribute to the range [−1, +1] or [0, 1]. Of course, we have to use the same normalization method to scale testing data before testing.

SELECT THE KERNEL TYPE AND KERNEL PARAMETERS Even though there are only four common kernels mentioned in the previous section, one must decide which one to use (or whether to try them all, one at a time, using a simple experimental design approach). Once the kernel type is selected, then one needs to select the value of penalty parameter C and kernel parameters. Generally speaking, RBF is a reasonable first choice for the kernel type. The RBF kernel aims to nonlinearly map data into a higher dimensional space; by doing so (unlike with a linear kernel) it handles the cases where the relation between

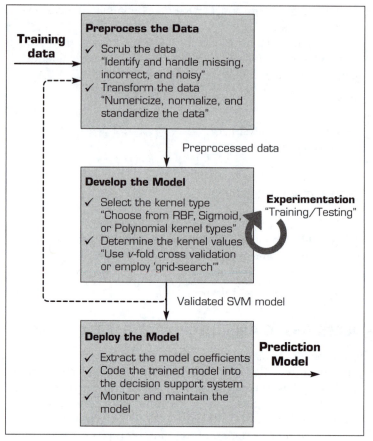

FIGURE 6.15 A Simple Process Description for Developing SVM Models.

input and output vectors is highly nonlinear. Besides, one should note that the linear kernel is just a special case of RBF kernel. There are two parameters to choose for RBF kernels: C and γ. It is not known beforehand which C and γ are the best for a given prediction problem; therefore, some kind of parameter search method needs to be used. The goal for the search is to identify optimal values for C and γ so that the classifier can accurately predict unknown data (i.e., testing data). The two most commonly used search methods are cross-validation and grid search.

DEPLOY THE MODEL Once an "optimal" SVM prediction model has been developed, the next step is to integrate it into the decision support system. For that, there are two options: (1) converting the model into a computational object (e.g., a Web service, Java Bean, or COM object) that takes the input parameter values and provides output prediction, (2) extracting the model coefficients and integrating them directly into the decision support system. The SVM models are useful (i.e., accurate, actionable) only if the behavior of the underlying domain stays the same. For some reason, if it changes, so does the accuracy of the model. Therefore, one should continuously assess the performance of the models, decide when they no longer are accurate, and, hence, need to be retrained.

Support Vector Machines Versus Artificial Neural Networks

Even though some people characterize SVMs as a special case of ANNs, most recognize them as two competing machine-learning techniques with different qualities. Here are a few points that help SVMs stand out against ANNs. Historically, the development of ANNs followed a heuristic path, with applications and extensive experimentation preceding theory. In contrast, the development of SVMs involved sound statistical learning theory first, then implementation and experiments. A significant advantage of SVMs is that while ANNs may suffer from multiple local minima, the solutions to SVMs are global and unique. Two more advantages of SVMs are that they have a simple geometric interpretation and give a sparse solution. The reason that SVMs often outperform ANNs in practice is that they successfully deal with the "over fitting" problem, which is a big issue with ANNs.

Besides these advantages of SVMs (from a practical point of view), they also have some limitations. An important issue that is not entirely solved is the selection of the kernel type and kernel function parameters. A second and perhaps more important limitation of SVMs are the speed and size, both in the training and testing cycles. Model building in SVMs involves complex and time-demanding calculations. From the practical point of view, perhaps the most serious problem with SVMs is the high algorithmic complexity and extensive memory requirements of the required quadratic programming in large-scale tasks. Despite these limitations, because SVMs are based on a sound theoretical foundation and the solutions they produce are global and unique in nature (as opposed to getting stuck in a suboptimal alternative such as a local minima), nowadays they are arguably one of the most popular prediction modeling techniques in the data mining arena. Their use and popularity will only increase as the popular commercial data mining tools start to incorporate them into their modeling arsenal.

SECTION 6.6 REVIEW QUESTIONS

1. What are the main steps and decision points in developing a SVM model?
2. How do you determine the optimal kernel type and kernel parameters?
3. Compared to ANN, what are the advantages of SVM?
4. What are the common application areas for SVM? Conduct a search on the Internet to identify popular application areas and specific SVM software tools used in those applications.

6.7 NEAREST NEIGHBOR METHOD FOR PREDICTION

Data mining algorithms tend to be highly mathematical and computationally intensive. The two popular ones that are covered in the previous section (i.e., ANNs and SVMs) involve time-demanding, computationally intensive iterative mathematical derivations. In contrast, the **k-nearest neighbor** algorithm (or kNN, in short) seems overly simplistic for a competitive prediction method. It is so easy to understand (and explain to others) what it does and how it does it. k-NN is a prediction method for classification- as well as regression-type prediction problems. k-NN is a type of instance-based learning (or lazy learning) where the function is only approximated locally and all computations are deferred until the actual prediction.

The k-nearest neighbor algorithm is among the simplest of all machine-learning algorithms: For instance, in the classification-type prediction, a case is classified by a majority vote of its neighbors, with the object being assigned to the class most common among its k nearest neighbors (where k is a positive integer). If $k = 1$, then the case is simply assigned to the class of its nearest neighbor. To illustrate the concept with an example, let us look at Figure 6.16, where a simple two-dimensional space represents the values for the two variables (x, y); the star represents a new case (or object); and circles and squares represent known cases (or examples). The task is to assign the new case to either circles or squares based on its closeness (similarity) to one or the other. If you set the value of k to 1 $(k = 1)$, the assignment should be made to square, because the closest example to star is a square. If you set the value of k to 3 $(k = 3)$, then the assignment should be made to

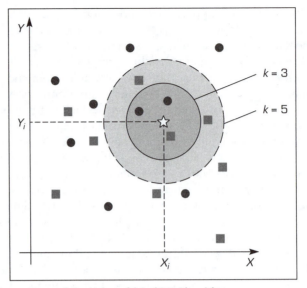

FIGURE 6.16 **The Importance of the Value of *k* in *k*NN Algorithm.**

circle, because there two circles and one square, and hence from the simple majority vote rule, circle gets the assignment of the new case. Similarly, if you set the value of *k* to 5 (*k* = 5), then the assignment should be made to square-class. This overly simplified example is meant to illustrate the importance of the value that one assigns to *k*.

The same method can also be used for regression-type prediction tasks, by simply averaging the values of its *k* nearest neighbors and assigning this result to the case being predicted. It can be useful to weight the contributions of the neighbors, so that the nearer neighbors contribute more to the average than the more distant ones. A common weighting scheme is to give each neighbor a weight of $1/d$, where *d* is the distance to the neighbor. This scheme is essentially a generalization of linear interpolation.

The neighbors are taken from a set of cases for which the correct classification (or, in the case of regression, the numerical value of the output value) is known. This can be thought of as the training set for the algorithm, even though no explicit training step is required. The *k*-nearest neighbor algorithm is sensitive to the local structure of the data.

Similarity Measure: The Distance Metric

One of the two critical decisions that an analyst has to make while using *k*NN is to determine the similarity measure (the other is to determine the value of *k*, which is explained next). In the *k*NN algorithm, the similarity measure is a mathematically calculable distance metric. Given a new case, *k*NN makes predictions based on the outcome of the *k* neighbors closest in distance to that point. Therefore, to make predictions with *k*NN, we need to define a metric for measuring the distance between the new case and the cases from the examples. One of the most popular choices to measure this distance is known as Euclidean (Equation 3), which is simply the linear distance between two points in a dimensional space; the other popular one is the rectilinear (a.k.a. City-block or Manhattan distance) (Equation 2). Both of these distance measures are special cases of Minkowski distance (Equation 1).

Minkowski distance

$$d(i, j) = \sqrt[q]{(|x_{i1} - x_{j1}|^q + |x_{i2} - x_{j2}|^q + \ldots + |x_{ip} - x_{jp}|^q)}$$

where $i = (x_{i1}, x_{i2}, ..., x_{ip})$ and $j = (x_{j1}, x_{j2}, ..., x_{jp})$ are two p-dimensional data objects (e.g., a new case and an example in the data set), and q is a positive integer.

If $q = 1$, then d is called Manhattan distance

$$d(i, j) = \sqrt{|x_{i1} - x_{j1}| + |x_{i2} - x_{j2}| + ... + |x_{ip} - x_{jp}|}$$

If $q = 2$, then d is called Euclidean distance

$$d(i, j) = \sqrt{(|x_{i1} - x_{j1}|^2 + |x_{i2} - x_{j2}|^2 + ... + |x_{ip} - x_{jp}|^2)}$$

Obviously, these measures apply only to numerically represented data. How about nominal data? There are ways to measure distance for non-numerical data as well. In the simplest case, for a multi-value nominal variable, if the value of that variable for the new case and that for the example case are the same, the distance would be zero, otherwise one. In cases such as text classification, more sophisticated metrics exist, such as the overlap metric (or Hamming distance). Often, the classification accuracy of kNN can be improved significantly if the distance metric is determined through an experimental design where different metrics are tried and tested to identify the best one for the given problem.

Parameter Selection

The best choice of k depends upon the data; generally, larger values of k reduce the effect of noise on the classification (or regression) but also make boundaries between classes less distinct. An "optimal" value of k can be found by some heuristic techniques, for instance, cross-validation. The special case where the class is predicted to be the class of the closest training sample (i.e., when $k = 1$) is called the nearest neighbor algorithm.

CROSS-VALIDATION Cross-validation is a well-established experimentation technique that can be used to determine *optimal* values for a set of unknown model parameters. It applies to most, if not all, of the machine-learning techniques, where there are a number of model parameters to be determined. The general idea of this experimentation method is to divide the data sample into a number of randomly drawn, disjointed sub-samples (i.e., v number of folds). For each potential value of k, the kNN model is used to make predictions on the vth fold while using the v-1 folds as the examples, and evaluate the error. The common choice for this error is the root-mean-squared-error (RMSE) for regression-type predictions and percentage of correctly classified instances (i.e., hit rate) for the classification-type predictions. This process of testing each fold against the remaining of examples repeats v times. At the end of the v number of cycles, the computed errors are accumulated to yield a goodness measure of the model (i.e., how well the model predicts with the current value of the k). At the end, the k value that produces the smallest overall error is chosen as the optimal value for that problem. Figure 6.17 shows a simple process where the training data is used to determine *optimal* values for k and *distance metric*, which are then used to predict new incoming cases.

As we observed in the simple example given earlier, the accuracy of the kNN algorithm can be significantly different with different values of k. Furthermore, the predictive power of the kNN algorithm degrades with the presence of noisy, inaccurate, or irrelevant features. Much research effort has been put into feature selection and normalization/scaling to ensure reliable prediction results. A particularly popular approach is the use of evolutionary algorithms (e.g., genetic algorithms) to optimize the set of features included in the kNN prediction system. In binary (two class) classification problems, it is helpful to choose k to be an odd number as this would avoid tied votes.

A drawback to the basic majority voting classification in kNN is that the classes with the more frequent examples tend to dominate the prediction of the new vector, as they

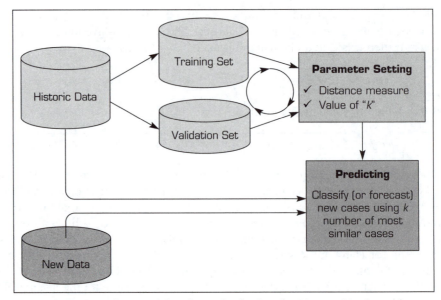

FIGURE 6.17 The Process of Determining the Optimal Values for Distance Metric and *k*.

tend to come up in the *k* nearest neighbors when the neighbors are computed due to their large number. One way to overcome this problem is to weigh the classification taking into account the distance from the test point to each of its *k* nearest neighbors. Another way to overcome this drawback is by one level of abstraction in data representation.

The naive version of the algorithm is easy to implement by computing the distances from the test sample to all stored vectors, but it is computationally intensive, especially when the size of the training set grows. Many nearest neighbor search algorithms have been proposed over the years; these generally seek to reduce the number of distance evaluations actually performed. Using an appropriate nearest neighbor search algorithm makes *k*NN computationally tractable even for large data sets. Application Case 6.5 talks about the superior capabilities of *k*NN in image recognition and categorization.

Application Case 6.5

Efficient Image Recognition and Categorization with *k*NN

Image recognition is an emerging data mining application field involved in processing, analyzing, and categorizing visual objects such as pictures. In the process of recognition (or categorization), images are first transformed into a multidimensional feature space and then, using machine-learning techniques, are categorized into a finite number of classes. Application areas of image recognition and categorization range from agriculture to homeland security, personalized marketing to environmental protection. Image recognition is an integral part of an artificial intelligence field called *computer vision*.

As a technological discipline, computer vision seeks to develop computer systems that are capable of "seeing" and reacting to their environment. Examples of applications of computer vision include systems for process automation (industrial robots), navigation (autonomous vehicles), monitoring/detecting (visual surveillance), searching and sorting visuals (indexing databases of images and image sequences), engaging (computer–human interaction), and inspection (manufacturing processes).

While the field of visual recognition and category recognition has been progressing rapidly, much remains to be done to reach human-level performance. Current approaches are capable of dealing with only a limited number of categories (100 or so categories) and are computationally expensive. Many machine-learning techniques (including ANN, SVM, and *k*NN) are used to develop computer systems for visual recognition and categorization. Though commendable results have been obtained, generally speaking, none of these tools in their current form is capable of developing systems that can compete with humans.

In a research project, several researchers from the Computer Science Division of the Electrical Engineering and Computer Science Department at the University of California, Berkeley, used an innovative ensemble approach to image categorization (Zhang et al., 2006). They considered visual category recognition in the framework of measuring similarities, or perceptual distances, to develop examples of categories. Their recognition and categorization approach was quite flexible, permitting recognition based on color, texture, and particularly shape. While nearest neighbor classifiers (i.e., *k*NN) are natural in this setting, they suffered from the problem of high variance (in bias-variance decomposition) in the case of limited sampling. Alternatively, one could choose to use support vector machines but they also involve time-consuming optimization and computations. They proposed a hybrid of these two methods, which deals naturally with the multiclass setting, has reasonable computational complexity both in training and at run time, and yields excellent results in practice. The basic idea was to find close neighbors to a query sample and train a local support vector machine that preserves the distance function on the collection of neighbors.

Their method can be applied to large, multiclass data sets where it outperforms nearest neighbor and support vector machines and remains efficient when the problem becomes intractable. A wide variety of distance functions were used, and their experiments showed state-of-the-art performance on a number of benchmark data sets for shape and texture classification (MNIST, USPS, CUReT) and object recognition (Caltech-101).

Another group of researchers (Boiman et al., 2008) argued that two practices commonly used in image classification methods (namely SVM- and ANN-type model-driven approaches and *k*NN type non-parametric approaches) have led to less-than-desired performance outcomes. They also claim that a hybrid method can improve the performance of image recognition and categorization. They propose a trivial Naïve Bayes *k*NN-based classifier, which employs *k*NN distances in the space of the local image descriptors (and not in the space of images). They claim that, although the modified *k*NN method is extremely simple, efficient, and requires no learning/training phase, its performance ranks among the top leading learning-based parametric image classifiers. Empirical comparisons of their method were shown on several challenging image categorization databases (Caltech-101, Caltech-256, and Graz-01).

In addition to image recognition and categorization, *k*NN is successfully applied to complex classification problems, such as content retrieval (handwriting detection, video content analysis, body and sign language, where communication is done using body or hand gestures), gene expression (this is another area where *k*NN tends to perform better than other state-of-the-art techniques; in fact, a combination of *k*NN-SVM is one of the most popular techniques used here), and protein-to-protein interaction and 3D structure prediction (graph-based *k*NN is often used for interaction structure prediction).

QUESTIONS FOR DISCUSSION

1. Why is image recognition/classification a worthy but difficult problem?
2. How can *k*NN be effectively used for image recognition/classification applications?

Sources: H. Zhang, A. C. Berg, M. Maire, and J. Malik, "SVM-KNN: Discriminative Nearest Neighbor Classification for Visual Category Recognition," *Proceedings of the 2006 IEEE Computer Society Conference on Computer Vision and Pattern Recognition (CVPR'06)*, Vol. 2, 2006, pp. 2126–2136; O. Boiman, E. Shechtman, and M. Irani, "In Defense of Nearest-Neighbor Based Image Classification," *IEEE Conference on Computer Vision and Pattern Recognition, 2008 (CVPR)*, 2008, pp.1–8.

SECTION 6.7 REVIEW QUESTIONS

1. What is special about the *k*NN algorithm?
2. What are the advantages and disadvantages of *k*NN as compared to ANN and SVM?

3. What are the critical success factors for a kNN implementation?

4. What is a similarity (or distance measure)? How can it be applied to both numerical and nominal valued variables?

5. What are the common applications of kNN?

Chapter Highlights

- Neural computing involves a set of methods that emulate the way the human brain works. The basic processing unit is a neuron. Multiple neurons are grouped into layers and linked together.
- In a neural network, the knowledge is stored in the weight associated with each connection between two neurons.
- Backpropagation is the most popular paradigm in business applications of neural networks. Most business applications are handled using this algorithm.
- A backpropagation-based neural network consists of an input layer, an output layer, and a certain number of hidden layers (usually one). The nodes in one layer are fully connected to the nodes in the next layer. Learning is done through a trial-and-error process of adjusting the connection weights.
- Each node at the input layer typically represents a single attribute that may affect the prediction.
- Neural network learning can occur in supervised or unsupervised mode.
- In supervised learning mode, the training patterns include a correct answer/classification/forecast.
- In unsupervised learning mode, there are no known answers. Thus, unsupervised learning is used for clustering or exploratory data analysis.
- The usual process of learning in a neural network involves three steps: (1) compute temporary outputs based on inputs and random weights, (2) compute outputs with desired targets, and (3) adjust the weights and repeat the process.

- The delta rule is commonly used to adjust the weights. It includes a learning rate and a momentum parameter.
- Developing neural network–based systems requires a step-by-step process. It includes data preparation and preprocessing, training and testing, and conversion of the trained model into a production system.
- Neural network software is available to allow easy experimentation with many models. Neural network modules are included in all major data mining software tools. Specific neural network packages are also available. Some neural network tools are available as spreadsheet add-ins.
- After a trained network has been created, it is usually implemented in end-user systems through programming languages such as C++, Java, and Visual Basic. Most neural network tools can generate code for the trained network in these languages.
- Many neural network models beyond backpropagation exist, including radial basis functions, support vector machines, Hopfield networks, and Kohonen's self-organizing maps.
- Neural network applications abound in almost all business disciplines as well as in virtually all other functional areas.
- Business applications of neural networks include finance, bankruptcy prediction, time-series forecasting, and so on.
- New applications of neural networks are emerging in healthcare, security, and so on.

Key Terms

artificial neural network (ANN)	k-nearest neighbor	parallel processing	supervised learning
axon	Kohonen's self-organizing feature map	pattern recognition	synapse
backpropagation	neural computing	perceptron	threshold value
connection weight	neural network	processing element (PE)	transformation (transfer) function
dendrite	neuron	sigmoid (logical activation) function	
hidden layer	nucleus	summation function	

Questions for Discussion

1. Compare artificial and biological neural networks. What aspects of biological networks are not mimicked by artificial ones? What aspects are similar?
2. The performance of ANN relies heavily on the summation and transformation functions. Explain the combined effects of the summation and transformation functions and how they differ from statistical regression analysis.
3. ANN can be used for both supervised and unsupervised learning. Explain how they learn in a supervised mode and in an unsupervised mode.
4. Explain the difference between a training set and a testing set. Why do we need to differentiate them? Can the same set be used for both purposes? Why or why not?
5. Say that a neural network has been constructed to predict the creditworthiness of applicants. There are two output nodes: one for yes (1 = yes, 0 = no) and one for no (1 = no, 0 = yes). An applicant receives a score of 0.83 for the "yes" output node and a 0.44 for the "no" output node. Discuss what may have happened and whether the applicant is a good credit risk.
6. Everyone would like to make a great deal of money on the stock market. Only a few are very successful. Why is using an ANN a promising approach? What can it do that other decision support technologies cannot do? How could it fail?

Exercises

Teradata University Network (TUN) and Other Hands-On Exercises

1. Go to the Teradata University Network Web site (**teradatauniversitynetwork.com**) or the URL given by your instructor. Locate Web seminars related to data mining and neural networks. Specifically, view the seminar given by Professor Hugh Watson at the SPIRIT2005 conference at Oklahoma State University; then, answer the following questions:
   a. Which real-time application at Continental Airlines may have used a neural network?
   b. What inputs and outputs can be used in building a neural network application?
   c. Given that Continental's data mining applications are in real time, how might Continental implement a neural network in practice?
   d. What other neural network applications would you propose for the airline industry?
2. Go to the Teradata University Network Web site (**teradatauniversitynetwork.com**) or the URL given by your instructor. Locate the Harrah's case. Read the case and answer the following questions:
   a. Which of the Harrah's data applications are most likely implemented using neural networks?
   b. What other applications could Harrah's develop using the data it is collecting from its customers?
   c. What are some concerns you might have as a customer at this casino?
3. The bankruptcy-prediction problem can be viewed as a problem of classification. The data set you will be using for this problem includes five ratios that have been computed from the financial statements of real-world firms. These five ratios have been used in studies involving bankruptcy prediction. The first sample includes data on firms that went bankrupt and firms that didn't. This will be your training sample for the neural network. The second sample of 10 firms also consists of some bankrupt firms and some nonbankrupt firms. Your goal is to use neural networks, support vector machines, and nearest neighbor algorithms to build a model, using the first 20 data points, and then test its performance on the other 10 data points. (Try to analyze the new cases yourself manually before you run the neural network and see how well you do.) The following tables show the training sample and test data you should use for this exercise.

Training Sample						
Firm	WC/TA	RE/TA	EBIT/TA	MVE/TD	S/TA	BR/NB
1	0.1650	0.1192	0.2035	0.8130	1.6702	1
2	0.1415	0.3868	0.0681	0.5755	1.0579	1
3	0.5804	0.3331	0.0810	1.1964	1.3572	1
4	0.2304	0.2960	0.1225	0.4102	3.0809	1
5	0.3684	0.3913	0.0524	0.1658	1.1533	1
6	0.1527	0.3344	0.0783	0.7736	1.5046	1
7	0.1126	0.3071	0.0839	1.3429	1.5736	1
8	0.0141	0.2366	0.0905	0.5863	1.4651	1
9	0.2220	0.1797	0.1526	0.3459	1.7237	1
10	0.2776	0.2567	0.1642	0.2968	1.8904	1
11	0.2689	0.1729	0.0287	0.1224	0.9277	0
12	0.2039	−0.0476	0.1263	0.8965	1.0457	0
13	0.5056	−0.1951	0.2026	0.5380	1.9514	0
14	0.1759	0.1343	0.0946	0.1955	1.9218	0
15	0.3579	0.1515	0.0812	0.1991	1.4582	0
16	0.2845	0.2038	0.0171	0.3357	1.3258	0
17	0.1209	0.2823	−0.0113	0.3157	2.3219	0
18	0.1254	0.1956	0.0079	0.2073	1.4890	0
19	0.1777	0.0891	0.0695	0.1924	1.6871	0
20	0.2409	0.1660	0.0746	0.2516	1.8524	0

Test Data

Firm	WC/TA	RE/TA	EBIT/TA	MVE/TD	S/TA	BR/NB
A	0.1759	0.1343	0.0946	0.1955	1.9218	?
B	0.3732	0.3483	−0.0013	0.3483	1.8223	?
C	0.1725	0.3238	0.1040	0.8847	0.5576	?
D	0.1630	0.3555	0.0110	0.3730	2.8307	?
E	0.1904	0.2011	0.1329	0.5580	1.6623	?
F	0.1123	0.2288	0.0100	0.1884	2.7186	?
G	0.0732	0.3526	0.0587	0.2349	1.7432	?
H	0.2653	0.2683	0.0235	0.5118	1.8350	?
I	0.1070	0.0787	0.0433	0.1083	1.2051	?
J	0.2921	0.2390	0.0673	0.3402	0.9277	?

Describe the results of the neural network, support vector machines, and nearest neighbor model predictions, including software, architecture, and training information.

4. The purpose of this exercise is to develop models to predict forest cover type using a number of cartographic measures. The given data set (Online File W6.1) includes four wilderness areas found in the Roosevelt National Forest of northern Colorado. A total of 12 cartographic measures were utilized as independent variables; seven major forest cover types were used as dependent variables. The following table provides a short description of these independent and dependent variables:

This is an excellent example for a multiclass classification problem. The data set is rather large (with 581,012 unique instances) and feature rich. As you will see, the data is also raw and skewed (unbalanced for different cover types). As a model builder, you are to make necessary decisions to preprocess the data and build the best possible predictor. Use your favorite tool to build the models for neural networks, support vector machines, and nearest neighbor algorithms, and document the details of your results and experiences in a written report. Use screenshots within your report to illustrate important and interesting findings. You are expected to discuss and justify any decision that you make along the way.

The reuse of this data set is unlimited with retention of copyright notice for Jock A. Blackard and Colorado State University.

Team Assignments and Role-Playing Projects

1. Consider the following set of data that relates daily electricity usage as a function of outside high temperature (for the day):

Temperature, X	Kilowatts, Y
46.8	12,530
52.1	10,800
55.1	10,180
59.2	9,730
61.9	9,750
66.2	10,230
69.9	11,160
76.8	13,910
79.7	15,110
79.3	15,690
80.2	17,020
83.3	17,880

Number	Name	Description
	Independent Variables	
1	Elevation	Elevation in meters
2	Aspect	Aspect in degrees azimuth
3	Slope	Slope in degrees
4	Horizontal_Distance_To_Hydrology	Horizontal distance to nearest surface-water features
5	Vertical_Distance_To_Hydrology	Vertical distance to nearest surface-water features
6	Horizontal_Distance_To_Roadways	Horizontal distance to nearest roadway
7	Hillshade_9am	Hill shade index at 9 A.M., summer solstice
8	Hillshade_Noon	Hill shade index at noon, summer solstice
9	Hillshade_3pm	Hill shade index at 3 P.M., summer solstice
10	Horizontal_Distance_To_Fire_Points	Horizontal distance to nearest wildfire ignition points
11	Wilderness_Area (4 binary variables)	Wilderness area designation
12	Soil_Type (40 binary variables)	Soil type designation

Number		Dependent Variable
1	Cover_Type (7 unique types)	Forest cover type designation

Note: More details about the data set (variables and observations) can be found in the online file.

a. Plot the raw data. What pattern do you see? What do you think is really affecting electricity usage?

b. Solve this problem with linear regression $Y = a + bX$ (in a spreadsheet). How well does this work? Plot your results. What is wrong? Calculate the sum-of-the-squares error and R^2.

c. Solve this problem by using nonlinear regression. We recommend a quadratic function, $Y = a + b_1X + b_2X^2$. How well does this work? Plot your results. Is anything wrong? Calculate the sum-of-the-squares error and R^2.

d. Break up the problem into three sections (look at the plot). Solve it using three linear regression models—one for each section. How well does this work? Plot your results. Calculate the sum-of-the-squares error and R^2. Is this modeling approach appropriate? Why or why not?

e. Build a neural network to solve the original problem. (You may have to scale the X and Y values to be between 0 and 1.) Train it (on the entire set of data) and solve the problem (i.e., make predictions for each of the original data items). How well does this work? Plot your results. Calculate the sum-of-the-squares error and R^2.

f. Which method works best and why?

2. Build a real-world neural network. Using demo software downloaded from the Web (e.g., NeuroSolutions at **neurodimension.com** or another site), identify real-world data (e.g., start searching on the Web at **ics.uci.edu/~mlearn/MLRepository.html** or use data from an organization with which someone in your group has a contact) and build a neural network to make predictions. Topics might include sales forecasts, predicting success in an academic program (e.g., predict GPA from high school rating and SAT scores, being careful to look out for "bad" data, such as GPAs of 0.0), or housing prices; or survey the class for weight, gender, and height and try to predict height based on the other two factors. You could also use U.S. Census data on this book's Web site or at **census.gov**, by state, to identify a relationship between education level and income. How good are your predictions? Compare the results to predictions generated using standard statistical methods (regression). Which method is better? How could your system be embedded in a DSS for real decision making?

3. For each of the following applications, would it be better to use a neural network or an expert system? Explain your answers, including possible exceptions or special conditions.

a. Diagnosis of a well-established but complex disease

b. Price-lookup subsystem for a high-volume merchandise seller

c. Automated voice-inquiry processing system

d. Training of new employees

e. Handwriting recognition

4. Consider the following data set, which includes three attributes and a classification for admission decisions into an MBA program:

GMAT	GPA	Quantitative GMAT	Decision
650	2.75	35	NO
580	3.50	70	NO
600	3.50	75	YES
450	2.95	80	NO
700	3.25	90	YES
590	3.50	80	YES
400	3.85	45	NO
640	3.50	75	YES
540	3.00	60	?
690	2.85	80	?
490	4.00	65	?

a. Using the data given here as examples, develop your own manual expert rules for decision making.

b. Build and test a neural network model using your favorite data mining tool. Experiment with different model parameters to "optimize" the predictive power of your model.

c. Build and test a support vector machine model using your favorite data mining tool. Experiment with different model parameters to "optimize" the predictive power of your model. Compare the results of ANN and SVM.

d. Report the predictions on the last three observations from each of the three classification approaches (ANN, SVM, and kNN). Comment on the results.

e. Comment on the similarity and differences of these three prediction approaches. What did you learn from this exercise?

5. You have worked on neural networks and other data mining techniques. Give examples of where each of these has been used. Based on your knowledge, how would you differentiate among these techniques? Assume that a few years from now you come across a situation in which neural network or other data mining techniques could be used to build an interesting application for your organization. You have an intern working with you to do the grunt work. How will you decide whether the application is appropriate for a neural network or for another data mining model? Based on your homework assignments, what specific software guidance can you provide to get your intern to be productive for you quickly? Your answer for this question might mention the specific software, describe how to go about setting up the model/neural network, and validate the application.

Internet Exercises

1. Explore the Web sites of several neural network vendors, such as California Scientific Software (**calsci.com**), NeuralWare (**neuralware.com**), and Ward Systems Group (**wardsystems.com**), and review some of their products. Download at least two demos and install, run, and compare them.

2. A very good repository of data that has been used to test the performance of neural network and other machine-learning algorithms can be accessed at **ics.uci.edu/~mlearn/MLRepository.html**. Some of the data sets are really meant to test the limits of current machine-learning algorithms and compare their performance against new approaches to learning. However, some of the smaller data sets can be useful for exploring the functionality of the software you might download in Internet Exercise 1 or the software that is available at **StatSoft.com** (i.e., Statistica Data Miner with extensive neural network capabilities). Download at least one data set from the UCI repository (e.g., Credit Screening Databases, Housing Database). Then apply neural networks as well as decision tree methods, as appropriate. Prepare a report on your results. (Some of these exercises could also be completed in a group or may even be proposed as semester-long projects for term papers and so on.)

3. Go to **calsci.com** and read about the company's various business applications. Prepare a report that summarizes the applications.

4. Go to **nd.com**. Read about the company's applications in investment and trading. Prepare a report about them.

5. Go to **nd.com**. Download the trial version of NeuroSolutions for Excel and experiment with it, using one of the data sets from the exercises in this chapter. Prepare a report about your experience with the tool.

6. Go to **neoxi.com**. Identify at least two software tools that have not been mentioned in this chapter. Visit Web sites of those tools and prepare a brief report on the tools' capabilities.

7. Go to **neuroshell.com**. Look at Gee Whiz examples. Comment on the feasibility of achieving the results claimed by the developers of this neural network model.

8. Go to **easynn.com**. Download the trial version of the software. After the installation of the software, find the sample file called **Houseprices.tvq**. Retrain the neural network and test the model by supplying some data. Prepare a report about your experience with this software.

9. Visit **statsoft.com**. Download at least three white papers of applications. Which of these applications may have used neural networks?

10. Go to **neuralware.com**. Prepare a report about the products the company offers.

End-of-Chapter Application Case

Coors Improves Beer Flavors with Neural Networks

Coors Brewers Ltd., based in Burton-upon-Trent, Britain's brewing capital, is proud of having the United Kingdom's top beer brands, a 20 percent share of the market, years of experience, and some of the best people in the business. Popular brands include Carling (the country's bestselling lager), Grolsch, Coors Fine Light Beer, Sol, and Korenwolf.

Problem

Today's customer has a wide variety of options regarding what he or she drinks. A drinker's choice depends on various factors, including mood, venue, and occasion. Coors' goal is to ensure that the customer chooses a Coors brand no matter what the circumstances are.

According to Coors, creativity is the key to long-term success. To be the customer's choice brand, Coors needs to be creative and anticipate the customer's ever so rapidly changing moods. An important issue with beers is the flavor; each beer has a distinctive flavor. These flavors are mostly determined through panel tests. However, such tests take time. If Coors could understand the beer flavor based solely on its chemical composition, it would open up new avenues to create beer that would suit customer expectations.

The relationship between chemical analysis and beer flavor is not clearly understood yet. Substantial data exist on the chemical composition of a beer and sensory analysis. Coors needed a mechanism to link those two together. Neural networks were applied to create the link between chemical composition and sensory analysis.

Solution

Over the years, Coors Brewers Ltd. has accumulated a significant amount of data related to the final product analysis, which has been supplemented by sensory data provided by the trained in-house testing panel. Some of the analytical inputs and sensory outputs are shown in the following table:

Analytical Data: Inputs	Sensory Data: Outputs
Alcohol	Alcohol
Color	Estery
Calculated bitterness	Malty
Ethyl acetate	Grainy
Isobutyl acetate	Burnt
Ethyl butyrate	Hoppy
Isoamyl acetate	Toffee
Ethyl hexanoate	Sweet

A single neural network, restricted to a single quality and flavor, was first used to model the relationship between the analytical and sensory data. The neural network was based on a package solution supplied by NeuroDimension, Inc. (**nd.com**). The neural network consisted of an MLP architecture with two hidden layers. Data were normalized within the network, thereby enabling comparison between the results for the various sensory outputs. The neural network was trained (to learn the relationship between the inputs and outputs) through the presentation of many combinations of relevant input/output combinations. When there was no observed improvement in the network error in the last 100 epochs, training was automatically terminated. Training was carried out 50 times to ensure that a considerable mean network error could be calculated for comparison purposes. Prior to each training run, a different training and cross-validation data set was presented by randomizing the source data records, thereby removing any bias.

This technique produced poor results, due to two major factors. First, concentrating on a single product's quality meant that the variation in the data was pretty low. The neural network could not extract useful relationships from the data. Second, it was probable that only one subset of the provided inputs would have an impact on the selected beer flavor. Performance of the neural network was affected by "noise" created by inputs that had no impact on flavor.

A more diverse product range was included in the training range to address the first factor. It was more challenging to identify the most important analytical inputs. This challenge was addressed by using a software switch that enabled the neural network to be trained on all possible combinations of inputs. The switch was not used to disable a significant input; if the significant input were disabled, we could expect the network error to increase. If the disabled input was insignificant, then the network error would either remain unchanged or be reduced due to the removal of noise. This approach is called an *exhaustive search* because all possible combinations are evaluated. The technique, although conceptually simple, was computationally impractical with the numerous inputs; the number of possible combinations was 16.7 million per flavor.

A more efficient method of searching for the relevant inputs was required. A genetic algorithm was the solution to the problem. A genetic algorithm was able to manipulate the different input switches in response to the error term from the neural network. The objective of the genetic algorithm was to minimize the network error term. When this minimum was reached, the switch settings would identify the analytical inputs that were most likely to predict the flavor.

Results

After determining what inputs were relevant, it was possible to identify which flavors could be predicted more skillfully. The network was trained using the relevant inputs previously identified multiple times. Before each training run, the network data were randomized to ensure that a different training and cross-validation data set was used. Network error was recorded after each training run. The testing set used for assessing the performance of the trained network contained approximately 80 records out of the sample data. The neural network accurately predicted a few flavors by using the chemical inputs. For example, "burnt" flavor was predicted with a correlation coefficient of 0.87.

Today, a limited number of flavors are being predicted by using the analytical data. Sensory response is extremely complex, with many potential interactions and hugely variable sensitivity thresholds. Standard instrumental analysis tends to be of gross parameters, and for practical and economical reasons, many flavor-active compounds are simply not measured. The relationship of flavor and analysis can be effectively modeled only if a large number of flavor-contributory analytes are considered. What is more, in addition to the obvious flavor-active materials, mouth-feel and physical contributors should also be considered in the overall sensory profile. With further development of the input parameters, the accuracy of the neural network models will improve.

QUESTIONS FOR THE END-OF-CHAPTER APPLICATION CASE

1. Why is beer flavor important to Coors' profitability?
2. What is the objective of the neural network used at Coors?
3. Why were the results of Coors' neural network initially poor, and what was done to improve the results?
4. What benefits might Coors derive if this project is successful?
5. What modifications would you make to improve the results of beer flavor prediction?

Sources: Compiled from C. I. Wilson and L. Threapleton, "Application of Artificial Intelligence for Predicting Beer Flavours from Chemical Analysis," *Proceedings of the 29th European Brewery Congress,* Dublin, Ireland, May 17–22, 2003, **neurosolutions.com/resources/apps/beer.html** (accessed February 2013); and R. Nischwitz, M. Goldsmith, M. Lees, P. Rogers, and L. MacLeod, "Developing Functional Malt Specifications for Improved Brewing Performance," The Regional Institute Ltd., **regional.org.au/au/abts/1999/nischwitz.htm** (accessed February 2013).

References

Ainscough, T. L., and J. E. Aronson. (1999). "A Neural Networks Approach for the Analysis of Scanner Data." *Journal of Retailing and Consumer Services,* Vol. 6.

Aizerman, M., E. Braverman, and L. Rozonoer. (1964). "Theoretical Foundations of the Potential Function Method in Pattern Recognition Learning." *Automation and Remote Control,* Vol. 25, pp. 821–837.

Altman, E. I. (1968). "Financial Ratios, Discriminant Analysis and the Prediction of Corporate Bankruptcy." *Journal of Finance,* Vol. 23.

California Scientific. "Maximize Returns on Direct Mail with BrainMaker Neural Networks Software." **calsci.com/DirectMail.html** (accessed August 2009).

Collard, J. E. (1990). "Commodity Trading with a Neural Net." *Neural Network News,* Vol. 2, No. 10.

Collins, E., S. Ghosh, and C. L. Scofield. (1988). "An Application of a Multiple Neural Network Learning System to Emulation of Mortgage Underwriting Judgments." *IEEE International Conference on Neural Networks,* Vol. 2, pp. 459–466.

Das, R., I. Turkoglu, and A. Sengur. (2009). "Effective Diagnosis of Heart Disease Through Neural Networks Ensembles." *Expert Systems with Applications,* Vol. 36, pp. 7675–7680.

Davis, J. T., A. Episcopos, and S. Wettimuny. (2001). "Predicting Direction Shifts on Canadian–U.S. Exchange Rates with Artificial Neural Networks." *International Journal of Intelligent Systems in Accounting, Finance and Management,* Vol. 10, No. 2.

Delen, D., and E. Sirakaya. (2006). "Determining the Efficacy of Data-Mining Methods in Predicting Gaming Ballot Outcomes." *Journal of Hospitality & Tourism Research,* Vol. 30, No. 3, pp. 313–332.

Delen, D., R. Sharda, and M. Bessonov. (2006). "Identifying Significant Predictors of Injury Severity in Traffic Accidents Using a Series of Artificial Neural Networks." *Accident Analysis and Prevention,* Vol. 38, No. 3, pp. 434–444.

Dutta, S., and S. Shakhar. (1988, July 24–27). "Bond-Rating: A Non-Conservative Application of Neural Networks." *Proceedings of the IEEE International Conference on Neural Networks,* San Diego, CA.

Estévez, P. A., M. H. Claudio, and C. A. Perez. "Prevention in Telecommunications Using Fuzzy Rules and Neural Networks." **cec.uchile.cl/~pestevez/RI0.pdf** (accessed May 2009).

Fadlalla, A., and C. Lin. (2001). "An Analysis of the Applications of Neural Networks in Finance." *Interfaces,* Vol. 31, No. 4.

Fishman, M., D. Barr, and W. Loick. (1991, April). "Using Neural Networks in Market Analysis." *Technical Analysis of Stocks and Commodities.*

Fozzard, R., G. Bradshaw, and L. Ceci. (1989). "A Connectionist Expert System for Solar Flare Forecasting." In D. S. Touretsky (ed.), *Advances in Neural Information Processing Systems,* Vol. 1. San Mateo, CA: Kaufman.

Francett, B. (1989, January). "Neural Nets Arrive." *Computer Decisions.*

Gallant, S. (1988, February). "Connectionist Expert Systems." *Communications of the ACM,* Vol. 31, No. 2.

Güler, I., Z. Gökçil, and E. Gülbandilar. (2009). "Evaluating Traumatic Brain Injuries Using Artificial Neural Networks." *Expert Systems with Applications,* Vol. 36, pp. 10424–10427.

Haykin, S. S. (2009). *Neural Networks and Learning Machines,* 3rd ed. Upper Saddle River, NJ: Prentice Hall.

Hill, T., T. Marquez, M. O'Connor, and M. Remus. (1994). "Neural Network Models for Forecasting and Decision Making." *International Journal of Forecasting,* Vol. 10.

Hopfield, J. (1982, April). "Neural Networks and Physical Systems with Emergent Collective Computational Abilities." *Proceedings of National Academy of Science,* Vol. 79, No. 8.

Hopfield, J. J., and D. W. Tank. (1985). "Neural Computation of Decisions in Optimization Problems." *Biological Cybernetics,* Vol. 52.

Iyer, S. R., and R. Sharda. (2009). "Prediction of Athletes' Performance Using Neural Networks: An Application in Cricket Team Selection." *Expert Systems with Applications,* Vol. 36, No. 3, pp. 5510–5522.

Kamijo, K., and T. Tanigawa. (1990, June 7–11). "Stock Price Pattern Recognition: A Recurrent Neural Network Approach." *International Joint Conference on Neural Networks,* San Diego.

Lee, P. Y., S. C. Hui, and A. C. M. Fong. (2002, September/October). "Neural Networks for Web Content Filtering." *IEEE Intelligent Systems.*

Liang, T. P. (1992). "A Composite Approach to Automated Knowledge Acquisition." *Management Science,* Vol. 38, No. 1.

Loeffelholz, B., E. Bednar, and K. W. Bauer. (2009). "Predicting NBA Games Using Neural Networks." *Journal of Quantitative Analysis in Sports,* Vol. 5, No. 1.

McCulloch, W. S., and W. H. Pitts. (1943). "A Logical Calculus of the Ideas Imminent in Nervous Activity." *Bulletin of Mathematical Biophysics,* Vol. 5.

Medsker, L., and J. Liebowitz. (1994). *Design and Development of Expert Systems and Neural Networks.* New York: Macmillan, p. 163.

Mighell, D. (1989). "Back-Propagation and Its Application to Handwritten Signature Verification." In D. S. Touretsky (ed.), *Advances in Neural Information Processing Systems.* San Mateo, CA: Kaufman.

Minsky, M., and S. Papert. (1969). *Perceptrons.* Cambridge, MA: MIT Press.

Neural Technologies. "Combating Fraud: How a Leading Telecom Company Solved a Growing Problem." **neuralt.com/iqs/dlsfa.list/dlcpti.7/downloads.html** (accessed March 2009).

Nischwitz, R., M. Goldsmith, M. Lees, P. Rogers, and L. MacLeod. "Developing Functional Malt Specifications for Improved Brewing Performance." The Regional Institute Ltd., **regional.org.au/au/abts/1999/nischwitz.htm** (accessed May 2009).

Olson, D. L., D. Delen, and Y. Meng. (2012). "Comparative Analysis of Data Mining Models for Bankruptcy Prediction." *Decision Support Systems,* Vol. 52, No. 2, pp. 464–473.

Piatesky-Shapiro, G. "ISR: Microsoft Success Using Neural Network for Direct Marketing." **kdnuggets.com/news/94/n9.txt** (accessed May 2009).

Principe, J. C., N. R. Euliano, and W. C. Lefebvre. (2000). *Neural and Adaptive Systems: Fundamentals Through Simulations.* New York: Wiley.

Rochester, J. (ed.). (1990, February). "New Business Uses for Neurocomputing." *I/S Analyzer.*

Sirakaya, E., D. Delen, and H-S. Choi. (2005). "Forecasting Gaming Referenda." *Annals of Tourism Research,* Vol. 32, No. 1, pp. 127–149.

Sordo, M., H. Buxton, and D. Watson. (2001). "A Hybrid Approach to Breast Cancer Diagnosis." In L. Jain and P. DeWilde (eds.), *Practical Applications of Computational Intelligence Techniques,* Vol. 16. Norwell, MA: Kluwer.

Surkan, A., and J. Singleton. (1990). "Neural Networks for Bond Rating Improved by Multiple Hidden Layers." *Proceedings of the IEEE International Conference on Neural Networks,* Vol. 2.

Tang, Z., C. de Almieda, and P. Fishwick. (1991). "Time-Series Forecasting Using Neural Networks vs. Box-Jenkins Methodology." *Simulation,* Vol. 57, No. 5.

Thaler, S. L. (2002, January/February). "AI for Network Protection: LITMUS:—Live Intrusion Tracking via Multiple Unsupervised STANNOs." *PC AI.*

Walczak, S., W. E. Pofahi, and R. J. Scorpio. (2002). "A Decision Support Tool for Allocating Hospital Bed Resources and Determining Required Acuity of Care." *Decision Support Systems,* Vol. 34, No. 4.

Wallace, M. P. (2008, July). "Neural Networks and Their Applications in Finance." *Business Intelligence Journal,* pp. 67–76.

Wen, U-P., K-M. Lan, and H-S. Shih. (2009). "A Review of Hopfield Neural Networks for Solving Mathematical Programming Problems." *European Journal of Operational Research,* Vol. 198, pp. 675–687.

Wilson, C. I., and L. Threapleton. (2003, May 17–22). "Application of Artificial Intelligence for Predicting Beer Flavours from Chemical Analysis." *Proceedings of the 29th European Brewery Congress,* Dublin, Ireland. **neurosolutions.com/resources/apps/beer.html** (accessed May 2009).

Wilson, R., and R. Sharda. (1994). "Bankruptcy Prediction Using Neural Networks." *Decision Support Systems,* Vol. 11.

Zahedi, F. (1993). *Intelligent Systems for Business: Expert Systems with Neural Networks.* Belmont, CA: Wadsworth.

Text Analytics, Text Mining, and Sentiment Analysis

LEARNING OBJECTIVES

- Describe text mining and understand the need for text mining
- Differentiate among text analytics, text mining, and data mining
- Understand the different application areas for text mining
- Know the process for carrying out a text mining project
- Appreciate the different methods to introduce structure to text-based data

- Describe sentiment analysis
- Develop familiarity with popular applications of sentiment analysis
- Learn the common methods for sentiment analysis
- Become familiar with speech analytics as it relates to sentiment analysis

This chapter provides a rather comprehensive overview of text mining and one of its most popular applications, sentiment analysis, as they both relate to business analytics and decision support systems. Generally speaking, sentiment analysis is a derivative of text mining, and text mining is essentially a derivative of data mining. Because textual data is increasing in volume more than the data in structured databases, it is important to know some of the techniques used to extract actionable information from this large quantity of unstructured data.

7.1 OPENING VIGNETTE: Machine Versus Men on *Jeopardy!*: The Story of Watson

Can machine beat the best of man in what man is supposed to be the best at? Evidently, yes, and the machine's name is Watson. Watson is an extraordinary computer system (a novel combination of advanced hardware and software) designed to answer questions posed in natural human language. It was developed in 2010 by an IBM Research team as part of a DeepQA project and was named after IBM's first president, Thomas J. Watson.

BACKGROUND

Roughly 3 years ago, IBM Research was looking for a major research challenge to rival the scientific and popular interest of Deep Blue, the computer chess-playing champion, which would also have clear relevance to IBM business interests. The goal was to advance computer science by exploring new ways for computer technology to affect science, business, and society. Accordingly, IBM Research undertook a challenge to build a computer system that could compete at the human champion level in real time on the American TV quiz show, *Jeopardy!* The extent of the challenge included fielding a real-time automatic contestant on the show, capable of listening, understanding, and responding—not merely a laboratory exercise.

COMPETING AGAINST THE BEST

In 2011, as a test of its abilities, Watson competed on the quiz show *Jeopardy!*, which was the first ever human-versus-machine matchup for the show. In a two-game, combined-point match (broadcast in three *Jeopardy!* episodes during February 14–16), Watson beat Brad Rutter, the biggest all-time money winner on *Jeopardy!*, and Ken Jennings, the record holder for the longest championship streak (75 days). In these episodes, Watson consistently outperformed its human opponents on the game's signaling device, but had trouble responding to a few categories, notably those having short clues containing only a few words. Watson had access to 200 million pages of structured and unstructured content consuming four terabytes of disk storage. During the game Watson was not connected to the Internet.

Meeting the *Jeopardy!* Challenge required advancing and incorporating a variety of QA technologies (text mining and natural language processing) including parsing, question classification, question decomposition, automatic source acquisition and evaluation, entity and relation detection, logical form generation, and knowledge representation and reasoning. Winning at *Jeopardy!* required accurately computing confidence in your answers. The questions and content are ambiguous and noisy and none of the individual algorithms are perfect. Therefore, each component must produce a confidence in its output, and individual component confidences must be combined to compute the overall confidence of the final answer. The final confidence is used to determine whether the computer system should risk choosing to answer at all. In *Jeopardy!* parlance, this confidence is used to determine whether the computer will "ring in" or "buzz in" for a question. The confidence must be computed during the time the question is read and before the opportunity to buzz in. This is roughly between 1 and 6 seconds with an average around 3 seconds.

HOW DOES WATSON DO IT?

The system behind Watson, which is called DeepQA, is a massively parallel, text mining–focused, probabilistic evidence-based computational architecture. For the *Jeopardy!* challenge, Watson used more than 100 different techniques for analyzing natural language, identifying sources, finding and generating hypotheses, finding and scoring evidence, and merging and ranking hypotheses. What is far more important than any particular technique that they used was how they combine them in DeepQA such that overlapping approaches can bring their strengths to bear and contribute to improvements in accuracy, confidence, and speed.

DeepQA is an architecture with an accompanying methodology, which is not specific to the *Jeopardy!* challenge. The overarching principles in DeepQA are massive parallelism, many experts, pervasive confidence estimation, and integration of the-latest-and-greatest in text analytics.

- ***Massive parallelism:*** Exploit massive parallelism in the consideration of multiple interpretations and hypotheses.
- ***Many experts:*** Facilitate the integration, application, and contextual evaluation of a wide range of loosely coupled probabilistic question and content analytics.
- ***Pervasive confidence estimation:*** No component commits to an answer; all components produce features and associated confidences, scoring different question and content interpretations. An underlying confidence-processing substrate learns how to stack and combine the scores.
- ***Integrate shallow and deep knowledge:*** Balance the use of strict semantics and shallow semantics, leveraging many loosely formed ontologies.

Figure 7.1 illustrates the DeepQA architecture at a very high level. More technical details about the various architectural components and their specific roles and capabilities can be found in Ferrucci et al. (2010).

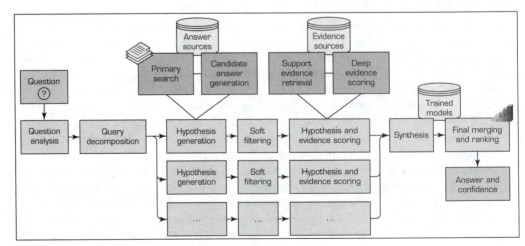

FIGURE 7.1 A High-Level Depiction of DeepQA Architecture.

CONCLUSION

The *Jeopardy!* challenge helped IBM address requirements that led to the design of the DeepQA architecture and the implementation of Watson. After 3 years of intense research and development by a core team of about 20 researchers, Watson is performing at human expert levels in terms of precision, confidence, and speed at the *Jeopardy!* quiz show.

IBM claims to have developed many computational and linguistic algorithms to address different kinds of issues and requirements in QA. Even though the internals of these algorithms are not known, it is imperative that they made the most out of text analytics and text mining. Now IBM is working on a version of Watson to take on surmountable problems in healthcare and medicine (Feldman et al., 2012).

QUESTIONS FOR THE OPENING VIGNETTE

1. What is Watson? What is special about it?
2. What technologies were used in building Watson (both hardware and software)?
3. What are the innovative characteristics of DeepQA architecture that made Watson superior?
4. Why did IBM spend all that time and money to build Watson? Where is the ROI?
5. Conduct an Internet search to identify other previously developed "smart machines" (by IBM or others) that compete against the best of man. What technologies did they use?

WHAT WE CAN LEARN FROM THIS VIGNETTE

It is safe to say that computer technology, on both the hardware and software fronts, is advancing faster than anything else in the last 50-plus years. Things that were too big, too complex, impossible to solve are now well within the reach of information technology. One of those enabling technologies is perhaps text analytics/text mining. We created databases to structure the data so that it can be processed by computers. Text, on the other hand, has always been meant for humans to process. Can machines do the things that require human creativity and intelligence, and which were not originally designed for machines? Evidently, yes! Watson is a great example of the distance that we have traveled in addressing the impossible. Computers are now intelligent enough to take on men at what we think men are the best at. Understanding the question that was posed in spoken human language, processing and digesting it, searching for an answer, and replying within a few seconds was something that we could not have imagined possible before Watson actually did it. In this chapter, you will learn the tools and techniques embedded in Watson and many other smart machines to create miracles in tackling problems that were once believed impossible to solve.

Sources: D. Ferrucci, E. Brown, J. Chu-Carroll, J. Fan, D. Gondek, A. A. Kalyanpur, A. Lally, J. W. Murdock, E. Nyberg, J. Prager, N. Schlaefer, and C. Welty, "Building Watson: An Overview of the DeepQA Project," AI Magazine, Vol. 31, No. 3, 2010; DeepQA, DeepQA Project: FAQ, IBM Corporation, 2011, research.ibm. com/deepqa/faq.shtml (accessed January 2013); and S. Feldman, J. Hanover, C. Burghard, and D. Schubmehl, "Unlocking the Power of Unstructured Data," IBM white paper, 2012, www-01.ibm.com/software/ebusiness/ jstart/downloads/unlockingUnstructuredData.pdf (accessed February 2013).

7.2   TEXT ANALYTICS AND TEXT MINING CONCEPTS AND DEFINITIONS

The information age that we are living in is characterized by the rapid growth in the amount of data and information collected, stored, and made available in electronic format. The vast majority of business data is stored in text documents that are virtually unstructured. According to a study by Merrill Lynch and Gartner, 85 percent of all corporate data is captured and stored in some sort of unstructured form (McKnight, 2005). The same study also stated that this unstructured data is doubling in size every 18 months. Because knowledge is power in today's business world, and knowledge is derived from data and information, businesses that effectively and efficiently tap into their text data sources will have the necessary knowledge to make better decisions, leading to a competitive advantage over those businesses that lag behind. This is where the need for text analytics and text mining fits into the big picture of today's businesses.

Even though the overarching goal for both text analytics and text mining is to turn unstructured textual data into actionable information through the application of natural language processing (NLP) and analytics, their definitions are somewhat different, at least to some experts in the field. According to them, text analytics is a broader concept that includes information retrieval (e.g., searching and identifying relevant documents for a given set of key terms) as well as information extraction, data mining, and Web mining, whereas text mining is primarily focused on discovering new and useful knowledge from the textual data sources. Figure 7.2 illustrates the relationships between text analytics and text mining along with other related application areas. The bottom of Figure 7.2 lists the main disciplines (the foundation of the house) that play a critical role in the development of these increasingly more popular application areas. Based on this definition of text analytics and text mining, one could simply formulate the difference between the two as follows:

$$\text{Text Analytics} = \text{Information Retrieval} + \text{Information Extraction} + \text{Data Mining} + \text{Web Mining},$$

or simply

$$\text{Text Analytics} = \text{Information Retrieval} + \text{Text Mining}$$

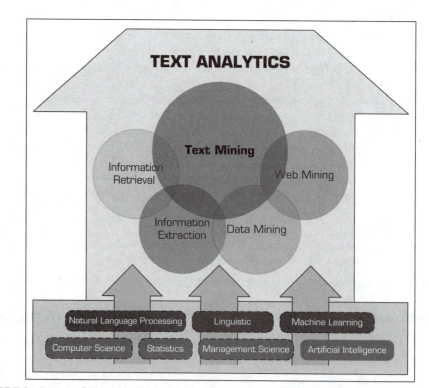

FIGURE 7.2 Text Analytics, Related Application Areas, and Enabling Disciplines.

Compared to text mining, text analytics is a relatively new term. With the recent emphasis on *analytics*, as has been the case in many other related technical application areas (e.g., consumer analytics, completive analytics, visual analytics, social analytics, and so forth), the text field has also wanted to get on the analytics bandwagon. While the term *text analytics* is more commonly used in a business application context, text mining is frequently used in academic research circles. Even though they may be defined somewhat differently at times, text analytics and text mining are usually used synonymously, and we (the authors of this book) concur with this.

Text mining (also known as *text data mining* or *knowledge discovery in textual databases*) is the semi-automated process of extracting patterns (useful information and knowledge) from large amounts of unstructured data sources. Remember that data mining is the process of identifying valid, novel, potentially useful, and ultimately understandable patterns in data stored in structured databases, where the data are organized in records structured by categorical, ordinal, or continuous variables. Text mining is the same as data mining in that it has the same purpose and uses the same processes, but with text mining the input to the process is a collection of unstructured (or less structured) data files such as Word documents, PDF files, text excerpts, XML files, and so on. In essence, text mining can be thought of as a process (with two main steps) that starts with imposing structure on the text-based data sources, followed by extracting relevant information and knowledge from this structured text-based data using data mining techniques and tools.

The benefits of text mining are obvious in the areas where very large amounts of textual data are being generated, such as law (court orders), academic research (research articles), finance (quarterly reports), medicine (discharge summaries), biology (molecular interactions), technology (patent files), and marketing (customer comments). For example, the free-form text-based interactions with customers in the form of complaints (or praises) and warranty claims can be used to objectively identify product and service characteristics that are deemed to be less than perfect and can be used as input to better product development and service allocations. Likewise, market outreach programs and focus groups generate large amounts of data. By not restricting product or service feedback to a codified form, customers can present, in their own words, what they think about a company's products and services. Another area where the automated processing of unstructured text has had a lot of impact is in electronic communications and e-mail. Text mining not only can be used to classify and filter junk e-mail, but it can also be used to automatically prioritize e-mail based on importance level as well as generate automatic responses (Weng and Liu, 2004). The following are among the most popular application areas of text mining:

- *Information extraction.* Identification of key phrases and relationships within text by looking for predefined objects and sequences in text by way of pattern matching. Perhaps the most commonly used form of information extraction is *named entity extraction*. Named entity extraction includes *named entity recognition* (recognition of known entity names—for people and organizations, place names, temporal expressions, and certain types of numerical expressions, using existing knowledge of the domain), *co-reference resolution* (detection of co-reference and anaphoric links between text entities), and *relationship extraction* (identification of relations between entities).
- *Topic tracking.* Based on a user profile and documents that a user views, text mining can predict other documents of interest to the user.
- *Summarization.* Summarizing a document to save time on the part of the reader.
- *Categorization.* Identifying the main themes of a document and then placing the document into a predefined set of categories based on those themes.
- *Clustering.* Grouping similar documents without having a predefined set of categories.

- *Concept linking.* Connects related documents by identifying their shared concepts and, by doing so, helps users find information that they perhaps would not have found using traditional search methods.
- *Question answering.* Finding the best answer to a given question through knowledge-driven pattern matching.

See Technology Insights 7.1 for explanations of some of the terms and concepts used in text mining. Application Case 7.1 describes the use of text mining in patent analysis.

TECHNOLOGY INSIGHTS 7.1   Text Mining Lingo

The following list describes some commonly used text mining terms:

- *Unstructured data (versus structured data).* Structured data has a predetermined format. It is usually organized into records with simple data values (categorical, ordinal, and continuous variables) and stored in databases. In contrast, **unstructured data** does not have a predetermined format and is stored in the form of textual documents. In essence, the structured data is for the computers to process while the unstructured data is for humans to process and understand.
- *Corpus.* In linguistics, a **corpus** (plural *corpora*) is a large and structured set of texts (now usually stored and processed electronically) prepared for the purpose of conducting knowledge discovery.
- *Terms.* A *term* is a single word or multiword phrase extracted directly from the corpus of a specific domain by means of natural language processing (NLP) methods.
- *Concepts.* *Concepts* are features generated from a collection of documents by means of manual, statistical, rule-based, or hybrid categorization methodology. Compared to terms, concepts are the result of higher level abstraction.
- *Stemming.* **Stemming** is the process of reducing inflected words to their stem (or base or root) form. For instance, *stemmer, stemming,* and *stemmed* are all based on the root *stem*.
- *Stop words.* **Stop words** (or *noise words*) are words that are filtered out prior to or after processing of natural language data (i.e., text). Even though there is no universally accepted list of stop words, most natural language processing tools use a list that includes articles (*a, am, the, of,* etc.), auxiliary verbs (*is, are, was, were,* etc.), and context-specific words that are deemed not to have differentiating value.
- *Synonyms and polysemes.* Synonyms are syntactically different words (i.e., spelled differently) with identical or at least similar meanings (e.g., *movie, film,* and *motion picture*). In contrast, **polysemes**, which are also called *homonyms*, are syntactically identical words (i.e., spelled exactly the same) with different meanings (e.g., *bow* can mean "to bend forward," "the front of the ship," "the weapon that shoots arrows," or "a kind of tied ribbon").
- *Tokenizing.* A *token* is a categorized block of text in a sentence. The block of text corresponding to the token is categorized according to the function it performs. This assignment of meaning to blocks of text is known as **tokenizing**. A token can look like anything; it just needs to be a useful part of the structured text.
- *Term dictionary.* A collection of terms specific to a narrow field that can be used to restrict the extracted terms within a corpus.
- *Word frequency.* The number of times a word is found in a specific document.
- *Part-of-speech tagging.* The process of marking up the words in a text as corresponding to a particular part of speech (such as nouns, verbs, adjectives, adverbs, etc.) based on a word's definition and the context in which it is used.
- *Morphology.* A branch of the field of linguistics and a part of natural language processing that studies the internal structure of words (patterns of word-formation within a language or across languages).
- *Term-by-document matrix (occurrence matrix).* A common representation schema of the frequency-based relationship between the terms and documents in tabular format

where terms are listed in rows, documents are listed in columns, and the frequency between the terms and documents is listed in cells as integer values.

- *Singular-value decomposition (latent semantic indexing).* A dimensionality reduction method used to transform the term-by-document matrix to a manageable size by generating an intermediate representation of the frequencies using a matrix manipulation method similar to principal component analysis.

Application Case 7.1
Text Mining for Patent Analysis

A patent is a set of exclusive rights granted by a country to an inventor for a limited period of time in exchange for a disclosure of an invention (note that the procedure for granting patents, the requirements placed on the patentee, and the extent of the exclusive rights vary widely from country to country). The disclosure of these inventions is critical to future advancements in science and technology. If carefully analyzed, patent documents can help identify emerging technologies, inspire novel solutions, foster symbiotic partnerships, and enhance overall awareness of business' capabilities and limitations.

Patent analysis is the use of analytical techniques to extract valuable knowledge from patent databases. Countries or groups of countries that maintain patent databases (e.g., the United States, the European Union, Japan) add tens of millions of new patents each year. It is nearly impossible to efficiently process such enormous amounts of semistructured data (patent documents usually contain partially structured and partially textual data). Patent analysis with semiautomated software tools is one way to ease the processing of these very large databases.

A Representative Example of Patent Analysis

Eastman Kodak employs more than 5,000 scientists, engineers, and technicians around the world. During the twentieth century, these knowledge workers and their predecessors claimed nearly 20,000 patents, putting the company among the top 10 patent holders in the world. Being in the business of constant change, the company knows that success (or mere survival) depends on its ability to apply more than a century's worth of knowledge about imaging science and technology to new uses and to secure those new uses with patents.

Appreciating the value of patents, Kodak not only generates new patents but also analyzes those created by others. Using dedicated analysts and state-of-the-art software tools (including specialized text mining tools from ClearForest Corp.), Kodak continuously digs deep into various data sources (patent databases, new release archives, and product announcements) in order to develop a holistic view of the competitive landscape. Proper analysis of patents can bring companies like Kodak a wide range of benefits:

- It enables competitive intelligence. Knowing what competitors are doing can help a company to develop countermeasures.
- It can help the company make critical business decisions, such as what new products, product lines, and/or technologies to get into or what mergers and acquisitions to pursue.
- It can aid in identifying and recruiting the best and brightest new talent, those whose names appear on the patents that are critical to the company's success.
- It can help the company to identify the unauthorized use of its patents, enabling it to take action to protect its assets.
- It can identify complementary inventions to build symbiotic partnerships or to facilitate mergers and/or acquisitions.
- It prevents competitors from creating similar products and it can help protect the company from patent infringement lawsuits.

Using patent analysis as a rich source of knowledge and a strategic weapon (both defensive as well as offensive), Kodak not only survives but excels in its market segment defined by innovation and constant change.

(Continued)

Application Case 7.1 (Continued)

QUESTIONS FOR DISCUSSION

1. Why is it important for companies to keep up with patent filings?
2. How did Kodak use text analytics to better analyze patents?
3. What were the challenges, the proposed solution, and the obtained results?

Sources: P. X. Chiem, "Kodak Turns Knowledge Gained About Patents into Competitive Intelligence," *Knowledge Management,* 2001, pp. 11–12; Y-H. Tsenga, C-J. Linb, and Y-I. Linc, "Text Mining Techniques for Patent Analysis," *Information Processing & Management,* Vol. 43, No. 5, 2007, pp. 1216–1247.

SECTION 7.2 QUESTIONS

1. What is text analytics? How does it differ from text mining?
2. What is text mining? How does it differ from data mining?
3. Why is the popularity of text mining as an analytics tool increasing?
4. What are some of the most popular application areas of text mining?

7.3 NATURAL LANGUAGE PROCESSING

Some of the early text mining applications used a simplified representation called *bag-of-words* when introducing structure to a collection of text-based documents in order to classify them into two or more predetermined classes or to cluster them into natural groupings. In the bag-of-words model, text, such as a sentence, paragraph, or complete document, is represented as a collection of words, disregarding the grammar or the order in which the words appear. The bag-of-words model is still used in some simple document classification tools. For instance, in spam filtering an e-mail message can be modeled as an unordered collection of words (a bag-of-words) that is compared against two different predetermined bags. One bag is filled with words found in spam messages and the other is filled with words found in legitimate e-mails. Although some of the words are likely to be found in both bags, the "spam" bag will contain spam-related words such as *stock, Viagra,* and *buy* much more frequently than the legitimate bag, which will contain more words related to the user's friends or workplace. The level of match between a specific e-mail's bag-of-words and the two bags containing the descriptors determines the membership of the e-mail as either spam or legitimate.

Naturally, we (humans) do not use words without some order or structure. We use words in sentences, which have semantic as well as syntactic structure. Thus, automated techniques (such as text mining) need to look for ways to go beyond the bag-of-words interpretation and incorporate more and more semantic structure into their operations. The current trend in text mining is toward including many of the advanced features that can be obtained using natural language processing.

It has been shown that the bag-of-words method may not produce good enough information content for text mining tasks (e.g., classification, clustering, association). A good example of this can be found in evidence-based medicine. A critical component of evidence-based medicine is incorporating the best available research findings into the clinical decision-making process, which involves appraisal of the information collected from the printed media for validity and relevance. Several researchers from the University of Maryland developed evidence assessment models using a bag-of-words method (Lin and Demner, 2005). They employed popular machine-learning methods along with more than half a million research articles collected from MEDLINE (Medical Literature Analysis and Retrieval System Online). In their models, they represented each abstract as a bag-of-words, where each stemmed term represented a feature. Despite using popular classification methods with proven experimental design methodologies, their prediction results were not much better than simple guessing, which may indicate that the bag-of-words is not generating a good enough representation of the research articles in this domain; hence, more advanced techniques such as natural language processing are needed.

Natural language processing (NLP) is an important component of text mining and is a subfield of artificial intelligence and computational linguistics. It studies the problem of "understanding" the natural human language, with the view of converting depictions of human language (such as textual documents) into more formal representations (in the form of numeric and symbolic data) that are easier for computer programs to manipulate. The goal of NLP is to move beyond syntax-driven text manipulation (which is often called "word counting") to a true understanding and processing of natural language that considers grammatical and semantic constraints as well as the context.

The definition and scope of the word "understanding" is one of the major discussion topics in NLP. Considering that the natural human language is vague and that a true understanding of meaning requires extensive knowledge of a topic (beyond what is in the words, sentences, and paragraphs), will computers ever be able to understand natural language the same way and with the same accuracy that humans do? Probably not! NLP has come a long way from the days of simple word counting, but it has an even longer way to go to really understanding natural human language. The following are just a few of the challenges commonly associated with the implementation of NLP:

- ***Part-of-speech tagging.*** It is difficult to mark up terms in a text as corresponding to a particular part of speech (such as nouns, verbs, adjectives, adverbs, etc.) because the part of speech depends not only on the definition of the term but also on the context within which it is used.
- ***Text segmentation.*** Some written languages, such as Chinese, Japanese, and Thai, do not have single-word boundaries. In these instances, the text-parsing task requires the identification of word boundaries, which is often a difficult task. Similar challenges in speech segmentation emerge when analyzing spoken language, because sounds representing successive letters and words blend into each other.
- ***Word sense disambiguation.*** Many words have more than one meaning. Selecting the meaning that makes the most sense can only be accomplished by taking into account the context within which the word is used.
- ***Syntactic ambiguity.*** The grammar for natural languages is ambiguous; that is, multiple possible sentence structures often need to be considered. Choosing the most appropriate structure usually requires a fusion of semantic and contextual information.
- ***Imperfect or irregular input.*** Foreign or regional accents and vocal impediments in speech and typographical or grammatical errors in texts make the processing of the language an even more difficult task.
- ***Speech acts.*** A sentence can often be considered an action by the speaker. The sentence structure alone may not contain enough information to define this action. For example, "Can you pass the class?" requests a simple yes/no answer, whereas "Can you pass the salt?" is a request for a physical action to be performed.

It is a longstanding dream of the artificial intelligence community to have algorithms that are capable of automatically reading and obtaining knowledge from text. By applying a learning algorithm to parsed text, researchers from Stanford University's NLP lab have developed methods that can automatically identify the concepts and relationships between those concepts in the text. By applying a unique procedure to large amounts of text, their algorithms automatically acquire hundreds of thousands of items of world knowledge and use them to produce significantly enhanced repositories for WordNet. **WordNet** is a laboriously hand-coded database of English words, their definitions, sets of synonyms, and various semantic relations between synonym sets. It is a major resource for NLP applications, but it has proven to be very expensive to build and maintain manually. By automatically inducing knowledge into WordNet, the potential exists to make WordNet an even greater and more comprehensive resource for NLP at a fraction of the cost. One prominent area where the benefits of NLP and WordNet are already being harvested is in customer relationship management (CRM). Broadly speaking, the goal of CRM is to maximize customer value by better understanding and effectively responding to their actual and perceived needs. An important area of CRM, where NLP is making a significant impact, is sentiment analysis. **Sentiment analysis** is a technique used to detect favorable and unfavorable opinions toward specific products and services using large numbers of textual data sources (customer feedback in the form of Web postings). A detailed coverage of sentiment analysis and WordNet is given in Section 7.7.

Text mining is also used in assessing public complaints. Application Case 7.2 provides an example where text mining is used to anticipate and address public complaints in Hong Kong.

Application Case 7.2

Text Mining Improves Hong Kong Government's Ability to Anticipate and Address Public Complaints

The 1823 Call Centre of the Hong Kong government's Efficiency Unit acts as a single point of contact for handling public inquiries and complaints on behalf of many government departments. 1823 operates round-the-clock, including during Sundays and public holidays. Each year, it answers about 2.65 million calls and 98,000 e-mails, including inquiries, suggestions, and complaints. "Having received so many calls and e-mails, we gather substantial volumes of data. The next step is to make sense of the data," says the Efficiency Unit's assistant director, W. F. Yuk. "Now, with SAS text mining technologies, we can obtain deep insights through uncovering the hidden relationship between words and sentences of complaints information, spot emerging trends and public concerns, and produce high-quality complaints intelligence for the departments we serve."

Building a "Complaints Intelligence System"

The Efficiency Unit aims to be the preferred consulting partner for all government bureaus and departments and to advance the delivery of world-class public services to the people of Hong Kong. The Unit launched the 1823 Call Centre in 2001. One of 1823's main functions is handling complaints—10 percent of the calls received last year were complaints. The Efficiency Unit recognized that there are social messages hidden in the complaints data, which provides important feedback on public service and highlights opportunities for service improvement. Rather than simply handling calls and e-mails, the Unit seeks to use the complaints information collected to gain a better understanding of daily issues for the public.

"We previously compiled some reports on complaint statistics for reference by government departments," says Yuk. "However, through 'eyeball' observations, it was absolutely impossible to effectively reveal new or more complex potential public issues and identify their root causes, as most of the complaints were recorded in unstructured textual format," says Yuk. Aiming to build a platform, called the Complaints Intelligence System, the Unit required a robust and powerful suite of text processing and mining solutions that could uncover the trends, patterns, and relationships inherent in the complaints.

Uncovering Root Causes of Issues from Unstructured Data

The Efficiency Unit chose to deploy SAS Text Miner, which can access and analyze various text formats, including e-mails received by the 1823 Call Centre. "The solution consolidates all information and uncovers hidden relationships through statistical modeling analyses," says Yuk. "It helps us understand hidden social issues so that government departments can discover them before they become serious, and thus seize the opportunities for service improvement."

Equipped with text analytics, the departments can better understand underlying issues and quickly respond even as situations evolve. Senior management can access accurate, up-to-date information from the Complaints Intelligence System.

Performance Reports at Fingertips

With the platform for SAS Business Analytics in place, the Efficiency Unit gets a boost from the system's ability to instantly generate reports. For instance, it previously took a week to compile reports on key performance indicators such as abandoned call rate, customer satisfaction rate, and first-time resolution rate. Now, these reports can be created at the click of a mouse through performance dashboards, as all complaints information is consolidated into the Complaints Intelligence System. This enables effective monitoring of the 1823 Call Centre's operations and service quality.

Strong Language Capabilities, Customized Services

Of particular importance in Hong Kong, SAS Text Miner has strong language capabilities—supporting English and traditional and simplified Chinese—and can perform automated spelling correction. The solution is also aided by the SAS capability of developing customized lists of synonyms such as the full and short forms of different government departments and to parse Chinese text for similar or identical terms whose meanings and connotations change, often dramatically, depending on the context in which they are used. "Also, throughout this 4-month project, SAS has proved to be our trusted partner," said Yuk. "We are satisfied with the comprehensive support provided by the SAS Hong Kong team."

Informed Decisions Develop Smart Strategies

"Using SAS Text Miner, 1823 can quickly discover the correlations among some key words in the complaints," says Yuk. "For instance, we can spot districts with frequent complaints received concerning public health issues such as dead birds found in residential areas. We can then inform relevant government departments and property management companies, so that they can allocate adequate resources to step up cleaning work to avoid spread of potential pandemics.

"The public's views are of course extremely important to the government. By decoding the 'messages' through statistical and root-cause analyses of complaints data, the government can better understand the voice of the people, and help government departments improve service delivery, make informed decisions, and develop smart strategies. This in turn helps boost public satisfaction with the government, and build a quality city," said W. F. Yuk, Assistant Director, Hong Kong Efficiency Unit.

QUESTIONS FOR DISCUSSION

1. How did the Hong Kong government use text mining to better serve its constituents?
2. What were the challenges, the proposed solution, and the obtained results?

Sources: SAS Institute, Customer Success Story, **sas.com/success/pdf/hongkongeu.pdf** (accessed February 2013); and **enterpriseinnovation.net/whitepaper/text-mining-improves-hong-kong-governments-ability-anticipate-and-address-public**.

NLP has successfully been applied to a variety of domains for a variety of tasks via computer programs to automatically process natural human language that previously could only be done by humans. Following are among the most popular of these tasks:

- ***Question answering.*** The task of automatically answering a question posed in natural language; that is, producing a human-language answer when given a human-language question. To find the answer to a question, the computer program may use either a prestructured database or a collection of natural language documents (a text corpus such as the World Wide Web).
- ***Automatic summarization.*** The creation of a shortened version of a textual document by a computer program that contains the most important points of the original document.
- ***Natural language generation.*** Systems convert information from computer databases into readable human language.
- ***Natural language understanding.*** Systems convert samples of human language into more formal representations that are easier for computer programs to manipulate.
- ***Machine translation.*** The automatic translation of one human language to another.
- ***Foreign language reading.*** A computer program that assists a nonnative language speaker to read a foreign language with correct pronunciation and accents on different parts of the words.
- ***Foreign language writing.*** A computer program that assists a nonnative language user in writing in a foreign language.
- ***Speech recognition.*** Converts spoken words to machine-readable input. Given a sound clip of a person speaking, the system produces a text dictation.
- ***Text-to-speech.*** Also called *speech synthesis*, a computer program automatically converts normal language text into human speech.
- ***Text proofing.*** A computer program reads a proof copy of a text in order to detect and correct any errors.
- ***Optical character recognition.*** The automatic translation of images of handwritten, typewritten, or printed text (usually captured by a scanner) into machine-editable textual documents.

The success and popularity of text mining depend greatly on advancements in NLP in both generation as well as understanding of human languages. NLP enables the extraction of features from unstructured text so that a wide variety of data mining techniques can be used to extract knowledge (novel and useful patterns and relationships) from it. In that sense, simply put, text mining is a combination of NLP and data mining.

SECTION 7.3 REVIEW QUESTIONS

1. What is natural language processing?

2. How does NLP relate to text mining?

3. What are some of the benefits and challenges of NLP?

4. What are the most common tasks addressed by NLP?

7.4 TEXT MINING APPLICATIONS

As the amount of unstructured data collected by organizations increases, so does the value proposition and popularity of text mining tools. Many organizations are now realizing the importance of extracting knowledge from their document-based data repositories through the use of text mining tools. Following are only a small subset of the exemplary application categories of text mining.

Marketing Applications

Text mining can be used to increase cross-selling and up-selling by analyzing the unstructured data generated by call centers. Text generated by call center notes as well as transcriptions of voice conversations with customers can be analyzed by text mining algorithms to extract novel, actionable information about customers' perceptions toward a company's products and services. Additionally, blogs, user reviews of products at independent Web sites, and discussion board postings are a gold mine of customer sentiments. This rich collection of information, once properly analyzed, can be used to increase satisfaction and the overall lifetime value of the customer (Coussement and Van den Poel, 2008).

Text mining has become invaluable for customer relationship management. Companies can use text mining to analyze rich sets of unstructured text data, combined with the relevant structured data extracted from organizational databases, to predict customer perceptions and subsequent purchasing behavior. Coussement and Van den Poel (2009) successfully applied text mining to significantly improve the ability of a model to predict customer churn (i.e., customer attrition) so that those customers identified as most likely to leave a company are accurately identified for retention tactics.

Ghani et al. (2006) used text mining to develop a system capable of inferring implicit and explicit attributes of products to enhance retailers' ability to analyze product databases. Treating products as sets of attribute–value pairs rather than as atomic entities can potentially boost the effectiveness of many business applications, including demand forecasting, assortment optimization, product recommendations, assortment comparison across retailers and manufacturers, and product supplier selection. The proposed system allows a business to represent its products in terms of attributes and attribute values without much manual effort. The system learns these attributes by applying supervised and semi-supervised learning techniques to product descriptions found on retailers' Web sites.

Security Applications

One of the largest and most prominent text mining applications in the security domain is probably the highly classified ECHELON surveillance system. As rumor has it, ECHELON is assumed to be capable of identifying the content of telephone calls, faxes, e-mails, and other types of data and intercepting information sent via satellites, public switched telephone networks, and microwave links.

In 2007, EUROPOL developed an integrated system capable of accessing, storing, and analyzing vast amounts of structured and unstructured data sources in order to track transnational organized crime. Called the Overall Analysis System for Intelligence Support (OASIS), this system aims to integrate the most advanced data and text mining technologies available in today's market. The system has enabled EUROPOL to make significant progress in supporting its law enforcement objectives at the international level (EUROPOL, 2007).

The U.S. Federal Bureau of Investigation (FBI) and the Central Intelligence Agency (CIA), under the direction of the Department for Homeland Security, are jointly developing a supercomputer data and text mining system. The system is expected to create a gigantic data warehouse along with a variety of data and text mining modules to meet the knowledge-discovery needs of federal, state, and local law enforcement agencies. Prior to this project, the FBI and CIA each had its own separate databases, with little or no interconnection.

Another security-related application of text mining is in the area of **deception detection**. Applying text mining to a large set of real-world criminal (person-of-interest) statements, Fuller et al. (2008) developed prediction models to differentiate deceptive statements from truthful ones. Using a rich set of cues extracted from the textual statements, the model predicted the holdout samples with 70 percent accuracy, which is believed to be a significant success considering that the cues are extracted only from textual statements (no verbal or visual cues are present). Furthermore, compared to other deception-detection techniques, such as polygraph, this method is nonintrusive and widely applicable to not only textual data, but also (potentially) to transcriptions of voice recordings. A more detailed description of text-based deception detection is provided in Application Case 7.3.

Application Case 7.3

Mining for Lies

Driven by advancements in Web-based information technologies and increasing globalization, computer-mediated communication continues to filter into everyday life, bringing with it new venues for deception. The volume of text-based chat, instant messaging, text messaging, and text generated by online communities of practice is increasing rapidly. Even e-mail continues to grow in use. With the massive growth of text-based communication, the potential for people to deceive others through computer-mediated communication has also grown, and such deception can have disastrous results.

Unfortunately, in general, humans tend to perform poorly at deception-detection tasks. This phenomenon is exacerbated in text-based communications. A large part of the research on deception detection (also known as *credibility assessment*) has involved face-to-face meetings and interviews. Yet, with the growth of text-based communication, text-based deception-detection techniques are essential.

Techniques for successfully detecting deception—that is, lies—have wide applicability. Law enforcement can use decision support tools and techniques to investigate crimes, conduct security screening in airports, and monitor communications of suspected terrorists. Human resources professionals might use deception detection tools to screen applicants. These tools and techniques also have the potential to screen e-mails to uncover fraud or other wrongdoings committed by corporate officers. Although some people believe that they can readily identify those who are not being truthful, a summary of deception research showed that, on average, people are only 54 percent accurate in making veracity determinations (Bond and DePaulo, 2006). This figure may actually be worse when humans try to detect deception in text.

Using a combination of text mining and data mining techniques, Fuller et al. (2008) analyzed person-of-interest statements completed by people involved in crimes on military bases. In these statements, suspects and witnesses are required to write their recollection of the event in their own words. Military law enforcement personnel searched archival data for statements that they could conclusively identify as being truthful or deceptive. These decisions were made on the basis of corroborating evidence and case resolution. Once labeled as truthful or deceptive, the law enforcement personnel removed identifying information and gave the statements to the research team. In total, 371 usable statements were received for analysis. The text-based deception-detection method used by Fuller et al. (2008) was based on a process known as *message feature mining*, which relies on elements of data and text mining techniques. A simplified depiction of the process is provided in Figure 7.3.

First, the researchers prepared the data for processing. The original handwritten statements had to be transcribed into a word processing file. Second, features (i.e., cues) were identified. The researchers identified 31 features representing categories or types of language that are relatively independent of the text content and that can be readily analyzed by automated means. For example, first-person pronouns such as *I* or *me* can be identified without analysis of the surrounding text. Table 7.1 lists the categories and an example list of features used in this study.

The features were extracted from the textual statements and input into a flat file for further processing. Using several feature-selection methods along with *10*-fold cross-validation, the researchers compared the prediction accuracy of three popular data mining methods. Their results indicated that neural network models performed the best, with 73.46 percent prediction accuracy on test data samples; decision trees performed second best, with 71.60 percent accuracy; and logistic regression was last, with 67.28 percent accuracy.

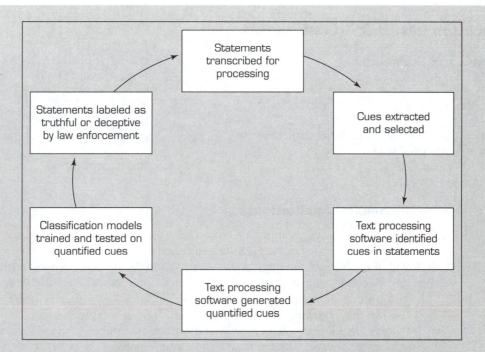

FIGURE 7.3 **Text-Based Deception-Detection Process.** *Source:* C. M. Fuller, D. Biros, and D. Delen, "Exploration of Feature Selection and Advanced Classification Models for High-Stakes Deception Detection," in *Proceedings of the 41st Annual Hawaii International Conference on System Sciences (HICSS),* January 2008, Big Island, HI, IEEE Press, pp. 80–99.

TABLE 7.1 **Categories and Examples of Linguistic Features Used in Deception Detection**

Number	Construct (Category)	Example Cues
1	Quantity	Verb count, noun-phrase count, etc.
2	Complexity	Average number of clauses, average sentence length, etc.
3	Uncertainty	Modifiers, modal verbs, etc.
4	Nonimmediacy	Passive voice, objectification, etc.
5	Expressivity	Emotiveness
6	Diversity	Lexical diversity, redundancy, etc.
7	Informality	Typographical error ratio
8	Specificity	Spatiotemporal information, perceptual information, etc.
9	Affect	Positive affect, negative affect, etc.

The results indicate that automated text-based deception detection has the potential to aid those who must try to detect lies in text and can be successfully applied to real-world data. The accuracy of these techniques exceeded the accuracy of most other deception-detection techniques even though it was limited to textual cues.

(Continued)

Application Case 7.3 (Continued)

QUESTIONS FOR DISCUSSION

1. Why is it difficult to detect deception?
2. How can text/data mining be used to detect deception in text?
3. What do you think are the main challenges for such an automated system?

Sources: C. M. Fuller, D. Biros, and D. Delen, "Exploration of Feature Selection and Advanced Classification Models for High-Stakes Deception Detection," in *Proceedings of the 41st Annual Hawaii International Conference on System Sciences (HICSS)*, 2008, Big Island, HI, IEEE Press, pp. 80–99; C. F. Bond and B. M. DePaulo, "Accuracy of Deception Judgments," *Personality and Social Psychology Reports*, Vol. 10, No. 3, 2006, pp. 214–234.

Biomedical Applications

Text mining holds great potential for the medical field in general and biomedicine in particular for several reasons. First, the published literature and publication outlets (especially with the advent of the open source journals) in the field are expanding at an exponential rate. Second, compared to most other fields, the medical literature is more standardized and orderly, making it a more "minable" information source. Finally, the terminology used in this literature is relatively constant, having a fairly standardized ontology. What follows are a few exemplary studies where text mining techniques were successfully used in extracting novel patterns from biomedical literature.

Experimental techniques such as DNA microarray analysis, serial analysis of gene expression (SAGE), and mass spectrometry proteomics, among others, are generating large amounts of data related to genes and proteins. As in any other experimental approach, it is necessary to analyze this vast amount of data in the context of previously known information about the biological entities under study. The literature is a particularly valuable source of information for experiment validation and interpretation. Therefore, the development of automated text mining tools to assist in such interpretation is one of the main challenges in current bioinformatics research.

Knowing the location of a protein within a cell can help to elucidate its role in biological processes and to determine its potential as a drug target. Numerous location-prediction systems are described in the literature; some focus on specific organisms, whereas others attempt to analyze a wide range of organisms. Shatkay et al. (2007) proposed a comprehensive system that uses several types of sequence- and text-based features to predict the location of proteins. The main novelty of their system lies in the way in which it selects its text sources and features and integrates them with sequence-based features. They tested the system on previously used data sets and on new data sets devised specifically to test its predictive power. The results showed that their system consistently beat previously reported results.

Chun et al. (2006) described a system that extracts disease–gene relationships from literature accessed via MedLine. They constructed a dictionary for disease and gene names from six public databases and extracted relation candidates by dictionary matching. Because dictionary matching produces a large number of false positives, they developed a method of machine learning–based named entity recognition (NER) to filter out false recognitions of disease/gene names. They found that the success of relation extraction is heavily dependent on the performance of NER filtering and that the filtering improved the precision of relation extraction by 26.7 percent, at the cost of a small reduction in recall.

Figure 7.4 shows a simplified depiction of a multilevel text analysis process for discovering gene–protein relationships (or protein–protein interactions) in the biomedical literature (Nakov et al., 2005). As can be seen in this simplified example that uses a simple sentence from biomedical text, first (at the bottom three levels) the text is tokenized

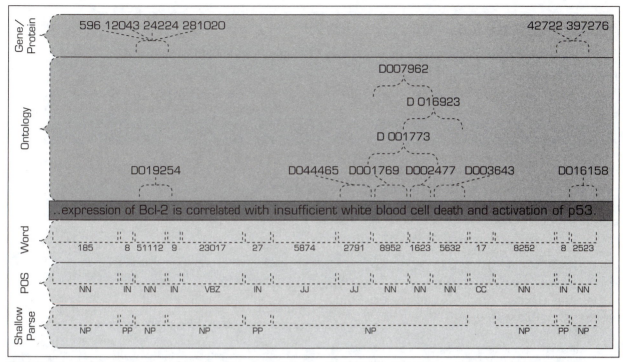

FIGURE 7.4 **Multilevel Analysis of Text for Gene/Protein Interaction Identification.** *Source:* P. Nakov, A. Schwartz, B. Wolf, and M. A. Hearst, "Supporting Annotation Layers for Natural Language Processing," *Proceedings of the Association for Computational Linguistics (ACL),* interactive poster and demonstration sessions, 2005, Ann Arbor, MI, Association for Computational Linguistics, pp. 65–68.

using **part-of-speech tagging** and shallow-parsing. The tokenized terms (words) are then matched (and interpreted) against the hierarchical representation of the domain ontology to derive the gene–protein relationship. Application of this method (and/or some variation of it) to the biomedical literature offers great potential to decode the complexities in the Human Genome Project.

Academic Applications

The issue of text mining is of great importance to publishers who hold large databases of information requiring indexing for better retrieval. This is particularly true in scientific disciplines, in which highly specific information is often contained within written text. Initiatives have been launched, such as *Nature*'s proposal for an Open Text Mining Interface (OTMI) and the National Institutes of Health's common Journal Publishing Document Type Definition (DTD), which would provide semantic cues to machines to answer specific queries contained within text without removing publisher barriers to public access.

Academic institutions have also launched text mining initiatives. For example, the National Centre for Text Mining, a collaborative effort between the Universities of Manchester and Liverpool, provides customized tools, research facilities, and advice on text mining to the academic community. With an initial focus on text mining in the biological and biomedical sciences, research has since expanded into the social sciences. In the United States, the School of Information at the University of California, Berkeley, is developing a program called BioText to assist bioscience researchers in text mining and analysis.

As described in this section, text mining has a wide variety of applications in a number of different disciplines. See Application Case 7.4 for an example of how a financial services firm is using text mining to improve its customer service performance.

Application Case 7.4

Text Mining and Sentiment Analysis Help Improve Customer Service Performance

The company is a financial services firm that provides a broad range of solutions and services to a global customer base. The company has a comprehensive network of facilities around the world, with over 5000 associates assisting their customers. Customers lodge service requests by telephone, email, or through an online chat interface.

As a B2C service provider, the company strives to maintain high standards for effective communication between their associates and customers, and tries to monitor customer interactions at every opportunity. The broad objective of this service performance monitoring is to maintain satisfactory quality of service over time and across the organization. To this end, the company has devised a set of standards for service excellence, to which all customer interactions are expected to adhere. These standards comprise different qualitative measures of service levels (e.g., associates should use clear and understandable language, associates should always maintain a professional and friendly demeanor, etc.) Associates' performances are measured based on compliance with these quality standards. Organizational units at different levels, like teams, departments, and the company as a whole, also receive scores based on associate performances. The evaluations and remunerations of not only the associates but also of management are influenced by these service performance scores.

Challenge

Continually monitoring service levels is essential for service quality control. Customer surveys are an excellent way of gathering feedback about service levels. An even richer source of information is the corpus of associate-customer interactions. Historically the company manually evaluated a sample of associate-customer interactions and survey responses for compliance with excellence standards. This approach, in addition to being subjective and error-prone, was time- and labor-intensive. Advances in machine learning and computational linguistics offer an opportunity to objectively evaluate all customer interactions in a timely manner.

The company needs a system for (1) automatically evaluating associate-customer interactions for compliance with quality standards and (2) analyzing survey responses to extract positive and negative feedback. The analysis must be able to account for the wide diversity of expression in natural language (e.g., pleasant and reassuring tone, acceptable language, appropriate abbreviations, addressing all of the customers' issues, etc.).

Solution

PolyAnalyst 6.5™ by Megaputer Intelligence is a data mining and analysis platform that provides a comprehensive set of tools for analyzing structured and unstructured data. PolyAnalyst's text analysis tools are used for extracting complex word patterns, grammatical and semantic relationships, and expressions of sentiment. The results of these text analyses are then classified into context-specific themes to identify actionable issues, which can be assigned to relevant individuals responsible for their resolution. The system can be programmed to provide feedback in case of insufficient classification so that analyses can be modified or amended. The relationships between structured fields and text analysis results are also established in order to identify patterns and interactions. The system publishes the results of analyses through graphical, interactive, web-based reports. Users create analysis scenarios using a drag-and-drop graphical user interface (GUI). These scenarios are reusable solutions that can be programmed to automate the analysis and report generation process.

A set of specific criteria were designed to capture and automatically detect compliance with the company's Quality Standards. The figure below displays an example of an associate's response, as well as the quality criteria that it succeeds or fails to match.

As illustrated above, this comment matches several criteria while failing to match one, and contributes accordingly to the associate's performance score. These scores are then automatically calculated and aggregated across various organizational units. It is relatively easy to modify the system in case of changes in quality standards, and the changes can be quickly applied to historical data. The system also has an integrated case management system, which generates email alerts in case of

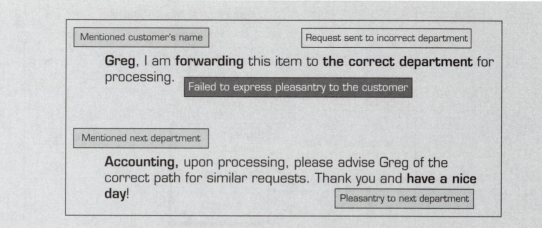

drops in service quality and allows users to track the progress of issue resolution.

Tangible Results

1. Completely automated analysis; saves time.
2. Analysis of entire dataset (> 1 million records per year); no need for sampling.
3. 45% cost savings over traditional analysis.
4. Weekly processing. In the case of traditional analysis, data could only be processed monthly due to time and resource constraints.
5. Analysis not subjective to the analyst.
   a. Increased accuracy.
   b. Increased uniformity.
6. Greater accountability. Associates can review the analysis and raise concerns in case of discrepancies.

Future Directions

Currently the corpus of associate-customer interactions does not include transcripts of phone conversations. By incorporating speech recognition capability, the system can become a one-stop destination for analyzing all customer interactions. The system could also potentially be used in real-time, instead of periodic analyses.

QUESTIONS FOR DISCUSSION

1. How did the financial services firm use text mining and text analytics to improve its customer service performance?
2. What were the challenges, the proposed solution, and the obtained results?

Source: Megaputer, Customer Success Story, megaputer.com (accessed September 2013).

SECTION 7.4 REVIEW QUESTIONS

1. List and briefly discuss some of the text mining applications in marketing.
2. How can text mining be used in security and counterterrorism?
3. What are some promising text mining applications in biomedicine?

7.5 TEXT MINING PROCESS

In order to be successful, text mining studies should follow a sound methodology based on best practices. A standardized process model is needed similar to CRISP-DM, which is the industry standard for data mining projects (see Chapter 5). Even though most parts of CRISP-DM are also applicable to text mining projects, a specific process model for text mining would include much more elaborate data preprocessing activities. Figure 7.5 depicts a high-level context diagram of a typical text mining process (Delen and Crossland, 2008). This context diagram presents the scope of the process, emphasizing its interfaces with the larger environment. In essence, it draws boundaries around the specific process to explicitly identify what is included in (and excluded from) the text mining process.

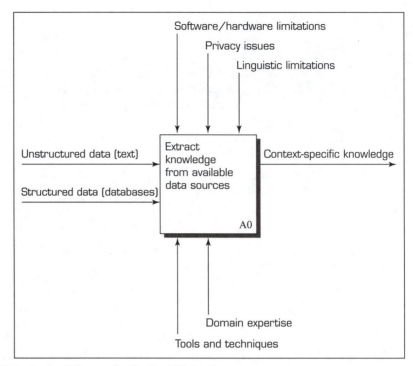

FIGURE 7.5 Context Diagram for the Text Mining Process.

As the context diagram indicates, the input (inward connection to the left edge of the box) into the text-based knowledge-discovery process is the unstructured as well as structured data collected, stored, and made available to the process. The output (outward extension from the right edge of the box) of the process is the context-specific knowledge that can be used for decision making. The controls, also called the *constraints* (inward connection to the top edge of the box), of the process include software and hardware limitations, privacy issues, and the difficulties related to processing the text that is presented in the form of natural language. The mechanisms (inward connection to the bottom edge of the box) of the process include proper techniques, software tools, and domain expertise. The primary purpose of text mining (within the context of knowledge discovery) is to process unstructured (textual) data (along with structured data, if relevant to the problem being addressed and available) to extract meaningful and actionable patterns for better decision making.

At a very high level, the text mining process can be broken down into three consecutive tasks, each of which has specific inputs to generate certain outputs (see Figure 7.6). If, for some reason, the output of a task is not what is expected, a backward redirection to the previous task execution is necessary.

Task 1: Establish the Corpus

The main purpose of the first task activity is to collect all of the documents related to the context (domain of interest) being studied. This collection may include textual documents, XML files, e-mails, Web pages, and short notes. In addition to the readily available textual data, voice recordings may also be transcribed using speech-recognition algorithms and made a part of the text collection.

Once collected, the text documents are transformed and organized in a manner such that they are all in the same representational form (e.g., ASCII text files) for computer processing. The organization of the documents can be as simple as a collection of digitized text excerpts stored in a file folder or it can be a list of links to a collection of Web pages in a specific domain. Many commercially available text mining software tools

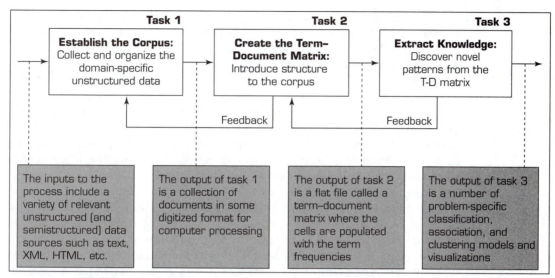

FIGURE 7.6 The Three-Step Text Mining Process.

could accept these as input and convert them into a flat file for processing. Alternatively, the flat file can be prepared outside the text mining software and then presented as the input to the text mining application.

Task 2: Create the Term–Document Matrix

In this task, the digitized and organized documents (the corpus) are used to create the **term–document matrix (TDM)**. In the TDM, rows represent the documents and columns represent the terms. The relationships between the terms and documents are characterized by indices (i.e., a relational measure that can be as simple as the number of occurrences of the term in respective documents). Figure 7.7 is a typical example of a TDM.

Documents \ Terms	Investment Risk	Project Management	Software Engineering	Development	SAP	. . .
Document 1	1			1		
Document 2		1				
Document 3			3		1	
Document 4		1				
Document 5			2	1		
Document 6	1			1		
. . .						

FIGURE 7.7 A Simple Term–Document Matrix.

The goal is to convert the list of organized documents (the corpus) into a TDM where the cells are filled with the most appropriate indices. The assumption is that the essence of a document can be represented with a list and frequency of the terms used in that document. However, are all terms important when characterizing documents? Obviously, the answer is "no." Some terms, such as articles, auxiliary verbs, and terms used in almost all of the documents in the corpus, have no differentiating power and therefore should be excluded from the indexing process. This list of terms, commonly called *stop terms* or *stop words,* is specific to the domain of study and should be identified by the domain experts. On the other hand, one might choose a set of predetermined terms under which the documents are to be indexed (this list of terms is conveniently called *include terms* or *dictionary*). Additionally, synonyms (pairs of terms that are to be treated the same) and specific phrases (e.g., "Eiffel Tower") can also be provided so that the index entries are more accurate.

Another filtration that should take place to accurately create the indices is *stemming*, which refers to the reduction of words to their roots so that, for example, different grammatical forms or declarations of a verb are identified and indexed as the same word. For example, stemming will ensure that *modeling* and *modeled* will be recognized as the word *model.*

The first generation of the TDM includes all of the unique terms identified in the corpus (as its columns), excluding the ones in the stop term list; all of the documents (as its rows); and the occurrence count of each term for each document (as its cell values). If, as is commonly the case, the corpus includes a rather large number of documents, then there is a very good chance that the TDM will have a very large number of terms. Processing such a large matrix might be time-consuming and, more importantly, might lead to extraction of inaccurate patterns. At this point, one has to decide the following: (1) What is the best representation of the indices? and (2) How can we reduce the dimensionality of this matrix to a manageable size?

REPRESENTING THE INDICES   Once the input documents are indexed and the initial word frequencies (by document) computed, a number of additional transformations can be performed to summarize and aggregate the extracted information. The raw term frequencies generally reflect on how salient or important a word is in each document. Specifically, words that occur with greater frequency in a document are better descriptors of the contents of that document. However, it is not reasonable to assume that the word counts themselves are proportional to their importance as descriptors of the documents. For example, if a word occurs one time in document *A*, but three times in document *B*, then it is not necessarily reasonable to conclude that this word is three times as important a descriptor of document *B* as compared to document *A*. In order to have a more consistent TDM for further analysis, these raw indices need to be normalized. As opposed to showing the actual frequency counts, the numerical representation between terms and documents can be normalized using a number of alternative methods. The following are a few of the most commonly used normalization methods (StatSoft, 2009):

- *Log frequencies.*   The raw frequencies can be transformed using the log function. This transformation would "dampen" the raw frequencies and how they affect the results of subsequent analysis.

$$f(wf) = 1 + \log(wf) \quad \text{for} \quad wf > 0$$

In the formula, *wf* is the raw word (or term) frequency and $f(wf)$ is the result of the log transformation. This transformation is applied to all of the raw frequencies in the TDM where the frequency is greater than zero.

- *Binary frequencies.*   Likewise, an even simpler transformation can be used to enumerate whether a term is used in a document.

$$f(wf) = 1 \quad \text{for} \quad wf > 0$$

The resulting TDM matrix will contain only 1s and 0s to indicate the presence or absence of the respective words. Again, this transformation will dampen the effect of the raw frequency counts on subsequent computations and analyses.

- ***Inverse document frequencies.*** Another issue that one may want to consider more carefully and reflect in the indices used in further analyses is the relative document frequencies (*df*) of different terms. For example, a term such as *guess* may occur frequently in all documents, whereas another term, such as *software,* may appear only a few times. The reason is that one might make *guesses* in various contexts, regardless of the specific topic, whereas *software* is a more semantically focused term that is only likely to occur in documents that deal with computer software. A common and very useful transformation that reflects both the specificity of words (document frequencies) as well as the overall frequencies of their occurrences (term frequencies) is the so-called **inverse document frequency** (Manning and Schutze, 2009). This transformation for the *i*th word and *j*th document can be written as:

$$idf(i, j) = \begin{cases} 0 & \text{if } wf_{ij} = 0 \\ (1 + \log(wf_{ij}))\log\dfrac{N}{df_i} & \text{if } wf_{ij} \geq 1 \end{cases}$$

In this formula, N is the total number of documents, and df_i is the document frequency for the *i*th word (the number of documents that include this word). Hence, it can be seen that this formula includes both the dampening of the simple-word frequencies via the log function (described here) and a weighting factor that evaluates to 0 if the word occurs in all documents [i.e., $\log(N/N = 1) = 0$], and to the maximum value when a word only occurs in a single document [i.e., $\log(N/1) = \log(N)$]. It can easily be seen how this transformation will create indices that reflect both the relative frequencies of occurrences of words as well as their semantic specificities over the documents included in the analysis. This is the most commonly used transformation in the field.

REDUCING THE DIMENSIONALITY OF THE MATRIX Because the TDM is often very large and rather sparse (most of the cells filled with zeros), another important question is "How do we reduce the dimensionality of this matrix to a manageable size?" Several options are available for managing the matrix size:

- A domain expert goes through the list of terms and eliminates those that do not make much sense for the context of the study (this is a manual, labor-intensive process).
- Eliminate terms with very few occurrences in very few documents.
- Transform the matrix using singular value decomposition.

Singular value decomposition (SVD), which is closely related to principal components analysis, reduces the overall dimensionality of the input matrix (number of input documents by number of extracted terms) to a lower dimensional space, where each consecutive dimension represents the largest degree of variability (between words and documents) possible (Manning and Schutze, 1999). Ideally, the analyst might identify the two or three most salient dimensions that account for most of the variability (differences) between the words and documents, thus identifying the latent semantic space that organizes the words and documents in the analysis. Once such dimensions are identified, the underlying "meaning" of what is contained (discussed or described) in the documents has been extracted. Specifically, assume that matrix A represents an $m \times n$ term occurrence matrix where m is the number of input documents and n is the number of terms selected for analysis. The SVD computes the $m \times r$ orthogonal matrix U, $n \times r$ orthogonal matrix V, and $r \times r$ matrix D, so that $A = UDV'$ and r is the number of eigen values of $A'A$.

Task 3: Extract the Knowledge

Using the well-structured TDM, and potentially augmented with other structured data elements, novel patterns are extracted in the context of the specific problem being addressed. The main categories of knowledge extraction methods are classification, clustering, association, and trend analysis. A short description of these methods follows.

CLASSIFICATION Arguably the most common knowledge-discovery topic in analyzing complex data sources is the **classification** (or categorization) of certain objects. The task is to classify a given data instance into a predetermined set of categories (or classes). As it applies to the domain of text mining, the task is known as *text categorization,* where for a given set of categories (subjects, topics, or concepts) and a collection of text documents the goal is to find the correct topic (subject or concept) for each document using models developed with a training data set that includes both the documents and actual document categories. Today, automated text classification is applied in a variety of contexts, including automatic or semiautomatic (interactive) indexing of text, spam filtering, Web page categorization under hierarchical catalogs, automatic generation of metadata, detection of genre, and many others.

The two main approaches to text classification are knowledge engineering and machine learning (Feldman and Sanger, 2007). With the knowledge-engineering approach, an expert's knowledge about the categories is encoded into the system either declaratively or in the form of procedural classification rules. With the machine-learning approach, a general inductive process builds a classifier by learning from a set of reclassified examples. As the number of documents increases at an exponential rate and as knowledge experts become harder to come by, the popularity trend between the two is shifting toward the machine-learning approach.

CLUSTERING **Clustering** is an unsupervised process whereby objects are classified into "natural" groups called *clusters.* Compared to categorization, where a collection of preclassified training examples is used to develop a model based on the descriptive features of the classes in order to classify a new unlabeled example, in clustering the problem is to group an unlabelled collection of objects (e.g., documents, customer comments, Web pages) into meaningful clusters without any prior knowledge.

Clustering is useful in a wide range of applications, from document retrieval to enabling better Web content searches. In fact, one of the prominent applications of clustering is the analysis and navigation of very large text collections, such as Web pages. The basic underlying assumption is that relevant documents tend to be more similar to each other than to irrelevant ones. If this assumption holds, the clustering of documents based on the similarity of their content improves search effectiveness (Feldman and Sanger, 2007):

- *Improved search recall.* Clustering, because it is based on overall similarity as opposed to the presence of a single term, can improve the recall of a query-based search in such a way that when a query matches a document its whole cluster is returned.
- *Improved search precision.* Clustering can also improve search precision. As the number of documents in a collection grows, it becomes difficult to browse through the list of matched documents. Clustering can help by grouping the documents into a number of much smaller groups of related documents, ordering them by relevance, and returning only the documents from the most relevant group (or groups).

The two most popular clustering methods are scatter/gather clustering and query-specific clustering:

- ***Scatter/gather.*** This document browsing method uses clustering to enhance the efficiency of human browsing of documents when a specific search query cannot be formulated. In a sense, the method dynamically generates a table of contents for the collection and adapts and modifies it in response to the user selection.
- ***Query-specific clustering.*** This method employs a hierarchical clustering approach where the most relevant documents to the posed query appear in small tight clusters that are nested in larger clusters containing less similar documents, creating a spectrum of relevance levels among the documents. This method performs consistently well for document collections of realistically large sizes.

ASSOCIATION A formal definition and detailed description of **association** was provided in the chapter on data mining (Chapter 5). Associations, or *association rule learning in data mining,* is a popular and well-researched technique for discovering interesting relationships among variables in large databases. The main idea in generating association rules (or solving market-basket problems) is to identify the frequent sets that go together.

In text mining, associations specifically refer to the direct relationships between concepts (terms) or sets of concepts. The concept set association rule $A \Rightarrow B$, relating two frequent concept sets A and C, can be quantified by the two basic measures of support and confidence. In this case, confidence is the percentage of documents that include all the concepts in C within the same subset of those documents that include all the concepts in A. Support is the percentage (or number) of documents that include all the concepts in A and C. For instance, in a document collection the concept "Software Implementation Failure" may appear most often in association with "Enterprise Resource Planning" and "Customer Relationship Management" with significant support (4%) and confidence (55%), meaning that 4 percent of the documents had all three concepts represented together in the same document and of the documents that included "Software Implementation Failure," 55 percent of them also included "Enterprise Resource Planning" and "Customer Relationship Management."

Text mining with association rules was used to analyze published literature (news and academic articles posted on the Web) to chart the outbreak and progress of bird flu (Mahgoub et al., 2008). The idea was to automatically identify the association among the geographic areas, spreading across species, and countermeasures (treatments).

TREND ANALYSIS Recent methods of trend analysis in text mining have been based on the notion that the various types of concept distributions are functions of document collections; that is, different collections lead to different concept distributions for the same set of concepts. It is therefore possible to compare two distributions that are otherwise identical except that they are from different subcollections. One notable direction of this type of analyses is having two collections from the same source (such as from the same set of academic journals) but from different points in time. Delen and Crossland (2008) applied **trend analysis** to a large number of academic articles (published in the three highest-rated academic journals) to identify the evolution of key concepts in the field of information systems.

As described in this section, a number of methods are available for text mining. Application Case 7.5 describes the use of a number of different techniques in analyzing a large set of literature.

Application Case 7.5

Research Literature Survey with Text Mining

Researchers conducting searches and reviews of relevant literature face an increasingly complex and voluminous task. In extending the body of relevant knowledge, it has always been important to work hard to gather, organize, analyze, and assimilate existing information from the literature, particularly from one's home discipline. With the increasing abundance of potentially significant research being reported in related fields, and even in what are traditionally deemed to be nonrelated fields of study, the researcher's task is ever more daunting, if a thorough job is desired.

In new streams of research, the researcher's task may be even more tedious and complex. Trying to ferret out relevant work that others have reported may be difficult, at best, and perhaps even near impossible if traditional, largely manual reviews of published literature are required. Even with a legion of dedicated graduate students or helpful colleagues, trying to cover all potentially relevant published work is problematic.

Many scholarly conferences take place every year. In addition to extending the body of knowledge of the current focus of a conference, organizers often desire to offer additional mini-tracks and workshops. In many cases, these additional events are intended to introduce the attendees to significant streams of research in related fields of study and to try to identify the "next big thing" in terms of research interests and focus. Identifying reasonable candidate topics for such mini-tracks and workshops is often subjective rather than derived objectively from the existing and emerging research.

In a recent study, Delen and Crossland (2008) proposed a method to greatly assist and enhance the efforts of the researchers by enabling a semi-automated analysis of large volumes of published literature through the application of text mining. Using standard digital libraries and online publication search engines, the authors downloaded and collected all of the available articles for the three major journals in the field of management information systems: *MIS Quarterly* (MISQ), *Information Systems Research* (ISR), and the *Journal of Management Information Systems* (JMIS). In order to maintain the same time interval for all three journals (for potential comparative longitudinal studies), the journal with the most recent starting date for its digital publication availability was used as the start time for this study (i.e., JMIS articles have been digitally available since 1994). For each article, they extracted the title, abstract, author list, published keywords, volume, issue number, and year of publication. They then loaded all of the article data into a simple database file. Also included in the combined data set was a field that designated the journal type of each article for likely discriminatory analysis. Editorial notes, research notes, and executive overviews were omitted from the collection. Table 7.2 shows how the data was presented in a tabular format.

In the analysis phase, they chose to use only the abstract of an article as the source of information extraction. They chose not to include the keywords listed with the publications for two main reasons: (1) under normal circumstances, the abstract would already include the listed keywords, and therefore inclusion of the listed keywords for the analysis would mean repeating the same information and potentially giving them unmerited weight; and (2) the listed keywords may be terms that authors would like their article to be associated with (as opposed to what is really contained in the article), therefore potentially introducing unquantifiable bias to the analysis of the content.

The first exploratory study was to look at the longitudinal perspective of the three journals (i.e., evolution of research topics over time). In order to conduct a longitudinal study, they divided the 12-year period (from 1994 to 2005) into four 3-year periods for each of the three journals. This framework led to 12 text mining experiments with 12 mutually exclusive data sets. At this point, for each of the 12 data sets they used text mining to extract the most descriptive terms from these collections of articles represented by their abstracts. The results were tabulated and examined for time-varying changes in the terms published in these three journals.

As a second exploration, using the complete data set (including all three journals and all four

TABLE 7.2 Tabular Representation of the Fields Included in the Combined Data Set

Journal	Year	Author(s)	Title	Vol/No	Pages	Keywords	Abstract
MISQ	2005	A. Malhotra, S. Gossain, and O. A. El Sawy	Absorptive capacity configurations in supply chains: Gearing for partner-enabled market knowledge creation	29/1	145–187	knowledge management supply chain absorptive capacity interorganizational information systems configuration approaches	The need for continual value innovation is driving supply chains to evolve from a pure transactional focus to leveraging interorganization partnerships for sharing
ISR	1999	D. Robey and M. C. Boudtreau	Accounting for the contradictory organizational consequences of information technology: Theoretical directions and methodological implications		165–185	organizational transformation impacts of technology organization theory research methodology intraorganizational power electronic communication misimplementation culture systems	Although much contemporary thought considers advanced information technologies as either determinants or enablers of radical organizational change, empirical studies have revealed inconsistent findings to support the deterministic logic implicit in such arguments. This paper reviews the contradictory…
JMIS	2001	R. Aron and E. K. Clemons	Achieving the optimal balance between investment in quality and investment in self-promotion for information products		65–88	information products Internet advertising product positioning signaling signaling games	When producers of goods (or services) are confronted by a situation in which their offerings no longer perfectly match consumer preferences, they must determine the extent to which the advertised features of…

(Continued)

Application Case 7.5 (Continued)

periods), they conducted a clustering analysis. Clustering is arguably the most commonly used text mining technique. Clustering was used in this study to identify the natural groupings of the articles (by putting them into separate clusters) and then to list the most descriptive terms that characterized those clusters. They used singular value decomposition to reduce the dimensionality of the term-by-document matrix and then an expectation-maximization algorithm to create the clusters. They conducted several experiments to identify the *optimal* number of clusters, which turned out to be nine. After the construction of the nine clusters, they analyzed the content of those clusters from two perspectives: (1) representation of the journal type (see Figure 7.8) and (2) representation of time. The idea was to explore the potential differences and/or commonalities among the three

journals and potential changes in the emphasis on those clusters; that is, to answer questions such as "Are there clusters that represent different research themes specific to a single journal?" and "Is there a time-varying characterization of those clusters?" They discovered and discussed several interesting patterns using tabular and graphical representation of their findings (for further information see Delen and Crossland, 2008).

QUESTIONS FOR DISCUSSION

1. How can text mining be used to ease the task of literature review?

2. What are the common outcomes of a text mining project on a specific collection of journal articles? Can you think of other potential outcomes not mentioned in this case?

FIGURE 7.8 **Distribution of the Number of Articles for the Three Journals over the Nine Clusters.** *Source:* D. Delen and M. Crossland, "Seeding the Survey and Analysis of Research Literature with Text Mining," *Expert Systems with Applications,* Vol. 34, No. 3, 2008, pp. 1707–1720.

SECTION 7.5 REVIEW QUESTIONS

1. What are the main steps in the text mining process?
2. What is the reason for normalizing word frequencies? What are the common methods for normalizing word frequencies?
3. What is singular value decomposition? How is it used in text mining?
4. What are the main knowledge extraction methods from corpus?

7.6 TEXT MINING TOOLS

As the value of text mining is being realized by more and more organizations, the number of software tools offered by software companies and nonprofits is also increasing. Following are some of the popular text mining tools, which we classify as commercial software tools and free (and/or open source) software tools.

Commercial Software Tools

The following are some of the most popular software tools used for text mining. Note that many companies offer demonstration versions of their products on their Web sites.

1. ClearForest offers text analysis and visualization tools.
2. IBM offers SPSS Modeler and data and text analytics toolkits.
3. Megaputer Text Analyst offers semantic analysis of free-form text, summarization, clustering, navigation, and natural language retrieval with search dynamic refocusing.
4. SAS Text Miner provides a rich suite of text processing and analysis tools.
5. KXEN Text Coder (KTC) offers a text analytics solution for automatically preparing and transforming unstructured text attributes into a structured representation for use in KXEN Analytic Framework.
6. The Statistica Text Mining engine provides easy-to-use text mining functionality with exceptional visualization capabilities.
7. VantagePoint provides a variety of interactive graphical views and analysis tools with powerful capabilities to discover knowledge from text databases.
8. The WordStat analysis module from Provalis Research analyzes textual information such as responses to open-ended questions, interviews, etc.
9. Clarabridge text mining software provides end-to-end solutions for customer experience professionals wishing to transform customer feedback for marketing, service, and product improvements.

Free Software Tools

Free software tools, some of which are open source, are available from a number of nonprofit organizations:

1. RapidMiner, one of the most popular free, open source software tools for data mining and text mining, is tailored with a graphically appealing, drag-and-drop user interface.
2. Open Calais is an open source toolkit for including semantic functionality within your blog, content management system, Web site, or application.
3. GATE is a leading open source toolkit for text mining. It has a free open source framework (or SDK) and graphical development environment.
4. LingPipe is a suite of Java libraries for the linguistic analysis of human language.
5. S-EM (Spy-EM) is a text classification system that learns from positive and unlabeled examples.
6. Vivisimo/Clusty is a Web search and text-clustering engine.

Often, innovative application of text mining comes from the collective use of several software tools. Application Case 7.6 illustrates a few customer case study synopses where text mining and advanced analytics are used to address a variety of business challenges.

Application Case 7.6

A Potpourri of Text Mining Case Synopses

1. Alberta's Parks Division gains insight from unstructured data

Business Issue:

Alberta's Parks Division was relying on manual processes to respond to stakeholders, which was time-consuming and made it difficult to glean insight from unstructured data sources.

Solution:

Using SAS Text Miner, the Parks Division is able to reduce a three-week process down to a couple of days, and discover new insights in a matter of minutes.

Benefits:

The solution has not only automated manual tasks, but also provides insight into both structured and unstructured data sources that was previously not possible.

"We now have opportunities to channel customer communications into products and services that meet their needs. Having the analytics will enable us to better support changes in program delivery," said Roy Finzel, Manager of Business Integration and Analysis, Alberta Tourism, Parks and Recreation.

For more details, please go to http://www.sas.com/success/alberta-parks2012.html

2. American Honda Saves Millions by Using Text and Data Mining

Business Issue:

One of the most admired and recognized automobile brands in the United States, American Honda wanted to detect and contain warranty and call center issues before they become widespread.

Solution:

SAS Text Miner helps American Honda spot patterns in a wide range of data and text to pinpoint problems early, ensuring safety, quality, and customer satisfaction.

Benefits:

"SAS is helping us make discoveries so that we can address the core issues before they ever become problems—and we can make sure that we are addressing the right causes. We're talking about hundreds of millions of dollars in savings," said Tracy Cermack, Project Manager in the Service Engineering Information Department, American Honda Motor Co.

For more details, please go to http://www.sas.com/success/honda.html

3. MaspexWadowice Group Analyzes Online Brand Image with Text Mining

Business Issue:

MaspexWadowice Group, a dominant player among food and beverage manufacturers in Central and Eastern Europe, wanted to analyze social media channels to monitor a product's brand image and see how it compares with its general perception in the market.

Solution:

MaspexWadowice Group choose to use SAS Text Miner, which is a part of the SAS Business Analytics capabilities, to tap into social media data sorces.

Benefits:

Maspex gained a competitive advantage through better consumer insights, resulting in more effective and efficient marketing efforts.

"This will allow us to plan and implement our marketing and communications activities more effectively, in particular those using a Web-based channel," said Marcin Lesniak, Research Manager, MaspexWadowice Group.

For more details, please go to http://www.sas.com/success/maspex-wadowice.html

4. Viseca Card Services Reduces Fraud Loss with Text Analytics

Business Issue:

Switzerland's largest credit card company aimed to prevent losses by detecting and preventing fraud on Viseca Card Services' 1 million credit cards and more than 100,000 daily transactions.

Solution:

They choose to use a suite of analytics tools from SAS including SAS® Enterprise Miner™, SAS® Enterprise Guide®, SAS Text Miner, and SAS BI Server.

Benefits:

Eighty-one percent of all fraud cases are found within a day, and total fraud loss has been reduced by 15 percent. Even as the number of fraud cases across the industry has doubled, Viseca Card Services has reduced loss per fraud case by 40 percent.

"Thanks to SAS Analytics our total fraud loss has been reduced by 15 percent. We have one of the best fraud prevention ratings in Switzerland and our business case for fraud prevention is straightforward: Our returns are simply more than our investment," said Marcel Bieler, Business Analyst, Viseca Card Services.

For more details, please go to http://www.sas. com/success/Visecacardsvcs.html

5. Improving Quality with Text Mining and Advanced Analytics

Business Issue:

Whirlpool Corp., the world's leading manufacturer and marketer of major home appliances, wanted to reduce service calls by finding defects through warranty analysis and correcting them quickly.

Solution:

SAS Warranty Analysis and early-warning tools on the SAS Enterprise BI Server distill and analyze warranty claims data to quickly detect product issues. The tools used in this project included SAS Enterprise BI Server, SAS Warranty Analysis, SAS Enterprise Guide, and SAS Text Miner.

Benefits:

Whirlpool Corp. aims to cut overall cost of quality, and SAS is playing a significant part in that objective. Expectations of the SAS Warranty Analysis solution include a significant reduction in Whirlpool's issue detection-to-correction cycle, a three-month decrease in initial issue detection, and a potential to cut overall warranty expenditures with significant quality, productivity and efficiency gains.

"SAS brings a level of analytics to business intelligence that no one else matches," said John Kerr, General Manager of Quality and Operational Excellence, Whirlpool Corp.

For more details, please go to http://www.sas. com/success/whirlpool.html

QUESTIONS FOR DISCUSSION

1. What do you think are the common characteristics of the kind of challenges these five companies were facing?
2. What are the types of solution methods and tools proposed in these case synopses?
3. What do you think are the key benefits of using text mining and advanced analytics (compared to the traditional way to do the same)?

Sources: SAS, **www.sas.com/success/** (accessed September 2013).

SECTION 7.6 REVIEW QUESTIONS

1. What are some of the most popular text mining software tools?
2. Why do you think most of the text mining tools are offered by statistics companies?
3. What do you think are the pros and cons of choosing a free text mining tool over a commercial tool?

7.7 SENTIMENT ANALYSIS OVERVIEW

We, humans, are social beings. We are adept at utilizing a variety of means to communicate. We often consult financial discussion forums before making an investment decision; ask our friends for their opinions on a newly opened restaurant or a newly released movie; and conduct Internet searches and read consumer reviews and expert reports before making a big purchase like a house, a car, or an appliance. We rely on others' opinions to make better decisions, especially in an area where we don't have a lot of knowledge or experience. Thanks to the growing availability and popularity of opinion-rich Internet resources such as social media outlets (e.g., Twitter, Facebook, etc.), online review sites, and personal blogs, it is now easier than ever to find opinions of others (thousands of them, as a matter of fact) on everything from the latest gadgets to political and public figures. Even though not everybody expresses opinions over the Internet, due mostly to the fast-growing numbers and capabilities of social communication channels, the numbers are increasing exponentially.

Sentiment is a difficult word to define. It is often linked to or confused with other terms like *belief, view, opinion,* and *conviction.* Sentiment suggests a settled opinion reflective of one's feelings (Mejova, 2009). Sentiment has some unique properties that set it apart from other concepts that we may want to identify in text. Often we want to categorize text by topic, which may involve dealing with whole taxonomies of topics. Sentiment classification, on the other hand, usually deals with two classes (positive versus negative), a range of polarity (e.g., star ratings for movies), or even a range in strength of opinion (Pang and Lee, 2008). These classes span many topics, users, and documents. Although dealing with only a few classes may seem like an easier task than standard text analysis, it is far from the truth.

As a field of research, sentiment analysis is closely related to computational linguistics, natural language processing, and text mining. Sentiment analysis has many names. It's often referred to as *opinion mining, subjectivity analysis,* and *appraisal extraction,* with some connections to affective computing (computer recognition and expression of emotion). The sudden upsurge of interest and activity in the area of sentiment analysis (i.e., opinion mining), which deals with the automatic extraction of opinions, feelings, and subjectivity in text, is creating opportunities and threats for businesses and individuals alike. The ones who embrace and take advantage of it will greatly benefit from it. Every opinion put on the Internet by an individual or a company will be accredited to the originator (good or bad) and will be retrieved and mined by others (often automatically by computer programs).

Sentiment analysis is trying to answer the question "What do people feel about a certain topic?" by digging into opinions of many using a variety of automated tools. Bringing together researchers and practitioners in business, computer science, computational linguistics, data mining, text mining, psychology, and even sociology, sentiment analysis aims to expand traditional fact-based text analysis to new frontiers, to realize opinion-oriented information systems. In a business setting, especially in marketing and customer relationship management, sentiment analysis seeks to detect favorable and unfavorable opinions toward specific products and/or services using large numbers of textual data sources (customer feedback in the form of Web postings, tweets, blogs, etc.).

Sentiment that appears in text comes in two flavors: explicit, where the subjective sentence directly expresses an opinion ("It's a wonderful day"), and implicit, where the text implies an opinion ("The handle breaks too easily"). Most of the earlier work done in sentiment analysis focused on the first kind of sentiment, since it was easier to analyze. Current trends are to implement analytical methods to consider both implicit and explicit sentiments. Sentiment polarity is a particular feature of text that sentiment analysis primarily focuses on. It is usually dichotomized into two—positive and negative—but polarity can also be thought of as a range. A document containing several opinionated statements would have a mixed polarity overall, which is different from not having a polarity at all (being objective) (Mejova, 2009).

Timely collection and analysis of textual data, which may be coming from a variety of sources—ranging from customer call center transcripts to social media postings—is a crucial part of the capabilities of proactive and customer-focused companies, nowadays.

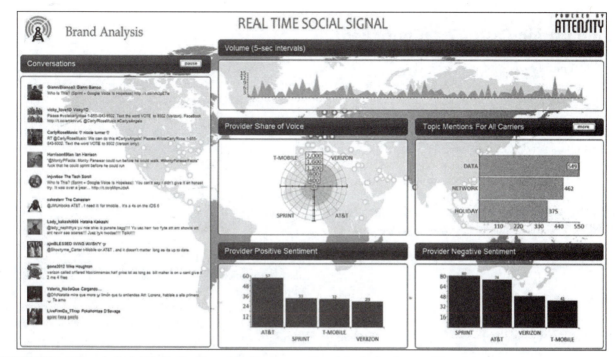

FIGURE 7.9 **A Sample Social Media Dashboard for Continuous Brand Analysis** *Source:* Attensity.

These real-time analyses of textual data are often visualized in easy-to-understand dashboards. Attensity is one of those companies that provide such end-to-end solutions to companies' text analytics needs (Figure 7.9 shows an example social media analytics dashboard created by Attensity). Application Case 7.7 provides an Attensity's customer success story, where a large consumer product manufacturer used text analytics and sentiment analysis to better connect with their customers.

Application Case 7.7
Whirlpool Achieves Customer Loyalty and Product Success with Text Analytics

Background

Every day, a substantial amount of new customer feedback data—rich in sentiment, customer issues, and product insights—becomes available to organizations through e-mails, repair notes, CRM notes, and online in social media. Within that data exists a wealth of insight into how customers feel about products, services, brands, and much more. That data also holds information about potential issues that could easily impact a product's long-term

success and a company's bottom line. This data is invaluable to marketing, product, and service managers across every industry.

Attensity, a premier text analytics solution provider, combines the company's rich text analytics applications within customer-specific BI platforms. The result is an intuitive solution that enables customers to fully leverage critical data assets to discover invaluable business insight and to foster better and faster decision making.

(Continued)

Application Case 7.7 (Continued)

Whirlpool is the world's leading manufacturer and marketer of major home appliances, with annual sales of approximately $19 billion, 67,000 employees, and nearly 70 manufacturing and technology research centers around the world. Whirlpool recognizes that consumers lead busy, active lives, and continues to create solutions that help consumers optimize productivity and efficiency in the home. In addition to designing appliance solutions based on consumer insight, Whirlpool's brand is dedicated to creating ENERGY STAR–qualified appliances like the Resource Saver side-by-side refrigerator, which recently was rated the #1 brand for side-by-side refrigerators.

Business Challenge

Customer satisfaction and feedback are at the center of how Whirlpool drives its overarching business strategy. As such, gaining insight into customer satisfaction and product feedback is paramount. One of Whirlpool's goals is to more effectively understand and react to customer and product feedback data, originating from blogs, e-mails, reviews, forums, repair notes, and other data sources. Whirlpool also strives to enable its managers to report on longitudinal data, and be able to compare issues by brand over time. Whirlpool has entrusted Attensity's text analytics solutions; and with that, Whirlpool listens and acts on customer data in their service department, their innovation and product developments groups, and in market every day.

Methods and the Benefits

To face its business requirements head-on, Whirlpool uses Attensity products for deep text analytics of their multi-channel customer data, which includes e-mails, CRM notes, repair notes, warranty data, and social media. More than 300 business users at Whirlpool use text analytics solutions every day to get to the root cause of product issues and receive alerts on emerging issues. Users of Attensity's analytics products at Whirlpool include product/service managers, corporate/product safety staff, consumer advocates, service quality staff, innovation managers, the Category Insights team, and all of Whirlpool's manufacturing divisions (across five countries).

Attensity's Text Analytics application has played a particularly critical role for Whirlpool. Whirlpool relies on the application to conduct deep analysis of the voice of the customer, with the goal of identifying product quality issues and innovation opportunities, and drive those insights more broadly across the organization. Users conduct in-depth analysis of customer data and then extend access to that analysis to business users all over the world.

Whirlpool has been able to more proactively identify and mitigate quality issues before issues escalate and claims are filed. Whirlpool has also been able to avoid recalls, which has the dual benefit of increased customer loyalty and reduced costs (realizing 80% savings on their costs of recalls due to early detection). Having insight into customer feedback and product issues has also resulted in more efficient customer support and ultimately in better products. Whirlpool's customer support agents now receive fewer product service support calls, and when agents do receive a call, it's easier for them to leverage the interaction to improve products and services.

The process of launching new products has also been enhanced by having the ability to analyze its customers' needs and fit new products and services to those needs appropriately. When a product is launched, Whirlpool can use external customer feedback data to stay on top of potential product issues and address them in a timely fashion.

Michael Page, development and testing manager for Quality Analytics at Whirpool Corporation affirms these types of benefits: "Attensity's products have provided immense value to our business. We've been able to proactively address customer feedback and work toward high levels of customer service and product success."

QUESTIONS FOR DISCUSSION

1. How did Whirlpool use capabilities of text analytics to better understand their customers and improve product offerings?
2. What were the challenges, the proposed solution, and the obtained results?

Source: Source: Attensity, Customer Success Story, **www.attensity. com/2010/08/21/whirlpool-2/** (accessed August 2013).

SECTION 7.7 REVIEW QUESTIONS

1. What is sentiment analysis? How does it relate to text mining?
2. What are the sources of data for sentiment analysis?
3. What are the common challenges that sentiment analysis has to deal with?

7.8 SENTIMENT ANALYSIS APPLICATIONS

Compared to traditional sentiment analysis methods, which were survey based or focus group centered, costly, and time-consuming (and therefore driven from small samples of participants), the new face of text analytics–based sentiment analysis is a limit breaker. Current solutions automate very large-scale data collection, filtering, classification, and clustering methods via natural language processing and data mining technologies that handle both factual and subjective information. Sentiment analysis is perhaps the most popular application of text analytics, tapping into data sources like tweets, Facebook posts, online communities, discussion boards, Web logs, product reviews, call center logs and recording, product rating sites, chat rooms, price comparison portals, search engine logs, and newsgroups. The following applications of sentiment analysis are meant to illustrate the power and the widespread coverage of this technology.

VOICE OF THE CUSTOMER (VOC)   **Voice of the customer (VOC)** is an integral part of an analytic CRM and customer experience management systems. As the enabler of VOC, sentiment analysis can access a company's product and service reviews (either continuously or periodically) to better understand and better manage the customer complaints and praises. For instance, a motion picture advertising/marketing company may detect the negative sentiments toward a movie that is about to open in theatres (based on its trailers), and quickly change the composition of trailers and advertising strategy (on all media outlets) to mitigate the negative impact. Similarly, a software company may detect the negative buzz regarding the bugs found in their newly released product early enough to release patches and quick fixes to alleviate the situation.

Often, the focus of VOC is individual customers, their service- and support-related needs, wants, and issues. VOC draw data from the full set of customer touch points, including e-mails, surveys, call center notes/recordings, and social media postings, and match customer voices to transactions (inquiries, purchases, returns) and individual customer profiles captured in enterprise operational systems. VOC, mostly driven by sentiment analysis, is a key element of **customer experience management** initiatives, where the goal is to create an intimate relationship with the customer.

VOICE OF THE MARKET (VOM)   **Voice of the market** is about understanding aggregate opinions and trends. It's about knowing what stakeholders—customers, potential customers, influencers, whoever—are saying about your (and your competitors') products and services. A well-done VOM analysis helps companies with competitive intelligence and product development and positioning.

VOICE OF THE EMPLOYEE (VOE)   Traditionally VOE has been limited to employee satisfaction surveys. Text analytics in general (and sentiment analysis in particular) is a huge enabler of assessing the VOE. Using rich, opinionated textual data is an effective and efficient way to listen to what employees are saying. As we all know, happy employees empower customer experience efforts and improve customer satisfaction.

BRAND MANAGEMENT   Brand management focuses on listening to social media where anyone (past/current/prospective customers, industry experts, other authorities) can post opinions that can damage or boost your reputation. There are a number of relatively newly launched start-up companies that offer analytics-driven brand management services for others. Brand management is product and company (rather than customer) focused. It attempts to shape perceptions rather than to manage experiences using sentiment analysis techniques.

FINANCIAL MARKETS Predicting the future values of individual (or a group of) stocks has been an interesting and seemingly unsolvable problem. What makes a stock (or a group of stocks) move up or down is anything but an exact science. Many believe that the stock market is mostly sentiment driven, making it anything but rational (especially for short-term stock movements). Therefore, use of sentiment analysis in financial markets has gained significant popularity. Automated analysis of market sentiments using social media, news, blogs, and discussion groups seems to be a proper way to compute the market movements. If done correctly, sentiment analysis can identify short-term stock movements based on the buzz in the market, potentially impacting liquidity and trading.

POLITICS As we all know, opinions matter a great deal in politics. Because political discussions are dominated by quotes, sarcasm, and complex references to persons, organizations, and ideas, politics is one of the most difficult, and potentially fruitful, areas for sentiment analysis. By analyzing the sentiment on election forums, one may predict who is more likely to win or lose. Sentiment analysis can help understand what voters are thinking and can clarify a candidate's position on issues. Sentiment analysis can help political organizations, campaigns, and news analysts to better understand which issues and positions matter the most to voters. The technology was successfully applied by both parties to the 2008 and 2012 American presidential election campaigns.

GOVERNMENT INTELLIGENCE Government intelligence is another application that has been used by intelligence agencies. For example, it has been suggested that one could monitor sources for increases in hostile or negative communications. Sentiment analysis can allow the automatic analysis of the opinions that people submit about pending policy or government-regulation proposals. Furthermore, monitoring communications for spikes in negative sentiment may be of use to agencies like Homeland Security.

OTHER INTERESTING AREAS Sentiments of customers can be used to better design e-commerce sites (product suggestions, upsell/cross-sell advertising), better place advertisements (e.g., placing dynamic advertisement of products and services that consider the sentiment on the page the user is browsing), and manage opinion- or review-oriented search engines (i.e., an opinion-aggregation Web site, an alternative to sites like Epinions, summarizing user reviews). Sentiment analysis can help with e-mail filtration by categorizing and prioritizing incoming e-mails (e.g., it can detect strongly negative or flaming e-mails and forward them to the proper folder), as well as citation analysis, where it can determine whether an author is citing a piece of work as supporting evidence or as research that he or she dismisses.

SECTION 7.8 REVIEW QUESTIONS

1. What are the most popular application areas for sentiment analysis? Why?
2. How can sentiment analysis be used for brand management?
3. What would be the expected benefits and beneficiaries of sentiment analysis in politics?
4. How can sentiment analysis be used in predicting financial markets?

7.9 SENTIMENT ANALYSIS PROCESS

Because of the complexity of the problem (underlying concepts, expressions in text, context in which the text is expressed, etc.), there is no readily available standardized process to conduct sentiment analysis. However, based on the published work in the field of sensitivity analysis so far (both on research methods and range of applications), a multi-step, simple logical process, as given in Figure 7.10, seems to be an appropriate methodology for sentiment analysis. These logical steps are iterative (i.e., feedback, corrections, and iterations are part of the discovery process) and experimental in nature, and once completed and combined, capable of producing desired insight about the opinions in the text collection.

STEP 1: SENTIMENT DETECTION   After the retrieval and preparation of the text documents, the first main task in sensitivity analysis is the detection of objectivity. Here the goal is to differentiate between a fact and an opinion, which may be viewed as classification of text as objective or subjective. This may also be characterized as calculation of O-S Polarity (Objectivity-Subjectivity Polarity, which may be represented with a numerical value ranging from 0 to 1). If the objectivity value is close to 1, then there is no opinion to mine (i.e., it is a fact); therefore, the process goes back and grabs the next text data to analyze. Usually opinion

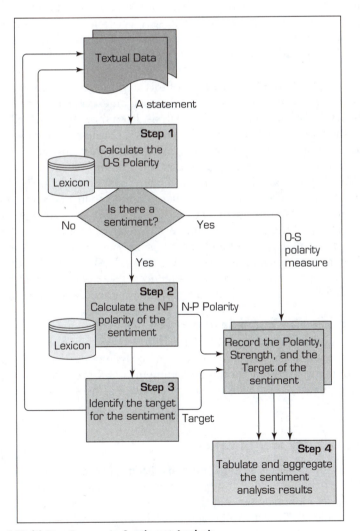

FIGURE 7.10   A Multi-Step Process to Sentiment Analysis.

detection is based on the examination of adjectives in text. For example, the polarity of "what a wonderful work" can be determined relatively easily by looking at the adjective.

STEP 2: N-P POLARITY CLASSIFICATION   The second main task is that of polarity classification. Given an opinionated piece of text, the goal is to classify the opinion as falling under one of two opposing sentiment polarities, or locate its position on the continuum between these two polarities (Pang and Lee, 2008). When viewed as a binary feature, polarity classification is the binary classification task of labeling an opinionated document as expressing either an overall positive or an overall negative opinion (e.g., thumbs up or thumbs down). In addition to the identification of N-P polarity, one should also be interested in identifying the strength of the sentiment (as opposed to just positive, it may be expressed as mildly, moderately, strongly, or very strongly positive). Most of this research was done on product or movie reviews where the definitions of "positive" and "negative" are quite clear. Other tasks, such as classifying news as "good" or "bad," present some difficulty. For instance an article may contain negative news without explicitly using any subjective words or terms. Furthermore, these classes usually appear intermixed when a document expresses both positive and negative sentiments. Then the task can be to identify the main (or dominating) sentiment of the document. Still, for lengthy texts, the tasks of classification may need to be done at several levels: term, phrase, sentence, and perhaps document level. For those, it is common to use the outputs of one level as the inputs for the next higher layer. Several methods used to identify the polarity and strengths of the polarity are explained in the next section.

STEP 3: TARGET IDENTIFICATION   The goal of this step is to accurately identify the target of the expressed sentiment (e.g., a person, a product, an event, etc.). The difficulty of this task depends largely on the domain of the analysis. Even though it is usually easy to accurately identify the target for product or movie reviews, because the review is directly connected to the target, it may be quite challenging in other domains. For instance, lengthy, general-purpose text such as Web pages, news articles, and blogs do not always have a predefined topic that they are assigned to, and often mention many objects, any of which may be deduced as the target. Sometimes there is more than one target in a sentiment sentence, which is the case in comparative texts. A subjective comparative sentence orders objects in order of preferences—for example, "This laptop computer is better than my desktop PC." These sentences can be identified using comparative adjectives and adverbs (more, less, better, longer), superlative adjectives (most, least, best), and other words (such as same, differ, win, prefer, etc.). Once the sentences have been retrieved, the objects can be put in an order that is most representative of their merits, as described in text.

STEP 4: COLLECTION AND AGGREGATION   Once the sentiments of all text data points in the document are identified and calculated, in this step they are aggregated and converted to a single sentiment measure for the whole document. This aggregation may be as simple as summing up the polarities and strengths of all texts, or as complex as using semantic aggregation techniques from natural language processing to come up with the ultimate sentiment.

Methods for Polarity Identification

As mentioned in the previous section, **polarity identification**—identifying the polarity of a text—can be made at the word, term, sentence, or document level. The most granular level for polarity identification is at the word level. Once the polarity identification is made at the word level, then it can be aggregated to the next higher level, and then the next until the level of aggregation desired from the sentiment analysis is reached. There seem to be two dominant techniques used for identification of polarity at the word/term level, each having its advantages and disadvantages:

1. Using a lexicon as a reference library (either developed manually or automatically, by an individual for a specific task or developed by an institution for general use)
2. Using a collection of training documents as the source of knowledge about the polarity of terms within a specific domain (i.e., inducing predictive models from opinionated textual documents)

Using a Lexicon

A lexicon is essentially the catalog of words, their synonyms, and their meanings for a given language. In addition to lexicons for many other languages, there are several general-purpose lexicons created for English. Often general-purpose lexicons are used to create a variety of special-purpose lexicons for use in sentiment analysis projects. Perhaps the most popular general-purpose lexicon is WordNet, created at Princeton University, which has been extended and used by many researchers and practitioners for sentiment analysis purposes. As described on the WordNet Web site (**wordnet. princeton.edu**), it is a large lexical database of English, including nouns, verbs, adjectives, and adverbs grouped into sets of cognitive synonyms (i.e., synsets), each expressing a distinct concept. Synsets are interlinked by means of conceptual-semantic and lexical relations.

An interesting extension of WordNet was created by Esuli and Sebastiani (2006) where they added polarity (Positive-Negative) and objectivity (Subjective-Objective) labels for each term in the lexicon. To label each term, they classify the synset (a group of synonyms) to which this term belongs using a set of ternary classifiers (a measure that attaches to each object exactly one out of three labels), each of them capable of deciding whether a synset is Positive, or Negative, or Objective. The resulting scores range from 0.0 to 1.0, giving a graded evaluation of opinion-related properties of the terms. These can be summed up visually as in Figure 7.11. The edges of the triangle represent one of the three classifications (positive, negative, and objective). A term can be located in this space as a point, representing the extent to which it belongs to each of the classifications.

A similar extension methodology is used to create SentiWordNet, a publicly available lexicon specifically developed for opinion mining (sentiment analysis) purposes.

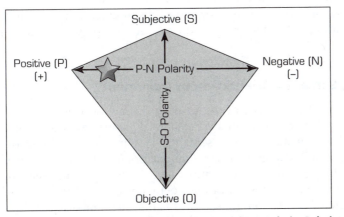

FIGURE 7.11   **A Graphical Representation of the P-N Polarity and S-O Polarity Relationship.**

SentiWordNet assigns to each synset of WordNet three sentiment scores: positivity, negativity, objectivity. More about SentiWordNet can be found at **sentiwordnet.isti.cnr.it**.

Another extension to WordNet is WordNet-Affect, developed by Strapparava and Valitutti (Strapparava and Valitutti, 2004). They label WordNet synsets using affective labels representing different affective categories like emotion, cognitive state, attitude, feeling, and so on. WordNet has also been directly used in sentiment analysis. For example, Kim and Hovy (Kim and Hovy, 2004) and Hu and Liu (Hu and Liu, 2005) generate lexicons of positive and negative terms by starting with a small list of "seed" terms of known polarities (e.g., love, like, nice, etc.) and then using the antonymy and synonymy properties of terms to group them into either of the polarity categories.

Using a Collection of Training Documents

It is possible to perform sentiment classification using statistical analysis and machine-learning tools that take advantage of the vast resources of labeled (manually by annotators or using a star/point system) documents available. Product review Web sites like Amazon, C-NET, ebay, RottenTomatoes, and the Internet Movie Database (IMDB) have all been extensively used as sources of annotated data. The star (or tomato, as it were) system provides an explicit label of the overall polarity of the review, and it is often taken as a gold standard in algorithm evaluation.

A variety of manually labeled textual data is available through evaluation efforts such as the Text REtrieval Conference (TREC), NII Test Collection for IR Systems (NTCIR), and Cross Language Evaluation Forum (CLEF). The data sets these efforts produce often serve as a standard in the text mining community, including for sentiment analysis researchers. Individual researchers and research groups have also produced many interesting data sets. Technology Insights 7.2 lists some of the most popular ones. Once an already labeled textual data set is obtained, a variety of predictive modeling and other machine-learning algorithms can be used to train sentiment classifiers. Some of the most popular algorithms used for this task include artificial neural networks, support vector machines, k-nearest neighbor, Naive Bayes, decision trees, and expectation maximization-based clustering.

Identifying Semantic Orientation of Sentences and Phrases

Once the semantic orientation of individual words has been determined, it is often desirable to extend this to the phrase or sentence the word appears in. The simplest way to accomplish such aggregation is to use some type of averaging for the polarities of words in the phrases or sentences. Though rarely applied, such aggregation can be as complex as using one or more machine-learning techniques to create a predictive relationship between the words (and their polarity values) and phrases or sentences.

Identifying Semantic Orientation of Document

Even though the vast majority of the work in this area is done in determining semantic orientation of words and phrases/sentences, some tasks like summarization and information retrieval may require semantic labeling of the whole document (REF). Similar to the case in aggregating sentiment polarity from word level to phrase or sentence level, aggregation to document level is also accomplished by some type of averaging. Sentiment orientation of the document may not make sense for very large documents; therefore, it is often used on small to medium-sized documents posted on the Internet.

TECHNOLOGY INSIGHTS 7.2   Large Textual Data Sets for Predictive Text Mining and Sentiment Analysis

Congressional Floor-Debate Transcripts: Published by Thomas et al. (Thomas and B. Pang, 2006); contains political speeches that are labeled to indicate whether the speaker supported or opposed the legislation discussed.

Economining: Published by Stern School at New York University; consists of feed-back postings for merchants at Amazon.com.

Cornell Movie-Review Data Sets: Introduced by Pang and Lee (Pang and Lee, 2008); contains 1,000 positive and 1,000 negative automatically derived document-level labels, and 5,331 positive and 5,331 negative sentences/snippets.

Stanford—Large Movie Review Data Set: A set of 25,000 highly polar movie reviews for training, and 25,000 for testing. There is additional unlabeled data for use as well. Raw text and already processed bag-of-words formats are provided. (See: **http://ai.stanford.edu/~amaas/data/sentiment.**)

MPQA Corpus: Corpus and Opinion Recognition System corpus; contains 535 manu-ally annotated news articles from a variety of news sources containing labels for opinions and private states (beliefs, emotions, speculations, etc.).

Multiple-Aspect Restaurant Reviews: Introduced by Snyder and Barzilay (Snyder and Barzilay, 2007); contains 4,488 reviews with an explicit 1-to-5 rating for five different aspects: food, ambiance, service, value, and overall experience.

SECTION 7.9 REVIEW QUESTIONS

1. What are the main steps in carrying out sentiment analysis projects?
2. What are the two common methods for polarity identification? What is the main dif-ference between the two?
3. Describe how special lexicons are used in identification of sentiment polarity.

7.10   SENTIMENT ANALYSIS AND SPEECH ANALYTICS

Speech analytics is a growing field of science that allows users to analyze and extract information from both live and recorded conversations. It is being used effectively to gather intelligence for security purposes, to enhance the presentation and utility of rich media applications, and perhaps most significantly, to deliver meaningful and quantitative business intelligence through the analysis of the millions of recorded calls that occur in customer contact centers around the world.

Sentiment analysis, as it applies to speech analytics, focuses specifically on assess-ing the emotional states expressed in a conversation and on measuring the presence and strength of positive and negative feelings that are exhibited by the participants. One common use of sentiment analysis within contact centers is to provide insight into a customer's feelings about an organization, its products, services, and customer service processes, as well as an individual agent's behavior. Sentiment analysis data can be used across an organization to aid in customer relationship management, agent training, and in identifying and resolving troubling issues as they emerge.

How Is It Done?

The core of automated sentiment analysis centers around creating a model to describe how certain features and content in the audio relate to the sentiments being felt and expressed by the participants in the conversation. Two primary methods have been deployed to predict sentiment within audio: acoustic/phonetic and linguistic modeling.

THE ACOUSTIC APPROACH The acoustic approach to sentiment analysis relies on extracting and measuring a specific set of features (e.g., tone of voice, pitch or volume, intensity and rate of speech) of the audio. These features can in some circumstances provide basic indicators of sentiment. For example, the speech of a surprised speaker tends to become somewhat faster, louder, and higher in pitch. Sadness and depression are presented as slower, softer, and lower in pitch (see Moore et al., 2008). An angry caller may speak much faster, much louder, and will increase the pitch of stressed vowels. There is a wide variety of audio features that can be measured. The most common ones are as follows:

- Intensity: energy, sound pressure level
- Pitch: variation of fundamental frequency
- Jitter: variation in amplitude of vocal fold movements
- Shimmer: variation in frequency of vocal fold movements
- Glottal pulse: glottal-source spectral characteristics
- HNR: harmonics-to-noise ratio
- Speaking rate: number of phonemes, vowels, syllables, or words per unit of time

When developing an acoustic analysis tool, the system must be built on a model that defines the sentiments being measured. The model is based on a database of the audio features (some of which are listed here) and how their presence may indicate each of the sentiments (as simple as positive, negative, neutral, or refined, such as fear, anger, sadness, hurt, surprise, relief, etc.) that are being measured. To create this database, each single-emotion example is preselected from an original set of recordings, manually reviewed, and annotated to identify which sentiment it represents. The final acoustic analysis tools are then trained (using data mining techniques) and a predictive model is tested and validated using a different set of the same annotated recordings.

As sophisticated as it sounds, the acoustic approach has its deficiencies. First, because acoustic analysis relies on identifying the audio characteristics of a call, the quality of the audio can significantly impact the ability to identify these features. Second, speakers often express blended emotions, such as both empathy and annoyance (as in "I do understand, madam, but I have no miracle solution"), which are extremely difficult to classify based solely on their acoustic features. Third, acoustic analysis is often incapable of recognizing and adjusting for the variety of ways that different callers may express the same sentiment. Finally, its time-demanding and laborious process make it impractical for use with live audio streams.

THE LINGUISTIC APPROACH Conversely, the linguistic approach focuses on the explicit indications of sentiment and context of the spoken content within the audio; linguistic models acknowledge that, when in a charged state, the speaker has a higher probability of using specific words, exclamations, or phrases in a particular order. The features that are most often analyzed in a linguistic model include:

- Lexical: words, phrases, and other linguistic patterns
- Disfluencies: filled pauses, hesitation, restarts, and nonverbals such as laughter or breathing
- Higher semantics: taxonomy/ontology, dialogue history, and pragmatics

The simplest method, in the linguistic approach, is to catch within the audio a limited number of specific keywords (a specific lexicon) that has domain-specific sentiment significance. This approach is perhaps the least popular due to its limited applicability and less-than-desired prediction accuracy. Alternatively, as with the acoustic approach, a model is built based on understanding which linguistic elements are predictors of particular sentiments, and this model is then run against a series of recordings to determine the sentiments that are contained therein. The challenge with this approach is in collecting the linguistic information contained in any corpus of audio. This has tradition-ally been done using a large vocabulary continuous speech recognition (LVCSR) system, often referred to as speech-to-text. However, LVCSR systems are prone to creating signifi-cant error in the textual indexes they create. In addition, the level of computational effort they require—that is, the amount of computer processing power needed to analyze large amounts of audio content—has made them very expensive to deploy for mass audio analysis.

Yet, another approach to linguistic analysis is that of phonetic indexing and search. Among the significant advantages associated with this approach to linguistic modeling is the method's ability to maintain a high degree of accuracy no matter what the quality of the audio source, and its incorporation of conversational context through the use of structured queries during analysis (Nexidia, 2009).

Application Case 7.8 is a great example to how analytically savvy companies find ways to better "listen" and improve their customers' experience.

Application Case 7.8

Cutting Through the Confusion: Blue Cross Blue Shield of North Carolina Uses Nexidia's Speech Analytics to Ease Member Experience in Healthcare

Introduction

With the passage of the healthcare law, many health plan members were perplexed by new rules and regulations and concerned about the effects man-dates would have on their benefits, copays, and providers. In an attempt to ease concerns, health plans such as Blue Cross Blue Shield of North Carolina (BCBSNC) published literature, updated Web sites, and sent various forms of communication to members to further educate them on the changes. However, members continued to reach out via the contact center, seeking answers regarding current claims and benefits and how their health insurance coverage might be affected in the future. As the law moves forward, members will be more engaged in making their own decisions about healthcare plans and about where to seek care, thus becoming better consumers. The transformation to healthcare con-sumerism has made it crucial for health plan contact centers to diligently work to optimize the customer experience.

BCBSNC became concerned that despite its best efforts to communicate changes, confusion remained among its nearly 4 million members, which was driving unnecessary calls into its contact center, which could lead to a decrease in member satisfaction. Also, like all plans, BCBSNC was look-ing to trim costs associated with its contact center,

as the health reform law mandates health plans spend a minimum of 80 percent of all premium pay-ments on healthcare. This rule leaves less money for administrative expenses, like the contact center.

However, BCBSNC saw an opportunity to leverage its partnership with Nexidia, a leading provider of customer interaction analytics, and use speech analytics to better understand the cause and depth of member confusion. The use of speech ana-lytics was a more attractive option for BCBSNC than asking their customer service professionals to more thoroughly document the nature of the calls within the contact center desktop application, which would have decreased efficiency and increased contact center administrative expenses. By iden-tifying the specific root cause of the interactions when members called the contact center, BCBSNC would be able to take corrective actions to reduce call volumes and costs and improve the members' experience.

Alleviating the Confusion

BCBSNC has been ahead of the curve on engaging and educating its members and providing exem-plary customer service. The health plan knew it needed to work vigorously to maintain its customer

(Continued)

Application Case 7.8   (Continued)

service track record as the healthcare mandates began. The first step was to better understand how members perceived the value they received from BCBSNC and their overall opinion of the company. To accomplish this, BCBSNC elected to conduct sentiment analysis to get richer insights into members' opinions and interactions.

When conducting sentiment analysis, two strategies can be used to garner results. The acoustic model relies on measuring specific characteristics of the audio, such as sound, tone of voice, pitch, volume, intensity, and rate of speech. The other strategy, used by Nexidia, is linguistic modeling, which focuses directly on spoken sentiment. Acoustic modeling results in inaccurate data because of poor recording quality, background noise, and a person's inability to change tone or cadence to reflect his or her emotion. The linguistic approach, which focuses directly on words or phrases used to convey a feeling, has proven to be most effective.

Since BCBSNC suspected its members may perceive their health coverage as confusing, BCBSNC utilized Nexidia to put together structured searches for words or phrases used by callers to express confusion: "I'm a little confused," "I don't understand," "I don't get it," and "Doesn't make sense." The results were the exact percentage of calls containing this sentiment and helped BCBSNC specifically isolate those circumstances and coverage instances where callers were more likely to be confused with a benefit or claim. BCBSNC filtered their "confusion calls" from their overall call volume so these calls were available for further analysis.

The next step was to use speech analytics to get to the root cause of what was driving the disconnection and develop strategies to alleviate the confusion. BCBSNC used Nexidia's dictionary independent phonetic indexing and search solution, allowing for all processed audio to be searched for any word or phrase, to create additional structured searches. These searches further classified the call drivers, and when combined with targeted listening, BCBSNC pinpointed the problems.

The findings revealed that literature created by BCBSNC used industry terms that members were unfamiliar with and didn't clearly explain their benefits, claims processes, and deductibles. Additionally, information on the Web site was neither easily located nor understood, and members were unable to "self-serve," resulting in unnecessary contact center interaction. Further, adding to BCBSNC's troubles, when Nexidia's speech analytics combined the unstructured call data with the structured data associated with the call, it showed "confusion calls" had a significantly higher average talk time (ATT), resulting in a higher cost to serve for BCBSNC.

The Results

By listening to, and more specifically understanding, the confusion of its members regarding benefits, BCBSNC began implementing strategies to improve member communication and customer experience. The health plan has developed more reader-friendly literature and simplified the layout to highlight pertinent information. BCBSNC also has implemented Web site redesigns to support easier navigation and education. As a result of the modifications, BCBSNC projects a 10 to 25 percent drop in "confusion calls," resulting in a better customer service experience and a lower cost to serve. Utilizing Nexidia's analytic solution to continuously monitor and track changes will be paramount to BCBSNC's continued success as a leading health plan.

"Because there is so much to do in healthcare today and because of the changes under way in the industry, you really want to invest in the consumer experience so that customers can get the most out of their health care coverage," says Gretchen Gray, director of Customer and Consumer Experience at BCBSNC. "I believe that unless you use [Nexidia's] approach, I don't know how you pick your priorities and focus. Speech analytics is one of the main tools we have where we can say, 'here is where we can have the most impact and here's what I need to do better or differently to assist my customers.'"

Questions for Discussion

1. For a large company like BCBSNC with a lot of customers, what does "listening to customer" mean?
2. What were the challenges, the proposed solution, and the obtained results for BCBSNC?

Source: Used with permission from **Nexidia.com**.

SECTION 7.10 REVIEW QUESTIONS

1. What is speech analytics? How does it relate to sentiment analysis?
2. Describe the acoustic approach to speech analytics.
3. Describe the linguistic approach to speech analytics.

Chapter Highlights

- Text mining is the discovery of knowledge from unstructured (mostly text-based) data sources. Given that a great deal of information is in text form, text mining is one of the fastest growing branches of the business intelligence field.
- Companies use text mining and Web mining to better understand their customers by analyzing their feedback left on Web forms, blogs, and wikis.
- Text mining applications are in virtually every area of business and government, including marketing, finance, healthcare, medicine, and homeland security.
- Text mining uses natural language processing to induce structure into the text collection and then uses data mining algorithms such as classification, clustering, association, and **sequence discovery** to extract knowledge from it.
- Successful application of text mining requires a structured methodology similar to the CRISP-DM methodology in data mining.
- Text mining is closely related to information extraction, natural language processing, and document summarization.
- Text mining entails creating numeric indices from unstructured text and then applying data mining algorithms to these indices.
- Sentiment can be defined as a settled opinion reflective of one's feelings.
- Sentiment classification usually deals with differentiating between two classes, positive and negative.
- As a field of research, sentiment analysis is closely related to computational linguistics, natural language processing, and text mining. It may be used to enhance search results produced by search engines.
- Sentiment analysis is trying to answer the question of "What do people feel about a certain topic?" by digging into opinions of many using a variety of automated tools.
- Voice of the customer is an integral part of an analytic CRM and customer experience management systems, and is often powered by sentiment analysis.
- Voice of the market is about understanding aggregate opinions and trends at the market level.
- Brand management focuses on listening to social media where anyone can post opinions that can damage or boost your reputation.
- Polarity identification in sentiment analysis is accomplished either by using a lexicon as a reference library or by using a collection of training documents.
- WordNet is a popular general-purpose lexicon created at Princeton University.
- SentiWordNet is an extension of WordNet to be used for sentiment identification.
- Speech analytics is a growing field of science that allows users to analyze and extract information from both live and recorded conversations.
- The acoustic approach to sentiment analysis relies on extracting and measuring a specific set of features (e.g., tone of voice, pitch or volume, intensity and rate of speech) of the audio.

Key Terms

association	customer experience	inverse document	part-of-speech tagging
classification	management (CEM)	frequency	polarity identification
clustering	deception detection	natural language	polyseme
corpus		processing (NLP)	sentiment

sentiment analysis	speech analytics	text mining	voice of the market
SentiWordNet	stemming	tokenizing	WordNet
sequence discovery	stop words	trend analysis	
singular value decomposition (SVD)	term–document matrix (TDM)	unstructured data voice of customer (VOC)	

Questions for Discussion

1. Explain the relationships among data mining, text mining, and sentiment analysis.
2. What should an organization consider before making a decision to purchase text mining software?
3. Discuss the differences and commonalities between text mining and sentiment analysis.
4. In your own words, define *text mining* and discuss its most popular applications.
5. Discuss the similarities and differences between the data mining process (e.g., CRISP-DM) and the three-step, high-level text mining process explained in this chapter.
6. What does it mean to introduce structure into the text-based data? Discuss the alternative ways of introducing structure into text-based data.
7. What is the role of natural language processing in text mining? Discuss the capabilities and limitations of NLP in the context of text mining.
8. List and discuss three prominent application areas for text mining. What is the common theme among the three application areas you chose?
9. What is sentiment analysis? How does it relate to text mining?

10. What are the sources of data for sentiment analysis?
11. What are the common challenges that sentiment analysis has to deal with?
12. What are the most popular application areas for sentiment analysis? Why?
13. How can sentiment analysis be used for brand management?
14. What would be the expected benefits and beneficiaries of sentiment analysis in politics?
15. How can sentiment analysis be used in predicting financial markets?
16. What are the main steps in carrying out sentiment analysis projects?
17. What are the two common methods for polarity identification? What is the main difference between the two?
18. Describe how special lexicons are used in identification of sentiment polarity.
19. What is speech analytics? How does it relate to sentiment analysis?
20. Describe the acoustic approach to speech analytics.
21. Describe the linguistic approach to speech analytics.

Exercises

Teradata University Network (TUN) and Other Hands-On Exercises

1. Visit **teradatauniversitynetwork.com**. Identify cases about text mining. Describe recent developments in the field. If you cannot find enough cases at the Teradata University network Web site, broaden your search to other Web-based resources.
2. Go to **teradatauniversitynetwork.com** or locate white papers, Web seminars, and other materials related to text mining. Synthesize your findings into a short written report.
3. Browse the Web and your library's digital databases to identify articles that make the natural linkage between text/Web mining and contemporary business intelligence systems.
4. Go to **teradatauniversitynetwork.com** and find a case study named "eBay Analytics." Read the case carefully, extend your understanding of the case by searching the Internet for additional information, and answer the case questions.
5. Go to **teradatauniversitynetwork.com** and find a sentiment analysis case named "How Do We Fix and App

Like That!" Read the description and follow the directions to download the data and the tool to carry out the exercise.

Team Assignments and Role-Playing Projects

1. Examine how textual data can be captured automatically using Web-based technologies. Once captured, what are the potential patterns that you can extract from these unstructured data sources?
2. Interview administrators in your college or executives in your organization to determine how text mining and Web mining could assist them in their work. Write a proposal describing your findings. Include a preliminary cost–benefits analysis in your report.
3. Go to your library's online resources. Learn how to download attributes of a collection of literature (journal articles) in a specific topic. Download and process the data using a methodology similar to the one explained in Application Case 7.5.
4. Find a readily available sentiment text data set (see Technology Insights 7.2 for a list of popular data sets) and

download it into your computer. If you have an analytics tool that is capable of text mining, use that; if not, download RapidMiner (**rapid-i.com**) and install it. Also install the text analytics add-on for RapidMiner. Process the downloaded data using your text mining tool (i.e., convert the data into a structured form). Build models and assess the sentiment detection accuracy of several classification models (e.g., support vector machines, decision trees, neural networks, logistic regression, etc.). Write a detailed report where you explain your finings and your experiences.

Internet Exercises

1. Survey some text mining tools and vendors. Start with **clearforest.com** and **megaputer.com**. Also consult with **dmreview.com** and identify some text mining products and service providers that are not mentioned in this chapter.
2. Find recent cases of successful text mining and Web mining applications. Try text and Web mining software vendors and consultancy firms and look for cases or success stories. Prepare a report summarizing five new case studies.
3. Go to **statsoft.com**. Select Downloads and download at least three white papers on applications. Which of these applications may have used the data/text/Web mining techniques discussed in this chapter?
4. Go to **sas.com**. Download at least three white papers on applications. Which of these applications may have used the data/text/Web mining techniques discussed in this chapter?
5. Go to **ibm.com**. Download at least three white papers on applications. Which of these applications may have used the data/text/Web mining techniques discussed in this chapter?
6. Go to **teradata.com**. Download at least three white papers on applications. Which of these applications may have used the data/text/Web mining techniques discussed in this chapter?
7. Go to **fairisaac.com**. Download at least three white papers on applications. Which of these applications may have used the data/text/Web mining techniques discussed in this chapter?
8. Go to **salfordsystems.com**. Download at least three white papers on applications. Which of these applications may have used the data/text/Web mining techniques discussed in this chapter?
9. Go to **clarabridge.com**. Download at least three white papers on applications. Which of these applications may have used text mining in a creative way?
10. Go to **kdnuggets.com**. Explore the sections on applications as well as software. Find names of at least three additional packages for data mining and text mining.

End-of-Chapter Application Case

BBVA Seamlessly Monitors and Improves its Online Reputation

BBVA is a global group that offers individual and corporate customers a comprehensive range of financial and nonfinancial products and services. It enjoys a solid leadership position in the Spanish market, where it first began its activities over 150 years ago. It also has a leading franchise in South America; it is the largest financial institution in Mexico; one of the 15 largest U.S. commercial banks and one of the few large international groups operating in China and Turkey. BBVA employs approximately 104,000 people in over 30 countries around the world, and has more than 47 million customers and 900,000 shareholders.

Looking for tools to reduce reputational risks

BBVA is interested in knowing what existing clients—and possible new ones—think about it through social media. Therefore, the bank has implemented an automated consumer insight solution to monitor and measure the impact of brand perception online—whether this be customer comments on social media sites (Twitter, Facebook, forums, blogs, etc.), the voices of experts in online articles about BBVA and its competitors, or references to BBVA on news sites—to detect possible risks to its reputation or to possible business opportunities.

Insights derived from this analytical tool give BBVA the opportunity to address reputational challenges and continue to build on positive opinions. For example, the bank can now respond to negative (or positive) brand perception by focusing its communication strategies on particular Internet sites, countering—or backing up—the most outspoken authors on Twitter, boards and blogs.

Finding a way forward

In 2009, BBVA began monitoring the web with an IBM social media research asset called Corporate Brand Reputation Analysis (COBRA), as a pilot between IBM and the bank's Innovation department. This pilot proved highly successful for different areas of the bank, including the Communications, Brand & Reputation, Corporate Social Responsibility, Consumer Insight, and Online Banking departments.

The BBVA Communication department then decided to tackle a new project, deploying a single tool that would enable the entire group to analyze online mentions of BBVA and monitor the bank's brand perception in various online communities.

The bank decided to implement IBM Cognos Consumer Insight to unify all its branches worldwide and allow them to use the same samples, models, and taxonomies. IBM Global Business Services is currently helping the bank to implement the solution, as well as design the focus of the analysis adapted to each country's requirements.

IBM Cognos Consumer Insight will allow BBVA to monitor the voices of current and potential clients on social media websites such as Twitter, Facebook and message boards, identify expert opinions about BBVA and its competitors on blogs, and control the presence of the bank in news channels to gain insights and detect possible reputational risks. All this new information will be distributed among the business departments of BBVA, enabling the bank to take a holistic view across all areas of its business.

Seamless focus on online reputation

The solution has now been rolled out in Spain, and BBVA's Online Communications team is already seeing its benefits.

"Huge amounts of data are being posted on Twitter every day, which makes it a great source of information for us," states the Online Communications Department of this bank. "To make effective use of this resource, we needed to find a way to capture, store and analyze the data in a better, faster and more detailed fashion. We believe that IBM Cognos Consumer Insight will help us to differentiate and categorize all the data we collect according to pre-established criteria, such as author, date, country and subject. This enables us to focus only on comments and news items that are actually relevant, whether in a positive, negative or neutral sense."

The content of the comments is subsequently analyzed using custom Spanish and English dictionaries, in order to identify whether the sentiments expressed are positive or negative. "What is great about this solution is that it helps us to focus our actions on the most important topics of online discussions and immediately plan the correct and most suitable reaction," adds the Department, "By building on what we accomplished in the initial COBRA project, the new solution enables BBVA to seamlessly monitor comments and postings, improve its decision-making processes, and thereby strengthen its online reputation."

"When BBVA detects a negative comment, a reputational risk arises," explains Miguel Iza Moreno, Business Analytics and Optimization Consultant at IBM Global Business Services. "Cognos Consumer Insight provides a reporting system which identifies the origin of a negative statement and BBVA sets up an internal protocol to decide how to react. This can happen through press releases, direct communication with users or, in some cases, no action is deemed to be required; the solution also highlights those cases in which the negative comment is considered 'irrelevant' or 'harmless'. The same procedure applies to positive comments—the solution allows the bank to follow a standard and structured process, which, based on positive insights, enables it to strengthen its reputation.

"Following the successful deployment in Spain, BBVA will be able to easily replicate the Cognos Consumer Insight solution in other countries, providing a single solution that will help to consolidate and reaffirm the bank's reputation management strategy," says the Department.

Tangible Results

Starting with the COBRA pilot project, the solution delivered visible benefits during the first half of 2011. Positive feedback about the company increased by more than one percent while negative feedback was reduced by 1.5 percent—suggesting that hundreds of customers and stakeholders across Spain are already enjoying a more satisfying experience from BBVA. Moreover, global monitoring improved, providing greater reliability when comparing results between branches and countries. Similar benefits are expected from the Cognos Consumer Insight project, and the initial results are expected shortly.

"BBVA is already seeing a remarkable improvement in the way that information is gathered and analyzed, which we are sure will translate into the same kind of tangible benefits we saw from the COBRA pilot project," states the bank, "For the time being, we have already achieved what we needed the most: a single tool which unifies the online measuring of our business strategies, enabling more detailed, structured and controlled online data analysis."

QUESTIONS FOR THE END-OF-CHAPTER APPLICATION CASE

1. How did BBVA use text mining?
2. What were BBVA's challenges? How did BBVA overcome them with text mining and social media analysis?
3. In what other areas, in your opinion, can BBVA use text mining?

Source: IBM Customer Success Story, "BBVA seamlessly monitors and improves its online reputation" at **http://www-01.ibm. com/software/success/cssdb.nsf/CS/STRD-8NUD29?Open Document&Site=corp&cty=en_us** (accessed August 2013).

References

Chun, H. W., Y. Tsuruoka, J. D. Kim, R. Shiba, N. Nagata, and T. Hishiki. (2006). "Extraction of Gene-Disease Relations from Medline Using Domain Dictionaries and Machine Learning." *Proceedings of the 11th Pacific Symposium on Biocomputing,* pp. 4–15.

Cohen, K. B., and L. Hunter. (2008). "Getting Started in Text Mining." *PLoS Compututional Biology,* Vol. 4, No. 1, pp. 1–10.

Coussement, K., and D. Van Den Poel. (2008). "Improving Customer Complaint Management by Automatic Email

Classification Using Linguistic Style Features as Predictors." *Decision Support Systems,* Vol. 44, No. 4, pp. 870–882.

Coussement, K., and D. Van Den Poel. (2009). "Improving Customer Attrition Prediction by Integrating Emotions from Client/Company Interaction Emails and Evaluating Multiple Classifiers." *Expert Systems with Applications,* Vol. 36, No. 3, pp. 6127–6134.

Delen, D., and M. Crossland. (2008). "Seeding the Survey and Analysis of Research Literature with Text Mining." *Expert Systems with Applications,* Vol. 34, No. 3, pp. 1707–1720.

Etzioni, O. (1996). "The World Wide Web: Quagmire or Gold Mine?" *Communications of the ACM,* Vol. 39, No. 11, pp. 65–68.

EUROPOL. (2007). "EUROPOL Work Program 2007." **statewatch.org/news/2006/apr/europol-work-pro-gramme-2007.pdf** (accessed October 2008).

Feldman, R., and J. Sanger. (2007). *The Text Mining Handbook: Advanced Approaches in Analyzing Unstructured Data.* Boston: ABS Ventures.

Fuller, C. M., D. Biros, and D. Delen. (2008). "Exploration of Feature Selection and Advanced Classification Models for High-Stakes Deception Detection." *Proceedings of the 41st Annual Hawaii International Conference on System Sciences (HICSS)*, Big Island, HI: IEEE Press, pp. 80–99.

Ghani, R., K. Probst, Y. Liu, M. Krema, and A. Fano. (2006). "Text Mining for Product Attribute Extraction." *SIGKDD Explorations,* Vol. 8, No. 1, pp. 41–48.

Grimes, S. (2011, February 17). "Seven Breakthrough Sentiment Analysis Scenarios." *InformationWeek.*

Han, J., and M. Kamber. (2006). *Data Mining: Concepts and Techniques,* 2nd ed. San Francisco: Morgan Kaufmann.

Kanayama, H., and T. Nasukawa. (2006). "Fully Automatic Lexicon Expanding for Domain-oriented Sentiment Analysis, EMNLP: Empirical Methods in Natural Language Processing." **trl.ibm.com/projects/textmining/takmi/sentiment_analysis_e.htm.**

Kleinberg, J. (1999). "Authoritative Sources in a Hyperlinked Environment." *Journal of the ACM,* Vol. 46, No. 5, pp. 604–632.

Lin, J., and D. Demner-Fushman. (2005). "'Bag of Words' Is Not Enough for Strength of Evidence Classification." *AMIA Annual Symposium Proceedings,* pp. 1031–1032. **pubmed-central.nih.gov/articlerender.fcgi?artid=1560897.**

Mahgoub, H., D. Rösner, N. Ismail, and F. Torkey. (2008). "A Text Mining Technique Using Association Rules Extraction." *International Journal of Computational Intelligence,* Vol. 4, No. 1, pp. 21–28.

Manning, C. D., and H. Schutze. (1999). *Foundations of Statistical Natural Language Processing.* Cambridge, MA: MIT Press.

Masand, B. M., M. Spiliopoulou, J. Srivastava, and O. R. Zaïane. (2002). "Web Mining for Usage Patterns and Profiles." *SIGKDD Explorations,* Vol. 4, No. 2, pp. 125–132.

McKnight, W. (2005, January 1). "Text Data Mining in Business Intelligence." *Information Management Magazine.* **information-management.com/issues/20050101/1016487-1.html** (accessed May 22, 2009).

Mejova, Y. (2009). "Sentiment Analysis: An Overview." Comprehensive exam paper. **www.cs.uiowa.edu/~ymejova/publications/CompsYelenaMejova.pdf** (accessed February 2013).

Miller, T. W. (2005). *Data and Text Mining: A Business Applications Approach.* Upper Saddle River, NJ: Prentice Hall.

Nakov, P., A. Schwartz, B. Wolf, and M. A. Hearst. (2005). "Supporting Annotation Layers for Natural Language Processing." *Proceedings of the ACL,* interactive poster and demonstration sessions, Ann Arbor, MI. Association for Computational Linguistics, pp. 65–68.

Nasraoui, O., M. Spiliopoulou, J. Srivastava, B. Mobasher, and B. Masand. (2006). "WebKDD 2006: Web Mining and Web Usage Analysis Post-Workshop Report." *ACM SIGKDD Explorations Newsletter*, Vol. 8, No. 2, pp. 84–89.

Nexidia (2009). "State of the art: Sentiment analysis" Nexidia White Paper, http://nexidia.com/files/resource_files/nexidia_sentiment_analysis_wp_8269.pdf (accessed February 2013).

Pang, B., and L. Lee. (2008). "Opinion Mining and Sentiment Analysis." Now Pub. **http://books.google.com**.

Peterson, E. T. (2008). "The Voice of Customer: Qualitative Data as a Critical Input to Web Site Optimization." **foreseeresults.com/Form_Epeterson_WebAnalytics.html** (accessed May 22, 2009).

Shatkay, H., A. Höglund, S. Brady, T. Blum, P. Dönnes, and O. Kohlbacher. (2007). "SherLoc: High-Accuracy Prediction of Protein Subcellular Localization by Integrating Text and Protein Sequence Data." *Bioinformatics,* Vol. 23, No. 11, pp. 1410–1417.

SPSS. "Merck Sharp & Dohme." **spss.com/success/template_view.cfm?Story_ID=185** (accessed May 15, 2009).

StatSoft. (2009). *Statistica Data and Text Miner User Manual.* Tulsa, OK: StatSoft, Inc.

Turetken, O., and R. Sharda. (2004). "Development of a Fisheye-Based Information Search Processing Aid (FISPA) for Managing Information Overload in the Web Environment." *Decision Support Systems,* Vol. 37, No. 3, pp. 415–434.

Weng, S. S., and C. K. Liu. (2004) "Using Text Classification and Multiple Concepts to Answer E-Mails." *Expert Systems with Applications,* Vol. 26, No. 4, pp. 529–543.

Zhou, Y., E. Reid, J. Qin, H. Chen, and G. Lai. (2005). "U.S. Domestic Extremist Groups on the Web: Link and Content Analysis." *IEEE Intelligent Systems,* Vol. 20, No. 5, pp. 44–51.

8

Web Analytics, Web Mining, and Social Analytics

LEARNING OBJECTIVES

- Define *Web mining* and understand its taxonomy and its application areas
- Differentiate between Web content mining and Web structure mining
- Understand the internals of Web search engines
- Learn the details about search engine optimization
- Define *Web usage mining* and learn its business application

- Describe the Web analytics maturity model and its use cases
- Understand social networks and social analytics and their practical applications
- Define *social network analysis* and become familiar with its application areas
- Understand social media analytics and its use for better customer engagement

This chapter is all about Web mining and its application areas. As you will see, Web mining is one of the fastest growing technologies in business intelligence and business analytics. Under the umbrella of Web mining, in this chapter, we will cover Web analytics, search engines, social analytics and their enabling methods, algorithms, and technologies.

8.1 OPENING VIGNETTE: Security First Insurance Deepens Connection with Policyholders

Security First Insurance is one of the largest homeowners' insurance companies in Florida. Headquartered in Ormond Beach, it employs more than 80 insurance professionals to serve its nearly 190,000 customers.

CHALLENGE

Being There for Customers Storm After Storm, Year After Year

Florida has more property and people exposed to hurricanes than any state in the country. Each year, the Atlantic Ocean averages 12 named storms and nine named hurricanes. Security First is one of a few Florida homeowners' insurance companies that has the financial strength to withstand multiple natural disasters. "One of our promises is to be there for our customers, storm after storm, year after year," says Werner Kruck, chief operating officer for Security First.

During a typical month, Security First processes 700 claims. However, in the aftermath of a hurricane, that number can swell to tens of thousands within days. It can be a challenge for the company to quickly scale up to handle the influx of customers trying to file post-storm insurance claims for damaged property and possessions. In the past, customers submitted claims primarily by phone and sometimes email. Today, policyholders use any means available to connect with an agent or claims representative, including posting a question or comment on the company's Facebook page or Twitter account.

Although Security First provides ongoing monitoring of its Facebook and Twitter accounts, as well as its multiple email addresses and call centers, the company knew that the communication volume after a major storm required a more aggressive approach. "We were concerned that if a massive number of customers contacted us through email or social media after a hurricane, we would be unable to respond quickly and appropriately," Kruck says. "We need to be available to our customers in whatever way they want to contact us." In addition, Security First recognized the need to integrate its social media responses into the claims process and document those responses to comply with industry regulations.

SOLUTION

Providing Responsive Service No Matter How Customers Get in Touch

Security First contacted IBM Business Partner Integritie for help with harnessing social media to improve the customer experience. Integritie configured a solution built on key IBM Enterprise Content Management software components, featuring IBM Content Analytics with Enterprise Search, IBM Content Collector for Email and IBM® FileNet® Content Manager software. Called Social Media Capture (SMC4), the Integritie solution offers four critical capabilities for managing social media platforms: capture, control, compliance and communication. For example, the SMC4 solution logs all social networking interaction for Security First, captures content, monitors incoming and outgoing messages and archives all communication for compliance review.

Because the solution uses open IBM Enterprise Content Management software, Security First can easily link it to critical company applications, databases and processes.

For example, Content Collector for Email software automatically captures email content and attachments and sends an email back to the policyholder acknowledging receipt. In addition, Content Analytics with Enterprise Search software sifts through and analyzes the content of customers' posts and emails. The software then captures information gleaned from this analysis directly into claims documents to begin the claims process. Virtually all incoming communication from the company's web, the Internet and emails is pulled into a central FileNet Content Manager software repository to maintain, control and link to the appropriate workflow. "We can bring the customer conversation and any pictures and attachments into our policy and claims management system and use it to trigger our claims process and add to our documentation," says Kruck.

Prioritizing Communications with Access to Smarter Content

People whose homes have been damaged or destroyed by a hurricane are often displaced quickly, with little more than the clothes on their backs. Grabbing an insurance policy on the way out the door is often an afterthought. They're relying on their insurance companies to have the information they need to help them get their lives back in order as quickly as possible. When tens of thousands of policyholders require assistance within a short period of time, Security First must triage requests quickly. The Content Analytics with Enterprise Search software that anchors the SMC4 solution provides the information necessary to help the company identify and address the most urgent cases first. The software automatically sifts through data in email and social media posts, tweets and comments using text mining, text analytics, natural language processing and sentiment analytics to detect words and tones that identify significant property damage or that convey distress. Security First can then prioritize the messages and route them to the proper personnel to provide reassurance, handle complaints or process a claim. "With access to smarter content, we can respond to our customers in a more rapid, efficient and personalized way," says Kruck. "When customers are having a bad experience, it's really important to get to them quickly with the level of assistance appropriate to their particular situations."

RESULTS

Successfully Addressing Potential Compliance Issues

Companies in all industries must stay compliant with new and emerging regulatory requirements regarding social media. The text analysis capabilities provided in the IBM software help Security First filter inappropriate incoming communications and audit outbound communications, avoiding potential issues with message content. The company can be confident that the responses its employees provide are compliant and controlled based on both Security First policies and industry regulations.

Security First can designate people or roles in the organization that are authorized to create and submit responses. The system automatically verifies these designations and analyzes outgoing message content, stopping any ineffective or questionable communications for further review. "Everything is recorded for compliance, so we can effectively track and maintain the process. We have the ability to control which employees respond, their level of authority and the content of their responses," says Kruck.

These capabilities give Security First the confidence to expand its use of social media. Because compliance is covered, the company can focus on additional opportunities for direct dialog with customers. Before this solution, Security First filtered customer communications through agents. Now it can reach out to customers directly and proactively as a company.

"We're one of the first insurance companies in Florida to make ourselves available to customers whenever, wherever and however they choose to communicate. We're also managing internal processes more effectively and proactively, reaching out to customers in a controlled and compliant manner," says Kruck.

Some of the prevailing business benefits of creative use of Web and social analytics include:

- Turns social media into an actionable communications channel during a major disaster
- Speeds claims processes by initiating claims with information from email and social media posts
- Facilitates prioritizing urgent cases by analyzing social media content for sentiments
- Helps ensure compliance by automatically documenting social media communications

QUESTIONS FOR THE OPENING VIGNETTE

1. What does Security First do?
2. What were the main challenges Security First was facing?
3. What was the proposed solution approach? What types of analytics were integrated in the solution?
4. Based on what you learn from the vignette, what do you think are the relationships between Web analytics, text mining, and sentiment analysis?
5. What were the results Security First obtained? Were any surprising benefits realized?

WHAT WE CAN LEARN FROM THIS VIGNETTE

Web analytics is becoming a way of life for many businesses, especially the ones that are directly facing the consumers. Companies are expected to find new and innovative ways to connect with their customers, understand their needs, wants, and opinions, and proactively develop products and services that fit well with them. In this day and age, asking customers to tell you exactly what they like and dislike is not a viable option. Instead, businesses are expected to deduce that information by applying advanced analytics tools to invaluable data generated on the Internet and social media sites (along with corporate databases). Security First realized the need to revolutionize their business processes to be more effective and efficient in the way that they deal with their customers and customer claims. They not only used what the Internet and social media have to offer, but also tapped into the customer call records/recordings and other relevant transaction databases. This vignette illustrates the fact that analytics technologies are advanced enough to bring together many different data sources to create a holistic view of the customer. And that is perhaps the greatest success criterion for today's businesses. In the following sections, you will learn about many of the Web-based analytical techniques that make it all happen.

Source: IBM Customer Success Story, "Security First Insurance deepens connection with policyholders" accessed at **http://www-01.ibm.com/software/success/cssdb.nsf/CS/SAKG-975H4N?OpenDocument&Site=default&cty=en_us** (accessed August 2013).*.*

8.2 WEB MINING OVERVIEW

The Internet has forever changed the landscape of business as we know it. Because of the highly connected, flattened world and broadened competitive field, today's companies are increasingly facing greater opportunities (being able to reach customers and markets that they may have never thought possible) and bigger challenge (a globalized and ever-changing competitive marketplace). Ones with the vision and capabilities to deal with such a volatile environment are greatly benefiting from it, while others who resist are having a hard time surviving. Having an engaged presence on the Internet is not a choice anymore: It is a business requirement. Customers are expecting companies to offer their products and/or services over the Internet. They are not only buying products and services but also talking about companies and sharing their transactional and usage experiences with others over the Internet.

The growth of the Internet and its enabling technologies has made data creation, data collection, and data/information/opinion exchange easier. Delays in service, manufacturing, shipping, delivery, and customer inquiries are no longer private incidents and are accepted as necessary evils. Now, thanks to social media tools and technologies on the Internet, everybody knows everything. Successful companies are the ones who embrace these Internet technologies and use them for the betterment of their business processes so that they can better communicate with their customers, understanding their needs and wants and serving them thoroughly and expeditiously. Being customer focused and keeping customers happy have never been as important a concept for businesses as they are now, in this age of the Internet and social media.

The World Wide Web (or, for short, the Web) serves as an enormous repository of data and information on virtually everything one can conceive—business, personal, you name it; an abundant amount of it is there. The Web is perhaps the world's largest data and text repository, and the amount of information on the Web is growing rapidly. A lot of interesting information can be found online: whose homepage is linked to which other pages, how many people have links to a specific Web page, and how a particular site is organized. In addition, each visitor to a Web site, each search on a search engine, each click on a link, and each transaction on an e-commerce site create additional data. Although unstructured textual data in the form of Web pages coded in HTML or XML is the dominant content of the Web, the Web infrastructure also contains hyperlink information (connections to other Web pages) and usage information (logs of visitors' interactions with Web sites), all of which provide rich data for knowledge discovery. Analysis of this information can help us make better use of Web sites and also aid us in enhancing relationships and value for the visitors to our own Web sites.

Because of its sheer size and complexity, mining the Web is not an easy undertaking by any means. The Web also poses great challenges for effective and efficient knowledge discovery (Han and Kamber, 2006):

- ***The Web is too big for effective data mining.*** The Web is so large and growing so rapidly that it is difficult to even quantify its size. Because of the sheer size of the Web, it is not feasible to set up a data warehouse to replicate, store, and integrate all of the data on the Web, making data collection and integration a challenge.
- ***The Web is too complex.*** The complexity of a Web page is far greater than a page in a traditional text document collection. Web pages lack a unified structure. They contain far more authoring style and content variation than any set of books, articles, or other traditional text-based document.
- ***The Web is too dynamic.*** The Web is a highly dynamic information source. Not only does the Web grow rapidly, but its content is constantly being updated. Blogs, news stories, stock market results, weather reports, sports scores, prices, company advertisements, and numerous other types of information are updated regularly on the Web.
- ***The Web is not specific to a domain.*** The Web serves a broad diversity of communities and connects billions of workstations. Web users have very different backgrounds, interests, and usage purposes. Most users may not have good knowledge of the structure of the information network and may not be aware of the heavy cost of a particular search that they perform.
- ***The Web has everything.*** Only a small portion of the information on the Web is truly relevant or useful to someone (or some task). It is said that 99 percent of the information on the Web is useless to 99 percent of Web users. Although this may not seem obvious,

it is true that a particular person is generally interested in only a tiny portion of the Web, whereas the rest of the Web contains information that is uninteresting to the user and may swamp desired results. Finding the portion of the Web that is truly relevant to a person and the task being performed is a prominent issue in Web-related research.

These challenges have prompted many research efforts to enhance the effectiveness and efficiency of discovering and using data assets on the Web. A number of index-based Web search engines constantly search the Web and index Web pages under certain keywords. Using these search engines, an experienced user may be able to locate documents by providing a set of tightly constrained keywords or phrases. However, a simple keyword-based search engine suffers from several deficiencies. First, a topic of any breadth can easily contain hundreds or thousands of documents. This can lead to a large number of document entries returned by the search engine, many of which are marginally relevant to the topic. Second, many documents that are highly relevant to a topic may not contain the exact keywords defining them. As we will cover in more detail later in this chapter, compared to keyword-based Web search, Web mining is a prominent (and more challenging) approach that can be used to substantially enhance the power of Web search engines because Web mining can identify authoritative Web pages, classify Web documents, and resolve many ambiguities and subtleties raised in keyword-based Web search engines.

Web mining (or Web data mining) is the process of discovering intrinsic relationships (i.e., interesting and useful information) from Web data, which are expressed in the form of textual, linkage, or usage information. The term *Web mining* was first used by Etzioni (1996); today, many conferences, journals, and books focus on Web data mining. It is a continually evolving area of technology and business practice. Web mining is essentially the same as data mining that uses data generated over the Web. The goal is to turn vast repositories of business transactions, customer interactions, and Web site usage data into actionable information (i.e., knowledge) to promote better decision making throughout the enterprise. Because of the increased popularity of the term *analytics,* nowadays many have started to call Web mining *Web analytics.* However, these two terms are not the same. Although Web analytics is primarily Web site usage data focused, Web mining is inclusive of all data generated via the Internet, including transaction, social, and usage data. While Web analytics aims to describe what has happened on the Web site (employing a predefined, metrics-driven descriptive analytics methodology), Web mining aims to discover previously unknown patterns and relationships (employing a novel predictive or prescriptive analytics methodology). From a big-picture perspective, Web analytics can be considered a part of Web mining. Figure 8.1 presents a simple taxonomy of Web mining, where it is divided into three main areas: Web content mining, Web structure mining, and Web usage mining. In the figure, the data sources used in these three main areas are also specified. Although these three areas are shown separately, as you will see in the following section, they are often used collectively and synergistically to address business problems and opportunities.

As Figure 8.1 indicates, Web mining relies heavily on data mining and text mining and their enabling tools and techniques, which we have covered in detail in the previous two chapters (Chapters 6 and 7). The figure also indicates that these three generic areas are further extended into several very well-known application areas. Some of these areas were explained in the previous chapters, and some of the others will be covered in detail in this chapter.

SECTION 8.2 REVIEW QUESTIONS

1. What are some of the main challenges the Web poses for knowledge discovery?
2. What is Web mining? How does it differ from regular data mining or text mining?
3. What are the three main areas of Web mining?
4. Identify three application areas for Web mining (at the bottom of Figure 8.1). Based on your own experiences, comment on their use cases in business settings.

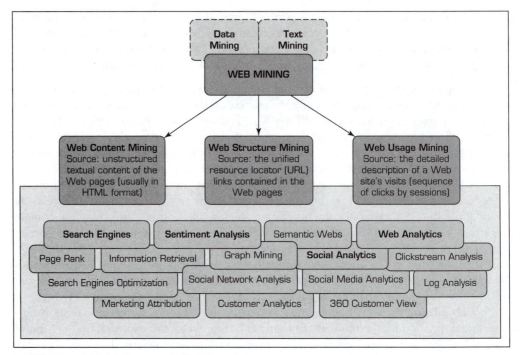

FIGURE 8.1 A Simple Taxonomy of Web Mining.

8.3 WEB CONTENT AND WEB STRUCTURE MINING

Web content mining refers to the extraction of useful information from Web pages. The documents may be extracted in some machine-readable format so that automated techniques can extract some information from these Web pages. **Web crawlers** (also called **spiders**) are used to read through the content of a Web site automatically. The information gathered may include document characteristics similar to what are used in text mining, but it may also include additional concepts, such as the document hierarchy. Such an automated (or semiautomated) process of collecting and mining Web content can be used for competitive intelligence (collecting intelligence about competitors' products, services, and customers). It can also be used for information/news/opinion collection and summarization, sentiment analysis, automated data collection, and structuring for predictive modeling. As an illustrative example to using Web content mining as an automated data collection tool, consider the following. For more than 10 years, two of the three authors of this book (Drs. Sharda and Delen) have been developing models to predict the financial success of Hollywood movies before their theatrical release. The data that they use for training the models come from several Web sites, each of which has a different hierarchical page structure. Collecting a large set of variables on thousands of movies (from the past several years) from these Web sites is a time-demanding, error-prone process. Therefore, they use Web content mining and spiders as an enabling technology to automatically collect, verify, validate (if the specific data item is available on more than one Web site, then the values are validated against each other and anomalies are captured and recorded), and store these values in a relational database. That way, they ensure the quality of the data while saving valuable time (days or weeks) in the process.

In addition to text, Web pages also contain hyperlinks pointing one page to another. Hyperlinks contain a significant amount of hidden human annotation that can potentially help to automatically infer the notion of centrality or *authority*. When a Web page developer includes a link pointing to another Web page, this may be regarded as the developer's endorsement of the other page. The collective endorsement of a given page by different developers on the Web may indicate the importance of the page and may naturally lead to the discovery of authoritative Web pages (Miller, 2005). Therefore, the vast amount of Web linkage information provides a rich collection of information about the relevance, quality, and structure of the Web's contents, and thus is a rich source for Web mining.

Web content mining can also be used to enhance the results produced by search engines. In fact, search is perhaps the most prevailing application of Web content mining and Web structure mining. A search on the Web to obtain information on a specific topic (presented as a collection of keywords or a sentence) usually returns a few relevant, high-quality Web pages and a larger number of unusable Web pages. Use of a relevance index based on keywords and authoritative pages (or some measure of it) will improve the search results and ranking of relevant pages. The idea of authority (or **authoritative pages**) stems from earlier information retrieval work using citations among journal articles to evaluate the impact of research papers (Miller, 2005). Though that was the origin of the idea, there are significant differences between the citations in research articles and hyperlinks on Web pages. First, not every hyperlink represents an endorsement (some links are created for navigation purposes and some are for paid advertisement). While this is true, if the majority of the hyperlinks are of the endorsement type, then the collective opinion will still prevail. Second, for commercial and competitive interests, one authority will rarely have its Web page point to rival authorities in the same domain. For example, Microsoft may prefer not to include links on its Web pages to Apple's Web sites, because this may be regarded as endorsement of its competitor's authority. Third, authoritative pages are seldom particularly descriptive. For example, the main Web page of Yahoo! may not contain the explicit self-description that it is in fact a Web search engine.

The structure of Web hyperlinks has led to another important category of Web pages called a **hub**. A hub is one or more Web pages that provide a collection of links to authoritative pages. Hub pages may not be prominent and only a few links may point to them; however, they provide links to a collection of prominent sites on a specific topic of interest. A hub could be a list of recommended links on an individual's homepage, recommended reference sites on a course Web page, or a professionally assembled resource list on a specific topic. Hub pages play the role of implicitly conferring the authorities on a narrow field. In essence, a close symbiotic relationship exists between good hubs and authoritative pages; a good hub is good because it points to many good authorities, and a good authority is good because it is being pointed to by many good hubs. Such relationships between hubs and authorities make it possible to automatically retrieve high-quality content from the Web.

The most popular publicly known and referenced algorithm used to calculate hubs and authorities is **hyperlink-induced topic search (HITS)**. It was originally developed by Kleinberg (1999) and has since been improved on by many researchers. HITS is a link-analysis algorithm that rates Web pages using the hyperlink information contained within them. In the context of Web search, the HITS algorithm collects a base document set for a specific query. It then recursively calculates the hub and authority values for each document. To gather the base document set, a root set that matches the query is fetched from a search engine. For each document retrieved, a set of documents that points to the original document and another set of documents that is pointed to by the original document are added to the set as the original document's neighborhood. A recursive process of document identification and link analysis continues until the hub and authority values converge. These values are then used to index and prioritize the document collection generated for a specific query.

Web structure mining is the process of extracting useful information from the links embedded in Web documents. It is used to identify authoritative pages and hubs, which are the cornerstones of the contemporary page-rank algorithms that are central to popular search engines such as Google and Yahoo!. Just as links going to a Web page may indicate a site's popularity (or authority), links within the Web page (or the compete Web site) may indicate the depth of coverage of a specific topic. Analysis of links is very important in understanding the interrelationships among large numbers of Web pages, leading to a better understanding of a specific Web community, clan, or clique. Application Case 8.1 describes a project that used both Web content mining and Web structure mining to better understand how U.S. extremist groups are connected.

SECTION 8.3 REVIEW QUESTIONS

1. What is Web content mining? How can it be used for competitive advantage?
2. What is an "authoritative page"? What is a "hub"? What is the difference between the two?
3. What is Web structure mining? How does it differ from Web content mining?

Application Case 8.1
Identifying Extremist Groups with Web Link and Content Analysis

We normally search for answers to our problems outside of our immediate environment. Often, however, the trouble stems from within. In taking action against global terrorism, domestic extremist groups often go unnoticed. However, domestic extremists pose a significant threat to U.S. security because of the information they possess, as well as their increasing ability, through the use of the Internet, to reach out to extremist groups around the world.

Keeping tabs on the content available on the Internet is difficult. Researchers and authorities need superior tools to analyze and monitor the activities of extremist groups. Researchers at the University of Arizona, with support from the Department of Homeland Security and other agencies, have developed a Web mining methodology to find and analyze Web sites operated by domestic extremists in order to learn about these groups through their use of the Internet. Extremist groups use the Internet to communicate, to access private messages, and to raise money online.

The research methodology begins by gathering a superior-quality collection of relevant extremist and terrorist Web sites. Hyperlink analysis is performed, which leads to other extremist and terrorist Web sites. The interconnectedness with other Web sites is crucial in estimating the similarity of the objectives of various groups. The next step is content analysis, which further codifies these Web sites based on various attributes, such as communications, fund raising, and ideology sharing, to name a few.

Based on link analysis and content analysis, researchers have identified 97 Web sites of U.S. extremist and hate groups. Often, the links between these communities do not necessarily represent any cooperation between them. However, finding numerous links between common interest groups helps in clustering the communities under a common banner. Further research using data mining to automate the process has a global aim, with the goal of identifying links between international hate and extremist groups and their U.S. counterparts.

QUESTIONS FOR DISCUSSION

1. How can Web link/content analysis be used to identify extremist groups?
2. What do you think are the challenges and the potential solution to such intelligence gathering activities?

Source: Y. Zhou, E. Reid, J. Qin, H. Chen, and G. Lai, "U.S. Domestic Extremist Groups on the Web: Link and Content Analysis," *IEEE Intelligent Systems*, Vol. 20, No. 5, September/October 2005, pp. 44–51.

8.4 SEARCH ENGINES

In this day and age, there is no denying the importance of Internet search engines. As the size and complexity of the World Wide Web increases, finding what you want is becoming a complex and laborious process. People use search engines for a variety of reasons. We use them to learn about a product or a service before committing to buy (including who else is selling it, what the prices are at different locations/sellers, the common issues people are discussing about it, how satisfied previous buyers are, what other products or services might be better, etc.) and search for places to go, people to meet, and things to do. In a sense, search engines have become the centerpiece of most Internet-based transactions and other activities. The incredible success and popularity of Google, the most popular search engine company, is a good testament to this claim. What is somewhat a mystery to many is how a search engine actually does what it is meant to do. In simplest terms, a **search engine** is a software program that searches for documents (Internet sites or files) based on the keywords (individual words, multi-word terms, or a complete sentence) that users have provided that have to do with the subject of their inquiry. Search engines are the workhorses of the Internet, responding to billions of queries in hundreds of different languages every day.

Technically speaking, *search engine* is the popular term for information retrieval system. Although Web search engines are the most popular, search engines are often used in a context other than the Web, such as desktop search engines or document search engines. As you will see in this section, many of the concepts and techniques that we covered in the text analytics and text mining chapter (Chapter 7) also apply here. The overall goal of a search engine is to return one or more documents/pages (if more than one documents/pages applies, a rank-order list is often provided) that best match the user's query. The two metrics that are often used to evaluate search engines are *effectiveness* (or quality—finding the right documents/pages) and *efficiency* (or speed—returning a response quickly). These two metrics tend to work in reverse direction; improving one tends to worsen the other. Often, based on user expectation, search engines focus on one at the expense of the other. Better search engines are the ones that excel in both at the same time. Because search engines not only search but, in fact, find and return the documents/pages, perhaps a more appropriate name for them would be "finding engines."

Anatomy of a Search Engine

Now let us dissect a search engine and look inside it. At the highest level, a search engine system is composed of two main cycles: a development cycle and a responding cycle (see the structure of a typical Internet search engine in Figure 8.2). While one is interfacing

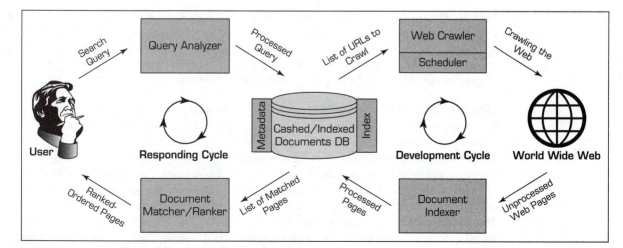

FIGURE 8.2 **Structure of a Typical Internet Search Engine.**

with the World Wide Web, the other is interfacing with the user. One can think of the development cycle as a production process (manufacturing and inventorying documents/pages) and the responding cycle as a retailing process (providing customers/users with what they want). In the following section these two cycles are explained in more detail.

1. Development Cycle

The two main components of the development cycle are the Web crawler and document indexer. The purpose of this cycle is to create a huge database of documents/pages organized and indexed based on their content and information value. The reason for developing such a repository of documents/pages is quite obvious: Due to its sheer size and complexity, searching the Web to find pages in response to a user query is not practical (or feasible within a reasonable time frame); therefore, search engines "cashes the Web" into their database, and uses the cashed version of the Web for searching and finding. Once created, this database allows search engines to rapidly and accurately respond to user queries.

Web Crawler

A Web crawler (also called a spider or a Web spider) is a piece of software that systematically browses (crawls through) the World Wide Web for the purpose of finding and fetching Web pages. Often Web crawlers copy all the pages they visit for later processing by other functions of a search engine.

A Web crawler starts with a list of URLs to visit, which are listed in the scheduler and often are called the seeds. These URLs may come from submissions made by Webmasters or, more often, they come from the internal hyperlinks of previously crawled documents/pages. As the crawler visits these URLs, it identifies all the hyperlinks in the page and adds them to the list of URLs to visit (i.e., the scheduler). URLs in the scheduler are recursively visited according to a set of policies determined by the specific search engine. Because there are large volumes of Web pages, the crawler can only download a limited number of them within a given time; therefore, it may need to prioritize its downloads.

Document Indexer

As the documents are found and fetched by the crawler, they are stored in a temporary staging area for the document indexer to grab and process. The document indexer is responsible for processing the documents (Web pages or document files) and placing them into the document database. In order to convert the documents/pages into the desired, easily searchable format, the document indexer performs the following tasks.

STEP 1: PREPROCESSING THE DOCUMENTS Because the documents fetched by the crawler may all be in different formats, for the ease of processing them further, in this step they all are converted to some type of standard representation. For instance, different content types (text, hyperlink, image, etc.) may be separated from each other, formatted (if necessary), and stored in a place for further processing.

STEP 2: PARSING THE DOCUMENTS This step is essentially the application of text mining (i.e., computational linguistic, natural language processing) tools and techniques to a collection of documents/pages. In this step, first the standardized documents are parsed into its components to identify index-worthy words/terms. Then, using a set of rules, the words/terms are indexed. More specifically, using tokenization rules, the words/terms/entities are extracted from the sentences in these documents. Using proper lexicons, the spelling errors and other anomalies in these words/terms are corrected. Not all the terms are discriminators. The nondiscriminating words/terms (also known as stop words) are eliminated from the list of index-worthy words/terms. Because the same word/term can be in many different forms, stemming is applied to reduce the words/terms to their root forms. Again, using lexicons and other language-specific resources (e.g., WordNet), synonyms and homonyms are identified and the word/term collection is processed before moving into the indexing phase.

STEP 3: CREATING THE TERM-BY-DOCUMENT MATRIX   In this step, the relationships between the words/terms and documents/pages are identified. The weight can be as simple as assigning 1 for presence or 0 for absence of the word/term in the document/page. Usually more sophisticated weight schemas are used. For instance, as opposed to binary, one may choose to assign frequency of occurrence (number of times the same word/term is found in a document) as a weight. As we have seen in Chapter 7, text mining research and practice have clearly indicated that the best weighting may come from the use of *term-frequency* divided by *inverse-document-frequency* (TF/IDF). This algorithm measures the frequency of occurrence of each word/term within a document, and then compares that frequency against the frequency of occurrence in the document collection. As we all know, not all high-frequency words/term are good document discriminators; and a good document discriminator in a domain may not be one in another domain. Once the weighing schema is determined, the weights are calculated and the term-by-document index file is created.

2. Response Cycle

The two main components of the responding cycle are the query analyzer and the document matcher/ranker.

Query Analyzer

The query analyzer is responsible for receiving a search request from the user (via the search engine's Web server interface) and converting it into a standardized data structure, so that it can be easily queried/matched against the entries in the document database. How the query analyzer does what it is supposed to do is quite similar to what the document indexer does (as we have just explained). The query analyzer parses the search string into individual words/terms using a series of tasks that include tokenization, removal of stop words, stemming, and word/term disambiguation (identification of spelling errors, synonyms, and homonyms). The close similarity between the query analyzer and document indexer is not coincidental. In fact, it is quite logical, because both are working off of the document database; one is putting in documents/pages using a specific index structures, and the other is converting a query string into the same structure so that it can be used to quickly locate most relevant documents/pages.

Document Matcher/Ranker

This is where the structured query data is matched against the document database to find the most relevant documents/pages and also rank them in the order of relevance/importance. The proficiency of this step is perhaps the most important component when different search engines are compared to one another. Every search engine has its own (often proprietary) algorithm that it uses to carry out this important step.

   The early search engines used a simple keyword match against the document database and returned a list of ordered documents/pages, where the determinant of the order was a function that used the number of words/terms matched between the query and the document along with the weights of those words/terms. The quality and the usefulness of the search results were not all that good. Then, in 1997, the creators of Google came up with a new algorithm, called PageRank. As the name implies, PageRank is an algorithmic way to rank-order documents/pages based on their relevance and value/importance. Technology Insights 8.1 provides a high-level description of this patented algorithm. Even

TECHNOLOGY INSIGHTS 8.1   PageRank Algorithm

PageRank is a link analysis algorithm—named after Larry Page, one of the two inventors of Google, which started as a research project at Stanford University in 1996—used by the Google Web search engine. PageRank assigns a numerical weight to each element of a hyperlinked set of documents, such as the ones found on the World Wide Web, with the purpose of measuring its relative importance within a given collection.

It is believed that PageRank has been influenced by citation analysis, where citations in scholarly works are examined to discover relationships among researchers and their research topics. The applications of citation analysis ranges from identification of prominent experts in a given field of study to providing invaluable information for a transparent review of academic achievements, which can be used for merit review, tenure, and promotion decisions. The PageRank algorithm aims to do the same thing: identifying reputable/important/valuable documents/pages that are highly regarded by other documents/pages. A graphical illustration of PageRank is shown in Figure 8.3.

How Does PageRank Work?

Computationally speaking, PageRank extends the citation analysis idea by not counting links from all pages equally and by normalizing by the number of links on a page. PageRank is defined as follows:

Assume page A has pages P_1 through P_n pointing to it (with *hyperlinks*, which is similar to *citations* in citation analysis). The parameter d is a damping/smoothing factor that can assume values between 0 and 1. Also $C(A)$ is defined as the number of links going out of page A. The simple formula for the PageRank for page A can be written as follows:

$$PageRank(A) = (1 - d) + d \sum_{i=1}^{n} \frac{PageRank(P_i)}{C(P_i)}$$

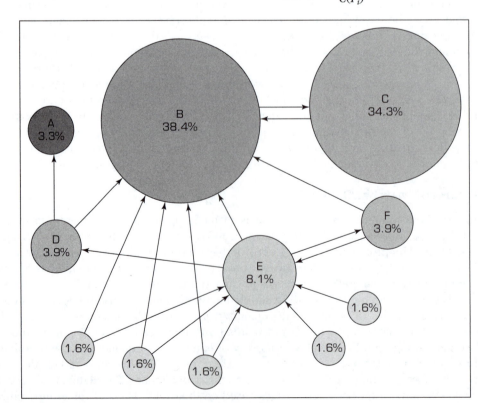

FIGURE 8.3   A Graphical Example for the PageRank Algorithm.

Note that the PageRanks form a probability distribution over Web pages, so the sum of all Web pages' PageRanks will be 1. *PageRank(A)* can be calculated using a simple iterative algorithm and corresponds to the principal eigenvector of the normalized link matrix of the Web. The algorithm is so computationally efficient that a PageRank for 26 million Web pages can be computed in a few hours on a medium-size workstation (Brin and Page, 2012). Of course, there are more details to the actual calculation of PageRank in Google. Most of those details are either not publicly available or are beyond the scope of this simple explanation.

Justification of the Formulation

PageRank can be thought of as a model of user behavior. It assumes there is a *random surfer* who is given a Web page at random and keeps clicking on hyperlinks, never hitting *back* but eventually getting bored and starting on another random page. The probability that the random surfer visits a page is its PageRank. And, the *d* damping factor is the probability at each page the *random surfer* will get bored and request another random page. One important variation is to only add the damping factor *d* to a single page, or a group of pages. This allows for personalization and can make it nearly impossible to deliberately mislead the system in order to get a higher ranking.

Another intuitive justification is that a page can have a high PageRank if there are many pages that point to it, or if there are some pages that point to it and have a high PageRank. Intuitively, pages that are well cited from many places around the Web are worth looking at. Also, pages that have perhaps only one citation from something like the Yahoo! homepage are also generally worth looking at. If a page was not high quality, or was a broken link, it is quite likely that Yahoo!'s homepage would not link to it. The formulation of PageRank handles both of these cases and everything in between by recursively propagating weights through the link structure of the Web.

---

though PageRank is an innovative way to rank documents/pages, it is an augmentation to the process of retrieving relevant documents from the database and ranking them based on the weights of the words/terms. Google does all of these collectively and more to come up with the most relevant list of documents/pages for a given search request. Once an ordered list of documents/pages is created, it is pushed back to the user in an easily digestible format. At this point, users may choose to click on any of the documents in the list, and it may not be the one at the top. If they click on a document/page link that is not at the top of the list, then can we assume that the search engine did not do a good job ranking them? Perhaps, yes. Leading search engines like Google monitor the performance of their search results by capturing, recording, and analyzing postdelivery user actions and experiences. These analyses often lead to more and more rules to further refine the ranking of the documents/pages so that the links at the top are more preferable to the end users.

How Does Google Do It?

Even though complex low-level computational details are trade secrets and are not known to the public, the high-level structure of the Google search system is well-known and quite simple. From the infrastructure standpoint, the Google search system runs on a distributed network of tens of thousands of computers/servers and can, therefore, carry out its heavy workload effectively and efficiently using sophisticated parallel processing algorithms (a method of computation in which many calculations can be distributed to many servers and performed simultaneously, significantly speeding up data processing). At the highest level, the Google search system has three distinct parts (**googleguide.com**):

1. Googlebot, a Web crawler that roams the Internet to find and fetch Web pages
2. The indexer, which sorts every word on every page and stores the resulting index of words in a huge database

3. The query processor, which compares your search query to the index and recommends the documents that it considers most relevant

1. ***Googlebot***   Googlebot is Google's Web crawling robot, which finds and retrieves pages on the Web and hands them off to the Google indexer. It's easy to imagine Googlebot as a little spider scurrying across the strands of cyberspace, but in reality Googlebot doesn't traverse the Web at all. It functions, much like your Web browser, by sending a request to a Web server for a Web page, downloading the entire page, and then handing it off to Google's indexer. Googlebot consists of many computers requesting and fetching pages much more quickly than you can with your Web browser. In fact, Googlebot can request thousands of different pages simultaneously. To avoid overwhelming Web servers, or crowding out requests from human users, Googlebot deliberately makes requests of each individual Web server more slowly than it's capable of doing.

When Googlebot fetches a page, it removes all the links appearing on the page and adds them to a queue for subsequent crawling. Googlebot tends to encounter little spam because most Web authors link only to what they believe are high-quality pages. By harvesting links from every page it encounters, Googlebot can quickly build a list of links that can cover broad reaches of the Web. This technique, known as *deep crawling,* also allows Googlebot to probe deep within individual sites. Because of their massive scale, deep crawls can reach almost every page in the Web. To keep the index current, Google continuously recrawls popular frequently changing Web pages at a rate roughly proportional to how often the pages change. Such crawls keep an index current and are known as *fresh crawls*. Newspaper pages are downloaded daily; pages with stock quotes are downloaded much more frequently. Of course, fresh crawls return fewer pages than the deep crawl. The combination of the two types of crawls allows Google to both make efficient use of its resources and keep its index reasonably current.

2. ***Google Indexer***   Googlebot gives the indexer the full text of the pages it finds. These pages are stored in Google's index database. This index is sorted alphabetically by search term, with each index entry storing a list of documents in which the term appears and the location within the text where it occurs. This data structure allows rapid access to documents that contain user query terms. To improve search performance, Google ignores common words, called *stop words* (such as *the, is, on, or, of, a, an,* as well as certain single digits and single letters). Stop words are so common that they do little to narrow a search, and therefore they can safely be discarded. The indexer also ignores some punctuation and multiple spaces, as well as converting all letters to lowercase, to improve Google's performance.

3. ***Google Query Processor***   The query processor has several parts, including the user interface (search box), the "engine" that evaluates queries and matches them to relevant documents, and the results formatter.

Google uses a proprietary algorithm, called PageRank, to calculate the relative rank order of a given collection of Web pages. PageRank is Google's system for ranking Web pages. A page with a higher PageRank is deemed more important and is more likely to be listed above a page with a lower PageRank. Google considers over a hundred factors in computing a PageRank and determining which documents are most relevant to a query, including the popularity of the page, the position and size of the search terms within the page, and the proximity of the search terms to one another on the page.

Google also applies machine-learning techniques to improve its performance automatically by learning relationships and associations within the stored data. For example, the *spelling-correcting system* uses such techniques to figure out likely alternative spellings. Google closely guards the formulas it uses to calculate relevance; they're tweaked to improve quality and performance, and to outwit the latest devious techniques used by spammers.

Indexing the full text of the Web allows Google to go beyond simply matching single search terms. Google gives more priority to pages that have search terms near each other and in the same order as the query. Google can also match multi-word phrases and sentences. Because Google indexes HTML code in addition to the text on the page, users can restrict searches on the basis of where query words appear (e.g., in the title, in the URL, in the body, and in links to the page, options offered by Google's Advanced Search Form and Using Search Operators).

Understanding the internals of popular search engines helps companies, who rely on search engine traffic, better design their e-commerce sites to improve their chances of getting indexed and highly ranked by search providers. Application Case 8.2 gives an illustrative example of such a phenomenon, where an entertainment company increased its search-originated customer traffic by 1500 percent.

Application Case 8.2
IGN Increases Search Traffic by 1500 Percent

IGN Entertainment operates the Internet's largest network of destinations for video gaming, entertainment, and community geared toward teens and 18- to 34-year-old males. The company's properties include IGN.com, GameSpy, AskMen.com, RottenTomatoes, FilePlanet, TeamXbox, 3D Gamers, VE3D, and Direct2Drive—more than 70 community sites and a vast array of online forums. IGN Entertainment is also a leading provider of technology for online game play in video games.

The Challenge

When this company contacted SEO Inc. in summer 2003, the site was an established and well-known site in the gaming community. The site also had some good search engine rankings and was getting approximately 2.5 million unique visitors per month. At the time IGN used proprietary in-house content management and a team of content writers. The pages that were generated when new game reviews and information were added to the site were not very well optimized. In addition, there were serious architectural issues with the site, which prevented search engine spiders from thoroughly and consistently crawling the site.

IGN's goals were to "dominate the search rankings for keywords related to any video games and gaming systems reviewed on the site." IGN

wanted to rank high in the search engines, and most specifically, Google, for any and all game titles and variants on those game titles' phrases. IGN's revenue is generated from advertising sales, so more traffic leads to more inventory for ad sales, more ads being sold, and therefore more revenue. In order to generate more traffic, IGN knew that it needed to be much more visible when people used the search engines.

The Strategy

After several conversations with the IGN team, SOE Inc. created a customized optimization package that was designed to achieve their ranking goals and also fit the client's budget. Because IGN.com had architectural problems and a proprietary CMS (content management system), it was decided that SEO Inc. would work with their IT and Web development team at their location. This allowed SEO to send their team to the IGN location for several days to learn how their system worked and partner with their in-house programmers to improve the system and, hence, improve search engine optimization. In addition, SEO created customized SEO best practices and architected these into their proprietary CMS. SEO also trained their content writers and page developers on SEO best practices. When new games and pages are added to the site, they are typically getting ranked within weeks, if not days.

(Continued)

Application Case 8.2 (Continued)

The Results

This was a true and quick success story. Organic search engine rankings skyrocketed and thousands of previously not-indexed pages were now being crawled regularly by search engine spiders. Some of the specific results were as follows:

- Unique visitors to the site doubled within the first 2 months after the optimization was completed.
- There was a 1500 percent increase in organic search engine traffic.
- Massive growth in traffic and revenues enabled acquisition of additional Web properties including Rottentomatoes.com and Askmen.com

IGN was acquired by News Corp in September 2005 for $650 million.

Questions for Discussion

1. How did IGN dramatically increase search traffic to its Web portals?
2. What were the challenges, the proposed solution, and the obtained results?

Source: SOE Inc., Customer Case Study, **seoinc.com/seo/case-studies/ign** (accessed March 2013).

SECTION 8.4 REVIEW QUESTIONS

1. What is a search engine? Why are they important for today's businesses?
2. What is the relationship between search engines and text mining?
3. What are the two main cycles in search engines? Describe the steps in each cycle.
4. What is a Web crawler? What is it used for? How does it work?
5. How does a query analyzer work? What is PageRank algorithm and how does it work?

8.5 SEARCH ENGINE OPTIMIZATION

Search engine optimization (SEO) is the intentional activity of affecting the visibility of an e-commerce site or a Web site in a search engine's natural (unpaid or organic) search results. In general, the higher ranked on the search results page, and more frequently a site appears in the search results list, the more visitors it will receive from the search engine's users. As an Internet marketing strategy, SEO considers how search engines work, what people search for, the actual search terms or keywords typed into search engines, and which search engines are preferred by their targeted audience. Optimizing a Web site may involve editing its content, HTML, and associated coding to both increase its relevance to specific keywords and to remove barriers to the indexing activities of search engines. Promoting a site to increase the number of backlinks, or inbound links, is another SEO tactic.

In the early days, in order to be indexed, all Webmasters needed to do was to submit the address of a page, or URL, to the various engines, which would then send a "spider" to "crawl" that page, extract links to other pages from it, and return information found on the page to the server for indexing. The process, as explained before, involves a search engine spider downloading a page and storing it on the search engine's own server, where a second program, known as an indexer, extracts various information about the page, such as the words it contains and where these are located, as well as any weight for specific words, and all links the page contains, which are then placed into a scheduler for crawling at a later date. Nowadays search engines are no longer relying on Webmasters submitting URLs (even though they still can); instead, they are proactively and continuously crawling the Web, and finding, fetching, and indexing everything about it.

Being indexed by search engines like Google, Bing, and Yahoo! is not good enough for businesses. Getting ranked on the most widely used search engines (see Technology Insights 8.2 for a list of most widely used search engines) and getting ranked higher than your competitors are what make the difference. A variety of methods can increase the ranking of a Web page within the search results. Cross-linking between pages of the same Web site to provide more links to the most important pages may improve its visibility. Writing content that includes frequently searched keyword phrases, so as to be relevant to a wide variety of search queries, will tend to increase traffic. Updating content so as to keep search engines crawling back frequently can give additional weight to a site. Adding relevant keywords to a Web page's metadata, including the title tag and metadescription, will tend to improve the relevancy of a site's search listings, thus increasing traffic. URL normalization of Web pages so that they are accessible via multiple URLs and using canonical link element and redirects can help make sure links to different versions of the URL all count toward the page's link popularity score.

Methods for Search Engine Optimization

In general, SEO techniques can be classified into two broad categories: techniques that search engines recommend as part of good site design, and those techniques of which search engines do not approve. The search engines attempt to minimize the effect of the latter, which is often called *spamdexing* (also known as *search spam, search engine spam,* or *search engine poisoning*). Industry commentators have classified these methods, and the practitioners who employ them, as either white-hat SEO or black-hat SEO

TECHNOLOGY INSIGHTS 8.2 Top 15 Most Popular Search Engines (March 2013)

Here are the 15 most popular search engines as derived from eBizMBA Rank **(ebizmba.com/ articles/search-engines)**, which is a constantly updated average of each Web site's Alexa Global Traffic Rank, and U.S. Traffic Rank from both Compete and Quantcast.

Rank	Name	Estimated Unique Monthly Visitors
1	Google	900,000,000
2	Bing	165,000,000
3	Yahoo! Search	160,000,000
4	Ask	125,000,000
5	AOL Search	33,000,000
6	MyWebSearch	19,000,000
7	blekko	9,000,000
8	Lycos	4,300,000
9	Dogpile	2,900,000
10	WebCrawler	2,700,000
11	Info	2,600,000
12	Infospace	2,000,000
13	Search	1,450,000
14	Excite	1,150,000
15	GoodSearch	1,000,000

(Goodman, 2005). White hats tend to produce results that last a long time, whereas black hats anticipate that their sites may eventually be banned either temporarily or permanently once the search engines discover what they are doing.

An SEO technique is considered white hat if it conforms to the search engines' guidelines and involves no deception. Because search engine guidelines are not written as a series of rules or commandments, this is an important distinction to note. White-hat SEO is not just about following guidelines, but about ensuring that the content a search engine indexes and subsequently ranks is the same content a user will see. White-hat advice is generally summed up as creating content for users, not for search engines, and then making that content easily accessible to the spiders, rather than attempting to trick the algorithm from its intended purpose. White-hat SEO is in many ways similar to Web development that promotes accessibility, although the two are not identical.

Black-hat SEO attempts to improve rankings in ways that are disapproved by the search engines, or involve deception. One black-hat technique uses text that is hidden, either as text colored similar to the background, in an invisible div, or positioned off-screen. Another method gives a different page depending on whether the page is being requested by a human visitor or a search engine, a technique known as *cloaking*. Search engines may penalize sites they discover using black-hat methods, either by reducing their rankings or eliminating their listings from their databases altogether. Such penalties can be applied either automatically by the search engines' algorithms, or by a manual site review. One example was the February 2006 Google removal of both BMW Germany and Ricoh Germany for use of unapproved practices (Cutts, 2006). Both companies, however, quickly apologized, fixed their practices, and were restored to Google's list.

For some businesses SEO may generate significant return on investment. However, one should keep in mind that search engines are not paid for organic search traffic, their algorithms change constantly, and there are no guarantees of continued referrals. Due to this lack of certainty and stability, a business that relies heavily on search engine traffic can suffer major losses if the search engine decides to change its algorithms and stop sending visitors. According to Google's CEO, Eric Schmidt, in 2010, Google made over 500 algorithm changes—almost 1.5 per day. Because of the difficulty in keeping up with changing search engine rules, companies that rely on search traffic practice one or more of the following: (1) Hire a company that specializes in search engine optimization (there seem to be an abundant number of those nowadays) to continuously improve your site's appeal to changing practices of the search engines; (2) pay the search engine providers to be listed on the paid sponsors sections; and (3) consider liberating yourself from dependence on search engine traffic.

Either originating from a search engine (organically or otherwise) or coming from other sites and places, what is most important for an e-commerce site is to maximize the likelihood of customer transactions. Having a lot of visitors without sales is not what a typical e-commerce site is built for. Application Case 8.3 is about a large Internet-based shopping mall where detailed analysis of customer behavior (using clickstreams and other data sources) is used to significantly improve the conversion rate.

SECTION 8.5 REVIEW QUESTIONS

1. What is "search engine optimization"? Who benefits from it?

2. Describe the old and new ways of indexing performed by search engines.

3. What are the things that help Web pages rank higher in the search engine results?

4. What are the most commonly used methods for search engine optimization?

Application Case 8.3

Understanding Why Customers Abandon Shopping Carts Results in $10 Million Sales Increase

Lotte.com, the leading Internet shopping mall in Korea with 13 million customers, has developed an integrated Web traffic analysis system using SAS for Customer Experience Analytics. As a result, Lotte.com has been able to improve the online experience for its customers, as well as generate better returns from its marketing campaigns. Now, Lotte.com executives can confirm results anywhere, anytime, as well as make immediate changes.

With almost 1 million Web site visitors each day, Lotte.com needed to know how many visitors were making purchases and which channels were bringing the most valuable traffic. After reviewing many diverse solutions and approaches, Lotte.com introduced its integrated Web traffic analysis system using the SAS for Customer Experience Analytics solution. This is the first online behavioral analysis system applied in Korea.

With this system, Lotte.com can accurately measure and analyze Web site visitor numbers (UV), page view (PV) status of site visitors and purchasers, the popularity of each product category and product, clicking preferences for each page, the effectiveness of campaigns, and much more. This information enables Lotte.com to better understand customers and their behavior online, and conduct sophisticated, cost-effective targeted marketing.

Commenting on the system, Assistant General Manager Jung Hyo-hoon of the Marketing Planning Team for Lotte.com said, "As a result of introducing the SAS system of analysis, many 'new truths' were uncovered around customer behavior, and some of them were 'inconvenient truths.'" He added, "Some site-planning activities that had been undertaken with the expectation of certain results actually had a low reaction from customers, and the site planners had a difficult time recognizing these results."

Benefits

Introducing the SAS for Customer Experience Analytics solution fully transformed the Lotte.com Web site. As a result, Lotte.com has been able to improve the online experience for its customers as well as generate better returns from its marketing campaigns. Now, Lotte.com executives can confirm results anywhere, anytime, as well as make immediate changes.

Since implementing SAS for Customer Experience Analytics, Lotte.com has seen many benefits:

A Jump in Customer Loyalty

A large amount of sophisticated activity information can be collected under a visitor environment, including quality of traffic. Deputy Assistant General Manager Jung said that "by analyzing actual valid traffic and looking only at one to two pages, we can carry out campaigns to heighten the level of loyalty, and determine a certain range of effect, accordingly." He added, "In addition, it is possible to classify and confirm the order rate for each channel and see which channels have the most visitors."

Optimized Marketing Efficiency Analysis

Rather than just analyzing visitor numbers only, the system is capable of analyzing the conversion rate (shopping cart, immediate purchase, wish list, purchase completion) compared to actual visitors for each campaign type (affiliation or e-mail, banner, keywords, and others), so detailed analysis of channel effectiveness is possible. Additionally, it can confirm the most popular search words used by visitors for each campaign type, location, and purchased products. The page overlay function can measure the number of clicks and number of visitors for each item in a page to measure the value for each location in a page. This capability enables Lotte.com to promptly replace or renew low traffic items.

Enhanced Customer Satisfaction and Customer Experience Lead to Higher Sales

Lotte.com built a customer behavior analysis database that measures each visitor, what pages are visited, how visitors navigate the site, and what activities are undertaken to enable diverse analysis and improve site efficiency. In addition, the database captures customer demographic information, shopping cart size and conversion rate, number of orders, and number of attempts.

By analyzing which stage of the ordering process deters the most customers and fixing those stages, conversion rates can be increased. Previously, analysis was done only on placed orders. By analyzing the movement pattern of visitors before ordering and at the point where breakaway occurs, customer

(Continued)

Application Case 8.3   (Continued)

behavior can be forecast, and sophisticated marketing activities can be undertaken. Through a pattern analysis of visitors, purchases can be more effectively influenced and customer demand can be reflected in real time to ensure quicker responses. Customer satisfaction has also improved as Lotte.com has better insight into each customer's behaviors, needs, and interests.

Evaluating the system, Jung commented, "By finding out how each customer group moves on the basis of the data, it is possible to determine customer service improvements and target marketing subjects, and this has aided the success of a number of campaigns." However, the most significant benefit of the system is gaining insight into individual customers and various customer groups. By understanding when customers will make purchases and the manner in which they navigate throughout the Web page, targeted channel marketing and better customer experience can now be achieved.

Plus, when SAS for Customer Experience Analytics was implemented by Lotte.com's largest overseas distributor, it resulted in a first-year sales increase of 8 million euros (US$10 million) by identifying the causes of shopping-cart abandonment.

Source: SAS, Customer Success Stories, **sas.com/success/lotte.html** (accessed March 2013).

8.6   WEB USAGE MINING (WEB ANALYTICS)

Web usage mining (also called **Web analytics**) is the extraction of useful information from data generated through Web page visits and transactions. Masand et al. (2002) state that at least three types of data are generated through Web page visits:

1. Automatically generated data stored in server access logs, referrer logs, agent logs, and client-side cookies
2. User profiles
3. Metadata, such as page attributes, content attributes, and usage data.

Analysis of the information collected by Web servers can help us better understand user behavior. Analysis of this data is often called **clickstream analysis**. By using the data and text mining techniques, a company might be able to discern interesting patterns from the clickstreams. For example, it might learn that 60 percent of visitors who searched for "hotels in Maui" had searched earlier for "airfares to Maui." Such information could be useful in determining where to place online advertisements. Clickstream analysis might also be useful for knowing *when* visitors access a site. For example, if a company knew that 70 percent of software downloads from its Web site occurred between 7 and 11 P.M., it could plan for better customer support and network bandwidth during those hours. Figure 8.4 shows the process of extracting knowledge from clickstream data and how the generated knowledge is used to improve the process, improve the Web site, and, most important, increase the customer value.

Web mining has wide a range of business applications. For instance, Nasraoui (2006) listed the following six most common applications:

1. Determine the lifetime value of clients.
2. Design cross-marketing strategies across products.
3. Evaluate promotional campaigns.
4. Target electronic ads and coupons at user groups based on user access patterns.
5. Predict user behavior based on previously learned rules and users' profiles.
6. Present dynamic information to users based on their interests and profiles.

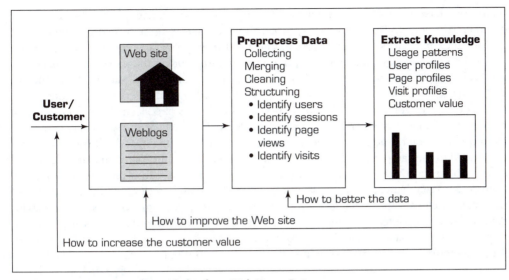

FIGURE 8.4 **Extraction of Knowledge from Web Usage Data.**

Amazon.com provides an excellent example of how Web usage history can be leveraged dynamically. A registered user who revisits Amazon.com is greeted by name. This is a simple task that involves recognizing the user by reading a cookie (i.e., a small text file written by a Web site on the visitor's computer). Amazon.com also presents the user with a choice of products in a personalized store, based on previous purchases and an association analysis of similar users. It also makes special "Gold Box" offers that are good for a short amount of time. All these recommendations involve a detailed analysis of the visitor as well as the user's peer group developed through the use of clustering, sequence pattern discovery, association, and other data and text mining techniques.

Web Analytics Technologies

There are numerous tools and technologies for Web analytics in the marketplace. Because of their power to measure, collect, and analyze Internet data to better understand and optimize Web usage, the popularity of Web analytics tools is increasing. Web analytics holds the promise to revolutionize how business is done on the Web. Web analytics is not just a tool for measuring Web traffic; it can also be used as a tool for e-business and market research, and to assess and improve the effectiveness of an e-commerce Web site. Web analytics applications can also help companies measure the results of traditional print or broadcast advertising campaigns. It can help estimate how traffic to a Web site changes after the launch of a new advertising campaign. Web analytics provides information about the number of visitors to a Web site and the number of page views. It helps gauge traffic and popularity trends, which can be used for market research.

There are two main categories of web analytics; off-site and on-site. Off-site Web analytics refers to Web measurement and analysis about you and your products that takes place outside your Web site. It includes the measurement of a Web site's potential audience (prospect or opportunity), share of voice (visibility or word-of-mouth), and buzz (comments or opinions) that is happening on the Internet.

What is more mainstream is on-site Web analytics. Historically, Web analytics has referred to on-site visitor measurement. However, in recent years this has blurred, mainly because vendors are producing tools that span both categories. On-site Web analytics measure a visitors' behavior once they are on your Web site. This includes its drivers and conversions—for example, the degree to which different landing pages are associated with online purchases. On-site Web analytics measure the performance of your Web site in a commercial context. This data collected on the Web site is then compared against key performance indicators for performance, and used to improve a Web site's or marketing campaign's audience response. Even though Google Analytics is the most widely-used on-site Web analytics service, there are others provided by Yahoo! and Microsoft, and newer and better tools are emerging constantly that provide additional layers of information.

For on-site Web analytics, there are two technical ways of collecting the data. The first and more traditional method is the server log file analysis, where the Web server records file requests made by browsers. The second method is page tagging, which uses JavaScript embedded in the site page code to make image requests to a third-party analytics-dedicated server whenever a page is rendered by a Web browser (or when a mouse click occurs). Both collect data that can be processed to produce Web traffic reports. In addition to these two main streams, other data sources may also be added to augment Web site behavior data. These other sources may include e-mail, direct-mail campaign data, sales and lead history, or social media–originated data. Application Case 8.4 shows how Allegro improved Web site performance by 500 percent with analysis of Web traffic data.

Application Case 8.4
Allegro Boosts Online Click-Through Rates by 500 Percent with Web Analysis

The Allegro Group is headquartered in Posnan, Poland, and is considered the largest non-eBay online marketplace in the world. Allegro, which currently offers over 75 proprietary Web sites in 11 European countries around the world, hosts over 15 million products and generates over 500 million page views per day. The challenge it faced was how to match the right offer to the right customer while still being able to support the extraordinary amount of data it held.

Problem

In today's marketplace, buyers have a wide variety of retail, catalog, and online options for buying their goods and services. Allegro is an e-marketplace with over 20 million customers who themselves buy from a network of over 30 thousand professional retail sellers using the Allegro network of e-commerce and auction sites. Allegro had been supporting its internal recommendation engine solely by applying rules provided by its re-sellers.

The challenge was for Allegro to increase its income and gross merchandise volume from its current network, as measured by two key performance indicators.

• ***Click-Thru Rates (CTR):*** The number of clicks on a product ad divided by the number of times the product is displayed.

• ***Conversion Rates:*** The number of completed sales transactions of a product divided by the number of customers receiving the product ad.

Solution

The online retail industry has evolved into the premier channel for personalized product recommendations. To succeed in this increasingly competitive e-commerce environment, Allegro realized that it needed to create a new, highly personalized solution integrating predictive analytics and campaign management into a real-time recommendation system.

Allegro decided to apply Social Network Analysis (SNA) as the analytic methodology underlying its product recommendation system. SNA focuses on the relationships or links between nodes (individuals or products) in a network, rather than the nodes' attributes as in traditional statistical methods. SNA was used to group similar products into communities based on their commonalities; then, communities were weighted based on visitor click paths, items placed in shopping carts, and purchases to create predictive attributes. The graph in Figure 8.5 displays a few of the product communities generated by Allegro using the KXEN's InfiniteInsight Social product for social network analysis (SNA).

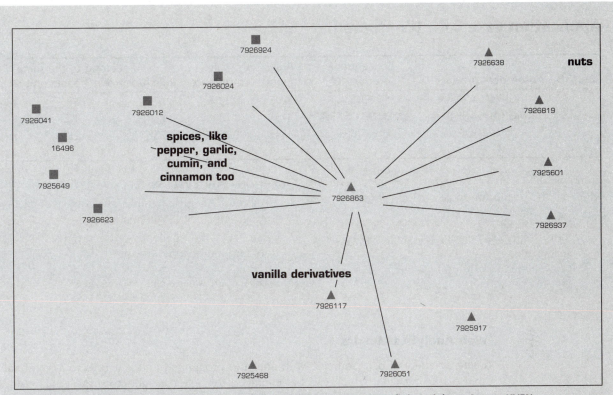

FIGURE 8.5 The Product Communities Generated by Allegro Using KXEN's InfiniteInsight . *Source:* KXEN.

Statistical classification models were then built using KXEN InfiniteInsight Modeler to predict conversion propensity for each product based on these SNA product communities and individual customer attributes. These conversion propensity scores are then used by Allegro to define personalized offers presented to millions of Web site visitors in real time.

Some of the challenges Allegro faced applying social network analysis included:

- Need to build multiple networks, depending on the product group categories
  - Very large differences in the frequency distribution of particular products and their popularity (clicks, transactions)
- Automatic setting of optimal parameters, such as the minimum number of occurrences of items (support)
- Automation through scripting
- Overconnected products (best-sellers, mega-hub communities).

Implementing this solution also presented its own challenges including:

- Different rule sets are produced per Web page placement
- Business owners decide appropriate weightings of rule sets for each type of placement / business strategy
- Building 160k rules every week
- Automatic conversion of social network analyses into rules and table-ization of rules

Results

As a result of implementing social network analysis in its automated real-time recommendation process, Allegro has seen a marked improvement in all areas.

Today Allegro offers 80 million personalized product recommendations daily, and its page views have increased by over 30 percent. But it's in the

(Continued)

Application Case 4.4   (Continued)

Rule ID	Antecedent product ID	Consequent product ID	Rule support	Rule confidence	Rule KI	Belong to the same product community?
1	DIGITAL CAMERA	LENS	21213	20%	0.76	YES
2	DIGITAL CAMERA	MEMORY CARD	3145	18%	0.64	NO
3	PINK SHOES	PINK DRESS	4343	38%	0.55	NO
…	…	…	…	…	…	…

numbers delivered by Allegro's two most critical KPIs that the results are most obvious:

- Click-through rate (CTR) has increased by more than 500 percent as compared to 'best seller' rules.
- Conversion rates are up by a factor of over 40X.

QUESTIONS FOR DISCUSSION

1. How did Allegro significantly improve click-through rates with Web analytics?
2. What were the challenges, the proposed solution, and the obtained results?

Source: **kxen.com/customers/allegro** (accessed July 2013).

Web Analytics Metrics

Using a variety of data sources, Web analytics programs provide access to a lot of valuable marketing data, which can be leveraged for better insights to grow your business and better document your ROI. The insight and intelligence gained from Web analytics can be used to effectively manage the marketing efforts of an organization and its various products or services. Web analytics programs provide nearly real-time data, which can document your marketing campaign successes or empower you to make timely adjustments to your current marketing strategies.

While Web analytics provides a broad range of metrics, there are four categories of metrics that are generally actionable and can directly impact your business objectives (TWG, 2013). These categories include:

- Web site usability: How were they using my Web site?
- Traffic sources: Where did they come from?
- Visitor profiles: What do my visitors look like?
- Conversion statistics: What does all this mean for the business?

Web Site Usability

Beginning with your Web site, let's take a look at how well it works for your visitors. This is where you can learn how "user-friendly" it really is or whether or not you are providing the right content.

1. *Page views.* The most basic of measurements, this metric is usually presented as the "average page views per visitor." If people come to your Web site and don't view many pages, then your Web site may have issues with its design or structure. Another explanation for low page views is a disconnect in the marketing messages that brought them to the site and the content that is actually available.

2. *Time on site.* Similar to page views, it's a fundamental measurement of a visitor's interaction with your Web site. Generally, the longer a person spends on your Web site, the better it is. That could mean they're carefully reviewing your content, utilizing interactive components you have available, and building toward an informed decision to buy, respond, or take the next step you've provided. On the contrary, the time on site also needs to be examined against the number of pages viewed to make sure the visitor isn't spending his or her time trying to locate content that should be more readily accessible.

3. Downloads.   This includes PDFs, videos, and other resources you make available to your visitors. Consider how accessible these items are as well as how well they're promoted. If your Web statistics, for example, reveal that 60 percent of the individuals who watch a demo video also make a purchase, then you'll want to strategize to increase viewership of that video.

4. Click map.   Most analytics programs can show you the percentage of clicks each item on your Web page received. This includes clickable photos, text links in your copy, downloads, and, of course, any navigation you may have on the page. Are they clicking the most important items?

5. Click paths.   Although an assessment of click paths is more involved, it can quickly reveal where you might be losing visitors in a specific process. A well-designed Web site uses a combination of graphics and information architecture to encourage visitors to follow "predefined" paths through your Web site. These are not rigid pathways but rather intuitive steps that align with the various processes you've built into the Web site. One process might be that of "educating" a visitor who has minimum understanding of your product or service. Another might be a process of "motivating" a returning visitor to consider an upgrade or repurchase. A third process might be structured around items you market online. You'll have as many process pathways in your Web site as you have target audiences, products, and services. Each can be measured through Web analytics to determine how effective they are.

Traffic Sources

Your Web analytics program is an incredible tool for identifying where your Web traffic originates. Basic categories such as search engines, referral Web sites, and visits from bookmarked pages (i.e., direct) are compiled with little involvement by the marketer. With a little effort, however, you can also identify Web traffic that was generated by your various offline or online advertising campaigns.

1. Referral Web sites.   Other Web sites that contain links that send visitors directly to your Web site are considered referral Web sites. Your analytics program will identify each referral site your traffic comes from, and a deeper analysis will help you determine which referrals produce the greatest volume, the highest conversions, the most new visitors, etc.

2. Search engines.   Data in the search engine category is divided between paid search and organic (or natural) search. You can review the top keywords that generated Web traffic to your site and see if they are representative of your products and services. Depending upon your business, you might want to have hundreds (or thousands) of keywords that draw potential customers. Even the simplest product search can have multiple variations based on how the individual phrases the search query.

3. Direct.   Direct searches are attributed to two sources. An individual who bookmarks one of your Web pages in their favorites and clicks that link will be recorded as a direct search. Another source occurs when someone types your URL directly into their browser. This happens when someone retrieves your URL from a business card, brochure, print ad, radio commercial, etc. That's why it's good strategy to use coded URLs.

4. Offline campaigns.   If you utilize advertising options other than Web-based campaigns, your Web analytics program can capture performance data if you'll include a mechanism for sending them to your Web site. Typically, this is a dedicated URL that you include in your advertisement (i.e., "**www.mycompany.com/offer50**") that delivers those visitors to a specific landing page. You now have data on how many responded to that ad by visiting your Web site.

5. *Online campaigns.* If you are running a banner ad campaign, search engine advertising campaign, or even e-mail campaigns, you can measure individual campaign effectiveness by simply using a dedicated URL similar to the offline campaign strategy.

Visitor Profiles

One of the ways you can leverage your Web analytics into a really powerful marketing tool is through segmentation. By blending data from different analytics reports, you'll begin to see a variety of user profiles emerge.

1. *Keywords.* Within your analytics report, you can see what keywords visitors used in search engines to locate your Web site. If you aggregate your keywords by similar attributes, you'll begin to see distinct visitor groups that are using your Web site. For example, the particular search phrase that was used can indicate how well they understand your product or its benefits. If they use words that mirror your own product or service descriptions, then they probably are already aware of your offerings from effective advertisements, brochures, etc. If the terms are more general in nature, then your visitor is seeking a solution for a problem and has happened upon your Web site. If this second group of searchers is sizable, then you'll want to ensure that your site has a strong education component to convince them they've found their answer and then move them into your sales channel.

2. *Content groupings.* Depending upon how you group your content, you may be able to analyze sections of your Web site that correspond with specific products, services, campaigns, and other marketing tactics. If you conduct a lot of trade shows and drive traffic to your Web site for specific product literature, then your Web analytics will highlight the activity in that section.

3. *Geography.* Analytics permits you to see where your traffic geographically originates, including country, state, and city locations. This can be especially useful if you use geo-targeted campaigns or want to measure your visibility across a region.

4. *Time of day.* Web traffic generally has peaks at the beginning of the workday, during lunch, and toward the end of the workday. It's not unusual, however, to find strong Web traffic entering your Web site up until the late evening. You can analyze this data to determine when people browse versus buy and also make decisions on what hours you should offer customer service.

5. *Landing page profiles.* If you structure your various advertising campaigns properly, you can drive each of your targeted groups to a different landing page, which your Web analytics will capture and measure. By combining these numbers with the demographics of your campaign media, you can know what percentage of your visitors fit each demographic.

Conversion Statistics

Each organization will define a "conversion" according to its specific marketing objectives. Some Web analytics programs use the term "goal" to benchmark certain Web site objectives, whether that be a certain number of visitors to a page, a completed registration form, or an online purchase.

1. *New visitors.* If you're working to increase visibility, you'll want to study the trends in your new visitors data. Analytics identifies all visitors as either new or returning.

2. *Returning visitors.* If you're involved in loyalty programs or offer a product that has a long purchase cycle, then your returning visitors data will help you measure progress in this area.

3. *Leads.* Once a form is submitted and a thank-you page is generated, you have created a lead. Web analytics will permit you to calculate a completion rate (or abandonment rate) by dividing the number of completed forms by the number of Web visitors that came to your page. A low completion percentage would indicate a page that needs attention.

4. *Sales/conversions.* Depending upon the intent of your Web site, you can define a "sale" by an online purchase, a completed registration, an online submission, or any number of other Web activities. Monitoring these figures will alert you to any changes (or successes!) that occur further upstream.

5. *Abandonment/exit rates.* Just as important as those moving through your Web site are those who began a process and quit or came to your Web site and left after a page or two. In the first case, you'll want to analyze where the visitor terminated the process and whether there are a number of visitors quitting at the same place. Then investigate the situation for resolution. In the latter case, a high exit rate on a Web site or a specific page generally indicates an issue with expectations. Visitors click to your Web site based on some message contained in an advertisement, a presentation, etc., and expect some continuity in that message. Make sure you're advertising a message that your Web site can reinforce and deliver.

Within each of these items are metrics that can be established for your specific organization. You can create a weekly dashboard that includes specific numbers or percentages that will indicate where you're succeeding—or highlight a marketing challenge that should be addressed. When these metrics are evaluated consistently and used in conjunction with other available marketing data, they can lead you to a highly quantified marketing program. Figure 8.6 shows a Web analytics dashboard created with freely available Google Analytics tools.

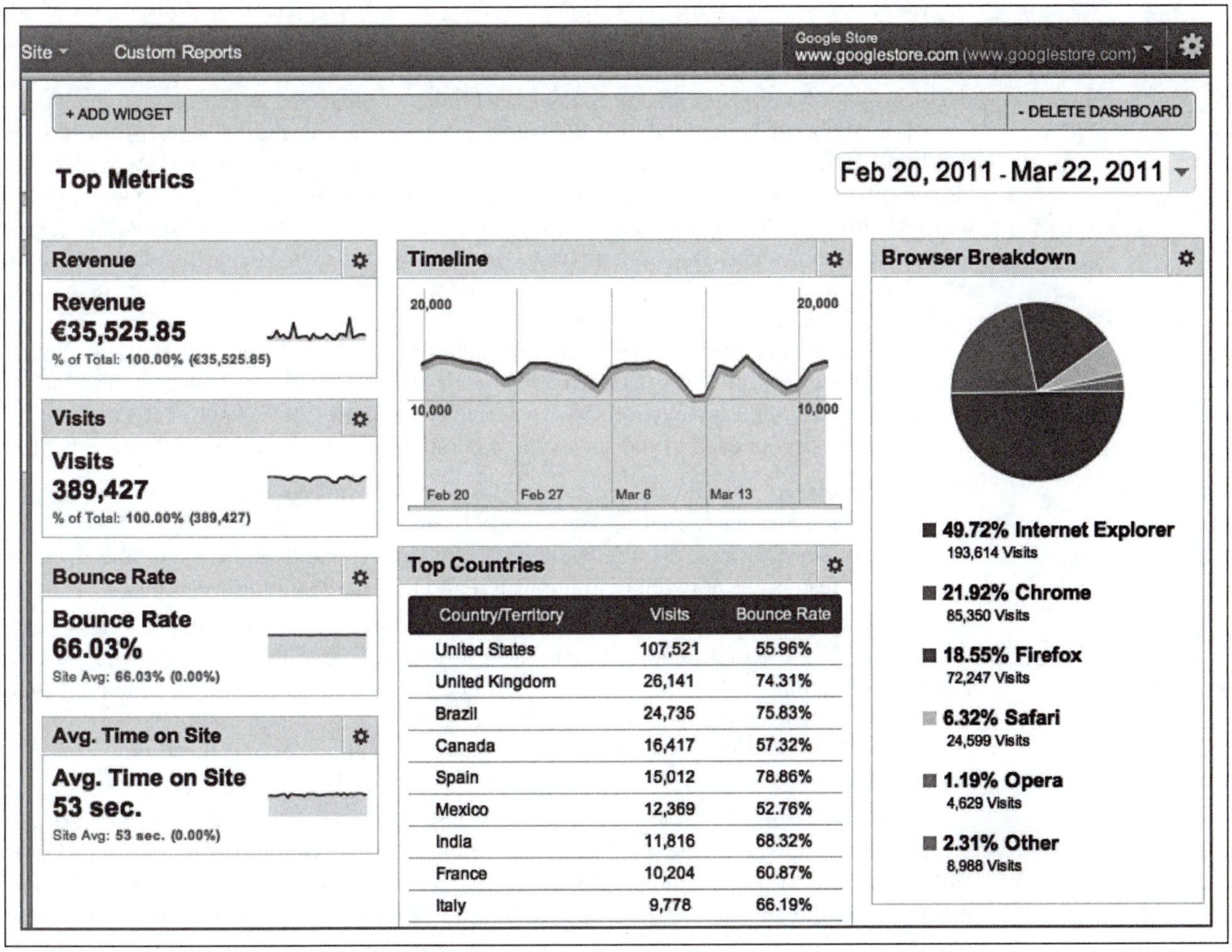

FIGURE 8.6   A Sample Web Analytics Dashboard.

SECTION 8.6 REVIEW QUESTIONS

1. What are the three types of data generated through Web page visits?
2. What is clickstream analysis? What is it used for?
3. What are the main applications of Web mining?
4. What are commonly used Web analytics metrics? What is the importance of metrics?

8.7 WEB ANALYTICS MATURITY MODEL AND WEB ANALYTICS TOOLS

The term "maturity" relates to the degree of proficiency, formality, and optimization of business models, moving "ad hoc" practices to formally defined steps and optimal business processes. A maturity model is a formal depiction of critical dimensions and their competency levels of a business practice. Collectively, these dimensions and levels define the maturity level of an organization in that area of practice. It often describes an evolutionary improvement path from ad hoc, immature practices to disciplined, mature processes with improved quality and efficiency.

A good example of maturity models is the BI Maturity Model developed by The Data Warehouse Institute (TDWI). In the TDWI BI Maturity Model the main purpose was to gauge where organization data warehousing initiatives are at a point in time and where it should go next. It was represented in a six-stage framework (Management Reporting → Spreadmarts → Data Marts → Data Warehouse → Enterprise Data Warehouse → BI Services). Another related example is the simple business analytics maturity model, moving from simple descriptive measures to predicting future outcomes, to obtaining sophisticated decision systems (i.e., Descriptive Analytics → Predictive Analytics → Prescriptive Analytics).

For Web analytics perhaps the most comprehensive model was proposed by Stéphane Hamel (2009). In this model, Hamel used six dimensions—(1) Management, Governance and Adoption, (2) Objectives Definition, (3) Scoping, (4) The Analytics Team and Expertise, (5) The Continuous Improvement Process and Analysis Methodology, (6) Tools, Technology and Data Integration—and for each dimension he used six levels of proficiency/competence. Figure 8.7 shows Hamel's six dimensions and the respective proficiency levels.

The proficiency/competence levels have different terms/labels for each of the six dimensions, describing specifically what each level means. Essentially, the six levels are indications of analytical maturity ranging from "0–Analytically Impaired" to "5–Analytical Competitor." A short description of each of the six levels of competencies is given here (Hamel, 2009):

1. *Impaired:* Characterized by the use of out-of-the-box tools and reports; limited resources lacking formal training (hands-on skills) and education (knowledge). Web analytics is used on an ad hoc basis and is of limited value and scope. Some tactical objectives are defined, but results are not well communicated and there are multiple versions of the truth.

2. *Initiated:* Works with metrics to optimize specific areas of the business (such as marketing or the e-commerce catalogue). Resources are still limited, but the process is getting streamlined. Results are communicated to various business stakeholders (often director level). However, Web analytics might be supporting obsolete business processes and, thus, be limited in the ability to push for optimization beyond the online channel. Success is mostly anecdotal.

3. *Operational:* Key performance indicators and dashboards are defined and aligned with strategic business objectives. A multidisciplinary team is in place and uses various sources of information such as competitive data, voice of customer, and social media or mobile analysis. Metrics are exploited and explored through segmentation and multivariate testing. The Internet channel is being optimized; personas are being defined.

Results start to appear and be considered at the executive level. Results are centrally driven, but broadly distributed.

4. Integrated: Analysts can now correlate online and offline data from various sources to provide a near 360-degree view of the whole value chain. Optimization encompasses complete processes, including back-end and front-end. Online activities are defined from the user perspective and persuasion scenarios are defined. A continuous improvement process and problem-solving methodologies are prevalent. Insight and recommendations reach the CXO level.

5. Competitor: This level is characterized by several attributes of companies with a strong analytical culture (Davenport and Harris, 2007):

a. One or more senior executives strongly advocate fact-based decision making and analytics

b. Widespread use of not just descriptive statistics, but predictive modeling and complex optimization techniques

c. Substantial use of analytics across multiple business functions or processes

d. Movement toward an enterprise-level approach to managing analytical tools, data, and organizational skills and capabilities.

6. Addicted: This level matches Davenport's "Analytical Competitor" characteristics: deep strategic insight, continuous improvement, integrated, skilled resources, top management commitment, fact-based culture, continuous testing, learning, and most important: far beyond the boundaries of the online channel.

In Figure 8.7, one can mark the level of proficiency in each of the six dimensions to create their organization's maturity model (which would look like a spider diagram).

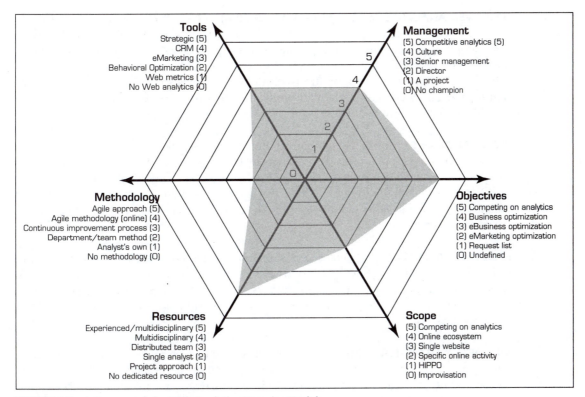

FIGURE 8.7 A Framework for Web Analytics Maturity Model.

Such an assessment can help organizations better understand at what dimensions they are lagging behind, and take corrective actions to mitigate it.

Web Analytics Tools

There are plenty of Web analytics applications (downloadable software tools and Web-based/on-demand service platforms) in the market. Companies (large, medium, or small) are creating products and services to grab their fair share from the emerging Web analytics marketplace. What is the most interesting is that many of the most popular Web analytics tools are free—yes, free to download and use for whatever reasons, commercial or nonprofit. The following are among the most popular free (or almost free) Web analytics tools:

GOOGLE WEB ANALYTICS (GOOGLE.COM/ANALYTICS) This is a service offered by Google that generates detailed statistics about a Web site's traffic and traffic sources and measures conversions and sales. The product is aimed at marketers as opposed to the Webmasters and technologists from which the industry of Web analytics originally grew. It is the most widely used Web analytics service. Even though the basic service is free of charge, the premium version is available for a fee.

YAHOO! WEB ANALYTICS (WEB.ANALYTICS.YAHOO.COM) Yahoo! Web analytics is Yahoo!'s alternative to the dominant Google Analytics. It's an enterprise-level, robust Web-based third-party solution that makes accessing data easy, especially for multiple-user groups. It's got all the things you'd expect from a comprehensive Web analytics tool, such as pretty graphs, custom-designed (and printable) reports, and real-time data tracking.

OPEN WEB ANALYTICS (OPENWEBANALYTICS.COM) Open Web Analytics (OWA) is a popular open source Web analytics software that anyone can use to track and analyze how people use Web sites and applications. OWA is licensed under GPL and provides Web site owners and developers with easy ways to add Web analytics to their sites using simple Javascript, PHP, or REST-based APIs. OWA also comes with built-in support for tracking Web sites made with popular content management frameworks such as WordPress and MediaWiki.

PIWIK (PIWIK.ORG) Piwik is the one of the leading self-hosted, decentralized, open source Web analytics platforms, used by 460,000 Web sites in 150 countries. Piwik was founded by Matthieu Aubry in 2007. Over the last 6 years, more talented and passionate members of the community have joined the team. As is the case in many open source initiatives, they are actively looking for new developers, designers, datavis architects, and sponsors to join them.

FIRESTAT (FIRESTATS.CC) FireStats is a simple and straightforward Web analytics application written in PHP/MySQL. It supports numerous platforms and set-ups including C# sites, Django sites, Drupal, Joomla!, WordPress, and several others. FireStats has an intuitive API that assists developers in creating their own custom apps or publishing platform components.

SITE METER (SITEMETER.COM) Site Meter is a service that provides counter and tracking information for Web sites. By logging IP addresses and using JavaScript or HTML to track visitor information, Site Meter provides Web site owners with information about their visitors, including how they reached the site, the date and time of their visit, and more.

WOOPRA (WOOPRA.COM) Woopra is a real-time customer analytics service that provides solutions for sales, service, marketing, and product teams. The platform is designed to help organizations optimize the customer life cycle by delivering live, granular behavioral data for individual Web site visitors and customers. It ties this individual-level data to aggregate analytics reports for a full life-cycle view that bridges departmental gaps.

AWSTATS (AWSTATS.ORG) AWStats is an open source Web analytics reporting tool, suitable for analyzing data from Internet services such as Web, streaming media, mail, and FTP servers. AWStats parses and analyzes server log files, producing HTML reports. Data is visually presented within reports by tables and bar graphs. Static reports can be created through a command line interface, and on-demand reporting is supported through a Web browser CGI program.

SNOOP (REINVIGORATE.NET) Snoop is a desktop-based application that runs on the Mac OS X and Windows XP/Vista platforms. It sits nicely on your system status bar/system tray, notifying you with audible sounds whenever something happens. Another outstanding Snoop feature is the Name Tags option, which allows you to "tag" visitors for easier identification. So when Joe over at the accounting department visits your site, you'll instantly know.

MOCHIBOT (MOCHIBOT.COM) MochiBot is a free Web analytics/tracking tool especially designed for Flash assets. With MochiBot, you can see who's sharing your Flash content, how many times people view your content, as well as help you track where your Flash content is to prevent piracy and content theft. Installing MochiBot is a breeze; you simply copy a few lines of ActionScript code in the .FLA files you want to monitor.

In addition to these free Web analytics tools, Table 8.1 provides a list of commercially available Web analytics tools.

TABLE 8.1 Commercial Web Analytics Software Tools

Product Name	Description	URL
Angoss Knowledge WebMiner	Combines ANGOSS Knowledge STUDIO and clickstream analysis	**angoss.com**
ClickTracks	Visitor patterns can be shown on Web site	**clicktracks.com, now at Lyris.com**
LiveStats from DeepMetrix	Real-time log analysis, live demo on site	**deepmetrix.com**
Megaputer WebAnalyst	Data and text mining capabilities	**megaputer.com/site/textanalyst.php**
MicroStrategy Web Traffic Analysis Module	Traffic highlights, content analysis, and Web visitor analysis reports	**microstrategy.com/Solutions/Applications/WTAM**
SAS Web Analytics	Analyzes Web site traffic	**sas.com/solutions/webanalytics**
SPSS Web Mining for Clementine	Extraction of Web events	**www-01.ibm.com/software/analytics/spss/**
WebTrends	Data mining of Web traffic information.	**webtrends.com**
XML Miner	A system and class library for mining data and text expressed in XML, using fuzzy logic expert system rules	**scientio.com**

Putting It All Together—A Web Site Optimization Ecosystem

It seems that just about everything on the Web can be measured—every click can be recorded, every view can be captured, and every visit can be analyzed—all in an effort to continually and automatically optimize the online experience. Unfortunately, the notions of "infinite measurability" and "automatic optimization" in the online channel are far more complex than most realize. The assumption that any single application of Web mining techniques will provide the necessary range of insights required to understand Web site visitor behavior is deceptive and potentially risky. Ideally, a holistic view to customer experience is needed that can only be captured using both quantitative and qualitative data. Forward-thinking companies have already taken steps toward capturing and analyzing a holistic view of the customer experience, which has led to significant gains, both in terms of incremental financial growth and increasing customer loyalty and satisfaction.

According to Peterson (2008), the inputs for Web site optimization efforts can be classified along two axes describing the nature of the data and how that data can be used. On one axis are data and information—data being primarily quantitative and information being primarily qualitative. On the other axis are measures and actions—measures being reports, analysis, and recommendations all designed to drive actions, the actual changes being made in the ongoing process of site and marketing optimization. Each quadrant created by these dimensions leverages different technologies and creates different outputs, but much like a biological ecosystem, each technological niche interacts with the others to support the entire online environment (see Figure 8.8).

Most believe that the Web site optimization ecosystem is defined by the ability to log, parse, and report on the clickstream behavior of site visitors. The underlying technology of this ability is generally referred to as *Web analytics*. Although Web analytics

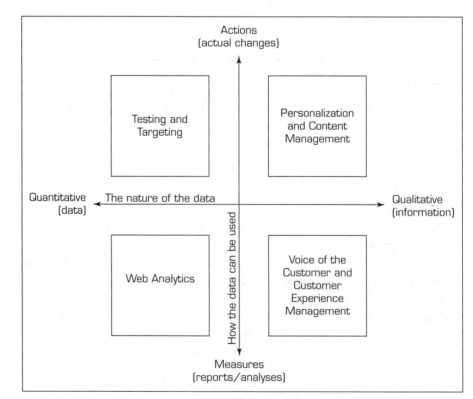

FIGURE 8.8 Two-Dimensional View of the Inputs for Web Site Optimization.

tools provide invaluable insights, understanding visitor behavior is as much a function of qualitatively determining interests and intent as it is quantifying clicks from page to page. Fortunately there are two other classes of applications designed to provide a more qualitative view of online visitor behavior designed to report on the overall user experience and report direct feedback given by visitors and customers: **customer experience management (CEM)** and **voice of customer (VOC)**:

- Web analytics applications focus on "where and when" questions by aggregating, mining, and visualizing large volumes of data, by reporting on online marketing and visitor acquisition efforts, by summarizing page-level visitor interaction data, and by summarizing visitor flow through defined multistep processes.
- Voice of customer applications focus on "who and how" questions by gathering and reporting direct feedback from site visitors, by benchmarking against other sites and offline channels, and by supporting predictive modeling of future visitor behavior.
- Customer experience management applications focus on "what and why" questions by detecting Web application issues and problems, by tracking and resolving business process and usability obstacles, by reporting on site performance and availability, by enabling real-time alerting and monitoring, and by supporting deep diagnosis of observed visitor behavior.

All three applications are needed to have a complete view of the visitor behavior where each application plays a distinct and valuable role. Web analytics, CEM, and VOC applications form the foundation of the Web site optimization ecosystem that supports the online business's ability to positively influence desired outcomes (a pictorial representation of this process view of the Web site optimization ecosystem is given in Figure 8.9). These similar-yet-distinct applications each contribute to a site operator's ability to recognize, react, and respond to the ongoing challenges faced by every Web site owner. Fundamental to the optimization process is measurement, gathering data and information that can then be transformed into tangible analysis, and recommendations for improvement using Web mining tools and techniques. When used properly, these applications allow for convergent validation—combining different sets of data collected for the same audience to provide a richer and deeper understanding of audience behavior. The convergent validation model—one

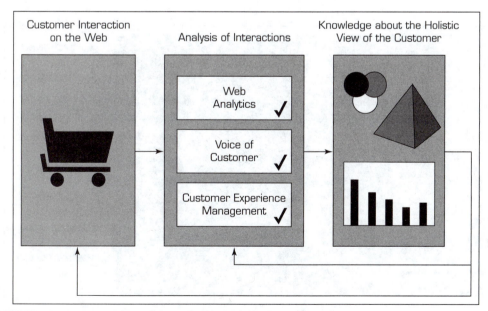

FIGURE 8.9   A Process View of the Web Site Optimization Ecosystem.

where multiple sources of data describing the same population are integrated to increase the depth and richness of the resulting analysis—forms the framework of the Web site optimization ecosystem. On one side of the spectrum are the primarily qualitative inputs from VOC applications; on the other side are the primarily quantitative inputs from CEM bridging the gap by supporting key elements of data discovery. When properly implemented, all three systems sample data from the same audience. The combination of these data—either through data integration projects or simply via the process of conducting good analysis—supports far more actionable insights than any of the ecosystem members individually.

A Framework for Voice of the Customer Strategy

Voice of the customer (VOC) is a term usually used to describe the analytic process of capturing a customer's expectations, preferences, and aversions. It essentially is a market research technique that produces a detailed set of customer wants and needs, organized into a hierarchical structure, and then prioritized in terms of relative importance and satisfaction with current alternatives. Attensity, one of the innovative service providers in the analytics marketplace, developed an intuitive framework for VOC strategy that they called LARA, which stands for Listen, Analyze, Relate, and Act. It is a methodology that outlines a process by which organizations can take user-generated content (UGC), whether generated by consumers talking in Web forums, on micro-blogging sites like Twitter and social networks like Facebook, or in feedback surveys, e-mails, documents, research, etc., and using it as a business asset in a business process. Figure 8.10 shows a pictorial depiction of this framework.

LISTEN   To "listen" is actually a process in itself that encompasses both the capability to listen to the open Web (forums, blogs, tweets, you name it) and the capability to seamlessly access enterprise information (CRM notes, documents, e-mails, etc.). It takes a listening post, deep federated search capabilities, scraping and enterprise class data integration, and a strategy to determine who and what you want to listen to.

ANALYZE   This is the hard part. How can you take all of this mass of unstructured data and make sense of it? This is where the "secret sauce" of text analytics comes into play. Look for solutions that include keyword, statistical, and natural language approaches

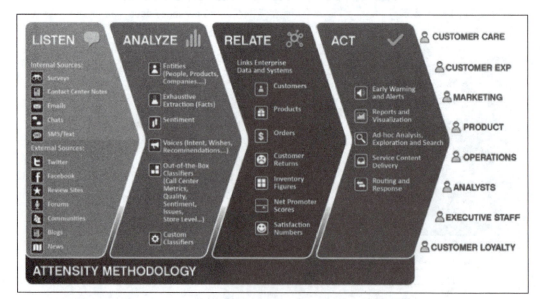

FIGURE 8.10   **Voice of the Customer Strategy Framework.**   *Source:* **Attensity.com.** Used with permission.

that will allow you to essentially tag or barcode every word and the relationships among words, making it data that can be accessed, searched, routed, counted, analyzed, charted, reported on, and even reused. Keep in mind that, in addition to technical capabilities, it has to be easy to use, so that your business users can focus on the insights, not the technology. It should have an engine that doesn't require the user to define keywords or terms that they want their system to look for or include in a rule base. Rather, it should *automatically* identify terms ("facts," people, places, things, etc.) *and their relationships with other terms or combinations of terms*—making it easy to use, maintain, and also be more accurate, so you can rely on the insights as actionable.

RELATE   Now that you have found the insights and can analyze the unstructured data, the real value comes when you can connect those insights to your "structured" data: your customers (which customer segment is complaining about your product most?); your products (which product is having the issue?); your parts (is there a problem with a specific part manufactured by a specific partner?); your locations (is the customer who is tweeting about wanting a sandwich near your nearest restaurant?); and so on. Now you can ask questions of your data and get deep, actionable insights.

ACT   Here is where it gets exciting, and your business strategy and rules are critical. What do you do with the new customer insight you've obtained? How do you leverage the problem resolution content created by a customer that you just identified? How do you connect with a customer who is uncovering issues that are important to your business or who is asking for help? How do you route the insights to the right people? And, how do you engage with customers, partners, and influencers once you understand what they are saying? You understand it; now you've got to act.

SECTION 8.7 REVIEW QUESTIONS

1. What is a maturity model?
2. List and comment on the six stages of TDWI's BI maturity framework.
3. What are the six dimensions used in Hamel's Web analytics maturity model?
4. Describe Attensity's framework for VOC strategy. List and describe the four stages.

8.8   SOCIAL ANALYTICS AND SOCIAL NETWORK ANALYSIS

Social analytics may mean different things to different people, based on their worldview and field of study. For instance, the dictionary definition of social analytics refers to a philosophical perspective developed by the Danish historian and philosopher Lars-Henrik Schmidt in the 1980s. The theoretical object of the perspective is *socius*, a kind of "commonness" that is neither a universal account nor a communality shared by every member of a body (Schmidt, 1996). Thus, social analytics differs from traditional philosophy as well as sociology. It might be viewed as a perspective that attempts to articulate the contentions between philosophy and sociology.

Our definition of social analytics is somewhat different; as opposed to focusing on the "social" part (as is the csae in its philosophical definition), we are more interested in the "analytics" part of the term. Gartner defined social analytics as "monitoring, analyzing, measuring and interpreting digital interactions and relationships of people, topics, ideas and content." Social analytics include mining the textual content created in social media (e.g., sentiment analysis, natural language processing) and analyzing socially established networks (e.g., influencer identification, profiling, prediction) for the purpose of gaining insight about existing and potential customers' current and future behaviors, and about the likes and dislikes toward a firm's products and services. Based on this definition and the current practices, social analytics can be classified into two different, but not necessarily mutually exclusive, branches: social network analysis and social media analytics.

Social Network Analysis

A **social network** is a social structure composed of individuals/people (or groups of individuals or organizations) linked to one another with some type of connections/relationships. The social network perspective provides a holistic approach to analyzing structure and dynamics of social entities. The study of these structures uses social network analysis to identify local and global patterns, locate influential entities, and examine network dynamics. Social networks and the analysis of them is essentially an interdisciplinary field that emerged from social psychology, sociology, statistics, and graph theory. Development and formalization of the mathematical extent of social network analysis dates back to the 1950s; the development of foundational theories and methods of social networks dates back to the 1980s (Scott and Davis, 2003). Social network analysis is now one of the major paradigms in business analytics, consumer intelligence, and contemporary sociology, and is also employed in a number of other social and formal sciences.

A social network is a theoretical construct useful in the social sciences to study relationships between individuals, groups, organizations, or even entire societies (social units). The term is used to describe a social structure determined by such interactions. The ties through which any given social unit connects represent the convergence of the various social contacts of that unit. In general, social networks are self-organizing, emergent, and complex, such that a globally coherent pattern appears from the local interaction of the elements (individuals and groups of individuals) that make up the system.

Following are a few typical social network types that are relevant to business activities.

COMMUNICATION NETWORKS   Communication studies are often considered a part of both the social sciences and the humanities, drawing heavily on fields such as sociology, psychology, anthropology, information science, biology, political science, and economics. Many communications concepts describe the transfer of information from one source to another, and thus can be represented as a social network. Telecommunication companies are tapping into this rich information source to optimize their business practices and to improve customer relationships.

COMMUNITY NETWORKS   Traditionally, community referred to a specific geographic location, and studies of community ties had to do with who talked, associated, traded, and attended social activities with whom. Today, however, there are extended "online" communities developed through social networking tools and telecommunications devices. Such tools and devices continuously generate large amounts of data, which can be used by companies to discover invaluable, actionable information.

CRIMINAL NETWORKS   In criminology and urban sociology, much attention has been paid to the social networks among criminal actors. For example, studying gang murders and other illegal activities as a series of exchanges between gangs can lead to better understanding and prevention of such criminal activities. Now that we live in a highly connected world (thanks to the Internet), many of the criminal networks' formations and their activities are being watched/pursued by security agencies using state-of-the-art Internet tools and tactics. Even though the Internet has changed the landscape for criminal networks and law enforcement agencies, the traditional social and philosophical theories still apply to a large extent.

INNOVATION NETWORKS   Business studies on diffusion of ideas and innovations in a network environment focus on the spread and use of ideas among the members of the social network. The idea is to understand why some networks are more innovative, and why some communities are early adopters of ideas and innovations (i.e., examining the impact of social network structure on influencing the spread of an innovation and innovative behavior).

Social Network Analysis Metrics

Social network analysis (SNA) is the systematic examination of social networks. Social network analysis views social relationships in terms of network theory, consisting of nodes (representing individuals or organizations within the network) and ties/connections (which represent relationships between the individuals or organizations, such as friendship, kinship, organizational position, etc.). These networks are often represented using social network diagrams, where nodes are represented as points and ties are represented as lines. Application Case 8.5 gets into the details of how SNA can be used to help telecommunication companies.

Over the years, various metrics (or measurements) have been developed to analyze social network structures from different perspectives. These metrics are often grouped into three categories: connections, distributions, and segmentation.

Application Case 8.5
Social Network Analysis Helps Telecommunication Firms

Because of the widespread use of free Internet tools and techniques (VoIP, video conferencing tools such as Skype, free phone calls within the United States by Google Voice, etc.), the telecommunication industry is going through a tough time. In order to stay viable and competitive, they need to make the right decisions and utilize their limited resources optimally. One of the key success factors for telecom companies is to maximize their profitability by listening and understanding the needs and wants of the customers, offering communication plans, prices, and features that they want at the prices that they are willing to pay.

These market pressures force telecommunication companies to be more innovative. As we all know, "necessity is the mother of invention." Therefore, many of the most promising use cases for social network analysis (SNA) are coming from the telecommunication companies. Using detailed call records that are already in their databases, they are trying to identify social networks and influencers. In order to identify the social networks, they are asking questions like "Who contacts whom?" "How often?" "How long?" "Both directions?" "On Net, off Net?" They are also trying to answer questions that lead to identification of influencers, such as "Who influenced whom how much on purchases?" "Who influences whom how much on churn?" and

"Who will acquire others?" SNA metrics like degree (how many people are directly in a person's social network), density (how dense is the calling pattern within the calling circle), betweenness (how essential you are to facilitate communication within your calling circle), and centrality (how "important" you are in the social network) are often used answer these questions.

Here are some of the benefits that can be obtained from SNA:

- Manage customer churn
  - Reactive (reduce collateral churn)—Identify subscribers whose loyalty is threatened by churn around them.
  - Preventive (reduce influential churn)— Identify subscribers who, should they churn, would take a few friends with them.
- Improve cross-sell and technology transfer
  - Reactive (leverage collateral adoption)— Identify subscribers whose affinity for products is increased due to adoption around them and stimulate them.
  - Proactive (identify influencers for this adoption)—Identify subscribers who, should they adopt, would push a few friends to do the same.

(Continued)

Application Case 8.5   (Continued)

- Manage viral campaigns—Understand what leads to high-scale spread of messages about products and services, and use this information to your benefit.
- Improve acquisition—Identify who are most likely to recommend a (off-Net) friend to become a new subscriber of the operator. The recommendation itself, as well as the subscription, is incentivized for both the subscriber and the recommending person.
- Identify households, communities, and close-groups to better manage your relationships with them.
- Identify customer life-stages—Identifying social network changes and from there identifying life-stage changes such as moving, changing a job, going to a university, starting a relationships, getting married, etc.
- Identifying pre-churners—Detecting potential churners during the process of leaving and motivating them to stay with you.
- Gain competitor insights—Track dynamic changes in social networks based on competitor's marketing activities

- Others inducing identifying rotational churners (switching between operators)—Facilitating re- to postmigration, and tracking customer's networks dynamics over his/her life cycle.

Actual cases indicate that proper implementation of SNA can significantly lower churn, improve cross-sell, boost new customer acquisition, optimize pricing and, hence, maximize profit, and improve overall competitiveness.

QUESTIONS FOR DISCUSSION

1. How can social network analysis be used in the telecommunications industry?
2. What do you think are the key challenges, potential solution, and probable results in applying SNA in telecommunications firms?

Source: Compiled from "More Things We Love About SNA: Return of the Magnificent 10," February 2013, presentation by Judy Bayer and Fawad Qureshi, Teradata.

Connections

Homophily: The extent to which actors form ties with similar versus dissimilar others. Similarity can be defined by gender, race, age, occupation, educational achievement, status, values, or any other salient characteristic.

Multiplexity: The number of content-forms contained in a tie. For example, two people who are friends and also work together would have a multiplexity of 2. Multiplexity has been associated with relationship strength.

Mutuality/reciprocity: The extent to which two actors reciprocate each other's friendship or other interaction.

Network closure: A measure of the completeness of relational triads. An individual's assumption of network closure (i.e., that their friends are also friends) is called *transitivity*. Transitivity is an outcome of the individual or situational trait of need for cognitive closure.

Propinquity: The tendency for actors to have more ties with geographically close others.

Distributions

Bridge: An individual whose weak ties fill a structural hole, providing the only link between two individuals or clusters. It also includes the shortest route when a longer one is unfeasible due to a high risk of message distortion or delivery failure.

Centrality: Refers to a group of metrics that aim to quantify the importance or influence (in a variety of senses) of a particular node (or group) within a network. Examples of common methods of measuring centrality include betweenness centrality, closeness centrality, eigenvector centrality, alpha centrality, and degree centrality.

Density: The proportion of direct ties in a network relative to the total number possible.

Distance: The minimum number of ties required to connect two particular actors.

Structural holes: The absence of ties between two parts of a network. Finding and exploiting a structural hole can give an entrepreneur a competitive advantage. This concept was developed by sociologist Ronald Burt and is sometimes referred to as an alternate conception of social capital.

Tie strength: Defined by the linear combination of time, emotional intensity, intimacy, and reciprocity (i.e., mutuality). Strong ties are associated with homophily, propinquity, and transitivity, while weak ties are associated with bridges.

Segmentation

Cliques and social circles: Groups are identified as *cliques* if every individual is directly tied to every other individual or *social circles* if there is less stringency of direct contact, which is imprecise, or as structurally cohesive blocks if precision is wanted.

Clustering coefficient: A measure of the likelihood that two members of a node are associates. A higher clustering coefficient indicates a greater *cliquishness*.

Cohesion: The degree to which actors are connected directly to each other by cohesive bonds. Structural cohesion refers to the minimum number of members who, if removed from a group, would disconnect the group.

SECTION 8.8 REVIEW QUESTIONS

1. What is meant by social analytics? Why is it an important business topic?
2. What is a social network? What is social network analysis?
3. List and briefly describe the most common social network types.
4. List and briefly describe the social network analysis metrics.

8.9 SOCIAL MEDIA DEFINITIONS AND CONCEPTS

Social media refers to the enabling technologies of social interactions among people in which they create, share, and exchange information, ideas, and opinions in virtual communities and networks. It is a group of Internet-based software applications that build on the ideological and technological foundations of Web 2.0, and that allow the creation and exchange of user-generated content (Kaplan and Haenlein, 2010). Social media depends on mobile and other Web-based technologies to create highly interactive platforms for individuals and communities to share, co-create, discuss, and modify user-generated content. It introduces substantial changes to communication between organizations, communities, and individuals.

Since their emergence in the early 1990s, Web-based social media technologies have seen a significant improvement in both quality and quantity. These technologies take on many different forms, including online magazines, Internet forums, Web logs, social blogs, microblogging, wikis, social networks, podcasts, pictures, video, and product/service evaluations/ratings. By applying a set of theories in the field of media research (social presence, media richness) and social processes (self-presentation, self-disclosure), Kaplan and Haenlein (2010) created a classification scheme with six different types of social media: collaborative projects (e.g., Wikipedia), blogs and microblogs (e.g., Twitter), content communities (e.g., YouTube), social networking sites (e.g., Facebook), virtual game worlds (e.g., World of Warcraft), and virtual social worlds (e.g., Second Life).

Web-based social media are different from traditional/industrial media, such as newspapers, television, and film, as they are comparatively inexpensive and accessible to enable anyone (even private individuals) to publish or access/consume information. Industrial media generally require significant resources to publish information, as in most cases the articles (or books) go through many revisions before being published (as was the case in the publication of this very book). Here are some of the most prevailing characteristics that help differentiate between social and industrial media (Morgan et al., 2010):

Quality: In industrial publishing—mediated by a publisher—the typical range of quality is substantially narrower than in niche, unmediated markets. The main challenge posed by content in social media sites is the fact that the distribution of quality has high variance: from very high-quality items to low-quality, sometimes abusive, content.

Reach: Both industrial and social media technologies provide scale and are capable of reaching a global audience. Industrial media, however, typically use a centralized framework for organization, production, and dissemination, whereas social media are by their very nature more decentralized, less hierarchical, and distinguished by multiple points of production and utility.

Frequency: Compared to industrial media, updating and reposting on social media platforms is easier, faster, and cheaper, and therefore practiced more frequently, resulting in fresher content.

Accessibility: The means of production for industrial media are typically government and/or corporate (privately owned), and are costly, whereas social media tools are generally available to the public at little or no cost.

Usability: Industrial media production typically requires specialized skills and training. Conversely, most social media production requires only modest reinterpretation of existing skills; in theory, anyone with access can operate the means of social media production.

Immediacy: The time lag between communications produced by industrial media can be long (weeks, months, or even years) compared to social media (which can be capable of virtually instantaneous responses).

Updatability: Industrial media, once created, cannot be altered (once a magazine article is printed and distributed, changes cannot be made to that same article), whereas social media can be altered almost instantaneously by comments or editing.

How Do People Use Social Media?

Not only are the numbers on social networking sites growing, but so is the degree to which they are engaged with the channel. Brogan and Bastone (2011) presented research results that stratify users according to how actively they use social media and tracked evolution of these user segments over time. They listed six different engagement levels (Figure 8.11).

According to the research results, the online user community has been steadily migrating upwards on this engagement hierarchy. The most notable change is among Inactives. Forty-four percent of the online population fell into this category. Two years

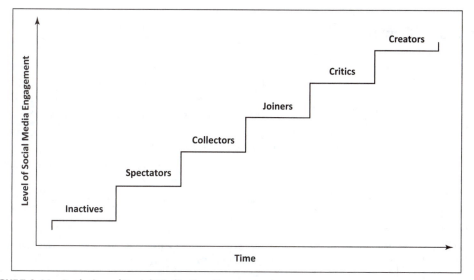

FIGURE 8.11 Evolution of Social Media User Engagement.

later, more than half of those Inactives had jumped into social media in some form or another. "Now roughly 82 percent of the adult population online is in one of the upper categories," said Bastone. "Social media has truly reached a state of mass adoption."

Application Case 8.6 shows the positive impact of social media at Lollapalooza.

Application Case 8.6

Measuring the Impact of Social Media at Lollapalooza

C3 Presents creates, books, markets, and produces live experiences, concerts, events, and just about anything that makes people stand up and cheer. Among others, they produce the Austin City Limits Music Festival, Lollapalooza, as well as more than 800 shows nationwide. They hope to see you up in front sometime.

An early adopter of social media as a way to drive event attendance, Lollapalooza organizer C3 Presents needed to know the impact of its social media efforts. They came to Cardinal Path for a social media measurement strategy and ended up with some startling insights.

The Challenge

When the Lollapalooza music festival decided to incorporate social media into their online marketing strategy, they did it with a bang. Using Facebook, MySpace, Twitter, and more, the Lollapalooza Web site was a first mover in allowing its users to engage and share through social channels that were integrated into the site itself.

After investing the time and resources in building out these integrations and their functionality, C3 wanted to know one simple thing: "Did it work?" To answer this, C3 Presents needed a measurement strategy that would provide a wealth of information about their social media implementation, such as:

- Which fans are using social media and sharing content?
- What social media is being used the most, and how?
- Are visitors that interact with social media more likely to buy a ticket?
- Is social media driving more traffic to the site? Is that traffic buying tickets?

The Solution

Cardinal Path was asked to architect and implement a solution based on an existing Google Analytics implementation that would to answer these questions.

A combination of customized event tracking, campaign tagging, custom variables, and a complex implementation and configuration was deployed to include the tracking of each social media outlet on the site.

(Continued)

Application Case 8.6   (Continued)

The Results

As a result of this measurement solution, it was easy to surface some impressive insights that helped C3 quantify the return on their social media investment:

- Users of the social media applications on Lollapalooza.com spent twice as much as non-users.
- Over 66 percent of the traffic referred from Facebook, MySpace, and Twitter was a result of sharing applications and Lollapalooza's messaging to its fans on those platforms.

- Fan engagement metrics such as time on site, bounce rate, page views per visit, and interaction goals improved significantly across the board as a result of social media applications.

QUESTIONS FOR DISCUSSION

1. How did C3 Presents use social media analytics to improve its business?
2. What were the challenges, the proposed solution, and the obtained results?

Source: **www.cardinalpath.com/case-study/social-media-measurement** (accessed March 2013).

SECTION 8.9 REVIEW QUESTIONS

1. What is social media? How does it relate to Web 2.0?
2. What are the differences and commonalities between Web-based social media and traditional/industrial media?
3. How do people use social media? What are the evolutionary levels of engagement?

8.10   SOCIAL MEDIA ANALYTICS

Social media analytics refers to the systematic and scientific ways to consume the vast amount of content created by Web-based social media outlets, tools, and techniques for the betterment of an organization's competitiveness. Social media analytics is rapidly becoming a new force in organizations around the world, allowing them to reach out to and understand consumers as never before. In many companies, it is becoming the tool for integrated marketing and communications strategies.

The exponential growth of social media outlets, from blogs, Facebook, and Twitter to LinkedIn and YouTube, and analytics tools that tap into these rich data sources offer organizations the chance to join a conversation with millions of customers around the globe every day. This aptitude is why nearly two-thirds of the 2,100 companies who participated in a recent survey by Harvard Business Review (HBR) Analytic Services said they are either currently using social media channels or have social media plans in the works (HBR, 2010). But many still say social media is an experiment, as they try to understand how to best use the different channels, gauge their effectiveness, and integrate social media into their strategy.

Despite the vast potential social media analytics brings, many companies seem focused on social media activity primarily as a one-way promotional channel and have yet to capitalize on the ability to not only listen to, but also analyze, consumer conversations and turn the information into insights that impact the bottom line. Here are some of the results from the HBR Analytic Services survey (HBR, 2010):

- Three-quarters (75%) of the companies in the survey said they did not know where their most valuable customers were talking about them.
- Nearly one-third (31%) do not measure effectiveness of social media.
- Less than one-quarter (23%) are using social media analytic tools.
- A fraction (7%) of participating companies are able to integrate social media into their marketing activities.

While still searching for best practice and measurements, two-thirds of the companies surveyed are convinced their use of social media will grow, and many anticipate investing more in it next year, even as spending in traditional media declines. So what is it specifically that the companies are interested in measuring in social media?

Measuring the Social Media Impact

For organizations, small or large, there is valuable insight hidden in all the user-generated content on social media sites. But how do you dig it out of dozens of review sites, thousands of blogs, millions of Facebook posts, and billions of tweets? Once you do that, how do you measure the impact of your efforts? These questions can be addressed by the analytics extension of the social media technologies. Once you decide on your goal for social media (what it is that you want to accomplish), there is a multitude of tools to help you get there. These analysis tools usually fall into three broad categories:

- *Descriptive analytics:* Uses simple statistics to identify activity characteristics and trends, such as how many followers you have, how many reviews were generated on Facebook, and which channels are being used most often.
- *Social network analysis:* Follows the links between friends, fans, and followers to identify connections of influence as well as the biggest sources of influence.
- *Advanced analytics:* Includes predictive analytics and text analytics that examine the *content* in online conversations to identify themes, sentiments, and connections that would not be revealed by casual surveillance.

Sophisticated tools and solutions to social media analytics use all three categories of analytics (i.e., descriptive, predictive, and prescriptive) in a somewhat progressive fashion.

Best Practices in Social Media Analytics

As an emerging tool, social media analytics is practiced by companies in a somewhat haphazard fashion. Because there are not well established methodologies, everybody is trying to create their own by trial and error. What follows are some of the field-tested best practices for social media analytics proposed by Paine and Chaves (2012).

THINK OF MEASUREMENT AS A GUIDANCE SYSTEM, NOT A RATING SYSTEM Measurements are often used for punishment or rewards; they should not be. They should be about figuring out what the most effective tools and practices are, what needs to be discontinued because it doesn't work, and what needs to be done more because it does work very well. A good analytics system should tell you where you need to focus. Maybe all that emphasis on Facebook doesn't really matter, because that is not where your audience is. Maybe they are all on Twitter, or vice versa. According to Paine and Chaves, channel preference won't necessarily be intuitive, "We just worked with a hotel that had virtually no activity on Twitter for one brand but lots of Twitter activity for one of their higher brands." Without an accurate measurement tool, you would not know.

TRACK THE ELUSIVE SENTIMENT Customers want to take what they are hearing and learning from online conversations and act on it. The key is to be precise in extracting and tagging their intentions by measuring their sentiments. As we have seen in Chapter 7, text analytic tools can categorize online content, uncover linked concepts, and reveal the sentiment in a conversation as "positive," "negative," or "neutral," based on the words people use. Ideally, you would like to be able to attribute sentiment to a specific product, service, and business unit. The more precise you can get in understanding the tone and perception that people express, the more actionable the information becomes, because you are mitigating concerns about mixed polarity. A mixed-polarity phrase, such as "hotel in great location but bathroom was smelly" should not be tagged as "neutral" because you have positives and negatives offsetting each other. To be actionable, these types of phrases are to be treated separately; "bathroom was smelly" is something someone can own and improve upon. One can classify and categorize these sentiments, look at trends over time, and see significant differences in the way people speak either positively or negatively about you. Furthermore, you can compare sentiment about your brand to your competitors.

CONTINUOUSLY IMPROVE THE ACCURACY OF TEXT ANALYSIS An industry-specific text analytics package will already know the vocabulary of your business. The system will have linguistic rules built into it, but it learns over time and gets better and better. Much as you would tune a statistical model as you get more data, better parameters, or new techniques to deliver better results, you would do the same thing with the natural language processing that goes into sentiment analysis. You set up rules, taxonomies, categorization, and meaning of words; watch what the results look like; and then go back and do it again.

LOOK AT THE RIPPLE EFFECT It is one thing to get a great hit on a high-profile site, but that's only the start. There's a difference between a great hit that just sits there and goes away versus a great hit that is tweeted, retweeted, and picked up by influential bloggers. Analysis should show you which social media activities go "viral" and which quickly go dormant—and why.

LOOK BEYOND THE BRAND One of the biggest mistakes people make is to be concerned only about their brand. To successfully analyze and act on social media, you need to understand not just what is being said about your brand, but the broader conversation about the spectrum of issues surrounding your product or service, as well. Customers don't usually care about a firm's message or its brand; they care about themselves. Therefore, you should pay attention to what they are talking about, where they are talking, and where their interests are.

IDENTIFY YOUR MOST POWERFUL INFLUENCERS Organizations struggle to identify who has the most power in shaping public opinion. It turns out, your most important influencers are not necessarily the ones who advocate specifically for your brand; they are the ones who influence the whole realm of conversation about your topic. You need to understand whether they are saying nice things, expressing support, or simply making observations or critiquing. What is the nature of their conversations? How is my brand being positioned relative to the competition in that space?

LOOK CLOSELY AT THE ACCURACY OF YOUR ANALYTIC TOOL Until recently, computer-based automated tools were not as accurate as humans for sifting through online content. Even now, accuracy varies depending on the media. For product review sites, hotel review sites, and Twitter, it can reach anywhere between 80 to 90 percent accuracy, because the context is more boxed in. When you start looking at blogs and discussion forums, where the conversation is more wide-ranging, the software can deliver 60 to 70 percent accuracy (Paine and Chaves, 2012). These figures will increase over time, because the analytics tools are continually upgraded with new rules and improved algorithms to reflect field experience, new products, changing market conditions, and emerging patterns of speech.

INCORPORATE SOCIAL MEDIA INTELLIGENCE INTO PLANNING Once you have big-picture perspective and detailed insight, you can begin to incorporate this information into your planning cycle. But that is easier said than done. A quick audience poll revealed that very few people currently incorporate learning from online conversations into their planning cycles (Paine and Chaves, 2012). One way to achieve this is to find time-linked associations between social media metrics and other business activities or market events. Social media is typically either organically invoked or invoked by something your organization does; therefore, if you see a spike in activity at some point in time, you want to know what was behind that.

Application Case 8.7 shows an interesting case where eHarmony, one of the most popular online relationship service providers, uses social media analytics to better listen, understand, and service its customers.

Application Case 8.7

eHarmony Uses Social Media to Help Take the Mystery Out of Online Dating

eHarmony launched in the United States in 2000 and is now the number-one trusted relationship services provider in the United States. Millions of people have used eHarmony's Compatibility Matching System to find compatible long-term relationships; an average of 542 eHarmony members marry every day in the United States, as a result of being matched on the site.

The Challenge

Online dating has continued to increase in popularity, and with the adoption of social media the social media team at eHarmony saw an even greater opportunity to connect with both current and future members. The team at eHarmony saw social media as a chance to dispel any myths and preconceived notions about online dating and, more importantly, have some fun with their social media presence. "For us it's about being human, and sharing great content that will help our members and our social media followers," says Grant Langston, director of social media at eHarmony. "We believe that if there are conversations happening around our brand, we need to be there and be a part of that dialogue."

The Approach

eHarmony started using Salesforce Marketing Cloud to listen to conversations around the brand and around keywords like "bad date" or "first date." They also took to Facebook and Twitter to connect with members, share success stories—including engagement and wedding videos—and answer questions from those looking for dating advice.

"We wanted to ensure our team felt comfortable using social media to connect with our community so we set up guidelines for how to respond and proceed," explains Grant Langston. "We try to use humor and have some fun when we reach out to people through Twitter or Facebook. We think it makes a huge difference and helps make people feel more comfortable."

The Results

By using social media to help educate and create awareness around the benefits of online dating, eHarmony has built a strong and loyal community. The social media team now has eight staff members working to respond to social interactions and posts, helping them reach out to clients and respond to hundreds of posts a week. They plan to start creating Facebook apps that celebrate their members' success, and they are looking to create some new videos around some common dating mistakes. The social team at eHarmony is making all the right moves and their hard work is paying off for their millions of happy members.

QUESTIONS FOR DISCUSSION

1. How did eHarmony use social media to enhance online dating?
2. What were the challenges, the proposed solution, and the obtained results?

Source: SalesForce Marketing Cloud, Case Study, **salesforcemarketingcloud.com; eharmony.com.**

Social Media Analytics Tools and Vendors

Monitoring social media, identifying interesting conversations among potential customers, and inferring what they are saying about your company, your products, and services is an essential yet a challenging task for many organizations. Generally speaking, there are two main paths that an organization can take to attain social media analytics (SMA) capabilities: in-house development or outsourcing. Because the SMA-related field is still evolving/maturing and because building an effective SMA system requires extensive knowledge in several related fields (e.g., Web, text mining, predictive analytics, reporting, visualization, performance management, etc.), with the exception of very large enterprises, most organizations choose the easier path: outsourcing.

Due to the astounding emphasis given to SMA, in the last few years we have witnessed an incredible emergence of start-up companies claiming to provide practical, cost-effective SMA solutions to organizations of all sizes and types. Because what they offered was not much more than just monitoring a few keywords about brands/products/services in social media, many of them did not succeed. While there still is a lot of uncertainty and churn in the marketplace, a significant number of them have survived and evolved to provide services that go beyond basic monitoring of a few brand names and keywords; they provide an integrated approach that helps many parts of the business, including product development, customer support, public outreach, lead generation, market research, and campaign management.

In the following section, we list and briefly define 10 SMA tools/vendors. This list is not meant to be "the absolute top 10" or the complete top-tier leaders in the market. It is to provide only 10 of the many successful SMA vendors and their respective tools/services with which we have some familiarity.

ATTENSITY360 Attensity360 operates on four key principles: listen, analyze, relate, and act. Attensity360 helps monitor trending topics, influencers, and the reach of your brand while recommending ways to join the conversation. Attensity Analyze applies text analytics to unstructured text to extract meaning and uncover trends. Attensity Respond helps automate the routing of incoming social media mentions into user-defined queues. Clients include Whirlpool, Vodofone, Versatel, TMobile, Oracle, and Wiley.

RADIAN6/SALESFORCE CLOUD Radian 6, purchased by Salesforce in 2011, works with brands to help them listen more intelligently to your consumers, competitors, and influencers with the goal of growing your business via detailed, real-time insights. Beyond their monitoring dashboard, which tracks mentions on more than 100 million social media sites, they offer an engagement console that allows you to coordinate your internal responses to external activity by immediately updating your blog, Twitter, and Facebook accounts all in one spot. Their clients include Red Cross, Adobe, AAA, Cirque du Soleil, H&R Block, March of Dimes, Microsoft, Pepsi, and Southwest Airlines.

SYSOMOS Managing conversations in real time, Sysomos's Heartbeat is a real-time monitoring and measurement tool that provides constantly updated snapshots of social media conversations delivered using a variety of user-friendly graphics. Heartbeat organizes conversations, manages workflow, facilitates collaboration, and provides ways to engage with key influencers. Their clients include IBM, HSBC, Roche, Ketchum, Sony Ericsson, Philips, ConAgra, Edelman, Shell Oil, Nokia, Sapient, Citi, and Interbrand. Owner: Marketwire.

COLLECTIVE INTELLECT Boulder, Colorado–based Collective Intellect, which started out by providing monitoring to financial firms, has evolved into a top-tier player in the marketplace of social media intelligence gathering. Using a combination of self-serve client dashboards and human analysis, Collective Intellect offers a robust monitoring and measurement tool suited to mid-size to large companies with its Social CRM Insights platform. Their clients include General Mills, NBC Universal, Pepsi, Walmart, Unilever, MillerCoors, Paramount, and Siemens.

WEBTRENDS Webtrends offers services geared toward monitoring, measuring, analyzing, profiling, and targeting audiences for a brand. The partner-based platform allows for crowd-sourced improvements and problem solving, creating transparency for their products and services. Their clients include CBS, NBC Universal, 20th Century Fox, AOL, Electronic Arts, Lifetime, and Nestle.

CRIMSON HEXAGON Cambridge, Massachusetts–based Crimson Hexagon taps into billions of conversations taking place in online media and turns them into actionable data for better brand understanding and improvement. Based on a technology licensed from Harvard, its VoxTrot Opinion is able to analyze vast amounts of qualitative information and determine quantitative proportion of opinion. Their clients include CNN, Hanes, AT&T, HP, Johnson & Johnson, Mashable, Microsoft, Monster, Thomson Reuters, Rubbermaid, Sybase, and *The Wall Street Journal.*

CONVERSEON New York–based social media consulting firm Converseon, named a leader in the social media monitoring sector by Forrester Research, builds tailored dashboards for its enterprise installations and offers professional services around every step of the social business intelligence process. Converseon starts with the technology and adds human analysis, resulting in high-quality data and impressive functionality. Their clients include Dow, Amway, Graco, and other major brands.

SPIRAL16 Spiral16 takes an in-depth look at who is saying what about a brand and compares results with those of top competitors. The goal is to help you monitor the effectiveness of your social media strategy, understand the sentiment behind conversations online, and mine large amounts of data. It uses impressive 3D displays and a standard dashboard. Their clients include Toyota, Lee, and Cadbury.

BUZZLOGIC BuzzLogic uses its technology platform to identify and organize the conversation universe, combining both conversation topic and audience to help brands reach audiences who are passionate on everything from the latest tech craze and cloud computing to parenthood and politics. Their clients include Starbucks, American Express, HBO, and HP.

SPROUTSOCIAL Founded in 2010 in Chicago, Illinois, SproutSocial is an innovative social media analytics company that provides social analytics services to many well-known firms and organizations. Their clients include Yahoo!, Nokia, Pepsi, St. Jude Children's Research Center, Hyatt Regency, McDonalds, and AMD. A sample screen shot of their social media solution dashboard is shown in Figure 8.12.

SECTION 8.10 REVIEW QUESTIONS

1. What is social media analytics? What type of data is analyzed with it?
2. What are the reasons/motivations behind the exponential growth of social media analytics?
3. How can you measure the impact of social media analytics?
4. List and briefly describe the best practices in social media analytics.
5. Why do you think social media analytics tools are usually offered as a service and not a tool?

FIGURE 8.12 A Social Media Analytics Screenshot. *Source:* Courtesy of **sproutsocial.com**.

Chapter Highlights

- Web mining can be defined as the discovery and analysis of interesting and useful information from the Web, about the Web, and usually using Web-based tools.
- Web mining can be viewed as consisting of three areas: Web content mining, Web structure mining, and Web usage mining.
- Web content mining refers to the automatic extraction of useful information from Web pages. It may be used to enhance search results produced by search engines.

- Web structure mining refers to generating interesting information from the links included in Web pages. This is used in Google's page rank algorithm to order the display of pages, for example.
- Web structure mining can also be used to identify the members of a specific community and perhaps even the roles of the members in the community.
- Web usage mining refers to developing useful information through analysis of Web server logs, user profiles, and transaction information.

- Web usage mining can assist in better CRM, personalization, site navigation modifications, and improved business models.
- Text and Web mining are emerging as critical components of the next generation of business intelligence tools, enabling organizations to compete successfully.
- A search engine is a software program that searches for documents (Internet sites or files), based on keywords (individual words, multi-word terms, or a complete sentence) users have provided that have to do with the subject of their inquiry.
- PageRank is a link analysis algorithm named after Larry Page, who is one of the two inventors of Google, which began as a research project at Stanford University in 1996. PageRank is used by the Google Web search engine.
- Search engine optimization (SEO) is the intentional activity of affecting the visibility of an e-commerce site or a Web site in a search engine's natural (unpaid or organic) search results.
- A maturity model is a formal depiction of critical dimensions and their competency levels of a business practice.

- Voice of the customer (VOC) is a term usually used to describe the analytic process of capturing a customer's expectations, preferences, and aversions.
- Social analytics is the monitoring, analyzing, measuring, and interpreting of digital interactions and relationships among people, topics, ideas, and content.
- A social network is a social structure composed of individuals/people (or groups of individuals or organizations) linked to one another with some type of connections/relationships.
- Social media refers to the enabling technologies of social interactions among people in which they create, share, and exchange information, ideas, and opinions in virtual communities and networks.
- Social media analytics refers to the systematic and scientific ways to consume the vast amount of content created by Web-based social media outlets, tools, and techniques for the betterment of an organization's competitiveness.

Key Terms

authoritative pages
clickstream analysis
customer experience management
  (CEM)
hubs
hyperlink-induced topic search
  (HITS)

search engine
social network
spiders
voice of customer (VOC)
Web analytics
Web content mining
Web crawler

Web mining
Web structure mining
Web usage mining

Questions for Discussion

1. Explain the relationship among data mining, text mining, and Web mining.
2. What should an organization consider before making a decision to purchase Web mining software?
3. Discuss the differences and commonalities between text mining and Web mining.
4. In your own words, define *Web mining* and discuss its importance.
5. What are the three main areas of Web mining? Discuss the differences and commonalities among these three areas.
6. What is Web content mining? How does it differ from text mining? Discuss and justify your answers with concrete examples.

7. What is Web structure mining? What are authoritative pages and hubs? How do they relate to Web structure mining?
8. Discuss the expected benefits of Web structure mining. Provide examples from real-world applications that you are familiar with.
9. What is Web usage mining? Draw a picture of the Web usage mining process and explain/discuss the major steps in the process.
10. Provide two exemplary business applications of Web usage mining; discuss their usage and business value.
11. What is a search engine? Why are they important for businesses?

12. What is search engine optimization? Who benefits from it? How?
13. What is Web analytics? What are the metrics used in Web analytics?
14. Define *social analytics, social network,* and *social network analysis.* What are the relationships among them?
15. What is social media analytics? How is it done? Who does it? What comes out of it?

Exercises

Teradata University Network (TUN) and Other Hands-on Exercises

1. Visit **teradatauniversitynetwork.com**. Identify cases about Web mining. Describe recent developments in the field. If you cannot find enough cases at the Teradata University network Web site, broaden your search to other Web-based resources.
2. Go to **teradatauniversitynetwork.com** or locate white papers, Web seminars, and other materials related to Web mining. Synthesize your findings into a short written report.
3. Browse the Web and your library's digital databases to identify articles that make the linkage between text/Web mining and contemporary business intelligence systems.

Team Assignments and Role-Playing Projects

1. Examine how Web-based data can be captured automatically using the latest technologies. Once captured, what are the potential patterns that you can extract from these content-rich, mostly unstructured data sources?
2. Interview administrators in your college or executives in your organization to determine how Web mining is assisting (or could assist) them in their work. Write a proposal describing your findings. Include a preliminary cost–benefit analysis in your report.
3. Go online, search for publicly available Web usage or social media data files, and download one of your choice. Then, download and use one of the free tools to analyze the data. Write your findings and experiences in a professionally organized report.

Internet Exercises

1. Survey some Web mining tools and vendors. Identify some Web mining products and service providers that are not mentioned in this chapter.
2. Find recent cases of successful Web mining applications. Try Web mining software vendors and consultancy firms and look for cases or success stories. Prepare a report summarizing five new case studies.
3. Go to **attensity.com**. Download at least three white papers on Web analytics applications. Which of these applications may have used a combination of data/text/Web mining techniques?
4. Go to **sas.com**. Find and download at least three case studies. Which of these studies may have used the Web mining techniques discussed in this chapter?
5. Go to **ibm.com**. Find and download at least three white papers on Web analytics. Write a summary of your findings.
6. Go to **teradata.com**. Download at least three white papers on applications. Which of these applications may have used the Web mining techniques discussed in this chapter?
7. Go to **kdnuggets.com**. Explore the sections on applications as well as software. Find names of at least three additional packages for Web mining and social media analytics.

End-of-Chapter Application Case

Keeping Students on Track with Web and Predictive Analytics

What makes a college student stay in school? Over the years, educators have held a lot of theories—from student demographics to attendance in college prep courses—but they've lacked the hard data to prove conclusively what really drives retention. As a result, colleges and universities have struggled to understand how to lower dropout rates and keep students on track all the way to graduation.

That situation is changing at American Public University System (APUS), an online university serving 70,000 distance learners from the United States and more than 100 countries.

APUS is breaking new ground by using analytics to zero in on those factors that most influence a student's decision to stay in school or drop out.

"By leveraging the power of predictive analytics, we can predict the probability that any given student will drop out," says Phil Ice, APUS' director of course design, research, and development. "This translates into actionable business intelligence that we can deploy across the enterprise to create and maintain the conditions for maximum student retention."

Rich Data Sources

As an online university, APUS has a rich store of student information available for analysis. "All of the activities are technology mediated here," says Ice, "so we have a very nice record of what goes on with the student. We can pull demographic data, registration data, course level data, and more." Ice and his colleagues then develop metrics that help APUS analyze and build predictive models of student retention.

One of the measures, for example, looks at the last time a student logged into the online system after starting a class. If too many days have passed, it may be a sign the student is about to drop out. Educators at APUS combine such online activity data with a sophisticated end-of-course survey to build a complete model of student satisfaction and retention.

The course survey yields particularly valuable data for APUS. Designed around a theoretical framework known as the Community of Inquiry, the survey seeks to understand the student's learning experience by analyzing three interdependent elements: social, cognitive, and teaching presence. Through the survey, Ice says, "We hone in on things such as a student's perception of being able to build effective community."

Increasing Accuracy

It turns out that the student's sense of being part of a larger community—his or her "social presence"—is one of the key variables affecting the student's likelihood of staying in school. Another one is the student's perception of the effectiveness of online learning. In fact, when fed into IBM SPSS Modeler and measured against disenrolment rates, these two factors together accounted for nearly 25 percent of the overall statistical variance, meaning they are strong predictors of student attrition. With the adoption of advanced analytics in its retention efforts, APUS predicts with approximately 80 percent certainty whether a given student is going to drop out.

Some of the findings generated by its predictive models actually came as a surprise to APUS. For example, it had long been assumed that gender and ethnicity were good predictors of attrition, but the models proved otherwise. Educators also assumed that a preparatory course called "College 100: Foundations of Online Learning" was a major driver of retention, but an in-depth analysis using Modeler came to a different conclusion. "When we ran the numbers, we found that students who took it were not retained the way we thought they were," says Dr. Frank McCluskey, provost and executive vice president at APUS. "IBM SPSS predictive analytics told us that our guess had been wrong."

Strategic Course Adjustments

The next step for APUS is to put its new-found predictive intelligence to work. Already the university is building online "dashboards" that are putting predictive analytics into the hands of deans and other administrators who can design and implement strategies for boosting retention. Specific action plans could include targeting individual at-risk students with special communications and counseling. Analysis of course surveys can also help APUS adjust course content to better engage students and provide feedback to instructors to help improve their teaching methods.

Survey and modeling results are reinforcing the university's commitment to enriching the student's sense of community—a key retention factor. Online courses, for example, are being refined to promote more interactions among students, and social media and online collaboration tools are being deployed to boost school spirit. "We have an online student lounge, online student clubs, online student advisors," says McCluskey. "We want to duplicate a campus fully and completely, where students can grow in all sorts of ways, learn things, exchange ideas—maybe even books—and get to know each other."

Smart Decisions

While predictive modeling gives APUS an accurate picture of the forces driving student attrition, tackling the problem means deciding among an array of possible intervention strategies. To help administrators sort out the options, APUS plans to implement a Decision Management System, a solution that turns IBM SPSS Modeler's predictive power into intelligent, data-driven decisions. The solution will draw from Modeler's analysis of at-risk students and suggest the best intervention strategies for any given budget.

APUS also plans to delve deeper into the surveys by mining the open-ended text responses that are part of each questionnaire (IBM SPSS Text Analytics for Surveys will help with that initiative). All of these data-driven initiatives aim to increase student learning, enhance the student's experience, and build an environment that encourages retention at APUS. It's no coincidence that achieving that goal also helps grow the university's bottom line. "Attracting and enrolling new students is expensive, so losing them is costly for us and for students as well," McCluskey says. "That is why we are excited about using predictive analytics to keep retention rates as high as possible."

QUESTIONS FOR THE END-OF-CHAPTER APPLICATION CASE

1. Describe challenges that APUS was facing. Discuss the ramifications of such challenges.
2. What types of data did APUS tap into? What do you think are the main obstacles one would have to overcome when using data that comes from different domains and sources?
3. What solutions did they pursue? What tools and technologies did they use?
4. What were the results? Do you think these results are also applicable to other educational institutions? Why? Why not?
5. What additional analysis are they planning on conducting? Can you think of other data analyses that they could apply and benefit from?

Source: IBM, Customer Success Stories, **www-01.ibm.com/software/ success/cssdb.nsf/CS/GREE-8F8M76** (accessed March 2013).

References

Brin, S., and L. Page. (2012). "Reprint of the Anatomy of a Large-Scale Hypertextual Web Search Engine." *Computer Networks,* Vol. 56, No. 18, pp. 3825–3833,

Brogan, C., and Bastone, J. (2011). "Acting on Customer Intelligence from Social Media: The New Edge for Building Customer Loyalty and Your Brand." SAS white paper. **sas.com/resources/whitepaper/wp_21122.pdf** (accessed March 2013).

Coussement, K., and D. Van Den Poel. (2009). "Improving Customer Attrition Prediction by Integrating Emotions from Client/Company Interaction Emails and Evaluating Multiple Classifiers." *Expert Systems with Applications,* Vol. 36, No. 3, pp. 6127–6134.

Cutts, M. (2006, February 4). "Ramping Up on International Webspam." **mattcutts.com/blog. mattcutts.com/blog/ramping-up-on-international-webspam** (accessed March 2013).

Etzioni, O. (1996). "The World Wide Web: Quagmire or Gold Mine?" *Communications of the ACM,* Vol. 39, No. 11, pp. 65–68.

Goodman, A. (2005). "Search Engine Showdown: Black Hats Versus White Hats at SES." SearchEngineWatch. **searchenginewatch.com/article/2066090/Search-Engine-Showdown-Black-Hats-vs.-White-Hats-at-SES** (accessed February 2013).

HBR. (2010). "The New Conversation: Taking Social Media from Talk to Action," A SAS-sponsored research report by Harvard Business Review Analytic Services. **sas.com/resources/whitepaper/wp_23348.pdf** (accessed March 2013).

Kaplan, A. M., and M. Haenlein. (2010). "Users of the World, Unite! The Challenges and Opportunities of Social Media." *Business Horizons,* Vol. 53, No. 1, pp. 59–68.

Kleinberg, J. (1999). "Authoritative Sources in a Hyperlinked Environment." *Journal of the ACM,* Vol. 46, No. 5, pp. 604–632.

Lars-Henrik, S. (1996). "Commonness Across Cultures," in Anindita Niyogi Balslev. *Cross-Cultural Conversation: Initiation.* Oxford University Press.

Liddy, E. (2012). "How a Search Engine Works." **www.infotoday.com/searcher/may01/liddy.htm** (accessed November 2012).

Masand, B. M., M. Spiliopoulou, J. Srivastava, and O. R. Zaïane. (2002). "Web Mining for Usage Patterns and Profiles." *SIGKDD Explorations,* Vol. 4, No. 2, pp. 125–132.

Morgan, N., G. Jones, and A. Hodges. (2010). "The Complete Guide to Social Media from the Social Media Guys." **thesocialmediaguys.co.uk/wp-content/uploads/downloads/2011/03/CompleteGuidetoSocialMedia.pdf** (accessed February 2013).

Nasraoui, O., M. Spiliopoulou, J. Srivastava, B. Mobasher, and B. Masand. (2006). "WebKDD 2006: Web Mining and Web Usage Analysis Post-Workshop Report." *ACM SIGKDD Explorations Newsletter,* Vol. 8, No. 2, pp. 84–89.

Paine, K. D., and M. Chaves. (2012). "Social Media Metrics." SAS white paper. **sas.com/resources/whitepaper/wp_19861.pdf** (accessed February 2013).

Peterson, E. T. (2008). "The Voice of Customer: Qualitative Data as a Critical Input to Web Site Optimization." **foreseeresults.com/Form_Epeterson_WebAnalytics.html** (accessed May 2009).

Scott, W. Richard, and Gerald F. Davis. (2003). "Networks In and Around Organizations." *Organizations and Organizing.* Upper Saddle River, NJ: Pearson Prentice Hall.

The Westover Group. (2013). "20 Key Web Analytics Metrics and How to Use Them." **www.thewestovergroup.com** (accessed February 2013).

Turetken, O., and R. Sharda. (2004). "Development of a Fisheye-Based Information Search Processing Aid (FISPA) for Managing Information Overload in the Web Environment." *Decision Support Systems,* Vol. 37, No. 3, pp. 415–434.

Zhou, Y., E. Reid, J. Qin, H. Chen, and G. Lai. (2005). "U.S. Domestic Extremist Groups on the Web: Link and Content Analysis." *IEEE Intelligent Systems,* Vol. 20, No. 5, pp. 44–51.

P A R T

IV

Prescriptive Analytics

LEARNING OBJECTIVES FOR PART IV

- Understand the applications of prescriptive analytics techniques in combination with reporting and predictive analytics

- Understand the concepts of analytical models for selected decision problems including linear programming and analytic hierarchy process

- Recognize the concepts of heuristic search methods and simulation models for decision support

- Understand the concepts and applications of automated rule systems and expert system technologies

- Gain familiarity with knowledge management and collaboration support systems

This part extends the decision support applications beyond reporting and data mining methods. It includes coverage of selected techniques that can be employed in combination with predictive models to help support decision making. We focus on techniques that can be implemented relatively easily using either spreadsheet tools or by using stand-alone software tools. Of course, there is much additional detail to be learned about management science models, but the objective of this part is to simply illustrate what is possible and how it has been implemented in some real settings. We also include coverage of automated decision systems that implement the results from various models described in this book, and expert system technologies. Finally, we conclude this part with a discussion of knowledge management issues and group support systems. Technologies and issues in knowledge management and group support systems directly impact the delivery and practice of prescriptive analytics.

CHAPTER 9

Model-Based Decision Making: Optimization and Multi-Criteria Systems

LEARNING OBJECTIVES

- Understand the basic concepts of analytical decision modeling
- Describe how prescriptive models interact with data and the user
- Understand some different, well-known model classes
- Understand how to structure decision making with a few alternatives
- Describe how spreadsheets can be used for analytical modeling and solution

- Explain the basic concepts of optimization and when to use them
- Describe how to structure a linear programming model
- Describe how to handle multiple goals
- Explain what is meant by sensitivity analysis, what-if analysis, and goal seeking
- Describe the key issues of multi-criteria decision making

I n this chapter we describe selected techniques employed in prescriptive analytics. We present this material with a note of caution: Modeling can be a very difficult topic and is as much an art as a science. The purpose of this chapter is not necessarily for you to *master the topics* of modeling and analysis. Rather, the material is geared toward *gaining familiarity* with the important concepts as they relate to DSS and their use in decision making. It is important to recognize that the modeling we discuss here is only cursorily related to the concepts of data modeling. You should not confuse the two. We walk through some basic concepts and definitions of modeling before introducing the influence diagrams, which can aid a decision maker in sketching a model of a situation and even solving it. We next introduce the idea of modeling directly in spreadsheets. We then discuss the structure and application of some successful time-proven models and methodologies: optimization, decision analysis, decision trees, and analytic hierarchy process. This chapter includes the following sections:

9.1 Opening Vignette: Midwest ISO Saves Billions by Better Planning of Power Plant Operations and Capacity Planning

9.2 Decision Support Systems Modeling

9.1 OPENING VIGNETTE: Midwest ISO Saves Billions by Better Planning of Power Plant Operations and Capacity Planning

INTRODUCTION

Midwest ISO (MISO) operates in 13 U.S. states as well as the province of Manitoba in Canada. It manages 35 transmission owners and 100 non-transmission owners, ensuring that all members of the organization have equal access to high-voltage power lines. Together, the United States and the province of Manitoba constitute one of the largest energy markets in the world, with yearly energy transactions amounting to about $23 billion. Before Midwest ISO existed, each transmission company operated independently. Now, after a company joins MISO, it still maintains control of its power plants and transmission lines, and shares in the responsibility of supplying and buying energy in a wholesale electricity market to meet demand. MISO, however, has the responsibility of deciding when and how much energy to produce and administer to the market in such a way as to increase benefit to society.

PRESENTATION OF PROBLEM

Individually, the companies had to make extra investments to manage risk. Their mode of operation resulted in inefficient use of transmission lines. Deregulation policies were introduced by Congress and were implemented by the Federal Energy Regulatory Commission (FERC) for the wholesale electricity industry. When MISO was formed, it first started an energy-only market in 2005 that ensured unbiased access to transmission lines. In 2009, it added ancillary services (regulation and contingency reserves) to its operations. Regulation was supposed to ensure that the frequency did not deviate from 60 hertz. Contingency reserves were supposed to help ensure that in the event of unexpected power loss, demand was met within 10 minutes of the power loss. Operations research methods were considered as means to provide the level of performance demanded by the ancillary services.

METHODOLOGY/SOLUTION

Sequentially, two optimization algorithms were used. These were the commitment algorithm and the dispatch algorithm. The commitment algorithm committed power plants to be either on or off. The dispatch algorithm determined the level of a power plant's output and price. With these two algorithms, facilities were given constraints on how much electricity to carry within their physical limits in order to avoid overload and damage to expensive equipment. The commitment problem for the energy-only market made use of the Lagrangian relaxation method. As mentioned earlier, it determined when each plant should turn on or off. The dispatch problem was solved with a linear programming model. It helped decide how much output should be produced by each power plant. It also helped determine the price of energy based on the location of the power plant. Even though these methods were just fine, they were not appropriate for the ancillary service market commitment problem. Rather, a mixed integer programming model was used as a result of its superior modeling capacity.

RESULTS/BENEFITS

Based on the improvements made, reliability of the transmission grid improved. Also, a dynamic transparent pricing structure was created. Value proposition studies show that Midwest ISO achieved about $2.1 billion and $3 billion dollars in net cumulative savings between 2007 and 2010. Future savings are expected to accrue to about $6.1 billion.

QUESTIONS FOR THE OPENING VIGNETTE

1. In what ways were the individual companies in Midwest ISO better off being part of MISO as opposed to operating independently?
2. The dispatch problem was solved with a linear programming method. Explain the need of such method in light of the problem discussed in the case.
3. What were the two main optimization algorithms used? Briefly explain the use of each algorithm.

LESSONS WE CAN LEARN FROM THIS VIGNETTE

Operations research (OR) methods were used by Midwest ISO to provide efficient and cheaper sources of energy for states in the midwestern region of the United States. A combination of linear programming and the Lagrangian relaxation methods was used to determine an optimized approach to generate and supply power. By extension, this methodology could be used by both government agencies and the private sector to optimize the cost and provision of services such as healthcare and education.

Source: Brian Carlson, Yonghong Chen, Mingguo Hong, Roy Jones, Kevin Larson, Xingwang Ma, Peter Nieuwesteeg, et al., "MISO Unlocks Billions in Savings Through the Application of Operations Research for Energy and Ancillary Services Markets," *Interfaces,* Vol. 42, No. 1, 2012, pp. 58–73.

9.2 DECISION SUPPORT SYSTEMS MODELING

Many readily accessible applications describe how the models incorporated in DSS contribute to organizational success. These include Pillowtex (see ProModel, 2013), Fiat (see ProModel, 2006), Procter & Gamble (see Camm et al., 1997), and others. INFORMS publications such as *Interfaces, ORMS Today,* and *Analytics* magazine all include stories that illustrate successful applications of decision models in real settings. This chapter includes many examples of such applications, as does the next chapter.

Simulation models can enhance an organization's decision-making process and enable it to see the impact of its future choices. Fiat (see ProModel, 2006) saves $1 million annually in manufacturing costs through simulation. IBM has predicted the behavior of the 230-mile-long Guadalupe River and its many tributaries. The prediction can be made several days before the imminent flood of the river. This is important as it would allow for enough time for disaster management and preparation. IBM used a combination of weather and sensor data to build a river system simulation application that could simulate thousands of river branches at a time. Besides flood prediction, the application could also be used for irrigation planning in such a way as to avoid the impact of droughts and surplus water. Even companies under financial stress need to invest in such solutions to squeeze more efficiency out of their limited resources—maybe even more so. Pillowtex, a $2 billion company that manufactures pillows, mattress pads, and comforters, had filed for bankruptcy and needed to reorganize its plants to maximize net profits from the company's operations. It employed a simulation model to develop a new lean manufacturing environment that would reduce the costs and increase throughput. The company estimated that the use of this model resulted in over $12 million savings immediately. (See **promodel.com**.) We will study simulation in the next chapter.

Modeling is a key element in most DSS and a necessity in a model-based DSS. There are many classes of models, and there are often many specialized techniques for solving each one. Simulation is a common modeling approach, but there are several others.

Applying models to real-world situations can save millions of dollars or generate millions of dollars in revenue. Christiansen et al. (2009) describe the applications of such models in shipping company operations. They describe applications of TurboRouter, a DSS for ship routing and scheduling. They claim that over the course of just a 3-week period, a company used this model to better utilize its fleet, generating additional profit of $1–2 million in just a short time. We provide another example of a model application in Application Case 9.1.

Application Case 9.1

Optimal Transport for ExxonMobil Downstream Through a DSS

ExxonMobil, a petroleum and natural gas company, operates in several countries worldwide. It provides several ranges of petroleum products including clean fuels, lubricants, and high-value products and feedstock to several customers. This is completed through a complex supply chain between its refineries and customers. One of the main products ExxonMobil transports is vacuum gas oil (VGO). ExxonMobil transports several shiploads of vacuum gas oil from Europe to the United States. In a year, it is estimated that ExxonMobil transports about 60–70 ships of VGO across the Atlantic Ocean. Hitherto, both ExxonMobil-managed vessels and third-party vessels were scheduled to transport VGO across the Atlantic through a cumbersome manual process. The whole process required the collaboration of several individuals across the supply chain organization. Several customized spreadsheets with special constraints, requirements, and economic trade-offs were used to determine the transportation schedule of the vessels. Some of the constraints included:

1. Constantly varying production and demand projections
2. Maximum and minimum inventory constraints
3. A pool of heterogeneous vessels (e.g., ships with varying speed, cargo size)

4. Vessels that load and discharge at multiple ports
5. Both ExxonMobil-managed and third-party supplies and ports
6. Complex transportation cost that includes variable overage and demurrage costs
7. Vessel size and draft limits for different ports

The manual process could not determine the actual routes of vessels, the timing of each vessel, and the quantity of VGO loaded and discharged. Additionally, consideration of the production and consumption data at several locations rendered the manual process burdensome and inefficient.

Methodology/Solution

A decision support tool that supported schedulers in planning an optimal schedule for ships to load, transport, and discharge VGO to and from multiple locations was developed. The problem was formulated as a mixed-integer linear programming problem. The solution had to satisfy requirements for routing, transportation, scheduling, and inventory management vis-à-vis varying production and demand profiles. A mathematical programming language, GAMS, was used for the problem formulation and Microsoft Excel was used as the

(Continued)

Application Case 9.1 (Continued)

user interface. When the solver (ILOG CPLEX) is run, an optimal solution is reached at a point when the objective value of the incumbent solution stops improving. This stopping criterion is determined by the user during each program run.

Results/Benefits

It was expected that using the optimization model will lead to reduced shipping cost and less demurrage expenses. These would be achieved because the tool would be able to support higher utilization of ships and help make ship selection (e.g., Panamax versus Aframax) and design more optimal routing schedules. The researchers expected to extend the research by exploring other alternate mathematical methods to solve the scheduling problem. They also

intended to give the DSS tool the capability to consider multiple products for a pool of vessels.

DISCUSSION QUESTIONS

1. List three ways in which manual scheduling of ships could result in more operational cost as compared to the tool developed.
2. In what other ways can ExxonMobil leverage the decision support tool developed to expand and optimize their other business operations?
3. What are some strategic decisions that could be made by decision makers using the tool developed.

Source: K. C. Furman, J. H. Song, G. R. Kocis, M. K. McDonald, and P. H. Warrick, "Feedstock Routing in the ExxonMobil Downstream Sector," *Interfaces*, Vol. 41, No. 2, 2011, pp. 149–163.

Current Modeling Issues

We next discuss some major modeling issues, such as problem identification and environmental analysis, variable identification, forecasting, the use of multiple models, model categories (or appropriate selection), model management, and knowledge-based modeling.

IDENTIFICATION OF THE PROBLEM AND ENVIRONMENTAL ANALYSIS One very important aspect of it is **environmental scanning and analysis,** which is the monitoring, scanning, and interpretation of collected information. No decision is made in a vacuum. It is important to analyze the scope of the domain and the forces and dynamics of the environment. A decision maker needs to identify the organizational culture and the corporate decision-making processes (e.g., who makes decisions, degree of centralization). It is entirely possible that environmental factors have created the current problem. BI/business analytics (BA) tools can help identify problems by scanning for them. The problem must be understood and everyone involved should share the same frame of understanding, because the problem will ultimately be represented by the model in one form or another. Otherwise, the model will not help the decision maker.

VARIABLE IDENTIFICATION Identification of a model's variables (e.g., decision, result, uncontrollable) is critical, as are the relationships among the variables. Influence diagrams, which are graphical models of mathematical models, can facilitate the identification process. A more general form of an influence diagram, a cognitive map, can help a decision maker develop a better understanding of a problem, especially of variables and their interactions.

FORECASTING (PREDICTIVE ANALYTICS) **Forecasting** is predicting the future. This form of predictive analytics is essential for construction and manipulating models, because when a decision is implemented the results usually occur in the future. Whereas DSS are typically designed to determine what will be, traditional MIS report what is or what was. There is no point in running a what-if (sensitivity) analysis on the past, because decisions made then have no impact on the future. Forecasting is getting easier as software vendors automate many of the complications of developing such models.

E-commerce has created an immense need for forecasting and an abundance of available information for performing it. E-commerce activities occur quickly, yet information about purchases is gathered and should be analyzed to produce forecasts. Part of the analysis involves simply predicting demand; however, forecasting models can use product life-cycle needs and information about the marketplace and consumers to analyze the entire situation, ideally leading to additional sales of products and services.

Many organizations have accurately predicted demand for products and services, using a variety of qualitative and quantitative methods. But until recently, most companies viewed their customers and potential customers by categorizing them into only a few, time-tested groupings. Today, it is critical not only to consider customer characteristics, but also to consider how to get the right product(s) to the right customers at the right price at the right time in the right format/packaging. The more accurately a firm does this, the more profitable the firm is. In addition, a firm needs to recognize when not to sell a particular product or bundle of products to a particular set of customers. Part of this effort involves identifying lifelong customer profitability. These customer relationship management (CRM) system and revenue management system (RMS) approaches rely heavily on forecasting techniques, which are typically described as *predictive analytics*. These systems attempt to predict who their best (i.e., most profitable) customers (and worst ones as well) are and focus on identifying products and services at appropriate prices to appeal to them. We describe an effective example of such forecasting at Harrah's Cherokee Casino and Hotel in Application Case 9.2.

Application Case 9.2

Forecasting/Predictive Analytics Proves to Be a Good Gamble for Harrah's Cherokee Casino and Hotel

Harrah's Cherokee Casino and Hotel uses a revenue management (RM) system to optimize its profits. The system helps Harrah's attain an average 98.6 percent occupancy rate 7 days a week all year, with the exception of December, and a 60 percent gross revenue profit margin. One aspect of the RM system is providing its customers with Total Rewards cards, which track how much money each customer gambles. The system also tracks reservations and overbookings, with the exception of those made through third parties such as travel agencies. The RM system calculates the opportunity cost of saving rooms for possible customers who gamble more than others, because gambling is Harrah's main source of revenue. Unlike the traditional method of company employees only tracking the "big spenders," the RM system also tracks the "mid-tier" spenders. This has helped increase the company's profits. Only customers who gamble over a certain dollar amount are recommended by the RM system to be given rooms at the hotel; those who spend less may be given complimentary rooms at nearby hotels in order to keep the bigger spenders close by. The RM system also tracks which gaming machines are most popular so that management can place them strategically throughout the casino in order to encourage customers to gamble more money. Additionally, the

system helps track the success of different marketing projects and incentives.

The casino collects demand data, which are then used by a forecasting algorithm with several components: smoothed values for base demand, demand trends, annual and day-of-the-week seasonality, and special event factors. The forecasts are used by overbooking and optimization models for inventory-control recommendations. The booking recommendation system includes a linear program (to be introduced later in the chapter). The model updates the recommendations for booking a room periodically or when certain events demand it. The bid-price model is updated or optimized after 24 hours have passed since the last optimization, when five rooms have been booked since the last optimization, or when the RM analyst manually starts a new optimization. The model is a good example of the process of forecasting demand and then using this information to employ a model-based DSS for making optimal decisions.

Source: Based on R. Metters, C. Queenan, M. Ferguson, L. Harrison, J. Higbie, S. Ward, B. Barfield, T. Farley, H. A. Kuyumcu, and A. Duggasani, "The 'Killer Application' of Revenue Management: Harrah's Cherokee Casino & Hotel," *Interfaces*, Vol. 38, No. 3, May/June 2008, pp. 161–175.

MODEL CATEGORIES   Table 9.1 classifies DSS models into seven groups and lists several representative techniques for each category. Each technique can be applied to either a **static** or a **dynamic model,** which can be constructed under assumed environments of certainty, uncertainty, or risk. To expedite model construction, we can use special decision analysis systems that have modeling languages and capabilities embedded in them. These include spreadsheets, data mining systems, OLAP systems, and modeling languages that help an analyst build a model. We will introduce one of these systems later in the chapter.

MODEL MANAGEMENT   Models, like data, must be managed to maintain their integrity, and thus their applicability. Such management is done with the aid of model base management systems (MBMS), which are analogous to database management systems (DBMS).

KNOWLEDGE-BASED MODELING   DSS uses mostly quantitative models, whereas expert systems use qualitative, knowledge-based models in their applications. Some knowledge is necessary to construct solvable (and therefore usable) models. Many of the predictive analytics techniques such as classification, clustering, and so on can be used in building knowledge-based models. As described, such models can also be built from analysis of expertise and incorporation of such expertise in models.

CURRENT TRENDS IN MODELING   One recent trend in modeling involves the development of model libraries and solution technique libraries. Some of these codes can be run directly on the owner's Web server for free, and others can be downloaded and run on a local computer. The availability of these codes means that powerful optimization and simulation packages are available to decision makers who may have only experienced these tools from the perspective of classroom problems. For example, the Mathematics and Computer Science Division at Argonne National Laboratory (Argonne, Illinois) maintains the NEOS Server for Optimization at **neos.mcs.anl.gov/neos/index.html**. You can find links to other sites by clicking the Resources link at **informs.org**, the Web site of the Institute for Operations Research and the Management Sciences (INFORMS). A wealth

TABLE 9.1   Categories of Models

Category	Process and Objective	Representative Techniques
Optimization of problems with few alternatives	Find the best solution from a small number of alternatives	Decision tables, decision trees, analytic hierarchy process
Optimization via algorithm	Find the best solution from a large number of alternatives, using a step-by-step improvement process	Linear and other mathematical programming models, network models
Optimization via an analytic formula	Find the best solution in one step, using a formula	Some inventory models
Simulation	Find a good enough solution or the best among the alternatives checked, using experimentation	Several types of simulation
Heuristics	Find a good enough solution, using rules	Heuristic programming, expert systems
Predictive models	Predict the future for a given scenario	Forecasting models, Markov analysis
Other models	Solve a what-if case, using a formula	Financial modeling, waiting lines

of modeling and solution information is available from INFORMS. The Web site for one of INFORMS' publications, *OR/MS Today,* at **lionhrtpub.com/ORMS.shtml** includes links to many categories of modeling software. We will learn about some of these shortly.

There is a clear trend toward developing and using Web tools and software to access and even run software to perform modeling, optimization, simulation, and so on. This has, in many ways, simplified the application of many models to real-world problems. However, to use models and solution techniques effectively, it is necessary to truly gain experience through developing and solving simple ones. This aspect is often overlooked. Another trend, unfortunately, involves the lack of understanding of what models and their solutions can do in the real world. Organizations that have key analysts who understand how to apply models indeed apply them very effectively. This is most notably occurring in the revenue management area, which has moved from the province of airlines, hotels, and automobile rental to retail, insurance, entertainment, and many other areas. CRM also uses models, but they are often transparent to the user. With management models, the amount of data and model sizes are quite large, necessitating the use of data warehouses to supply the data and parallel computing hardware to obtain solutions in a reasonable time frame.

There is a continuing trend toward making analytics models completely transparent to the decision maker. For example, **multidimensional analysis (modeling)** involves data analysis in several dimensions. In multidimensional analysis (modeling) and some other cases, data are generally shown in a spreadsheet format, with which most decision makers are familiar. Many decision makers accustomed to slicing and dicing data cubes are now using OLAP systems that access data warehouses. Although these methods may make modeling palatable, they also eliminate many important and applicable model classes from consideration, and they eliminate some important and subtle solution interpretation aspects. Modeling involves much more than just data analysis with trend lines and establishing relationships with statistical methods.

There is also a trend to build a model of a model to help in its analysis. An **influence diagram** is a graphical representation of a model; that is, it is a model of a model. Some influence diagram software packages are capable of generating and solving the resultant model.

SECTION 9.2 REVIEW QUESTIONS

1. List three lessons learned from modeling.

2. List and describe the major issues in modeling.

3. What are the major types of models used in DSS?

4. Why are models not used in industry as frequently as they should or could be?

5. What are the current trends in modeling?

9.3 STRUCTURE OF MATHEMATICAL MODELS FOR DECISION SUPPORT

In the following sections, we present the topics of analytical mathematical models (e.g., mathematical, financial, engineering). These include the components and the structure of models.

The Components of Decision Support Mathematical Models

All **quantitative models** are typically made up of four basic components (see Figure 9.1): result (or outcome) variables, decision variables, uncontrollable variables (and/or parameters), and intermediate result variables. Mathematical relationships link these components together. In non-quantitative models, the relationships are symbolic or qualitative. The results of decisions are determined based on the decision made (i.e., the values of the decision variables), the factors that cannot be controlled by the decision maker (in the

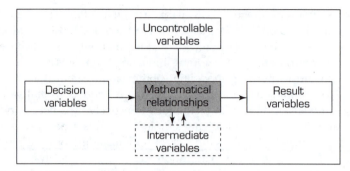

FIGURE 9.1 The General Structure of a Quantitative Model.

environment), and the relationships among the variables. The modeling process involves identifying the variables and relationships among them. Solving a model determines the values of these and the result variable(s).

RESULT (OUTCOME) VARIABLES **Result (outcome) variables** reflect the level of effectiveness of a system; that is, they indicate how well the system performs or attains its goal(s). These variables are outputs. Examples of result variables are shown in Table 9.2. Result variables are considered *dependent variables*. Intermediate result variables are sometimes used in modeling to identify intermediate outcomes. In the case of a dependent variable, another event must occur first before the event described by the variable can occur. Result variables depend on the occurrence of the decision variables and the uncontrollable variables.

DECISION VARIABLES **Decision variables** describe alternative courses of action. The decision maker controls the decision variables. For example, for an investment problem, the amount to invest in bonds is a decision variable. In a scheduling problem, the decision variables are people, times, and schedules. Other examples are listed in Table 9.2.

TABLE 9.2 **Examples of the Components of Models**

Area	Decision Variables	Result Variables	Uncontrollable Variables and Parameters
Financial investment	Investment alternatives and amounts	Total profit, risk Rate of return on investment (ROI) Earnings per share Liquidity level	Inflation rate Prime rate Competition
Marketing	Advertising budget Where to advertise	Market share Customer satisfaction	Customer's income Competitor's actions
Manufacturing	What and how much to produce Inventory levels Compensation programs	Total cost Quality level Employee satisfaction	Machine capacity Technology Materials prices
Accounting	Use of computers Audit schedule	Data processing cost Error rate	Computer technology Tax rates Legal requirements
Transportation	Shipments schedule Use of smart cards	Total transport cost Payment float time	Delivery distance Regulations
Services	Staffing levels	Customer satisfaction	Demand for services

UNCONTROLLABLE VARIABLES, OR PARAMETERS   In any decision-making situation, there are factors that affect the result variables but are not under the control of the decision maker. Either these factors can be fixed, in which case they are called **uncontrollable variables,** or **parameters,** or they can vary, in which case they are called *variables*. Examples of factors are the prime interest rate, a city's building code, tax regulations, and utilities costs. Most of these factors are uncontrollable because they are in and determined by elements of the system environment in which the decision maker works. Some of these variables limit the decision maker and therefore form what are called the *constraints* of the problem.

INTERMEDIATE RESULT VARIABLES   **Intermediate result variables** reflect intermediate outcomes in mathematical models. For example, in determining machine scheduling, spoilage is an intermediate result variable, and total profit is the result variable (i.e., spoilage is one determinant of total profit). Another example is employee salaries. This constitutes a decision variable for management: It determines employee satisfaction (i.e., intermediate outcome), which, in turn, determines the productivity level (i.e., final result).

The Structure of Mathematical Models

The components of a quantitative model are linked together by mathematical (algebraic) expressions—equations or inequalities.

A very simple financial model is

$$P = R - C$$

where P = profit, R = revenue, and C = cost. This equation describes the relationship among the variables. Another well-known financial model is the simple present-value cash flow model, where P = present value, F = a future single payment in dollars, i = interest rate (percentage), and n = number of years. With this model, it is possible to determine the present value of a payment of $100,000 to be made 5 years from today, at a 10 percent (0.1) interest rate, as follows:

$$P = 100,000/(1 + 0.1)^5 = 62,092$$

We present more interesting and complex mathematical models in the following sections.

SECTION 9.3 REVIEW QUESTIONS

1. What is a decision variable?

2. List and briefly discuss the three major components of linear programming.

3. Explain the role of intermediate result variables.

9.4 CERTAINTY, UNCERTAINTY, AND RISK[1]

Part of Simon's decision-making process described in Chapter 2 involves evaluating and comparing alternatives; during this process, it is necessary to predict the future outcome of each proposed alternative. Decision situations are often classified on the basis of what the decision maker knows (or believes) about the forecasted results. We customarily classify this knowledge into three categories (see Figure 9.2), ranging from complete knowledge to complete ignorance:

- Certainty
- Risk
- Uncertainty

---

[1]Some parts of the original versions of these sections were adapted from Turban and Meredith (1994).

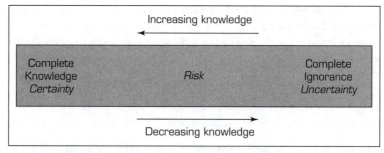

FIGURE 9.2 The Zones of Decision Making.

When we develop models, any of these conditions can occur, and different kinds of models are appropriate for each case. Next, we discuss both the basic definitions of these terms and some important modeling issues for each condition.

Decision Making Under Certainty

In decision making under **certainty,** it is *assumed* that complete knowledge is available so that the decision maker knows exactly what the outcome of *each course of action* will be (as in a deterministic environment). It may not be true that the outcomes are 100 percent known, nor is it necessary to really evaluate *all* the outcomes, but often this assumption simplifies the model and makes it tractable. The decision maker is viewed as a perfect predictor of the future because it is assumed that there is only one outcome for each alternative. For example, the alternative of investing in U.S. Treasury bills is one for which there is complete availability of information about the future return on the investment if it is held to maturity. A situation involving decision making under certainty occurs most often with structured problems with short time horizons (up to 1 year). Certainty models are relatively easy to develop and solve, and they can yield optimal solutions. Many financial models are constructed under assumed certainty, even though the market is anything but 100 percent certain.

Decision Making Under Uncertainty

In decision making under **uncertainty,** the decision maker considers situations in which several outcomes are possible for each course of action. In contrast to the risk situation, in this case, the decision maker does not know, or cannot estimate, the probability of occurrence of the possible outcomes. Decision making under uncertainty is more difficult than decision making under certainty because there is insufficient information. Modeling of such situations involves assessment of the decision maker's (or the organization's) attitude toward risk.

Managers attempt to avoid uncertainty as much as possible, even to the point of assuming it away. Instead of dealing with uncertainty, they attempt to obtain more information so that the problem can be treated under certainty (because it can be "almost" certain) or under calculated (i.e., assumed) risk. If more information is not available, the problem must be treated under a condition of uncertainty, which is less definitive than the other categories.

Decision Making Under Risk (Risk Analysis)

A decision made under **risk**[2] (also known as a *probabilistic* or *stochastic* decision-making situation) is one in which the decision maker must consider several possible outcomes for each alternative, each with a given probability of occurrence.

---

[2]Our definitions of the terms *risk* and *uncertainty* were formulated by F. H. Knight of the University of Chicago in 1933. Other, comparable definitions also are in use.

The long-run probabilities that the given outcomes will occur are assumed to be known or can be estimated. Under these assumptions, the decision maker can assess the degree of risk associated with each alternative (called *calculated* risk). Most major business decisions are made under assumed risk. **Risk analysis** (i.e., calculated risk) is a decision-making method that analyzes the risk (based on assumed known probabilities) associated with different alternatives. Risk analysis can be performed by calculating the expected value of each alternative and selecting the one with the best expected value. Application Case 9.3 illustrates one application to reduce uncertainty.

Application Case 9.3
American Airlines Uses Should-Cost Modeling to Assess the Uncertainty of Bids for Shipment Routes

Introduction

American Airlines, Inc. (AA) is one of the world's largest airlines. Its core business is passenger transportation but it has other vital ancillary functions that include full-truckload (FTL) freight shipment of maintenance equipment and in-flight shipment of passenger service items that could add up to over $1 billion in inventory at any given time. AA receives numerous bids from suppliers in response to request for quotes (RFQs) for inventories. AA's RFQs could total over 500 in any given year. Bid quotes vary significantly as a result of the large number of bids and resultant complex bidding process. Sometimes, a single contract bid could deviate by about 200 percent. As a result of the complex process, it is common to either overpay or underpay suppliers for their services. To this end, AA wanted a should-cost model that would streamline and assess bid quotes from suppliers in order to choose bid quotes that were fair to both them and their suppliers.

Methodology/Solution

In order to determine fair cost for supplier products and services, three steps were taken:

1. Primary (e.g., interviews) and secondary (e.g., Internet) sources were scouted for base-case and range data that would inform cost variables that affect an FTL bid.
2. Cost variables were chosen so that they were mutually exclusive and collectively exhaustive.
3. The DPL decision analysis software was used to model the uncertainty.

Furthermore, Extended Swanson-Megill (ESM) approximation was used to model the probability distribution of the most sensitive cost variables used. This was done in order to account for the high variability in the bids in the initial model.

Results/Benefits

A pilot test was done on an RFQ that attracted bids from six FTL carriers. Out of the six bids presented, five were within three standard deviations from the mean while one was considered an outlier. Subsequently, AA used the should-cost FTL model on more than 20 RFQs to determine what a fair and accurate cost of goods and services should be. It is expected that this model will help in reducing the risk of either overpaying or underpaying its suppliers.

QUESTIONS FOR DISCUSSION

1. Besides reducing the risk of overpaying or underpaying suppliers, what are some other benefits AA would derive from its "should be" model?
2. Can you think of other domains besides air transportation where such a model could be used?
3. Discuss other possible methods with which AA could have solved its bid overpayment and underpayment problem.

Source: M. J. Bailey, J. Snapp, S. Yetur, J. S. Stonebraker, S. A. Edwards, A. Davis, and R. Cox, "Practice Summaries: American Airlines Uses Should-Cost Modeling to Assess the Uncertainty of Bids for Its Full-Truckload Shipment Routes," *Interfaces*, Vol. 41, No. 2, 2011, pp. 194–196.

SECTION 9.4 REVIEW QUESTIONS

1. Define what it means to perform decision making under assumed certainty, risk, and uncertainty.
2. How can decision-making problems under assumed certainty be handled?
3. How can decision-making problems under assumed uncertainty be handled?
4. How can decision-making problems under assumed risk be handled?

9.5 DECISION MODELING WITH SPREADSHEETS

Models can be developed and implemented in a variety of programming languages and systems. These range from third-, fourth-, and fifth-generation programming languages to computer-aided software engineering (CASE) systems and other systems that automatically generate usable software. We focus primarily on *spreadsheets* (with their add-ins), modeling languages, and transparent data analysis tools. With their strength and flexibility, spreadsheet packages were quickly recognized as easy-to-use implementation software for the development of a wide range of applications in business, engineering, mathematics, and science. Spreadsheets include extensive statistical, forecasting, and other modeling and database management capabilities, functions, and routines. As spreadsheet packages evolved, add-ins were developed for structuring and solving specific model classes. Among the add-in packages, many were developed for DSS development. These DSS-related add-ins include Solver (Frontline Systems Inc., **solver.com**) and What's*Best!* (a version of Lindo, from Lindo Systems, Inc., **lindo.com**) for performing linear and nonlinear optimization; Braincel (Jurik Research Software, Inc., **jurikres.com**) and NeuralTools (Palisade Corp., **palisade.com**) for artificial neural networks; Evolver (Palisade Corp.) for genetic algorithms; and @RISK (Palisade Corp.) for performing simulation studies. Comparable add-ins are available for free or at a very low cost. (Conduct a Web search to find them; new ones are added to the marketplace on a regular basis.)

The spreadsheet is clearly the most popular *end-user modeling tool* because it incorporates many powerful financial, statistical, mathematical, and other functions. Spreadsheets can perform model solution tasks such as linear programming and regression analysis. The spreadsheet has evolved into an important tool for analysis, planning, and modeling (see Farasyn et al., 2008; Hurley and Balez, 2008; and Ovchinnikov and Milner, 2008). Application Case 9.4 describes an interesting application of a spreadsheet-based optimization model in a small business.

Application Case 9.4

Showcase Scheduling at Fred Astaire East Side Dance Studio

The Fred Astaire East Side Dance Studio in New York City presents two ballroom showcases a year. The studio wanted a cheap, user-friendly, and quick computer program to create schedules for its showcases that involved heats lasting around 75 seconds and solos lasting around 3 minutes. The program was created using an integer programming optimization model in Visual Basic and Excel. The employees just have to enter the students' names, the types of dances the students want to participate in, the teachers the students want to dance with, how many times the students want to do each type of dance, what times the students are unavailable, and what times the teachers are unavailable. This is entered into an Excel spreadsheet. The program then uses guidelines provided by the business to design the schedule. The guidelines include a dance type not being performed twice in a row if possible, a student participating in each quarter of the showcase in order to keep him/her active throughout, all participants in each heat performing the same type of dance (with a maximum of seven couples per heat), eliminating as many one-couple heats as possible, each student and teacher only being scheduled once per heat, and allowing students and teachers to dance multiple times per dance type if desired. A two-step heuristic method was used to help minimize the number of one-couple heats. In the end, the program cut down the time the employees spent creating the schedule and allowed for changes to be calculated and made quickly as compared to when made manually. For the summer 2007 showcase, the system scheduled 583 heat entries, 19 dance types, 18 solo entries, 28 students, and 8 teachers. This combination of Microsoft Excel and Visual Basic enabled the studio to use a model-based decision support system for a problem that could be time-consuming to solve.

Source: Based on M. A. Lejeune and N. Yakova, "Showcase Scheduling at Fred Astaire East Side Dance Studio," *Interfaces,* Vol. 38, No. 3, May/June 2008, pp. 176–186.

Other important spreadsheet features include what-if analysis, goal seeking, data management, and programmability (i.e., macros). With a spreadsheet, it is easy to change a cell's value and immediately see the result. Goal seeking is performed by indicating a target cell, its desired value, and a changing cell. Extensive database management can be performed with small data sets, or parts of a database can be imported for analysis (which is essentially how OLAP works with multidimensional data cubes; in fact, most OLAP systems have the look and feel of advanced spreadsheet software after the data are loaded). Templates, macros, and other tools enhance the productivity of building DSS.

Most spreadsheet packages provide fairly seamless integration because they read and write common file structures and easily interface with databases and other tools. Microsoft Excel is the most popular spreadsheet package. In Figure 9.3, we show a simple loan calculation model in which the boxes on the spreadsheet describe the contents of the cells, which contain formulas. A change in the interest rate in cell E7 is immediately reflected in the monthly payment in cell E13. The results can be observed and analyzed immediately. If we require a specific monthly payment, we can use goal seeking to determine an appropriate interest rate or loan amount.

Static or dynamic models can be built in a spreadsheet. For example, the monthly loan calculation spreadsheet shown in Figure 9.3 is static. Although the problem affects the borrower over time, the model indicates a single month's performance, which is replicated. A dynamic model, in contrast, represents behavior over time. The loan calculations in the spreadsheet shown in Figure 9.4 indicate the effect of prepayment on the principal over time. Risk analysis can be incorporated into spreadsheets by using built-in random-number generators to develop simulation models (see the next chapter).

Spreadsheet applications for models are reported regularly. We will learn how to use a spreadsheet-based optimization model in the next section.

SECTION 9.5 REVIEW QUESTIONS

1. What is a spreadsheet?

2. What is a spreadsheet add-in? How can add-ins help in DSS creation and use?

3. Explain why a spreadsheet is so conducive to the development of DSS.

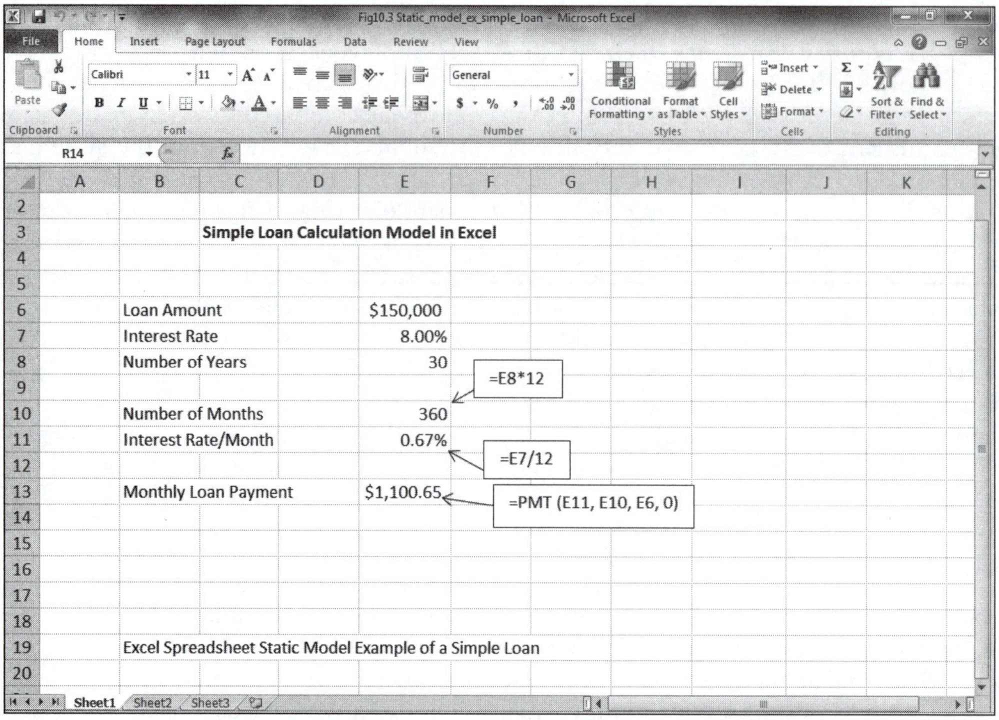

FIGURE 9.3   Excel Spreadsheet Static Model Example of a Simple Loan Calculation of Monthly Payments.

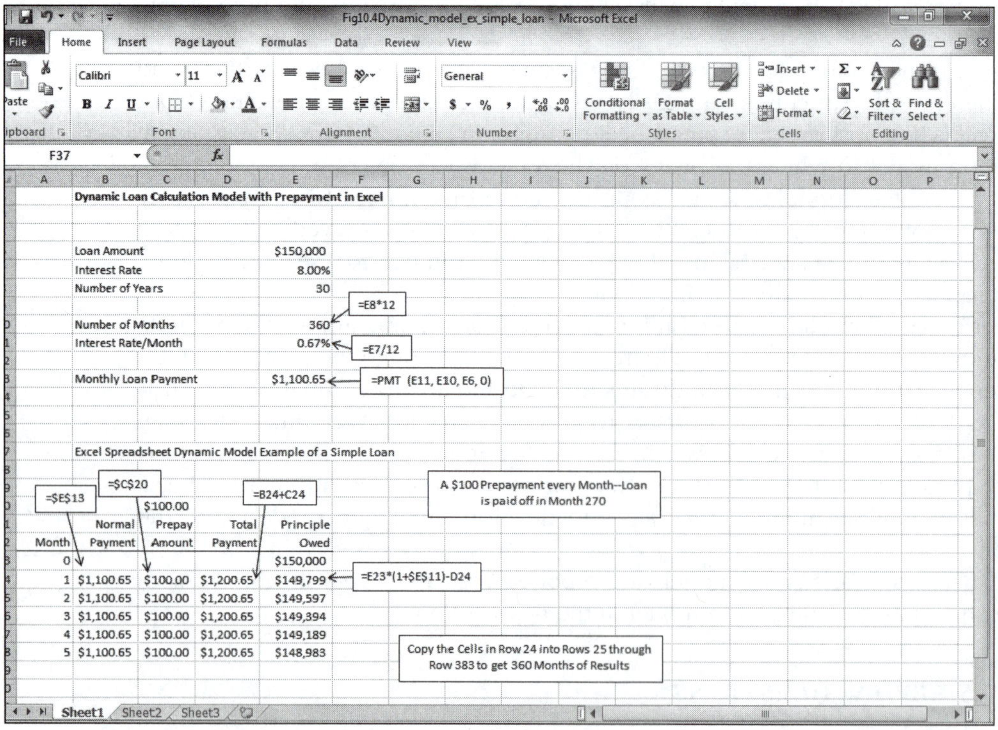

FIGURE 9.4   Excel Spreadsheet Dynamic Model Example of a Simple Loan Calculation of Monthly Payments and the Effects of Prepayment.

9.6 MATHEMATICAL PROGRAMMING OPTIMIZATION

The basic idea of optimization was introduced in Chapter 2. **Linear programming (LP)** is the best-known technique in a family of optimization tools called *mathematical programming*; in LP, all relationships among the variables are linear. It is used extensively in DSS (see Application Case 9.5). LP models have many important applications in practice. These include supply chain management, product mix decisions, routing, and so on. Special forms of the models can be used for specific applications. For example, Application Case 9.5 describes a spreadsheet model that was used to create a schedule for medical interns.

Application Case 9.5

Spreadsheet Model Helps Assign Medical Residents

Fletcher Allen Health Care (FAHC) is a teaching hospital that works with the University of Vermont's College of Medicine. In this particular case, FAHC employs 15 residents with hopes of adding 5 more in the diagnostic radiology program. Each year the chief radiology resident is required to make a year-long schedule for all of the residents in radiology. This is a time-consuming process to do manually because there are many limitations on when each resident is and is not allowed to work. During the weekday working hours, the residents work with certified radiologists, but nights, weekends, and holidays are all staffed by residents only. The residents are also required to take the "emergency rotations," which involve taking care of the radiology needs of the emergency room, which is often the busiest on weekends. The radiology program is a 4-year program, and there are different rules for the work schedules of the residents for each year they are there. For example, first- and fourth-year residents cannot be on call on holidays, second-year residents cannot be on call or assigned ER shifts during 13-week blocks when they are assigned to work in Boston, and third-year residents must work one ER rotation during only one of the major winter holidays (Thanksgiving or Christmas/New Year's). Also, first-year residents cannot be on call until after January 1, and fourth-year residents cannot be on call after December 31, and so on. The goal that the various chief residents have each year is to give each person the maximum number of days between on-call days as is possible. Manually, only 3 days between on-call days

was the most a chief resident had been able to accomplish.

In order to create a more efficient method of creating a schedule, the chief resident worked with an MS class of MBA students to develop a spreadsheet model to create the schedule. To solve this multiple-objective decision-making problem, the class used a constraint method made up of two stages. The first stage was to use the spreadsheet created in Excel as a calculator and to not use it for optimizing. This allowed the creators "to measure the key metrics of the residents' assignments, such as the number of days worked in each category." The second stage was an optimization model, which was layered on the calculator spreadsheet. Assignment constraints and the objective were added. The Solver engine in Excel was then invoked to find a feasible solution. The developers used Premium Solver by Frontline and the Xpress MP Solver engine by Dash Optimization to solve the yearlong model. Finally, using Excel functions, the developers converted the solution for a yearlong schedule from zeros and ones to an easy-to-read format for the residents. In the end, the program could solve the problem of a schedule with 3 to 4 days in between on calls instantly and with 5 days in between on calls (which was never accomplished manually).

Source: Based on A. Ovchinnikov and J. Milner, "Spreadsheet Model Helps to Assign Medical Residents at the University of Vermont's College of Medicine," *Interfaces,* Vol. 38, No. 4, July/August 2008, pp. 311–323.

Mathematical Programming

Mathematical programming is a family of tools designed to help solve managerial problems in which the decision maker must allocate scarce resources among competing activities to optimize a measurable goal. For example, the distribution of machine time (the resource) among various products (the activities) is a typical allocation problem. LP allocation problems usually display the following characteristics:

- A limited quantity of economic resources is available for allocation.
- The resources are used in the production of products or services.
- There are two or more ways in which the resources can be used. Each is called a *solution* or a *program.*
- Each activity (product or service) in which the resources are used yields a return in terms of the stated goal.
- The allocation is usually restricted by several limitations and requirements, called *constraints.*

The LP allocation model is based on the following rational economic assumptions:

- Returns from different allocations can be compared; that is, they can be measured by a common unit (e.g., dollars, utility).
- The return from any allocation is independent of other allocations.
- The total return is the sum of the returns yielded by the different activities.
- All data are known with certainty.
- The resources are to be used in the most economical manner.

Allocation problems typically have a large number of possible solutions. Depending on the underlying assumptions, the number of solutions can be either infinite or finite. Usually, different solutions yield different rewards. Of the available solutions, at least one is the best, in the sense that the degree of goal attainment associated with it is the highest (i.e., the total reward is maximized). This is called an **optimal solution,** and it can be found by using a special algorithm.

Linear Programming

Every LP problem is composed of *decision variables* (whose values are unknown and are searched for), an *objective function* (a linear mathematical function that relates the decision variables to the goal, measures goal attainment, and is to be optimized), *objective function coefficients* (unit profit or cost coefficients indicating the contribution to the objective of one unit of a decision variable), *constraints* (expressed in the form of linear inequalities or equalities that limit resources and/or requirements; these relate the variables through linear relationships), *capacities* (which describe the upper and sometimes lower limits on the constraints and variables), and *input/output (technology) coefficients* (which indicate resource utilization for a decision variable).

Let us look at an example. MBI Corporation, which manufactures special-purpose computers, needs to make a decision: How many computers should it produce next month at the Boston plant? MBI is considering two types of computers: the CC-7, which requires 300 days of labor and $10,000 in materials, and the CC-8, which requires 500 days of labor and $15,000 in materials. The profit contribution of each CC-7 is $8,000, whereas that of each CC-8 is $12,000. The plant has a capacity of 200,000 working days per month, and the material budget is $8 million per month. Marketing requires that at least 100 units of the CC-7 and at least 200 units of the CC-8 be produced each month. The problem is to maximize the company's profits by determining how many units of the CC-7 and how many units of the CC-8 should be produced each month. Note that in a real-world environment, it could possibly take months to obtain the data in the problem statement, and while gathering the data the decision maker would no doubt uncover facts about how to structure the model to be solved. Web-based tools for gathering data can help.

Modeling in LP: An Example

A standard LP model can be developed for the MBI Corporation problem just described. As discussed in Technology Insights 9.1, the LP model has three components: decision variables, result variables, and uncontrollable variables (constraints).

The decision variables are as follows:

$$X_1 = \text{unit of CC-7 to be produced}$$
$$X_2 = \text{unit of CC-8 to be produced}$$

The result variable is as follows:

$$\text{Total profit} = Z$$

The objective is to maximize total profit:

$$Z = 8{,}000X_1 + 12{,}000X_2$$

The uncontrollable variables (constraints) are as follows:

$$\text{Labor constraint: } 300X_1 + 500X_2 \leq 200{,}000 \text{ (in days)}$$
$$\text{Budget constraint: } 10{,}000X_1 + 15{,}000X_2 \leq 8{,}000{,}000 \text{ (in dollars)}$$
$$\text{Marketing requirment for CC-7: } X_1 \geq 100 \text{ (in units)}$$
$$\text{Marketing requirment for CC-8: } X_2 \geq 200 \text{ (in units)}$$

This information is summarized in Figure 9.5.

The model also has a fourth, hidden component. Every LP model has some internal intermediate variables that are not explicitly stated. The labor and budget constraints may each have some slack in them when the left-hand side is strictly less than the right-hand side. This slack is represented internally by slack variables that indicate excess resources available. The marketing requirement constraints may each have some surplus in them when the left-hand side is strictly greater than the right-hand side. This surplus is represented internally by surplus variables indicating that there is some room to adjust the right-hand sides of these constraints. These slack and surplus variables are intermediate. They can be of great value to a decision maker because LP solution methods use them in establishing sensitivity parameters for economic what-if analyses.

TECHNOLOGY INSIGHTS 9.1   Linear Programming

LP is perhaps the best-known optimization model. It deals with the optimal allocation of resources among competing activities. The allocation problem is represented by the model described here.

The problem is to find the values of the decision variables X_1, X_2, and so on, such that the value of the result variable Z is maximized, subject to a set of linear constraints that express the technology, market conditions, and other uncontrollable variables. The mathematical relationships are all linear equations and inequalities. Theoretically, any allocation problem of this type has an infinite number of possible solutions. Using special mathematical procedures, the LP approach applies a unique computerized search procedure that finds a best solution(s) in a matter of seconds. Furthermore, the solution approach provides automatic sensitivity analysis.

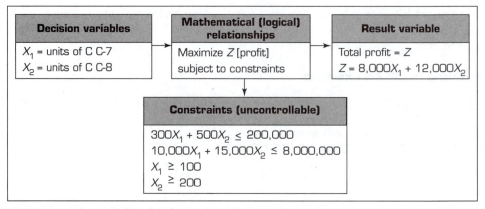

FIGURE 9.5 Mathematical Model of a Product-Mix Example.

The product-mix model has an infinite number of possible solutions. Assuming that a production plan is not restricted to whole numbers—which is a reasonable assumption in a monthly production plan—we want a solution that maximizes total profit: an optimal solution. Fortunately, Excel comes with the add-in Solver, which can readily obtain an optimal (best) solution to this problem. Although the location of Solver Add-in has moved from one version of Excel to another, it is still available as a free Add-in. Look for it under Data tab and on the Analysis ribbon. If it is not there, you should be able to enable it by going to Excel's Options Menu and selecting Add-ins.

We enter these data directly into an Excel spreadsheet, activate Solver, and identify the goal (by setting Target Cell equal to Max), decision variables (by setting By Changing Cells), and constraints (by ensuring that Total Consumed elements is less than or equal to Limit for the first two rows and is greater than or equal to Limit for the third and fourth rows). Cells C7 and D7 constitute the decision variable cells. Results in these cells would be filled after running the Solver Add-in. Target Cell is Cell E7, which is also the result variable, representing a product of decision variable cells and their per unit profit coefficients (in Cells C8 and D8). Note that all the numbers have been divided by 1,000 to make it easier to type (except the decision variables). Rows 9–12 describe the constraints of the problem: the constraints on labor capacity, budget, and the desired minimum production of the two products X_1 and X_2. Columns C and D define the coefficients of these constraints. Column E includes the formulae that multiply the decision variables (Cells C7 and D7) with their respective coefficients in each row. Column F defines the right-hand side value of these constraints. Excel's matrix multiplication capabilities (e.g., SUMPRODUCT function) can be used to develop such row and column multiplications easily.

After the model's calculations have been set up in Excel, it is time to invoke the Solver Add-in. Clicking on the Solver Add-in (again under the Analysis group under Data Tab) opens a dialog box (window) that lets you specify the cells or ranges that define the objective function cell, decision/changing variables (cells), and the constraints. Also, in Options, we select the solution method (usually Simplex LP), and then we solve the problem. Next, we select all three reports—Answer, Sensitivity, and Limits—to obtain an optimal solution of $X_1 = 333.33$, $X_2 = 200$, and Profit = \$5,066,667, as shown in Figure 9.6. Solver produces three useful reports about the solution. Try it. Solver now also includes the ability to solve nonlinear programming problems and integer programming problems by using other solution methods available within it.

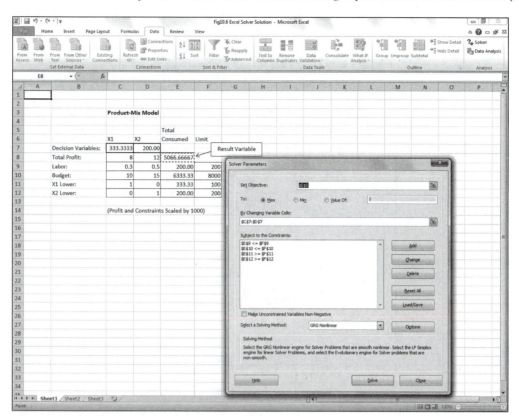

FIGURE 9.6   **Excel Solver Solution to the Product-Mix Example.**

The following example was created by Prof. Rick Wilson of Oklahoma State University to further illustrate the power of spreadsheet modeling for decision support.

The table in Figure 9.7 describes some estimated data and attributes of nine "swing states" for the 2012 election. Attributes of the nine states include their number of electoral votes, two regional descriptors (note that three states are classified as neither North or South), and an estimated "influence function," which relates to increased candidate support per unit of campaign financial investment in that state.

For instance, influence function F1 shows that for every financial unit invested in that state, there will be a total of a 10-unit increase in voter support (units will stay general here), made up of an increase in young men support by 3 units, old men support by 1 unit, and young and old women each by 3 units.

The campaign has 1,050 financial units to invest in the 9 states. It must invest at least 5 percent in each state of the total overall invested, but no more than 25 percent of the overall total invested can be in any one state. All 1,050 units do not have to be invested (your model must correctly deal with this).

The campaign has some other restrictions as well. From a financial investment standpoint, the West states (in total) must have campaign investment at levels that are at least 60 percent of the total invested in East states. In terms of people influenced, the decision to allocate financial investments to states must lead to at least 9,200 total people influenced. Overall, the total number of females influenced must be greater than or equal to the total number of males influenced. Also, at least 46 percent of all people influenced must be "old."

			Electoral			Influence	
		State	Votes	W/E	N/S	Function	
		NV	6	West		F1	
		CO	9	West		F2	
		IA	6	West	North	F3	
		WI	10	West	North	F1	
		OH	18	East	North	F2	
		VA	13	East	South	F2	
		NC	15	East	South	F1	
		FL	29	East	South	F3	
		NH	4	East		F3	

F1	Young	Old		
Men	3	1	4	
Women	3	3	6	
	6	4	10	Total

F2	Young	Old		
Men	1.5	2.5	4	
Women	2.5	1	3.5	
	4	3.5	7.5	Total

F3	Young	Old		
Men	2.5	2.5	5	
Women	1	2	3	
	3.5	4.5	8	Total

FIGURE 9.7 Data for Election Resource Allocation Example.

Our task is to create an appropriate integer programming model that determines the optimal integer (i.e., whole number) allocation of financial units to states that maximizes the sum of the products of the electoral votes times units invested subject to the other aforementioned restrictions. (Thus, indirectly, this model is giving preference to states with higher numbers of electoral votes). Note that for ease of implementation by the campaign staff, all decisions for allocation in the model should lead to integer values.

The three aspects of the models can be categorized based on the following questions that they answer:

1. ***What do we control?*** The amount invested in advertisements across the nine states, Nevada, Colorado, Iowa, Wisconsin, Ohio, Virginia, North Carolina, Florida, and New Hampshire, which are represented by the nine decision variables, NV, CO, IA, WI, OH, VA, NC, FL, and NH

2. ***What do we want to achieve?*** We want to maximize the total number of electoral votes gains. We know the value of each electoral vote in each state (EV), so this amounts to EV*Investments aggregated over the nine states, i.e.,

Max(6NV + 9CO + 6IA + 10WI + 18OH + 13VA + 15NC + 29FL + 4NH)

3. ***What constrains us?*** Following are the constraints as given in the problem description:

a. No more than 1,050 financial units to invest into, i.e., NV + CO + IA + WI + OH + VA + NC + FL + NH <= 1050.

b. Invest at least 5 percent of the total in each state, i.e.,

$$NV >= 0.05(NV + CO + IA + WI + OH + VA + NC + FL + NH)$$

$$CO >= 0.05(NV + CO + IA + WI + OH + VA + NC + FL + NH)$$

$$IA >= 0.05(NV + CO + IA + WI + OH + VA + NC + FL + NH)$$

$$WI >= 0.05(NV + CO + IA + WI + OH + VA + NC + FL + NH)$$

$$OH >= 0.05(NV + CO + IA + WI + OH + VA + NC + FL + NH)$$

$$VA >= 0.05(NV + CO + IA + WI + OH + VA + NC + FL + NH)$$

$$NC >= 0.05(NV + CO + IA + WI + OH + VA + NC + FL + NH)$$

$$FL >= 0.05(NV + CO + IA + WI + OH + VA + NC + FL + NH)$$

$$NH >= 0.05(NV + CO + IA + WI + OH + VA + NC + FL + NH)$$

We can implement these nine constraints in a variety of ways using Excel.

c. Invest no more than 25 percent of the total in each state.
As with (b) we need nine individual constraints again since we do not know how much of the 1,050 financial units we will invest. We must write the constraints on "general" terms.

$$NV <= 0.25(NV + CO + IA + WI + OH + VA + NC + FL + NH)$$

$$CO <= 0.25(NV + CO + IA + WI + OH + VA + NC + FL + NH)$$

$$IA <= 0.25(NV + CO + IA + WI + OH + VA + NC + FL + NH)$$

$$WI <= 0.25(NV + CO + IA + WI + OH + VA + NC + FL + NH)$$

$$OH <= 0.25(NV + CO + IA + WI + OH + VA + NC + FL + NH)$$

$$VA <= 0.25(NV + CO + IA + WI + OH + VA + NC + FL + NH)$$

$$NC <= 0.25(NV + CO + IA + WI + OH + VA + NC + FL + NH)$$

$$FL <= 0.25(NV + CO + IA + WI + OH + VA + NC + FL + NH)$$

$$NH <= 0.25(NV + CO + IA + WI + OH + VA + NC + FL + NH)$$

d. Western states must have investment levels that are at least 60 percent of the Eastern states.

West States = NV + CO + IA + WI

East States = OH + VA + NC + FL + NH

So, (NV + CO + IA + WI) >= 0.60(OH + VA + NC + FL + NH). Again we can implement this constraint in a variety of ways using Excel.

e. Influence at least 9,200 total people.

$$(10NV + 7.5CO + 8IA + 10WI + 7.5OH + 7.5VA + 10NC + 8\ FL + 8\ NH) >= 9200$$

f. Influence at least as many females as males. This requires transition of influence functions.

F1 = 6 women influenced, F2 = 3.5 women
F3 = 3 women influenced
F1 = 4 men influenced, F2 = 4 men
F3 = 5 men influenced
So implementing females >= males, we get:

$$(6NV + 3.5CO + 3\ IA + 6WI + 3.5OH + 3.5VA + 6NC + 3FL + 3NH) > = (4NV + 4CO + 5IA + 4WI + 4OH + 4VA + 4NC + 5FL + 5NH)$$

As before, we can implement this in Excel in a couple of different ways.

g. At least 46 percent of all people influenced must be old.
All people influenced was on the left-hand side of the constraint (e). So, old people influenced would be:

$$(4NV + 3.5CO + 4.5IA + 4WI + 3.5OH + 3.5VA + 4NC + 4.5FL + 4.5NH)$$

This would be set >= 0.46* the left-hand side of constraint (e) (10NV + 7.5CO + 8IA + 10WI + 7.5OH + 7.5VA + 10NC + 8FL + 8NH), which would give a right-hand side of 0.46NV + 3.45CO + 3.68IA + 4.6WI + 3.45OH + 3.45VA + 4.6NC + 3.68FL + 3.68NH
This is the last constraint other than to force all variables to be integers.

All told in algebraic terms, this integer programing model would have 9 decision variables and 24 constraints (one constraint for integer requirements).

Implementation

One approach would be to implement the model in strict "standard form," or a row-column form, where all constraints are written with decision variables on the left-hand side, and a number on the right-hand side. Figure 9.8 shows such an implementation and displays the solved model.

Alternatively, we could use the spreadsheet to calculate different parts of the model in a less rigid manner as well as uniquely implementing the repetitive constraints (b) and (c), and have a much more concise (but not as transparent) spreadsheet. This is shown in Figure 9.9.

LP models (and their specializations and generalizations) can be also specified directly in a number of other user-friendly modeling systems. Two of the best known are Lindo and Lingo (Lindo Systems, Inc., **lindo.com**; demos are available). Lindo is an LP and integer programming system. Models are specified in essentially the same way that they are defined algebraically. Based on the success of Lindo, the company developed Lingo, a modeling language that includes the powerful Lindo optimizer and extensions for solving nonlinear problems. Many other modeling languages such as AMPL, AIMMS, MPL, XPRESS, and others are available.

The most common optimization models can be solved by a variety of mathematical programming methods, including the following:

- Assignment (best matching of objects)
- Dynamic programming
- Goal programming
- Investment (maximizing rate of return)
- Linear and integer programming
- Network models for planning and scheduling
- Nonlinear programming
- Replacement (capital budgeting)
- Simple inventory models (e.g., economic order quantity)
- Transportation (minimize cost of shipments)

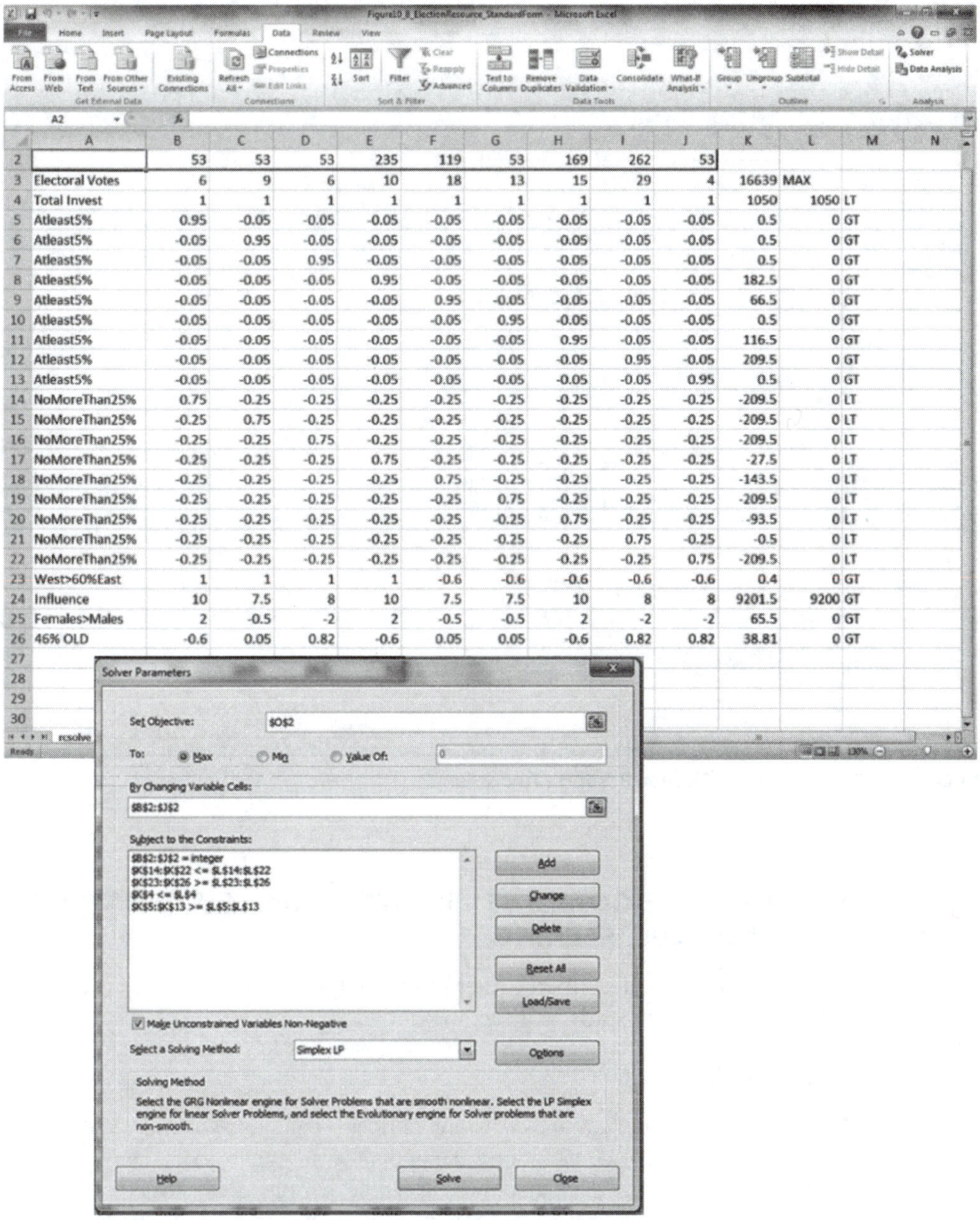

	A	B	C	D	E	F	G	H	I	J	K	L	M	N
2		53	53	53	235	119	53	169	262	53				
3	Electoral Votes	6	9	6	10	18	13	15	29	4	16639	MAX		
4	Total Invest	1	1	1	1	1	1	1	1	1	1050	1050	LT	
5	Atleast5%	0.95	-0.05	-0.05	-0.05	-0.05	-0.05	-0.05	-0.05	-0.05	0.5	0	GT	
6	Atleast5%	-0.05	0.95	-0.05	-0.05	-0.05	-0.05	-0.05	-0.05	-0.05	0.5	0	GT	
7	Atleast5%	-0.05	-0.05	0.95	-0.05	-0.05	-0.05	-0.05	-0.05	-0.05	0.5	0	GT	
8	Atleast5%	-0.05	-0.05	-0.05	0.95	-0.05	-0.05	-0.05	-0.05	-0.05	182.5	0	GT	
9	Atleast5%	-0.05	-0.05	-0.05	-0.05	0.95	-0.05	-0.05	-0.05	-0.05	66.5	0	GT	
10	Atleast5%	-0.05	-0.05	-0.05	-0.05	-0.05	0.95	-0.05	-0.05	-0.05	0.5	0	GT	
11	Atleast5%	-0.05	-0.05	-0.05	-0.05	-0.05	-0.05	0.95	-0.05	-0.05	116.5	0	GT	
12	Atleast5%	-0.05	-0.05	-0.05	-0.05	-0.05	-0.05	-0.05	0.95	-0.05	209.5	0	GT	
13	Atleast5%	-0.05	-0.05	-0.05	-0.05	-0.05	-0.05	-0.05	-0.05	0.95	0.5	0	GT	
14	NoMoreThan25%	0.75	-0.25	-0.25	-0.25	-0.25	-0.25	-0.25	-0.25	-0.25	-209.5	0	LT	
15	NoMoreThan25%	-0.25	0.75	-0.25	-0.25	-0.25	-0.25	-0.25	-0.25	-0.25	-209.5	0	LT	
16	NoMoreThan25%	-0.25	-0.25	0.75	-0.25	-0.25	-0.25	-0.25	-0.25	-0.25	-209.5	0	LT	
17	NoMoreThan25%	-0.25	-0.25	-0.25	0.75	-0.25	-0.25	-0.25	-0.25	-0.25	-27.5	0	LT	
18	NoMoreThan25%	-0.25	-0.25	-0.25	-0.25	0.75	-0.25	-0.25	-0.25	-0.25	-143.5	0	LT	
19	NoMoreThan25%	-0.25	-0.25	-0.25	-0.25	-0.25	0.75	-0.25	-0.25	-0.25	-209.5	0	LT	
20	NoMoreThan25%	-0.25	-0.25	-0.25	-0.25	-0.25	-0.25	0.75	-0.25	-0.25	-93.5	0	LT	
21	NoMoreThan25%	-0.25	-0.25	-0.25	-0.25	-0.25	-0.25	-0.25	0.75	-0.25	-0.5	0	LT	
22	NoMoreThan25%	-0.25	-0.25	-0.25	-0.25	-0.25	-0.25	-0.25	-0.25	0.75	-209.5	0	LT	
23	West>60%East	1	1	1	1	-0.6	-0.6	-0.6	-0.6	-0.6	0.4	0	GT	
24	Influence	10	7.5	8	10	7.5	7.5	10	8	8	9201.5	9200	GT	
25	Females>Males	2	-0.5	-2	2	-0.5	-0.5	2	-2	-2	65.5	0	GT	
26	46% OLD	-0.6	0.05	0.82	-0.6	0.05	0.05	-0.6	0.82	0.82	38.81	0	GT	

Solver Parameters

Se_t Objective: $O$2

To: ● Ma_x ○ Mi_n ○ _Value Of: 0

_By Changing Variable Cells:
$B$2:$J$2

S_ubject to the Constraints:
$B$2:$J$2 = integer
$K$14:$K$22 <= $L$14:$L$22
$K$23:$K$26 >= $L$23:$L$26
$K$4 <= $L$4
$K$5:$K$13 >= $L$5:$L$13

Add
Change
_Delete
_Reset All
_Load/Save

☑ Ma_ke Unconstrained Variables Non-Negative

S_elect a Solving Method: Simplex LP   Options

Solving Method
Select the GRG Nonlinear engine for Solver Problems that are smooth nonlinear. Select the LP Simplex engine for linear Solver Problems, and select the Evolutionary engine for Solver problems that are non-smooth.

Help   Solve   Close

FIGURE 9.8 Model for Election Resource Allocation—Standard Version.

SECTION 9.6 REVIEW QUESTIONS

1. List and explain the assumptions involved in LP.
2. List and explain the characteristics of LP.
3. Describe an allocation problem.
4. Define the product-mix problem.
5. Define the blending problem.
6. List several common optimization models.

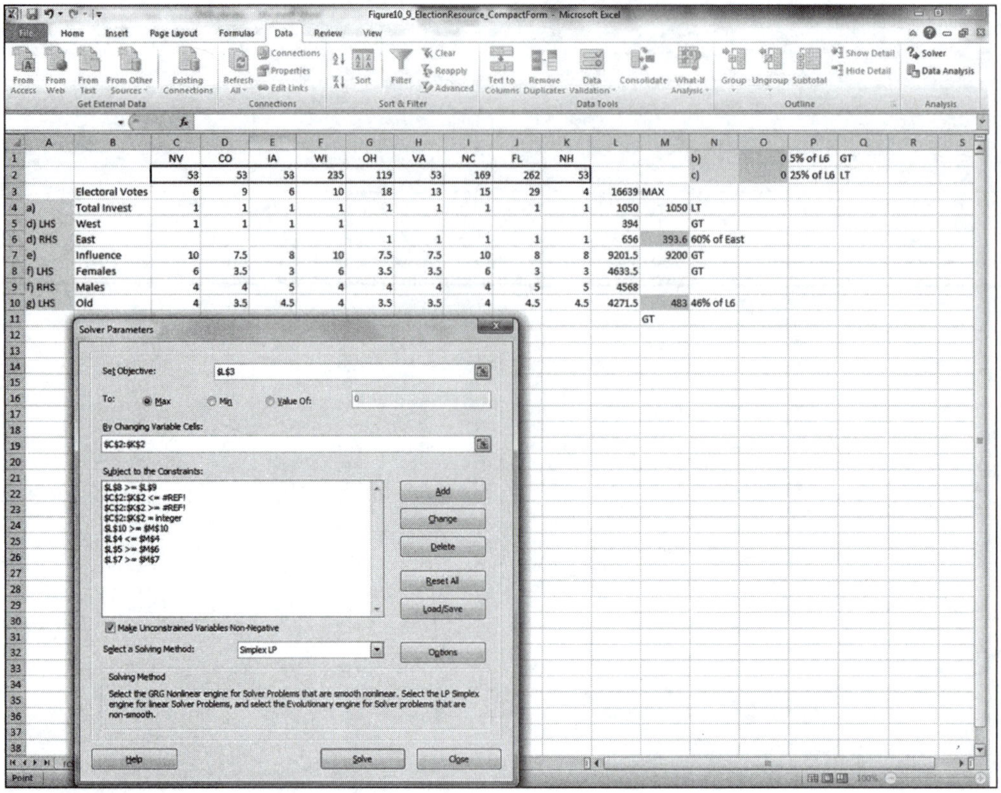

FIGURE 9.9 A Compact Formulation for Election Resource Allocation.

9.7 MULTIPLE GOALS, SENSITIVITY ANALYSIS, WHAT-IF ANALYSIS, AND GOAL SEEKING

The search process described earlier in this chapter is coupled with evaluation. Evaluation is the final step that leads to a recommended solution.

Multiple Goals

The analysis of management decisions aims at evaluating, to the greatest possible extent, how far each alternative advances managers toward their goals. Unfortunately, managerial problems are seldom evaluated with a single simple goal, such as profit maximization. Today's management systems are much more complex, and one with a single goal is rare. Instead, managers want to attain *simultaneous goals*, some of which may conflict. Different stakeholders have different goals. Therefore, it is often necessary to analyze each alternative in light of its determination of each of several goals (see Koksalan and Zionts, 2001).

For example, consider a profit-making firm. In addition to earning money, the company wants to grow, develop its products and employees, provide job security to its workers, and serve the community. Managers want to satisfy the shareholders and at the same time enjoy high salaries and expense accounts, and employees want to increase their take-home pay and benefits. When a decision is to be made—say, about an investment project—some of these goals complement each other, whereas others conflict. Kearns (2004) described how the analytic hierarchy process (AHP), which we will introduce in Section 9.9, combined with integer programming, addressed multiple goals in evaluating IT investments.

Many quantitative models of decision theory are based on comparing a single measure of effectiveness, generally some form of utility to the decision maker. Therefore, it is usually necessary to transform a multiple-goal problem into a single-measure-of-effectiveness problem before comparing the effects of the solutions. This is a common method for handling multiple goals in an LP model.

Certain difficulties may arise when analyzing multiple goals:

- It is usually difficult to obtain an explicit statement of the organization's goals.
- The decision maker may change the importance assigned to specific goals over time or for different decision scenarios.
- Goals and sub-goals are viewed differently at various levels of the organization and within different departments.
- Goals change in response to changes in the organization and its environment.
- The relationship between alternatives and their role in determining goals may be difficult to quantify.
- Complex problems are solved by groups of decision makers, each of whom has a personal agenda.
- Participants assess the importance (priorities) of the various goals differently.

Several methods of handling multiple goals can be used when working with MSS. The most common ones are:

- Utility theory
- Goal programming
- Expression of goals as constraints, using LP
- A points system

Sensitivity Analysis

A model builder makes predictions and assumptions regarding input data, many of which deal with the assessment of uncertain futures. When the model is solved, the results depend on these data. **Sensitivity analysis** attempts to assess the impact of a change in the input data or parameters on the proposed solution (i.e., the result variable).

Sensitivity analysis is extremely important in MSS because it allows flexibility and adaptation to changing conditions and to the requirements of different decision-making situations, provides a better understanding of the model and the decision-making situation it attempts to describe, and permits the manager to input data in order to increase the confidence in the model. Sensitivity analysis tests relationships such as the following:

- The impact of changes in external (uncontrollable) variables and parameters on the outcome variable(s)
- The impact of changes in decision variables on the outcome variable(s)
- The effect of uncertainty in estimating external variables
- The effects of different dependent interactions among variables
- The robustness of decisions under changing conditions

Sensitivity analyses are used for:

- Revising models to eliminate too-large sensitivities
- Adding details about sensitive variables or scenarios
- Obtaining better estimates of sensitive external variables
- Altering a real-world system to reduce actual sensitivities
- Accepting and using the sensitive (and hence vulnerable) real world, leading to the continuous and close monitoring of actual results

The two types of sensitivity analyses are automatic and trial-and-error.

AUTOMATIC SENSITIVITY ANALYSIS Automatic sensitivity analysis is performed in standard quantitative model implementations such as LP. For example, it reports the range within which a certain input variable or parameter value (e.g., unit cost) can vary without having any significant impact on the proposed solution. Automatic sensitivity analysis is usually limited to one change at a time, and only for certain variables. However, it is very powerful because of its ability to establish ranges and limits very fast (and with little or no additional computational effort). For example, automatic sensitivity analysis is part of the LP solution report for the MBI Corporation product-mix problem described earlier. Sensitivity analysis is provided by both Solver and Lindo. Sensitivity analysis could be used to determine that if the right-hand side of the marketing constraint on CC-8 could be decreased by one unit, then the net profit would increase by $1,333.33. This is valid for the right-hand side decreasing to zero. For details, see Hillier and Lieberman (2005) and Taha (2006) or later editions of these textbooks.

TRIAL-AND-ERROR SENSITIVITY ANALYSIS The impact of changes in any variable, or in several variables, can be determined through a simple trial-and-error approach. You change some input data and solve the problem again. When the changes are repeated several times, better and better solutions may be discovered. Such experimentation, which is easy to conduct when using appropriate modeling software, such as Excel, has two approaches: what-if analysis and goal seeking.

What-If Analysis

What-if analysis is structured as *What will happen to the solution if an input variable, an assumption, or a parameter value is changed?* Here are some examples:

- What will happen to the total inventory cost if the cost of carrying inventories increases by 10 percent?
- What will be the market share if the advertising budget increases by 5 percent?

With the appropriate user interface, it is easy for managers to ask a computer model these types of questions and get immediate answers. Furthermore, they can perform multiple cases and thereby change the percentage, or any other data in the question, as desired. The decision maker does all this directly, without a computer programmer.

Figure 9.10 shows a spreadsheet example of a what-if query for a cash flow problem. When the user changes the cells containing the initial sales (from 100 to 120) and the sales growth rate (from 3% to 4% per quarter), the program immediately recomputes the value of the annual net profit cell (from $127 to $182). At first, initial sales were 100, growing at 3 percent per quarter, yielding an annual net profit of $127. Changing the initial sales cell to 120 and the sales growth rate to 4 percent causes the annual net profit to rise to $182. What-if analysis is common in expert systems. Users are given the opportunity to change their answers to some of the system's questions, and a revised recommendation is found.

Goal Seeking

Goal seeking calculates the values of the inputs necessary to achieve a desired level of an output (goal). It represents a backward solution approach. The following are some examples of goal seeking:

- What annual R&D budget is needed for an annual growth rate of 15 percent by 2018?
- How many nurses are needed to reduce the average waiting time of a patient in the emergency room to less than 10 minutes?

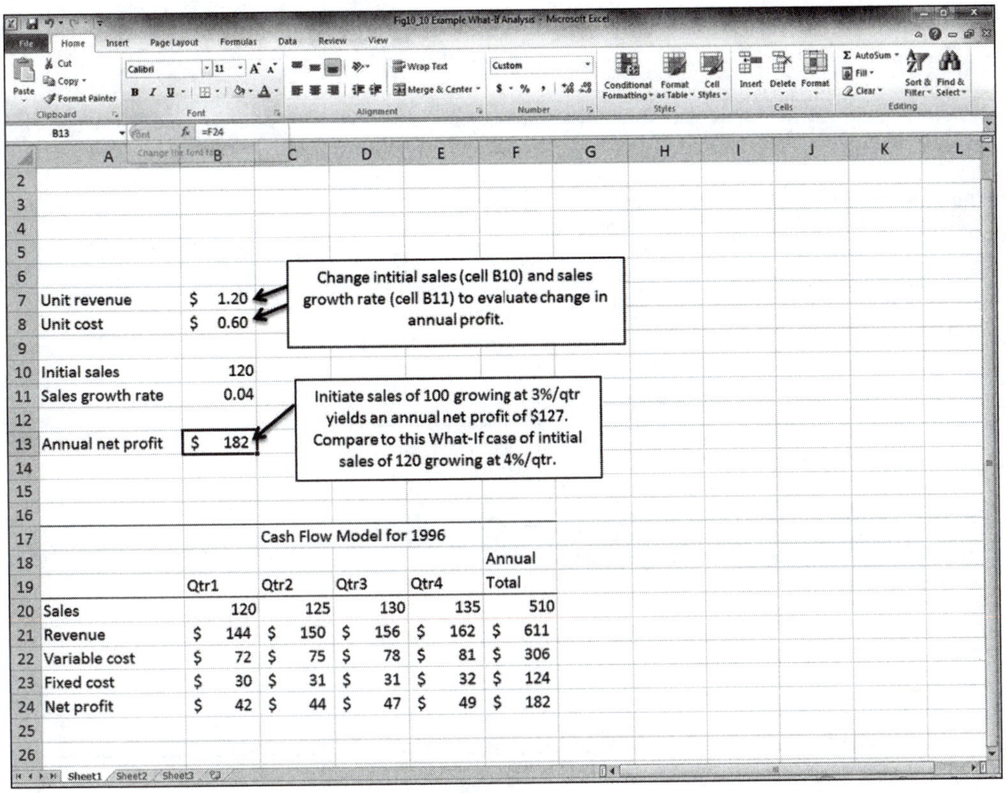

FIGURE 9.10 **Example of a What-If Analysis Done in an Excel Worksheet.**

An example of goal seeking is shown in Figure 9.11. For example, in a financial planning model in Excel, the internal rate of return is the interest rate that produces a net present value (NPV) of zero. Given a stream of annual returns in Column E, we can compute the net present value of planned investment. By applying goal seeking, we can determine the internal rate of return where the NPV is zero. The goal to be achieved is NPV equal to zero, which determines the internal rate of return (IRR) of this cash flow, including the investment. We set the NPV cell to the value 0 by changing the interest rate cell. The answer is 38.77059 percent.

COMPUTING A BREAK-EVEN POINT BY USING GOAL SEEKING Some modeling software packages can directly compute break-even points, which is an important application of goal seeking. This involves determining the value of the decision variables (e.g., quantity to produce) that generate zero profit.

In many general applications programs, it can be difficult to conduct sensitivity analysis because the prewritten routines usually present only a limited opportunity for asking what-if questions. In a DSS, the what-if and the goal-seeking options must be easy to perform.

SECTION 9.7 REVIEW QUESTIONS

1. List some difficulties that may arise when analyzing multiple goals.

2. List the reasons for performing sensitivity analysis.

3. Explain why a manager might perform what-if analysis.

4. Explain why a manager might use goal seeking.

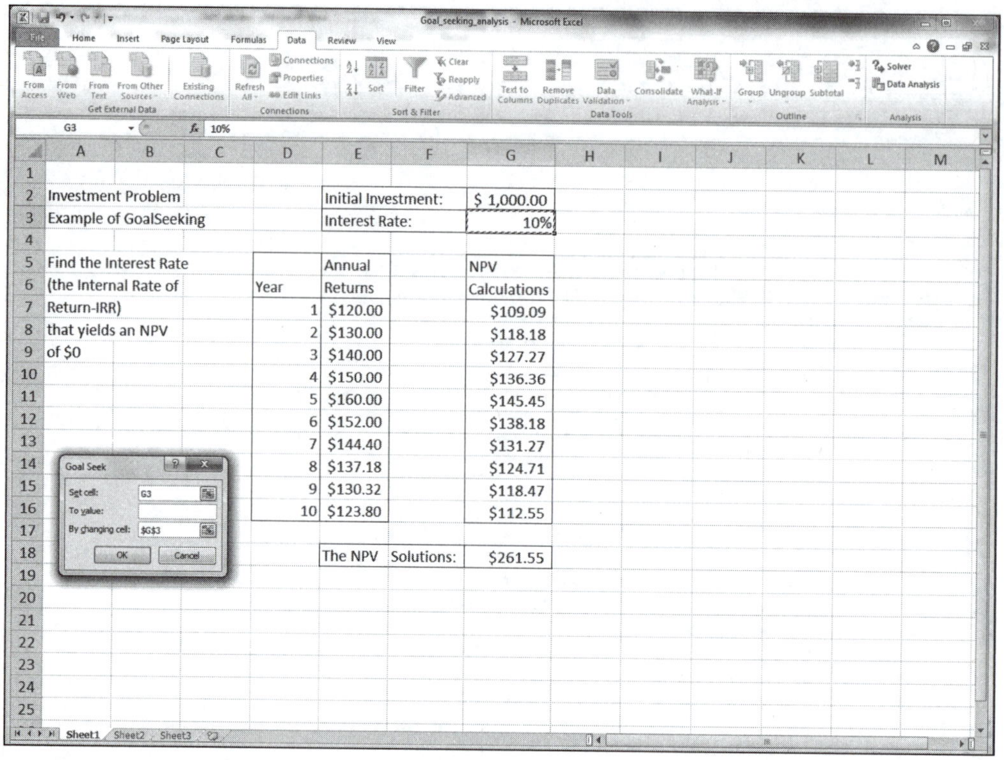

FIGURE 9.11 Goal-Seeking Analysis.

9.8 DECISION ANALYSIS WITH DECISION TABLES AND DECISION TREES

Decision situations that involve a finite and usually not too large number of alternatives are modeled through an approach called **decision analysis** (see Arsham, 2006a, 2006b; and Decision Analysis Society, **decision-analysis.society.informs.org**). Using this approach, the alternatives are listed in a table or a graph, with their forecasted contributions to the goal(s) and the probability of obtaining the contribution. These can be evaluated to select the best alternative.

Single-goal situations can be modeled with *decision tables* or *decision trees*. Multiple goals (criteria) can be modeled with several other techniques, described later in this chapter.

Decision Tables

Decision tables conveniently organize information and knowledge in a systematic, tabular manner to prepare it for analysis. For example, say that an investment company is considering investing in one of three alternatives: bonds, stocks, or certificates of deposit (CDs). The company is interested in one goal: maximizing the yield on the investment after one year. If it were interested in other goals, such as safety or liquidity, the problem would be classified as one of *multi-criteria decision analysis* (see Koksalan and Zionts, 2001).

The yield depends on the state of the economy sometime in the future (often called the *state of nature*), which can be in solid growth, stagnation, or inflation. Experts estimated the following annual yields:

- If there is solid growth in the economy, bonds will yield 12 percent, stocks 15 percent, and time deposits 6.5 percent.

- If stagnation prevails, bonds will yield 6 percent, stocks 3 percent, and time deposits 6.5 percent.
- If inflation prevails, bonds will yield 3 percent, stocks will bring a loss of 2 percent, and time deposits will yield 6.5 percent.

The problem is to select the one best investment alternative. These are assumed to be discrete alternatives. Combinations such as investing 50 percent in bonds and 50 percent in stocks must be treated as new alternatives.

The investment decision-making problem can be viewed as a *two-person game* (see Kelly, 2002). The investor makes a choice (i.e., a move), and then a state of nature occurs (i.e., makes a move). Table 9.3 shows the payoff of a mathematical model. The table includes *decision variables* (the alternatives), *uncontrollable variables* (the states of the economy; e.g., the environment), and *result variables* (the projected yield; e.g., outcomes). All the models in this section are structured in a spreadsheet framework.

If this were a decision-making problem under certainty, we would know what the economy will be and could easily choose the best investment. But that is not the case, so we must consider the two situations of uncertainty and risk. For uncertainty, we do not know the probabilities of each state of nature. For risk, we assume that we know the probabilities with which each state of nature will occur.

TREATING UNCERTAINTY Several methods are available for handling uncertainty. For example, the *optimistic approach* assumes that the best possible outcome of each alternative will occur and then selects the best of the best (i.e., stocks). The *pessimistic approach* assumes that the worst possible outcome for each alternative will occur and selects the best of these (i.e., CDs). Another approach simply assumes that all states of nature are equally possible. (See Clemen and Reilly, 2000; Goodwin and Wright, 2000; and Kontoghiorghes et al., 2002.) Every approach for handling uncertainty has serious problems. Whenever possible, the analyst should attempt to gather enough information so that the problem can be treated under assumed certainty or risk.

TREATING RISK The most common method for solving this risk analysis problem is to select the alternative with the greatest expected value. Assume that experts estimate the chance of solid growth at 50 percent, the chance of stagnation at 30 percent, and the chance of inflation at 20 percent. The decision table is then rewritten with the known probabilities (see Table 9.4). An expected value is computed by multiplying the results (i.e., outcomes) by their respective probabilities and adding them. For example, investing in bonds yields an expected return of 12(0.5) + 6(0.3) + 3(0.2) = 8.4 percent.

This approach can sometimes be a dangerous strategy because the utility of each potential outcome may be different from the value. Even if there is an infinitesimal chance of a catastrophic loss, the expected value may seem reasonable, but the investor may not be willing to cover the loss. For example, suppose a financial advisor presents you with an "almost sure" investment of $1,000 that can double your money in one day, and then

TABLE 9.3 Investment Problem Decision Table Model

	State of Nature (Uncontrollable Variables)		
Alternative	Solid Growth (%)	Stagnation (%)	Inflation (%)
Bonds	12.0	6.0	3.0
Stocks	15.0	3.0	–2.0
CDs	6.5	6.5	6.5

TABLE 9.4	Multiple Goals		
Alternative	**Yield (%)**	**Safety**	**Liquidity**
Bonds	8.4	High	High
Stocks	8.0	Low	High
CDs	6.5	Very high	High

the advisor says, "Well, there is a .9999 probability that you will double your money, but unfortunately there is a .0001 probability that you will be liable for a $500,000 out-of-pocket loss." The expected value of this investment is as follows:

$$0.9999(\$2,000 - \$1,000) + .0001(-\$500,000 - \$1,000) = \$999.90 - \$50.10$$
$$= \$949.80$$

The potential loss could be catastrophic for any investor who is not a billionaire. Depending on the investor's ability to cover the loss, an investment has different expected utilities. Remember that the investor makes the decision only *once*.

Decision Trees

An alternative representation of the decision table is a decision tree (for examples, see Mind Tools Ltd., **mindtools.com**). A **decision tree** shows the relationships of the problem graphically and can handle complex situations in a compact form. However, a decision tree can be cumbersome if there are many alternatives or states of nature. TreeAge Pro (TreeAge Software Inc., **treeage.com**) and PrecisionTree (Palisade Corp., **palisade. com**) include powerful, intuitive, and sophisticated decision tree analysis systems. These vendors also provide excellent examples of decision trees used in practice. Note that the phrase *decision tree* has been used to describe two different types of models and algorithms. In the current context, decision trees refer to scenario analysis. On the other hand, some classification algorithms in predictive analysis (see Chapters 5 and 6) also are called decision tree algorithms.

A simplified investment case of **multiple goals** (a decision situation in which alternatives are evaluated with several, sometimes conflicting, goals) is shown in Table 9.4. The three goals (criteria) are yield, safety, and liquidity. This situation is under assumed certainty; that is, only one possible consequence is projected for each alternative; the more complex cases of risk or uncertainty could be considered. Some of the results are qualitative (e.g., low, high) rather than numeric.

See Clemen and Reilly (2000), Goodwin and Wright (2000), and Decision Analysis Society (**faculty.fuqua.duke.edu/daweb**) for more on decision analysis. Although doing so is quite complex, it is possible to apply mathematical programming directly to decision-making situations under risk. We discuss several other methods of treating risk in the next few chapters. These include simulation and certainty factors.

SECTION 9.8 REVIEW QUESTIONS

1. What is a decision table?
2. What is a decision tree?
3. How can a decision tree be used in decision making?
4. Describe what it means to have multiple goals.

9.9 MULTI-CRITERIA DECISION MAKING WITH PAIRWISE COMPARISONS

Multi-criteria (goal) decision making was introduced in Chapter 2. One of the most effective approaches is to use weights based on decision-making priorities. However, soliciting weights (or priorities) from managers is a complex task, as is calculation of the weighted averages needed to choose the best alternative. The process is complicated further by the presence of qualitative variables. One method of multi-criteria decision making is the analytic hierarchy process developed by Saaty.

The Analytic Hierarchy Process

The **analytic hierarchy process (AHP),** developed by Thomas Saaty (1995, 1996), is an excellent modeling structure for representing *multi-criteria* (multiple goals, multiple objectives) *problems*—with sets of criteria and alternatives (choices)—commonly found in business environments. The decision maker uses AHP to decompose a decision-making problem into relevant criteria and alternatives. The AHP separates the analysis of the criteria from the alternatives, which helps the decision maker to focus on small, manageable portions of the problem. The AHP manipulates quantitative and qualitative decision-making criteria in a fairly structured manner, allowing a decision maker to make trade-offs quickly and "expertly." Application Case 9.6 gives an example of an application of AHP in selection of IT projects.

Application Case 9.6

U.S. HUD Saves the House by Using AHP for Selecting IT Projects

The U.S. Department of Housing and Urban Development's (HUD) mission is to increase home-ownership, support community development, and increase access to affordable housing free from discrimination. HUD's total annual budget is $32 billion with roughly $400 million allocated to IT spending each year. HUD was annually besieged by requests for IT projects by its program areas, but had no rational process that allowed management to select and monitor the best projects within its budgetary constraints. Like most federal agencies, HUD was required by congressional act to hire a CIO and develop an IT capital planning process. However, it wasn't until the Office of Management and Budget (OMB) threatened to cut agency budgets in 1999 that an IT planning process was actually developed and implemented at HUD. There had been a great deal of wasted money and manpower in the duplication of efforts by program areas, a lack of a sound project prioritization process, and no standards or guidelines for the program areas to follow.

For example, in 1999 there were requests for over $600 million in HUD IT projects against an IT budget of less than $400 million. There were over 200 approved projects but no process for selecting, monitoring, and evaluating these projects. HUD could not determine whether its selected IT projects were properly aligned with the agency's mission and objectives and were thus the most effective projects.

The agency determined from best practices and industry research that it needed both a rational process and a tool to support this process to meet OMB's requirements. Using the results from this research, HUD recommended that a process and guidelines be developed that would allow senior HUD management to select and prioritize the objectives and selection criteria while allowing the program teams to score specific project requests. HUD now uses the analytic hierarchy process through Expert Choice software with its capital planning process to select, manage, and evaluate its IT portfolio in real time, while the selected IT programs are being implemented.

The results have been staggering: With the new methodology and Expert Choice, HUD has reduced the preparation and meeting time for the

(Continued)

424 Part IV • Prescriptive Analytics

Application Case 9.5 (Continued)

annual selection and prioritization of IT projects from months to mere weeks, saving time and management hours. Program area requests of recent IT budgets dropped from the 1999 level of over $600 million to less than $450 million as managers recognized that the selection criteria for IT projects were going to be fairly and stringently applied by senior management, and that the number of projects funded had dropped from 204 to 135. In the first year of implementation, HUD reallocated $55 million of its IT budget to more effective projects that were better aligned with the agency's objectives.

In addition to saving time, the fair and transparent process has increased buy-in at all levels of management. There are few opportunities or incentives, if any, for an "end run" around the process. HUD now requires that each assistant secretary for the program areas sign off on the weighted selection criteria, and managers now know that special requests are likely fruitless if they cannot be supported by the selection criteria.

Source: **http://expertchoice.com/xres/uploads/resource-center-documents/HUD_casestudy.pdf** (accessed February 2013).

Expert Choice (**expertchoice.com**; a demo is available directly on its Web site) is an excellent commercial implementation of AHP. A problem is represented as an inverted tree with a goal node at the top. All the weight of the decision is in the goal (1.000). Directly beneath and attached to the goal node are the criteria nodes. These are the factors that are important to the decision maker. The goal is decomposed into criteria, to which 100 percent of the weight of the decision from the goal is distributed. To distribute the weight, the decision maker conducts pairwise comparisons of the criteria: first criterion to second, first to third,..., first to last; then, second to third,..., second to last;...; and then the next-to-last criterion to the last one. This establishes the importance of each criterion; that is, how much of the goal's weight is distributed to each criterion (how *important* each criterion is). This objective method is performed by internally manipulating matrices mathematically. The manipulations are transparent to the user because the operational details of the method are *not* important to the decision maker. Finally, an inconsistency index indicates how consistent the comparisons were, thus identifying inconsistencies, errors in judgment, or simply errors. The AHP method is consistent with decision theory.

The decision maker can make comparisons verbally (e.g., one criterion is moderately more important than another), graphically (with bar and pie charts), or numerically (with a *matrix*—comparisons are scaled from 1 to 9). Students and business professionals generally prefer graphical and verbal approaches over matrices (based on an informal sample).

Beneath each criterion are the same sets of choices (alternatives) in the simple case described here. Like the goal, the criteria decompose their weight into the choices, which capture 100 percent of the weight of each criterion. The decision maker performs a pairwise comparison of choices in terms of *preferences,* as they relate to the specific criterion under consideration. Each set of choices must be pairwise compared as they relate to each criterion. Again, all three modes of comparison are available, and an inconsistency index is derived for each set and reported.

Finally, the results are synthesized and displayed on a bar graph. The choice with the most weight is the correct choice. However, under some conditions the correct decision may not be the right one. For example, if there are two "identical" choices (e.g., if you are selecting a car for purchase and you have two identical cars), they may split the weight and neither will have the most weight. Also, if the top few choices are very close, there may be a missing criterion that could be used to differentiate among these choices.

Expert Choice also has a sensitivity analysis module. A newer version of the product, called Comparion, also synthesizes the results of a group of decision makers using the same model. This version can work on the Web. Overall, AHP as implemented in Expert Choice attempts to derive a decision maker's preference (utility) structure in terms of the criteria and choices and help him or her to make an expert choice.

In addition to Expert Choice, other software packages allow for weighting of pairwise choices. For example, Web-HIPRE (**hipre.aalto.fi**), an adaptation of AHP and several other weighting schemes, enables a decision maker to create a decision model, enter pairwise preferences, and analyze the optimal choice. These weightings can be computed using AHP as well as other techniques. It is available as a Java applet on the Web so it can be easily located and run online, free for noncommercial use. To run Web-HIPRE, one has to access the site and leave a Java applet window running. The user can enter a problem by providing the general labels for the decision tree at each node level and then entering the problem components. After the model has been specified, the user can enter pairwise preferences at each node level for criteria/subcriteria/alternative. Once that is done, the appropriate analysis algorithm can be used to determine the model's final recommendation. The software can also perform sensitivity analysis to determine which criteria/subcriteria play a dominant role in the decision process. Finally, the Web-HIPRE can also be employed in group mode. In the following paragraphs, we provide a tutorial on using AHP through Web-HIPRE.

Tutorial on Applying Analytic Hierarchy Process Using Web-HIPRE

The following paragraphs give an example of application of the analytic hierarchy process in making a decision to select a movie that suits an individual's interest. Phrasing the decision problem in AHP terminology:

1. The goal is to select the most appropriate movie of interest.
2. Let us identify some criteria for making this decision. To get started, let us agree that the main criteria for movie selection are genre, language, day of release, user/critics rating.
3. The subcriteria for each of main criteria are listed here:
   a. Genre: Action, Comedy, Sci-Fi, Romance
   b. Language: English, Hindi
   c. Day of Release: week day, weekend
   d. User/Critics Rating: High, Average, Low
4. Let us assume that the alternatives are the following current movies: *SkyFall, The Dark Knight Rises, The Dictator, Dabaang, Alien,* and *DDL.*

The following steps enable setting up the AHP using Web-HIPRE. The same can be done using commercial strength software such as Expert Choice/Comparion and many other tools. As mentioned earlier, Web-HIPRE can be accessed online at **hipre.aalto.fi**

Step 1 Web-HIPRE allows the users to create the goal, associated main criteria, subcriteria and the alternatives, and establish appropriate relationships among each of them. Once the application is opened, double-clicking on the diagram space allows users to create all the elements, which are renamed as the goal, criteria, and alternatives. Selecting an element and right-clicking on the desired element will create a relationship between these two elements.

    Figure 9.12 shows the entire view of the sample decision problem of selecting a movie: a sequence of goal, main criteria, subcriteria, and the alternatives.

Step 2 All of the main criteria related to the goal are then ranked with their relative importance over each other using a comparative ranking scale ranging from 1 to 9, with ascending order of importance. To begin entering your pairwise

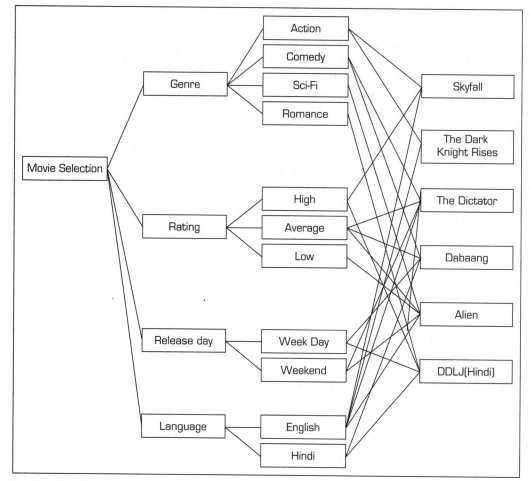

FIGURE 9.12 Main AHP Diagram.

priorities for any element's children nodes, you click on the Priorities Menu, and then select AHP as the method of ranking. Again, note that each comparison is made between just two competing criteria/subcriteria or alternatives with respect to the parent node. For example, in the current problem, the rating of the movie was considered to be the most important criterion, followed by genre, release day, and language. The criteria are ranked or rated in a pairwise mode with respect to the parent node—the goal of selecting a movie. The tool readily normalizes the rankings of each of the main criteria over one another to a scale ranging from 0 to 1 and then calculates the row averages to arrive at an overall importance rating ranging from 0 to 1.

Figure 9.13 shows the main criteria ranked over one another and the final ranking of each of the main criteria.

Step 3 All of the subcriteria related to each of the main criteria are then ranked with their relative importance over one another. In the current example, one of the main criteria, Genre, the subcriterion Comedy is ranked with higher importance followed by Action, Romance, and Sci-Fi. The ranking is normalized and averaged to yield a final score ranging between 0 and 1. Likewise, for each of the main criteria, all subcriteria are relatively ranked over one another.

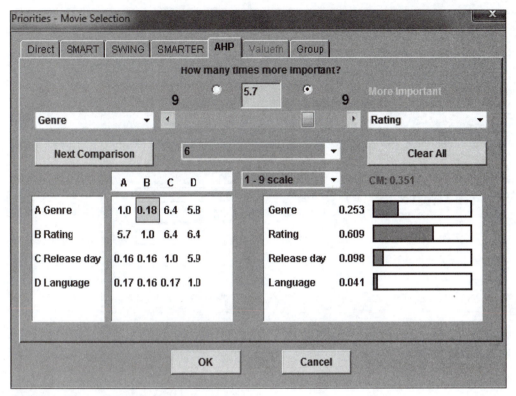

FIGURE 9.13 Ranking Main Criteria.

Figure 9.14 shows the subcriteria ranked over one another and the final ranking of each of the subcriteria with respect to the main criterion, Genre.

Step 4 Each alternative is ranked with respect to all of the subcriteria that are linked with the alternatives in a similar fashion using the relative scale of 0–9. Then the overall importance of each alternative is calculated using normalization and row averages of rankings of each of the alternatives.

Figure 9.15 shows the alternatives specific to Comedy–Sub-Genre being ranked over each other.

Step 5 The final result of the relative importance of each of the alternatives, with respect to the weighted scores of subcriteria, as well as the main criteria, is obtained from the composite priority analysis involving all the subcriteria and main criteria associated with each of the alternatives. The alternative with the highest composite score, in this case, the movie *The Dark Knight Rises,* is then selected as the right choice for the main goal.

Figure 9.16 shows the composite priority analysis.

Note that this example follows a top-down approach of choosing alternatives by first setting up priorities among the main criteria and subcriteria, eventually evaluating the relative importance of alternatives. Similarly, a bottom-up approach of first evaluating the alternatives with respect to the subcriteria and then setting up priorities among subcriteria and main criteria can also be followed in choosing a particular alternative.

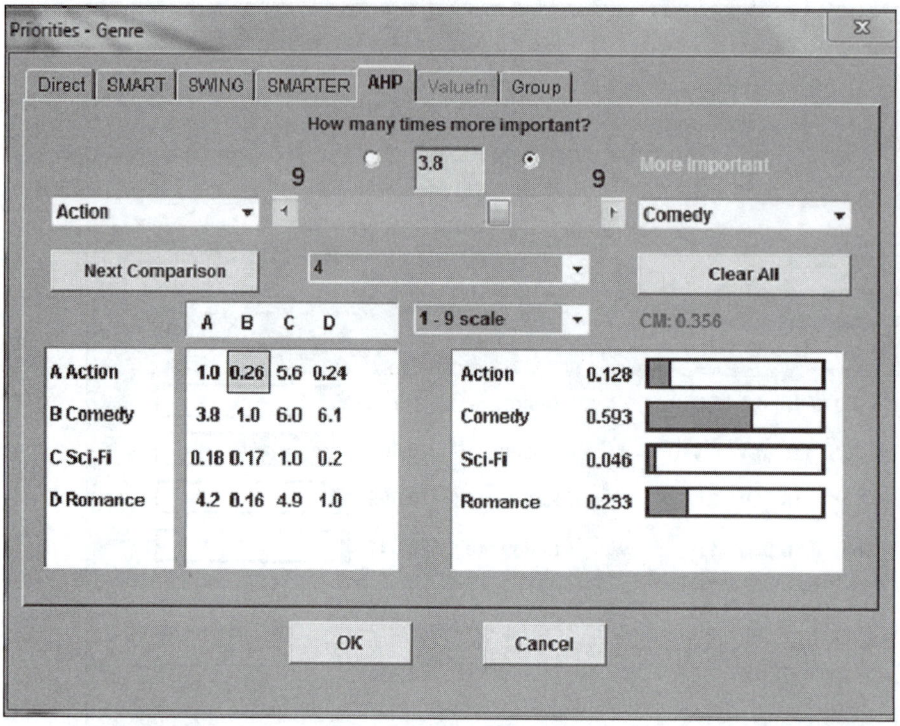

FIGURE 9.14 Ranking Subcriteria.

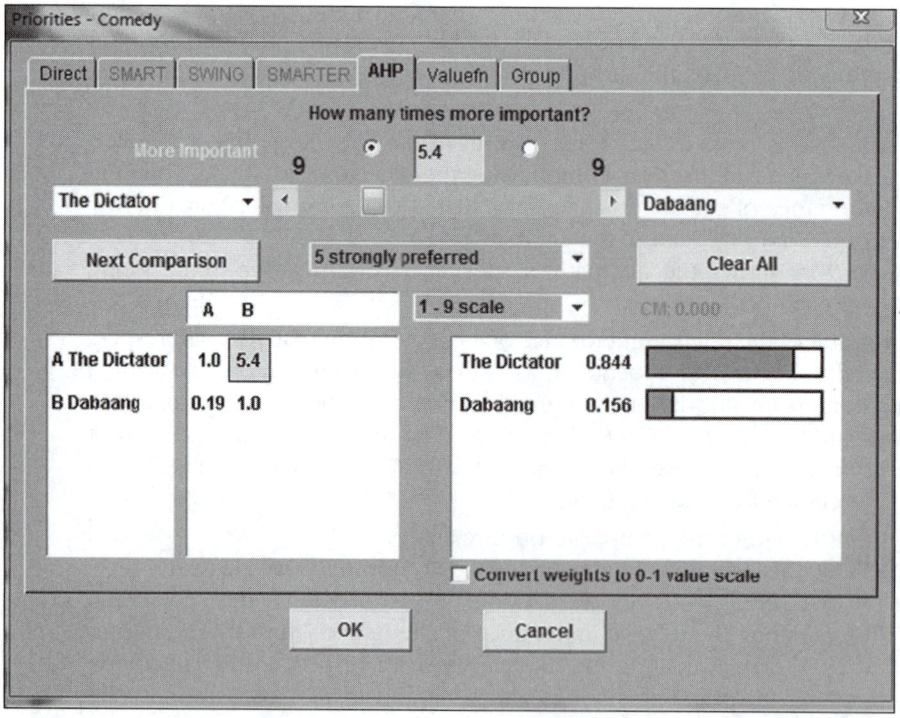

FIGURE 9.15 Ranking Alternatives.

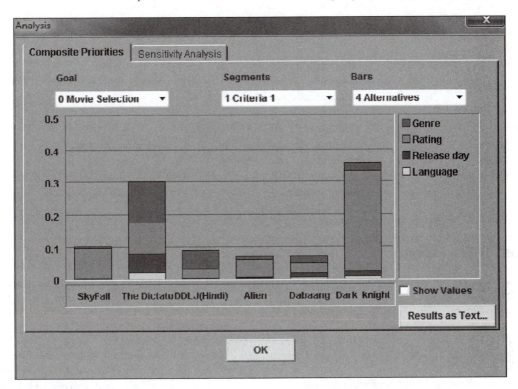

FIGURE 9.16 **Final Composite Scores.**

You can try to build the model in Figure 9.12 yourself and then enter your own pairwise comparisons to make decisions. Do you agree with the choice of the movie?

SECTION 9.9 REVIEW QUESTIONS

1. What is analytic hierarchy process?

2. What steps are needed in applying AHP?

3. What software can be used for AHP?

Chapter Highlights

- Models play a major role in DSS because they are used to describe real decision-making situations. There are several types of models.
- Models can be static (i.e., a single snapshot of a situation) or dynamic (i.e., multiperiod).
- Analysis is conducted under assumed certainty (which is most desirable), risk, or uncertainty (which is least desirable).
- Influence diagrams graphically show the inter-relationships of a model. They can be used to enhance the use of spreadsheet technology.
- Spreadsheets have many capabilities, including what-if analysis, goal seeking, programming, data-base management, optimization, and simulation.
- Decision tables and decision trees can model and solve simple decision-making problems.

- Mathematical programming is an important opti-mization method.
- LP is the most common mathematical programming method. It attempts to find an optimal allocation of limited resources under organizational constraints.
- The major parts of an LP model are the objective function, the decision variables, and the constraints.
- Multi-criteria decision-making problems are difficult but not impossible to solve.
- The AHP is a leading method for solving multi-criteria decision-making problems.
- What-if and goal seeking are the two most com-mon methods of sensitivity analysis.
- Many DSS development tools include built-in quantitative models (e.g., financial, statistical) or can easily interface with such models.

Key Terms

analytic hierarchy process (AHP)
certainty
decision analysis
decision table
decision tree
decision variable
dynamic models
environmental scanning and
   analysis
forecasting

goal seeking
influence diagram
intermediate result variable
linear programming (LP)
mathematical (quantitative) model
mathematical programming
multidimensional analysis
   (modeling)
multiple goals
optimal solution

parameter
result (outcome) variable
risk
risk analysis
sensitivity analysis
static models
uncertainty
uncontrollable variable
what-if analysis

Questions for Discussion

1. What is the relationship between environmental analysis and problem identification?
2. Explain the differences between static and dynamic models. How can one evolve into the other?
3. What is the difference between an optimistic approach and a pessimistic approach to decision making under assumed uncertainty?
4. Explain why solving problems under uncertainty sometimes involves assuming that the problem is to be solved under conditions of risk.
5. Excel is probably the most popular spreadsheet software for PCs. Why? What can we do with this package that makes it so attractive for modeling efforts?
6. Explain how decision trees work. How can a complex problem be solved by using a decision tree?

7. Explain how LP can solve allocation problems.
8. What are the advantages of using a spreadsheet package to create and solve LP models? What are the disadvantages?
9. What are the advantages of using an LP package to create and solve LP models? What are the disadvantages?
10. What is the difference between decision analysis with a single goal and decision analysis with multiple goals (i.e., criteria)? Explain in detail the difficulties that may arise when analyzing multiple goals.
11. Explain how multiple goals can arise in practice.
12. Compare and contrast what-if analysis and goal seeking.
13. Does Simon's four-phase decision-making model fit into most of the modeling methodologies described? Explain.

Exercises

Teradata UNIVERSITY NETWORK (TUN) and Other Hands-on Exercises

1. Explore **teradatauniversitynetwork.com** and determine how models are used in the BI cases and papers.
2. Create the spreadsheet models shown in Figures 9.3 and 9.4.
   a. What is the effect of a change in the interest rate from 8 percent to 10 percent in the spreadsheet model shown in Figure 9.3?
   b. For the original model in Figure 9.3, what interest rate is required to decrease the monthly payments by 20 percent? What change in the loan amount would have the same effect?
   c. In the spreadsheet shown in Figure 9.4, what is the effect of a prepayment of $200 per month? What prepayment would be necessary to pay off the loan in 25 years instead of 30 years?
3. Solve the MBI product-mix problem described in this chapter, using either Excel's Solver or a student version of an LP solver, such as Lindo. Lindo is available from Lindo Systems, Inc., at **lindo.com**; others are also available—search the

Web. Examine the solution (output) reports for the answers and sensitivity report. Did you get the same results as reported in this chapter? Try the sensitivity analysis outlined in the chapter; that is, lower the right-hand side of the CC-8 marketing constraint by 1 unit, from 200 to 199. What happens to the solution when you solve this modified problem? Eliminate the CC-8 lower-bound constraint entirely (this can be done easily by either deleting it in Solver or setting the lower limit to zero) and re-solve the problem. What happens? Using the original formulation, try modifying the objective function coefficients and see what happens.

4. Go to **orms-today.com** and access the article "The 'Sound' Science of Scheduling," by L. Gordon and E. Erkut from *OR/ MS Today*, Vol. 32, No. 2, April 2005. Describe the overall problem, the DSS developed to solve it, and the benefits.
5. Investigate via a Web search how models and their solutions are used by the U.S. Department of Homeland Security in the "war against terrorism." Also investigate how other governments or government agencies are using models in their missions.

6. Have a group meeting and discuss how you chose a place to live when you relocated to start your college program (or relocated to where you are now). What factors were important for each individual then, and how long ago was it? Have the criteria changed? As a group, identify the five to seven most important criteria used in making the decision. Using the current group members' living arrangements as choices, develop an AHP model that describes this decision-making problem. Do not put your judgments in yet. You should each solve the AHP model independently. Be careful to keep the inconsistency ratio less than 0.1. How many of the group members selected their current home using the software? For those who did, was it a close decision, or was there a clear winner? If some group members did not choose their current homes, what criteria made the result different? (In this decision-making exercise, you should not consider spouses or parents, even those who cook really well, as part of the home.) Did the availability of better choices that meet their needs become known? How consistent were your judgments? Do you think you would really prefer to live in the winning location? Why or why not? Finally, average the results for all group members (by adding the synthesized weights for each choice and dividing by the number of group members). This is one way AHP works. Is there a clear winner? Whose home is it, and why did it win? Were there any close second choices? Turn in your results in a summary report (up to two typed pages), with copies of the individual AHP software runs.

7. Consider a problem with the following goal, main criteria, and subcriteria. Assume relative importance that is most appropriate to your personal experience when ranking the main criteria and subcriteria across various alternatives.

   a. Goal: To select the right university for pursuing your current academic program

   b. Main criteria: Location, weather, cost of the program, reputation, student life, duration

   c. Subcriteria:

   Location → City Proximity, Part-Time Jobs, Full-Time Industry Proximity

   Weather → Hot, Cold, Snow

   Cost of the program → Dollar Amount, Scholarship, Living Expenses

   Reputation → Rank, Public Image

   Student life → Cultural Events, Athletics

   Duration → Length of Course, Flexibility in Changing Duration

d. Choose various alternatives that you have considered.

   Solve the problem using the AHP methodology and any AHP software. Write a report on how best AHP matched your decision of choice.

8. Consider a problem with the following goal, main criteria, and subcriteria. Assume relative importance that is most appropriate to your personal experience when ranking the main criteria and subcriteria across various alternatives.

   a. Goal: To promote the most deserved candidate to a higher position either at your current work location or your previous work location

   b. Main criteria: Performance, Managerial Skill, Team Orientation

   c. Subcriteria:

   Performance → Subject Knowledge, Quality of work, Responsibility, Accountability

   Managerial skill → Leadership Abilities, Interpersonal Skills, Communication

   Team orientation → Outgoing Behavior, Work Load Distribution, Issue Resolution Ability

   d. Choose various alternatives as the persons that you have considered.

   Solve the problem using the AHP methodology and any AHP software. Write a report on how best AHP matched your decision of choice.

9. This problem was contributed by Dr. Rick Wilson of Oklahoma State University.

   The recent drought has hit farmers hard. Cows are eating candy corn! (**healthyliving.msn.com/blogs/daily-apple-blog-post?post=bdb849dd-ad6c-4868-b3c6-22c6e1817a08#scptmd**)

   You are interested in creating a feed plan for the next week for your cattle using the following 7 nontraditional feeding products: Chocolate Lucky Charms cereal, Butterfinger bars, Milk Duds, Vanilla Ice Cream, Cap'n Crunch cereal, Candy Corn (since the real corn is all dead), and Chips Ahoy cookies.

   Their per pound cost is shown, as is the protein units per pound they contribute, their total digestible nutrients (TDN) they contribute per pound, and the calcium units per pound.

   You estimate that total amount of nontraditional feeding products contribute the following amount of nutrients: at least 20,000 units of protein, at least 4,025 units of TDN, at least 1,000 but no more than 1,200 units of calcium.

	Choc Lucky Charms	Butterfinger	Milk Duds	Vanilla Ice Cream	Cap'n Crunch	Candy Corn	Chips Ahoy
$$/lb	2.15	7	4.25	6.35	5.25	4	6.75
choc	YES	YES	YES	NO	NO	NO	YES
Protein	75	80	45	65	72	26	62
TDN	12	20	18	6	11	8	12
Calcium	3	4	4.5	12	2	1	5

There are some other miscellaneous requirements as well.

- The chocolate in your overall feed plan (in pounds) cannot exceed the amount of non-chocolate poundage. Whether a product is considered chocolate or not is shown in the table (YES = chocolate, NO = not chocolate).
- No one feeding product can make up more than 25 percent of the total pounds needed to create an acceptable feed mix.
- There are two cereals (Choco Lucky Charms and Cap'n Crunch). Combined, they can be no more than 40 percent (in pounds) of the total mix required to meet the mix requirements.

Determine the optimal levels of the 7 products to create your weekly feed plan that minimizes cost. Note that all amounts of products must NOT have fractional values (whole numbered pounds only).

10. This exercise was contributed by Dr. Rick Wilson of Oklahoma State University to illustrate the modeling capabilities of Excel Solver.

You are working with a large set of temporary workers (collection of interns, retirees, etc.) to create a draft plan to staff a nighttime call center (for the near future). You also have a handful of full-time workers who are your "anchors"—but you have already placed them in the schedule and this has led to your staffing requirements. They (full-time workers) are of no concern to you in the model.

These staffing requirements are by day: You need 15, 20, 19, 22, 7, 32, and 35 staff for M, T, W, Th, F, Sat, Sun (respectively).

You have between 8 and 10 of the pool who cannot work on the weekend (Saturday or Sunday).

For these "Weekday Only" folks, there are 3 shifts possible: They will work 4 of the 5 weekdays, one shift will have Tuesday off, one shift will have Wednesday off, and one shift will have Thursday off.

You must have at least eight people total assigned to these "Weekday Only" shifts.

For all other shifts (and you are not constrained by size of employee pool), a person works 4 of the 7 days each week. Workers will work 2 weekdays and both weekend days (a "2/2" shift). All possible "2" day combinations of days are relevant shifts—except any combinations where workers have three consecutive days off; those are not allowed and should not be in the model.

We are going with a very simple model—no costs. The objective of our model is to find the fewest number of workers that meet stated minimum call center daily requirements *and* not have more than 4 extra workers (above min requirements) assigned during any one day.

Also, all shifts ("Weekday Only" or the 2/2 shifts) can have no more than 6 people "allocated" to them.

Create a core model that satisfies these constraints and minimizes the total number of people needed to meet the minimum requirements. If it's an issue, yes, assume that number of people are integers (whole).

11. This exercise was also contributed by Dr. Rick Wilson of Oklahoma State University. The following simple scenario mimics the "Black Book" described in a *Business Week* article (**http://www.businessweek.com/articles/2013-01-31/coke-engineers-its-orange-juice-with-an-algorithm,** accessed February 2013) about Coca-Cola's production of orange juice. Create an appropriate LP model for this scenario.

For the next production period, there are five different batches of raw orange juice that can be blended together to make orange juice products SunnyQ, GlowMorn, and OrenthalJames. In creating the optimal blend of the three products from the five different batches, an LP model should seek to maximize the net of the sales price per gallon of the products less the assessed per gallon cost of the raw juice.

The 5 raw batches of orange juice are described here. Brix is a measure of sweetness, pulp, available stock, and cost—all self-explanatory:

Batch 1—Pineapple Orange A, brix = 16, pulp = 1.2, 250 gallons, $2.01/gallon

Batch 2—Pineapple Orange B, brix = 17, pulp = 0.9, 200 gallons, $2.32/gallon

Batch 3—Mid Sweet, brix = 20, pulp = 0.8, 175 gallons, $3.14/gallon

Batch 4—Valencia, brix = 18, pulp = 2.1, 300 gallons, $2.41/gallon

Batch 5—Temple Orange, brix = 14, pulp = 1.6, 265 gallons, $2.55/gallon

Note that in order to make sure that the raw juice doesn't get too "old" over time, one production requirement is that at least 50 percent of each batch's available stock must be used in blending the three orange juice products (obviously, more than what is available cannot be used).

From a product perspective, there must be at least 100 gallons of SunnyQ blended, and at least 125 gallons each of GlowMorn and OrenthalJames. Likewise, the projected future demand for the products indicates that in this period, there should be a maximum of 400 gallons of SunnyQ, a maximum of 375 gallons of GlowMorn, and a maximum of 300 gallons of OrenthalJames produced. Also, when blending the products from the five batches, an individual batch can provide no more than 40 percent of the total amount of a given product. This is to be enforced individually on each product.

Attributes of the three products include sales price, the maximum average brix of the final mixed product, the minimum average brix of the final mixed product, and the maximum average pulp content. In the three "average" requirements, this implies the weighted average of all juice mixed together for that product must meet that specification.

SunnyQ—Sales = $3.92/gallon, Max Brix = 19, Min Brix = 18.5, Max Pulp = 1.6

GlowMorn—Sales = $4.13/gallon, Max Brix = 17, Min Brix = 16.75, Max Pulp = 1.8

OrenthalJames—Sales = $3.77/gallon, Max Brix = 17.75, Min Brix = 17.55, Max Pulp = 1.1

End-of-Chapter Application Case

Pre-Positioning of Emergency Items for CARE International

Problem

CARE International is a humanitarian organization that provides relief aid to areas that are affected by natural disasters such as earthquakes and hurricanes. The organization has relief programs in over 65 countries worldwide. Just like other humanitarian organizations, CARE International faces challenges in offering the needed help to affected areas in the event of natural disasters. In the event of a disaster, CARE International identifies suppliers that could provide the needed relief items. Arrangements are then made regarding the acquisition of warehouses to transport the items. With respect to the transportation of the items, a third-party company transports the items by air to the affected country from where they are further transported by road to CARE International's warehouse and distribution center. This mode of response to disasters could be slow, not to mention the unreliability of the transportation network used. Hitherto, CARE has preferred purchasing relief items from local suppliers since they are closer to the disaster areas and, also, it helps reinvigorate the local economy after a disaster. However, in the wake of a disaster, there are always issues with availability, price, and quality of needed items.

Specifically, CARE International's challenges are two-fold as identified by the authors of the research. First, the organization wanted the ability to gather supplies and relief items from both local and international suppliers in an agile manner so they could better serve people affected by disasters. Second, once the supplies are mobilized, they wanted to be able to effectively distribute them in the most timely and cost-efficient manner to affected regions.

Methodology/Solution

In collaboration with Georgia Institute of Technology, CARE developed a model in which relief items were placed in a pre-positioned network to serve as a complement to the existing mode of supplying relief items to disaster areas. Using a mixed-integer programming (MIP) inventory-location model, a pre-positioning network was designed based on two main factors. The first factor was up-front investment related to initial stocking of inventory and warehouse setup. The second factor was related to the average response time it takes to get relief items to affected regions. Basically, the main concern was to determine a configuration that would allow for the least response time given an up-front investment value. Demand data for the model was based on historical records of previous operations. Supply data was estimated hypothetically since historical data was not present. It was assumed

that any supplier would be able to ship relief items within 2 weeks. The model for warehouse establishment was built based on 12 locations CARE considered as low or no-cost, as well as seven relief items necessary for most disaster relief operations. The object function was to reduce the total response time in moving items to affected areas. The capacity constraints employed were the number of warehouses to maintain and the amount of items to keep in them. The MIP model consisted of 470,000 variables and 56,000 constraints. It took the ILOG OPL Studio with CPLEX solver application about 4 hours to produce an optimal solution.

Results/Benefits

The main purpose of the model was to increase the capacity and swiftness to respond to sudden natural disasters like earthquakes, as opposed to other slow-occurring ones like famine. Based on up-front cost, the model is able to provide the best optimized configuration of where to locate a warehouse and how much inventory should be kept. It is able to provide an optimization result based on estimates of frequency, location, and level of potential demand that is generated by the model. Based on this model, CARE has established three warehouses in the warehouse pre-positioning system in Dubai, Panama, and Cambodia. In fact, during the Haiti earthquake crises in 2010, water purification kits were supplied to the victims from the Panama warehouse. In the future, the pre-positioning network is expected to be expanded.

QUESTIONS FOR THE END-OF-CHAPTER APPLICATION CASE

1. What were the main challenges encountered by CARE International before they created their warehouse pre-positioning model?
2. How does the objective function relate to the organization's need to improve relief services to affected areas?
3. Conduct online research and suggest at least three other applications or types of software that could handle the magnitude of variable and constraints CARE International used in their MIP model.
4. Elaborate on some benefits CARE International stands to gain from implementing their pre-positioning model on a large scale in future.

Source: S. Duran, M. A. Gutierrez, and P. Keskinocak, "Pre-Positioning of Emergency Items for CARE International," *Interfaces*, Vol. 41, No. 3, 2011, pp. 223–237.

References

Arsham, H. (2006a). "Modeling and Simulation Resources." **home.ubalt.edu/ntsbarsh/Business-stat/RefSim.htm** (accessed February 2013).

Arsham, H. (2006b). "Decision Science Resources." **home.ubalt.edu/ntsbarsh/Business-stat/Refop.htm** (accessed February 2013).

Bailey, M. J., J. Snapp, S. Yetur, J. S. Stonebraker, S. A. Edwards, A. Davis, and R. Cox. (2011). "Practice Summaries: American Airlines Uses Should-Cost Modeling to Assess the Uncertainty of Bids for Its Full-Truckload Shipment Routes." *Interfaces*, Vol. 41, No. 2, pp. 194–196.

Businessweek.com. "Coke Engineers Its Orange Juice—With an Algorithm." **www.businessweek.com/articles/2013-01-31/coke-engineers-its-orange-juice-with-an-algorithm** (accessed February 2013).

Camm, J. D., T. E. Chorman, F. A. Dill, J. R. Evans, D. J. Sweeney, and G. W. Wegryn. (1997, January/February). "Blending OR/MS, Judgment, and GIS: Restructuring P&G's Supply Chain." *Interfaces*, Vol. 27, No. 1, pp. 128–142.

Carlson, Brian, Yonghong Chen, Mingguo Hong, Roy Jones, Kevin Larson, Xingwang Ma, Peter Nieuwesteeg, et al. (2012). "MISO Unlocks Billions in Savings Through the Application of Operations Research for Energy and Ancillary Services Markets." *Interfaces*, Vol. 42, No. 1 pp. 58–73.

Christiansen, M., K. Fagerholt, G. Hasle, A. Minsaas, and B. Nygreen. (2009, April). "Maritime Transport Optimization: An Ocean of Opportunities." *OR/MS Today*, Vol. 36, No. 2, pp. 26–31.

Clemen, R. T., and T. Reilly. (2000). *Making Hard Decisions with Decision Tools Suite*. Belmont, MA: Duxbury Press.

Duran, S., M. A. Gutierrez, and P. Keskinocak. (2011). "Pre-Positioning of Emergency Items for CARE International." *Interfaces*, Vol. 41, No. 3, pp. 223–237.

Expertchoice.com. "U.S. Department of Housing and Urban Development (HUD) Case Study." **http://expertchoice.com/xres/uploads/resource-center-documents/HUD_casestudy.pdf** (accessed February 2013).

Farasyn, I., K. Perkoz, and W. Van de Velde. (2008, July/August). "Spreadsheet Models for Inventory Target Setting at Procter and Gamble." *Interfaces*, Vol. 38, No. 4, pp. 241–250.

Furman, K. C., J. H. Song, G. R. Kocis, M. K. McDonald, and P. H. Warrick. (2011). "Feedstock Routing in the ExxonMobil Downstream Sector." *Interfaces*, Vol. 41, No. 2, pp. 49–163.

Goodwin, P., and G. Wright. (2000). *Decision Analysis for Management Judgment*, 2nd ed. New York: Wiley.

Healthyliving.msn.com. "Cows Eating 'Candy' Corn." **http://healthyliving.msn.com/blogs/daily-apple-blog-post?post=bdb849dd-ad6c-4868-b3c6-22c6e1817a08#scptmd** (accessed February 2013).

Hillier, F. S., and G. J. Lieberman. (2005). *Introduction to Operations Research*, 8th ed. New York: McGraw-Hill.

Hurley, W. J., and M. Balez. (2008, July/August). "A Spreadsheet Implementation of an Ammunition Requirements Planning Model for the Canadian Army." *Interfaces*, Vol. 38, No. 4, pp. 271–280.

Kearns, G. S. (2004, January–March). "A Multi-Objective, Multi-Criteria Approach for Evaluating IT Investments: Results from Two Case Studies." *Information Resources Management Journal*, Vol. 17, No. 1, pp. 37–62.

Kelly, A. (2002). *Decision Making Using Game Theory: An Introduction for Managers*. Cambridge, UK: Cambridge University Press.

Koksalan, M., and S. Zionts (eds.). (2001). *Multiple Criteria Decision Making in the New Millennium*. Berlin: Springer-Verlag.

Kontoghiorghes, E. J., B. Rustem, and S. Siokos. (2002). *Computational Methods in Decision Making, Economics, and Finance*. Boston: Kluwer.

Lejeune, M. A., and N. Yakova. (2008, May/June). "Showcase Scheduling at Fred Astaire East Side Dance Studio." *Interfaces*, Vol. 38, No. 3, pp. 176–186.

Metters, M., C. Queenan, M. Ferguson, L. Harrison, J. Higbie, S. Ward, B. Barfield, T. Farley, H. A. Kuyumcu, and A. Duggasani. (2008, May/June). "The 'Killer Application' of Revenue Management: Harrah's Cherokee Casino & Hotel." *Interfaces*, Vol. 38, No. 3, pp. 161–175.

Ovchinnikov, A., and J. Milner. (2008, July/August). "Spreadsheet Model Helps to Assign Medical Residents at the University of Vermont's College of Medicine." *Interfaces*, Vol. 38, No. 4, pp. 311–323.

ProModel. (2006, March). "Fiat Case." **promodel.com** (accessed February 2013).

ProModel. (2009). "Throughput, Cycle Time, and Bottleneck Analysis with ProModel Simulation Solutions for Manufacturing." **promodel.com** (accessed February 2013).

ProModel. (2013). "Pillowtex Case." **promodel.com** (accessed February 2013).

Saaty, T. L. (1995). *Decision Making for Leaders: The Analytic Hierarchy Process for Decisions in a Complex World*, Rev. ed. Pittsburgh, PA: RWS Publishers.

Saaty, T. L. (1996). *Decision Making for Leaders*, Vol. II. Pittsburgh, PA: RWS Publishers.

Saaty, T. L. (1999). *The Brain: Unraveling the Mystery of How It Works (The Neural Network Process)*. Pittsburgh, PA: RWS Publishers.

Taha, H. (2006). *Operations Research: An Introduction*, 8th ed. Upper Saddle River, NJ: Prentice Hall.

TreeAge Software, Inc. (2009). "Dr. Victor Grann Uses Decision Analysis to Weigh Treatment Options for Patients at High Risk of Developing Cancer." (accessed February 2013).

CHAPTER

10

Modeling and Analysis: Heuristic Search Methods and Simulation

LEARNING OBJECTIVES

- Explain the basic concepts of simulation and heuristics, and when to use them
- Understand how search methods are used to solve some decision support models
- Know the concepts behind and applications of genetic algorithms
- Explain the differences among algorithms, blind search, and heuristics

- Understand the concepts and applications of different types of simulation
- Explain what is meant by system dynamics, agent-based modeling, Monte Carlo, and discrete event simulation
- Describe the key issues of model management

In this chapter, we continue to explore some additional concepts related to the model base, one of the major components of decision support systems (DSS). As pointed out in the last chapter, we present this material with a note of caution: The purpose of this chapter is not necessarily for you to *master the topics* of modeling and analysis. Rather, the material is geared toward *gaining familiarity* with the important concepts as they relate to DSS and their use in decision making. We discuss the structure and application of some successful time-proven models and methodologies: search methods, heuristic programming, and simulation. Genetic algorithms mimic the natural process of evolution to help find solutions to complex problems. The concepts and motivating applications of these advanced techniques are described in this chapter, which is organized into the following sections:

10.1 OPENING VIGNETTE: System Dynamics Allows Fluor Corporation to Better Plan for Project and Change Management

INTRODUCTION

Fluor is an engineering and construction company with over 36,000 employers spread over several countries worldwide. The company's net income in 2009 amounted to about $680 million based on total revenue of $22 billion. As part of its operations, Fluor manages varying sizes of projects that are subject to scope changes, design changes, and schedule changes.

PRESENTATION OF PROBLEM

Fluor estimated that changes accounted for about 20 to 30 percent of revenue. Most changes were due to secondary impacts like ripple effects, disruptions, and productivity loss. Previously, the changes were collated and reported at a later period and the burden of cost allocated to the stakeholder responsible. In certain instances when late surprises about cost and project schedule are attributed to clients, it causes friction between clients and Fluor, which eventually affect future business dealings. Sometimes, cost impacts occur in such a time and fashion when it is difficult to take preventive measures. The company determined that to improve on its efficiency, reduce legal ramification with clients, and keep them happy it had to review its method of handling changes to projects. One challenge the company faced was the fact that changes stayed extremely remote from the situation, which warranted the change. In such a case, it is difficult to determine the cause of a change, and it affects subsequent measures to handle related change issues.

METHODOLOGY/SOLUTION

For sure, Fluor knew that one way of combating the issue was to foresee and avoid the events that might lead to changes. However, that alone would not be enough to solve the problem. The company needed to understand the dynamics of the different situations that could warrant changes to project plans. Systems dynamics was used as a base method in a three-part analytical solution for understanding the dynamics between different factors that could cause changes to be made. System dynamics is a methodology and simulation-modeling technique for analyzing complex systems using principles of cause and effect, feedback loops, and time-delayed and nonlinear effects. Building tools for rapidly tailoring a solution to different situations form the next part of the three-part analytical solution. In this part, industry standards and company references are embedded. The project plan is also embedded as an input. The model is then converged to simulate the correct amounts and timing of other factors like staffing, project progress, productivity, and effects on productivity. The last part of the analytical solution was to deploy the project models to nonmodelers. Basically, the system takes inputs that are specific to a particular project being worked and its environment, such as the labor market. Some other input parameters, transformed into numerical data, are related to progress curves, expenses, and labor laws and constraints.

The resultant system provides reports on project impacts as well as helps perform cause–effect diagnostics.

RESULTS/BENEFITS

With this system, customers are able to perform "what-if" analysis even before a project is started so the project performance can be gauged. Through diagnostics, the system also helps explain why certain effects are realized based on impact to the project plan. Since its development, Fluor has recorded over 100 extensive uses of their system dynamics model and project simulation system. As an example, the model was used to analyze and save $10 million in the future impact of changes to a mining project. Also, based on the what-if capability of Fluor's model, a company saved $10 million when the project team used the model to redesign the process of reviewing changes so that the speed of the company's definition and approval procedures was increased.

QUESTIONS FOR THE OPENING VIGNETTE

1. Explain the use of system dynamics as a simulation tool for solving complex problems.
2. In what ways was it applied in Fluor Corporation to solve complex problems?
3. How does a what-if analysis help a decision maker to save on cost?
4. In your own words, explain the factors that might have triggered the use of system dynamics to solve change management problems in Fluor Corporation.
5. Pick a geographic region and business domain and list some corresponding relevant factors that would be used as inputs in building such a system.

WHAT WE CAN LEARN FROM THIS VIGNETTE

Changes to project plans and timelines are a major contributing factor to upward increase in cost from initial amount budgeted for projects. In this case, Fluor relied on system dynamics to understand what, why, when, and how changes occurred to project plans. The models that the system dynamics model produced helped them correctly quantify the cost of projects even before they started. The vignette demonstrates that system dynamics is still a credible and robust methodology in understanding business processes and creating "what-if" analyses of the impact of both expected and unexpected changes in project plans.

Source: E. Godlewski, G. Lee, and K. Cooper, "System Dynamics Transforms Fluor Project and Change Management," *Interfaces*, Vol. 42, No. 1, 2012, pp. 17–32.

10.2 PROBLEM-SOLVING SEARCH METHODS

We next turn to several well-known search methods used in the choice phase of problem solving. These include analytical techniques, algorithms, blind searching, and heuristic searching.

The choice phase of problem solving involves a search for an appropriate course of action (among those identified during the design phase) that can solve the problem. Several major search approaches are possible, depending on the criteria (or criterion) of choice and the type of modeling approach used. These search approaches are shown in Figure 10.1. For normative models, such as mathematical programming-based ones, either an analytical approach is used or a complete, exhaustive enumeration (comparing the outcomes of all the alternatives) is applied. For descriptive models, a comparison of a limited number of alternatives is used, either blindly or by employing heuristics. Usually the results guide the decision maker's search.

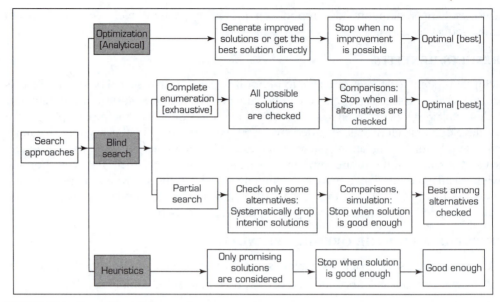

FIGURE 10.1 Formal Search Approaches.

Analytical Techniques

Analytical techniques use mathematical formulas to derive an optimal solution directly or to predict a certain result. Analytical techniques are used mainly for solving structured problems, usually of a tactical or operational nature, in areas such as resource allocation or inventory management. Blind or heuristic search approaches generally are employed to solve more complex problems.

Algorithms

Analytical techniques may use algorithms to increase the efficiency of the search. An algorithm is a step-by-step search process for obtaining an optimal solution (see Figure 10.2). (Note: There may be more than one optimum, so we say *an* optimal solution rather than

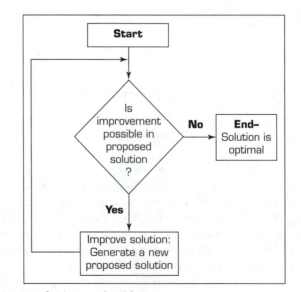

FIGURE 10.2 The Process of Using an Algorithm.

the optimal solution.) Solutions are generated and tested for possible improvements. An improvement is made whenever possible, and the new solution is subjected to an improvement test, based on the principle of choice (i.e., objective value found). The process continues until no further improvement is possible. Most mathematical programming problems are solved by using efficient algorithms. Web search engines use various algorithms to speed up searches and produce accurate results.

Blind Searching

In conducting a search, a description of a desired solution may be given. This is called a *goal*. A set of possible steps leading from initial conditions to the goal is called the *search steps*. Problem solving is done by searching through the possible solutions. The first of these search methods is blind searching. The second is heuristic searching.

Blind search techniques are arbitrary search approaches that are not guided. There are two types of blind searches: a *complete enumeration*, for which all the alternatives are considered and therefore an optimal solution is discovered; and an *incomplete*, or partial, search, which continues until a good-enough solution is found. The latter is a form of suboptimization.

There are practical limits on the amount of time and computer storage available for blind searches. In principle, blind search methods can eventually find an optimal solution in most search situations, and, in some situations, the scope of the search can be limited; however, this method is not practical for solving very large problems because too many solutions must be examined before an optimal solution is found.

Heuristic Searching

For many applications, it is possible to find rules to guide the search process and reduce the number of necessary computations through heuristics. **Heuristics** are the informal, judgmental knowledge of an application area that constitute the rules of good judgment in the field. Through domain knowledge, they guide the problem-solving process. **Heuristic programming** is the process of using heuristics in problem solving. This is done via heuristic search methods, which often operate as algorithms but limit the solutions examined either by limiting the search space or stopping the method early. Usually, rules that have either demonstrated their success in practice or are theoretically solid are applied in heuristic searching. In Application Case 10.1, we provide an example of a DSS in which the models are solved using heuristic searching.

Application Case 10.1
Chilean Government Uses Heuristics to Make Decisions on School Lunch Providers

The Junta Nacional de Auxilio Escolar y Becas (JUNAEB), an agency of the Chilean government, promotes integration and retention of socially vulnerable children in the country's school system. JUNAEB's school meal program provides meals for approximately 10,000 schools. Decisions on meal providers are made through an annual tender using a combinatorial auction, where food industry firms bid on supply contracts, based on a series of disjoint, compact geographical areas called territorial units (TUs). These territorial units consist of districts spanning the country.

When the Chilean economy suffered a downturn, many competing meal service providers ceased their operations. Thus, the number of suppliers participating in the combinatorial auction was reduced.

(Continued)

Application Case 10.1 (Continued)

The entire school meal policy was called into question. The central problem was in defining TUs. JUNAEB divided Chile's 13 official regions, consisting of several districts, into 136 TUs based on geographical criteria, which attempted to equalize the number of meals to be served in each TU. This process led to severe disparities as the districts in regions requiring large numbers of meals were assigned to a single TU; the remaining districts were combined into TUs requiring similar quantities of numbers of meals but for a possibly larger geographical area and number of schools in each district. Sometimes, a firm that ended up bagging an attractive TU was paired with another unattractive TU and, hence, was unable to fulfill its contract.

With realization of the need to determine new configurations of territorial units, homogenization of characteristics across territorial units was achieved based on a score that considered each constituent district's four characteristics: number of meals, number of schools, geographic area, and accessibility. A series of operating research methodologies was applied toward reaching the goal of homogenization of TUs.

The analytic hierarchy process was first applied to determine the relative weight of each of four characteristics for each TU in each region, and then total scores for each TU were calculated. Then a local search heuristic was employed to find a set of homogenously attractive TUs within each region. The TU's attractiveness was calculated using the values derived from the AHP process for each characteristic, and the TU's criterion weights were calculated for the local search heuristic's assessment in each region. The degree of homogeneity was measured as the standard deviation, which measures the dispersion of a TU's attractiveness level by quantifying the divergence of each TU in a region from the regional average. The heuristic attempts to minimize this measure by exchanging the combination of districts in each TU with the districts in other TUs existing in the same region. The initial set of TUs in the region are defined based on expert opinions. Then heuristics proceeds by searching the local minima and approaching the best solution by transferring districts from one TU to another until a local minima is reached where the combination of districts across all TUs separate the TUs with lowest standard deviation.

The new configuration limited the minimum and maximum number of meals for each TU between 15,000 and 40,000, and each of the 13 geographical regions was assigned TUs accordingly. The districts belonging to the TUs served as the basic units in homogenizing the TUs. Each district in the TU that served more than 10,000 meals was again divided into an equal number of subdistricts.

An integer linear programming (ILP) model was applied to the results generated by a cluster enumeration algorithm, which formed TUs as clusters created by grouping contiguous districts and subdistricts into a TU. For each region, the ILP model selected a set of clusters constituting a partition of region that minimizes the difference between the most and least attractive clusters based on the TU scores that were calculated using the weights of criteria used in a cluster.

Finally, a combination of ILP and heuristics was applied in which the results obtained from ILP were used as the initial solution on which local search heuristics were applied. This further aimed to reduce the standard deviation of attractiveness scores of TUs.

Existing data about the TUs from 2007 was used as the baseline, and the results from each of three methodologies showed a significant level of homogeneity that did not exist in the 2007 data.

QUESTIONS FOR DISCUSSION

1. What were the main challenges faced by JUNAEB?
2. What operation research methodologies were employed in achieving homogeneity across territorial units?
3. What other approaches could you use in this case study?

What We Can Learn from This Application Case

Heuristic methods can work best in providing solutions for problems that involve exhaustive, repetitive processes to arrive at a solution. The application case also shows that combinations of operations research methodologies can play a vital role in solving a particular problem.

Source: D. M. G. Alfredo, E. N. R. David, M. Cristian, and Z. V. G. Andres, "Quantitative Methods for a New Configuration of Territorial Units in a Chilean Government Agency Tender Process," *Interfaces,* 2011.

SECTION 10.2 REVIEW QUESTIONS

1. What is a search approach?
2. List the different problem-solving search methods.
3. What are the practical limits to blind searching?
4. How are algorithms and heuristic search methods similar? How are they different?

10.3 GENETIC ALGORITHMS AND DEVELOPING GA APPLICATIONS

Genetic algorithms (GA) are a part of global search techniques used to find approximate solutions to optimization-type problems that are too complex to be solved with traditional optimization methods (which are guaranteed to produce the best solution to a specific problem). Genetic algorithms have been successfully applied to a wide range of highly complex real-world problems, including vehicle routing (Baker and Syechew, 2003), bankruptcy prediction (Shin and Lee, 2002), and Web searching (Nick and Themis, 2001).

Genetic algorithms are a part of the machine-learning family of methods under artificial intelligence. Because they cannot guarantee the truly optimal solution, genetic algorithms are considered to be heuristic methods. Genetic algorithms are sets of computational procedures that conceptually follow the steps of the biological process of evolution. That is, better and better solutions evolve from the previous generation of solutions until an optimal or near-optimal solution is obtained.

Genetic algorithms (also known as **evolutionary algorithms**) demonstrate self-organization and adaptation in much the same way that biological organisms do by following the chief rule of evolution, *survival of the fittest*. The method improves the solutions by producing offspring (i.e., a new collection of feasible solutions) using the best solutions of the current generation as "parents." The generation of offspring is achieved by a process modeled after biological reproduction whereby mutation and crossover operators are used to manipulate genes in constructing newer and "better" chromosomes. Notice that a simple analogy between genes and decision variables and between chromosomes and potential solutions underlies the genetic algorithm terminology.

Example: The Vector Game

To illustrate how genetic algorithms work, we describe the classical Vector game (see Walbridge, 1989). This game is similar to MasterMind. As your opponent gives you clues about how good your guess is (i.e., the outcome of the fitness function), you create a new solution, using the knowledge gained from the recently proposed solutions and their quality.

Description of The Vector Game   Vector is played against an opponent who secretly writes down a string of six digits (in a genetic algorithm, this string consists of a *chromosome*). Each digit is a decision variable that can take the value of either 0 or 1. For example, say that the secret number that you are to figure out is 001010. You must try to guess this number as quickly as possible (with the least number of trials). You present a sequence of digits (a guess) to your opponent, and he or she tells you how many of the digits (but not which ones) you guessed are correct (i.e., the fitness function or quality of your guess). For example, the guess 110101 has no correct digits (i.e., the score = 0). The guess 111101 has only one correct digit (the third one, and hence the score = 1).

Default Strategy: Random Trial and Error   There are 64 possible six-digit strings of binary numbers. If you pick numbers at random, you will need, on average, 32 guesses to obtain the right answer. Can you do it faster? Yes, if you can interpret the feedback provided to you by your opponent (a measure of the goodness or fitness of your guess). This is how a genetic algorithm works.

Improved Strategy: Use of Genetic Algorithms The following are the steps in solving the Vector game with genetic algorithms:

1. Present to your opponent four strings, selected at random. (Select four arbitrarily. Through experimentation, you may find that five or six would be better.) Assume that you have selected these four:

   (A) 110100; score = 1 (i.e., one digit guessed correctly)
   (B) 111101; score = 1
   (C) 011011; score = 4
   (D) 101100; score = 3

2. Because none of the strings is entirely correct, continue.
3. Delete (A) and (B) because of their low scores. Call (C) and (D) parents.
4. "Mate" the parents by splitting each number as shown here between the second and third digits (the position of the split is randomly selected):

   (C) 01:1011
   (D) 10:1100

   Now combine the first two digits of (C) with the last four of (D) (this is called crossover). The result is (E), the first offspring:

   (E) 011100; score = 3

   Similarly, combine the first two digits of (D) with the last four of (C). The result is (F), the second offspring:

   (F) 101011; score = 4

   It looks as though the offspring are not doing much better than the parents.

5. Now copy the original (C) and (D).
6. Mate and crossover the new parents, but use a different split. Now you have two new offspring, (G) and (H):

   (C) 0110:11
   (D) 1011:00
   (G) 0110:00; score = 4
   (H) 1011:11; score = 3

   Next, repeat step 2: Select the best "couple" from all the previous solutions to reproduce. You have several options, such as (G) and (C). Select (G) and (F). Now duplicate and crossover. Here are the results:

   (F) 1:01011
   (G) 0:11000
   (I) 111000; score = 3
   (J) 001011; score = 5

   You can also generate more offspring:

   (F) 101:011
   (G) 011:000
   (K) 101000; score = 4
   (L) 011011; score = 4

   Now repeat the processes with (J) and (K) as parents, and duplicate the crossover:

   (J) 00101:1
   (K) 10100:0
   (M) 001010; score = 6

   That's it! You have reached the solution after 13 guesses. Not bad compared to the expected average of 32 for a random-guess strategy.

Terminology of Genetic Algorithms

A genetic algorithm is an iterative procedure that represents its candidate solutions as strings of genes called **chromosomes** and measures their viability with a fitness function. The fitness function is a measure of the objective to be obtained (i.e., maximum or minimum). As in biological systems, candidate solutions combine to produce offspring in each algorithmic iteration, called a *generation*. The offspring themselves can become candidate solutions. From the generation of parents and children, a set of the fittest survive to become parents that produce offspring in the next generation. Offspring are produced using a specific genetic reproduction process that involves the application of crossover and mutation operators. Along with the offspring, some of the best solutions are also migrated to the next generation (a concept called **elitism**) in order to preserve the best solution achieved up until the current iteration. Following are brief definitions of these key terms:

- *Reproduction.* Through **reproduction**, genetic algorithms produce new generations of potentially improved solutions by selecting parents with higher fitness ratings or by giving such parents a greater probability of being selected to contribute to the reproduction process.
- *Crossover.* Many genetic algorithms use a string of binary symbols (each corresponding to a decision variable) to represent chromosomes (potential solutions), as was the case in the Vector game described earlier. **Crossover** means choosing a random position in the string (e.g., after the first two digits) and exchanging the segments either to the right or the left of that point with those of another string's segments (generated using the same splitting schema) to produce two new offspring.
- *Mutation.* This genetic operator was not shown in the Vector game example. **Mutation** is an arbitrary (and minimal) change in the representation of a chromosome. It is often used to prevent the algorithm from getting stuck in a local optimum. The procedure randomly selects a chromosome (giving more probability to the ones with better fitness value) and randomly identifies a gene in the chromosome and inverses its value (from 0 to 1 or from 1 to 0), thus generating one new chromosome for the next generation. The occurrence of mutation is usually set to a very low probability (0.1 percent).
- *Elitism.* An important aspect in genetic algorithms is to preserve a few of the best solutions to evolve through the generations. That way, you are guaranteed to end up with the best possible solution for the current application of the algorithm. In practice, a few of the best solutions are migrated to the next generation.

How Do Genetic Algorithms Work?

Figure 10.3 is a flow diagram of a typical genetic algorithm process. The problem to be solved must be described and represented in a manner amenable to a genetic algorithm. Typically, this means that a string of 1s and 0s (or other more recently proposed complex representations) are used to represent the decision variables, the collection of which represents a potential solution to the problem. Next, the decision variables are mathematically and/or symbolically pooled into a *fitness function* (or *objective function*). The fitness function can be one of two types: maximization (something that is more is better, such as profit) or minimization (something that is less is better, such as cost). Along with the fitness function, all of the constraints on decision variables that collectively

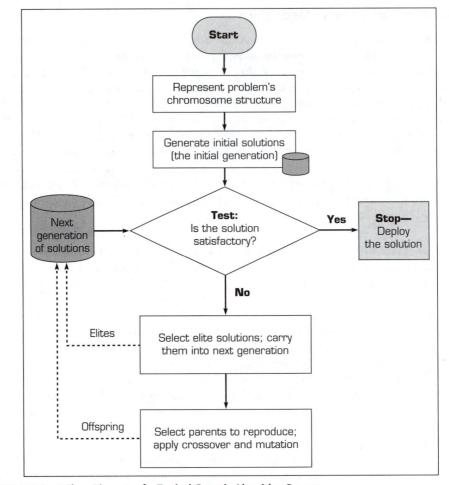

FIGURE 10.3 A Flow Diagram of a Typical Genetic Algorithm Process.

dictate whether a solution is a feasible one should be demonstrated. Remember that only feasible solutions can be a part of the solution population. Infeasible ones are filtered out before finalizing a generation of solutions in the iterations process. Once the representation is complete, an initial set of solutions is generated (i.e., the initial population). All infeasible solutions are eliminated, and fitness functions are computed for the feasible ones. The solutions are rank-ordered based on their fitness values; those with better fitness values are given more probability (proportional to their relative fitness value) in the random selection process.

A few of the best solutions are migrated to the next generation. Using a random process, several sets of parents are identified to take part in the generation of offspring. Using the randomly selected parents and the genetic operators (i.e., crossover and mutation), offspring are generated. The number of potential solutions to generate is determined by the population size, which is an arbitrary parameter set prior to the evolution of solutions. Once the next generation is constructed, the solutions go through the evaluation and generation of new populations for a number of iterations. This iterative process continues until a good-enough solution is obtained (an optimum is not guaranteed), no improvement occurs over several generations, or the time/iteration limit is reached.

As mentioned, a few parameters must be set prior to the execution of the genetic algorithm. Their values are dependent on the problem being solved and are usually determined through trial and error:

- Number of initial solutions to generate (i.e., the initial population)
- Number of offspring to generate (i.e., the population size)
- Number of parents to keep for the next generation (i.e., elitism)
- Mutation probability (usually a very low number, such as 0.1 percent)
- Probability distribution of crossover point occurrence (generally equally weighted)
- Stopping criteria (time/iteration based or improvement based)
- The maximum number of iterations (if the stopping criteria are time/iteration based)

Sometimes these parameters are set and frozen beforehand, or they can be varied systematically while the algorithm is running for better performance.

Limitations of Genetic Algorithms

According to Grupe and Jooste (2004), the following are among the most important limitations of genetic algorithms:

- Not all problems can be framed in the mathematical manner that genetic algorithms demand.
- Development of a genetic algorithm and interpretation of the results require an expert who has both the programming and statistical/mathematical skills demanded by the genetic algorithm technology in use.
- It is known that in a few situations the "genes" from a few comparatively highly fit (but not optimal) individuals may come to dominate the population, causing it to converge on a local maximum. When the population has converged, the ability of the genetic algorithm to continue to search for better solutions is effectively eliminated.
- Most genetic algorithms rely on random-number generators that produce different results each time the model runs. Although there is likely to be a high degree of consistency among the runs, they may vary.
- Locating good variables that work for a particular problem is difficult. Obtaining the data to populate the variables is equally demanding.
- Selecting methods by which to evolve the system requires thought and evaluation. If the range of possible solutions is small, a genetic algorithm will converge too quickly on a solution. When evolution proceeds too quickly, thereby altering good solutions too quickly, the results may miss the optimum solution.

Genetic Algorithm Applications

Genetic algorithms are a type of machine learning for representing and solving complex problems. They provide a set of efficient, domain-independent search heuristics for a broad spectrum of applications, including the following:

- Dynamic process control
- Induction of optimization of rules
- Discovery of new connectivity topologies (e.g., neural computing connections, neural network design)
- Simulation of biological models of behavior and evolution
- Complex design of engineering structures
- Pattern recognition
- Scheduling
- Transportation and routing

- Layout and circuit design
- Telecommunication
- Graph-based problems

A genetic algorithm interprets information that enables it to reject inferior solutions and accumulate good ones, and thus it learns about its universe. Genetic algorithms are also suitable for parallel processing.

Because the kernels of genetic algorithms are pretty simple, it is not difficult to write computer codes to implement them. For better performance, software packages are available.

Several genetic algorithm codes are available for fee or for free (try searching the Web for research and commercial sites). In addition, a number of commercial packages offer online demos. Representative commercial packages include Microsoft Solver and XpertRule GenAsys, an ES shell with an embedded genetic algorithm (see **xpertrule.com**). Evolver (from Palisade Corp., **palisade.com**) is an optimization add-in for Excel. It uses a genetic algorithm to solve complex optimization problems in finance, scheduling, manufacturing, and so on.

SECTION 10.3 REVIEW QUESTIONS

1. Define *genetic algorithm*.
2. Describe the evolution process in genetic algorithms. How is it similar to biological evolution?
3. Describe the major genetic algorithm operators.
4. List major areas of genetic algorithm application.
5. Describe in detail three genetic algorithm applications.
6. Describe the capability of Evolver as an optimization tool.

We now turn our attention to simulation, a class of modeling method that has enjoyed significant actual use in decision making.

10.4 SIMULATION

Simulation is the appearance of reality. In MSS, simulation is a technique for conducting experiments (e.g., what-if analyses) with a computer on a model of a management system.

Typically, real decision-making situations involve some randomness. Because DSS deals with semistructured or unstructured situations, reality is complex, which may not be easily represented by optimization or other models but can often be handled by simulation. Simulation is one of the most commonly used DSS methods. See Application Cases 10.2 and 10.3 for examples. Application Case 10.3 illustrates the value of simulation in a setting where sufficient time is not available to perform clinical trials.

Application Case 10.2
Improving Maintenance Decision Making in the Finnish Air Force Through Simulation

The Finnish Air Force wanted to gain efficiency in its maintenance system in order to keep as many aircraft as possible safely available at all times for training, missions, and other tasks, as needed. A discrete event simulation program similar to those used in manufacturing was developed to accommodate workforce issues, task times, material handling delays, and the likelihood of equipment failure.

The developers had to consider aircraft availability, resource requirements for international operations, and the periodic maintenance program. The information for normal conditions and conflict conditions was input into the simulation program because the maintenance schedule could be altered from one situation to another.

The developers had to estimate some information due to confidentiality, especially with regards to conflict scenarios (no data of battle-damage probabilities was available). They used several methods to acquire and secure data, such as asking experts in aircraft maintenance fields at different levels for their opinions and designing a model that allowed the confidential data to be input into the system. Also, the simulations were compared to actual performance data to make sure the simulated results were accurate.

The maintenance program was broken into three levels:

1. The organizational level, in which the fighter squadron takes care of preflight checks, turn-around checks (which occur when an aircraft returns), and other minor repairs at the main command airbase in normal conditions
2. The intermediate level, in which more complicated periodic maintenance and failure repairs are taken care of at the air command repair shop at the main airbase in normal conditions
3. The depot level, in which all major periodic maintenance is taken care of and is located away from the main airbase

During conflict conditions, the system is decentralized from the main airbase. The maintenance levels just described may continue to do the exact same repairs, or periodic maintenance may be eliminated. Additionally, depending on need, supplies, and capabilities, any of these levels may take care of any maintenance and repairs needed at any time during conflict conditions.

The simulation model was implemented using Arena software based on the SIMAN language and involved using a graphical user interface (GUI) that was executed using Visual Basic for Applications (VBA). The input data included simulation parameters and the initial system state: characteristics of the air commands, maintenance needs, and flight operations; accumulated flight hours; and the location of each aircraft. Excel spreadsheets were used for data input and output. Additionally, parameters of some of the input data were estimated from statistical data or based on information from subject matter experts. These included probabilities for time between failures, damage sustained during a single-flight mission, the duration of each type of periodic maintenance, failure repair, damage repair, the times between flight missions, and the duration of a mission. This simulation model was so successful that the Finnish Army, in collaboration with the Finnish Air Force, has now devised a simulation model for the maintenance for some of its new transport helicopters.

Source: Based on V. Mattila, K. Virtanen, and T. Raivio, "Improving Maintenance Decision Making in the Finnish Air Force Through Simulation," *Interfaces*, Vol. 38, No. 3, May/June 2008, pp. 187–201.

Application Case 10.3
Simulating Effects of Hepatitis B Interventions

Although the United States has made significant investments in healthcare, some problems seem to defy solution. For example, a sizable proportion of the Asian population in the United States is more prone than others to the Hepatitis B viral disease. In addition to the social problems associated with the disease (like isolation), one out of every four chronically infected individuals stands the risk of suffering from liver cancer or cirrhosis if the disease is not treated effectively. Managing this disease could be very costly. There are a number of control measures, including screening, vaccination, and treatment procedures. The government is reluctant to spend money on any method of control if it is not cost-effective and there is no proof of increased health for people afflicted with the disease. Even though not all the control measures are optimal for all situations, the best method or combination of methods for combatting the disease are not yet known.

(Continued)

Application Case 10.3 (Continued)

Methodology/Solution

A multidisciplinary team consisting of those with medical, management science, and engineering backgrounds developed a mathematical model using operations research (OR) methods that determined the right combination of control measures to be used to combat Hepatitis B in the Asian and Pacific Island populations. Normally, clinical trials are used in the medical field to determine the best course of action in disease treatment and prevention. Complicating this situation is the unusually long period of time it takes Hepatitis B to progress. Because of the high cost that would accompany clinical trials in this situation, operations research models and methods were used. A combination of Markov and decision models offered a more cost-effective way for determining what combination of control measures to use at any point in time. The decision model helps measure the economic and health benefits of various possibilities of screening, treatment, and vaccination. The Markov model was used to model the progression of Hepatitis B. The new model was created based on past literature and expertise from one of the researchers and draws from actual current infection and treatment data. Policymakers built the new model using Microsoft Excel because it is user friendly.

Results/Benefits

The resultant model was analyzed vis-à-vis existing control programs in both the United States and China. In the United States four strategies were developed and compared to the existing strategy. The four strategies are:

a. All individuals are vaccinated.
b. Individuals are first screened to determine whether they have a chronic infection. If yes, then they are treated.
c. Individuals are first screened to determine whether they have a chronic infection. If they have the infection, they are treated. In addition, close associates of those infected are also screened and vaccinated, if necessary.
d. Individuals are first screened to determine whether they have a chronic infection or need vaccination. If they are infected, they are treated. If they need vaccination, they are vaccinated.

Results of the simulations indicated that performing blood tests to determine chronic infection and vaccinating associates of infected people are cost-effective.

In China, the model helped design a catch-up vaccination policy for children and adolescents. This catch-up policy was compared with current coverage levels of Hepatitis B vaccination. It was concluded that when individuals under the age of 19 years are vaccinated, the health outcomes are improved in the long run. In fact, this policy was more financially cost-effective than the current disease control policy in place at the time of the evaluation.

QUESTIONS FOR DISCUSSION

1. Explain the advantage of operations research methods such as simulation over clinical trial methods in determining the best control measure for Hepatitis B.
2. In what ways do the decision and Markov models provide cost-effective ways of combating the disease?
3. Discuss how multidisciplinary background is an asset in finding a solution for the problem described in the case.
4. Besides healthcare, in what other domain could such a modeling approach help reduce cost?

Source: D. W. Hutton, M. L. Brandeau, and S. K. So, "Doing Good with Good OR: Supporting Cost-Effective Hepatitis B Interventions," *Interfaces,* Vol. 41, No. 3, 2011, pp. 289–300.

Major Characteristics of Simulation

Simulation is not strictly a type of model; models generally *represent* reality, whereas simulation typically *imitates* it. In a practical sense, there are fewer simplifications of reality in simulation models than in other models. In addition, simulation is a technique for *conducting experiments*. Therefore, it involves testing specific values of the decision or uncontrollable variables in the model and observing the impact on the output variables. At DuPont, decision makers had initially chosen to purchase more railcars; however, an alternative involving better scheduling of the existing railcars was developed, tested, and found to have excess capacity, and it ended up saving money.

Simulation is a *descriptive* rather than a *normative* method. There is no automatic search for an optimal solution. Instead, a simulation model describes or predicts the characteristics of a given system under different conditions. When the values of the characteristics are computed, the best of several alternatives can be selected. The simulation process usually repeats an experiment many times to obtain an estimate (and a variance) of the overall effect of certain actions. For most situations, a computer simulation is appropriate, but there are some well-known manual simulations (e.g., a city police department simulated its patrol car scheduling with a carnival game wheel).

Finally, simulation is normally used only when a problem is too complex to be treated using numerical optimization techniques. Complexity in this situation means either that the problem cannot be formulated for optimization (e.g., because the assumptions do not hold), that the formulation is too large, that there are too many interactions among the variables, or that the problem is stochastic in nature (i.e., exhibits risk or uncertainty).

Advantages of Simulation

Simulation is used in decision support modeling for the following reasons:

- The theory is fairly straightforward.
- A great amount of *time compression* can be attained, quickly giving a manager some feel as to the long-term (1- to 10-year) effects of many policies.
- Simulation is descriptive rather than normative. This allows the manager to pose what-if questions. Managers can use a trial-and-error approach to problem solving and can do so faster, at less expense, more accurately, and with less risk.
- A manager can experiment to determine which decision variables and which parts of the environment are really important, and with different alternatives.
- An accurate simulation model requires an intimate knowledge of the problem, thus forcing the MSS builder to constantly interact with the manager. This is desirable for DSS development because the developer and manager both gain a better understanding of the problem and the potential decisions available.
- The model is built from the manager's perspective.
- The simulation model is built for one particular problem and typically cannot solve any other problem. Thus, no generalized understanding is required of the manager; every component in the model corresponds to part of the real system.
- Simulation can handle an extremely wide variety of problem types, such as inventory and staffing, as well as higher-level managerial functions, such as long-range planning.
- Simulation generally can include the real complexities of problems; simplifications are not necessary. For example, simulation can use real probability distributions rather than approximate theoretical distributions.
- Simulation automatically produces many important performance measures.
- Simulation is often the only DSS modeling method that can readily handle relatively unstructured problems.
- Some relatively easy-to-use simulation packages (e.g., Monte Carlo simulation) are available. These include add-in spreadsheet packages (e.g., @RISK), influence diagram software, Java-based (and other Web development) packages, and the visual interactive simulation systems to be discussed shortly.

Disadvantages of Simulation

The primary disadvantages of simulation are as follows:

- An optimal solution cannot be guaranteed, but relatively good ones generally are found.
- Simulation model construction can be a slow and costly process, although newer modeling systems are easier to use than ever.
- Solutions and inferences from a simulation study are usually not transferable to other problems because the model incorporates unique problem factors.
- Simulation is sometimes so easy to explain to managers that analytic methods are often overlooked.
- Simulation software sometimes requires special skills because of the complexity of the formal solution method.

The Methodology of Simulation

Simulation involves setting up a model of a real system and conducting repetitive experiments on it. The methodology consists of the following steps, as shown in Figure 10.4:

1. ***Define the problem.*** We examine and classify the real-world problem, specifying why a simulation approach is appropriate. The system's boundaries, environment, and other such aspects of problem clarification are handled here.
2. ***Construct the simulation model.*** This step involves determination of the variables and their relationships, as well as data gathering. Often the process is described by using a flowchart, and then a computer program is written.
3. ***Test and validate the model.*** The simulation model must properly represent the system being studied. Testing and validation ensure this.
4. ***Design the experiment.*** When the model has been proven valid, an experiment is designed. Determining how long to run the simulation is part of this step. There are two important and conflicting objectives: accuracy and cost. It is also prudent to identify typical (e.g., mean and median cases for random variables), best-case (e.g., low-cost, high-revenue), and worst-case (e.g., high-cost, low-revenue) scenarios. These help establish the ranges of the decision variables and environment in which to work and also assist in debugging the simulation model.
5. ***Conduct the experiment.*** Conducting the experiment involves issues ranging from random-number generation to result presentation.

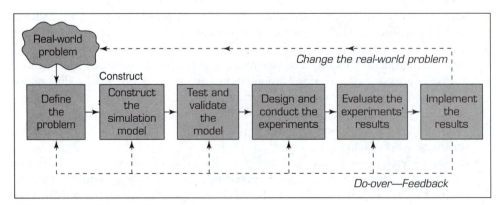

FIGURE 10.4 The Process of Simulation.

6. ***Evaluate the results.*** The results must be interpreted. In addition to standard statistical tools, sensitivity analyses also can be used.

7. ***Implement the results.*** The implementation of simulation results involves the same issues as any other implementation. However, the chances of success are better because the manager is usually more involved with the simulation process than with other models. Higher levels of managerial involvement generally lead to higher levels of implementation success.

Banks and Gibson (2009) presented some useful advice about simulation practices. For example, they list the following seven issues as the common mistakes committed by simulation modelers. The list, though not exhaustive, provides general directions for professionals working on simulation projects.

- Focusing more on the model than on the problem
- Providing point estimates
- Not knowing when to stop
- Reporting what the client wants to hear rather than what the model results say
- Lack of understanding of statistics
- Confusing cause and effect
- Failure to replicate reality

In a follow-up article they provide additional guidelines. The reader should consult this article: **analytics-magazine.org/spring-2009/205-software-solutions-the-abcs-of-simulation-practice.html**

Simulation Types

As we have seen, simulation and modeling are used when pilot studies and experimenting with real systems are expensive or sometimes impossible. Simulation models allow us to investigate various interesting scenarios before making any investment. In fact, in simulations, the real-world operations are mapped into the simulation model. The model consists of relationships and, consequently, equations that all together present the real-world operations. The results of a simulation model, then, depend on the set of parameters given to the model as inputs.

There are various simulation paradigms such as Monte Carlo simulation, discrete event, agent based, or system dynamics. One of the factors that determine the type of simulation technique is the level of abstraction in the problem. Discrete events and agent-based models are usually used for middle or low levels of abstraction. They usually consider individual elements such as people, parts, and products in the simulation models, whereas systems dynamics is more appropriate for aggregate analysis.

In the following sections, we introduce several major types of simulation: probabilistic simulation, time-dependent and time-independent simulation, visual simulation, system dynamics modeling, and agent-based modeling.

PROBABILISTIC SIMULATION   In probabilistic simulation, one or more of the independent variables (e.g., the demand in an inventory problem) are probabilistic. They follow certain probability distributions, which can be either discrete distributions or continuous distributions:

- *Discrete distributions* involve a situation with a limited number of events (or variables) that can take on only a finite number of values.
- *Continuous distributions* are situations with unlimited numbers of possible events that follow density functions, such as the normal distribution.

The two types of distributions are shown in Table 10.1.

TABLE 10.1 Discrete Versus Continuous Probability Distributions

Daily Demand	Discrete Probability	Continuous Probability
5	.10	Daily demand is normally distributed with a mean of 7 and a standard deviation of 1.2.
6	.15	
7	.30	
8	.25	
9	.20	

TIME-DEPENDENT VERSUS TIME-INDEPENDENT SIMULATION   *Time-independent* refers to a situation in which it is not important to know exactly when the event occurred. For example, we may know that the demand for a certain product is three units per day, but we do not care *when* during the day the item is demanded. In some situations, time may not be a factor in the simulation at all, such as in steady-state plant control design. However, in waiting-line problems applicable to e-commerce, it is important to know the precise time of arrival (to know whether the customer will have to wait). This is a *time-dependent* situation.

Monte Carlo Simulation

In most business decision problems, we usually employ one of the following two types of probabilistic simulations. The most common simulation method for business decision problems is **Monte Carlo simulation**. This method usually begins with building a model of the decision problem without having to consider the uncertainty of any variables. Then we recognize that certain parameters or variables are uncertain or follow an assumed or estimated probability distribution. This estimation is based upon analysis of past data. Then we begin running sampling experiments. Running sampling experiments consists of generating random values of uncertain parameters and then computing values of the variables that are impacted by such parameters or variables. These sampling experiments essentially amount to solving the same model hundreds or thousands of times. Then we can analyze the behavior of these dependent or performance variables by examining their statistical distributions. This method has been used in simulations of physical as well as business systems. A good public tutorial on the Monte Carlo simulation method is available on **Palisade.com** (**palisade.com/risk/monte_carlo_simulation.asp**). Palisade markets @RISK, a popular spreadsheet-based Monte Carlo simulation software. Another popular software in this category has been Crystal Ball, now marketed by Oracle as Oracle Crystal Ball. Of course, it is also possible to build and run Monte Carlo experiments within an Excel spreadsheet without using any add-on software such as the two just mentioned. But these tools make it more convenient to run such experiments in Excel-based models. Monte Carlo simulation models have been used in many commercial applications. Examples include Procter & Gamble using these models to determine hedging foreign-exchange risks; Lilly using the model for deciding optimal plant capacity; Abu Dhabi Water and Electricity Company using @Risk for forecasting water demand in Abu Dhabi; and literally thousands of other actual case studies. Each of the simulation software companies' Web sites includes many such success stories.

One DSS modeling language Planners Lab that was mentioned in Chapter 2 (and is available online for free for academic use) also includes significant Monte Carlo simulation capabilities. The reader is urged to review the online tutorial for Planners Lab to appreciate how easy it can be to build and run Monte Carlo simulation models for analyzing the uncertainty in a problem.

Discrete Event Simulation

Discrete event simulation refers to building a model of a system where the interaction between different entities is studied. The simplest example of this is a shop consisting of a server and customers. By modeling the customers arriving at various rates and the server serving at various rates, we can estimate the average performance of the system, waiting time, the number of waiting customers, etc. Such systems are viewed as collections of customers, queues, and servers. There are thousands of documented applications of discrete event simulation models in engineering, business, etc. Tools for building discrete event simulation models have been around for a long time, but these have evolved to take advantage of developments in graphical capabilities for building and understanding the results of such simulation models. We will discuss this modeling method further in the next section.

VISUAL SIMULATION The graphical display of computerized results, which may include animation, is one of the most successful developments in computer–human interaction and problem solving. We describe this in the next section.

SECTION 10.4 REVIEW QUESTIONS

1. List the characteristics of simulation.
2. List the advantages and disadvantages of simulation.
3. List and describe the steps in the methodology of simulation.
4. List and describe the types of simulation.

10.5 VISUAL INTERACTIVE SIMULATION

We next examine methods that show a decision maker a representation of the decision-making situation in action as it runs through scenarios of the various alternatives. These powerful methods overcome some of the inadequacies of conventional methods and help build trust in the solution attained because they can be visualized directly.

Conventional Simulation Inadequacies

Simulation is a well-established, useful, descriptive, mathematics-based method for gaining insight into complex decision-making situations. However, simulation does not usually allow decision makers to see how a solution to a complex problem evolves over (compressed) time, nor can decision makers interact with the simulation (which would be useful for training purposes and teaching). Simulation generally reports statistical results at the end of a set of experiments. Decision makers are thus not an integral part of simulation development and experimentation, and their experience and judgment cannot be used directly. If the simulation results do not match the intuition or judgment of the decision maker, a *confidence gap* in the results can occur.

Visual Interactive Simulation

Visual interactive simulation (VIS), also known as **visual interactive modeling (VIM)** and *visual interactive problem solving*, is a simulation method that lets decision makers see what the model is doing and how it interacts with the decisions made, as they are made. The technique has been used with great success in operations management DSS. The user can employ his or her knowledge to determine and try different decision strategies while interacting with the model. Enhanced learning, about both the problem and the impact of the alternatives tested, can and does occur. Decision makers also contribute to model validation. Decision makers who use VIS generally support and trust their results.

VIS uses animated computer graphic displays to present the impact of different managerial decisions. It differs from regular graphics in that the user can adjust the decision-making process and see the results of the intervention. A visual model is a graphic used as an integral part of decision making or problem solving, not just as a communication device. Some people respond better than others to graphical displays, and this type of interaction can help managers learn about the decision-making situation.

VIS can represent static or dynamic systems. Static models display a visual image of the result of one decision alternative at a time. Dynamic models display systems that evolve over time, and the evolution is represented by animation. The latest visual simulation technology has been coupled with the concept of virtual reality, where an artificial world is created for a number of purposes, from training to entertainment to viewing data in an artificial landscape. For example, the U.S. military uses VIS systems so that ground troops can gain familiarity with terrain or a city in order to very quickly orient themselves. Pilots also use VIS to gain familiarity with targets by simulating attack runs. The VIS software can also include GIS coordinates.

Visual Interactive Models and DSS

VIM in DSS has been used in several operations management decisions. The method consists of priming (like priming a water pump) a visual interactive model of a plant (or company) with its current status. The model then runs rapidly on a computer, allowing managers to observe how a plant is likely to operate in the future.

Waiting-line management (queuing) is a good example of VIM. Such a DSS usually computes several measures of performance for the various decision alternatives (e.g., waiting time in the system). Complex waiting-line problems require simulation. VIM can display the size of the waiting line as it changes during the simulation runs and can also graphically present the answers to what-if questions regarding changes in input variables. Application Case 10.4 gives an example of a visual simulation that was used to explore the applications of RFID technology in developing new scheduling rules in a manufacturing setting.

Application Case 10.4

Improving Job-Shop Scheduling Decisions Through RFID: A Simulation-Based Assessment

A manufacturing services provider of complex optical and electro-mechanical components seeks to gain efficiency in its job-shop scheduling decision because the current shop-floor operations suffer from a few issues:

- There is no system to record when the work-in-process (WIP) items actually arrive at or leave operating workstations and how long those WIPs actually stay at each workstation.

- The current system cannot monitor or keep track of the movement of each WIP in the production line in real time.

As a result, the company is facing two main issues at this production line: high backlogs and high costs of overtime to meet the demand. Additionally, the upstream cannot respond to unexpected incidents such as changes in demand or material shortages quickly enough and revise schedules in a cost-effective manner. The company is considering implementing RFID on a production line. A discrete event simulation program is then developed to examine how track and traceability through RFID can facilitate job-shop production scheduling activities.

The visibility-based scheduling (VBS) rule that utilizes the real-time traceability systems to track those WIPs, parts and components, and raw materials in shop-floor operations is proposed. A simulation approach is applied to examine the benefit of the VBS rule against the classical scheduling rules: the first-in-first-out (FIFO) and earliest due date (EDD) dispatching rules. The simulation model is developed using Simio™. Simio is a 3D simulation modeling software package that employs an object-oriented approach to modeling and has recently been used in many areas such as factories, supply chains, healthcare, airports, and service systems.

Figure 10.5 presents a screenshot of the SIMIO interface panel of this production line. The parameter estimates used for the initial state in the simulation model include weekly demand and forecast, process flow, number of workstations, number of shop-floor operators, and operating time at each workstation. Additionally, parameters of some of the input data such as RFID tagging time, information retrieving time, or system updating time are estimated from a pilot study and from the subject matter experts. Figure 10.6 presents the process view of the simulation model where specific simulation commands are implemented and coded. Figures 10.7 and 10.8 present the standard report view and pivot grid report of the simulation model. The standard report and pivot grid format provide a very quick method to find specific statistical results such as average, percent, total, maximum, or minimum values of variables assigned and captured as an output of the simulation model.

The results of the simulation suggest that an RFID-based scheduling rule generates better performance compared to traditional scheduling rules with regard to processing time, production time, resource utilization, backlogs, and productivity.

Source: Based on J. Chongwatpol and R. Sharda, "RFID-Enabled Track and Traceability in Job-Shop Scheduling Environment," *European Journal of Operational Research*, Vol. 227, No. 3 , pp. 453–463, **2013 http://dx.doi.org/10.1016/j.ejor.2013.01.009**.

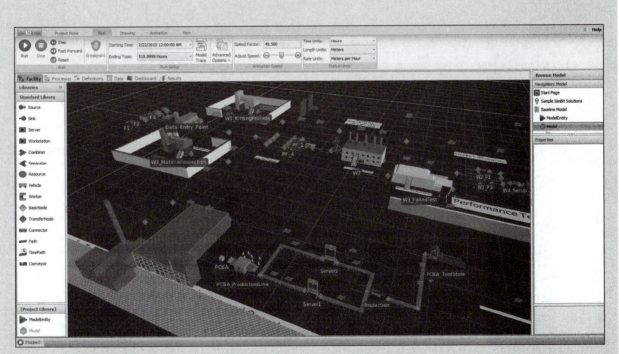

FIGURE 10.5 SIMIO Interface View of the Simulation System.

(Continued)

Application Case 10.4 (Continued)

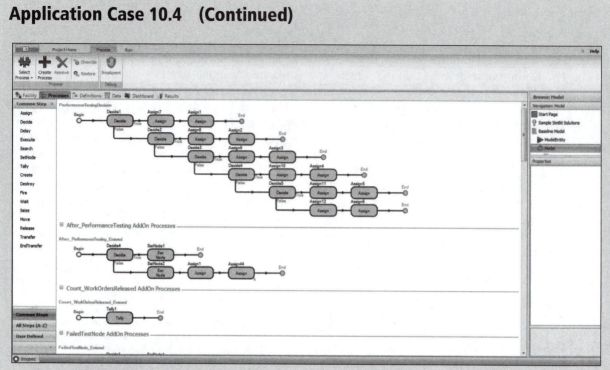

FIGURE 10.6 Process View of the Simulation Model.

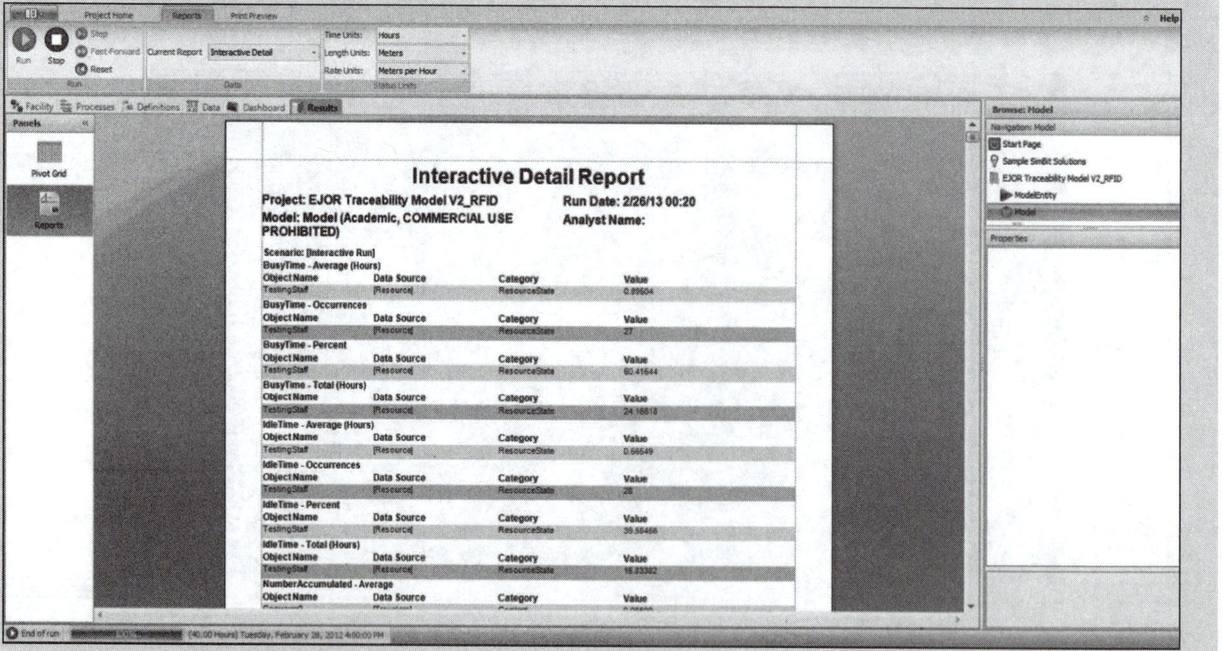

FIGURE 10.7 Standard Report View.

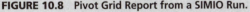

Object Type	Object Name	Data Source	Category	Data Item	Statistic	Average Total
Combiner	PCBABoardAssembl...	[Resource]	Capacity	ScheduledUtiliz...	Percent	30.2941
				UnitsAllocated	Total	291.0000
				UnitsScheduled	Average	1.0000
					Maximum	1.0000
				UnitsUtilized	Average	0.3029
					Maximum	1.0000
			ResourceState	ProcessingTime	Average (Hours)	0.0416
					Occurrences	291.0000
					Percent	30.2941
					Total (Hours)	12.1176
				StarvedTime	Average (Hours)	0.0955
					Occurrences	292.0000
					Percent	69.7059
					Total (Hours)	27.8824
		Batching	MemberQueue	NumberWaiting	Average	0.6816
					Maximum	1.0000
				TimeWaiting	Average (Hours)	0.0904
					Maximum (Hours)	1.9591
					Minimum (Hours)	0.0000
			ParentQueue	NumberWaiting	Average	38.1148
					Maximum	260.0000
				TimeWaiting	Average (Hours)	5.2391
					Maximum (Hours)	11.5623
					Minimum (Hours)	0.0000
		MemberInputBuffer	Content	NumberInStation	Average	0.6816
					Maximum	1.0000
			HoldingTime	TimeInStation	Average (Hours)	0.0904
					Maximum (Hours)	1.9591

FIGURE 10.8   Pivot Grid Report from a SIMIO Run.

The VIM approach can also be used in conjunction with artificial intelligence. Integration of the two techniques adds several capabilities that range from the ability to build systems graphically to learning about the dynamics of the system. These systems, especially those developed for the military and the video-game industry, have "thinking" characters who can behave with a relatively high level of intelligence in their interactions with users.

Simulation Software

Hundreds of simulation packages are available for a variety of decision-making situations. Many run as Web-based systems. *ORMS Today* publishes a periodic review of simulation software. One recent review is located at **orms-today.org/surveys/Simulation/ Simulation.html** (accessed February 2013). PC software packages include Analytica

(Lumina Decision Systems, **lumina.com**) and the Excel add-ins Crystal Ball (now sold by Oracle as Oracle Crystal Ball, **oracle.com**) and @RISK (Palisade Corp., **palisade. com**). A major commercial software for discrete event simulation has been Arena (sold by Rockwell Intl., **arenasimulation.com**). Original developers of Arena have now developed Simio (**simio.com**), which was used in the screens shown above. Another popular discrete event VIS software is ExtendSim (**extendsim.com**). SAS has a graphical analytics software package called JMP that also includes a simulation component in it.

For information about simulation software, see the Society for Modeling and Simulation International (**scs.org**) and the annual software surveys at *ORMS Today* (**orms-today.com**).

SECTION 10.5 REVIEW QUESTIONS

1. Define *visual simulation* and compare it to conventional simulation.
2. Describe the features of VIS (i.e., VIM) that make it attractive for decision makers.
3. How can VIS be used in operations management?
4. How is an animated film like a VIS application?

10.6 SYSTEM DYNAMICS MODELING

System dynamics was introduced in the opening vignette as a powerful method of analysis. System dynamics models are macro-level simulation models in which aggregate values and trends are considered. The objective is to study the overall behavior of a system over time, rather than the behavior of each individual participant or player in the system. The other major key dimension is the evolution of the various components of the system over time and as a result of interplay between the components over time. System dynamics (SD) was first introduced by Forrester (1958) to address problems in industrial systems. He later expanded his work and used system dynamics to model and simulate a classic supply chain (1961). Since then, system dynamics has contributed to theory building, problem solving, and research methodology. SD has been used with operations research and management science approaches (Angerhofer & Angelides, 2000) where SD and operations research are considered complementary techniques in which SD can provide a more qualitative analysis for understanding a system, while operations research techniques build analytical models of the problem. System dynamics has been used extensively in the area of information technology, which usually changes an organization's business processes and behavior. Using system dynamics, possible changes in organizations are projected and analyzed through conceptual models and simulations. The SD technique also has been used in evaluating IT investments: Marquez and Blanchar (2006) developed a system dynamics model to analyze a variety of investment strategies in a high-tech company. Their simulation allows them to analyze strategies and trade-offs that are hard to investigate in real cases. A system dynamics model can capture IT benefits that are sometimes nonlinear and achieved over years.

To create an SD model, we need to draw causal loop diagrams for all processes that lead to some benefits. This is a qualitative step in which the processes, variables, and relationships within the conceptual model are identified. These causal loop diagrams are then transformed into mathematical equations that represent the relations among variables. The equations and stock and flow diagrams are then used to simulate different practical and theoretical scenarios.

Causal loop diagrams show the relationships between variables in a system. A link between two elements shows that changes in one element lead to changes in the other one. The direction of the link shows the direction of influence between two elements. The sign of each arrow shows the direction of change between each pair of elements.

A positive sign means both elements change in the same direction while a negative sign means the elements change in opposite directions. Feedback processes in the **causal loops** are the key components by which a variable re-affects itself over time through a chain of causal relationships.

We illustrate a basic application of system dynamics modeling through a partial model of the impact of electronic health record (EHR) systems. This is based on Kasiri, Sharda, and Asamoah (2010). Implementing electronic health record (EHR) systems is on the agenda for many healthcare organizations in the next few years. Before investing in an EHR system, however, decision makers need to identify and measure the benefits of such systems. Using a system dynamics approach, it is possible to map complex relationships among healthcare processes into a model by which one can dynamically measure the effect of any changes in the parameters over time. Simulation of EHR implementations using a system dynamics model produces useful data on the benefits of EHRs that are hard to obtain through empirical data collection methods. The results of an SD model can then be transformed into economic values to estimate financial performance.

Let us consider some of the factors that impact healthcare delivery in the hospital as a result of the implementation of an electronic health records system. The causal loop diagram in Figure 10.9 shows how different processes and variables interrelate in an electronic health records system to offer significant benefits to healthcare delivery. The sign on each arrow indicates the direction of change between each pair of elements. A positive relationship means both elements change in the same direction while a negative relationship means the elements change in opposite directions.

Electronic notes (e-notes) and electronic prescribing (e-Rx) are shown as two common processes in EHRs that contribute to an increase in the amount of staff time saved

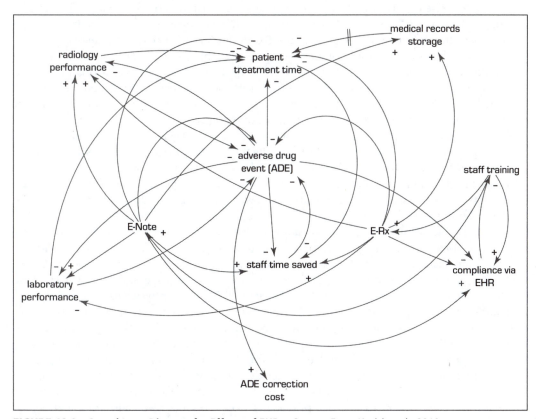

FIGURE 10.9 **Causal Loop Diagram for Effects of EHR.** *Source:* From Kasiri et al., 2010.

(McGowan et al., 2008). They also contribute to a decrease in patient treatment time, which is the time it takes for a patient to receive medical assistance starting from initial contact with the receptionist to the time he or she leaves the hospital after receiving medical care from the physician and other hospital staff. The average increase in patient treatment time as a result of adverse drug events (ADEs) is 1.74 per occurrence (Classen et al., 1997). According to Anderson (2002), entering records directly entered into computer-based medical information systems contributes to increased quality of care and reduces costs related to ADEs. Hence, instead of paper notes and paper prescriptions, doctors can reduce costs when notes on patients and prescriptions are entered directly into the EHR system. Quality of care is directly affected by the amount of time a patient spends at the hospital. Based on the diagram in Figure 10.9, there is a positive link between e-note and staff time saved as well as e-Rx and staff time saved. This indicates that the more physicians use the EHR system, the less time nurses and other staff need to manually retrieve records and files on patients in order to offer medical support to them; in fact, there is no need to transfer files and paper documents from one department to another physically. Staff can therefore transfer the time saved on dealing with documentation to having direct contact with the patients and, hence, improve the quality of healthcare given to patients and decrease ADEs.

E-note and e-Rx also impact the occurrence of adverse drug events (Garrido, 2005; McGowan et al., 2008). The more the system is utilized to record notes on patients and to write prescriptions, the fewer the mistakes in the administration of drugs that stem directly from inefficiencies in manual drug administration processes. Hence, patients spend less time at the hospital as a result of not having to deal with delays related to complications that could occur with paper notes and paper prescriptions. Also, "staff time saved" is increased because the time needed to correct the mistakes related to ADEs is eliminated. The occurrence of ADEs in hospitals is estimated to be an average of 6.5 events per 100 hospitals (Bates et al., 1995; Leape et al., 1995). Subsequently, when the ADE rate decreases through the use of e-note and e-Rx, ADE correction costs also decrease.

The electronic records storage (e-storage) variable refers to the capability to store records in the hospital that otherwise would have been stored in paper format. E-storage is important because it helps in easy retrieval of medical records of patients even after many years. For instance, EHR enables the use of e-note and e-Rx, electronic forms of paper notes and paper prescriptions, which are easier to store and retrieve than are data in hard-copy formats. Hence, EHR helps facilitate the storage and retrieval of health records. Access to the patient's electronic health records helps physicians easily make decisions and diagnoses based on past records. The delay link from e-storage to patient treatment time indicates that patients can be taken care of much faster if electronic data that offer quicker retrieval are available. Uncertainty in clinical decision making on the part of physicians is greatly reduced as a result of e-storage capability (Garrido, 2005). Of course, electronic storage of this data is enhanced by greater use of e-Rx and e-note.

Hospitals are required to comply with certain standards regarding the administration of medication and other related healthcare administration processes (Sidorov, 2006). Certain drugs may be restricted, and the amount given to a particular patient must be closely watched at any period in time by staff. With EHR, physicians can easily track patients' records to know how much has been given and what amount is yet to be given. If an attempt is made to prescribe an amount that is more than the requisite amount for that particular patient, a "red flag message" can be generated to warn the physician of the imminent breach in compliance. In this way, it is easier to comply with regulations regarding the dispensing of a particular medicine and ensure that the maximum amount that is supposed to be given to the patient is not exceeded. Also, rules can be set in the EHR system to prevent physicians from prescribing certain combinations of drugs because of negative reactions such combinations may cause. If a particular rule is violated during e-prescribing, a warning message can be immediately generated to warn the physician of the imminent danger. ADEs that may occur as a result of incorrect amounts and combinations of drugs given can hence be minimized.

The likelihood that any information system in an organization will be used is closely related to how well the users are trained in using the system. Hence, when staff, including nurses, physicians, and lab assistants, are given adequate periodic training, the use and acceptance of e-Rx, e-note, and the EHR system in general increases. Training also leads to greater compliance with standards.

In addition, when EHR is integrated with other healthcare delivery departments such as the radiology and laboratory departments, their performance level is increased. Greater efficiency in the radiology and laboratory departments leads to fewer ADEs and shorter patient treatment times. Also, using EHR reduces the rate of duplication in radiology work and provides quicker access to radiology records and, hence, directly increases the savings in staff time. With the EHR system, a functional department like the radiology department can directly access the patient's x-ray order through the e-note functionality. Hence, mistakes related to incorrect interpretation of physicians' handwritten orders can be avoided, leading to a decrease in patient treatment time at the hospital.

The causal loop diagram shows various benefits of EHRs such as lower rate of ADEs, higher amounts of staff time saved, and lower patient treatment times. In the next section, we develop a stock and flow diagram with loops that reflect some of the most important factors that impact the flows. These relationships and effects can be translated into mathematical equations for simulation purposes. Based on estimated parameters and initial values, we simulate the model and discuss the results.

Because the goal of this section is only to introduce some concepts of system dynamics simulation, we will not go into all the details of the technique. Once the causal loop diagrams are built, one can build the stock and flow diagrams, which lead to developing the mathematical equations for simulating the behavior of the underlying system under study. Results can provide considerable insight into the growing behavior of the system under consideration. In another project, Kasiri and Sharda (2012), for example, studied the effects of introducing radio-frequency identification (RFID) tags in retail stores on each item. They built system dynamics models to identify impacts of such technology in a retail store—increased visibility of information about what is on the shelves leading to a decrease in inventory inaccuracy, better pricing management, etc. Industry participants were able to provide inputs on such effects to be able to build models for investment decisions.

Many software tools are now available for building system dynamics models. Such listings are usually updated on Wikipedia and other sites. Some of the popular tools that include academic and commercial pricings include VenSim, Vissim, and many others. One free software, Insightmaker, appears to offer both system dynamics and agent-based modeling capabilities in its Web version.

SECTION 10.6 REVIEW QUESTIONS

1. What is the key difference between system dynamics simulation and other simulation types?
2. What is the purpose of a causal loop diagram?
3. How are relationships between two variables represented in a causal loop diagram?

10.7 AGENT-BASED MODELING

The term *agent* is derived from the concept of agency, referring to employing someone to act on one's behalf. A human agent represents a person and interacts with others to accomplish a predefined task. The concept of agents goes surprisingly far back.

More than 60 years ago, Vannevar Bush envisioned a machine called a *memex*. He imagined the memex assisting humans to manage and process huge amounts of data and information.

Agent-based modeling (ABM) is a simulation modeling technique to support complex decision systems where a system or network is modeled as a set of autonomous decision-making units called *agents* that individually evaluate their situation and make decisions on the basis of a set of predefined behavior and interaction rules. This technique is a bottom-up approach to modeling complex systems particularly suitable for understanding evolving and dynamic systems. An ABM approach focuses on modeling an "adaptive learning" property rather than "optimizing" nature. Characteristics such as heterogeneity, rule of thumb, or optimization strategies and adaptive learning leading to new capabilities in the system can be defined as a set of rules and behaviors. Also, ABM is able to capture emergent phenomena that exhibit as a result of interacting components of a system with each other, and influencing each other through these interactions. These kinds of characteristics make a system difficult to understand and predict and inherently more unstable. Flocks of birds, social dynamics of science, and the birth and decline of disciplines (Sun, Kaur, et al., 2013), traffic jams and crowds simulation, ant colony, financial contagion, movements of ancient societies (2005), housing segregation and other urban issues (Crooks, 2010), disease propagation (Carley, Altman, et al., 2004), and operations management problems (Caridi and Cavalieri, 2004; Allwood and Lee, 2005, 2008) are some past applications of ABMs. For business problems in which many interrelated factors, irregular data, and high uncertainty and emergent behaviors exist, interactions between agents are complex, discrete, or nonlinear, the population is heterogeneous, agents exhibit learning and adaptive behaviors and also spatial issues, or social networks are of interest, agent-based modeling can be used.

According to the framework developed by Macal and North (2005), to build an agent-based model, the following steps should be taken. First of all, it should be questioned what specific problem should be solved by the model, and particularly what values agent-based modeling brings to the problem that the other problem-solving approaches cannot bring. The second step includes identifying the agents and getting a theory of agent behavior. What agents should be included in the model, who are the decision makers in the system, which agents have behaviors? What kinds of data on agents are available? Is it simply descriptive (static attributes)? Or does it have to be calculated endogenously by the model and informed to the agents (dynamic attributes)? Third, the agent relationships should be identified and a theory of agent interaction should be taken into account. That is, the agents' environment should be studied to determine how the agents interact with the environment, what agent behaviors are of interest, what behavior and interaction rules the agent creates and follows, what decisions the agents make, and what behaviors or actions are being acted upon by the agents. Next, the required agent-related data should be collected. Finally, the performance of the agent-based system should be validated against reality either at the individual agent level or the model as a whole; particularly, the agent behaviors should be examined.

Agent-based modeling can be implemented either using general programing languages or through some specially designed applications that address the requirements of agent modeling. Among agent-based platforms, SWARM (**www.swarms.org**), Netlogo (**http://ccl.northwestern.edu/netlogo**), RePast/Sugarscape (**www.repast.sourceforge.net**), and Escape (**www.metascapeabm.com**) provide an appropriate graphical user interface and comprehensive documentation (Railsback, Lytinen, et al., 2006). Application Case 10.5 describes a really useful application of agent-based modeling to simulate effects of disease mitigation strategies.

Application Case 10.5

Agent-Based Simulation Helps Analyze Spread of a Pandemic Outbreak

Knowledge about the spread of a disease plays an important role in both preparing for and responding to a pandemic outbreak. Previous models for such analyses are mostly homogenous and make use of simplistic assumptions about transmission and the infection rates. These models assume that each individual in the population is identical and typically has the same number of potential contacts with an infected individual in the same time period. Also each infected individual is assumed to have the same probability to transmit the disease. Using these models, implementing any mitigation strategies to vaccinate the susceptible individuals and treating the infected individuals become extremely difficult under limited resources.

In order to effectively choose and implement a mitigation strategy, modeling of the disease spread has to be done across the specific set of individuals, which enables researchers to prioritize the selection of individuals to be treated first and also gauge the effectiveness of mitigation strategy.

Although nonhomogenous models for spread of a disease can be built based on individual characteristics using the interactions in a contact network, such individual levels of infectivity and vulnerability require complex mathematics to obtain the information needed for such models.

Simulation techniques can be used to generate hypothetical outcomes of disease spread by simulating events on the basis of hourly, daily, or other periods and tallying the outcomes throughout the simulation. A nonhomogenous agent-based simulation approach allows each member of the population to be simulated individually, considering the unique individual characteristics that affect the transmission and infection probabilities. Furthermore, individual behaviors that affect the type and length of contact between individuals, and the possibility of infected individuals recovering and becoming immune, can also be simulated via **agent-based models**.

One such simulation model, built for the Ontario Agency for Health Protection and Promotion (OAHPP) following the global outbreak of severe acute respiratory syndrome (SARS) in 2002–2003, simulated the spread of disease by applying various

mitigation strategies. The simulation models each state of an individual in each time unit, based on the individual probabilities to transition from susceptible state to infected stage and then to recovered state and back to susceptible state. The simulation model also uses an individual's duration of contact with infected individuals. The model also accounts for the rate of disease transmission per time unit based on the type of contact between individuals and for behavioral changes of individuals in a disease progression (being quarantined or treated or recovered). It is flexible enough to consider several factors affecting the mitigation strategy, such as an individual's age, residence, level of general interaction with other members of population, number of individuals in each household, distribution of households, and behavioral aspects involving daily commutes, attendance at schools, and asymptotic time period of disease.

The simulation model was tested to measure the effectiveness of a mitigation strategy involving an advertising campaign that urged individuals who have symptoms of disease to stay at home rather than commute to work or school. The model was based on a pandemic influenza outbreak in the greater Toronto area. Each individual agent, generated from the population, was sequentially assigned to households. Individuals were also assigned to different ages based on census age distribution; all other pertinent demographic and behavioral attributes were assigned to the individuals.

The model considered two types of contact: close contact, which involved members of the same household or commuters on the public transport; and causal contact, which involved random individuals among the same census tract. Influenza pandemic records provided past disease transmission data, including transmission rates and contact time for both close and causal contacts. The effect of public transportation was simplified with an assumption that every individual of working age used the nearest subway line to travel. An initial outbreak of infection was fed into the model. A total of 1,000 such simulations was conducted.

The results from the simulation indicated that there was a significant decrease in the levels of infected

(Continued)

Application Case 10.5 (Continued)

and deceased persons as an increasing number of infected individuals followed the mitigation strategy of staying at home. The results were also analyzed by answering questions that sought to verify issues such as the impact of 20 percent of infected individuals staying at home versus 10 percent staying at home. The results from each of the simulation outputs were fed into geographic information system software, ESRI ArcGIS, and detailed shaded maps of the greater Toronto area, showing the spread of disease based on the average number of cumulative infected individuals. This helped to determine the effectiveness of a particular mitigation strategy. This agent-based simulation model provides a what-if analysis tool that can be used to compare relative outcomes of different disease scenarios and mitigation strategies and help in choosing the effective mitigation strategy.

QUESTIONS FOR DISCUSSION

1. What are the characteristics of an agent-based simulation model?

2. List the various factors that were fed into the agent-based simulation model described in the case.
3. Elaborate on the benefits of using agent-based simulation models.
4. Besides disease prevention, in which other situations could agent-based simulation be employed?

What We Can Learn from This Application Case

Advancements in computing technology allow for building advanced simulation models that are nonhomogeneous in nature and factor for many socio-demographic and behavioral factors. These simulation models further enhance the support for policy decision making by hypothetically simulating many real-time complex problem situations.

Source: D. M. Aleman, T. G. Wibisono, and B. Schwartz, "A Nonhomogeneous Agent-Based Simulation Approach to Modeling the Spread of Disease in a Pandemic Outbreak," *Interfaces*, Vol. 41, No. 3, 2011, pp. 301–315.

Chapter Highlights

- Heuristic programming involves problem solving using general rules or intelligent search.
- Genetic algorithms are search techniques that emulate the natural process of biological evolution. They utilize three basic operations: reproduction, crossover, and mutation.
- Reproduction is a process that creates the next-generation population based on the performance of different cases in the current population.
- Crossover is a process that allows elements in different cases to be exchanged to search for a better solution.
- Mutation is a process that changes an element in a case to search for a better solution.

- Simulation is a widely used DSS approach that involves experimentation with a model that represents the real decision-making situation.
- Simulation can deal with more complex situations than optimization, but it does not guarantee an optimal solution.
- There are many different simulation methods. Some that are important for DSS include Monte Carlo simulation, discrete event simulation, systems dynamics modeling, and agent-based simulations.
- VIS/VIM allows a decision maker to interact directly with a model and shows results in an easily understood manner.

Key Terms

agent-based models
causal loops
discrete event simulation
chromosome
crossover

elitism
evolutionary algorithm
genetic algorithm
heuristic programming
heuristics

Monte Carlo simulation
mutation
reproduction
simulation
system dynamics

visual interactive
    modeling (VIM)
visual interactive
    simulation (VIS)

Questions for Discussion

1. Compare the effectiveness of genetic algorithms against standard methods for problem solving, as described in the literature. How effective are genetic algorithms?
2. Describe the general process of simulation.
3. List some of the major advantages of simulation over optimization and vice versa.
4. What are the advantages of using a spreadsheet package to perform simulation studies? What are the disadvantages?
5. Compare the methodology of simulation to Simon's four-phase model of decision making. Does the methodology of simulation map directly into Simon's model? Explain.
6. Many computer games can be considered visual simulation. Explain why.
7. Explain why VIS is particularly helpful in implementing recommendations derived by computers.

Exercises

Teradata University Network (TUN) and Other Hands-on Exercises

1. Each group in the class should access a different online Java-based Web simulation system (especially those systems from visual interactive simulation vendors) and run it. Write up your experience and present it to the class.
2. Solve the knapsack problem from Section 10.3 manually, and then solve it using Evolver. Try another code (find one on the Web). Finally, develop your own genetic algorithm code in Visual Basic, C++, or Java.
3. Search online to find vendors of genetic algorithms and investigate the business applications of their products. What kinds of applications are most prevalent?
4. Go to **palisade.com** and examine the capabilities of Evolver. Write a summary about your findings.
5. Each group should review, examine, and demonstrate in class a different state-of-the-art DSS software product. The specific packages depend on your instructor and the group interests. You may need to download a demo from a vendor's Web site, depending on your instructor's directions. Be sure to get a running demo version, not a slideshow. Do a half-hour in-class presentation, which should include an explanation of why the software is appropriate for assisting in decision making, a hands-on demonstration of selected important capabilities of the software, and your critical evaluation of the software. Try to make your presentation interesting and instructive to the whole class. The main purpose of the class presentation is for class members to see as much state-of-the-art software as possible, both in breadth (through the presentations by other groups) and in depth (through the experience you have in exploring the ins and outs of one particular software product). Write a 5- to 10-page report on your findings and comments regarding this software. Include screenshots in your report. Would you recommend this software to anyone? Why or why not?

End-of-Chapter Application Case

HP Applies Management Science Modeling to Optimize Its Supply Chain and Wins a Major Award

HP's groundbreaking use of operations research not only enabled the high-tech giant to successfully transform its product portfolio program and return $500 million to the bottom line over a 3-year period, but it also earned HP the coveted 2009 Edelman Award from INFORMS for outstanding achievement in operations research. "This is not the success of just one person or one team," said Kathy Chou, vice president of Worldwide Commercial Sales at HP, in accepting the award on behalf of the winning team. "It's the success of many people across HP who made this a reality, beginning several years ago with mathematics and imagination and what it might do for HP."

To put HP's product portfolio problem into perspective, consider these numbers: HP generates more than $135 billion annually from customers in 170 countries by offering tens of thousands of products supported by the largest supply chain in the industry. You want variety? How about 2,000 laser printers and more than 20,000 enterprise servers and storage products? Want more? HP offers more than 8 million configure-to-order combinations in its notebook and desktop product line alone.

The something-for-everyone approach drives sales, but at what cost? At what point does the price of designing, manufacturing, and introducing yet another new product, feature, or option exceed the additional revenue it is likely to generate? Just as important, what are the costs associated with too much or too little inventory for such a product, not to mention additional supply chain complexity, and how does all of that impact customer satisfaction? According to Chou, HP didn't have good answers to any of those questions before the Edelman award–winning work.

"While revenue grew year over year, our profits were eroded due to unplanned operational costs," Chou said in

HP's formal Edelman presentation. "As product variety grew, our forecasting accuracy suffered, and we ended up with excesses of some products and shortages of others. Our suppliers suffered due to our inventory issues and product design changes. I can personally testify to the pain our customers experienced because of these availability challenges." Chou would know. In her role as VP of Worldwide Commercial Sales, she's "responsible and on the hook" for driving sales, margins, and operational efficiency.

Constantly growing product variety to meet increasing customer needs was the HP way—after all, the company is nothing if not innovative—but the rising costs and inefficiency associated with managing millions of products and configurations "took their toll," Chou said, "and we had no idea how to solve it."

Compounding the problem, Chou added, was HP's "organizational divide." Marketing and sales always wanted more—more SKUs, more features, more configurations—and for good reason. Providing every possible product choice was considered an obvious way to satisfy more customers and generate more sales.

Supply chain managers, however, always wanted less. Less to forecast, less inventory, and less complexity to manage. "The drivers (on the supply chain side) were cost control," Chou said. "Supply chain wanted fast and predictable order cycle times. With no fact-based, data-driven tools, decision making between different parts of the organization was time-consuming and complex due to these differing goals and objectives."

By 2004, HP's average order cycle times in North America were nearly twice that of its competition, making it tough for the company to be competitive despite its large variety of products. Extensive variety, once considered a plus, had become a liability.

It was then that the Edelman prize–winning team—drawn from various quarters both within the organization (HP Business Groups, HP Labs, and HP Strategic Planning and Modeling) and out (individuals from a handful of consultancies and universities) and armed with operations research thinking and methodology—went to work on the problem. Over the next few years, the team: (1) produced an analytically driven process for evaluating new products for introduction, (2) created a tool for prioritizing existing products in a portfolio, and (3) developed an algorithm that solves the problem many times faster than previous technologies, thereby advancing the theory and practice of network optimization.

The team tackled the product variety problem from two angles: prelaunch and postlaunch. "Before we bring a new product, feature, or option to market, we want to evaluate return on investment in order to drive the right investment decisions and maximize profits," Chou said. To do that, HP's Strategic Planning and Modeling Team (SPaM) developed "complexity return on investment screening calculators" that took into account downstream impacts across the HP product line and supply chain that were never properly accounted for before.

Once a product is launched, variety product management shifts from screening to managing a product portfolio as sales data become available. To do that, the Edelman award–winning team developed a tool called revenue coverage optimization (RCO) to analyze more systematically the importance of each new feature or option in the context of the overall portfolio.

The RCO algorithm and the complexity ROI calculators helped HP improve its operational focus on key products, while simultaneously reducing the complexity of its product offerings for customers. For example, HP implemented the RCO algorithm to rank its Personal Systems Group offerings based on the interrelationship between products and orders. It then identified the "core offering," which is composed of the most critical products in each region. This core offering represented about 30 percent of the ranked product portfolio. All other products were classified as HP's "extended offering."

Based on these findings, HP adjusted its service level for each class of products. Core offering products are now stocked in higher inventory levels and are made available with shorter lead times, and extended offering products are offered with longer lead times and are either stocked at lower levels or not at all. The net result: lower costs, higher margins, and improved customer service.

The RCO software algorithm was developed as part of HP Labs' "analytics" theme, which applies mathematics and scientific methodologies to help decision making and create better-run businesses. Analytics is one of eight major research themes of HP Labs, which last year refocused its efforts to address the most complex challenges facing technology customers in the next decade.

"Smart application of analytics is becoming increasingly important to businesses, especially in the areas of operational efficiency, risk management, and resource planning," says Jaap Suermondt, director, Business Optimization Lab, HP Labs. "The RCO algorithm is a fantastic example of an innovation that helps drive efficiency with our businesses and our customers."

In accepting the Edelman Award, Chou emphasized not only the company-wide effort in developing elegant technical solutions to incredibly complex problems, but also the buy-in and cooperation of managers and C-level executives and the wisdom and insight of the award-winning team to engage and share their vision with those managers and executives. "For some of you who have not been a part of a very large organization like HP, this might sound strange, but it required tenacity and skill to bring about major changes in the processes of a company of HP's size," Chou said. "In many of our business [units], project managers took the tools and turned them into new processes and programs that fundamentally changed the way HP manages its product portfolios and bridged the organizational divide."

QUESTIONS FOR THE END-OF-CHAPTER APPLICATION CASE

1. Describe the problem that a large company such as HP might face in offering many product lines and options.
2. Why is there a possible conflict between marketing and operations?
3. Summarize your understanding of the models and the algorithms.
4. Perform an online search to find more details of the algorithms.
5. Why would there be a need for such a system in an organization?
6. What benefits did HP derive from implementation of the models?

Source: Adapted with permission, P. Horner, "Less Is More for HP," *ORMS Today,* Vol. 36, No. 3, June 2009, pp. 40–44.

References

Aleman, D. M., T. G. Wibisono, and B. Schwartz. (2011). "A Nonhomogeneous Agent-Based Simulation Approach to Modeling the Spread of Disease in a Pandemic Outbreak." *Interfaces,* Vol. 41, No. 3, pp. 301–315.

Alfredo, D. M. G., E. N. R. David, M. Cristian, and Z. V. G. Andres. (2011, May/June). "Quantitative Methods for a New Configuration of Territorial Units in a Chilean Government Agency Tender Process." *Interfaces,* Vol. 41, No. 3, pp. 263–277.

Allwood, J. M., and J. H. Lee. (2005). "The Design of an Agent for Modelling Supply Chain Network Dynamics." *International Journal of Production Research,* Vol. 43, No. 22, pp. 4875–4898.

Angerhofer, B. J., and M. C. Angelides. (2000, Winter). "System Dynamics Modeling in Supply Chain Management: Research Review." IEEE, *Simulation Conference, 2000,* Vol. 1, pp. 342–351.

Baker, B. M., and M. A. Syechew. (2003). "A Genetic Algorithm for the Vehicle Routing Problem." *Computers and Operations Research,* Vol. 30, No. 5, pp. 787–800.

Banks, J., and R. R. Gibson. (2009). "Seven Sins of Simulation Practice." *INFORMS Analytics,* pp. 24–27. **www.analytics-magazine.org/summer-2009/193-strategic-problems-modeling-the-market-space** (accessed February 2013).

Bates, D. W., Cullen, D. J., Laird, N., Petersen, L. A., Small, S. D., Servi, D.,… & Edmondson, A. (1995). Incidence of adverse drug events and potential adverse drug events. JAMA: the journal of the American Medical Association, 274(1), 29–34.

Caridi, M., and S. Cavalieri. (2004). "Multi-Agent Systems in Production Planning and Control: An Overview." *Production Planning & Control,* Vol. 15, No. 2, pp. 106–118.

Carley, K. M., et al. (2004). "BioWar: A City-Scale Multi-Agent Network Model of Weaponized Biological Attacks." **http://handle.dtic.mil/100.2/ADA459122.**

Chongwatpol, J., and R. Sharda. (2013). "RFID-Enabled Track and Traceability in Job-Shop Scheduling Environment." *European Journal of Operational Research.*

Classen, D., M. Pestotnik, R. Evans, J. Lloyd, and J. Burke. (1997). "Adverse Drug Events in Hospitalized Patients: Excessive Length of Stay, Extra Cost, and Attributable Mortality." *The Journal of the American Medical Association,* Vol. 277, No. 4, pp. 301–311.

Crooks, A. T. (2010). "Constructing and Implementing an Agent-Based Model of Residential Segregation Through Vector GIS." *International Journal of Geographical Information Science,* Vol. 24, No. 5, pp. 661–675.

Dardan, S., et al. (2006). "An Application of the Learning Curve and the Nonconstant-Growth Dividend Model: IT Investment Valuations at Intel Corporation." *Decision Support Systems,* Vol. 41, No. 4, pp. 688–697.

Garrido, Anderson J. (2002). "Evaluation in Health Informatics: Computer Simulation." *Computers in Biology and Medicine,* Vol. 32, No. 3, pp. 151–164.

Garrido, T., L. Jamieson, Y. Zhou, A. Wiesenthal, and L. Liang. (2005). "Effect of Electronic Health Records in Ambulatory Care: Retrospective, Serial, Cross-Sectional study." *Information in Practice, BJM,* Vol. 330, No. 7491, pp. 1–5.

Godlewski, E., G. Lee, and K. Cooper. (2012). "System Dynamics Transforms Fluor Project and Change Management." *Interfaces,* Vol. 42, No. 1, pp. 17–32.

Grupe, F. H., and S. Jooste. (2004, March). "Genetic Algorithms: A Business Perspective." *Information Management and Computer Security,* Vol. 12, No. 3, pp. 288–297.

Horner, P. (2009, June). "Less Is More for HP." *ORMS Today,* Vol. 36, No. 3, pp. 40–44.

Hutton, D. W., M. L. Brandeau, and S. K. So. (2011). "Doing Good with Good OR: Supporting Cost-Effective Hepatitis B Interventions." *Interfaces,* Vol. 41, No. 3, pp. 289–300.

Kasiri, N., R. Sharda, and D. Asamoah. (2012, June). "Evaluating Electronic Health Record Systems: A System Dynamics Simulation." *SIMULATION,* Vol. 88, No. 6, pp. 639–648.

Leape, L., D. Bates, D. Cullen, J. Cooper, H. Demonaco, T. Gallivan, R. Hallisey, J. Ives, N. Laird, G. Laffel, R. Nemeskal, L. Petersen, K. Porter, D. Servi, B. Shea, S. Small, B. Sweitzer, C. M. Macal, and M. J. North. (2005). "Tutorial on Agent-Based Modeling and Simulation." *Proceedings of the 37th Conference on Winter Simulation.* Orlando, Florida, Winter Simulation Conference, pp. 2–15.

Marquez, A. C., and C. Blanchar. (2006). "A Decision Support System for Evaluating Operations Investments in High-Technology Business." *Decision Support Systems*, Vol. 41, No. 2, pp. 472–487.

Mattila, V., K. Virtanen, and T. Raivio. (2008, May/June). "Improving Maintenance Decision Making in the Finnish Air Force Through Simulation." *Interfaces*, Vol. 38, No. 3, pp. 187–201.

McGowan, J., C. Cusack, and E. Poon. (2008). "Formative Evaluation: A Critical Component in EHR Implementation." *Journal of the American Medical Informatics Association*, Vol. 15, No. 3, pp. 297–301.

Nick, Z., and P. Themis. (2001). "Web Search Using a Genetic Algorithm." *IEEE Internet Computing*, Vol. 5, No. 2.

Railsback, S., et al. (2006). "Agent-Based Simulation Platforms: Review and Development Recommendations." *Simulation*, Vol. 82, No. 9, pp. 609–623.

Shin, K., and Y. Lee. (2002). "A Genetic Algorithm Application in Bankruptcy Prediction Modeling." *Expert Systems with Applications*, Vol. 23, No. 3.

Sidorov, J. (2006). "It Ain't Necessarily So: The Electronic Health Record and the Unlikely Prospect of Reducing Health Care Costs." *Health Affairs*, Vol. 25, No. 4, pp. 1079–1085.

Thompson, B., and M. Vliet. (1995). "Systems Analysis of Adverse Drug Events." *The Journal of the American Medical Association,* Vol. 274, No. 1, pp. 35–43.

Thompson, D. I., J. Osheroff, D. Classen, and D. F. Sittig. (2007). "A Review of Methods to Estimate the Benefits of Electronic Medical Records in Hospitals and the Need for a National Benefits Database." *Healthcare Information and Management Systems Society (HIMSS)*, Vol. 21, No. 1, pp. 62–68.

Walbridge, C. T. (1989, June). "Genetic Algorithms: What Computers Can Learn from Darwin." *Technology Review (USA),* Vol. 92, No. 1.

Xiaoling, S., J. Kaur, S. Milojević, A. Flammini, and F. Menczer. (2013). "Social Dynamics of Science." *Scientific Reports,* Vol. 3, p. 1069.

11

Automated Decision Systems and Expert Systems

LEARNING OBJECTIVES

- Understand the concept and applications of automated rule-based decision systems
- Understand the importance of knowledge in decision support
- Describe the concept and evolution of rule-based expert systems (ES)
- Understand the architecture of rule-based ES

- Learn the knowledge engineering process used to build ES
- Explain the benefits and limitations of rule-based systems for decision support
- Identify proper applications of ES
- Learn about tools and technologies for developing rule-based DSS

This chapter addresses two issues. First, how do some of the analytics technologies including predictive and optimization models get used in practice? In many cases, results of predictive models or even optimization models get simplified as rules that are then implemented in other applications. We call these automated decision systems. Second, in addition to the use of data and mathematical models, some managerial decisions require qualitative information and the judgmental knowledge that resides in the minds of human experts. Therefore, it is necessary to find effective ways to incorporate such information and knowledge into decision support systems (DSS). A system that integrates knowledge from experts is commonly called a knowledge-based decision support system (KBDSS) or an intelligent decision support system (IDSS). A KBDSS can enhance the capabilities of decision support not only by supplying a tool that directly supports a decision maker, but also by enhancing various computerized DSS environments. The foundation for building such systems is the techniques and tools that have been developed in the area of artificial intelligence—rule-based expert systems being the primary one. This chapter introduces the essentials of automated decision systems and provides a detailed description of expert systems.

11.1 OPENING VIGNETTE: InterContinental Hotel Group Uses Decision Rules for Optimal Hotel Room Rates

With 4,437 hotels and 647,161 rooms, InterContinental Hotel Group (IHG) is the world's largest hotel group in terms of number of rooms. About 85 percent of its hotels are franchised, 14 percent are managed, and 1 percent are owned directly by the InterContinental Hotel group. Some of the hotel brands that belong to this group are Holiday Inn, Holiday Express, Staybridge Suites, and Crowne Plaza. Revenue generated from their rooms amounts to around $20 billion. Before the optimization model was implemented, pricing decisions were made based on a complex myriad of variables, some of which were day of the week, seasonality, occupancy level, competition, and customer feedback. These decisions were made without the use of analytics. Price decisions were made with the assumption that demand was independent of the price charged for a room. This fundamental flaw worked well in normal economic conditions. However, when the hospitality industry suffered a decline in revenue, with the challenge posed by the widespread use of the Internet, which introduced multiple distribution channels, IHG started considering and exploring alternative and effective revenue generation methods. The main aim was to increase the revenue per available room (RevPAR).

METHODOLOGY/SOLUTION

IHG rolled out their retail price optimization system to help increase their RevPAR. The large number of hotels was a big challenge to this task. Pricing decisions numbered over 273 million (or 76,000 per hotel) per day. The project resulted in a change of their fundamental business flow. The final model included a demand forecast model, market response model, competitor rates model, and an optimization price model. For each hotel, a price response is calculated by the market response model based on historical data. Price and competitor rates were used to estimate the demand for rooms. The objective function used in this computation turned out to be nonlinear. The input data for the competitor rates model were derived from third-party sources. Decision variables used to determine the best rates for each hotel were based on factors like estimated demand, hotel capacity, current bookings, and prices being charged by competitors. IHG's price optimization system is packaged in a Web application called PERFORM^{sm}.

RESULTS/BENEFITS

There has been widespread adoption of the retail price optimization model by hotel managers globally. PERFORM is used by over 4,000 users worldwide. The retail price optimization model was tested in a couple of IHG's hotels and the results were compared with hotels where the model had not been implemented yet. It was recognized that there was a 2.7 percent increase in RevPAR for hotels where the optimization model had been implemented.

QUESTIONS FOR THE OPENING VIGNETTE

1. Describe the challenges faced by IHG during development of their retail price optimization system.

2. Besides the hotel business in the hospitality industry, explain at least three other areas where an optimization model could be used.

3. What other methods could be used to solve IHG's price optimization problem?

WHAT WE CAN LEARN FROM THIS VIGNETTE

IHG has been doing business using manual price optimization methods for a long time and it seems to have worked for them. However, sometimes business environments change, which renders existing methods of running a business obsolete. IHG used data analytics and mathematical optimization methods to revolutionize revenue management. The price optimization model was a combination of different operations research methods. What is also important is that such decisions are eventually implemented using a decision system that is available to each client hotel. They do not have to know anything about the underlying decision methods to be able to use the recommendations made by the system.

Source: Dev Koushik, Jon A. Higbie, and Craig Eister, "Retail Price Optimization at InterContinental Hotels Group." *Interfaces,* Vol. 42, No. 1, 2012, pp. 45–57.

11.2 AUTOMATED DECISION SYSTEMS

A relatively new approach to supporting decision making is called **automated decision systems (ADS)**, sometimes also known as **decision automation systems** (DAS; see Davenport and Harris, 2005). An ADS is a rule-based system that provides a solution, usually in one functional area (e.g., finance, manufacturing), to a specific repetitive managerial problem, usually in one industry (e.g., to approve or not to approve a request for a loan, to determine the price of an item in a store).

Application Case 11.1 shows an example of applying automated decision systems to a problem that every organization faces—how to price its products or services. In contrast with management science approaches, which provide a model-based solution to generic structured problems (e.g., resource allocation, inventory level determination), ADS provide rule-based solutions. The following are examples of business rules: "If only 70 percent of the seats on a flight from Los Angeles to New York are sold 3 days prior to departure, offer a discount of x to nonbusiness travelers," "If an applicant owns a house and makes over $100,000 a year, offer a $10,000 credit line," and "If an item costs more than $2,000, and if your company buys it only once a year, the purchasing agent does not need special approval." Such rules, which are based on experience or derived through data mining, can be combined with mathematical models to form solutions that can be automatically and instantly applied to problems (e.g., "Based on the information provided and subject to verification, you will be admitted to our university"), or they can be provided to a human, who will make the final decision (see Figure 11.1). ADS attempt to automate highly repetitive decisions (in order to justify the computerization cost), based on business rules. ADS are mostly suitable for frontline employees who can see

Application Case 11.1

Giant Food Stores Prices the Entire Store

Giant Food Stores, LLC, a regional U.S. supermarket chain based in Carlisle, Pennsylvania, had a narrow Every Day Low Price strategy that it applied to most of the products in its stores. The company had a 30-year-old pricing and promotion system that was very labor intensive and that could no longer keep up with the pricing decisions required in the fast-paced grocery market. The system also limited the company's ability to execute more sophisticated pricing strategies.

Giant was interested in executing its pricing strategy more consistently based on a definitive set of pricing rules (pricing rules in retail might include relationships between national brands and private-label brands, relationships between sizes, ending digits such as "9," etc.). In the past, many of the rules were kept on paper, others were kept in people's heads, and some were not documented well enough for others to understand and ensure continuity. The company also had no means of reliably forecasting the impact of rule changes before prices hit the store shelves.

Giant Foods worked with DemandTec to deploy a system for its pricing decisions. The system is able to handle massive amounts of point-of-sale and competitive data to model and forecast consumer demand, as well as automate and streamline complex rules-based pricing schemes. It can handle large numbers of price changes, and it can do so without increasing staff. The system allows Giant Foods to codify pricing rules with "natural language" sentences rather than having to go through a technician. The system also has forecasting capabilities. These capabilities allow Giant Foods to predict the impact of pricing changes and new promotions before they hit the shelves. Giant Foods decided to implement the system for the entire store chain.

The system has allowed Giant Foods to become more agile in its pricing. It is now able to react to competitive pricing changes or vendor cost changes on a weekly basis rather than when resources become available. Giant's productivity has doubled because it no longer has to increase staff for pricing changes. Giant now focuses on "maintaining profitability while satisfying its customer and maintaining its price image."

Source: "Giant Food Stores Prices the Entire Store with DemandTec," DemandTec, **https://mydt.demandtec.com/mydemandtec/c/ document_library/get_file?uuid=3151a5e4-f3e1-413e-9cd7-333289eeb3d5&groupId=264319** (accessed February 2013).

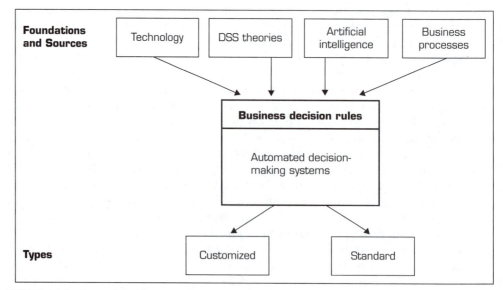

FIGURE 11.1 **General Architecture of Automated Decision Systems.**

the customer information online and frequently must make quick decisions. Davenport and Harris (2005) provide a good introduction to such systems. Dan Power started a Web site **decisionautomation.com** to compile information on such systems. He argues that decision automation systems are really not decision support systems. These types of systems make the decisions in real time or near–real time. Systems that provide credit approval decisions for loan approvals, or quote fares for the next airline flight reservation for a particular flight request, or deal with any other pricing issues are the most common examples of such systems. Application Case 11.1 illustrates use of such systems at many retailers that use such technologies. **Demandtec.com** is now an IBM Company.

ADS initially appeared in the airline industry, where they were called *revenue* (or *yield*) *management* (or revenue optimization) systems. Airlines use these systems to dynamically price tickets based on actual demand. Today, many service industries use similar pricing models.

The building blocks of such intelligent systems are business rules. A business rule can be as simple as saying—"Offer a discount if average sales drop by 10 percent." Once a set of rules are in place governing a decision, a model is built and implemented that is capable of making decisions autonomously. This removes the need for human intervention in making decisions. There might be some external factors or parameters that can cause the model to fail. However, advances in artificial intelligence have led to the creation of adaptable models, capable of adjusting to changes in external parameters.

To put this in perspective, almost all airlines have automated decision systems to assign dynamic prices based on demand. If it were left to a human being to analyze trends and travel patterns to generate prices, it would probably take a very long time, and the price would not cater to the trend.

All airlines have three major information systems closely integrated together: (1) pricing and accounting systems, (2) aircraft scheduling systems, and (3) inventory management systems. To manage this whole ecosystem, skilled individuals are hired possessing skillsets varying from operations management to business analytics to data warehousing. These individuals are assigned one of the most important tasks in running a successful airline—revenue management.

How does an airline go from processing inventory data, airport schedules, and customer demand to aircraft selection/scheduling and boarding? Revenue management planners (RM Planners) play a key role in running this whole process of keeping the airline profitable, while offering best possible prices and customer service. The most important entity in this process is the customer. In an ideal situation, prices and schedules are driven by customer demand. However, forecasting customer demand is an extremely complex process involving thousands of possibilities. As a general practice, past demand is used to predict future demand, which is not always accurate. With the growth of low-cost carriers (LCCs), booking patterns change drastically from time to time. Customers are able to purchase tickets at low prices, within a week of departure, which creates a forecasting nightmare. The airlines use average demand levels to decide prices and make adjustments whenever necessary.

Recognizing the nature of a customer is extremely important to an airline. Leisure passengers are price sensitive but are willing to adapt to a flexible schedule for a lower price. These passengers are willing to commit to a reservation in advance. Business passengers, on the other hand, are extremely time sensitive and are willing to pay a higher price to get to the destination on time. Also, they are not likely to commit to a reservation in advance, and they prefer last-minute availability. Moreover, business passengers do not make purchases themselves, and they have their company pay for the trip. Both these types of customers have different needs and preferences. Catering to their specific preferences separately is extremely important.

Recognizing customer segments is extremely useful in determining the total revenue generated by a flight. Fares for leisure and business passengers are considerably different. As an example, if fares for business passengers are in the $200–$350 range, fares for leisure passengers are in the $90–$150 range. This distinction creates a need to balance the seats sold for both these classes for a certain flight to be profitable. Generally, revenue maximization is done over a network of airports operated by the airline, and not for a single flight. The objective is to generate overall revenues exceeding the minimum standards set by the airline. Empty seats on a flight are equivalent to lost revenue. Seats on a flight may be left empty due to a variety of reasons: last-minute cancellations, late arrival, and multiple bookings due to uncertainty of travel plans. As a precaution, most flights are overbooked, based on historical demand economics and human behavior. This is done to minimize lost revenue and allows more passengers to book their preferred flight. But overbooking can also lead to passengers being denied boarding, which creates ill-will. Airlines often try to compensate with attractive incentives to customers in exchange for moving to an alternate flight.

All of this process is done with the help of the revenue management system with inputs from RM Planners. Figure 11.2 presents a general architecture of such airline **revenue management systems**. This figure has been developed by Dr. Mukund Shankar, an airline revenue management specialist who has worked for/with several airlines in developing such systems. The pricing and accounting system handles ticket data, published fares, and pricing rules. The aircraft scheduling system handles flight schedules based on customer demand; finally, the inventory management system handles bookings, cancellations, and changes in departure data.

Customer demand is estimated at various price levels before prices are published. This accommodates seasonal- and weekday-based changes in customer demand. However, prices can be adjusted on-the-fly to reactively cater to changes in demand. Simultaneously, a change in the demand forecast calls for changes in aircraft scheduling

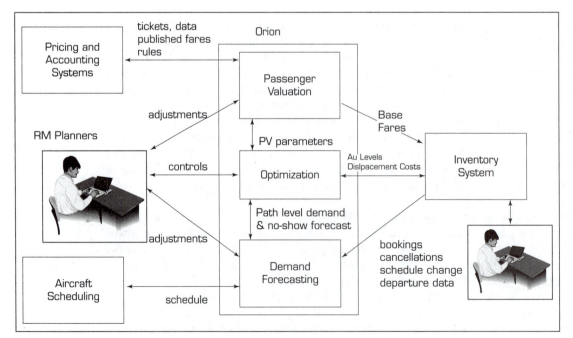

FIGURE 11.2 **Architecture of Airline Revenue Management Systems.** Courtesy: Mukund Shankar.

as empty or overbooked flights are a challenge to handle, and come at an expense of lost revenue. Moreover, optimization is done at each price level to operate flights at the lowest possible cost. This means that the whole information ecosystem of the airline needs to be extremely versatile, if it is to maximize profits. However, there is a limitation to how flexible this system can get as any airline has a limited inventory of flights at their disposal. Extreme demand cannot be accommodated with a limited fleet and often leads to losing customers to other airlines.

Because of the complexity involved in managing airlines, they invest heavily in building better predictive models for forecasting demand; analyzing the customer base more carefully to generate better segments of customers; operations research for optimizing flight routes, demand, and scheduling; and extremely fast hardware to process all this information as fast as possible. Virtually every major airline uses such automated decision systems. What is important to recognize is that similar systems also exist and are in use in many other industries. Although our examples are from business decision making, similar systems exist in engineering applications as well. For example, smart grid depends upon automated decisions to trigger specific activities whenever supply and demand of electricity demands switching of electricity generation or distributions. As we will discuss in the last chapter, we believe that these types of systems present a major future entrepreneurial opportunity in the consumer sector.

We next turn our attention to another class of **rule-based systems** that have been popular and in use since the mid-1980s. These systems have their roots in artificial intelligence, so we will first do an extremely quick overview of artificial intelligence.

SECTION 11.2 REVIEW QUESTIONS

1. Define *decision automation systems*.

2. What are the key components of a decision automation system?

3. Which industries are big users of decision automation systems?

4. How could decision automation systems assist consumers?

11.3 THE ARTIFICIAL INTELLIGENCE FIELD

Artificial intelligence (AI) is a collection of concepts and ideas that are related to the development of intelligent systems. These concepts and ideas may be developed in different areas and be applied to different domains. In order to understand the scope of AI, therefore, we need to see a group of areas that may be called the AI family. Figure 11.3 shows the major branches of AI applications. These applications are built on the foundation of many disciplines and technologies, including computer science, philosophy, electrical engineering, management science, psychology, and linguistics. Artificial intelligence (AI) is an area of computer science. Even though the term has many different definitions, most experts agree that AI is concerned with two basic ideas: (1) the study of human thought processes (to understand what intelligence is) and (2) the representation and duplication of those thought processes in machines (e.g., computers, robots).

One well-publicized, classic definition of AI is "behavior by a machine that, if performed by a human being, would be called intelligent." Rich and Knight (1991) provided a thought-provoking definition: "Artificial intelligence is the study of how to make computers do things at which, at the moment, people are better." To understand what artificial intelligence is, we need to examine those abilities that are considered to be signs of intelligence:

- Learning or understanding from experience
- Making sense out of ambiguous or contradictory messages

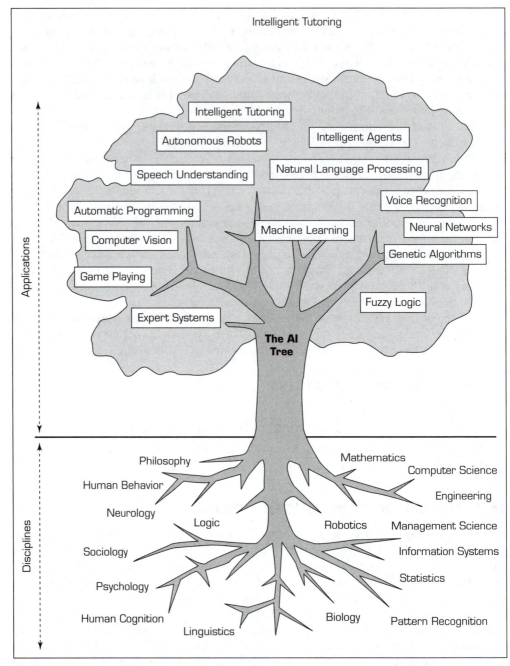

FIGURE 11.3   The Disciplines and Applications of AI.

- Responding quickly and successfully to a new situation (i.e., different responses, flexibility)
- Using reasoning in solving problems and directing conduct effectively
- Dealing with perplexing situations
- Understanding and inferring in a rational way
- Applying knowledge to manipulate the environment
- Thinking and reasoning
- Recognizing and judging the relative importance of different elements in a situation

Alan Turing designed an interesting test to determine whether a computer exhibits intelligent behavior; the test is called the *Turing test*. According to this test, a computer can be considered smart only when a human interviewer cannot identify the computer while conversing with both an unseen human being and an unseen computer.

As Figure 11.3 shows, there are many application areas of artificial intelligence. We will only focus on the expert systems because these relate to the automated rule-based decision systems described in the previous section.

SECTION 11.3 REVIEW QUESTIONS

1. What is the definition of artificial intelligence?

2. What are some of the major applications areas of artificial intelligence?

3. Identify some key characteristics of AI.

11.4 BASIC CONCEPTS OF EXPERT SYSTEMS

Expert systems (ES) are computer-based information systems that use expert knowledge to attain high-level decision performance in a narrowly defined problem domain. MYCIN, developed at Stanford University in the early 1980s for medical diagnosis, is the most well-known ES application. ES has also been used in taxation, credit analysis, equipment maintenance, help desk automation, environmental monitoring, and fault diagnosis. ES have been popular in large and medium-sized organizations as a sophisticated tool for improving productivity and quality.

The basic concepts of ES include how to determine who experts are, the definition of expertise, how expertise can be extracted and transferred from a person to a computer, and how the expert system should mimic the reasoning process of human experts. We describe these concepts in the following sections.

Experts

An **expert** is a person who has the special knowledge, judgment, experience, and skills to put his or her knowledge in action to provide sound advice and to solve complex problems in a narrowly defined area. It is an expert's job to provide knowledge about how he or she performs a task that a KBS will perform. An expert knows which facts are important and also understands and explains the dependency relationships among those facts. In diagnosing a problem with an automobile's electrical system, for example, an expert mechanic knows that a broken fan belt can be the cause for the battery to discharge.

There is no standard definition of *expert*, but decision performance and the level of knowledge a person has are typical criteria used to determine whether a particular person is an expert. Typically, experts must be able to solve a problem and achieve a performance level that is significantly better than average. In addition, experts are relative (and not absolute). An expert at a time or in a region may not be an expert in another time or region. For example, an attorney in New York may not be a legal expert in Beijing, China. A medical student may be an expert compared to the general public but may not be considered an expert in brain surgery. Experts have expertise that can help solve problems and explain certain obscure phenomena within a specific problem domain. Typically, human experts are capable of doing the following:

- Recognizing and formulating a problem
- Solving a problem quickly and correctly
- Explaining a solution

- Learning from experience
- Restructuring knowledge
- Breaking rules (i.e., going outside the general norms), if necessary
- Determining relevance and associations
- Declining gracefully (i.e., being aware of one's limitations)

Expertise

Expertise is the extensive, task-specific knowledge that experts possess. The level of expertise determines the performance of a decision. Expertise is often acquired through training, reading, and experience in practice. It includes explicit knowledge, such as theories learned from a textbook or in a classroom, and implicit knowledge, gained from experience. The following is a list of possible knowledge types:

- Theories about the problem domain
- Rules and procedures regarding the general problem domain
- Heuristics about what to do in a given problem situation
- Global strategies for solving these types of problems
- Metaknowledge (i.e., knowledge about knowledge)
- Facts about the problem area

These types of knowledge enable experts to make better and faster decisions than nonexperts when solving complex problems.

Expertise often includes the following characteristics:

- Expertise is usually associated with a high degree of intelligence, but it is not always associated with the smartest person.
- Expertise is usually associated with a vast quantity of knowledge.
- Expertise is based on learning from past successes and mistakes.
- Expertise is based on knowledge that is well stored, organized, and quickly retrievable from an expert who has excellent recall of patterns from previous experiences.

Features of ES

ES must have the following features:

- ***Expertise.*** As described in the previous section, experts differ in their level of expertise. An ES must possess expertise that enables it to make expert-level decisions. The system must exhibit expert performance with adequate robustness.
- ***Symbolic reasoning.*** The basic rationale of artificial intelligence is to use symbolic reasoning rather than mathematical calculation. This is also true for ES. That is, knowledge must be represented symbolically, and the primary reasoning mechanism must be symbolic. Typical symbolic reasoning mechanisms include backward chaining and forward chaining, which are described later in this chapter.
- ***Deep knowledge.*** Deep knowledge concerns the level of expertise in a knowledge base. The knowledge base must contain complex knowledge not easily found among nonexperts.
- ***Self-knowledge.*** ES must be able to examine their own reasoning and provide proper explanations as to why a particular conclusion was reached. Most experts have very strong learning capabilities to update their knowledge constantly. ES also need to be able to learn from their successes and failures as well as from other knowledge sources.

The development of ES is divided into two generations. Most first-generation ES use if-then rules to represent and store their knowledge. The second-generation ES are more flexible in adopting multiple knowledge representation and reasoning methods. They may integrate fuzzy logic, neural networks, or genetic algorithms with rule-based inference to achieve a higher level of decision performance. A comparison between conventional systems and ES is given in Table 11.1. Application Case 11.2 illustrates an application of such systems in the sports industry. We will review several applications in the next section.

TABLE 11.1 Comparison of Conventional Systems and Expert Systems

Conventional Systems	Expert Systems
Information and its processing are usually combined in one sequential program.	The knowledge base is clearly separated from the processing (inference) mechanism (i.e., knowledge rules are separated from the control).
The program does not make mistakes (programmers or users do).	The program may make mistakes.
Conventional systems do not (usually) explain why input data are needed or how conclusions are drawn.	Explanation is a part of most ES.
Conventional systems require all input data. They may not function properly with missing data unless planned for.	ES do not require all initial facts. ES can typically arrive at reasonable conclusions with missing facts.
Changes in the program are tedious (except in DSS).	Changes in the rules are easy to make.
The system operates only when it is completed.	The system can operate with only a few rules (as the first prototype).
Execution is done on a step-by-step (algorithmic) basis.	Execution is done by using heuristics and logic.
Large databases can be effectively manipulated.	Large knowledge bases can be effectively manipulated.
Conventional systems represent and use data.	ES represent and use knowledge.
Efficiency is usually a major goal.	
Effectiveness is important only for DSS.	Effectiveness is the major goal.
Conventional systems easily deal with quantitative data.	ES easily deal with qualitative data.
Conventional systems use numeric data representations.	ES use symbolic and numeric knowledge representations.
Conventional systems capture, magnify, and distribute access to numeric data or information.	ES capture, magnify, and distribute access to judgment and knowledge.

Application Case 11.2

Expert System Helps in Identifying Sport Talents

In the world of sports, recruiters are constantly looking for new talent and parents want to identify the sport that is the most appropriate for their child. Identifying the most plausible match between a person (characterized by a large number of unique qualities and limitations) and a specific sport is anything but a trivial task. Such a matching process requires adequate information about the specific person (i.e., values of certain characteristics), as well as the deep knowledge of what this information should include (i.e., the types of characteristics). In other words, expert knowledge is what is needed in order to accurately predict the right sport (with the highest success possibility) for a specific individual.

It is very hard (if not impossible) to find the true experts for this difficult matchmaking problem. Because the domain of the specific knowledge is divided into various types of sports, the experts have in-depth knowledge of the relevant factors only for a specific sport (that they are an expert of), and beyond the limits of that sport they are not any better than an average spectator. In an ideal case, you would need experts from a wide range of sports brought together into a single room to collectively create a matchmaking decision. Because such a setting is not feasible in the real world, one might consider creating it in the computer world using expert systems. Because expert systems are known to incorporate knowledge from multiple experts, this situation seems to fit well with an expert system–type solution.

In a recent publication Papic et al. (2009) reported on an expert system application for the identification of sports talents. Tapping into the knowledge of a large number of sports experts, they have built a knowledge base of a comprehensive set of rules that maps the expert-driven factors (e.g., physical and cardiovascular measurement, performance test, skill assessments) to different sports. Taking advantage of the inexact representation capabilities of fuzzy logic, they managed to incorporate the exact natural reasoning of the expert knowledge into their advising system.

The system was built as a Web-based DSS using the ASP.NET development platform. Once the system development was completed, it was tested for verification and validation purposes. The system's prediction results were evaluated by experts using real cases collected from the past several years. Comparison was done between the sport proposed by the expert system and the actual outcome of the person's sports career. Additionally, the expert system output and the human expert suggestions were compared using a large number of test cases. All tests showed high reliability and accuracy of the developed system.

Source: V. Papic, N. Rogulj, and V. Pletina, "Identification of Sport Talents Using a Web-Oriented Expert System with a Fuzzy Module," *Expert Systems with Applications,* Vol. 36, 2009, pp. 8830–8838.

SECTION 11.4 REVIEW QUESTIONS

1. What is an ES?
2. Explain why we need ES.
3. What are the major features of ES?
4. What is expertise? Provide an example.
5. Define *deep knowledge* and give an example of it.

11.5 APPLICATIONS OF EXPERT SYSTEMS

ES have been applied to many business and technological areas to support decision making. Application Case 11.3 shows a recent real-world application of ES. Table 11.2 shows some representative ES and their application domains.

Application Case 11.3

Expert System Aids in Identification of Chemical, Biological, and Radiological Agents

Terrorist attacks using chemical, biological, or radiological agents (CBR) are of great concern due to the potential for widespread loss of life. The United States and other nations have spent billions of dollars on plans and protocols in defense against acts of terrorism that could involve CBR. However, CBR covers a wide range of agents with many specific chemicals and biological organisms that could be used in multiple subcategories. Timely response requires rapid identification of the agent involved. This can be a difficult process involving different methods and instruments.

The U.S. Environmental Protection Agency (EPA) along with Dr. Lawrence H. Keith, president of Instant Reference Sources Inc., and others from an extensive team incorporated their knowledge, experience, and expertise, plus information in publicly available EPA documents, to develop the CBR Advisor using Exsys Inc.'s Corvid® software.

One of the most important parts of the CBR Advisor is advice in logical step-by-step procedures to determine the identity of a toxic agent when little or no information is available, which is typical at the beginning of a terrorism incident. The systems help response staff proceed according to a well-established action plan—even in the highly stressful environment of a terrorist attack. The system's dual screens present three levels of information: (1) a top/executive level with brief answers, (2) an educational level with in-depth information, and (3) a research level with links to other documents, slide shows, forms, and Internet sites. Content includes:

- How to classify threat warnings
- How to conduct initial threat evaluation
- Immediate response actions
- How to perform site characterization
- Initial site evaluation and safe entry
- Where and how to best collect samples
- How to package and ship samples for analysis

Restricted content includes CBR agents and methods for analyzing them. The CBR Advisor can be used for incident response and/or training. It has two different menus, one for emergency response and another longer menu for training. The CBR Advisor is a restricted software program and is not publicly available.

QUESTIONS FOR DISCUSSION

1. How can CBR Advisor assist in making quick decisions?
2. What characteristics of CBR Advisor make it an expert system?
3. What could be other situations where such expert systems can be employed?

What We Can Learn from This Application Case

Expert systems are now widely being used in high-pressure situations where the human decision makers often struggle to take quick actions involving both the subjective as well as the objective perspectives in responding to the situations.

Source: **www.exsys.com** "Identification of Chemical, Biological and Radiological Agents," **http://www.exsyssoftware.com/ CaseStudySelector/casestudies.html** accessed February 2013.

Classical Applications of ES

Early ES applications, such as DENDRAL for molecular structure identification and MYCIN for medical diagnosis, were primarily in the science domain. XCON for configuration of the VAX computer system at Digital Equipment Corp. (a major producer of minicomputers around 1990 that was later taken over by Compaq) was a successful example in business.

DENDRAL The DENDRAL project was initiated by Edward Feigenbaum in 1965. It used a set of knowledge- or rule-based reasoning commands to deduce the likely molecular structure of organic chemical compounds from known chemical analyses and mass spectrometry data.

TABLE 11.2 Sample Applications of Expert Systems

Expert System	Organization	Application Domain
Classical Applications		
MYCIN	Stanford University	Medical diagnosis
XCON	DEC	System configuration
Expert Tax	Coopers & Lybrand	Tax planning
Loan Probe	Peat Marwick	Loan evaluation
La-Courtier	Cognitive Systems	Financial planning
LMOS	Pacific Bell	Network management
PROSPECTOR	Stanford Research Institute	Discovery of new mineral deposits
Reported Applications		
Fish-Expert	North China	Disease diagnosis in fish
HelpDeskIQ	BMC Remedy	Help desk management
Authorete	Haley	Business rule automation
eCare	CIGNA	Insurance claims
SONAR	NSAD	Stock market monitoring

DENDRAL proved to be fundamentally important in demonstrating how rule-based reasoning could be developed into powerful knowledge engineering tools and led to the development of other rule-based reasoning programs at the Stanford Artificial Intelligence Laboratory (SAIL). The most important of those programs was MYCIN.

MYCIN   MYCIN is a rule-based ES that diagnoses bacterial infections of the blood. It was developed by a group of researchers at Stanford University in the 1970s. By asking questions and backward chaining through a rule base of about 500 rules, MYCIN can recognize approximately 100 causes of bacterial infections, which allows the system to recommend effective drug prescriptions. In a controlled test, its performance was rated to be equal that of human specialists. The reasoning and uncertainty processing methods used in MYCIN are pioneers in the area and have generated long-term impact in ES development.

XCON   XCON, a rule-based system developed at Digital Equipment Corp., used rules to help determine the optimal system configuration that fit customer requirements. The system was able to handle a customer request within 1 minute that typically took the sales team 20 to 30 minutes. With the ES, service accuracy increased to 98 percent, from a manual approach with an accuracy of 65 percent, saving millions of dollars every year.

Newer Applications of ES

More recent applications of ES include risk management, pension fund advising, business rule automation, automated market surveillance, and homeland security. There are literally thousands of publications reporting applications of expert systems. We mention just a few here.

CREDIT ANALYSIS SYSTEMS   ES have been developed to support the needs of commercial lending institutions. ES can help a lender analyze a customer's credit record and determine a proper credit line. Rules in the knowledge base can also help assess risk and risk-management policies. These kinds of systems are used in over one-third of the top 100 commercial banks in the United States and Canada.

PENSION FUND ADVISORS   Nestlé Foods Corporation has developed an ES that provides information on an employee's pension fund status. The system maintains an up-to-date knowledge base to give participants advice concerning the impact of regulation changes and conformance with new standards. A system offered on the Internet at the Pingtung Teacher's College in Taiwan has functions that allow participants to plan their retirement through a what-if analysis that calculates their pension benefits under different scenarios.

AUTOMATED HELP DESKS   BMC Remedy (**remedy.com**) offers HelpDeskIQ, a rule-based help desk solution for small businesses. This browser-based tool enables small businesses to deal with customer requests more efficiently. Incoming e-mails automatically pass into HelpDeskIQ's business rule engine. The messages are sent to the proper technician, based on defined priority and status. The solution assists help desk technicians in resolving problems and tracking issues more effectively.

Areas for ES Applications

As indicated in the preceding examples, ES have been applied commercially in a number of areas, including the following:

- *Finance.*   Finance ES include insurance evaluation, credit analysis, tax planning, fraud prevention, financial report analysis, financial planning, and performance evaluation.
- *Data processing.*   Data processing ES include system planning, equipment selection, equipment maintenance, vendor evaluation, and network management.
- *Marketing.*   Marketing ES include customer relationship management, market analysis, product planning, and market planning.
- *Human resources.*   Examples of human resources ES are human resources planning, performance evaluation, staff scheduling, pension management, and legal advising.
- *Manufacturing.*   Manufacturing ES include production planning, quality management, product design, plant site selection, and equipment maintenance and repair.
- *Homeland security.*   Homeland security ES include terrorist threat assessment and terrorist finance detection.
- *Business process automation.*   ES have been developed for help desk automation, call center management, and regulation enforcement.
- *Healthcare management.*   ES have been developed for bioinformatics and other healthcare management issues.

Now that you are familiar with a variety of different ES applications, it is time to look at the internal structure of an ES and how the goals of the ES are achieved.

SECTION 11.5 REVIEW QUESTIONS

1. What is MYCIN's problem domain?
2. Name two applications of ES in finance and describe their benefits.
3. Name two applications of ES in marketing and describe their benefits.
4. Name two applications of ES in homeland security and describe their benefits.

11.6 STRUCTURE OF EXPERT SYSTEMS

ES can be viewed as having two environments: the development environment and the consultation environment (see Figure 11.4). An ES builder uses the **development environment** to build the necessary components of the ES and to populate the knowledge base with appropriate representation of the expert knowledge. A nonexpert uses the **consultation environment** to obtain advice and to solve problems using the expert knowledge embedded into the system. These two environments can be separated at the end of the system development process.

The three major components that appear in virtually every ES are the knowledge base, the inference engine, and the user interface. In general, though, an ES that interacts with the user can contain the following additional components:

- Knowledge acquisition subsystem
- Blackboard (workplace)
- Explanation subsystem (justifier)
- Knowledge-refining system

Currently, most ES do not contain the knowledge refinement component. A brief description of each of these components follows.

Knowledge Acquisition Subsystem

Knowledge acquisition is the accumulation, transfer, and transformation of problem-solving expertise from experts or documented knowledge sources to a computer

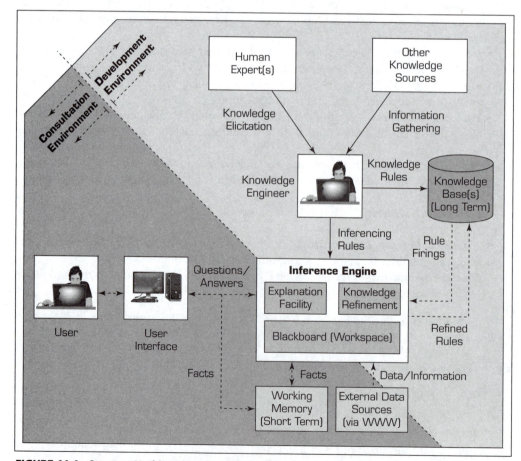

FIGURE 11.4 Structure/Architecture of an Expert System.

program for constructing or expanding the knowledge base. Potential sources of knowledge include human experts, textbooks, multimedia documents, databases (public and private), special research reports, and information available on the Web.

Currently, most organizations have collected a large volume of data, but the organization and management of organizational knowledge are limited. Knowledge acquisition deals with issues such as making tacit knowledge explicit and integrating knowledge from multiple sources.

Acquiring knowledge from experts is a complex task that often creates a bottleneck in ES construction. In building large systems, a knowledge engineer, or knowledge elicitation expert, needs to interact with one or more human experts in building the knowledge base. Typically, the **knowledge engineer** helps the expert structure the problem area by interpreting and integrating human answers to questions, drawing analogies, posing counterexamples, and bringing conceptual difficulties to light.

Knowledge Base

The **knowledge base** is the foundation of an ES. It contains the relevant knowledge necessary for understanding, formulating, and solving problems. A typical knowledge base may include two basic elements: (1) facts that describe the characteristics of a specific problem situation (or *fact base*) and the theory of the problem area and (2) special heuristics or rules (or *knowledge nuggets*) that represent the deep expert knowledge to solve specific problems in a particular domain. Additionally, the inference engine can include general-purpose problem-solving and decision-making rules (or *meta-rules*— rules about how to process production rules).

It is important to differentiate between the knowledge base of an ES and the knowledge base of an organization. The knowledge stored in the knowledge base of an ES is often represented in a special format so that it can be used by a software program (i.e., an expert system shell) to help users solve a particular problem. The organizational knowledge base, however, contains various kinds of knowledge in different formats (most of which is represented in a way that it can be consumed by people) and may be stored in different places. The knowledge base of an ES is a special case and only a very small subset of an organization's knowledge base.

Inference Engine

The "brain" of an ES is the inference engine, also known as the *control structure* or the *rule interpreter* (in rule-based ES). This component is essentially a computer program that provides a methodology for reasoning about information in the knowledge base and on the blackboard to formulate appropriate conclusions. The inference engine provides directions about how to use the system's knowledge by developing the agenda that organizes and controls the steps taken to solve problems whenever a consultation takes place. It is further discussed in Section 11.7.

User Interface

An ES contains a language processor for friendly, problem-oriented communication between the user and the computer, known as the **user interface**. This communication can best be carried out in a natural language. Due to technological constraints, most existing systems use the graphical or textual question-and-answer approach to interact with the user.

Blackboard (Workplace)

The **blackboard** is an area of working memory set aside as a database for description of the current problem, as characterized by the input data. It is also used for recording intermediate results, hypotheses, and decisions. Three types of decisions can be recorded on the blackboard: a plan (i.e., how to attack the problem), an agenda (i.e., potential actions awaiting execution), and a solution (i.e., candidate hypotheses and alternative courses of action that the system has generated thus far).

Consider this example. When your car fails to start, you can enter the symptoms of the failure into a computer for storage in the blackboard. As the result of an intermediate hypothesis developed in the blackboard, the computer may then suggest that you do some additional checks (e.g., see whether your battery is connected properly) and ask you to report the results. This information is also recorded in the blackboard. Such an iterative process of populating the blackboard with values of hypotheses and facts continues until the reason for the failure is identified.

Explanation Subsystem (Justifier)

The ability to trace responsibility for conclusions to their sources is crucial both in the transfer of expertise and in problem solving. The **explanation subsystem** can trace such responsibility and explain the ES behavior by interactively answering questions such as these:

- Why was a certain question asked by the ES?
- How was a certain conclusion reached?
- Why was a certain alternative rejected?
- What is the complete plan of decisions to be made in reaching the conclusion? For example, what remains to be known before a final diagnosis can be determined?

In most ES, the first two questions (why and how) are answered by showing the rule that required asking a specific question and showing the sequence of rules that were used (fired) to derive the specific recommendations, respectively.

Knowledge-Refining System

Human experts have a **knowledge-refining system**; that is, they can analyze their own knowledge and its effectiveness, learn from it, and improve on it for future consultations. Similarly, such evaluation is necessary in expert systems so that a program can analyze the reasons for its success or failure, which could lead to improvements resulting in a more accurate knowledge base and more effective reasoning.

The critical component of a knowledge refinement system is the self-learning mechanism that allows it to adjust its knowledge base and its processing of knowledge based on the evaluation of its recent past performances. Such an intelligent component is not yet mature enough to appear in many commercial ES tools. Application Case 11.4 illustrates another application of expert systems in healthcare.

Application Case 11.4

Diagnosing Heart Diseases by Signal Processing

Auscultation is the science of listening to the sounds of internal body organs, in this case the heart. Skilled experts can make diagnoses using this technique. It is a noninvasive screening method of providing valuable information about the conditions of the heart and its valves, but it is highly subjective and depends on the skills and experience of the listener. Researchers from the Department of Electrical & Electronic Engineering at Universiti Teknologi Petronas have developed an Exsys Corvid expert system, SIPMES (Signal Processing Module Integrated Expert System) to analyze digitally processed heart sound.

The system utilizes digitized heart sound algorithms to diagnose various conditions of the heart. Heart sounds are effectively acquired using a digital electronic stethoscope. The heart sounds were collected from the Institut Jantung Negara (National Heart Institute) in Kuala Lumpur and the Fatimah Ipoh Hospital in Malaysia. A total of 40 patients age 16 to 79 years old with various pathologies were used as the control group, and to test the validity of the system using their abnormal heart sound samples and other patient medical data.

The heart sounds are transmitted using a wireless link to a nearby workstation that hosts the Signal Processing Module (SPM). The SPM has the capability to segment the stored heart sounds into individual cycles and identifies the important cardiac events.

The SPM data was then integrated with the Exsys Corvid knowledge automation expert system. The rules in the system use expert physician reasoning knowledge, combined with information acquired from medical journals, medical textbooks, and other noted publications on cardiovascular diseases (CVD). The system provides the diagnosis and generates a list of diseases arranged in descending order of their probability of occurrence.

SIPMES was designed to diagnose all types of cardiovascular heart diseases. The system can help general physicians diagnose heart diseases at the earliest possible stages under emergency situations where expert cardiologists and advanced medical facilities are not readily available.

The diagnosis made by the system has been counterchecked by senior cardiologists, and the results coincide with these heart experts. A high coincidence factor of 74 percent has been achieved using SIPMES.

QUESTIONS FOR DISCUSSION

1. List the major components involved in building SIPMES and briefly comment on them.
2. Do expert systems like SIPMES eliminate the need for human decision making?
3. How often do you think that the existing expert systems, once built, should be changed?

What We Can Learn from This Application Case

Many expert systems are prominently being used in the field of medicine. Many traditional diagnostic procedures are now being built into logical rule-based systems, which can readily assist the medical staff in quickly diagnosing the patient's condition of disease. These expert systems can help in saving the valuable time of the medical staff and increase the number of patients being served.

Source: **www.exsys.com,** "Diagnosing Heart Diseases," **exsys http://www.exsyssoftware.com/CaseStudySelector/ casestudies.html** (accessed February 2013).

SECTION 11.6 REVIEW QUESTIONS

1. Describe the ES development environment.
2. List and define the major components of an ES.
3. What are the major activities performed in the ES blackboard (workplace)?
4. What are the major roles of the explanation subsystem?
5. Describe the difference between a knowledge base of an ES and an organizational knowledge base.

11.7 KNOWLEDGE ENGINEERING

The collection of intensive activities encompassing the acquisition of knowledge from human experts (and other information sources) and conversion of this knowledge into a repository (commonly called a *knowledge base*) are called **knowledge engineering**. The term *knowledge engineering* was first defined in the pioneering work of Feigenbaum and McCorduck (1983) as the art of bringing the principles and tools of artificial intelligence research to bear on difficult application problems requiring the knowledge of experts for their solutions. Knowledge engineering requires cooperation and close communication between the human experts and the knowledge engineer to successfully codify and explicitly represent the rules (or other knowledge-based procedures) that a human expert uses to solve problems within a specific application domain. The knowledge possessed by human experts is often unstructured and not explicitly expressed. A major goal of knowledge engineering is to help experts articulate *how they do what they do* and to document this knowledge in a reusable form.

Knowledge engineering can be viewed from two perspectives: narrow and broad. According to the narrow perspective, knowledge engineering deals with the steps necessary to build expert systems (i.e., knowledge acquisition, knowledge representation, knowledge validation, inferencing, and explanation/justification). Alternatively, according to the broad perspective, the term describes the entire process of developing and maintaining any intelligent systems. In this book, we use the narrow definition. Following are the five major activities in knowledge engineering:

- ***Knowledge acquisition.*** Knowledge acquisition involves the acquisition of knowledge from human experts, books, documents, sensors, or computer files. The knowledge may be specific to the problem domain or to the problem-solving procedures, it may be general knowledge (e.g., knowledge about business), or it may be metaknowledge (knowledge about knowledge). (By *metaknowledge,* we mean information about how experts use their knowledge to solve problems and about problem-solving procedures in general.)
- ***Knowledge representation.*** Acquired knowledge is organized so that it will be ready for use, in an activity called knowledge representation. This activity involves preparation of a knowledge map and encoding of the knowledge in the knowledge base.
- ***Knowledge validation.*** Knowledge validation (or verification) involves validating and verifying the knowledge (e.g., by using test cases) until its quality is acceptable. Test results are usually shown to a domain expert to verify the accuracy of the ES.
- ***Explanation and justification.*** This step involves the design and programming of an explanation capability (e.g., programming the ability to answer questions such as why a specific piece of information is needed by the computer or how a certain conclusion was derived by the computer).

Figure 11.5 shows the process of knowledge engineering and the relationships among the knowledge engineering activities. Knowledge engineers interact with human experts or collect documented knowledge from other sources in the knowledge acquisition stage. The acquired knowledge is then coded into a representation scheme to create a knowledge base. The knowledge engineer can collaborate with human experts or use test cases to verify and validate the knowledge base. The validated knowledge can be used in a **knowledge-based system** to solve new problems via machine inference and to explain the generated recommendation. Details of these activities are discussed in the following sections.

Knowledge Acquisition

Knowledge is a collection of specialized facts, procedures, and judgment usually expressed as rules. Knowledge can come from one or from many sources, such as books, films, computer databases, pictures, maps, stories, news articles, and sensors, as well as from human experts. Acquisition of knowledge from human experts (often called *knowledge elicitation*) is arguably the most valuable and most challenging task in knowledge acquisition. Technology Insights 11.1 lists some of the difficulties of knowledge acquisition. The classical knowledge elicitation methods, which are also called *manual methods*, include interviewing (i.e., structured, semistructured, unstructured), tracking the reasoning process, and observing. Because these manual methods are slow, expensive, and sometimes inaccurate, the ES community has been developing semiautomated and fully automated means to acquire knowledge. These techniques, which rely on computers

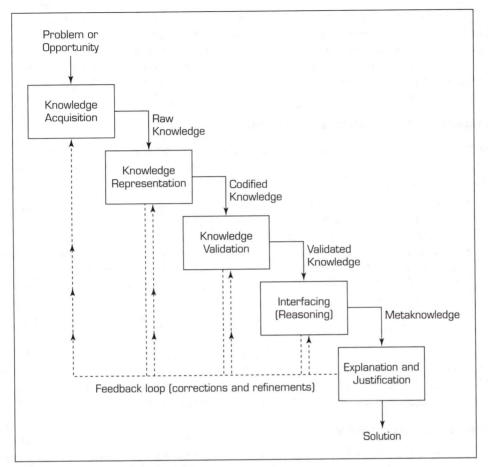

FIGURE 11.5   The Process of Knowledge Engineering.

and AI techniques, aim to minimize the involvement of the knowledge engineer and the human experts in the process. Despite its disadvantages, in real-world ES projects the traditional knowledge elicitation techniques still dominate.

TECHNOLOGY INSIGHTS 11.1   Difficulties in Knowledge Acquisition

Acquiring knowledge from experts is not an easy task. The following are some factors that add to the complexity of knowledge acquisition from experts and its transfer to a computer:

- Experts may not know how to articulate their knowledge or may be unable to do so.
- Experts may lack time or may be unwilling to cooperate.
- Testing and refining knowledge are complicated.
- Methods for knowledge elicitation may be poorly defined.
- System builders tend to collect knowledge from one source, but the relevant knowledge may be scattered across several sources.
- System builders may attempt to collect documented knowledge rather than use experts. The knowledge collected may be incomplete.
- It is difficult to recognize specific knowledge when it is mixed up with irrelevant data.
- Experts may change their behavior when they are observed or interviewed.
- Problematic interpersonal communication factors may affect the knowledge engineer and the expert.

A critical element in the development of an ES is the identification of experts. The usual approach to mitigate this problem is to build ES for a very narrow application domain in which expertise is more clearly defined. Even then, there is a very good chance that one might find more than one expert with different (sometime conflicting) expertise. In such situations, one might choose to use multiple experts in the knowledge elicitation process.

Knowledge Verification and Validation

Knowledge acquired from experts needs to be evaluated for quality, including evaluation, validation, and verification. These terms are often used interchangeably. We use the definitions provided by O'Keefe et al. (1987):

- *Evaluation* is a broad concept. Its objective is to assess an ES's overall value. In addition to assessing acceptable performance levels, it analyzes whether the system would be usable, efficient, and cost-effective.
- *Validation* is the part of evaluation that deals with the performance of the system (e.g., as it compares to the expert's). Simply stated, validation is building the right system (i.e., substantiating that a system performs with an acceptable level of accuracy).
- *Verification* is building the system right or substantiating that the system is correctly implemented to its specifications.

In the realm of ES, these activities are dynamic because they must be repeated each time the prototype is changed. In terms of the knowledge base, it is necessary to ensure that the right knowledge base (i.e., that the knowledge is valid) is used. It is also essential to ensure that the knowledge base has been constructed properly (i.e., verification).

Knowledge Representation

Once validated, the knowledge acquired from experts or induced from a set of data must be represented in a format that is both understandable by humans and executable on computers. A variety of knowledge representation methods is available: production rules, semantic networks, frames, objects, decision tables, decision trees, and predicate logic. Next, we explain the most popular method—production rules.

PRODUCTION RULES **Production rules** are the most popular form of knowledge representation for expert systems. Knowledge is represented in the form of condition/ action pairs: IF this condition (or premise or antecedent) occurs, THEN some action (or result or conclusion or consequence) will (or should) occur. Consider the following two examples:

- If the stop light is red AND you have stopped, THEN a right turn is okay.
- If the client uses purchase requisition forms AND the purchase orders are approved and purchasing is separate from receiving AND accounts payable AND inventory records, THEN there is strongly suggestive evidence (90 percent probability) that controls to prevent unauthorized purchases are adequate. (This example from an internal control procedure includes a probability.)

Each production rule in a knowledge base implements an autonomous chunk of expertise that can be developed and modified independently of other rules. When combined and fed to the inference engine, the set of rules behaves synergistically, yielding better results than the sum of the results of the individual rules. In some sense, rules can be viewed as a simulation of the cognitive behavior of human experts. According to this view, rules are not just a neat formalism to represent knowledge in a computer; rather, they represent a model of actual human behavior.

KNOWLEDGE AND INFERENCE RULES Two types of rules are common in artificial intelligence: knowledge and inference. **Knowledge rules**, or *declarative rules,* state all the facts and relationships about a problem. **Inference rules**, or *procedural rules,* offer advice on how to solve a problem, given that certain facts are known. The knowledge engineer separates the two types of rules: Knowledge rules go to the knowledge base, whereas inference rules become part of the inference engine that was introduced earlier as a component of an expert system. For example, assume that you are in the business of buying and selling gold. The knowledge rules might look like this:

Rule 1: IF an international conflict begins, THEN the price of gold goes up.

Rule 2: IF the inflation rate declines, THEN the price of gold goes down.

Rule 3: IF the international conflict lasts more than 7 days and IF it is in the Middle East, THEN buy gold.

Inference rules contain rules about rules and thus are also called meta-rules. They pertain to other rules (or even to themselves). Inference (procedural) rules may look like this:

Rule 1: IF the data needed are not in the system, THEN request them from the user.

Rule 2: IF more than one rule applies, THEN deactivate any rules that add no new data.

Inferencing

Inferencing (or reasoning) is the process of using the rules in the knowledge base along with the known facts to draw conclusions. Inferencing requires some logic embedded in a computer program to access and manipulate the stored knowledge. This program is an algorithm that, with the guidance of the inferencing rules, controls the reasoning process and is usually called the **inference engine**. In rule-based systems, it is also called the *rule interpreter*.

The inference engine directs the search through the collection of rules in the knowledge base, a process commonly called *pattern matching*. In inferencing, when all of the hypotheses (the "IF" parts) of a rule are satisfied, the rule is said to be fired. Once a rule is fired, the new knowledge generated by the rule (the conclusion or the validation of the THEN part) is inserted into the memory as a new fact. The inference engine checks every rule in the knowledge base to identify those that can be fired based on what is known at that point in time (the collection of known facts), and keeps doing so until the goal is achieved. The most popular inferencing mechanisms for rule-based systems are forward and backward chaining:

- **Backward chaining** is a goal-driven approach in which you start from an expectation of what is going to happen (i.e., hypothesis) and then seek evidence that supports (or contradicts) your expectation. Often, this entails formulating and testing intermediate hypotheses (or subhypotheses).
- **Forward chaining** is a data-driven approach. We start from available information as it becomes available or from a basic idea, and then we try to draw conclusions. The ES analyzes the problem by looking for the facts that match the IF part of its IF-THEN rules. For example, if a certain machine is not working, the computer checks the electricity flow to the machine. As each rule is tested, the program works its way toward one or more conclusions.

FORWARD AND BACKWARD CHAINING EXAMPLE Here we discuss an example involving an investment decision about whether to invest in IBM stock. The following variables are used:

A = Have $10,000

B = Younger than 30

C = Education at college level

D = Annual income of at least $40,000

E = Invest in securities

F = Invest in growth stocks

G = Invest in IBM stock (the potential goal)

Each of these variables can be answered as true (yes) or false (no).

We assume that an investor has $10,000 (i.e., that A is true) and that she is 25 years old (i.e., that B is true). She would like advice on investing in IBM stock (yes or no for the goal).

Our knowledge base includes the following five rules:

R1: IF a person has $10,000 to invest and she has a college degree,

THEN she should invest in securities.

R2: IF a person's annual income is at least $40,000 and she has a college degree,

THEN she should invest in growth stocks.

R3: IF a person is younger than 30 and she is investing in securities,

THEN she should invest in growth stocks.

R4: IF a person is younger than 30,

THEN she has a college degree.

R5: IF a person wants to invest in a growth stock,

THEN the stock should be IBM.

These rules can be written as follows:

R1: IF A and C, THEN E.

R2: IF D and C, THEN F.

R3: IF B and E, THEN F.

R4: IF B, THEN C.

R5: IF F, THEN G.

Backward Chaining   Our goal is to determine whether to invest in IBM stock. With backward chaining, we start by looking for a rule that includes the goal (G) in its conclusion (THEN) part. Because R5 is the only one that qualifies, we start with it. If several rules contain G, then the inference engine dictates a procedure for handling the situation. This is what we do:

1. Try to accept or reject G. The ES goes to the assertion base to see whether G is there. At present, all we have in the assertion base is A is true. B is true. Therefore, the ES proceeds to step 2.
2. R5 says that if it is true that we invest in growth stocks (F), then we should invest in IBM (G). If we can conclude that the premise of R5 is either true or false, then we have solved the problem. However, we do not know whether F is true. What shall we do now? Note that F, which is the premise of R5, is also the conclusion of R2 and R3. Therefore, to find out whether F is true, we must check either of these two rules.
3. We try R2 first (arbitrarily); if both D and C are true, then F is true. Now we have a problem. D is not a conclusion of any rule, nor is it a fact. The computer can either move to another rule or try to find out whether D is true by asking the investor for whom the consultation is given if her annual income is above $40,000. What the ES does depends on the search procedures used by the inference engine. Usually, a user is asked for additional information only if the information is not available or

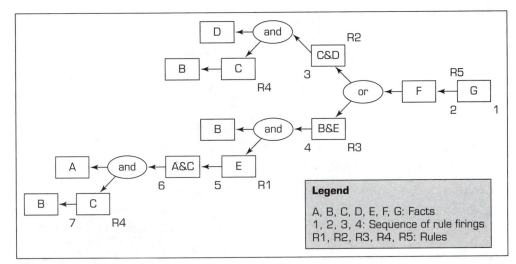

FIGURE 11.6   **A Graphical Depiction of Backward Chaining.**

cannot be deduced. We abandon R2 and return to the other rule, R3. This action is called *backtracking* (i.e., knowing that we are at a dead end, we try something else; the computer must be preprogrammed to handle backtracking).

4. Go to R3; test B and E. We know that B is true because it is a given fact. To prove E, we go to R1, where E is the conclusion.
5. Examine R1. It is necessary to determine whether A and C are true.
6. A is true because it is a given fact. To test C, it is necessary to test R4 (where C is the conclusion).
7. R4 tells us that C is true (because B is true). Therefore, C becomes a fact (and is added to the assertion base). Now E is true, which validates F, which validates our goal (i.e., the advice is to invest in IBM).

Note that during the search, the ES moved from the THEN part to the IF part, back to the THEN part, and so on (see Figure 11.6 for a graphical depiction of the backward chaining).

Forward Chaining   Let us use the same example we examined in backward chaining to illustrate the process of forward chaining. In forward chaining, we start with known facts and derive new facts by using rules having known facts on the IF side. The specific steps that forward chaining would follow in this example are as follows (also see Figure 11.7 for a graphical depiction of this process):

1. Because it is known that A and B are true, the ES starts deriving new facts by using rules that have A and B on the IF side. Using R4, the ES derives a new fact C and adds it to the assertion base as true.
2. R1 fires (because A and C are true) and asserts E as true in the assertion base.
3. Because B and E are both known to be true (they are in the assertion base), R3 fires and establishes F as true in the assertion base.
4. R5 fires (because F is on its IF side), which establishes G as true. So the ES recommends an investment in IBM stock. If there is more than one conclusion, more rules may fire, depending on the inferencing procedure.

INFERENCING WITH UNCERTAINTY   Although uncertainty is widespread in the real world, its treatment in the practical world of artificial intelligence is very limited. One could argue that because the knowledge provided by experts is often inexact an ES that mimics

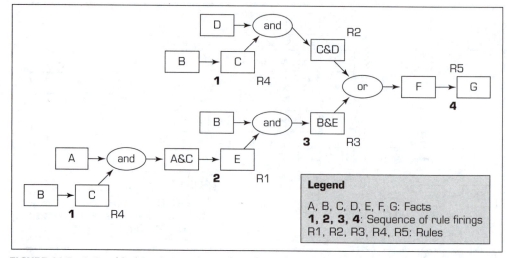

FIGURE 11.7 **A Graphical Depiction of Forward Chaining.**

the reasoning process of experts should represent such uncertainty. ES researchers have proposed several methods to incorporate uncertainty into the reasoning process, including probability ratios, the Bayesian approach, fuzzy logic, the Dempster–Shafer theory of evidence, and the theory of certainty factors. Following is a brief description of the theory of certainty factors, which is the most commonly used method to accommodate uncertainty in ES.

The **theory of certainty factors** is based on the concepts of belief and disbelief. The standard statistical methods are based on the assumption that an uncertainty is the probability that an event (or fact) is true or false, whereas certainty theory is based on the *degrees of belief* (not the calculated probability) that an event (or fact) is true or false.

Certainty theory relies on the use of certainty factors. **Certainty factors (CF)** express belief in an event (or a fact or a hypothesis) based on the expert's assessment. Certainty factors can be represented by values ranging from 0 to 100; the smaller the value, the lower the probability that the event (or fact) is true or false. Because certainty factors are not probabilities, when we say that there is a certainty value of 90 for rain, we do not mean (or imply) any opinion about no rain (which is not necessarily 10). Thus, certainty factors do not have to sum up to 100.

Combining Certainty Factors Certainty factors can be used to combine estimates by different experts in several ways. Before using any ES shell, you need to make sure that you understand how certainty factors are combined. The most acceptable way of combining them in rule-based systems is the method used in EMYCIN. In this approach, we distinguish between two cases, described next.

Combining Several Certainty Factors in One Rule Consider the following rule with an AND operator:

IF inflation is high, CF = 50 (A)

AND unemployment rate is above 7 percent, CF = 70 (B)

AND bond prices decline, CF = 100 (C),

THEN stock prices decline.

For this type of rule, all IFs must be true for the conclusion to be true. However, in some cases, there is uncertainty as to what is happening. Then the CF of the conclusion is the minimum CF on the IF side:

$$CF(A, B, C) = minimum [CF(A), CF(B), CF(C)]$$

Thus, in our case, the CF for stock prices to decline is 50 percent. In other words, the chain is as strong as its weakest link.

Now look at this rule with an OR operator:

IF inflation is low, CF = 70 percent

OR bond prices are high, CF = 85,

THEN stock prices will be high.

In this case, it is sufficient that only one of the IFs is true for the conclusion to be true. Thus, if both IFs are believed to be true (at their certainty factor), then the conclusion will have a CF with the maximum of the two:

$$CF \text{ (A or B)} = \text{maximum } [CF \text{ (A)}, CF \text{ (B)}]$$

In our case, CF must be 85 for stock prices to be high. Note that both cases hold for any number of IFs.

Combining Two or More Rules Why might rules be combined? There may be several ways to reach the same goal, each with different certainty factors for a given set of facts. When we have a knowledge-based system with several interrelated rules, each of which makes the same conclusion but with a different certainty factor, each rule can be viewed as a piece of evidence that supports the joint conclusion. To calculate the certainty factor (or the confidence) of the conclusion, it is necessary to combine the evidence. For example, let us assume that there are two rules:

R1: IF the inflation rate is less than 5 percent,

THEN stock market prices go up (CF = 0.7).

R2: IF the unemployment level is less than 7 percent,

THEN stock market prices go up (CF = 0.6).

Now let us assume a prediction that during the next year, the inflation rate will be 4 percent and the unemployment level will be 6.5 percent (i.e., we assume that the premises of the two rules are true). The combined effect is computed as follows:

$$CF(R1, R2) = CF(R1) + CF(R2) \times [1 - CF(R1)]$$
$$= CF(R1) + CF(R2) - [CF(R1) \times CF(R2)]$$

In this example, given CF(R1) = 0.7 and CF(R2) = 0.6

$$CF(R1, R2) = 0.7 + 0.6 - [(0.7) \times (0.6)] = 0.88$$

If we add a third rule, we can use the following formula:

$$CF(R1, R2, R3) = CF(R1, R2) + CF(R3) \times [1 - CF(R1, R2)]$$
$$= CF(R1, R2) + CF(R3) - [CF(R1, R2) \times CF(R3)]$$

In our example:

R3: IF bond price increases,

THEN stock prices go up (CF = 0.85)

$$CF(R1, R2, R3) = 0.88 + 0.85 - [(0.88) \times (0.85)] = 0.982$$

Note that CF(R1,R2) was computed earlier as 0.88. For a situation with more rules, we can apply the same formula incrementally.

Explanation and Justification

A final feature of expert systems is their interactivity with users and their capacity to provide an explanation consisting of the sequence of inferences that were made by the system in arriving at a conclusion. This feature offers a means of evaluating the integrity of the system when it is to be used by the experts themselves. Two basic types of explanations are the why and the how. Metaknowledge is knowledge about knowledge. It is a structure within the system using the domain knowledge to accomplish the system's problem-solving strategy. This section deals with different methods used in ES for generating explanations.

Human experts are often asked to explain their views, recommendations, or decisions. If ES are to mimic humans in performing highly specialized tasks, they, too, need to justify and explain their actions. An explanation is an attempt by an ES to clarify its reasoning, recommendations, or other actions (e.g., asking a question). The part of an ES that provides explanations is called an *explanation facility* (or *justifier*). The explanation facility has several purposes:

- Make the system more intelligible to the user.
- Uncover the shortcomings of the rules and knowledge base (i.e., debugging of the systems by the knowledge engineer).
- Explain situations that were unanticipated by the user.
- Satisfy psychological and social needs by helping the user feel more assured about the actions of the ES.
- Clarify the assumptions underlying the system's operations to both the user and the builder.
- Conduct sensitivity analyses. (Using the explanation facility as a guide, the user can predict and test the effects of changes on the system.)

Explanation in rule-based ES is usually associated with a way of tracing the rules that are fired during the course of a problem-solving session. This is about the closest to a real explanation that today's systems come, given that their knowledge is usually represented almost exclusively as rules that do not include basic principles necessary for a human-type explanation. Though many explanations have been proposed, in the following section we provide brief descriptions for the two most common types: the why and the how explanations.

WHY EXPLANATIONS   A user poses a typical "why?" question to a computer after the computer asks the user to provide some information. For example, using our earlier investment example, we might have the following dialogue:

COMPUTER: What is your annual income?

CLIENT: Why? (Why do you need to know?)

COMPUTER: R2; meaning "In checking R2, I need to know whether your income is above $40,000. If this is true, I will conclude that because you have a college degree, you should invest in growth stocks."

HOW EXPLANATIONS   A user poses a typical "how?" question when he or she would like to know how a certain conclusion or recommendation was reached. Simple systems are limited to the final conclusion. More complex systems can handle intermediate conclusions as well. The system can explain why a certain rule was fired; that is, it shows the chain of rules used to reach the conclusion. In the investment problem, the how explanation might look like this:

COMPUTER: Invest in IBM stocks.

CLIENT: How? (How was the conclusion reached?)

COMPUTER: R5–R3–R7–R4; meaning "Given that you have $10,000 to invest and you are younger than 30, then according to R4, you have a college degree. If this is the case, then according to R1, you should invest in securities. For a young investor like you, according to R3, you should invest in growth stocks if you are going to invest at all. Finally, according to R5, if you need to invest in growth stocks, then IBM is your best bet."

The why and how explanations often show the rules as they were programmed and not in a natural language. However, some systems have the capability to present these rules in natural language.

SECTION 11.7 REVIEW QUESTIONS

1. State two production rules that can represent the knowledge of repairing your car.

2. Describe how ES perform inference.

3. Describe the reasoning procedures of forward chaining and backward chaining.

4. List the three most popular methods to deal with uncertainty in ES.

5. Why do we need to incorporate uncertainty in ES solutions?

6. What are the ways by which ES justify their knowledge?

11.8 PROBLEM AREAS SUITABLE FOR EXPERT SYSTEMS

ES can be classified in several ways. One way is by the general problem areas they address. For example, diagnosis can be defined as "inferring system malfunctions from observations." *Diagnosis* is a generic activity performed in medicine, organizational studies, computer operations, and so on. The generic categories of ES are listed in Table 11.3. Some ES belong to two or more of these categories. A brief description of each category follows:

- *Interpretation systems.* Systems that infer situation descriptions from observations. This category includes surveillance, speech understanding, image analysis, signal interpretation, and many kinds of intelligence analyses. An interpretation system explains observed data by assigning them symbolic meanings that describe the situation.

TABLE 11.3 Generic Categories of Expert Systems

Category	Problem Addressed
Interpretation	Inferring situation descriptions from observations
Prediction	Inferring likely consequences of given situations
Diagnosis	Inferring system malfunctions from observations
Design	Configuring objects under constraints
Planning	Developing plans to achieve goals
Monitoring	Comparing observations to plans and flagging exceptions
Debugging	Prescribing remedies for malfunctions
Repair	Executing a plan to administer a prescribed remedy
Instruction	Diagnosing, debugging, and correcting student performance
Control	Interpreting, predicting, repairing, and monitoring system behaviors

- **Prediction systems.** These systems include weather forecasting; demographic predictions; economic forecasting; traffic predictions; crop estimates; and military, marketing, and financial forecasting.
- **Diagnostic systems.** These systems include medical, electronic, mechanical, and software diagnoses. Diagnostic systems typically relate observed behavioral irregularities to underlying causes.
- **Design systems.** These systems develop configurations of objects that satisfy the constraints of the design problem. Such problems include circuit layout, building design, and plant layout. Design systems construct descriptions of objects in various relationships with one another and verify that these configurations conform to stated constraints.
- **Planning systems.** These systems specialize in planning problems, such as automatic programming. They also deal with short- and long-term planning in areas such as project management, routing, communications, product development, military applications, and financial planning.
- **Monitoring systems.** These systems compare observations of system behavior with standards that seem crucial for successful goal attainment. These crucial features correspond to potential flaws in the plan. There are many computer-aided monitoring systems for topics ranging from air traffic control to fiscal management tasks.
- **Debugging systems.** These systems rely on planning, design, and prediction capabilities for creating specifications or recommendations to correct a diagnosed problem.
- **Repair systems.** These systems develop and execute plans to administer a remedy for certain diagnosed problems. Such systems incorporate debugging, planning, and execution capabilities.
- **Instruction systems.** Systems that incorporate diagnosis and debugging subsystems that specifically address students' needs. Typically, these systems begin by constructing a hypothetical description of the student's knowledge that interprets her or his behavior. They then diagnose weaknesses in the student's knowledge and identify appropriate remedies to overcome the deficiencies. Finally, they plan a tutorial interaction intended to deliver remedial knowledge to the student.
- **Control systems.** Systems that adaptively govern the overall behavior of a system. To do this, a control system must repeatedly interpret the current situation, predict the future, diagnose the causes of anticipated problems, formulate a remedial plan, and monitor its execution to ensure success.

Not all the tasks usually found in each of these categories are suitable for ES. However, thousands of decisions do fit into these categories.

SECTION 11.8 REVIEW QUESTIONS

1. Describe a sample ES application for prediction.
2. Describe a sample ES application for diagnosis.
3. Describe a sample ES application for the rest of the generic ES categories.

11.9 DEVELOPMENT OF EXPERT SYSTEMS

The development of ES is a tedious process and typically includes defining the nature and scope of the problem, identifying proper experts, acquiring knowledge, selecting the building tools, coding the system, and evaluating the system.

Defining the Nature and Scope of the Problem

The first step in developing an ES is to identify the nature of the problem and to define its scope. Some domains may not be appropriate for the application of ES. For example, a problem that can be solved by using mathematical optimization algorithms is often inappropriate for ES. In general, rule-based ES are appropriate when the nature of the problem is qualitative, knowledge is explicit, and experts are available to solve the problem effectively and provide their knowledge.

Another important factor is to define a feasible scope. The current technology is still very limited and is capable of solving relatively simple problems. Therefore, the scope of the problem should be specific and reasonably narrow. For example, it may be possible to develop an ES for detecting abnormal trading behavior and possible money laundering, but it is not possible to use an ES to determine whether a particular transaction is criminal.

Identifying Proper Experts

After the nature and scope of the problem have been clearly defined, the next step is to find proper experts who have the knowledge and are willing to assist in developing the knowledge base. No ES can be designed without the strong support of knowledgeable and supportive experts. A project may identify one expert or a group of experts. A proper expert should have a thorough understanding of problem-solving knowledge, the role of ES and decision support technology, and good communication skills.

Acquiring Knowledge

After identifying helpful experts, it is necessary to start acquiring decision knowledge from them. The process of eliciting knowledge is called *knowledge engineering*. The person who is interacting with experts to document the knowledge is called a *knowledge engineer*.

Knowledge acquisition is a time-consuming and risky process. Experts may be unwilling to provide their knowledge for various reasons. First, their knowledge may be proprietary and valuable. Experts may not be willing to share their knowledge without a reasonable payoff. Second, even though an expert is willing to share, certain knowledge is tacit, and the expert may not have the skill to clearly dictate the decision rules and considerations. Third, experts may be too busy to have enough time to communicate with the knowledge engineer. Fourth, certain knowledge may be confusing or contradictory in nature. Finally, the knowledge engineer may misunderstand the expert and inaccurately document knowledge.

The result of knowledge acquisition is a knowledge base that can be represented in different formats. The most popular one is if-then rules. The knowledge may also be represented as decision trees or decision tables. The knowledge in the knowledge base must be evaluated for its consistency and applicability.

Selecting the Building Tools

After the knowledge base is built, the next step is to choose a proper tool for implementing the system. There are three different kinds of development tools, as described in the following sections.

GENERAL-PURPOSE DEVELOPMENT ENVIRONMENT The first type of tool is general-purpose computer languages, such as C++, Prolog, and LISP. Most computer programming languages support the if-then statement. Therefore, it is possible to use C++ to develop an ES for a particular problem domain (e.g., disease diagnosis). Because these programming languages do not have built-in inference capabilities, using them in this way is often very costly and time-consuming. Prolog and LISP are two languages for developing intelligent systems. It is easier to use them than to use C++, but they are still specifically designed for professional programmers and are not very friendly. For recent Web-based applications, Java and computer languages that support Web services (such as the Microsoft .NET platform) are also useful. Companies such as Logic Programming Associates (**www.lpa.co.uk**) offer Prolog-based tools.

ES SHELLS The second type of development tool, the **expert system (ES) shell**, is specifically designed for ES development. An ES shell has built-in inference capabilities and a user interface, but the knowledge base is empty. System development is therefore a process of feeding the knowledge base with rules elicited from the expert.

A popular ES shell is the Corvid system developed by Exsys (**exsys.com**). The system is an object-oriented development platform that is composed of three types of operations: variables, logic blocks, and command blocks. Variables define the major factors considered in problem solving. Logic blocks are the decision rules acquired from experts. Command blocks determine how the system interacts with the user, including the order of execution and the user interface. Figure 11.8 shows a screenshot of a logic block that shows the decision rules under Exys Corvid. More products are available from business rules management vendors, such as LPA's VisiRule (**www.lpa.co.uk/vsr.htm**), which is based on a general-purpose tool called Micro-Prolog.

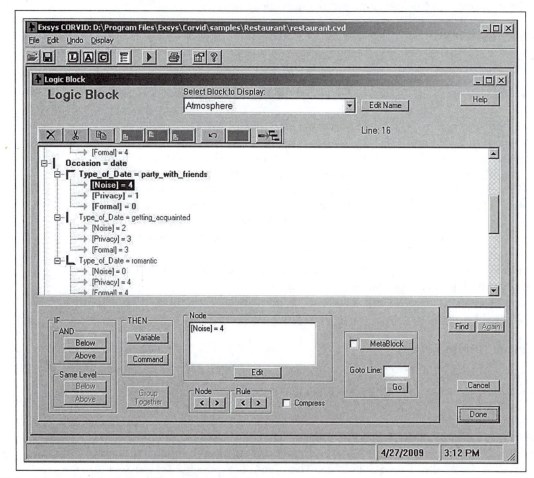

FIGURE 11.8   A Screenshot from Corvid Expert System Shell.

TAILORED TURN-KEY SOLUTIONS   The third tool, a tailored turn-key tool, is tailored to a specific domain and can be adapted to a similar application very quickly. Basically, a tailored turn-key tool contains specific features often required for developing applications in a particular domain. This tool must adjust or modify the base system by tailoring the user interface or a relatively small portion of the system to meet the unique needs of an organization.

CHOOSING AN ES DEVELOPMENT TOOL   Choosing among these tools for ES development depends on a few criteria. First, you need to consider the cost benefits. Tailored turn-key solutions are the most expensive option. However, you need to consider the total cost, not just the cost of the tool. Second, you need to consider the technical functionality and flexibility of the tool; that is, you need to determine whether the tool provides the function you need and how easily it allows the development team to make necessary changes. Third, you need to consider the tool's compatibility with the existing information infrastructure in the organization. Most organizations have many existing applications, and the tool must be compatible with those applications and needs to be able to be integrated as part of the entire information infrastructure. Finally, you need to consider the reliability of the tool and vendor support. The vendor's experiences in similar domains and training programs are critical to the success of an ES project.

Coding the System

After choosing a proper tool, the development team can focus on coding the knowledge based on the tool's syntactic requirements. The major concern at this stage is whether the coding process is efficient and properly managed to avoid errors. Skilled programmers are helpful and important.

Evaluating the System

After an ES system is built, it must be evaluated. Evaluation includes both verification and validation. Verification ensures that the resulting knowledge base contains knowledge exactly the same as that acquired from the expert. In other words, verification ensures that no error occurred at the coding stage. Validation ensures that the system can solve the problem correctly. In other words, validation checks whether the knowledge acquired from the expert can indeed solve the problem effectively. Application Case 11.5 illustrates a case where evaluation played a major role.

Application Case 11.5

Clinical Decision Support System for Tendon Injuries

Flexor tendon injuries in the hand continue to be one of the greatest challenges in hand surgery and hand therapy. Despite the advances in surgical techniques, better understanding is needed of the tendon anatomy, healing process and suture strength, edema, scarring, and stiffness. The Clinical Decision Support System (CDSS) system focuses on flexor tendon injuries in Zone II, which is technically the most demanding in both surgical and rehabilitation areas. This zone is considered a "No Man's Land" in which not many surgeons feel comfortable repairing. It is very difficult and time-consuming for both the hand surgeon and hand therapist working with tendon injury patients to keep up with the ongoing advances in this field. However, it is essential to be aware of all the information that would be

(Continued)

Application Case 11.5   (Continued)

potentially useful in making optimal clinical judgments. Major functions of the system include supporting clinical diagnosis, treatment plan processes, promoting the use of best practices, condition-specific guidelines, and population-based management. In the medical field, knowledge automation expert systems are a widely used type of CDSS.

The Clinical Decision Support System, developed using Exsys Knowledge Automation Software for Zone II flexor tendon injuries, encompasses the continuum from injury to complete rehabilitation of the tendon. The system architecture uses rule-based logic blocks to create a decision support system, which takes the user (hand surgeon, hand therapist, and other medical personnel) through a series of questions. Based on the users' input, the system's analysis will make recommendations for repair and rehabilitation for each particular situation. The CDSS takes the user through the entire process of a person's hand injury involving the flexor tendon from the emergency room encounter to full recovery, including rehabilitation of the tendon.

With combined experience of 45 years, this system was tested by hand therapists, and plastic hand and orthopedic surgeons. Two out of three concurred that this system works well, encompassing the entire continuum of the flexor tendon injury and rehabilitation. They also agreed that the system is a good support tool making good decisions, and can be used by nonexpert healthcare personnel.

Questions for Discussion

1. Research other expert systems in other domains and list a few of them.
2. Why is important to evaluate the expert systems before they are put into use?

What We Can Learn from This Application Case

The need for expert systems is continuously increasing in various fields. Many individuals are now imparting their knowledge and useful experience for future generations by building the expert systems. Also, expert systems having interactive capabilities and abilities to provide ready information based on the user inputs provide an ideal platform for expediting human decision making.

Source: **www.exsys.com,** "Advanced Clinical Advice for Tendon Injuries," **http://www.exsyssoftware.com/CaseStudySelector/ casestudies.html** (accessed February 2013).

SECTION 11.9 REVIEW QUESTIONS

1. Describe the major steps in developing rule-based ES.
2. What are the necessary conditions for a good expert?
3. Compare three different types of tools for developing ES.
4. List the criteria for choosing a development tool.
5. What is the difference between verification and validation of an ES?

11.10   CONCLUDING REMARKS

Rule-based systems have become extremely useful and important in practice. As seen in this chapter, there are systems that implement the results of other analytical models through a rule-based system, and then there are systems that are built to take advantage of the subjective knowledge of human experts. Collectively, these technologies enable an organization to pull its expertise together and use it in decision making. Sometimes, it is customer-facing; at other times, it plays an internal decision-making role. But these technologies are now quite practicable and in use in organizations. Confluence of artificial intelligence, Web development technologies, and analytical methods makes it possible for systems to be deployed that collectively give an organization a major competitive advantage or allow for better social welfare.

Chapter Highlights

- Artificial intelligence (AI) is a discipline that investigates how to build computer systems to perform tasks that can be characterized as intelligent.
- The major characteristics of AI are symbolic processing, the use of heuristics instead of algorithms, and the application of inference techniques.
- Knowledge, rather than data or information, is the major focus of AI.
- Major areas of AI include expert systems, natural language processing, speech understanding, intelligent robotics, computer vision, fuzzy logic, intelligent agents, intelligent computer-aided instruction, automatic programming, neural computing, game playing, and language translation.
- Expert systems (ES) are the most often applied AI technology. ES attempt to imitate the work of experts. They capture human expertise and apply it to problem solving.
- For an ES to be effective, it must be applied to a narrow domain, and the knowledge must include qualitative factors.
- The power of an ES is derived from the specific knowledge it possesses, not from the particular knowledge representation and inference schemes it uses.
- Expertise is task-specific knowledge acquired through training, reading, and experience.
- ES technology can transfer knowledge from experts and documented sources to the computer and make it available for use by nonexperts.

- The major components of an ES are the knowledge acquisition subsystem, knowledge base, inference engine, user interface, blackboard, explanation subsystem, and knowledge-refinement subsystem.
- The inference engine provides reasoning capability for an ES.
- ES inference can be done by using forward chaining or backward chaining.
- Knowledge engineers are professionals who know how to capture the knowledge from an expert and structure it in a form that can be processed by the computer-based ES.
- ES development process includes defining the nature and scope of the problem, identifying proper experts, acquiring knowledge, selecting the building tools, coding the system, and evaluating the system.
- ES are popular in a number of generic categories: interpretation, prediction, diagnosis, design, planning, monitoring, debugging, repair, instruction, and control.
- The ES shell is an ES development tool that has the inference engine and building blocks for the knowledge base and the user interface. Knowledge engineers can easily develop a prototype system by entering rules into the knowledge base.

Key Terms

artificial intelligence (AI)
automated decision systems (ADS)
backward chaining
blackboard
certainty factors (CF)
consultation environment
decision automation systems
development environment
expert
expert system (ES)

expert system (ES) shell
expertise
explanation subsystem
forward chaining
inference engine
inference rules
knowledge acquisition
knowledge base
knowledge engineer
knowledge engineering

knowledge rules
knowledge-based system (KBS)
knowledge-refining system
production rules
revenue management systems
rule-based systems
theory of certainty factors
user interface

Questions for Discussion

1. Why are automated decision systems so important for business applications?
2. It is said that powerful computers, inference capabilities, and problem-solving heuristics are necessary but not sufficient for solving real problems. Explain.
3. Explain the relationship between the development environment and the consultation (i.e., runtime) environment.
4. Explain the difference between forward chaining and backward chaining and describe when each is most appropriate.

5. What kinds of mistakes might ES make and why? Why is it easier to correct mistakes in ES than in conventional computer programs?
6. An ES for stock investment is developed and licensed for $1,000 per year. The system can help identify the most undervalued securities on the market and the best timing for buying and selling the securities. Will you order a copy as your investment advisor? Explain why or why not.

Exercises

Teradata UNIVERSITY NETWORK (TUN) and Other Hands-on Exercises

1. Go to **teradatauniversitynetwork.com** and search for stories about Chinatrust Commercial Bank's (CTCB's) use of the Teradata Relationship Manager and its reported benefits. Study the functional demo of the Teradata Relationship Manager to answer the following questions:
   a. What functions in the Teradata Relationship Manager are useful for supporting the automation of business rules? In CTCB's case, identify a potential application that can be supported by rule-based ES and solicit potential business rules in the knowledge base.
   b. Access Haley and compare the Teradata Relationship Manager and Haley's Business Rule Management System. Which tool is more suitable for the application identified in the previous question?
2. We list 10 categories of ES applications in the chapter. Find 20 sample applications, 2 in each category, from the various functional areas in an organization (i.e., accounting, finance, production, marketing, and human resources).
3. Download Exsys' Corvid tool for evaluation. Identify an expert (or use one of your teammates) in an area where experience-based knowledge is needed to solve problems, such as buying a used car, selecting a school and major, selecting a job from many offers, buying a computer, diagnosing and fixing computer problems, etc. Go through the knowledge-engineering process to

acquire the necessary knowledge. Using the evaluation version of the Corvid tool, develop a simple expert system application on the expertise area of your choice. Report on your experiences in a written document; use screenshots from the software as necessary.
4. Search to find applications of artificial intelligence and ES. Identify an organization with which at least one member of your group has a good contact who has a decision-making problem that requires some expertise (but is not too complicated). Understand the nature of its business and identify the problems that are supported or can potentially be supported by rule-based systems. Some examples include selection of suppliers, selection of a new employee, job assignment, computer selection, market contact method selection, and determination of admission into graduate school.
5. Identify and interview an expert who knows the domain of your choice. Ask the expert to write down his or her knowledge. Choose an ES shell and build a prototype system to see how it works.
6. Go to **exsys.com** to play with the restaurant selection example in its demo systems. Analyze the variables and rules contained in the example's knowledge base.
7. Access the Web site of the American Association for Artificial Intelligence (**aaai.org**). Examine the workshops it has offered over the past year and list the major topics related to intelligent systems.

End-of-Chapter Application Case

Tax Collections Optimization for New York State

Introduction

Tax collection in the State of New York is under the mandate of the New York State Department of Taxation and Finance's Collections and Civil Enforcement Division (CCED). Between 1995 and 2005, CCED changed and improved on its operations

in order to make tax collection more efficient. Even though the division's staff strength decreased from over 1,000 employees in 1995 to about 700 employees, its tax collection revenue increased from $500 million to over $1 billion within the same period as a result of the improved systems and procedures they used.

Presentation of Problem

The State of New York found it a challenge to reverse its growing budget deficit, partly due to the unfavorable economic conditions prior to 2009. A key part of the state's budget is revenue from tax collection, which forms about 40 percent of their yearly revenue. Tax collection mechanism was therefore seen as one key area that would help decrease the state's budget deficit if improved. The goal was to optimize tax collection in a very efficient way. The existing rigid and manual rules took too long to implement and also required too many personnel and resources to be used. This was not going to be feasible any longer because the resources allocated to the CCED for tax collection were in line to be reduced. This meant the tax collection division had to find ways of doing more with fewer resources.

Methodology/Solution

Out of all the improvements CCED made to their work process between 1995 and 2005, one area that remained unchanged was the process of collection of delinquent taxes. The existing method for tax collection employed a linear approach to identify, initiate, and collect delinquent taxes. This approach emphasized what should be done, rather than what could be done, by tax collection officers. A "one-size-fits-all" procedure for data collection was used within the constraints of allowable laws. However, the challenge of a complex legal tax system, and the less than optimal results produced by their existing scoring system, made the approach deficient. When 70 percent of delinquent cases relate to individuals and 30 percent relate to business, it is difficult to operate at an optimal level by taking on delinquent cases based on whether it is allowable or not. Better processes that would allow smarter decisions about which delinquent cases to pursue had to be developed within a constrained Markov Decision Process (MDP) framework.

Analytics and optimization processes were coupled with a Constrained Reinforcement Learning (C-RL) method. This method helped develop rules for tax collection based on taxpayer characteristics. That is, they determined that the past behavior of a taxpayer was a major predictor of a taxpayer's future behavior, and this discovery was leveraged by the method used. Basically, data analytics and optimization process were performed based on the following inputs: a list of business rules for collecting taxes, the state of the tax collection process, and resources available. These inputs produced rules for allocating actions to be taken in each tax delinquency situation.

Results/Benefits

The new system, implemented in 2009, enabled the tax agency to only collect delinquent tax when needed as opposed to when allowed within the constraints of the law. The year-to-year increase in revenue between 2007 and 2010 was 8.22 percent ($83 million). As a result of more efficient tax collection rules, fewer personnel were needed both at their contact center and on the field. The average age of cases, even with fewer employees, dropped by 9.3 percent; however, the amount of dollars collected per field agent increased by about 15 percent. Overall, there was a 7 percent increase in revenue from 2009 to 2010. As a result, more revenue was generated to support state programs.

QUESTIONS FOR THE END-OF-CHAPTER APPLICATION CASE

1. What is the key difference between the former tax collection system and the new system?
2. List at least three benefits that were derived from implementing the new system.
3. In what ways do analytics and optimization support the generation of an efficient tax collection system?
4. Why was tax collection a target for decreasing the budget deficit in the State of New York?

What We Can Learn from This End-of-Chapter Application Case

This case presents a scenario that depicts the dual use of predictive analytics and optimization in solving real-world problems. Predictive analytics was used to determine the future tax behavior of taxpayers based on their past behavior. Based on the delinquency status of the individual's or corporate body's tax situation, different courses of action are followed based on established rules. Hence, the tax agency was able to sidestep the "one-size-fits-all" policy and initiate tax collection procedures based on what they should do to increase tax revenue, and not just what they could lawfully do. The rule-based system was implemented using the information derived from optimization models.

Source: Gerard Miller, Melissa Weatherwax, Timothy Gardinier, Naoki Abe, Prem Melville, Cezar Pendus, David Jensen, et al., "Tax Collections Optimization for New York State." *Interfaces*, Vol. 42, No. 1, 2012, pp. 74–84.

References

DemandTec. "Giant Food Stores Prices the Entire Store with DemandTec." **https://mydt.demandtec.com/ mydemandtec/c/document_library/ get_file?uuid=3151a5e4-f3e1-413e-9cd7-** **333289eeb3d5&groupId=264319** (accessed February 2013).

Exsyssoftware.com. "Advanced Clinical Advice for Tendon Injuries." **exsyssoftware.com/CaseStudySelector/**

AppDetailPages/ExsysCaseStudiesMedical.html (accessed February 2013).

Exsyssoftware.com. "Diagnosing Heart Diseases." **exsyssoftware.com/CaseStudySelector/ AppDetailPages/Exsys CaseStudiesMedical.html** (accessed February 2013).

Exsyssoftware.com. "Identification of Chemical, Biological and Radiological Agents." **exsyssoftware.com/Case StudySelector/AppDetailPages/ExsysCase StudiesMedical.html** (accessed February 2013).

Koushik, Dev, Jon A. Higbie, and Craig Eister. (2012). "Retail Price Optimization at InterContinental Hotels Group." *Interfaces,* Vol. 42, No. 1, pp. 45–57.

Miller, G., M. Weatherwax, T. Gardinier, N. Abe, P. Melville, C. Pendus, D. Jensen, et al. (2012). "Tax Collections Optimization for New York State." *Interfaces,* Vol. 42, No. 1, pp. 74–84.

Papic, V., N. Rogulj, and V. Pleština. (2009). "Identification of Sport Talents Using a Web-Oriented Expert System with a Fuzzy Module." *Expert Systems with Applications,* Vol. 36, pp. 8830–8838.

CHAPTER 12

Knowledge Management and Collaborative Systems

LEARNING OBJECTIVES

- Define knowledge and describe the different types of knowledge
- Describe the characteristics of knowledge management
- Describe the knowledge management cycle
- Describe the technologies that can be used in a knowledge management system (KMS)
- Describe different approaches to knowledge management
- Understand the basic concepts and processes of groupwork, communication, and collaboration

- Describe how computer systems facilitate communication and collaboration in an enterprise
- Explain the concepts and importance of the time/place framework
- Explain the underlying principles and capabilities of groupware, such as group support systems (GSS)
- Understand how the Web enables collaborative computing and group support of virtual meetings
- Describe the role of emerging technologies in supporting collaboration

In this chapter, we study two major IT initiatives related to decision support. First, we describe the characteristics and concepts of knowledge management. We explain how firms use information technology (IT) to implement knowledge management (KM) systems and how these systems are transforming modern organizations. Knowledge management, although conceptually ancient, is a relatively new business philosophy. The goal of knowledge management is to identify, capture, store, maintain, and deliver useful knowledge in a meaningful form to anyone who needs it, anyplace and anytime, within an organization. Knowledge management is about sharing and collaborating at the organization level. People work together, and groups make most of the complex decisions in organizations. The increase in organizational decision-making complexity increases the need for meetings and groupwork. Supporting groupwork, where team members may be in different locations and working at different times, emphasizes the important aspects of communications, computer-mediated collaboration, and work methodologies.

Group support is a critical aspect of decision support systems (DSS). Effective computer-supported group support systems have evolved to increase gains and decrease losses in task performance and underlying processes. So this chapter covers both knowledge management and collaborative systems. It consists of the following sections:

12.1   OPENING VIGNETTE: Expertise Transfer System to Train Future Army Personnel

A major problem for organizations implementing knowledge management systems such as lessons-learned capabilities is the lack of success of such systems or poor service of the systems to their intended goal of promoting knowledge reuse and sharing. Lessons-learned systems are part of the broad organizational and knowledge management systems that have been well studied by IS researchers. The objective of lessons-learned systems is to support the capture, codification, presentation, and application of expertise in organizations. Lesson-learned systems have been a failure mainly for two reasons—inadequate representation and lack of integration into an organization's decision-making process.

The expertise transfer system (ETS) is a knowledge transfer system developed by the Spears School of Business at Oklahoma State University as a prototype for the Defense Ammunition Center (DAC) in McAlester, Oklahoma, for use in Army ammunition career fields. The ETS is designed to capture the knowledge of experienced ammunition personnel leaving the Army (i.e., retirements, separations, etc.) and those who have been recently deployed to the field. This knowledge is captured on video, converted into units of actionable knowledge called "nuggets," and presented to the user in a number of learning-friendly views.

ETS begins with an audio/video–recorded (A/V) interview between an interviewee and a "knowledge harvester." Typically, the recording lasts between 60 and 90 minutes. Faculty from the Oklahoma State University College of Education trained DAC knowledge harvesters on effective interviewing techniques, methods of eliciting tacit information from the interviewees, and ways to improve recorded audio quality in the interview process. Once the videos have been recorded, the meat of the ETS process takes place, as depicted in Figure 12.1. First, the digital A/V files are converted to text. Currently, this is accomplished with human transcriptionists, but we have had promising results using voice recognition (VR) technologies for transcription and foresee a day when most of the transcription will be automated. Second, the transcriptions are parsed into small units and organized into knowledge nuggets (KN). Simply put, a knowledge nugget is a significant experience the interviewee had during his/her career that is worth sharing. Then these

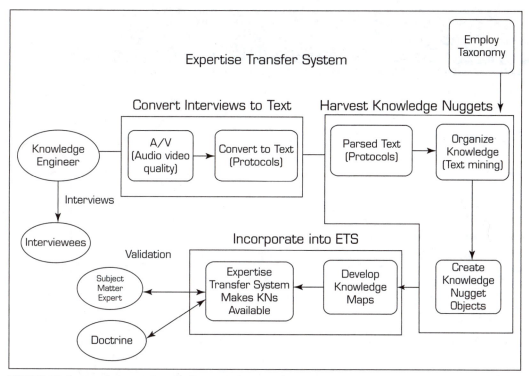

FIGURE 12.1   **Development Process for Expertise Transfer System.**

KNs are incorporated into the expertise transfer system. Finally, additional features are added to the KNs to make them easy to find, more user friendly, and more effective in the classroom.

KNOWLEDGE NUGGETS

We chose to call the harvested knowledge assets *knowledge nuggets* (KN). Of the many definitions or explanations provided by a thesaurus for *nugget*, two explanations stand out: (1) a lump of precious metal, and (2) anything of great value or significance. A knowledge nugget assumes even more importance because knowledge already is of great value. A KN can be just one piece of knowledge like a video or text. However, a KN can also be a combination of video, text, documents, figures, maps, and so forth. The tools used to transfer knowledge have a central theme, which is the knowledge itself. In our DAC repository, we have a combination of knowledge statements, videos, corresponding transcripts, causal maps, and photographs. The knowledge nugget is a specific lesson learned on a particular topic that has been developed for future use. It consists of several components. Figure 12.2 displays a sample knowledge nugget. A summary page provides the user with the title or "punchline" of the KN, the name and deployment information of the interviewee, and a bulleted summary of the KN. Clicking on the video link will bring the users to the KN video clip, whereas clicking on the transcript link will provide them with a complete transcript of the nugget. The KN text is linked back to the portion of the A/V interview from which it was harvested. The result is a searchable 30- to 60-second video clip (with captions) of the KN. A causal map function gives the user an opportunity to see and understand the thought process of the interviewee as they describe the situation captured by the nugget. The related links feature provides users with a list of regulatory guidance associated with the KN, and the related nuggets link lists all KNs within the same knowledge domain. Also provided is information about the interviewee, recognized subject matter experts (SMEs) in the KN domain, and supporting images related to the nugget.

FIGURE 12.2 A Sample Knowledge Nugget.

One of the primary objectives of the ETS is to quickly capture knowledge from the field and incorporate it into the training curriculum. This is accomplished with the My URL feature. This function allows course developers and instructors to use ETS to identify a specific nugget for sharing, and then generate a URL that can be passed directly into a course curriculum and lesson plans. When an instructor clicks on the URL, it brings him/her directly to the KN. As such, the "war story" captured in the nugget becomes the course instructor's war story and provides a real-world decision-making or problem-solving scenario right in the classroom.

The summary page also includes capabilities for users to rate the KN and make any comments about its accuracy. This makes the knowledge nugget a live and continously updated piece of knoweldge. These nuggets can then be sorted on the basis of higher ratings, if so desired. Each nugget intially includes keywords created by the nugget developer. These are presented as tags. A user can also suggest their own tags. These user-specified tags make future searching faster and easier. This brings Web 2.0 concepts of user participation to knowledge management.

In its initial conceptualization, the ETS was supposed to capture the "lesson learned" of the interviews. However, we quickly learned that the ETS process often captures "lessons to be learned." That is, the interviewees often found themselves in situations where they had to improvise and be innovative while deployed. Many of their approaches and solutions are quite admirable, but sometimes they may not be appropriate or suitable for everyone. In light of that finding, a vetting process was developed for the KNs. Each KN is reviewed by recognized subject matter experts (SME). If the SMEs find the approach acceptable, it is noted as "vetted." If guidance for the KN situation already exists, it is identified and added to the related links. The KN is then noted as "doctrine." If the KN has yet to be reviewed, it is noted as "not reviewed." In this way, the user always has an idea of the quality of each KN viewed. Additionally, if the site must be brought down for any reason, the alerts feature is used to relay that information.

The ETS is designed for two primary types of users: DAC instructors and ammunition personnel. As such, a "push/pull" capability was developed. Tech training instructors do not have the time to search the ETS to find those KNs that are related to the courses they teach. To provide some relief to instructors, the KNs are linked to DAC courses and topics, and can be *pushed* to instructors' e-mail accounts as the KNs come online. Instructors can opt-in or opt-out of courses and topics at will, and they can arrange for new KNs to be pushed as often as they like. Ammunition personnel are the other primary users of the ETS. These users need the ability to quickly locate and *pull* KNs related to their immediate knowledge needs. To aid them, the ETS organizes the nuggets in various views and has a robust search engine. These views include courses and topics; interviewee names; chronological; and by user-created tags. The goal of the ETS is to provide the user with the KNs they need in 5 minutes or less.

KNOWLEDGE HARVESTING PROCESS

The knowledge harvesting process began with videotaping interviews with DAC employees regarding their deployment experience. Speech in the interviews, in some cases, was converted manually to text. In other cases, the knowledge harvesting team (hereinafter referred to as the "team") employed voice recognition technologies to convert the speech to text. The text was checked for accuracy and then passed through the text mining division of the team. The text mining group read through the transcript and employed text mining software to extract some preliminary knowledge from the transcript. The text mining process provided a one-sentence summary for the knowledge nugget, which became the knowledge statement, commonly known among the team as the "punchline." The punchline created from the transcripts along with the excerpts, relevant video from the interview, and causal maps make up the entire knowledge nugget. The knowledge nugget is further refined by checking for quality of general appearance, errors in text, and so on.

IMPLEMENTATION AND RESULTS

The ETS system was built as a prototype for demonstration of its potential use at the Defense Ammunition Center. It was built using a MySQL database for the collection of knowledge nuggets and the related content, and PHP and JavaScript as the Web language platform. The system also incorporated necessary security and access control precautions. It was made available to several groups of trainees who really liked using this type of tacit knowledge presentation. The feedback was very positive. However, some internal issues as well as the challenge of having the tacit knowledge be shared as official knowledge resulted in the system being discontinued. However, the application was developed to be more of a general knowledge–sharing system as opposed to just this specific use. The authors are exploring other potential users for this platform.

QUESTIONS FOR THE OPENING VIGNETTE

1. What are the key impediments to the use of knowledge in a knowledge management system?
2. What features are incorporated in a knowledge nugget in this implementation?
3. Where else could such a system be implemented?

WHAT WE CAN LEARN FROM THIS VIGNETTE

Knowledge management initiatives in many organizations have not succeeded. Although many studies have been conducted on this issue and we will learn more about this topic in future sections, two major issues seem to be critical. Compilation of a lot of user-generated information in a large Web compilation by itself does not present the needed information in the right format to the user. Nor does it make it easy to find the right knowledge at the right time. So developing a friendly knowledge presentation format that includes audio, video, text summary, and Web 2.0 features such as tagging, sharing, comments, and ratings makes it more likely that users will actually use the KM content. Second, organizing the knowledge to be visible in specific taxonomies as well as search and enabling the users to tag the content enable this knowledge to be more easily discovered within a knowledge management system.

Sources: Based on our own documents and S. Iyer, R. Sharda, D. Biros, J. Lucca, and U. Shimp, "Organization of Lessons Learned Knowledge: A Taxonomy of Implementation," *International Journal of Knowledge Management*, Vol. 5, No. 3 (2009).

12.2 INTRODUCTION TO KNOWLEDGE MANAGEMENT

Humans learn effectively through stories, analogies, and examples. Davenport and Prusak (1998) argue that knowledge is communicated effectively when it is conveyed with a convincing narrative. Family-run businesses transfer the secrets of business learned through experience to the next generation. Knowledge through experience does not necessarily reside in any business textbook, but the transfer of such knowledge facilitates its profitable use. Nonaka (1991) used the term *tacit knowledge* for the knowledge that exists in the head but not on paper. Tacit knowledge is difficult to capture, manage, and share. He also observes that organizations that use tacit knowledge as a strategic weapon are innovators and leaders in their respective business domains. There is no substitute for the substantial value that tacit knowledge can provide. Therefore, it is necessary to capture and codify tacit knowledge to the greatest extent possible.

In the 2000s knowledge management was considered to be one of the cornerstones of business success. Despite spending billions of dollars on knowledge management both by industry and government, success has been mixed. Usually it is the successful projects that see the limelight. Much research has focused on successful knowledge management initiatives as well as factors that could lead to a successful knowledge management project (Davenport et al., 1998). But a few researchers have presented case studies of knowledge management failures (Chua and Lam, 2005). One of the causes for such failures is that the prospective users of such knowledge cannot easily locate relevant information. Knowledge compiled in a knowledge management system is no good to the organization if it cannot be easily found by the likely end users. On the other hand, although their worth is difficult to measure, organizations recognize the value of their intellectual assets. Fierce global competition drives companies to better use their intellectual assets by transforming themselves into organizations that foster the development and sharing of knowledge. In the next few sections we cover the basic concepts of knowledge management.

Knowledge Management Concepts and Definitions

With roots in **organizational learning** and innovation, the idea of KM is not new (see Ponzi, 2004; and Schwartz, 2006). However, the application of IT tools to facilitate the creation, storage, transfer, and application of previously uncodifiable organizational knowledge is a new and major initiative in many organizations. Successful managers have long used intellectual assets and recognized their value. But these efforts were not systematic, nor did they ensure that knowledge gained was shared and dispersed appropriately for maximum organizational benefit. Knowledge management is a process that helps organizations identify, select, organize, disseminate, and transfer important information and expertise that are part of the organization's memory and that typically reside within the organization in an unstructured manner. **Knowledge management (KM)** is the systematic and active management of ideas, information, and knowledge residing in an organization's employees. The structuring of knowledge enables effective and efficient problem solving, dynamic learning, strategic planning, and decision making. KM initiatives focus on identifying knowledge, explicating it in such a way that it can be shared in a formal manner, and leveraging its value through reuse. The information technologies that make KM available throughout an organization are referred to as *KM systems*.

Through a supportive organizational climate and modern IT, an organization can bring its entire organizational memory and knowledge to bear on any problem, anywhere in the world, and at any time (see Bock et al., 2005). For organizational success, knowledge, as a form of capital, must be exchangeable among persons, and it must be able to grow. Knowledge about how problems are solved can be captured so that KM can promote organizational learning, leading to further knowledge creation.

Knowledge

Knowledge is very distinct from data and information (see Figure 12.3). Data are facts, measurements, and statistics; information is organized or processed data that is timely (i.e., inferences from the data are drawn within the time frame of applicability) and accurate (i.e., with regard to the original data) (Kankanhalli et al., 2005). **Knowledge** is information that is contextual, relevant, and actionable. For example, a map that gives detailed driving directions from one location to another could be considered data. An up-to-the-minute traffic bulletin along the freeway that indicates a traffic slowdown due to construction several miles ahead could be considered information. Awareness of an alternative, back-road route could be considered knowledge. In this case, the map is considered data because it does not contain current relevant information that affects the driving time and conditions from one location to the other. However, having the current conditions as information is useful only if you have knowledge that enables you to avert the construction zone. The implication is that knowledge has strong experiential and reflective elements that distinguish it from information in a given context.

Having knowledge implies that it can be exercised to solve a problem, whereas having information does not carry the same connotation. An ability to act is an integral part of being knowledgeable. For example, two people in the same context with the same information may not have the same ability to use the information to the same degree of success. Hence, there is a difference in the human capability to add value. The differences in ability may be due to different experiences, different training, different perspectives, and other factors. Whereas data, information, and knowledge may all be viewed as assets of an organization, knowledge provides a higher level of meaning about data and information. It conveys meaning and hence tends to be much more valuable, yet more ephemeral.

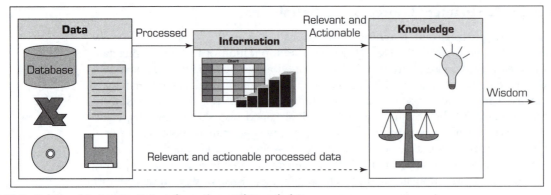

FIGURE 12.3 Relationship Among Data, Information, and Knowledge.

Unlike other organizational assets, knowledge has the following characteristics (see Gray, 1999):

- ***Extraordinary leverage and increasing returns.*** Knowledge is not subject to diminishing returns. When it is used, it is not decreased (or depleted); rather, it is increased (or improved). Its consumers can add to it, thus increasing its value.
- ***Fragmentation, leakage, and the need to refresh.*** As knowledge grows, it branches and fragments. Knowledge is dynamic; it is *information in action*. Thus, an organization must continually refresh its knowledge base to maintain it as a source of competitive advantage.
- ***Uncertain value.*** It is difficult to estimate the impact of an investment in knowledge. There are too many intangible aspects that cannot be easily quantified.
- ***Value of sharing.*** It is difficult to estimate the value of sharing one's knowledge or even who will benefit most from it.

Over the past few decades, the industrialized economy has been going through a transformation from being based on natural resources to being based on intellectual assets (see Alavi, 2000; and Tseng and Goo, 2005). The **knowledge-based economy** is a reality (see Godin, 2006). Rapid changes in the business environment cannot be handled in traditional ways. Firms are much larger today than they used to be, and, in some areas, turnover is extremely high, fueling the need for better tools for collaboration, communication, and knowledge sharing. Firms must develop strategies to sustain competitive advantage by leveraging their intellectual assets for optimal performance. Competing in the globalized economy and markets requires quick response to customer needs and problems. To provide service, managing knowledge is critical for consulting firms spread out over wide geographical areas and for virtual organizations.

There is a vast amount of literature about what knowledge and knowing mean in epistemology (i.e., the study of the nature of knowledge), the social sciences, philosophy, and psychology. Although there is no single definition of what knowledge and KM specifically mean, the business perspective on them is fairly pragmatic. Information as a resource is not always valuable (i.e., information overload can distract from what is important); knowledge as a resource is valuable because it focuses attention back toward what is important (see Carlucci and Schiuma, 2006; and Hoffer et al., 2002). Knowledge implies an implicit understanding and experience that can discriminate between its use and misuse. Over time, information accumulates and decays, whereas knowledge evolves. Knowledge is dynamic in nature. This implies, though, that today's knowledge may well become tomorrow's ignorance if an individual or organization fails to update knowledge as environmental conditions change.

Knowledge evolves over time with experience, which puts connections among new situations and events in context. Given the breadth of the types and applications of knowledge, we adopt the simple and elegant definition that knowledge is information in action.

Explicit and Tacit Knowledge

Polanyi (1958) first conceptualized the difference between an organization's explicit and tacit knowledge. **Explicit knowledge** deals with more objective, rational, and technical knowledge (e.g., data, policies, procedures, software, documents). **Tacit knowledge** is usually in the domain of subjective, cognitive, and experiential learning; it is highly personal and difficult to formalize. Alavi and Leidner (2001) provided a taxonomy (see Table 12.1), where they defined a spectrum of different types of knowledge, going beyond the simple binary classification of explicit versus tacit. However, most KM research has been (and still is) debating over the dichotomous classification of knowledge.

Explicit knowledge comprises the policies, procedural guides, white papers, reports, designs, products, strategies, goals, mission, and core competencies of an enterprise and its IT infrastructure. It is the knowledge that has been codified (i.e., documented) in a form that can be distributed to others or transformed into a process or strategy without requiring interpersonal interaction. For example, a description of how to process a job application would be documented in a firm's human resources policy manual. Explicit knowledge has also been called **leaky knowledge** because of the ease with which it can leave an individual, a document, or an organization due to the fact that it can be readily and accurately documented (see Alavi, 2000).

TABLE 12.1 Taxonomy of Knowledge

Knowledge Type	Definition	Example
Tacit	Knowledge is rooted in actions, experience, and involvement in specific context	Best means of dealing with a specific customer
Cognitive tacit:	Mental models	Individual's belief on cause-effect relationships
Technical tacit:	Know-how applicable to specific work	Surgery skills
Explicit	Articulated, generalized knowledge	Knowledge of major customers in a region
Individual	Created by and inherent in the individual	Insights gained from completed project
Social	Created by and inherent in collective actions of a group	Norms for intergroup communication
Declarative	Know-about	What drug is appropriate for an illness
Procedural	Know-how	How to administer a particular drug
Causal	Know-why	Understanding why the drug works
Conditional	Know-when	Understanding when to prescribe the drug
Relational	Know-with	Understanding how the drug interacts with other drugs
Pragmatic	Useful knowledge for an organization	Best practices, treatment protocols, case analyses, postmortems

Tacit knowledge is the cumulative store of the experiences, mental maps, insights, acumen, expertise, know-how, trade secrets, skillsets, understanding, and learning that an organization has, as well as the **organizational culture** that has embedded in it the past and present experiences of the organization's people, processes, and values. Tacit knowledge, also referred to as *embedded knowledge* (see Tuggle and Goldfinger, 2004), is usually either localized within the brain of an individual or embedded in the group interactions within a department or a branch office. Tacit knowledge typically involves expertise or high skill levels.

Sometimes tacit knowledge could easily be documented but has remained tacit simply because the individual housing the knowledge does not recognize its potential value to other individuals. Other times, tacit knowledge is unstructured, without tangible form, and therefore difficult to codify. It is difficult to put some tacit knowledge into words. For example, an explanation of how to ride a bicycle would be difficult to document explicitly and thus is tacit. Successful transfer or sharing of tacit knowledge usually takes place through associations, internships, apprenticeship, conversations, other means of social and interpersonal interactions, or even simulations (see Robin, 2000). Nonaka and Takeuchi (1995) claimed that intangibles such as insights, intuitions, hunches, gut feelings, values, images, metaphors, and analogies are the often-overlooked assets of organizations. Harvesting these intangible assets can be critical to a firm's bottom line and its ability to meet its goals. Tacit knowledge sharing requires a certain context or situation in order to be facilitated because it is less commonly shared under normal circumstances (see Shariq and Vendelø, 2006).

Historically, management information systems (MIS) departments have focused on capturing, storing, managing, and reporting explicit knowledge. Organizations now recognize the need to integrate both types of knowledge in formal information systems. For centuries, the mentor–apprentice relationship, because of its experiential nature, has been a slow but reliable means of transferring tacit knowledge from individual to individual. When people leave an organization, they take their knowledge with them. One critical goal of knowledge management is to retain the valuable know-how that can so easily and quickly leave an organization. **Knowledge management systems (KMS)** refer to the use of modern IT (e.g., the Internet, intranets, extranets, Lotus Notes, software filters, agents, data warehouses, Web 2.0) to systematize, enhance, and expedite intra- and interfirm KM.

KM systems are intended to help an organization cope with turnover, rapid change, and downsizing by making the expertise of the organization's human capital widely accessible. They are being built, in part, because of the increasing pressure to maintain a well-informed, productive workforce. Moreover, they are built to help large organizations provide a consistent level of customer service.

SECTION 12.2 REVIEW QUESTIONS

1. Define *knowledge management* and describe its purposes.
2. Distinguish between knowledge and data.
3. Describe the knowledge-based economy.
4. Define *tacit knowledge* and *explicit knowledge*.
5. Define *KMS* and describe the capabilities of KMS.

12.3 APPROACHES TO KNOWLEDGE MANAGEMENT

The two fundamental approaches to knowledge management are the process approach and the practice approach (see Table 12.2). We next describe these two approaches as well as hybrid approaches.

TABLE 12.2 The Process and Practice Approaches to Knowledge Management

	Process Approach	Practice Approach
Type of knowledge supported	Explicit knowledge—codified in rules, tools, and processes	Mostly tacit knowledge—unarticulated knowledge not easily captured or codified
Means of transmission	Formal controls, procedures, and standard operating procedures, with heavy emphasis on information technologies to support knowledge creation, codification, and transfer of knowledge	Informal social groups that engage in storytelling and improvisation
Benefits	Provides structure to harness generated ideas and knowledge Achieves scale in knowledge reuse Provides spark for fresh ideas and responsiveness to changing environment	Provides an environment to generate and transfer high-value tacit knowledge
Disadvantages	Fails to tap into tacit knowledge May limit innovation and forces participants into fixed patterns of thinking	Can result in inefficiency Abundance of ideas with no structure to implement them
Role of information technology (IT)	Requires heavy investment in IT to connect people with reusable codified knowledge	Requires moderate investment in IT to facilitate conversations and transfer of tacit knowledge

Source: Compiled from M. Alavi, T. R. Kayworth, and D. E. Leidner, "An Empirical Examination of the Influence of Organizational Culture on Knowledge Management Practices," *Journal of Management Information Systems,* Vol. 22, No. 3, 2006, pp. 191–224.

The Process Approach to Knowledge Management

The **process approach** to knowledge management attempts to codify organizational knowledge through formalized controls, processes, and technologies (see Hansen et al., 1999). Organizations that adopt the process approach may implement explicit policies governing how knowledge is to be collected, stored, and disseminated throughout the organization. The process approach frequently involves the use of IT, such as intranets, data warehousing, knowledge repositories, decision support tools, and groupware to enhance the quality and speed of knowledge creation and distribution in the organization. The main criticisms of the process approach are that it fails to capture much of the tacit knowledge embedded in firms and it forces individuals into fixed patterns of thinking (see Kiaraka and Manning, 2005). This approach is favored by firms that sell relatively standardized products that fill common needs. Most of the valuable knowledge in these firms is fairly explicit because of the standardized nature of the products and services. For example, a kazoo manufacturer has minimal product changes or service needs over the years, and yet there is steady demand and a need to produce the item. In these cases, the knowledge may be typically static in nature.

The Practice Approach to Knowledge Management

In contrast to the process approach, the **practice approach** to knowledge management assumes that a great deal of organizational knowledge is tacit in nature and that formal controls, processes, and technologies are not suitable for transmitting this type of understanding. Rather than build formal systems to manage knowledge, the focus of this approach is to build the social environments or communities of practice necessary to facilitate the sharing of tacit understanding (see Hansen et al., 1999; Leidner et al., 2006; and Wenger and Snyder, 2000). These communities are informal social groups that meet regularly to share ideas, insights, and best practices. This approach is typically adopted by companies that provide highly customized solutions to unique problems. For these firms, knowledge is shared mostly through person-to-person contact. Collaborative computing methods (e.g., group support systems [GSS], e-mail) help people communicate. The valuable knowledge for these firms is tacit in nature, which is difficult to express, capture, and manage. In this case, the environment and the nature of the problems being encountered are extremely dynamic. Because tacit knowledge is difficult to extract, store, and manage, the explicit knowledge that points to how to find the appropriate tacit knowledge (i.e., people contacts, consulting reports) is made available to an appropriate set of individuals who might need it. Consulting firms generally fall into this category. Firms adopting the codification strategy implicitly adopt the network storage model in their initial KMS (see Alavi, 2000).

Hybrid Approaches to Knowledge Management

Many organizations use a hybrid of the process and practice approaches. Early in the development process, when it may not be clear how to extract tacit knowledge from its sources, the practice approach is used so that a repository stores only explicit knowledge that is relatively easy to document. The tacit knowledge initially stored in the repository is contact information about experts and their areas of expertise. Such information is listed so that people in the organization can find sources of expertise (e.g., the process approach). From this start, best practices can eventually be captured and managed so that the **knowledge repository** will contain an increasing amount of tacit knowledge over time. Eventually, a true process approach may be attained. But if the environment changes rapidly, only some of the best practices will prove useful. Regardless of the type of KMS developed, a storage location for the knowledge (i.e., a knowledge repository) of some kind is needed.

Certain highly skilled, research-oriented industries exhibit traits that require nearly equal efforts with both approaches. For example, Koenig (2001) argued that the pharmaceutical firms in which he has worked require about a 50/50 split. We suspect that industries that require both a lot of engineering effort (i.e., how to create products) and heavy-duty research effort (where a large percentage of research is unusable) would fit the 50/50 hybrid category. Ultimately, any knowledge that is stored in a knowledge repository must be reevaluated; otherwise, the repository will become a knowledge landfill.

Knowledge Repositories

A knowledge repository is neither a database nor a knowledge base in the strictest sense of the terms. Rather, a knowledge repository stores knowledge that is often text based and has very different characteristics. It is also referred to as an organizational knowledge base. Do not confuse a knowledge repository with the knowledge base of an expert system. They are very different mechanisms: A knowledge base of an expert system contains knowledge for solving a specific problem. An organizational knowledge base contains all the organizational knowledge.

Capturing and storing knowledge are the goals for a knowledge repository. The structure of the repository is highly dependent on the types of knowledge it stores. The repository can range from simply a list of frequently asked (and obscure) questions and solutions, to a listing of individuals with their expertise and contact information, to detailed best practices for a large organization. Figure 12.4 shows a comprehensive KM architecture designed around an all-inclusive knowledge repository (Delen and

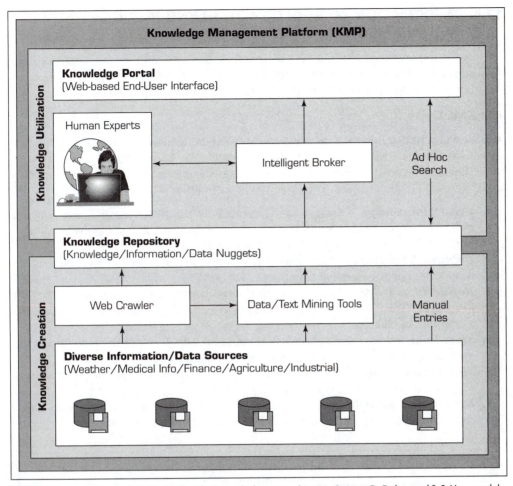

FIGURE 12.4   A Comprehensive View of a Knowledge Repository. *Source:* D. Delen and S. S. Hawamdeh, "A Holistic Framework for Knowledge Discovery and Management," *Communications of the ACM*, Vol. 52, No. 6, 2009, pp. 141–145.

Hawamdeh, 2009). Most knowledge repositories are developed using several different storage mechanisms, depending on the types and amount of knowledge to be maintained and used. Each has strengths and weaknesses when used for different purposes within a KMS. Developing a knowledge repository is not an easy task. The most important aspects and difficult issues are making the contribution of knowledge relatively easy for the contributor and determining a good method for cataloging the knowledge. The users should not be involved in running the storage and retrieval mechanisms of the knowledge repository. Typical development approaches include developing a large-scale Internet-based system or purchasing a formal electronic document management system or a knowledge management suite. The structure and development of the knowledge repository are a function of the specific technology used for the KMS.

SECTION 12.3 REVIEW QUESTIONS

1. Describe the process approach to knowledge management.
2. Describe the practice approach to knowledge management.
3. Why is a hybrid approach to KM desirable?
4. Define *knowledge repository* and describe how to create one.

12.4 INFORMATION TECHNOLOGY (IT) IN KNOWLEDGE MANAGEMENT

The two primary functions of IT in knowledge management are retrieval and communication. IT also extends the reach and range of knowledge use and enhances the speed of knowledge transfer. Networks facilitate collaboration in KM.

The KMS Cycle

A functioning KMS follows six steps in a cycle (see Figure 12.5). The reason for the cycle is that knowledge is dynamically refined over time. The knowledge in a good KMS is never finished because the environment changes over time, and the knowledge must be updated to reflect the changes. The cycle works as follows:

1. *Create knowledge.* Knowledge is created as people determine new ways of doing things or develop know-how. Sometimes external knowledge is brought in. Some of these new ways may become best practices.
2. *Capture knowledge.* New knowledge must be identified as valuable and be represented in a reasonable way.
3. *Refine knowledge.* New knowledge must be placed in context so that it is actionable. This is where human insights (i.e., tacit qualities) must be captured along with explicit facts.
4. *Store knowledge.* Useful knowledge must be stored in a reasonable format in a knowledge repository so that others in the organization can access it.
5. *Manage knowledge.* Like a library, a repository must be kept current. It must be reviewed to verify that it is relevant and accurate.
6. *Disseminate knowledge.* Knowledge must be made available in a useful format to anyone in the organization who needs it, anywhere and anytime.

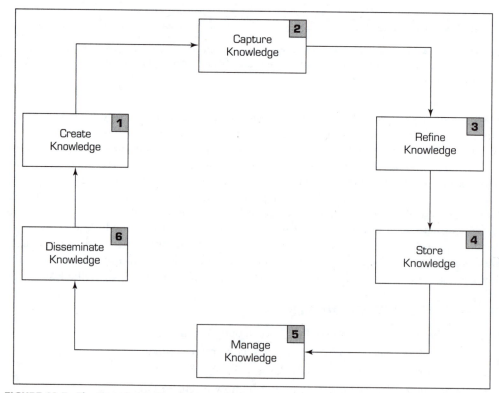

FIGURE 12.5 The Knowledge Management Cycle.

Components of KMS

Knowledge management is more a methodology applied to business practices than a technology or a product. Nevertheless, IT is crucial to the success of every KMS. IT enables knowledge management by providing the enterprise architecture on which it is built. KMS are developed using three sets of technologies: communication, collaboration, and storage and retrieval.

Communication technologies allow users to access needed knowledge and to communicate with each other—especially with experts. E-mail, the Internet, corporate intranets, and other Web-based tools provide communication capabilities. Even fax machines and telephones are used for communication, especially when the practice approach to knowledge management is adopted.

Collaboration technologies (next several sections) provide the means to perform groupwork. Groups can work together on common documents at the same time (i.e., synchronous) or at different times (i.e., asynchronous); they can work in the same place or in different places. Collaboration technologies are especially important for members of a **community of practice** working on knowledge contributions. Other collaborative computing capabilities, such as electronic brainstorming, enhance group-work, especially for knowledge contribution. Additional forms of groupwork involve experts working with individuals trying to apply their knowledge; this requires collaboration at a fairly high level. Other collaborative computing systems allow an organization to create a virtual space so that individuals can work online anywhere and at any time (see Van de Van, 2005).

Storage and retrieval technologies originally meant using a database management system (DBMS) to store and manage knowledge. This worked reasonably well in the early days for storing and managing most explicit knowledge—and even explicit knowledge about tacit knowledge. However, capturing, storing, and managing tacit knowledge usually requires a different set of tools. Electronic document management systems and specialized storage systems that are part of collaborative computing systems fill this void. These storage systems have come to be known as knowledge repositories.

We describe the relationship between these knowledge management technologies and the Web in Table 12.3.

Technologies That Support Knowledge Management

Several technologies have contributed to significant advances in knowledge management tools. Artificial intelligence, intelligent agents, knowledge discovery in databases, eXtensible Markup Language (XML), and Web 2.0 are examples of technologies that enable advanced functionality of modern KMS and form the basis for future innovations in the knowledge management field. Following is a brief description of how these technologies are used in support of KMS.

ARTIFICIAL INTELLIGENCE In the definition of knowledge management, artificial intelligence (AI) is rarely mentioned. However, practically speaking, AI methods and tools are embedded in a number of KMS, either by vendors or by system developers. AI methods can assist in identifying expertise, eliciting knowledge automatically and semiautomatically, interfacing through natural language processing, and intelligently searching through intelligent agents. AI methods—notably expert systems, neural networks, fuzzy logic, and intelligent agents—are used in KMS to do the following:

- Assist in and enhance searching knowledge (e.g., intelligent agents in Web searches)
- Help establish knowledge profiles of individuals and groups

TABLE 12.3 Knowledge Management Technologies and Web Impacts		
Knowledge Management	**Web Impacts**	**Impacts on the Web**
Communication	Consistent, friendly graphical user interface (GUI) for client units Improved communication tools Convenient, fast access to knowledge and knowledgeable individuals Direct access to knowledge on servers	Knowledge captured and shared is used in improving communication, communication management, and communication technologies.
Collaboration	Improved collaboration tools Enables anywhere/anytime collaboration Enables collaboration between companies, customers, and vendors Enables document sharing Improved, fast collaboration and links to knowledge sources Makes audio- and videoconferencing a reality, especially for individuals not using a local area network	Knowledge captured and shared is used in improving collaboration, collaboration management, and collaboration technologies (i.e., SharePoint, wiki, GSS).
Storage and retrieval	Consistent, friendly GUI for clients Servers provide for efficient and effective storage and retrieval of knowledge	Knowledge captured and shared is utilized in improving data storage and retrieval systems, database management/ knowledge repository management, and database and knowledge repository technologies.

- Help determine the relative importance of knowledge when it is contributed to and accessed from the knowledge repository
- Scan e-mail, documents, and databases to perform knowledge discovery, determine meaningful relationships, glean knowledge, or induce rules for expert systems
- Identify patterns in data (usually through neural networks)
- Forecast future results by using existing knowledge
- Provide advice directly from knowledge by using neural networks or expert systems
- Provide a natural language or voice command–driven user interface for a KMS

WEB 2.0 The Web has evolved from a tool for disseminating information and conducting business to a platform for facilitating new ways of information sharing, collaboration, and communication in the digital age. A new vocabulary has emerged, as mashups, social networks, media-sharing sites, RSS, blogs, and wikis have come to characterize the genre of interactive applications collectively known as Web 2.0. These technologies have given knowledge management a strong boost by making it easy and natural for everyone to share knowledge. In some ways this has occurred to the point of perhaps making the term *knowledge management* almost redundant. Indeed, Davenport (2008) characterized Web 2.0 (and its reflection to the enterprise world, Enterprise 2.0) as "new, new knowledge management." One of the bottlenecks for knowledge management practices has been the difficulty for nontechnical people to natively share their knowledge. Therefore, the ultimate value of Web 2.0 is its ability to foster greater responsiveness, better knowledge capture and sharing, and ultimately, more effective collective intelligence.

SECTION 12.4 REVIEW QUESTIONS

1. Describe the KMS cycle.

2. List and describe the components of KMS.

3. Describe how AI and intelligent agents support knowledge management.

4. Relate Web 2.0 to knowledge management

Web 2.0 also engenders collaborative inputs. Whether these collaborations are for knowledge management activities or other organizational decision making, the overall principles are the same. We study some basic collaborative mechanisms and systems in the next several sections.

12.5 MAKING DECISIONS IN GROUPS: CHARACTERISTICS, PROCESS, BENEFITS, AND DYSFUNCTIONS

Managers and other knowledge workers continuously make decisions, design and manufacture products, develop policies and strategies, create software systems, and so on. When people work in groups (i.e., teams), they perform groupwork (i.e., teamwork). **Groupwork** refers to work done by two or more people together.

Characteristics of Groupwork

The following are some of the functions and characteristics of groupwork:

- A group performs a task (sometimes decision making, sometimes not).
- Group members may be located in different places.
- Group members may work at different times.
- Group members may work for the same organization or for different organizations.
- A group can be permanent or temporary.
- A group can be at one managerial level or span several levels.
- It can create synergy (leading to process and task gains) or conflict.
- It can generate productivity gains and/or losses.
- The task may have to be accomplished very quickly.
- It may be impossible or too expensive for all the team members to meet in one place, especially when the group is called for emergency purposes.
- Some of the needed data, information, or knowledge may be located in many sources, some of which may be external to the organization.
- The expertise of no team members may be needed.
- Groups perform many tasks; however, groups of managers and analysts frequently concentrate on decision making.
- The decisions made by a group are easier to implement if supported by all (or at least most) members.

The Group Decision-Making Process

Even in hierarchical organizations, decision making is usually a shared process. A group may be involved in a decision or in a decision-related task, such as creating a short list of acceptable alternatives or choosing criteria for evaluating alternatives and prioritizing them. The following activities and processes characterize meetings:

- The decision situation is important, so it is advisable to make it in a group in a meeting.
- A meeting is a joint activity engaged in by a group of people typically of equal or nearly equal status.
- The outcome of a meeting depends partly on the knowledge, opinions, and judgments of its participants and the support they give to the outcome.
- The outcome of a meeting depends on the composition of the group and on the decision-making process the group uses.
- Differences in opinions are settled either by the ranking person present or, often, through negotiation or arbitration.
- The members of a group can be in one place, meeting face-to-face, or they can be a **virtual team**, in which case they are in different places while in a meeting.
- The process of group decision making can create benefits as well as dysfunctions.

The Benefits and Limitations of Groupwork

Some people endure meetings (the most common form of groupwork) as a necessity; others find them to be a waste of time. Many things can go wrong in a meeting. Participants may not clearly understand their goals, they may lack focus, or they may have hidden agendas. Many participants may be afraid to speak up, while a few may dominate the discussion. Misunderstandings occur through different interpretations of language, gesture, or expression. Table 12.4 provides a comprehensive list of factors that can hinder the effectiveness of a meeting (Nunamaker, 1997). Besides being challenging, teamwork is also expensive. A meeting of several managers or executives may cost thousands of dollars per hour in salary costs alone.

Groupwork may have both potential benefits (process gains) and potential drawbacks (process losses). **Process gains** are the benefits of working in groups. The unfortunate dysfunctions that may occur when people work in groups are called **process losses**. Examples of each are listed in Technology Insights 12.1.

TABLE 12.4 Difficulties Associated with Groupwork

• Waiting to speak	• Wrong composition of people
• Dominating the discussion	• Groupthink
• Fear of speaking	• Poor grasp of problem
• Fear of being misunderstood	• Ignored alternatives
• Inattention	• Lack of consensus
• Lack of focus	• Poor planning
• Inadequate criteria	• Hidden agendas
• Premature decisions	• Conflicts of interest
• Missing information	• Inadequate resources
• Distractions	• Poorly defined goals
• Digressions	

TECHNOLOGY INSIGHTS 12.1   Benefits of Working in Groups and Dysfunctions of the Group Process

Benefits of Working in Groups (Process Gains)	Dysfunctions of the Group Process (Process Losses)
• It provides learning. Groups are better than individuals at understanding problems.	• Social pressures of conformity may result in **groupthink** (i.e., people begin to think alike and do not tolerate new ideas; they yield to *conformance pressure*).
• People readily take ownership of problems and their solutions. They take responsibility.	• It is a time-consuming, slow process (i.e., only one member can speak at a time).
• Group members have their egos embedded in the decision, so they are committed to the solution.	• There can be lack of coordination of the meeting and poor meeting planning.
• Groups are better than individuals at catching errors.	• Inappropriate influences (e.g., domination of time, topic, or opinion by one or few individuals; fear of contributing because of the possibility of *flaming*).
• A group has more *information* (i.e., knowledge) than any one member. Group members can combine their knowledge to create new knowledge. More and more creative alternatives for problem solving can be generated, and better solutions can be derived (e.g., through *stimulation*).	• There can be a tendency for group members to either dominate the agenda or rely on others to do most of the work (free-riding).
• A group may produce *synergy* during problem solving. The effectiveness and/ or quality of groupwork can be greater than the sum of what is produced by independent individuals.	• Some members may be afraid to speak up.
• Working in a group may stimulate the creativity of the participants and the process.	• There can be a tendency to produce compromised solutions of poor quality.
• A group may have better and more precise communication working together.	• There is often nonproductive time (e.g., socializing, preparing, waiting for latecomers; i.e., *air-time fragmentation*).
• Risk propensity is balanced. Groups moderate high-risk takers and encourage conservatives.	• There can be a tendency to repeat what has already been said (because of failure to remember or process).
	• Meeting costs can be high (e.g., travel, participation time spent).
	• There can be incomplete or inappropriate use of information.
	• There can be too much information (i.e., information overload).
	• There can be incomplete or incorrect task analysis.

(Continued)

Benefits of Working in Groups (Process Gains)	Dysfunctions of the Group Process (Process Losses)
	• There can be inappropriate or incomplete representation in the group.
	• There can be attention blocking.
	• There can be concentration blocking.

SECTION 12.5 REVIEW QUESTIONS

1. Define *groupwork.*

2. List five characteristics of groupwork.

3. Describe the process of a group meeting for decision making.

12.6 SUPPORTING GROUPWORK WITH COMPUTERIZED SYSTEMS

When people work in teams, especially when the members are in different locations and may be working at different times, they need to communicate, collaborate, and access a diverse set of information sources in multiple formats. This makes meetings, especially virtual ones, complex, with a greater chance for process losses. It is important to follow a certain process for conducting meetings.

Groupwork may require different levels of coordination (Nunamaker, 1997). Sometimes a group may operate at the individual work level, with members making individual efforts that require no coordination. As with a team of sprinters representing a country participating in a 100-meter dash, group productivity is simply the best of the individual results. Other times group members may interact at the coordinated work level. At this level, as with a team in a relay race, the work requires careful coordination between otherwise independent individual efforts. Sometimes a team may operate at the concerted work level. As in a rowing race, teams working at this level must make a continuous concerted effort to be successful. Different mechanisms support groupwork at different levels of coordination.

It is almost trite to say that all organizations, small and large, are using some computer-based communication and collaboration methods and tools to support people working in teams or groups. From e-mails to mobile phones and SMS as well as conferencing technologies, such tools are an indispensable part of one's work life today. We next highlight some related technologies and applications.

An Overview of Group Support Systems (GSS)

For groups to collaborate effectively, appropriate communication methods and technologies are needed. The Internet and its derivatives (i.e., intranets and extranets) are the infrastructures on which much communication for collaboration occurs. The Web supports intra- and interorganizational collaborative decision making through collaboration tools and access to data, information, and knowledge from inside and outside the organization.

Intra-organizational networked decision support can be effectively supported by an intranet. People within an organization can work with Internet tools and procedures through enterprise information portals. Specific applications can include important internal documents and procedures, corporate address lists, e-mail, tool access, and software distribution.

An *extranet* links people in different organizations. For example, **covisint.com** focuses on providing such collaborative mechanisms in diverse industries such as manufacturing, healthcare, and energy. Other extranets are used to link teams together to design products when several different suppliers must collaborate on design and manufacturing techniques.

Computers have been used for several decades to facilitate groupwork and group decision making. Lately, collaborative tools have received even greater attention due to their increased capabilities and ability to save money (e.g., on travel cost) as well as their ability to expedite decision making. Such computerized tools are called groupware.

Groupware

Many computerized tools have been developed to provide group support. These tools are called **groupware** because their primary objective is to support groupwork. Groupware tools can support decision making directly or indirectly, and they are described in the remainder of this chapter. For example, generating creative solutions to problems is a direct support. Some e-mail programs, chat rooms, instant messaging (IM), and teleconferencing provide indirect support.

Groupware provides a mechanism for team members to share opinions, data, information, knowledge, and other resources. Different computing technologies support groupwork in different ways, depending on the purpose of the group, the task, and the time/place category in which the work occurs.

Time/Place Framework

The effectiveness of a collaborative computing technology depends on the location of the group members and on the time that shared information is sent and received. DeSanctis and Gallupe (1987) proposed a framework for classifying IT communication support technologies. In this framework, communication is divided into four cells, which are shown together with representative computerized support technologies in Figure 12.6. The four cells are organized along two dimensions—time and place.

When information is sent and received almost simultaneously, the communication is **synchronous (real time)**. Telephones, IM, and face-to-face meetings are examples of synchronous communication. **Asynchronous** communication occurs when the receiver

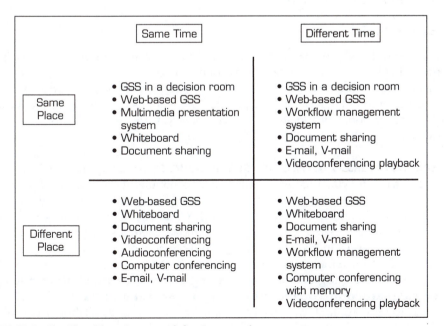

FIGURE 12.6   The Time/Place Framework for Groupwork.

gets the information at a different time than it was sent, such as in e-mail. The senders and the receivers can be in the same room or in different places.

As shown in Figure 12.6, time and place combinations can be viewed as a four-cell matrix, or framework. The four cells of the framework are as follows:

- *Same time/same place.* Participants meet face-to-face in one place at the same time, as in a traditional meeting or decision room. This is still an important way to meet, even when Web-based support is used, because it is sometimes critical for participants to leave the office to eliminate distractions.
- *Same time/different place.* Participants are in different places, but they communicate at the same time (e.g., with videoconferencing).
- *Different time/same place.* People work in shifts. One shift leaves information for the next shift.
- *Different time/different place (any time, any place).* Participants are in different places, and they also send and receive information at different times. This occurs when team members are traveling, have conflicting schedules, or work in different time zones.

Groups and groupwork (also known as *teams* and *teamwork*) in organizations are proliferating. Consequently, groupware continues to evolve to support effective groupwork, mostly for communication and collaboration.

SECTION 12.6 REVIEW QUESTIONS

1. Why do companies use computers to support groupwork?

2. Describe the components of the time/place framework.

12.7 TOOLS FOR INDIRECT SUPPORT OF DECISION MAKING

A large number of tools and methodologies are available to facilitate e-collaboration, communication, and decision support. The following sections present the major tools that support decision making indirectly.

Groupware Tools

Groupware products provide a way for groups to share resources and opinions. Groupware implies the use of networks to connect people, even if they are in the same room. Many groupware products are available on the Internet or an intranet to enhance the collaboration of a large number of people. The features of groupware products that support commutation, collaboration, and coordination are listed in Table 12.5. What follows are brief definitions of some of those features.

SYNCHRONOUS VERSUS ASYNCHRONOUS PRODUCTS Notice that the features in Table 12.5 may be synchronous, meaning that communication and collaboration are done in real time, or asynchronous, meaning that communication and collaboration are done by the participants at different times. Web conferencing and IM as well as Voice over IP (VoIP) are associated with synchronous mode. Methods that are associated with asynchronous modes include e-mail, wikilogs, and online workspaces, where participants can collaborate, for example, on joint designs or projects, but work at different times. Google Drive (**drive.google.com**) and Microsoft SharePoint (**http://office.microsoft. com/en-us/SharePoint/collaboration-software-SharePoint-FX103479517.aspx**) allow users to set up online workspaces for storing, sharing, and collaboratively working on different types of documents.

TABLE 12.5 Groupware Products and Features

General (Can Be Either Synchronous or Asynchronous)

- Built-in e-mail, messaging system
- Browser interface
- Joint Web-page creation
- Sharing of active hyperlinks
- File sharing (graphics, video, audio, or other)
- Built-in search functions (by topic or keyword)
- Workflow tools
- Use of corporate portals for communication, collaboration, and search
- Shared screens
- Electronic decision rooms
- Peer-to-peer networks

Synchronous (Same Time)

- Instant messaging (IM)
- Videoconferencing, multimedia conferencing
- Audioconferencing
- Shared whiteboard, smart whiteboard
- Instant video
- Brainstorming
- Polling (voting), and other decision support (consensus builder, scheduler)

Asynchronous (Different Times)

- Workspaces
- Threaded discussions
- Users can receive/send e-mail, SMS
- Users can receive activity notification alerts via e-mail or SMS
- Users can collapse/expand discussion threads
- Users can sort messages (by date, author, or read/unread)
- Auto responder
- Chat session logs
- Bulletin boards, discussion groups
- Use of blogs, wikis, and wikilogs
- Collaborative planning and/or design tools
- Use of bulletin boards

Companies such as **Dropbox.com** provide an easy way to share documents. Of course, similar systems are evolving for consumer and home use such as photo sharing (e.g., Picasa, Flicker, Facebook).

Groupware products are either stand-alone products that support one task (such as videoconferencing) or integrated kits that include several tools. In general, groupware technology products are fairly inexpensive and can easily be incorporated into existing information systems.

VIRTUAL MEETING SYSTEMS The advancement of Web-based systems opens the door for improved, electronically supported **virtual meetings**, where members are in different locations and even in different countries. For example, online meetings and presentation tools are provided by **webex.com, gotomeeting.com, Adobe.com, Skype.com**, and many others. Microsoft Office also includes a built-in virtual meeting capability. These systems feature Web seminars (popularly called Webinars), screen sharing, audioconferencing, videoconferencing, polling, question–answer sessions, and so on. Even mobile phones now have sufficient interaction capabilities to allow live meetings through applications such as Facetime.

Groupware

Although many of the technologies that enable group decision support are merging in common office productivity software tools such as Microsoft Office, it is instructive to learn about one specific software that illustrates some unique capabilities of groupware. GroupSystems (**groupsystems.com**) MeetingRoom was one of the first comprehensive same time/same place electronic meeting packages. The follow-up product, GroupSystems OnLine, offered similar capabilities, and it ran in asynchronous mode (anytime/anyplace) over the Web (MeetingRoom ran only over a local area network [LAN]). GroupSystems' latest product is ThinkTank, which is a suite of tools that significantly shortens cycle time for brainstorming, strategic planning, product development, problem solving, requirements gathering, risk assessments, team decision makings, and other collaborations. ThinkTank moves face-to-face or virtual teams through customizable processes toward their goals faster and more effectively than its predecessors. ThinkTank offers the following capabilities:

- ThinkTank builds in the discipline of an agenda, efficient participation, workflow, prioritization, and decision analysis.
- ThinkTank's anonymous brainstorming for ideas and comments is an ideal way to capture the participants' creativity and experience.
- ThinkTank Web 2.0's enhanced user interface ensures that participants do not need prior training to join, so they can focus 100 percent on solving problems and making decisions.
- With ThinkTank, all of the knowledge shared by participants is captured and saved in documents and spreadsheets and automatically converted to the meeting minutes and made available to all participants at the end of the session.

Another specialized product is eRoom (now owned by EMC/Documentum at **http://www.emc.com/enterprise-content-management/centerstage.htm**). This comprehensive Web-based suite of tools can support a variety of collaboration scenarios. Yet another product is Team Expert Choice (Comparion), which is an add-on product for Expert Choice (**expertchoice.com**). It has limited decision support capabilities, mainly supporting one-room meetings, but focuses on developing a model and process for decision making using the analytic hierarchy process that was covered in Chapter 9.

Collaborative Workflow

Collaborative workflow refers to software products that address project-oriented and collaborative types of processes. They are administered centrally yet are capable of being accessed and used by workers from different departments and even from different physical locations. The goal of collaborative workflow tools is to empower knowledge workers. The focus of an enterprise solution for collaborative workflow is on allowing workers to communicate, negotiate, and collaborate within an integrated environment. Some leading vendors of collaborative workflow applications are Lotus, EpicData, FileNet, and Action Technologies.

Web 2.0

The term *Web 2.0* refers to what is perceived to be the second generation of Web development and Web design. It is characterized as facilitating communication, information sharing, interoperability, user-centered design, and collaboration on the World Wide Web. It has led to the development and evolution of Web-based communities, hosted services, and novel Web applications. Example Web 2.0 applications include social-networking sites (e.g., LinkedIn, Facebook), video-sharing sites (e.g., YouTube, Flickr, Vimeo), wikis, blogs, mashups, and folksonomies.

Web 2.0 sites typically include the following features/techniques, identified by the acronym SLATES:

- **Search.** The ease of finding information through keyword search.
- **Links.** Ad hoc guides to other relevant information.
- **Authoring.** The ability to create content that is constantly updated by multiple users. In wikis, the content is updated in the sense that users undo and redo each other's work. In blogs, content is updated in that posts and comments of individuals are accumulated over time.
- **Tags.** Categorization of content by creating tags. Tags are simple, one-word, user-determined descriptions to facilitate searching and avoid rigid, premade categories.
- **Extensions.** Powerful algorithms leverage the Web as an application platform as well as a document server.
- **Signals.** RSS technology is used to rapidly notify users of content changes.

Wikis

A **wiki** is a piece of server software available at a Web site that allows users to freely create and edit Web page content through a Web browser. (The term *wiki* means "quick" or "to hasten" in the Hawaiian language; e.g., "Wiki Wiki" is the name of the shuttle bus at Honolulu International Airport.) A wiki supports hyperlinks and has a simple text syntax for creating new pages and cross-links between internal pages on-the-fly. It is especially suited for collaborative writing.

Wikis are unusual among group communication mechanisms in that they allow the organization of the contributions to be edited as well as the content itself. The term *wiki* also refers to the collaborative software that facilitates the operation of a wiki Web site.

A wiki enables documents to be written collectively in a very simple markup, using a Web browser. A single page in a wiki is referred to as a "wiki page," and the entire body of pages, which are usually highly interconnected via hyperlinks, is "the wiki"; in effect, it is a very simple, easy-to-use database. For further details, see **en.wikipedia. org/wiki/Wiki** and **wiki.org**.

Collaborative Networks

Traditionally, collaboration took place among supply chain members, frequently those that were close to each other (e.g., a manufacturer and its distributor, a distributor and a retailer). Even if more partners were involved, the focus was on the optimization of information and product flow between existing nodes in the traditional supply chain. Advanced approaches, such as collaborative planning, forecasting, and replenishment, do not change this basic structure.

Traditional collaboration results in a vertically integrated supply chain. However, Web technologies can fundamentally change the shape of the supply chain, the number of players in it, and their individual roles. In a collaborative network, partners at any point in the network can interact with each other, bypassing traditional partners. Interaction may occur among several manufacturers or distributors, as well as with new players, such as software agents that act as aggregators, business-to-business (B2B) exchanges, or logistics providers.

SECTION 12.7 REVIEW QUESTIONS

1. List the major groupware tools and divide them into synchronous and asynchronous types.
2. Identify specific tools for Web conferencing and their capabilities.
3. Define *wiki* and *wikilog*.
4. Define *collaborative hub.*

12.8 DIRECT COMPUTERIZED SUPPORT FOR DECISION MAKING: FROM GROUP DECISION SUPPORT SYSTEMS TO GROUP SUPPORT SYSTEMS

Decisions are made at many meetings, some of which are called in order to make one specific decision. For example, the federal government meets periodically to decide on the short-term interest rate. Directors may be elected at shareholder meetings, organizations allocate budgets in meetings, a company decides on which candidate to hire, and so on. Although some of these decisions are complex, others can be controversial, as in resource allocation by a city government. Process gains and dysfunctions can be significantly large in such situations; therefore, computerized support has often been suggested to mitigate these complexities. These computer-based support systems have appeared in the literature under different names, including *group decision support systems* (GDSS), *group support systems* (GSS), *computer-supported collaborative work* (CSCW), and *electronic meeting systems* (EMS). These systems are the subject of this section.

Group Decision Support Systems (GDSS)

During the 1980s, researchers realized that computerized support to managerial decision making needed to be expanded to groups because major organizational decisions are made by groups such as executive committees, special task forces, and departments. The result was the creation of group decision support systems (see Powell et al., 2004).

A **group decision support system (GDSS)** is an interactive computer-based system that facilitates the solution of semistructured or unstructured problems by a group of decision makers. The goal of GDSS is to improve the productivity of decision-making meetings by speeding up the decision-making process and/or by improving the quality of the resulting decisions.

The following are the major characteristics of a GDSS:

- Its goal is to support the process of group decision makers by providing automation of subprocesses, using information technology tools.
- It is a specially designed information system, not merely a configuration of already-existing system components. It can be designed to address one type of problem or a variety of group-level organizational decisions.
- It encourages generation of ideas, resolution of conflicts, and freedom of expression. It contains built-in mechanisms that discourage development of negative group behaviors, such as destructive conflict, miscommunication, and groupthink.

The first generation of GDSS was designed to support face-to-face meetings in a decision room. Today, support is provided mostly over the Web to virtual groups. The group can meet at the same time or at different times by using e-mail, sending documents, and reading transaction logs. GDSS is especially useful when controversial decisions have to be made (e.g., resource allocation, determining which individuals to lay off). GDSS applications require a facilitator when done in one room or a coordinator or leader when done using virtual meetings.

GDSS can improve the decision-making process in various ways. For one, GDSS generally provide structure to the planning process, which keeps the group on track, although some applications permit the group to use unstructured techniques and methods for **idea generation**. In addition, GDSS offer rapid and easy access to external and stored information needed for decision making. GDSS also support parallel processing of information and idea generation by participants and allow asynchronous computer discussion. They make possible larger meetings that would otherwise be unmanageable;

having a larger group means that more complete information, knowledge, and skills will be represented in the meeting. Finally, voting can be anonymous, with instant results, and all information that passes through the system can be recorded for future analysis (producing *organizational memory*).

Initially, GDSS were limited to face-to-face meetings. To provide the necessary technology, a special facility (i.e., room) was created. Also, groups usually had a clearly defined, narrow task, such as allocation of scarce resources or prioritization of goals in a long-range plan.

Over time, it became clear that support teams' needs were broader than that supported by GDSS. Furthermore, it became clear that what was really needed was support for virtual teams, both in different place/same time and different place/different time situations. Also, it became clear that teams needed indirect support in most decision-making cases (e.g., help in searching for information or collaboration) rather than direct support for the decision making. Although GDSS expanded to virtual team support, they were unable to meet all the other needs. Thus, a broader term, *GSS*, was created. We use the terms interchangeably in this book.

Group Support Systems

A **group support system (GSS)** is any combination of hardware and software that enhances groupwork either in direct or indirect support of decision making. GSS is a generic term that includes all forms of collaborative computing. GSS evolved after information technology researchers recognized that technology could be developed to support the many activities normally occurring at face-to-face meetings (e.g., idea generation, consensus building, anonymous ranking).

A complete GSS is still considered a specially designed information system, but since the mid-1990s many of the special capabilities of GSS have been embedded in standard productivity tools. For example, Microsoft Office can embed the Lync tool for Web conferences. Most GSS are easy to use because they have a Windows-based graphical user interface (GUI) or a Web browser interface. Most GSS are fairly general and provide support for activities such as idea generation, conflict resolution, and voting. Also, many commercial products have been developed to support only one or two aspects of teamwork (e.g., videoconferencing, idea generation, screen sharing, wikis).

GSS settings range from a group meeting at a single location for solving a specific problem to virtual meetings conducted in multiple locations and held via telecommunication channels for the purpose of addressing a variety of problem types. Continuously adopting new and improved methods, GSS are building up their capabilities to effectively operate in asynchronous as well as synchronous modes.

How GDSS (or GSS) Improve Groupwork

The goal of GSS is to provide support to meeting participants to improve the productivity and effectiveness of meetings by streamlining and speeding up the decision-making process (i.e., efficiency) or by improving the quality of the results (i.e., effectiveness). GSS attempts to increase process and task gains and decrease process and task losses. Overall, GSS have been successful in doing just that (see Holt, 2002); however, some process and task gains may decrease, and some process and task losses may increase. Improvement is achieved by providing support to group members for the generation and exchange of ideas, opinions, and preferences. Specific features such as **parallelism** (i.e., the ability of participants in a group to work simultaneously on a task, such as brainstorming or voting) and anonymity produce this improvement. The following are some specific GDSS support activities:

- GDSS support parallel processing of information and idea generation (parallelism).
- GDSS enable the participation of larger groups with more complete information, knowledge, and skills.
- GDSS permit the group to use structured or unstructured techniques and methods.
- GDSS offer rapid, easy access to external information.
- GDSS allow parallel computer discussions.
- GDSS help participants frame the big picture.
- Anonymity allows shy people to contribute to the meeting (i.e., get up and do what needs to be done).
- Anonymity helps prevent aggressive individuals from driving a meeting.
- GDSS provide for multiple ways to participate in instant, anonymous voting.
- GDSS provide structure for the planning process to keep the group on track.
- GDSS enable several users to interact simultaneously (i.e., conferencing).
- GDSS record all information presented at a meeting (i.e., **organizational memory**).

For GSS success stories, look for sample cases at vendors' Web sites. As you will see, in many of these cases, collaborative computing led to dramatic process improvements and cost savings.

Facilities for GDSS

There are three options for deploying GDSS/GSS technology: (1) as a special-purpose decision room, (2) as a multiple-use facility, and (3) as Internet- or intranet-based groupware, with clients running wherever the group members are.

DECISION ROOMS The earliest GDSS were installed in expensive, customized, special-purpose facilities called **decision rooms** (or electronic meeting rooms) with PCs and large public screens at the front of each room. The original idea was that only executives and high-level managers would use the facility. The software in a special-purpose electronic meeting room usually runs over a LAN, and these rooms are fairly plush in their furnishings. Electronic meeting rooms can be constructed in different shapes and sizes. A common design includes a room equipped with 12 to 30 networked PCs, usually recessed into the desktop (for better participant viewing). A server PC is attached to a large-screen projection system and connected to the network to display the work at individual workstations and aggregated information from the facilitator's workstation. Breakout rooms equipped with PCs connected to the server, where small subgroups can consult, are sometimes located adjacent to the decision room. The output from the subgroups can also be displayed on the large public screen.

INTERNET-/INTRANET-BASED SYSTEMS Since the late 1990s, the most common approach to GSS facilities has been to use Web- or intranet-based groupware that allows group members to work from any location at any time (e.g., WebEx, GotoMeeting, Adobe Connect, Microsoft Lync, GroupSystems). This groupware often includes audioconferencing and videoconferencing. The availability of relatively inexpensive groupware (for purchase or for subscription), combined with the power and low cost of computers and mobile devices, makes this type of system very attractive.

SECTION 12.8 REVIEW QUESTIONS

1. Define *GDSS* and list the limitations of the initial GDSS software.
2. Define *GSS* and list its benefits.

3. List process gain improvements made by GSS.

4. Define *decision room*.

5. Describe Web-based GSS.

This chapter has served to provide a relatively quick overview of knowledge management and collaborative systems, two movements that were really prominent in the past 20 years but have now been subsumed by other technologies for information sharing and decision making. It helps to see where the roots of many of the technologies today might have come from, although the names may have changed.

Chapter Highlights

- Knowledge is different from information and data. Knowledge is information that is contextual, relevant, and actionable.
- Knowledge is dynamic in nature. It is information in action.
- Tacit (i.e., unstructured, sticky) knowledge is usually in the domain of subjective, cognitive, and experiential learning; explicit (i.e., structured, leaky) knowledge deals with more objective, rational, and technical knowledge, and it is highly personal and difficult to formalize.
- Organizational learning is the development of new knowledge and insights that have the potential to influence behavior.
- The ability of an organization to learn, develop memory, and share knowledge is dependent on its culture. Culture is a pattern of shared basic assumptions.
- Knowledge management is a process that helps organizations identify, select, organize, disseminate, and transfer important information and expertise that typically reside within the organization in an unstructured manner.
- The knowledge management model involves the following cyclical steps: create, capture, refine, store, manage, and disseminate knowledge.
- Two knowledge management approaches are the process approach and the practice approach.
- Standard knowledge management initiatives involve the creation of knowledge bases, active process management, knowledge centers, collaborative technologies, and knowledge webs.
- A KMS is generally developed using three sets of technologies: communication, collaboration, and storage.
- A variety of technologies can make up a KMS, including the Internet, intranets, data warehousing, decision support tools, and groupware. Intranets are the primary vehicles for displaying and distributing knowledge in organizations.
- People collaborate in their work (called *groupwork*). Groupware (i.e., collaborative computing software) supports groupwork.
- Group members may be in the same organization or may span organizations; they may be in the same location or in different locations; they may work at the same time or at different times.
- The time/place framework is a convenient way to describe the communication and collaboration patterns of groupwork. Different technologies can support different time/place settings.
- Working in groups may result in many benefits, including improved decision making.
- Communication can be synchronous (i.e., same time) or asynchronous (i.e., sent and received in different times).
- Groupware refers to software products that provide collaborative support to groups (including conducting meetings).
- Groupware can support decision making/problem solving directly or can provide indirect support by improving communication between team members.
- The Internet (Web), intranets, and extranets support decision making through collaboration tools and access to data, information, and knowledge.
- Groupware for direct support such as GDSS typically contains capabilities for electronic brainstorming, electronic conferencing or meeting, group scheduling, calendaring, planning, conflict resolution, model building, videoconferencing, electronic document sharing, stakeholder identification, topic commentator, voting, policy formulation, and enterprise analysis.
- Groupware can support anytime/anyplace groupwork.

- A GSS is any combination of hardware and software that facilitates meetings. Its predecessor, GDSS, provided direct support to decision meetings, usually in a face-to-face setting.
- GDSS attempt to increase process and task gains and reduce process and task losses of groupwork.
- Parallelism and anonymity provide several GDSS gains.

- GDSS may be assessed in terms of the common group activities of information retrieval, information sharing, and information use.
- GDSS can be deployed in an electronic decision room environment, in a multipurpose computer lab, or over the Web.
- Web-based groupware is the norm for anytime/anyplace collaboration.

Key Terms

asynchronous
community of
   practice
decision room
explicit knowledge
group decision support
   system (GDSS)
group support system
   (GSS)

groupthink
groupware
groupwork
idea generation
knowledge
knowledge-based
   economy
knowledge management
   (KM)

knowledge management
   system (KMS)
knowledge repository
leaky knowledge
organizational culture
organizational learning
organizational memory
parallelism
practice approach

process approach
process gain
process loss
synchronous (real-time)
tacit knowledge
virtual meeting
virtual team
wiki

Questions for Discussion

1. Why is the term *knowledge* so difficult to define?
2. Describe and relate the different characteristics of knowledge to one another.
3. Explain why it is important to capture and manage knowledge.
4. Compare and contrast tacit knowledge and explicit knowledge.
5. Explain why organizational culture must sometimes change before knowledge management is introduced.
6. How does knowledge management attain its primary objective?
7. How can employees be motivated to contribute to and use KMS?
8. What is the role of a knowledge repository in knowledge management?
9. Explain the importance of communication and collaboration technologies to the processes of knowledge management.

10. List the three top technologies most frequently used for implementing KMS and explain their importance.
11. Explain why it is useful to describe groupwork in terms of the time/place framework.
12. Describe the kinds of support that groupware can provide to decision makers.
13. Explain why most groupware is deployed today over the Web.
14. Explain why meetings can be so inefficient. Given this, explain how effective meetings can be run.
15. Explain how GDSS can increase some of the benefits of collaboration and decision making in groups and eliminate or reduce some of the losses.
16. The original term for group support system (GSS) was group decision support system (GDSS). Why was the word *decision* dropped? Does this make sense? Why or why not?

Exercises

Teradata UNIVERSITY NETWORK (TUN) and Other Hands-on Exercises

1. Make a list of all the knowledge management methods you use during your day (work and personal). Which are the most effective? Which are the least effective? What kinds of work or activities does each knowledge management method enable?

2. Describe how to ride a bicycle, drive a car, or make a peanut butter and jelly sandwich. Now have someone else try to do it based solely on your explanation. How can you best convert this knowledge from tacit to explicit (or can't you)?
3. Examine the top five reasons that firms initiate KMS and investigate why they are important in a modern enterprise.

4. Read *How the Irish Saved Civilization* by Thomas Cahill (New York: Anchor, 1996) and describe how Ireland became a knowledge repository for Western Europe just before the fall of the Roman Empire. Explain in detail why this was important for Western civilization and history.

5. Examine your university, college, or company and describe the roles that the faculty, administration, support staff, and students have in the creation, storage, and dissemination of knowledge. Explain how the process works. Explain how technology is currently used and how it could potentially be used.

6. Search the Internet for knowledge management products and systems and create categories for them. Assign one vendor to each team. Describe the categories you created and justify them.

7. Consider a decision-making project in industry for this course or from another class or from work. Examine some typical decisions in the project. How would you extract the knowledge you need? Can you use that knowledge in practice? Why or why not?

8. How does knowledge management support decision making? Identify products or systems on the Web that help organizations accomplish knowledge management. Start with **brint.com** and **knowledgemanagement.com**. Try one out and report your findings to the class.

9. Search the Internet to identify sites that deal with knowledge management. Start with **google.com, kmworld.com, kmmag.com**, and **km-forum.org**. How many did you find? Categorize the sites based on whether they are academic, consulting firms, vendors, and so on. Sample one of each and describe the main focus of the site.

10. Make a list of all the communications methods (both work and personal) you use during your day. Which are the most effective? Which are the least effective? What kind of work or activity does each communications method enable?

11. Investigate the impact of turning off every communication system in a firm (i.e., telephone, fax, television, radio, all computer systems). How effective and efficient would the following types of firms be: airline, bank, insurance company, travel agency, department store, grocery store? What would happen? Do customers expect 100 percent uptime? (When was the last time a major airline's reservation system was down?) How long would it be before each type of firm would not be functioning at all? Investigate what organizations are doing to prevent this situation from occurring.

12. Investigate how researchers are trying to develop collaborative computer systems that portray or display nonverbal communication factors.

13. For each of the following software packages, check the trade literature and the Web for details and explain how computerized collaborative support system capabilities are included: Lync, GroupSystems, and WebEx.

14. Compare Simon's four-phase decision-making model to the steps in using GDSS.

15. A major claim in favor of wikis is that they can replace e-mail, eliminating its disadvantages (e.g., spam). Go to **socialtext.com** and review such claims. Find other supporters of switching to wikis. Then find counterarguments and conduct a debate on the topic.

16. Search the Internet to identify sites that describe methods for improving meetings. Investigate ways that meetings can be made more effective and efficient.

17. Go to **groupsystems.com** and identify its current GSS products. List the major capabilities of those products.

18. Go to the Expert Choice Web site (**expertchoice.com**) and find information about the company's group support products and capabilities. Team Expert Choice is related to the concept of the AHP described. Evaluate this product in terms of decision support. Do you think that keypad use provides process gains or process losses? How and why? Also prepare a list of the product analytical capabilities. Examine the free trial. How can it support groupwork?

END-OF-CHAPTER APPLICATION CASE

Solving Crimes by Sharing Digital Forensic Knowledge

Digital forensics has become an indispensable tool for law enforcement. This science is not only applied to cases of crime committed with or against digital assets, but is used in many physical crimes to gather evidence of intent or proof of prior relationships. The volume of digital devices that might be explored by a forensic analysis, however, is staggering, including anything from a home computer to a videogame console, to an engine module from a getaway vehicle. New hardware, software, and applications are being released into public use daily, and analysts must create new methods to deal with each of them.

Many law enforcement agencies have widely varying capabilities to do forensics, sometimes enlisting the aid of other agencies or outside consultants to perform analyses. As new techniques are developed, internally tested, and ultimately scrutinized by the legal system, new forensic hypotheses are born and proven. When the same techniques are applied to other cases, the new proceeding is strengthened by the precedent of a prior case. Acceptance of a methodology in multiple proceedings makes it more acceptable for future cases.

Unfortunately, new forensic discoveries are rarely formally shared—sometimes even among analysts within the same agency. Briefings may be given to other analysts within the same agency, although caseloads often dictate immediately moving on to the next case. Even less is shared between different agencies, or even between different offices of some federal law enforcement communities. The result of this lack of sharing is duplication of significant effort to re-discover the same or similar approaches to prior cases and a failure to take consistent advantage of precedent rulings that may strengthen the admission of a certain process.

The Center for Telecommunications and Network Security (CTANS), a center of excellence that includes faculty from Oklahoma State University's Management Science and Information Systems Department, has developed, hosted, and is continuously evolving Web-based software to support law enforcement digital forensics investigators (LEDFI) via access to forensics resources and communication channels for the past 6 years. The cornerstone of this initiative has been the National Repository of Digital Forensics Information (NRDFI), a collaborative effort with the Defense Cyber Crime Center (DC3), which has evolved into the Digital Forensics Investigator Link (DFILink) over the past 2 years.

Solution

The development of the NRDFI was guided by the theory of the egocentric group and how these groups share knowledge and resources among one another in a community of practice (Jarvenpaa & Majchrzak, 2005). Within an egocentric community of practice, experts are identified through interaction, knowledge remains primarily tacit, and informal communication mechanisms are used to transfer this knowledge from one participant to the other. The informality of knowledge transfer in this context can lead to local pockets of expertise

as well as redundancy of effort across the broader community as a whole. For example, a digital forensics (DF) investigator in Washington, DC, may spend 6 hours to develop a process to extract data hidden in slack space in the sectors of a hard drive. The process may be shared among his local colleagues, but other DF professionals in other cities and regions will have to develop the process on their own.

In response to these weaknesses, the NRDFI was developed as a hub for knowledge transfer between local law enforcement communities. The NRDFI site was locked down so that only members of law enforcement were able to access content, and members were provided the ability to upload knowledge documents and tools that may have developed locally within their community, so that the broader law enforcement community of practice could utilize their contributions and reduce redundancy of efforts. The Defense Cyber Crime Center, a co-sponsor of the NRDFI initiative, provided a wealth of knowledge documents and tools in order to seed the system with content (see Figure 12.7).

Results

Response from the LEDFI community was positive, and membership to the NRDFI site quickly jumped to over 1,000 users. However, the usage pattern for these members was almost exclusively unidirectional. LEDFI members would periodically log on, download a batch of tools and knowledge documents, and then not log on again until the knowledge content on the site was extensively refreshed. The mechanisms in place for local LEDFI communities to share their own knowledge and tools sat largely unused. From here, CTANS began to explore the literature with regard to motivating knowledge sharing, and began a redesign of NRDFI

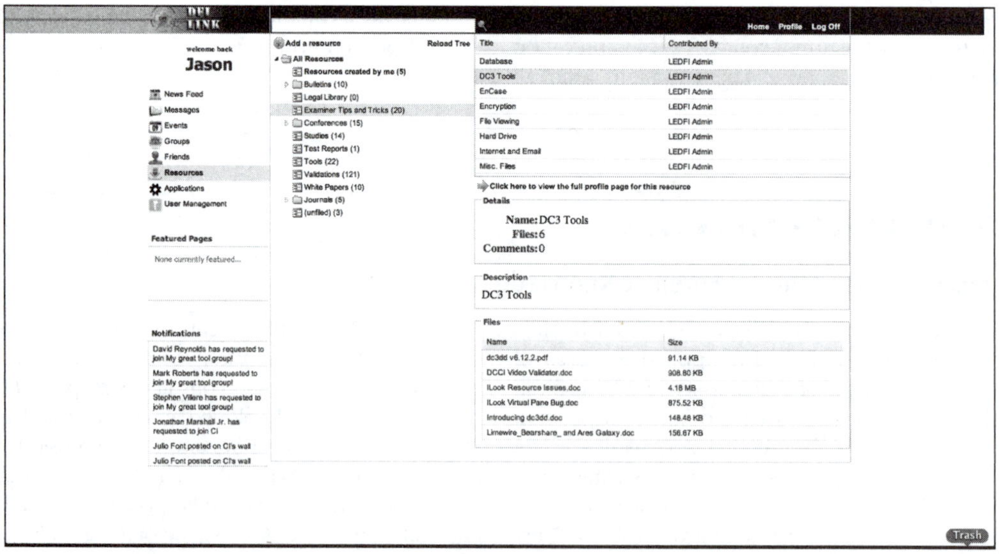

FIGURE 12.7 DFI-Link Resources.

driven by the extant literature; they focused on promoting sharing within the LEDFI community through the NRDFI.

Some additional capabilities include new applications such as a "Hash Link," which can provide DFI Link members with a repository of hash values that they would otherwise need to develop on their own and a directory to make it easier to contact colleagues in other departments and jurisdictions. A calendar of events and a newsfeed page were integrated into the DFI Link in response to requests from the users. Increasingly, commercial software is also being hosted. Some were licensed through grants and others were provided by vendors, but all are free to vetted users of the law enforcement community.

The DFI Link has been a positive first step toward getting LEDFI to better communicate and share knowledge with colleagues in other departments. Ongoing research is helping to shape the DFI Link to better meet the needs of its customers and promote even greater knowledge, sharing. Many LEDFI are inhibited from sharing such knowledge, as policies and culture in the law enforcement domain often promote the protection of information at the cost of knowledge sharing. However, by working with DC3 and the law enforcement community, researchers are beginning to knock down these barriers and create a more productive knowledge sharing environment.

QUESTIONS FOR THE END-OF-CHAPTER APPLICATION CASE

1. Why should digital forensics information be shared among law enforcement communities?
2. What does egocentric theory suggest about knowledge sharing?
3. What behavior did the developers of NRDFI observe in terms of use of the system?
4. What additional features might enhance the use and value of such a KMS?

Sources: Harrison et al., "A Lessons Learned Repository for Computer Forensics," *International Journal of Digital Evidence*, Vol. 1, No. 3, 2002; S. Jarvenpaa and A. Majchrzak, *Developing Individuals' Transactive Memories of their Ego-Centric Networks to Mitigate Risks of Knowledge Sharing: The Case of Professionals Protecting CyberSecurity*. Paper presented at the Proceedings of the Twenty-Sixth International Conference on Information Systems, 2005; J. Nichols, D. P. Biros, and M. Weiser, "Toward Alignment Between Communities of Practice and Knowledge-Based Decision Support," *Journal of Digital Forensics, Security, and Law*, Vol. 7, No. 2, 2012; M. Weiser, D. P. Biros, and G. Mosier, "Building a National Forensics Case Repository for Forensic Intelligence," *Journal of Digital Forensics, Security, and Law*, Vol. 1, No. 2, May 2006 (This case was contributed by David Biros, Jason Nichols, and Mark Weiser).

References

Alavi, M. (2000). "Managing Organizational Knowledge." Chapter 2 in W. R. Zmud (ed.). *Framing the Domains of IT Management: Projecting the Future*. Cincinnati, OH: Pinnaflex Educational Resources.

Alavi, M., T. Kayworth, and D. Leidner. (2005/2006). "An Empirical Examination of the Influence of Organizational Culture on Knowledge Management Practice." *Journal of Management Information Systems*, Vol. 22, No. 3.

Alavi, M., and D. Leidner. (2001). "Knowledge Management and Knowledge Management Systems: Conceptual Foundations and Research Issues." *MIS Quarterly*, Vol. 25, No. 1, pp. 107–136.

Bock, G.-W., R. Zmud, Y. Kim, and J. Lee. (2005). "Behavioural Intention Formation in Knowledge Sharing: Examining the Roles of Extrinsic Motivators, Social Psychological Forces and Organizational Climate." *MIS Quarterly Journal*, Vol. 29, No. 1.

Carlucci, D., and G. Schiuma. (2006). "Knowledge Asset Value Spiral: Linking Knowledge Assets to Company's Performance." *Knowledge and Process Management*, Vol. 13, No. 1.

Chua, A., and W. Lam. (2005). "Why KM Projects Fail: A Multi-Case Analysis." *Journal of Knowledge Management*, Vol. 9, No. 3, pp. 6–17.

Davenport, D. (2008). "Enterprise 2.0: The New, New Knowledge Management?" **http://blogs.hbr.org/ davenport/2008/02/enterprise_20_the_new_new_ know.html** (accessed Sept. 2013).

Davenport, T., D. W. DeLong, and M. C. Beers. (1998, Winter). "Successful Knowledge Management Projects." *Sloan Management Review*, Vol. 39, No. 2.

Davenport, T., and L. Prusak. (1998). "How Organizations Manage What They Know." Boston: Harvard Business School Press.

Delen, D., and S. S. Hawamdeh. (2009). "A Holistic Framework for Knowledge Discovery and Management." *Communications of the ACM*, Vol. 52, No. 6, pp. 141–145.

DeSanctis, G., and R. B. Gallupe. (1987). "A Foundation for the Study of Group Decision Support Systems." *Management Science*, Vol. 33, No. 5.

Godin, B. (2006). "Knowledge-Based Economy: Conceptual Framework or Buzzword." *The Journal of Technology Transfer*, Vol. 31, No. 1.

Gray, P. (1999). "Tutorial on Knowledge Management." *Proceedings of the Americas Conference of the Association for Information Systems*, Milwaukee.

Hall, M. (2002, July 1). "Decision Support Systems." *Computerworld*, Vol. 36, No. 27.

Hansen, M., et al. (1999, March/April). "What's Your Strategy for Managing Knowledge?" *Harvard Business Review,* Vol. 77, No. 2.

Harrison, et al. (2002, Fall). "A Lessons Learned Repository for Computer Forensics." *International Journal of Digital Evidence,* Vol. 1, No. 3.

Hoffer, J., M. Prescott, and F. McFadden. (2002). *Modern Database Management,* 6th ed. Upper Saddle River, NJ: Prentice Hall.

Holt, K. (2002, August 5). "Nice Concept: Two Days' Work in a Day." *Meeting News,* Vol. 26, No. 11.

Iyer, S., R. Sharda, D. Biros, J. Lucca, and U. Shimp. (2009). "Organization of Lessons Learned Knowledge: A Taxonomy of Implementation." *International Journal of Knowledge Management,* Vol. 5, No. 3.

Jarvenpaa, S., and A. Majchrzak. (2005). *Developing Individuals' Transactive Memories of their Ego-Centric Networks to Mitigate Risks of Knowledge Sharing: The Case of Professionals Protecting CyberSecurity.* Paper presented at the Proceedings of the Twenty-Sixth International Conference on Information Systems.

Kankanhalli, A., and B. C. Y. Tan. (2005). "Knowledge Management Metrics: A Review and Directions for Future Research." *International Journal of Knowledge Management,* Vol. 1, No. 2.

Kiaraka, R. N., and K. Manning. (2005). "Managing Organizations Through a Process-Based Perspective: Its Challenges and Rewards." *Knowledge and Process Management,* Vol. 12, No. 4.

Koenig, M. (2001, September). "Codification vs. Personalization." *KMWorld.*

Konicki, S. (2001, November 12). "Collaboration Is the Cornerstone of $19B Defense Contract." *InformationWeek.*

Leidner, D., M. Alavi, and T. Kayworth. (2006). "The Role of Culture in Knowledge Management: A Case Study of Two Global Firms." *International Journal of eCollaboration,* Vol. 2, No. 1.

Nichols, J., D. P. Biros, and M. Weiser. (2012). "Toward Alignment Between Communities of Practice and Knowledge-Based Decision Support." *Journal of Digital Forensics, Security, and Law,* Vol. 7, No. 2.

Nonaka, I. (1991). "The Knowledge-Creating Company." *Harvard Business Review,* Vol. 69, No. 6, pp. 96–104.

Nunamaker, J. F., R. O. Briggs, D. D. Mittleman, D. T. Vogel, and P. A. Balthazard. (1997). "Lessons from a Dozen Years of Group Support Systems Research: A Discussion of Lab and Field Findings." *Journal of Management Information Systems,* Vol. 13, pp. 163–207.

Polanyi, M. (1958). *Personal Knowledge.* Chicago: University of Chicago Press.

Ponzi, L. J. (2004). "Knowledge Management: Birth of a Discipline." In M. E. D. Koenig and T. K. Srikantaiah (eds.). *Knowledge Management Lessons Learned: What Works and What Doesn't.* Medford, NJ: Information Today.

Powell, A., G. Piccoli, and B. Ives. (2004, Winter). "Virtual Teams: A Review of Current Literature and Directions for Future Research." *Data Base.*

Robin, M. (2000, March). "Learning by Doing." *Knowledge Management.*

Ruggles, R. (1998). "The State of the Notion: Knowledge Management in Practice." *California Management Review,* Vol. 40, No. 3.

Schwartz, D. G. (ed.). (2006). *Encyclopedia of Knowledge Management.* Hershey, PA: Idea Group Reference.

Shariq, S. G., and M. T. Vendelø. (2006). "Tacit Knowledge Sharing." In D. G. Schwartz (ed.). *Encyclopedia of Knowledge Management.* Hershey, PA: Idea Group Reference.

Tseng, C., and J. Goo. (2005). "Intellectual Capital and Corporate Value in an Emerging Economy: Empirical Study of Taiwanese Manufacturers." *R&D Management,* Vol. 35, No. 2.

Tuggle, F. D., and W. E. Goldfinger. (2004). "A Methodology for Mining Embedded Knowledge from Process Maps." *Human Systems Management,* Vol. 23, No. 1.

Van de Van, A. H. (2005, June). "Running in Packs to Develop Knowledge-Intensive Technologies." *MIS Quarterly,* Vol. 29, No. 2.

Weiser, M, D. P. Biros, and G. Mosier. (2006, May). "Building a National Forensics Case Repository for Forensic Intelligence." *Journal of Digital Forensics, Security, and Law,* Vol. 1, No. 2.

Wenger, E. C., and W. M. Snyder. (2000, January/ February). "Communities of Practice: The Organizational Frontier." *Harvard Business Review,* pp. 139–145.

Big Data and Future Directions for Business Analytics

LEARNING OBJECTIVES FOR PART V

- Understand the concepts, definitions, and potential use cases for Big Data and analytics
- Learn the enabling technologies, methods, and tools used to derive value from Big Data
- Explore some of the emerging technologies that offer interesting application and development opportunities for analytic systems in general and business

intelligence in particular. These include geospatial data, location-based analytics, social networking, Web 2.0, reality mining, and cloud computing.

- Describe some personal, organizational, and societal impacts of analytics
- Learn about major ethical and legal issues of analytics

This part consists of two chapters. Chapter 13 introduces Big Data analytics, a hot topic in the analytics world today. It provides a detailed description of Big Data, the benefits and challenges that it brings to the world of analytics, and the methods, tools, and technologies developed to turn Big Data into immense business value. The primary purpose of Chapter 14 is to introduce several emerging technologies that will provide new opportunities for application and extension of business analytics techniques and support systems. This part also briefly explores the individual, organizational, and societal impacts of these technologies, especially the ethical and legal issues in analytics implementation. After describing many of the emerging technologies or application domains, we will focus on organizational issues.

13

Big Data and Analytics

LEARNING OBJECTIVES

- Learn what Big Data is and how it is changing the world of analytics
- Understand the motivation for and business drivers of Big Data analytics
- Become familiar with the wide range of enabling technologies for Big Data analytics
- Learn about Hadoop, MapReduce, and NoSQL as they relate to Big Data analytics

- Understand the role of and capabilities/ skills for data scientist as a new analytics profession
- Compare and contrast the complementary uses of data warehousing and Big Data
- Become familiar with the vendors of Big Data tools and services
- Understand the need for and appreciate the capabilities of stream analytics
- Learn about the applications of stream analytics

Big Data, which means many things to many people, is not a new technological fad. It is a business priority that has the potential to profoundly change the competitive landscape in today's globally integrated economy. In addition to providing innovative solutions to enduring business challenges, Big Data and analytics instigate new ways to transform processes, organizations, entire industries, and even society all together. Yet extensive media coverage makes it hard to distinguish hype from reality. This chapter aims to provide a comprehensive coverage of Big Data, its enabling technologies, and related analytics concepts to help understand the capabilities and limitations of this emerging paradigm. The chapter starts with the definition and related concepts of Big Data, followed by the technical details of the enabling technologies, including Hadoop, MapReduce, and NoSQL. After describing "data scientist" as a new, fashionable organizational role/job, we provide a comparative analysis between data warehousing and Big

Data analytics. The last part of the chapter is dedicated to stream analytics, which is one of the most promising value propositions of Big Data analytics. This chapter contains the following sections:

13.1 OPENING VIGNETTE: Big Data Meets Big Science at CERN

The European Organization for Nuclear Research, known as CERN (which is derived from the acronym for the French "Conseil Européen pour la Recherche Nucléaire"), is playing a leading role in fundamental studies of physics. It has been instrumental in many key global innovations and breakthrough discoveries in theoretical physics and today operates the world's largest particle physics laboratory, home to the Large Hadron Collider (LHC) nestled under the mountains between Switzerland and France. Founded in 1954, CERN, one of Europe's first joint ventures, now has 20 member European states. At the beginning, their research primarily concentrated on understanding the inside of the atom, hence, the word "nuclear" in its name.

At CERN physicists and engineers are probing the fundamental structure of the universe. They use the world's largest and the most sophisticated scientific instruments to study the basic constituents of matter—the fundamental particles. These instruments include purpose-built particle accelerators and detectors. Accelerators boost the beams of particles to very high energies before the beams are forced to collide with each other or with stationary targets. Detectors observe and record the results of these collisions, which are happening at or near the speed of light. This process provides the physicists with clues about how the particles interact, and provides insights into the fundamental laws of nature. The LHC and its various experiments have received media attention following the discovery of a new particle strongly suspected to be the elusive Higgs Boson—an elementary particle initially theorized in 1964 and tentatively confirmed at CERN on March 14, 2013. This discovery has been called "monumental" because it appears to confirm the existence of the Higgs field, which is pivotal to the major theories within particle physics.

THE DATA CHALLENGE

Forty million times per second, particles collide within the LHC, each collision generating particles that often decay in complex ways into even more particles. Precise electronic circuits all around LHC record the passage of each particle via a detector as a series of electronic signals, and send the data to the CERN Data Centre (DC) for recording and digital reconstruction. The digitized summary of data is recorded as a "collision event." Physicists must sift through the 15 petabytes or so of digitized summary data produced annually to determine if the collisions have thrown up any interesting physics. Despite the state-of-the-art instrumentation and computing infrastructure, CERN does not have the capacity to process all of the data that it generates, and therefore relies on numerous other research centers all around the world to access and process the data.

The Compact Muon Solenoid (CMS) is one of the two general-purpose particle physics detectors operated at the LHC. It is designed to explore the frontiers of physics and provide physicists with the ability to look at the conditions presented in the early stages of our universe. More than 3,000 physicists from 183 institutions representing 38 countries are involved in the design, construction, and maintenance of the experiments. An experiment of this magnitude requires an enormously complex distributed computing and data management system. CMS spans more than a hundred data centers in a three-tier model and generates around 10 petabytes (PB) of summary data each year in real data, simulated data, and metadata. This information is stored and retrieved from relational and nonrelational data sources, such as relational databases, document databases, blogs, wikis, file systems, and customized applications.

At this scale, the information discovery within a heterogeneous, distributed environment becomes an important ingredient of successful data analysis. The data and associated metadata are produced in variety of forms and digital formats. Users (within CERN and scientists all around the world) want to be able to query different services (at dispersed data servers and at different locations) and combine data/information from these varied sources. However, this vast and complex collection of data means they don't necessarily know where to find the right information or have the domain knowledge to extract and merge/combine this data.

SOLUTION

To overcome this Big Data hurdle, CMS's data management and workflow management (DMWM) created the Data Aggregation System (DAS), built on MongoDB (a Big Data management infrastructure) to provide the ability to search and aggregate information across this complex data landscape. Data and metadata for CMS come from many different sources and are distributed in a variety of digital formats. It is organized and managed by constantly evolving software using both relational and nonrelational data sources. The DAS provides a layer on top of the existing data sources that allows researchers and other staff to query data via free text-based queries, and then aggregates the results from across distributed providers—while preserving their integrity, security policy, and data formats. The DAS then represents that data in defined format.

"The choice of an existing relational database was ruled out for several reasons—namely, we didn't require any transactions and data persistency in DAS, and as such can't have a pre-defined schema. Also the dynamic typing of stored metadata objects was one of the requirements. Amongst other reasons, those arguments forced us to look for alternative IT solutions," explained Valentin Kuznetsov, a research associate from Cornell University who works at CMS.

"We considered a number of different options, including file-based and in-memory caches, as well as key-value databases, but ultimately decided that a document database would best suit our needs. After evaluating several applications, we chose MongoDB, due to its support of dynamic queries, full indexes, including inner objects and embedded arrays, as well as auto-sharding."

ACCESSING THE DATA VIA FREE-FORM QUERIES

All DAS queries can be expressed in a free text-based form, either as a set of keywords or key-value pairs, where a pair can represent a condition. Users can query the system using a simple, SQL-like language, which is then transformed into the MongoDB query syntax, which is itself a JSON record. "Due to the schema-less nature of the underlying

MongoDB back-end, we are able to store DAS records of any arbitrary structure, regardless of whether it's a dictionary, lists, key-value pairs, etc. Therefore, every DAS key has a set of attributes describing its JSON structure," added Kuznetsov.

DATA AGNOSTIC

Given the number of different data sources, types, and providers that DAS connects to, it is imperative that the system itself be data agnostic and allow us to query and aggregate the metadata information in customizable ways. The MongoDB architecture easily integrates with existing data services while preserving their access, security policy, and development cycles. This also provides a simple plug-and-play mechanism that makes it easy to add new data services as they are implemented and configure DAS to connect to specific domains.

CACHING FOR DATA PROVIDERS

As well as providing a way for users to easily access a wide range of data sources in a simple and consistent manner, DAS uses MongoDB as a dynamic cache, collating the information fed back from the data providers—feedback in a variety of formats and file structures. "When a user enters a query, it checks if the MongoDB database has the aggregation the user is asking for and, if it does, returns it; otherwise, the system does the aggregation and saves it to MongoDB," said Kuznetsov. "If the cache does not contain the requested query, the system contacts distributed data providers that could have this information and queries them, gathering their results. It then merges all of the results, doing a sort of 'group by' operation based on predefined identifying keys and inserts the aggregated information into the cache."

The deployment specifics are as follows:

- The CMS DAS currently runs on a single eight-core server that processes all of the queries and caches the aggregated data.
- OS: Scientific Linux
- Server hardware configuration: 8-core CPU, 40GB RAM, 1TB storage (but data set usually around 50–100GB)
- Application Language: Python
- Other database technologies: Aggregates data from a number of different databases including Oracle, PostGreSQL, CouchDB, and MySQL

RESULTS

"DAS is used 24 hours a day, seven days a week, by CMS physicists, data operators, and data managers at research facilities around the world. The average query may resolve into thousands of documents, each a few kilobytes in size. The performance of MongoDB has been outstanding, with a throughput of around 6,000 documents a second for raw cache population," concluded Kuznetsov. "The ability to offer a free text query system that is fast and scalable, with a highly dynamic and scalable cache that is data agnostic, provides an invaluable two-way translation mechanism. DAS helps CMS users to easily find and discover information they need in their research, and it represents one of the many tools that physicists use on a daily basis toward great discoveries. Without help from DAS, information lookup would have taken orders of magnitude longer." As the data collected by the various experiments grows, CMS is looking into horizontally scaling the system with sharding (i.e., distributing a single, logical database system across a cluster of machines) to meet demand. Similarly the team are spreading the word beyond CMS and out to other parts of CERN.

QUESTIONS FOR THE OPENING VIGNETTE

1. What is CERN? Why is it important to the world of science?

2. How does Large Hadron Collider work? What does it produce?

3. What is essence of the data challenge at CERN? How significant is it?

4. What was the solution? How did Big Data address the challenges?

5. What were the results? Do you think the current solution is sufficient?

WHAT WE CAN LEARN FROM THIS VIGNETTE

Big Data is big, and much more. Thanks largely to the technological advances, it is easier to create, capture, store, and analyze very large quantities of data. Most of the Big Data is generated automatically by machines. The opening vignette is an excellent example to this testament. As we have seen, LHC at CERN creates very large volumes of data very fast. The Big Data comes in varied formats and is stored in distributed server systems. Analysis of such a data landscape requires new analytical tools and techniques. Regardless of its size, complexity, and velocity, data need to be made easy to access, query, and analyze if promised value is to be derived from it. CERN uses Big Data technologies to make it easy to analyze vast amount of data created by LHC to scientists all over the world, so that the promise of understanding the fundamental building blocks of the universe is realized. As organizations like CERN hypothesize new means to leverage the value of Big Data, they will continue to invent newer technologies to create and capture even Bigger Data.

Sources: Compiled from N. Heath, "Cern: Where the Big Bang Meets Big Data," TechRepublic, 2012, **techrepublic.com/blog/european-technology/cern-where-the-big-bang-meets-big-data/636** (accessed February 2013); **home.web.cern.ch/about/computing;** and 10gen Customer Case Study, "Big Data at the CERN Project," **10gen.com/customers/cern-cms** (accessed March 2013).

13.2 DEFINITION OF BIG DATA

Using data to understand customers/clients and business operations to sustain (and foster) growth and profitability is an increasingly more challenging task for today's enterprises. As more and more data becomes available in various forms and fashions, timely processing of the data with traditional means becomes impractical. This phenomenon is nowadays called Big Data, which is receiving substantial press coverage and drawing increasing interest from both business users and IT professionals. The result is that Big Data is becoming an overhyped and overused marketing buzzword.

Big Data means different things to people with different backgrounds and interests. Traditionally, the term "Big Data" has been used to describe the massive volumes of data analyzed by huge organizations like Google or research science projects at NASA. But for most businesses, it's a relative term: "Big" depends on an organization's size. The point is more about finding new value within and outside conventional data sources. Pushing the boundaries of data analytics uncovers new insights and opportunities, and "big" depends on where you start and how you proceed. Consider the popular description of Big Data: Big Data exceeds the reach of commonly used hardware environments and/or capabilities of software tools to capture, manage, and process it within a tolerable time span for its user population. Big Data has become a popular term to describe the exponential growth, availability, and use of information, both structured and unstructured. Much has been written on the Big Data trend and how it can serve as the basis for innovation, differentiation, and growth.

Where does the Big Data come from? A simple answer is "everywhere." The sources of data that were ignored because of technical limitations are now being treated like gold mines. Big Data may come from Web logs, RFID, GPS systems, sensor networks, social networks, Internet-based text documents, Internet search indexes, detailed call records, astronomy, atmospheric science, biological, genomics, nuclear physics, biochemical experiments, medical records, scientific research, military surveillance, photography archives, video archives, and large-scale ecommerce practices.

Big Data is not new. What is new is that the definition and the structure of Big Data constantly change. Companies have been storing and analyzing large volumes of data since the advent of the data warehouses in the early 1990s. While terabytes used to be synonymous with Big Data warehouses, now it's petabytes, and the rate of growth in data volumes continues to escalate as organizations seek to store and analyze greater levels of transaction details, as well as Web- and machine-generated data, to gain a better understanding of customer behavior and business drivers.

Many (academics and industry analysts/leaders alike) think that "Big Data" is a misnomer. What it says and what it means are not exactly the same. That is, Big Data is not just "big." The sheer volume of the data is only one of many characteristics that are often associated with Big Data, such as variety, velocity, veracity, variability, and value proposition, among others.

The Vs That Define Big Data

Big Data is typically defined by three "V"s: volume, variety, velocity. In addition to these three, we see some of the leading Big Data solution providers adding other Vs, such as veracity (IBM), variability (SAS), and value proposition.

VOLUME   Volume is obviously the most common trait of Big Data. Many factors contributed to the exponential increase in data volume, such as transaction-based data stored through the years, text data constantly streaming in from social media, increasing amounts of sensor data being collected, automatically generated RFID and GPS data, and so forth. In the past, excessive data volume created storage issues, both technical and financial. But with today's advanced technologies coupled with decreasing storage costs, these issues are no longer significant; instead, other issues emerge, including how to determine relevance amidst the large volumes of data and how to create value from data that is deemed to be relevant.

As mentioned before, big is a relative term. It changes over time and is perceived differently by different organizations. With the staggering increase in data volume, even the naming of the next Big Data echelon has been a challenge. The highest mass of data that used to be called petabytes (PB) has left its place to zettabytes (ZB), which is a trillion gigabytes (GB) or a billion terabytes (TB). Technology Insights 13.1 provides an overview of the size and naming of Big Data volumes.

TECHNOLOGY INSIGHTS 13.1   The Data Size Is Getting Big, Bigger, and Bigger

The measure of data size is having a hard time keeping up with new names. We all know kilobyte (KB, which is 1,000 bytes), megabyte (MB, which is 1,000,000 bytes), gigabyte (GB, which is 1,000,000,000 bytes), and terabyte (TB, which is 1,000,000,000,000 bytes). Beyond that, the names given to data sizes are relatively new to most of us. The following table shows what comes after terabyte and beyond.

Name	Symbol	Value
Kilobyte	kB	10^3
Megabyte	MB	10^6
Gigabyte	GB	10^9
Terabyte	TB	10^{12}
Petabyte	PB	10^{15}
Exabyte	EB	10^{18}
Zettabyte	ZB	10^{21}
Yottabyte	YB	10^{24}
Brontobyte*	BB	10^{27}
Gegobyte*	GeB	10^{30}

*Not an official SI (International System of Units) name/symbol, yet.

Consider that an exabyte of data is created on the Internet each day, which equates to 250 million DVDs' worth of information. And the idea of even larger amounts of data—a zettabyte—isn't too far off when it comes to the amount of info traversing the Web in any one year. In fact, industry experts are already estimating that we will see a 1.3 zettabytes of traffic annually over the Internet by 2016—and soon enough, we might start talking about even bigger volumes. When referring to yottabytes, some of the Big Data scientists often wonder about how much data the NSA or FBI have on people altogether. Put in terms of DVDs, a yottabyte would require 250 trillion of them. A brontobyte, which is not an official SI prefix but is apparently recognized by some people in the measurement community, is a 1 followed by 27 zeros. Size of such magnitude can be used to describe the amount of sensor data that we will get from the Internet in the next decade, if not sooner. A gegobyte is 10 to the power of 30. With respect to where the Big Data comes from, consider the following:

- The CERN Large Hadron Collider generates 1 petabyte per second.
- Sensors from a Boeing jet engine create 20 terabytes of data every hour.
- 500 terabytes of new data per day are ingested in Facebook databases.
- On YouTube, 72 hours of video are uploaded per minute, translating to a terabyte every 4 minutes.
- The proposed Square Kilometer Array telescope (the world's proposed biggest telescope) will generate an exabyte of data per day.

Sources: S. Higginbotham, "As Data Gets Bigger, What Comes After a Yottabyte?" 2012, **gigaom. com/2012/10/30/as-data-gets-bigger-what-comes-after-a-yottabyte** (accessed March 2013); and **en. wikipedia.org/wiki/Petabyte** (accessed March 2013).

From a short historical perspective, in 2009 the world had about 0.8ZB of data; in 2010, it exceeded the 1ZB mark; at the end of 2011, the number was 1.8ZB. Six or seven years from now, the number is estimated to be 35ZB (IBM, 2013). Though this number is astonishing in size, so are the challenges and opportunities that come with it.

VARIETY   Data today comes in all types of formats—ranging from traditional databases to hierarchical data stores created by the end users and OLAP systems, to text documents, e-mail, XML, meter-collected, sensor-captured data, to video, audio, and stock ticker data. By some estimates, 80 to 85 percent of all organizations' data is in some sort of unstructured or semistructured format (a format that is not suitable for traditional database schemas). But there is no denying its value, and hence it must be included in the analyses to support decision making.

VELOCITY   According to Gartner, velocity means both how fast data is being produced and how fast the data must be processed (i.e., captured, stored, and analyzed) to meet the need or demand. **RFID** tags, automated sensors, GPS devices, and smart meters are driving an increasing need to deal with torrents of data in near–real time. Velocity is perhaps the most overlooked characteristic of Big Data. Reacting quickly enough to deal with velocity is a challenge to most organizations. For the time-sensitive environments, the opportunity cost clock of the data starts ticking the moment the data is created. As the time passes, the value proposition of the data degrades, and eventually becomes worthless. Whether the subject matter is the health of a patient, the well-being of a traffic system, or the health of an investment portfolio, accessing the data and reacting faster to the circumstances will always create more advantageous outcomes.

In the Big Data storm that we are witnessing now, almost everyone is fixated on at-rest analytics, using optimized software and hardware systems to mine large quantities of variant data sources. Although this is critically important and highly valuable, there is another class of analytics driven from the velocity nature of Big Data, called "data stream analytics" or "in-motion analytics," which is mostly overlooked. If done correctly, data stream analytics can be as valuable, and in some business environments more valuable, than at-rest analytics. Later in this chapter we will cover this topic in more detail.

VERACITY   Veracity is a term that is being used as the fourth "V" to describe Big Data by IBM. It refers to the conformity to facts: accuracy, quality, truthfulness, or trustworthiness of the data. Tools and techniques are often used to handle Big Data's veracity by transforming the data into quality and trustworthy insights.

VARIABILITY   In addition to the increasing velocities and varieties of data, data flows can be highly inconsistent, with periodic peaks. Is something big trending in the social media? Perhaps there is a high-profile IPO looming. Maybe swimming with pigs in the Bahamas is suddenly the must-do vacation activity. Daily, seasonal, and event-triggered peak data loads can be challenging to manage—especially with social media involved.

VALUE PROPOSITION   The excitement around Big Data is its value proposition. A preconceived notion about "big" data is that it contains (or has a greater potential to contain) more patterns and interesting anomalies than "small" data. Thus, by analyzing large and feature rich data, organizations can gain greater business value that they may not have otherwise. While users can detect the patterns in small data sets using simple statistical and machine-learning methods or ad hoc query and reporting tools, Big Data means "big" analytics. Big analytics means greater insight and better decisions, something that every organization needs nowadays.

Since the exact definition of Big Data is still a matter of ongoing discussion in academic and industrial circles, it is likely that more characteristics (perhaps more Vs) are likely to be added to this list. Regardless of what happens, the importance and value proposition of Big Data are here to stay. Figure 13.1 shows a conceptual architecture where big data (at the left side of the figure) is converted to business insight through the use of a combination of advanced analytics and delivered to a variety of different users/ roles for faster/better decision making.

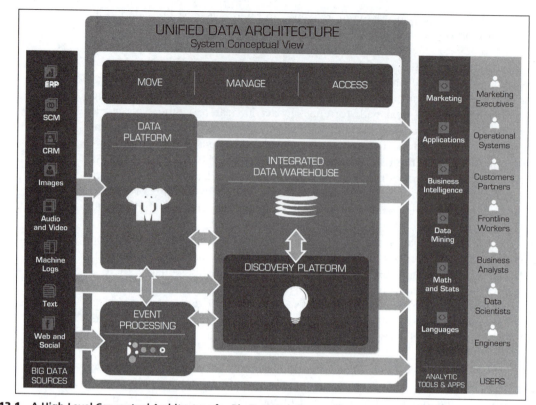

FIGURE 13.1 **A High-Level Conceptual Architecture for Big Data Solutions.** (*Source:* AsterData—a Teradata Company)

Application Case 13.1 shows the creative use of Big Data analytics in the ever-so-popular social media industry.

Application Case 13.1

Big Data Analytics Helps Luxottica Improvement Its Marketing Effectiveness

Based in Mason, Ohio, Luxottica Retail North America (Luxottica) is a wholly owned retail arm of Milan-based Luxottica Group S.p.A, the world's largest designer, manufacturer, distributer and seller of luxury and sports eyewear. Employing more than 65,000 people worldwide, the company reported net sales of EUR6.2 billion in 2011.

Problem - Disconnected Customer Data

Nearly 100 million customers purchase eight house brands from Luxottica through the company's numerous websites and retail chain stores. The big data captured from those customer interactions (in the form of transactions, click streams, product reviews, and social media postings) constitutes a massive source of business intelligence for potential product, marketing, and sales opportunities.

Luxottica, however, outsourced both data storage and promotional campaign development and management, leading to a disconnect between data analytics and marketing execution. The outsource model hampered access to current, actionable data, limiting its marketing value and the analytic value of the IBM PureData System for Analytics appliance that Luxottica used for a small segment of its business.

Luxottica's competitive posture and strategic growth initiatives were compromised for lack of an individualized view of its customers and an inability to act decisively and consistently on the different types of information generated by each retail channel. Luxottica needed to be able to exploit all data regardless of source or which internal or external application it resided on. Likewise, the company's marketing team wanted more control over promotional campaigns, including the capacity to gauge campaign effectiveness.

Solution - Fine-tuned Marketing

To integrate all data from its multiple internal and external application sources and gain visibility into its customers, Luxottica deployed the Customer Intelligence Appliance (CIA) from IBM Business Partner Aginity LLC.

CIA is an integrated set of adaptable software, hardware, and embedded analytics built on the IBM PureData System for Analytics solution. The combined technologies help Luxottica highly segment customer behavior and provide a platform and smart database for marketing execution systems, such as campaign management, e-mail services and other forms of direct marketing.

IBM® PureData™ for Analytics, which is powered by Netezza data warehousing technology, is one of the leading data appliances for large-scale, real-time analytics. Because of its innovative data storage mechanisms and massively parallel processing capabilities, it simplifies and optimizes performance of data services for analytic applications, enabling very complex algorithms to run in minutes, not hours or days, rapidly delivering invaluable insight to decision makers when they need it.

The IBM and Aginity platform provides Luxottica with unprecedented visibility into a class of customer that is of particular interest to the company: the omni-channel customer. This customer purchases merchandise both online and in-store and tends to shop and spend more than web-only or in-store customers.

"We've equipped their team with tools to gain a 360-degree view of their most profitable sales channel, the omni-channel customers, and individualize the way they market to them," says Ted Westerheide, chief architect for Aginity. "With the Customer Intelligence Appliance and PureData System for Analytics platform, Luxottica is a learning organization, connecting to customer data across multiple channels and improving marketing initiatives from campaign to campaign."

Benefits

Successful implementation of such an advanced big data analytics solution brings about numerous business benefits. In the case of Luxottica, the top three benefits were:

- Anticipates a 10 percent improvement in marketing effectiveness
- Identifies the highest-value customers out of nearly 100 million
- Targets individual customers based on unique preferences and histories

QUESTIONS FOR DISCUSSION

1. What does Big Data mean to Luxottica?
2. What were their main challenges?
3. What was the proposed solution, and the obtained results?

Source: IBM Customer Case, "Luxottica anticipates 10 percent improvement in marketing effectiveness" **http://www-01.ibm.com/software/success/cssdb.nsf/CS/KPES-9BNNKV?OpenDocument&Site=default&cty=en_us** (accessed October 2013).

SECTION 13.2 REVIEW QUESTIONS

1. Why is Big Data important? What has changed to put it in the center of the analytics world?
2. How do you define Big Data? Why is it difficult to define?
3. Out of the Vs that are used to define Big Data, in your opinion, which one is the most important? Why?
4. What do you think the future of Big Data will be like? Will it leave its popularity to something else? If so, what will it be?

13.3 FUNDAMENTALS OF BIG DATA ANALYTICS

Big Data by itself, regardless of the size, type, or speed, is worthless unless business users do something with it that delivers value to their organizations. That's where "big" analytics comes into the picture. Although organizations have always run reports and dashboards against data warehouses, most have not opened these repositories to in-depth on-demand exploration. This is partly because analysis tools are too complex for the average user but also because the repositories often do not contain all the data needed by the power user. But this is about to change (and had already changed for some) in a dramatic fashion, thanks to the new Big Data analytics paradigm.

With the value proposition, Big Data also brought about big challenges for organizations. The traditional means for capturing, storing, and analyzing data are not capable of dealing with Big Data effectively and efficiently. Therefore, new breeds of technologies need to be developed (or purchased/hired/outsourced) to take on the Big Data challenge. Before making such an investment, organizations should justify the means. Here are some questions that may help shed light on this situation. If any of the following statements are true, then you need to seriously consider embarking on a Big Data journey.

- You can't process the amount of data that you want to because of the limitations posed by your current platform or environment.
- You want to involve new/contemporary data sources (e.g., social media, RFID, sensory, Web, GPS, textual data) into your analytics platform, but you can't because it does not comply with the data storage schema-defined rows and columns without sacrificing fidelity or the richness of the new data.
- You need to (or want to) integrate data as quickly as possible to be current on your analysis.
- You want to work with a schema-on-demand (as opposed to the predetermined schema used in RDBMS) data storage paradigm because the nature of the new data may not be known, or there may not be enough time to determine it and develop a schema for it.
- The data is arriving so fast at your organization's doorstep that your traditional analytics platform cannot handle it.

As is the case with any other large IT investment, the success in **Big Data analytics** depends on a number of factors. Figure 13.2 shows a graphical depiction of the most critical success factors (Watson 2012).

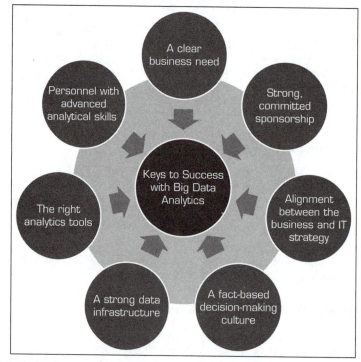

FIGURE 13.2 Critical Success Factors for Big Data Analytics. (*Source:* AsterData—a Teradata Company)

Following are the most critical success factors for Big Data analytics (Watson et al., 2012):

1. *A clear business need (alignment with the vision and the strategy).* Business investments ought to be made for the good of the business, not for the sake of mere technology advancements. Therefore the main driver for Big Data analytics should be the needs of the business at any level—strategic, tactical, and operations.

2. *Strong, committed sponsorship (executive champion).* It is a well-known fact that if you don't have strong, committed executive sponsorship, it is difficult (if not impossible) to succeed. If the scope is a single or a few analytical applications, the sponsorship can be at the departmental level. However, if the target is enterprise-wide organizational transformation, which is often the case for Big Data initiatives, sponsorship needs to be at the highest levels and organization-wide.

3. *Alignment between the business and IT strategy.* It is essential to make sure that the analytics work is always supporting the business strategy, and not other way around. Analytics should play the enabling role in successful execution of the business strategy.

4. *A fact-based decision making culture.* In a fact-based decision-making culture, the numbers rather than intuition, gut feeling, or supposition drive decision making. There is also a culture of experimentation to see what works and doesn't. To create a fact-based decision-making culture, senior management needs to:
   - Recognize that some people can't or won't adjust
   - Be a vocal supporter
   - Stress that outdated methods must be discontinued
   - Ask to see what analytics went into decisions
   - Link incentives and compensation to desired behaviors

5. *A strong data infrastructure.* Data warehouses have provided the data infrastructure for analytics. This infrastructure is changing and being enhanced in the Big Data era with new technologies. Success requires marrying the old with the new for a holistic infrastructure that works synergistically.

As the size and the complexity increase, the need for more efficient analytical systems is also increasing. In order to keep up with the computational needs of Big Data, a number of new and innovative computational techniques and platforms have been developed. These techniques are collectively called *high-performance computing,* which includes the following:

- *In-memory analytics:* Solves complex problems in near–real time with highly accurate insights by allowing analytical computations and Big Data to be processed in-memory and distributed across a dedicated set of nodes.
- *In-database analytics:* Speeds time to insights and enables better data governance by performing data integration and analytic functions inside the database so you won't have to move or convert data repeatedly.
- *Grid computing:* Promotes efficiency, lower cost, and better performance by processing jobs in a shared, centrally managed pool of IT resources.
- *Appliances:* Bringing together hardware and software in a physical unit that is not only fast but also scalable on an as-needed basis.

Computational requirement is just a small part of the list of challenges that Big Data imposes upon today's enterprises. Following is a list of challenges that are found by business executives to have a significant impact on successful implementation of Big Data analytics. When considering Big Data projects and architecture, being mindful of these challenges could make the journey to analytics competency a less stressful one.

- **Data volume:** The ability to capture, store, and process the huge volume of data at an acceptable speed so that the latest information is available to decision makers when they need it.
- **Data integration:** The ability to combine data that is not similar in structure or source and to do so quickly and at reasonable cost.
- **Processing capabilities:** The ability to process the data quickly, as it is captured. The traditional way of collecting and then processing the data may not work. In many situations data needs to be analyzed as soon as it is captured to leverage the most value (this is called *stream analytics*, which will be covered later in this chapter).
- **Data governance:** The ability to keep up with the security, privacy, ownership, and quality issues of Big Data. As the volume, variety (format and source), and velocity of data change, so should the capabilities of governance practices.
- **Skills availability:** Big Data is being harnessed with new tools and is being looked at in different ways. There is a shortage of people (often called data scientists, covered later in this chapter) with the skills to do the job.
- **Solution cost:** Since Big Data has opened up a world of possible business improvements, there is a great deal of experimentation and discovery taking place to determine the patterns that matter and the insights that turn to value. To ensure a positive ROI on a Big Data project, therefore, it is crucial to reduce the cost of the solutions used to find that value.

Though challenges are real, so is the value proposition of Big Data analytics. Anything that you can do as business analytics leaders to help prove the value of new data sources to the business will move your organization beyond experimenting and exploring Big Data into adapting and embracing it as a differentiator. There is nothing wrong with exploration, but ultimately the value comes from putting those insights into action.

Business Problems Addressed by Big Data Analytics

The top business problems addressed by Big Data overall are process efficiency and cost reduction as well as enhancing customer experience, but different priorities emerge when it is looked at by industry. Process efficiency and cost reduction are common business problems that can be addressed by analyzing Big Data, which are perhaps among the top-ranked problems that can be addressed with Big Data analytics for the manufacturing, government, energy and utilities, communications and media, transport, and healthcare sectors. Enhanced customer experience may be at the top of the list of problems addressed by insurance companies and retailers. Risk management usually is at the top of the list for companies in banking and education. Here is a list of problems that can be addressed using Big Data analytics:

- Process efficiency and cost reduction
- Brand management
- Revenue maximization, cross-selling, and up-selling
- Enhanced customer experience
- Churn identification, customer recruiting
- Improved customer service
- Identifying new products and market opportunities
- Risk management
- Regulatory compliance
- Enhanced security capabilities

Application Case 13.2 illustrates an excellent example in the banking industry, where disparate data sources are integrated into a Big Data infrastructure to achieve a single source of the truth.

Application Case 13.2

Top 5 Investment Bank Achieves Single Source of Truth

The Bank's highly respected derivatives team is responsible for over one-third of the world's total derivatives trades. Their derivatives practice has a global footprint with teams that support credit, interest rate, and equity derivatives in every region of the world. The Bank has earned numerous industry awards and is recognized for its product innovations.

Challenge

With its significant derivatives exposure the Bank's management recognized the importance of having a real-time global view of its positions. The existing system, based on a relational database, was comprised of multiple installations around the world. Due to the gradual expansions to accommodate the increasing data volume varieties, the legacy system was not fast enough to respond to growing business needs and requirements. It was unable to deliver real-time alerts to manage market and counterparty credit positions in the desired timeframe.

Solution

The Bank built a derivatives trade store based on the MarkLogic (a Big Data analytics solution provider)

Server, replacing the incumbent technologies. Replacing the 20 disparate batch-processing servers with a single operational trade store enabled the Bank to know its market and credit counterparty positions in real time, providing the ability to act quickly to mitigate risk. The accuracy and completeness of the data allowed the Bank and its regulators to confidently rely on the metrics and stress test results it reports.

The selection process included upgrading existing Oracle and Sybase technology. Meeting all the new regulatory requirements was also a major factor in the decision as the Bank looked to maximize its investment. After the Bank's careful investigation, the choice was clear—only MarkLogic could meet both needs plus provide better performance, scalability, faster development for future requirements and implementation, and a much lower total cost of ownership (TCO). Figure 13.3 illustrates the transformation from the old fragmented systems to the new unified system.

Results

MarkLogic was selected because existing systems would not provide the sub-second updating and analysis response times needed to effectively

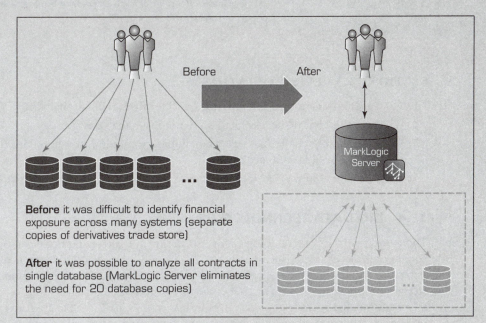

Before it was difficult to identify financial exposure across many systems (separate copies of derivatives trade store)

After it was possible to analyze all contracts in single database (MarkLogic Server eliminates the need for 20 database copies)

FIGURE 13.3   Moving from Many Old Systems to a Unified New System.   *Source:* MarkLogic.

(*Continued*)

Application Case 13.2 (Continued)

manage a derivatives trade book that represents nearly one-third of the global market. Trade data is now aggregated accurately across the Bank's entire derivatives portfolio, allowing risk management stakeholders to know the true enterprise risk profile, to conduct predictive analyses using accurate data, and to adopt a forward-looking approach. Not only are hundreds of thousands of dollars of technology costs saved each year, but the Bank does not need to add resources to meet regulators' escalating demands for more transparency and stress-testing frequency. Here are the highlights from the obtained results:

- An alerting feature keeps users appraised of up-to-the-minute market and counterparty credit changes so they can take appropriate actions.
- Derivatives are stored and traded in a single MarkLogic system requiring no downtime for maintenance, a significant competitive advantage.
- Complex changes can be made in hours versus days, weeks, and even months needed by competitors.
- Replacing Oracle and Sybase significantly reduced operations costs: one system versus 20, one database administrator instead of up to 10, and lower costs per trade.

Next Steps

The successful implementation and performance of the new system resulted in the Bank's examination of other areas where it could extract more value from its Big Data—structured, unstructured, and/or poly-structured. Two applications are under active discussion. Its equity research business sees an opportunity to significantly boost revenue with a platform that provides real-time research, repurposing, and content delivery. The Bank also sees the power of centralizing customer data to improve onboarding, increase cross-sell opportunities, and support know your customer requirements.

QUESTIONS FOR DISCUSSION

1. How can Big Data benefit large-scale trading banks?
2. How did MarkLogic infrastructure help ease the leveraging of Big Data?
3. What were the challenges, the proposed solution, and the obtained results?

Source: MarkLogic, Customer Success Story, **marklogic.com/resources/top-5-derivatives-trading-bank-achieves-single-source-of-truth** (accessed March 2013).

SECTION 13.3 REVIEW QUESTIONS

1. What is Big Data analytics? How does it differ from regular analytics?
2. What are the critical success factors for Big Data analytics?
3. What are the big challenges that one should be mindful of when considering implementation of Big Data analytics?
4. What are the common business problems addressed by Big Data analytics?

13.4 BIG DATA TECHNOLOGIES

There are a number of technologies for processing and analyzing Big Data, but most have some common characteristics (Kelly 2012). Namely, they take advantage of commodity hardware to enable scale-out, parallel processing techniques; employ nonrelational data storage capabilities in order to process unstructured and semistructured data; and apply advanced analytics and data visualization technology to Big Data to convey insights to end users. There are three Big Data technologies that stand out, that most believe will transform the business analytics and data management markets: MapReduce, Hadoop, and NoSQL.

MapReduce

MapReduce is a technique popularized by Google that distributes the processing of very large multi-structured data files across a large cluster of machines. High performance is achieved by breaking the processing into small units of work that can be run in parallel across the hundreds, potentially thousands, of nodes in the cluster. To quote the seminal paper on MapReduce:

"MapReduce is a programming model and an associated implementation for processing and generating large data sets. Programs written in this functional style are automatically parallelized and executed on a large cluster of commodity machines. This allows programmers without any experience with parallel and distributed systems to easily utilize the resources of a large distributed system" (Dean and Ghemawat, 2004).

The key point to note from this quote is that MapReduce is a programming model, not a programming language, that is, it is designed to be used by programmers, rather than business users. The easiest way to describe how MapReduce works is through the use of an example—see the geometric shape counter in Figure 13.4.

The input to the MapReduce process in Figure 13.4 is a set of geometric shapes. The objective is to count the number of geometric shapes of each type (diamond, circle, square, star, and triangle). The programmer in this example is responsible for coding the map and reducing programs; the remainder of the processing is handled by the software system implementing the MapReduce programming model.

The MapReduce system first reads the input file and splits it into multiple pieces. In this example, there are two splits, but in a real-life scenario, the number of splits would typically be much higher. These splits are then processed by multiple map programs

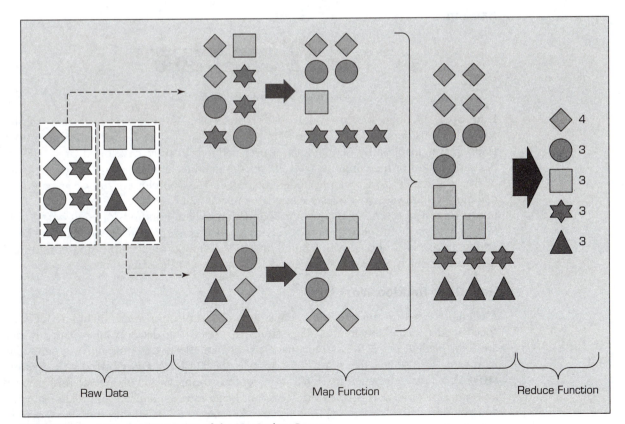

FIGURE 13.4 **A Graphical Depiction of the MapReduce Process.**

running in parallel on the nodes of the cluster. The role of each map program in this case is to group the data in a split by the type of geometric shape. The MapReduce system then takes the output from each map program and merges (shuffles/sorts) the results for input to reduce the program, which calculates the sum of the number of different types of geometric shapes. In this example, only one copy of the reduce program is used, but there may be more in practice. To optimize performance, programmers can provide their own shuffle/sort program and can also deploy a combiner that combines local map output files to reduce the number of output files that have to be remotely accessed across the cluster by the shuffle/sort step.

Why Use MapReduce?

MapReduce aids organizations in processing and analyzing large volumes of multi-structured data. Application examples include indexing and search, graph analysis, text analysis, machine learning, data transformation, and so forth. These types of applications are often difficult to implement using the standard SQL employed by relational DBMSs.

The procedural nature of MapReduce makes it easily understood by skilled programmers. It also has the advantage that developers do not have to be concerned with implementing parallel computing—this is handled transparently by the system. Although MapReduce is designed for programmers, non-programmers can exploit the value of prebuilt MapReduce applications and function libraries. Both commercial and open source MapReduce libraries are available that provide a wide range of analytic capabilities. Apache Mahout, for example, is an open source machine-learning library of "algorithms for clustering, classification, and batch-based collaborative filtering" that are implemented using MapReduce.

Hadoop

Source: Hadoop. Used with permission.

Hadoop is an open source framework for processing, storing, and analyzing massive amounts of distributed, unstructured data. Originally created by Doug Cutting at Yahoo!, Hadoop was inspired by MapReduce, a user-defined function developed by Google in the early 2000s for indexing the Web. It was designed to handle petabytes and exabytes of data distributed over multiple nodes in parallel. Hadoop clusters run on inexpensive commodity hardware so projects can scale-out without breaking the bank. Hadoop is now a project of the Apache Software Foundation, where hundreds of contributors continuously improve the core technology. Fundamental concept: Rather than banging away at one, huge block of data with a single machine, Hadoop breaks up Big Data into multiple parts so each part can be processed and analyzed at the same time.

How Does Hadoop Work?

A client accesses unstructured and semistructured data from sources including log files, social media feeds, and internal data stores. It breaks the data up into "parts," which are then loaded into a file system made up of multiple nodes running on commodity hardware. The default file store in Hadoop is the **Hadoop Distributed File System (HDFS)**. File systems such as HDFS are adept at storing large volumes of unstructured and semistructured data as they do not require data to be organized into relational rows and columns. Each "part" is replicated multiple times and loaded into the file system, so that if a node fails, another node has a copy of the data contained on the failed node.

A Name Node acts as facilitator, communicating back to the client information such as which nodes are available, where in the cluster certain data resides, and which nodes have failed.

Once the data is loaded into the cluster, it is ready to be analyzed via the MapReduce framework. The client submits a "Map" job—usually a query written in Java—to one of the nodes in the cluster known as the Job Tracker. The Job Tracker refers to the Name Node to determine which data it needs to access to complete the job and where in the cluster that data is located. Once determined, the Job Tracker submits the query to the relevant nodes. Rather than bringing all the data back into a central location for processing, processing then occurs at each node simultaneously, or in parallel. This is an essential characteristic of Hadoop.

When each node has finished processing its given job, it stores the results. The client initiates a "Reduce" job through the Job Tracker in which results of the map phase stored locally on individual nodes are aggregated to determine the "answer" to the original query, and then loaded onto another node in the cluster. The client accesses these results, which can then be loaded into one of a number of analytic environments for analysis. The MapReduce job has now been completed.

Once the MapReduce phase is complete, the processed data is ready for further analysis by data scientists and others with advanced data analytics skills. **Data scientists** can manipulate and analyze the data using any of a number of tools for any number of uses, including searching for hidden insights and patterns or use as the foundation for building user-facing analytic applications. The data can also be modeled and transferred from Hadoop clusters into existing relational databases, data warehouses, and other traditional IT systems for further analysis and/or to support transactional processing.

Hadoop Technical Components

A Hadoop "stack" is made up of a number of components, which include:

- *Hadoop Distributed File System (HDFS):* The default storage layer in any given Hadoop cluster
- *Name Node:* The node in a Hadoop cluster that provides the client information on where in the cluster particular data is stored and if any nodes fail
- *Secondary Node:* A backup to the Name Node, it periodically replicates and stores data from the Name Node should it fail
- *Job Tracker:* The node in a Hadoop cluster that initiates and coordinates MapReduce jobs, or the processing of the data
- *Slave Nodes:* The grunts of any Hadoop cluster, slave nodes store data and take direction to process it from the Job Tracker

In addition to these components, the Hadoop ecosystem is made up of a number of complimentary sub-projects. NoSQL data stores like Cassandra and HBase are also used to store the results of MapReduce jobs in Hadoop. In addition to Java, some MapReduce jobs and other Hadoop functions are written in Pig, an open source language designed specifically for Hadoop. Hive is an open source data warehouse originally developed by Facebook that allows for analytic modeling within Hadoop. Here are the most commonly referenced sub-projects for Hadoop.

HIVE **Hive** is a Hadoop-based data warehousing–like framework originally developed by Facebook. It allows users to write queries in an SQL-like language called HiveQL, which are then converted to MapReduce. This allows SQL programmers with no MapReduce experience to use the warehouse and makes it easier to integrate with business intelligence and visualization tools such as MicroStrategy, Tableau, Revolutions Analytics, and so forth.

PIG   **Pig** is a Hadoop-based query language developed by Yahoo!. It is relatively easy to learn and is adept at very deep, very long data pipelines (a limitation of SQL.)

HBASE   HBase is a nonrelational database that allows for low-latency, quick lookups in Hadoop. It adds transactional capabilities to Hadoop, allowing users to conduct updates, inserts, and deletes. eBay and Facebook use HBase heavily.

FLUME   Flume is a framework for populating Hadoop with data. Agents are populated throughout one's IT infrastructure—inside Web servers, application servers, and mobile devices, for example—to collect data and integrate it into Hadoop.

OOZIE   Oozie is a workflow processing system that lets users define a series of jobs written in multiple languages—such as Map Reduce, Pig, and Hive—and then intelligently link them to one another. Oozie allows users to specify, for example, that a particular query is only to be initiated after specified previous jobs on which it relies for data are completed.

AMBARI   Ambari is a Web-based set of tools for deploying, administering, and monitoring Apache Hadoop clusters. Its development is being led by engineers from Hortonworks, which include Ambari in its Hortonworks Data Platform.

AVRO   Avro is a data serialization system that allows for encoding the schema of Hadoop files. It is adept at parsing data and performing removed procedure calls.

MAHOUT   Mahout is a data mining library. It takes the most popular data mining algorithms for performing clustering, regression testing, and statistical modeling and implements them using the MapReduce model.

SQOOP   Sqoop is a connectivity tool for moving data from non-Hadoop data stores—such as relational databases and data warehouses—into Hadoop. It allows users to specify the target location inside of Hadoop and instructs Sqoop to move data from Oracle, Teradata, or other relational databases to the target.

HCATALOG   HCatalog is a centralized metadata management and sharing service for Apache Hadoop. It allows for a unified view of all data in Hadoop clusters and allows diverse tools, including Pig and Hive, to process any data elements without needing to know physically where in the cluster the data is stored.

Hadoop: The Pros and Cons

The main benefit of Hadoop is that it allows enterprises to process and analyze large volumes of unstructured and semistructured data, heretofore inaccessible to them, in a cost- and time-effective manner. Because Hadoop clusters can scale to petabytes and even exabytes of data, enterprises no longer must rely on sample data sets but can process and analyze *all* relevant data. Data scientists can apply an iterative approach to analysis, continually refining and testing queries to uncover previously unknown insights. It is also inexpensive to get started with Hadoop. Developers can download the Apache Hadoop distribution for free and begin experimenting with Hadoop in less than a day.

The downside to Hadoop and its myriad components is that they are immature and still developing. As with any young, raw technology, implementing and managing

Hadoop clusters and performing advanced analytics on large volumes of unstructured data require significant expertise, skill, and training. Unfortunately, there is currently a dearth of Hadoop developers and data scientists available, making it impractical for many enterprises to maintain and take advantage of complex Hadoop clusters. Further, as Hadoop's myriad components are improved upon by the community and new components are created, there is, as with any immature open source technology/approach, a risk of forking. Finally, Hadoop is a batch-oriented framework, meaning it does not support real-time data processing and analysis.

The good news is that some of the brightest minds in IT are contributing to the Apache Hadoop project, and a new generation of Hadoop developers and data scientists is coming of age. As a result, the technology is advancing rapidly, becoming both more powerful and easier to implement and manage. An ecosystems of vendors, both Hadoop-focused start-ups like Cloudera and Hortonworks and well-worn IT stalwarts like IBM and Microsoft, are working to offer commercial, enterprise-ready Hadoop distributions, tools, and services to make deploying and managing the technology a practical reality for the traditional enterprise. Other bleeding-edge start-ups are working to perfect NoSQL (Not Only SQL) data stores capable of delivering near– real-time insights in conjunction with Hadoop. Technology Insights 13.2 provides a few facts to clarify some misconceptions about Hadoop.

TECHNOLOGY INSIGHTS 13.2   A Few Demystifying Facts About Hadoop

Although Hadoop and related technologies have been around for more than 5 years now, most people still have several misconceptions about Hadoop and related technologies such as MapReduce and Hive. The following list of 10 facts intends to clarify what Hadoop is and does relative to BI, as well as in which business and technology situations Hadoop-based BI, data warehousing, and analytics can be useful (Russom, 2013).

Fact #1. Hadoop consists of multiple products. We talk about Hadoop as if it's one monolithic thing, whereas it's actually a family of open source products and technologies overseen by the Apache Software Foundation (ASF). (Some Hadoop products are also available via vendor distributions; more on that later.)

The Apache Hadoop library includes (in BI priority order) the Hadoop Distributed File System (HDFS), MapReduce, Hive, Hbase, Pig, Zookeeper, Flume, Sqoop, Oozie, Hue, and so on. You can combine these in various ways, but HDFS and MapReduce (perhaps with Hbase and Hive) constitute a useful technology stack for applications in BI, DW, and analytics.

Fact #2. Hadoop is open source but available from vendors, too. Apache Hadoop's open source software library is available from ASF at apache.org. For users desiring a more enterprise-ready package, a few vendors now offer Hadoop distributions that include additional administrative tools and technical support.

Fact #3. Hadoop is an ecosystem, not a single product. In addition to products from Apache, the extended Hadoop ecosystem includes a growing list of vendor products that integrate with or expand Hadoop technologies. One minute on your favorite search engine will reveal these.

Fact #4. HDFS is a file system, not a database management system (DBMS). Hadoop is primarily a distributed file system and lacks capabilities we'd associate with a DBMS, such as indexing, random access to data, and support for SQL. That's okay, because HDFS does things DBMSs cannot do.

Fact #5. Hive resembles SQL but is not standard SQL. Many of us are handcuffed to SQL because we know it well and our tools demand it. People who know SQL can quickly learn to hand code Hive, but that doesn't solve compatibility issues with SQL-based tools. TDWI feels that over time, Hadoop products will support standard SQL, so this issue will soon be moot.

Fact #6. Hadoop and MapReduce are related but don't require each other. Developers at Google developed MapReduce before HDFS existed, and some variations of MapReduce work with a variety of storage technologies, including HDFS, other file systems, and some DBMSs.

Fact #7. MapReduce provides control for analytics, not analytics per se. MapReduce is a general-purpose execution engine that handles the complexities of network communication, parallel programming, and fault tolerance for any kind of application that you can hand code—not just analytics.

Fact #8. Hadoop is about data diversity, not just data volume. Theoretically, HDFS can manage the storage and access of any data type as long as you can put the data in a file and copy that file into HDFS. As outrageously simplistic as that sounds, it's largely true, and it's exactly what brings many users to Apache HDFS.

Fact #9. Hadoop complements a DW; it's rarely a replacement. Most organizations have designed their DW for structured, relational data, which makes it difficult to wring BI value from unstructured and semistructured data. Hadoop promises to complement DWs by handling the multi-structured data types most DWs can't.

Fact #10. Hadoop enables many types of analytics, not just Web analytics. Hadoop gets a lot of press about how Internet companies use it for analyzing Web logs and other Web data, but other use cases exist. For example, consider the Big Data coming from sensory devices, such as robotics in manufacturing, RFID in retail, or grid monitoring in utilities. Older analytic applications that need large data samples—such as customer-base segmentation, fraud detection, and risk analysis—can benefit from the additional Big Data managed by Hadoop. Likewise, Hadoop's additional data can expand 360-degree views to create a more complete and granular view.

NoSQL

A related new style of database called **NoSQL** (Not Only SQL) has emerged to, like Hadoop, process large volumes of multi-structured data. However, whereas Hadoop is adept at supporting large-scale, batch-style historical analysis, NoSQL databases are aimed, for the most part (though there are some important exceptions), at serving up discrete data stored among large volumes of multi-structured data to end-user and automated Big Data applications. This capability is sorely lacking from relational database technology, which simply can't maintain needed application performance levels at Big Data scale.

In some cases, NoSQL and Hadoop work in conjunction. The aforementioned HBase, for example, is a popular NoSQL database modeled after Google BigTable that is often deployed on top of HDFS, the Hadoop Distributed File System, to provide low-latency, quick lookups in Hadoop. The downside of most NoSQL databases today is that they trade ACID (atomicity, consistency, isolation, durability) compliance for performance and scalability. Many also lack mature management and monitoring tools. Both these shortcomings are in the process of being overcome by both the open source NoSQL communities and a handful of vendors that are attempting to commercialize the various NoSQL databases. NoSQL databases currently available include HBase, Cassandra, MongoDB, Accumulo, Riak, CouchDB, and DynamoDB, among others. Application Case 13.3 shows the use of NoSQL databases at eBay.

Application Case 13.3

eBay's Big Data Solution

eBay is the world's largest online marketplace, enabling the buying and selling of practically anything. Founded in 1995, eBay connects a diverse and passionate community of individual buyers and sellers, as well as small businesses. eBay's collective impact on e-commerce is staggering: In 2012, the total value of goods sold on eBay was $75.4 billion. eBay currently serves over 112 million active users and has 400+ million items for sale.

The Challenge: Supporting Data at Extreme Scale

One of the keys to eBay's extraordinary success is its ability to turn the enormous volumes of data it generates into useful insights that its customers can glean directly from the pages they frequent. To accommodate eBay's explosive data growth—its data centers perform billions of reads and writes each day—and the increasing demand to process data at blistering speeds, eBay needed a solution that did not have the typical bottlenecks, scalability issues, and transactional constraints associated with common relational database approaches. The company also needed to perform rapid analysis on a broad assortment of the structured and unstructured data it captured.

The Solution: Integrated Real-Time Data and Analytics

Its Big Data requirements brought eBay to NoSQL technologies, specifically Apache Cassandra and DataStax Enterprise. Along with Cassandra and its high-velocity data capabilities, eBay was also drawn to the integrated Apache Hadoop analytics that come with DataStax Enterprise. The solution incorporates a scale-out architecture that enables eBay to deploy multiple DataStax Enterprise clusters across several different data centers using commodity hardware. The end result is that eBay is now able to more cost effectively process massive amounts of data at very high speeds, at very high velocities, and achieve far more than they were able to with the higher cost propriety system they had been using. Currently, eBay is managing a sizable portion of its data center needs—250TBs+ of storage—in Apache Cassandra and DataStax Enterprise clusters.

Additional technical factors that played a role in eBay's decision to deploy DataStax Enterprise so widely include the solution's linear scalability, high availability with no single point of failure, and outstanding write performance.

Handling Diverse Use Cases

eBay employs DataStax Enterprise for many different use cases. The following examples illustrate some of the ways the company is able to meet its Big Data needs with the extremely fast data handling and analytics capabilities the solution provides. Naturally, eBay experiences huge amounts of write traffic, which the Cassandra implementation in DataStax Enterprise handles more efficiently than any other RDBMS or NoSQL solution. eBay currently sees 6 billion+ writes per day across multiple Cassandra clusters and 5 billion+ reads (mostly offline) per day as well.

One use case supported by DataStax Enterprise involves quantifying the social data eBay displays on its product pages. The Cassandra distribution in DataStax Enterprise stores all the information needed to provide counts for "like," "own," and "want" data on eBay product pages. It also provides the same data for the eBay "Your Favorites" page that contains all the items a user likes, owns, or wants, with Cassandra serving up the entire "Your Favorites" page. eBay provides this data through Cassandra's scalable counters feature.

Load balancing and application availability are important aspects to this particular use case. The DataStax Enterprise solution gave eBay architects the flexibility they needed to design a system that enables any user request to go to any data center, with each data center having a single DataStax Enterprise cluster spanning those centers. This design feature helps balance the incoming user load and eliminates any possible threat to application downtime. In addition to the line of business data powering the Web pages its customers visit, eBay is also able to perform high-speed analysis with the ability to maintain a separate data center running

(Continued)

Application Case 13.3 (Continued)

Hadoop nodes of the same DataStax Enterprise ring (see Figure 13.5).

Another use case involves the Hunch (an eBay sister company) "taste graph" for eBay users and items, which provides custom recommendations based on user interests. eBay's Web site is essentially a graph between all users and the items for sale. All events (bid, buy, sell, and list) are captured by eBay's systems and stored as a graph in Cassandra. The application sees more than 200 million writes daily and holds more than 40 billion pieces of data.

eBay also uses DataStax Enterprise for many time-series use cases in which processing high-volume, real-time data is a foremost priority. These include mobile notification logging and tracking (every time eBay sends a notification to a mobile phone or device it is logged in Cassandra), fraud detection, SOA request/response payload logging, and RedLaser (another eBay sister company) server logs and analytics.

Across all of these use cases is the common requirement of uptime. eBay is acutely aware of the need to keep their business up and open for business, and DataStax Enterprise plays a key part in that through its support of high availability clusters. "We have to be ready for disaster recovery all the time. It's really great that Cassandra allows for active-active multiple data centers where we can read and write data anywhere, anytime," says eBay architect Jay Patel.

QUESTIONS FOR DISCUSSION

1. Why Big Data is a big deal for eBay?
2. What were the challenges, the proposed solution, and the obtained results?
3. Can you think of other e-commerce businesses that may have Big Data challenges comparable to that of eBay?

Source: DataStax, Customer Case Studies, **datastax.com/resources/casestudies/eBay** (accessed January 2013).

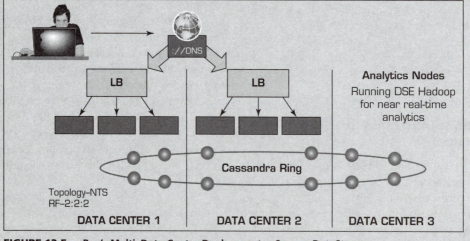

FIGURE 13.5 **eBay's Multi–Data-Center Deployment.** *Source:* DataStax.

SECTION 13.4 REVIEW QUESTIONS

1. What are the common characteristics of emerging Big Data technologies?

2. What is MapReduce? What does it do? How does it do it?

3. What is Hadoop? How does it work?

4. What are the main Hadopp components? What functions do they perform?

5. What is NoSQL? How does it fit into the Big Data analytics picture?

13.5   DATA SCIENTIST

Data scientist is a role or a job frequently associated with Big Data or data science. In a very short time it has become one of the most sought-out roles in the marketplace. In a recent article published in the October 2012 issue of the *Harvard Business Review,* authors Thomas H. Davenport and D. J. Patil called data scientist "The Sexiest Job of the 21st Century." In that article they specified data scientists' most basic, universal skill as the ability to write code (in the latest Big Data languages and platforms). Although this may be less true in the near future, when many more people will have the title "data scientist" on their business cards, at this time it seems to be the most fundamental skill required from data scientists. A more enduring skill will be the need for data scientists to communicate in a language that all their stakeholders understand—and to demonstrate the special skills involved in storytelling with data, whether verbally, visually, or—ideally—both (Davenport and Patil, 2012).

Data scientists use a combination of their business and technical skills to *investigate* Big Data looking for ways to improve current business analytics practices (from descriptive to predictive and prescriptive) and hence to improve decisions for new business opportunities. One of the biggest differences between a data scientist and a business intelligence user—such as a business analyst—is that a data scientist investigates and looks for new possibilities, while a BI user analyzes existing business situations and operations.

One of the dominant traits expected from data scientists is an intense curiosity—a desire to go beneath the surface of a problem, find the questions at its heart, and distill them into a very clear set of hypotheses that can be tested. This often entails the associative thinking that characterizes the most creative scientists in any field. For example, we know of a data scientist studying a fraud problem who realized that it was analogous to a type of DNA sequencing problem (Davenport and Patil, 2012). By bringing together those disparate worlds, he and his team were able to craft a solution that dramatically reduced fraud losses.

Where Do Data Scientists Come From?

Although there still is disagreement about the use of "science" in the name, it is becoming less of a controversial issue. Real scientists use tools made by other scientists, or make them if they don't exist, as a means to expand knowledge. That is exactly what data scientists are expected to do. Experimental physicists, for example, have to design equipment, gather data, and conduct multiple experiments to discover knowledge and communicate their results. Even though they may not be wearing white coats, and may not be living in a sterile lab environment, that is exactly what data scientists do: use creative tools and techniques to turn data into actionable information for others to use for better decision making.

There is no consensus on what educational background a data scientist has to have. The usual suspects like Master of Science (or Ph.D.) in Computer Science, MIS, Industrial Engineering, or the newly popularized postgraduate analytics degrees may be necessary but not sufficient to call someone a data scientist. One of the most sought-out characteristics of a data scientist is expertise in both technical and business application domains. In that sense, it somewhat resembles to the professional engineer (PE) or project management professional (PMP) roles, where experience is valued as much as (if not more than) the technical skills and educational background. It would not be a huge surprise to see within the next few years a certification specifically designed for data scientists (perhaps called "Data Science Professional" or "DSP," for short).

Because it is a profession for a field that is still being defined, many of its practices are still experimental and far from being standardized; companies are overly sensitive about the experience dimension of data scientist. As the profession matures, and

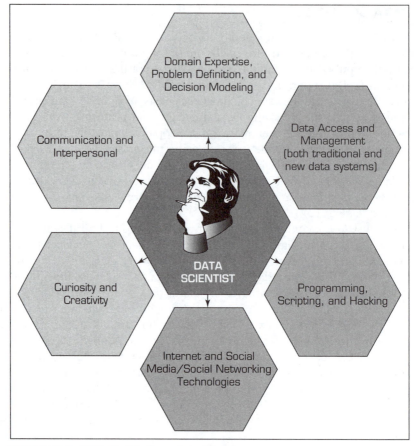

FIGURE 13.6 Skills That Define a Data Scientist.

practices are standardized, experience will be less of an issue when defining a data scientist. Nowadays, companies looking for people who have extensive experience in working with complex data have had good luck recruiting among those with educational and work backgrounds in the physical or social sciences. Some of the best and brightest data scientists have been Ph.D.s in esoteric fields like ecology and systems biology (Davenport and Patil, 2012). Even though there is no consensus on where data scientists come from, there is a common understanding of what skills and qualities they are expected to possess. Figure 13.6 shows a high-level graphical illustration of these skills.

Data scientists are expected to have soft skills such as creativity, curiosity, communication/interpersonal, domain expertise, problem definition, and managerial (shown with light background hexagons on the left side of the figure) as well as sound technical skills such as data manipulation, programming/hacking/scripting, and Internet and social media/networking technologies (shown with darker background hexagons on the right side of the figure). Technology Insights 13.3 is about a typical job advertisement for a data scientist.

TECHNOLOGY INSIGHTS 13.3   A Typical Job Post for Data Scientists

[Some company] is seeking a Data Scientist to join our Big Data Analytics team. Individuals in this role are expected to be comfortable working as a software engineer and a quantitative researcher. The ideal candidate will have a keen interest in the study of an online social network and a passion for identifying and answering questions that help us build the best products.

Responsibilities

- Work closely with a product engineering team to identify and answer important product questions
- Answer product questions by using appropriate statistical techniques on available data
- Communicate findings to product managers and engineers
- Drive the collection of new data and the refinement of existing data sources
- Analyze and interpret the results of product experiments
- Develop best practices for instrumentation and experimentation and communicate those to product engineering teams

Requirements

- M.S. or Ph.D. in a relevant technical field, or 4+ years of experience in a relevant role
- Extensive experience solving analytical problems using quantitative approaches
- Comfort with manipulating and analyzing complex, high-volume, high-dimensionality data from varying sources
- A strong passion for empirical research and for answering hard questions with data
- A flexible analytic approach that allows for results at varying levels of precision
- Ability to communicate complex quantitative analysis in a clear, precise, and actionable manner
- Fluency with at least one scripting language such as Python or PHP
- Familiarity with relational databases and SQL
- Expert knowledge of an analysis tool such as R, Matlab, or SAS
- Experience working with large data sets, experience working with distributed computing tools a plus (Map/Reduce, Hadoop, Hive, etc.)

People with this range of skills are rare, which explains why data scientists are in short supply. Because of the high demand for these relatively fewer individuals, the starting salaries for data scientists are well above six figures, and for ones with ample experience and specific domain expertise, salaries are pushing near seven figures. For most organizations, rather than looking for individuals with all these capabilities, it will be necessary instead to build a team of people that collectively have these skills. Here are some recent anecdotes about data scientists:

- Data scientists turn Big Data into big value, delivering products that delight users and insight that informs business decisions.
- A data scientist is not only proficient to work with data, but also appreciates data itself as an invaluable asset.
- By 2020 there will be 4.5 million new data scientist jobs, of which only one-third will be filled because of the lack of available personnel.
- Today's data scientists are the quants of the financial markets of the 1980s.

Data scientists are not limited to high-tech Internet companies. Many of the companies that do not have much Internet presence are also interested in highly qualified Big Data analytics professionals. For instance, as described in the End-of-Chapter Application Case, Volvo is leveraging data scientists to turn data that comes from its corporate transaction databases and from sensors (placed in its cars) into actionable insight. An interesting area where we have seen the use of data scientists in the recent past is in politics. Application Case 13.4 describes the use of Big Data analytics in the world of politics and presidential elections.

Application Case 13.4

Big Data and Analytics in Politics

One of the application areas where Big Data and analytics promise to make a big difference is arguably the field of politics. Experiences from the recent presidential elections illustrated the power of Big Data and analytics to acquire and energize millions of volunteers (in the form of a modern-era grassroots movement) to not only raise hundreds of millions of dollars for the election campaign but to optimally organize and mobilize potential voters to get out and vote in large numbers, as well. Clearly, the 2008 and 2012 presidential elections made a mark on the political arena with the creative use of Big Data and analytics to improve chances of winning. Figure 13.7 illustrates a graphical depiction of the analytical process of converting a wide variety of data into the ingredients for winning an election.

As Figure 13.7 illustrates, data is the source of information; the richer and deeper it is, the better and more relevant the insights. The main characteristics of Big Data, namely volume, variety, and velocity (the three Vs), readily apply to the kind of data that is used for political campaigns. In addition to the structured data (e.g., detailed records of previous campaigns, census data, market research, and poll data) vast volumes and a variety of **social media** (e.g., tweets at Twitter, Facebook wall posts, blog posts) and Web data (Web pages, news articles, newsgroups) are used to learn more about voters and obtain deeper insights to enforce or change their opinions. Often, the search and browsing histories of individuals are captured and made available to customers (political analysts) who can use such data for better insight and behavioral targeting. If done correctly, Big Data and analytics can provide invaluable information to manage political campaigns better than ever before.

From predicting election outcomes to targeting potential voters and donors, Big Data and analytics have a lot to offer to modern-day election campaigns. In fact, they have changed the way presidential election campaigns are run. In the 2008 and 2012 presidential elections, the major political parties (Republican and Democratic) employed social media and data-driven analytics for a more effective and efficient campaign, but as many agree, the Democrats clearly had the competitive advantage (Issenberg, 2012). Obama's 2012 data and analytics-driven operation was far more sophisticated and more efficient than its much-heralded 2008 process, which was primarily social media driven. In the 2012

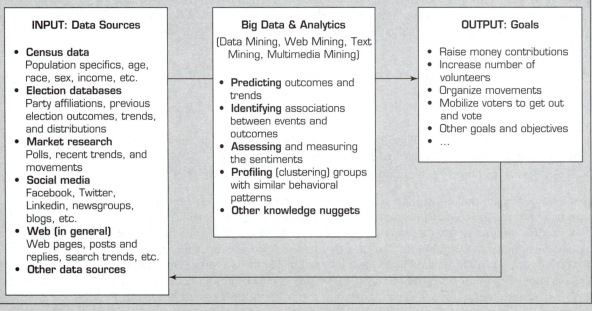

FIGURE 13.7 Leveraging Big Data and Analytics for Political Campaigns.

campaign, hundreds of analysts applied advanced analytics on very large and diverse data sources to pinpoint exactly who to target, for what reason, with what message, on a continuous basis. Compared to 2008, they had more expertise, hardware, software, data (e.g., Facebook and Twitter were orders of magnitude bigger in 2012 than they had been in 2008), and computational resources to go over and beyond what they had accomplished previously (Shen, 2013). Before the 2012 election, in June of last year, a *Politico* reporter claimed that Obama had a data advantage and went on to say that the depth and breadth of the campaign's digital operation, from political and demographic data mining to voter sentiment and behavioral analysis, reached beyond anything politics had ever seen (Romano, 2012).

According to Shen, the real winner of the 2012 elections was analytics (Shen, 2013). While most people, including the so-called political experts (who often rely on gut feelings and experiences), thought the 2012 presidential election would be very close, a number of analysts, based on their data-driven analytical models, predicted that Obama would win easily with close to 99 percent certainty. For example, Nate Silver at FiveThirtyEight, a popular political blog published by *The New York Times*, predicted not only that Obama would win but also by exactly how much he would win.

Simon Jackman, professor of political science at Stanford University, accurately predicted that Obama would win 332 electoral votes and that North Carolina and Indiana—the only two states that Obama won in 2008—would fall to Romney.

In short, Big Data and analytics have become a critical part of political campaigns. The usage and expertise gap between the party lines may disappear, but the importance of analytical capabilities will continue to evolve for the foreseeable future.

QUESTIONS FOR DISCUSSION

1. What is the role of analytics and Big Data in modern-day politics?
2. Do you think Big Data Analytics could change the outcome of an election?
3. What do you think are the challenges, the potential solution, and the probable results of the use of Big Data Analytics in politics?

Sources: Compiled from G. Shen, "Big Data, Analytics and Elections," INFORMS' *Analytics Magazine,* January–February 2013; L. Romano, "Obama's Data Advantage," *Politico,* June 9, 2012; M. Scherer, "Inside the Secret World of the Data Crunchers Who Helped Obama Win," *Time,* November 7, 2012; S. Issenberg, "Obama Does It Better" (from "Victory Lab: The New Science of Winning Campaigns"), *Slate,* October 29, 2012; and D. A. Samuelson, "Analytics: Key to Obama's Victory," INFORMS' *ORMS Today,* February 2013 Issue, pp. 20–24.

SECTION 13.5 REVIEW QUESTIONS

1. Who is a data scientist? What makes them so much in demand?
2. What are the common characteristics of data scientists? Which one is the most important?
3. Where do data scientists come from? What educational backgrounds do they have?
4. What do you think is the path to becoming a great data scientist?

13.6 BIG DATA AND DATA WAREHOUSING

There is doubt that the emergence of Big Data has changed and will continue to change data warehousing in a significant way. Until recently, enterprise data warehouses were the centerpiece of all decision support technologies. Now, they have to share the spotlight with the newcomer, Big Data. The question that is popping up everywhere is whether Big Data and its enabling technologies such as Hadoop will replace data warehousing and its core technology relational data base management systems (RDBMS). Are we witnessing a data warehouse versus Big Data challenge (or from the technology standpoint, Hadoop versus RDBMS)? In this section we will explain why these questions have no basis—and at least justify that such an either-or choice is not the reflection of the reality at this point in time.

In the last decade or so, we have seen a significant improvement in the area of computer-based decision support systems, which can largely be credited to data warehousing and technological advancements in both software and hardware to capture, store, and analyze data. As the size of the data increased, so did the capabilities of data warehouses. Some of these data warehousing advances included massively parallel processing (moving from one or few to many parallel processors), storage area networks (easily scalable storage solutions), solid-state storage, in-database processing, in-memory processing, and columnar (column oriented) databases, just to name a few. These advancements helped keep the increasing size of data under control, while effectively serving analytics needs of the decision makers. What has changed the landscape in recent years is the variety and complexity of data, which made data warehouses incapable of keeping up. It is not the volume of the structured data but the variety and the velocity that forced the world of IT to develop a new paradigm, which we now call "Big Data." Now that we have these two paradigms, data warehousing and Big Data, seemingly competing for the same job—turning data into actionable information—which one will prevail? Is this a fair question to ask? Or are we missing the big picture? In this section, we try to shed some light on this intriguing question.

As has been the case for many previous technology innovations, hype about Big Data and its enabling technologies like Hadoop and MapReduce is rampant. Both non-practitioners as well as practitioners are overwhelmed by diverse opinions. According to Awadallah and Graham (2012), people are missing the point in claiming that Hadoop replaces relational databases and is becoming the new data warehouse. It is easy to see where these claims originate since both Hadoop and data warehouse systems can run in parallel, scale up to enormous data volumes, and have shared-nothing architectures. At a conceptual level, it is easy to think they are interchangeable. The reality is that they are not, and the differences between the two overwhelm the similarities. If they are not interchangeable, then how do we decide when to deploy Hadoop and when to use a data warehouse?

Use Case(s) for Hadoop

As we have covered earlier in this chapter, Hadoop is the result of new developments in computer and storage grid technologies. Using commodity hardware as a foundation, Hadoop provides a layer of software that spans the entire grid, turning it into a single system. Consequently, some major differentiators are obvious in this architecture:

- Hadoop is the repository and refinery for raw data.
- Hadoop is a powerful, economical, and active archive.

Thus, Hadoop sits at both ends of the large-scale data life cycle—first when raw data is born, and finally when data is retiring, but is still occasionally needed.

1. ***Hadoop as the repository and refinery.*** As volumes of Big Data arrive from sources such as sensors, machines, social media, and clickstream interactions, the first step is to capture all the data reliably and cost effectively. When data volumes are huge, the traditional single-server strategy does not work for long. Pouring the data into the Hadoop Distributed File System (HDFS) gives architects much needed flexibility. Not only can they capture hundreds of terabytes in a day, but they can also adjust the Hadoop configuration up or down to meet surges and lulls in data ingestion. This is accomplished at the lowest possible cost per gigabyte due to open source economics and leveraging commodity hardware.

   Since the data is stored on local storage instead of SANs, Hadoop data access is often much faster, and it does not clog the network with terabytes of data movement. Once the raw data is captured, Hadoop is used to refine it. Hadoop can act as a parallel "ETL engine on steroids," leveraging handwritten or commercial data transformation technologies. Many of these raw data transformations require the unraveling of complex free-form data into structured formats. This is particularly true with clickstreams (or Web logs) and complex sensor data formats. Consequently, a programmer needs to tease the wheat from the chaff, identifying the valuable signal in the noise.

2. ***Hadoop as the active archive.*** In a 2003 interview with ACM, Jim Gray claimed that hard disks can be treated as tape. While it may take many more years for magnetic tape archives to be retired, today some portions of tape workloads are already being redirected to Hadoop clusters. This shift is occurring for two fundamental reasons. First, while it may appear inexpensive to store data on tape, the true cost comes with the difficulty of retrieval. Not only is the data stored offline, requiring hours if not days to restore, but tape cartridges themselves are also prone to degradation over time, making data loss a reality and forcing companies to factor in those costs. To make matters worse, tape formats change every couple of years, requiring organizations to either perform massive data migrations to the newest tape format or risk the inability to restore data from obsolete tapes.

   Second, it has been shown that there is value in keeping historical data online and accessible. As in the clickstream example, keeping raw data on a spinning disk for a longer duration makes it easy for companies to revisit data when the context changes and new constraints need to be applied. Searching thousands of disks with Hadoop is dramatically faster and easier than spinning through hundreds of magnetic tapes. Additionally, as disk densities continue to double every 18 months, it becomes economically feasible for organizations to hold many years' worth of raw or refined data in HDFS. Thus, the Hadoop storage grid is useful in both the pre-processing of raw data and the long-term storage of data. It's a true "active archive" since it not only stores and protects the data, but also enables users to quickly, easily, and perpetually derive value from it.

Use Case(s) for Data Warehousing

After nearly 30 years of investment, refinement, and growth, the list of features available in a data warehouse is quite staggering. Built upon relational database technology using schemas and integrating business intelligence (BI) tools, the major differences in this architecture are:

- Data warehouse performance
- Integrated data that provides business value
- Interactive BI tools for end users

1. ***Data warehouse performance.*** Basic indexing, found in open source databases, such as MySQL or Postgres, is a standard feature used to improve query response times or enforce constraints on data. More advanced forms such as materialized views, aggregate join indexes, cube indexes, and sparse join indexes enable numerous performance gains in data warehouses. However, the most important performance enhancement to date is the cost-based optimizer. The optimizer examines incoming SQL and considers multiple plans for executing each query as fast as possible. It achieves this by comparing the SQL request to the database design and extensive data statistics that help identify the best combination of execution steps. In essence, the optimizer is like having a genius programmer examine every query and tune it for the best performance. Lacking an optimizer or data demographic statistics, a query that could run in minutes may take hours, even with many indexes.

For this reason, database vendors are constantly adding new index types, partitioning, statistics, and optimizer features. For the past 30 years, every software release has been a performance release.

2. ***Integrating data that provides business value.*** At the heart of any data warehouse is the promise to answer essential business questions. Integrated data is the unique foundation required to achieve this goal. Pulling data from multiple subject areas and numerous applications into one repository is the *raison d'être* for data warehouses. Data model designers and ETL architects armed with metadata, data-cleansing tools, and patience must rationalize data formats, source systems, and semantic meaning of the data to make it understandable and trustworthy. This creates a common vocabulary within the corporation so that critical concepts such as "customer," "end of month," or "price elasticity" are uniformly measured and understood. Nowhere else in the entire IT data center is data collected, cleaned, and integrated as it is in the data warehouse.

3. ***Interactive BI tools.*** BI tools such as MicroStrategy, Tableau, IBM Cognos, and others provide business users with direct access to data warehouse insights. First, the business user can create reports and complex analysis quickly and easily using these tools. As a result, there is a trend in many data warehouse sites toward end-user self-service. Business users can easily demand more reports than IT has staffing to provide. More important than self-service, however, is that the users become intimately familiar with the data. They can run a report, discover they missed a metric or filter, make an adjustment, and run their report again all within minutes. This process results in significant changes in business users' understanding the business and their decision-making process. First, users stop asking trivial questions and start asking more complex strategic questions. Generally, the more complex and strategic the report, the more revenue and cost savings the user captures. This leads to some users becoming "power users" in a company. These individuals become wizards at teasing business value from the data and supplying valuable strategic information to the executive staff. Every data warehouse has anywhere from two to 20 power users.

The Gray Areas (Any One of the Two Would Do the Job)

Even though there are several areas that differentiate one from the other, there are also gray areas where the data warehouse and Hadoop cannot be clearly discerned. In these areas either tool could be the right solution—either doing an equally good or a not-so-good job on the task at hand. Choosing the one over the other depends on the requirements and the preferences of the organization. In many cases, Hadoop and the data warehouse work together in an information supply chain, and just as often, one tool is better for a specific workload (Awadallah and Graham, 2012). Table 13.1 illustrates the preferred platform (one versus the other, or equally likely) under a number of commonly observed requirements.

Coexistence of Hadoop and Data Warehouse

There are several possible scenarios under which using a combination of Hadoop and relational DBMS-based data warehousing technologies makes more sense. Here are some of those scenarios (White, 2012):

1. ***Use Hadoop for storing and archiving multi-structured data.*** A connector to a relational DBMS can then be used to extract required data from Hadoop for analysis by the relational DBMS. If the relational DBMS supports MapReduce functions, these functions can be used to do the extraction. The Aster-Hadoop adaptor,

TABLE 13.1 When to Use Which Platform—Hadoop Versus DW

Requirement	Data Warehouse	Hadoop
Low latency, interactive reports, and OLAP	☑	
ANSI 2003 SQL compliance is required	☑	☑
Preprocessing or exploration of raw unstructured data		☑
Online archives alternative to tape	☑	
High-quality cleansed and consistent data	☑	☑
100s to 1,000s of concurrent users	☑	☑
Discover unknown relationships in the data		☑
Parallel complex process logic	☑	☑
CPU intense analysis	☑	
System, users, and data governance		☑
Many flexible programming languages running in parallel		☑
Unrestricted, ungoverned sandbox explorations		☑
Analysis of provisional data	☑	
Extensive security and regulatory compliance	☑	☑

for example, uses SQL-MapReduce functions to provide fast, two-way data loading between HDFS and the Aster Database. Data loaded into the Aster Database can then be analyzed using both SQL and MapReduce.

2. ***Use Hadoop for filtering, transforming, and/or consolidating multi-structured data.***   A connector such as the Aster-Hadoop adaptor can be used to extract the results from Hadoop processing to the relational DBMS for analysis.

3. ***Use Hadoop to analyze large volumes of multi-structured data and publish the analytical results***   to the traditional data warehousing environment, a shared workgroup data store, or a common user interface.

4. ***Use a relational DBMS that provides MapReduce capabilities as an investigative computing platform.***   Data scientists can employ the relational DBMS (the Aster Database system, for example) to analyze a combination of structured data and multi-structured data (loaded from Hadoop) using a mixture of SQL processing and MapReduce analytic functions.

5. ***Use a front-end query tool to access and analyze data***   that is stored in both Hadoop and the relational DBMS.

These scenarios support an environment where the Hadoop and relational DBMS systems are separate from each other and connectivity software is used to exchange data between the two systems (see Figure 13.8). The direction of the industry over the next few years will likely be moving toward more tightly coupled Hadoop and relational DBMS-based data warehouse technologies—software as well as hardware. Such integration provides many benefits, including eliminating the need to install and maintain multiple systems, reducing data movement, providing a single metadata store for application development, and providing a single interface for both business users and analytical tools.

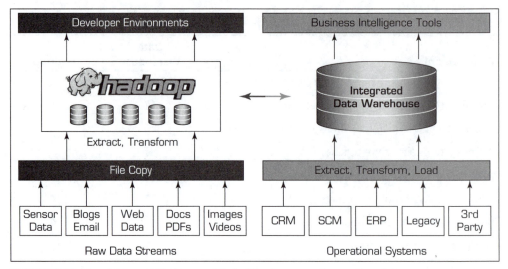

FIGURE 13.8 **Coexistence of Hadoop and Data Warehouses.** *Source:* Teradata.

SECTION 13.6 REVIEW QUESTIONS

1. What are the challenges facing data warehousing and Big Data? Are we witnessing the end of the data warehousing era? Why or why not?
2. What are the use cases for Big Data and Hadoop?
3. What are the use cases for data warehousing and RDBMS?
4. In what scenarios can Hadoop and RDBMS coexist?

13.7 BIG DATA VENDORS

As a relatively new technology area, the Big Data vendor landscape is developing very rapidly. A number of vendors have developed their own Hadoop distributions, most based on the Apache open source distribution but with various levels of proprietary customization. The clear market leader in terms of distribution seems to be Cloudera (**cloudera.com**), a Silicon Valley start-up with an all-star lineup of Big Data experts, including Hadoop creator Doug Cutting and former Facebook data scientist Jeff Hammerbacher. In addition to distribution, Cloudera offers paid enterprise-level training/services and proprietary Hadoop management software. MapR (**mapr.com**), another Valley start-up, offers its own Hadoop distribution that supplements HDFS with its proprietary NFS for improved performance. EMC Greenplum partnered with MapR to release a partly proprietary Hadoop distribution of its own in May 2011. Hortonworks (**hortonworks.com**), which was spun-out of Yahoo! in summer 2011, released its 100 percent open source Hadoop distribution, called Hortonworks Data Platform, and related support services in November 2011. These are just a few of the many companies (established and start-ups) that are crowding the competitive landscape of tool and service providers for Hadoop technologies.

In the NoSQL world, a number of start-ups are working to deliver commercially supported versions of the various flavors of NoSQL. DataStax, for example, offers a commercial version of Cassandra that includes enterprise support and services, as well as integration with Hadoop and open source enterprise search via Lucene Solr. As mentioned, proprietary data integration vendors, including Informatica, Pervasive Software, and Syncsort, are making inroads into the Big Data market with Hadoop connectors and complementary tools aimed at making it easier for developers to move data around and within Hadoop clusters.

The analytics layer of the Big Data stack is also experiencing significant development. A start-up called Datameer, for example, is developing what it says is an "all-in-one" business intelligence platform for Hadoop, while data visualization specialist Tableau Software has added Hadoop and Next Generation Data Warehouse connectivity to its product suite. EMC Greenplum, meanwhile, has Chorus, a sort of playground for data scientists where they can mash-up, experiment with, and share large volumes of data for analysis. Other vendors focus on specific analytic use cases, such as ClickFox with its customer experience analytics engine. A number of traditional business intelligence vendors, most notably MicroStrategy, are working to incorporate Big Data analytic and reporting capabilities into their products.

Less progress has been made in the Big Data application space, however. There are few off-the-shelf Big Data applications currently on the market. This void leaves enterprises with the task of developing and building custom Big Data applications with internal or outsourced teams of application developers. There are exceptions. Namely, a start-up called Treasata offers Big-Data-as-a-service applications for the financial services vertical market, and Google makes its internal Big Data analytics application, called BigQuery, available as a service.

Meanwhile, the next-generation data warehouse market has experienced significant consolidation since 2010. Four leading vendors in this space—Netezza, Greenplum, Vertica, and Aster Data—were acquired by IBM, EMC, HP, and Teradata, respectively. Just a handful of niche independent players remain, among them Kognitio and ParAccel. These vendors, by and large, position their products as complementary to Hadoop and NoSQL deployments, providing real-time analytic capabilities on large volumes of structured data.

Mega-vendors Oracle and IBM also play in the Big Data space. IBM's Big Insights platform is based on Apache Hadoop, but includes numerous proprietary modules including the Netezza database, InfoSphere Warehouse, Cognos business intelligence tools, and SPSS data mining capabilities. It also offers IBM InfoSphere Streams, a platform designed for streaming Big Data analysis. Oracle, meanwhile, has embraced the appliance approach to Big Data with its Exadata, Exalogic, and Big Data appliances. Its Big Data appliance incorporates Cloudera's Hadoop distribution with Oracle's NoSQL database and data integration tools. Application Case 6.5 provides an interesting case where Dublin City council used Big Data Analytics to reduce city's traffic congestion.

The cloud is increasingly playing a role in the Big Data market as well. Amazon and Google support Hadoop deployments in their public cloud offerings, Amazon Elastic

Application Case 13.5

Dublin City Council Is Leveraging Big Data to Reduce Traffic Congestion

Employing 6,000 people, Dublin City Council (DCC) delivers housing, water and transport services to 1.2 million citizens across the Irish capital. To keep the city moving, the council's traffic control center (TCC) works together with local transport operators to manage an extensive network of roads, tramways and bus lanes. Using operational data from the TCC, the council's roads and traffic department is responsible for predicting Dublin's future transport requirements, and developing effective strategies to meet them.

Like local governments in many large European cities, DCC has a wide array of technology at its disposal. Sensors such as inductive-loop traffic detectors, rain gauges and closed-circuit television (CCTV) cameras collect data from across Dublin,

and each of the city's 1,000 buses transmits a GPS update every 20 seconds.

Tackling Traffic Congestion

In the past, only a small proportion of this Big Data was available to controllers at Dublin's TCC–reducing their ability to identify, anticipate and address the causes of traffic congestion.

As Brendan O'Brien, Head of Technical Services–Roads and Traffic Department at Dublin City Council, explains: "Previously, our TCC systems only offered a narrow window on the overall status of our transport network–for example, controllers could only view the status of individual bus routes. Our legacy systems were also unable to monitor the

(Continued)

Application Case 13.5 (Continued)

geospatial location of Dublin's bus fleet, which further complicated the traffic control process." He continues: "Because we couldn't see the 'health' of the whole transport network in real time, it was very difficult to identify traffic congestion in its early stages. This meant that the causes of delays had often moved on by the time our TCC operators were able to select the appropriate CCTV feed–making it hard to determine and mitigate the factors causing congestion."

DCC wanted to ease traffic congestion across Dublin. To achieve this, the council needed to find a way to integrate, process and visualize large amounts of structured and unstructured data from its network of sensor arrays–all in real time.

Becoming a Smarter City

To help develop a smarter approach to traffic control, DCC entered into a research partnership with IBM Research–Ireland. Francesco Calabrese, Research Manager–Smarter Urban Dynamics at IBM Research, comments: "Smarter Cities are cities with the tools to extract actionable insights from massive amounts of constantly changing data, and deliver those insights instantly to decision-makers. At the IBM Smarter Cities Technology Centre in Dublin, our goal is to develop innovative solutions to enable cities like Dublin to support smarter ways of working–delivering a better quality of life for their citizens. "

Today, DCC makes all of its data available to the IBM Smarter Cities Technology Centre in Dublin. Using Big Data analytics technologies, IBM Research is developing new solutions for Smarter Cities, and making the deep insights it discovers available to the council's roads and traffic department.

"From our first discussion with the IBM Research team, we realized that our goals were perfectly aligned," says O'Brien. "Using our data, the IBM Smarter Cities Technology Centre can both drive its own research, and deliver innovative solutions to help us visualize transport data from sensor arrays across the city."

Analyzing the Transport Network

As a first step, IBM integrated geospatial data from buses and data on bus timetables into a central geographic information system. Using IBM InfoSphere Streams and mapping software, IBM researchers created a digital map of the city, overlaid with the real-time positions of Dublin's 1,000 buses. "In the past, our TCC operators could only see the status of individual bus corridors," says O'Brien. "Now, each TCC operator gets a twin-monitor setup–one displaying a dashboard, and the other a real-time map of all buses across the city.

"Using the dashboard screen, operators can drill down to see the number of buses that are on-time or delayed on each route. This information is also displayed visually on the map screen, allowing operators to see the current status of the entire bus network at a glance. Because the interface is so intuitive, our operators can rapidly home in on emerging areas of traffic congestion, and then use CCTV to identify the causes of delays before they move further downstream."

Taking Action to Ease Congestion

By enriching its data with GPS tracking, DCC can produce detailed reports on areas of the network where buses are frequently delayed, and take action to ease congestion. "The IBM Smarter Cities Technology Centre has provided us with a lot of valuable insights," says O'Brien. "For example, the IBM team created trace reports on bus journeys, which showed that at rush hour, some buses were being overtaken by buses that set off later.

"Working with the city's bus operators, we are looking at why the headways are diverging in that way, and what we can do to improve traffic flow at these peak times. Thanks to the work of the IBM team, we can now start answering questions such as: 'Are the bus lane start times correct?', and 'Where do we need to add additional bus lanes and bus-only traffic signals?'"

O'Brien continues: "Over the next two years, we are starting a project team for bus priority measures and road-infrastructure improvements. Without the ability to visualize our transport data, this would not have been possible."

Planning For the Future

Based on the success of the traffic control project for the city's bus fleet, DCC and IBM Research are working together to find ways to further augment traffic control in Dublin. "Our relationship with IBM is quite fluid–we offer them our expertise about how the city operates, and their researchers use that input to extract valuable insights from our Big Data," says O'Brien. "Currently, the IBM team is working on ways to integrate data from rain and flood gauges into the traffic control solution–alerting controllers to potential hazards presented by extreme weather conditions, and allowing them to take timely action to reduce the impact on road users."

In addition to meteorological data, IBM is investigating the possibility of incorporating data from the under-road sensor network to better understand the impact of private motor vehicles on traffic congestion.

The IBM team is also developing a predictive analytics solution combining data from the city's tram network with electronic docks for the city's free bicycle scheme. This project aims to optimize the distribution of the city's free bicycles according to anticipated demand–ensuring that citizens can seamlessly continue their journey after stepping off a tram.

"Working with IBM Research has allowed us to take a fresh look at our transport strategy,"

concludes O'Brien. "Thanks to the continuing work of the IBM team, we can see how our transport network is working as a whole–and develop innovative ways to improve it for Dublin's citizens."

QUESTIONS FOR DISCUSSION

1. Is there a strong case to make for large cities to use Big Data Analytics and related information technologies? Identify and discuss examples of what can be done with analytics beyond what is portrayed in this application case.

2. How can a big data analytics help ease the traffic problem in large cities?

3. What were the challenges Dublin City was facing; what were the proposed solution, initial results, and future plans?

Source: **IBM Customer Story, "Dublin City Council - Leveraging the leading edge of IBM Smarter Cities research to reduce traffic congestion" public.dhe.ibm.com/common/ssi/ecm/en/ imc14829ieen/IMC14829IEEN.PDF** (accessed October 2013).

MapReduce and Google Compute Engine, respectively, enabling users to easily scale up and scale down clusters as needed. Microsoft abandoned its own internal Big Data platform and will support Hortonworks' Hadoop distribution on its Azure cloud.

As part of its market-sizing efforts, Wikibon (Kelly, 2013) tracked and/or modeled the 2012 Big Data revenue of more than 60 vendors. The list included both Big Data pure-plays—those vendors that derive close to if not all their revenue from the sale of Big Data products and services—and vendors for whom Big Data sales is just one of multiple revenue streams. Table 13.2 shows the top 20 vendors in order of Big Data revenues in 2012, and Figure 13.9 shows the top 10 pure players in the Big Data marketplace.

The services side of the Big Data market is small but growing. The established services providers like Accenture and IBM are just starting to build Big Data practices, while just a few smaller providers focus strictly on Big Data, among them Think Big Analytics. EMC is also investing heavily in Big Data training and services offerings, particularly around data science. Similarly, Hadoop distribution vendors Hortonworks and Cloudera offer a number of training classes aimed at both Hadoop administrators and data scientists.

There are also other vendors approaching Big Data from the visual analytics angle. As Gartner's latest Magic Quadrant indicated, a significant growth in business intelligence and analytics is in visual exploration and visual analytics. Large companies like SAS, SAP, and IBM, along with small but stable companies like Tableau, TIBCO, and QlikView, are making a strong case for high performance analytics built into information visualization platforms. Technology Insights 13.4 provides a few key enablers to succeed with Big Data and visual analytics. SAS is perhaps the one pushing it harder than any other with its recently launched SAS Visual Analytics platform. Using a multitude of computational enhancements, the SAS Visual Analytics platform is capable of turning tens of millions of data records into informational graphics in just a few seconds by using massively parallel processing (MPP) and in-memory computing. Application Case 13.6 is a customer case where the SAS Visual Analytics platform is used for accurate and timely credit decisions.

TABLE 13.2 Top 20 Vendors in Big Data Market

		2012 Worldwide Big Data Revenue by Vendor ($US millions)				
Vendor	**Big Data Revenue**	**Total Revenue**	**Big Data Revenue as % of Total Revenue**	**% Big Data Hardware Revenue**	**% Big Data Software Revenue**	**% Big Data Services Revenue**
IBM	$1,352	$103,930	1%	22%	33%	44%
HP	$664	$119,895	1%	34%	29%	38%
Teradata	$435	$2,665	16%	31%	28%	41%
Dell	$425	$59,878	1%	83%	0%	17%
Oracle	$415	$39,463	1%	25%	34%	41%
SAP	$368	$21,707	2%	0%	67%	33%
EMC	$336	$23,570	1%	24%	36%	39%
Cisco Systems	$214	$47,983	0%	80%	0%	20%
Microsoft	$196	$$71,474	0%	0%	67%	33%
Accenture	$194	$29,770	1%	0%	0%	100%
Fusion-io	$190	$439	43%	71%	0%	29%
PwC	$189	$31,500	1%	0%	0%	100%
SAS Institute	$187	$2,954	6%	0%	59%	41%
Splunk	$186	$186	100%	0%	71%	29%
Deloitte	$173	$31,300	1%	0%	0%	100%
Amazon	$170	$56,825	0%	0%	0%	100%
NetApp	$138	$6,454	2%	77%	0%	23%
Hitachi	$130	$112,318	0%	0%	0%	100%
Opera Solutions	$118	$118	100%	0%	0%	100%
Mu Sigma	$114	$114	100%	0%	0%	100%

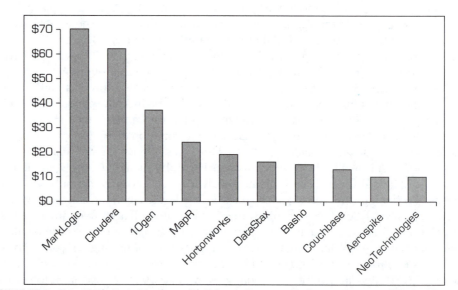

FIGURE 13.9 Top 10 Big Data Vendors with Primary Focus on Hadoop. *Source:* **wikibon.org.**

TECHNOLOGY INSIGHTS 13.4   How to Succeed with Big Data

What a year 2012 was for Big Data! From the White House to your house, it's hard to find an organization or consumer who has less data today than a year ago. Database options proliferate, and business intelligence evolves to a new era of organization-wide analytics. And everything's mobile. Organizations that successfully adapt their data architecture and processes to address the three characteristics of Big Data—volume, variety, and velocity—are improving operational efficiency, growing revenues, and empowering new business models. With all the attention organizations are placing on innovating around data, the rate of change will only increase. So what should companies do to succeed with Big Data? Here are some of the industry testaments:

1. **Simplify.**   It is hard to keep track of all of the new database vendors, open source projects, and Big Data service providers. It will even be more crowded and complicated in the years ahead. Therefore, there is a need for simplification. It is essential to take a strategic approach by extending your relational and online transaction processing (OLTP) systems to one or more of the new on-premise, hosted, or service-based database options that best reflect the needs of your industry and your organization, and then picking a real-time business intelligence platform that supports direct connections to many databases and file formats. Choosing the best mix of solution alternatives for every project (between connecting live to fast databases and importing data extracts into an in-memory analytics engine to offset the performance of slow or overburdened databases) is critical to the success of any Big Data projects. For instance, eBay's Big Data analytics architecture comprises Teradata (one of the most popular data warehousing companies), Hadoop (most promising solution to Big Data challenge), and Tableau (one of the prolific visual analytics solution providers). eBay employees can visualize insights from more than 52 petabytes of data. eBay uses a visual analytics solution by Tableau to analyze search relevance and quality of the **eBay.com** site; monitor the latest customer feedback and meter sentiments on **eBay.com**; and achieve operational reporting for the data warehouse systems, all of which helped an analytic culture flourish within eBay.

2. **Coexist.**   Using the strengths of each database platform and enabling them to coexist in your organization's data architecture is essential. There is ample literature that talks about the necessity of maintaining and nurturing the coexistence of traditional data warehouses with the capabilities of new platforms.

3. **Visualize.**   According to leading analytics research companies like Forrester and Gartner, enterprises find advanced data visualization platforms to be essential tools that enable them to monitor business, find patterns, and take action to avoid threats and snatch opportunities. Visual analytics help organizations uncover trends, relationships, and anomalies by visually shifting through very large quantities of data. A visual analysis experience has certain characteristics. It allows you to do two things at any moment:
   • Instantly change what data you are looking at. This is important because different questions require different data.
   • Instantly change the way you are looking at it. This is important because each view may answer different questions.

      This combination creates the exploratory experience required for anyone to answer questions quickly. In essence, visualization becomes a natural extension of your experimental thought process.

4. **Empower.**   Big Data and self-service business intelligence go hand in hand, according to Aberdeen Group's recently published "Maximizing the Value of Analytics and Big Data." Organizations with Big Data are over 70 percent more likely than other organizations to have BI/BA projects that are driven primarily by the business community, not by the IT group. Across a range of uses—from tackling new business problems, developing entirely new products and services, finding actionable intelligence in less than an hour, and blending data from disparate sources—Big Data has fired the imagination of what is possible through the application of analytics.

5. **Integrate.**   Integrating and blending data from disparate sources for your organization is an essential part of Big Data analytics. Organizations that can blend different relational,

semistructured, and raw data sources in real time, without expensive up-front integration costs, will be the ones that get the best value from Big Data. Once integrated and blended, the structure of the data (e.g., spreadsheets, a database, a data warehouse, an open source file system like Hadoop, or all of them at the same time) becomes unimportant; that is, you don't need to know the details of how data is stored to ask and answer questions against it. As we saw in Application Case 13.4, the Obama campaign found a way to integrate social media, technology, e-mail databases, fundraising databases, and consumer market data to create competitive advantage.

6. ***Govern.*** Data governance has always been a challenging issue in IT, and is getting even more puzzling with the advent of Big Data. More than 80 countries have data privacy laws. The European Union (EU) defines seven "safe harbor privacy principles" for the protection of their citizens' personal data. In Singapore, the personal data protection law took effect January 2013. In the United States, Sarbanes-Oxley affects all publicly listed companies, and HIPAA (Health Insurance Portability and Accountability Act) sets national standards in healthcare. The right balance between control and experimentation varies depending on the organization and industry. Use of master data management (MDM) best practices seems to help manage the governance process.

7. ***Evangelize.*** With the backing of one or more executive sponsors, evangelists like yourself can get the ball rolling and instill a virtuous cycle: Tthe more departments in your organization that realize actionable benefits, the more pervasive analytics becomes across your organization. Fast, easy-to-use visual analytics is the key that opens the door to organization-wide analytics adoption and collaboration.

Sources: Compiled from A. Lampitt, "Big Data Visualization: A Big Deal for eBay," *InfoWorld,* December 6, 2012, **infoworld.com/d/big-data/big-data-visualization-big-deal-ebay-208589** (accessed March 2013); Tableau white paper, **cdnlarge.tableausoftware.com/sites/default/files/whitepapers/7-tips-to-succeed-with-big-data-in-2013.pdf** (accessed January 2013).

Application Case 13.6

Creditreform Boosts Credit Rating Quality with Big Data Visual Analytics

Founded as a credit agency in Mainz, Germany, in 1879, Creditreform has grown to now serve more than 163,000 members from 177 offices across Europe and China as one of the leading international providers of business information and receivables management services. Creditreform provides a comprehensive spectrum of integrated credit risk management solutions and services worldwide, provides members with more than 16 million commercial reports a year, and helps them recover billions in outstanding debts.

Challenge

Via its online database, Creditreform makes more than 24 million credit reports from 26 countries in Europe and from China that are available around the clock. Using high-performance solutions Creditreform wants to quickly detect anomalies and relationships within those high data volumes and present results in easy-to-read graphics. Already Germany's top provider of quality business information and debt collection services, Creditreform wants to maintain its leadership and widen its market lead through better and faster analytics.

Solution and the Results

Creditreform decided to use SAS Visual Analytics to simplify the analytics process, so that every Creditreform employee can use the software to make smart decisions without needing extensive training. The new high-performance solution, obtained from one of the business analytics leaders in the market place (SAS Institute), makes Creditreform better at providing the highest quality financial information and credit ratings to its client businesses.

"SAS Visual Analytics makes it faster and easier for our analysts to detect correlations in our business data," said Bernd Bütow, managing director at Creditreform. "That, in turn, improves the quality and forecasting accuracy of our credit ratings."

"Creditreform saw SAS Visual Analytics as a compelling solution," remarked Mona Beck, financial services sales director at SAS Germany. "SAS Visual Analytics advances business analytics by combining Big Data analysis with excellent usability, making it a breeze to represent data graphically. As a company known for providing top-quality information on businesses, Creditreform is a perfect match for the very latest in business analytics technology."

SAS Visual Analytics is a high-performance, in-memory solution for exploring massive amounts of data very quickly. Users can explore all data, execute analytic correlations on billions of rows of data in just minutes or seconds, and visually present results. With SAS Visual Analytics, executives can make quicker, better decisions with instant access,

via PC or tablet, to insights based on the latest data. By integrating corporate and consumer data, bank executives gain real-time insights for risk management, customer development, product marketing, and financial management.

QUESTIONS FOR DISCUSSION

1. How did Creditreform boost credit rating quality with Big Data and visual analytics?
2. What were the challenges, proposed solution, and initial results?

Source: SAS, Customer Stories, "With SAS, Creditreform Boosts Credit Rating Quality, Forecasting: SAS Visual Analytics, High-Performance Analytics Speed Decisions, Increase Efficiency," **sas.com/news/preleases/banking-visual-analytics.html** (accessed March 2013).

SECTION 13.7 REVIEW QUESTIONS

1. What is special about the Big Data vendor landscape? Who are the big players?
2. How do you think the Big Data vendor landscape will change in the near future? Why?
3. What is the role of visual analytics in the world of Big Data?

13.8 BIG DATA AND STREAM ANALYTICS

Along with volume and variety, as we have seen earlier in this chapter, one of the key characteristics that define Big Data is velocity, which refers to the speed at which the data is created and streamed into the analytics environment. Organizations are looking for new means to process this streaming data as it comes in to react quickly and accurately to problems and opportunities to please their customers and to gain competitive advantage. In situations where data streams in rapidly and continuously, traditional analytics approaches that work with previously accumulated data (i.e., data at arrest) often either arrive at the wrong decisions because of using too much out-of-context data, or they arrive at the correct decisions but too late to be of any use to the organization. Therefore it is critical for a number of business situations to analyze the data soon after it is created and/or as soon as it is streamed into the analytics system.

The presumption that the vast majority of modern-day businesses are currently living by is that it is important and critical to record every piece of data because it might contain valuable information now or sometime in the near future. However, as long as the number of data sources increases, the "store-everything" approach becomes harder and harder and, in some cases, not even feasible. In fact, despite technological advances, current total storage capacity lags far behind the digital information being generated in the world. Moreover, in the constantly changing business environment, real-time detection of meaningful changes in data as well as of complex pattern variations within a given short time window are essential in order to come up with the actions that better fit with the new environment. These facts become the main triggers for a paradigm that we call *stream analytics*. The stream analytics paradigm was born as an answer to these challenges, namely, the unbounded flows of data that cannot be permanently stored in order to be subsequently analyzed, in a timely and efficient manner, and complex pattern variations that need to be detected and acted upon as soon as they happen.

Stream analytics (also called *data in-motion analytics* and *real-time data analytical,* among others) is a term commonly used for the analytic process of extracting actionable information from continuously flowing/streaming data. A stream can be defined as a continuous sequence of data elements (Zikopoulos et al., 2013). The data elements in a stream are often called *tuples*. In a relational database sense, a tuple is similar to a row of data (a record, an object, an instance). However in the context of semistructured or unstructured data, a tuple is an abstraction that represents a package of data, which can be characterized as a set of attributes for a given object. If a tuple by itself is not sufficiently informative for analysis, a correlation—or other collective relationships among tuples are needed—then a window of data that includes a set of tuples is used. A window of data is a finite number/sequence of tuples, where the windows are continuously updated as new data become available. The size of the window is determined based on the system being analyzed. Stream analytics is becoming increasingly more popular because of two things. First, time-to-action has become an ever decreasing value, and second, we have the technological means to capture and process the data while it is being created.

Some of the most impactful applications of stream analytics were developed in the energy industry, specifically for smart grid (electric power supply chain) systems. The new smart grids are capable of not only real-time creation and processing of multiple streams of data in order to determine optimal power distribution to fulfill real customer needs, but also generating accurate short-term predictions aimed at covering unexpected demand and renewable energy generation peaks. Figure 13.10 shows a depiction of a generic use case for streaming analytics in energy industry (a typical smart grid application). The goal is to accurately predict electricity demand and production in real time by using streaming data that is coming from smart meters, production system sensors, and meteorological models. The ability to predict near future consumption/production trends and detect anomalies in real time can be used to optimize supply decisions (how much to produce, what sources of production to use, optimally adjust production capacities) as well as to adjust smart meters to regulate consumption and favorable energy pricing.

Stream Analytics Versus Perpetual Analytics

The terms "streaming" and "perpetual" probably sound like the same thing to most people, and in many cases they are used synonymously. However, in the context of intelligent systems, there is a difference (Jonas, 2007). Streaming analytics involves applying transaction-level logic to real-time observations. The rules applied to these observations take into account previous observations as long as they occurred in the prescribed window; these windows have some arbitrary size (e.g., last 5 seconds, last 10,000 observations, etc.). **Perpetual analytics**, on the other hand, evaluates every incoming observation against all prior observations, where there is no window size. Recognizing how the new observation relates to all prior observations enables the discovery of real-time insight.

Both streaming and perpetual analytics have their pros and cons, and their respective places in the business analytics world. For example, sometimes transactional volumes are high and the time-to-decision is too short, favoring nonpersistence and small window sizes, which translates into using streaming analytics. However, when the mission is critical and transaction volumes can be managed in real time, then perpetual analytics is a better answer. That way, one can answer questions such as "How does what I just learned relate to what I have known?" "Does this matter?" and "Who needs to know?"

Critical Event Processing

Critical event processing is a method of capturing, tracking, and analyzing streams of data to detect events (out of normal happenings) of certain types that are worthy of the effort. Complex event processing is an application of stream analytics that combines data from multiple sources to infer events or patterns of interest either before they actually

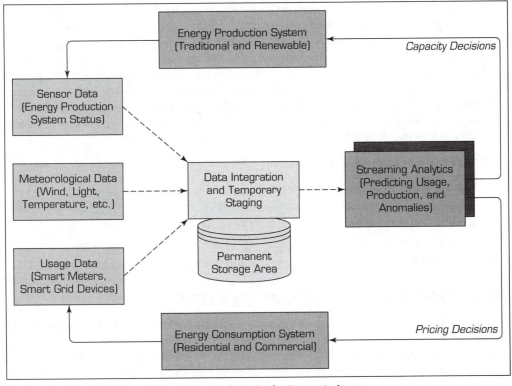

FIGURE 13.10 **A Use Case of Streaming Analytics in the Energy Industry.**

occur or as soon as they happen. The goal is to take rapid actions to either prevent (or mitigate the negative effects of) these events (e.g., fraud or network intrusion), or in the case of a short window of opportunity, take full advantage of the situation within the allowed time (based on user behavior on a e-commerce site, create promotional offers that they are more likely to respond to).

These critical events may be happening across the various layers of an organization such as sales leads, orders, or customer service calls. Or, more broadly, they may be news items, text messages, social media posts, stock market feeds, traffic reports, weather conditions, or other kinds of anomalies that may have a significant impact on the well-being of the organization. An event may also be defined generically as a "change of state," which may be detected as a measurement exceeding a predefined threshold of time, temperature, or some other value. Even though there is no denying the value proposition of critical event processing, one has to be selective in what to measure, when to measure, and how often to measure. Because of the vast amount of information available about events, which is sometimes referred to as the *event cloud,* there is a possibility of overdoing it, in which case as opposed to helping the organization, it may hurt the operational effectiveness.

Data Stream Mining

Data stream mining, as an enabling technology for stream analytics, is the process of extracting novel patterns and knowledge structures from continuous, rapid data records. As we have seen in the data mining chapter (Chapter 5), traditional data mining methods require the data to be collected and organized in a proper file format, and then processed in a recursive manner to learn the underlying patterns. In contrast, a data stream is a continuous flow of ordered sequence of instances that in many applications of data stream mining can be read/processed only once or a small number of times using limited computing and storage capabilities. Examples of data streams include sensor data, computer network traffic, phone conversations, ATM transactions, web searches, and financial data. Data stream mining can be considered a subfield of data mining, machine learning, and knowledge discovery.

In many data stream mining applications, the goal is to predict the class or value of new instances in the data stream given some knowledge about the class membership or values of previous instances in the data stream. Specialized machine learning techniques (mostly derivative of traditional machine learning techniques) can be used to learn this prediction task from labeled examples in an automated fashion. An example of such a prediction method is developed by Delen et al. (2005), where they gradually built and refined a decision tree model by using a subset of the data at a time.

SECTION 13.8 REVIEW QUESTIONS

1. What is a stream (in Big Data world)?
2. What are the motivations for stream analytics?
3. What is stream analytics? How does it differ from regular analytics?
4. What is critical event processing? How does it relate to stream analytics?
5. Define data stream mining? What are the additional challenges that are posed?

13.9 APPLICATIONS OF STREAM ANALYTICS

Because of its power to create insight instantly, helping decision makers to be on top of events as they unfold and allowing organizations to address issues before they become problems, the use of streaming analytics is on an exponentially increasing trend. Following are some of the application areas that have already benefited from stream analytics.

e-Commerce

Companies like Amazon and eBay (among many others) are trying to make the most out of the data that they collect while the customer is on their Web sites. Every page visit, every product looked at, every search conducted, and every click made is recorded and analyzed to maximize the value gained from a user's visit. If done quickly, analysis of such a stream of data can turn browsers into buyers and buyers into shopaholics. When we visit an e-commerce Web site, even one where we are not a member, after a few clicks here and there we start to get very interesting product and bundle price offers. Behind the scenes, advanced analytics are crunching the real-time data coming from our clicks, and the clicks of thousands of others, to "understand" what it is that we are interested in (in some cases, even we do not know that) and make the most of that information by creative offerings.

Telecommunications

The volume of data that comes from call detail records (CDR) for telecommunications companies is astounding. Although this information has been used for billing purposes for quite some time now, there is a wealth of knowledge buried deep inside this Big Data that the telecommunications companies are just now realizing to tap. For instance, CDR data can be analyzed to prevent churn by identifying networks of callers, influencers, leaders, and followers within those networks and proactively acting on this information. As we all know, influencers and leaders have the effect of changing the perception of the followers within their network toward the service provider, either positively or negatively. Using social network analysis techniques, telecommunication companies are identifying the leaders and influencers and their network participants to better manage their customer base. In addition to churn analysis, such information can also be used to recruit new members and maximize the value of the existing members.

Continuous stream of data that comes from CDR can be combined with social media data (sentiment analysis) to assess the effectiveness of marketing campaigns. Insight gained from these data streams can be used to rapidly react to adverse effects (which may lead to loss of customers) or boost the impact of positive effects (which may lead to maximizing purchases of existing customers and recruitment of new customers) observed in these campaigns. Furthermore, the process of gaining insight from CDR can be replicated for data networks using Internet protocol detail records. Since most telecommunications companies provide both of these service types, a holistic optimization of all offerings and marketing campaigns could lead to extraordinary market gains. Application Case 13.7 is an example of how telecommunication companies are using stream analytics to boost customer satisfaction and competitive advantage.

Application Case 13.7

Turning Machine-Generated Streaming Data into Valuable Business Insights

This case study is about one of the largest U.S. telecommunications organizations, which offers a variety of services, including digital voice, high-speed Internet, and cable, to more than 24 million customers. As a subscription-based business, its success depends on its IT infrastructure to deliver a high-quality customer experience. When application failures or network latencies negatively impact the customer experience, they adversely impact company revenue as well. That's why this leading telecommunications organization demands robust and timely information from its operational telemetry to ensure data integrity, stability, application quality, and network efficiency.

Challenges

The environment generates over a billion daily events running on a distributed hardware/software infrastructure supporting millions of cable, online, and interactive media customers. It was overwhelming to even gather and view this data in one place, much less to perform any diagnostics, or hone in on the real-time intelligence that lives in the machine-generated data. Using time-consuming and error-prone traditional search methods, the company's roster of experts would shuffle through mountains of data to uncover issues threatening data integrity, system stability, and applications performance—all necessary components of delivering a quality customer experience.

Solution

In order to bolster operational intelligence, the company selected to work with Splunk, one of the leading analytics service providers in the area of turning machine-generated streaming data into valuable business insights. Here are some of the results.

Application troubleshooting. Before Splunk developers had to ask the operations team to FTP log files to them. And then they waited ... sometimes 16+ hours to get the data they needed while the operations teams had to step away from their primary duties to assist the developers. Now, because Splunk aggregates all relevant machine data into one place, developers can be more proactive about troubleshooting code and improving the user experience. When they first deployed Splunk, they started with a simple search for 404 errors. Splunk revealed up to 1,600 404s per second for a particular service. The team identified latencies in a flash player download as the primary blocker, causing viewers to navigate away from the page without viewing any content. Just one search in Splunk has helped to boost video views by 3 percent over the last year. In a business where eyes equal dollars, that's real money to the business. Now when the applications team sees 404s spiking on custom dashboards they've built in Splunk, they can dig in to see what's happening upstream and align appropriate resources to recapture those viewers—and that revenue.

Operations. Splunk's ability to model systems and examine patterns in real time helped the operations team avoid critical downtime. Using Splunk, they spotted the potential for failure in a vendor-provided infrastructure. Modeling the proposed architecture in Splunk, they were able to predict system imbalance

(Continued)

Application Case 13.7 (Continued)

and how it might fail based on inability to distribute load. "My team provides guidance to our executives on mission-critical media systems and strategic systems architecture," said Matt Stevens, director of software architecture. "This is just one instance where Splunk paid for itself by helping us avoid deployment of vulnerable systems, which would inevitably result in downtime and upset customers." In day-to-day operations, teams use Splunk to identify and drill into events to identify activity patterns leading to outages. Once they've identified signatures or patterns, they create alerts to proactively avoid future problems.

Compliance. Once seen as a foe, many organizations are looking to compliance mandates as an opportunity to implement best practices in log consolidation and IT systems management. This organization is no different. As Sarbanes-Oxley (SOX) and other compliance mandates evolve, the company uses Splunk to audit its systems, generate scheduled and ad hoc reports, and share information with business executives, auditors, and partners.

Security. When you're a content provider, DNS attacks simply can't be tolerated. By consolidating logs across data centers, the security team has improved the effectiveness of its threat assessments and security monitoring. Dashboards allow analysts to detect system vulnerabilities or attacks on both its content delivery network and critical applications. Trend reports spanning long timeframes also identify recurring threats and known attackers. And alerts for bad actors trigger immediate responses.

Conclusion

No longer does the sheer volume of machine-generated data overwhelm the operations team. The more data that the company's enormous infrastructure generates, the more lurking issues and security threats are revealed. The team even seeks out historical data—going back years—to identify trends and unique patterns. As the discipline of investigating anomalies and creating alerts based on unmasked event signatures spreads throughout the IT organization, the growing knowledge base and awareness fortify the cable provider's ability to deliver continuous quality customer experiences.

Even more valuable than this situational awareness has been the predictive capability gained. When testing a new technology, the decision-making team sees how a solution will work in production—determining the potential for instability by observing reactions to varying loads and traffic patterns. Splunk's predictive analytics capabilities help this leading cable provider make the right decisions, avoiding costly delays and downtime.

QUESTIONS FOR DISCUSSION

1. Why is stream analytics becoming more popular?
2. How did the telecommunication company in this case use stream analytics for better business outcomes? What additional benefits can you foresee?
3. What were the challenges, proposed solution, and initial results?

Source: Splunk, Customer Case Study, **splunk.com/view/SP-CAAAFAD** (accessed March 2013).

Law Enforcement and Cyber Security

Streams of Big Data provide excellent opportunities for improved crime prevention, law enforcement, and enhanced security. They offer unmatched potential when it comes to security applications that can be built in the space, such as real-time situational awareness, multimodal surveillance, cyber-security detection, legal wire taping, video surveillance, and face recognition (Zikopoulos et al., 2013). As an application of information assurance, enterprises can use streaming analytics to detect and prevent network intrusions, cyber attacks, and malicious activities by streaming and analyzing network logs and other Internet activity monitoring resources.

Power Industry

Because of the increasing use of smart meters, the amount of real-time data collected by power utilities is increasing exponentially. Moving from once a month to every 15 minutes (or more frequent), meter read accumulates large quantities of invaluable data for power utilities. These smart meters and other sensors placed all around the power grid are sending information back to the control centers to be analyzed in real time. Such analyses help utility companies to optimize their supply chain decision (e.g., capacity adjustments, distribution network options, real-time buying or selling) based on the up-to-the-minute consumer usage and demand patterns. Additionally, utility companies can integrate weather and other natural condition data into their analytics to optimize power generation from alternative sources (e.g., wind, solar, etc.) and to better forecast energy demand on different geographic granulations. Similar benefits also apply to other utilities such as water and natural gas.

Financial Services

Financial service companies are among the prime examples where analysis of Big Data streams can provide faster and better decisions, competitive advantage, and regulatory oversight. The ability to analyze fast-paced, high volumes of trading data at very low latency across markets and countries offers tremendous advantage to making the split-second buy/sell decisions that potentially translate into big financial gains. In addition to optimal buy/sell decisions, stream analytics can also help financial service companies in real-time trade monitoring to detect fraud and other illegal activities.

Health Sciences

Modern era medical devices (e.g., electrocardiograms and equipment that measures blood pressure, blood oxygen level, blood sugar level, body temperature, and so on) are capable of producing invaluable streaming diagnostic/sensory data at a very fast rate. Harnessing this data and analyzing it in real time offers benefits—the kind that we often call "life and death"—unlike any other field. In addition to helping healthcare companies become more effective and efficient (and hence more competitive and profitable), stream analytics is also improving patient conditions, saving lives.

Many hospital systems all around the world are developing care infrastructures and health systems that are futuristic. These systems aim to take full advantage of what the technology has to offer, and more. Using hardware devices that generate high-resolution data at a very rapid rate, coupled with super-fast computers that can synergistically analyze multiple streams of data, increases the chances of keeping patients safe by quickly detecting anomalies. These systems are meant to help human decision makers make faster and better decisions by being exposed to a multitude of information as soon as it becomes available.

Government

Governments all around the world are trying to find ways to be more efficient (via optimal use of limited resources) and effective (providing the services that people need and want). As the practices for e-government become mainstream, coupled with widespread use and access to social media, very large quantities of data (both structured and unstructured) are at the disposal of government agencies. Proper and timely use of these Big Data streams differentiates proactive and highly efficient agencies from the ones that are still using traditional methods to react to situations as they unfold. Another way in which government agencies can leverage real-time analytics capabilities is to manage natural disasters such as snowstorms, hurricanes, tornados, and wildfires through surveillance of streaming data coming from radars, sensors, and other smart detection devices. They can also use similar approaches to monitor water quality, air quality, and consumption patterns, and detect anomalies before they become significant problems. Yet another area where government agencies use stream analytics is in traffic management in congested cities. By using the data coming from traffic flow cameras, GPS data coming from commercial vehicles, and traffic sensors embedded in roadways, agencies are able to change traffic light sequences and traffic flow lanes to ease the pain caused by traffic congestion problems.

SECTION 13.9 REVIEW QUESTIONS

1. What are the most fruitful industries for stream analytics?
2. How can stream analytics be used in e-commerce?
3. In addition to what is listed in this section, can you think of other industries and/or application areas where stream analytics can be used?
4. Compared to regular analytics, do you think stream analytics will have more (or fewer) use cases in the era of Big Data analytics? Why?

Chapter Highlights

- Big Data means different things to people with different backgrounds and interests.
- Big Data exceeds the reach of commonly used hardware environments and/or capabilities of software tools to capture, manage, and process it within a tolerable time span.
- Big Data is typically defined by three "V"s: volume, variety, velocity.
- MapReduce is a technique to distribute the processing of very large multi-structured data files across a large cluster of machines.
- Hadoop is an open source framework for processing, storing, and analyzing massive amounts of distributed, unstructured data.
- Hive is a Hadoop-based data warehousing–like framework originally developed by Facebook.
- Pig is a Hadoop-based query language developed by Yahoo!.
- NoSQL, which stands for Not Only SQL, is a new paradigm to store and process large volumes of unstructured, semistructured, and multi-structured data.

- Data scientist is a new role or a job commonly associated with Big Data or data science.
- Big Data and data warehouses are complementary (not competing) analytics technologies.
- As a relatively new area, the Big Data vendor landscape is developing very rapidly.
- Stream analytics is a term commonly used for extracting actionable information from continuously flowing/streaming data sources.
- Perpetual analytics evaluates every incoming observation against all prior observations.
- Critical event processing is a method of capturing, tracking, and analyzing streams of data to detect certain events (out of normal happenings) that are worthy of the effort.
- Data stream mining, as an enabling technology for stream analytics, is the process of extracting novel patterns and knowledge structures from continuous, rapid data records.

Key Terms

Big Data	data stream mining	Hive	Pig
Big Data analytics	Hadoop	MapReduce	RFID
critical event processing	Hadoop Distributed File	NoSQL	stream analytics
data scientist	System (HDFS)	perpetual analytics	social media

Questions for Discussion

1. What is Big Data? Why is it important? Where does Big Data come from?
2. What do you think the future of Big Data will be? Will it leave its popularity to something else? If so, what will it be?
3. What is Big Data analytics? How does it differ from regular analytics?
4. What are the critical success factors for Big Data analytics?

5. What are the big challenges that one should be mindful of when considering implementation of Big Data analytics?

6. What are the common business problems addressed by Big Data analytics?

7. Who is a data scientist? What makes them so much in demand?

8. What are the common characteristics of data scientists? Which one is the most important?

9. In the era of Big Data, are we about to witness the end of data warehousing? Why?

10. What are the use cases for Big Data/Hadoop and data warehousing/RDBMS?

11. What is stream analytics? How does it differ from regular analytics?

12. What are the most fruitful industries for stream analytics? What is common to those industries?

13. Compared to regular analytics, do you think stream analytics will have more (or fewer) use cases in the era of Big Data analytics? Why?

Exercises

Teradata University Network (TUN) and Other Hands-On Exercises

1. Go to **teradatauniversitynetwork.com** and search for case studies. Read cases and white papers that talk about Big Data analytics. What is the common theme in those case studies?

2. At **teradatauniversitynetwork.com**, find the SAS Visual Analytics white papers, case studies, and hands-on exercises. Carry out the visual analytics exercises on large data sets and prepare a report to discuss your findings.

3. At **teradatauniversitynetwork.com**, go to the podcasts library. Find podcasts about Big Data analytics. Summarize your findings.

4. Go to **teradatauniversitynetwork.com** and search for BSI videos that talk about Big Data. Review these BSI videos and answer case questions related to them.

5. Go to the **teradata.com** and/or **asterdata.com** Web sites. Find at least three customer case studies on Big Data, and write a report where you discuss the commonalities and differences of these cases.

6. Go to **IBM.com**. Find at least three customer case studies on Big Data, and write a report where you discuss the commonalities and differences of these cases.

7. Go to **cloudera.com.** Find at least three customer case studies on Hadoop implementation, and write a report where you discuss the commonalities and differences of these cases.

8. Go to **MapR.com**. Find at least three customer case studies on Hadoop implementation, and write a report where you discuss the commonalities and differences of these cases.

9. Go to **hortonworks.com**. Find at least three customer case studies on Hadoop implementation, and write a report where you discuss the commonalities and differences of these cases.

10. Go to **marklogic.com**. Find at least three customer case studies on Hadoop implementation, and write a report where you discuss the commonalities and differences of these cases.

11. Go to **youtube.com**. Search for videos on Big Data computing. Watch at least two. Summarize your findings.

12. Go to **google.com/scholar** and search for articles on stream analytics. Find at least three related articles. Read and summarize your findings.

13. Enter **google.com/scholar** and search for articles on data stream mining. Find at least three related articles. Read and summarize your findings.

14. Search the job search sites like **monster.com**, **careerbuilder.com**, and so forth. Find at least five job postings for data scientist. Identify the key characteristics and skills expected from the applicants.

15. Enter **google.com/scholar** and search for articles that talk about Big Data versus data warehousing. Find at least five articles. Read and summarize your findings.

End-of-Chapter Application Case

Discovery Health Turns Big Data into Better Healthcare

Introduction—Business Context

Founded in Johannesburg more than 20 years ago, Discovery now operates throughout the country, with offices in most major cities to support its network of brokers. It employs more than 5,000 people and offers a wide range of health, life and other insurance services.

In the health sector, Discovery prides itself on offering the widest range of health plans in the South African market. As one of the largest health scheme administrators in the country, its is able to keep member contributions as low as possible, making it more affordable to a wider cross-section of the population. On a like-for-like basis, Discovery's plan contributions are as much as 15 percent lower than those of any other South African medical scheme.

Business Challenges

When your health schemes have 2.7 million members, your claims system generates a million new rows of data daily, and you are using three years of historical data in your analytics environment, how can you identify the key insights that your business and your members' health depend on?

This was the challenge facing Discovery Health, one of South Africa's leading specialist health scheme administrators. To find the needles of vital information in the big data haystack, the company not only needed a sophisticated data-mining and predictive modeling solution, but also an analytics infrastructure with the power to deliver results at the speed of business.

Solutions—Big Data Analytics

By building a new accelerated analytics landscape, Discovery Health is now able to unlock the true potential of its data for the first time. This enables the company to run three years' worth of data for its 2.7 million members through complex statistical models to deliver actionable insights in a matter of minutes. Discovery is constantly developing new analytical applications, and has already seen tangible benefits in areas such as predictive modeling of members' medical needs and fraud detection.

Predicting and preventing health risks

Matthew Zylstra, Actuary, Risk Intelligence Technical Development at Discovery Health, explains: "We can now combine data from our claims system with other sources of information such as pathology results and members' questionnaires to gain more accurate insight into their current and possible future health.

"For example, by looking at previous hospital admissions, we can now predict which of our members are most likely to require procedures such as knee surgery or lower back surgery. By gaining a better overview of members' needs, we can adjust our health plans to serve them more effectively and offer better value."

Lizelle Steenkamp, Divisional Manager, Risk Intelligence Technical Development, adds: "Everything we do is an attempt to lower costs for our members while maintaining or improving the quality of care. The schemes we administer are mutual funds–non-profit organizations–so any surpluses in the plan go back to the members we administer, either through increased reserves or lowered contributions. "One of the most important ways we can simultaneously reduce costs and improve the well-being of our members is to predict and prevent health problems before they need treatment. We are using the results of our predictive modeling to design preventative programs that can help our members stay healthier."

Identifying and eliminating fraud

Estiaan Steenberg, Actuary at Discovery Health, comments: "From an analytical point of view, fraud is often a small intersection between two or more very large data-sets. We now have the tools we need to identify even the tiniest anomalies and trace suspicious transactions back to their source."

For example, Discovery can now compare drug prescriptions collected by pharmacies across the country with healthcare providers' records. If a prescription seems to have been issued by a provider, but the person fulfilling it has not visited

that provider recently, it is a strong indicator that the prescription may be fraudulent. "We used to only be able to run this kind of analysis for one pharmacy and one month at a time," says Estiaan Steenberg. "Now we can run 18 months of data from all the pharmacies at once in two minutes. There is no way we could have obtained these results with our old analytics landscape."

Similar techniques can be used to identify coding errors in billing from healthcare providers–for example, if a provider "upcodes" an item to charge Discovery for a more expensive procedure than it actually performed, or "unbundles" the billing for a single procedure into two or more separate (and more expensive) lines. By comparing the billing codes with data on hospital admissions, Discovery is alerted to unusual patterns, and can investigate whenever mistakes or fraudulent activity are suspected.

The Results—Transforming Performance

To achieve this transformation in its analytics capabilities, Discovery worked with BITanium, an IBM Business Partner with deep expertise in operational deployments of advanced analytics technologies. "BITanium has provided fantastic support from so many different angles," says Matthew Zylstra. "Product evaluation and selection, software license management, technical support for developing new models, performance optimization and analyst training are just a few of the areas they have helped us with."

Discovery is an experienced user of IBM SPSS® predictive analytics software, which forms the core of its data-mining and predictive analytics capability. But the most important factor in embedding analytics in day-to-day operational decision-making has been the recent introduction of the IBM PureData™ System for Analytics, powered by Netezza® technology–an appliance that transforms the performance of the predictive models.

"BITanium ran a proof of concept for the solution that rapidly delivered useful results," says Lizelle Steenkamp. "We were impressed with how quickly it was possible to achieve tremendous performance gains." Matthew Zylstra adds: "Our data warehouse is so large that some queries used to take 18 hours or more to process–and they would often crash before delivering results. Now, we see results in a few minutes, which allows us to be more responsive to our customers and thus provide better care."

From an analytics perspective, the speed of the solution gives Discovery more scope to experiment and optimize its models. "We can tweak a model and re-run the analysis in a few minutes," says Matthew Zylstra "This means we can do more development cycles faster–and release new analyses to the business in days rather than weeks."

From a broader business perspective, the combination of SPSS and PureData technologies gives Discovery the ability to put actionable data in the hands of its decision-makers faster. "In sensitive areas such as patient care and fraud investigation, the details are everything," concludes Lizelle Steenkamp. "With the IBM solution, instead of inferring a 'near enough' answer from high-level summaries of data, we can get the right information, develop the right models, ask the right questions, and provide accurate analyses that meet the precise needs of the business."

Looking to the future, Discovery is also starting to analyze unstructured data, such as text-based surveys and comments from online feedback forms.

About BITanium

BITanium believes that the truth lies in data. Data does not have its own agenda, it does not lie, it is not influenced by promotions or bonuses. Data contains the only accurate representation of what has and is actually happening within a business. BITanium also believes that one of the few remaining differentiators between mediocrity and excellence is how a company uses its data.

BITanium is passionate about using technology and mathematics to find patterns and relationships in data. These patterns provide insight and knowledge about problems, transforming them into opportunities. To learn more about services and solutions from BITanium, please visit bitanium.co.za.

About IBM Business Analytics

IBM Business Analytics software delivers data-driven insights that help organizations work smarter and outperform their peers. This comprehensive portfolio includes solutions for business intelligence, predictive analytics and decision management, performance management, and risk management. Business Analytics solutions enable companies to identify and visualize trends and patterns in areas, such as customer analytics, that can have a profound effect on business performance. They can compare scenarios, anticipate potential threats and opportunities, better plan, budget and forecast resources, balance risks against expected returns and work to meet regulatory requirements. By making analytics widely available, organizations can align tactical and strategic decision-making to achieve business goals. For more information, you may visit ibm.com/business-analytics.

QUESTIONS FOR THE END-OF-CHAPTER APPLICATION CASE

1. How big is Big Data for Discovery Health?
2. What big data sources did Discovery Health use for their analytic solutions?
3. What were the main data/analytics challenges Discovery Health was facing?
4. What were the main solutions they have produced?
5. What were the initial results/benefits? What do you think will be the future of Big Data analytics at Discovery?

Source: IBM Customer Story, **"Discovery Health turns big data into better healthcare"** public.dhe.ibm.com/common/ssi/ecm/en/ytc03619zaen/YTC03619ZAEN.PDF (accessed October 2013).

References

Awadallah, A., and D. Graham. (2012). "Hadoop and the Data Warehouse: When to Use Which." White paper by Cloudera and Teradata. **teradata.com/white-papers/Hadoop-and-the-Data-Warehouse-When-to-Use-Which** (accessed March 2013).

Davenport, T. H., and D. J. Patil. (2012, October). "Data Scientist." *Harvard Business Review,* pp. 70–76.

Dean, J., and S. Ghemawat. (2004). "MapReduce: Simplified Data Processing on Large Clusters." **research.google.com/archive/mapreduce.html** (accessed March 2013).

Delen, D., M. Kletke, and J. Kim. (2005). "A Scalable Classification Algorithm for Very Large Datasets." *Journal of Information and Knowledge Management,* Vol. 4, No. 2, pp. 83–94.

Ericsson. (2012). "Proof of Concept for Applying Stream Analytics to Utilities." Ericsson Labs, Research Topics, **labs.ericsson.com/blog/proof-of-concept-for-applying-stream-analytics-to-utilities** (accessed March 2013).

Issenberg, S. (2012, October 29). "Obama Does It Better" (from "Victory Lab: The New Science of Winning Campaigns"), *Slate.*

Jonas, J. (2007). "Streaming Analytics vs. Perpetual Analytics (Advantages of Windowless Thinking)." **jeffjonas.typepad.com/jeff_jonas/2007/04/streaming_analy.html** (accessed March 2013).

Kelly, L. (2012). "Big Data: Hadoop, Business Analytics and Beyond." **wikibon.org/wiki/v/Big_Data:_Hadoop,_Business_Analytics_and_Beyond** (accessed January 2013).

Kelly, L. (2013). "Big Data Vendor Revenue and Market Forecast 2012–2017." **wikibon.org/wiki/v/Big_Data_Vendor_Revenue_and_Market_Forecast_2012-2017** (accessed March 2013).

Romano, L. (2012, June 9). "Obama's Data Advantage." *Politico.*

Russom, P. (2013). "Busting 10 Myths about Hadoop: The Big Data Explosion." TDWI's *Best of Business Intelligence,* Vol. 10, pp. 45–46.

Samuelson, D. A. (2013, February). "Analytics: Key to Obama's Victory." INFORMS' *ORMS Today,* pp. 20–24.

Scherer, M. (2012, November 7). "Inside the Secret World of the Data Crunchers Who Helped Obama Win." *Time.*

Shen, G. (2013, January–February). "Big Data, Analytics, and Elections." INFORMS' *Analytics Magazine.*

Watson, H. (2012). "The Requirements for Being an Analytics-Based Organization." *Business Intelligence Journal,* Vol. 17, No. 2, pp. 42–44.

Watson, H., R. Sharda, and D. Schrader. (2012). "Big Data and How to Teach It." Workshop at AMCIS. Seattle, WA.

White, C. (2012). "MapReduce and the Data Scientist." Teradata Aster white paper. **teradata.com/white-paper/MapReduce-and-the-Data-Scientist** (accessed February 2013).

Zikopoulos, P., D. DeRoos, K. Parasuraman, T. Deutsch, D. Corrigan, and J. Giles. (2013). *Harness the Power of Big Data.* New York: MacGraw Hill Publishing.

14

Business Analytics: Emerging Trends and Future Impacts

LEARNING OBJECTIVES

■ Explore some of the emerging technologies that may impact analytics, BI, and decision support

■ Describe how geospatial and location-based analytics are assisting organizations

■ Describe how analytics are powering consumer applications and creating a new opportunity for entrepreneurship for analytics

■ Describe the potential of cloud computing in business intelligence

■ Understand Web 2.0 and its characteristics as related to analytics

■ Describe organizational impacts of analytics applications

■ List and describe the major ethical and legal issues of analytics implementation

■ Understand the analytics ecosystem to get a sense of the various types of players in the analytics industry and how one can work in a variety of roles

This chapter introduces several emerging technologies that are likely to have major impacts on the development and use of business intelligence applications. Many other interesting technologies are also emerging, but we have focused on some trends that have already been realized and others that are about to impact analytics further. Using a crystal ball is always a risky proposition, but this chapter provides a framework for analysis of emerging trends. We introduce and explain some emerging technologies and explore their current applications. We then discuss the organizational, personal, legal, ethical, and societal impacts of support systems that may affect their implementation. We conclude with a description of the analytics ecosystem. This section should help readers appreciate different career possibilities within the realm of analytics. This chapter contains the following sections:

14.1   OPENING VIGNETTE: Oklahoma Gas and Electric Employs Analytics to Promote Smart Energy Use

Oklahoma Gas and Electric (OG&E) serves over 789,000 customers in Oklahoma and Arkansas. OG&E has a strategic goal to delay building new fossil fuel generation plants until the year 2020. OG&E forecasts a daily system demand of 5,864 megawatts in 2020, a reduction of about 500 megawatts.

One of the ways to optimize this demand is to engage the consumers in managing their energy usage. OG&E has completed installation of smart meters and other devices on the electronic grid at the consumer end that enable it to capture large amounts of data. For example, currently it receives about 52 million meter reads per day. Apart from this, OG&E expects to receive close to 2 million event messages per day from its advanced metering infrastructure, data networks, meter alarms, and outage management systems. OG&E employs a three-layer information architecture involving data warehouse, improved and expanded integration and data management, and new analytics and presentation capabilities to support the Big Data flow.

With this data, OG&E has started working on consumer-oriented efficiency programs to shift the customer's usage out of peak demand cycles. OG&E is targeting customers with its smart hours plan. This plan encourages customers to choose a variety of rate options sent via phone, text, or e-mail. These rate options offer attractive summer rates for all other hours apart from the peak hours of 2 P.M. to 7 P.M. OG&E is making an investment in customers by supplying a communicating thermostat that will respond to the price signals sent by OG&E and help customers in managing their utility consumption. OG&E also educates its customers on their usage habits by providing 5-minute interval data every 15 minutes to the demand-responsive customers.

OG&E has developed consumer analytics and customer segmentation analytics that will enhance their understanding about individuals' responses to the price signals and identify the best customers to be targeted with specific marketing campaigns. It also uses demand-side management analytics for peak load management/load shed. With Teradata's platform, OG&E has combined its smart meter data, outage data, call center data, rate data, asset data, price signals, billing, and collections into one integrated data platform. The platform also incorporates geospatial mapping of the integrated data using the in-database geospatial analytics that add onto the OG&E's dynamic segmentation capabilities.

Using geospatial mapping and visual analytics, OG&E now views a near–real-time version of data about its energy-efficient prospects spread over geographic areas and comes up with marketing initiatives that are most suitable for these customers. OG&E now has an easy way to narrow down to the specific customers in a geographic region based on their meter usage; OG&E can also find noncommunicating smart meters. Furthermore, OG&E can track the outage, with the deployed crew supporting outages as well as the weather overlay of their services. This combination of filed infrastructure, geospatial data, enterprise data warehouse, and analytics has enabled OG&E to manage its customer demand in such a way that it can optimize its long-term investments.

QUESTIONS FOR THE OPENING VIGNETTE

1. Why perform consumer analytics?

2. What is meant by dynamic segmentation?

3. How does geospatial mapping help OG&E?

4. What types of incentives might the consumers respond to in changing their energy use?

WHAT WE CAN LEARN FROM THIS VIGNETTE

Many organizations are now integrating the data from the different internal units and turning toward analytics to convert the integrated data into value. The ability to view the operations/customer-specific data using in-database geospatial analytics gives organizations a broader perspective and aids in decision making.

Sources: **Teradata.com**, "Utilities Analytic Summit 2012 Oklahoma Gas & Electric," **teradata.com/video/ Utilities-Analytic-Summit-2012-Oklahoma-Gas-and-Electric** (accessed March 2013); **ogepet.com**, "Smart Hours," **ogepet.com/programs/smarthours.aspx** (accessed March 2013); **IntellidentUtility.com**, "OGE's Three-Tiered Architecture Aids Data Analysis," **intelligentutility.com/article/12/02/oges-three-tiered- architecture-aids-data-analysis&utm_medium=eNL&utm_campaign=IU_DAILY2&utm_term=Original- Magazine** (accessed March 2013).

14.2 LOCATION-BASED ANALYTICS FOR ORGANIZATIONS

This goal of this chapter is to illustrate the potential of new technologies when innovative uses are developed by creative minds. Most of the technologies described in this chapter are nascent and have yet to see widespread adoption. Therein lies the opportunity to create the next "killer" application. For example, use of RFID and sensors is growing, with each company exploring its use in supply chains, retail stores, manufacturing, or service operations. The chapter argues that with the right combination of ideas, networking, and applications, it is possible to develop creative technologies that have the potential to impact a company's operations in multiple ways, or to create entirely new markets and make a major difference to the world. We also study the analytics ecosystem to better understand which companies are the players in this industry.

Thus far, we have seen many examples of organizations employing analytical techniques to gain insights into their existing processes through informative reporting, predictive analytics, forecasting, and optimization techniques. In this section, we learn about a critical emerging trend—incorporation of location data in analytics. Figure 14.1 gives our classification of location-based analytic applications. We first review applications that make use of static location data that is usually called *geospatial data*. We then examine the explosive growth of applications that take advantage of all the location data being generated by today's devices. This section focuses on analytics applications that are being developed by organizations to make better decisions in managing operations (as was illustrated in the opening vignette), targeting customers, promotions, and so forth. In the following section we will explore analytics applications that are being developed to be used directly by a consumer, some of which also take advantage of the location data.

Geospatial Analytics

A consolidated view of the overall performance of an organization is usually represented through the visualization tools that provide actionable information. The information may include current and forecasted values of various business factors and key performance indicators (KPIs). Looking at the key performance indicators as overall numbers via

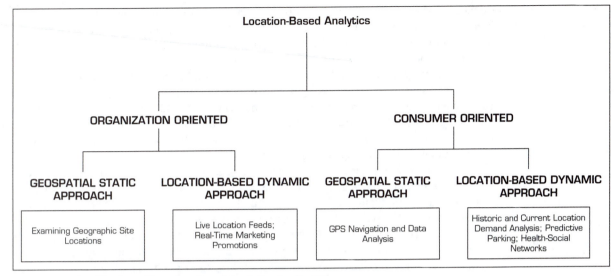

FIGURE 14.1 Classification of Location-Based Analytics Applications.

various graphs and charts can be overwhelming. There is a high risk of missing potential growth opportunities or not identifying the problematic areas. As an alternative to simply viewing reports, organizations employ visual maps that are geographically mapped and based on the traditional location data, usually grouped by the postal codes. These map-based visualizations have been used by organizations to view the aggregated data and get more meaningful location-based insights. Although this approach has advantages, the use of postal codes to represent the data is more of a static approach suitable for achieving a higher level view of things.

The traditional location-based analytic techniques using geocoding of organizational locations and consumers hampers the organizations in understanding "true location-based" impacts. Locations based on postal codes offer an aggregate view of a large geographic area. This poor granularity may not be able to pinpoint the growth opportunities within a region. The location of the target customers can change rapidly. An organization's promotional campaigns might not target the right customers. To address these concerns, organizations are embracing location and spatial extensions to analytics (Gnau, 2010). Addition of location components based on latitudinal and longitudinal attributes to the traditional analytical techniques enables organizations to add a new dimension of "where" to their traditional business analyses, which currently answer questions of "who," "what," "when," and "how much."

Location-based data are now readily available from geographic information systems (GIS). These are used to capture, store, analyze, and manage the data linked to a location using integrated sensor technologies, global positioning systems installed in smartphones, or through radio-frequency identification deployments in retail and healthcare industries.

By integrating information about the location with other critical business data, organizations are now creating location intelligence (LI) (Krivda, 2010). LI is enabling organizations to gain critical insights and make better decisions by optimizing important processes and applications. Organizations now create interactive maps that further drill down to details about any location, offering analysts the ability to investigate new trends and correlate location-specific factors across multiple KPIs. Analysts in the organizations can now pinpoint trends and patterns in revenues, sales, and profitability across geographical areas.

By incorporating demographic details into locations, retailers can determine how sales vary by population level and proximity to other competitors; they can assess the demand and efficiency of supply chain operations. Consumer product companies can identify the specific needs of the customers and customer complaint locations, and easily trace them back to the products. Sales reps can better target their prospects by analyzing their geography (Krivda, 2010).

Integrating detailed global intelligence, real-time location information, and logistics data in a visual, easy-to-access format, U.S. Transportation Command (USTRANSCOM) could easily track the information about the type of aircraft, maintenance history, complete list of crew, the equipment and supplies on the aircraft, and location of the aircraft. Having this information will enable it to make well-informed decisions and coordinate global operations, as noted in Westholder (2010).

Additionally, with location intelligence, organizations can quickly overlay weather and environmental effects and forecast the level of impact on critical business operations. With technology advancements, geospatial data is now being directly incorporated in the enterprise data warehouses. Location-based in-database analytics enable organizations to perform complex calculations with increased efficiency and get a single view of all the spatially oriented data, revealing the hidden trends and new opportunities. For example, Teradata's data warehouse supports the geospatial data feature based on the SQL/MM standard. The geospatial feature is captured as a new geometric data type called ST_GEOMETRY. It supports a large spectrum of shapes, from simple points, lines, and curves to complex polygons in representing the geographic areas. They are converting the nonspatial data of their operating business locations by incorporating the latitude and longitude coordinates. This process of geocoding is readily supported by service companies like NAVTEQ and Tele Atlas, which maintain worldwide databases of addresses with geospatial features and make use of address-cleansing tools like Informatica and Trillium, which support mapping of spatial coordinates to the addresses as part of extract, transform, and load functions.

Organizations across a variety of business sectors are employing geospatial analytics. We will review some examples next. Sabre Airline Solutions' application, Traveler Security, uses a geospatial-enabled dashboard that alerts the users to assess the current risks across global hotspots displayed in interactive maps. Using this, airline personnel can easily find current travelers and respond quickly in the event of any travel disruption. Application Case 14.1 provides an example of how location-based information was used in making site selection decisions in expanding a company's footprint.

Application Case 14.1

Great Clips Employs Spatial Analytics to Shave Time in Location Decisions

Great Clips, the world's largest and fastest growing salon, has more than 3,000 salons throughout United States and Canada. Great Clips' franchise success depends on a growth strategy that is driven by rapidly opening new stores in the right locations and markets. The company needed to analyze the locations based on the requirements for a potential customer base, demographic trends, and sales impact on existing franchises in the target location. Choosing a good site is of utmost importance. The current processes took a long time to analyze a single site and a great deal of labor requiring intensive analyst resources was needed to manually assess the data from multiple data sources.

With thousands of locations analyzed each year, the delay was risking the loss of prime sites to competitors and was proving expensive: Great Clips employed external contractors to cope with the delay. Great Clips created a site-selection workflow application to evaluate the new salon site locations by using the geospatial analytical capabilities of Alteryx. A new site location was evaluated by its drive-time proximity and convenience for serving all the existing customers of the Great Clips Salon network in the area. The Alteryx-based solution also enabled evaluation of each new location based on demographics and consumer behavior data, aligning with existing Great Clip's customer profiles and the potential revenue impact of the new site on the existing sites. As a result of using location-based analytic techniques, Great Clips was able to reduce the time to assess new locations by nearly 95 percent. The labor-intensive analysis was automated and developed into a data collection analysis, mapping, and reporting application that could be easily used by the nontechnical real estate

managers. Furthermore, it enabled the company to implement proactive predictive analytics for a new franchise location because the whole process now took just a few minutes.

QUESTIONS FOR DISCUSSION

1. How is geospatial analytics employed at Great Clips?
2. What criteria should a company consider in evaluating sites for future locations?
3. Can you think of other applications where such geospatial data might be useful?

Source: **alteryx.com**, "Great Clips," **alteryx.com/sites/default/files/resources/files/case-study-great-chips.pdf** (accessed March 2013).

In addition to the retail transaction analysis applications highlighted here, there are many other applications of combining geographic information with other data being generated by an organization. The opening vignette described a use of such location information in understanding location-based energy usage as well as outage. Similarly, network operations and communication companies often generate massive amounts of data every day. The ability to analyze the data quickly with a high level of location-specific granularity can better identify the customer churn and help in formulating strategies specific to locations for increasing operational efficiency, quality of service, and revenue.

Geospatial analysis can enable communication companies to capture daily transactions from a network to identify the geographic areas experiencing a large number of failed connection attempts of voice, data, text, or Internet. Analytics can help determine the exact causes based on location and drill down to an individual customer to provide better customer service. You can see this in action by completing the following multimedia exercise.

A Multimedia Exercise in Analytics Employing Geospatial Analytics

Teradata University Network includes a BSI video on the case of dropped mobile calls. Please watch the video that appears on YouTube at the following link: **teradatauniversitynetwork.com/teach-and-learn/library-item/?LibraryItemId=893**

A telecommunication company launches a new line of smartphones and faces problems of dropped calls. The new rollout is in trouble, and the northeast region is the worst hit region as they compare effects of dropped calls on the profit for the geographic region. The company hires BSI to analyze the problems arising due to defects in smartphone handsets, tower coverage, and software glitches. The entire northeast region data is divided into geographic clusters, and the problem is solved by identifying the individual customer data. The BSI team employs geospatial analytics to identify the locations where network coverage was leading to the dropped calls and suggests installing a few additional towers where the unhappy customers are located. They also work with companies on various actions that ensure that the problem is addressed.

After the video is complete, you can see how the analysis was prepared on a slide set at: **slideshare.net/teradata/bsi-teradata-the-case-of-the-dropped-mobile-calls** This multimedia excursion provides an example of a combination of geospatial analytics along with Big Data analytics that assist in better decision making.

Real-Time Location Intelligence

Many devices in use by consumers and professionals are constantly sending out their location information. Cars, buses, taxis, mobile phones, cameras, and personal navigation devices all transmit their locations thanks to network-connected positioning technologies such as GPS, wifi, and cell tower triangulation. Millions of consumers and businesses use location-enabled devices for finding nearby services, locating friends and family, navigating, tracking of assets and pets, dispatching, and engaging in sports, games, and hobbies. This surge in location-enabled services has resulted in a massive database of historical and real-time streaming location information. It is, of course, scattered and by itself not very useful. Indeed, a new name has been given to this type of data mining—**reality mining**. Eagle and Pentland (2006) appear to have been the first to use this term. Reality mining builds on the idea that these location-enabled data sets could provide remarkable real-time insight into aggregate human activity trends. For example, a British company called Path Intelligence (**pathintelligence.com**) has developed a system called Footpath that ascertains how people move within a city or even within a store. All of this is done by automatically tracking movement without any cameras recording the movement visually. Such analysis can help determine the best layout for products or even public transportation options. The automated data collection enabled through capture of cell phone and wifi hotspot access points presents an interesting new dimension in nonintrusive market research data collection and, of course, microanalysis of such massive data sets.

By analyzing and learning from these large-scale patterns of movement, it is possible to identify distinct classes of behaviors in specific contexts. This approach allows a business to better understand its customer patterns and also to make more informed decisions about promotions, pricing, and so on. By applying algorithms that reduce the dimensionality of location data, one can characterize places according to the activity and movement between them. From massive amounts of high-dimensional location data, these algorithms uncover trends, meaning, and relationships to eventually produce human-understandable representations. It then becomes possible to use such data to automatically make intelligent predictions and find important matches and similarities between places and people.

Location-based analytics finds its application in consumer-oriented marketing applications. Quiznos, a quick-service restaurant, used Sense Networks' platform to analyze location trails of mobile users based on the geospatial data obtained from the GPS and target tech-savvy customers with coupons. See Application Case 14.2. This case illustrates the emerging trend in retail space where companies are looking to improve efficiency of marketing campaigns—not just by targeting every customer based on real-time location, but by employing more sophisticated predictive analytics in real time on consumer behavioral profiles and finding the right set of consumers for the advertising campaigns.

Many mobile applications now enable organizations to target the right customer by building the profile of customers' behavior over geographic locations. For example, the Radii app takes the customer experience to a whole new level. The Radii app collects

Application Case 14.2

Quiznos Targets Customers for its Sandwiches

Quiznos, a franchised, quick-service restaurant, implemented a location-based mobile targeting campaign that targeted the tech-savvy and busy consumers of Portland, Oregon. It made use of Sense Networks' platform, which analyzed the location trails of mobile users over detailed time periods and built anonymous profiles based on the behavioral attributes of shopping habits.

With the application of predictive analytics on the user profiles, Quiznos employed location-based behavioral targeting to narrow the characteristics of users who are most likely to eat at a quick-service restaurant. Its advertising campaign ran for 2 months—November and December, 2012—and targeted only potential customers who had been to quick-service restaurants over the past 30 days, within a 3-mile radius of Quiznos, and between the ages of 18 and 34. It used relevant mobile advertisements of local coupons based on the customer's location. The campaign resulted in over 3.7 million new customers and had a 20 percent increase in coupon redemptions within the Portland area.

QUESTIONS FOR DISCUSSION

1. How can location-based analytics help retailers in targeting customers?
2. Research similar applications of location-based analytics in the retail domain.

Source: **Mobilemarketer.com**, "Quiznos Sees 20pc Boost in Coupon Redemption via Location-Based Mobile Ad Campaign," **mobilemarketer.com/cms/news/advertising/14738.html** (accessed February 2013).

information about the user's habits, interests, spending patterns, and favorite locations to understand their personality. Radii uses the Gimbal Context Awareness SDK to gather location and geospatial information. Gimbal SDK's Geofencing functionality enables Radii to pick up the user's interests and habits based on the time they spend at a location and how often they visit it. Depending on the number of users who visit a particular location, and based on their preferences, Radii assigns a personality to that location, which changes based on which type of user visits the location, and their preferences. New users are given recommendations that are closer to their personality, making this process highly dynamic.

Users who sign up for Radii receive 10 "Radii," which is their currency. Users can use this currency at select locations to get discounts and special offers. They can also get more Radii by inviting their friends to use the app. Businesses who offer these discounts pay Radii for bringing customers to their location, as this in turn translates into more business. For every Radii exchanged between users, Radii is paid a certain amount. Radii thus creates a new direct marketing platform for business and enhances the customer experience by providing recommendations, discounts, and coupons.

Yet another extension of location-based analytics is to use augmented reality. Cachetown has introduced a location-sensing augmented reality-based game to encourage users to claim offers from select geographic locations. The user can start anywhere in a city and follow markers on the Cachetown app to reach a coupon, discount, or offer from a business. Virtual items are visible through the Cachetown app when the user points a phone's camera toward the virtual item. The user can then claim this item by clicking on it through the Cachetown app. On claiming the item, the user is given a certain free good/discount/offer from a nearby business, which he can use just by walking into their store.

Cachetown's business-facing app allows businesses to place these virtual items on a map using Google Maps. The placement of this item can be fine-tuned by using Google's Street View. Once all virtual items have been configured with information and location, the business can submit items, after which the items are visible to the user in real time. Cachetown also provides usage analytics to the business to enable better targeting of virtual items. The virtual reality aspect of this app improves the experience of users, providing them with a "gaming"-type environment in real life. At the same time, it provides a powerful marketing platform for businesses to reach their customers better. More information on Cachetown is at **candylab.com/ augmented-reality/**.

As is evident from this section, location-based analytics and ensuing applications are perhaps the most important front in the near future for organizations. A common theme in this section was the use of operational or marketing data by organizations. We will next explore analytics applications that are directly targeted at the users and sometimes take advantage of location information.

SECTION 14.2 REVIEW QUESTIONS

1. How does traditional analytics make use of location-based data?
2. How can geocoded locations assist in better decision making?
3. What is the value provided by geospatial analytics?
4. Explore the use of geospatial analytics further by investigating its use across various sectors like government census tracking, consumer marketing, and so forth.

14.3 ANALYTICS APPLICATIONS FOR CONSUMERS

The explosive growth of the apps industry for smartphone platforms (iOS, Android, Windows, Blackberry, Amazon, and so forth) and the use of analytics are also creating tremendous opportunities for developing apps that the consumers can use directly. These apps differ from the previous category in that these are meant for direct use by a consumer rather than an organization that is trying to mine a consumer's usage/purchase data to create a profile for marketing specific products or services to them. Predictably, these apps are meant for enabling consumers to do their job better. We highlight two of these in the following examples.

Sense Networks has built a mobile application called CabSense that analyzes large amounts of data from the New York City Taxi and Limousine Commission and helps New Yorkers and visitors in finding the best corners for hailing a taxi based on the person's location, day of the week, and time. CabSense rates the street corners on a 5-point scale by making use of machine-learning algorithms applied to the vast amounts of historical location points obtained from the pickups and drop-offs of all New York City cabs. Although the app does not give the exact location of cabs in real time, its data-crunching predictions enable people to get to a street corner that has the highest probability of finding a cab.

CabSense provides an interactive map based on current user location obtained from the mobile phone's GPS locator to find the best street corners for finding an open cab. It also provides a radar view that automatically points the right direction toward the best street corner. The application also allows users to plan in advance, set up date and time of travel, and view the best corners for finding a taxi. Furthermore, CabSense distinguishes New York's Yellow Cab services from the for-hire vehicles and readily prompts the users with relevant details of private service providers that can be used in case no Yellow Cabs are available.

Another transportation-related app that uses predictive analytics has been deployed in Pittsburgh, Pennsylvania. Developed in collaboration with Carnegie Mellon University, this app includes predictive capabilities to estimate parking availability. ParkPGH directs drivers to parking lots in the area where parking is available. It calculates the number of parking spaces available in 10 lots—over 5,300 spaces, and 25 percent of the garage parking in downtown Pittsburgh. Available spaces are updated every 30 seconds, keeping the driver as close to the current availability as possible. The app is also capable of predicting parking availability by the time the driver reaches the destination. Depending on historical demand and current events, the app is able to provide information on which lots will have free space by the time the driver gets to the destination. The app's underlying algorithm uses data on current events around the area—for example, a basketball game—to predict an increase in demand for parking spaces later that day, thus saving commuters valuable time searching for parking spaces in the busy city. Both of these examples show consumer-oriented examples of location-based analytics in transportation. Application Case 14.3 illustrates another consumer-oriented application, but in the health domain. There are many more health-related apps.

Application Case 14.3

A Life Coach in Your Pocket

Most people today are finding ways to stay active and healthy. Although everyone knows it's best to follow a healthy lifestyle, people often lack the motivation needed to keep them on track. 100Plus, a start-up company, has developed a personalized, mobile prediction platform called Outside that keeps users active. The application is based on the quantified self-approach, which makes use of technology to self-track the data on a person's habits, analyze it, and make personalized recommendations.

100 Plus posited that people are most likely to succeed in changing their lifestyles when they are given small, micro goals that are easier to achieve. They built Outside as a personalized product that engages people in these activities and enables them to understand the long-term impacts of short-term activities.

After the user enters basic data such as gender, age, weight, height, and the location where he or she lives, a behavior profile is built and compared with data from Practice Fusion and CDC records. A life score is calculated using predictive analytics. This score gives the estimated life expectancy of the user. Once registered, users can begin discovering health opportunities, which are categorized as "missions" on the mobile interface. These missions are specific to the places based on the user's location. Users can track activities, complete them, and get a

score that is credited back to a life score. Outside also enables its users to create diverse, personalized suggestions by keeping track of photographs of them doing each activity. These can be used for suggestions to others, based on their location and preferences. A leader board allows a particular user to find how other people with similar characteristics are completing their missions and inspires the current user to resort to healthier living. In that sense it also combines social media with predictive analytics.

Today, most smartphones are equipped with accelerometers and gyroscopes to measure jerk, orientation, and sense motion. Many applications use this data to make the user's experience on the smartphone better. Data on accelerometer and gyroscope readings is publicly available and can be used to classify various activities like walking, running, lying down, and climbing. Kaggle (**kaggle.com**), a platform that hosts competitions and research for predictive modeling and analytics, recently hosted a competition aimed at identifying muscle motions that may be used to predict the progression of Parkinson's disease. Parkinson's disease is caused by a failure in the central nervous system, which leads to tremors, rigidity, slowness of movement, and postural instability. The objective of the competition is to best identify markers that can lead

(Continued)

Application Case 14.3   (Continued)

to predicting the progression of the disease. This particular application of advanced technology and analytics is an example of how these two can come together to generate extremely useful and relevant information.

Questions for Discussion

1. Search online for other applications of consumer-oriented analytical applications.
2. How can location-based analytics help individual consumers?

3. How can smartphone data be used to predict medical conditions?
4. How is ParkPGH different from a "parking space–reporting" app?

Source: Institute of Medicine of the National Academies, "Health Data Initiative Forum III: The Health Datapalooza," **iom.edu/Activities/PublicHealth/HealthData/2012-JUN-05/Afternoon-Apps-Demos/outside-100plus.aspx** (accessed March 2013).

Analytics-based applications are emerging not just for fun and health, but also to enhance one's productivity. For example, Cloze is an app that manages in-boxes from multiple e-mail accounts in one place. It integrates social networks with e-mail contacts to learn which contacts are important and assigns a score—a higher score for important contacts. E-mails with a higher score are shown first, thus filtering less important and irrelevant e-mails out of the way. Cloze stores the context of each conversation to save time when catching up with a pending conversation. Contacts are organized into groups based on how frequently they interact, helping users keep in touch with people with whom they may be losing contact. Users are able to set a Cloze score for people they want to get in touch with and work on improving that score. Cloze marks up the score whenever an attempt at connecting is made.

On opening an e-mail, Cloze provides several options, such as now, today, tomorrow, and next week, which automatically reminds the user to initiate contact at the scheduled time. This serves as a reminder for getting back to e-mails at a later point without just forgetting about them or marking them as "unread," which often leads to a cluttered in-box.

As is evident from these examples of consumer-centric apps, predictive analytics is beginning to enable development of software that is directly used by a consumer. *The Wall Street Journal* (**wsj.com/apps**) estimates that the app industry has already become a $25 billion industry with more growth expected. We believe that the growth of consumer-oriented analytic applications will grow and create many entrepreneurial opportunities for the readers of this book.

One key concern in employing these technologies is the loss of privacy. If someone can track the movement of a cell phone, the privacy of that customer is a big issue. Some of the app developers claim that they only need to gather aggregate flow information, not individually identifiable information. But many stories appear in the media that highlight violations of this general principle. Both users and developers of such apps have to be very aware of the deleterious effect of giving out private information as well as collecting such information. We discuss this issue a little bit further in Section 14.8.

SECTION 14.3 REVIEW QUESTIONS

1. What are the various options that CabSense provides to users?
2. Explore more transportation applications that may employ location-based analytics.
3. Briefly describe how the data are used to create profiles of users.
4. What other applications can you imagine if you were able to access cell phone location data? Do a search on location-enabled services.

14.4 RECOMMENDATION ENGINES

In most decision situations, people rely on recommendations gathered either directly from other people or indirectly through the aggregated recommendations made by others in the form of reviews and ratings posted either in newspapers, product guides, or online. Such information sharing is considered one of the major reasons for the success of online retailers such as **Amazon.com**. In this section we briefly review the common terms and technologies of such systems as these are becoming key components of any analytic application.

The term *recommender systems* refers to a Web-based information filtering system that takes the inputs from users and then aggregates the inputs to provide recommendations for other users in their product or service selection choices. Some recommender systems now even try to predict the rating or preference that a user would give for a particular product or service.

The data necessary to build a recommendation system are collected by Web-based systems where each user is specifically asked to rate an item on a rating scale, rank the items from most favorite to least favorite, and/or ask the user to list the attributes of the items that the user likes. Other information such as the user's textual comments, feedback reviews, amount of time that the user spends on viewing an item, and tracking the details of the user's social networking activity provides behavioral information about the product choices made by the user.

Two basic approaches that are employed in the development of recommendation systems are collaborative filtering and content filtering. In collaborative filtering, the recommendation system is built based on the individual user's past behavior by keeping track of the previous history of all purchased items. This includes products, items that are viewed most often, and ratings that are given by the users to the items they purchased. These individual profile histories with item preferences are grouped with other similar user-item profile histories to build a comprehensive set of relations between users and items, which are then used to predict what the user will like and recommend items accordingly.

Collaborative filtering involves aggregating the user-item profiles. It is usually done by building a user-item ratings matrix where each row represents a unique user and each column gives the individual item rating made by the user. The resultant matrix is a dynamic, sparse matrix with a huge dimensionality; it gets updated every time the existing user purchases a new item or a new user makes item purchases. Then the recommendation task is to predict what rating a user would give to a previously unranked item. The predictions that result in higher item rankings are then presented as recommendations to the users. The user-item based approach employs techniques like matrix factorization and low-rank matrix approximation to reduce the dimensionality of the sparse matrix in generating the recommendations.

Collaborative filtering can also take a user-based approach in which the users take the main role. Similar users sharing the same preferences are combined into a group, and recommendations of items to a particular user are based on the evaluation of items by other users in the same group. If a particular item is ranked high by the entire community, then it is recommended to the user. Another collaborative filtering approach is based on the item-set similarity, which groups items based on the user ratings provided by various users. Both of these collaborative filtering approaches employ many algorithms, such as KNN (*K*-Nearest Neighborhood) and Pearson Correlation, in measuring user and behavior similarity of ratings among the items.

The collaborative filtering approaches often require huge amounts of existing data on user-item preferences to make appropriate recommendations; this problem is most often referred to as *cold start* in the process of making recommendations. Also, in the typical Web-based environment, tapping each individual's ratings and purchase behavior generates large amounts of data, and applying collaborative filtering algorithms requires separate high-end computation power to make the recommendations.

Collaborative filtering is widely employed in e-commerce. Customers can rate books, songs, or movies and then get recommendations regarding those issues in future. It is also being utilized in browsing documents, articles, and other scientific papers and magazines. Some of the companies using this type of recommender system are **Amazon. com** and social networking Web sites like Facebook and LinkedIn.

Content-based recommender systems overcome one of the disadvantages of collaborative filtering recommender systems, which completely rely on the user ratings matrix, by considering specifications and characteristics of items. In the content-based filtering approach, the characteristics of an item are profiled first and then content-based individual user profiles are built to store the information about the characteristics of specific items that the user has rated in the past. In the recommendation process, a comparison is made by filtering the item information from the user profile for which the user has rated positively and compares these characteristics with any new products that the user has not rated yet. Recommendations are made if there are similarities found in the item characteristics.

Content-based filtering involves using information tags or keywords in fetching detailed information about item characteristics and restricts this process to a single user, unlike collaborative filtering, which looks for similarities between various user profiles. This approach makes use of machine-learning and classification techniques like Bayesian classifiers, cluster analysis, decision trees, and artificial neural networks in order to estimate the probability of recommending similar items to the users that match the user's existing ratings for an item.

Content-based filtering approaches are widely used in recommending textual content such as news items and related Web pages. It is also used in recommending similar movies and music based on the existing individual profile. One of the companies employing this technique is Pandora, which builds a user profile based on the musicians/stations that a particular user likes and makes recommendations of other musicians following the similar genres an individual profile contains. Another example is an app called Patients Like Me, which builds individual patient profiles and recommends patients registered with Patients Like Me to contact other patients suffering from similar diseases.

SECTION 14.4 REVIEW QUESTIONS

1. List the types of approaches used in recommendation engines.
2. How do the two approaches differ?
3. Can you identify specific sites that may use one or the other type of recommendation system?

14.5   WEB 2.0 AND ONLINE SOCIAL NETWORKING

Web 2.0 is the popular term for describing advanced Web technologies and applications, including blogs, wikis, RSS, mashups, user-generated content, and social networks. A major objective of Web 2.0 is to enhance creativity, information sharing, and collaboration.

One of the most significant differences between Web 2.0 and the traditional Web is the greater collaboration among Internet users and other users, content providers, and enterprises. As an umbrella term for an emerging core of technologies, trends, and principles, Web 2.0 is not only changing what is on the Web, but also how it works. Web 2.0 concepts have led to the evolution of Web-based virtual communities and their hosting services, such as social networking sites, video-sharing sites, and more. Many believe that companies that understand these new applications and technologies—and apply the capabilities early on—stand to greatly improve internal business processes and marketing. Among the biggest advantages is better collaboration with customers, partners, and suppliers, as well as among internal users.

Representative Characteristics of Web 2.0

The following are representative characteristics of the Web 2.0 environment:

- Web 2.0 has the ability to tap into the collective intelligence of users. The more users contribute, the more popular and valuable a Web 2.0 site becomes.
- Data is made available in new or never-intended ways. Web 2.0 data can be remixed or "mashed up," often through Web service interfaces, much the way a dance-club DJ mixes music.
- Web 2.0 relies on user-generated and user-controlled content and data.
- Lightweight programming techniques and tools let nearly anyone act as a Web site developer.
- The virtual elimination of software-upgrade cycles makes everything a *perpetual beta* or work-in-progress and allows rapid prototyping, using the Web as an application development platform.
- Users can access applications entirely through a browser.
- An architecture of participation and *digital democracy* encourages users to add value to the application as they use it.
- A major emphasis is on social networks and computing.
- There is strong support for information sharing and collaboration.
- Web 2.0 fosters rapid and continuous creation of new business models.

Other important features of Web 2.0 are its dynamic content, rich user experience, metadata, scalability, open source basis, and freedom (net neutrality).

Most Web 2.0 applications have a rich, interactive, user-friendly interface based on Ajax or a similar framework. Ajax (Asynchronous JavaScript and XML) is an effective and efficient Web development technique for creating interactive Web applications. The intent is to make Web pages feel more responsive by exchanging small amounts of data with the server behind the scenes so that the entire Web page does not have to be reloaded each time the user makes a change. This is meant to increase the Web page's interactivity, loading speed, and usability.

A major characteristic of Web 2.0 is the global spread of innovative Web sites and start-up companies. As soon as a successful idea is deployed as a Web site in one country, other sites appear around the globe. This section presents some of these sites. For example, approximately 120 companies specialize in providing Twitter-like services in dozens of countries. An excellent source for material on Web 2.0 is Search CIO's *Executive Guide: Web 2.0* (see **searchcio.techtarget.com/general/0,295582,sid19_ gci1244339,00.html#glossary**).

Social Networking

Social networking is built on the idea that there is structure to how people know each other and interact. The basic premise is that social networking gives people the power to share, making the world more open and connected. Although social networking is usually practiced in social networks such as LinkedIn, Facebook, or Google+, aspects of it are also found in Wikipedia and YouTube.

We first briefly define *social networks* and then look at some of the services they provide and their capabilities.

A Definition and Basic Information

A *social network* is a place where people create their own space, or homepage, on which they write blogs (Web logs); post pictures, videos, or music; share ideas; and link to other Web locations they find interesting. In addition, members of social networks can tag the content they create and post it with keywords they choose themselves, which makes the content searchable. The mass adoption of social networking Web sites points to an evolution in human social interaction.

Mobile social networking refers to social networking where members converse and connect with one another using cell phones or other mobile devices. Virtually all major social networking sites offer mobile services or apps on smartphones to access their services. The explosion of mobile Web 2.0 services and companies means that many social networks can be based from cell phones and other portable devices, extending the reach of such networks to the millions of people who lack regular or easy access to computers.

Facebook (**facebook.com**), which was launched in 2004 by former Harvard student Mark Zuckerberg, is the largest social network service in the world, with almost 1 billion users worldwide as of February 2013. A primary reason why Facebook has expanded so rapidly is the network effect—more users means more value. As more users become involved in the social space, more people are available to connect with. Initially, Facebook was an online social space for college and high school students that automatically connected students to other students at the same school. Expanding to a global audience has enabled Facebook to become the dominant social network.

Today, Facebook has a number of applications that support photos, groups, events, marketplaces, posted items, games, and notes. A special feature on Facebook is the News Feed, which enables users to track the activities of friends in their social circles. For example, when a user changes his or her profile, the updates are broadcast to others who subscribe to the feed. Users can also develop their own applications or use any of the millions of Facebook applications that have been developed by other users.

Orkut (**orkut.com**) was the brainchild of a Turkish Google programmer of the same name. Orkut was to be Google's homegrown answer to Facebook. Orkut follows a format similar to that of other major social networking sites: a homepage where users can display every facet of their personal life they desire using various multimedia applications. It is more popular in countries such as Brazil than in the United States. Google has introduced another social network called Google+ that takes advantage of the popular e-mail service from Google, Gmail, but it is still a much smaller competitor of Facebook.

Implications of Business and Enterprise Social Networks

Although advertising and sales are the major EC activities in public social networks, there are emerging possibilities for commercial activities in business-oriented networks such as LinkedIn and in enterprise social networks.

USING TWITTER TO GET A PULSE OF THE MARKET   Twitter is a popular social networking site that enables friends to keep in touch and follow what others are saying. An analysis of "tweets" can be used to determine how well a product/service is doing in the market. Previous chapters on Web analytics included a significant coverage of social media analytics. This continues to grow in popularity and business use. Analysis of posts on social media sites such as Facebook and Twitter has become a major business. Many companies provide services to monitor and manage such posts on behalf of companies and individuals. One good example is **reputation.com**.

SECTION 14.5 REVIEW QUESTIONS

1. Define *Web 2.0.*

2. List the major characteristics of Web 2.0.

3. What new business model has emerged from Web 2.0?

4. Define *social network.*

5. List some major social network sites.

14.6 CLOUD COMPUTING AND BI

Another emerging technology trend that business intelligence users should be aware of is cloud computing. Wikipedia (**en.wikipedia.org/wiki/cloud_computing**) defines **cloud computing** as "a style of computing in which dynamically scalable and often virtualized resources are provided over the Internet. Users need not have knowledge of, experience in, or control over the technology infrastructures in the cloud that supports them." This definition is broad and comprehensive. In some ways, cloud computing is a new name for many previous, related trends: utility computing, application service provider, grid computing, on-demand computing, *software as a service* (SaaS), and even older, centralized computing with dumb terminals. But the term *cloud computing* originates from a reference to the Internet as a "cloud" and represents an evolution of all of the previously shared/centralized computing trends. The Wikipedia entry also recognizes that cloud computing is a combination of several information technology components as services. For example, *infrastructure as a service* (IaaS) refers to providing computing *platforms as a service* (PaaS), as well as all of the basic platform provisioning, such as management administration, security, and so on. It also includes SaaS, which includes applications to be delivered through a Web browser while the data and the application programs are on some other server.

Although we do not typically look at Web-based e-mail as an example of cloud computing, it can be considered a basic cloud application. Typically, the e-mail application stores the data (e-mail messages) and the software (e-mail programs that let us process and manage e-mails). The e-mail provider also supplies the hardware/software and all of the basic infrastructure. As long as the Internet is available, one can access the e-mail application from anywhere in the Internet cloud. When the application is updated by the e-mail provider (e.g., when Gmail updates its e-mail application), it becomes available to all the customers without them having to download any new programs. Thus, any Web-based general application is in a way an example of a cloud application. Another example of a general cloud application is Google Docs and Spreadsheets. This application allows a user to create text documents or spreadsheets that are stored on Google's servers and are available to the users anywhere they have access to the Internet. Again, no programs need to be installed, "the application is in the cloud." The storage space is also "in the cloud."

A very good general business example of cloud computing is Amazon.com's Web services. Amazon.com has developed an impressive technology infrastructure for e-commerce as well as for business intelligence, customer relationship management, and supply chain management. It has built major data centers to manage its own operations. However, through Amazon.com's cloud services, many other companies can employ these very same facilities to gain advantages of these technologies without having to make a similar investment. Like other cloud-computing services, a user can subscribe to any of the facilities on a pay-as-you-go basis. This model of letting someone else own the hardware and software but making use of the facilities on a pay-per-use basis is the cornerstone of cloud computing. A number of companies offer cloud-computing services, including Salesforce.com, IBM, Sun Microsystems, Microsoft (Azure), Google, and Yahoo!

Cloud computing, like many other IT trends, has resulted in new offerings in business intelligence. White (2008) and Trajman (2009) provided examples of BI offerings related to cloud computing. Trajman identified several companies offering cloud-based data warehouse options. These options permit an organization to scale up its data warehouse and pay only for what it uses. Companies offering such services include 1010data, LogiXML, and Lucid Era. These companies offer feature extract, transform, and load capabilities as well as advanced data analysis tools. These are examples of SaaS as well as *data as a service* (DaaS) offerings. Other companies, such as Elastra and Rightscale, offer dashboard and data management tools that follow the SaaS and DaaS models, but they also employ IaaS from other providers, such as Amazon.com or Go Grid. Thus, the end user of a cloud-based BI service may use one organization for analysis applications that, in turn, uses another firm for the platform or infrastructure.

The next several paragraphs summarize the latest trends in the interface of cloud computing and business intelligence/decision support systems. These are excerpted from a paper written by Haluk Demirkan and one of the co-authors of this book (Demirkan and Delen, 2013).

Service-oriented thinking is one of the fastest growing paradigms in today's economy. Most of the organizations have already built (or are in a process of building) decision support systems that support agile data, information, and analytics capabilities as services. Let's look at the implications of service-orientation on DSS. One of the main premises of service orientation is that service-oriented decision support systems will be developed with a component-based approach that is characterized by reusability (services can be reused in many workflows), substitutability (alternative services can be used), extensibility and scalability (ability to extend services and scale them, increase capabilities of individual services), customizability (ability to customize generic features, and composability—easy construction of more complex functional solutions using basic services), reliability, low cost of ownership, economy of scale, and so on.

In a service-oriented DSS environment, most of the services are provided with distributed collaborations. Various DSS services are produced by many partners, and consumed by end users for decision making. In the meantime, partners play the role of producer and consumer in a given time.

Service-Oriented DSS

In a SODSS environment, there are four major components: information technology as enabler, process as beneficiary, people as user, and organization as facilitator. Figure 14.2 illustrates a conceptual architecture of service-oriented DSS.

In service-oriented DSS solutions, operational systems (1), data warehouses (2), online analytic processing (3), and end-user components (4) can be individually or bundled provided to the users as service. Some of these components and their brief descriptions are listed in Table 14-1.

In the following subsections we provide brief descriptions of the three service models (i.e., data-as-a-service, information-as-a-service, and analytics-as-a-service) that underlie (as its foundational enablers) the service-oriented DSS.

Data-as-a-Service (DaaS)

In the service-oriented DSS environment (such as cloud environment), the concept of data-as-services basically advocates the view that—with the emergence of service-oriented business processes, architecture, and infrastructure, which includes standardized processes for accessing data "where it lives"—the actual platform on which the data resides doesn't matter (Dyche, 2011). Data can reside in a local computer or in a server at a server farm inside a cloud-computing environment. With data-as-a-service, any business

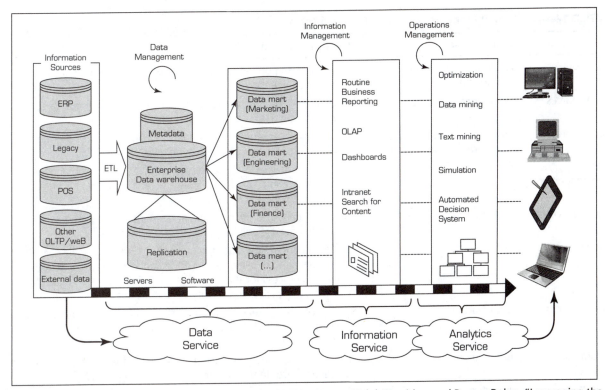

FIGURE 14.2 **Conceptual Architecture of Service-Oriented DSS.** *Source:* Haluk Demirkan and Dursun Delen, "Leveraging the Capabilities of Service-Oriented Decision Support Systems: Putting Analytics and Big Data in Cloud," *Decision Support Systems,* Vol. 55, No. 1, April 2013, pp. 412–421.

process can access data wherever it resides. Data-as-a-service began with the notion that data quality could happen in a centralized place, cleansing and enriching data and offering it to different systems, applications, or users, irrespective of where they were in the organization, computers, or on the network. This has now been replaced with master data management (MDM) and customer data integration (CDI) solutions, where the record of the customer (or product, or asset, etc.) may reside anywhere and is available as a service to any application that has the services allowing access to it. By applying a standard set of transformations to the various sources of data (for example, ensuring that gender fields containing different notation styles [e.g., M/F, Mr./Ms.] are all translated into male/female) and then enabling applications to access the data via open standards such as SQL, XQuery, and XML, service requestors can access the data regardless of vendor or system.

With DaaS, customers can move quickly thanks to the simplicity of the data access and the fact that they don't need extensive knowledge of the underlying data. If customers require a slightly different data structure or have location-specific requirements, the implementation is easy because the changes are minimal (agility). Second, providers can build the base with the data experts and outsource the presentation layer (which allows for very cost-effective user interfaces and makes change requests at the presentation layer much more feasible—cost-effectiveness), and access to the data is controlled through the data services, which tends to improve data quality because there is a single point for updates. Once those services are tested thoroughly, they only need to be regression tested if they remain unchanged for the next deployment (better data quality). Another important point is that DaaS platforms use NoSQL (sometimes expanded to "not only SQL"), which is a broad class of database management system that differs from classic relational database management systems (RDBMSs) in some significant ways. These data

TABLE 14-1   Major Components of Service-Oriented DSS

	Component	Brief Description
Data sources	Application programming interface	Mechanism to populate source systems with raw data and to pull operational reports.
Data sources	Operational transaction systems	Systems that run day-to-day business operations and provide source data for the data warehouse and DSS environment.
Data sources	Enterprise application integration/staging area	Provides an integrated common data interface and interchange mechanism for real-time and source systems.
Data management	Extract, transform, load (ETL)	The processes to extract, transform, cleanse, reengineer, and load source data into the data warehouse, and move data from one location to another.
Data services	Metadata management	Data that describes the meaning and structure of business data, as well as how it is created, accessed, and used.
Data services	Data warehouse	Subject-oriented, integrated, time-variant, and nonvolatile collection of summary and detailed data used to support the strategic decision-making process for the organization. This is also used for ad hoc and exploratory processing of very large data sets.
Data services	Data marts	Subset of data warehouse to support specific decision and analytical needs and provide business units more flexibility, control, and responsibility.
Information services	Information	Such as ad hoc query, reporting, OLAP, dashboards, intra- and Internet search for content, data, and information mashups.
Analytics services	Analytics	Such as optimization, data mining, text mining, simulation, automated decision system.
Information delivery to end users	Information delivery portals	Such as desktop, Web browser, portal, mobile devices, e-mail.
Information management	Information services with library and administrator	Optimizes the DSS environment use by organizing its capabilities and knowledge, and assimilating them into the business processes. Also includes search engines, index crawlers, content servers, categorization servers, application/content integration servers, application servers, etc.
Data management	Ongoing data management	Ongoing management of data within and across the environment (such as backup, aggregate, retrieve data from near-line and off-line storage).
Operations management	Operations and administration	Activities to ensure daily operations, and optimize to allow manageable growth (systems management, data acquisition management, service management, change management, scheduling, monitor, security, etc.).
Information sources	Internal and external databases	Databases and files.
Servers	Operations	Database, application, Web, network, security, etc.
Software	Operations	Applications, integration, analytics, portals, ETL, etc.

stores may not require fixed table schemas, usually avoid join operations, and typically scale horizontally (Stonebraker, 2010). Amazon offers such a service, called SimpleDB (**http://aws.amazon.com/simpledb**). Google's AppEngine (**http://code.google.com/appengine**) provides its DataStore API around BigTable. But apart from these two proprietary offerings, the current landscape is still open for prospective service providers.

Information-as-a-Service (Information on Demand) (IaaS)

The overall idea of IaaS is making information available quickly to people, processes, and applications across the business (agility). Such a system promises to eliminate silos of data that exist in systems and infrastructure today, to enable sharing real-time information for emerging apps, to hide complexity, and to increase availability with virtualization. The main idea is to bring together diverse sources, provide a "single version of the truth," make it available 24/7, and by doing so, reduce proliferating redundant data and the time it takes to build and deploy new information services. The IaaS paradigm aims to implement and sustain predictable qualities of service around information delivery at runtime and leverage and extend legacy information resources and infrastructure immediately through data and runtime virtualization, and thereby reduce ongoing development efforts. IaaS is a comprehensive strategy for the delivery of information obtained from information services, following a consistent approach using SOA infrastructure and/or Internet standards. Unlike enterprise information integration (EII), enterprise application integration (EAI), and extract, transform, and load (ETL) technologies, IaaS offers a flexible data integration platform based on a newer generation of service-oriented standards that enables ubiquitous access to any type of data, on any platform, using a wide range of interface and data access standards (Yuhanna, Gilpin, and Knoll, The Forrester Wave: Information-as-a-Service, Q1 2010, Forrester Research, 2010). Forrester Research names IaaS as Information Fabric and proposes a new, logical view to better characterize it. Two examples of such products are IBM's Web Sphere Information Integration and BEAs AquaLogic Data Services. These products can take the messy underlying data and present them as elemental services—for example, a service that presents a single view of a customer from the underlying data. These products can be used to enable real-time, integrated access to business information regardless of location or format by means of semantic integration. They also provide models-as-services (MaaS) to provide a collection of industry-specific business processes, reports, dashboards, and other service models for key industries (e.g., banking, insurance, and financial markets) to accelerate enterprise business initiatives for business process optimization and multi-channel transformation. They also provide master data management services (MDM) to enable the creation and management of multiform master data, provided as a service, for customer information across heterogeneous environments, content management services, and business intelligence services to perform powerful analysis from integrated data.

Analytics-as-a-Service (AaaS)

Analytics and data-based managerial solutions—the applications that query data for use in business planning, problem solving, and decision support—are evolving rapidly and being used by almost every organization. Gartner predicts that by 2013, 33 percent of BI functionality will be consumed via handheld devices; by 2014, 30 percent of analytic applications will use in-memory functions to add scale and computational speed, and will use proactive, predictive, and forecasting capabilities; and by 2014, 40 percent of spending on business analytics will go to system integrators, not software vendors (Tudor and Pettey, 2011).

The concept of analytics-as-a-service (AaaS)—by some referred to as Agile Analytics—is turning utility computing into a service model for analytics. AaaS is not limited to a single database or software; rather, it has the ability to turn a general-purpose analytical platform into a shared utility for an enterprise with the focus on virtualization of analytical services (Ratzesberger, 2011). With the needs of Enterprise Analytics growing rapidly, it is imperative that traditional hub-and-spoke architectures are not able to satisfy the demands driven by increasingly complex business analysis and analytics. New and improved architectures are needed to be able to process very large amounts of structured and unstructured data in a very short time to produce accurate and actionable results. The "analytics-as-a-service" model is already being facilitated by Amazon, MapReduce, Hadoop, Microsoft's Dryad/SCOPE, Opera Solutions, eBay, and others. For example, eBay employees access a virtual slice of the main data warehouse server where they can store and analyze their own data sets. eBay's virtual private data marts have been quite successful—hundreds have been created, with 50 to 100 in operation at any one time. They have eliminated the company's need for new physical data marts that cost an estimated $1 million apiece and require the full-time attention of several skilled employees to provision (Winter, 2008).

AaaS in the cloud has economies of scale and scope by providing many virtual analytical applications with better scalability and higher cost savings. With growing data volumes and dozens of virtual analytical applications, chances are that more of them leverage processing at different times, usage patterns, and frequencies (Kalakota, 2011). A number of database companies such as Teradata, Netezza, Greenplum, Oracle, IBM DB2, DATAllegro, Vertica, and AsterData that provide shared-nothing (scalable) database management applications are well-suited for AaaS in cloud deployment.

Data and text mining is another very promising application of AaaS. The capabilities that a service orientation (along with cloud computing, pooled resources, and parallel processing) brings to the analytic world are not limited to data/text mining. It can also be used for large-scale optimization, highly-complex multi-criteria decision problems, and distributed simulation models. These prescriptive analytics require highly capable systems that can only be realized using service-based collaborative systems that can utilize large-scale computational resources.

We also expect that there will be significant interest in conducting service science research on cloud computing in Big Data analysis. With Web 2.0, more than enough data has been collected by organizations. We are entering the "petabyte age," and traditional data and analytics approaches are beginning to show their limits. Cloud analytics is an emerging alternative solution for large-scale data analysis. Data-oriented cloud systems include storage and computing in a distributed and virtualized environment. These solutions also come with many challenges, such as security, service level, and data governance. Research is still limited in this area. As a result, there is ample opportunity to bring analytical, computational, and conceptual modeling into the context of service science, service orientation, and cloud intelligence.

These types of cloud-based offerings are continuing to grow in popularity. A major advantage of these offerings is the rapid diffusion of advanced analysis tools among the users, without significant investment in technology acquisition. However, a number of concerns have been raised about cloud computing, including loss of control and privacy, legal liabilities, cross-border political issues, and so on. Nonetheless, cloud computing is an important initiative for a BI professional to watch.

SECTION 14.6 REVIEW QUESTIONS

1. Define *cloud computing*. How does it relate to PaaS, SaaS, and IaaS?
2. Give examples of companies offering cloud services.
3. How does cloud computing affect business intelligence?
4. What are the three service models that provide the foundation to service-oriented DSS?
5. How does DaaS change the way data is handled?
6. What is MaaS? What does it offer to businesses?
7. Why is AaaS cost-effective?
8. Why is MapReduce mentioned in the context of Aaas?

14.7 IMPACTS OF ANALYTICS IN ORGANIZATIONS: AN OVERVIEW

Analytic systems are important factors in the information, Web, and knowledge revolution. This is a cultural transformation with which most people are only now coming to terms. Unlike the slower revolutions of the past, such as the Industrial Revolution, this revolution is taking place very quickly and affecting every facet of our lives. Inherent in this rapid transformation are a host of managerial, economic, and social issues.

Separating the impact of analytics from that of other computerized systems is a difficult task, especially because of the trend toward integrating, or even embedding, analytics with other computer-based information systems. Analytics can have both micro and macro implications. Such systems can affect particular individuals and jobs, and they can also affect the work structures of departments and units within an organization. They can also have significant long-term effects on total organizational structures, entire industries, communities, and society as a whole (i.e., a macro impact).

The impact of computers and analytics can be divided into three general categories: organizational, individual, and societal. In each of these, computers have had many impacts. We cannot possibly consider all of them in this section, so in the next paragraphs we touch upon topics we feel are most relevant to analytics.

New Organizational Units

One change in organizational structure is the possibility of creating an analytics department, a BI department, or a knowledge management department in which analytics play a major role. This special unit can be combined with or replace a quantitative analysis unit, · or it can be a completely new entity. Some large corporations have separate decision support units or departments. For example, many major banks have such departments in their financial services divisions. Many companies have small decision support or BI/data warehouse units. These types of departments are usually involved in training in addition to consulting and application development activities. Others have empowered a chief technology officer over BI, intelligent systems, and e-commerce applications. Companies such as Target and Walmart have major investments in such units, which are constantly analyzing their data to determine the efficiency of marketing and supply chain management by understanding their customer and supplier interactions.

Growth of the BI industry has resulted in the formation of new units within IT provider companies as well. For example, a few years back IBM formed a new business unit focused on analytics. This group includes units in business intelligence, optimization models, data mining, and business performance. As noted in Sections 14.2 and 14.3, the enormous growth of the app industry has created many opportunities for new companies that can employ analytics and deliver innovative applications in any specific domain.

There is also consolidation through acquisition of specialized software companies by major IT providers. For example, IBM acquired Demandtec, a revenue and promotion optimization software company, to build their offerings after having acquired SPSS for predictive analytics and ILOG to build their prescriptive analytics capabilities. Oracle acquired Hyperion some time back. Finally, there are also collaborations to enable companies to work cooperatively in some cases while also competing elsewhere. For example, SAS and Teradata announced a collaboration to let Teradata users develop BI applications using SAS analytical modeling capabilities. Teradata acquired Aster to enhance their Big Data offerings and Aprimo to add to their customer campaign management capabilities.

Section 14.9 describes the ecosystem of the analytics industry and recognizes the career paths available to analytics practitioners. It introduces many of the industry clusters, including those in user organizations.

Restructuring Business Processes and Virtual Teams

In many cases, it is necessary to restructure business processes before introducing new information technologies. For example, before IBM introduced e-procurement, it restructured all related business processes, including decision making, searching inventories, reordering, and shipping. When a company introduces a data warehouse and BI, the information flows and related business processes (e.g., order fulfillment) are likely to change. Such changes are often necessary for profitability, or even survival. Restructuring is especially necessary when major IT projects such as ERP or BI are undertaken. Sometimes an organization-wide, major restructuring is needed; then it is referred to as *reengineering*. Reengineering involves changes in structure, organizational culture, and processes. In a case in which an entire (or most of an) organization is involved, the process is referred to as **business process reengineering (BPR)**.

The Impacts of ADS Systems

As indicated in Chapter 1 and other chapters, ADS systems, such as those for pricing, scheduling, and inventory management, are spreading rapidly, especially in industries such as airlines, retailing, transportation, and banking. These systems will probably have the following impacts:

- Reduction of middle management
- Empowerment of customers and business partners
- Improved customer service (e.g., faster reply to requests)
- Increased productivity of help desks and call centers

The impact goes beyond one company or one supply chain, however. Entire industries are affected. The use of profitability models and optimization are reshaping retailing, real estate, banking, transportation, airlines, and car rental agencies, among other industries.

Job Satisfaction

Although many jobs may be substantially enriched by analytics, other jobs may become more routine and less satisfying. For example, more than 40 years ago, Argyris (1971) predicted that computer-based information systems would reduce managerial discretion in decision making and lead to managers being dissatisfied. In their study about ADS, Davenport and Harris (2005) found that employees using ADS systems, especially those who are empowered by the systems, were more satisfied with their jobs. If the routine and mundane work can be done using an analytic system, then it should free up the managers and knowledge workers to do more challenging tasks.

Job Stress and Anxiety

An increase in workload and/or responsibilities can trigger job stress. Although computerization has benefited organizations by increasing productivity, it has also created an ever-increasing and changing workload on some employees—many times brought on by downsizing and redistributing entire workloads of one employee to another. Some workers feel overwhelmed and begin to feel anxious about their jobs and their performance. These feelings of anxiety can adversely affect their productivity. Management must alleviate these feelings by redistributing the workload among workers or conducting appropriate training.

One of the negative impacts of the information age is information anxiety. This disquiet can take several forms, such as frustration with the inability to keep up with the amount of data present in our lives. Constant connectivity afforded through mobile devices, e-mail, and instant messaging creates its own challenges and stress. Research on e-mail response strategies (**iris.okstate.edu/REMS**) includes many examples of studies conducted to recognize such stress. Constant alerts about incoming e-mails lead to interruptions, which eventually result in loss of productivity (and then an increase in stress). Systems have been developed to provide decision support to determine how often a person should check his or her e-mail (see Gupta and Sharda, 2009).

Analytics' Impact on Managers' Activities and Their Performance

The most important task of managers is making decisions. Analytics can change the manner in which many decisions are made and can consequently change managers' jobs. Some of the most common areas are discussed next.

According to Perez-Cascante et al. (2002), an ES/DSS was found to improve the performance of both existing and new managers as well as other employees. It helped managers gain more knowledge, experience, and expertise, and it consequently enhanced the quality of their decision making. Many managers report that computers have finally given them time to get out of the office and into the field. (BI can save an hour a day for every user.) They have also found that they can spend more time planning activities instead of putting out fires because they can be alerted to potential problems well in advance, thanks to intelligent agents, ES, and other analytical tools.

Another aspect of the managerial challenge lies in the ability of analytics to support the decision-making process in general and strategic planning and control decisions in particular. Analytics could change the decision-making process and even decision-making styles. For example, information gathering for decision making is completed much more quickly when analytics are in use. Enterprise information systems are extremely useful in supporting strategic management (see Liu et al., 2002). Data, text, and Web mining technologies are now used to improve external environmental scanning of information. As a result, managers can change their approach to problem solving and improve on their decisions quickly. It is reported that Starbucks recently introduced a new coffee beverage and made the decision on pricing by trying several different prices and monitoring the social media feedback throughout the day. This implies that data collection methods for a manager could be drastically different now than in the past.

Research indicates that most managers tend to work on a large number of problems simultaneously, moving from one to another as they wait for more information on their current problem (see Mintzberg et al., 2002). Analytics technologies tend to reduce the time required to complete tasks in the decision-making process and eliminate some of the nonproductive waiting time by providing knowledge and information. Therefore, managers work on fewer tasks during each day but complete more of them. The reduction in start-up time associated with moving from task to task could be the most important source of increased managerial productivity.

Another possible impact of analytics on the manager's job could be a change in leadership requirements. What are now generally considered good leadership qualities may be significantly altered by the use of analytics. For example, face-to-face communication is frequently replaced by e-mail, wikis, and computerized conferencing; thus, leadership qualities attributed to physical appearance could become less important.

The following are some potential impacts of analytics on managers' jobs:

- Less expertise (experience) is required for making many decisions.
- Faster decision making is possible because of the availability of information and the automation of some phases in the decision-making process.
- Less reliance on experts and analysts is required to provide support to top executives; managers can do it by themselves with the help of intelligent systems.

- Power is being redistributed among managers. (The more information and analysis capability they possess, the more power they have.)
- Support for complex decisions makes them faster to make and be of better quality.
- Information needed for high-level decision making is expedited or even self-generated.
- Automation of routine decisions or phases in the decision-making process (e.g., for frontline decision making and using ADS) may eliminate some managers.

In general, it has been found that the job of middle managers is the most likely job to be automated. Midlevel managers make fairly routine decisions, which can be fully automated. Managers at lower levels do not spend much time on decision making. Instead, they supervise, train, and motivate nonmanagers. Some of their routine decisions, such as scheduling, can be automated; other decisions that involve behavioral aspects cannot. However, even if we completely automate their decisional role, we could not automate their jobs. The Web provides an opportunity to automate certain tasks done by frontline employees; this empowers them, thus reducing the workload of approving managers. The job of top managers is the least routine and therefore the most difficult to automate.

SECTION 14.7 REVIEW QUESTIONS

1. List the impacts of analytics on decision making.
2. List the impacts of analytics on other managerial tasks.
3. Describe new organizational units that are created because of analytics.
4. How can analytics affect restructuring of business processes?
5. Describe the impacts of ADS systems.
6. How can analytics affect job satisfaction?

14.8 ISSUES OF LEGALITY, PRIVACY, AND ETHICS

Several important legal, privacy, and ethical issues are related to analytics. Here we provide only representative examples and sources.

Legal Issues

The introduction of analytics may compound a host of legal issues already relevant to computer systems. For example, questions concerning liability for the actions of advice provided by intelligent machines are just beginning to be considered.

In addition to resolving disputes about the unexpected and possibly damaging results of some analytics, other complex issues may surface. For example, who is liable if an enterprise finds itself bankrupt as a result of using the advice of an analytic application? Will the enterprise itself be held responsible for not testing the system adequately before entrusting it with sensitive issues? Will auditing and accounting firms share the liability for failing to apply adequate auditing tests? Will the software developers of intelligent systems be jointly liable? Consider the following specific legal issues:

- What is the value of an expert opinion in court when the expertise is encoded in a computer?
- Who is liable for wrong advice (or information) provided by an intelligent application? For example, what happens if a physician accepts an incorrect diagnosis made by a computer and performs an act that results in the death of a patient?
- What happens if a manager enters an incorrect judgment value into an analytic application and the result is damage or a disaster?
- Who owns the knowledge in a knowledge base?
- Can management force experts to contribute their expertise?

Privacy

Privacy means different things to different people. In general, **privacy** is the right to be left alone and the right to be free from unreasonable personal intrusions. Privacy has long been a legal, ethical, and social issue in many countries. The right to privacy is recognized today in every state of the United States and by the federal government, either by statute or by common law. The definition of *privacy* can be interpreted quite broadly. However, the following two rules have been followed fairly closely in past court decisions: (1) The right of privacy is not absolute. Privacy must be balanced against the needs of society. (2) The public's right to know is superior to the individual's right to privacy. These two rules show why it is difficult, in some cases, to determine and enforce privacy regulations (see Peslak, 2005). Privacy issues online have specific characteristics and policies. One area where privacy may be jeopardized is discussed next. For privacy and security issues in the data warehouse environment, see Elson and LeClerc (2005).

COLLECTING INFORMATION ABOUT INDIVIDUALS The complexity of collecting, sorting, filing, and accessing information manually from numerous government agencies was, in many cases, a built-in protection against misuse of private information. It was simply too expensive, cumbersome, and complex to invade a person's privacy. The Internet, in combination with large-scale databases, has created an entirely new dimension of accessing and using data. The inherent power in systems that can access vast amounts of data can be used for the good of society. For example, by matching records with the aid of a computer, it is possible to eliminate or reduce fraud, crime, government mismanagement, tax evasion, welfare cheating, family-support filching, employment of illegal workers, and so on. However, what price must the individual pay in terms of loss of privacy so that the government can better apprehend criminals? The same is true on the corporate level. Private information about employees may aid in better decision making, but the employees' privacy may be affected. Similar issues are related to information about customers.

The implications for online privacy are significant. The USA PATRIOT Act also broadens the government's ability to access student information and personal financial information without any suspicion of wrongdoing by attesting that the information likely to be found is pertinent to an ongoing criminal investigation (see Electronic Privacy Information Center, 2005). Location information from devices has been used to locate victims as well as perpetrators in some cases, but at what point is the information not the property of the individual?

Two effective tools for collecting information about individuals are cookies and spyware. Single-sign-on facilities that let a user access various services from a provider are beginning to raise some of the same concerns as cookies. Such services (Google, Yahoo!, MSN) let consumers permanently enter a profile of information along with a password and use this information and password repeatedly to access services at multiple sites. Critics say that such services create the same opportunities as cookies to invade an individual's privacy.

The use of artificial intelligence technologies in the administration and enforcement of laws and regulations may increase public concern regarding privacy of information. These fears, generated by the perceived abilities of artificial intelligence, will have to be addressed at the outset of almost any artificial intelligence development effort.

MOBILE USER PRIVACY Many users are unaware of the private information being tracked through mobile PDA or cell phone use. For example, Sense Networks' models are built using data from cell phone companies that track each phone as it moves from one cell tower to another, from GPS-enabled devices that transmit users' locations, and from PDAs transmitting information at wifi hotspots. Sense Networks claims that it is extremely careful and protective of users' privacy, but it is interesting to note how much information is available through just the use of a single device.

HOMELAND SECURITY AND INDIVIDUAL PRIVACY Using analytics technologies such as mining and interpreting the content of telephone calls, taking photos of people in certain places and identifying them, and using scanners to view your personal belongings are considered by many to be an invasion of privacy. However, many people recognize that analytic tools are effective and efficient means to increase security, even though the privacy of many innocent people is compromised.

The U.S. government applies analytical technologies on a global scale in the war on terrorism. In the first year and a half after September 11, 2001, supermarket chains, home improvement stores, and other retailers voluntarily handed over massive amounts of customer records to federal law enforcement agencies, almost always in violation of their stated privacy policies. Many others responded to court orders for information, as required by law. The U.S. government has a right to gather corporate data under legislation passed after September 11, 2001. The FBI now mines enormous amounts of data, looking for activity that could indicate a terrorist plot or crime.

Privacy issues abound. Because the government is acquiring personal data to detect suspicious patterns of activity, there is the prospect of improper or illegal use of the data. Many see such gathering of data as a violation of citizens' freedoms and rights. They see the need for an oversight organization to "watch the watchers," to ensure that the Department of Homeland Security does not mindlessly acquire data. Instead, it should acquire only pertinent data and information that can be mined to identify patterns that potentially could lead to stopping terrorists' activities. This is not an easy task.

Recent Technology Issues in Privacy and Analytics

Most providers of Internet services such as Google, Facebook, Twitter, and others depend upon monetizing their users' actions. They do so in many different ways, but all of these approaches in the end amount to understanding a user's profile or preferences on the basis of their usage. With the growth of Internet users in general and mobile device users in particular, many companies have been founded to employ advanced analytics to develop profiles of users on the basis of their device usage, movement, and the contacts of the users. *The Wall Street Journal* has an excellent collection of articles titled "What They Know" (**wsj.com/wtk**). These articles are constantly updated to highlight the latest technology and privacy/ethical issues. Some of the companies that have been mentioned in this series include companies such as Rapleaf (**rapleaf. com**). Rapleaf claims to be able to provide a profile of a user by just knowing their e-mail address. Clearly, their technology enables them to gather significant information. Similar technology is also marketed by X+1 (**xplusone.com**). Another company that aims to identify devices on the basis of their usage is Bluecava (**bluecava.com**). All of these companies employ technologies such as clustering and association mining to develop profiles of users. Such analytics applications definitely raise thorny questions of privacy violation for the users. Of course, many of the analytics start-ups in this space claim to honor user privacy, but violations are often reported. For example, a recent story reported that Rapleaf was collecting unauthorized user information from Facebook users and was banned from Facebook. A column in *Time Magazine* by Joel Stein (2011) reports that an hour after he gave his e-mail address to a company that specializes in user information monitoring (**reputation.com**), they had already been able to discover his Social Security number. This number is a key to accessing much private information about a user and could lead to identity theft. So, violations of privacy create fears of criminal conduct based on user information. This area is a big concern overall and needs careful study. The book's Web site will constantly update new developments. *The Wall Street Journal* site "What They Know" is a resource that ought to be consulted periodically.

Another application area that combines organizational IT impact, Big Data, sensors, and privacy concerns is analyzing employee behaviors on the basis of data collected from sensors that the employees wear in a badge. One company **Sociometric Solutions** (**sociometricsolutions.com**) has reported several such applications of their sensor-embedded badges that the employees wear. These sensors track all movement of an employee. **Sociometric Solutions** has reportedly been able to assist companies in predicting which types of employees are likely to stay with the company or leave on the basis of these employees' interactions with other employees. For example, those employees who stay in their own cubicles are less likely to progress up the corporate ladder than those who move about and interact with other employees extensively. Similar data collection and analysis have helped other companies determine the size of conference rooms needed or even the office layout to maximize efficiency. This area is growing really fast and has resulted in another term—people analytics. Of course, this creates major privacy issues. Should the companies be able to monitor their employees this intrusively? Sociometric has reported that its analytics are only reported on an aggregate basis to their clients. No individual user data is shared. They have noted that some employers want to get individual employee data, but their contract explicitly prohibits this type of sharing. In any case, sensors are leading to another level of surveillance and analytics, which poses interesting privacy, legal, and ethical questions.

Ethics in Decision Making and Support

Several ethical issues are related to analytics. Representative ethical issues that could be of interest in analytics implementations include the following:

- Electronic surveillance
- Ethics in DSS design (see Chae et al., 2005)
- Software piracy
- Invasion of individuals' privacy
- Use of proprietary databases
- Use of intellectual property such as knowledge and expertise
- Exposure of employees to unsafe environments related to computers
- Computer accessibility for workers with disabilities
- Accuracy of data, information, and knowledge
- Protection of the rights of users
- Accessibility to information
- Use of corporate computers for non–work-related purposes
- How much decision making to delegate to computers

Personal values constitute a major factor in the issue of ethical decision making. The study of ethical issues is complex because of its multi-dimensionality. Therefore, it makes sense to develop frameworks to describe ethics processes and systems. Mason et al. (1995) explained how technology and innovation expand the size of the domain of ethics and discuss a model for ethical reasoning that involves four fundamental focusing questions: Who is the agent? What action was actually taken or is being contemplated? What are the results or consequences of the act? Is the result fair or just for all stakeholders? They also described a hierarchy of ethical reasoning in which each ethical judgment or action is based on rules and codes of ethics, which are based on principles, which in turn are grounded in ethical theory. For more on ethics in decision making, see Murali (2004).

SECTION 14.8 REVIEW QUESTIONS

1. List some legal issues of analytics.
2. Describe privacy concerns in analytics.

3. Explain privacy concerns on the Web.

4. List ethical issues in analytics.

14.9 AN OVERVIEW OF THE ANALYTICS ECOSYSTEM

So, you are excited about the potential of analytics, and want to join this growing industry. Who are the current players, and what do they do? Where might you fit in? The objective of this section is to identify various sectors of the analytics industry, provide a classification of different types of industry participants, and illustrate the types of opportunities that exist for analytics professionals. The section (indeed the book) concludes with some observations about the opportunities for professionals to move across these clusters.

First, we want to remind the reader about the three types of analytics introduced in Chapter 1 and described in detail in the intervening chapters: descriptive or reporting analytics, predictive analytics, and prescriptive or decision analytics. In the following sections we will assume that you already know these three categories of analytics.

Analytics Industry Clusters

This section is aimed at identifying various analytics industry players by grouping them into sectors. We note that the list of company names included is not exhaustive. These merely reflect our own awareness and mapping of companies' offerings in this space. Additionally, the mention of a company's name or its capability in one specific group does not mean that is the only activity/offering of that organization. We use these names simply to illustrate our descriptions of sectors. Many other organizations exist in this industry. Our goal is not to create a directory of players or their capabilities in each space, but to illustrate to the students that many different options exist for playing in the analytics industry. One can start in one sector and move to another role altogether. We will also see that many companies play in multiple sectors within the analytics industry and, thus, offer opportunities for movement within the field both horizontally and vertically.

Figure 14.3 illustrates our view of the analytics ecosystem. It includes nine key sectors or clusters in the analytics space. The first five clusters can be broadly termed technology providers. Their primary revenue comes from developing technology, solutions, and training to enable the user organizations employ these technologies in the most effective and efficient manner. The accelerators include academics and industry organizations whose goal is to assist both technology providers and users. We describe each of these next, briefly, and give some examples of players in each sector.

Data Infrastructure Providers

This group includes all of the major players in the data hardware and software industry. These organizations provide hardware and software targeted at providing the basic foundation for all data management solutions. Obvious examples of these would include all major hardware players that provide the infrastructure for database computing—IBM, Dell, HP, Oracle, and so forth. We would also include storage solution providers such as EMC and NetApp in this sector. Many companies provide both hardware and software platforms of their own (e.g., IBM, Oracle, and Teradata). On the other hand, many data solution providers offer database management systems that are hardware independent and can run on many platforms. Perhaps Microsoft's SQL Server family is the most common example of this. Specialized integrated software providers such as SAP also are in this family of companies. Because this group of companies is well known and represents

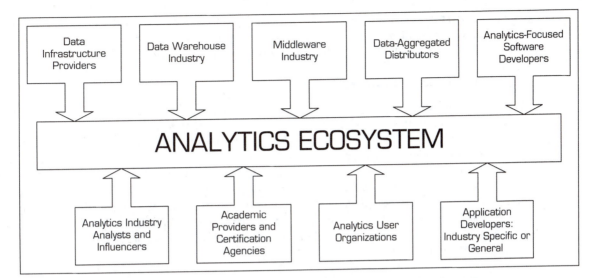

FIGURE 14.3   Analytic Industry Clusters.

a massive overall economic activity, we believe it is sufficient to recognize the key roles all these companies play. By inference, we also include all the other organizations that support each of these companies' ecosystems. These would include database appliance providers, service providers, integrators, and developers.

Several other companies are emerging as major players in a related space, thanks to the network infrastructure enabling cloud computing. Companies such as Amazon and **Salesforce.com** pioneered to offer full data storage (and more) solutions through the cloud. This has now been adopted by several of the players already identified.

Another group of companies that can be included here are the recent crop of companies in the Big Data space. Companies such as Cloudera, Hortonworks, and many others do not necessarily offer their own hardware but provide infrastructure services and training to create the Big Data platform. This would include Hadoop clusters, MapReduce, NoSQL, and other related technologies for analytics. Thus, they could also be grouped under industry consultants or trainers. We include them here because their role is aimed at enabling the basic infrastructure.

Bottom line, this group of companies provides the basic data and computing infrastructure that we take for granted in the practice of any analytics.

Data Warehouse Industry

We distinguish between this group and the preceding group mainly due to differences in their focus. Companies with data warehousing capabilities focus on providing integrated data from multiple sources so an organization can derive and deliver value from its data assets. Many companies in this space include their own hardware to provide efficient data storage, retrieval, and processing. Recent developments in this space include performing analytics on the data directly in memory. Companies such as IBM, Oracle, and Teradata are major players in this arena. Because this book includes links to Teradata University Network (TUN), we note that their platform software is available to TUN participants to explore data warehousing concepts (Chapter 3). In addition, all major players (EMC, IBM, Microsoft, Oracle, SAP, Teradata) have their own academic alliance programs through which much data warehousing software can be obtained so that students can develop familiarity and experience with the software. These companies clearly work with all the other sector players to provide data warehouse solutions and services within their ecosystem. Because players in this industry are covered extensively by technology media as well as textbooks and have their own ecosystems in many cases, we will just recognize them as a backbone of the analytics industry and move to other clusters.

Middleware Industry

Data warehousing began with the focus on bringing all the data stores into an enterprise-wide platform. By making sense of this data, it becomes an industry in itself. The general goal of this industry is to provide easy-to-use tools for reporting and analytics. Examples of companies in this space include MicroStrategy, Plum, and many others. A few of the major players that were independent middleware players have been acquired by companies in the first two groups. For example, Hyperion became a part of Oracle. SAP acquired Business Objects. IBM acquired Cognos. This segment is thus merging with other players or at least partnering with many others. In many ways, the focus of these companies has been to provide descriptive analytics and reports, identified as a core part of BI or analytics.

Data Aggregators/Distributors

Several companies realized the opportunity to develop specialized data collection, aggregation, and distribution mechanisms. These companies typically focus on a specific industry sector and build upon their existing relationships. For example, Nielsen provides data sources to their clients on retail purchase behavior. Another example is Experian, which includes data on each household in the United States. (Similar companies exist outside the United States, as well.) Omniture has developed technology to collect Web clicks and share such data with their clients. Comscore is another major company in this space. Google compiles data for individual Web sites and makes a summary available through Google Analytics services. There are hundreds of other companies that are developing niche platforms and services to collect, aggregate, and share such data with their clients.

Analytics-Focused Software Developers

Companies in this category have developed analytics software for general use with data that has been collected in a data warehouse or is available through one of the platforms identified earlier (including Big Data). It can also include inventors and researchers in universities and other organizations that have developed algorithms for specific types of analytics applications. We can identify major industry players in this space along the same lines as the three types of analytics outlined in Chapter 1.

Reporting/Analytics

As seen in Chapters 1 and 4, the focus of reporting analytics is on developing various types of reports, queries, and visualizations. These include general visualizations of data or dashboards presenting multiple performance reports in an easy-to-follow style. These are made possible by the tools available from the middleware industry players or unique capabilities offered by focused providers. For example, Microsoft's SQL Server BI toolkit includes reporting as well as predictive analytics capabilities. On the other hand, specialized software is available from companies such as Tableau for visualization. SAS also offers a visual snalytics tool for similar capacity. Both are linked through TUN. There are many open source visualization tools as well. Literally hundreds of data visualization tools have been developed around the world. Many such tools focus on visualization of data from a specific industry or domain. A Google search will show the latest list of such software providers and tools.

Predictive Analytics

Perhaps the biggest recent growth in analytics has been in this category. Many statistical software companies such as SAS and SPSS embraced predictive analytics early on and developed the software capabilities as well as industry practices to employ data mining techniques, as well as classical statistical techniques, for analytics. SPSS was purchased by IBM and now sells IBM SPSS Modeler. SAS sells its software called Enterprise Miner. Other players in this space include KXEN, Statsoft, Salford Systems, and scores of other companies that may sell their software broadly or use it for their own consulting practices (next group of companies).

Two open source platforms (R and RapidMiner) have also emerged as popular industrial-strength software tools for predictive analytics and have companies that support training and implementation of these open sources tools. A company called Alteryx uses R extensions for reporting and predictive analytics, but its strength is in delivery of analytics solutions processes to customers and other users. By sharing the analytics process stream in a gallery where other users can see what data processing and analytic steps were used to arrive at a result from multiple data sources, other users can understand the logic of the analysis, even change it, and share the updated process with other users if they so choose.

In addition, many companies have developed specialized software around a specific technique of data mining. A good example includes a company called Rulequest, which sells proprietary variants of decision tree software. Many neural network software companies such as NeuroDimensions would also fall under this category. It is important to note that such specific software implementations may also be part of the capability offered by general predictive analytics tools identified earlier. The number of companies focused on predictive analytics is so large that it would take several pages to identify even a partial set.

Prescriptive Analytics

Software providers in this category offer modeling tools and algorithms for optimization of operations. Such software is typically available as management science/operations research (MS/OR) software. The best source of information for such providers is through *OR/MS Today*, a publication of INFORMS. Online directories of software in various categories are available on their Web site at **orms-today.org**. This field has had its own set of major software providers. IBM, for example, has classic linear and mixed-integer programming software. IBM also acquired a company (ILOG) that provides prescriptive analysis software and services to complement their other offerings. Analytics providers such as SAS have their own OR/MS tools—SAS/OR. FICO acquired another company, XPRESS, that offers optimization software. Other major players in this domain include companies such as AIIMS, AMPL, Frontline, GAMS, Gurobi, Lindo Systems, Maximal, and many others. A detailed delineation and description of these companies' offerings is beyond the scope of our goals here. Suffice it to note that this industry sector has seen much growth recently.

Of course, many techniques fall under the category of prescriptive analytics. Each group has its own set of providers. For example, simulation software is a category in its own right. Major companies in this space include Rockwell (ARENA) and Simio, among others. Palisade provides tools that include many software categories. Similarly, Frontline offers tools for optimization with Excel spreadsheets as well as predictive analytics. Decision analysis in multiobjective settings can be performed using tools such as Expert Choice. There are also tools from companies such as Exsys, XpertRule, and others for generating rules directly from data or expert inputs.

Some new companies are evolving to combine multiple analytics models in the Big Data space. For example, Teradata Aster includes its own predictive and prescriptive analytics capabilities in processing Big Data streams. We believe there will be more opportunities for companies to develop specific applications that combine Big Data and optimization techniques.

As noted earlier, all three categories of analytics have a rich set of providers, offering the user a wide set of choices and capabilities. It is worthwhile to note again that these groups are not mutually exclusive. In most cases a provider can play in multiple components of analytics.

Application Developers or System Integrators: Industry Specific or General

The organizations in this group focus on using solutions available from the data infrastructure, data warehouse, middleware, data aggregators, and analytics software providers to develop custom solutions for a specific industry. They also use their analytics expertise to develop specific applications for a user. Thus, this industry group makes it possible for the analytics technology to be truly useful. Of course, such groups may also exist in specific user organizations. We discuss those next, but distinguish between the two because the latter group is responsible for analytics within an organization whereas these application developers work with a larger client base. This sector presents excellent opportunities for someone interested in broadening their analytics implementation experience across industries. Predictably, it also represents a large group, too numerous to identify. Most major analytics technology providers clearly recognize the opportunity to connect to a specific industry or client. Virtually every provider in any of the groups identified earlier includes a consulting practice to help their clients employ their tools. In many cases, revenue from such engagements may far exceed the technology license revenue. Companies such as IBM, SAS, Teradata, and most others identified earlier have significant consulting practices. They hire graduates of analytics programs to work on different client projects. In many cases the larger technology providers also run their own certification programs to ensure that the graduates and consultants are able to claim a certain amount of expertise in using their specific tools.

Companies that have traditionally provided application/data solutions to specific sectors have recognized the potential for the use of analytics and are developing industry-specific analytics offerings. For example, Cerner provides electronic medical records (EMR) solutions to medical providers. Their offerings now include many analytics reports and visualizations. This has now extended to providing athletic injury reports and management services to sports programs in college and professional sports. Similarly, IBM offers a fraud detection engine for the health insurance industry and is working with an insurance company to employ their famous Watson analytics platform (which is known to have won against humans in the popular TV game show *Jeopardy!*) in assisting medical providers and insurance companies with diagnosis and disease management. Another example of a vertical application provider is Sabre Technologies, which provides analytical solutions to the travel industry including fare pricing for revenue optimization, dispatch planning, and so forth.

This group also includes companies that have developed their own domain-specific analytics solutions and market them broadly to a client base. For example, Axiom has developed clusters for virtually all households in the United States based upon all the data they collect about households from many different sources. These cluster labels allow a client organization to target a marketing campaign more precisely. Several companies provide this type of service. Credit score and classification reporting companies (such as FICO and Experian) also belong in this group. Demandtec (a company now owned by IBM) provides pricing optimization solutions in the retail industry. They employ predictive analytics to forecast price-demand sensitivity and then recommend prices for thousands of products for retailers. Such analytics consultants and application providers are emerging to meet the needs of specific industries and represent an entrepreneurial opportunity to develop industry-specific applications. One area with many emerging start-ups is Web/social media/location analytics. By analyzing data available from Web clicks/smartphones/app uses, companies are trying to profile users and their interests to be better able to target promotional campaigns in real time. Examples of such companies and their activities include Sense Networks, which employs location data for developing user/group profiles; X+1 and Rapleaf, which profile users on the basis of e-mail usage; Bluecava, which aims to identify users through all device usage; and Simulmedia, which targets advertisements on TV on the basis of analysis of a user's TV-watching habits.

Another group of analytics application start-ups focuses on very specific analytics applications. For example, a popular smartphone app called Shazam is able to identify a song on the basis of the first few notes and then let the user select it from their song base to play/download/purchase. Voice-recognition tools such as Siri on iPhone and Google Now on Android are likely to create many more specialized analytics applications for very specific purposes in analytics applied to images, videos, audio, and other data that can be captured through smartphones and/or connected sensors.

This start-up activity and space is growing and in major transition due to technology/venture funding and security/privacy issues. Nevertheless, the application developer sector is perhaps the biggest growth industry within analytics at this point.

Analytics User Organizations

Clearly, this is the economic engine of the whole analytics industry. If there were no users, there would be no analytics industry. Organizations in every other industry, size, shape, and location are using analytics or exploring use of analytics in their operations. These include the private sector, government, education, and the military. It includes organizations around the world. Examples of uses of analytics in different industries abound. Others are exploring similar opportunities to try and gain/retain a competitive advantage. We will not identify specific companies in this section. Rather, the goal here is to see what types of roles analytics professionals can play within a user organization.

Of course, the top leadership of an organization is critically important in applying analytics to its operations. Reportedly, Forrest Mars of the Mars Chocolate Empire said that all management boiled down to applying mathematics to a company's operations and economics. Although not enough senior managers seem to subscribe to this view, the awareness of applying analytics within an organization is growing everywhere. Certainly the top leadership in information technology groups within a company (such as chief information officer) need to see this potential. For example, a health insurance company executive once told me that his boss (the CEO) viewed the company as an IT-enabled organization that collected money from insured members and distributed it to the providers. Thus, efficiency in this process was the premium they could earn over a competitor. This led the company to develop several analytics applications to reduce fraud and overpayment to providers and promote wellness among those insured so they would use the providers less often. Virtually all major organizations in every industry we are aware of are considering hiring analytical professionals. Titles of these professionals vary across industries. Table 14-2 includes selected titles of the MS graduates in our MIS program as well as graduates of our SAS Data Mining Certificate program (courtesy of Dr. G. Chakbraborty). This list indicates that most titles are indeed related to analytics. A "word cloud" of all of the titles of our analytics graduates, included in Figure 14-4, confirms the general results of these titles. It shows that analytics is already a popular title in the organizations hiring graduates of such programs.

TABLE 14-2 Selected Titles of Analytics Program Graduates

Advanced Analytics Math Modeler	Media Performance Analyst
Analytics Software Tester	Operation Research Analyst
Application Developer/Analyst	Operations Analyst
Associate Director, Strategy and Analytics	Predictive Modeler
Associate Innovation Leader	Principal Business Analyst
Bio Statistical Research Analyst	Principal Statistical Programmer
Business Analysis Manager	Procurement Analyst
Business Analyst	Project Analyst
Business Analytics Consultant	Project Manager
Business Data Analyst	Quantitative Analyst
Business Intelligence Analyst	Research Analyst
Business Intelligence Developer	Retail Analytics
Consultant Business Analytics	Risk Analyst—Client Risk and Collections
Credit Policy and Risk Analyst	SAS Business Analyst
Customer Analyst	SAS Data Analyst
Data Analyst	SAS Marketing Analyst
Data Mining Analyst	SAS Predictive Modeler
Data Mining Consultant	Senior Business Intelligence Analyst
Data Scientist	Senior Customer Intelligence Analyst
Decision Science Analyst	Senior Data Analyst
Decision Support Consultant	Senior Director of Analytics and Data Quality
ERP Business Analyst	Senior Manager of Data Warehouse, BI, and Analytics
Financial/Business Analyst	Senior Quantitative Marketing Analyst
Healthcare Analyst	Senior Strategic Marketing Analyst
Inventory Analyst	Senior Strategic Project Marketing Analyst
IT Business Analyst	Senior Marketing Database Analyst
Lead Analyst—Management Consulting Services	Senior Data Mining Analyst
Manager of Business Analytics	Senior Operations Analyst
Manager Risk Management	Senior Pricing Analyst
Manager, Client Analytics	Senior Strategic Marketing Analyst
Manager, Decision Support Analysis	Senior Strategy and Analytics Analyst
Manager, Global Customer Strategy and Analytics	Statistical Analyst
Manager, Modeling and Analytics	Strategic Business Analyst
Manager, Process Improvement, Global Operations	Strategic Database Analyst
Manager, Reporting and Analysis	Supply Chain Analyst
Managing Consultant	Supply Chain Planning Analyst
Marketing Analyst	Technical Analyst
Marketing Analytics Specialist	

FIGURE 14.4   Word Cloud of Titles of Analytics Program Graduates.

Of course, user organizations include career paths for analytics professionals moving into management positions. These titles include project managers, senior managers, directors … all the way up to chief information officer or chief executive officer. Our goal is here is to recognize that user organizations exist as a key cluster in the analytics ecosystem.

Analytics Industry Analysts and Influencers

The next cluster includes three types of organizations or professionals. The first group is the set of professional organizations that provides advice to analytics industry providers and users. Their services include marketing analyses, coverage of new developments, evaluation of specific technologies, and development of training/white papers, and so forth. Examples of such players include organizations such as the Gartner Group, The Data Warehousing Institute, and many of the general and technical publications and Web sites that cover the analytics industry. The second group includes professional societies or organizations that also provide some of the same services but are membership based and organized. For example, INFORMS, a professional organization, has now focused on promoting analytics. The Special Interest Group on Decision Support Systems (SIGDSS), a subgroup of the Association for Information Systems, also focuses on analytics. Most of the major vendors (e.g., Teradata and SAS) also have their own membership-based user groups. These entities promote the use of analytics and enable sharing of the lessons learned through their publications and conferences. They may also provide placement services.

A third group of analytics industry analysts is what we call analytics ambassadors, influencers, or evangelists. These folks have presented their enthusiasm for analytics through their seminars, books, and other publications. Illustrative examples include Steve Baker, Tom Davenport, Charles Duhigg, Wayne Eckerson, Bill Franks, Malcolm

Gladwell, Claudia Imhoff, Bill Inman, and many others. Again, the list is not inclusive. All of these ambassadors have written books (some of them bestsellers!) and/or given presentations to promote the analytics applications. Perhaps another group of evangelists to include here is the authors of textbooks on business intelligence/analytics (such as us, humbly) who aim to assist the next cluster to produce professionals for the analytics industry.

Academic Providers and Certification Agencies

In any knowledge-intensive industry such as analytics, the fundamental strength comes from having students who are interested in the technology and choose that industry as their profession. Universities play a key role in making this possible. This cluster, then, represents the academic programs that prepare professionals for the industry. It includes various components of business schools such as information systems, marketing, and management sciences. It also extends far beyond business schools to include computer science, statistics, mathematics, and industrial engineering departments across the world. The cluster also includes graphics developers who design new ways of visualizing information. Universities are offering undergraduate and graduate programs in analytics in all of these disciplines, though they may be labeled differently. A major growth frontier has been certificate programs in analytics to enable current professionals to retrain and retool themselves for analytics careers. Certificate programs enable practicing analysts to gain basic proficiency in specific software by taking a few critical courses. Power (2012) published a partial list of the graduate programs in analytics, but there are likely many more such programs, with new ones being added daily.

Another group of players assists with developing competency in analytics. These are certification programs to award a certificate of expertise in specific software. Virtually every major technology provider (IBM, Microsoft, MicroStrategy, Oracle, SAS, Teradata) has its own certification programs. These certificates ensure that potential new hires have a certain level of tool skills. On the other hand, INFORMS has just introduced a Certified Analytics Professional (CAP) certificate program that is aimed at testing an individual's general analytics competency. Any of these certifications give a college student additional marketable skills.

The growth of academic programs in analytics is staggering. Only time will tell if this cluster is overbuilding the capacity that can be consumed by the other eight clusters, but at this point the demand appears to outstrip the supply of qualified analytics graduates.

The purpose of this section has been to create a map of the landscape of the analytics industry. We identified nine different groups that play a key role in building and fostering this industry. It is possible for professionals to move from one industry cluster to another to take advantage of their skills. For example, expert professionals from providers can sometimes move to consulting positions, or directly to user organizations. Academics have provided consulting or have moved to industry. Overall, there is much to be excited about the analytics industry at this point.

SECTION 14.9 REVIEW QUESTIONS

1. Identify the nine clusters in the analytics ecosystem.
2. Which clusters represent technology developers?
3. Which clusters represent technology users?
4. Give examples of an analytics professional moving from one cluster to another.

Chapter Highlights

- Geospatial data can enhance analytics applications by incorporating location information.
- Real-time location information of users can be mined to develop promotion campaigns that are targeted at a specific user in real time.
- Location information from mobile phones and PDAs can be used to create profiles of user behavior and movement. Such location information can enable users to find other people with similar interests and advertisers to customize their promotions.
- Location-based analytics can also benefit consumers directly rather than just businesses. Mobile apps are being developed to enable such innovative analytics applications.
- Web 2.0 is about the innovative application of existing technologies. Web 2.0 has brought together the contributions of millions of people and has made their work, opinions, and identity matter.
- User-created content is a major characteristic of Web 2.0, as is the emergence of social networking.
- Large Internet communities enable the sharing of content, including text, videos, and photos, and promote online socialization and interaction.
- Business-oriented social networks concentrate on business issues both in one country and around the world (e.g., recruiting, finding business partners).

- Business-oriented social networks include LinkedIn and Xing.
- Cloud computing offers the possibility of using software, hardware, platform, and infrastructure, all on a service-subscription basis. Cloud computing enables a more scalable investment on the part of a user.
- Cloud-computing–based BI services offer organizations the latest technologies without significant upfront investment.
- Analytics can affect organizations in many ways, as stand-alone systems or integrated among themselves, or with other computer-based information systems.
- The impact of analytics on individuals varies; it can be positive, neutral, or negative.
- Serious legal issues may develop with the introduction of intelligent systems; liability and privacy are the dominant problem areas.
- Many positive social implications can be expected from analytics. These range from providing opportunities to disabled people to leading the fight against terrorism. Quality of life, both at work and at home, is likely to improve as a result of analytics. Of course, there are also negative issues to be concerned about.
- Analytics industry consists of many different types of stakeholders.

Key Terms

business process reengineering (BPR)
cloud computing
mobile social networking

privacy
reality mining
Web 2.0

Questions for Discussion

1. What are the potential benefits of using geospatial data in analytics? Give examples.
2. What type of new applications can emerge from knowing locations of users in real time? What if you also knew what they have in their shopping cart, for example?
3. How can consumers benefit from using analytics, especially based on location information?
4. "Location-tracking–based profiling (reality mining) is powerful but also poses privacy threats." Comment.

5. Is cloud computing "just an old wine in a new bottle"? How is it similar to other initiatives? How is it different?
6. Discuss the relationship between mobile devices and social networking.
7. Some say that analytics in general, and ES in particular, dehumanize managerial activities, and others say they do not. Discuss arguments for both points of view.
8. Diagnosing infections and prescribing pharmaceuticals are the weak points of many practicing physicians

(according to E. H. Shortliffe, one of the developers of MYCIN). It seems, therefore, that society would be better served if MYCIN (and other ES, see Chapter 11) were used extensively, but few physicians use ES. Answer the following questions:

a. Why do you think such systems are little used by physicians?

b. Assume that you are a hospital administrator whose physicians are salaried and report to you. What would you do to persuade them to use ES?

c. If the potential benefits to society are so great, can society do something that will increase doctors' use of such analytic systems?

9. Discuss the potential impacts of ADS systems on various types of employees and managers.

10. What are some of the major privacy concerns in employing analytics on mobile data?

11. How can one move from a technology provider cluster to a user cluster?

Exercises

Teradata University Network (TUN) and Other Hands-on Exercises

1. Go to **teradatauniversitynetwork.com** and search for case studies. Read the Continental Airlines cases written by Hugh Watson and his colleagues. What new applications can you imagine with the level of detailed data an airline can capture today.

2. Also review the Mycin case at **teradatauniversitynetwork.com**. What other similar applications can you envision?

3. At **teradatauniversitynetwork.com**, go to the podcasts library. Find podcasts of pervasive BI submitted by Hugh Watson. Summarize the points made by the speaker.

4. Go to **teradatauniversitynetwork.com** and search for BSI videos. Review these BSI videos and answer case questions related to them.

5. Location-tracking–based clustering provides the potential for personalized services but challenges for privacy. Divide the class in two parts to argue for and against such applications.

6. Identify ethical issues related to managerial decision making. Search the Internet, join chat rooms, and read articles from the Internet. Prepare a report on your findings.

7. Search the Internet to find examples of how intelligent systems (especially ES and intelligent agents) facilitate activities such as empowerment, mass customization, and teamwork.

8. Investigate the American Bar Association's Technology Resource Center (**abanet.org/tech/ltrc/techethics.html**) and **nolo.com**. What are the major legal and societal concerns and advances addressed there? How are they being dealt with?

9. Explore several sites related to healthcare (e.g., **WebMD.com, who.int**). Find issues related to analytics and privacy. Write a report on how these sites improve healthcare.

10. Go to **computerworld.com** and find five legal issues related to BI and analytics.

11. Enter **youtube.com**. Search for videos on cloud computing. Watch at least two. Summarize your findings.

12. Enter **pandora.com**. Find out how you can create and share music with friends. Why is this a Web 2.0 application?

13. Enter **mashable.com** and review the latest news regarding social networks and network strategy. Write a report.

14. Enter **sociometricsolutions.com**. Review various case studies and summarize one interesting application of sensors in understanding social exchanges in organizations.

15. The objective of the exercise is to familiarize you with the capabilities of smartphones to identify human activity. The data set is available at **archive.ics.uci.edu/ml/datasets/Human+Activity+Recognition+Using+Smartphones**

It contains accelerometer and gyroscope readings on 30 subjects who had the smartphone on their waist. The data is available in a raw format, and involves some data preparation efforts. Your objective is to identify and classify these readings into activities like walking, running, climbing, and such. More information on the data set is available on the download page. You may use clustering for initial exploration and gain an understanding on the data. You may use tools like R to prepare and analyze this data.

End-of-Chapter Application Case

Southern States Cooperative Optimizes Its Catalog Campaign

Southern States Cooperative is one of the largest farmer-owned cooperatives in the United States, with over 300,000 farmer members being served at over 1,200 retail locations across 23 states. It manufactures and purchases farm supplies like feed, seed, and fertilizer and distributes the products to farmers and other rural American customers.

Southern States Cooperative wanted to maintain and extend their success by better targeting the right customers in its direct-marketing campaigns. It realized the need to continually optimize marketing activities by gaining insights into its customers. Southern States employed Alteryx modeling tools, which enabled the company to solve the main business challenges of determining the right set of customers to be targeted for mailing the catalogs, choosing the right combination of storage keeping units (SKUs) to be included in the catalog, cutting down mailing costs, and increasing customer response, resulting in increased revenue generation, ultimately enabling it to provide better services to its customers.

SSC first built a predictive model to determine which catalogs the customer was most likely to prefer. The data for the analysis included Southern States' historical customer transaction data; the catalog data including the SKU information; farm-level data corresponding to the customers; and geocoded customer locations—as well as Southern States outlets. In performing the analysis, data from one year was analyzed on the basis of recency, frequency, and monetary value of customer transactions. In marketing, this type of analysis is commonly known as RFM analysis. The number of unique combinations of catalog SKUs and the customer purchase history of particular items in SKUs were used to predict the customers who were most likely to use the catalogs and the SKUs that ought to be included for the customers to respond to the catalogs. Preliminary exploratory analysis revealed that all the RFM measures and the measure of previous catalog SKU purchases had a diminishing marginal effect. As a result, these variables were natural-log transformed for logistic regression models. In addition to the logistic regression models, both a decision tree (based on a recursive partitioning algorithm) and a random forest model were also estimated using an estimation sample. The four different models (a "full" logistic regression model, a reduced version of the "full" logistic regression model based on the application of both forward and backward stepwise variable selection, the decision tree model, and the random forest model) were then compared using a validation sample via a gains (cumulative captured) response chart. A model using logistic regression was selected in which the most significant predictive factor was customers' past purchase of items contained in the catalog.

Based on the predictive modeling results, an incremental revenue model was built to estimate the effect of a customer's catalog use and the percentage revenues generated from the customer who used a particular catalog in a particular catalog period. Linear regression was the main technique applied in estimating the revenue per customer responding to the catalog. The model indicated that there was an additional 30 percent revenue per individual who used the catalog as compared to the non-catalog customers.

Furthermore, based on the results of the predictive model and the incremental revenue model, an optimization model was developed to maximize the total income from mailing the catalogs to customers. The optimization problem jointly maximizes the selection of catalog SKUs and customers to be sent the catalog, taking into account the expected response rate from mailing the catalog to specific customers and the expected profit margin in percentage from the purchases by that customer. It also considers the mailing cost. This formulation represents a constrained non-linear programming problem. This model was solved using genetic algorithms, aiming to maximize the combined selection of the catalog SKUs and the customers to whom the catalog should be sent to result in increased response, at the same time increasing the revenues and cutting down the mailing costs.

The Alteryx-based solution involved application of predictive analytics as well as prescriptive analytics techniques. The predictive model aimed to determine the customer's catalog use in purchasing selected items and then prescriptive analytics was applied to the results generated by predictive models to help the marketing department prepare the customized catalogs containing the SKUs that suited the targeted customer needs, resulting in better revenue generation.

From the model-based counterfactual analysis of the 2010 catalogs, the models quantified that the people who responded to the catalogs spent more in purchasing goods than those who had not used a catalog. The models indicated that in the year 2010, targeting the right customers with catalogs containing customized SKUs, Southern States Cooperative would have been able to reduce the number of catalogs sent by 63 percent, while improving the response rate by 34 percent, for an estimated incremental gross margin, less mailing cost, of $193,604—a 24 percent increase. The models were also applied toward the analysis of 2011 catalogs, and they estimated that with right combination and targeting of the 2011 catalogs, the total incremental gross margin would have been $206,812. With the insights derived from results of the historical data analysis, Southern States Cooperative is now planning to make use of these models in their future direct-mail marketing campaigns to target the right customers.

QUESTIONS FOR THE END-OF-CHAPTER APPLICATION CASE

1. What is main business problem faced by Southern States Cooperative?
2. How was predictive analytics applied in the application case?
3. What problems were solved by the optimization techniques employed by Southern States Cooperative?

What We Can Learn from This End-of-Chapter Application Case

Predictive models built on historical data can be used to help quantify the effects of new techniques employed, as part of a retrospective assessment that otherwise cannot be quantified. The quantified values are estimates, not hard numbers, but obtaining hard numbers simply isn't possible. Often in a real-world scenario, many business problems require application of more than one type of analytics solution. There is often a chain of actions associated in solving problems where each stage relies on the outputs of the previous stages. Valuable insights can be derived by application of each type of analytic technique, which can be further applied to reach the optimal solution. This application case illustrates a combination of predictive and prescriptive analytics where geospatial data also played a role in developing the initial model.

Sources: **Alteryx.com**, "Southern States Cooperative Case Study," and direct communication with Dr. Dan Putler, **alteryx.com/default/files/resources/files/case-study-southern-states.pdf** (accessed February 2013).

References

Alteryx.com. "Great Clips." **alteryx.com/sites/default/files/resources/files/case-study-great-chips.pdf** (accessed March 2013).

Alteryx.com. "Southern States Cooperative Case Study." Direct communication with Dr. Dan Putler. **alteryx.com/sites/default/files/resources/files/case-study-southern-states.pdf** (accessed February 2013).

Anandarajan, M. (2002). "Internet Abuse in the Workplace." *Communications of the ACM*, Vol. 45, No. 1, pp. 53–54.

Argyris, C. (1971). "Management Information Systems: The Challenge to Rationality and Emotionality." *Management Science*, Vol. 17, No. 6, pp. B-275.

Chae, B., D. B. Paradice, J. F. Courtney, and C. J. Cagle. (2005). "Incorporating an Ethical Perspective into Problem Formulation." *Decision Support Systems*, Vol. 40, No. 2, pp. 197–212.

Davenport, T. H., and J. G. Harris. (2005). "Automated Decision Making Comes of Age." *MIT Sloan Management Review*, Vol. 46, No. 4, p. 83.

Delen, D., B. Hardgrave, and R. Sharda. (2007). "RFID for Better Supply-Chain Management Through Enhanced Information Visibility." *Production and Operations Management,* Vol. 16, No. 5, pp. 613–624.

Dyche, J. (2011). "Data-as-a-Service, Explained and Defined." **searchdatamanagement.techtarget.com/answer/Data-as-a-service-explained-and-defined** (accessed March 2013).

Eagle, N., and A. Pentland. (2006). "Reality Mining: Sensing Complex Social Systems." *Personal and Ubiquitous Computing*, Vol. 10, No. 4, pp. 255–268.

Electronic Privacy Information Center. (2005). "USA PATRIOT Act." **epic.org/privacy/terrorism/usapatriot** (accessed March 2013).

Elson, R. J., and R. LeClerc. (2005). "Security and Privacy Concerns in the Data Warehouse Environment." *Business Intelligence Journal*, Vol. 10., No. 3, p. 51.

Emc.com. "Data Science Revealed: A Data-Driven Glimpse into the Burgeoning New Field." **emc.com/collateral/about/news/emc-data-science-study-wp.pdf** (accessed February 2013).

Fritzsche, D. (1995, November). "Personal Values: Potential Keys to Ethical Decision Making." *Journal of Business Ethics*, Vol. 14, No. 11.

Gnau, S. (2010). "Find Your Edge." *Teradata Magazine Special Edition Location Intelligence.* **teradata.com/articles/Teradata-Magazine-Special-Edition-Location-Intelligence-AR6270/?type=ART** (accessed March 2013).

Gupta, A., and R. Sharda. (2009). "SIMONE: A Simulator for Interruptions and Message Overload in Network Environments." *International Journal of Simulation and Process Modeling*, Vol. 4, Nos. 3/4, pp. 237–247.

Institute of Medicine of the National Academies. "Health Data Initiative Forum III: The Health Datapalooza." **iom.edu/Activities/PublicHealth/HealthData/2012-JUN-05/Afternoon-Apps-Demos/outside-100plus.aspx** (accessed February 2013).

IntellidentUtility.com. "OGE's Three-Tiered Architecture Aids Data Analysis." **intelligentutility.com/article/12/02/oges-three-tiered-architecture-aids-data-analysis&utm_medium=eNL&utm_campaign=IU_DAILY2&utm_term=Original-Magazine** (accessed March 2013).

Kalakota, R. (2011). "Analytics-as-a-Service: Understanding How **Amazon.com** Is Changing the Rules." **practicalanalytics.wordpress.com/2011/08/13/analytics-as-a-service-understanding-how-amazon-com-is-changing-the-rules** (accessed March 2013).

Krivda, C. D. (2010). "Pinpoint Opportunity." *Teradata Magazine Special Edition Location Intelligence.* **teradata.com/articles/Teradata-Magazine-Special-Edition-Location-Intelligence-AR6270/?type=ART** (accessed March 2013).

Liu, S., J. Carlsson, and S. Nummila. (2002, July). "Mobile E-Services: Creating Added Value for Working Mothers." *Proceedings DSI AGE 2002*, Cork, Ireland.

Mason, R. O., F. M. Mason, and M. J. Culnan. (1995). *Ethics of Information Management*. Thousand Oaks, CA: Sage.

Mintzberg, H., et al. (2002). *The Strategy Process,* 4th ed. Upper Saddle River, NJ: Prentice Hall.

Mobilemarketer.com. "Quiznos Sees 20pc Boost in Coupon Redemption via Location-Based Mobile Ad Campaign." **mobilemarketer.com/cms/news/advertising/14738.html** (accessed February 2013).

Murali, D. (2004). "Ethical Dilemmas in Decision Making." *BusinessLine*.

Ogepet.com. "Smart Hours." **ogepet.com/programs/smarthours.aspx** (accessed March 2013).

Perez-Cascante, L. P., M. Plaisent, L. Maguiraga, and P. Bernard. (2002). "The Impact of Expert Decision Support Systems on the Performance of New Employees." *Information Resources Management Journal*.

Peslak, A. P. (2005). "Internet Privacy Policies." *Information Resources Management Journal*.

Power, D. P. (2012). "What Universities Offer Master's Degrees in Analytics and Data Science?" **dssresources. com/faq/index.php?action=artikel&id=250** (accessed February 2013).

Ratzesberger, O. (2011). "Analytics as a Service." **xlmpp. com/articles/16-articles/39-analytics-as-a-service** (accessed September 2011).

Sensenetworks.com. "CabSense New York: The Smartest Way to Find a Cab." **sensenetworks.com/products/ macrosense-technology-platform/cabsense** (accessed February 2013).

Stein, J. "Data Mining: How Companies Now Know Everything About You." *Time Magazine.* **time.com/time/ magazine/article/0,9171,2058205,00.html** (accessed March 2013).

Stonebraker, M. (2010). "SQL Databases V. NoSQL Databases." *Communications of the ACM*, Vol. 53, No. 4, pp. 10–11.

Teradata.com. "Sabre Airline Solutions." **teradata.com/t/ case-studies/Sabre-Airline-Solutions-EB6281** (accessed March 2013).

Teradata.com. "Utilities Analytic Summit 2012 Oklahoma Gas & Electric." **teradata.com/video/Utilities-Analytic-Summit-2012-Oklahoma-Gas-and-Electric** (accessed March 2013).

Trajman, O. (2009, March). "Business Intelligence in the Clouds." *InfoManagement Direct.* **information-management.**

com/infodirect/2009_111/10015046-1.html (accessed July 2009).

Tudor, B., and C. Pettey. (2011, January 6). "Gartner Says New Relationships Will Change Business Intelligence and Analytics." *Gartner Research.*

Tynan, D. (2002, June). "How to Take Back Your Privacy (34 Steps)." *PC World.*

WallStreetJournal.com. (2010). "What They Know." **online. wsj.com/public/page/what-they-know-2010.html** (accessed March 2013).

Westholder, M. (2010). "Pinpoint Opportunity." *Teradata Magazine Special Edition Location Intelligence.* **teradata. com/articles/Teradata-Magazine-Special-Edition-Location-Intelligence-AR6270/?type=ART** (accessed March 2013).

White, C. (2008, July 30). "Business Intelligence in the Cloud: Sorting Out the Terminology." **BeyeNetwork.b-eye-network.com/channels/1138/view/8122** (accessed March 2013).

Winter, R. (2008). "E-Bay Turns to Analytics as a Service." **informationweek.com/news/software/info_ management/210800736** (accessed March 2013).

Yuhanna, N., M. Gilpin, and A. Knoll. (2010). "The Forrester Wave: Information-as-a-Service, Q1 2010." **forrester. com/rb/Research/wave%26trade%3B_information-as-a-service%2C_q1_2010/q/id/55204/t/2** (accessed March 2013).

GLOSSARY

active data warehousing *See* real-time data warehousing.

ad hoc DSS A DSS that deals with specific problems that are usually neither anticipated nor recurring.

ad hoc query A query that cannot be determined prior to the moment the query is issued.

agency The degree of autonomy vested in a software agent.

agent-based models A simulation modeling technique to support complex decision systems where a system or network is modeled as a set of autonomous decision-making units called agents that individually evaluate their situation and make decisions on the basis of a set of predefined behavior and interaction rules.

algorithm A step-by-step search in which improvement is made at every step until the best solution is found.

analog model An abstract, symbolic model of a system that behaves like the system but looks different.

analogical reasoning The process of determining the outcome of a problem by using analogies. It is a procedure for drawing conclusions about a problem by using past experience.

analytic hierarchy process (AHP) A modeling structure for representing *multi-criteria* (multiple goals, multiple objectives) *problems*—with sets of criteria and alternatives (choices)—commonly found in business environments.

analytical models Mathematical models into which data are loaded for analysis.

analytical techniques Methods that use mathematical formulas to derive an optimal solution directly or to predict a certain result, mainly in solving structured problems.

analytics The science of analysis—to use data for decision making.

application service provider (ASP) A software vendor that offers leased software applications to organizations.

Apriori algorithm The most commonly used algorithm to discover association rules by recursively identifying frequent itemsets.

area under the ROC curve A graphical assessment technique for binary classification models where the true positive rate is plotted on the *Y*-axis and the false positive rate is plotted on the *X*-axis.

artificial intelligence (AI) The subfield of computer science concerned with symbolic reasoning and problem solving.

artificial neural network (ANN) Computer technology that attempts to build computers that operate like a human brain. The machines possess simultaneous memory storage and work with ambiguous information. Sometimes called, simply, a *neural network. See* neural computing.

association A category of data mining algorithm that establishes relationships about items that occur together in a given record.

asynchronous Occurring at different times.

authoritative pages Web pages that are identified as particularly popular based on links by other Web pages and directories.

automated decision support (ADS) A rule-based system that provides a solution to a repetitive managerial problem. Also known as *enterprise decision management (EDM)*.

automated decision system (ADS) A business rule–based system that uses intelligence to recommend solutions to repetitive decisions (such as pricing).

autonomy The capability of a software agent acting on its own or being empowered.

axon An outgoing connection (i.e., terminal) from a biological neuron.

backpropagation The best-known learning algorithm in neural computing where the learning is done by comparing computed outputs to desired outputs of training cases.

backward chaining A search technique (based on if-then rules) used in production systems that begins with the action clause of a rule and works backward through a chain of rules in an attempt to find a verifiable set of condition clauses.

balanced scorecard (BSC) A performance measurement and management methodology that helps translate an organization's financial, customer, internal process, and learning and growth objectives and targets into a set of actionable initiatives.

best practices In an organization, the best methods for solving problems. These are often stored in the knowledge repository of a knowledge management system.

Big Data Data that exceeds the reach of commonly used hardware environments and/or capabilities of software tools to capture, manage, and process it within a tolerable time span.

blackboard An area of working memory set aside for the description of a current problem and for recording intermediate results in an expert system.

black-box testing Testing that involves comparing test results to actual results.

bootstrapping A sampling technique where a fixed number of instances from the original data is sampled (with replacement) for training and the rest of the data set is used for testing.

bot An intelligent software agent. Bot is an abbreviation of robot and is usually used as part of another term, such as knowbot, softbot, or shopbot.

business (or system) analyst An individual whose job is to analyze business processes and the support they receive (or need) from information technology.

business analytics (BA) The application of models directly to business data. Business analytics involve using DSS tools, especially models, in assisting decision makers. *See also* business intelligence (BI).

business intelligence (BI) A conceptual framework for decision support. It combines architecture, databases (or data warehouses), analytical tools, and applications.

business network A group of people who have some kind of commercial relationship; for example, sellers and buyers, buyers among themselves, buyers and suppliers, and colleagues and other colleagues.

business performance management (BPM) An advanced performance measurement and analysis approach that embraces planning and strategy.

business process reengineering (BPR) A methodology for introducing a fundamental change in specific business processes. BPR is usually supported by an information system.

case library The knowledge base of a case-based reasoning system.

case-based reasoning (CBR) A methodology in which knowledge or inferences are derived from historical cases.

categorical data Data that represent the labels of multiple classes used to divide a variable into specific groups.

causal loops A way for relating different factors in a system dynamics model to define evolution of relationships over time.

certainty A condition under which it is assumed that future values are known for sure and only one result is associated with an action.

certainty factors (CF) A popular technique for representing uncertainty in expert systems where the belief in an event (or a fact or a hypothesis) is expressed using the expert's unique assessment.

chief knowledge officer (CKO) The leader typically responsible for knowledge management activities and operations in an organization.

choice phase The third phase in decision making, in which an alternative is selected.

chromosome A candidate solution for a genetic algorithm.

classification Supervised induction used to analyze the historical data stored in a database and to automatically generate a model that can predict future behavior.

clickstream analysis The analysis of data that occur in the Web environment.

clickstream data Data that provide a trail of the user's activities and show the user's browsing patterns (e.g., which sites are visited, which pages, how long).

cloud computing Information technology infrastructure (hardware, software, applications, platform) that is available as a service, usually as virtualized resources.

clustering Partitioning a database into segments in which the members of a segment share similar qualities.

cognitive limits The limitations of the human mind related to processing information.

collaboration hub The central point of control for an e-market. A single collaboration hub (c-hub), representing one e-market owner, can host multiple collaboration spaces (c-spaces) in which trading partners use c-enablers to exchange data with the c-hub.

collaborative filtering A method for generating recommendations from user profiles. It uses preferences of other users with similar behavior to predict the preferences of a particular user.

collaborative planning, forecasting, and replenishment (CPFR) A project in which suppliers and retailers collaborate in their planning and demand forecasting to optimize the flow of materials along the supply chain.

community of practice (COP) A group of people in an organization with a common professional interest, often self-organized, for managing knowledge in a knowledge management system.

complexity A measure of how difficult a problem is in terms of its formulation for optimization, its required optimization effort, or its stochastic nature.

confidence In association rules, the conditional probability of finding the RHS of the rule present in a list of transactions where the LHS of the rule already exists.

connection weight The weight associated with each link in a neural network model. Neural networks learning algorithms assess connection weights.

consultation environment The part of an expert system that a non-expert uses to obtain expert knowledge and advice. It includes the workplace, inference engine, explanation facility, recommended action, and user interface.

content management system (CMS) An electronic document management system that produces dynamic versions of documents and automatically maintains the current set for use at the enterprise level.

content-based filtering A type of filtering that recommends items for a user based on the description of previously evaluated items and information available from the content (e.g., keywords).

corporate (enterprise) portal A gateway for entering a corporate Web site. A corporate portal enables communication, collaboration, and access to company information.

corpus In linguistics, a large and structured set of texts (now usually stored and processed electronically) prepared for the purpose of conducting knowledge discovery.

CRISP-DM A cross-industry standardized process of conducting data mining projects, which is a sequence of six steps that starts with a good understanding of the business and the need for the data mining project (i.e., the application domain) and ends with the deployment of the solution that satisfied the specific business need.

critical event processing (CEP) A method of capturing, tracking, and analyzing streams of data to detect certain events (out of normal happenings) that are worthy of the effort.

critical success factors (CSF) Key factors that delineate the things that an organization must excel at to be successful in its market space.

crossover The combination of parts of two superior solutions by a genetic algorithm in an attempt to produce an even better solution.

cube A subset of highly interrelated data that is organized to allow users to combine any attributes in a cube (e.g., stores, products, customers, suppliers) with any metrics in the cube (e.g., sales, profit, units, age) to create various two-dimensional views, or *slices*, that can be displayed on a computer screen.

customer experience management (CEM) Applications designed to report on the overall user experience by detecting Web application issues and problems, by tracking and resolving business process and usability obstacles, by reporting on site performance and availability, by enabling real-time alerting and monitoring, and by supporting deep-diagnosis of observed visitor behavior.

dashboard A visual presentation of critical data for executives to view. It allows executives to see hot spots in seconds and explore the situation.

data Raw facts that are meaningless by themselves (e.g., names, numbers).

data cube A two-dimensional, three-dimensional, or higher-dimensional object in which each dimension of the data represents a measure of interest.

data integration Integration that comprises three major processes: data access, data federation, and change capture. When these three processes are correctly implemented, data can be accessed and made accessible to an array of ETL, analysis tools, and data warehousing environments.

data integrity A part of data quality where the accuracy of the data (as a whole) is maintained during any operation (such as transfer, storage, or retrieval).

data mart A departmental data warehouse that stores only relevant data.

data mining A process that uses statistical, mathematical, artificial intelligence, and machine-learning techniques to extract and identify useful information and subsequent knowledge from large databases.

data quality (DQ) The holistic quality of data, including their accuracy, precision, completeness, and relevance.

data scientist A new role or a job commonly associated with Big Data or data science.

data stream mining The process of extracting novel patterns and knowledge structures from continuously streaming data records. *See* stream analytics.

data visualization A graphical, animation, or video presentation of data and the results of data analysis.

data warehouse (DW) A physical repository where relational data are specially organized to provide enterprise-wide, cleansed data in a standardized format.

data warehouse administrator (DWA) A person responsible for the administration and management of a data warehouse.

database A collection of files that are viewed as a single storage concept. The data are then available to a wide range of users.

database management system (DBMS) Software for establishing, updating, and querying (e.g., managing) a database.

deception detection A way of identifying deception (intentionally propagating beliefs that are not true) in voice, text, and/or body language of humans.

decision analysis Methods for determining the solution to a problem, typically when it is inappropriate to use iterative algorithms.

decision automation systems Computer systems that are aimed at building rule-oriented decision modules.

decision making The action of selecting among alternatives.

decision room An arrangement for a group support system in which PCs are available to some or all participants. The objective is to enhance groupwork.

decision style The manner in which a decision maker thinks and reacts to problems. It includes perceptions, cognitive responses, values, and beliefs.

decision support systems (DSS) A conceptual framework for a process of supporting managerial decision making, usually by modeling problems and employing quantitative models for solution analysis.

decision tables Information and knowledge conveniently organized in a systematic, tabular manner, often prepared for further analysis.

decision tree A graphical presentation of a sequence of interrelated decisions to be made under assumed risk. This technique classifies specific entities into particular classes based upon the features of the entities; a root is followed by internal nodes, each node (including root) is labeled with a question, and arcs associated with each node cover all possible responses.

decision variable A variable in a model that can be changed and manipulated by the decision maker. Decision variables correspond to the decisions to be made, such as quantity to produce, amounts of resources to allocate, etc.

defuzzification The process of creating a crisp solution from a fuzzy logic solution.

Delphi method A qualitative forecasting methodology that uses anonymous questionnaires. It is effective for technological forecasting and for forecasting involving sensitive issues.

demographic filtering A type of filtering that uses the demographic data of a user to determine which items may be appropriate for recommendation.

dendrite The part of a biological neuron that provides inputs to the cell.

dependent data mart A subset that is created directly from a data warehouse.

descriptive model A model that describes things as they are.

design phase The second decision-making phase, which involves finding possible alternatives in decision making and assessing their contributions.

development environment The part of an expert system that a builder uses. It includes the knowledge base and the inference engine, and it involves knowledge acquisition and improvement of reasoning capability. The knowledge engineer and the expert are considered part of the environment.

diagnostic control system A cybernetic system that has inputs, a process for transforming the inputs into outputs, a standard or benchmark against which to compare the outputs, and a feedback channel to allow information on variances between the outputs and the standard to be communicated and acted on.

dimensional modeling A retrieval-based system that supports high-volume query access.

directory A catalog of all the data in a database or all the models in a model base.

discovery-driven data mining A form of data mining that finds patterns, associations, and relationships among data in order to uncover facts that were previously unknown or not even contemplated by an organization.

discrete event simulation Building a model of a system where the interaction between different entities is studied. The simplest example of this is a shop consisting of a server and customers.

distance measure A method used to calculate the closeness between pairs of items in most cluster analysis methods. Popular distance measures include Euclidian distance (the ordinary distance between two points that one would measure with a ruler) and Manhattan distance (also called the rectilinear distance, or taxicab distance, between two points).

distributed artificial intelligence (DAI) A multiple-agent system for problem solving. DAI involves splitting a problem into multiple cooperating systems to derive a solution.

DMAIC A closed-loop business improvement model that includes these steps: defining, measuring, analyzing, improving, and controlling a process.

document management systems (DMS) Information systems (e.g., hardware, software) that allow the flow, storage, retrieval, and use of digitized documents.

drill-down The investigation of information in detail (e.g., finding not only total sales but also sales by region, by product, or by salesperson). Finding the detailed sources.

DSS application A DSS program built for a specific purpose (e.g., a scheduling system for a specific company).

dynamic models Models whose input data are changed over time (e.g., a 5-year profit or loss projection).

effectiveness The degree of goal attainment. Doing the right things.

efficiency The ratio of output to input. Appropriate use of resources. Doing things right.

electronic brainstorming A computer-supported methodology of idea generation by association. This group process uses analogy and synergy.

electronic document management (EDM) A method for processing documents electronically, including capture, storage, retrieval, manipulation, and presentation.

electronic meeting systems (EMS) An information technology–based environment that supports group meetings (groupware), which may be distributed geographically and temporally.

elitism A concept in genetic algorithms where some of the better solutions are migrated to the next generation in order to preserve the best solution.

end-user computing Development of one's own information system. Also known as *end-user development*.

Enterprise 2.0 Technologies and business practices that free the workforce from the constraints of legacy communication and productivity tools such as e-mail. Provides business managers with access to the right information at the right time through a Web of interconnected applications, services, and devices.

enterprise application integration (EAI) A technology that provides a vehicle for pushing data from source systems into a data warehouse.

enterprise data warehouse (EDW) An organizational-level data warehouse developed for analytical purposes.

enterprise decision management (EDM) *See* automated decision support (ADS).

enterprise information integration (EII) An evolving tool space that promises real-time data integration from a variety of sources, such as relational databases, Web services, and multidimensional databases.

enterprise knowledge portal (EKP) An electronic doorway into a knowledge management system.

enterprise-wide collaboration system A group support system that supports an entire enterprise.

entropy A metric that measures the extent of uncertainty or randomness in a data set. If all the data in a subset belong to just one class, then there is no uncertainty or randomness in that data set, and therefore the entropy is zero.

environmental scanning and analysis A process that involves conducting a search for and an analysis of information in external databases and flows of information.

evolutionary algorithm A class of heuristic-based optimization algorithms modeled after the natural process of biological evolution, such as genetic algorithms and genetic programming.

expert A human being who has developed a high level of proficiency in making judgments in a specific, usually narrow, domain.

expert location system An interactive computerized system that helps employees find and connect with colleagues who have expertise required for specific problems—whether they are across the county or across the room—in order to solve specific, critical business problems in seconds.

expert system (ES) A computer system that applies reasoning methodologies to knowledge in a specific domain to render advice or recommendations, much like a human expert. An ES is a computer system that achieves a high level of performance in task areas that, for human beings, require years of special education and training.

expert system (ES) shell A computer program that facilitates relatively easy implementation of a specific expert system. Analogous to a DSS generator.

expert tool user A person who is skilled in the application of one or more types of specialized problem-solving tools.

expertise The set of capabilities that underlines the performance of human experts, including extensive domain knowledge, heuristic rules that simplify and improve approaches to problem solving, metaknowledge and metacognition, and compiled forms of behavior that afford great economy in a skilled performance.

explanation subsystem The component of an expert system that can explain the system's reasoning and justify its conclusions.

explanation-based learning A machine-learning approach that assumes that there is enough existing theory to rationalize why one instance is or is not a prototypical member of a class.

explicit knowledge Knowledge that deals with objective, rational, and technical material (e.g., data, policies, procedures, software, documents). Also known as *leaky knowledge*.

extraction The process of capturing data from several sources, synthesizing them, summarizing them, determining which of them are relevant, and organizing them, resulting in their effective integration.

extraction, transformation, and load (ETL) A data warehousing process that consists of extraction (i.e., reading data from a database), transformation (i.e., converting the extracted data from its previous form into the form in which it needs to be so that it can be placed into a data warehouse or simply another database), and load (i.e., putting the data into the data warehouse).

facilitator (in a GSS) A person who plans, organizes, and electronically controls a group in a collaborative computing environment.

forecasting Predicting the future.

forward chaining A data-driven search in a rule-based system.

functional integration The provision of different support functions as a single system through a single, consistent interface.

fuzzification A process that converts an accurate number into a fuzzy description, such as converting from an exact age into categories such as young and old.

fuzzy logic A logically consistent way of reasoning that can cope with uncertain or partial information. Fuzzy logic is characteristic of human thinking and expert systems.

fuzzy set A set theory approach in which set membership is less precise than having objects strictly in or out of the set.

genetic algorithm A software program that learns in an evolutionary manner, similar to the way biological systems evolve.

geographic information system (GIS) An information system capable of integrating, editing, analyzing, sharing, and displaying geographically referenced information.

Gini index A metric that is used in economics to measure the diversity of the population. The same concept can be used to determine the purity of a specific class as a result of a decision to branch along a particular attribute/variable.

global positioning systems (GPS) Wireless devices that use satellites to enable users to detect the position on earth of items (e.g., cars or people) the devices are attached to, with reasonable precision.

goal seeking Analyzing a model (usually in spreadsheets) to determine the level an independent variable should take in order to achieve a specific level/value of a goal variable.

grain A definition of the highest level of detail that is supported in a data warehouse.

graphical user interface (GUI) An interactive, user-friendly interface in which, by using icons and similar objects, the user can control communication with a computer.

group decision support system (GDSS) An interactive computer-based system that facilitates the solution of semistructured and unstructured problems by a group of decision makers.

group support system (GSS) Information system, specifically DSS, that supports the collaborative work of groups.

group work Any work being performed by more than one person.

groupthink In a meeting, continual reinforcement of an idea by group members.

groupware Computerized technologies and methods that aim to support the work of people working in groups.

groupwork Any work being performed by more than one person.

Hadoop An open source framework for processing, storing, and analyzing massive amounts of distributed, unstructured data.

heuristic programming The use of heuristics in problem solving.

heuristics Informal, judgmental knowledge of an application area that constitutes the rules of good judgment in the field. Heuristics also encompasses the knowledge of how to solve problems efficiently and effectively, how to plan steps in solving a complex problem, how to improve performance, and so forth.

hidden layer The middle layer of an artificial neural network that has three or more layers.

Hive A Hadoop-based data warehousing–like framework originally developed by Facebook.

hub One or more Web pages that provide a collection of links to authoritative pages.

hybrid (integrated) computer system Different but integrated computer support systems used together in one decision-making situation.

hyperlink-induced topic search (HITS) The most popular publicly known and referenced algorithm in Web mining used to discover hubs and authorities.

hyperplane A geometric concept commonly used to describe the separation surface between different classes of things within a multidimensional space.

hypothesis-driven data mining A form of data mining that begins with a proposition by the user, who then seeks to validate the truthfulness of the proposition.

IBM SPSS Modeler A very popular, commercially available, comprehensive data, text, and Web mining software suite developed by SPSS (formerly Clementine).

iconic model A scaled physical replica.

idea generation The process by which people generate ideas, usually supported by software (e.g., developing alternative solutions to a problem). Also known as *brainstorming*.

implementation phase The fourth decision-making phase, involving actually putting a recommended solution to work.

independent data mart A small data warehouse designed for a strategic business unit or a department.

inductive learning A machine-learning approach in which rules are inferred from facts or data.

inference engine The part of an expert system that actually performs the reasoning function.

influence diagram A diagram that shows the various types of variables in a problem (e.g., decision, independent, result) and how they are related to each other.

influences rules In expert systems, a collection of if-then rules that govern the processing of knowledge rules acting as a critical part of the inferencing mechanism.

information Data organized in a meaningful way.

information gain The splitting mechanism used in ID3 (a popular decision-tree algorithm).

information overload An excessive amount of information being provided, making processing and absorbing tasks very difficult for the individual.

institutional DSS A DSS that is a permanent fixture in an organization and has continuing financial support. It deals with decisions of a recurring nature.

integrated intelligent systems A synergistic combination (or hybridization) of two or more systems to solve complex decision problems.

intellectual capital The know-how of an organization. Intellectual capital often includes the knowledge that employees possess.

intelligence A degree of reasoning and learned behavior, usually task or problem-solving oriented.

intelligence phase The initial phase of problem definition in decision making.

intelligent agent (IA) An expert or knowledge-based system embedded in computer-based information systems (or their components) to make them smarter.

intelligent computer-aided instruction (ICAI) The use of AI techniques for training or teaching with a computer.

intelligent database A database management system exhibiting artificial intelligence features that assist the user or designer; often includes ES and intelligent agents.

intelligent tutoring system (ITS) Self-tutoring systems that can guide learners in how best to proceed with the learning process.

interactivity A characteristic of software agents that allows them to interact (communicate and/or collaborate) with each other without having to rely on human intervention.

intermediary A person who uses a computer to fulfill requests made by other people (e.g., a financial analyst who uses a computer to answer questions for top management).

intermediate result variable A variable that contains the values of intermediate outcomes in mathematical models.

Internet telephony *See* Voice over IP (VoIP).

interval data Variables that can be measured on interval scales.

inverse document frequency A common and very useful transformation of indices in a term-by-document matrix that reflects both the specificity of words (document frequencies) as well as the overall frequencies of their occurrences (term frequencies).

iterative design A systematic process for system development that is used in management support systems (MSS). Iterative design involves producing a first version of MSS, revising it, producing a second design version, and so on.

kernel methods A class of algorithms for pattern analysis that approaches the problem by mapping highly nonlinear data into a high dimensional feature space, where the data items are transformed into a set of points in a Euclidean space for better modeling.

kernel trick In machine learning, a method for using a linear classifier algorithm to solve a nonlinear problem by mapping the original nonlinear observations onto a higher-dimensional space, where the linear classifier is subsequently used; this makes a linear classification in the new space equivalent to nonlinear classification in the original space.

kernel type In kernel trick, a type of transformation algorithm used to represent data items in a Euclidean space. The most commonly used kernel type is the radial basis function.

key performance indicator (KPI) Measure of performance against a strategic objective and goal.

k-fold cross-validation A popular accuracy assessment technique for prediction models where the complete data set is randomly split into k mutually exclusive subsets of approximately equal size. The classification model is trained and tested k times. Each time it is trained on all but one fold and then tested on the remaining single fold. The cross-validation estimate of the overall accuracy of a model is calculated by simply averaging the k individual accuracy measures.

k-nearest neighbor (k-NN) A prediction method for classification as well as regression type prediction problems where the prediction is made based on the similarity to k neighbors.

knowledge Understanding, awareness, or familiarity acquired through education or experience; anything that has been learned, perceived, discovered, inferred, or understood; the ability to use information. In a knowledge management system, knowledge is information in action.

knowledge acquisition The extraction and formulation of knowledge derived from various sources, especially from experts.

knowledge audit The process of identifying the knowledge an organization has, who has it, and how it flows (or does not) through the enterprise.

knowledge base A collection of facts, rules, and procedures organized into schemas. A knowledge base is the assembly of all the information and knowledge about a specific field of interest.

knowledge discovery in databases (KDD) A machine-learning process that performs rule induction or a related procedure to establish knowledge from large databases.

knowledge engineer An artificial intelligence specialist responsible for the technical side of developing an expert system. The knowledge engineer works closely with the domain expert to capture the expert's knowledge in a knowledge base.

knowledge engineering The engineering discipline in which knowledge is integrated into computer systems to solve complex problems that normally require a high level of human expertise.

knowledge management The active management of the expertise in an organization. It involves collecting, categorizing, and disseminating knowledge.

knowledge management system (KMS) A system that facilitates knowledge management by ensuring knowledge flow from the person(s) who knows to the person(s) who needs to know throughout the organization; knowledge evolves and grows during the process.

knowledge repository The actual storage location of knowledge in a knowledge management system. A knowledge repository is similar in nature to a database but is generally text oriented.

knowledge rules A collection of if-then rules that represents the deep knowledge about a specific problem.

knowledge-based economy The modern, global economy, which is driven by what people and organizations know rather than only by capital and labor. An economy based on intellectual assets.

knowledge-based system (KBS) Typically, a rule-based system for providing expertise. A KBS is identical to an expert system, except that the source of expertise may include documented knowledge.

knowledge-refining system A system that is capable of analyzing its own performance, learning, and improving itself for future consultations.

knowware Technology tools that support knowledge management.

Kohonen self-organizing feature map A type of neural network model for machine learning.

leaky knowledge *See* explicit knowledge.

lean manufacturing Production methodology focused on the elimination of waste or non-value-added features in a process.

learning A process of self-improvement where the new knowledge is obtained through a process by using what is already known.

learning algorithm The training procedure used by an artificial neural network.

learning organization An organization that is capable of learning from its past experience, implying the existence of an organizational memory and a means to save, represent, and share it through its personnel.

learning rate A parameter for learning in neural networks. It determines the portion of the existing discrepancy that must be offset.

linear programming (LP) A mathematical model for the optimal solution of resource allocation problems. All the relationships among the variables in this type of model are linear.

linguistic cues A collection of numerical measures extracted from the textual content using linguistic rules and theories.

link analysis The linkage among many objects of interest is discovered automatically, such as the link between Web pages and referential relationships among groups of academic publication authors.

literature mining A popular application area for text mining where a large collection of literature (articles, abstracts, book excerpts, and commentaries) in a specific area is processed using semiautomated methods in order to discover novel patterns.

machine learning The process by which a computer learns from experience (e.g., using programs that can learn from historical cases).

management science (MS) The application of a scientific approach and mathematical models to the analysis and solution of managerial decision situations (e.g., problems, opportunities). Also known as *operations research* (OR).

management support system (MSS) A system that applies any type of decision support tool or technique to managerial decision making.

MapReduce A technique to distribute the processing of very large multi-structured data files across a large cluster of machines.

mathematical (quantitative) model A system of symbols and expressions that represent a real situation.

mathematical programming An optimization technique for the allocation of resources, subject to constraints.

maturity model A formal depiction of critical dimensions and their competency levels of a business practice.

mental model The mechanisms or images through which a human mind performs sense-making in decision making.

metadata Data about data. In a data warehouse, metadata describe the contents of a data warehouse and the manner of its use.

metasearch engine A search engine that combines results from several different search engines.

middleware Software that links application modules from different computer languages and platforms.

mobile agent An intelligent software agent that moves across different system architectures and platforms or from one Internet site to another, retrieving and sending information.

mobile social networking Members converse and connect with one another using cell phones or other mobile devices.

mobility The degree to which agents travel through a computer network.

model base A collection of preprogrammed quantitative models (e.g., statistical, financial, optimization) organized as a single unit.

model base management system (MBMS) Software for establishing, updating, combining, and so on (e.g., managing) a DSS model base.

model building blocks Preprogrammed software elements that can be used to build computerized models. For example, a random-number generator can be employed in the construction of a simulation model.

model mart A small, generally departmental repository of knowledge created by using knowledge-discovery techniques on past decision instances. Model marts are similar to data marts. *See* model warehouse.

model warehouse A large, generally enterprise-wide repository of knowledge created by using knowledge-discovery techniques on past decision instances. Model warehouses are similar to data warehouses. *See* model mart.

momentum A learning parameter in backpropagation neural networks.

Monte Carlo simulation A method of simulation whereby a model is built and then sampling experiments are run to collect and analyze the performance of interesting variables.

MSS architecture A plan for organizing the underlying infrastructure and applications of an MSS project.

MSS suite An integrated collection of a large number of MSS tools that work together for applications development.

MSS tool A software element (e.g., a language) that facilitates the development of an MSS or an MSS generator.

multiagent system A system with multiple cooperating software agents.

multidimensional analysis (modeling) A modeling method that involves data analysis in several dimensions.

multidimensional database A database in which the data are organized specifically to support easy and quick multidimensional analysis.

multidimensional OLAP (MOLAP) OLAP implemented via a specialized multidimensional database (or data store) that summarizes transactions into multidimensional views ahead of time.

multidimensionality The ability to organize, present, and analyze data by several dimensions, such as sales by region, by product, by salesperson, and by time (four dimensions).

multiple goals Refers to a decision situation in which alternatives are evaluated with several, sometimes conflicting, goals.

mutation A genetic operator that causes a random change in a potential solution.

natural language processing (NLP) Using a natural language processor to interface with a computer-based system.

neural computing An experimental computer design aimed at building intelligent computers that operate in a manner modeled on the functioning of the human brain. *See* artificial neural network (ANN).

neural (computing) networks A computer design aimed at building intelligent computers that operate in a manner modeled on the functioning of the human brain.

neural network *See* artificial neural network (ANN).

neuron A cell (i.e., processing element) of a biological or artificial neural network.

nominal data A type of data that contains measurements of simple codes assigned to objects as labels, which are not measurements. For example, the variable *marital status* can be generally categorized as (1) single, (2) married, and (3) divorced.

nominal group technique (NGT) A simple brainstorming process for nonelectronic meetings.

normative model A model that prescribes how a system should operate.

NoSQL (which stands for Not Only SQL) A new paradigm to store and process large volumes of unstructured, semistructured, and multi-structured data.

nucleus The central processing portion of a neuron.

numeric data A type of data that represent the numeric values of specific variables. Examples of numerically valued variables include age, number of children, total household income (in U.S. dollars), travel distance (in miles), and temperature (in Fahrenheit degrees).

object A person, place, or thing about which information is collected, processed, or stored.

object-oriented model base management system (OOMBMS) An MBMS constructed in an object-oriented environment.

online analytical processing (OLAP) An information system that enables the user, while at a PC, to query the system, conduct an analysis, and so on. The result is generated in seconds.

online (electronic) workspace Online screens that allow people to share documents, files, project plans, calendars, and so on in the same online place, though not necessarily at the same time.

oper mart An operational data mart. An oper mart is a small-scale data mart typically used by a single department or functional area in an organization.

operational data store (ODS) A type of database often used as an interim area for a data warehouse, especially for customer information files.

operational models Models that represent problems for the operational level of management.

operational plan A plan that translates an organization's strategic objectives and goals into a set of well-defined tactics and initiatives, resource requirements, and expected results.

optimal solution A best possible solution to a modeled problem.

optimization The process of identifying the best possible solution to a problem.

ordinal data Data that contains codes assigned to objects or events as labels that also represent the rank order among them. For example, the variable *credit score* can be generally categorized as (1) low, (2) medium, and (3) high.

organizational agent An agent that executes tasks on behalf of a business process or computer application.

organizational culture The aggregate attitudes in an organization concerning a certain issue (e.g., technology, computers, DSS).

organizational knowledge base An organization's knowledge repository.

organizational learning The process of capturing knowledge and making it available enterprise-wide.

organizational memory That which an organization knows.

ossified case A case that has been analyzed and has no further value.

PageRank A link analysis algorithm, named after Larry Page—one of the two founders of Google as a research project at Stanford University in 1996, and used by the Google Web search engine.

paradigmatic case A case that is unique that can be maintained to derive new knowledge for the future.

parallel processing An advanced computer processing technique that allows a computer to perform multiple processes at once, in parallel.

parallelism In a group support system, a process gain in which everyone in a group can work simultaneously (e.g., in brainstorming, voting, ranking).

parameter *See* uncontrollable variable (parameter).

part-of-speech tagging The process of marking up the words in a text as corresponding to a particular part of speech (such as nouns, verbs, adjectives, adverbs, etc.) based on a word's definition and context of its use.

pattern recognition A technique of matching an external pattern to a pattern stored in a computer's memory (i.e., the process of classifying data into predetermined categories). Pattern recognition is used in inference engines, image processing, neural computing, and speech recognition.

perceptron An early neural network structure that uses no hidden layer.

performance measurement system A system that assists managers in tracking the implementations of business strategy by comparing actual results against strategic goals and objectives.

personal agent An agent that performs tasks on behalf of individual users.

physical integration The seamless integration of several systems into one functioning system.

Pig A Hadoop-based query language developed by Yahoo!.

polysemes Words also called *homonyms*, they are syntactically identical words (i.e., spelled exactly the same) with different meanings (e.g., *bow* can mean "to bend forward," "the front of the ship," "the weapon that shoots arrows," or "a kind of tied ribbon").

portal A gateway to Web sites. Portals can be public (e.g., Yahoo!) or private (e.g., corporate portals).

practice approach An approach toward knowledge management that focuses on building the social environments or communities of practice necessary to facilitate the sharing of tacit understanding.

prediction The act of telling about the future.

predictive analysis Use of tools that help determine the probable future outcome for an event or the likelihood of a situation occurring. These tools also identify relationships and patterns.

predictive analytics A business analytical approach toward forecasting (e.g., demand, problems, opportunities) that is used instead of simply reporting data as they occur.

principle of choice The criterion for making a choice among alternatives.

privacy In general, the right to be left alone and the right to be free of unreasonable personal intrusions. Information privacy is the right to determine when, and to what extent, information about oneself can be communicated to others.

private agent An agent that works for only one person.

problem ownership The jurisdiction (authority) to solve a problem.

problem solving A process in which one starts from an initial state and proceeds to search through a problem space to identify a desired goal.

process approach An approach to knowledge management that attempts to codify organizational knowledge through formalized controls, processes, and technologies.

process gain In a group support system, improvements in the effectiveness of the activities of a meeting.

process loss In a group support system, degradation in the effectiveness of the activities of a meeting.

processing element (PE) A neuron in a neural network.

production rules The most popular form of knowledge representation for expert systems where atomic pieces of knowledge are represented using simple if-then structures.

prototyping In system development, a strategy in which a scaled-down system or portion of a system is constructed in a short time, tested, and improved in several iterations.

public agent An agent that serves any user.

quantitative software package A preprogrammed (sometimes called *ready-made*) model or optimization system. These packages sometimes serve as building blocks for other quantitative models.

query facility The (database) mechanism that accepts requests for data, accesses them, manipulates them, and queries them.

rapid application development (RAD) A development methodology that adjusts a system development life cycle so that parts of the system can be developed quickly, thereby enabling users to obtain some functionality as soon as possible. RAD includes methods of phased development, prototyping, and throwaway prototyping.

RapidMiner A popular, open source, free-of-charge data mining software suite that employs a graphically enhanced user interface, a rather large number of algorithms, and a variety of data visualization features.

ratio data Continuous data where both differences and ratios are interpretable. The distinguishing feature of a ratio scale is the possession of a nonarbitrary zero value.

real-time data warehousing The process of loading and providing data via a data warehouse as they become available.

real-time expert system An expert system designed for online dynamic decision support. It has a strict limit on response time; in other words, the system always produces a response by the time it is needed.

reality mining Data mining of location-based data.

recommendation system (agent) A computer system that can suggest new items to a user based on his or her revealed preference. It may be content based or use collaborative filtering to suggest items that match the preference of the user. An example is **Amazon.com**'s "Customers who bought this item also bought …" feature.

regression A data mining method for real-world prediction problems where the predicted values (i.e., the output variable or dependent variable) are numeric (e.g., predicting the temperature for tomorrow as 68°F).

reinforcement learning A sub-area of machine learning that is concerned with learning-by-doing-and-measuring to maximize some notion of long-term reward. Reinforcement learning differs from supervised learning in that correct input/output pairs are never presented to the algorithm.

relational database A database whose records are organized into tables that can be processed by either relational algebra or relational calculus.

relational model base management system (RMBMS) A relational approach (as in relational databases) to the design and development of a model base management system.

relational OLAP (ROLAP) The implementation of an OLAP database on top of an existing relational database.

report Any communication artifact prepared with the specific intention of conveying information in a presentable form.

reproduction The creation of new generations of improved solutions with the use of a genetic algorithm.

result (outcome) variable A variable that expresses the result of a decision (e.g., one concerning profit), usually one of the goals of a decision-making problem.

revenue management systems Decision-making systems used to make optimal price decisions in order to maximize revenue, based upon previous demand history as well as forecasts of demand at various pricing levels and other considerations.

RFID A generic technology that refers to the use of radio-frequency waves to identify objects.

risk A probabilistic or stochastic decision situation.

risk analysis A decision-making method that analyzes the risk (based on assumed known probabilities) associated with different alternatives.

robot A machine that has the capability of performing manual functions without human intervention.

rule-based system A system in which knowledge is represented completely in terms of rules (e.g., a system based on production rules).

SAS Enterprise Miner A comprehensive, commercial data mining software tool developed by SAS Institute.

satisficing A process by which one seeks a solution that will satisfy a set of constraints. In contrast to optimization, which seeks the best possible solution, satisficing simply seeks a solution that will work well enough.

scenario A statement of assumptions and configurations concerning the operating environment of a particular system at a particular time.

scorecard A visual display that is used to chart progress against strategic and tactical goals and targets.

screen sharing Software that enables group members, even in different locations, to work on the same document, which is shown on the PC screen of each participant.

search engine A program that finds and lists Web sites or pages (designated by URLs) that match some user-selected criteria.

search engine optimization (SEO) The intentional activity of affecting the visibility of an e-commerce site or a Web site in a search engine's natural (unpaid or organic) search results.

self-organizing A neural network architecture that uses unsupervised learning.

semantic Web An extension of the current Web, in which information is given well-defined meanings, better enabling computers and people to work in cooperation.

semantic Web services An XML-based technology that allows semantic information to be represented in Web services.

semistructured problem A category of decision problems where the decision process has some structure to it but still requires subjective analysis and an iterative approach.

SEMMA An alternative process for data mining projects proposed by the SAS Institute. The acronym "SEMMA" stands for "sample, explore, modify, model, and assess."

sensitivity analysis A study of the effect of a change in one or more input variables on a proposed solution.

sentiment A settled opinion reflective of one's feelings.

sentiment analysis The technique used to detect favorable and unfavorable opinions toward specific products and services using a large number of textual data sources (customer feedback in the form of Web postings).

SentiWordNet An extension of WordNet to be used for sentiment identification. *See* WordNet.

sequence discovery The identification of associations over time.

sequence mining A pattern discovery method where relationships among the things are examined in terms of their order of occurrence to identify associations over time.

sigmoid (logical activation) function An *S*-shaped transfer function in the range of 0 to 1.

simple split Data is partitioned into two mutually exclusive subsets called a *training set* and a *test set* (or *holdout set*). It is common to designate two-thirds of the data as the training set and the remaining one-third as the test set.

simulation An imitation of reality in computers.

singular value decomposition (SVD) Closely related to principal components analysis, reduces the overall dimensionality of the input matrix (number of input documents by number of extracted terms) to a lower dimensional space, where each consecutive dimension represents the largest degree of variability (between words and documents).

Six Sigma A performance management methodology aimed at reducing the number of defects in a business process to as close to zero defects per million opportunities (DPMO) as possible.

social analytics The monitoring, analyzing, measuring, and interpreting digital interactions and relationships of people, topics, ideas, and content.

social media The online platforms and tools that people use to share opinions, experiences, insights, perceptions, and various media, including photos, videos, or music, with each other. The enabling technologies of social interactions among people in which they create, share, and exchange information, ideas, and opinions in virtual communities and networks.

social media analytics The systematic and scientific ways to consume the vast amount of content created by Web-based social media outlets, tools, and techniques for the betterment of an organization's competitiveness.

social network analysis (SNA) The mapping and measuring of relationships and information flows among people, groups, organizations, computers, and other information- or knowledge-processing entities. The nodes in the network are the people and groups, whereas the links show relationships or flows between the nodes.

software agent A piece of autonomous software that persists to accomplish the task it is designed for (by its owner).

software-as-a-service (SaaS) Software that is rented instead of sold.

speech analytics A growing field of science that allows users to analyze and extract information from both live and recorded conversations.

speech (voice) understanding An area of artificial intelligence research that attempts to allow computers to recognize words or phrases of human speech.

staff assistant An individual who acts as an assistant to a manager.

static models Models that describe a single interval of a situation.

status report A report that provides the most current information on the status of an item (e.g., orders, expenses, production quantity).

stemming A process of reducing words to their respective root forms in order to better represent them in a text mining project.

stop words Words that are filtered out prior to or after processing of natural language data (i.e., text).

story A case with rich information and episodes. Lessons may be derived from this kind of case in a case base.

strategic goal A quantified objective that has a designated time period.

strategic models Models that represent problems for the strategic level (i.e., executive level) of management.

strategic objective A broad statement or general course of action that prescribes targeted directions for an organization.

strategic theme A collection of related strategic objectives, used to simplify the construction of a strategic map.

strategic vision A picture or mental image of what the organization should look like in the future.

strategy map A visual display that delineates the relationships among the key organizational objectives for all four balanced scorecard perspectives.

stream analytics A term commonly used for extracting actionable information from continuously flowing/streaming data sources.

structured problem A decision situation where a specific set of steps can be followed to make a straightforward decision

Structured Query Language (SQL) A data definition and management language for relational databases. SQL front ends most relational DBMS.

suboptimization An optimization-based procedure that does not consider all the alternatives for or impacts on an organization.

summation function A mechanism to add all the inputs coming into a particular neuron.

supervised learning A method of training artificial neural networks in which sample cases are shown to the network as input, and the weights are adjusted to minimize the error in the outputs.

support The measure of how often products and/or services appear together in the same transaction; that is, the proportion of transactions in the data set that contain all of the products and/or services mentioned in a specific rule.

support vector machines (SVM) A family of generalized linear models, which achieve a classification or regression decision based on the value of the linear combination of input features.

synapse The connection (where the weights are) between processing elements in a neural network.

synchronous (real time) Occurring at the same time.

system architecture The logical and physical design of a system.

system development lifecycle (SDLC) A systematic process for the effective construction of large information systems.

systems dynamics Macro-level simulation models in which aggregate values and trends are considered. The objective is to study the overall behavior of a system over time, rather than the behavior of each individual participant or player in the system

tacit knowledge Knowledge that is usually in the domain of subjective, cognitive, and experiential learning. It is highly personal and difficult to formalize.

tactical models Models that represent problems for the tactical level (i.e., midlevel) of management.

teleconferencing The use of electronic communication that allows two or more people at different locations to have a simultaneous conference.

term–document matrix (TDM) A frequency matrix created from digitized and organized documents (the corpus) where the columns represent the terms while rows represent the individual documents.

text analytics A broader concept that includes information retrieval (e.g., searching and identifying relevant documents for a given set of key terms) as well as information extraction, data mining, and Web mining.

text mining The application of data mining to nonstructured or less structured text files. It entails the generation of meaningful numeric indices from the unstructured text and then processing those indices using various data mining algorithms.

theory of certainty factors A theory designed to help incorporate uncertainty into the representation of knowledge (in terms of production rules) for expert systems.

threshold value A hurdle value for the output of a neuron to trigger the next level of neurons. If an output value is smaller than the threshold value, it will not be passed to the next level of neurons.

tokenizing Categorizing a block of text (token) according to the function it performs.

topology The way in which neurons are organized in a neural network.

transformation (transfer) function In a neural network, the function that sums and transforms inputs before a neuron fires. It shows the relationship between the internal activation level and the output of a neuron.

trend analysis The collecting of information and attempting to spot a pattern, or *trend*, in the information.

Turing test A test designed to measure the "intelligence" of a computer.

uncertainty In expert systems, a value that cannot be determined during a consultation. Many expert systems can accommodate uncertainty; that is, they allow the user to indicate whether he or she does not know the answer.

uncontrollable variable (parameter) A factor that affects the result of a decision but is not under the control of the decision maker. These variables can be internal (e.g., related to technology or to policies) or external (e.g., related to legal issues or to climate).

unstructured data Data that does not have a predetermined format and is stored in the form of textual documents.

unstructured problem A decision setting where the steps are not entirely fixed or structured, but may require subjective considerations.

unsupervised learning A method of training artificial neural networks in which only input stimuli are shown to the network, which is self-organizing.

user interface The component of a computer system that allows bidirectional communication between the system and its user.

user interface management system (UIMS) The DSS component that handles all interaction between users and the system.

user-developed MSS An MSS developed by one user or by a few users in one department, including decision makers and professionals (i.e., knowledge workers, e.g., financial analysts, tax analysts, engineers) who build or use computers to solve problems or enhance their productivity.

utility (on-demand) computing Unlimited computing power and storage capacity that, like electricity, water, and telephone services, can be obtained on demand, used, and reallocated for any application and that are billed on a pay-per-use basis.

vendor-managed inventory (VMI) The practice of retailers making suppliers responsible for determining when to order and how much to order.

video teleconferencing (videoconferencing) Virtual meeting in which participants in one location can see participants at other locations on a large screen or a desktop computer.

virtual (Internet) community A group of people with similar interests who interact with one another using the Internet.

virtual meeting An online meeting whose members are in different locations, possibly even in different countries.

virtual team A team whose members are in different places while in a meeting together.

virtual worlds Artificial worlds created by computer systems in which the user has the impression of being immersed.

visual analytics The combination of visualization and predictive analytics.

visual interactive modeling (VIM) *See* visual interactive simulation (VIS).

visual interactive simulation (VIS) A simulation approach used in the decision-making process that shows graphical animation in which systems and processes are presented dynamically to the decision maker. It enables visualization of the results of different potential actions.

visual recognition The addition of some form of computer intelligence and decision making to digitized visual information, received from a machine sensor such as a camera.

voice of customer (VOC) Applications that focus on "who and how" questions by gathering and reporting direct feedback from site visitors, by benchmarking against other sites and offline channels, and by supporting predictive modeling of future visitor behavior.

voice (speech) recognition Translation of human voice into individual words and sentences that are understandable by a computer.

Voice over IP (VoIP) Communication systems that transmit voice calls over Internet Protocol (IP)–based networks. Also known as *Internet telephony*.

voice portal A Web site, usually a portal, that has an audio interface.

voice synthesis The technology by which computers convert text to voice (i.e., speak).

Web 2.0 The popular term for advanced Internet technology and applications, including blogs, wikis, RSS, and social bookmarking. One of the most significant differences between Web 2.0 and the traditional World Wide Web is greater collaboration among Internet users and other users, content providers, and enterprises.

Web analytics The application of business analytics activities to Web-based processes, including e-commerce.

Web content mining The extraction of useful information from Web pages.

Web crawlers An application used to read through the content of a Web site automatically.

Web mining The discovery and analysis of interesting and useful information from the Web, about the Web, and usually through Web-based tools.

Web services An architecture that enables assembly of distributed applications from software services and ties them together.

Web structure mining The development of useful information from the links included in Web documents.

Web usage mining The extraction of useful information from the data being generated through Web page visits, transactions, and so on.

Weka A popular, free-of-charge, open source suite of machine-learning software written in Java, developed at the University of Waikato.

what-if analysis A process that involves asking a computer what the effect of changing some of the input data or parameters would be.

wiki A piece of server software available in a Web site that allows users to freely create and edit Web page content, using any Web browser.

wikilog A Web log (blog) that allows people to participate as peers; anyone can add, delete, or change content.

WordNet A popular general-purpose lexicon created at Princeton University.

work system A system in which humans and/or machines perform a business process, using resources to produce products or services for internal or external customers.

INDEX

Note: 'A', 'f', 'n' and 't' refer to application cases, figures, notes and tables respectively